HANDBOOK OF LATIN AMERICAN STUDIES: No. 47

A Selective and Annotated Guide to Recent Publications in Anthropology, Economics, Education, Geography, Government and Politics, International Relations, and Sociology

VOLUME 48 WILL BE DEVOTED TO THE HUMANITIES: ART, FILM, HISTORY, LANGUAGE, LITERATURE, MUSIC, AND PHILOSOPHY

EDITORIAL NOTE: Comments concerning the *Handbook of Latin American Studies* should be sent directly to the Editor, *Handbook of Latin American Studies*, Hispanic Division, Library of Congress, Washington, D.C. 20540.

HANDBOOK OF LATIN AMERICAN STUDIES NO. 47

SOCIAL SCIENCES

Prepared by a Number of Scholars
for the Hispanic Division of The Library of Congress

Edited by DOLORES MOYANO MARTIN

1985

UNIVERSITY OF TEXAS PRESS   *Austin*

International Standard Book Number 0-292-73038-1
International Standard Serial Number 0072-9833
Library of Congress Catalog Card Number 36-32633
Copyright © 1987 by the University of Texas Press
Printed in the United States of America

Requests for permission to reproduce material
from this work should be sent to
Permissions, University of Texas Press,
Box 7819, Austin, Texas 78713-7819.

First Edition, 1987

IN MEMORIAM

BRYCE WOOD (March 13, 1908–January 23, 1986)

Bryce Wood was one of the most influential shapers of scholars and scholarship in Latin American studies in the post World War II period. During his years at the Social Science Research Council and in the Foreign Area Fellowship program, he sponsored dissertation research and field work for many young scholars who are now leaders in many fields of Latin American studies. He was a strong supporter of the movement to establish the Latin American Studies Association.

Trained at Reed College and Columbia University, Wood also served as a Latin American specialist at the Department of State during World War II. In spite of heavy commitments, he wrote many important books. His most publicized book, often cited among the best scholarly studies of Latin America, was *The Making of the Good Neighbor Policy* (1962), a work based on US diplomatic archives. Shortly before his death he published a sequel, *Dismantling the Good Neighbor Policy* (1985), a study which chartered the collapse of that policy in Argentina and Guatemala. Other important works included *The United States and Latin American wars: 1932–1942* (1966) and *Aggression and history: the case of Ecuador and Peru* (1978).

Wood's association with the Hispanic Division of the Library of Congress was of long duration and significance. He began serving as contributing editor of the *Handbook* with volume 7 in 1941, an association that would last for almost half a century, practically the life span of the *Handbook* itself. He covered the international relations section until 1962. In that year, he became a member of the *Handbook*'s Advisory Board where he served until his death. He was a dedicated Board member, a meticulous editor and a sensitive and generous adviser. Few individuals have worked with more care or greater devotion to enhance the quality of the *Handbook* than Bryce Wood. His enthusiasm and dedication will be deeply missed by all of us who had the privilege to know him and work with him.

Cole Blasier
University of Pittsburgh

CONTRIBUTING EDITORS

SOCIAL SCIENCES

Michael B. Anderson, *Inter-American Development Bank*, ECONOMICS
Roderic A. Camp, *Central College, Pella, Iowa*, GOVERNMENT AND POLITICS
Lyle Campbell, *State University of New York at Albany*, ANTHROPOLOGY
William L. Canak, *Tulane University*, SOCIOLOGY
Charlotte Jones Carroll, *The World Bank*, ECONOMICS
Thomas F. Carroll, *George Washington University*, ECONOMICS
Manuel J. Carvajal, *Florida International University*, ECONOMICS
Donald V. Coes, *University of Illinois, Urbana*, ECONOMICS
Lambros Comitas, *Columbia University*, ANTHROPOLOGY
David W. Dent, *Towson State College*, GOVERNMENT AND POLITICS
Clinton R. Edwards, *University of Wisconsin, Milwaukee*, GEOGRAPHY
Everett Egginton, *University of Louisville*, EDUCATION
Robert C. Eidt, *University of Wisconsin, Milwaukee*, GEOGRAPHY
Gary S. Elbow, *Texas Tech University*, GEOGRAPHY
Yale H. Ferguson, *Rutgers University, Newark*, INTERNATIONAL RELATIONS
Michael J. Francis, *University of Notre Dame*, INTERNATIONAL RELATIONS
William R. Garner, *Southern Illinois University*, GOVERNMENT AND POLITICS
Dennis Gilbert, *Cornell University*, SOCIOLOGY
George W. Grayson, *College of William and Mary*, INTERNATIONAL RELATIONS
Norman Hammond, *Rutgers University, New Brunswick*, ANTHROPOLOGY
Kevin Healy, *Inter-American Foundation*, SOCIOLOGY
John R. Hébert, *Library of Congress*, BIBLIOGRAPHY AND GENERAL WORKS
Mario Hiraoka, *Millersville State College*, GEOGRAPHY
John M. Hunter, *Michigan State University*, ECONOMICS
John M. Ingham, *University of Minnesota*, ANTHROPOLOGY
W. Jerald Kennedy, *Florida Atlantic University*, ANTHROPOLOGY
Waud H. Kracke, *University of Illinois at Chicago Circle*, ANTHROPOLOGY
Thomas J. La Belle, *University of Pittsburgh*, EDUCATION
Barbara Deutsch Lynch, *Cornell University*, SOCIOLOGY
Robert Malina, *University of Texas at Austin*, ANTHROPOLOGY
Markos Mamalakis, *University of Wisconsin, Milwaukee*, ECONOMICS
Tom L. Martinson, *Ball State University*, GEOGRAPHY
Betty J. Meggers, *Smithsonian Institution*, ANTHROPOLOGY
Ernesto Migliazza, *Hyattsville, Md.*, ANTHROPOLOGY
Andrew M. Modelski, *Library of Congress*, GEOGRAPHY
Raúl Moncarz, *Florida International University*, ECONOMICS
Lisandro Pérez, *Florida International University*, SOCIOLOGY
Jorge F. Pérez-López, *U.S. Department of Labor*, ECONOMICS
Roger N. Rasnake, *Goucher College*, ANTHROPOLOGY

Steve C. Ropp, *University of Wyoming*, GOVERNMENT AND POLITICS
Jorge Salazar-Carrillo, *Florida International University*, ECONOMICS
Margaret Sarles, *University of Maryland, College Park*, GOVERNMENT AND POLITICS
Stephen M. Smith, *University of Idaho, Moscow*, ECONOMICS
Barbara L. Stark, *Arizona State University*, ANTHROPOLOGY
Andrés Suárez, *University of Florida*, GOVERNMENT AND POLITICS
Francisco E. Thoumi, *Inter-American Development Bank*, ECONOMICS
Antonio Ugalde, *University of Texas at Austin*, SOCIOLOGY
Robert E. Verhine, *Universidade Federal da Bahia, Salvador, Brazil*, EDUCATION
Carlos H. Waisman, *University of California, San Diego*, SOCIOLOGY
Gary W. Wynia, *University of Minnesota*, GOVERNMENT AND POLITICS

HUMANITIES

Jean A. Barman, *University of British Columbia*, HISTORY
Roderick J. Barman, *University of British Columbia*, HISTORY
María Luisa Bastos, *Lehman College-CUNY*, LITERATURE
Judith Ishmael Bissett, *Miami University, Ohio*, LITERATURE
David Bushnell, *University of Florida*, HISTORY
D. Lincoln Canfield, *Southern Illinois University at Carbondale*, LANGUAGES
Sara Castro-Klarén, *Library of Congress*, LITERATURE
Donald E. Chipman, *North Texas State University, Denton*, HISTORY
Flora Clancy, *University of New Mexico, Albuquerque*, ART
S.L. Cline, *University of California, Santa Barbara*, HISTORY
Don M. Coerver, *Texas Christian University*, HISTORY
Michael L. Conniff, *University of New Mexico, Albuquerque*, HISTORY
René de Costa, *University of Chicago*, LITERATURE
Edith B. Couturier, *National Endowment for the Humanities*, HISTORY
Joseph T. Criscenti, *Boston College*, HISTORY
Ethel O. Davie, *West Virginia State College*, LITERATURE
Ralph E. Dimmick, *Organization of American States*, LITERATURE
Leonard Folgarait, *Vanderbilt University*, ART
Fernando García Núñez, *University of Texas at El Paso*, LITERATURE
Magdalena García Pinto, *University of Missouri, Columbia*, LITERATURE
Naomi M. Garrett, *West Virginia State College*, LITERATURE
Jaime Giordano, *State University of New York at Stony Brook*, LITERATURE
Cedomil Goić, *University of Michigan*, LITERATURE
Richard E. Greenleaf, *Tulane University*, HISTORY
Oscar Hahn, *University of Iowa*, LITERATURE
Michael T. Hamerly, *Latin American Bibliographic Foundation*, HISTORY
John R. Hébert, *Library of Congress*, BIBLIOGRAPHY AND GENERAL WORKS
Carlos R. Hortas, *Hunter College*, LITERATURE
Regina Igel, *University of Maryland, College Park*, LITERATURE
Randal Johnson, *University of Florida*, FILM
Djelal Kadir, *Purdue University*, LITERATURE
Norma Klahn, *Columbia University*, LITERATURE
Pedro Lastra, *State University of New York at Stony Brook*, LITERATURE
Asunción Lavrin, *Howard University*, HISTORY
Suzanne Jill Levine, *University of Washington*, LITERATURE
Maria Angélica Guimarães Lopes, *University of South Carolina, Columbia*, LITERATURE

William Luis, *Dartmouth College*, LITERATURE
Murdo J. MacLeod, *University of Arizona*, HISTORY
Wilson Martins, *New York University*, LITERATURE
Robert J. Mullen, *University of Texas at San Antonio*, ART
José Neistein, *Brazilian American Cultural Institute, Washington*, ART
Julio Ortega, *University of Texas at Austin*, LITERATURE
José Miguel Oviedo, *University of California, Los Angeles*, LITERATURE
Colin Palmer, *University of North Carolina, Chapel Hill*, HISTORY
Vincent C. Peloso, *Howard University*, HISTORY
Anne Pérotin-Dumon, *Institut des hautes études de l'Amérique latine, Paris*,
   HISTORY
Richard A. Preto-Rodas, *University of South Florida, Tampa*, LITERATURE
Jane M. Loy Rausch, *University of Massachusetts-Amherst*, HISTORY
Daniel R. Reedy, *University of Kentucky*, LITERATURE
James D. Riley, *Catholic University of America*, HISTORY
Rubén Ríos Avila, *University of Puerto Rico*, LITERATURE
Frank Salomon, *University of Wisconsin, Madison*, HISTORY
John F. Scott, *University of Florida*, ART
Rebecca Scott, *University of Michigan*, HISTORY
Nicolas Shumway, *Yale University*, LITERATURE
Blanca G. Silvestrini, *University of Puerto Rico*, HISTORY
Susan M. Socolow, *Emory University*, HISTORY
Saúl Sosnowski, *University of Maryland, College Park*, LITERATURE
Robert Stevenson, *University of California, Los Angeles*, MUSIC
Juan Carlos Torchia-Estrada, *Organization of American States*, PHILOSOPHY
Kathryn Waldron, *New York City*, HISTORY
George Woodyard, *University of Kansas*, LITERATURE
Thomas C. Wright, *University of Nevada*, HISTORY
Winthrop R. Wright, *University of Maryland, College Park*, HISTORY
George Yudice, *Emory University*, LITERATURE

Foreign Corresponding Editors

Lino G. Canedo, *Franciscan Academy, Bethesda, Md.*, COLONIAL HISTORY
Marcello Carmagnani, *Università Degli Studi ai Torino, Italy*, ITALIAN LANGUAGE
Krystian Complak, *Wroclaw University, Wroclaw, Poland*, POLISH SOCIAL SCIENCE
   MATERIAL
Magnus Mörner, *Göteborgs Universitet, Sweden*, SCANDINAVIAN LANGUAGES
Wilhelm Stegmann, *Ibero-Amerikanisches Institut, Berlin, Federal Republic of
   Germany*, GERMAN LANGUAGE
Hasso von Winning, *Southwest Museum, Los Angeles*, GERMAN MATERIAL ON
   MESOAMERICAN ARCHAEOLOGY

Special Contributing Editors

Robert V. Allen, *Library of Congress*, RUSSIAN LANGUAGE
Marie-Louise H. Bernal, *Library of Congress*, SCANDINAVIAN LANGUAGES
Georgette M. Dorn, *Library of Congress*, GERMAN AND HUNGARIAN LANGUAGES
George J. Kovtun, *Library of Congress*, CZECH LANGUAGE
Norine I. Vicenti, *Library of Congress*, DUTCH LANGUAGE

CONTENTS

ECONOMICS

EDUCATION

GEOGRAPHY

GOVERNMENT AND POLITICS

INTERNATIONAL RELATIONS

SOCIOLOGY

INDEXES

EDITOR'S NOTE

I. GENERAL AND REGIONAL TRENDS

The most striking fact about the literature annotated in this volume of the *Handbook* is *increase* or, in the words of one of our contributors, "increase in quantity, quality, indigenous origin, and scope" (p. 233)—an increase which is the direct result of the reestablishment of liberal democracy throughout most of South America (the exceptions being Paraguay, Chile and Surinam).

The return to civilian rule has led to a widespread interest in and concern with the issue of redemocratization and one contributor to this volume notes the desire of these new democratic governments to distance themselves "from traditional bureaucratic patrimonialism" and to move towards "more participatory" rule (p. 556). Less sanguine scholars, however, remind us of the "ancient" corporatist "currents" (item **7109**) and "dominant authoritarian" traditions that undermine these democracies (p. 570). The return to civilian rule also has brought a shift in the choice of political topics of study including less attention to military rule and bureaucratic authoritarianism, and more attention to political parties, electoral behavior, and presidential leadership (p. 522). Although there is also less emphasis on the issue of human rights, the political role played by the Catholic Church in their protection is especially evident in writings about Central America and Chile (items **6103, 6113, 6115, 6460, 6470,** and **6492**).

The turmoil in Central America has "spawned a new growth industry of books" many of which, unfortunately, "suffer from overbreadth, superficiality, paucity of original research, lack of comparative studies among countries, the quest for instant topicality, and podium-pounding dogmatism that often substitutes sloganeering for analysis" (p. 593). Nevertheless, a few rigorous works have appeared that attempt to examine the Central American predicament as well as "the ill-defined goals" of US policy therein (p. 593 and items **7187, 7221,** and **7252**).

Several contributors to this volume remark on the decline of dependency theory as the explanation of Latin American underdevelopment (pp. 546, 569, and 617) and one work analyzes why nations subject in equal measure to dependency, neo-colonialism, and multinational corporations such as Denmark, Cyprus, Malta, South Korea, and Singapore have nevertheless managed to achieve "conspicuous progress" (item **7252**).

The emergence of several prosperous Asian nations in addition to Japan has led to the formulation of "the notion of a Pacific Basin" (p. 617), a unit of extraordinary economic dynamism which will be of much relevance to Latin American countries which are Pacific nations as well (see items **7144** and **7263**).

Undoubtedly, the reestablishment of liberal democracy has been the leading factor in the upsurge of quality publications in the social sciences, especially in sociology and anthropology, fields regarded as "subversive" by the deposed military regimes. As is stated elsewhere in this volume these "suspect" disciplines are once again operating in the open having relegated the circulation of "underground or *zamisdat* social science literature" to a "thing of the past" (p. 679). In Bolivia, for example, "a remarkable development" has been "the steady stream of sociological literature" (p. 674) issued in 1984. Many of these Bolivian works offer a more contemporary and sophisticated view of the 1950s–80s period, in particular of events such as the agrarian reform and evolution of "peasant syndicates which have resumed their political role as a national pressure group in the new democratic order" (p. 675). In Argentina, the renaissance of the social sciences is exemplified by the return of two publishers: "Editorial de Belgrano which began issuing social science monographs in earnest in 1982 and the Centro Editor de América Latina, a prolific little operation run by the people who directed the EUDEBA national university press in the early 1960s before they were expelled by Gen. Onganía in 1966" (p. 545). In Peru, social scientists have published numerous works on the anthropology and sociology of the Andean highlands (pp. 166 and 668). In Brazil, "the technical competence" of the nation's "academic economists is reflected in the approach and level" of many of these scholars' articles while their monographs make up "a substantial proportion" of works on the Brazilian economy that are featured in this volume (pp. 349–350). The significance of Brazilian anthropology is reflected in the number of outstanding works issued by the nation's social scientists (p. 129). In Mexico, there has been a notable "increase in regional studies which probably reflects the decentralization and expansion of universities and research centers" throughout the country (p. 639). And in Chile, despite the dictatorship "a remarkable network of research centers exists allowing" social scientists "not only to remain in the country but to turn out high quality work" (p. 679). "Paradoxically," as one contributor notes, "some of the most interesting research in the Southern Cone is being conducted in Pinochet's Chile" (p. 679 and items **8338–8352**). Indeed, the limitations confronting social science research in the above mentioned countries are not merely political but economic: "stagnant, debt-ridden economies that can hardly support a solid research establishment" (p. 679).

A "sense of crisis" permeates much of the writings about the Latin American economies, "especially after the severity of the external debt" (p. 348) became apparent in the early 1980s. These writings often reflect much ambivalence about the International Monetary Fund's role in the alleviation of the crisis, a role which the debtor nations both request and resent. When "governments hesitate to impose harsh and consequently unpopular measures to correct balance-of-payment disequilibria and ease their external debt (items **3284** and **3334**), the IMF forces them to succumb to pressures of fiscal austerity, wage controls, and devaluation, all of which are bound to bruise nationalist pride" (p. 276).

The economic crisis is thus indirectly to blame for the fact, that, although the number and competence of social scientists in Latin America continue to grow, publication and distribution of their works are hindered by high costs (p. 64). Nevertheless, this *HLAS* volume features a surprisingly "large number of publications on the subject of book production in Latin America" (p. 5), a subject raised in *HLAS 46* (p. xiii) where we noted that the Brazilian publishing business was not merely the most active in Latin America but well on the way to becoming "the premier book industry of the Third World" (see *HLAS 46:3461*). Surprisingly, contributions by US authors, usually the leading group of non Latin-American scholars writing about the region, have declined in some important areas and topics. This is especially the case in sociological works about Central America (p. 640), ethnological studies of the Andean peoples (p. 166), and economic works about Venezuela (p. 312) and Colombia (p. 301). On the other hand, the interest of extra-hemispheric scholars in Latin America, noted in previous volumes, continues unabated. The Japanese have made important contributions to Andean anthropology (see items **1471, 1483, 1486, 1487, 1493, 1515,** and **1516**). Significant works by German authors have enhanced "our understanding of contemporary Central America" (p. 419), and French writers continue to publish valuable studies of South America (p. 429). Finally, as one contributor notes, "the Soviet Union's 'presence' in the Western Hemisphere—in terms of more diplomatic relations, trade, economic and military assistance, and ships at sea—is undeniable" (p. 571). This presence is reflected in the upsurge of Soviet writings on Latin America, writings which "unfortunately shed little light on the USSR's official perspective on the Latin American region" (p. 572). Nevertheless, in addition to the usual polemics, there appears to be a slight increase in the number of works concerned with serious analysis, particularly of the declining hegemony of the US in Latin America (see items **7043** and **7056**).

Another striking trend of the social sciences in the last biennium is the overwhelming reliance on history and use of the historical record to illuminate cultural patterns and socioeconomic issues. One geographer observes how "the dominant theme" among all works examined is "historical" (p. 419). An anthropologist emphasizes the "spectacular expansion of interest" in the "history of indigenous peoples" (p. 132). An archaeologist notes how "ethnohistoric studies continue to provide a rich fund of information concerning social structure" (p. 27). An ethnologist observes how "many scholars are using history" to shed light on cultural questions (p. 97). Thus, the present rise of interest in history among social scientists, especially anthropologists, and the concurrent rise of interest in indigenous peoples among historians reflects "the rapprochement of anthropologists and historians spurred in the US by symbolic anthropology and in France by structural history" (p. 132). Indeed, a "perceptive book" (item **940**) describes the emergence of historical structuralism as "the dominant perspective among Mexican anthropologists in the 1970s and early 1980s" (p. 96).

Concern with this aspect of Latin American history has also been spurred by "the indigenous people's own rising interest in their own past as they seek to redefine their identity" (pp. 132–133, and see items **1214, 1237, 1330,** and **1363**). In fact, "a major development of the last few years has been the strengthening identity and growing self-awareness of indigenous peoples," an attainment which is "reflected in the appearance of writings on indigenous cultures by members of those cultures themselves, on the initiative of indigenous authors, with an anthropologist (if any) acting merely as a go-between" (p. 129, and see items **1237** and **1363**). Sociologists in Mexico and Central America have also shown much concern in involving "the peasantry in the study of its own social conditions" by collecting numerous "peasant autobiographies or lengthy narrations" (p. 640). Such writings constitute an unprecedented social development and most likely herald a more active political participation by these indigenous and peasant groups who, having redefined their own past, will most likely go on to play an increasingly larger role in shaping their own future.

This is already the case in Brazil and other Amazonian countries where "the increasing sophistication of the pro-indigenous movement" is evident in its keen "interest in legal issues" (p. 132). The latter are carefully examined in the published proceedings of several conferences held to study native populations and national legislation (see items **1173, 1206, 1235, 1338,** and **1352**).

Interest in population movements, especially migration, continues to command much attention. In the Andes, migration studies focus on movements to colonization areas and cities (p. 167 and items **1421** and **1422**). In the Caribbean, "international migration continues to be the topic of greatest interest among sociologists" (p. 654). In Brazil, many works have appeared that attempt to analyze regional, rural-urban, and rural-rural population shifts, all of them based on the 1980 census (see items **5231, 5262, 5281**, and **5317**). Emigration is the principal interest of Uruguayan sociologists (p. 679) and migration to the US continues as a leading concern of Mexican social scientists (p. 639). There is, nevertheless, a decline in demographic studies of Mexico which coincides with the beginning of serious research into the question of drug addiction. This may be an indication that perhaps "drug abuse is becoming a social problem in Mexico" (p. 639 and see items **8051, 8085**, and **8093**). In Colombia, the literature on the nation's politics is "heavily influenced," among other things, by "the politics of drug trafficking" (p. 521). Moreover, efforts of the nation's military to eradicate the illicit drug trade worries one social scientist who anticipates that such a growing military role will move Colombia closer to "bureaucratic authoritarian rule" (p. 521 and see item **6360**).

A subject which continues to monopolize the attention of Mexican political scientists is organized labor (items **6049, 6052, 6090**, and **6093**). In Brazil there is much interest in the political role and participation of non-organized labor, particularly among agricultural workers (p. 555).

The establishment of "Women's Studies" as a legitimate field is most apparent in Colombia where "a well trained, insightful and productive group of women sociologists has made a mark" (p. 663). An example of the emergence of these female sociologists is their three-volume study of Colombian women (item **8228**). In the Caribbean, "studies on the status of women continue to proliferate" (p. 654 and see items **8160, 8173, 8177, 8198, 8202**, and **8220**). The organized impulse for such women's studies in this area can be attributed to a multidisciplinary project entitled "Women in the Caribbean" sponsored by the Institute of Social and Economic Research of the Univ. of the West Indies. Many research monographs examine themes such as "perceptions and stereotypes of Caribbean women (item **1023**), women and politics in Barbados (item **1050**), women, work and development (item **1058**), the demographics of employed women (item **1084**), women and education (item **1148**), and women and the family (item **1149**)" (p. 110).

To conclude we should note how one of the most important undertakings of the last decade has finally come to fruition during the last few years, the decoding of Maya hieroglyphic writing, an achievement that is generating unprecedented excitement in several fields: anthrolinguistics (items **1525, 1531, 1560, 1563, 1580**, and **1670**), archaeology (items **277, 284, 327, 503, 510, 519, 522, 523, 524, 530, 532**, and **533**) and ethnohistory (see our next volume, *HLAS 48*). The light such findings shed on this enigmatic and extraordinary culture has unprecedented implications for understanding the rise and fall of civilizations in the Americas. The significance of this breakthrough is not unlike Champollion's decoding of the Rosetta stone in the 1820s when the illumination of another mysterious culture on the banks of the Nile contributed much towards understanding the rise and fall of civilizations in Europe.

II. CHANGES IN VOLUME 47

Anthropology
Roger N. Rasnake, Goucher College, contributed the section on ethnology of the Andean highlands.

Economics

Raúl Moncarz, Florida International Univ., annotated the literature on the economy of Mexico. Charlotte Jones Carroll, The World Bank, and Thomas F. Carroll, George Washington Univ., collaborated with Francisco Thoumi by preparing the subsection on the economy of Ecuador. Mostafa Hassan, Florida International Univ., collaborated with Jorge Salazar-Carrillo in annotating the literature on the economy of Venezuela.

Government and Politics

Steve C. Ropp, University of Wyoming, reviewed materials on Central America.

Sociology

Dennis Gilbert, Barbara Deutsch Lynch and Patricia Garrett, Cornell University, collaborated in preparing the section on Peru and Ecuador.

Table of Contents

As of this volume, the table of contents of the *Handbook* will be expanded to feature not merely the disciplinary and regional breakdowns as has been customary (e.g., Archaeology, Mesoamerica) but all subsections within such breakdowns wherever they appear (e.g., I. Archaeology; 1) Mesoamerica; a) General, b) Fieldwork and Artifacts, c) Native Sources and Epigraphy). The reasons for the expansion of our table of contents are related to the reduction of our subject index as is explained in the following paragraph.

Subject Index

As stated in previous volumes, the policy of the *HLAS* Subject Index is to use the Library of Congress Subject Headings as much as possible but when necessary to adapt them to terms that predominate in the literature as familiar and useful ones to Latin Americanists. In 1984–85, as is noted on the title page of this volume, the *HLAS* editorial staff was reduced from five to four individuals. As a result, the *HLAS* subject index of this volume was also reduced by excluding geographic index terms. The next volume or *HLAS 48*, however, will once again feature city, state, and regional geographic terms. Cross references ("see also" terms) have also been eliminated from this volume but subject terms have remained the same to insure consistency with previous volumes and facilitate research. For related subject terms, the user should consult the *Library of Congress Subject Headings* or the subject indexes of previous *HLAS* volumes. Finally, subject headings which appear in our newly expanded table of contents will no longer appear in the subject index.

Other Changes

Changes in the editorial staff of the *Handbook*, the administrative officers of the Library of Congress, and membership of the Advisory Board are reflected in the title page of the present volume.

Dolores Moyano Martin

HANDBOOK OF
LATIN AMERICAN STUDIES:
No. 47

BIBLIOGRAPHY AND GENERAL WORKS

JOHN R. HEBERT, *Assistant Chief, Hispanic Division, Library of Congress*

THE NUMBER OF TIMELY and useful bibliographies and general works did not diminish during the period in which materials were surveyed for this section. Indeed, the quality of these research aids has improved so that simple listings of bibliographical citations unaided by critical review constitute a minority. One cannot but consider such a development a critical indication that, at long last, scholarly demands for more than simple listings have been heeded by those who prepare research aids; of course, it is likely that those demanding quality research works may be the same individuals who compile them.

As in previous volumes of *HLAS*, this section contains examples of a variety of publications that appear as general bibliographies, national bibliographies, subject bibliographies, personal and collective bibliographies, catalogs, works on library science, research and reference works, general works, and selected new serial titles. The quantity of publications that falls within any of these categories is so vast that it would be impossible to be all inclusive and review them all. One hopes that those selected and annotated below are representative of the whole and of use to researchers who consult this volume.

Occasionally, well presented general bibliographies appear and their contributions are noted. Of those appearing recently, the Institut des hautes études de l'Amérique latine's (Paris) semiannual *Bibliographie latinoaméricaine d'articles* (item 1) contains listings from 175 journals from the Hispanic world. The *CARICOM Bibliography* (item 2), produced by the Caribbean Community Secretariat's library, includes items listed in the national bibliographies of Barbados, Guyana, Jamaica, Trinidad and Tobago and entries from other English-speaking areas of the Caribbean. In the CLIO Press's World Bibliographical Series, offerings on Haiti, Panama, and Mexico serve as useful introductions to these countries. Equally useful as a national listing, but more comprehensive, is Beverley Steele's 1983 *Grenada bibliography* (item 3) which is a welcome addition to the literature. Among this group one must recognize the *Hispanic American Periodical Index, 1970–74* (item 5) which contains references to articles, reports, original literary works, and other works found in 229 journal titles with material on Latin America.

The appearance of national bibliographies is always welcomed. While those produced in the English-speaking Caribbean (e.g., the national bibliographies of Jamaica, Barbados, Trinidad and Tobago, Guyana) appear regularly, those on other parts of the region appear from time to time and should be noted. The *Bibliográfia Brasileira* (item 10) is the new format and title for the *Boletim Bibliográfico da Biblioteca Nacional*, a work that the Brazilian national library has issued for several years; the *Bibliografía Uruguaya* (item 11) produced by the Biblioteca del Poder Legislativo Nacional, provides a listing of Uruguayan publications produced 1973–77. Its appearance reintroduces the publication of a much desired record for Uruguay.

While the number and utility of subject bibliographies vary in this *HLAS*, a number of themes are dominant and include studies of the Antilles, Argentina, education, and economics.

Bibliografía económica de México (item **17**) by the Banco de México and the Banco Central de la República Dominicana's *Bibliografía económica dominicana, 1978–1982* (item **18**) provide extensive information on each country's economy. Of international interest is the *Guía bancaria latinoamericana* (item **91**), produced by the Federación Latinoamericana de Bancos, which provides capsule information on member banks throughout Latin America. The Seminar for the Acquisition of Latin American Library Materials XXVI concentrated on Latin American economic issues. Selected papers (item **63**) from that 1981 meeting, held in New Orleans, provide information on public and private sector interests on economic issues.

A growing interest in the history and the current direction of the varied Caribbean nations and entities is evident in the publication of bibliographies and other reference resources. Philip Boucher and Gabriel Debien's "Chronique bibliographique de l'histoire des Antilles françaises, 1979–1982" (item **24**) lists current articles and monographs on the subject; Rosemary Brana-Shute's *A bibliography of Caribbean migration and Caribbean immigrant communities* (item **22**) provides nearly 2600 citations on the topic; Stephen Glazier's article "An Annotated Ethnographic Bibliography of Trinidad" (item **32**) is more specifically related to national interests in that major Caribbean nation; Phillip Jeffrey's and Maureen Newton's *Selected annotated bibliography of studies on the Caribbean Community* (item **45**) was published by the Caribbean Community in Georgetown, Guyana; Marianne Ramesar's *A select bibliography on publications and studies relating to human resources in the Commonwealth Caribbean* (item **46**) provides access to materials available in the Institute of Social and Economic Research, University of the West Indies, Trinidad; and Enriqueta Vila Vilar's "Bibliografía Básica para la Historia de Puerto Rico" (item **48**) covers the period from prehispanic to the present. A number of general publications on the Caribbean are found in this section. *Les années trente à Cuba* (item **116**) contains 16 articles on the Cuban economy and social movements during the 1930s; the publication contains the papers presented during a November 1980 colloquium sponsored by the Centre interuniversitaire d'études cubaines and the Université de la Sorbonne-Nouvelle, Paris. *Ten years of CARICOM* (item **128**) publishes papers presented at a seminar on economic integration in the Caribbean, held in Bridgetown, Barbados, July 1983. Two useful biographical studies include the 7th ed. of *Personalities Caribbean* (item **107**), an international guide to who's who in the West Indies, providing biographical descriptions of selected individuals in the English and Dutch-speaking countries of the Caribbean, as well as Puerto Rico; *Who's Who in Jamaica*, 15th ed., (item **115**) provides information on selected individuals in Jamaican life.

Although not impressive in number, the bibliographies, on education in Latin America annotated below, should be useful to the researcher. The UNESCO's regional office on Education has produced *Bibliografía sobre educación en Perú: años 1980 a 1983* (item **19**). Alicia Castro de Salmerón *et al.*'s *Bibliografía sobre educación superior en América Latina* (item **20**) lists 940 entries on higher education.

A noteworthy number of publications in this section provide references to Argentine history and literature. Roberto Etchepareborda's *Historiografía militar argentina* (item **28**) provides an overview of the Argentine military; Luis Alberto Musso Ambrosio's "Anotaciones de Bibliografía Uruguaya sobre Historia Argentina en el Período 1831–1852: Epoca de Rosas" (item **40**) is a useful addition to the references on the Rosas period; Graciela Barcala de Moyano's "Bibliografía del Doctor Ricardo R. Caillet-Bois" (item **50**) lists 426 publications by the noted Argentine historian; and Julián Cáceres Freyre's "Bibliografía del Profesor Milcíades Acejo Vignati" (item **52**) lists publications by the author between 1916 and 1973.

Several recent guides to archival and library collections have appeared. Vol. 13 of the *Anais da Biblioteca e Arquivo Públicos do Pará* (1983, item **57**) is devoted to a description of Pará's archives and collections. Norma García Mainieri's "Situación Archivística Actual en Guatemala" (item **73**) includes a brief description of the state of archival training in that Central American nation. Roy Boland's 1984 publication, *A select bibliography of serials relating to Hispanic language, literature, and civilization held by libraries in Australia and New Zealand* (item **112**) describes holdings in 146 libraries. Rodolfo Ruz Menéndez's brief article "Los Archivos del Estado de Yucatán" (item **111**) provides a description of the contents and the history of seven archives in Yucatán.

Equally valuable to the researcher are the numerous reference works that have appeared in this volume. Three works of particular interest are worthy of note: Enrique Carrizosa Argáez's *Linajes y bibliografías de nuestros gobernantes, 1830–1982* (item **79**) contains information on Colombia's chief executives and their families since Domingo Caicedo in 1830; *Estudios fronterizos México-Estados Unidos: directorio general de investigadores* (item **87**) compiled by the Centro de Estudios Fronterizos del Norte de México in Tijuana, contains information on research in progress on a broad range of themes concerning US-Mexican border studies; the Instituto de Fomento Industrial's *Inventario de estudios e informes existentes en las agencias regionales del IFI* (item **99**) lists the publications of the seven regional agencies of this institute.

I was pleasantly surprised by the large number of publications on the subject of book production in Latin America. The variety of themes covered should be of interest to this *Handbook*'s varied audience. Among the noteworthy volumes were the Centro Regional para el Fomento del Libro en América Latina y el Caribe (CERLAL)'s 1982 *Políticas nacionales del libro* (item **126**) which is part of a group of studies prepared in response to a demand by UNESCO to provide profiles of national publishing industries of Latin America issued at the 1982 International Book Congress in London. The final report of the Regional Congress on Books for Latin America and the Caribbean (item **127**), held in Rio de Janeiro (Dec. 1982), serves to diffuse in Latin America and the Caribbean the UNESCO program of action to promote a reading society. With these, a number of items on national publishing appeared, including Bernardo Subercaseaux's *La industria editorial y el libro en Chile, 1930–1984* (item **129**); a brief article "La Actividad Editorial en Cuba" (item **19**) which provides an overview of book publishing and distribution in Cuba since Castro; an article in of *El Libro Español* (Feb. 1983), "En América Latina se Produce 36,300 Titulos por Año" (item **122**) contains a concise overview on current Latin American book production by country; another issue of *El Libro Español* (Feb. 1984) featured an article by Alvaro Garzón López, "La Libre Circulación del Libro en América Latina" (item **120**), which addresses a Spanish proposal to improve the circulation of Iberian imprints in Latin America. Finally, Pedro Grases' 1967 *La Imprenta en Venezuela* (item **121**) reappeared in 1981.

Growing interest in automation, computerization, and library network development is evident in the number of publications devoted to these topics. Several studies examine areas of political upheaval (e.g., Central America and the Caribbean) as well as the Latin American economies. The problem of national bibliographies continues to loom as large as ever in the sense that new publications and/or advances in some countries are offset by reversals in others. As a result, most Latin American national bibliographies are more often than not either unreliable or inconsistent or both. The preparation and execution of these crucial tools should become a key priority of the governments and national book systems of each country.

The purpose of this introductory statement is to highlight the more important works and trends among publications annotated below. Individual researchers should bear in mind that many more works are published and available than those selected for this HLAS section. Therefore, if a particular topic or specific publication does not appear below, the reasons are neither neglect nor unavailability but the strict space limitations of *HLAS* which is, above all, a "selective" bibliography.

GENERAL BIBLIOGRAPHIES

1 *Bibliographie latinoaméricaine d'articles*. Institut des hautes études de l'Amérique latine, Centre de documentation. No. 17, nov. 1984– . Paris.

Work does not include articles in French, Swiss, Belgium or Quebecan periodicals related to Latin America (such items are found in *Bulletin bibliographique Amérique latine* issued by GREC 26, CNRS), but contains articles appearing in 175 journals, mainly Spanish, issued between 1980–84. Entries appear in sections arranged by country and within specific subject areas per country.

2 *The CARICOM Bibliography*. Caribbean Community Secretariat, Information and Documentation Section. Vol. 5, No. 2, 1981– . Georgetown, Guyana.

Cumulated subject list of current national imprints of Caribbean Community member countries arranged by Dewey Decimal Classification order. Items listed are compiled from the national bibliographies of Barbados, Guyana, Jamaica, and Trinidad and Tobago along with entries from the territories which do not yet produce national bibliographies.

3 **Grenada bibliography.** Compiled by Beverley A. Steele. St. George's, Grenada: Extra Mural Dept., Univ. of West Indies, 1983. 119 p. (Marryshow House publications; 2)

Groundbreaking effort presents publications on Grenada in two separate sections (i.e., by subject and author). Newspaper and magazine articles selectively appear. Location of items not given.

4 **Haiti.** Frances Chambers, compiler. Oxford, England: Clio Press, 1983. 177 p., 1 leaf of plates: index, map (World bibliographical series; 39)

This publication, part of the World Bibliographical Series of ABC-Clio, contains annotated entries on works dealing with Haiti's history, geography, economy, politics, culture, customs, religion, and social organization of its people. It is intended for the general reader, undergraduate student, and librarian interested in building a library collection. Contains over 550 citations, articles and monographs, in 37 categories; English language publications predominate. General index appears.

5 *HAPI: Hispanic American Periodicals Index*: 1970–1974. v. 1, A-I. v. 2, J-Z. v. 3, Authors. Edited by Barbara G. Valk. Los Angeles: UCLA, Latin American Center, 1984. 3 v. (1545 p.)

Three-vol. work designed to provide a bridge between the *Index to Latin American Periodical Literature* and its supplement, which ceased publication in 1970 and the annual *Hispanic American Periodicals Index* which commenced with articles appearing in 1975. Lists by subject and author, articles, documents, reports, bibliographies, original literary works, and other items appearing in 229 journal titles published throughout the world, which regularly contain information on Latin America.

6 **Meeting microcomputers and bibliographic information systems in Latin America:** problems, experiences and projections, Santiago, Chile, 24 to 27 April, 1984. Santiago: ECLA, International Development Research Centre: UNESCO, 1984. 54 p.

The 1984 meeting was convened to discuss the relationship of microcomputers and bibliographic information systems, to discuss the basic functional specifications to be met by software used, to review methodologies for analyzing the advantages and disadvantages of existing software suitable for the retrieval and dissemination of bibliographic information, to examine the feasibility of creating new software or adapting existing software, to analyze the problems raised by data exchange and software set up in different microcomputers with emphasis on standards, and to begin to identify cooperative schemes. A limited number of participants was invited to exchange views.

7   Mexico. Naomi C. Robbins, compiler. Edited by Sheila R. Herstein. Oxford, England: Clio Press, 1984. 165 p., 1 leaf of plates: index, map (World bibliographical series; 48)

Contains 640 entries arranged into 48 subject categories. Includes primarily publications in English. As most bibliographies in World Bibliographical Series, work is intended for the general public, reference librarian, and undergraduate student interested in Mexico. Publications listed are contemporary 20th-century works.

8   Moraes, Rubens Borba de. Bibliographia brasiliana: rare books about Brazil published from 1504 to 1900 and works by Brazilian authors of the colonial period. Rev. and enl. ed. Los Angeles: UCLA, Latin American Center Publications; Rio de Janeiro: Livraria Kosmos Editôra, 1983. 2 v. (1074 p.): bibl., ill., index (Reference series; 10)

Revised and enlarged ed. of Moraes appears more than 20 years after 1958 ed. Contains over 50 percent more material than first ed. and its more than 10,000 citations describe works published abroad (1504–1900) and works of Brazilian authors published before Brazil's independence in 1822. Contains general index.

9   Panama. Eleanor DeSelms Langstaff, compiler. Edited by Sheila R. Herstein. Oxford, England: Clio Press, 1982. 184 p.: index, map (World bibliographical series; 14)

World Bibliographical Series of ABC-Clio, publication provides introduction to the literature of Panama for general English-speaking audience, although Spanish language publications do appear. Includes general index.

NATIONAL BIBLIOGRAPHIES

10   Bibliografia Brasileira. Biblioteca Nacional. Vol. 1, No. 1/2, 1983– . Rio de Janeiro.

This is a new format to the *Boletim Bibliográfico da Biblioteca Nacional;* also available in microfiche. Same information is provided on current publications in Brazil, with entries appearing in Dewey Decimal Classification order. Includes author, title, and subject indexes.

11   Bibliografía Uruguaya. Biblioteca del Poder Legislativo. Vol. 1/2, 1983– . Montevideo.

Provides a listing of Uruguayan publications produced from 1973–77. Includes title, subject, classification, publisher, imprint, and onomastic indexes.

12   Jamaican National Bibliography. National Library of Jamaica. Vol. 9, No. 4, Jan./Dec. 1983 [i.e. 1984]– . Kingston.

Subject list of Jamaican materials received in the National Library, arranged according to the Dewey Decimal Classification. Includes author-title index, publishers list, selected Jamaican serial list, Ministry papers list, and articles in selected Jamaican serials.

13   National Bibliography of Barbados. Public Library. Jan./Dec. 1982 [i.e. 1984]– . Bridgetown.

Cumulative listing of 1982 works published in Barbados or authored by Barbadians. Excludes periodicals (except first issues) and certain government publications. Provides 1982 statuatory measures, bills, and congressional debates.

SUBJECT BIBLIOGRAPHIES

14   Artesanato brasileiro: uma contribuição à sua bibliografia. Organizada por Inalda Monteiro Silvestre, Sylvia Pereira de Holanda Cavalcanti. Recife: Fundação Joaquim Nabuco, Instituto de Documentação, Biblioteca Central Blanche Knopf: Editora Massangana, 1981. 114 p.: index (Série Obras de consulta; 2)

Contains a broad range of items, both monographic and periodical titles, on the theme of the artisan in Brazil. Includes separate author-subject index. Identifies library location of items.

15 **Azócar, Jesús Napoleón.** Bibliografía del Estado Monagas. Maturín, Venezuela: Gobernación del Estado Monagas, Instituto Autónoma Biblioteca Nacional y de Servicios de Bibliotecas, 1982. 262 p. (Col. Guanipa. Ensayos e investigaciones)

Lists 778 citations related to state of Monagas, Venezuela. Entries are organized according to categories (i.e., reference works, publications on the state, official publications, periodical publications of the state, and articles on Monagas). Includes separate title, geographic, and onomastic indexes. Provides names of state authors and towns they are from. Brief introductory essay on the state describes administrative history and cultural and publishing interests.

16 **Bibliografía anotada sobre población/planificación familiar:** Colombia. Coordinación y edición, Adriana de Barella. Resúmenes, localización y ordenamiento del material, Piedad Pérez García-Herreros et al. Bogotá: Asociación Colombiana para el Estudio de la Población: Corporación Centro Regional de Población, 1984. 284 p.: indexes.

Contains nearly 600 annotated entries on population and family planning in Colombia. Citations are found in 13 separate sections, including entries on mortality, birth control, migration, geographic distribution of the population, family and marriage, economy, education, health, employment, housing and transportation, fertility. Includes author, title, subject, and institutional indexes.

17 **Bibliografía económica de México:** libros, 1979–1980. México: Banco de México, Biblioteca, 1984. 1 v.: index.

Listing of current publications arranged by topic (e.g., methodology, economic development, production, balance of payments, money and banking, public finances, social economy, statistics, and legislation). Items are not described. Includes author index.

18 **Bibliografía económica dominicana, 1978–1982.** Santo Domingo: Banco Central de la República Dominicana, 1983. 125 p.: index.

Prepared on the 36th anniversary of the Banco Central. Includes all references to publications on the economy of the Dominican Republic located in the Biblioteca Juan Pablo Duarte of the Banco Central. Entries appear in alphabetical order by author. Includes subject index.

19 **Bibliografía sobre educación en Perú:** años 1980 a 1983. Santiago: Centro de Documentación e Información, Oficina Regional de Educación de la UNESCO para América Latina y el Caribe, 1984. 10 p.

Lists 112 articles and monographs and 18 periodical titles on the theme. Items appear in alphabetical order by author. Provides introductory information on contemporary research.

20 **Bibliografía sobre educación superior en América Latina.** Compilada por Alicia Castro de Salmerón, María Elena Saucedo Lugo, María Graciela Alvarez de Pérez. México: UNAM, 1983. 197 p.: indexes.

Selected listing of 940 entries considered of greatest interest for the study of higher education in Latin America. Compilation based on information found in the Asociación Nacional de Universidades e Instituciones de Educación Superior (ANUIES), Centro de Documentación Legislativa Universitaria (CDLU), and Unión de Universidades de América Latina (UDUAL). Entries were published 1975–81. Includes subject and country and region indexes.

21 **Bibliografía sobre las Islas Malvinas.** Buenos Aires: Ministerio de Educación, Centro Nacional de Documentación e Información Educativa, 1982. 14 p.: map (Nueva serie divulgación; 24)

Lists 64 publications from five Argentine libraries, intended for use by students and teachers. Items appear in alphabetical order by author.

22 **A Bibliography of Caribbean migration and Caribbean immigrant communities.** Compiled and edited by Rosemary Brana-Shute with the assistance of Rosemarijn Hoefte. Gainesville: Reference and Bibliographic Dept., Univ. of Florida Libraries in cooperation with the Center for Latin American Studies, Univ. of Florida, 1983. 339 p.: appendices, index (Bibliographic series; 9)

Provides 2585 citations on the topic, with the exclusion of works on the African slave trade and precolumbian migrations which the author feels have been treated elsewhere. Entries appear in alphabetical order by author; appendices provide separately list of computerized databases consulted, list of periodicals cited, list of second or joint authors, indexes on the origin and destination of migrants, and topical index.

23 **Bonfiglio, Giovanni.** Desarrollo de la comunidad y trabajo social: ensayo: bibliografía. Lima: Celats Ediciones, 1982. 269 p.: bibl., indexes.

Contains over 2000 entries devoted to the subject of social work and community development; over 70 percent of titles were published between 1950–69. Another 26 percent of the works have appeared since 1970. Entries are presented in alphabetical order by author; separate subject, author, geographic, and journal indexes appear. Includes introductory essay.

24 **Boucher, Philip** and **Gabriel Debien.** Chronique bibliographique de l'histoire des Antilles françaises, 1979–1982. Aubenas, France: Imprimerie Leinhart, 1985. 75 p. (Notes d'histoire coloniale; 230. Extrait du *Bulletin de la Société d'histoire de la Guadeloupe*; 59)

Provides bibliographical citations to current publications, articles and monographs, concerning history of French Antilles. Includes not only French islands and Caribbean mainland (i.e., Guyane) but also refers to French in Louisiana. Important assessment of current research.

25 **Caspar, Dale E.** The urban development of Latin America: recent writings, 1977–1983. Monticello, Ill.: Vance Bibliographies, 1984. 14 p. (Public administration series. Bibliography, O193–970X; P-1486)

Brief, selected bibliography on topic; items, both articles and monographs, are arranged in categories by region (e.g., general works, Mexico, West Indies, South America). Items appear in alphabetical order by author in each section. Useful introductory work on relatively current publishing.

26 **Devas, Esmond.** A check list of Caribbean tourism studies. Rev. Barbados, West Indies: Caribbean Tourism Research and Development Centre, 1983. 20 p.

Although not comprehensive, the publication does provide coverage of works on tourism in the wider Caribbean, with emphasis on publications appearing since 1970. Items appear by country arrangement; general works are listed in the regional studies section.

27 **Durand, Francisco.** La industria en el Perú: bibliografía (UP/EA, 9:17/18, p. 195–246)

Identifies more than 1200 citations found in a review of 28 Peruvian libraries and research institutions covering fields of industry and industrialization. Publications identified include theses, articles, and monographs; locations of each item are indicated. Entries appear in alphabetical order by author.

28 **Etchepareborda, Roberto.** Historiografía militar argentina. Buenos Aires: Círculo Militar, 1984. 205 p.: bibl.

Author provides fine overview, historiographically, of the military in Argentina through an essay fully supplemented by a bibliography—divided by chronology and events—of key works on the subject. Etchepareborda has provided an excellent source for information on resources for the study of the field. Includes works published in 1980.

29 **Fernández, José B.** and **Roberto G. Fernández.** Indice bibliográfico de autores cubanos: diáspora, 1959–1979: literatura = Bibliographical index of Cuban authors: diaspora, 1959–1979: literature. Miami, Fla.: Ediciones Universal, 1983. 106 p.: appendix, bibl., index.

Main objective of bibliography is to list works produced by Cuban authors and critics living abroad with the hope that it would serve as a source of information to those interested in the Cuban diaspora and especially its literary figures. Entries appear in the following categories: short story, novel, poetry, theater, folklore, literary criticism and culture, and linguistics. A total of 971 entries appear. Appendix provides location of Cuban imprints. Includes author index.

30 **Foster, David William.** Bibliografía literaria hispanoamericana, 1980–1981 (IILI/RI, 49:122, enero/marzo 1983, p. 235–241)

Describes recent publications of bibliographic studies on Spanish-American literature, divided into brief references to general bibliographies, special/subject bibliographies such as those on literary themes (e.g., women writers, ethnic influences), indexes, guides to theses and dissertations, and special or personal bibliographies on key authors. Author provides a good contemporary update of key works.

31 Garst, Rachel. Bibliografía anotada de obras de referencia sobre Centroamérica y Panamá en el campo de las ciencias sociales. San José: Instituto de Investigaciones Sociales, Univ. de Costa Rica; s.l.: Friends World College, Latin American Center, 1983. 2 v. (662 p.): indexes.

Identifies sources by subject area and by location of publication. Lists over 1400 citations. Includes author, title, and subject indexes. Provides description of resource centers by country.

32 Glazier, Stephen D. An annotated ethnographic bibliography of Trinidad (HRAF/BSR, 17:1/2, Spring/Summer 1982, p. 31–58, bibl.)

Provides annotated citations (i.e., articles, books, and dissertations) on the ethnographic literature of Trinidad with special attention to the island's ethnic diversity. Entries appear in alphabetical order by author. Also includes selected, unannotated list of master's theses.

González, José Luis and Teresa María van Ronzelen. Religiosidad popular en el Perú: bibliografía: antropología, historia, sociología y pastoral. See item 8276

33 Hernández G., María Magdalena. Bibliografía colombiana sobre pequeña y mediana industria, 1960–1980. Bogotá: Ministerio de Educación Nacional, Fondo Colombiano de Investigaciones Científicas y Proyectos Especiales Francisco José de Caldas, 1982 [i.e. 1983]. 90 p.: indexes.

Contains over 1000 citations on the theme. Provides subject, co-author, and geographic indexes and indicates library location of items cited.

34 Human services in postrevolutionary Cuba: an annotated international bibliography. Compiled by Larry R. Oberg. Westport, Conn.: Greenwood Press, 1984. 433 p.: indexes.

Contains over 2000 citations, some annotated, of works published 1959–82 on Cuban education, public health, housing, sports, youth, women, and ethnic minorities appearing in books, chapters in books, pamphlets, articles, government agency publications, dissertations, and some newspaper and encyclopedia articles. Includes separate author, title, and subject indexes.

35 Hux, Meinrado. El indio en la llanura del Plata: guía bibliográfica. La Plata, Argentina: Dirección General de Escuelas, Archivo Histórico Ricardo Levene, 1984. 262 p.: indexes.

Lists over 5100 monographs and articles and nearly 500 maps related to the theme. Provides contents of separate journal issues selectively. Includes separate subject, foreign traveler, and expedition indexes. Uses separate geographical index for map segment.

36 Klementeva, N.M. Razvitie sviazei mezhdu SSSR i riadom stran Latinskoi Ameriki v oblasti kultury, 1965–1975: bibliograficheskii ukazatel = Developments of relations between the USSR and a number of countries in Latin America in the sphere of culture, 1965–1975: bibliographic guide. Otvetstvennyi redaktor i avtor vstupitelnoi stati, A.I. Sizonenko. Moskva: Vses. gos. biblioteka inostrannoi lit-ry, 1983. 172 p.: index.

Covers development of such relations, with principal interest lying in two sections, Soviet culture in Latin America and Latin American culture in Soviet Union. 870 entries. Index by country and by subject. [R.V. Allen]

37 Latin American politics: a historical bibliography. Santa Barbara, Calif.: ABC-Clio Information Services, 1984. 290 p.: indexes (Clio bibliography series; 16)

Entries are drawn from ABC Clio's history data base from which every abstract on Latin American politics was selected. Publication represents a decade (1973–82) of journal literature on Latin America and the Caribbean since 1914 found in approximately 2000 journals from 90 countries in ABC Clio data base. Provides author and subject indexes and periodical listing.

38 McKanna, Clare V. The frontier in comparative view: a bibliography (PCCLAS/P, 1980/1981, p. 149–168)

Selected, annotated listing of 155 items (i.e., articles, monographs) on theme of the frontier in history. Substantial listings of publications on the frontier in the Spanish Americas.

39 Martins, Antonio J. Etat et société en Amérique latine: éléments de bibliographie (ULB/RIS, 1/2, 1981, p. 397–426)

Author provides selected listing of current publications (i.e., primarily 1970s) related to theme of the State and society in Latin America. Publications are grouped into three themes: 1) state and society: the populist relations; 2) state and society: the authoritarian relations; 3) statism and the bureaucracy of the State. Bibliographical essay on multiple themes precedes listing.

40 Musso, Luis Alberto. Anotaciones de bibliografía uruguaya sobre historia argentina en el período 1831–1852: época de Rosas (EEHA/HBA, 23, 1979, p. 121–138, bibl.)

Lists Uruguayan books and pamphlets on Rosas period in Argentina. Annotated entries appear in alphabetical order by author. Useful, selected compilation drawn from vast corpus of writings on subject.

————. Bibliografía básica de la historia de la República Oriental del Uruguay hasta 1973: pt. 2. See *HLAS 46:3434.*

41 Noticia para la bibliografía anarquista en México (CEHSMO, 5:20, sept. 1980, p. 20–26)

Reproduction of work prepared in 1927 by José C. Valades, in Mexico. Contains random collection of publications, journal titles, articles, and monographs, that were published in 19th and early 20th century that the compiler felt related to the study of anarchism in Mexico.

Oberg, Larry R. Human services in postrevolutionary Cuba: an annotated international bibliography. See item 8206

42 Oquelí, Ramón. Bibliografía sociopolítica de Honduras. Tegucigalpa: Univ. Nacional Autónoma de Honduras, Editorial Universitaria, 1981. 106 p. (Col. Cuadernos universitarios; 15)

Provides listing of 1332 entries on the theme, presented in alphabetical order by author. No indexes or division of works by subject appears.

43 Osán de Pérez Sáez, Fanny and **Iris Rossi.** Contribución a la bibliografía de la literatura saltena. Salta, Argentina: Univ. Nacional de Salta, 1982. 52 p.: indexes.

Contains 560 items related to literature in or on Salta, Argentina. Entries are grouped by subject (i.e., under anthologies, essays, folklore, poetry, poetic prose, narrative prose, theater, and various). Includes separate onomastic and titles indexes.

44 The Perceptual and socio-cultural dimensions of the tourism environment: an annotated bibliography. Washington: International Trade and Tourism Division, Dept. of Economic Affairs, OAS: Travel and Tourism Program, George Washington Univ., 1983. 123 p.: indexes.

Bibliography, containing nearly 500 annotated entries, is divided into three sections (i.e., tourism, environmental perception, tourism and environmental perception). Although work provides broad variety of international examples, it emphasizes the Caribbean, where tourism affects a diversity of social, cultural, and environmental conditions, often in the context of small, physically contained island environments. Includes subject and geographical location indexes.

Podestá, Bruno. Estudios latinoamericanos en Italia: el caso peruano, 1960–1979. See *HLAS 46:3008.*

Rey Balmaceda, Raúl. Comunidades extranjeras en la Argentina: contribución a una bibliografía. See *HLAS 46:3331.*

Seiferheld, Alfredo M. El Paraguay visto a través del idioma alemán: un intento de bibliografía en alemán sobre el Paraguay. See *HLAS 46:3402.*

45 Select annotated bibliography of studies on the Caribbean Community. Compiled by Phillip Jeffrey and Maureen Newton. Georgetown, Guyana: Information and Documentation Section, Caribbean Community Secretariat, 1983. 17 p.

Selected annotated bibliography prepared on the occasion of the symposium "Ten Years of the CARICOM Integration Experience" (Barbados, July 1983). Entries appear in varied sections devoted to: theories and concepts of integration and their Third World applications, studies of the Caribbean community, legal aspects, trade aspects, monetary and financial aspects, LDCs and CARICOM, and external relations.

46 A Select bibliography of publications and studies relating to human resources in the Commonwealth Caribbean:

material available in Trinidad and Tobago. Compiled by Marianne Ramesar. St. Augustine, Trinidad: Institute of Social and Economic Research, Univ. of the West Indies, 1981. 127 p.: index (Occasional papers. Human resources; 3)

Bibliography intended as a guide for researchers in the ongoing Human Resources and other programs of the Institute of Social and Economic Research at the Univ. of the West Indies, St. Augustine, Trinidad. Publication is divided into chapters on manpower and employment, industrial relations, attitudes to work, education and training, and population. Entries in each chapter are divided by geographic area. Includes author index.

Soares, Maria Regina de Lima and **Gerson Moura.** Brasil-Argentina: fontes bibliográficas. See *HLAS 46:3355.*

47 Tesauros, bibliografia, 1970/1982 = Thesauri, bibliography, 1970/1982. Compilada por Suly Cambraia Alves. Organizada, revista e ampliada por Marisa Bräscher Basílio, Simone Bastos. Brasília: Conselho Nacional de Desenvolvimento Científico e Tecnológico, Instituto Brasileiro de Informação em Ciência e Tecnologia, Centro de Informação em Ciência da Informação, 1983. 163 p.: bibl., indexes.

Contains listings of thesauri and national and international literature about them. Publication's objective is to provide fundamental information to allow the control of terminology in the creation and presentation of bibliographies. Cites over 800 publications with author, subject, and title indexes provided.

Vieira Filho, Domingos. Populário maranhense: bibliografia. See *HLAS 46:1039.*

48 Vila Vilar, Enriqueta. Bibliografía básica para la historia de Puerto Rico (EEHA/HBA, 23, 1979, p. 97–116, bibl.)

Useful annotated listing of key works on the history of Puerto Rico from the prehispanic period to the 20th century. Selected bibliographies and history journals are given.

COLLECTIVE AND PERSONAL BIBLIOGRAPHIES

Agosin, Marjorie. Bibliografía de Violeta Parra. See *HLAS 46:1071.*

49 Agraz García de Alba, Gabriel. Biobibliografía general de Don José María Vigil. México: UNAM, 1981. 286 p., 69 p. of plates: ill., index.

Provides a variety of information on José María Vigil (1829–1909), noted Mexican writer and head of the National Library for over 29 years. Includes general index.

50 Barcala de Moyano, Graciela G. Bibliografía del Doctor Ricardo R. Caillet-Bois (ANH/B, 52, 1979, p. 279–315)

Lists 426 publications, articles, books, reviews, introductions, presentations, by the noted Argentine historian. Subject and title indexes are given. Compilation is most useful in identifying Caillet-Bois's long interest in the history of the Malvinas and in the influence of the French Revolution on Spanish America and especially the La Plata region.

51 Becco, Horacio Jorge. Bibliografía de Pedro Grases. Caracas: Talleres de Cromotip, 1984. 102 p.: indexes, plate.

Lists publications by the noted Venezuelan author including books, pamphlets, prologues, compilations, works in collaboration, and contributions in collected works. Includes general and chronological indexes for Grases works (1931–84).

52 Cáceres Freyre, Julián. Bibliografía del Profesor Milcíades Alejo Vignati (ANH/B, 52, 1979, p. 263–278)

Provides a listing of 225 publications by the Argentine author (1916–73).

53 Espejo Beshers, Olga. Clarice Lispector: a bibliography (RIB, 34:3/4, 1984, p. 385–402)

Provides listing of works by the Brazilian author and publications (i.e., books, dissertations, chapters of books, and critical articles) about her writings. Most entries about Lispector are annotated.

54 Monzón M. de Velásquez, Imelda. Biografía y bibliografía de y sobre Carlos Samayoa Chinchilla (Letras de Guatemala [San Carlos, Guatemala] 2, dic. 1980, p. 63–73)

Provides listing of publications (i.e., monographs, introductions, articles) prepared by the noted Guatemalan author (1898–1973). Also includes writings about him. Samayoa Chinchilla was involved for many years in Guatemalan newspaper work as well as holding high level governmental positions, including Director of the National Library of Guatemala (1947–48).

55 Peri Rossi, Cristina. Julio Cortázar: bibliografía (El Libro Español [Instituto Nacional del Libro Español (INLE), Madrid] 309, marzo 1984, p. 82–84, plate)

Provides useful biographical and bibliographical essay on noted Argentine author (d. 1984).

56 Vargas e os anos cinqüenta: bibliografia. Compilada por Ana Lígia Silva Medeiros, Maria Celina Soares d'Araújo. Rio de Janeiro: Instituto de Documentação, Editôra Fundação Getúlio Vargas, 1983. 155 p.: ill., index.

Listing of works that follows the lines of research developed in the Center of Research and Documentation of Contemporary Brazilian History (CPDOC) which intends to provide information that facilitates study of recent Brazilian history. With a listing of 1095 items, this reference to the former Brazilian president provides separate listings for political party activity, populism, energy matters, international relations, the military, the 1954 crisis, administration of government, speeches and messages of Getúlio Vargas, and biographical references. Library location of items cited appears. Includes general index.

Tesler, Mario. Aportes de Diego Luis Molinari a la cultura hispanoamericana: ensayo bibliográfico. See *HLAS 46:3361.*

LIBRARY SCIENCE AND SERVICES

57 *Anais da Biblioteca e Arquivo Públicos do Pará.* Vol. 13, 1983– . Belém.

Contains series of articles on Pará archives and its collections. Articles list works cataloged during 1979–82, catalog of exhibits of rare works, listing of manuscript codes referring to the colonial period in the Amazon region, demographic information for the area of Amazonas and Rio Negro after the 17th century, summary of the correspondence of Grão-Pará Bishop Miguel de Bulhões (18th century) and listing of microfilm of collections on the area located in Lisbon.

58 Caldeira, Paulo da Terra. O controle bibliográfico na área da biblioteconomia no Brasil (Revista de Biblioteconomia de Brasília [Associação dos Bibliotecários do

Distrito Federal *com a colaboração do* Depto. de Biblioteconomia, Faculdade de Estudos Sociais Aplicados, Univ. de Brasília] 9:2, julho/dez. 1981, p. 77–88)

Provides descriptive analysis of tools for bibliographic control and directories for library science and documentation in Brazil. Discusses factors that influence the emergence of information in the country (i.e., university professors, researchers, librarians, and students). Calls for greater efforts to coordinate activities of publishers of bibliographic tools to achieve rationalization.

59 Carvalho, Thereza de Sá. A cooperação a nível das bibliotecas (Universitas [Revista de cultura da Univ. Federal da Bahia] 29, jan./abril 1982, p. 67–73, bibl.)

Article dwells upon problems that face Brazilian university libraries, particularly in the Northeast. Emphasizes need for existing programs for inter-library cooperation and for even stronger efforts at cooperation, to avoid unnecessary duplication of resources.

60 Keren, Carl. A National Library and Information Service System in Barbados: report of a consultancy mission, September, 1981. Ottawa: International Development Research Centre, Information Science Division, 1981. 52 p.: bibl., ill.

Special study prepared in cooperation with the Barbadian Ministry of Information intended to assess existing information activities and planning and to determine areas of strength and weaknesses.

61 Lacerda, Célia Maria Peres et al. Avaliação de experiências de controle bibliográfico em Curitiba: 1970–1980 (Revista de Biblioteconomia de Brasília [Associação dos Bibliotecários do Distrito Federal *com a colaboração do* Depto. de Biblioteconomia, Faculdade de Estudos Sociais Aplicados, Univ. de Brasília] 9:2, julho/dez. 1981, p. 95–102, chart)

Provides examination of some basic activities of bibliographic control performed in Curitiba: editing, in-source-cataloging, standardization, and legal deposit of publications. Discusses production of bibliographic catalogs and bibliographies.

62 Nocetti, Milton A. Bibliografia brasileira sobre automação de serviços bibliotecários: 1968–1981. Brasília: Empresa Brasileira de Pesquisa Agropecuária, Depto.

de Informação e Documentação, 1982. 75 p.: indexes.

Identifies 240 titles on the subject with author and subject indexes provided. Publication is intended for the use of the library community, automation specialists, and professors and students of library science schools.

63 Seminar on the Acquisition of Latin American Library Materials, *26th, Tulane University, 1981.* Latin American economic issues: information needs and sources. Madison: SALALM Secretariat, Univ. of Wisconsin; Los Angeles: Latin American Center Publications, UCLA, 1984. 354 p: bibl.

Provides record of April 1981 SALALM meeting in New Orleans, La., which addressed Latin American economic issues. Selected papers from that conference relating to public and private sector interests in economic issues appear. Much attention is given to the identification of sources of information in both sectors for the study of the Latin American economies. For economist's comment, see item 2988.

64 ———, *27th, Washington, D.C. 1982.* Public policy issues and Latin American library sources. Madison: SALALM Secretariat, Univ. of Wisconsin; Los Angeles: Latin American Center Publications, UCLA, 1984. 234 p.: bibl., indexes.

Provides record of March 1982 SALALM meeting held in Washington, D.C. Selected presentations from its sessions include papers on censorship and propaganda, national policies and cultural patrimony, networks and databases in Latin America, scholarly communication and public policy, the role of quantitative data in the formulation of public policy, and a national plan for Latin American library collections in the US.

65 Silva, Edna Lúcia da and Vera Ingrid Hobold. Projeto para implantação de um banco de dados manual sobre Santa Catarina (Revista de Biblioteconomia de Brasília [Associação dos Bibliotecários do Distrito Federal *com a colaboração do* Depto. de Biblioteconomia, Faculdade de Estudos Sociais Aplicados, Univ. de Brasília] 6 : 2, julho/dez. 1981, p. 103–110, charts)

Addresses the development of a Santa Catarina data bank based on formal cooperation. Implementation of the system includes enrollment of institutions, collection/storage/and indexing of data, establishment of guidelines for retrieval and dissemination of information, and cost estimates.

ACQUISITIONS, COLLECTIONS, AND CATALOGS

66 Anthropology: a catalog of selected doctoral dissertation research. Ann Arbor, Mich.: Univ. Microfilms International, 1984? 14 p.

Entries appear in subject order under general broad terms with separate entries for Central America, the Caribbean, and South America in certain categories. No index.

67 *Boletín Bibliográfico de Obras Inscriptas.* Ministerio de Justicia, Dirección Nacional del Derecho de Autor. No. 34, julio/sept. 1981– . Buenos Aires.

Lists 1981 Argentine imprints received by legal deposit. Individual publications appear in alphabetical order by author within distinct literary, art, and scientific categories.

68 Borisovna, Liudmila *et al.* Fuentes para la historia de México de 1810 a 1920 en la Biblioteca José María Lafragua de la Universidad Autónoma de Puebla. Puebla, México: Univ. Autónoma de Puebla, Instituto de Ciencias, Centro de Investigaciones Históricas y Sociales, 1982. 189 p. (Fuentes y documentos para la historia de Puebla; 1)

Provides description of 19th- and 20th-century materials, to 1920, in the Lafragua Library that pertain to Mexico in general and to Puebla in particular. List is divided into a general section and a Puebla section; no index or subject arrangement to the material appears.

69 Catálogo de obras raras. Recife: Governo do Estado de Pernambuco, Secretaria de Turismo, Cultura e Esportes, Arquivo Público Estadual, 1982. 57 p.: index (Série Col. especiais; 2)

Contains listing of 16th to 20th-century rarities found in the collections of Pernambuco's state archives. Includes author index.

70 Catálogo de publicaciones de la UNSJ. San Juan, Argentina: Univ. Nacional de San Juan, Dirección General de Bibliotecas, 1981. 185 p.: indexes.

Lists 739 publications of faculties of pure sciences, social sciences, philosophy-humanities-arts, and engineering-architecture. Cites indexes to authors, periodicals, and scientific meetings.

71 Colomar Albajar, María. Catálogo de uniformes. Archivo General de Indias, Sección de Mapas y Planos. Madrid: Ministerio de Cultura, Dirección General de Bellas Artes, Archivos y Bibliotecas, Subdirección General de Archivos, 1981. 99 p.: ill., index.

Cites 133 items in collections of Archivo General de Indias that contain illustrations of Spanish military uniforms in Spanish America. Shows 18th- and 19th-century uniforms worn in Bolivia, Colombia, Cuba, Ecuador, Spanish United States, Philippines, Mexico, Panama, Puerto Rico, Santo Domingo, and Venezuela.

72 Filmografia do habitat. Brasília: SEPLAN (Secretaria de Planejamento), CNPq (Conselho Nacional de Desenvolvimento Científico de Tecnológico), Coordenação Editorial, 1982. 198 p.

Lists nearly 600 films related to urban living. Includes subject, distributor, and names (film name) indexes.

73 García Mainieri, Norma. Situación archivística actual en Guatemala (PAIGH/H, 89, enero/junio 1980, p. 91–162, charts)

Contains description of colonial and national period materials in Guatemalan archives. Holdings, by total legajo count, are provided for colonial government, captaincy general, royal treasury, ecclesiastical affairs, and independent sections of society. References are to materials found in Archivo General de Centroamérica, ecclesiastical archives, and departamental archives of the country. Includes enabling legislation providing for the creation of these archives. Finally, devotes considerable space to a discussion of the current state of archival development in Guatemala and to programs in existence or required to develop qualified Guatemalan archivists.

74 Grupo de trabalho do arquivo permanente do AN: Convênio MJ/FGV: histórico das instalações do Arquivo Nacional (MAN, 13:6, junho 1982, p. 183–195, tables)

Provides chronology of development of the National Archives of Brazil and lists key publications that serve to describe its functions, contents, and development.

Lassegue, J.B. and F. Letona. Catálogo general del Archivo del Monasterio de Santa Catalina del Cusco, Perú. See *HLAS 46:2711.*

75 Latin America: a catalog of selected doctoral dissertation research. Ann Arbor, Mich.: Univ. Microfilms International, 1984. 32 p.

Contains citations to 1321 doctoral dissertations and 47 masters theses published 1981–84. Items are arranged in alphabetical order by author within discreet subject arrangements.

Liehr, Reinhard. El Fondo Quesada en el Instituto Ibero-Americano de Berlín. See *HLAS 46:3283.*

76 Seminario de Publicaciones Seriadas, *2nd, Bogotá, Colombia, 1983.* Memorias. Univ. de los Andes, Biblioteca General. Bogotá: Instituto Colombiano para el Fomento de la Educación Superior (ICFES), Sub dirección de Fomento, División de Recursos Bibliográficos, Grupo Recursos de Información, 1983. 2 v. (722 p.): bibl., ill.

Contains series of presentations on the theme (e.g., papers on the acquisition of periodicals at the national level in Colombia, a national policy for cataloging periodicals, analytic data bank in the Colombian system for bibliographic information, the ISSN in Colombia, service and reader use in a serial library, national exchange of periodicals in science and technology, and development of serial collections). Recommendations were forwarded in order to promote a national plan for serial acquisition, control, and utilization.

REFERENCE WORKS AND RESEARCH

77 Argueta, Mario R. Guía para el investigador de la historia colonial hondureña: un ensayo temático bibliográfico (Boletín del Sistema Bibliotecario de la UNAH [Univ. Nacional Autónoma de Honduras, Tegucigalpa] 12:4, oct./dic. 1983, p. 3–17, plate)

Author provides flowing review of scholarship on Honduran colonial history and indicates areas of that history in need of further research.

78 Cardozo, Lubio. Los repertorios bibliográficos venezolanos del siglo diecinueve. Caracas: Univ. Central de Venezuela, Facultad de Humanidades y Educación, Instituto de Investigaciones Literarias, 1982. 52 leaves, 4 leaves of plates: index (Col. Prepublicaciones)

Provides brief review of 19th-century research on Venezuela. Author presents bibliographical essay of key publications from the past century and includes a full bibliographical description of these important works. Title index appears.

79 Carrizosa Argáez, Enrique. Linajes y bibliografías de nuestros gobernantes, 1830–1982. Bogotá: Banco de la República, 1983. 623 p.: bibl., indexes.

Contains useful biographical information on Colombia's executives from Domingo Caicedo (1830) to Belisario Betancur Cuartas (1982-). Familial relations of these leaders, updated to present, are especially useful and the publication's main purpose.

80 Catálogo de dissertações e teses da Universidade Federal de Pernambuco. Recife: Univ. Federal de Pernambuco, Biblioteca Central, 1981. 1 v.: index.

Dissertations and theses are presented by department and encompass 1917–81 period. Includes author index.

81 Catálogo de publicaciones periódicas BAC. Martha Guevara de Bejarano y Francisco A. Salazar Alonso, compiladores. 3a ed. Bogotá: Instituto Colombiano Agropecuario, Subgerencia de Desarrollo Rural, División de Comunicación, Biblioteca Agropecuaria de Colombia, 1981. 424 p.: indexes.

Revision of 1975 and 1976 eds. Lists nearly 2000 periodical titles, mainly in the field of agriculture, contained in the Biblioteca Agropecuaria de Colombia (BAC). Indicates holdings.

82 Catálogo nacional de instituções que atuam na área de meio ambiente: 1981–1982. Brasília: Ministerio do Interior, Secretaria Especial do Meio Ambiente, Secretaria Adjunta de Planejamento, 1982. 1 v.: ill., indexes.

Updated ed. of work previously published in 1980 contains extensive list of institutions and services whose work relates

directly to environmental issues. In addition to listing addresses, fields of endeavor, and juridical jurisdiction, includes statement as to the objectives of the entity. Indexes to institutions, subjects of endeavor, and acronyms appear.

83 Congresso Nacional de Informática, *14th, São Paulo, 1981.* Anais. São Paulo: Sociedade dos Usuários de Computadores e Equipamentos Subsidiários, 1981. 852 p.: bibls., ill., index.

Proceedings of conference devoted exclusively to use of computers and electronic data processing. Separate sections cover various categories such as the administration of data processing, data banks, software for online systems, computer networks, software for micro and mini computers, the development of software, design of computers, and information and society.

84 Demografische data. Paramaribo: Algemeen Bureau voor de Statistiek, 1981. 43 leaves: ill. (Suriname in cijfers; no. 135/81/05)

Contains statistical data projected to 1980.

85 Dissertações de mestrado nas áreas de ciências sociais e humanidades defendidas na UFPE. Federação Brasileira de Associações de Bibliotecários, Comissão Brasileira de Documentação em Ciências Sociais e Humanidades. Recife: Univ. Federal de Pernambuco, Editora Universitária, 1983. 77 leaves: indexes.

Lists 263 theses by discipline defended at Pernambuco between 1971 and Aug. 1983. Includes author, mentor, and subject indexes.

86 Documentos relativos a la independencia de Norteamérica existentes en archivos españoles. v. 10, Archivo Histórico Nacional: expedientes, años 1821–1850. Compiled by P. León Tello. Madrid: Ministerio de Asuntos Exteriores, Dirección General de Relaciones Culturales, 1984. 1 v.

Vol. 10 is latest release of Spanish series begun in 1976 and refers to documents in Archivo Histórico Nacional containing items of interest to the independence period in Latin America as well as to early 18th-century events in the US borderlands.

87 Estudios fronterizos México-Estados Unidos: directorio general de investigadores. Editado por Jorge A. Bustamante,

Alberto Hernández y Francisco Malagamba. Tijuana: Centro de Estudios Fronterizos del Norte de México, 1984. 234 p.: indexes.

Provides information on research in progress among scholars involved in border studies; research information is provided by institution within each state of Mexico or US. Researcher, subject, and institution indexes appear. Major themes of research include public administration, economic development, bibliographic studies, education and culture, women's studies, historical and linguistic studies, urban studies, US-Mexican relations, sociopolitical organizations, Mexican population in the US, and migration and demography.

88   Farac, Sergio and **Blasio H. Hickmann.** Quem é quem nas letras rio-grandenses: dicionário de autores contemporâneos. 2a ed. Porto Alegre: Secretaria Municipal de Educação e Cultura, Divisão de Cultura, 1983. 270 p.

Second ed. of work first published in 1982. Provides brief biobibliographical information on 248 contemporary authors of Rio Grande do Sul, Brazil.

89   Fontes de informação em meio ambiente no Brasil. Brasília: CNPq (Conselho Nacional de Desenvolvimento Científico e Tecnologia), IBICT (Instituto Brasileiro de Informação em Ciência e Tecnologia), 1983. 147 p.: indexes.

Lists entities, libraries, research centers, publications and data bases. Location and subject of specialization of centers are given. Separate alphabetical, subject, acronym, and geographic indexes facilitate use of this reference work. Over 200 references are identified.

90   Guatemala: a country study. Edited by Richard F. Nyrop. 2nd ed. Washington: Foreign Area Studies, American Univ., 1984. 261 p.: bibl., ill., index, map (Area handbook series. DA pam; 550–78)

Second ed. of work which first appeared in 1970. Attempts to treat in a compact and objective manner the dominant social, political, economic, and national security aspects of contemporary Guatemalan society. Useful introduction to the country.

91   Guía bancaria latinoamericana = Latin American banking guide. 3a ed. Bogotá: Federación Latinoamericana de Bancos (FLB), 1984. 301 p.: ill. (some col.)

Provides capsule information on member banks throughout Latin America; indicates staffing and financial status of each bank.

92   Guia das bibliotecas públicas brasileiras conveniadas com o Instituto Nacional do Livro. Brasília: O Instituto, Fundação Nacional Pró-Memória, Ministério da Educação e Cultura, 1983. 341 p.

Lists public libraries by state with information on location, collection size and book budget.

93   A guide to official gazettes and their contents. Compiled by John E. Roberts. Washington: Law Library, Library of Congress, 1985. 1 v.

Work attempts to assist researchers unfamiliar with legal publications of foreign jurisdictions to identify and use official gazettes. The official gazettes serve national governments to disseminate new legislation, regulations, orders and decisions of government bodies, and official announcements. Indicates titles of official gazettes, frequency of publication, and description of contents.

94   Hartness-Kane, Ann. Governments as publishers of reference materials: Mexico and Brazil, 1970–1980 (LARR, 17:2, 1982, p. 142–155, bibl.)

Article suggests official publications of both governments that serve as useful reference tools. Cited publications include directories of official printers, a listing of governmental acronyms, product or industry legislative compendia, guides to archives and collections therein, etc. Includes bibliography of works cited.

95   Hernández Casas de Benenati, Elena. Algunos aspectos de los estudios latinoamericanos de Francia (IPGH/RHI, 3, 1982, p. 175–186)

Brief article speaks to the study of Latin America in France, student interest in the subject, diverse problems of studying it in Paris, need to develop such studies in France, and need for coordination of French programs wth European and Latin American institutes. Describes various programs throughout France in single paragraph entries.

96   Imprensa Oficial do Estado: 90 anos de produção gráfica, 1891–1981. Coordenação, Ivone Tálamo. São Paulo: Governo do Estado de São Paulo, Imprensa Oficial do

Estado, Divisão de Biblioteca, 1983. 295 p.: bibl., ill. (some col.), indexes.

Lists official publications of state of São Paulo since 1891. Indicates locations of copies. Separate author, title, and legislation indexes appear.

97 Indice del Boletín del Instituto de Historia Argentina y Americana, 1922–1980. Buenos Aires: El Instituto, 1982. 140 p.

Provides author, chronology to theme, reviewed author, notes, illustrations, extract of documents indexes to the Boletín del Instituto de Investigaciones Históricas (1922–45), the Boletín del Instituto de Historia Argentina Doctor Emilio Ravignani (1956–71), and the Boletín del Instituto de Historia Argentina y Americana Doctor Emilio Ravignani (1973 and 1980).

98 Indice general de los números 1 al 11: 1962–1974. Compilador, Manuel Hernández. Mérida, Venezuela: Univ. de los Andes, Facultad de Humanidades y Educación, Hemeroteca y Sala de Referencias Dr. Carlos E. Muñoz Oraa, 1983. 17 leaves: indexes (Col. bibliográfica; 2)

This index to Anuario de Filología of the Univ. del Zulia, Maracaibo, provides access to several works of research in the fields of philology and general literature that appear in this journal. Includes separate author and subject indexes.

99 Inventario de estudios de informes existentes en las agencias regionales del IFI. Bogotá: Centro de Documentación, Instituto de Fomento Industrial, Ministerio de Desarrollo Económico, 1983. 92 p.: index (Información documentaria; no. 4)

Lists publications of each of seven regional agencies of the Colombian Instituto de Fomento Industrial (IFI). Lists over 500 items arranged by subject within each agency. General index provides access to all publications.

100 Investigaciones en curso = research in progress (RIB, 34:3/4, 1984, p. 436–496)

Provides indication of work in progress with probable completion date. Entries are grouped by discipline.

101 Johnson, Peter T. Bibliography: current practices and future trends (LARR, 18:1, 1983, p. 254–263)

Author reviews 10 relatively current bibliographic publications (i.e., since 1977)

which he considers as ranging from the traditional to the futuristic in approach. All publications reviewed were published in the US; one item, Bibliographic Guide to Latin American Studies, is an annual publication. Encourages utilization of consistent bibliographic style in the preparation of research aids.

102 Lavrov, Nicolai M. El estudio de la historia de América Latina en la U.R.S.S. (IPGH/RHI, 3, 1982, p. 169–174)

Provides brief history of the development of Latin American studies in the Soviet Union. Although initially the study of Latin America was concentrated in Moscow and Leningrad, there are now centers in Ivanovo, Jaroslav, Kiev, Kishinev, and Grosniy.

103 León Pinelo, Antonio de. Epítome. Edición y estudio introductorio por Horacio Capel. Barcelona: Publicacions Edicions Universitat de Barcelona, 1982? 3 v. in 2: bibl., indexes.

Facsimile of León Pinelo's 1629 publication reproduces in full the 1737–38 ed. of that major bibliographic work. The Epítome was the first specific bibliography on the New World as well as one of the first geographic bibliographies published in Europe. Includes citations on all parts of the world (i.e., the work is divided into four major sections: Asia and Africa; Spanish America; nautical; and geographic). A brief introduction describes the history of the publication. This is a fine reference tool.

104 López de Díaz, Aura. Glosario de siglas de los medios de comunicación social. Río Piedras: Biblioteca, Escuela de Comunicación Pública, Depto. de Bibliotecas Graduadas, Univ. de Puerto Rico, 1984. 23, 22 leaves.

List is organized to provide two points of access: 1) alphabetical order by acronyms; and 2) alphabetical order by name of organization. Also lists acronyms appearing in newspapers or other printed materials and related to Latin America and the Third World.

105 Mac.Pherson, Telasco A. Diccionario del Estado Lara: histórico, geográfico, estadístico y biográfico. 3a ed. Caracas: Ediciones de la Presidencia de la República, 1981. 558 p. (Biblioteca de autores larenses; 3)

Third ed., appearing over 40 years after previous one, contains references to individuals, locations, and other historical facts about the state of Lara. Information, however, has not been updated.

106 **Pérez, Lisandro.** The holdings of the Library of Congress on the population of Cuba (UP/CSEC, 13:1, Winter 1983, p. 69–76)

Identifies 19th- and 20th-century demographic publications in the Library of Congress. Although the Library's holdings are strong for all periods, they are especially so for 1899–1958.

107 **Personalities Caribbean:** the international guide to who's who in the West Indies. Kingston: Personalities, 1982–1983. 1027 p.: ill.

Provides biographical descriptions of selected individuals in the English- and Dutch-speaking countries of the Caribbean as well as a listing for Puerto Rico, Bermuda, and the Bahamas.

108 **Peters, Gertrud.** Fuentes para el estudio del comercio de los Estados Unidos con Costa Rica: siglos XIX y XX (UNCR/R, 4:8, enero/julio 1979, p. 83–107, bibl., tables)

Provides excellent introduction to US and Costa Rican sources for the study of trade between them. Includes titles of publications and coverage as well as their location. Primary and secondary source materials are given in accompanying brief bibliography.

109 **Raten Amerika kenkyūsha meikan.** S.l: s.n., 1983. 104 p.

Useful reference work published only in Japanese, provides information on Japanese Latin Americanists and their major publications.

110 **Reber, Vera Blinn.** Utilizing French sources in Paris for Latin American historical research (LARR, 17:2, 1982, p. 171–177)

Brief description of major archives and libraries in Paris that contain the greatest amount of material on Latin America.

111 **Ruz Menéndez, Rodolfo.** Los archivos del estado de Yucatán (UY/R, 22:128, marzo/abril 1980, p. 12–19)

Provides brief description of contents and history of seven archives in Yucatán (i.e., Archivo General del Estado, Archivo Notarial del Estado, Archivo General de la Arquidiócesis de Yucatán, Archivo de la Mitra

Emeritense, Biblioteca Carlos R. Menéndez, Biblioteca Central de la Universidad de Yucatán, and the Junta Facultativa de Campeche).

112 **A Select bibliography of serials relating to Hispanic language, literature, and civilizations held by libraries in Australia and New Zealand.** Compiled by Roy Boland and Alun Kenwood. Auckland, New Zealand: Auckland Univ. Library, 1984. 64 p. (Bibliographical bulletin; 0067–0499; 13)

Lists original as well as microfilm holdings of Hispanic language serials, both peninsular and Latin American, in 146 libraries (i.e., university, institutional, and public) in New Zealand and Australia.

Sidel, Mark. Latin American studies in the People's Republic of China. See item 4361.

Sizonenko, Alexandr. La latinoamericanística en las Repúblicas Federadas de la URSS. See item 4363.

113 **Suriname directory of commerce, industry and tourism.** Paramaribo: Publico, 1983–1984. 1 v.

Provides useful statistical and narrative information related to commerce, industry, and tourism in Surinam. Includes city plan of Paramaribo.

114 **Thèses souteneus sur l'Amérique latine en 1979–1980** (CDAL, 24, 1981, p. 3–135)

Provides abstracts of 21 doctoral theses prepared in French universities from 1979–80. Subjects and geographical concentrations are quite varied; works on the French possessions in the Antilles or on the Caribbean in general, except for Haiti, are not noted. The subjects of research are primarily contemporary development issues or technology (e.g., oil exploration in Mexico).

Toledo, María I. Revisión de la literatura arqueológica de la cuenca del Lago de Maracaibo. See item **878.**

Tulchin, Joseph S. Emerging patterns of research in the study of Latin America. See item **4370.**

115 **Who's who in Jamaica.** Kingston: Who's Who Publications, 1981–1982. 1 v.: ill., indexes.

This is 15th ed. of useful source of information on selected individuals in Jamaican life. Entries appear in alphabetical order; separate indexes for various categories of endeavor (i.e., art and culture; industry and commerce; medicine and science; judiciary and law enforcement; religion and philosophy; politics and government; and sports and physical culture).

GENERAL WORKS

116 Les Années trente à Cuba: actes du colloque international. Organisé à Paris en novembre 1980 par le Centre interuniversitaire d'études cubaines et l'Université de la Sorbonne-Nouvelle, Paris III. Paris: Harmattan, 1982. 309 p.: bibl.

Includes 16 separate articles on the Cuban economy and social movement, theory and ideology, and arts and literature during the 1930s. Contributions by: B. Alvarez, A. García Garcés, R. Labarre, G. Fournial, J. Le Riverend, J. Lamore, A. Guy, C. Serrano, O. Cabrera, M.S. Ramón de Armas Delamaster-Scott, P.P. Rodríguez, A. Demichel, A. Melon, M. Tollis-Guicharnaud, A. Cairo Ballester, and M. Poumier-Taquechel.

117 Country profile: business travel and security report. v. 4, Guatemala. Tysons Corner, Va.: Overseas Security Management, 1984. 1 v.: ill., index.

Intended for the traveling executive and the corporate security officer concerned with terrorism and criminal violence around the world; book attempts to cover practical information relating to travel, security, and temporary work in Guatemala. In addition to practical information for the new arrival, provides information on security (e.g., which city areas to avoid, reliable security firms, local laws and policies regarding weapons, payment of ransoms).

118 ———. v. 5, Costa Rica. Tysons Corner, Va.: Overseas Security Management, 1984. 1 v.: ill., index.

As in the case of other country profiles prepared by the Overseas Security Management Inc. (e.g., similar analyses of Bolivia, Chile, Panama, Guatemala, Peru, and Brazil, as well as future publications on Mexico, countries of Central and South America), work is directly related to safety of the executive, as the title implies. Nevertheless, useful information for businessmen and travelers is found in this work.

119 Cuba. Ministerio de Cultura. Dirección de Editoriales. La actividad editorial en Cuba (in La Cultura en Cuba socialista. La Habana: Editorial Letras Cubanas, 1982, p. 91–102, tables)

Provides brief overview of book publishing and distribution in Cuba since Castro. Describes organizations established to promote book production and identifies publishers of textbooks and research works in contemporary Cuba.

120 Garzón López, Alvaro. La libre circulación del libro en América Latina: una estrategia para afrontar la crisis (El Libro Español [Instituto Nacional del Libro Español, Madrid] 308, feb. 1984, p. 36–40, plates, table)

Spanish proposal to improve the circulation of Iberian imprint books in Latin America.

121 Grases, Pedro. La imprenta en Venezuela. Barcelona: Editorial Seix Barral, 1981. 1 v.: ill. (Obras de Pedro Grases; 8)

Reproduces Grases's 1967 treatment of the subject. Contains information on the history of book printing and publishing in Venezuela with a concentration on the initial years of the 19th century.

122 Grupo Interamericano de Editores. En América Latina se producen 36,300 títulos por año: encuesta realizada durante 1983 (El Libro Español [Instituto Nacional del Libro Español, Madrid] 308, feb. 1983, p. 50–54, plates)

Provides brief overview of book production in Latin America, with a description of the book industry in each country.

123 Kline, Harvey F. Colombia: portrait of unity and diversity. Boulder, Colo.: Westview Press, 1983. 169 p.: bibl., ill., index (Westview profiles. Nations of contemporary Latin America)

Brief general work on Colombia with the contemporary (i.e., post-1930 period). Provides an introduction to the people, politics, economics, history, and international relations of the country. Concluding chapter looks to future developments. Brief bibliography and general index appear.

124 Latin America, its problems and its promise: a multidisciplinary introduction. Edited by Jan Knippers Black. Boulder,

Colo.: Westview Press, 1984. 549 p.: bibl., ill., index.

Anthology of special articles addressing specific Latin American themes (e.g., the land and people, historical setting, cultural expression, economic and social structures, political processes and trends, external relations, Mexico, Central America and Panama, Cuba and the Caribbean, the Andes, the Southern Cone, and Brazil). Contributors are: Peter Bakewell, E. Bradford Burns, Fred Strum, William P. Glade, Gilbert Merkx, Larman Wilson, Martin Needler, Richard Millett, Steve Ropp, Nelson Valdés, Anthony Maingot, John Martz, Peter Snow, Michael Conniff, and Brady Tyson.

125 Paladines, Carlos. Notas sobre "modelos" de conocimiento de la cultura latinoamericana en la tradición universitaria alemana (IPGH/RHI, 3, 1982, p. 141–157)

Excellent review of German thinking and study of Latin America and of those who influenced such models (e.g., Humboldt, Hegel, the educational realism school of the period of Kaiser Wilhelm II, and the regional studies approach). Article points out that 121 Latin American institutes have been established in Germany with 33 in existence before 1945, with the first institute in Hamburg in 1916. A survey of Latin American research in Germany shows that the fields of anthropology, political science, and geography predominate.

126 Políticas nacionales del libro. v. 2, Colombia, Chile. Bogotá: Centro Regional para el Fomento del Libro en América Latina y el Caribe (CERLAL), 1982. 1 v.: ill. (Monografías)

Present vol. is part of a group of studies prepared by CERLAL in response to a demand by UNESCO to provide profiles of national publishing industries of Latin America for the International Book Congress (London, 1982). This study of Colombia and Chile provides information on production, distribution, imports, exports, costs, etc. of book industry in these countries. The reader will find information on the national policy for the book, legal aspects, rights of authors, fiscal regulations related to production and sale of books, and finally, current problems and future prospects for the industry.

127 Regional Congress on Books for Latin America and the Caribbean, Rio de Janeiro, Brazil, 1982. Relatorio final = Informe final = Final report. Rio de Janeiro: Biblioteca Nacional, 1984. 91 p.

Objectives of this Rio Congress (Dec. 1982) were: 1) to promote in Latin America and the Caribbean a program of action that would lead to a reading society as approved by UNESCO's World Congress on Books (London, June 1982); and 2) to approve a plan of action for the 1980s based on targets proposed in London but adapting them to the realities of Latin America and the Caribbean, and outlining guidelines for future action.

128 Seminar on Economic Integration in the Caribbean, Bridgetown, Barbados, 1983. Ten Years of CARICOM: papers presented at a seminar sponsored by the Inter-American Development Bank. Washington: The Bank; Georgetown: Caribbean Community (CARICOM) Secretariat, 1984. 351 p.: bibls.

Symposium's objective was to evaluate the experience of CARICOM in the working and improvement of integration movement as an instrument for the rapid social and economic development of the peoples of the Caribbean Community (CARICOM). Separate papers discuss integration movements in the Third World, the Caribbean Community, historical and cultural background of the Caribbean Community experience, geopolitical realities in the Caribbean, CARICOM and Latin American integration experiences, evolving structure of CARICOM trade, record of CARICOM and EEC relations, and LDCs in CARICOM.

129 Subercaseaux, Bernardo. La industria editorial y el libro en Chile, 1930–1984: ensayo de interpretación de una crisis. Santiago: Centro de Indagación y Expresión Cultural y Artística (CENECA), 1984. 118 p.: appendices, indexes.

Describes Chile's book industry through three distinct periods: 1) 1930–70, the enlightenment and mesocratic; 2) 1970–73, state run and popular; and 3) 1973–84, authoritarian and the changing of editorial design. Each section describes book production, promotion, and consumption. Concludes that the Chilean book industry is in need of much help and assistance; only a program of integral development can reverse the negative trend in publishing that Chile has experienced since 1930.

NEW SERIAL TITLES

130 *Anuario de Historia de la Iglesia en Chile.* Seminario Pontificio Mayor. Vol. 1, No. 1, 1983– . Santiago.

This publication on the Church in Chile is the result of a collaboration between the Seminario and the Sociedad de Historia de la Iglesia en Chile. Includes articles on particular priests, parishes, and Church and politics (i.e., Marciano Barrios Valdés's "La Historiografía Eclesiástica Chilena como Instrumento Político, 1848–1918"). Sections related to documents, archives, and current publications related to the subject of the Church in Chile appear. The journal is edited by Antonio Rehbein Pesce and is available from the Seminario Pontificio Mayor, Casilla 3-D, Santiago, Chile.

131 *Carbet.* Revue martiniquaise de sciences sociales. Edition Désormeaux. No. 1, nov. 1983– . Fort de France, Martinique.

Triannual publication printed by Edition Désormeaux, Rue Galiéni, 97200 Fort de France, Martinique, contains a variety of social science studies of Martinique and the French Antilles. The editor is Serge Domi.

132 *Carta Informativa.* Junta de Gobierno de Reconstrucción Nacional (JGRN), Dirección General de Divulgación y Prensa, Dirección Sectorial de Comunicación y Propaganda (DISCOP). 1983 [i.e. 1984]– . Managua.

Annual report of the government of Nicaragua contains reports from various sectors of the government (e.g., economic, commercial, social services, governmental, defense, and production).

Encuentro. Ciencias sociales y humanidades. Revista trimestral. El Colegio de Jalisco. See *HLAS 46:1917.*

133 *Latin American Monitor.* Latin American Monitor Ltd. Vol. l, No. l, 1984– . London.

Under this title are found five separate regional publications reflecting the activities of social, economic, and political forces. Separate monthly (i.e., 10 times a year) reports are issued for Mexico and Brazil, Central America, Andean Group, Southern Cone, and Caribbean. The reports are compiled from over 100 local and international news and radio sources. Subscriptions can be requested from Latin American Monitor Ltd., London House, 266 Fulham Road, London SW10 9EL, England.

134 *Revista Andina.* Centro Bartolomé de las Casas. Tomo 1, No. 1, 1. semestre 1983– . Cusco, Perú.

Centro de Estudios Rurales Andinos Bartolomé de las Casas will issue the publication by semester. Articles related specifically to the Andes will appear. First issue contains two long articles with commentary on the themes of transport in the development of an internal colonial market and the problems of employment in Cusco's campesino communities. Review articles, guides to collections, and general commentary fill the pages of the new impressive journal.

JOURNAL ABBREVIATIONS BIBLIOGRAPHY AND GENERAL WORKS

ANH/B Boletín de la Academia Nacional de Historia. Buenos Aires.

CDAL Cahiers des Amériques latines. Paris.

CEHSMO Historia Obrera. Centro de Estudios Históricos del Movimiento Obrero Mexicano. México.

EEHA/HBA Historiografía y Bibliografía Americanista. Escuela de Estudios Hispano-Americanos de Sevilla. Sevilla.

HRAF/BSR Behavior Science Research. HRAF journal of comparative studies. Human Relations Area Files. New Haven.

IILI/RI Revista Iberoamericana. Instituto Internacional de Literatura Latinoamericana. Patronicada por la Univ. de Pittsburgh. Pittsburgh, Pa.

IPGH/RHI Revista de Historia de las Ideas. Instituto Panamericano de Geografía e Historia. Editorial Casa de la Cultura Ecuatoriana. Quito.

LARR Latin American Research Review. Univ. of North Carolina Press *for the* Latin American Studies Association (LASA). Chapel Hill.

MAN Mensário do Arquivo Nacional. Ministério da Justiça, Arquivo Nacional, Divisão de Publicações. Rio de Janeiro.

PAIGH/H   Revista de Historia de América. Instituto Panamericano de Geografía e Historia, Comisión de Historia. México.

PCCLAS/P   Proceedings of the Pacific Coast Council on Latin American Studies. Univ. of California. Los Angeles.

ULB/RIS   Revue de l'Institut de sociologie. Univ. libre de Bruxelles. Bruxelles.

UNCR/R   Revista de Historia. Univ. Nacional de Costa Rica, Escuela de Historia. Heredia, Costa Rica.

UP/CSEC   Cuban Studies/Estudios Cubanos. Univ. of Pittsburgh, Univ. Center for International Studies, Center for Latin American Studies. Pittsburgh, Pa.

UP/EA   Estudios Andinos. Univ. of Pittsburgh, Latin American Studies Center. Pittsburgh, Pa.

UY/R   Revista de la Universidad de Yucatán. Mérida, México.

ANTHROPOLOGY

GENERAL

251 Arqueología de rescate: ponencias presentadas en la Primera Conferencia de Arqueología de Rescate del Nuevo Mundo. Edición de Rex L. Wilson y Gloria Loyola. Washington: Preservation Press: Fondo Nacional para la Preservación Histórica, Organización de los Estados Americanos, 1982. 322 p.: bibl.

Selection of papers delivered at the 1st New World Conference on Rescue Archaeology, dealing with policy, philosophies, and principles; economics and legislation; professional standards; the status of the rescue archaeology in Mexico, Chile, Costa Rica; and general problems of gaining support for archaeology in development projects. [B.J. Meggers]

252 Boglár, Lajos and **Tamás Kovács.** Indian art from Mexico to Peru. Covina Kaidó, Budapest: s.n., 1983. 26 p.: ill. (40 col., 211 b/w plates)

Excellent photographs of pottery, stone, metal, and wooden objects mainly in previously unpublicized collections in Hungary, Poland, Switzerland, and Belgium. [B.J. Meggers]

Calendars in Mesoamerica and Peru: native American computations of time. See item **505.**

253 Conrad, Geoffrey W. and **Arthur A. Demarest.** Religion and empire: the dynamics of Aztec and Inca expansionism. Cambridge, England: Cambridge Univ. Press, 1984. 266 p.: bibl., ill., index.

After separately reviewing the formation, expansion, and decline of the Aztec and Inca empires, authors consider and reject environmental, climatic change, population pressure, external pressure, and other explanations in favor of changes in the traditional religion and elaboration of specialized forms of ideology as the driving force for both expansions. [B.J. Meggers]

254 Drained field agriculture in Central and South America. Edited by J.P. Darch. Oxford, England: British Archaeological Reports, 1983. 263 p.: bibl., ill., maps, tables (BAR International series; 189)

Introductory chapter by Darch is followed by descriptions of specific areas where "raised" or "ridged" fields were constructed. Chapters deal with Veracruz (Siemens, Wilkerson); the Maya lowlands (Turner II; Gliessman, Turner II, Rosado, and Amador; Lambert and Arnason; Scarborough); the Valley of Mexico (Rojas Rabiela); coastal Ecuador (Denevan and Mathewson); highland Ecuador (Knapp and Ryder); the Titicaca basin (Lennon); highland Peru (Farrington); and coastal Suriname (Versteeg). Extent, form, purpose, soil, crops, and construction are among topics discussed. Concluding chapter (Smith) identifies soil limitations associated with swamps, which help to explain the geographical distribution of these features. [B.J. Meggers]

255 Gordon, Michael W. The Third World and the protection of national patrimony: oil, art and orchid (HICLR, 2:2, Summer 1979, p. 281–306)

Useful comparative legal essay in which cultural and natural resources are treated as valuable assets of countries open to illegal exploitation. [N. Hammond]

256 Healy, Paul F. Archaeology abroad: ethical considerations of fieldwork in foreign countries (in Ethics and values in archaeology. Edited by Ernestene L. Green. New York: Free Press, 1984, p. 123–132)

Discusses the ethical, political, and practical problems of dealing with host governments and scholars. [N. Hammond]

Highwater, Jamake. Arts of the Indian Americas, North-Central-South: leaves from the sacred tree. See item **560.**

257 Ibarra Grasso, Dick Edgar. América en la prehistoria mundial: difusión greco-fenicia. Buenos Aires: Tipografía Editora Argentina, 1982. 420 p.: bibl., ill. (some col.)

A self-identified "ultradiffusionist" details the theoretical basis for his position and provides numerous illustrations of evidence for significant transoceanic introductions to the Americas. Foci include ancient maps and evidence of navigation; pottery, metallurgy, and recording; astronomy and calendars. Significant Asiatic introductions are concentrated around 3000 BC, 1800 BC, and AD 500; Hellenistic introduction of astronomical and calendric ideas occurred 200–100 BC. Elements of architecture were introduced to Indochina from Central America about AD 500. Important synthesis of the position of a leading advocate of precolumbian transoceanic contact. [B.J. Meggers]

258 International Congress for the Study of the Pre-Columbian Cultures of the Lesser Antilles, 9th, Santo Domingo, 1981. Proceedings. Edited by Louis Allaire and Francine-M. Mayer. Montréal, Canada: Univ. de Montréal, Centre de recherches caraibes, 1983. 574 p.: bibl., ill., maps, plates, tables.

Consists of 40 articles dealing with varied aspects of Caribbean archaeology and ethnohistory. For individual annotations of articles on South America, see items **603, 793, 796, 797, 873, 875, 876, 877,** and **879.** [B.J. Meggers]

259 Kinship, ideology, and practice in Latin America. Edited by Raymond T. Smith. Chapel Hill: Univ. of North Carolina Press, 1984. 341 p.: bibl., index, tables.

Collection of original articles on kinship in Latin America by anthropologists, historians, and sociologists with differing theoretical perspectives. Organized into four sections: 1) kinship ideology in slave societies; 2) establishing colonial hierarchies; 3) hierarchies and enterprise, the use of kinship in adversity and prosperity; and 4) sex roles and economic change. Specific countries or regions covered include: the Andes; Brazil; British West Indies; colonial New Mexico; Jamaica; Mexico; and Peru. Editor's introduction contains useful critiques of major approaches to the study of kinship. For individual annotations of articles by the following authors, see item numbers in parentheses: J.M. Ossio (item **1500**); J. Alexander (item **1008**); G. de la Peña (item **8089**); and F. Wilson (item **1514**). [L. Comitas]

260 Mangelsdorf, Paul C. The mystery of corn: new perspectives (APS/P, 127:4, 1983, p. 215–247, ill., plates)

Survey article takes account of new work but does not shift Mangelsdorf's basic position on the teosinte controversy. [N. Hammond]

261 Matheny, Ray T. and **Deanne L. Gurr.** Variation in prehistoric agricultural systems of the New World (Annual Review of Anthropology [Annual Reviews Inc., Palo Alto, Calif.] 12, 1983, p. 79–103, bibl.)

Review of agricultural systems focusing on Mesoamerica and the Central Andes. Variability is stressed in technology as well as organizational requirements. [Scott Fedick]

262 Müller, Wolfgang. Die Indianer Lateinamerikas; ein ethnostatistischer Überblick. Berlin, FRG: Dietrich Reimer Verlag, 1984. 179 p.: maps, tables.

Thorough statistical overview of indigenous groups in Latin America, in the form of a register. Provides basic facts on each group, such as location, linguistic family, type of social structure, and approximate numbers. Maps enhance the usefulness of this guide which will be invaluable to ethnologists. [G.M. Dorn]

263 Núñez-Regueiro, Víctor A. Sistema de documentación y registros del Programa Arqueología de Rescate (Boletín del Programa Arqueología de Rescate [Corpozulia, Univ. del Zulia, Maracaibo, Venezuela] 2:2, enero/dic. 1980, p. 57–96, facsim., ill., maps, tables)

Discussion and illustration of forms used for recording activities, sites, excavations, petroglyphs, artifact tabulations, conservation procedures, and negatives to standardize information obtained in rescue archaeological efforts in the Venezuelan state of Zulia. [B.J. Meggers]

264 Oliveira, Roberto Cardoso de. Os povos indígenas e o seus direitos: a Declaração de San José (Anuario Antropológico [Edições Tempo Brasileiro, Rio de Janeiro] 81, 1983, p. 13–20)

Text of the Declaration of San José on

indigenous rights, with an editorial enumerating other recent human rights declarations. [W. Kracke]

265 Precolumbian plant migration. Edited by Doris Stone. Cambridge, Mass.: Peabody Museum of Archaeology and Ethnology, Harvard Univ., 1984. 183 p.: bibl., ill., maps, tables (Papers of the Peabody Museum of Archaeology and Ethnology; 76)

Nine papers evaluate the origin and spread of Amazonian cultigens, maize, cacao, manioc, peach palms, papaya, chili peppers, and coca. Essays by Roosevelt and Ford evaluate kinds of evidence. Volume is more "state of the art" than definitive. [B.L. Stark]

266 Text and image in Precolumbian art: essays on the interrelationship of the verbal and visual arts. Oxford, England: British Archaeological Reports, 1983. 212 p.: bibl., ill., tables (BAR international series; 180)

Eight papers (six Mexican, two Peruvian) on "the interrelationship of the verbal and visual arts." [N. Hammond]

267 The Transition to statehood in the New World. Edited by Grant D. Jones and Robert R. Kautz. Cambridge, England: Cambridge Univ. Press, 1981. 254 p.: bibl., ill., index (New directions in archaeology)

Following an introduction reviewing the issues, seven chapters by different authors are grouped under three headings: Sociopolitical Factors; Environmental Factors; and Ideological Factors. More theoretical than substantive, volume deals with criteria differentiating chiefdoms into states, using examples from Asia, Africa, and Oceania to support or reject models based on New World archaeology. General consensus is that no explanation yet suggested separates groups that made the transition to statehood from those that did not. [B.J. Meggers]

ARCHAEOLOGY: Mesoamerica

NORMAN HAMMOND, *Professor of Archaeology, Rutgers University*
BARBARA L. STARK, *Associate Professor of Anthropology, Arizona State University*

AS AN AFTERMATH OF THE SPECTACULAR Aztec Templo Mayor project in Mexico City, papers continue to appear discussing the excavations (items **423, 431, 432,** and **461**) or reviewing research about Tenochtitlan-Tlatelolco (items **357** and **489**). The US benefitted from a major exhibit of Aztec artifacts at the National Gallery, which included some items recovered in that project (item **442**). In addition, a major study of Aztec art appeared (item **448**), as did another semipopular book about the Aztecs (item **292**).

Ethnohistoric studies of contact period societies continue to provide a rich fund of information concerning social structure and processes of change and interaction within and among states, primarily in the Central Highlands (items **291, 299, 300, 311, 501, 504, 516, 517, 526,** and **512**). These highly anthropological studies are extremely informative for archaeologists. They provide short time depth data that are a provocative complement to the "coarse grained" archaeological chronologies in use for Central Mexico. A bibliography entirely devoted to Mesoamerican ethnohistory and compiled by S.L. Cline, appeared in *HLAS 46* (p. 81−90) and will appear again in *HLAS 48* scheduled for publication in 1987.

In addition to prolific late postclassic research, studies of preclassic era societies in the Central Highlands were numerous in the past two years (items **388, 390, 429,** and **444**), although no major revolutions in syntheses about that era have ensued. A volume about trade and exchange sets forth interpretations about economic factors in the preclassic (item **306**), and two important papers describe some of the limiting parameters for long-distance food transport (items **287** and **288**).

In addition to preclassic Chalcatzingo (items **388** and **389**), a variety of other key sites have been published in greater detail. A synthetic volume on Tula has been needed for some time (item **374**), and monographs with more technical studies about the city appeared (items **400** and **429**). Several papers and monographs deal with Teotihuacan (items **339, 356, 366, 372, 416, 464,** and **481**), some providing excavation data which complement an earlier mapping and survey project. A project began at Matacapan, Veracruz, long known as a site with intriguing Teotihuacan associations (item **468**).

Cantona, Puebla, a previously nearly unknown site, has proven to be another major urban center (item **422**). A synthetic study of Xochicalco updates information from that center using results from a survey project (item **408**).

The Valley of Oaxaca and the Monte Albán state continue to be major subjects represented in recent publications (items **309, 380, 384, 409, 418, 449, 449** and **457**). An important synthetic volume for the region (item **368**) is complemented by studies of an adjacent small valley conquered by the Zapotec (items **457** and **495**).

The Archaic period and the study of domesticated plants are crucial subjects which have been somewhat neglected in the last few years in Mesoamerica, following the surge of publications associated with Richard MacNeish's projects in highland valleys. Three contributions help redress this situation (items **315, 334,** and **368**).

Among general contributions that synthesize research are overviews: of agricultural systems (items **261** and **286**); of the role of regional scale surveys (item **270**); of the study of cultural evolution (item **280**); and of the nature of Mesoamerica (items **319** and **322**). An effort to reexamine and untangle "highland-lowland interaction" in Mesoamerica is represented in a volume mainly devoted to Teotihuacan-lowland Maya relationships (item **305**).

A new volume on the Olmecs (item **332**) and a popular paperbound survey of Mesoamerican prehistory (item **285**) constitute substantive syntheses. Other new resources are a history of Mesoamerican research (item **279**), new editions of two readers (items **271** and **324**), and a guide to library materials for Mesoamerican archaeology (item **316**). In addition, Dumbarton Oaks has produced a number of thematic volumes slanted toward cognitive interpretations (items **328, 343, 378** and **436**).

It is a pleasure to report two new series. The Consejo of the INAH has begun an annual publication about current projects in Mexico (item **360**). The reporting is more substantial than that included in the *American Antiquity* Current Research section (item **312, 316,** and **417**). However, the President of the Consejo reports that the first contents did not cover many projects and expansion is anticipated. In addition, the Facultad de Arquitectura of UNAM has begun issuing a monographic series entitled "Cuadernos de Arquitectura Mesoamericana," which contain excellent architectural drawings (items **295** and **297**).

For the Maya area there are further excellent books of synthesis (item **321**), and a synoptic critical article (item **317**) stimulating several comments and correctives (items **272, 398,** and **454**). The preceramic period is discussed in a Mesoamerica-wide article (item **315**) and in a summary of MacNeish's work in Belize (item **497**): the evidence on both the local and the general scales is still ambiguous in many respects. Preclassic work has included reports on major sites such as Mirador (item **373**) and Edzná (item **430**), smaller centers such as Tzutzuculi (item **424**), and minor but early sites including Paso de la Amada (item 367) and Playa de los Muertos (item 413). At the other end of the Maya prehispanic period there are monographs on settlement on Cozumel in the postclassic (item 383) and on the finds from the Sacred Cenote at Chichén Itzá (item 364), and papers on work in the Petén (item 459) and in Belize (items 450 and 451). There are numerous reports on work at some important classic period sites, particularly in the southern portion of the Maya area where the first of the monographs on work at Copán appeared (item 411) together with articles on subsequent work (items 284, 379, 427, 428, 460, 465, 473, 479, 490, and 494) and a monograph on pottery (item 354). For Quirigua there are two monographs (items 344 and 456) and several papers (items 344, 345, 456, and 472), and sites in El Salvador have yielded a final monograph (item 342) and papers (items 359 and 382). Belize continues to generate a large body of material, including a book (item 371) and papers on the chert workshops of Colha (items 405, 406, 407 and 471), papers on the offshore trading and fishing station of Moho Cay (items 402 and 425) and the nearby preclassic through postclassic and colonial site of Lamanai (items 450 and 451), and on sites in the Caracol region of the Maya Mountains (items 401, 403, and 499). Monograph coverage of a 1974 survey of northern Belize (item 474) and the 1979 work at Pulltrouser Swamp (item 455) was published. Small sites were studied in several parts of the country (items 420 and 484). A small number of papers was published on the neighboring Petén (items 459, 510, 514 and 530), including Tikal (item 314) on which there is another volume in the final monographic series (item 486).

Additional monographs on the northern lowlands have appeared such as the Becan work of the 1970s (items 482 and 487) and the first reports on the Edzná project (item 430), together with a book on Cobá (item 381) and two shorter studies (items 278 and 355) of the site. The Cozumel Project of 1972–73 yielded two further books (items 383 and 395) and Dzibilchaltun another monograph (item 370).

In Chiapas, partly Maya lowland, partly highland and partly Pacific coast, there are several publications on Toniná (items 277, 522, and 523). Vol. 1 of an important series on the sculptures of Palenque also appeared (item 387).

Maya trade is discussed by a number of authors (items 272, 273, 287, 288, 336, 399, 402, 406, 439, 460, and 480), mainly in terms of salt and obsidian, with a concentration on long-distance exchange also brought out in the study of the Sacred Cenote material (item 364). The role of water management is discussed by several authors (items 401, 455, 469, and 476), and there is a considerable number of books and papers devoted to subsistence, including agricultural techniques, species grown (items 322, 337, 338, 403, 425, 455, and 487), and animal use (items 395 and 453).

Further developments in the study of Maya hieroglyphic writing included a major work on the verbs (item 534), a further installment of the *Corpus of hieroglyphic inscriptions* (item 522), a treatise on the codices (item 519), and a number of discussions of individual sites, monuments and writing elements (items 277, 284, 327, 503, 506, 510, 523, 524, 530, 532, and 533).

The history of Maya archaeology was dealt with in a two-volume *festschrift* for Gordon Willey, which contains a plethora of papers that are especially strong on settlement patterns of the Maya (items 283 and 325). The history of Maya archaeology is dealt with in another paper (item 303). Finally, the present threat to monuments from looting is chillingly documented for a particular area of the Maya lowlands (item 301).

Many of the following annotations were prepared by Scott Fedick, who assisted Stark, and by Hasso von Winning, a prior contributor to this section. The authors thank the many colleagues and publishers who generously assisted us by providing reprints and publications. Of course, in some cases items were not available for examination and could not be included. Regrettably, limitations of space imposed by *HLAS* which is, above all, a "selective" bibliography, required that we list several volumes below without separately annotating each individual paper they contain.

GENERAL

268 Ackerly, Neal W. and Dennis L. Young. Formative period political differentiation in the Southern Valley of Mexico: a comment on Steponaitis (AAA/AA, 86:4, Dec. 1984, p. 976–985, bibl., tables)
An earlier paper about agricultural productivity and political differentiation is critiqued in regard to the efficacy of its statistical analysis. [BLS]

269 Adams, R.E.W. Rank size analysis of Northern Belize Maya sites (BISRA/BS, 11:6, 1983, p. 1–8, bibl.)
Regional application of the method used more widely (see *HLAS 45:263*); Nohmul, Lamanai and Aventura are the largest centers on this method. [NH]

270 Ammerman, Albert J. Surveys and archaeological research (Annual Review of Anthropology [Annual Reviews Inc., Palo Alto, Calif.] 10, 1981, p. 63–88, bibl.)
Reviews the contribution of regional scale surveys within the US Southwest, Valley of Mexico, and Mesopotamia. [SF]

271 Ancient Mesoamerica: selected readings. Edited by John A. Graham. 2nd ed. Palo Alto, Calif.: Peek Publications, 1981. 366 p.: bibl., ill., maps, tables.
The contents (all reprinted) are considerably changed from the 1966 title. Only six of 27 papers are the same. Subsistence, art history, decipherment, unusual discoveries, and key sites are featured. [BLS]

272 Andrews, Anthony P. Long-distance exchange among the Maya: a comment on Marcus (SAA/AA, 49:4, Oct. 1984, p. 826–828)
Suggests that Marcus (item **317**) underestimates the importance of trade in perishable goods such as salt, and thereby the impact of long-distance trade in general. [NH]

273 ———. Maya salt production and trade. Tucson: Univ. of Arizona Press, 1983. 1 v.: bibl., index.
Competent survey of archaeological and ethnographic evidence for coastal and inland salt production, with emphasis on Yucatan and Chiapas but extending to El Salvador. [NH]

274 Andrews, George F. Xkichmook revisited: Puuc vs. Chenes architecture (Cuadernos de Arquitectura Mesoamericana [UNAM, México] 1, feb. 1984, p. 49–87, bibl., ill.)
Reviews the architecture of a key site for the understanding of chronology and cultural history of the Chenes and Puuc regions. Copiously illustrated. [HvW]

275 Barthel, Thomas S. Tohil, der Feuerbringer (IAI/I, 1984, p. 207–219, bibl., ill.)
Detailed analysis of text and motifs on a polychrome late classic vase from highland Guatemala, referring to the Quichean deities Tohil (the Fire Giver) and Balamquitze (the Fire Receiver). Concludes that the vase is the first reported evidence of prehispanic Quiché rebus writing. [HvW]

276 ———. Von Mexiko zum Indus (MLV/T, 33, 1984, p. 75–79, bibl., ill.)
Preliminary report on investigation of analogies among calendar animals on copper plates from Mohenjodaro (Indus Valley) and those of the Chinese zodiac with the Mexican day signs. [HvW]

277 Becquelin, Pierre and Eric Taladoire. Informe de la cuarta temporada de excavaciones en Toniná, Chiapas, 1979 (CEM/ECM, 13, 1981, p. 349–371, bibl., ill., tables)
Preliminary report on work at the main center and subsidiary ruins in surrounding valley. The most important find reported is Monument 101 with an Initial Series of 10.4.0.0.0. (AD 909). [NH]

278 Benavides Castillo, Antonio. Cobá y Tulum: adaptación al medio ambiente y control del medio social (CEM/ECM, 13, 1981, p. 205–222, bibl., ill., tables)

Reports recent settlement pattern work (up to 1979) at Cobá and Tulum, Q.R., with definition of urban zones and a discussion of Maya urbanism. [NH]

279 Bernal, Ignacio. A history of Mexican archaeology: the vanished civilizations of Middle America. London: Thames and Hudson, 1980. 208 p.: bibl., ill., index.

Fine, well written history that goes up to 1950. Well illustrated. [BLS]

280 Blanton, Richard E. Advances in the study of cultural evolution in prehispanic highland Mesoamerica (Advances in World Archaeology [Academic Press, New York] 2, 1983, p. 245–288, bibl., maps)

Overview of domestication, first villages, early social hierarchies, origins of states and cities, and late period reorganization. Critiques cultural ecological explanations founded on population pressure, irrigation, and economic symbiosis. Brief sketch of future research topics. [BLS]

281 ———. The ecological perspective in highland Mesoamerican archaeology (in Archaeological hammers and theories. Edited by James A. Moore and Arthur S. Keene. New York: Academic Press, 1983, p. 221–231, bibl. [Studies in archaeology])

Critiques "population determinism" as an explanation for cultural evolution. An alternative approach involving social and demographic dynamics among communities is discussed with reference to the Valley of Oaxaca. [SF and BLS]

282 ——— and Gary Feinman. The Mesoamerican world system (AAA/AA, 86:3, Sept. 1984, p. 673–682, bibl.)

An argument that interregional relations are critical to understand Mesoamerica. A "world system" model is useful, but with more emphasis on luxury trade than admitted by I. Wallerstein. [BLS]

Calendars in Mesoamerica and Peru: native American computations of time. See item **505.**

283 Civilization in the ancient Americas: essays in honor of Gordon R. Willey. Edited by Richard M. Leventhal and Alan L. Kolata. Albuquerque: Univ. of New Mexico Press; Cambridge, Mass.: Peabody Museum of Archaeology and Ethnology, Harvard Univ., 1983. 487 p.: bibl., ill., index.

Series of tributary essays from Willey's students, mostly on Maya topics. [NH]

284 Closs, Michael P.; Anthony F. Aveni; and Bruce Crowley. The planet Venus and Temple 22 at Copan (IAI/I, 1984, p. 221–247, bibl., ill., tables)

Discussion of the cosmological-mythical role of Venus and its apparition in a window of Temple 22 whose iconography is related to the planet. "The northern extremes of Venus and the apparition in the window are complementary and can be combined to yield a scheme for making (almost) annual observations of Venus at or near the beginning of the rainy season," the beginning of the agricultural cycle. [HvW]

285 Davies, Nigel. The ancient kingdoms of Mexico: a magnificent recreation of their art and life. New York: Penguin Books, 1982. 272 p.: bibl., ill., index, maps.

"Readable" synthesis is weak on archaeology of earlier periods, but strong on Toltec and Aztec developments. [BLS]

286 Denevan, William M. Tipología de configuraciones agrícolas prehispánicas (III/AI, 40:4, 1980, p. 619–652, bibl.)

Different agricultural constructions are described for the New World, and their functions and prehistoric occurrences are noted. Valuable survey. [BLS]

287 Drennan, Robert D. Long-distance movement of goods in the Mesoamerican formative and classic (SAA/AA, 49:1, Jan. 1984, p. 27–43, bibl., maps, tables)

An evaluation of long-distance exchange in the development of complex societies. Concludes there was a geographically restricted role for food transport and a delayed major role for long-distance movement of other goods. [SF]

288 ———. Long-distance transport costs in prehispanic Mesoamerica (AAA/AA, 86:1, March 1984, p. 105–112, bibl., map, tables)

Calculates economic limits for effective tributary food transport given foot travel: 275 km. High value, light weight luxury goods may travel further. Aztec data constitute a case example. [BLS]

289 Dütting, Dieter. Venus, the moon and the gods of the Palenque triad (DGV/ZE, 109, 1984, p. 7–74, bibl., ill.)

Author (aided by Matthias Schramm in the computation of astronomical positions) investigates if the timing of some historical events (accession of rulers, etc.) was influenced by significant celestial phenomena. Dates, particularly from Palenque, appear to be linked by full multiples of sidereal lunar months (and triple sidereal months), implying comparable lunar mansions. Analysis of the 2 Cib 14 Mol event at Palenque indicates rituals were performed to evoke rebirth or resurrection of Pacal. Deities intimately connected with resurrection process are the Moon Goddess and gods of Palenque triad that correspond to the descending Evening Star and Night-Sun (GIII), Morning Star (GI) and reborn Sun (GII). Data strongly support the 584285 variant of the GMT correlation, first proposed by Thompson in 1935. [HvW]

290   Essays in Otomanguean culture history. Edited by J. Kathryn Josserand, Marcus Winter, and Nicholas Hopkins. Nashville: Vanderbilt Univ., 1984. 225 p.: bibl., ill., maps, tables (Publications in anthropology; 31)

Two papers emphasize relationships between linguistics and archaeology. Another considers Mixtec dialects. Byland's paper deviates in that it concentrates on archaeological ceramic boundaries compared with ethnohistoric records. [BLS]

291   Explorations in ethnohistory: Indians of Central Mexico in the sixteenth century. Edited by H.R. Harvey and Hanns J. Prem. Albuquerque: Univ. of New Mexico Press, 1983. 311 p.: ill., maps, tables.

Excellent array of detailed studies. Subjects include: royal marriages, land tenure, cadastral registers, household organization, labor requirements, agricultural implements, and toponyms. For ethnohistorian's comment, see *HLAS 46:1530.* [BLS]

292   Fagan, Brian M. The Aztecs. New York: W.H. Freeman, 1984. 322 p.: bibl., ill., index, maps.

A highly "readable" introduction covering the history of Aztec studies, the antecedents and rise of the Aztec state, the economic and governmental base of the imperial state, social organization, cosmology, and the Spanish conquest and aftermath. [SF]

293   Flora and fauna imagery in precolumbian cultures: iconography and function. Edited by Jeanette F. Peterson. Oxford, England: British Archaeological Reports, 1983. 178 p.: bibl., ill., maps (BAR International series; 171)

Eight chapters of interdisciplinary studies which associate fauna and flora with their original ecological and cultural contexts. Only two papers are non-Mesoamerican in content. [SF]

294   Folan, William J. Mining and quarrying techniques of the lowland Maya (Anthropology [Dept. of Anthropology, SUNY, Stony Brook] 6:1/2, May/Dec. 1982, p. 149–174, bibl., ill.)

Survey of techniques for extracting building stone, potters' clay and attapulgite, using data from Cobá, Quintana Roo, for illustration. [NH]

295   Gendrop, Paul. La crestería maya y su posible simbolismo dinástico (Cuadernos de Arquitectura Mesoamericana [UNAM, México] 1, feb. 1984, p. 24–38, bibl., ill.)

Useful overview of Maya roof combs. Those enshrining effigies of rulers and deity masks, as well as the emblem towers in the Chenes region, are probably dynastic displays of power. [HvW]

296   ———. Los estilos Río Bec, Chenes y Puuc en la arquitectura maya. México: UNAM, Facultad de Arquitectura, 1983. 248 p.: bibl., ill, maps, plans.

First comprehensive treatise of the late classic regional architectural styles of northern Yucatan. [HvW]

297   ——— et al. El tablero-talud y otros perfiles arquitectónicos: pt. l (Cuadernos de Arquitectura Mesoamericana [UNAM, Facultad de Arquitectura, México] 2, julio 1984, p. 1–96 p., bibl., ill.)

Contains eight profusely illustrated articles on external architectural features in Mesoamerica. Also Spanish translation of George Kubler's "Renascence and Disjunction in the Art of Mesoamerican Antiquity" (see *HLAS 41:312*). [HvW]

298   Giesing, Kornelia. Rudra-Śiva und Tezcatlipoca: ein Beitrag zur Indo-Mexikanistik. Tübingen, FRG: Verlag Science & Fiction, 1984. 347 p.: bibl., ill., tables (Reihe, Ethnologische Studien; 1)

The polytheism of Greater India and Mexico, the various manifestations of Rudra (Śiva) and of Tezcatlipoca have similar functions. Each deity complex is scrutinized to evaluate and expand previously postulated equivalences (by T.S. Barthel) between Tezcatlipoca in the Borgia group manuscripts and his Hinduistic prototype in copious Sanskrit sources. Under strict methodological guidelines, author examines, in particular, honorific name lists in terms of their historical and thematic components and their relevance for the structural analysis of Codex Borgia, in progress at Tübingen Univ. [HvW]

299 Gledhill, John and **Mogens Larsen.** The Polanyi paradigm and a dynamic analysis of archaic states (*in* Theory and explanation in archaeology: the Southampton conference. Edited by Colin Renfrew, Michael J. Rowlands, and Barbara Abbott Segraves. New York: Academic Press, 1982, p. 197–229, bibl., ill., map)

Dynamic cycles of state political and economic centralization are viewed as interacting with decentralized interests in the Aztec case. Markets, merchants, landholding, and state level political actions are dissected. [BLS]

300 Gorenstein, Shirley and **Helen Perlstein Pollard.** The Tarascan civilization: a late prehispanic cultural system. Nashville, Tenn.: Vanderbilt Univ., 1983. 199 p.: bibl., ill. (Publications in anthropology; 28)

Uses ethnohistoric, modern, and limited archaeological survey data (noncollection strategy employed) to examine regional integration, economy, transport networks, and population-resource relations. Emphasis is on nature of the Tarascan state, especially in comparison to Aztecs. [BLS]

301 Gutchen, Mark. The destruction of archaeological resources in Belize, Central America (AFA/JFA, 10, 1983, p. 217–228)

Sobering and meticulous tabulation of the ravages of looting of Maya sites. [NH]

302 Hammond, Norman. The development of Belizean archaeology (AT/A, 57:219, March 1983, p. 19–58, bibl., map)

In a general context of the history of Maya archaeology, describes progress of archaeological work in the Crown Colony of British Honduras from 1895 through independence to present-day Belize. [NH]

303 ———. Nineteenth-century drawings of Maya monuments in the Society's library (Antiquaries Journal [Society of Antiquaries, London] 64:1, 1984, p. 84–103, ill.)

Identifies drawings of monuments at Tikal, Ixkun and Ixtutz as copies of those made for Modesto Méndez in 1848 and 1852 expeditions. [NH]

304 Hartung, Horst. Alignments in architecture and sculpture of Maya centers: notes on Piedras Negras, Copan and Chichen Itza (IAA, 10:2, 1984, p. 223–240, bibl., ill.)

Convergence of astronomical and/or geometric reference lines indicates a sophisticated network governing the planning design, alignments, and relations between structures and hieroglyphic monuments at these sites. [HvW]

305 Highland-lowland interaction in Mesoamerica: interdisciplinary approaches: a conference at Dumbarton Oaks, October 18th and 19th, 1980. Edited by Arthur G. Miller. Washington: Dumbarton Oaks, Trustees for Harvard Univ., 1983. 263 p.: bibl., ill., maps, tables.

Agricultural and astronomical technology, obsidian and ceramic trade, and linguistic borrowings are among the topics examined. Teotihuacan's impact on the lowland Maya is the major theme investigated, but other regions or sites, such as Cacaxtla, figure in some papers. [BLS]

306 Hirth, Kenneth G. Catchment analysis and formative settlement in the Valley of Mexico (AAA/AA, 86:1, March 1984, p. 136–143, bibl., tables)

Questions utility of catchment analysis by Steponaitis (see *HLAS 45:357*). [BLS]

307 Iglesias Ponce de León, María Josefa and **Andrés Ciudad Ruiz.** Informe preliminar sobre la cerámica funeraria de Agua Tibia, Totonicapán, Guatemala (CEM/ECM, 13, 1981, p. 251–264, bibl., ill.)

Description of excavations of small cemetery of 19 burials in western highlands of Guatemala, dating to late classic. [NH]

308 *Jahrbuch für Geschichte von Staat, Wirtschaft und Gesellschaft Lateinamerikas.* Vol. 20, 1983– . Köln, FRG.

Entire issue consists of *Festschrift*

for Erwin Palm and contains following articles on archaeology: Angel García Cook "Capulac-Concepción, P-211: un Juego de Pelota Temprano en el Altiplano Central de México" (p. 1–16); Eduardo Matos Moctezuma "Notas sobre Algunas Urnas Funerarias del Templo Mayor" (p. 17–32); Ignacio Bernal "Un Tipo de Pectorales de Oaxaca" (p. 33–40); Horst Hartung "La Estructuración de los Alzados en la Arquitectura Precolombina de Mitla" (p. 41–60); Franz Tichy "El Patrón de Asentamientos con Sistema Radical en la Meseta Central de México: ¿'Sistema Ceque' en Mesoamérica?" (p. 61–84); Dieter Klaus and Wilhelm Lauer "Humanökologische Aspekte der vorspanischen Besiedlungsgeschichte, Bevölkerungsentwicklung und Gesellschaftsstruktur im mexikanischen Hochland" (p. 85–120); Klaus Heine "Outline of Man's Impact on the Natural Environment in Central Mexico" (p. 121–131); and Bodo Spranz "Berichte über die im 18. Jahrhundert entdeckten Ruinen von Palenque, Mexiko, in einer deutschen Veröffentlichung von 1832" (p. 239–256). [HvW]

309 Kowalewski, Stephen A.; Richard E. Blanton; Gary Feinman; and Laura Finsten. Boundaries, scale, and internal organization (Journal of Anthropological Archaeology [Academic Press, New York] 2 : 1, March 1983, p. 32–56, bibl., ill., map, tables)
Archaeological measures for social system size, centralization, and boundary permeability are applied to regional survey data from the Valley of Oaxaca. [SF]

310 Kubler, George. Portales con columnas-serpiente en Yucatán y el altiplano (Anales del Instituto de Investigaciones Estéticas [UNAM, México] 52, 1983, p. 21–45, bibl., ill., tables)
Discussion of iconography, function, and chronological development of serpent-column portals at Chichén Itzá, Mayapan, Tulum and Tula with reference to mythographic serpents. Points out the ideological and political changes affecting these sculptures in Toltec and pre-Toltec art. [HvW]

311 Lameiras, Brigitte B. de. El mercado y el Estado en el México prehispánico (III/AI, 42 : 3, julio/sept. 1982, p. 381–407, bibl.
Discussion of Marxist and formalist views of Aztec economy. For the Aztecs, po-

litical and economic changes were complexly related. [BLS]

312 Laporte Molina, Juan Pedro. Bibliografía de la arqueología guatemalteca. Guatemala: Dirección General de Antropología, 1981. 271 p.
Useful compilation of works on Maya research in Guatemala. [NH]

313 Lauer, Wilhelm and Enno Seele. Geographische Beobachtungen zu einer frühen Besiedelung in Quintana Roo, Mexiko (MLV/T, 33, 1984, p. 133–142, bibl, maps)
Investigation of geomorphological conditions and the availability of raw material for stone tools and of food procurement to determine the environmental adequacy for preceramic settlement locations. [HvW]

314 MacKinnon, J. Jefferson. The nature of residential Tikal: a spatial analysis (CEM/ECM, 13, 1981, p. 223–249, bibl., tables)
Suggests that residence was in family units, with little evidence of hierarchy or pervasive political control of settlement. [NH]

315 MacNeish, Richard S. and Antoinette Nelken-Terner. The preceramic of Mesoamerica (AFA/JFA, 10, 1983, p. 71–84)
Summary of the extant evidence, with a perhaps overconfident identification of some doubtful sites and uncertain chronologies, organized into four Early Man substages and three Archaic substages; a provocative paper with an even chance of proving its authors correct. [NH]

316 Magee, Susan Forston. Mesoamerican archaeology: a guide to the literature and other information sources. Austin: Univ. of Texas, Institute of Latin American Studies, 1981. 71 p.: bibl., index (Guides and bibliographies series; 12)
Paperback introduction to library materials which is valuable for students and professionals alike. [BLS]

317 Marcus, Joyce. Lowland Maya archaeology at the crossroads (SAA/AA, 48 : 3, 1983, p. 454–488)
Examination, by specialist in highland (Oaxacan) archaeology, of the current state of knowledge in Maya lowland studies. Critical polemic with an emphasis on site hierarchy

and correlation with dynastic texts (see also items **272, 398,** and **454**). [NH]

318 ———. Mesoamerican territorial boundaries: reconstructions from archaeology and hieroglyphic writing (Archaeological Reviews from Cambridge [Dept. of Archaeology] 3:2, 1984, p. 48–62, bibl., ill., maps)

Complementary classes of data differentially define territorial boundaries between the Aztecs and Tarascans, for the Monte Albán state, and among classic Maya polities. [SF]

319 **Matos Moctezuma, Eduardo.** El proceso de desarrollo en Mesoamérica (Boletín de Antropología Americana [Instituto Panamericano de Geografía e Historia, México] 5, julio 1982, p. 117–131, charts, map)

Essay on the intellectual history of concepts regarding Mesoamerica—spatial, cultural, and especially temporal (stages of development). Groups developmental schemes into two schools of thought. [BLS]

320 **Melgarejo Vivanco, José Luis.** Antigua ecología indígena en Veracruz. Xalapa, México: Gobierno del Estado de Veracruz, Dirección de Asuntos Ecológicos, 1980. 125 p.: bibl., ill.

Rather speculative and dated treatment of archaeological data. Overview relies mainly on documents and geography. [BLS]

321 **Morley, Sylvanus Griswold** and **George W. Brainerd.** The ancient Maya. Revised by Robert J. Sharer. 4th ed. Stanford, Calif.: Stanford Univ. Press, 1983. 708 p.: bibl., ill., index.

Excellent revision and recasting of a classic popular work. [NH]

322 **Pasztory, Esther.** The function of art in Mesoamerica (AIA/A, 37:1, Jan./Feb. 1984, p. 18–25, ill.)

Highlights art in societies as a communication system, form of wealth, competitive display of political power, religious symbols, and a factor in state legitimation. [SF]

323 **Peters, Charles M.** Observations on Maya subsistence and the ecology of a tropical tree (SAA/AA, 48:3, 1983, p. 610–615)

Continues debate on use of *ramón* (*Brosimum alicastrum*) by the Maya initiated by Reina and Hill (see *HLAS 43:407*) and continued by Miksicek *et al* (see *HLAS 45:574*). Argues that distribution is mainly edaphic, not economic, but that at Tikal density is such that artificial selection by the Maya may have been practiced. [NH]

324 **Precolumbian art history:** selected readings. Edited by Alana Cordy-Collins. Palo Alto, Calif.: Peek Publications, 1982. 343 p.: bibl., ill., maps.

Although bearing the same title as an earlier "reader," contents do not overlap. Ten articles pertain to Mesoamerica, and all are new. Includes topics on Pacific coast of Guatemala, lowland Maya, Teotihuacan, Veracruz, the Mixtec, and Aztec. [BLS]

325 **Prehistoric settlement patterns:** essays in honor of Gordon R. Willey. Edited by Evon Z. Vogt and Richard M. Leventhal. Albuquerque: Univ. of New Mexico Press; Cambridge, Mass.: Peabody Museum of Archaeology and Ethnology, Harvard Univ., 1983. 519 p.: bibl., ill., index.

Fourteen of 21 chapters deal with Mesoamerican topics ranging in scale from households through communities, cities, and regions. Several chapters are devoted to general concepts and methods. [SF]

326 **Prem, Hanns J.** Chronologische Miszellen IV: Die Herrscherfolge von Colhuacan (Mexicon [Berlin] 6:6, Nov. 1984, p. 86–89, bibl., tables)

Clarifies the sequence of early rulers of Colhuacan. [HvW]

327 **Riese, Berthold.** Kriegsberichte der klassischen Maya (MV/BA, 30, 1982, p. 255–321, bibl., ill., map)

Glyph compounds that refer to war (e.g., prisoner, capture, victor, etc.) are analyzed in terms of their structure, semantics, and iconographic contexts. Compilation of numerous occurrences reveals the bellicose expeditions by the classic Maya in the lowlands which are mapped. [HvW]

328 **Ritual human sacrifice in Mesoamerica:** a conference at Dumbarton Oaks, October 13th and 14th, 1979. Organized by Elizabeth P. Benson. Edited by Elizabeth H. Boone. Washington: Dumbarton Oaks Research Library and Collection, 1984. 247 p.: bibl., ill.

Examines Gulf coast, Maya, and Aztec sacrificial practices. Also contains analysis of the Aztec Templo Mayor. Most papers stress the cultural meaning of sacrifice. [BLS]

329 Shao, Paul. The origin of ancient American cultures. Ames: Iowa State Univ. Press, 1983. 374 p.: bibl., ill., maps.

Non-scientific attempt to derive Meso-american cultures from East Asia. [BLS]

330 Sodi, Demetrio. Los mayas, el tiempo capturado. Editado por Beatrice True-blood. México: Bancomer, 1980. 312 p.: appendices, bibl., charts, ill., index, maps.

Elegant and well illustrated volume on the history, arts and architecture, and ethnology of the Maya, with contributions by Merle Green Robertson on glyphic texts. Edition of 20,000 copies distributed (privately) by Bancomer. [HvW]

331 Soustelle, Jacques. Les Maya. Paris: Flammarion, 1982. 253 p.: bibl., ill. (some col.) (L'Odyssée)

Popular account by veteran authority on Mesoamerica, embracing ancient and modern Maya culture. [NH]

332 ———. The Olmecs: the oldest civilization in Mexico. Garden City, N.Y.: Doubleday, 1984. 214 p.: bibl., ill., index, maps.

Well written synthesis considers both Gulf coast Olmecs and their relation to other regions. Considerable emphasis on sculptural interpretation. [BLS]

333 Space and time in the cosmovision of Mesoamerica. Edited by Franz Tichy. Munich, FRG: Wilhelm Fink Verlag, 1982. 195 p.: bibl., ill. (Lateinamerika-Studien; 10)

Contains: Anthony F. Aveni and Horst Hartung "New Observations of the Pecked Cross Petroglyph" (p. 25–42); John B. Carlson "The Structure of Mayapan: a Major Post-classic Site in Northern Yucatan" (p. 43–62); Franz Tichy "The Axial Direction of Meso-american Ceremonial Centers on 17° North of West and Their Associations to Calendar and Cosmovision" (p. 63–83); Maarten E.R.G.N. Jansen "The Four Quarters of the Mixtec World" (p. 85–96); Anneliese Mön-nich "The *Tonalpohualli* of *Codex Tudela* and the Four Quarters of the World" (p. 97–110); Ulrich Köhler "On the Significance of the Aztec Day Sign *Olin*" (p. 111–128); Johanna Broda "La Fiesta Azteca del Fuego

Nuevo y el Culto de las Pléyades" (p. 129–158); Michel Graulich "Quecholli et Pan-quetzaliztli: une Nouvelle Interprétation" (p. 159–174); Anthony F. Aveni "Horizontal Astronomy in Incaic Cuzco" (p. 175–194). [HvW]

334 Spranz, Bodo. Sesshafte Wildbeuter in Mesoamerika (PMK, 30, 1984, p. 331–337, bibl., map)

Reviews recent data on the transition from nomadic hunter-gatherers to settled plant domesticators. But varied regional ecological conditions led to permanent settlements without practice of agriculture. [HvW]

335 Steponaitis, Vincas P. Some further remarks on catchments, nonproducers, and tribute flow in the Valley of Mexico (AAA/AA, 86:1, March 1984, p. 143–148, bibl., tables)

Effort to rebut Hirth's criticisms (see item **306**). Further discussion of catchment assumptions. [BLS]

336 Trade and exchange in early Meso-america. Edited by Kenneth G. Hirth. Albuquerque: Univ. of New Mexico Press, 1984. 338 p.: bibl., ill., index.

Useful conference volume with emphasis on the formation of the economy and relationships between economic and social structure. Papers cover central Mexico, Oaxaca, Chiapas and highland Guatemala, omitting the Maya lowlands and the Gulf coast. Introductory and theoretical papers concentrate on regional exchange systems, and the time frame is more or less restricted to the middle and late formative 1000 BC-AD 300. [NH]

337 Turner, B.L., II. Agricultura y desar-rollo del Estado en las tierras bajas mayas (CEM/ECM, 13, 1981, p. 285–306, bibl.)

Paper (from the 1979 Vancouver Congress of Americanists) summarizing Turner's views at the time (with addendum updating them) on the role of intensive agriculture in lowland Maya society. [NH]

338 ——— and Charles H. Miksicek. Economic plant species associated with prehistoric agriculture in the Maya lowlands (Economic Botany [New Botanical Garden *for the* Society for Economic Botany, New York] 38:2, 1984, p. 179–193, tables)

Evaluates evidence for staple crops and

examines problems such as *ramón*, cacao, root crops and amaranth. Notes concentration of data from northern Belize, and absence of material from some commonly consumed species such as bean, tomato, and roots. [NH]

339 von Winning, Hasso. Insignias de oficio en la iconografía de Teotihuacan (Pantoc [Publicaciones antropológicas de Occidente, Instituto de Investigaciones Antropológicas, Univ. Autónoma de Guadalajara, México] 8, junio/dic. 1984, p. 5–54, bibl., ill.)

Analyzes headdresses and emblems that denote occupation and social status among the elite of Teotihuacan at home and abroad. [HvW]

FIELDWORK AND ARTIFACTS

340 Agurcía Fasquelle, Ricardo. Asentamientos del clásico tardío en el Valle de Comayagua (YAXKIN, 3:4, dic. 1980, p. 249–264, bibl., maps)

Description, based on six sites south of Comayagua, of settlement in a highland Honduras valley. [NH]

341 Alvarez A., Carlos. Las esculturas de Teotenango (UNAM/ECN, 16, 1983, p. 233–264, bibl., ill.)

Numerous sculptures from large hilltop site (AD 700-1521) and environs include calendric inscriptions with human and animal low reliefs, with Teotihuacan and, mainly, Xochicalco influences. Rock art (1162–1476) is attributed to Matlatzinca expansion, followed by Mexica domination with fine Aztec sculptures. [HvW]

343 The Art and iconography of late postclassic Central Mexico. Edited by Elizabeth Hill Boone. Washington: Dumbarton Oaks, Trustees for Harvard Univ., 1982. 254 p.: bibl., ill., maps, tables.

Highly eclectic volume which includes several iconographic analyses of Aztec and Mixtec documents and a formal study of Aztec sculpture. There also are papers on Malinalco, Texcocan legal processes, and the Mixteca-Puebla concept. [BLS]

344 Ashmore, Wendy. Classic Maya wells at Quirigua, Guatemala: household facilities in a water-rich setting (SAA/AA, 49:1, 1984, p. 147–153)

Reports ceramic-lined tube wells with expanded base and stone filter bed in the Motagua flood-plain. [NH]

345 ———. Quirigua archaeology and history revised (AFA/JFA, 11, 1984, p. 365–386)

Reports later work (1978–79) at this Motagua Valley site, concentrating on settlement pattern studies; most data comes from the period AD 400–800, and the nature of Quirigua as a terminal classic center of Peten-inspired origin is discussed (see *HLAS 41:440*). [NH]

346 Aspects of the Mixteca-Puebla style and Mixtec and central Mexican culture in Southern Mesoamerica: papers from a symposium. Organized by Doris Stone. John Paddock *et al.* New Orleans, La.: Middle American Research Institute, Tulane Univ., 1982. 76 p.: bibl., ill. (some col.) (Occasional paper; 4)

Seven papers discuss several topics: 1) this style in Oaxaca, especially in ceramics; 2) Mixtec historical manuscripts, especially the Codex *Nuttall*; 3) Mixtec iconography; 4) the Santa Rita murals; and 5) Mexican highland impact on Costa Rica. [BLS]

347 Aveni, A. and H. Hartung. The observation of the sun at the time of passage through the zenith in Mesoamerica (Archaeoastronomy [Supplement to the Journal for the History of Astronomy, Giles, England] 12:3, 1981, p. 51–70, bibl., ill.)

Stresses the importance of the zenith sun in Mesoamerican astronomy. Describes astronomical devices at Xochicalco and Monte Albán, suggesting them to be "zenith tubes." [SF]

348 Bankmann, Ulf. Eine Jadeitmaske aus Tizatlan, Tlaxcala (Mexicon [Berlin, FRG] 5:5, Sept. 1984, p. 80–84, bibl., ill.)

Clarifies that this magnificent mask, now in the Basel Völkerkunde Museum, was found in Tizatlan by Dupaix in 1807. [HvW]

349 ———. Ometochtecomatl, ein altmexikanisches Pulquegefäss im Museum zu Basel (Verhandlungen der Naturf. Gessellschaft [Basel, Switzerland] 94, 1984, p. 307–320, bibl., ill.)

Commentary on stone and ceramic vessels with attributes of pulque gods. [HvW]

350 Baquedano, Elizabeth. Aztec sculpture. London: British Museum Publications, 1984. 96 p.: bibl., ill., index.
Descriptive catalogue of over 50 sculptures in the British Museum. Omits references to earlier interpretative articles (e.g., by Seler, Nicholson, etc.). Includes glossary. [HvW]

351 Barba de Piña Chán, Beatriz. Tlapacoya: los principios de la teocracia en la cuenca de México. Prefacio por Julio Cesar Olivé. 2a ed. México: Biblioteca Enciclopédica del Estado de México, 1980. 198, 77 p.: appendices, bibls., ill., maps, plans (Biblioteca Enciclopédica del Estado de México; 103)
Reprinting of 1956 monograph (see *HLAS 20:91*). [BLS]

352 Barrera Rubio, Alfredo. Los relieves dinámico-narrativos de San Diego, Yucatán, México (Mexicon [Berlin, FRG] 5:4, July 1983, p. 63–68)
Illustrated description of six extraordinary low-reliefs characterized by free movement and figures in lively scenes including wrestling, dancing, and playing musical instruments. [NH]

353 Baus de Czitrom, Carolyn. Tecuexes y cocas: dos grupos de la región Jalisco en el siglo XVI. México: INAH, 1982. 107 p.: bibl., ill., maps, tables (Colección científica. Serie etnohistoria; 112)
Primarily an ethnohistoric description of the two groups, but includes a review of extant archaeological data from the two zones. [BLS]

354 Beaudry, Marilyn P. Ceramic production and distribution in the Southeastern Maya periphery: late classic painted serving vessels. Oxford, England: British Archaeological Reports, 1984. 1 v.: ill., tables (BAR international series; 203)
Dissertation-based study of pottery in the Copán region, divided into stylistic classes. [NH]

355 Benavides C., Antonio. Cobá, una ciudad prehispánica de Quintana Roo: guía oficial. México: Instituto Nacional de Antropología e Historia, Centro Regional del Sureste, 1981. 143, 6 p.: bibl., ill.
Useful short guide to the major classic Maya site in the northeastern Yucatan Peninsula. [NH]

356 Berlo, Janet Catherine. Teotihuacan art abroad: a study of metropolitan style and provincial transformation in incensario workshops. Oxford, England: British Archaeological Reports, 1984. 2 v. (255, 297 p.): appendix, bibl., plates (BAR international series; 199)
Comprehensive analysis of elaborate figural clay censers from the Valley of Mexico, Escuintla and Lake Amatitlan, Guatemala. Discusses their stylistic and iconographic variations through time and space within the broad context of Teotihuacan art and its influence in southern Mesoamerica. [HvW]

357 Bernal, Ignacio. Los arqueólogos de Tenochtitlán (UNAM/AA, 18:1, julio 1981, p. 57–71)
Discussion of the contributors to archaeological study of Tenochtitlan-Tlatelolco, noting attitudes toward study of the capital. Salvage and accident have dominated archaeological study of it. [BLS]

358 Beyer, Bernd Fahmel. Continuidad y cambio en dos tradiciones cerámicas posclásicas de Mesoamérica: anaranjada fina y plomiza (UNAM/AA, 18:1, julio 1981, p. 85–97, bibl., maps)
Questions the traditional use of X Fine Orange and Tohil plumbate as early postclassic diagnostics since earlier and later associations are found. [BLS]

359 Boggs, Stanley H. A pottery cayuco model from El Salvador (SEM/E, 48:3/4, 1983, p. 205–209, ill., map)
Purchased piece shows two figures in and one on the prow of a long canoe similar to those illustrated on engraved bones from Tikal (see *HLAS 43:303*). [NH]

360 Boletín del Consejo de Arqueología. Instituto Nacional de Antropología e Historia. Vol. 1, 1984- . México.
Vol. 1 inaugurates journal which will give brief annual synopses of current projects. Vol. 1 includes 33. Types of information are: names of participants, support, aims, key results, and bibliography derived from the project. [BLS]

361 Bryant, Douglas Donne. A recently discovered amber source near Totolapa, Chiapas, Mexico (SAA/AA, 48:2, 1983, p. 354–357)

Reports the second amber source known in the Maya highland zone. [NH]

362 Cabrero G., María Teresa. Entre chinampas y bosques: estudio arqueológico de Topilejo, D.F. México: UNAM, Instituto de Investigaciones Antropológicas, 1980. 96 p., 22 p. of plates (some folded): bibl., facsims., ill., maps (Serie antropológica; 33. Arqueología)

Reports on the study of 43 rural sites in the southwest Valley of Mexico, using survey, surface collection, and test pits. Terrace agriculture supporting urban centers was economically predominant. Dates were mainly Aztec III (late postclassic). [BLS]

363 Carrasco, Ramón. Informe del sitio arqueológico Nuevo Jalisco, Chiapas (CEM/ECM, 13, 1981, p. 339–348, bibl., ill.)

Brief report on site near Bonampak, with a single plaza and four standing temples on a terrace at north end. [NH]

364 Cenote of sacrifice: Maya treasures from the sacred well at Chichén Itzá. Edited by Clemency Chase Coggins and Orrin C. Shane III. Catalogue by Clemency Chase Coggins. Contributions by Gordon R. Willey and Linnea H. Wren. Foreword by C.C. Lamberg-Karlovsky and Wendell A. Mordy. Photographs by Hillel Burger. Austin: Univ. of Texas Press, 1984. 1 v.: bibl., index, photos.

Useful and scholarly catalogue assigns Cenote material to two major phases, each subdivided, beginning in the terminal classic ca. AD 800 and ending in the late postclassic. Contact with Costa Rica and Panama is demonstrated, and the importance of established long-distance trade underscored by pieces apparently made specifically for the Maya market. Rarely-preserved objects of wood and textiles enlarge the usual repertory of artifacts. Several heirloom pieces include fine Olmec and classic Maya jades. [NH]

365 Cerámica de Cultura Maya. Temple Univ. No. 13, 1984–. Philadelphia.

Latest issue of periodical journal contains type-lists and descriptions for sites in Belize, Peten, Chiapas and Yucatan, and an article on the protoclassic pottery of Holmul and Nohmul. [NH]

366 Chiu, B.C. and **Philip Morrison.** Astronomical origin of the offset street grid at Teotihuacan (Archaeoastronomy [Supplement to the Journal for the History of Astronomy, Giles, England] 11:2, 1980, p. 55–64, bibl., ill., maps)

The offset alignment of the Teotihuacan plan is hypothetically associated with observation of 12 Aug. sunsets, a datum related in some views to the origin of the Mesoamerican calendar. [SF and BLS]

367 Clark, John E. The early preclassic obsidian industry of Paso de la Amada, Chiapas, México (CEM/ECM, 13, 1981, p. 265–284, bibl., ill., tables)

Describes an early flake industry made using hard hammer and bipolar percussion on cores from the Tajumulco, Rio Pixcaya and El Chayal sources in the highlands east from the site. Author suggests on the basis of this sample of nearly 19,000 fragments that flake industries preceded blade technology in preclassic Mesoamerica. [NH]

368 The Cloud people: divergent evolution of the Zapotec and Mixtec civilizations. Edited by Kent V. Flannery and Joyce Marcus. New York: Academic Press, 1973. 391 p.: bibl., ill., index, maps, tables.

Facets of Oaxacan prehistory are analyzed by 15 contributors. Notable integration of linguistic, documentary archaeological, and environmental data covering the full sequence of occupation. [BLS]

369 Coe, Michael D. Old gods and young heroes: the Pearlman Collection of Maya Ceramics. Photographs by Justin Kerr. Jerusalem: Israel Museum, Maremont Pavilion of Ethnic Arts, 1982. 128 p.: bibl., plates.

Minimal text, numerous illustrations of Maya-style pottery of unknown provenance and uncertain authenticity. [NH]

370 Coggins, Clemency. The stucco decoration and architectural assemblange of structure 1-Sub Dzibilchaltun, Yucatan, Mexico. New Orleans, La.: Middle American Research Institue, Tulane Univ., 1984. 70 p.: bibl., ill. (Publication; 49)

Descriptive and analytical reconstruction of the complex iconography of the decorated façades of this classic period temple. [NH]

371 Colha e i maya dei bassipiani. Edited by Gilda Majani Ronzoni and M. Luisa Greggio. Illustrations by Piero Basaglia, Gianluigi Casini, and Renzo Zanetti. Venezia, Italy: Erizzo, 1983. 240 p.: ill. (Esplorazioni e ricerche; v. 8)

Well illustrated Italian popular book on the major chert-working center in northern Belize. Extraneous but attractive introductory and peripheral material. Good complement to the scientific papers on Colha (items **405, 406, 407** and **471**). [NH]

372 Cowgill, George L.; Jeffrey H. Altschul; and Rebecca S. Sload. Spatial analysis of Teotihuacan: a Mesoamerican metropolis (*in* Intrasite spatial analysis in archaeology. Edited by Harold J. Hietala. Cambridge, Mass.: Cambridge Univ. Press, 1984, p. 154–195, bibl., ill., maps, tables [New directions in archaeology])

Explains character of current work with Teotihuacan computerized surface data and offers examples of analyses. Social status, barrios, and pyramid functions are explored in a carefully reasoned style. [BLS]

373 Dahlin, Bruce H. A colossus in Guatemala: the preclassic Maya city of El Mirador (AIA/A, 37, Sept./Oct. 1984, p. 18–25)

General summary of work at the largest known preclassic Maya site, with colossal architecture. [NH]

374 Diehl, Richard A. Tula: the Toltec capital of ancient Mexico. London: Thames and Hudson, 1983. 184 p.: bibl., ill., index (New aspects of antiquity)

Overview of Toltec economy, trade, social organization, religion, and impact on the rest of Mesoamerica, based on archaeological and ethnohistoric sources. Best single source on the city. [SF and BLS]

375 Doolittle, William E. Settlements and the development of "statelets" in Sonora, Mexico (AFA/JFA, 11:1, Spring 1984, p. 13–24, bibl., ill., maps, tables)

In the Valley of Sonora, sites from AD 1350–1550 contrast with earlier occupation because two regional centers are added to village, hamlet, and *ranchería* sites. Local exchanges are viewed as important in this social development. [BLS]

377 Epstein, Jeremiah F. Fechando el complejo del policromo del ulua (YAXKIN, 3:4, dic. 1980, p. 237–248, bibl., ill.)

Confirms on archaeological grounds the accepted late classic date for the Ulua Polychrome ceramic style of northwestern Honduras. [NH]

378 Falsifications and misreconstructions of precolumbian art: a conference at Dumbarton Oaks, October 14th and 15th, 1978. Edited by Elizabeth H. Boone. Washington: Dumbarton Oaks, Trustees for Harvard Univ., 1982. 142 p.: bibl., ill., tables.

Contains three Mesoamerican papers, Pasztory's on three Aztec masks, Taylor's on Maya vase painting, and Molina-Montes's on Mexican architectural "restoration." Conservation ethics are explored. [BLS]

379 Fash, William L.; Ricardo Agurcia Fasquelle; and Elliot M. Abrams. Excavaciones en el Sitio CV 36, 1980–1981 (YAXKIN, 4:2, dic. 1981, p. 111–132, ill.)

Summary of excavations in a large residential group at Copán which yielded sculptures and other important artifacts including "ball-players yokes." [NH]

380 Feinman, Gary; Stephen A. Kowalewski; and Richard E. Blanton. Modeling ceramic production and organizational change in the prehispanic Valley of Oaxaca, Mexico (*in* The Many dimensions of pottery: ceramics in archaeology and anthropology. Edited by S.E. van der Leeuw and A.C. Pritchard. Amsterdam: Universiteit van Amsterdam, 1984, p. 296–337, bibl., ill., maps, tables [Albert Egges van Giffen Instituut Voor Prae-En Protohistorie Cingvla; 7])

Diachronic shifts in pottery production strategies are traced and are related to sociopolitical and demographic factors. [SF]

381 Folan, William J.; Ellen R. Kintz; and Laraine Fletcher. Cobá: a classic Maya metropolis. New York: Academic Press, 1983. 244 p.: ill., maps.

Ambitious but imperfect attempt to define and analyze the city-state of Cobá; numerous editorial errors make the basic data less useful. Includes 22 boxed maps. [NH]

382 Fowler, William R., Jr. Late preclassic mortuary patterns and evidence of human sacrifice at Chalchuapa, El Salvador (SAA/AA, 49:3, July 1984, p. 603–618, bibl., ill., map)

Remains of 33 individuals from construction fill of Str. E3–7 are interpreted as evidence of sacrifice; all identifiable remains were adult males, with the possible inference that war captives were used. [NH]

383 Freidel, David A. and Jeremy A. Sabloff. Cozumel: late Maya settlement patterns. Orlando, Fla.: Academic Press, 1984. 208 p.: bibl., ill., index (Studies in archaeology)

Dissertation-based description of post-classic settlement on an island off Yucatan. Includes useful factual descriptions, but too small a sample for the typology employed, and too little evidence for the ceremonial circuits proposed. [NH]

384 Fuente, Beatriz de la. Figura humana olmeca de jade (IIE/A, 52, 1983, p. 7–19, bibl., ill.)

Comparative description of an Olmec figure with glyphic inscription probably added later in Oaxaca. Critical observations on the alleged continuity of Olmec symbolism and its meaning in Monte Albán period I. [HvW]

385 Gandelman, Claude. Problemas del *non finito* en el arte mexicano: sobre una cabeza totonaca del Museo de Antropología de Jalapa (IIE/A, 52, 1983, p. 59–68, ill.)

Observations of an intentionally unfinished stone head (only the right half of the face is sculpted) with comparisons in classical and modern art. [HvW]

386 Garber, James F. Patterns of jade consumption and disposal at Cerros, Northern Belize (SAA/AA, 48:4, 1983, p. 800–807)

Late preclassic jades include complete specimens in caches and shattered examples associated with the abandonment of buildings. This is interpreted as a valedictory ritual. [NH]

387 Greene Robertson, Merle. The sculpture of Palenque. v. 1, The Temple of the Inscriptions. Princeton, N.J.: Princeton Univ. Press, 1983. 1 v.: bibl., ill., index, map (folded in pocket)

Superbly illustrated account of the funerary temple of the ruler Pacal (AD 615–683). [NH]

388 Grove, David C. Chalcatzingo: excavations on the Olmec frontier. New York: Thames and Hudson, 1984. 184 p.: bibl., ill., index, maps, table.

The role of this key Olmec era site is exposed by consideration of monuments, buildings, goods, regional setting, and comparisons to other data. Argues chiefly for a local emphasis. Local productive factors and long-distance trade are stressed as causal factors. [BLS]

389 ———— and Susan D. Gillespie. Chalcatzingo's portrait figurines and the cult of the ruler (AIA/A, 37:4, July/Aug. 1984, p. 27–33, ill.)

Analysis of middle formative period figurines suggests some were portraits of rulers, associated with a ruler-cult derived from the Gulf coast. [SF]

390 Guillén, Ann Cyphers. Asentamientos humanos en el norte del Valle de México (UNAM/AA, 18:1, julio 1981, p. 73–83, bibl.)

Overview of the roles of Tlatilco, Zacatenco, and El Arbolillo in the Valley of Mexico. Synthesizes prior evidence. [BLS]

391 Gutiérrez Solana, Nelly. La bolsas ceremoniales en el arte mesoamericano (IIE/A, 53, 1983, p. 17–29, bibl., ill.)

Representations of ceremonial pouches in sculpture, murals, and codices, from Olmec to early colonial times. [HvW]

392 ————. Objectos ceremoniales en piedra de la cultura mexica. México: UNAM, Instituto de Investigaciones Estéticas, 1983. 226 p.: bibl., ill. (Estudios y fuentes del arte en México; 44)

Descriptive analytical catalogue of relief-decorated rectangular and circular Aztec stone sculptures, mostly in the Museo de Antropología, Mexico. Discusses formal, stylistic, and iconographical features with reference to codices and ethnohistorical data. [HvW]

393 ————. Sobre un fémur con grabados pertenecientes a la cultura mexica (IIE/A, 52, 1983, p. 47–57, bibl., ill.)

Interpretation of the solar-sacrificial symbolism engraved on a femur rasp from the Metro excavations in Mexico City. [HvW]

394 Haberland, Wolfgang. Zwei Xipe-Köpfe aus Stein im Hamburgischen Museum für Völkerkunde (MLV/T, 33, 1984, p. 89–96, bibl., ill.)

Description of two Xipe stone heads with notes on comparable but scarce sculptures. [HvW]

395 Hamblin, Nancy L. Animal use by the Cozumel Maya. Tucson: Univ. of Arizona Press, 1983. 206 p.

Dissertation-based summary of faunal exploitation by mainly postclassic occupants of an offshore island. [NH]

396 Hammond, Norman. Archäologische Untersuchungen 1983 in Nohmul, Belize (Mexicon [Berlin] 5:6, Nov. 1983, p. 106–113, ill.)

Summary of 1983 fieldwork, including the excavation of a late preclassic "acropolis" topped by a larger timber "palace" forming part of a major coeval ceremonial precinct. [NH]

397 ——. Nohmul, Belize: 1982 investigations (AFA/JFA, 10, 1983, p. 245–254)

This large Maya center has an occupation span of two millennia, with major florescences in the terminal formative (ca. AD 200–300) and terminal classic early postclassic (AD 800-1000) periods. Excavations revealed a large timber building of the former period and completed the exposure of a circular structure of the latter one. Settlement pattern mapping located a focus of early formative occupation. [NH]

398 ——. Two roads diverged: a brief comment on "Lowland Maya Archaeology at the Crossroads" (SAA/AA, 49:4, Oct. 1984, p. 821–826)

Corrects and comments on Marcus's article (item **317**) with particular reference to the site of Cuello. [NH]

399 ——; Mary E. Neivens; and Garman Harbottle. Trace element analysis of obsidian artifacts from a classic Maya residential group at Nohmul, Belize (SAA/AA, 49:4, Oct. 1984, p. 815–820, bibl., ill., table)

Analysis of 49 artifacts suggests a shift towards Ixtepeque as the dominant source for Nohmul obsidian after AD 800. [NH]

400 Healan, Dan M.; Janet M. Kerley; and George J. Bey III. Excavation and preliminary analysis of an obsidian workshop in Tula, Hidalgo, Mexico (AFA/JFA, 10:2, Summer 1983, p. 127–145, bibl., ill., maps, tables)

A Tollan phase workshop associated with habitations reveals preformed core importation and technological steps prior to prismatic pressure blade removal. [BLS]

401 Healy, Paul F. An ancient Maya dam in the Cayo District, Belize (AFA/JFA, 10, 1983, p. 147–154)

A dam near Blue Hope Camp in the Vaca Plateau (Maya Mountains) is of dressed stone and rubble fill, blocks a narrow creek, and is probably of late classic date. [NH]

402 ——; Heather I. McKillop; and Bernie Walsh. Analysis of obsidian from Moho Cay, Belize: new evidence on classic Maya trade routes (AAAS/S, 225, 1984, p. 414–417, map)

Most obsidian at this site on the Belize coast comes from El Chayal source and is of middle classic (AD 400–700) date; a coastal as well as interior trade route for Chayal obsidian is suggested. [NH]

403 ——; John D.H. Lambert; J.T. Arnason; and Richard J. Hebda. Caracol, Belize: evidence on ancient Maya agricultural terraces (AFA/JFA, 10, 1983, p. 397–410)

Agricultural terraces of the late classic period, and perhaps earlier, indicate high population densities (up to 1610/sq. km on 100 percent occupancy of recorded housemounds) around this classic center (see item **499**). [NH]

404 Hers, Marie-Areti. Santuarios huicholes en la sierra de Tenzompa: Jalisco (IIE/A, 50:1, 1982, p. 35–41, ill.)

Current, colonial, and possibly prehispanic sanctuary sites are discussed in connection with both change and continuity in Huichol rituals. [BLS]

405 Hester, Thomas R. and Harry J. Shafer. Exploitation of chert resources by the ancient Maya of Northern Belize, Central America (World Archaeology [Routledge and Kegan, London[16:2, Oct. 984, p. 157–173, ill.)

Survey of chert resources and their utilization from the preceramic onwards, with emphasis on the preclassic-classic site of Colha. [NH]

406 ——; ——; Jack D. Eaton; and Giancarlo Ligabue. Colha's stone tool industry (AIA/A, 36, Nov./Dec. 1983, p. 46–52)

Summary of work at an important preclassic and classic chert tool workshop in northern Belize with regional trade contacts. [NH]

407 —— et al. Archaeological investigations at Colha, Belize: the 1981 season

(BISRA/BS, 11:5, 1983, p. 1–22, bibl., ill., maps)

Further work at the major chert workshop site in Northern Belize shows occupation by the early first millennium BC, and a late preclassic florescence with the establishment of production on an industrial scale (items 371, 405, 406, and 471). [NH]

408 Hirth, Kenneth. Xochicalco: urban growth and state formation in Central Mexico (AAAS/S, 225:4662, 10 Aug. 1984, p. 579–586, bibl., ill., maps)

Report of mapping project, summarizing growth, internal organization, and regional socioeconomic domain of this epiclassic period urban center. It emerged during the waning of Teotihuacán's influence. [SF]

409 Hopkins, Joseph W., II. Irrigation & [i.e. and] the Cuicatec ecosystem: study of agriculture & civilization in North Central Oaxaca. Ann Arbor: Museum of Anthropology, Univ. of Michigan, 1984. 148 p.: bibl., ill., maps, tables (Memoirs; 17. Studies in Latin American ethnohistory and archaeology; 2)

Ethnohistorical, ethnographic, and archaeological evidence are integrated to examine change in subsistence, especially irrigation, in relation to settlement pattern. Aztec period and historic data are emphasized. [SF and BLS]

410 Hosler, Dorothy. Copper tin bronzes in Mesoamerica (UNAM/AA, 18:1, julio 1981, p. 99–132, bibl., ill., map, tables)

Suggests bronze working to have been first introduced into west Mexico from the southern Andes, prior to Inca expansion. [SF]

411 Introducción a la arqueología de Copán, Honduras. Edited by Claude Baudez. Tegucigalpa: Instituto Hondureño de Antropología e Historia, 1983. 3 v.: ill., maps.

Vol. 1 contains seven papers exploring the background of Copán archaeology, including ecology and survey work in the valley. Vol. 2 has 11 papers on excavations in the ceremonial precinct. Vol. 3 consists of maps. [NH]

412 Journal of New World Archaeology. Institute of Archaeology, Univ. of California. Vol. 6, No. 2, Feb. 1984- . Los Angeles.

Issue devoted to ethnoarchaeology includes papers on Mesoamerican, Central American, and Caribbean topics. Most are only indirectly informative to archaeologists except Lewenstein's on experiments with obsidian chips and root grating and Abrams' on tuff sculpting in relation to Copán monuments. [BLS]

413 Kennedy, Nedenia C. La cronología cerámica del formativo de Playa de los Muertos, Honduras (YAXKIN, 3:4, dic. 1980, p. 265–272, bibl.)

Suggests that the sequence runs from ca. 650 BC onwards, and not from the early preclassic as originally suggested, with comparisons in highland Honduras at Los Naranjos in the middle preclassic. Late middle preclassic comparisons can be made with the Maya Xe horizon, and there is a late preclassic complex also. Ties formerly suggested to Tlatilco do not exist, and links to the east with lower Central America/South America are stronger than hitherto thought. [NH]

414 Köhler, Ulrich. Das Felsbild von Maltrata in seiner Beziehung zu mexikanischen Bilderhandschriften (MLV/T, 33, 1984, p. 125–132, bibl., ill.)

Stylistic comparisons of the temple ritual on a 7th to 9th-century rock carving from the Veracruz-Puebla border with motifs on Xochicalco monuments and in Codex Borgia. Similarities in theme and iconography tend to support that Codex Borgia originated in a south-eastern style province of Puebla. [HvW]

415 Kolb, Charles C. Ceramic technology and problems and prospects of provenience in specific ceramics from Mexico and Afghanistan (in Archaeological ceramics. Edited by Jacqueline S. Olin and Alan D. Franklin. Washington: Smithsonian Institution, 1982, p. 193–208, bibl., ill., maps, tables)

Includes petrographic analysis of "Thin Orange" ceramics from Central Mexico which was intended to identify loci of manufacture and sociocultural mechanisms of distribution. [SF]

416 ———. Technological and cultural aspects of Teotihuacán period "Thin Orange" ware (in Pots and potters: current approaches in ceramic archaeology. Edited by Prudence M. Rice. Los Angeles: Institute of Archaeology, Univ. of California, 1984, p. 209–226, bibl., maps, tables)

Summarizes past studies of "Thin Orange" wares and discusses sociological implications of an expanded petrographic study. [BLS]

417 Kowalewski, Stephen A. Current research: Mesoamerica (SAA/AA, 48:1, Jan. 1983, p. 178–181; 48:4, Oct. 1983, p. 853–856; 49:4, Oct. 1984, p. 868–871)
Synopses of current research, appearing in three issues, not yet in the publication stage.

418 ――― and Laura Finsten. The economic system of ancient Oaxaca: a regional perspective (UC/CA 24:4, Aug./Oct. 1983, p. 413–441, bibl., graphs)
Regional survey data are utilized to examine shifting access to goods and resources among communities and subregions. Argues that a degree of political-administrative control affected these changes. [SF]

419 Latocha, Hartwig. Der Hund in den alten Kulturen Mittel- und Südamerikas (in Zur frühen Mensch-Tier-Symbiose. Komm. für Allg. u. Vergleichende Archäologie d. Dt. Archäolog. Inst. Bonn. Hrsg. von Hermann Müller-Karpe. München: Beck, 1983, p. 219–241, bibl., ill. [Kolloquien zur Allgemeinen und Vergleichenden Archäologie; 4])
Comparisons of the ritual and mythological significance of dog representations in Mesoamerica and South America during two millennia. [HvW]

420 Lewenstein, Suzanne. The Ramonal ruins, Corozal District (BISRA/BS, 11:2, 1983, p. 13–22, ill., maps)
Map and preliminary description of small early classic center in northern Belize. [NH]

421 Limón, Morrison and Luis Barba. Prospección arqueológica en San José, Ixtapa (UNAM/AA, 18:1, julio 1981, p. 151–171, bibl., maps, plates)
Provocative surface study of San José Ixtapa in the Temascalcingo Valley (Estado de México). A combination of seven surface techniques suggested structure locations and outdoor areas possibly involved in pottery firing, with the pottery itself used in producing another product. [BLS]

422 López Molina, Diana. Cantona: una urbe prehispánica mesoamericana (BBAA, 5, julio 1982, p. 133–136, ill., map)

This city in northern Puebla was mapped with a combination of air photography and ground survey. Covering 30 km², with a dense core of 16 km², it rivals Teotihuacán in area, but its chronology is uncertain. [BLS]

423 Macazaga Ordoño, César. El Templo Mayor. México: Editorial Innovación, 1981. 79 p.: bibl., ill., index (Colección Religión del México antiguo; 2)
Popular discussion of Aztec religion as represented in the Templo Mayor in Tenochtitlan. Emphasis on agricultural connotations. [BLS]

424 McDonald, Andrew J. Tzutzuculi: a middle preclassic site on the Pacific coast of Chiapas, Mexico. Provo, Utah: New World Archaeological Foundation, Brigham Young Univ., 1983. 73 p.: ill., maps (Papers; 47)
Summary of excavations and ceramic sequence at small Olmec-related site on the littoral plain. [NH]

425 McKillop, Heather. Prehistoric Maya reliance on marine resources: analysis of a midden from Moho Cay, Belize (AFA/JFA, 11, 1984, p. 25–35)
Reports analysis of animal/shell remains demonstrating a middle classic (AD 400–700) occupation concentrating on manatee hunting and offshore fishing. Manatee provided 89 percent of meat, and marine species altogether 99.6 percent. [NH]

426 Maggetti, Marino; Harold Westley; and Jacqueline S. Olin. Provenance and technical studies of Mexican majolica using elemental and phase analysis (in Archaeological chemistry. Joseph B. Lambert, vol. editor. Washington: American Chemical Society, 1984, v. 3, p. 151–191, bibl., charts, ill., tables [Advances in chemistry series, 0065–2393; 205])
In addition to successful detection of contrasts between New World and Spanish made majolicas, two groups of Mexican majolicas were distinguished. [BLS]

427 Mallory, John K. Especialización económica en el Valle de Copán: excavaciones en "El Duende" (YAXKIN, 4:2, dic. 1981, p. 171–185, bibl., ill.)
Description of small late classic obsidian workshop 2.5 km from Copán. [NH]

428 ———. Excavaciones en el complejo residencial de Las Sepulturas, Copán (YAXKIN, 4:2, dic. 1981, p. 145–158, ill.)

Description of excavations in CV–30, a small elite residence group close to the Copán center. [NH]

429 **Mastache, Alba Guadalupe; Ana María Crespo; Robert H. Cobean; and Dan M. Healan.** Estudios sobre la antigua ciudad de Tula. México: INAH, 1982. 149 p.: bibl., ill., maps, tables (Colección científica. Arqueología; 121)

Three papers treat the plan of Tula, excavations and ceramic analysis at Tula Chico, and residential plans at Tula. Important volume for analysis of the early history of the site. [BLS]

430 **Matheny, Ray T.** *et al.* Investigations at Edzná, Campeche, Mexico. v. l, pts. 1–2, The Hydraulic System. v. 2, Ceramics. Provo, Utah: New World Archaeological Foundation, Brigham Young Univ., 1980–1983. 2 v. in 3: bibl., col. maps, ill. (Papers; 46)

Important report on a major middle preclassic and classic Maya city. Vol. 1 describes the unique water control systems used for drainage, transportation, and defense; vol. 2 describes ceramic sequence from middle preclassic through terminal classic/early postclassic. [NH]

431 **Matos Moctezuma, Eduardo.** The great temple of Tenochtitlán (SA, 251:2, Aug. 1984, p. 80–90, ill., maps)

Overview of discoveries, grouped by building epochs and tied to historical reigns. Takes note of over 100 offerings. Well illustrated. [BLS]

432 ———. Una visita al Templo Mayor de Tenochtitlán. México: INAH, 1981. 77 p., 1 folded leaf of plates: bibl., ill. (some col.)

Semi-popular summary of construction history of Templo Mayor. Excellent photographs, including several of offerings. [BLS]

433 **Mayer, Karl Herbert.** Gewölbedecksteine mit Dekor der Maya-Kultur (MWV/AV, 37, 1983, p. 1–62, bibl., ill.)

Comprehensive and well researched account of 29 published and 14 unpublished capstones with polychrome or relief decoration. [HvW]

434 ———. Major Maya art in a Mérida collection (Cuadernos de Arquitectura Mesoamericana [UNAM, México] 1, feb. 1984, p. 41–47, bibl., ill.)

Ten hitherto unpublished, much eroded limestone sculptures are tentatively assigned to the northern lowlands (ca. AD 800-1000). [HvW]

435 ———. Maya monuments: sculptures of unknown provenance in Middle America. Berlin, FRG: Verlag Karl-Friedrich von Flemming, 1984. 122 p.: appendices, bibl., ill., tables.

Well annotated catalogue of 190 sculptures (204 plates) of monuments in Mexico and Central America. Includes addenda for previous volumes on monuments in Europe (see *HLAS 41:417*) and in the US (*HLAS 43:364*). [HvW]

436 **Mesoamerican sites and world-views:** a conference at Dumbarton Oaks, October 16th and 17th, 1976. Edited by Elizabeth P. Benson. Washington: Dumbarton Oaks, Trustees for Harvard Univ., 1981. 245 p.: bibl., ill., maps, tables.

Topics such as symbolic meanings and astronomical bases of site locations, orientations, and arrangements are considered for Teotihuacán, Monte Albán, Tenochtitlán, Palenque, and highland Chiapas (ethnographic). Spatial symbolism is emphasized. [BLS]

437 **Michelet, Dominique.** Río Verde, San Luis Potosí, Mexique. Mexico: Centre d'études mexicaines et centroaméricaines, 1984. 436 p.: bibl., ill., maps, tables (Collection Etudes mésoaméricaines; 9)

Descriptive report of regional survey, mapping of nine sites, and excavation of seven. Synthetic chapters cover the ecological setting, way of life, social organization, and "marginality" of the region. Three phases span the classic period and most of the early postclassic. [BLS]

438 **Mining and mining techniques in ancient Mesoamerica.** Edited by Phil C. Weigand and Gretchen Gwynne (Anthropology [SUNY at Stony Brook] 6:2/3, May/Dec. 1982, p. 1–222, bibl., ill., maps, tables)

Seven chapters cover mining methods and techniques, with particular reference to associated political and economic organization. Areas discussed include the Valley of

Mexico, Zacatecas, Jalisco, Querétaro, and the lowland Maya region. [SF]

439 Moholy-Nagy, Hattula; Frank Asaro; and Fred H. Stross. Tikal obsidian: sources and typology (SAA/AA, 49:1, 1984, 104–117)

Obsidian was imported from highland Guatemala, with El Chayal dominance in the early and middle classic, and from Central Mexico, in small proportion and mainly in the early classic. Central Mexican grey obsidian was used for points/knives, green obsidian for blades, and Guatemalan obsidian for ceremonial objects. Source and artifact typology are correlated. [NH]

440 Mountjoy, Joseph B. Investigaciones arqueológicas en la cuenca del Río Tomatlán, Jalisco, 1975–1977 (Pantoc [Publicaciones antropológicas de Occidente, Univ. Autónoma de Guadalajara, México] 5, junio 1983, p. 21–50, bibl., ill.)

Summary of results of salvage explorations on the Jalisco coast which yielded significant data on postclassic settlements and artifacts. Full account to be published by INAH, Col. Científica: Arqueología, of which the first of three fascicles appeared 1982 (No. 122). [HvW]

441 Müller, Florencia. Estudio de la cerámica hispánica y moderna de Tlaxcala-Puebla. México: INAH, Depto. de Salvamento Arqueológico, 1981. 78 p.: bibl., ill., index, map, tables (Col. científica. Arqueología; 103)

Primarily a typology of historic postconquest pottery produced in Puebla-Tlaxcala, but includes discussion of the industry in relation to changing circumstances. Includes settlement pattern data from a survey. [BLS]

442 Nicholson, Henry B. and **Eloise Quiñones Keber.** Art of Aztec Mexico: treasures of Tenochtitlan. Washington: National Gallery of Art, 1983. 188 p.: bibl., ill.

The catalog of this unusually large exhibit includes a history of the discovery of Aztec sculpture. Each piece illustrated has lengthy descriptive commentary. Included are mainly stone sculptures, but also wooden drums and a few pottery vessels and other items. [BLS]

443 Nickel, Helmut. A note on the macquauitl (IAI/I, 9, 1984, p. 159–173, bibl.)

The only two prehispanic obsidian-studded swords from central Mexico were destroyed by fire in Madrid, 1884. Such weapons are known only from pictorial and manuscript sources. [HvW]

444 Ochoa Castillo, Patricia. Secuencia cronológica de Tlatilco, Estado de México: Temporada IV. México: Secretaría de Educación, Cultura y Bienestar Social del Gobierno del Estado de México, 1982. 212 p.: bibl., ill. (Biblioteca enciclopédica del Estado de México; 115)

A classification of ceramics, lithics, and other artifacts, presented in a three-phase, stratigraphic analysis. Sequence is proposed to begin about 1400 BC. [BLS]

445 Olin, Jacquelin S.; Garman Harbottle; and Edward V. Sayre. Elemental compositions of Spanish and Spanish-colonial majolica ceramics in the identification of provenience (in Archaeological chemistry. Giles F. Carter, vol. editor. Washington: American Chemical Society, 1978, v. 2, p. 201–229, bibl., ill., tables [Advances in chemistry series, 0065–2393; 171])

Mexican and Spanish majolicas are distinguishable using neutron activation analysis, also confirmed by other methods. [BLS]

446 Ortiz de Montellano, Bernard R. Counting skulls: comment on the Aztec cannibalism theory of Harner-Harris (AAA/AA, 85:2, June 1983, p. 403–406, bibl., table)

Skull rack and skull dimensions preclude Tapia's estimate of the number of sacrificed persons exhibited. [BLS]

447 Parsons, Jeffrey R.; Keith W. Kintigh; and Susan A. Gregg. Archaeological settlement pattern data from the Chalco, Xochimilco, Ixtapalapa, Texcoco and Zumpango regions, Mexico. Ann Arbor: Museum of Anthropology, Univ. of Michigan, 1983. 222 p.: bibl., ill., maps, tables (Technical reports; 14. Research reports in archaeology; 9)

Supplementary data are tabulated for earlier Valley of Mexico survey reports. Includes data on chronology, environmental zone, site classification, UTM coordinates, and other variables. [BLS]

448 Pasztory, Esther. Aztec art. New York: H.N. Abrams, 1983. 335 p.: bibl., ill., index.

Includes coverage of Aztecs' place in Mesoamerican prehistory, sources of information, Aztec culture, and explication of the principal "art" corpus. Illustrations are excellent. Most pieces in item 442 are included. [BLS]

449 Payne, William O. Kiln and ceramic technology of ancient Mesoamerica (*in* Archaeological ceramics. Edited by Jaqueline S. Olin and Alan D. Franklin. Washington: Smithsonian Institution Press, 1982, p. 189–192, bibl., ill.)

Focuses on technology of Oaxacan prehistoric and ethnographic pottery making. [BLS]

450 Pendergast, David M. Excavations at Lamanai, Belize, 1983 (Mexicon [Berlin, FRG] 6:1, Jan. 1984, p. 5–10, ill)

Reports discoveries of the postclassic/colonial periods, the most important being a Tulum-style building converted to a church in 1567. [NH]

451 ———. The Hunchback tomb (Rotunda [Royal Ontario Museum, Toronto, Canada] 16:4, 1984, p. 5–11, ill.)

Burial of 15th/16th-century date contained 12 vessels including large hunchback effigy on stool. [NH]

452 Piña Chan, Román and Kuniakí Oi. Exploraciones arqueológicas en Tingambato, Michoacán. México: INAH, 1982. 101 p.: bibl., ill., maps.

Excavation and restoration at the center of Tinganio uncovered a ballcourt with sculptures and a tomb with copious ceramic offerings. A two-stage chronology is placed within the classic period. A weak case is made for Teotihuacán influence. [BLS]

453 Pohl, Mary and John Pohl. Ancient Maya cave rituals (AIA/A, 36, May/June 1983, p. 28–32, 50–51)

Presents evidence for rituals involving animals and executed in caves. [NH]

454 Potter, Daniel R.; Thomas R. Hester; Stephen L. Black; and Fred Valdez, Jr. Relationships between early preclassic and early middle preclassic phases in Northern Belize: a comment on "Lowland Maya Archaeology at the Crossroads" (SAA/AA, 49:3, July 1984, p. 628–631, bibl., ill.)

Comment on and corrections to the survey article by Marcus (item 317), on the basis of evidence from the site of Colha, Belize. [NH]

455 Pulltrouser Swamp: ancient Maya habitat, agriculture and settlement in Northern Belize. Edited by B.L. Turner II and Peter D. Harrison. Austin: Univ. of Texas Press, 1983. 226 p.: ill., tables.

Report on first season (1979) of study of raised and channelized fields in a swamp between the site of Nohmul and the Río Nuevo (into which it drains). Construction and use of fields began in the late preclassic; crops grown may have included maize. [NH]

456 Quirigua reports. v. 1, Papers 1–5: site map. Wendy Ashmore, vol. editor. v. 2, Papers 6–15. Edward M. Schortman, Patricia A. Urban, vol. editors. Robert J. Sharer, general editor. Philadelphia: Univ. Museum, Univ. of Pennsylvania, 1979–1983. 2 v.: bibl., ill. (Univ. Museum monograph; 37, 49)

Initial volumes of final report on excavations and restoration work at important southeastern Maya lowland center of Quirigua. Ceremonial center work, including monument conservation, settlement pattern study and general context are among topics covered in a series of chapters in each volume. [NH]

457 Redmond, Elsa M. A fuego y sangre: early Zapotec imperialism in the Cuicatlán Cañada, Oaxaca. Ann Arbor: Univ. of Michigan, Museum of Anthropology, 1983. 216 p.: appendix, bibl., graphs, ill., maps, photos, tables (Memoirs of the Museum of Anthropology; 16. Studies in Latin American ethnohistory and archaeology; 1)

Ethnohistoric models of Zapotec militaristic activity are applied to prehistoric Oaxaca. Monte Albán's expansionist strategy is examined through survey and excavation in the Cañada frontier area. [SF]

458 Las Representaciones de arquitectura en la arqueología de América. v. 1, Mesoamérica. Coordinador, Daniel Schávelzon. México: UNAM, Coordinación de Extensión Universitaria, 1982. 1 v.: bibl., ill.

Consists of 36 papers which discuss representations of buildings on pottery, in graffiti, models, stelae, paintings, tombs forms, and codices. [BLS]

459 Rice, Don S. and Prudence M. Rice. Collapse to contact: postclassic archaeology of the Petén Maya (AIA/A, 37, March/April 1984, p. 46–51)

Summarizes authors' fieldwork and current knowledge of this period for the "lake district" of Central Petén, Guatemala. [NH]

460 Rice, Prudence M. Obsidian procurement in the Central Petén Lakes Region, Guatemala (AFA/JFA, 11:2, 1984, p. 181–194, ill., tables)

Documents changing reliance on three major sources of obsidian from the middle preclassic through late postclassic periods, with early prominence of Río Pixcaya and El Chayal, and significant use of Ixtepeque from the late classic onwards. [NH]

461 Riese, Berthold. Coyolxauhqui: eine aztekische skulptur vom Haupttempel in Mexico-Tenochtitlan. Berlin, FRG: Colloquium-Verlag, 1982. 16 p.: ill., tables (Miscellanea Ibero-Americana; 4)

Ethnohistorical confirmation of the iconography of the monumental low-relief portraying Huitzilopochtli's dismembered sister at the Templo Mayor. [HvW]

462 Rodríguez, François. Outillage lithique de chasseurs-collecteurs du Nord du Mexique: le Sud-Ouest de l'état de San Luis Potosí. Avec les collaborations de Henri Puig, Carlos Serrano et Rosa María Ramos. Paris: Editions Recherches sur les civilisations, 1983. 223 p., 1 p. of plates: ill. (Etudes méso-américaines; II–6. Cahier; no. 13)

Lithics from four sites either excavated or surface collected in 1965–66 by Jean LeSage are classified. Three "traditions" are seen as contributing to the lithic complexes. No data are included about the sites themselves or the fieldwork. [BLS]

463 Romaine, Marianne. Ikonographie und Verwendung der klassischen und postklassischen Tonfigurinen der Maya. Hohenschäftlarn, FRG: Klaus Renner Verlag, 1984. 308 p.: bibl., ill. (Münchener Beiträge zur Amerikanistik; 16)

Iconography and function of classic and postclassic Maya figurines, the significance of deity icons in ceremonies according to ethnohistorical sources, and their cult among the modern Maya. [HvW]

464 Ruiz Aguilar, María Elena. Distribución de obsidiana en Teotihuacán: una muestra representativa (UNAM/AA, 18:1, julio 1981, p. 133–149, folded maps, maps, tables)

Obsidian excavated from five locations in central Teotihuacán revealed two groups of artifacts differing in manufacturing technique and predominant raw material. Reasons for the patterns are noted. [BLS]

465 Sanders, Williams T. Proyecto Copán: segunda fase (YAXKIN, 4:2, dic. 1981, p. 79–88, ill.)

Brief summary of work as of late 1981. [NH]

466 ——and David Webster. El reconocimiento del Valle de Copán (YAXKIN, 4:2, dic. 1981, p. 89–99, bibl., maps, tables)

Description of the environment of the Copán valley, survey methods used, and a preliminary estimate of 12–15,000 inhabitants for the "Copán pocket" in the late classic. [NH]

467 Santley, Robert S. and Philip J. Arnold III. Obscured by clouds (UNM/JAR, 40:1, Spring 1984, p. 211–230, bibl., map, tables)

This review article concerning a recent book on Oaxacan prehistory (item **368**) reanalyzes: 1) chronology; and 2) a small part of the data used to identify pottery production locations. [BLS]

468 ——et al. Final field report of the Matacapan Archaeological Project: the 1982 season. Albuquerque: Latin American Institute, Univ. of New Mexico, 1984. 91 p.: bibl., ill., maps, tables (Research paper series; 15)

Site map and organization of surface collections and text excavations presented. Contains obsidian analysis and discussion of workshops in relation to Teotihuacán. [BLS]

469 Scarborough, Vernon. A preclassic Maya water system (SAA/AA, 48:4, 1983, p. 720–744)

Describes canal system for drainage and possibly defense/demarcation of the site core at the late preclassic center of Cerros, Belize. A few drained fields are associated with the drainage system. [NH]

470 Schöndube B., Otto. Hallazgos en el Hospital de Belén, 1789–1982 (Pantoc [Publicaciones antropológicas de Occidente, Univ. Autónoma de Guadalajara, México] 5, junio 1983, p. 51–68, bibl., ill.)

Description of painted vessels from salvage excavations of a tomb in Guadalajara. [HvW]

471 Shafer, Harry J. and **Thomas R. Hester.**
Ancient Maya chert workshops in Northern Belize, Central America (SAA/AA, 48:3, 1983, p. 519–543)

Describes the industrial-scale workshops at Colha and associated sites. Colha has major florescences in the late preclassic and late terminal classic, with specialized production of tanged macroblades, tranchet adzes and teardrop-shaped axes in the former phase, and a range of bifaces in the latter. Important demonstration of the regional organization of Maya production economics from the late preclassic onwards. [NH]

472 Sharer, Robert J. Sucesos terminales en las tierras bajas del Sureste: perspectiva desde Quirigua (Mesoamérica [Centro de Investigaciones Regionales de Mesoamérica, Antigua, Guatemala] 3:4, dic. 1982, p. 356–364, ill.)

Summarizes evidence for terminal classic (AD 800–900) occupation at Quirigua. [NH]

473 Sheehy, James J. Notas preliminares sobre las excavaciones en CV 26, Copán (YAXKIN, 4:2, dic. 1981, p. 133–143, bibl., ill.)

Short report on excavations in a major residential group close to the Copán center. [NH]

474 Sidrys, Raymond V. Archaeological excavations in Northern Belize, Central America. Los Angeles: Institute of Archaeology, Univ. of California, 1983. 434 p.: ill., maps, plates, tables (Monograph; 17)

Reports fieldwork at sites in Corozal District in 1974, including mapping and test excavations. [NH]

475 Siemens, Alfred H. Oriented raised fields in central Veracruz (SAA/AA, 48:1, Jan. 1983, p. 85–102, bibl., ill., map)

Patches of seasonal wetlands near the coast of central Veracruz show from the air artificial drainage marks and possibly field constructions. These are compared environmentally to the southern Gulf coast and Yucatan. The orientation of fields is hypothesizes to reflect Teotihuacán control. [BLS]

476 ———. Wetland agriculture in prehispanic Mesoamerica (AGS/GR, 73:2, April 1983, p. 166–181, bibl., ill., maps)

Hydrological principles and substantive discoveries pertaining to Maya practices are summarized and related to recent research on the topic in Veracruz. [BLS]

477 Sisson, Edward B. La Venta: ubicación estratégica de un sitio olmeca (Mesoamérica [Centro de Investigaciones Regionales de Mesoamérica, Antigua, Guatemala] 4:5, junio 1983, p. 195–202, maps)

La Venta's geomorphological position is argued to have been strategic for riverine and coastal trade. Shifts in river courses have produced its modern setting. [BLS]

478 Smith, C. Earle, Jr. and **Paul Tolstoy.**
Vegetation and man in the Basin of Mexico (SEB/EB, 35:4, 1981, p. 415–433, bibl., ill., maps, tables)

Reconstruction of early natural vegetation patterns is accompanied by report on macroflora recovered at four early ceramic period sites. [BLS]

479 Spink, Mary L. and **Charles D. Cheek.**
Excavaciones en el Grupo 3, Grupo Principal, Copán (YAXKIN, 4:2, dic. 1981, p. 159–169, ill.)

Description of the long architectural sequence in Str. 10L–223, between AD 650 and 736. The final building may have been a youths' house. [NH]

480 Stross, Fred H.; Payson Sheets; Frank Asaro; and **Helen V. Michel.** Excavations/artifacts precise characterization of Guatemalan obsidian sources, and source determination of artifacts from Quirigua (SAA/AA, 48:2, 1983, p. 323–346)

Reviews analytical methods and source characteristics, and reports analysis of 30 Quirigua artifacts, of which 24 were from the Ixtepeque source and four from El Chayal. [NH]

481 Teotihuacán, 80–82: primeros resultados. Coordinación: Rubén Cabrera, Ignacio Rodríguez y Noel Morelos. México: INAH, 1982. 155 p., 14 folded leaves of plates: bibl., ill.

Preliminary results of explorations mainly in the Ciudadela and Street of the Dead. Includes most of the papers presented at a symposium on Teotihuacán, "Nuevos Datos, Nuevas Síntesis y Nuevos Problemas" (Mexico, Oct. 1981). [HvW]

482 Thomas, Prentice M., Jr. Prehistoric Maya settlement: patterns at Becan, Campeche, Mexico. New Orleans, La.:

Middle American Research Institute, Tulane Univ., 1981. 116 p.: bibl., ill., maps (Publication; 45)

Final report, with excellent maps, on the community surrounding the major late preclassic through terminal classic center of Becan in the central Maya lowlands. [NH]

483 **Thouvenot, Marc.** Chalchihuitl: le jade chez les Aztèques. Paris: Institut d'ethnologie, Musée de l'homme, 1982. 357 p.: bibl., ill., map, tables (Musée national d'histoire naturelle: Mémoires de l'Institut d'ethnologie; 21)

Exhaustive survey of Aztec jadeite using documents. Covers linguistic data, function, trade, tribute, manufacture, and symbolism. [BLS]

484 **Topsey, H.; J. Awe; J. Morris;** and **A. Moore.** Belmopan before Pauling (BISRA/BS, 11:3, 1983, p. 12–20, bibl., maps)

Reports work at a small late classic site in the area of the Belizean capital. [NH]

485 **Torres, Luis M.; Anna W. Arie;** and **Beatriz Sandoval.** Provenance determination of fine orange Maya ceramic figurines by flame atomic absorption spectrometry: a preliminary study of objects from Jaina, Campeche, and Jonuta, Tabasco, Mexico (in Archaeological chemistry. Joseph B. Lambert, vol. editor. Washington: American Chemical Society, 1984, v. 3, p. 193–213, bibl., graphs, ill., tables [Advances in chemistry series, 0065–2393; 205])

There was a source contrast between several Jaina figurines and ones from Jonuta, Tabasco, but samples were too few for conclusive results. [BLS]

486 **Trik, Helen** and **Michael E. Kampen.** The graffiti of Tikal. Philadelphia: Univ. Museum, Univ. of Pennsylvania, 1983. 11 p.: 105 p. of plates (1 folded): bibl., ill. (Univ. Museum monograph; 57)

Illustrated catalogue of incised designs, narrative and abstract, on plaster walls of temples and other buildings at this Maya center. [NH]

487 **Turner, B.L., II.** Once beneath the forest: prehistoric terracing in the Río Bec Region of the Maya lowlands. Boulder, Colo.: Westview Press, 1983. 209 p.: ill., tables.

Dissertation-based account of late classic landscape modification in the Becan area of the Central Maya lowlands, involving erosion control and silt-trap terracing with access routes. Evidence of permanent land demarcation suggests perennial cultivation on a rotation system rather than the traditional *milpa* swiddening. Important evidence for permanent intensive agricultural facilities. [NH]

488 **Uriarte, María Teresa.** Pintura rupestre en Baja California: algunos métodos para su apreciación artística. México: INAH, Depto. de Investigaciones Históricas, 1981. 160 p.: bibl., ill., maps, tables (Colección científica. Cuadernos del México prehispánico; 106)

Well illustrated analysis of cave paintings, using computerized variables for compositional analysis. Defines a style and evaluates its antiquity. [BLS]

489 **Valverde, Adrián.** Algunos hallazgos arqueológicos en el centro de la Ciudad de México (UNAM/AA, 19, 1982, p. 45–49, ill.)

Summary of discoveries in Tenochtitlán since 1790, primarily in the central precinct. [BLS]

490 **Viel, René.** Cronología cerámica de Copán (YAXKIN, 4:2, dic. 1981, p. 103–109, ill.)

Seven ceramic complexes span the period from early middle preclassic (900–600 BC) through early postclassic ca. AD 900-1200, with links ranging from Olmec through highland Guatemala, to lowland Maya and Central America in the late classic reflecting Copán's location on the frontier of Mesoamerica. [NH]

491 **von Schuler-Schömig, Immina.** Ein chinesisches Porzellanfigürchen aus Oaxaca, Mexico (IAI/I, 9, 1984, p. 147–157, bibl., ill.)

A Ming period figurine (1550–1600), since 1852 in the Berlin Museum, reportedly excavated at Monte Albán, is attributed to early colonial trade between China and Spain via Mexico. [HvW]

492 **von Winning, Hasso.** Der Jaguar und sein Menschenopfer auf Reliefgefässen aus Veracruz (MLV/T, 33, 1983, p. 183–191, bibl., ill.)

Sequential elaboration of the jaguar theme as decapitator with severed human heads on five late classic relief-decorated bowls from Río Blanco. [HvW]

493 ———. Der westmexikanische equipal-Stuhl; ein ethnologisch-archäologischer Vergleich (IAI/I, 9, 1984, p. 175–187, bibl., ill.)

Late postclassic Colima figures seated on a round stool are compared with similarly constructed Huichol shaman seats and the modern *equipal*. Prehispanic origin of the latter is apparent. [HvW]

494 Webster, David and Elliot M. Abrams. An elite compound at Copán, Honduras (AFA/JFA, 10, 1983, p. 285–296)

Plaza A in Group CV36 of the Sepultura residential zone at Copán had elaborate stone buildings, of which Str. 82 had an elaborate hieroglyphic bench/throne dated to AD 780 (see item 411). [NH]

495 Whalen, Michael E. Reconstructing early formative village organization in Oaxaca, Mexico (SAA/AA, 48:1, Jan. 1983, p. 17–43, bibl., ill., maps, tables)

The social organization of Tomaltepec in the early preclassic is analyzed using house architecture, associated artifacts, and burials from a cemetery. While not completely egalitarian, the community shows scant formal status differentiation. [BLS]

496 Worthy, Morgan; Roy S. Dickens, Jr.; and Thomas W. Whitaker. The Mesoamerican pecked cross as a calendrical device (SAA/AA, 48:3, July 1983, p. 573–576, bibl., ill.)

The pecked-cross motif could have been used as a 365-day or 365 1/4-day calendar in addition to other previously suggested functions. [SF]

497 Zeitlin, Robert N. A summary report on three seasons of field investigations into the archaic period prehistory of lowland Belize (AAA/AA, 86:2, June 1984, p. 358–369, ill., map)

Suggests that in spite of ambiguous evidence and lack of stratified material there is enough to prove the existence of a preceramic occupation between 9000 and 2000 BC in the Maya lowlands; an honest appraisal which does as much with the evidence as is credible. [NH]

NATIVE SOURCES AND EPIGRAPHY

498 Anderson, Arthur J.O. and Charles E. Dibble. *Florentine Codex*: introductions and indices. Salt Lake City: Univ. of Utah: School of American Research, 1982. 137 p.: bibl., ill., index (Monographs of the School of American Research; 14:1)

Last volume in a magnificent series. [BLS]

499 Beetz, Carl P. and Linton Satterthwaite. The monuments and inscriptions of Caracol, Belize. Philadelphia: Univ. Museum, Univ. of Pennsylvania, 1981. 132 p., 53 p. of plates: bibl., ill. (Univ. Museum monograph; 45)

Final report, with excellent drawings, on Satterthwaite's 1950–53 work at Caracol, which recovered numerous classic period monuments. Beetz has transcribed inscriptions, analyzed iconography, and proposed a dynastic succession. [NH]

500 Bricker, Victoria R. Directional glyphs in Maya inscriptions and codices (SAA/AA, 48:2, 1983, p. 347–353)

Confirms on phonetic evidence that the Maya directional glyphs refer to rising and setting sun, zenith and nadir, and not the cardinal directions. Corroborates the thesis of Coggins (see *HLAS 43:289*). [NH]

501 Broda, Johanna. Metodología en el estudio de culto y sociedad mexica (UNAM/AA, 19, 1982, p. 123–137, bibl.)

Argues Aztec myths and rituals express class differences as well as an ideology of reciprocity. [BLS]

502 Brotherston, Gordon. Year 13 reed equals 3113 BC: a clue to Mesoamerican chronology (UCSB/NS, 8, 1982, p. 75–84, bibl., ill.)

Suggests that the base date ascribed to the long-count calendar system of the lowland Maya was more widespread than previously suspected, appearing in "Mixtec-Aztec" documents. [SF]

503 Bruhns, Karen Olsen. The ladies of Cotzumalhuapa (Mexicon [Berlin, FRG] 6:3, Mai 1984, p. 38–39, ill.)

Argues that some Bilbao and El Baúl monuments depict women and commemorate dynastic events. [NH]

504 Brumfiel, Elizabeth M. Aztec state making: ecology, structure, and the origin of the State (AAA/AA, 85:2, June 1983, p. 261–284, bibl., map, table)

Political factionalism and competition are stressed as causal factors in late central Mexican history, including a series of changes in Aztec state organization. Other theories are disputed. [BLS]

505 Calendars in Mesoamerica and Peru: native American computations of time. Edited by Anthony F. Aveni and Gordon Brotherston. Oxford, England: British Archaeological Reports, 1983. 263 p.: bibl., ill., maps, tables (BAR international series; 174)

In the eight Mesoamerican papers (among 10), Mayan, Zapotec, and Mexica calendrics are considered, among other topics. [BLS]

506 Closs, Michael P. A truncated initial series from Xcalumkin (SAA/AA, 48:1, 1983, p. 115–122)

Reports an initial series truncated by suppression of the *uinal-kin* coefficients into a *tun-Ahau* statement, and new head variants for Nos. 2 and 16. [NH]

507 Dibble, Charles E. Sahagun's tonalpohualli (IAI/I, 9, 1984, p. 115–122)

Subtle distinctions in the 20 13-day groups between Sahagún's Tepepulco informants and those of Tlatelolco. [HvW]

508 Diccionario maya Cordemex: mayaespañol, español-maya. Director: Alfredo Barrera Vásquez. Redactores: Juan Ramón Bastarrachea Manzano, William Brito Sansores. Colaboradores: Refugio Vermont Salas, David Dzul Góngora, Domingo Dzul Poot. Mérida, México: Ediciones Cordemex, 1980. 1 v. (69, 984, 360 p.): bibl.

Compilation of terms and phrases contained in over 13 published and unpublished Yucatec-Maya dictionaries most of which are not readily accessible. [HvW]

509 Dyckerhoff, Ursula and Hanns J. Prem. Aztec place-names and ethnonyms and their interaction (MLV/T, 33, 1984, p. 81–88, bibl.)

Systematic study of the structure and grammatical rules governing 16th-century Nahuatl names for places and ethnic groups. Summary of results of a forthcoming monograph. [HvW]

510 Fahsen, Federico. Notes for a sequence of rulers at Machaquila (SAA/AA, 49:1, 1984, p. 94–104)

Proposes six rulers between 9.14.0.0.0. and 10.0.15.0.0. and relates them to 17 stelae at this east Peten center. [NH]

511 Faivre, Jean-Baptiste. Trois peintres Techialoyan: peintres du Zempoala, du Tepotztlan et du Calpulalpan (IAI/I, 9, 1984, p. 137–146, bibl., ill.)

Comparisons in style and content of different post-conquest Techialoyan codices and their relationships to other manuscripts. [HvW]

512 Five centuries of law and politics in Central Mexico. Edited by Ronald Spores and Ross Hassig. Nashville: Vanderbilt Univ., 1984. 286 p.: bibl., ill., tables (Publications in anthropology; 30)

Within this volume three skillful papers pertain to late prehispanic society: Offner's on Texcoco legal councils in relation to factionalism; Hassig's suggestion that the Aztecs had a "hegemonic" empire; and J. Zeitlin's comparison of pre- and post-conquest Isthmus Zapotec society. [BLS]

513 Foncerrada de Molina, Marta. Signos glíficos relacionados con Tláloc en murales de la batalla en Cacaxtla (IIE/A, 50:1, 1982, p. 23–33, ill.)

Well illustrated account of Tlaloc iconography at Cacaxtla, suggesting the victory of Tlaloc-Jaguar group in the battle scene, the presence of Olmeca-Xicalanca at Teotihuacan, and a Teotihuacan promotion of the cult of Tlaloc-Jaguar as a war god. [NH]

514 Gaida, Maria. Die Inschriften von Naranjo, Petén, Guatemala. Hamburg, FRG: Hamburgisches Museum für Völkerkunde; Hohenschäftlarn bei München, FRG: Im Kommissionsverlag K. Renner, 1983. 158 p. (some folded): bibl. (Beiträge zur mittelamerikanischen Völkerkunde; 17)

Inscriptions contain biographical, dynastic and regional-political information spanning 300 years. All pertinent glyphs are transcribed and elucidated, including full transcriptions of texts on 43 monuments. Indispensable supplement to drawings in the *Corpus of Maya hieroglyphic inscriptions* (for vol. 2, pts. 1–3, see *HLAS 41:465*). [HvW]

515 **Houston, Stephen D.** An example of homophony in Maya script (SAA/AA, 49:4, Oct. 1984, p. 790–805, bibl., ill., tables)

Notes that the sound *kan/kaan*, meaning "sky," "four" and "snake" can be represented by substitution of glyphs, and appears in a spelling of the deity name *Kukulcan*. [NH]

516 **Isaac, Barry L.** The Aztec "Flowery War:" a geopolitical explanation (UNM/JAR, 39:4, Winter 1983, p. 415–432, bibl., table)

Ritual and ecological arguments for the Aztec failure to conquer the Tlaxcalans are rejected in favor of the idea that Puebla-Tlaxcala region had a history of successful armed resistence. [BLS]

517 ———. Aztec warfare: goals and battlefield comportment (UP/E, 22:2, April 1983, p. 121–131, bibl.)

Marshalls evidence that Aztec warfare had practical aims (political and economic), rather than solely ritual ones. [BLS]

518 **Kelley, David H.** Astronomical identities of Mesoamerican gods (Archaeoastronomy [Supplement to Journal for the History of Astronomy, Giles, England] 11:2, 1980, p. 1–54, bibl., ill., tables)

Certain deity calendric names occur in an order in Mesoamerican calendars which reflects the astronomical cycles of planets. A general calendric base date is assumed. The interpretation implies a more extensive Mesoamerican astronomical knowledge than previous scholarship allowed. [BLS]

519 **Knorozov, Yurii V.** Maya hieroglyphic codices. Translated from the Russian by Sophie D. Coe. Albany: Institute for Mesoamerican Studies, SUNY, 1982. 429 p.: bibl., index (Publication; 8)

English version of important work by a Russian pioneer in Maya linguistics and epigraphy. [NH]

520 **Kubler, George.** An Aztec calendar of 20,176 non-repeating years in *Codex Borbonicus*, p. 21–22 (IAI/I, 9, 1984, p. 123–136, bibl., ill., tables)

Ingenious solution to account for the meshing of an uninterrupted and continuous sequence of the Nine Lords of the Night with the 52 year-bearer days (as in the Maya count) in a newly proposed expanded cycle that repeats itself indefinitely after the first 20,176 years. [HvW]

521 **Kurtz, Donald V.** Strategies of legitimation and the Aztec state (UP/E, 23:4, Oct. 1984, p. 301–314, bibl.)

Strategies for state legitimation include economic development, greater social distance of rulers, elaboration of state religion, consolidation of power and authority, and political socialization. [SF and BLS]

522 **Mathews, Peter.** Corpus of Maya hieroglyphic inscriptions. v. 6, pt. 1, Toniná. Cambridge, Mass.: Peabody Museum, Harvard Univ., 1983. 63 p.: ill., maps.

Further addition to this admirable project, covering monuments at a center in highland Chiapas with links to Palenque. [NH]

523 **Mayer, Karl Herbert** and **Berthold Riese.** Monument 134 aus Toniná, Chiapas (Mexicon [Berlin, FRG] 5:5, Sept. 1983, p. 87–90, ill.)

A new inscription of Ruler III on his statue, linked to Monument 29 and Fragment 88, gives the ruler's accession date and birth date. [NH]

524 **Miller, Mary Ellen** and **David S. Stuart.** Dumbarton Oaks relief panel 4 (CEM/ECM, 13, 1981, p. 197–204, bibl., ill.)

Analysis of a looted panel of AD 800 (9.18.10.0.0.), suggesting that it may come from Pomona, Tabasco, and relating it to another looted panel now at Tuxtla, Chiapas. [NH]

525 **The Native sources and the history of the Valley of Mexico.** Edited by J. de Durand-Forest. Oxford, England: British Archaeological Reports, 1984. 268 p.: bibl., ill., tables (BAR international series; 204)

Most of the 10 papers pertain to the central highlands of Mexico although the Maya are included as well. Chronology and emic views of history are among the many topics. [SF and BLS]

526 **Offner, Jerome A.** Law and politics in Aztec Texcoco. Cambridge, England: Cambridge Univ. Press, 1983. 340 p.: bibl., ill., index (Cambridge Latin American studies; 44)

Although the book focuses on Texcocan law, political and social organization are evaluated as well. Includes history of development of Texcocan legal system. [BLS]

527 **Paddock, John.** Lord 5 Flower's family: rulers of Zaachila and Cuilapan. Nashville: Vanderbilt Univ., 1983. 112 p.: bibl., ill., tables (Publications in anthropology; 29)

Analysis of ethnohistoric documents suggests a much earlier prominent Mixtec role in the Valley of Oaxaca than previously recognized. [SF]

528 **Prem, Hanns J.** Das Chronologieproblem in der autochthonen Tradition Zentralamerikas (DGV/ZE, 108:1, 1983, p. 133–161, bibl, ill., tables)

Commentary, with methodological guidelines toward solutions, on discrepancies in ethnohistorical sources concerning the correlation of the central Mexican calendar with the Julian calendar, the divergent names for the beginning of the year, the proposed but dubious existence of several regional calendar styles, intercalary corrections, and the dates for various episodes of the Spanish conquest (see also: "The Chronological Dilemma,: in International Congress of Americanists, 44th, Manchester, England, 1982. Oxford, England: 1984, p. 5–25, bibl., tables [British Archaeological Reports (BAR) international series; 204] and "Las Fechas Calendáricas Completas en los Textos de Iztlilxochitl" in *Estudios de Cultura Náhuatl* [UNAM, México] 16, 1983, p. 225–231, bibl., tables). [HvW]

529 ——— and **Berthold Riese.** Autochthonous American writing systems: the Aztec and Maya examples (*in* Writing in focus. Edited by Florian Coulmas and Konrad Ehlich. Berlin, FRG: Mouton, 1983, p. 167–186, bibl., ill. (Trends in linguistics. Studies and monographs; 24)

Important analytical study of the constituents and functions of graphic communication systems and their spatial and temporal developments. [HvW]

530 **Riese, Berthold.** Dynastiegeschichtliche und kalendarische Beobachtungen an den Maya-Inschriften von Machaquila, Petén, Guatemala (MLV/T, 33, 1984, p. 149–154, bibl., ill.)

Identification of six rulers according to name glyphs on stelae and observations on unusual calendric computations (see also

item 510 for a different approach but similar results). [HvW]

531 ———. Eine mexikanische Gottheit im Venuskapitel der Mayahandschrift *Codex Dresdensis* (SSA/B, 46, 1982, p. 37–39, bibl.)

The blind-folded image of ixquimilli, a variant of Tezcatlipoca, in Dresden 29 is identified by his name sign *ce acatl* which the Maya scribe rendered phonetically in a glyph compound. [HvW]

532 ———. Zur Chronologie der Maya-Dynastie von Piedras Negras, Guatemala (Jahrbuch Preussischer Kulturbesitz [Berlin, FRG] 19, 1982, p. 231–247, bibl., ill.)

Hieroglyphic analysis of Stelae 3 which commemorates the enthronement of a female ruler, and further comments on dynastic records for which Maler's 1898 photographs remain a primary source. [HvW]

533 ——— and **Karl Herbert Mayer.** Altar 10 von Uxmal, Yukatan, Mexico (Mexicon [Berlin, FRG] 6:5, Sept. 1984, p. 70–73, ill.)

First complete publication and interpretation of the glyphic text which contains genealogical information. [HvW]

534 **Schele, Linda.** Maya glyphs: the verbs. Austin: Univ. of Texas Press, 1982. 427 p.: ill.

Copiously illustrated treatise on the decipherment of a major class of Maya glyphs of great importance for the study of the Maya writing system. [NH]

535 ——— and **Jeffrey H. Miller.** The mirror, the rabbit, and the bundle: "accession" expressions from the classic Maya inscriptions. Washington: Dumbarton Oaks, Trustees for Harvard Univ., 1983. 1 v.: bibl. (Studies in precolumbian art & archaeology; 25)

Argues that three glyphs used in accession statements are metaphors. [NH]

536 **Smith, Michael E.** The Aztlán migrations of the Náhuatl chronicles: myth or history? (ASE/E, 31:3, 1984, p. 153–186, bibl., tables)

Chichimec and Aztec migration accounts are dissected anew to give a chronology, which is compared to glottochronology and to archaeological ceramic sequences. Considerable historical veracity is attributed to migration accounts. [BLS]

537 **Tedlock, Barbara.** Time and the high-land Maya. Albuquerque: Univ. of

New Mexico Press, 1982. 245 p.: bibl., ill., index.

Descriptive analysis of Quiché ritual in Momostenango, emphasizing the role of the 260-day ritual calendar. [NH]

ARCHAEOLOGY: Caribbean Area

W. JERALD KENNEDY, Associate Professor of Anthropology, Florida Atlantic University

PUBLICATIONS INCLUDED IN THIS SECTION cover a broad range of topics and numerous countries in the Caribbean and Central America.

CENTRAL AMERICA

Two landmark publications dealing with a variety of topics in Lower Central American prehistory makes compiling this section of the *Handbook* an especially enjoyable task (items **540** and **569**).

Publications were reviewed dealing with every country in Lower Central America. The majority dealt with Costa Rican and Panamanian archaeology. As the pace in archaeological investigations of this region has picked up, especially in this area, the levels of analysis far exceed the simple description of the past. Articles dealing with interregional trade and the testing of trade models are noted in several articles (items **549–551, 563–564,** and **571**) as are analyses of zooarchaeological materials (items **544–545** and **547–548**).

Especially valuable are the selections which give recent overviews of the archaeology in this area (items **544, 554–555, 563, 571–573,** and **579**). In contrast to previous *HLAS* volumes, there are very few articles dealing with historical archaeology (item **570**).

Considerable activity in archaeological research albeit not yet in publication has been noted in this region over the last biennium. Richard G. Cooke in the "Current Research" section of *American Antiquity* (48:1, Jan. 1983, p. 176–178) notes numerous excavations in progress both in Costa Rica and Panama.

Four important symposia and conferences were held during the past two-year period: 1) in April 1983, the Society for American Archaeology on "Interregional Ties in Costa Rican Prehistory;" 2) in Aug. 1984, the "Tercer Congreso Sobre la Cerámica de La Nicoya: Panorama Actual de la Arqueología de Costa Rica" in Costa Rica; 3) in Oct. 1984, the "Simposia Sobre la Biografía de América Central," in Merida, Yucatán; and 4) in July 1985, the 45th International Congress of Americanists, in Bogotá, Colombia. Publications are forthcoming from all of the above.

CARIBBEAN ISLANDS

Geographically, publications covered nine islands. The bulk of the articles reviewed, however, were more general, dealing with Antillean archaeology on a broader scope.

A variety of research projects underway in the Greater and Lesser Antilles are reported by Charles Hoffman in the "Current Research" section of *American Antiquity* (50:1, Jan. 1985, p. 173–175; 49:1, Jan. 1984, p. 184–185; 47:4, Oct. 1982, p. 883–884). Of significant interest are the numerous investigations being conducted by various scientific teams on a number of islands in the Bahamas.

A new journal *Before Columbus: Indian Traditions of the Bahamas* will be published seminannually by the Florida Gulf Coast Archaeological Program, Horseshoe Creek, Florida. Beginning Feb. 1985, a traveling exhibit on Taino Art from the Dominican Republic premiered at the Univ. of Florida before appearances at the Museum of Art in New York and the Miami-Bacardí Gallery in Miami.

RECENT DOCTORAL DISSERTATIONS

Creamer, Winifred. Production and exchange in two islands in the Gulf of Nicoya: Costa Rica, AD 1200–1550. Tulane Univ., 1983.

Einhaus, Catherine Shelton. Formative settlement in Western Chiriquí, Panama: ceramic chronology and phase relationships. Temple Univ., 1984.

Piperno, Dolores. The application of phytolith analysis to the reconstruction of plant subsistence and environment in Panama. Temple Univ., 1983.

CENTRAL AMERICA

538 Acuña Coto, Víctor. Algunos sitios arqueológicos en el Valle de Turrialba (Boletín de la Asociación Costarricense de Arqueólogos [San José] 2, 1983, p. 16–21)

Summary discussion of three archaeological sites in the Turrialba Valley of Costa Rica (i.e., Margot, Zapote-2, Florencia-1) which have been studied by the Univ. of Costa Rica and Museo Nacional de Costa Rica. Preliminary investigations suggest these sites will offer valuable information for the archaeology of the region.

539 Archaeology and volcanism in Central America: the Zapotitlan Valley of El Salvador. Edited by Payson D. Sheets. Austin: Univ. of Texas Press, 1983. 307 p.: appendices.

Extremely valuable collection of original articles, consisting of 13 chapters and appendices. Considers both beneficial as well as detrimental aspects of volcanic activity in relation to El Salvador's culture history, especially in the Zapotitlan Valley.

540 The Archaeology of Lower Central America. Edited by Frederick W. Lange and Doris Z. Stone. Albuquerque: Univ. of New Mexico Press, School of American Research, 1984. 476 p.: appendices.

Extremely valuable publication for archaeologists and scholars working in the Intermediate area. Outgrowth of the 1980 advanced seminar on Lower Central American archaeology held at the School of American Research, Santa Fe, N.M. Contributors to this work are among the most prominent archaeologists in the field. A "state of the art" summary of the archaeology of the region.

The book is divided into five parts: Introduction; The Northern Frontier of Lower Central America; The Lower Central American Core; The Southern Frontier of Lower Central America; and Summary Statement. Appendices with C14 dates. The following articles are annotated separately in this section as indicated by the item number in parenthesis: Doris Z. Stone, "A History of Lower Central American Archaeology" (item 576); Frederick W. Lange, "Cultural Geography of Pre-Columbian Lower Central America" (item 562) and "The Greater Nicoya Archaeological Subarea" (item 563); Robert J. Sharer, "Lower Central America as seen from Mesoamerica" (item 571); Payson D. Sheets, "The Prehistory of El Salvador: an Interpretive Summary" (item 572); Paul F. Healy, "The Archaeology of Honduras" (item 555); Michael J. Snarskis, "Central America: the Lower Caribbean" (item 573); Wolfgang Haberland, "The Archaeology of Greater Chiriqui" (item 554); Richard Cooke, "Archaeological Research in Central and Eastern Panama: a Review of Some Problems" (item 544); Warwick Bray, "Across the Darien Gap: a Colombian View of Isthmian Archaeology (item 541); Gordon Willey, "A Summary of the Archaeology of Lower Central America" (item 579).

541 Bray, Warwick. Across the Darien Gap: a Colombian view of Isthmian archaeology (*in* The Archaeology of Lower Central America [see item 540] p. 305–340)

Emphasizes local adaptation and cultural adaptability as primary stimulus for cultural development in lowland Colombia from Gulf of Uraba to Venezuela. Extremely interesting "chain model" applied to examine the cultural dynamics between neighboring cultures of the region.

542 Bruhns, Karen Olsen. A view from the bridge: intermediate area sculpture in thematic perspective (MV/BA, 30, 1982, p. 147–182, ill.)

Excellent article in which author analyzes shared artistic themes found in the Intermediate Area and Mesoamerica. Concludes that despite similarities, the basic forms were quite different. Common motifs are explained by contact, early beliefs and paralellism rather than the imposition of religion (religious art) by migration.

543 Cabello Carro, Paz. Desarrollo cultural en Costa Rica precolombina: con el catálogo de las piezas arqueológicas de Costa Rica del Museo de América. Madrid: Museo de América, 1980. 165 p.: ill.

Brief overview of Costa Rican culture history. Final chapter describes Costa Rican ceramics by provenience and culture period which comprise the permanent collection in the Museum of America, Madrid.

544 Cooke, Richard G. Archaeological research in Central and Eastern Panama: a review of some problems (in The Archaeology of Lower Central America [see item **540**] p. 263–304)

Incorporating the most current data, author focuses on the following themes: Paleo-Indian adaptation; beginnings of agriculture; early ceramic period in Parita Bay; establishment of sedentary villages and social ranking; and insights gained from faunal analysis.

545 ———. Birds and men in prehistoric Central Panama (in Recent developments in Isthmian archaeology [see item **569**] p. 243–281)

Analyzes relationship between men and birds in the central Pacific region of Panama between 5000 BC and Spanish conquest. Examines and identifies iconography of artifacts with avian motifs. Symbolism suggests possible social metaphors and certain species are closely associated with myth and kinship structure. Author also presents an economic assessment of bone samples taken from archaeological sites.

546 ——— and Anthony J. Ranere. The "Proyecto Santa María:" a multidisciplinary analysis of prehistoric adaptations to a tropical watershed in Panama (in Recent developments in Isthmian archaeology [see item **569**] p. 3–30)

Background and progress to date of the energetic "Proyecto Santa María" which aims to reconstruct pre-AD 500 environments, settlement patterns, and subsistence systems in the Santa María River basin on the Pacific coast of Central Panama. Extremely informative results thus far from this multidisciplinary project.

547 ——— and Storrs L. Olson. An archaeological record for the white-faced whistling-duck—*Dendrocygna Viduata*—in Central Panama (The Condor [The Cooper Ornithological Society, Berkeley, Calif.] 86, 1984, p. 493–494)

Brief report on 400 avian bone specimens found at several central Panamanian archaeological sites. Identification provides information on the disjunctured range of several species as well as suggesting possible domestication of *Dendrocygna* and *Carina*.

548 Creamer, Winifred. Archaeological faunal remains as indicators of territory size and subsistence strategy (Brenesia [San José] 21, 1983, p. 395–401)

Comparative study of zooarchaeological remains from two island sites in the Gulf of Nicoya, Costa Rica. Data suggests that as long as similar faunal resources were available to both island populations; the smaller island was more specialized in its procurement of marine resources. Author concludes that the existence of trade networks made specialization advantageous to its inhabitants.

549 ———. Sistemas de intercambio en el Golfo de Nicoya, Costa Rica, 1200–1550 BC (MNCR/V, 8:1, 1982, p. 13–38)

Focuses on trade patterns during the Late Polychrome Period in the Gulf of Nicoya, Costa Rica. Artifacts are analyzed from two island sites. Both regional and interregional trade networks were present. Evidence suggests that regional trade activity was more common. Notes that, although less frequent, there was long distance trade both north and south, well beyond the Gulf of Nicoya.

550 Day, Jane Stevenson. Decorated ceramic types from the Late Polychrome Period: 1200–1500 AD, Hacienda Tempisque,

Guanacaste Province, Costa Rica (MNCR/V, 8:2, 1982, p. 39–64)

Stylistic analysis of 400 decorated ceramic vessels obtained from burials at Hacienda Tempisque, Guanacaste, is used to clarify temporal and spatial distribution of Late Polychrome Period ceramics. The author concludes that Hacienda Tempisque was part of larger interaction sphere running along the Tempisque River drainage and north to Rivas and lake area of southwestern Nicaragua. Site is seen as long-distance way station between Northern South America and Nicaragua.

551 ――――. New approaches in stylistic analysis: the ceramics at Hacienda Tempisque (in Recent developments in Isthmian archaeology [see item 569] p. 199–214)

Results from detailed analysis of Late Polychrome Period (AD 1200–1500) ceramics from Hacienda Tempisque in northwestern Costa Rica. Specific centers of manufacture are suggested for various ceramic types and local copies of imported polychrome ritual vessels are among some of the interesting findings.

552 Drolet, Robert P. Community life in a Late Phase agricultural village, Southeastern Costa Rica (in Recent developments in Isthmian archaeology [see item 569] p. 123–152)

Significant inroads into better understanding the politico-organizational structure of a Chiriqui Phase (AD 1000–1500) agricultural village (Murciélago) in the Disquis Valley of Costa Rica.

553 Fonseca Zamora, Oscar and Luis Hurtado de Mendoza. Algunos resultados de las investigaciones en la región de Guayabo de Turrialba (UCR/RCS, edición especial no. 1, julio 1984, p. 37–52)

Excellent article discusses results of long-term archaeological research in the Guayabo region and the administrative-ceremonial center of Guayabo in the Atlantic Watershed area of Costa Rica. Authors favor modification of temporal spans of the three ceramic phases in this area and note their findings suggest that a Chiefdom level of sociocultural complexity appeared in the La Cabaña phase (AD 800-1550). Long-term goals favor a better understanding of the dynamic processes taking place through time in this area.

554 Haberland, Wolfgang. The archaeology of Greater Chiriquí (in The Archaeology of Lower Central America [see item 540] p. 233–253)

Summary of cultural development in the Grand Chiriquí region from ca. 6000 BC (Period II) to 1550 BC (Period IV). Interesting addition is Haberland's report of Richard Drolet's recent year-long survey of the region. Although many substantive issues raised in the article are not changed by the research, many of its views are enhanced by data from 50 additional archaeological sites.

555 Healy, Paul F. The archaeology of Honduras (in The Archaeology of Lower Central America [see item 540] p. 113–164)

Archaeologically, Honduras remains one of the least known Central American countries. Author capably sketches out its archaeological zones and provides us with the most accurate cultural chronology to date. Concludes there are numerous gaps in our knowledge and many questions remain to be answered.

556 ――――. Northeast Honduras: a precolumbian frontier zone (in Recent developments in Isthmian archaeology [see item 569] p. 227–242)

Based on author's regional survey and excavations during the years 1973–76 in Colón Dept, northeastern Honduras. Article examines prehistoric linkages with other regions and their implications for cultural change in this area. Preliminary results point to a cultural frontier that is increasingly stimulated by cultures from Lower Central America over time.

557 Helms, Mary W. Miskito slaving and culture contact: ethnicity and opportunity in an expanding population (UNM/JAR, 39:2, 1983, p. 179–197)

Ethnohistoric material provides considerable detail regarding slave trade along the Miskito coast of Nicaragua. Considers ecological relationships, both human and cultural. Analysis provides insights into settlement patterns and subsistence modes which will be of interest to historical archaeologists.

558 ――――. Precious metals and politics: style and ideology in the Intermediate Area and Peru (UCLA/JLAL, 7:2, 1981, p. 215–238)

Interesting thesis presented by author in which the complex interplay between metallurgical traditions and political organization is investigated. A comparison is made between the metallurgical traditions and styles of chiefdoms in the Isthmian area and statal societies in Peru.

559 Herra, Carlos E. Sitio Nosarita de Nicoya: informe propuesta de la excavación (MNCR/V, 8;2, 1982, p. 65–74)

Preliminary report based on site visitations at Nosarita, Nicoya. Notes archaeological features, most likely being burial mounds for this Early Polychrome Period occupation. Proposes several hypotheses for future research at this site.

560 Highwater, Jamake. Arts of the Indian Americas, North-Central-South: leaves from the sacred tree. New York: Harper and Row, 1983. 372 p.: bibl., index.

A somewhat flawed but nonetheless well written book on American Indian art. Some slight attention given to prehistoric art of Lower Central America. Includes glossary.

561 Hurtado de Mendoza, Luis. La historia antigua de Turrialba: proposiciones generales (Boletín de la Asociación Costarricense de Arqueólogos [San José] 2, 1983, p. 10–15)

Very generalized three-stage developmental scheme for the culture history of the canton of Turrialba, Costa Rica.

562 Lange, Frederick W. Cultural geography of precolumbian Lower Central America (in The Archaeology of Lower Central America [see item **540**] p. 33–62)

Provides geographical/ecological focus for better understanding of cultural developments in Lower Central American prehistory. When considering settlement patterns and trade networks in natural commodities, stresses the fact of the region's being relatively small in size but geographically diverse.

563 ———. The Greater Nicoya archaeological subarea (in The Archaeology of Lower Central America [see item **540**] p. 165–194)

Summary of current archaeological data, period by period, for this region. Notes similarities and differences among sites. Delineates northern and southern sectors within the Gran Nicoya subarea. Discusses

influence of trade, ecological adaptation and general cultural evolutionary developments.

564 ———. La participación de personas de alto rango social en el traspaso de cerámica precolombina en Costa Rica (Boletín de la Asociación Costarricense de Arqueólogos [San José] 2, 1983, p. 22–43)

Extremely interesting article presents the distribution of ceramics in the Gran Nicoya and Meseta Central archaeological zones. Applies various trade models in order to explain differential frequency distribution of trade wares through time.

565 Matillo Vila, Joaquín. Trilogía arqueológica rupestre: máscaras, magos y hechiceros, danzas y danzantes en el arte rupestre de Nicaragua. Managua: Fundación Científica Hermano Hildeberto María, 1981. 63 p., 16 p. of plates: ill.

Book divided into three parts: Masks, Magical Practitioners, and Dances. Attempts to interpret numerous petroglyphs and rock carvings found in Nicaragua. Author perceives the study of rock art as indispensable in understanding rituals and ceremonies. Representations are seen as religious symbols found on ritual masks and gestures of dancers associated with specific magico-religious ceremonies.

566 Moreau, Jean-François. Subsistence et évolution socio-culturelle au Sitio Vidor, Costa Rica (in Recent developments in Isthmian archaeology [see item **569**] p. 179–198)

Data from excavations at the Vidor site provides useful insights into the social and cultural changes that take place during the Polychrome Periods in northeastern Costa Rica.

567 Olien, Michael. The Miskito Kings and the line of succession (UNM/JAR, 39:2, 1983, p. 198–241)

Article of interest to those concerned with Nicaraguan archaeology of the historic period. Author uses ethnohistoric material in order to document the 239 year political succession of kings among the Miskito Indians of lowland eastern Nicaragua (1655–1894).

568 Piperno, Dolores R. and **Karen Husum Clary.** Early plant use and cultivation in the Santa María Basin, Panama: data from phytoliths and pollen (in Recent developments in Isthmian archaeology [see item 569] p. 85–122)

Informative article deals with analysis of modern plants and archaeological sediments in Central Pacific Panama. Analyzes preceramic and ceramic period sites in order to provide insights into prehistoric plant subsistence through time.

569 Recent developments in Isthmian archaeology: advances in the prehistory of Lower Central America. Edited by Frederick W. Lange. Oxford, England: British Archaeological Reports, 1984. 315 p.: ill. (BAR international series; 212)

Consists of 12 papers on varied topics dealing with Lower Central America prehistory delivered at the 44th International Congress of Americanists (Manchester, England, 1984) and edited by Norman Hammond. For those which are individually annotated elsewhere in this section, see item number in parenthesis: Frederick W. Lange "Introduction" (p. 1–2); Richard C. Cooke and Anthony J. Ranere "The 'Proyecto Santa María': a Multidisciplinary Analysis of Prehistoric Adaptations to a Tropical Watershed in Panama" (item 546); Doris Weiland "Prehistoric Settlement Patterns in the Santa María Drainage of Central Pacific Panama" (item 578); James H. Clary, Patricia Hansell, Anthony J. Ranere, and Thomas Buggey "The Holocene Geology of the Western Parita Bay Coastline of Central Panama" (p. 55–84); Dolores P. Piperno and Karen Husum Clary "Early Plant Use and Cultivation in the Santa María Basin, Panama: Data from Phytoliths and Pollen" (item 568); Robert P. Drolet "Community Life in a Late Phase Agricultural Village, Southeastern Costa Rica" (item 552); Michael J. Snarskis "Prehistoric Microsettlement Patterns in the Central Highlands-Atlantic Watershed of Costa Rica" (item 575); Jean-François Moreau "Subsistence et Evolution Socio-Culturelle au Sitio Vidor, Costa Rica" (item 566); Frederick W. Lange et al "New Approaches to Greater Nicoya Ceramics" (p. 199–214); Jane S. Day "New Approaches in Stylistic Analysis: the Ceramics of Hacienda Tempisque" (item 551); Paul F. Healy "Northeast Honduras: a Precolumbian Frontier Zone" (item 556); Richard C. Cooke "Birds and Men in Prehistoric Central Panama" (item 545); and Beatriz Rovira "La Cerámica Histórica en la

Ciudad de Panamá: Tres Contextos Estratigráficos" (item 570).

570 Rovira, Beatriz E. La cerámica histórica en la Ciudad de Panamá: tres contextos estratigráficos (in Recent developments in Isthmian archaeology [see item 569] p. 283–215)

Results derived from archaeological excavations and analysis of ceramics from two historic period sites: Convento de Santo Domingo and Iglesia de la Compañía de Jesús in the city of Panama.

571 Sharer, Robert J. Lower Central America as seen from Mesoamerica (in The Archaeology of Lower Central America [see item 540] p. 63–84)

Outlines the development of exchange networks, subsistence systems, and trade routes in Lower Central America with a focus on relationships with Mesoamerica. Many useful suggestions regarding directions for future research.

572 Sheets, Payson D. The prehistory of El Salvador: an interpretive summary (in The Archaeology of Lower Central America [see item 540] p. 85–112)

Excellent review of El Salvador's prehistory. Focus is on effects of external relationships, ecological adaptation, vulcanism and regional economics. Demonstrates close relationships with Mesoamerica.

573 Snarskis, Michael J. Central America: the Lower Caribbean (in The Archaeology of Lower Central America [see item 540] p. 195–232)

This is the most comprehensive treatment to date of coastal Atlantic Central America, from Nicaragua to Panama. Includes cultural chronology. Presents series of thought provoking hypotheses that need to be tested.

574 ———. Cien años de arqueología en la Vertiénte Atlántica de Costa Rica (Boletín de la Asociación Costarricense de Arqueólogos [San José] 2, 1983, p. 2–9)

Brief article traces the development of archaeological research in the Atlantic Watershed zone of Costa Rica. Notes priorities for future research.

575 ———. Prehistoric microsettlement patterns in the Central Highlands-Atlantic Watershed of Costa Rica (in Recent developments in Isthmian archaeology [see item **569**] p. 153–175)

Draws several significant generalizations for this archaeological zone on the basis of excavation data from several recent Museo Nacional de Costa Rica projects. Sedentary villages in central and eastern Costa Rica were present by the time of Christ. Variability of individual structures suggest hierarchical sociopolitical organization at least by AD 1–500. Changes in house shapes from rectangular to circular after AD 500 suggest northern (Mesoamerican) influences for earlier rectangular house types and southern influence for circular ones. Indicates corresponding changes in community demographic patterns.

576 Stone, Doris Z. A history of Lower Central American archaeology (in The Archaeology of Lower Central America [see item **540**] p. 13–32)

Excellent detailed overview by country provides readers with a historic perspective on the development of archaeology in Lower Central America.

577 Velarde B., Oscar A. Arquitectura precolombina panameña (LNB/L, 100, marzo 1981, p. 41–52)

Author discusses similarities and differences in settlement patterns and archaeological features found among ceremonial and habitational sites from shortly after AD 1 until the contact period in Panama.

578 Weiland, Doris. Prehistoric settlement patterns in the Santa María Drainage of Central Pacific Panama: a preliminary analysis (in Recent developments in Isthmian archaeology [see item **569**] p. 31–54)

Discussion of results in ongoing regional survey of archaeological sites in the Santa María drainage basin. To date 200 sites have been located. Notes widespread preceramic occupations from 5000–2500 BC as well as appearance of large nucleated agricultural settlements by the first millenium BC. Discusses implications drawn from exploitation of coastal resources.

579 Willey, Gordon R. A summary of the archaeology of Lower Central America (in The Archaeology of Lower Central America [see item **540**] p. 341–380)

The difficult task of "pulling it all together" with clarity is ably done by the author. Article organized into four parts: 1) Lower Central America: Archaeological and Natural Settings; 2) Archaeological Cultures, Space, and Time; 3)Chronological-Developmental Scheme of Lower Central America; and 4) Interpretations. This synthesis and insightful interpretive overview provides numerous intellectual challenges to students of Lower Central America prehistory.

ANTILLES

580 Aarons, G.A. Archaeological sites in the Hellshire area (IJ/JJ, 16:1, Feb. 1983, p. 76–87, bibl., ill., maps, photos)

Brief survey of prehistoric, historic, and marine sites in the Hellshire Hills and Bay region of Jamaica.

581 Alegría, Ricardo E. El uso de gases nocivos como arma bélica por los indios taínos y caribes de la Antillas (ICP/R, 22:82, enero/marzo 1982, p. 51–55, ill.)

Presents ethnohistoric evidence to document previously unreported use of poison gas (Family Solanaceae; Capsicum annum and Capsicum frutescens) as a weapon used by both Taino and Carib.

582 ———. El uso de la incrustación en la escultura de los indios antillanos. San Juan: Centro de Estudios Avanzados de Puerto Rico y el Caribe con la colaboración de la Fundación Guardia Arévalo, Santo Domingo, 1981. 79 p.: ill.

Well illustrated article deals with the application, use, and distribution of crustations in Antillean sculpture. Initially appearing in Puerto Rico with the Saladoid culture (ca. AD 120), the spread of this artistic technique is traced throughout the Antilles to historic times.

583 ———. El uso de la terminología etnohistórica para designar las culturas aborígenes de las Antillas (ICP/R, 21:80, julio/sept. 1978, p. 22–32, ill.)

Interesting article uses ethnohistoric sources which trace initial occurrences of vocabulary denoting precolumbian cultures of the Caribbean. On the basis of these early documents, author concludes that the indigenous groups that inhabited the islands at contact comprised three great traditions: preceramic/preagricultural; agricultural Arawakan; and historical Carib.

584 Allaire, Louis. A reconstruction of early historical Island Carib pottery (Southeastern Archaeology [Southeastern Archaeological Conference, Gainesville, Fla.] 3:2, Winter 1984, p. 121–133)

Interesting analysis of Island Carib ceramics shortly after contact.

585 Caba Fuentes, Angel and **Harold Olsen Bogaert.** Descripción de tipos cerámicos de Cueva de Collantes, Distrito Nacional (MHD/B, 11:18, 1983, p. 91–109, bibl., ill., plates)

Detailed description of ceramic and non-ceramic artifacts found at Collantes Cave, a historic period site in the Dominican Republic. Five ceramic types, well decorated and specialized in shape, suggest ceremonial use of this cave. Author believes that the unfired clay balls found were part of a ritual which included geophagy.

Crónicas francesas de los indios caribes. See HLAS 46:2488.

586 Handler, Jerome S. An African pipe from a slave cemetery in Barbados, West Indies (in The Archaeology of the clay tobacco pipe, VIII America. Edited by P. Davey. Oxford, England: British Archaeological Reports, 1983, p. 245–253 [Bar international series; 175])

Discussion centers on 22 clay pipes excavated in 92 burials from a slave cemetery in Barbados. This comprises the largest number of complete pipes found in any New World colonial period site. Using ethnohistoric data, author convincingly points to African stylistic features and manufacturing techniques. Clay pipes are seen as grave goods which resemble African burial ceremonies. This provides another example of African traditions which influenced slave cultures in the New World.

587 Journal of New World Archaeology. The Institute of Archaeology, Univ. of California. Vol. 5, No. 2, April 1982– . Los Angeles.

Excellent series of articles treating a wide variety of topics on Antillean archaeology: David Watters, "Relating Oceanography to Antillean Archaeology: Implications from Oceania" (p. 3–12); Elizabeth Wing and Elizabeth Reitz, "Prehistoric Fishing Communities of the Caribbean" (p. 13–32); Marcio Veloz Maggiolo and Bernardo Vega "The Antillean Preceramic: a New Approximation" (p. 33–44); Irving Rouse "Ceramic and Religious Development in the Greater Antilles" (p. 45–56); William F. Keegan "Lucayan Cave Burials from the Bahamas" (p. 57–66); Charles H. Fairbanks and Rochelle A. Merrinan, "The Puerto Rico Project: Haiti" (p. 67–72); Edwin Dethlefsen "The Historical Archaeology of St. Eustatius" (p. 73–86); Douglas V. Armstrong "The 'Old Village' at Drax Hall: an Archaeological Process Report" (p. 87).

588 Keegan, William F. Lucayan fishing practices: an experimental approach (FAS/FA, 35:4, 1982, p. 146)

Short report on ongoing research in the Bahamas which focuses on subsistence behavior of the aboriginal Lucayan population (AD 800–1500).

589 López y Sebastián, Lorenzo Eladio. Arqueología de Jamaica: Sevilla la Nueva (IGFO/RI, 42:167/168, enero/junio 1982, p. 223–242, bibl., ill., maps)

Report on successive occupations (Arawak, Spanish, and English) of Sevilla la Nueva, first capital of Jamaica, founded in 1509.

590 Navarrete Pujol, Ramón. El sitio cubano de Caimanes III (MHD/B, 11:18, 1983, p. 111–113)

Brief report on the Caimanes III site near Santiago de Cuba, intially excavated in 1978. Includes short history of ceramic and lithic artifacts. Site has C14 date of 1745± BP. A need for further investigations at this site and elsewhere in Cuba is critical for understanding the relationship of this early ceramic group with others in the Antilles.

591 Pagán Perdomo, Dato and **Abelardo Jiménez Lamberetus.** Reconocimiento arqueológico y espeleológico de la región de Samaná: reporte de más de 45 nuevos sitios (MHD/B, 11:18, 1983, p. 39–71, ill., maps, plates)

Brief report on 45 archaeological sites in southeastern Dominican Republic. Comprising mostly cave sites, petroglyphs are noted at several.

592 Ratch, Christian and **Andrew R. Craston.** Ultsheimer's remarks on the

Caribs in the years 1599–1601 (BISRA/BS, 11:1, 1983, p. 16–25, bibl.)

Short article referring to Andrew Ultsheimer's manuscripts (1616) whose remarks on the Caribs of St. Vincent and Dominica are likely the oldest ethnohistoric sources for these islands.

593 Rimoli, Renato O. and Joaquín E. Nadel. El horizonte ceramista temprano en Santo Domingo y otras Antillas. Santo Domingo: Editora de la Univ. Autónoma de Santo Domingo, 1983. 353 p.: ill. (Publicaciones; v. 317. Col. Historia y sociedad; no. 57)

Until recently there has been little to suggest the appearance of ceramics in the Greater Antilles much earlier than AD 120 as evidenced at the Hacienda Grande site in Puerto Rico. This coincides approximately with the Saladoid expansion from South America. Authors discuss recent investigations in the Dominican Republic and Cuba which point to the appearance of earlier ceramics that are not linked to the Saldero tradition. The work is an excellent synthesis of what is known of the early ceramic complex and an attempt made to establish broader relationships. Further research is required.

594 Robiou Lamarche, Sebastián. Del mito al tiempo sagrado: un posible calendario agrícola-ceremonial taíno (MHD/B, 11:18, 1983, p. 117–140, bibl., ill., plates, tables)

Through a study of Taino mythology, author suggests importance of the Sun and Moon as well as Pleiades, Orion and Venus in certain rituals of precolumbian Antilleans. Ceremonial plazas and artifacts from several archaeological sites lend credence to the theory that a complex agricultural-ceremonial calendar was part of Taino society.

595 Rose, Richard. The Pigeon Creek site, San Salvador Bahamas (FAS/FA, 35:4, 1982, p. 129–145)

Brief but excellent description of the Pigeon Creek site excavated by author. Approximately 12 acres, it is an important site providing information on settlement patterns, subsistence, ceramics and other artifacts in the Bahamas. C14 dates.

596 Steedman, David; David R. Watters; Elizabeth Reitz; and Gregory Pregill. Vertebrates from archaeological sites on Montserrat, West Indies (Annals of Carnegie Museum [Pittsburgh, Pa.] 53, 1984, p. 1–29)

Excellent, detailed zooarchaeological study from two sites, Trant's and Radio Antilles on Montserrat, West Indies. Findings show that Saladoid people used primarily local marine and terrestrial vertebrates. Agouti and dog appear to have been brought in by the Saladoids.

597 Veloz Maggiolo, Marcio and Carlos Alberto Martin. Las técnicas unifaciales de los yacimientos del Jobo y sus similitudes con el Paleo-Arcaico antillano (MHD/B, 11:18, 1983, p. 13–37, map, ill.)

Excellent summary of similarities and differences of unifacially worked lithic artifacts from El Jobo, Venezuela, and early lithic industries of the Paleo Archaic in the Antilles. Notes spatial distribution of four distinct types. Investigators do not believe that connections exist between the unifacial lithic tradition of mainland Venezuela and Caribbean traditions. All agree more research is necessary.

598 ———; Renato O. Rimoli; and Fernando Luna Calderón. Investigaciones arqueológicas en Cueva Collantes, D.N.: informe preliminar (MHD/B, 11:18, 1983, p. 73–96, bibl., plates)

Complex of caves in the city of Santo Domingo, investigated by authors who conclude that it is a Taino ceremonial site occupied ca. AD 1000–1300.

599 Watters, David R.; Elizabeth Reitz; David Steedman; and Gregory Pregill. Vertebrates from archaeological sites on Barbuda, West Indies (Annals of Carnegie Museum [Pittsburgh, Pa.] 53, 1984, p. 383–412)

Excellent article in which authors identify various fish, reptile, bird, and mammalian bones from three archaeological sites (Indiantown Trail, Sufferers and Overview) on Barbuda, West Indies. Distribution studies from basically uncontaminated units are extremely informative.

ARCHAEOLOGY: South America

BETTY J. MEGGERS, *Research Associate, Department of Anthropology, Smithsonian Institution*

ALTHOUGH THE NUMBER AND COMPETENCE of archaeologists in South America continues to increase, publication is hindered by high costs. Distribution has also been affected, with the consequence that a number of works published since *HLAS 45* are not included among the annotated titles that follow.

In spite of economic difficulties, progress is occurring in several areas. Concern for the destruction of archaeological sites is becoming more widespread (items **674, 675, 676, 697** and **852**) and the Second New World Congress on Rescue Archaeology (Dallas, Tx., Nov. 1984) passed a resolution urging Latin American governments and development agencies to fund archaeological investigation wherever sites are endangered. Growing awareness of the potential contribution of precolumbian history to defining national identity is reflected in greater support for archaeology throughout Latin America and in general works directed toward informing the public (items **680, 788** and **822**). Concomitantly, efforts to stem the traffic in antiquities have been strengthened. The repatriations of two large collections, one of Peruvian objects illegally exported to the US and the other of Ecuadorian objects sent to Italy, are significant precedents. Catalogs to accompany exhibitions in Washington, D.C., of selected specimens from both seizures were sponsored by the Dept. of Cultural Affairs of the Organization of American States. Both are noteworthy for their emphasis on the damage to the cultural heritages of the countries of origin inflicted by such illicit international traffic (items **768** and **848**).

Among successful efforts to improve dissemination of information is the *Gaceta Arqueológica Andina* initiated in 1982, which has expanded from 12 to 16 pp. Published bimonthly, it provides summaries of ongoing or recently completed projects conducted by North American as well as Latin American archaeologists in Andean countries. Two new journals have appeared. The *Revista de Arqueología*, sponsored jointly by the Conselho Nacional de Desenvolvimento Científico e Tecnológico and the Museu Paraense Emílio Goeldi, is scheduled for two issues a year; Vol. 1, No. 1 was published in late 1983. *Paleoetnológica*, sponsored by the Centro Argentino de Etnología Americana, reflects the growing interest in "humanizing" archaeological data; Vol. 1, No. 1 appeared in April 1985. The Sociedade de Arqueologia Brasileira has circumvented high costs of publication by duplicating Master's and Doctoral dissertations by Brazilians for distribution to members. The BAR International Series, Oxford, England, restricted to Old World topics since its inception in 1976, has begun accepting volumes on New World archaeology, including the proceedings of the 44th International Congress of Americanists held in Manchester in 1982 (item **805**).

GENERAL

600 Andean ecology and civilization.
Edited by Shozo Masuda, Izumi Shimada, and Craig Morris. Tokyo: Univ. of Tokyo Press, 1985. 550 p.: bibl., glossary, index (Papers from Wenner-Gren Foundation for Anthropological Research; Symposium no. 9)

Consists of articles by 21 Andeanists from Chile, Great Britain, Japan, Peru, and the US who met in 1983 to examine Murra's "vertical archipelago model" from archaeological, ethnohistoric, ecological, economic, social, and temporal perspectives. The antiquity and importance of vertical and horizontal complementarity were reaffirmed, along with social organization associated with discontinuous territories. The breadth of treatment of the general approach and the variety of perspectives offered by the contributors make this volume essential for Andean scholars.

601 Bryan, Alan L. South America (*in* Early man in the New World. Edited by Richard Shutler, Jr. Beverly Hills, Calif.: Sage Publications, 1983, p. 137–146, bibl., map)

Postulates earliest immigrants brought a unifacial core and flake tradition prior to 20,000 BP. Fishtail bifacial points developed in Patagonia by 11,000 BP and spread northward; leaf-shaped and tanged point traditions originated independently during the Paleo-Indian stage. Wooden points may also have been used commonly; pleistocene fauna are not necessarily associated with Paleo-Indian sites.

602 Cuesta Domingo, Mariano and **Salvador Rovira Llorens.** Los trabajos en metal en el área andina. Madrid: Ministerio de Cultura, Dirección General de Bellas Artes, Archivos y Bibliotecas, Subdirección General de Museos, Patronato Nacional de Museos, 1982? 258 p.: bibl., ill. (some col.)

Introductory chapters reviewing the general chronology and characteristics of metallurgy in Colombia, Ecuador, and Peru precede illustrated catalogs of specimens in the Museo de América of Madrid, which have not been published previously.

603 Dubelaar, C.N. The distribution of Im Thurn's elaborate type petroglyphs in South America (*in* International Congress for the Study of the Pre-Columbian Cultures of the Lesser Antilles, 9th, Santo Domingo, 1981. Proceedings [see item **258**] p. 375–397, bibl., ill., map)

Review of the occurrence of anthropomorphic, stylized figures with rectanguloid bodies and semi-lunar heads; treatment of the body resembles "swaddling" of Antillean petroglyphs and probably symbolizes ritual costume.

604 Errázuriz, Jaime. Tumaco-La Tolita: una cultura precolombina desconocida: an unknown precolumbian culture. Fotografía, Ricardo Gamboa et al. Traducción al inglés, Susan Cowles. Bogotá: C. Valencia Editores, 1980. 316 p.: bibl., ill. (some col.)

Based on examining some 80,000 artifacts, author divides the sequence into three periods: 1) Oriental (400–100 BC); 2) Transitional (100 BC-AD 100); and 3) Mesoamerican (AD 100–500). The first incorporates Asiatic influence and the latter Mesoamerican. Discussions of daily life, sexual life, illness, and mythology are based on pottery depictions. Liberally illustrated.

605 Hyslop, John. The Inka road system. Orlando, Fla.: Academic Press, 1984. 377 p.: bibl., ill., maps (Studies in archaeology)

Selects 12 segments from 100–200 km long in order to sample environmental, historical, political, cultural, and functional variables incorporated into the Inca highway. A chapter reviews historical sources, describes the road and associated structures, and includes a map. Pt. 2 discusses special topics, such as types of construction, kinds of use, lodging and storage facilities, bridges, and incorporation of earlier paths. Bibliography contains over 600 entries. These data permit a new estimate of the road's magnitude at about 23,139 km.

606 Lumbreras, Luis Guillermo. Las sociedades nucleares de Suramérica. Caracas: Academia Nacional de la Historia de Venezuela, 1983. 429 p.: bibl., ill. (some col.): indexes (Historia general de América. Período indígena; 4)

Overview of cultural development in the region dominated by the Incas at European contact, from the introduction of pottery making about 3000 BC. Chapters discuss transition from wild to domesticated subsistence, appearance and diffusion of pottery making, advent of the State; regional developments, the expansive states, and the Inca empire. Use as a general reference is hampered by the bibliography's lacking most publications cited in the text.

607 Lynch, Thomas F. Camelid pastoralism and the emergence of Tiwanaku civilization in the South-Central Andes (World Archaeology [London] 15, June 1983, p. 1–14, bibl.)

Affirms the distinctiveness of the culture area around and south Lake Titicaca, and reviews several models accounting for the emergence of integration, all based on dependence on camelids and their products.

608 Ravines, Rogger. Panorama de la arqueología andina. Lima: Instituto de Estudios Peruanos, 1982. 334 p.: 12 p. of plates: bibl., ill., index (Fuentes e investigaciones para la historia del Perú; 6)

Overview of 15,000 years of Andean prehistory by cultural areas: north (Ecuador), central (Peru), altiplano (Bolivia), and south (Chile), and 10 chronological periods. Chronological charts, maps, and lists of C14 dates supplement the text for each area. Although author discounts importance of Mesoamerican influences, he provides a useful summary of principal developments within the region embraced by the Inca Empire.

609 Reinhard, Johan. Las montañas sagradas: un estudio etnoarqueológico de ruinas en las altas cumbres andinas (Cuadernos de Historia [Depto. de Ciencias Históricas, Univ. de Chile, Santiago] 3, julio 1983, p. 27–62, bibl., ill.)

Notes 63 mountains recorded as having stone structures on summits above 5200 m elevation in the Andes of southern Peru, Argentina, and Chile. After reviewing hypotheses concerning their origin and purpose, and presenting ethnographic and ethnohistorical evidence, author concludes they reflect religious concepts centering on the role of mountains in ensuring rainfall essential to productive agriculture.

610 Social and economic organization in the prehispanic Andes. Edited by David L. Browman, Richard L. Burger, and Mario A. Rivera. Oxford, England: British Archaeological Reports, 1982. 247 p.: bibl., ill., maps, tables (BAR international series; 194)

Consists of 12 articles that discuss various forms of evidence for interaction between highland and lowland groups and kinds of social relations involved. Topics include the role of La Plata island in spondylus trade (Marcos and Norton); decorated stone bowls in Ecuador and Peru (Peterson); coastal-highland connections during the late period in Peru (Thompson); the vertical economy in the Cusco region (Farrington); trade and economic expansion by Tiwanaku (Browman); altiplano-tropical lowland contacts in northern Chile (Rivera); interregional relationships in the southern Andes (Serracino); relations between the Argentine puna and the eastern border zone (Krapovickas); elaboration of an alkaline substance from a local cactus in northwest Argentina (Fernández Distel); and late prehistoric relations between northwest Argentina and north Chile (Pollard). Two papers describe stable boundaries between culture areas, where interaction was minimal: Peru and Ecuador (Burger) and Chupachu / Serrano cultures in the Huánuco region of highland Peru (Bird).

611 Stierlin, Henri. Art of the Incas and its origins. Translated from the French by Betty and Peter Ross. New York: Rizzoli, 1984. 240 p.: bibl., ill. (some col.): index.

This historical synthesis traces artistic styles during 5000 years, beginning with Valdivia in Ecuador, continuing with Chorrera, Chavín, Moche, Jama-Coaque, Paracas-Nazca, Tiahuanaco, and Chimu, concluding with Inca. Public works, pottery, metallurgy, and textiles are the primary sources, beautifully illustrated. The well written text provides environmental, social, and contextual information. Controversies and discrepancies are avoided in the interest of a coherent picture. Noteworthy for the attention paid to the Ecuadorian contribution to prehistoric cultural and artistic developments in the central Andes.

612 Whitaker, Thomas W. Cucurbits in Andean prehistory (SAA/AA, 48, 1983, p. 576–585, bibl., ill.)

Lagenaria and *Cucurbita maxima* occur by 2000 BC on the Peruvian coast; *C. moschata* and *C. ficifolia* were introduced from Mesoamerica shortly after 2000 BC. Scarcity at high elevations reflects climatic constraints. *C. maxima* occurs preceramically in northwestern Argentina.

ARGENTINA

613 Aguerre, Ana M. Los niveles inferiores de la Cueva Grande, Arroyo Feo, área Río Pinturas, Provincia de Santa Cruz (SAA/R, 14:2, 1981/1982, p. 211–239, bibl., ill., tables)

Examination of the spatial relationships between materials from levels 9-11 permits recognizing activity areas and seasonal indicators; these suggest the shelter was used during a period of the year favorable to guanaco hunting. C14 dates extended from about 4900 to 9300 BP.

614 Albeck, María Ester. Riego prehispánico en Casabindo, Provincia de Jujuy: nota preliminar (UNLPM/R, 8:60, 1984, p. 265–278, bibl., ill.)

Air photographs and ground survey permit reconstructing the prehispanic irrigation system and zones of cultivation in the puna of central Jujuy. Six types of canal construction are distinguished.

615 Alfaro, Lidia C. Investigación arqueológica en la cuenca del Río Doncellas, Provincia de Jujuy: integración de la puna jujeña a los centros cúlticos andinos (SAA/R, 15, 1983, p. 25–47, bibl., ill., map)

The characteristics of the large and diversified site of Doncellas suggest it was occupied sporadically or seasonally over some 500 years. Survey of the surrounding region revealed sites with specialized functions (ritual, residential, agricultural) compatible with this hypothesis.

616 Arqueología del Chubut: el Valle de Piedra Parada. Coordinador, Carlos A. Aschero. Rawson, Argentina: Gobierno de la Provincia del Chubut, 1983. 103 p.: bibl., ill. (Serie Humanidades)

Survey and excavations in northwestern Chubut permit defining a sequence of three periods: Casapedrense, Tehuelchense nonceramic, and Tehuelchense ceramic. Pictographs and lithics are the principal remains. Includes 44 illustrations.

617 Aschero, Carlos A. Nuevos datos sobre la arqueología del Cerro Casa de Piedra, Sitio CCP 5, Parque Nacional Perito Moreno, Santa Cruz, Argentina (SAA/R, 14:2, 1981/1982, p. 267–284, bibl., ill.)

Description of excavations, artifacts, and wall paintings in a cave occupied by representatives of the Toldense tradition between about 4900 and 3000 BP.

618 Baldini, Lidia. Dispersión y cronología de las urnas de tres cinturas en el noroeste Argentino (SAA/R, 14:1, 1980, p. 49–61, bibl, ill., map)

Tabulation of elements of morphology and decoration permits recognizing two types: anthropomorphic and non-anthropomorphic. The two variants have slightly different geographical distributions. Two C14 dates place their inception by AD 1100.

619 Bárcena, J. Roberto and **Fidel A. Roig.** Investigaciones arqueológicas en el área puneña de Mendoza, con especial referencia a *Tephrocactus andicola*, Cactáceae, como nuevo elemento alimentario (SAA/R, 14:2, 1981/1982, p. 85–107, bibl., ill., tables)

The abundance of fruits, seeds, and roots of a species of cactus in rock shelters occupied intermittently from 1500 BC to AD attests to the importance of this plant in the diet.

620 Borrero, Luis Alberto; Marcela Casiraghi; and **Hugo Daniel Yacobaccio.** First guanaco-processing site in southern South America (UC/CA, 26, 1985, p. 273–276, bibl, map, tables)

Description of lithics and faunal remains from a site on the coast of northern Tierra del Fuego, C14 dated at 785 ± 120 BP, believed to represent a kill and processing site, the first encountered outside a cave.

621 Caggiano, María Amanda. Prehistoria del noroeste argentino y sus vinculaciones con la República Oriental del Uruguay y sur de Brasil. São Leopoldo, Brazil: Instituto Anchietano de Pesquisas, 1984. 109 p.: bibl., ill., index, table (Anthroplogía; 38)

A time-space framework for the provinces of Misiones, Corrientes, and Entre Ríos and adjacent portions of Uruguay and Brazil is established using available stratigraphic and C14 evidence. The Cultura Entrerriana with three contemporary phases marks the inception of pottery making about 500 BC characterized by punctation, drag-and-jab, and zig-zag incisions. The Cultura Ribereños Plásticos elaborates these techniques and adds modeling and painting beginning about AD 500. The Tupiguarani Tradition expanded down the Río Uruguay about AD 1300.

622 Cardich, Augusto and **Andrés Laguens.** Fractura intencional y posterior utilización del material óseo arqueológico de la Cueva 3 de Los Toldos, Provincia de Santa Cruz, Argentina (UNLPM/R, 8:63, 1984, p. 329–384, bibl., charts, ill.)

Of 8329 bone fragments from eight levels extending from 11000 to 4500 BP, only 6.37 percent appear to have been broken intentionally. Detailed analysis of attributes shows no significant change throughout the sequence.

623 —— and Laura Miotti. Recursos faunísticos en la economía de los cazadores-recolectores de Los Toldos, Provincia de Santa Cruz, Argentina (SAA/R, 15, 1983, p. 145–157, bibl.)

Three of the four cultural units emphasize guanaco; the Toldense period exhibits high variation, including birds. Evidence for method of preparation, portions of the animal represented, and other details are provided.

624 ———; **María Estela Mansur-Franchomme; Martín Giesso; and Víctor Alberto Durán.** Arqueología de las cuevas de El Ceibo, Provincia de Santa Cruz, Argentina (SAA/R, 14:2, 1981/1982, p. 173–209, bibl., ill.)

Description of excavations at a site 150 km south of Los Toldos, and detailed analysis of artifacts from Level 12 associated with horse bones. Wear analysis indicates stone tools were used principally for working skins and secondarily for working wood and for butchering. The scarcity of animal bones and other kinds of evidence suggest only skins and certain portions of meat were brought to the rock shelter, where domestic activities took place.

625 **Casamiquela, Rodolfo M.** El arte rupuestre de la Patagonia. Neuquén, Argentina: Siringa Libros, 1981. 135 p.: bibl., ill.

Principal motifs of rock art are analyzed using the seven styles defined by Menghin, and inferences made about their significance. Style No. 2 (scenes) is associated with hunting magic; styles Nos. 5 (frets) and 6 (miniatures) with male initiation rites; styles Nos. 1 (hands) and 3 (footprints) with female or mixed puberty rites. A variety of other interpretations is also presented.

626 **Casiraghi, Marcela.** Análisis de los artefactos óseos de la Cueva Huachichocana III, Provincia de Jujuy, República Argentina (Paleoetnológica [Buenos Aires] 1, 1985, p. 19–33, bibl., ill.)

Description of bone objects from three layers; camelids and deer are the principal animals used.

627 **Castro, Alicia S.** Noticia preliminar sobre un yacimiento en la Sierra de la Ventana, Sierras Australes de la Provincia de Buenos Aires (SAA/R, 15, 1983, p. 91–107, bibl., ill., map, table)

Description of lithic and faunal remains from excavations in a small cave. Two occupations were distinguished, the earliest with a C14 date of 6230 ± 90 BP.

628 **Ceballos, Rita** and **Antonia Peronja.** Informe preliminar sobre el arte rupestre

de la Cueva Visconti, Provincia de Río Negro (SAA/R, 5, 1983, p. 109–119, bibl., ill.)

Classification and description of naturalistic and geometric elements produced by abrasion or pecking. The former predominate and are equally divided between animals (guanaco, puma, emu) and humans. The petroglyphs obscured by occupational debris, extend from 15 cm below the present surface downward. A C14 date of 2526 ± 93 BP was obtained from Level 8.

629 **Dougherty, Bernardo** and **Elsa Leonor Zagaglia.** Problemas generales de la arqueología del Chaco occidental (UNLPM/R, 8:54, p. 107–110, bibl.)

Presence of the same distinctive traits on both sides of the Chaco implies communication, raising the question whether environmental conditions may have been more uniform than today.

630 **Fernández, Jorge.** Cronología y tecnología de las hachas salineras de Truquico, Neuquén (SAA/R, 14:2, 1981/1982, p. 109–120, bibl., ill., tables)

Demonstrates that the hypothesis these celts were hafted by inserting them into a living tree and allowing the wood to grow around the butt is invalid. Eight C14 dates extend between 710 and 550 BP.

631 **Flegenheimer, Nora.** Hallazgos de puntas "cola de pescado" en la Provincia de Buenos Aires (SAA/R, 14:1, 1980, p. 169–176, bibl., ill.)

Excavations at two sites 85 m apart reveals two occupational levels, the earliest of which contained a basal fragment and a complete fluted "fishtail" projectile point. A C14 date of 10,720 ± 150 BP was obtained.

632 **García, Lidia Clara.** Los instrumentos para hacer fuego del sitio Huachichocana, Depto. de Purmamarca, Provincia de Jujuy, República Argentina (Paleoetnológica [Buenos Aires] 1, 1985, p. 13–17, bibl., ill.)

Fire making by rotary friction was employed at least by 2100 BC in northwest Argentina, based on evidence provided by 12 active and 17 passive components from two rock shelters.

633 **González, Alberto Rex.** Inca settlement patterns in a marginal province of the empire: sociocultural implications (*in* Prehistoric settlement patterns [see item **325**] p. 337–360, ill.)

Classifies 42 northwest Argentine sites exhibiting Inca influence into six functional categories: production, redistribution, communication, military, religious, and administration. Exploitation of metal and turquoise sources was the chief goal; adaptation rather than replacement of local facilities and customs was the mechanism.

634 ———. Las "provincias" incas del antiguo Tucumán (PEMN/R, 46, 1982 [i.e. 1984] p. 317–380, bibl.)

Presents evidence to support the existence of four provinces of the Inca Empire: Chicoana with its capital in La Paya; Quire-Quire with its capital at Tolombón; Humahuaca with its center at the Pucará de Tilcara; and a southern province implied by archaeological information.

635 **Gradin, Carlos J.** Las pinturas de la Cueva Grande, Arroyo Feo, Area Río Pinturas, Provincia de Santa Cruz (SAA/R, 14:2, 1981/1982, p. 241–265, bibl., ill., tables)

Biomorphic and abstract motifs on seven sections of the cave wall are classified by element and color. Tabulation of superpositions permits distinguishing three periods, the earliest consisting of black figures, the second using reds, and the third white and polychrome. Total of 83 samples of pigment from excavations allowed refining the chronology, estimated to extend from 7300 BC to AD 300. Comparing measurements on hand prints with living populations indicates that two-thirds are assignable to individuals under age 13.

636 ——— and **Ana M. Aguerre.** Arte rupestre del Area la Martita, Sección A del Departamento Magallanes, Provincia de Santa Cruz (SAA/R, 15, 1983, p. 195–223, bibl., ill., map)

Description of locations with pictographs, including details of color, motif, and association, investigated between 1976 and 1982. Three zones were differentiated; their characteristics and affiliations are discussed.

637 **Gramajo de Martínez Moreno, Amalia J.** Posible influencias incaicas en Santiago del Estero (in Museo Arqueológico Emilio y Duncan Wagner. Santiago del Estero, Argentina: Imprenta Oficial de la Provincia, 1982, p. 35–48, bibl., ill. [Serie Estudio; 3])

Evidence of Inca acculturation in pottery and metal objects of the Averías culture.

638 ——— and **Hugo N. Martínez Moreno.** Otros aportes al arte rupestre del este catamarqueño (in Museo Arqueológico Emilio y Duncan Wagner. Santiago del Estero, Argentina: Imprenta Oficial de la Provincia, 1982, p. 77–88, ill., map [Serie Estudio; 3])

Predominantly zoomorphic pictographs executed in white on the walls of four rockshelters are tentatively assigned to La Aguada culture (AD 700-1000).

639 **Hyslop, John** and **Pío Pablo Díaz.** El camino incaico: Calchaquí-Tastil, noroeste argentino (Gaceta Arqueológica Andina [Instituto Andino de Estudios Arqueológicas, Lima] 1:6, marzo 1983, p. 6–8, bibl., ill., map)

Establishes the Inca origin of the road at elevations between 3000 and 4400 m, and describes associated structures.

640 **Krapovickas, Pedro.** Hallazgos incaicos en Tilcara y Yacoraite: una reinterpretación (SAA/R, 14:2, 1981/1982, p. 67–80, bibl.)

Review of investigations at two sites in the Quebrada de Humahuaca in the context of more recent ethnohistoric information reveals aspects of economic and social importance to the Inca empire overlooked in the original interpretation of their function.

641 **Llamazares, Ana María.** El arte rupestre del Abrigo de Pilcaniyeu, Provincia de Río Negro (SAA/R, 14:1, 1980, p. 103–120, bibl., ill., tables)

Two categories of depictions, human and animal footprints and geometric elements, are tabulated and correlated with methods of production. The footprints are carved; the geometric elements painted or carved. Superpositions imply the latter are more recent.

642 **Lorandi, Ana María.** Olleros del Inka en Catamarca, Argentina (Gaceta Arqueológica Andina [Lima] 2:8, nov. 1983, p. 6–7, 10, ill., map)

High frequency of pottery from the Tucumano-Santiagueña complex to the east suggests transfer of potters from that region to an extensive Inca center in the Depto. de Aldalgalá.

643 Navamuel, Leonor. El mensaje de los petroglifos. Salta, Argentina: Univ. Nacional de Salta, Depto. de Humanidades, 1980. 179 p., 8 p. of plates: ill.

Focussing on petroglyphs of northwestern Argentina, author elaborates the thesis that they represent profound and intimate sentiments and applies comparative sociological theory to their interpretation.

644 Onetto, María. Arte rupestre de Campo Cretton, Valle de Piedra Parada, Provincia del Chubut (SAA/R, 14:2, 1981/1982, p. 159–172, bibl., ill.)

Detailed analysis of motifs in five sectors of a rock shelter, executed by painting (yellow and three tones of red) and/or engraving, allows defining four styles. Their occurrence at other sites in the region is noted.

645 Orquera, Luis Abel; Ernesto Luis Piana; and Arturo Emilio Sala. La antigüedad de la ocupación humana de la Gruta del Oro, Partido de Juárez, Provincia de Buenos Aires: un problema resuelto (SAA/R, 14:1, 1980, p. 83–101, bibl., ill.)

Disagreement over the antiquity of occupation was resolved by reexcavation, which verified the existence of a buried humus layer and produced a C14 date of 6560 ± 80 BP.

646 Politis, Gustavo and **Eduardo P. Tonni.** Arqueología de la región pampeana: el sitio 2 de Zanjón Seco, Partido de Necochea, Provincia de Buenos Aires, República Argentina (Revista de Pré-História [Univ. de São Paulo, Instituto de Pré-História] 3:4, 1982, p. 109–139, bibl., ill., map)

Lithics, faunal remains, and pottery from excavations are described and interpreted as indicating the site was occupied briefly and served as a "terminal processing" locus.

647 Pollard, Gordon C. The prehistory of NW Argentina: the Calchaquí Valley Project, 1977–1981 (AFA/JFA, 10, 1983, p. 11–32, bibl., ill., tables)

Seriation of 24 sites using 84 associations of surface finish, decorative technique and motif provides a regional chronology between about AD 1000–1300. Independent analysis by ware showed geographical as well as chronological differences. Although minor differences exist with the sequence in the Santa María Valley, retention of the estab-

lished tradition name is recommended pending more precise information.

648 Raffino, Rodolfo A. Excavaciones en El Churcal, Valle Calchaquí, República Argentina (UNLPM/R, 8:59, 1984, p. 223–263, bibl., ill.)

The history of a complex containing 530 stone-walled units is reconstructed from excavation, architecture, burials, and artifacts. Decorated pottery belongs to the Santa María tradition. Occupation is estimated between AD 1100 and 1350.

649 Rolandi de Perrot, Diana and **Cecilia Pérez de Micou.** Los materiales textiles y cesteros de Huachichocana III y IV, Departamento de Tumbaya, Jujuy (Paleoetnológica [Buenos Aires] 1, 1985, p. 35–41, bibl., ill.)

Cords, knots, basketry, and fabric remains associated with six periods extending from 7600 BC to post-Spanish are described. A tendency to increasing complexity was observed.

650 Schobinger, Juan. Estudios de arqueología sudamericana: arte rupestre y santuarios incaicos en el oeste de la Argentina. San Antonio de Padua, Argentina: Ediciones Castañeda, 1982. 133 p., 14 p. of plates: bibl., ill. (Col. Estudios antropológicas y religiosos; 5)

Collection of papers previously published in obscure non-Argentine contexts; topics are rock art, high-altitude Inca shrines, an anthropomorphic vessel, and a general overview of New World prehistory from the 9th to the 2nd millennium BC.

651 Sempe, Carlota. Punto Colorado, un sitio Aguada, Depto. de Tinogasta, Pcia. de Catamarca (UNLPM/R, 8:55, 1983, p. 111–138, bibl., ill., tables)

Punto Colorado was occupied throughout the duration of the Aguada culture, from 650 BC to its incorporation into the Late Period phases. In addition to structures and ceramics, plant remains are described, including Cucurbita, Lagenaria, and three varieties of maize.

652 Williams, Verónica I. Evidencia de actividad textil en el establecimiento incaico Potrero-Chaquiago, Provincia de Catamarca (SAA/R, 15, 1983, p. 49–59, bibl., ill.)

Typological analysis of 38 spindle whorls from three structures revealed higher concentration in one, implying a difference in function. This inference is also supported by greater abundance of food remains and potsherds.

BOLIVIA

653 Arellano López, Jorge. La cultura Tarija: aporte al conocimiento de los señoríos regionales del sur boliviano (Arqueología Boliviana [Instituto Nacional de Arqueología, La Paz] 1, 1984, p. 73–82, bibl., ill., map)

Resumé of characteristics of a local chiefdom that developed near the Argentine border between the Tiwanaku decline and Inca expansion, under the influence of the Mollo culture to the south.

654 ———. Mollo: investigaciones arqueológicas. La Paz: s.n., 1985. 80 p.: bibl., ill., maps.

Summary of the characteristics of the Mollo culture, centering on the Llika valley east of Lake Titicaca, based on excavations at Iskanwaya, Pukanwaya, and Pukarilla, and survey of the region with the greater concentration of remains of this culture. Discusses habitat, settlement pattern, architecture, burial practices, economy, and social organization. Recognizes three stages of development: a village stage with a median date of AD 1050, an urban stage with a median date of AD 1145, and a colonizing stage with a median date of AD 1416.

655 Byrne de Caballero, Geraldine. El Tiwanaku en Cochabamba (Arqueología Boliviana [Instituto Nacional de Arqueología, La Paz] 1, 1984, p. 67–71, bibl., map)

More than 60 percent of the pottery from Cochabamba is influenced by Tiwanaku. Reviews problems in defining the nature of the relationship with the highland center.

656 Claure Callaú, Omar. El templo mágico-religioso de Samaipata: una mirada retrospectiva a una cultura lejana. Santa Cruz de la Sierra, Bolivia: Alcaldía Municipal de Santa Cruz de la Sierra, 1981. 81 p.: bibl., ill.

Very generalized discussion of a little known site in the vicinity of Santa Cruz termed "El Fuerte," consisting of ceremonial precincts, terraces, platforms, habitations, canals, and other features. Tripod vessels are characteristic, as well as anthropomorphic ones.

657 Cordero Miranda, Gregorio. Reconocimiento arqueológico en las márgenes del Río Beni (Arqueología Boliviana [Instituto Nacional de Arqueología, La Paz] 1, 1984, p. 15–38, ill.)

Description and illustration of pottery and stone objects from sites in the vicinity of Rurrenabaque and along the Beni for a distance of about 65 km to the north.

658 Dougherty, Bernardo and Horacio Calandra. Excavaciones arqueológicas en la Loma Alta de Casarabe, Llanos de Moxos, Departamento del Beni, Bolivia (SAA/R, 14:2, 1981/1982, p. 9–48, bibl., ill., map)

Analysis of ceramics obtained from a stratigraphic excavation 10 m in depth permits defining three chronological phases. Eight C14 dates extend from AD 335 to 1195. Pottery and other artifacts are described; affiliations are suggested with the south as well as Amazonia.

659 Erickson, Clark L. Sistemas agrícolos prehispánicos en los Llanos de Mojos (III/AI, 40:4, oct./dic. 1980, p. 731–755, bibl., ill.)

Survey along a transect provided by the Trinidad-San Borja road revealed a variety of types of earthworks, including mounds, causeways, canals, and reservoirs. In addition to facilitating agriculture, these may have served to conserve sufficient water to sustain fish during the dry season. The surface collections of pottery exhibit high diversity, which is compatible with historic information on ethnic heterogeneity and archaeological indications of multicomponent occupations of sites.

660 Faldín A., J.D. La arqueología beniana y su panorama interpretativo (Arqueología Boliviana [Instituto Nacional de Arqueología, La Paz] 1, 1984, p. 83–90, bibl., maps)

Review of investigation in the vicinity of Trinidad on the Río Mamoré, including preliminary results of recent fieldwork by the Misión del Museo de La Plata, Argentina.

661 Oakland, Amy. Tejidos preincaicos en Cochabamba (*in* Los Tejidos precolombinos en el Museo Arqueológico de la Universidad Mayor de San Simón, Cochabamba. Cochabamba, Bolivia: s.n., 1981, p. 4–9)

Highlights of a collection of more than 300 textiles from several sites. Affinities with coastal Chile, northwestern Argentina and south coastal Peru were noted.

662 Pereira Herrera, Dávid M. Introducción a la arqueología de la cuenca del Río Cotacajes (Historia Boliviana [La Paz] 4:1, 1984, p. 1–14, bibl., ill., map)

Terraces, canals, compounds, and other constructions are restricted to the Depto. de Cochabamba and imply complex sociopolitical development in pre-Inca times.

663 Querejazu Lewis, Roy. El mundo arqueológico del Cnl. Federico Diez de Medina. La Paz: Editorial Los Amigos del Libro, 1983. 248 p., 26 leaves of plates: bibl., ill. (some col.)

Compilation of essays by retired military officer and amateur archaeologist, liberally illustrated with specimens from his collection focussing on Tiwanaku. Symbolism of trophy heads and pumas, relations with Atlantis, pottery art, deities, music, and funerary practices are among themes discussed.

664 Rivera Sundt, Oswaldo. La Horca del Inka (Arqueología Boliviana [Instituto Nacional de Arqueología, La Paz] 1, 1984, p. 90–106, bibl., ill.)

Investigations and observations at a partly natural, partly artificial arrangement of large stones by a summit above Cochabamba indicate its use for marking the solstice and equinox. A pre-Inca dating is inferred.

665 Tapia Pineda, Félix. Excavaciones arqueológicas en el sector habitacional de El Fuerte de Samaipata, Santa Cruz (Arqueología Boliviana [Instituto Nacional de Arqueología, La Paz] 1, 1984, p. 49–66, bibl., ill., map)

Pottery obtained from excavations verifies the predominantly Inca affiliation of this large (ca. 18 ha.) ceremonial-habitation site at 1950 m elevation.

666 ———. Informe preliminar sobre las excavaciones arqueológicas en Camata, Provincia Omasuyos, Departamento de La Paz (Arqueología Boliviana [Instituto Nacional de Arqueología, La Paz] 1, 1984, p. 39–48, ill., map)

Exploratory excavations in a site on the northeast side of Lake Titicaca produced remains of structures, tombs, and pottery assignable to Chiripa, Tiwanaku, and post-Tiwanaku periods.

BRAZIL

667 Alemany, F. Pavia. Estudio de la insolación del abrigo arqueológico Sarandí (Revista de Pré-História [Univ. de São Paulo, Instituto de Pré-História] 5:5, 1983, p. 125–143)

Measurements of insolation reveal none entering the rock shelter between March 21 and Sept. 21, indicating that the location was selected for occupation for other reasons than warmth during the winter months.

668 Barbosa, Altair Sales. O período arqueológico "arcaico" em Goiás (Anuário de Divulgação Científica [Instituto Goiano de Pré-História e Antropologia, Univ. Católica de Goiás, Goiânia, Brazil] 10, 1981/1984, p. 85–97, bibl.)

Although the lithic industry appears not to change, settlement pattern differences and climatic alteration affecting subsistence permit dividing the Archaic into two periods. The earlier extends from 9000 to 6690 BP and the later from 6690 to 1000 BP.

669 ———; Avelino Fernandes de Miranda; and Pedro Ignácio Schmitz. Sítios précerámicos de superfície no programa arqueológico de Goiás: alguns elementos para discussão dos fenômenos adaptativos (Anuário de Divulgação Científica [Instituto Goiano de Pré-História e Antropologia, Univ. Católica de Goiás, Goiânia, Brazil] 10, 1981/1984, p. 43–60, bibl., ill.)

Comparison of habitat, lithic sources, and categories of artifacts and debitage from surface sites in two environmentally distinct regions: Alto Araguaia and Serra Geral. The Alto Araguaia sites are assigned to the Paleo-Indian Phase (Itaparica Tradition); the Serra Geral sites may belong to this tradition but exhibit a distinct settlement pattern.

670 Caldarelli, Solange Bezerra. Aldeias Tupiguarani no Vale do Rio Mogiguaçu, Estado de São Paulo (Revista de Pré-

História [Univ. de São Paulo, Instituto de Pré-História] 5 : 5 , 1983, p. 37–124, bibl., ill.)
Description and detailed illustration of vessel shapes represented at four habitation sites of the Tupiguarani tradition, Painted subtradition.

671 ——— and **Walter Alves Neves.** Programa de pesquisas arqueológicas no Vale Médio do Rio Tieté: 1980/1982 (Revista de Pré-História [Univ. de São Paulo, Instituto de Pré-História] 3 : 4, 1982, p. 19–81, bibl., ill., map)
Description of nine prehistoric and two historic lithic open sites. Scrapers and projectile points are the principal stone artifacts in the former; gun flints in the latter. A rock shelter (Sarandi) produced a C14 date of 5540 BP.

672 Carvalho, Eliana Teixeira de. Estudo arqueológico do sítio Corondó: missão de 1978. Rio de Janeiro: Instituto de Arqueologia Brasileira, 1984. 243 p.: bibl., ill., tables (Série Monografias; No. 2)
Multi-year excavations at an Archaic period site of the Itaipu tradition on the coast of Rio de Janeiro permit defining a way of life between 4000–3000 BP supported by hunting, fishing, and consumption of plants in amounts compatible with dependence on agriculture (possibly sweet manioc). Stone, bone, and shell artifacts are described and interpreted, postholes permit reconstruction of habitations.

673 Chmyz, Igor. Estado atual das pesquisas arqueológicas na margem esquerda do Rio Paraná: Projeto Arqueológico Itaipú (UFP/EB, 8, 1982, p. 5–39, bibl., maps)
Summary of the time-space framework constructed after six seasons of salvage investigations on the Brazilian side of the Itaipú reservoir (see items **674** and **675** for more detailed information).

674 ———. Projeto Arqueológico Itaipú: sétimo relatório das pesquisas realizadas na área de Itaipú, 1981–1983. Curitiba, Brazil: Projeto Arqueológico Itaipú, 1983. 106 p.: bibl., charts, ill., maps.
Final monograph on investigations in the area inundated by the Itaipú dam, reporting 27 sites at the northern extreme of the reservoir. Three preceramic and two ceramic (Tupiguarani) traditions are described. Sum-

mary of the chronological sequence incorporates a large number of C14 dates.

675 ———. Projeto Arqueológico Itaipú: sexto relatório das pesquisas realizadas na área de Itaipú, 1980–1981. Curitiba, Brazil: Projeto Arqueológico Itaipú, 1981. 69 p.: bibl., charts, ill., maps.
Continuing survey of the area to be inundated produced 23 sites, representing two preceramic and two ceramic phases, the latter assigned to the Painted and Corrugated subtraditions of the Tupiguarani tradition. Detailed descriptions of sites, lithics, and ceramic are provided by phase.

676 ———. Relatorio das pesquisas arqueológicas realizadas nas áreas das usinas hidroelétricas de Rosana e Taquaruçu, 1982–3, Curitiba, Paraná, Brasil. São Paulo: Companhia Energética de São Paulo and Depto. de Meio Ambiente e Recursos Naturais, 1984. 80 p.: bibl., ill.
Rescue archaeology in the region to be inundated by hydroelectric dams on the left bank of the lower 200 km of the Rio Parapanema produced six sites representing one preceramic tradition, the Tupiguarani tradition, and the Neobrazilian tradition. Sites and artifacts are described and the regional chronology summarized.

677 Dias, Ondemar and **Eliana Carvalho.** Un possível foco de domesticação de plantas no Estado do Rio de Janeiro: RJ-JC-64, Sítio Corondó (Boletim Série Ensaios [Instituto de Arqueologia Brasileira] 1, 1983, p. 1–19, bibl.)
Analysis of artifacts, fauna, plant, and human remains from a habitation site dating 4000–3000 BP indicates intensive use of plants, possibly including domesticated sweet manioc. Text in English and Portuguese.

678 Ferrari, Jussara Louzada. O povoamento Tupiguarani no baixo Ijuí, RS, Brasil (IAP/P [Antropologia] 35, 1983, p. 1–131, p., bibl., ill., maps)
Survey of the Ijuí and adjacent portions of the Uruguai produced 70 sites, representing the preceramic Umbu and Humaitá traditions and the Ijuí and Comandaí phases of the Tupiguarani tradition. Seriated sequences of the ceramic phases and comparative data provide a basis for reconstructing human occupation from Paleo-Indian to European times.

679 Figueiredo, Napoleão. Notes concerning the lithic statuette found on the River Parú, Pará State, Brazil, belonging to the Federal University of Pará collection (EM/A, 1981/1982, p. 30–38, bibl., ill.)
History and description of a remarkable alter-ego stone sculpture encountered in the late 19th century.

680 Herança: a expressão visual do brasileiro antes da influência do europeu. s.l.: Empresas Dow-Brazil, 1984. 152 p.: plates (col. and b/w)
Selection of beautiful stone and pottery artifacts from coastal and Amazonian archaeological sites, and of pictographs and petroglyphs, aimed at increasing appreciation of the precolumbian heritage of Brazil and concern for its conservation.

681 Kneip, Lina Maria. A aldeia préhistórica de Três Vendas: uma tentativa de reconstituição (Revista de Arqueologia [Museu Paraense Emílio Goeldi, Belém, Brazil] 1:1, julho/dez. 1983, p. 46–52, bibl., ill.)
Description of excavations at a habitation site in the State of Rio de Janeiro occupied by groups of the Tupiguarani and Neobrazilian traditions.

682 Laroche, Armand François Gaston. Ensaios de classificações tipológicas sobre pontas de arremissos e outros objetos líticos da tradição Potiguar do Rio Grande do Norte. Mossoró, Brazil: Escola Superior de Agricultura de Mossoró [and] Fundação Guimarães Duque, 1983. 46 p.: ill., tables (Coleção Mossoroense. Série B; 412)
Projectile points ca. 6–12 cm long, with serrated margins and parallel-sided or tapering stems, sometimes with concave base, define the Portiguar tradition. All are surface finds.

683 Lima, Jeannette Maria Dias de. Pesquisas arqueológica no Município do Brejo da Madre de Deus, Pernambuco (Revista da Universidade Católica de Pernambuco [Recife, Brazil] 26:1, 1984, p. 9–60, ill., maps)
Excavations in the rock shelter, Furna do Estrago, produced evidence of occupation during some eight millennia. Perishable materials are well preserved; recent levels contained 53 burials.

684 Lima, Tânia Andrade and Regina Coeli Pinheiro da Silva. Zoo-arqueologia: alguns resultados para a pré-história da Ilha de Santana (Revista de Arqueologia [Museu Paraense Emílio Goeldi, Belém, Brazil] 2:2, julho/dez. 1984, p. 10–40, bibl., ill., tables)
Identification of fish, crustacea, equinoderms, mollusks, birds, reptiles, and mammals from a site on the coast of Rio de Janeiro with a C14 date of 1260 ± 330 BP. Minimal number of individuals and biomass are calculated for some groups.

685 Martin, Gabriela; Alice Aguiar; and Jacionira Rocha. O sítio arqueológico Peri-Peri em Pernambuco (Revista de Arqueologia [Museo Paraense Emílio Goeldi, Belém, Brazil] 1:1, julho/dez. 1983, p. 30–39, bibl., ill.)
Excavation in a rock shelter with paintings in white, yellow, and red revealed a hearth associated with lithics and pigment; a C14 date of 1790 BP was obtained.

686 Morais, José Luiz de. A utilização dos afloramentos litológicos pelo homem pré-histórico brasileiro: análise do tratamento da matéria-prima. São Paulo: Museu Paulista, 1983. 212 p.: bibl., ill., maps (Coleção Museu Paulista. Arqueologia; 7)
Three sites associated with different raw materials—quartzite, chert, and quartz—provide samples for comparison. Experimental stone working revealed correlations between form and workmanship of the artifacts and the fracture patterns of the types of stone.

687 Pallestrini, Luciana. "Superfícies amplas" em arqueologia pré-histórica no Brasil (Revista de Arqueologia [Museu Paraense Emílio Goeldi, Belém, Brazil] 1:1, julho/dez. 1983, p. 7–18, bibl., ill.)
Argues that reconstruction of past behavior can be accomplished only by exposure of large and strategically located sectors of prehistoric occupational sites.

688 Prous, André and Fabiano Lopes de Paula. Informações preliminares sobre grafismos de tipo "nordestino" no Estado de Minas Gerais (Revista de Pré-História [Univ. de São Paulo, Instituto de Pré-História] 5:5, 1983, p. 145–153, bibl., ill.)
Discussion of significance of the presence of rare anthropomorphic rock art representations in northern Minas Gerais.

689 *Revista de Pré-História.* Univ. de São Paulo, Instituto de Pré-História. Vol. 6, 1984- . São Paulo.

Special issue (477 p.) consists of summaries of papers delivered during the Semana de Estudos sobre Pré-História e Arqueologia, dealing with shell middens, field methods, evidence for structures, lithic technology, sea-level change, and paleobiology.

690   Ribeiro, Maira Barberi. Aspetos ambentais e arte rupestre na área do projeto Alto Araguaia (Anuário de Divulgação Científica [Instituto Goiano de Pré-História e Antropologia, Univ. Católica de Goiás, Goiânia, Brazil] 10, 1981/1984, p. 61–70, bibl.)

Combination of geological criteria was used to identify a region likely to contain archaeological sites. Exploration revealed 17 sites. Two categories of rock art were defined: geometric figures on walls with irregular surfaces or difficult access, and large scenes of humans and animals on even, vertical walls.

691   Ribeiro, Pedro Augusto Mentz. Sítios arqueológicos numa microregião de área alagadiça na depressão central do Rio Grande do Sul, Brasil (Revista de CEPA [Associação Pró-Ensino em Santa Cruz do Sul, Brazil] 10:12, 1983, p. 1–121, bibl., ill., map, tables)

Investigations in the Rio Pardo valley permitted establishing a sequence beginning with the preceramic Pardinho Phase (Umbu tradition) with C14 dates of 2920 and 1425 BP; continuing through the Pinhal Phase of the Humaitá tradition, the Eveiras Phase of the Taquara tradition (ceramic), and unnamed phase of the Vieira tradition, and ending with the Trombudo Phase of the Tupiguarani tradition.

692   ───── and José Soloviy Féris. Sítios com petróglifos na Campanha do Rio Grande do Sul, Brasil (Revista do CEPA [Associação Pró-Ensino em Santa Cruz do Sul, Brazil] 11:13, 1984, p. 7–32, bibl., ill.)

Petroglyphs in the form of abstract rectilinear and stylized biomorphic elements are associated with nonceramic habitation, workshop and ceremonial sites; dating is estimated within the Christian Era.

693   Schmitz, Pedro Ignácio; Altair Sales Barbosa; Maira Barberi Ribeiro; and Ivone Verardi. Arte rupestre no centro do

Brasil: pinturas e gravuras da pré-história de Goiás e oeste da Bahia. São Leopoldo: Instituto Anchietano de Pesquisas, 1984. 80 p.: bibl., ill., maps.

Brief explanation of rock art classification precedes description of the environmental and archaeological contexts of examples from six regions in Goiás and one region in Bahia. Excellent illustrations substantiate the contrast between the Bahia examples and those from adjacent Goiás.

694   Simões, Mário F. Pesquisa e cadastro de sítios arqueológicos na Amazônia Legal Brasileira, 1978–1982. Belém, Brazil: Museu Paraense Emílio Goeldi, 1983. 100 p.: bibl. (Publicações avulsas; 38)

Reports 334 archaeological sites since publication of the previous list (see *HLAS 41:682*) and describes them in geographical and numerical order. Information includes location, area, condition, functions, and investigator.

695   Sítios arqueológicos do Rio Grande do Sul. Edited by Valter Augusto Goldmeier. São Leopoldo: Instituto Anchietano de Pesquisas, 1983. 166 p.: maps.

Archaeological sites recorded by investigators from the Instituto Anchietano de Pesquisas up to 1983 are listed in numerical order and cross-referenced by phase and municipality. Summary descriptions of phases and traditions are provided. Maps show the locations of sites by municipality.

696   Uchôa, Dorath Pinto and **Caio Del Rio Garcia.** Cadastramento dos sítios arqueológicos da Baixada Cananéia-Iguape, litoral sul do Estado de São Paulo, Brasil (Revista de Arqueologia [Museu Paraense Emílio Goeldi, Belém, Brazil] 1:1, julho/dez. 1983, p. 19–29, bibl., ill., table)

Data on 107 shell middens on the coast and offshore islands include dimensions, shell species, state of preservation, and C14 dates. Tables identify number of sites in each location by millennium, predominant composition, and relative state of preservation. One hundred seven C14 dates from 27 sites extend from 5170 to 920 BP.

697   ─────; Maria Cristina M. Scatamacchia; and Caio del Rio Garcia. O sítio cerâmico do Itaguá: um sítio de contacto no litoral do Estado de São Paulo, Brasil (Revista de Arqueologia [Museu Paraense

Emílio Goeldi, Belém, Brazil] 2:2, julho/dez. 1984, p. 51–60, bibl., ill.)

Salvage excavation of a habitation on the north coast of São Paulo produced pottery and objects of European origin (four glass beads, one copper disk). The pottery is assigned to the Painted subtradition of the Tupiguarani tradition. A C14 date of AD 1290 is rejected as incompatible with the presence of European materials.

CHILE

698 Aldunate del S., Carlos; José Berenguer R; and Victoria Castro R. La función de las chullpas en Likán (*in* Congreso de Arqueología Chilena, 8th, Valdivia, Chile, 1979. Actas [see item **704**] p. 129–174, bibl., ill.)

Investigations at the largest concentration of chullpas in northern Chile, containing more than 70 structures, and observation of funerary rituals still practiced in the region suggested that the chullpas were "adoratorios." Eleven predictions developed to test this hypothesis confirmed their ceremonial function.

699 Allison, Marvin J.; Bernardo Arriaza T.; Guillermo Focacci A.; and Iván Muñoz O. Los orejones de Arica (UN/C, 11, 1983, p. 167–172, bibl., ill.)

Of a sample of 615 mummies from Playa Miller and the Azapa valley, 21 had perforations of the earlobe. All were male, between ages 14 and 50. Describes and illustrates four types of perforations, three types of ornaments and their compositions. Four pre-Inca complexes are represented.

700 Berenguer R., José. Hallazgos La Aguada en San Pedro de Atacama, Norte de Chile (Gaceta Arqueológica Andina [Instituto Andino de Estudios Arqueológicos, Lima] 3:12, dic. 1984, p. 12–14, bibl., ill.)

A basket and a female wooden figurine of Aguada style from a cemetery confirm contacts between Aguada and San Pedro around AD 700.

701 Briones Morales, Luis. Fundamentos para una metodología aplicada al relevamiento de los geoglifos del Norte de Chile (UN/C, 11, agosto 1984, p. 41–56, bibl., ill.

Aspects relevant to complete description of geoglyphs are discussed, forms for recording data are presented, and importance of systematic and standardized methods for comparison and interpretation of the figures is stressed.

702 Castillo G., Gastón. Sacrificios de camélidos en la costa de Coquimbo, Chile (Gaceta Arqueológica Andina [Instituto Andino de Estudios Arqueológicos, Lima] 2:7, agosto 1983, p. 6–7, ill.)

Presence of one to five camelid skeletons in burials of adults and children in a cemetery of Las Animas phase (900-1100 AD) implies the existence of domesticated herds in pre-Inca times.

703 Chacón, Sergio and Mario Orellana. El Tambo Chungará (*in* Congreso de Arqueología Chilena, 8th, Valdivia, Chile, 1979. Actas [see item **704**] p. 247–255, ill.)

Description of a well preserved Inca tambo 205 m from Arica at 4350 m elevation, consisting of platform, patio, corridors, nine rooms, and corrals.

704 Congreso de Arqueología Chilena, 8th, Valdivia, Chile, 1979. Actas. Sociedad Chilena de Arqueologia, Universidad Austral de Chile. Valdivia: Ediciones Kultrun, 1982. 324 p., 41 p. of plates: bibl., ill., maps, port.

For individual annotations of papers delivered at this congress, see items **698, 703, 710, 713, 715–716, 722,** and **731**).

705 Dauelsberg H., Percy. Investigaciones arqueológicas en la Sierra de Arica, sector Belén (UN/C, 11, 1983, p. 63–83, bibl., ill., map)

Architecture and pottery from five *pucaras* are compared to define Inca occupation of the highland region around Belén; extensive agricultural terraces imply great agricultural productivity.

706 ————. Taltape: definición de un tipo cerámico (UN/C, 11, agosto 1984, p. 19–39, bibl., ill.)

Four complete vessels and eight fragments are described individually and then generalized into a type description, characterized by black painting on a thin white slip. Examples are distributed between Azapa and Chiu-Chiu and are rare, suggesting the type is intrusive.

707 ————. Tojo-Tojone, un paradero de cazadores arcaicos: características y secuencias (UN/C, 11, 1983, p. 11–30, bibl., ill.)

Excavations at a rock shelter at 3600 m elevation permitted defining three periods. Tojo-Tojone I, characterized by thick lanceolate points, has a C14 date of 7630 BC; Tojo-Tojone II, with thinner and shorter points, is estimated to date about 4000 BC; Tojo-Tojone III has no cultural remains but is assigned to the Archaic based on a C14 date of 1790 BC.

708 Dillehay, Tom D. A late ice-age settlement in southern Chile (SA, 251:4, Oct. 1984, p. 106–112, 117, ill., map)

Unusual preservation permits defining a complex of rectangular rooms constructed of wood and probably draped with skins. Associated are cut logs, stone tools with wooden hafts, remains of wild plants, hearths, and mastodon bones. Several C14 dates extend from 13,000 to 12,500 BP.

709 ———. Monteverde: aportes al conocimiento del paleoindio en el extremo sur (Gaceta Arqueológico Andino [Instituto Andino de Estudios Arqueológicos, Lima] 1:4/5, nov. 1982, p. 6–7, 10, ill.)

A site south of Valdivia on the coast of Chile has produced wooden artifacts, grooved bola stones, and remains of dwellings with C14 dates about 12,000 BP.

710 Durán Serrano, Eliana. El complejo cultural Aconcagua y su material ergológico (in Congreso de Arqueología Chilena, 8th, Valdivia, Chile 1979. Actas [see item **704**] p. 5–18, bibl., ill., map)

Summary of sites and artifacts characteristic of the late pre-Inca complex between the Río Aconcagua and Río Cochapoal. A map shows location of sites.

711 Falabella, F.; M.T. Planella; and P. Szmulewicz. Los Puquios: sitio arqueológico en la costa de Chile central (SCHG/R, 149, 1981, p. 85–107, bibl.)

Description of burials and offerings from a shell midden south of Valparaíso representing the Llolleo complex.

712 Focacci Aste, Guillermo. El Tiwanaku Clásico en el Valle de Azapa (Documentos de Trabajo [Univ. de Tarapacá, Instituto de Antropología y Arqueología, Arica, Chile] 3, 1983, p. 94–124, bibl., ill.)

Suggests that Tiwanaku influence began several centuries earlier than generally accepted.

713 Kaltwasser P., Jorge; Alberto Medina R.; and Juan R. Munizaga V. Cementerio del período arcaico en Cuchipuy (in Congreso de Arqueología Chilena, 8th, Valdivia, Chile, 1979. Actas [see item **704**] p. 275–280, bibl., ill.)

Preliminary information on human, faunal, and cultural remains from a large cemetery on the north edge of former Lake Taguatagua. Eleven C14 dates extend from 8070 to 5060 BP.

714 ———; ———; and ———. Estudio de once fechas de R.C. 14 relacionadas con el hombre de Cuchipuy (UC/BPC, 9, 1983, p. 9–13, bibl., ill.)

An extensive zone on the margin of former Lake Taguatagua has produced skeletal remains representing more than 100 individuals along with abundant artifacts and fauna. Differences in the physical characteristics and artifacts permit recognizing four periods. Eleven C14 dates are evaluated. An age of 5760 BP is accepted for Cemetery 2, 7610 to 6160 BP for Cemetery 3, and 8070 to 7610 BP for Cemetery 4.

715 Llagostera M., Agustín. Tres dimensiones en la conquista prehistórica del mar: un aporte para el estudio de las formaciones pescadores de la costa sur andina (in Congreso de Arqueología Chilena, 8th, Valdivia, Chile, 1979. Actas [see item **704**] p. 217–245, bibl.)

Three stages of exploitation of marine resources are defined: 1) longitudinal (along the shore); 2) "batitudinal" (deep water); and 3) latitudinal (navigation). Each enhanced the food supply obtained from the sea, permitting larger populations. A major limiting factor on the Chilean coast is the scarcity of fresh water, which placed a ceiling on cultural development.

716 Massone M., Mauricio. Investigaciones arqueológicas en la costa nororiental del Estrecho de Magallanes (in Congreso de Arqueología Chilena, 8th, Valdivia, Chile, 1979. Actas [see item **704**] p. 257–274, bibl., ill.)

Comparison of artifacts, faunal remains, and dates for 10 sites on the north margin of the Strait of Magellan indicates all represent loci visited for brief periods at different times of the year by hunters from the interior. Numerous C14 dates were obtained, the majority between the 4th and 6th centuries AD.

717 Mostny Glaser, Grete and **Hans Niemeyer Fernández.** Arte rupestre chileno. Santiago: Ministerio de Educación, Depto. de Extensión Cultura, s.d. 150 p.: bibl., ill., maps [Serie El patromino cultural chileno. Colección Historia del arte chileno]

Introduction to rock art in Chile for the layman. Discusses geographical distribution, techniques, and motifs; reviews nine local styles from different parts of the country; compares representations of humans, animals, and geometric figures in different styles, and explains methods of inferring chronology. Beautifully illustrated in color.

718 Mujica, Elías J; Mario A. Rivera; and **Thomas F. Lynch.** Proyecto de estudio sobre la complementariedad económica Tiwanaku en los valles occidentales del centro-sur andino (UN/C, 11, 1983, p. 85–109, bibl., ill., map)

Design of research to clarify economic complementarity, routes of communication, ethnic relationships, colonization, and other aspects of interaction and integration of northern Chilean and Tiwanaku populations.

719 Muñoz Ovalle, Iván. La fase Alto Ramírez en los valles del extremo norte de Chile (Documentos de Trabajo [Univ. de Tarapacá, Instituto de Antropología y Arqueología, Arica, Chile] 3, 1983, p. 3–42, bibl., ill.)

Interprets the Alto Ramírez phase, between about 500 BC and AD 350, as an amalgamation between invaders from the highlands and local incipient agriculturalists with maritime orientation.

720 ———. Hallazgo de un *Alouatta seniculus* en el Valle de Azapa: estudio preliminar de la iconografía de simios de Arica (UN/C, 10, marzo 1983, p. 39–46, bibl., ill.)

Child's burial assigned to the San Miguel phase (about AD 1000) contained among offerings a small monkey accompanied by a small basket. This is in keeping with representations in late contexts on textiles, pottery, and stone, and reflects trade with the eastern side of the Andes.

721 ———. El poblamiento aldeano en el Valle de Azapa y su vinculación con Tiwanaku, Arica, Chile (Documentos de Tra-

bajo [Univ. de Tarapacá, Instituto de Antropología y Arqueología, Arica, Chile] 3, 1983, p. 43–93, bibl., ill.)

Evidence for contemporaneity of local and intrusive Tiwanakoid populations in the Azapa Valley supports Murra's model of verticality.

722 Niemeyer F., Hans. Cultura El Molle de Río Huasco: revisión y síntesis (*in* Congreso de Arqueología Chilena, 8th, Valdivia, Chile, 1979. Actas [see item **704**] p. 295–316, bibl., ill.)

Description of two tombs and their contents, attributable to El Molle culture.

723 ——— and **Mario Rivera A.** El camino del Inca en el despoblado de Atacama (UC/BPC, 9, 1983, p. 91–193, bibl, ill.)

Description of the Inca highway and associated structures mapped and sampled between Aguada de Puquios and Vaquillas. Describes and classifies pottery samples by cultural affiliation. This section of the highway is attributable to Inca construction, no earlier remains being associated.

724 ———; **Miguel Cervellino G.;** and **Eduardo Muñoz.** Viña del Cerro: metalurgia Inka en Copiapó, Chile (Gaceta Arqueológica Andina [Instituto Andino de Estudios Arqueológicos, Lima] 3 : 9, marzo 1984, p. 6–7, ill.)

Characteristics of an Inca center for processing copper ore.

725 Núñez Atencio, Lautaro. Paleoindio y arcaico en Chile: diversidad, secuencia y procesos. México: Instituto Nacional de Antropología e Historia, 1983. 205 p.: bibl., ill., map (Serie Monografías; 3)

Review of evidence for early man in Chile by environmental zones permits recognizing differences in adaptation. Regions discussed are the arid and semiarid north, the fertile center, and the semiarid south. A useful table lists C14 dates through Oct. 1980. A synthesis by periods highlights variations. Important contribution by Chile's leading authority on the Paleo-Indian and Archaic cultures.

726 ———. Pircas: ocupación temprana en el Norte de Chile (Gaceta Arqueológica Andina [Instituto Andino de Estudios Arqueológicos, Lima] 3 : 11, sept. 1984, p. 8–9, 12, ill., map)

Identification of a cultural complex in

the Quebrada de Tarapacá with distinctive double-walled dwellings, cemeteries, geoglyphs, and agriculture featuring maize, C14 dates between AD 70–500.

727 —— and **Cora Moragas W.** Cerámica temprana en Cáñamo, costa desértica del norte de Chile: análisis y evaluación regional (UN/C, 11, 1983, p. 31–61, bibl., ill., map)

Characteristics of pottery from a site near Iquique on the north coast, petrographic analysis, and comparison with ceramic complexes from adjacent regions shows closest affiliation with the Wanakarani culture of the southern altiplano. C14 and thermolumensence dating places its appearance at about 860 BC. Maize and algarroba are associated.

728 ——; **Juan Varela;** and **Rodolfo Casamiquela.** Ocupación paleoindia en Quereo: reconstrucción multidisciplinaria en el territorio semiárido de Chile. Antofagasta, Chile: Univ. del Norte, 1983. 169 p.: bibl., charts, ill., tables.

Final report on investigations at a coastal site with five C14 dates of 11,000+ BP. Details are provided on excavation, stratigraphy, fauna, artifacts, and chronology, including paleoenvironmental reconstruction. Appendices deal with wood and pollen, fossil molluscs, and microfossils. Important contribution to Paleo-Indian studies in southern South America.

729 **Núñez Henríquez, Patricio.** Aldeas tarapaqueñas: notas y comentarios (UN/C, 10, marzo 1983, p. 29–37, bibl., maps)

Interpretation of social organization of six settlements on the lower quebrada of Tarapacá, and their evolution between AD 1000–1500.

730 **Orellana Rodríguez, Mario.** Investigaciones y teorías en la arqueología de Chile. Santiago: Centro de Estudios Humanísticos, Facultad de Ciencias Físicas y Matemáticas, Univ. de Chile, 1982. 189 p.: ill., ports (Ediciones del Centro; 16)

The development of Chilean archaeology is divided into 5 periods: 1) 1842–82; 2) 1882–1911; 3) 1911–40; 4) 1940–60; and 5) 1960 to present. The contributions of principal figures and the development of theory during periods 1–3 are reviewed. The significance of early work is demonstrated in a concluding chapter on the impact of Tiawanaku on the cultures of northern Chile.

731 **Pinto, Andrés** and **Rubén Stehberg.** Las ocupaciones alfareras prehispánicas del Cordón de Chacabuco, con especial referencia a la Caverna de El Carrizo (in Congreso de Arqueología Chilena, 8th, Valdivia, Chile, 1979. Actas [see item **704**] p. 19–32, bibl., ill., map)

Lithic and bone artifacts and faunal remains from a deposit 1.6 cm deep permit reconstructing three successive ceramic occupations during the Christian era.

732 **Santoro Vargas, Calogero.** Camino del Inca en la sierra de Arica (UN/C, 10, marzo 1983, p. 47–56, bibl., ill.)

Description of a 22 km segment of Inca road at Socoroma in the head of the Lluta valley, probably improved from an earlier trail.

733 **Schiappacasse F., Virgilio** and **Hans Niemeyer F.** Descripción y análisis interpretativo de un sitio arcaico temprano en la Quebrada de Camarones. Santiago: Museo Nacional de Historia Natural, 1984. 187 p.: bibl., ill. (Publicación ocasional; 41)

Description of excavations, artifacts, faunal remains, and burials from a habitation site with four C14 dates extending from 5440 to 4665 BC, representing the Chinchorro culture known principally from cemeteries. Inferences are drawn concerning subsistence, settlement permanence, and paleodemography.

734 **Standen R., Vivien** and **Lautaro Núñez A.** Indicadores antropológico-físico y culturales del cementerio precerámico Tiliviche-2, norte de Chile (UN/C, 11, agosto 1984, p. 135–154, bibl., ill., tables)

The 25 graves containing 34 individuals represent an Archaic population dating about 1830 BC. Reports on grave goods manufactured from hide, stone, wood, plant fiber, wool, and shell and compares them with occurrences at four other coastal sites. Cranial deformation was more common in children, suggesting it was a recently introduced practice.

735 **Stehberg L., Rubén.** Arqueología de Chile central (Gaceta Arqueológica Andina [Instituto Andino de Estudios Arqueológicos, Lima] 3:12, dic. 1984, p. 4–5, 15, bibl., ill.)

Summarizes evidence justifying inclusion of central Chile in the southern Andean area, rather than the marginal extreme southern Andean area.

736 ———. El complejo prehispánico Aconcagua en la Rinconada de Huechún. Santiago: Museo Nacional de Historia Natural, 1981. 87 p., 2 folded leaves of plates: ill. (Publicación ocasional; 35)

Excavations in a village and cemetery provide evidence for more detailed definition of the Aconcagua Complex of central Chile. Two irrigation canals of pre-Inca date are reported.

737 Zlatar, Vjera. Replanteamiento sobre el problema Caleta Huelén 42 (UN/C, 10, marzo 1983, p. 21–28, bibl., maps)

During the millennium between 2800 and 1800 BC, this site was occupied intermittently by groups making the transition from terrestrial hunting to marine exploitation, and gathering to agriculture.

COLOMBIA

738 Angulo Valdés, Carlos. Arqueología del Valle de Santiago, norte de Colombia. Bogotá: Banco de la República, 1983. 196 p.: bibl, ill. (Publiaciones de la Fundación de Investigaciones Arqueológicas Nacionales; 19)

Extensive stratigraphic excavation at three sites in different environments within the Santiago Valley west of Barranquilla permitted defining three archaeological phases: Palmar in the foothills; Tocahagua around the ciénagas; and La Isla on the coast. Contemporaneity is implied by C14 dates between AD 1535 and 1695 for the late portions of each phase, and supported by historical accounts. Settlements were small; subsistence was based on hunting, fishing, and maize cultivation. Pottery types are described in detail; two phases employ shell temper.

739 Ardila C., Gerardo Ignacio. Chía: un sitio precerámico en la Sabana de Bogotá. Bogotá: Banco de la República, 1984. 128 p.: bibl., ill., maps, tables (Publicaciones de la Fundación de Investigaciones Arqueológicas Nacionales; 26)

Excavations in two rock shelters and one open site indicate the region was inhabited between 7500 and 5000 BP by hunter-gatherers who occupied rock shelters. Between 5000 and 3000 BP, population increased, rock shelters were abandoned for open sites, and root crops were probably cultivated. A C14 date of 2090 ± 60 BP associated with pottery implies a third period in which rock shelters were used for temporary camps. Pottery and agriculture are inferred to have been introduced from the Magdalena Valley.

740 Castaño Uribe, Carlos and Carmen Lucía Dávita. Investigación arqueológica en el Magdalena Medio: sitios Colorados y Mayaca. Bogotá: Banco de la República, 1984. 178 p.: bibl., ill. (Publicaciones de la Fundación de Investigaciones Arqueológicas Nacionales; 22)

Excavations at two habitation sites and a cemetery permit defining the late ceramic complex associated with urns with seated figures on the lids. Distribution of this style in South America and possible affiliation with Cariban speakers are discussed.

741 Castillo Espitia, Neyla. Arqueología de Tunja. Bogotá, Banco de la República, 1984. 237 p.: bibl., ill. (Publicaciones de la Fundación de Investigaciones Arqueológicas Nacionales; 21)

Surface collections and stratigraphic excavations at sites in and around the city of Tunja, Depto. de Boyacá, permitted constructing a sequence of two ceramic periods. The earliest, characterized by incised decoration, has a single C14 date of AD 690. Period II, characterized by painted decoration, has a date of AD 1170. Some 300 years of transition imply gradual incorporation of new techniques, rather than replacement. Pottery is described and illustrated in detail, other remains more briefly.

742 Correal Urrego, Gonzalo and María Pinto Nolla. Investigación arqueológica en el Municipio de Zipacón, Cundinamarca. Bogotá: Banco de la República, 1983. 202 p.: bibl., ill. (Publicaciones de la Fundación de Investigaciones Arqueológicas Nacionales; 18)

Detailed description of stratigraphy, faunal remains, lithic, bone artifacts, and pottery from a rock shelter north of Bogotá. Percussion-made stone artifacts continue the preceramic tradition; a C14 date of 1300 BC is the earliest for pottery on the Sabana de Bogotá. An appendix reports discovery of a fragmentary fishtail projectile point in the Depto. de Chocó.

743 —— and ——. Investigaciones arqueológicas en el Municipio de Zipacón, Cundinamarca (Boletín [Museo del Oro, Banco de la República, Bogotá] 5, enero/abril 1982, p. 24–34, bibl., ill.)

Excavations at the Zipacón rock shelter indicate that maize, potatoes, and avocados were being cultivated by 1320 BC. Associated pottery resembles the Herrera Period types of the Magdalena Valley.

744 Cubillos Ch., Julio César. Arqueología del Valle del Río Cauca: asentamientos prehispánicos en la Suela Plana del Río Cauca. Bogotá: Banco de la República, 1984. 204 p.: bibl., ill. (Publicaciones del Fundación de Investigaciones Arqueológicas Nacionales; 25)

Survey of the southern Cauca basin produced 12 habitation sites representing three archaeological phases: Sachamate, Tinajas, and Quebrada Seca. Pottery types, figurines, spindle whorls, and lithics are described in detail and illustrated. C14 dates of AD 1170 and 1200 correspond to the beginning of the seriated sequence, supporting paleoenvironmental evidence that the plain became habitable about the 10th century AD.

745 Duque Gómez, Luis and **César Cubillos.** Arqueología de San Agustín: La Estación. Bogotá: Banco de la República, 1981. 155 p.: bibl., ill. (some col.) (Publicaciones de la Fundación de Investigaciones Arqueológicas Nacionales; 8)

Investigations during 1976–77 at a habitation site in the Parque Arqueológico de San Agustín revealed rings of postholes defining houses, burials, roads, and channels for providing water. Associated pottery and stone artifacts are described and illustrated, as well as plant remains including maize. Stratigraphic and cultural evidence indicates a single occupation between the 9th and 11th centuries AD.

746 Eden, Michael J.; Warwick Bray; Leonor Herrera; and **Colin McEwan.** *Terra preta* soils and their archaeological context in the Caquetá Basin of southeast Colombia (SAA/AA, 49, 1984, p. 125–140, bibl., ill., map)

Description of black soils characteristic of precolumbian sites, confirming their origin through accumulation of domestic waste products. Characteristics of the Camami and Nofurei archaeological ceramic styles are summarized.

747 Legast, Anne. La fauna mítica Tairona (Boletín [Museo del Oro, Banco de la República, Bogotá] 5, enero/abril 1982, p. 1–18, bibl., ill.)

Tabulation of categories of animals represented in gold, pottery, stone, bone, shell, and wood in the collections of the Museo del Oro shows that amphibians predominate (61 percent) in gold, stone (93 percent), shell and bone (63 percent), whereas mammals (31 percent) and birds (37 percent) are most common in pottery.

748 Llanos Vargas, Héctor and **Anabella Durán de Gómez.** Asentamientos prehispánicos de Quinchana, San Agustín. Bogotá: Banco de la República, 1983. 157 p.: bibl., ill. (Publicaciones de la Fundación de Investigaciones Arqueológicas Nacionales; 20)

Extensive excavations in three habitational terraces revealed pit-and-chamber tombs and postholes defining circular houses. Ridges and drainage channels on adjacent slopes mark locations of associated prehistoric fields. Details of the pottery imply dating about AD 800.

749 Méndez Gutiérrez, Miguel. Puntas de proyectil de Cajibío, Cauca, Colombia: indicios de pobladores tempranos en el Valle de Pubenza. Popayán, Colombia: s.n., 1984. 47 p.: ill.

Description of five stemmed points 4.2–9.9 cm long from the vicinity of Popayán and comparison with Paleo-Indian projectile points. Dating is estimated prior to 5000 BC although the earliest C14 date from the excavation is about 1100 BC.

750 Morales G., Jorge and **Gilberto Cadavid Camargo.** Investigaciones etnohistóricas y arqueológicas en el área Guane. Bogotá: Banco de la República, 1984. 163 p.: bibl., ill. (Publicaciones de la Fundación de Investigaciones Arqueológicas Nacionales; 24)

Pt. 2 describes survey and excavations on the Mesa de Los Santos, Depto. de Santander. The principal types of sites are rings of stones outlining habitations, terraces probably used for cultivation, large middens, and pictographs. Details of the pottery and motifs of the pictographs are compatible with ethnohistorical information in Pt. 1 on the Guane, providing time depth to their occupation of the region.

751 Ochoa de Molina, Blanca. Colombia prehispánica: arte e imaginería. Bogotá: Ediciones Tercer Mundo, 1983. 227 p.: bibl., ill.

The principal animals depicted on metal objects in the Banco de la República collection and the functions of the items provide a basis for inferring symbolism. Chapters summarize the principal archaeological zones: southeast, Calima, Quimbaya, Tolima, Sinú, Tairona, and Muisca.

752 Ponzellini, Maria Luisa Castelli. Simbolismo e fantasia nelle fusaiole de terracotta precolombiana (AISA/TA, 43, ott. 1984, p. 51–74, ill.)

Describes and illustrates individually 105 spindle whorls attributed to the Quimbaya culture.

753 Pro Calima: Archäologisches Projekt im westlichen Kolumbien/Südamerika. Basel, Switzerland: s.n., 1983. 60 p.: ill. (Periodische Publikation der Vereinigung Pro Calima; no. 3)

Survey and excavation in El Dorado Valley between the Cauca and Calima rivers revealed platforms, ditches, "field lines," burial chambers, and drainage systems. Results of physiographic and soil phosphate studies are reported. Most of the features are attributable to the Sonso (late) period.

754 Regional archaeology in the Valle de la Plata, Colombia: a preliminary report on the 1984 season of the Proyecto Arqueológico Valle de la Plata. Edited by Robert D. Drennan. Ann Arbor: Univ. of Michigan, Museum of Anthropology, 1985. 195 p.: bibl., ill. (Technical reports; no. 16)

The Valle de la Plata, a headwater tributary of the Río Magdalena, was selected for intensive survey to obtain data relevant to estimating changes in population density and cultural complexity and identifying their causes. During the initial field season, data were collected on geology, soils, vegetation, paleoecology, and settlement pattern. Survey methodology and pottery wares are described. Early, Middle, and Late periods are defined and population changes estimated on the

basis of calculations of sherd density and occupied area for each period.

755 Scott, D.A. and N.J. Seeley. The examination of prehispanic gold chisel from Colombia (Journal of Archaeological Science [London] 10, 1983, p. 153–163, bibl., ill.)

Metallographic, atomic absorption spectophotometry, electron probe, and microhardness methods identified a chisel from the Dept. of Antioquia as tumbaga. Composition and method of manufacture are compared with previously analyzed examples.

756 Tello Cifuentes, Hernán. Geología de algunos sitios arqueológicos. Bogotá: Banco de la República, 1981. 112 p.: bibl., ill. (some col.) (Publicaciones de la Fundación de Investigaciones Arqueológicas Nacionales; 13)

Petrographic analysis of stone sculptures from San Agustín, Tierradentro, Quinchana, Aguabonita, and Moscopán establishes the origin of the raw material in situ.

ECUADOR

757 Alcina Franch, José. Tomebamba y el problema de los indios cañaris de la Sierra Sur del Ecuador (EEHA/AEA, 37, 1983, p. 403–433, bibl., maps)

Review of conflicting archival and historical sources pertinent to identifying the boundaries and "towns" associated with the Cañaris. For ethnohistorian's comment, see *HLAS 46:1580.*

758 Almeida, Napoleón. El período de Integración en el sur de la provincia de Loja (IFEA/B, 11, 1982, p. 29–37, bibl., ill.)

A single relatively uniform cultural tradition is indicated by settlement pattern and ceramics in a sample of over 100 sites and is assigned to the ethnohistoric Paltas.

759 Almeida Reyes, Eduardo and Holguer Jara Chávez. El Pucará de Rumicucho. Quito: Museos del Banco Central del Ecuador, 1984. 156 p.: bibl., ill. (Miscelanea antropológica ecuatoriana. Serie monográfica; 1)

Pt. 1 describes excavations, artifacts, faunal remains, and structures. The data support construction by the Inca as a military-religious center. Pt. 2 summarizes the evidence and techniques used in the architectural reconstruction.

760 Batchelor, Bruce E. Los camellones de Cayambe en la Sierra de Ecuador (III/AI, 40:4, 1980, p. 671–689, bibl., ill.)
Description of system of canals and fields defined on the downhill border by arc-shaped embankments and divided internally into ridges, irrigated by tapping natural streams. In the absence of archaeological evidence, construction is attributed to the Cara, of Chibcha affiliation.

761 Berenguer R., José. Figurillas post-Formativas en la Sierra Norte del Ecuador (Gaceta Arqueológica Andina [Instituto Andino de Estudios Arqueológicos, Lima] 3:10, junio 1984, p. 4–5, bibl., ill., map)
Figurine fragments from a site northwest of Ibarra represent a distinctive style, dated tentatively about the beginning of the Christian Era.

762 ——— and José Echeverría. La cerámica de Tababuela, Sierra Norte del Ecuador (Gaceta Arqueológica Andina [Instituto Andino de Estudios Arqueológicos, Lima] 3:11, sept. 1984, p. 7, ill.)
Vessels with incised, punctate, and applique-pellet decoration associated with figurines (see item 761) are assigned to the Middle Chimba period.

763 Bodenhorst, Benno. Los sellos cerámicos de Manabí (Antropología Ecuatoriana [Casa de la Cultura Ecuatoriana, Quito] 2/3, 1983–1984, p. 23–56, bibl., ill.)
After considering various functions for the flat and cylindrical pottery stamps, author assigns highest probability to decorating the human skin.

764 Damp, Jonathan E. Architecture of the early Valdivia village (SAA/AA, 49, 1984, p. 573–585, bibl., ill.)
Postholes define ovoid structures used for sleeping; cooking and other activities took place outside. Evidence from Loma Alta and Real Alto suggests a U-shaped village layout.

765 ———. Ceramic art and symbolism in the early Valdivia community (UCLA/JLAL, 8, 1982, p. 155–178, bibl., ill.)
Argues that hatched triangles and interlocking T elements represent snakes and felines, and that these animals were important in ritual and cosmology.

766 Di Capua, Costanza. Consideraciones sobre una exposición de sellos arqueológicos (Antropología Ecuatoriana [Casa de la Cultura Ecuatoriana, Quito] 2/3, 1983/1984, p. 79–103, bibl., ill.)
Attributes of 60 pottery stamps imply their function was ceremonial. Comparison with motifs on spindle whorls, metal, and other kinds of pottery objects should offer a basis for inferring symbolic significance.

767 Echeverría A., José. Area septentrional andina oeste, formas de producción concretas en la cultura Valdivia: el control racionalizado del manglar (Antropología Ecuatoriana [Casa de la Cultura Ecuatoriana, Quito] 2/3, 1983–1984, p. 7–21, bibl., maps)
Suggests that the shell middens of the Valdivia culture reflect specialized utilization of mangrove resources, which are traded to groups in the interior.

768 Ecuador al rescate de su pasado= Ecuador regains its past. Quito: Ministerio de Relaciones Exteriores del Ecuador: Ministerio de Relaciones Exteriores del Ecuador: Museo del Banco del Ecuador: Organización de los Estados Americanos, 1984. 1 v.: ill.
Catalog accompanying the exhibit of a selection of 9236 precolumbian objects smuggled to Italy and recuperated by Ecuador after seven years of litigation. Lists events in the process of repatriation and provides summary of Ecuadorian prehistory as well as photographs and identifications of 64 objects.

769 Fresco, Antonio. La arqueología de Ingapirca, Ecuador: costumbres funerarias, cerámica y otros materiales. Cuenca: Comisión del Castillo de Ingapirca, Consejo de Gobierno del Museo Arqueológico del Banco Central del Ecuador, 1984. 223 p., 99 p. of plates: bibl., ill., maps.
Monograph reporting excavations in three sectors of Ingapirca during 1974–75. Describes one collective and 31 individual burials as well as pottery (figurines, spoon), bone (*atlatl* hooks, tubular containers, punch, ornaments, needles, flutes), stone (axes, mortars, pounders, balls), shell artifacts and pottery types. Eight C14 dates range from AD 990-1400. With minor exceptions, the pottery belongs to the Cashaloma tradition.

770 ———. Arquitectura de Ingapirca (Miscelánea Antropológica Ecuatoriana [Guayaquil] 3, 1983 [i.e. 1984] p. 195–212, bibl., ill.)

Excavations conducted between 1978–82 permit describing the groups of structures composing the site of Ingapirca and inferring their functions. Cañari structures and pottery underlie most of the Inca occupation, indicating the site was an important administrative, military, and religious center prior to the Inca conquest.

771 ———. El tambo incaico de Paredones de Culebrillas (CCE/RA, 7, nov. 1981, p. 137–177, ill.)

Details of the plan of a tambo in the southern highlands of Ecuador are comparable to Tunsucancha, Dept. of Huánuco, Peru, indicating standardization of construction and use.

772 **Gardner, Joan S.** Textiles precolombinos del Ecuador (Miscelánea Antropológica Ecuatoriana [Guayaquil] 2:2, 1982, p. 9–23, bibl., ill.)

Spanish version of *HLAS 43:700*, with additional illustrations.

773 **Gondard, Pierre** and **Freddy López.** Inventario arqueológico preliminar de los Andes septentrionales del Ecuador. Libro 1, Texto. Libro 2, Material de investigación. Quito: Ministerio de Agricultura y Ganadería: Office de la recherche scientifique et technique Outre Mer *con el auspicio del Museo del Banco Central del Ecuador,* 1983. 274 p.: bibl., ill., maps.

While mapping present land use between Cayambe and the Colombian border, authors observed mounds, terraces, ridges, and other aberrant features. Their distributions and relations to the topography and soils raised questions about their origin and function which are addressed from a geographical perspective. The data constitute a significant resource for archaeologists concerned with reconstructing and understanding prehistoric adaptation.

774 **González C., Celiano.** Petroglifos de la Provincia de El Oro: ensayo de estudio y comprensión. Ambato: Editorial Pío XII, 1982. 107 p., 18 p. of plates: bibl.

After reviewing the petroglyphs recorded in the southern province of El Oro, author discusses origin, development, and significance of rock art in general. Comparison with other parts of northern South America leads him to attribute them to the Caribs.

775 **Guffroy, Jean.** Inhumations tardives dans la région de Macará (IFEA/B, 11, 1982, p. 39–49, ill.)

Description of burials at four locations north of the town of Macará in southern Loja, assigned to the period of Inca occupation.

776 ———. Les traditions culturelles formatives de la Vallée de Catamayo (IFEA/B, 11, 1982, p. 3–11, bibl., ill., map)

Foundation walls of two stone structures were encountered at a Formative period site west of Loja excavated during 1981. Associated pottery is decorated by incision filled with red or white, red bands, and punctation.

777 **Guinea Bueno, Mercedes.** Patrones de asentamiento en la arqueología de Esmeraldas, Ecuador. Madrid: Misión Arqueológica Española en el Ecuador, 1984. 243 p.: bibl., ill., maps (Memorias; 8)

Annual production of pottery per family, daily protein consumption per person, population size per refuse mound, and duration of occupation were calculated from archaeological remains using conversions employed by investigators in other regions to reconstruct demography on the north coast of Ecuador between about AD 100 and 1500. A chiefdom level is inferred for the Regional Developmental period and much greater population density and sociopolitical complexity during the Integration period.

778 **Lecoq, Patrice.** La période de Développment Régional dans le sud de la province de Loja (IFEA/B, 11, 1982, p. 13–27, bibl., ill.)

Ceramics characterizing three complexes of the Regional Developmental period are briefly described and serve as a basis for observing an increase in settlement density.

779 **Ledergerber C., Paulina.** El origen de más de un cuarto de siglo de investigaciones sobre la cultura Valdivia (EANH/B, 65:139/140, 1982, p. 25–44, bibl.)

Appraisal of effects of the thesis of transpacific origin of Valdivia pottery suggested in 1965 on subsequent archaeological investigations in Ecuador and review of principal objections to the thesis.

780 Lippi, Ronald D.; Robert McK. Bird; and David M. Stemper. Maíz primitivo encontrado en La Ponga, en un contexto Machalilla (Miscelánea Antropológica Ecuatoriana [Guayaquil] 3, 1983 [i.e. 1984] p. 143–154, bibl., ill., map)

Description of 15 examples of grains or cupulas from Machalilla tradition contexts, providing the first direct evidence of maize from the Formative period of coastal Ecuador.

781 ——; ——; and ——. Maize recovered at La Ponga, an early Ecuadorian site (SAA/AA, 49, 1984, p. 118–124, bibl., ill.)

Description of charred maize kernels and cupules from Machalilla levels, dating ca. 1200–800 BC.

782 Ortiz, Lenin. Pasado antigua del Ecuador: evolución social. Quito: Consejo Provincial de Pichincha: Publitécnica, 1981. 246 p., 4 folded leaves of plates: bibl., ill., index, maps.

Divides Ecuadorian prehistory into four periods on the basis of modes of production: 1) Hunting, fishing, and gathering; 2) Agricultural; 3) Surplus agricultural; and 4) Commercial agricultural. The principal subsistence resources, social and ideological characteristics, and technological achievements are summarized for cultures assigned to each period. Prepared for student use, this volume is most valuable for 221 plates illustrating pottery, stone, and metal objects.

783 Parsons, James J. and Roy Shiemon. Nuevo informe sobre los campos elevados prehistóricos de la Cuenca del Guayas, Ecuador (Miscelánea Antropológica Ecuatoriana [Guayaquil] 2:2, 1982, p. 31–37, bibl., ill.)

Additional information on the location and density of earth platforms and ridged fields in the Guayas basin based on study of air photographs.

784 Porras Garcés, Pedro I. Arqueología: Palenque, Los Ríos, La Ponga, Guayas. Auxiliares, Patricio Moncayo E. y Luis Zúñiga P. Quito: Centro de Investigaciones Arqueológicas, Pontificia Univ. Católica del Ecuador (PUCE), 1983. 238 p.: bibl., ill.

Description of excavations and artifacts from two coastal sites. Palenque is a complex of artificial mounds; comparative

analysis of the pottery indicates closest affiliations with the Guayaquil Phase of the Regional Developmental period. La Ponga, in the Valdivia Valley, is assigned to the Machalilla tradition on the basis of ceramic evidence. C14 dates of 1000 and 890 BC were obtained.

785 ——. Arte rupestre del Alto Napo, Valle del Misagualli, Ecuador. Quito: s.n., 1985. 393 p.: bibl., ill.

Description, classification, and interpretation of petroglyphs on boulders in the vicinity of the Río Misagualli between Cotundo and Tena. Four styles are recognized: "matchstick," outline, abstract, and representational or naturalistic. Tables present the frequencies of styles, substyles, and transitional forms. Evolutionary elaborations are suggested. The styles are estimated to be of different ages: respectively dating prior to 300 BC, 300 BC to AD 300, AD 300 to 1200, and post AD 1200. Abundant illustrations permit evaluating the author's interpretations.

786 ——. Petroglifos del Alto Napo. Guayaquil, Ecuador: Edición Huancavilca, 1983. 1 v. (unpaged): ill., map.

Illustrations of spirals, anthropomorphic figures, and miscellaneous other petroglyphs from the valley of the Misagualí, a left-bank tributary of the upper Napo.

787 Reinoso Hermida, Gustavo. El periódico precerámico de la costa ecuatoriana (CCE/RA, 7, nov. 1981, p. 144–175, bibl., ill., photos)

Detailed description of the Vegas complex based on excavations by Stothert, followed by brief references to other preceramic remains from the Santa Elena peninsula.

788 Salazar, Ernesto. Cazadores recolectores del antiguo Ecuador. Quito: Banco Central del Ecuador, 1984. 100 p.: bibl., ill. (Serie Nuestro pasado. Guía didáctica; no. 1)

Review of Paleo-Indian and Archaic complexes designed for the layman, prepared in conjunction with an exhibition at the Museo del Banco Central in Cuenca.

789 Salomon, Frank and Clark Erickson. Tulipe, un recinto sagrado en la montaña ecuatoriana (Antropología Ecuatoriana [Casa de la Cultura Ecuatoriana, Quito] 2/3, 1983/1984, p. 57–78, ill., map)

Description of platform mounds and sunken plazas some 40 km north of Quito and speculations about their function and possible affiliation with the Yumbos.

790 Stothert, Karen E. Review of the early preceramic complexes of the Santa Elena Peninsula, Ecuador (SAA/AA, 48:1, Jan. 1983, p. 122–127, bibl., map)

Among four preceramic complexes defined by Lanning, only the Vegas complex can be confirmed. The others were based on misinterpreted evidence.

791 Temme, Mathilde. Excavaciones en el sitio precerámico de Cubilan (Miscelánea Antropológica Ecuatoriana [Guayaquil] 2:2, 1983, p. 135–164, bibl., ill.)

Excavations at two sites on the headwaters of the Río Oña, tributary of the Río Jubones, at 3100 m elevation produced percussion-flaked tools, including projectile points with contracting stems. Two C14 dates for each site are nearly identical: 10,500 and 10,300 BP for Cu 27 and 9100 and 9160 BP for Cu 26.

792 Wurster, Wolfgang W. Zur Rekonstruktion von Rundbauten auf der Rampenpyramiden von Cochasquí, Ecuador (Allgemeine und Vergleichende Archäologie Beitrage [München, FRG] 2, 1980, p. 459–486, ill.)

Excavations on the summit of a rectangular platform mound revealed evidence of two circular buildings of perishable construction, with clay floors and clay-plastered walls and central posts. A pottery vessel from the north highlands shows a similar structure. Associated lithic debris suggests function as elite dwellings.

THE GUIANAS

793 Boomert, Aad. The Saladoid occupation of Wonotobo Falls, western Surinam (in International Congress for the Study of the Pre-Columbian Cultures of the Lesser Antilles, 9th, Santo Domingo, 1981. Proceedings [see item **258**] p. 97–120, bibl., ill., map)

Description of pottery representing the Saladoid tradition with a C14 date of 1900 BP, which constitutes the easternmost known occurrence of this tradition on the South American continent.

794 ——. The Taruma Phase of southern Suriname (Archaeology and Anthropology [Journal of the Walter Roth Museum of Archaeology and Anthropology [Georgetown] 4:1/2, 1981 [i.e. 1985] p. 104–157, bibl., ill., map)

Detailed review of historical information on indigenous populations of the upper Corantijn and Essequibo regions precedes descriptions of five forest and 13 savanna sites with Taruma Phase pottery. Discusses relations with the Guyana complex described by Meggers and Evans and complexes from the Parú savanna of adjacent Brazil described by Frikel. Characteristics of stone alignments from the Guianas region are analyzed and considered too diverse to belong to a single tradition. An origin for the Taruma on the lower Río Negro is accepted.

795 Dubelaar, C.N. Petroglyphs in Suriname: a survey (Archaeology and Anthropology [Journal of the Walter Roth Museum of Archaeology and Anthropology, Georgetown] 4:1/2, 1981 [i.e. 1985], p. 65–80, bibl., ill.)

Describes petroglyphs from 25 locations, the majority along the Corantyn River.

796 Petitjean-Roget, Hugues. Evolution et décadence de l'art funéraire des sites pré et post-colombiens de la baie de l'Oyapock (in International Congress for the Study of the Pre-Columbian Cultures of the Lesser Antilles, 9th, Santo Domingo, 1981. Proceedings [see item **258**] p. 183–199, bibl., ill.)

Comparison of funerary urns from two precontact and three postcontact cemetery sites of the Aristé Phase shows a decline in the frequency of anthropomorphic vessels and a simplication of the body contours after European contact.

797 Toutouri, Christian. La roche gravée de l'Inipi, Guyana Française (in International Congress for the Study of the Pre-Columbian Cultures of the Lesser Antilles, 9th, Santo Domingo, 1981. Proceedings [see item **258**] p. 363–374, bibl., ill., map)

Description of biomorphic petroglyphs 186 km south of Cayenne and a myth explaining their origin.

798 Williams, Denis. Excavation of the Barabina shell mound northwest district: an interim report (Archaeology and Anthropology [Journal of the Walter Roth

Museum of Archaeology and Anthropology, Georgetown] 4:1/2, 1981 [i.e. 1985] p. 13–34, bibl., ill., table)

History of investigations at Barabina shell mound and description of faunal remains, artifacts, and burials from two excavations by the author. Lithics correspond to the Alaka Phase inventory, but the only pottery was of Mabaruma Phase types in a disturbed context. C14 dates of 4115 ± 50 (SI-4332) and 5960 ± 50 (SI-4333) are consistent with the cultural information.

799 ———. Three sites of the Taruma Phase in southeast and east Guyana (Archaeology and Anthropology [Journal of the Walter Roth Museum of Archaeology and Anthropology, Georgetown] 4:1/2, 1981 [i.e. 1985] p. 81–103, bibl., ill., tables)

Investigations at three locations permit elaborating the previous descriptions of pottery types and stone implements of the Taruma Phase. The sites seriate in the upper third of the Meggers-Evans sequence.

PERU

800 Benavides Calle, Mario. Carácter del Estado wari. Ayacucho, Perú: Univ. Nacional de San Cristóbal de Huamanga, 1984. 194 p.: appendices, bibl., ill.

Evidence obtained during 1977 excavations in the Cheqo Wasi sector in the center of Wari is described as a basis for reconstructing the development of the Wari state and tracing its expansion and decline.

801 Bonavia, Duccio. El complejo Chivateros: una aproximación tecnológica (PEMN/R, 46, 1982 [i.e. 1984] p. 19–37, bibl., ill.)

Presents evidence that the Chivateros site is a quarry and workshop; all the "artifacts" are preforms of waste flakes.

802 ———. Los Gavilanes: mar, desierto y oasis en la historia del hombre precerámico peruano. Con la colaboración de Ramiro Castro de la Mata et al. Lima: Corporación Financiera de Desarrollo, Oficina de Asuntos Culturales: Instituto Arqueológico Alemán, Comisión de Arqueología General y Comparada, 1982. 512 p., 5 folded leaves of plates: bibl., ill., index.

Five C14 dates place occupation of Los Gavilanes in the Huarmey Valley between 2200 and 1300 BC. Lithics, textiles, wood, bone, and shell artifacts are described, as well as remains of cultivated maize, cotton and beans, and fauna. A long and critical review of information from the principal late preceramic sites provides a basis for assessing the origins of agriculture and attributing specialized function to Los Gavilanes.

803 Bonnier, Elizabeth. Piruru: nuevas evidencias de ocupación temprana en Tantamayo, Perú (Gaceta Arqueológica Andina [Instituto Andino de Estudios Arqueológicas, Lima] 2:8, nov. 1983, p. 8–10, ill., map)

Three sequential phases characterized by different forms and techniques of construction are identified and assigned to preceramic and early Formative occupations.

804 Bueno Mendoza, Alberto. Arquitectura y sociedad prechavín en los Andes Centrales (Boletín de Antropología Americana [Instituto Panamericano de Geografía e Historia, México] 6, dic. 1982, p. 119–140, bibl., ill.)

Review of evidence for permanent settlement places the transition to semisedentary life between 7000–5000 BP. The first monumental constructions, ca. 3500 BP, incorporate U-shaped platforms characteristic of later Chavín centers. Sociopolitical and religious implications of the locations and compositions of structures are discussed.

805 Burger, Richard L. Archaeological areas and prehistoric frontiers: the case of Formative Peru and Ecuador (in International Congress of Americanists, 44th, Manchester, 1982. Proceedings. Oxford, England: British Archaeological Reports, 1984, p. 33–71, bibl., maps [BAR international series; 194])

Presents evidence that a cultural frontier existed in the vicinity of the modern international boundary as far back as the Peruvian Early Horizon, corresponding to the Ecuadorian Late Formative.

806 Campana D., Cristóbal. La vivienda mochica. Trujillo, Perú: Varese, 1983. 72 p.: bibl., ill.

Architect discusses Mochica domestic structures in terms of architecture, function, material, climatization, spatial organization, and context, drawing on pottery models and archaeological sites, and traces survivals among modern peasant dwellings in the region.

807 Cuesta Domingo, Mariano. Arqueología andina, Perú. Madrid: Ministerio de Cultura, Dirección General del Patrimonio Artístico, Archivos y Museos, 1980. 444 p.: bibl., ill. (some col.)

Chronological overview of principal Peruvian cultures emphasizing specimens in the Museo de América de Madrid, acquired principally from 1771–1934. Most useful for illustrations of pottery, stone, metal, and textiles from the collections.

808 Current archaeological projects in the Central Andes: some approaches and results. Edited by Ann Kendall. Oxford, England: British Archaeological Reports, 1984. 375 p.: bibl., ill., maps (BAR international series; 210)

Consists of 15 articles that discuss data, especially settlement pattern, from ongoing projects in the Lurín valley (Feltham), Carahuarazo valley (Schreiber), Chicha-Soras valley (Meddens), Huari urban prehistory (Isbell); the Inca sites of Cochabamba (Schjellerup), Ollantaytambo (Gibajade Valencia), towns near Cusco (Gonzales Corrales, Niles); and aspects of the Cusichaca project (Kendall, Hey, Lunt, Keeley, Drew).

809 D'Altroy, Terence N. and **Christine A. Hastorf.** The distribution and contents of Inca state storehouses in the Xauxa region of Peru (SAA/AA, 49:2, April 1984, p. 334–349, ill., tables)

Excavations and flotation sampling from six storehouses revealed evidence of all major highland crops and predominantly Inca pottery, inferred as storage jars. Absence of evidence of manufactured goods is attributed to poor conditions for preservation.

810 ——— and Timothy K. Earle. Staple finance, wealth finance, and storage in the Inka political economy (UC/CA, 26, 1985, p. 187–206, bibl.)

The development and functioning of the Inca state economy are examined by distinguishing staple finance (direct mobilization of food and utilitarian goods) from wealth finance (manufacture and procurement of valuables). The former buffers variable supply and demand, whereas the latter integrates managerial personnel. By mixing

the two concepts, the Inca achieved the flexibility necessary for extending the empire and meeting disparate economic requirements.

811 Davidson, Judith R. El Spondylus en la cosmología chimú (PEMN/R, 45, 1981 [i.e. 1983] p. 75–88, bibl., ill.)

After reviewing the ethnohistorical evidence for the importance of Spondylus in Andean cosmology, author suggests four characteristics responsible for its prominence. Two (alteration between edibility and toxicity, and difference in size and function of the valves) objectified the dualities (male/female, life/death, human/god) basic to Chimú myth and ritual in a unique and obvious fashion.

812 Dillehay, Tom D. and **Patricia J. Netherly.** Exploring the upper Zaña Valley in Peru (AIA/A, 36:4, July/Aug. 1983, p. 22–30, ill.)

Human settlement from early preceramic to Inca times, reveals changes in intensity of exploitation of the various habitats, ranging from desert to tropical forest. Access to local tropical forest products has bearing on hypotheses of Amazonian influences on coastal Peruvian cultures.

813 Donnan, Christopher B. Ancient murals from Chornancap, Peru (AIA/A, 37:3, May/June 1984, p. 32–37, ill.)

Remarkably preserved polychrome murals on the wall of a courtyard at Chornancap in the lower Lambayeque valley depict human figures, trophy heads, anthropomorphized birds, plants, and other elements. Similarities to depictions on textiles from Pacatnamu indicate common origin. Both date between AD 600–900.

814 ———. La caza del venado en el arte mochica (PEMN/R, 46, 1982 [i.e. 1984] p. 235–251, bibl., ill.)

A sample of 120,000 designs in the "Moche Archive" includes 53 scenes of deer hunting. Analysis of the iconography suggests they are ritual rather than secular activities.

815 Early ceremonial architecture in the Andes: a conference at Dumbarton Oaks, 26 and 27 October 1982. Christopher B. Donnan, editor. Washington: Dumbarton Oaks Research Library and Collection, 1985. 289 p.: bibl.

The widespread occurrence of substantial ceremonial structures during the Initial Period, beginning about 3000 BC, undercuts previous views of Chavín as the earliest significant Andean religious development. Chapters describe early architecture at Huaca La Florida, La Galgada, Huaricoto, Huaca Los Reyes, Cerro Sechín, and in the Cajamarca and Jequetepeque valleys, and discuss their implications for subsistence, social organization, ideology, and the development of Andean civilization. A useful synthesis of data that has forced abandonment of the traditional view of Chavín as the basis for Peruvian civilization.

816 Epstein, S.M. The prehistoric copper smelting industry at Cerro de los Cementerios, Peru: analysis of the product (MASCA Journal [Museum Applied Science Center for Archaeology, Univ. Museum, Univ. of Pennsylvania, Philadelphia] 2, 1982, p. 58–62, bibl., ill.)

Excavation of 24 of more than 100 smelting furnaces permits reconstructing precolumbian methods. Composition of prills and ingots is consistent with smelting of local oxide ores and addition of arsenic in the form of imported sulfide ores in a pyritic smelting process.

817 Erickson, Clark L. Los waru-waru de Huatta, Puno (Gaceta Arqueológicas Andina [Instituto Andino de Estudios Arqueológicos, Lima] 2:7, agosto 1983, p. 4–5, ill., map)

Experimental cultivation of precolumbian ridged fields northwest of Lake Titicaca demonstrated their potential productivity with relatively low labor input.

818 Farrington, I.S. Un entendimiento de sistemas de riego prehistórico en Perú (III/AI, 40:4, 1980, p. 691–711, bibl., graphs, tables)

Applying principles of hydrology to open canals in the Moche and Cusichaca valleys establishes that the precolumbian engineers employed the concepts of velocity and discharge in designing methods of delivering water in the amounts necessary for successful agriculture.

819 Fleming, S.J.; W.T. Miller; and J.L. Brahin. The mummies of Pachacamac, Peru (MASCA Journal [Museum Applied Science Center for Archaeology, Univ. Museum, Univ. of Pennsylvania, Philadelphia] 2, 1983, p. 138–156, bibl., ill.)

The career of Max Uhle and the history of Pachacamac are summarized as background to technical studies on two mummy bundles in the Univ. Museum's Uhle collection. X-ray revealed one to contain a female about age 12 who died from brain disease and the other to contain a sacrificed (by decapitation) child about a year old. Ethnohistoric data pertinent to interpretation are reviewed.

820 Fung Pineda, Rosa. Sobre el origen selvático de la civilización Chavín (CAAAP/AP, 4:8, enero 1983, p. 77–92, bibl.)

Supports Tello's hypothesis of an "Amazonian" origin of Chavín and accepts Lathrap's "evidence" in confirmation.

821 Gibaja O., Arminda. Excavaciones en Ollantaytambo, Cusco (Gaceta Arqueológicos Andina [Instituto Andino de Estudios Arqueológicos, Lima] 3:9, marzo 1984, p. 4–5, ill.)

Identifies the loci of stabilization and restoration conducted since 1981.

822 González Carré, Enrique. Historia prehispánica de Ayacucho. Ayacucho, Perú: Univ. Nacional de San Cristóbal de Huamanga, 1982. 174 p.: bibl., ill.

Synthesis of cultural development in Ayacucho from Paleo-Indian to Inca times, directed toward interested layman, particularly Peruvians, concerned with knowing their antecedents.

823 ———; Jorge Cosmópolis A.; and Jorge Levano P. La ciudad inca de Vilcashuamán. Ayacucho, Perú: Univ. Nacional de San Cristóbal de Huamanga, 1981. 85 p., 31 leaves of plates (some folded): bibl., ill.

Investigations from 1977–80 at Vilcashuamán, south of Ayacucho, defined the extent and composition of the Inca city and identified important buildings, permitting production of a tentative map and recommendations for conservation. Liberally illustrated with plans showing present and reconstructed appearances of sectors and structures.

Helms, Mary W. Precious metals and politics: style and ideology in the Intermediate Area and Peru. See item **558.**

824 Hemming, John. Monuments of the Incas. Photographs by Edward Ranney. Boston: Little, Brown, 1982. 228 p.: bibl., ill., index (A New York Graphic Society book)

Magnificent photographs of Inca buildings, architectural details, and landscapes, accompanied by plans and an informative text. Lesser known sites are included, as well as Sacsahuaman, Machu Picchu, Pisac, and Ollantaytambo.

825 Hocquenghem, Anne-Marie. Les cerfs et les morts dans l'iconographie Mochica (SA/J, 69, 1983, p. 71–83, bibl., ill.)

Mythology, rituals, and traditions of recent Andean agriculturalists provide clues to interpreting scenes involving deer, implying considerable antiquity for the ritual calendar and permitting speculations on its function.

826 Hurtado de Mendoza, Luis. Patrones prehispánicos de uso de diversos tipos de piedra en la región del Río Cunas, Huancayo (PEMN/R, 46, 1982 [i.e. 1984] p. 39–53, bibl., map, tables)

Differences in frequency of use of eight types of raw material characterize the cultural sequence, permitting assignment of chronological positions to archaeological sites. Discusses method of quantification of data and problems of analysis.

827 ——— and Carlos Chahud Gutiérrez. Algunos datos adicionales acerca del sitio Callavallauri: Abrigo Rocoso No. 1 de Tschopik (Guaman-Poma [Centro de Investigación de Ciencias Sociales, Económicas, Administrativas y Humanidades, Univ. Nacional del Centro del Perú, Huancayo] 2, 1983, p. 9–33, bibl.)

Compositions of four surface collections, representing the interior of the rock shelter, adjacent slope, terraces above and below the shelter, are compared, providing a relative chronology from preceramic to Late Horizon. Dimensions of land mollusca, which correlate with ambient temperature, indicate that the preceramic occupation occurred when the climate was cooler than today.

828 Illescas Cook, Guillermo. El Candelabro de Paracas y la Cruz del Sur. Lima: Talleres Garcilaso, 1982. 88 p.: bibl., ill. (some col.).

Argues that the geoglyph in the form of a candelabra on the slope facing the sea represents the constellation known as the Southern Cross.

829 Kauffmann Doig, Federico. Pucullo y figures antropomorfas de madera en el Antisuyo (Cielo Abierto [Lima] 10:29, julio/sept. 1984, p. 45–52, bibl., ill.)

Description of cylindrical towers in a rock shelf near Pajatén, tropical highlands of north Peru, one of them ornamented by six wooden human figures averaging 60 cm tall, hanging from roof projections, also of wood. Inca pottery was encountered.

830 Keatinge, Richard W. and Geoffrey W. Conrad. Imperialist expansion in Peruvian prehistory: Chimu administration of a conquered territory (AFA/JFA, 10, 1983, p. 254–283, ill., bibl.)

Incorporation of the Jequetepeque Valley into the Chimu Empire is attested by the intrusive administrative centers, Farfán and Talambo, which channeled tribute and labor to the capital at Chan Chan in the Moche Valley.

831 Kendall, Ann. Middle stages of the Cusichaca archaeological project, Peru (Bulletin [Institute of Archaeology, Univ. of London] 20, 1983, p. 43–71, ill.)

Summary of goals, methods, and progress of long-term archaeological investigations of Inca and Late Intermediate period sites in the region between Machu Picchu and Ollantaytambo.

832 Lavallée, Danièle and Michèle Julien. Asto: curacazgo prehispánico de los Andes Centrales. Lima: Instituto de Estudios Peruanos, 1983. 150 p.: bibl., ill., map.

Characteristics of settlements, habitations, subsistence, technology, and other archaeological evidence are employed to reconstruct the demography and social aspects of a Late period chiefdom in the Vilca-Mantaro basin.

833 ———; ———; and Jane Wheeler. Telarmachay: niveles precerámicos de ocupación (PEMN/R, 46, 1982 [i.e. 1984] p. 55–133, bibl., ill,. tables)

Excavations from 1975–80 permitted distinguishing six preceramic levels dating from about 7000 to 1700 BC. Stratigraphy, faunal remains, lithics, and other evidence are summarized; periods of occupation are tentatively correlated with climatic changes.

Appendix provides functional analysis of lithic artifacts from Level IV.

834 Lechtman, Heather. Andean value systems and the development of prehistoric metallurgy (Technology and Culture [i.e. Society for the History of Technology, Detroit, Mich.] 25, 1984, p. 1–36, bibl., ill.)

In contrast to significant uses of metal in the Old World for warfare and transport, their role in the Andes was primarily symbolic of status, power, ideology, and ritual. Emphasis was placed on color, encouraging development of techniques for alloying, depletion, and enrichment based on gold and silver.

835 ———. Pre-columbian surface metallurgy (SA, 250:6, June 1984, p. 56–63, ill.)

Description of the techniques of electrochemical replacement and depletion gilding used in Peru as early as the second millennium BC to produce objects appearing to be gold but actually copper of copper-rich alloys.

836 McEwan, Gordon. Investigaciones en la cuenca del Lucre, Cusco (Gaceta Arqueológica Andina [Instituto Andino de Estudios Arqueológicas, Lima] 3:9, marzo 1984, p. 12–15, bibl., ill.)

Distinct ceramic styles imply at least two local groups in the Cuzco Valley at the time of Wari occupation; their influence can be discerned on Inca pottery.

837 ———. Investigaciones en Pikillaqta: una ocupación Wari en el Cusco (Gaceta Arqueológica Andina [Instituto Andino de Estudios Arqueológicas, Lima] 2:8, nov. 1983, p. 4–5, ill.)

Summary of characteristics of an urban center constructed and occupied between AD 600 and 900.

838 MacNeish, Richard S. et al. Prehistory of the Ayacucho Basin, Peru. v. 4, The preceramic way of life. Ann Arbor: Univ. of Michigan Press for the Robert S. Peabody Foundation for Archaeology, 1983. 300 p.: bibl., ill.

The data presented in vols. 1–3 are assembled into chronological records of adaptation to the Puna, Humid Woodland, Thorn Forest Scrub, and Thorn Forest Riverine ecological zones. Activity areas are identified by occupation layers and their assemblages used to infer band size, duration of occupation, subsistence, seasonality, and probable activities. Floor plots show the locations of every object. The final chapter converts the data into energy-flow systems for each phase, which reveal a steady reduction in leisure with increasing cultural complexity. This pioneering effort to reveal the process of cultural change should be consulted by everyone concerned with its explanation.

839 Moseley, Michael E. The good old days were better: agrarian collapse and tectonics (AAA/AA, 85:4, 1983, p. 773–799, bibl., maps)

Slow elevation of the Peruvian coast altered drainage conditions, which changed the slopes of irrigation channels and destroyed the subsistence basis for the societies dependent upon them. The evidence from Chan Chan of expansion and collapse becomes intelligible in this context.

840 ———. Patterns of settlement and preservation in the Virú and Moche Valleys (in Prehistoric settlement patterns [see item 325] p. 423–442)

The archaeological record on the north coast of Peru is distorted by landscape remodelling resulting from tectonic uplift, sea-level changes, and El Niño episodes, which have destroyed sites, altered the area and characteristics of the land available for exploitation and led to erroneous interpretations of precolumbian cultural development.

841 ———; Robert A. Feldman; Charles R. Ortloff; and Alfredo Narvaez. Principles of agrarian collapse in the Cordillera Negra, Peru (Annals of the Carnegie Museum [Pittsburgh, Pa.] 52, 1983, p. 299–327, bibl., ill.)

Continental uplift combined with erosional downcutting during the past 1000 years are responsible for reduction of land under cultivation by 35–40 percent by altering the topography so as to decrease the scope of irrigation. Data from the Moche Valley document this process.

842 Mujica B., Elías. Cerro Arena-Layzon: relaciones costa-sierra en el norte del Perú (Gaceta Arqueológico Andina [Instituto Andino de Estudios Arqueológicas, Lima] 3:10, junio 1984, p. 12–13, 15, bibl., ill.)

Atypical pottery from a late Formative site in the Moche Valley, excavated in 1973, is derived from the Layzón period occupation of the Cajamarca Valley.

843 Mulvany de Peñaloza, Eleonora. Motivos fitomorfos de alucinógenos en Chavín (UN/C, 11, agosto 1984, p. 57–80, bibl., ill.)

Representations on the Tello Obelisk are identified as three genera of plants with hallucinogenic properties, which are still used by indigenous groups. Similarities between representations in Chavín art and visions experienced during use of these drugs suggests a relationship.

844 Negro, Sandra. Uquira: arquitectura Tawantinsuyo en la costa central del Perú (USP/RA, 26, 1983, p. 129–150, bibl., ill., map)

An Inca administrative center on the lower Río Onas exemplifies adoption of local architectural elements and building materials while conserving the Inca composition and arrangement of structures.

845 Netherly, Patricia J. The management of late Andean irrigation systems of the north coast of Peru (SAA/AA, 49:2, April 1984, p. 227–254, bibl., maps, table)

Documentary evidence and field investigations indicate that the irrigation systems of Lambayeque and La Leche valleys were maintained by sociopolitical groups occupying levels in the hierarchy corresponding to the size of the canal they administered, rather than by the centralized state bureaucracy. This has implications for assessing the efficiency and equity of water distribution and the role of irrigation as a prime mover for development of the state.

846 Oehm, Victor P. Investigaciones sobre minería y metalurgia en el Perú prehispánico: una visión actualizada. Bonn: Univ. Bonn, 1984. 107 p.: bibl., ill., maps, tables (Bonner Amerikanistische Studien; 12)

Compilation on information from literary sources on geological evidence for presence of gold, silver, copper, tin, arsenic, antimony, and zinc; precolumbian sites of extraction; processing sites; and results of analytic studies. Tables summarize principal additional elements in objects with primary compositions of gold, silver, and copper.

847 Pereyra Parra, A.; E. López Carranza; and Danièle Lavallée. Datación por termoluminiscencia de tiestos cerámicos antiguos provenientes de Telarmachay (IFEA/B, 11:1/2, 1982, p. 91–95, tables)

TL results from four samples agreed with C14 determinations, whereas two gave younger results than expected.

848 Peruvian antiquities: a manual for United States Customs. Washington: Dept. of Cultural Affairs, OAS, 1983. 74 p.: ill.

Prepared in conjunction with an exhibition of examples from a collection illicitly brought to the US and returned to Peru, this manual endeavors to provide information useful to US Customs agents in recognizing precolumbian objects. Chapters discussing aspects of Peruvian cultures are illustrated with examples of the artifacts.

849 Petersen G., Georg. Evolución y desaparición de las altas culturas Paracas-Cahuachi, Nasca. Lima: Univ. Nacional Federico Villarreal, Dirección Universitaria de Investigación, 1980. 86 p.: bibl., ill.

Reconstruction of cultural development in the Nasca region from Paracas-Cahuachi to Inca periods, supplemented by tables listing sites by period.

850 Prehistoric Andean ecology: man, settlement and environment in the Andes. v. 3, Stone typology. v. 4, Chilca. Edited by Frédéric André Engel. New York: Hunter College of the CUNY, 1983. 2 v. (185, 183 p.): bibl., ill., photos.

Vol. 3 consists of three parts: pt. 1 discusses typology and taxonomy of flaked stone artifacts; pt. 2 describes and compares fishhooks and other devices; pt. 3 provides plans, photographs, and brief descriptions of three Inca sites on the west slope: Huaytara, Incahuasi, and Tambo Colorado. Extensive illustration of artifacts makes this volume an important reference. Vol. 4 provides catalog of sites near streams in four sectors of the Chilca Valley, increasing in aridity from the rainy highlands to the dry lower valley; lists of C14 dates, plants collected, pollen identified; a complex analytical chart of ceramics, and numerous plans and photographs of structures and features. A brief introduction offers the observation that population density was considerably higher during several periods than can be sustained today. The final section provides the atlas of archaeological sites in Sector II, Pisco to Lurín.

851 **Quilter, Jeffrey** and **Terry Stocker.** Subsistence economies and the origins of Andean complex societies (AAA/AA, 85, 1983, p. 545–562, bibl.)

Argues that the combination of seafood and domesticated plants, rather than the primacy of either resource, permitted the development of complex societies by the late preceramic period on the Peruvian coast.

852 **Ravines, Rogger.** Arqueología del Valle Medio del Jequetepeque. Colaboradores: César Alva Velásquez *et al.* Lima: Proyecto de Rescate Arqueológico Jequetepeque, 1983. 225 p.: ill. (Materiales para la arqueología del Perú; 2)

Profiles of excavations, plans of structures, details of ceramics and other artifacts from 17 of 645 recorded sites impacted by expansion and irrigation. Irrigation canals of Chimú-Inca date and associated fields between Tembladera and Montegrande are also reported with profiles, dimensions, and other details.

853 ——. Prácticas funerarias en Ancón (PEMN/R, 45, 1981 [i.e. 1983] p. 89–166, bibl., ill.)

Pt. 2 of detailed description of burials (for pt. 1, see *HLAS 43:793*) including 21 tombs of Epochs B-D. Conclusion summarizes changes and continuities from preceramic to Inca times.

854 ——; **Helen Engelstad; Victoria Palomino;** and **Daniel H. Sandweiss.** Materiales arqueológicos de la Garagay (PEMN/R, 46, 1982 [i.e. 1984] p. 135–233, bibl., ill., tables)

Four periods are defined, extending from about 1500 to 600 BC. Pottery, textiles, plant remains, and molluscs are described in detail. The site is the largest monumental complex in the Rímac Valley.

855 **Reinhard, Johan.** Las líneas de Nazca, montañas y fertilidad (Boletín de Lima, 26, 1983, p. 29–50, bibl., ill., map)

Proposes the hypothesis that the geoglyphs of the Nazca plain are associated with worship of mountains, the source of water for agriculture, and thus with insuring the fertility of crops.

856 **Richardson, James B., III.** The Chira beach ridges, sea level change, and the origins of maritime economies on the Peruvian coast (Annals of the Carnegie Museum [Pittsburgh, Pa.] 52, 1983, p. 265–276, bibl., ill.)

Stabilization of sea level and a change in ocean currents about 5000 BP enriched marine food resources, enabling the subsequent rise of complex preceramic maritime societies.

857 **Rick, John W.** Cronología, clima y subsistencia en el precerámico peruano. Lima: Instituto Andino de Estudios Arqueológicos, 1983. 208 p.: bibl., ill. (Biblioteca mínima INDEA. América andina; 1)

Following a review of sites assigned dates prior to about 4000 BC and of evidence for climatic alterations subsequent to 10,000 years ago, Rick presents his thesis for sedentary occupation rather than transhumance in the central puna. Support comes from his investigations in the punas of Junín (see *HLAS 43:796*), which imply an equilibrium adaptation by early hunter-gatherers exploiting wild vicuña.

858 **Sandweiss, Daniel H.; Harold B. Rollins;** and **James B. Richardson III.** Landscape alteration and prehistoric human occupation on the north coast of Peru (Annals of the Carnegie Museum [Pittsburgh, Pa.] 52, 1983, p. 277–298, bibl., ill.)

Major episodes of tectonic uplift about 5000 and 4000 BP must be incorporated into explanations of changing human adaptation on the north Peruvian coast.

859 **Scholten de D'Ebneth, María.** Chavín de Huantar. v. 2, Piedras esculpidas. v. 3, Observatorio? Lima: Editorial Juan Mejía Baca, 1982. 2 v.: bibl., ill., plans.

Vol. 2 provides calculations and diagrams to support thesis that structures and sculptures at Chavín de Huántar employ a unit of measurement based on the "Unidad Americana." Different mathematical ratios permit distinguishing early and late periods. Vol. 3 presents arguments for the function of the "dwellings" on the terrace of the principal temple at Chavín as astronomical observatories and the importance of the Pleiades in the cosmology.

860 **Shimada, Izumi; Stephen Epstein;** and **Alan K. Craig.** The metallurgical process of ancient north Peru (AIA/A, 36:5, Sept./Oct. 1983, p. 38–45, ill.)

Description of smelting process reconstructed from archaeological features and artifacts in excavations at Cerro de los Cementerios. Primary copper source was within three km, but arsenic-sulfide ore seems to have been imported from the north highlands. Social and political inferences are drawn (see items **816** and **861**).

861 Shimada, Melody and **Izumi Shimada.** Explotación y manejo de los recursos naturales en Pampa Grande, sitio Moche V: significado del análisis orgánico (PEMN/R, 45, 1981 [i.e. 1983] p. 19–73, bibl., ill.)

Assemblages of organic remains from deposits least likely to be distorted are compared with their archaeological contexts to reconstruct production, storage, and distribution of goods and food. Reviews social, economic, and political implications of the pattern.

862 —— and ——. Prehistoric llama breeding and herding on the north coast of Peru (SAA/AA, 50, 1985, p. 3–26, bibl., ill.)

Presents ethnographic, archaeozoological, physiological, and ethnohistoric evidence for breeding llamas by AD 600 and perhaps earlier on the northern Peruvian coast.

863 Stierlin, Henri. Une nouvelle hypothèse sur les tracés géants du désert de Nazca, Pérou (SSA/B, 47, 1983, p. 45–59, bibl., ill.)

Departing from the high value placed on textiles and the immense length of threads required for constructing large pieces, author suggests the zig-zag lines of Nazca served as guides to produce threads of required lengths, and that the animals associated represent deities under whose protection the sacred textiles were placed.

864 ——. Nazca: la clé du mystère: le déchiffrement d'une énigme archéologique. Plans, cartes et dessins par José Conesa. Paris: Albin Michel, 1983. 258 p.: ill. (some col.), index.

Exposition of the thesis that the Nazca lines and figures were used in preparing the extremely long threads needed to produce the immense textiles employed for funerary bundles, and that the same religious symbolism is incorporated in both.

865 Terada, Kazuo. El formativo en el Valle de Cajamarca (Gaceta Arqueológica

Andina [Instituto Andino de Estudios Arqueológicos, Lima] 4/5, nov. 1982, p. 4–5, ill.)

The site of Layzón at 3200 m elevation produced platforms and carvings of mythical beings reminiscent of Chavín, indicating late Formative occupation.

866 Thomas, Mary Jean. The reconstruction and analysis of a Peruvian Middle Horizon tapestry fragment (Syracuse Scholar [An interdisciplinary journal of ideas, Syracuse Univ., Syracuse, NY] 4:2, Fall 1983, p. 25–54, graphs, ill., plate)

Systematic sequences of colors on a Wari textile in the Syracuse Univ. Art Collections imply that the existing fragment, measuring 1.27 by 1.60 m, was originally 3.89 m long. Technical details suggest a vertical loom and four weavers. Felines and staff-bearing deities are the repeated motifs.

867 Thompson, Donald E. Buildings are for people: speculations on the aesthetics and cultural impact of structures and their arrangement (*in* Prehistoric settlement patterns [see item **325**] p. 115–127, ill.)

The locations of large, densely compacted, stone-walled settlements on the summits of ridges in the upper Marañón and Huallaga drainages, occupied from about AD 900 to 1570, are evaluated in practical, social, political, and aesthetic perspectives.

868 Topic, Theresa L. and **John R. Topic.** Huamachuco archaeological project: preliminary report on the third season, June-August 1983. Peterborough, N.H.: Trent Univ., 1984. 94 p.: bibl., ill. (Occasional papers in anthropology; 1)

Describes contents of a Wari burial structure and Inca storage facilities at Cerro Amaru. The 200+ storerooms were designed to provide low humidity conditions for goods such as seed crops and higher humidity conditions suitable for storing tubers.

869 Wassén, S. Henry. Some notes on faked and copied ceramic so-called Paracas trophy head jars (EM/A, 1981/1982, p. 70–80, bibl., ill.)

Account of a 30-year "detective story" establishing the origins of falsified Paracas vessels, conducted by the author and Junius Bird.

870 Williams, Carlos and **José Pineda.** La arquitectura temprana en Cajamarca (Gaceta Arqueológica Andina [Instituto

Andino de Estudios Arqueológicos, Lima] 1 : 6 marzo 1983, p. 4–5, bibl., ill.)

Argues that large Formative period structures and the Cumbemayo artificial canal represent an integrated hydraulic-ceremonial system.

871 Wurster, Wolfgang W. Modelos arquitectónicos peruanos: ensayo de interpretación (PEMN/R, 46, 1982 [i.e. 1984] p. 253–266, bibl., ill.)

Illustrates pottery vessels and models showing dwellings and argues they provide a valuable supplement to information from archaeological sites and chronicles.

872 ———. Zur Interpretation von peruanischen Architekturmodellen (Beiträge zur Allgemeinen und Vergleichenden Archäologie [München, FRG] 3, 1981, p. 437–463, ill.)

House models in pottery from Chavín, Nazca, Mochica, Chancay, and Inca cultures are compared to assess concepts of space, variation in size, and forms of construction among these cultures. Symbolic elements and transfer to the pottery medium are distorting factors that must be considered. Function as architectural models is rejected.

VENEZUELA

873 Molina, Luis E. El área arqueológica de Sicarigua, Venezuela: investigaciones en curso (Boletín de Antropología Americana [Instituto Panamericano de Geografía e Historia, México] 5, julio 1982, p. 137–149, bibl.)

Excavations at a site estimated to date between AD 1000–1500, supplemented by ethnohistorical accounts, indicate sedentary agricultural (maize, manioc) and wild animal subsistence. Canals and reservoirs suggest irrigation may have been practiced; social stratification had not developed.

874 Nieves de Galicia, Fulvia. Ocupaciones ceramistas de la llanada barloventeña: consideraciones en torno de la investigación arqueológica de la costa centro-oriental de Venezuela (in International Congress for the Study of Pre-Columbian Cultures of the Lesser Antilles, 9th, Santo Domingo, 1981. Proceedings [see item 258] p. 131–144, bibl., map)

General discussion of environment

and ceramic complexes from eastern part of the state of Miranda.

875 Peñalver Gómez, Henriqueta. "Protectores genitales" de los pobladores precolombinos que habitaron la cuenca del Lago de Valencia, Venezuela (in International Congress for the Study of the Pre-Columbian Cultures of the Lesser Antilles, 9th, Santo Domingo, 1981. Proceedings [see item 258] p. 291–299, ill.)

Type and occurrence of snail shells used as genital coverings from two sites with C14 dates of 4500 and 350 BP.

876 Rouse, Irving. Diffusion and interaction in the Orinoco Valley and the coast (in International Congress for the Study of the Pre-Columbian Cultures of the Lesser Antilles, 9th, Santo Domingo, 1981. Proceedings [see item 258] p. 3–13, bibl., map)

Adjustment of author's earlier alignment of Barrancoid and Saladoid complexes to accomodate early C14 dates from the middle Orinoco, and speculations on mechanisms of dispersal.

877 Sanoja, Mario. Tipología de concheros precerámicos del noreste de Venezuela (in International Congress for the Study of the Pre-Columbian Cultures of the Lesser Antilles, 9th, Santo Domingo, 1981. Proceedings [see item 258] p. 15–26, bibl., ill.)

Two periods appear distinguishable: period 1 with lithic and period 2 with shell artifacts.

878 Toledo, María I. Revisión de la literatura arqueológica de la cuenca del Lago de Maracaibo (Boletín del Programa Arqueología de Rescate [Corpozulia, Univ. de Zulia, Maracaibo, Venezuela] 2 : 2, enero/dic. 1980, p. 11–56, bibl., tables)

Annotated bibliography and list of sites in the Lake Maracaibo basin, providing location, absolute and comparative dating, investigator, and publication.

879 Vargas Arenas, Iraida. Nuevas evidencias de sitios saladoides en la costa oriental de Venezuela, el sitio Playa Grande-S9 (in International Congress for the Study of the Pre-Columbian Cultures of the Lesser Antilles, 9th, Santo Domingo, 1981. Proceeding [see item 258] p. 57–71, bibl., ill.)

Excavations reveal two occupations, the earlier by shellfish gatherers lacking pottery and the later by representatives of the coastal Saladoid tradition.

880 Voorhies, Barbara; Erika Wagner; and Lillian Arvelo. Mora: un yacimiento arqueológico en el Bajo Delta del Orinoco, Venezuela (FSCN/A, 55, 1981, p. 31–50, bibl., ill., map)

Decorated sherds collected from a site in the Orinoco delta identify it as a late (AD 1000–1500) representative of the Barrancoid tradition.

881 Wagner, Erika. Arqueología de los Andes venezolanos: los páramos y la tierra fría (*in* El medio ambiente páramo. Editado por M.L. Salgado. Caracas: CEA-IVIC/UNESCO, 1979, p. 207–218, ill., map, tables)

Summary of subsistence, dwellings, commerce, ceramics, and cultural relationships of groups occupying the *tierra fría* zone of western Venezuela between AD 1000–1500.

882 ——. Los pobladores palafíticos de la cuenca de Maracaibo. Caracas: Lagoven, 1980. 68, 4 p.: bibl,. ill. (Cuadernos Lagoven. El Hombre y su ambiente)

Excavations on the east margin of Lake Maracaibo revealed remains of a pile village. Five C14 dates range from 480 to 210 BC. Modeled, incised, and punctated pottery decoration is affiliated with the Osoid tradition.

883 Zucchi, Alberta. Alternative interpretations of precolumbian water management in the western llanos of Venezuela (IAI/I, 9, 1984, p. 309–327, bibl., ill., map)

Natural levees, drainages, and other features of the topography may have been exploited similarly to artificially constructed ridges for agriculture. Features commonly considered causeways may have functioned instead as dikes in water management.

884 —— and Kay Tarble. Los Cedeñoides: un nuevo grupo prehispánico del Orinoco medio (AVAC/ACV, 35, 1984, p. 293–309, bibl., ill.)

The Cedeñoid series is proposed to accommodate pottery characterized by dried-clay pellet temper, incised and painted decoration, and diagnostic vessel shapes, reported from various sites on the middle Orinoco. C14 and TL dates extend from 1000 BC to AD 1400, making this series contemporary or antecedent to the Saladoid occupation.

885 —— and ——. Evolución y antigüedad de la alfarería con esponjilla en Agüerito: un yacimiento del Orinoco medio (AIA/I, 7, 1982, p. 183–199, bibl., ill.)

Analysis of stratigraphic changes in temper, form, and decoration suggests that sponge spicule temper may be earlier than previously assumed on the middle Orinoco, although C14 dates from the site are ambiguous.

886 ——; ——; and J. Eduardo Vaz. The ceramic sequence and new TL and C14 dates from the Agüerito site of the middle Orinoco, Venezuela (AFA/JFA, 11, 1984, p. 155–180, bibl., ill.)

Six stratigraphic excavations provide the basis for reconstructing habitation of the site and distinguishing four cultural components. The reliability of extremely early C14 dates for the initial component was evaluated using thermoluminescence. The results indicate they do not correspond to period 1, which equates with the Ronquin Sombra Phase, but the possibility exists that they represent a pre-Saladoid occupation.

ETHNOLOGY: Middle America

JOHN M. INGHAM, *Associate Professor of Anthropology, University of Minnesota*

SEVERAL ITEMS IN THE FOLLOWING review look at the history of Middle American anthropology. Medina and García Mora (item **976**) anthologize earlier papers on anthropological theory and indigenismo. In a perceptive book, Hewitt de Alcántara (item **940**) describes the emergence of historical structuralism, the dominant perspective among Mexican anthropologists in the 1970s and early 1980s. The assessment of the research by Northamerican scholars in *Heritage of conquest: thirty years later* (item **939**) is complementary. Several papers share the Mexicans' concern with regional and national political economy; many others exemplify an interest in symbols and meanings in local traditions. The various efforts at intellectual history, in fact, highlight the hiatus between political-economic and ideational approaches (see item **984**).

Both approaches have adherents although in recent years there are increasing signs of convergence between sociological and culturalist perspectives. Many scholars are using history to illuminate cultural patterns (items **902, 930, 937, 942, 973, 974, and 1001**). Some studies focus more explicitly on ritual and cosmology (items **895, 899, 907, 912, 933, 948, 956, 963, 982, 983, and 1002**), myth (items **901, 903, 962, and 991**), women's roles (items **892, 897, and 947a**), and illness and health care (items **890, 897, 904, 916, 921, 922, 936, 951, 954, 979, 999, and 1003**), although often indicating at least some concern with socioeconomic conditions. Studies of interethnic relations (items **888, 905, 906, 934, 980, and 983**) and political culture (item **951**) evince an even more explicit interest in the connection between expressive culture and economic and political relations. Some publications imply that the family is the mediating link between economic conditions and expressive culture (items **928, 947a, 957, 965, 989, 991, and 994**; see also *HLAS 45 : 1093*).

Two new journals will be of interest to Middle Americanists: *Mesoamérica* (Revista del Centro de Investigaciones Regionales de Mesoamérica, Guatemala) and *Mexican Studies/Estudios Mexicanos* (Univ. of California, Berkeley).

887 Acheson, James M. Limitations on firm size in a Tarascan pueblo (SAA/HO, 41 : 4, Winter 1982, p. 323–329, bibl., table)

Suggests that specialization in carpentry firms is influenced by internal and external transaction costs. Training unskilled labor, lack of supervisors and accounting skills, and irregular production increase internal costs; the structural position of Indian carpenters in the wider society increases external costs.

888 Aguilar, John L. Shame, acculturation and ethnic relations: a psychological "process of domination" in southern Mexico (Psychoanalytic Anthropology [s.n., s.l.] 5 : 2, Spring 1982, p. 155–171, bibl.)

Proposes that a sense of shame among Indians in highland Chiapas reinforces compliance with ladino demands and expectations, and suggests that in part shame represents an internalization of ladino racial attitudes.

889 ———. Trust and exchange: expressive and instrumental dimensions of reciprocity in a peasant community (Ethos [Univ. of California, Berkeley] 12 : 1, Spring 1984, p. 3–29, bibl.)

Intentional trust-making is seen as a rational response to widespread "psychologi-

cal distrust" in a biethnic community in the Chiapas highlands. Insightfully describes strategies of conflict avoidance and network building.

890 Alcorn, Janis B. Huastec Mayan ethnobotany. Austin: Univ. of Texas Press, 1984. 982 p.: appendix, bibl., ill., map, plates, tables.

Offers exceptionally rich material on cosmology, illness beliefs, shamanism, and subsistence patterns, with emphasis on plant-human interrelations. An appendix contains information on plant names and uses for 965 taxa.

891 Barba de Piña Chán, Beatriz. Notas de antropología e historia del Valle de Guadalupe, Jalisco. México: INAH, 1980. 122 p., 1 folded leaf of plates: bibl,. ill. (Estudios especiales de la Dirección General del INAH)

Brief ethnography of a criollo community in the highlands of Jalisco with notes on prehistory, demography, economy, and social organization.

892 Bossen, Laurel Herbenar. The redivision of labor: women and economic choice in four Guatemalan communities. Albany: SUNY Press, 1984. 396 p., 8 p. of plates: bibl., ill., index (SUNY series in the anthropology of work)

Purports to show that social equality between the sexes varies with economic equality and degree of integration into the market economy. Concludes that economic independence reinforces machismo among ladino men.

893 ———. Sexual stratification in Mesoamerica (in Heritage of conquest: thirty years later [see item 939] p. 35–71)

Reviews the literature on the position of women in Middle America as well as the author's work in Guatemala; concludes that macroeconomic changes are promoting sexual inequality.

894 **Brandes, Stanley.** Animal metaphors and social control in Tzintzuntzan (UP/E, 23 : 3, July 1984, p. 207–215, bibl.)

Describes use of animal terms to mark both the difference between culture and nature and social distance.

895 ———. The posadas in Tzintzuntzan: structure and sentiment in a Mexican Christmas festival (AFS/JAF, 96 : 381, July/ Sept. 1983, p. 259–280, bibl., plate)

Thorough description of Christmas festivities with discussion of cooperation, conflict, and disorderly conduct.

896 **Bricker, Victoria R.** The meaning of masking in San Pedro Chenalho (in The power of symbols: masks and masquerade in the Americas [see item 975] p. 111–115)

Argues that the content of Chenalho ritual refers not to present Indian-ladino relations but rather to conditions during the Tzeltal Revolt of 1712.

897 **Browner, C. H.** Criteria for selecting herbal remedies (UP/E, 24 : 1, Jan. 1985, p. 13–32, bibl., tables)

Presents excellent data on Chinantec techniques for alleviating uterine ailments: some remedies are thought to facilitate childbirth, menstruation, and abortion, whereas others are used to aid postpartum recovery, avert excessive uterine bleeding, and treat infertility.

898 **Burgess, Don; Willett Kempton; and Robert E. MacLaury.** Tarahumara color modifiers: category structure presaging evolutionary change (AES/AE, 10 : 1, Feb. 1983, p. 133–149, bibl., graphs, tables)

Finds that modifiers specify an object's grade of membership in a color category. Supports Kay and McDaniel's view of the fuzziness of color categories and concludes that skewing precedes splitting in Tarahumara linguistic change.

899 **Cabarrús, Carlos Rafael.** La cosmovisión k'ekchi' en proceso de cambio. San Salvador: UCA/Editores, 1979. 168 p.: bibl. (Col. Estructuras y Procesos; 5)

Study of religious tradition and change in Alta Verapaz, Guatemala, describes images of God and the devil, the concept of guilt, family and public rituals, and witchcraft, also Acción Católica and the Word of God movement.

900 **Cámara, Luis Millet.** Logwood and archaeology in Campeche (UNM/JAR, 40 : 2, Summer 1984, p. 324–328, bibl., map)

Proposes that large-scale logging in the 19th century may account for earthworks, ditches, etc., better than does the hypothesis of precolumbian origin.

901 **Campos, Julieta.** La herencia obstinada: análisis de cuentos nahuas. México: Fondo de Cultura Económica, 1982. 271 p.: bibl., maps (Col. popular; 233)

Innovative study of 18 tales from Nahua communities in Mecayapan, Veracruz, draws for analytical frameworks on Freudian psychoanalysis, Propp's lack-reparation schema, and Lévi-Strauss's opposition between culture and nature.

902 **Careaga Viliesid, Lorena.** Chan Santa Cruz: historia de un comunidad cimarrona de Quintana Roo. México: Univ. Iberoamericana, 1981. 189 p.: bibl., graphs, maps.

Reconstructs the social history of Chan Santa Cruz and compares it with those of other runaway and reconstituted communities.

903 **Chapman, Anne.** Los hijos de la muerte: el universo mítico de los tolupan-jicaques, Honduras. México: INAH, 1982. 324 p.: bibl., map, plates, tables.

Jicaque social organization and traditional folklore are said to evince an east-west dualism on the horizontal plane and a notion of ownership on the vertical plane.

904 **Cohen, Milton.** The ethnomedicine of the Garifuna, Black Caribs, of Río Tinto, Honduras (CUA/AQ, 57 : 1, Jan. 1984, p. 16–27, bibl.)

Informative overview of medical beliefs, healing practices, and attitudes toward modern medicine.

905 Collin Harguindeguy, Laura. Respuestas alternativas frente a la relación interétnica: fiestas religiosas. Toluca, México: Univ. Autónoma del Estado de México, Coordinación de Investigación Científica, 1983. 74 p.: bibl., tables (Cuadernos de investigación; 2)

Comparison of Holy Week celebrations in Mexico and festival organization in an Otomí community indicate that ritual elements vary with ethnicity, ethnic conflict, and fiesta organization.

906 Constantino, Emilio and Daniela Tozzi. Libertad personal y norma social: algunas tesis sobre la Semana Santa en los tarahumaras de Monérachi (UNAM/AA, 18, 1981, p. 101–113, ill., map)

Examines the symbolization of ethnic unity and social differentiation in Holy Week festivities.

907 Cook, Scott. Peasant capitalist industry: piecework and enterprise in southern Mexican brickyards. Lanham, Md.: Univ. Press of America, 1984. 240 p.: bibl., maps, plates, tables.

Empirically rich and theoretically informed study of small-scale commodity production in a Oaxacan community describes the historical and economic context, the careers of representative workers, tools and techniques, forms of ownership, and worker ideology.

908 ———. Peasant economy, ritual industry and capitalist development in the Oaxaca Valley, Mexico (JPS, 12:1, Oct. 1984, p. 3–40, bibl., tables)

Observations suggest that labor intensive rural industries in Oaxaca have a potential for becoming more capital intensive.

909 Corbett, Jack and Scott Whiteford. State penetration and development in Mesoamerica, 1950–1980 (in Heritage of conquest: thirty years later [see item **939**] p. 9–33)

Describes the growing influence of federal government and national economy in local communities, with special attention to politics in Oaxaca and sugarcane cultivation in the Tehuacán Valley.

910 Cosminsky, Sheila. Medical pluralism in Mesoamerica (in Heritage of conquest: thirty years later [see item **939**] p. 159–173)

Surveys work on medical treatment in rural areas, particularly statistically-oriented studies.

911 Crumrine, N. Ross. Mask use and meaning in Easter ceremonialism: the Mayo *parisero* (in The power of symbols: masks and masquerade in the Americas [see item **975**] p. 93–101)

Compares and contrasts mestizo Carnival masking and Mayo Lenten masking to show that the latter is a means of establishing ethnic distance.

912 ———. Mayo social organization, ceremonial and ideological systems, Sonora, northwestern Mexico. Greeley: Museum of Anthropology, Univ. of Northern Colorado, 1982. 80 leaves: bibl., ill. (Occasional publications in anthropology. Ethnology series; 41)

In four separate essays, author surveys contemporary social and ritual organization, examines wet-vs.-dry symbolism in the ceremonial cycle, and offers various structuralist interpretations of myths.

913 ———. Symbolic structure and ritual symbolism in northwest and west Mexico (in Heritage of conquest: thirty years later [see item **939**] p. 247–266)

Innovative, plausible paper holds the Holy Family to be the root metaphor for Mayo ritual and myth.

914 Dennis, Philip A. and Michael D. Olien. Kingship among the Miskito (AES/AE, 11:4, Nov. 1984, p. 718–737, bibl., ill., map, plate)

Concludes that Miskito kingship was based on an indigenous, lower Central American leadership pattern comprising apprenticeship to powerful outsiders, control of a secret language, trade contacts, and symbols of external connection.

915 The Don Juan papers: further Castañeda controversies. Edited by Richard de Mille. Santa Barbara, Calif: Ross-Erikson, 1980. 518 p.: appendices, bibl., ill., index.

The authenticity of Don Juan is examined in 43 essays, many by de Mille. Apart from Mary Douglas's hasty acceptance, most of the collection is a witty and convincing unmasking of Castañeda's outrageous hoax.

916 Dow, James. Symbols, soul, and magical healing among the Otomí Indians (UCLA/JLAL, 10:1, Summer 1984, p. 3–21, bibl., ill.)

Otomí paper figures represent *zaki*, the life force. Cultural understandings about the life force, in turn, are said to account for the efficacy of the figures in curing ritual.

917 Early, John D. A demographic survey of contemporary Guatemalan Maya: some methodological implications for anthropological research (*in* Heritage of conquest: thirty years later [see item **939**] p. 73–91)

Uses the 1950, 1964, and 1973 national censuses to estimate the Maya population and describe the distribution of ladinoization.

918 Engle, Patricia L.; Susan C. M. Scrimshaw; and Robert Smidt. Sex differences in attitudes towards newborn infants among women of Mexican origin (Medical Anthropology [Redgrave Press, South Salem, N.Y.] 8:2, Spring 1984, p. 133–144, bibl., table)

Finds that factors other than sex shape attitudes toward children.

919 Esser, Janet Brody. Tarascan masks of women as agents of social control (*in* The Power of symbols: masks and masquerade in the Americas [see item **975**] p. 116–127)

Interesting discussion of the figures of the Beautiful Woman, Grandfather, and Ugly Ones in Tarascan masking, with informed speculation about their prehispanic antecedents.

920 Falla, Ricardo. El tesoro de San Blas: turismo en San Blas. Panamá: Ediciones Centro de Capacitación Social, 1979. 143 p.: bibl., ill., maps, plates (Serie El indio panameño; 5)

An examination of tourism among the Kuna notes changes in domestic organization and increasing stratification. Describes the Centro Turístico del IPAT, and politics of Kuna reactions to tourism.

921 Finkler, Kaja. Spiritualist healers in Mexico: successes and failures of alternative therapeutics. Foreword by Arthur Kleinman. New York: Praeger: Bergin & Garvey Publishers, 1985. 256 p.: bibl., tables.

Impressive study based on participant observation covers ideology and ritual, illness etiologies, patterns of resorting to medical care, and therapeutic techniques and outcomes. Shows that the efficacy of spiritualist healing, such as it is, depends more on the power of symbols than on the patient-practitioner relationship.

922 Foster, George M. How to stay well in Tzintzuntzan (Social Science Medicine/Great Britain [Pergamon Press, Elmsford, N.Y.] 19:5, s.d. p. 523–533, bibl.)

Describes elements of folk pathology in unusual detail (e.g., *aire* and *frío*, gradations within the hot-cold dichotomy, the sources of hot and cold, concepts about internal organs, and beliefs and practices related to prevention as well as curing). Makes special note of the practice of avoiding extremes to prevent disease.

923 Furbee, Louanna and Robert A. Benfer. Cognitive and geographic maps: study of individual variation among Tojolabal Mayans (AAA/AA, 85:2, June 1983, p. 305–334, bibl., ill., map, tables)

Multivariate statistical approach purports to show that informants' maps of the environment and disease classification are interrelated.

924 García Ruiz, Jesús. El defensor y el defendido: dialéctica de la agresión entre los mochó (Cuicuilco [Revista de la Escuela Nacional de Antropología e Historia, México] 2:8, abril 1982, p. 12–21, bibl., plates)

Examines ritual expressions of aggression and defense against evil and sickness in the municipio de Motozintla, Guatemala.

925 Garma Navarro, Carlos. Liderazgo protestante en una lucha campesina en México (III/AI, 44:1, enero/marzo 1984, p. 127–141, bibl.)

Describes and analyzes a local insurrection in which Totonac pentecostals, coffee growers, and peasant wage earners occupied the municipal building of Ixtepec, Puebla, under the banner of the Partido Socialista Unificado de México.

926 **Gillmor, Frances.** Symbolic representation in Mexican combat plays (in The Power of symbols: masks and masquerade in the Americas [see item 975] p. 102–110)

Contains symbolically rich material on the dances of La Conquista, Los Moros y Cristianos, and Los Tastoanes (a dance found in Jalisco and Zacatecas).

927 **Gjording, Chris N.** The Cerro Colorado Copper Project and the Guaymi Indians of Panama. Cambridge, Mass.: Cultural Survival, 1981. 50 p.: bibl., ill., tables (Occasional paper. Cultural Survival Inc.; 3)

Assessment of the actual and potential impact of the Cerro Colorado project on the Guaymi, with discussion of Guaymi attitudes toward the project. Concludes that there is an urgent need for formal recognition of Guaymi land rights and provision for Guaymi control in impact studies.

928 **González, Nancie Loudon.** Rethinking the consanguineal household and matrifocality (UP/E, 23:1, Jan. 1984, p. 1–12, bibl., tables)

Suggests that Garifuna household structure and membership depend on immediate economic circumstances. The article in effect questions the validity of typological approaches in family studies.

929 **Gossen, Gary H.** Una diáspora maya moderna: desplazamiento y persistencia cultural de San Juan Chamula, Chiapas (Mesoamérica [Publicaciones del Centro de Investigaciones Regionales de Mesoamérica, Antigua, Guatemala] 4:5, junio 1983, p. 253–276)

Discusses plans and rationale for the study of nine migrant Chamula communities.

930 **Gouy-Gilbert, Cécile.** Une résistance indienne: les Yaquis du Sonora. Introduction de Michel Antochiw K. Lyon, France: Fédérop, 1983. 204, 11 p.: bibl., ill., maps.

Historical study of Yaqui relations with the wider society, including Yaqui participation in the Revolution, and analysis of social, political, and ceremonial organization.

931 **Gregory, James R.** Cooperatives: "failures" versus "success" (BISRA/BS, 12:5, 1984, p. 1–15)

Cooperatives in a Belizean community were not in themselves especially successful but they affected the distribution of political power and initiated new economic activities.

932 **Gross, Joseph J.** and **Carl Kendall.** The analysis of domestic organization in Mesoamerica: the case of postmarital residence in Santiago Atitlan, Guatemala (in Heritage of conquest: thirty years later [see item 939] p. 201–228)

Argues intelligently that predominant virilocality reflects the concerns of household heads with support in old age and actual economic assistance and political-ritual ambition. Questions the assumption that virilocal residence expresses patrilineal tendencies.

933 **Hanks, William F.** Sanctification, structure, and experience in a Yucatec ritual event (AFS/JAF, 97:384, April/June 1984, p. 131–166, bibl., plate

Ethnographically solid paper contends that shamanic prayer is part of a paradigmatic system in which spirits are defined by vertical, temporal, directional, and agentive qualities.

934 **Hawkins, John.** Inverse images: the meaning of culture, ethnicity and family in postcolonial Guatemala. Foreword by Manning Nash. Albuquerque: Univ. of New Mexico Press, 1984. 470 p.: bibl., ill., maps, plates, tables.

Ambitious, semiotic interpretation of Guatemalan ethnicity theorizes that the cultural ideologies of Indians and ladinos are inverted images of each other. Illustrates the argument with a comparison of economic activity, conceptions of status and ethnicity, life cycle, and the developmental cycle of the domestic group in two adjacent communities.

935 ———. Robert Redfield's culture concept and Mesoamerican anthropology (in Heritage of conquest: thirty years later [see item 939] p. 299–336).

Faults Redfield for a behavioral view of culture and traces its influence on subsequent research. Offers a summary of the author's inverse image theory of Middle American ethnicity (see item 934) to illustrate the advantages of an ideational approach.

936 **Helbig, Jörg Wolfgang.** Religion und Medizinmannwesen bei den Cuna. Hohenschäftlarn, FRG: K. Renner, 1983. 249

p.: bibl. (Münchner Beiträge zur Amerikanistik; 5)
Modern culturalist study of shamanism and healing among the Cuna.

937 Helms, Mary W. Miskito slaving and
culture contact: ethnicity and opportunity in an expanding population (UNM/
JAR, 39:2, Summer 1983, p. 179–197, bibl.,
ill., maps)
Demographic expansion and ecological
conditions in the 18th century encouraged
Miskito aggressiveness, whereas slave trading
with the British influenced prestige symbols
and ethnicity.

938 Hendricks, Janet and **Arthur D.
Murphy.** From poverty to poverty: the
adaptation of young migrant households in
Oaxaca, México (UA, 10:1, Spring 1981,
p. 53–70, bibl., tables)
Migrants in the city of Oaxaca tend to
come from surrounding rural areas; they
are not evenly distributed throughout the labor force; they are less educated and have
lower family incomes than comparable non-
migrants; and their situations may decline
rather than improve with time.

939 Heritage of conquest: thirty years
later. Edited by Carl Kendall, John
Hawkins, and Laurel Bossen. Foreword by Sol
Tax. Albuquerque: Univ. of New Mexico
Press, 1983. 368 p.: bibl., maps, tables.)
This volume contains sections on regional perspectives, institutions, and ideology, each with an introduction by the
editors. For individual annotations of articles,
see items 893, 909, 910, 913, 917, 932, 935,
947, 955, 959, 981, 984, and 992).

940 Hewitt de Alcántara, Cynthia. Anthropological perspectives on rural Mexico.
London: Routledge & Kegan Paul, 1984.
224 p.: bibl.
Readable history of Mexican anthropology traces the dialectic of theoretical paradigms from ethnographic particularism,
functionalism, and indigenismo to various
expressions of historical structuralism (e.g.,
dependency theory, Marxism, and cultural
ecology).

941 Horcasitas de Barros, María Luisa.
Una artesanía con raíces prehispánicas
en Santa Clara del Cobre: addenda 1980, proceso de cambio de la artesanía en el lapso de
doce años y genealogía de una familia de ar-

tesanos del cobre. México: Instituto Nacional
de Antropología e Historia, Depto. de Etnohistoria, 1981. 168 p.: bibl., ill., plates, tables
(some folded) (Col. científica. Etnología; 97)
Revised and expanded version of earlier publication contains material on copper
working and marketing, a discussion of recent change, and the genealogy of an artisan
family.

942 Hu-DeHart, Evelyn. Yaqui resistance
and survival: the struggle for land and
autonomy, 1821–1910. Madison: Univ. of
Wisconsin Press, 1984. 293 p.: bibl., index,
maps.
Argues that Yaqui strength during the
national period resided in land and high demand for Yaqui labor. The situation changed
during the early 20th century as the government abandoned the traditional land-for-
labor trade-off and post-Revolution agrarian
policy increased Yaqui dependency.

943 Huerta Ríos, César. Organización
socio-política de una minoría nacional,
los triquis de Oaxaca. México: Instituto Nacional Indigenista, 1981. 282 p., 1 folded leaf
of plates: bibl., ill. (Col. INI; 62. Serie de
antropología social)
Contains valuable material on lineage
and clan organization, land tenure, and the
social relations of production as well as interesting observations on religion and social
power, including unusual data on beliefs
about naguales and lineage organization.

944 Irigoyen Rascón, Fructuoso. Cero-
cahuí: una comunidad en la Tarahumara. 2a ed. rev. por el autor. Chihuahua,
México: Centro Librero La Prensa, 1979.
206 p.: bibl., ill., maps, plates.
Rev. ed. of 1974 publication covers cultural practices, folklore, alcohol consumption, and use of traditional and modern
medicine.

945 Kemper, Robert V. Obstacles and opportunities: household economics of
Tzintzuntzan migrants in Mexico City (UA,
10:3, Fall 1981, p. 212–229)
Study of household economies of
Tzintzuntzan migrants in Mexico City
shows that the most successful migrants
combine employment in the "formal" economy with entrepreneurship in the "informal"
economy.

946 ——. Urbanization and development in the Tarascan region since 1940 (UA, 10:1, Spring 1981, p. 89–119, bibl., tables)

Overview of demographic, linguistic, and economic conditions finds that what little economic development has occurred in the Tarascan area has been a mixed blessing; the Tarascan language is disappearing and traditional culture is being commercialized to attract tourism.

947 —— and **Anya Peterson Royce.** Urbanization in Mexico: beyond the heritage of conquest (*in* Heritage of conquest: thirty years later [see item **939**] p. 93–128)

Reviews the history of urbanization in Middle America and scholarly concern with the subject.

947a **Kerns, Virginia.** Women and the ancestors: Black Carib kinship and ritual. Urbana: Univ. of Illinois Press, 1983. 229 p., 24 p. of plates: bibl., ill., maps, tables.

Demonstrates the strength of the mother-child relationship and women's importance in the social reproduction of culture. Ritual, the author suggests, instills moral principles and gratitude toward older lineals and ancestors.

948 **Kuroda, Etsuko.** Under Mt. Zempoaltépetl: highland Mixe society and ritual. Osaka, Japan: National Museum of Ethnology, 1984. 246 p.: bibl., ill., maps, plates (Senri ethnological studies; 12)

Compares two Mixe communities with special attention to continuity and change in family rituals, religious fiestas, and national secular festivities.

949 **Los Legítimos hombres:** aproximación antropológica al grupo tojolabal. Edición de Mario Humberto Ruz. México: UNAM, Instituto de Investigaciones Filológicas, Centro de Estudios Mayas, 1983. 3 v. (178, 323, 234 p.): bibl., ill., maps, plates, tables.)

Substantial contribution to the literature on the Tojolabal of southern Mexico. Vols. 1 and 3 include interesting articles by Ruz and others on cultural geography and ecology, physical anthropology, language, and folk medicine. Vol. 2, a comprehensive ethnography by Ruz, covers subsistence techniques, life cycle, social and ritual organization, and external relations.

950 **Logan, Kathleen.** Getting by with less: economic strategies of lower income households in Guadalajara (UA, 10:3, Fall 1981, p. 231–246, bibl.)

Describes economic coping strategies among lower income families in Guadalajara: maximizing economic opportunities, utilizing rural resources, establishing reciprocal exchanges with neighbors, and minimizing waste through recycling and conservation.

951 ——. The role of pharmacists and over-the-counter medications in the health care system of a Mexican city (Medical Anthropology [Redgrave Press, South Salem, N.Y.] 7:3, Summer 1983, p. 68–87, bibl., tables)

Observes that the importance of self-diagnosis, pharmacists, and over-the-counter drugs in health care in Juárez, Mexico, although finds that other curing modalities are apt to figure in the treatment of *susto*.

952 **Lomnitz-Adler, Claudio.** Evolución de una sociedad rural. México: Fondo de Cultura Económica 1982. 317 p.: bibl., ill. (SEP; 80/27)

Insightful restudy of Tepoztlán, Morelos, focuses on political history and culture. Particularly interesting is the discussion of interbarrio politics and their ritual expressions.

953 **Lutes, Steven V.** The mask and magic of the Yaqui *paskola* clowns (*in* The power of symbols: masks and masquerade in the Americas [see item **975**] p. 81–92)

Suggests that playing the role of the demonic *paskola* is an exercise in "making, containing, and using power" and, thus, an expression of the general theme of restraint in Yaqui culture.

954 **Méndez Domínguez, Alfredo.** Illness and medical theory among Guatemalan Indians (*in* Heritage of conquest: thirty years later [see item **939**] p. 267–298)

Unusual country-wide survey of beliefs about *hijillo*, *aire*, and *susto*.

955 **Menéndez, Eduardo L.** Poder, estratificación y salud: análisis de las condiciones sociales y económicas de la enfermedad en Yucatán. México: Centro de Investigaciones y Estudios Superiores en Antropología Social, 1981. 590 p.: bibl., tables (Ediciones de la Casa Chata; 13)

Examines morbidity and traditional and modern health care delivery in the context of regional political and socioeconomic relations. Includes some interesting observations on mortality decline but also much theorizing about the virtues of historical structuralism.

956 Merrill, William L. God's saviors in the Sierra Madre (AMNH/NH, 92:3, March 1983, p. 58–67, ill.)

Describes Easter ceremonies and syncretic ideas about God, the Devil, and the afterlife in a conservative Tarahumara community. During Holy Week the Tarahumara try to strengthen God so that he can prevent the Devil from destroying the world.

957 Miller, Richard W. Class, politics, and family organization in San Cosme Xalostoc, Mexico (UP/E, 23:4, Oct. 1984, p. 289–300, bibl., table)

Finds that the extended family is positively correlated with landholding, wealth, and secular orientation in a mestizo community in southern Tlaxcala, but argues that class and political factors are even more important in encouraging extended families.

958 Moberg, Mark A. From individuals to class: the dynamics of peasant cooperatives in revolutionary Nicaragua (Dialectical Anthropology [The New School of Social Research, New York] 8:3, Dec. 1983, p. 217–236)

Describes the organization and operation of cooperatives, and attributes their current success to the pre-revolution proletarianization and revolutionary ideology of many peasants. Thus questions the view that peasants are typically uncooperative.

959 Moore, G. Alexander. Anthropology and education in Mesoamerica today (in Heritage of conquest: thirty years later [see item **939**]) p. 135–158)

Examines the literature on socialization, including Ivan Illich's critique of schooling.

960 ———. From council to legislature: democracy, parliamentarianism, and the San Blas Cuna (AAA/AA, 86:1, March 1984, p. 28–42, bibl.)

Places the Cuna general congress on a continuum between the Cuna local congress and the Panamanian National Assembly: the tribal congress is more formal and rational than the indigenous model but less so than the western legislature; the National Assembly, however, is not more democratic than the Cuna institutions.

961 Murphy, Arthur D. and Henry A. Selby. A comparison of household income and budgetary patterns in four Mexican cities (UA, 10:3, Fall 1981, p. 247–267, bibl., graph, tables)

Discriminant function analysis of household budgets in Oaxaca, San Luis Potosí, Tampico, and Mexicali shows that for the poor the most important factor distinguishing cities is income, whereas for middle and upper-income families the cities differ with respect to the proportion of income that must be spent to maintain a middle-class lifestyle.

962 Musgrave-Portilla, L. Marie. The *nahualli* or transforming wizard in pre- and postconquest Mesoamerica (UCLA/ JLAL, 8:1, Summer 1982, p. 3–62, bibl., ill., plates)

Tour de force synthesizes 16th-century and recent material on the were-animal. Clarifies, among other things, concepts of *nahualli, tonalli, tonal,* and *ihiyotl.*

963 Navarrete, Carlos. San Pascualito Rey y el culto a la muerte en Chiapas. México: UNAM, Instituto de Investigaciones Antropológicas, 1982. 146 p., 74 p. of plates: bibl., ill. (some col.) (Serie antropológica; 46. Etnohistoria)

Account of the cult of San Pascual in Tuxtla includes fascinating material on ritual and oral tradition as well as many marvelous photographs. Also examines origins of the cult and its relation to recent social conditions.

964 Nolasco Armas, Margarita. De nómadas cazadores y recolector a aldeas agrícolas indiferenciadas: el caso del noroeste de México (UNAM/AA, 19, 1982, p. 59–72, bibl.)

Examines culture and subsistence activities in the desert cultures of northwest Mexico in the 16th and 17th centuries with the aim of elucidating the role of agriculture in the development of civilization.

965 Nutini, Hugo. Ritual kinship. v. 2, Ideological and structural integration of the compadrazgo system in rural Tlaxcala.

Princeton: Princeton Univ. Press, 1984. 505 p.: appendices, bibl., map.

Theoretically oriented work completes a two-volume study (see *HLAS 45:996*). Claims compadrazgo is sacred and symmetrical in traditional contexts and predicts that it will become secular and asymmetrical with urbanization and modernization.

966 Oettinger, Marion. Una comunidad tlapaneca: sus linderos sociales y territoriales. México: Instituto Nacional Indigenista, 1980. 338 p.: bibl., ill., maps, plates, tables (Col. INI; 61. Serie de antropología social)

Shows that the boundaries of the social commuinty coincide with the limits of communal land, and argues that socioreligious organization is geared to reinforcing cohesion in the face of external threat. The Tlapanecas, however, are not ignorant of external influences; rather they rework them in keeping with their own purposes.

967 Olien, Michael D. The Miskito kings and the line of succession (UNM/JAR, 39:2, Summer 1983, p. 198–241, bibl., ill., maps)

Contrary to the view that they were puppets installed by the British, Miskito kings formed a single line of succession from 1655–1894. In general, kings were succeeded by the eldest sons of their primary wives.

968 Ornes, Mayobanex. Los caminos del indigenismo. San José: Editorial Costa Rica, 1980. 221 p.: bibl.

Comprehensive treatise on Indianism in Costa Rica. Gives a brief history of Indians in Costa Rica and an overview of both the conditions in Indian communities and government Indian policies and programs.

969 Palacio, Joseph. Food and social relations in Belizean Garifuna village (BISRA/BS, 12:3, 1984, p. 1–35, tables)

Finds that "caring with food" defines and legitimizes the roles of mother and father, and that cash and non-cash food exchanges express relations between families, including hierarchical relations.

970 Papousek, Dick Allard. Alfareros-campesinos mazahuas: situación de estímulo y procesos de adaptación. Traducción del inglés por Mercedes Barquet. Toluca, México: Secretaría de Educación, Cultura y Bienestar Social del Gobierno del Estado de México, 1982. 300 p.: bibl., ill., maps, plates, tables.

Describes pottery production and change in three Mazahua communities. Author criticizes Foster's explanation for peasant mistrust and conservativism and emphasizes instead the conjunction of necessity and opportunity, particularly as they are shaped by ecological conditions, patronage systems, and the developmental cycle of the domestic group.

971 Parrish, Timothy C. Class and social reproduction in New Spain/Mexico (Dialectical Anthropology [The New School for Social Research, New York] 7:2, Nov. 1982, p. 137–153)

Argues that dependency theory overlooks regional variations. In several parts of Mexico (e.g., Yucatán, Oaxaca, and northern Mexico), economic change is better understood in terms of local economic conditions, class structures, and patterns of biological and social reproduction.

972 Perera, Victor and Robert D. Bruce. The last lords of Palenque: the Lacandon Mayas of the Mexican rain forest. Boston: Little, Brown, 1982. 311 p.: ill., maps, plates.

Pastiche of Lacandon lore and life, rambling snippets of personal experience, and distressing observations on the effects of missionaries and mahogany exploitation.

973 Pérez Castro, Ana Bella. Duraznal: situación actual de una comunidad indígena (UNAM/AA, 18, 1981, p. 173–186, bibl., tables)

Traces the effect of coffee production on subsistence activities and religious and political organization in the community of Duraznal, Chiapas, an immigrant population originally from San Andrés Larraizar.

974 Pintado Cervera, Oscar M. Estructura productiva y pérdida de la indianidad en Yucatán en el proceso henequenero: dos ensayos. México: Centro de Investigaciones y Estudios Superiores en Antropología Social, 1982. 116 p. (Cuadernos de la casa chata; 71)

Surveys history of the henequen plantation and its effects on Indian society and culture. Also criticizes Redfield for ignoring the plantations in his work on the folk-urban continuum.

975 **The Power of symbols:** masks and masquerade in the Americas. Edited by N. Ross Crumrine and Marjorie Halpin. Vancouver, Canada: Univ. of British Columbia Press, 1983. 244 p.: bibl., ill., plates.

Contains a number of articles on Middle America which are annotated separately (see items **896, 911, 919, 926,** and **953**).

976 **La Quiebra política de la antropología social en México:** antología de una polémica. t. 1, La impugnación. Edición de Andrés Medina y Carlos García Mora. México: UNAM, 1983. 422 p.: bibl.

Anthologizes and comments upon the debate over social theory, politics, and indigenismo in Mexican anthropology. In addition to introductory essays by the editors, includes previously published papers by Cazés, Aldama Zapiain, Villa Rojas, Bonfil, Romano Delgado, Aguirre Beltran, Palerm, Montoya Briones, and Comas, and new commentaries by Warman and Olivera.

977 **Rohner, Ronald P.; Samuel Roll; and Evelyn C. Rohner.** Perceived parental acceptance-rejection and personality organization among Mexican and American elementary school children (HRAF/BSR, 15:1, 1980, p. 23–39, bibl., tables)

Reports that children in Monterrey, Mexico, perceive themselves to be more rejected than children in Washington, D.C.; also finds that perceived rejection is correlated with emotional and behavioral disturbance.

978 **Royce, Anya Peterson.** Isthmus Zapotec households: economic responses to scarcity and abundance (UA, 10:3, Fall 1981, p. 269–286, bibl.)

The Zapotec people of Juchitán, Oaxaca have evolved strategies for coping with alternating periods of good and bad economic fortune, among them intra- and inter-family cooperation, investment, and multiple employment.

979 **Rubel, Arthur J.; Carl W. O'Nell; and Rolando Collado-Ardon.** *Susto:* a folk illness. With the assistance of John Krejci and Jean Krejci. Berkeley: Univ. of California Press, 1984. 186 p.: bibl., map, plates, tables.

Statistically-oriented study of *susto* among Chinantecs, Zapotecs, and mestizos finds that the condition is associated with so-cial stress and organic disorders but not psychiatric disorders.

980 **Salazar Peralta, Ana María.** Variabilidad cultural entre dos grupos mayas de Chiapas: tzotziles y choles (UNAM/AA, 19, 1982, p. 231–240, bibl.)

Compares and contrasts the Tzotziles of the Chiapas highlands and the Choles to their immediate north, noting that the latter are less traditional even though more isolated. The difference is attributed to the nature of Indian-ladino interaction in the two cases.

981 **Salovesh, Michael.** Person and polity in Mexican cultures: another view of social organization (*in* Heritage of conquest: thirty years later [see item **939**] p. 175–199)

Thoughtful paper on kinship studies in Mexican cultures identifies regional trends in kinship terminology, naming, marriage and residence, and compadrazgo. Avers that kinship is the basic idiom of Mexican social organization.

982 **Schackt, Jon.** The Tzuultak'a: religious lore and cultural processes among the Kekchi (BISRA/BS, 12:5, 1984, p. 16–29, bibl.)

Describes the revival of a traditional ceremony to appease the divine owners of the hills and valleys in a period of economic crisis.

983 **Schwartz, Norman B.** San Simón: ambiguity and identity in Petén, Guatemala (SOCIOL, 33:2, 1983, p. 152–173, ill., tables)

Interesting paper suggests that the ethnically ambiguous rain-making figure of San Simón in the Lake Petén Itza area of Guatemala symbolically resolves ethnic tensions while providing a focus for anxieties about drought.

984 ———. The second heritage of conquest: some observations (*in* Heritage of conquest: thirty years later [see item **939**] p. 339–362)

Lucid, effective summary of the volume, with remarks on continuities and discontinuities in Middle American research. Comments insightfully on the rift between political-economic analysis and ideational approaches.

985 Sewastynowicz, James. Community and power brokers and national political parties in rural Costa Rica (CUA/AQ, 56:3, July 1983, p. 107–115, bibl.)

Notes that Costa Rica's democratic organization is an anomaly in peasant studies, and suggests that brokerage reflects the convergence between local and national interests.

986 Sherzer, Joel. Kuna ways of speaking: an ethnographic perspective. Austin: Univ. of Texas Press, 1983. 260 p.: bibl., ill., plates, tables.

Marvelous ethnography of Kuna speaking. Grammar, vocabulary, and metaphor are described, as are linguistic styles and varieties peculiar to politics, curing, magic, and puberty rites.

987 Smith, Carol A. Does a commodity economy enrich the few while ruining the masses?: differentiation among petty commodity producers in Guatemala (JPS, 11:3, April 1984, p. 60–95, bibl., tables)

Finds that high wages among artisans in Tononicapan prevent class differentiation (high wages are said to be related to both subsistence and capitalist production in the social formation). Thus reasons that commodity production is not a sufficient condition for labor-capital polarization.

988 Stavenhagen, Rodolfo. Problemas étnicos y campesinos: ensayos. México: Instituto Nacional Indigenista, 1980. 198 p.: bibl., ill., tables (Colección INI; 60. Serie de antropología social)

Collection of author's previously published essays on pluralism, ethnicity, bilingualism, collectivization, and regional development.

989 Stier, Frances. Domestic economy: land, labor, and wealth in a San Blas community (AES/AE, 9:3, Aug. 1982, p. 519–537, map, tables)

Methodologically sophisticated treatment of household composition and agricultural production argues that technical difficulties in Sahlins's use of Chayanov can be resolved with multiple regression and path analysis. Finds that relative wealth has more influence on cultivated area than household dependents and workforce.

990 Suárez, Orozco and Alan Dundes. The piropo and the dual image of women in the Spanish-speaking world (UCLA/JLAL, 10:1, Summer 1984, p. 111–133, bibl.)

Shows that piropos are mixtures of flattery and insult and, hence, expressions of men's ambivalence toward women: they imply that women are fallen angels—part virgin, part harlot.

991 Taggart, James M. Nahuat myth and social structure. Austin: Univ. of Texas Press, 1983. 287 p.: bibl., ill., index (The Texas Pan American series)

Demonstrates that the same stories— Men Who Enter the Forest, Adam and Eve, and Lightning-bolts who Punish Sin—differ in two Sierra Nahuat communities according to variations in land inheritance, postmarital residence, and median age difference between spouses.

992 Tedlock, Barbara. A phenomenological approach to religious change in highland Guatemala (in Heritage of conquest: thirty years later [see item 939] p. 235–246)

Makes an interesting argument for dialectical approach to religious syncretism.

993 Thomas, John S. and Michael C. Robbins. The limits to growth in a Mexican ejido (SAA/HO, 42:1, Spring 1983, p. 69–71, bibl.)

Land disputes between a Tojolabal community and neighboring Tojolabales and ladino ranchers are related to population pressure. In contrast to Carneiro, however, authors suggest that farmers respond to resource pressure when about half their land is in use.

994 Tripp, Robert. Domestic organization and access to property in a town in eastern El Salvador (CUA/AQ, 56:1, Jan. 1983, p. 24–34, bibl., tables)

Household composition in a coffee-growing region is explained by community-wide values and disaggregated data on renting, house ownership, caretaking, and house and land ownership.

995 Vandervelde, Marjorie Mills and Marvel Iglesias. Born primitive. Emmetsburg, Iowa: Velde Press, 1982. 184 p.: bibl., maps, plates.

Informal biography of Lonnie (Alcibiades) Iglesias, a Kuna leader.

996 Varela, Roberto. Expansión de sistemas y relaciones de poder. México: Univ. Autónoma Metropolitana, 1984. 288 p.: bibl., map, tables.

Comparative study of political process in nine communities in Morelos suggests that the concentration of power evolves in conjunction with social complexity and, to some extent, with energy systems.

997 ———. Procesos políticos en Tlayacapan, Morelos. México: Univ. Autónoma Metropolitana, 1984. 138 p.: bibl., map, tables (Cuadernos universitarios; 11)

Yet another work in a growing list of publications on Tlayacapan analyzes political organization and describes political activity during 1970–71, particularly as it related to the issue of potable water.

998 Varela-Ruiz, Leticia T. Die Musik im Leben der Yaqui: Beitrag zum Studium der Tradition einer mexikanischen Ethnie. Regensburg, FRG: Bosse, 1982. 2 v. (217, 167 p.): bibl., disc., ill., music (Kölner Beiträge zur Musikforschung; 127)

Describes types and ceremonial uses of musical forms, musical instruments, and technical features of music. Short but interesting section relates Yaqui music to cosmological ideas.

999 Villa Rojas, Alfonso. Breves consideraciones sobre la creencia del mal de ojo (UNAM/AA, 19, 1982, p. 147–161, bibl., map)

Although the evil eye in Middle America is usually thought to have an Old World provenience, some features of the complex indicate that it may also have prehispanic antecedents.

1000 Wagley, Charles. Learning fieldwork: Guatemala (in Fieldwork: the human experience. Edited by Robert Lawless, Vinson H. Sutlive, Jr., and Mario D. Zamora. New York: Gordon and Breach Science Publishers, 1983, p. 1–17, bibl.)

Distinguished anthropologist recalls fieldwork in Guatemala in the 1930s. Describes learning about the advantages of taking a vacation from fieldwork, and admits that what most anthropologists do in the field is really "passive participant observation."

1001 Wasserstrom, Robert. Class and society in central Chiapas. Berkeley: Univ. of California Press, 1983. 357 p., 8 p. of plates: bibl., ill., index, maps, tables.

Maintains that ethnicity and communal organization are not the vestiges of precolumbian customs but rather the outcome of socioeconomic processes, some recent. Lay Christianity is seen as a continuation of tendencies in the late Middle Ages and Las Casas's efforts to create and defend Christian communities in the face of ladino exploitation.

1002 Watanabe, John M. In the world of the sun: a cognitive model of Mayan cosmology (RAI/M, 18:4, Dec. 1983, p. 710–728, bibl., map, ill.)

Analysis of contemporary Mam words for time and direction suggests that Mayan cosmology is based on daily and annual movements of the sun.

1003 Weller, Susan C. New data on intracultural variability: the hot-cold concept of medicine and illness (SAA/HO, 42:3, Fall 1983, p. 249–257, tables)

Uses multidimensional scaling and multivariate statistics to represent and analyze the structure of illness concepts in urban and rural Guatemala. The results imply that the hot-cold system has little salience.

1004 Zúñiga, Rosa María. Nombres de lugar en Oaxaca (Cuicuilco [Escuela Nacional de Antropología e Historia, México] 3:7, enero 1982, p. 15–19, plates)

Preliminary report on Zapotec toponyms.

ETHNOLOGY: West Indies

LAMBROS COMITAS, *Professor of Anthropology and Education, Teachers College, Columbia University, and Director, Research Institute for the Study of Man, New York*

IN THIS VOLUME OF *HLAS*, I have annotated publications in social and cultural anthropology or other closely related disciplines. They cover 29 distinct Caribbean territories: Antigua, Aruba, Barbados, Barbuda, Belize, Cuba, Curaçao, Dominica, Dominican Republic, Grand Cayman, Grenada, Guadeloupe, Guyana, Haiti, Jamaica, Martinique, Montserrat, Nevis, Panama, Puerto Rico, Saba, St. Barthelemy, St. John, St. Kitts, St. Vincent, Surinam, Tobago, Trinidad, and Venezuela. Also included are some 36 annotations of publications that deal generally with the Caribbean region, the Commonwealth Caribbean, or with units such as the US Virgin Islands. The territory receiving by far the most attention from researchers during this two-year report period has been Jamaica followed by Haiti and then by Belize and Surinam. As in the past, the cited publications cover a wide range of subject matter, methodological approaches, and theoretical perspectives. Numerically, however, the foci of scholarly inquiry for Caribbeanists during this period have been the subjects of religion and magic, and ethnicity.

In the first category, interest in Rastafarianism is particularly marked (item **1018**), with various researchers probing such diverse dimensions of that religio-political movement as personal discovery and conversion (item **1055**), its history and belief structure (item **1025**), dread talk (item **1105**), musical style (item **1094**), and cultural identity (item **1117**). For the moment, it appears that the Rastafarian phenomenon is in anthropological fashion. Other specialists on aspects of religion and magic deal with Jamaican Kumina (item **1020**), Spiritual Baptists in Trinidad (item **1061**), Gagá in the Dominican Republic (item **1119**) as well as *salve* music in that country (item **1041**), the Jonestown tragedy (item **1026**), Voodoo (item **1086**) as well as zombie phenomena in Haiti (items **1040, 1045, 1047,** and **1123**), Surinamese religious specialists (item **1145**), and Bush Negro religious movements in Surinam during the late 19th and early 20th centuries (item **1139a**).

Ethnicity in the Caribbean, as a general topic, is well represented largely by a special issue of *Ethnic Groups* (6 : 2 / 3). Its eight articles cover ethnicity in Cuba and Puerto Rico in the 18th and 19th centuries (item **1049**), race and ethnicity in the US Virgin Islands (item **1007**), differential expressions of Chinese ethnicity in the British West Indies (item **1125**), ethnic participation in rural Belizean economic development (item **1022**), Carib structural position in Dominica (item **1081**) as well as with two broader discussions of "new ethnicity" (item **1075**) and the meaning of ethnicity in the Caribbean (item **1062**). Other publications on this theme center on Belizean mating patterns (item **1033**), ethnic references in Haitian folktales (item **1043**), schooling in the US Virgin Islands (item **1057**), and on the relationship of economy and revolt to ethnicity in Haiti (item **1099**). Anthropological interest remains high for specific ethnic groups—particularly those most removed, geographically and culturally, from the mainstream of West Indian life. For example, eight articles cited in this section (items **1039, 1064, 1065, 1069, 1073, 1074, 1100,** and **1101**) deal with the Black Caribs or Garifuna (several of these appear in the collection *Black Caribs: a case study of biocultural adaptation,* edited by Michael H. Crawford for Plenum Press). The Bush Negroes of Surinam have received even more attention: Richard and Sally Price have contributed five publications, including three books, on Saramaka Maroon ethnohistory and contemporary life (items

1107–1111); a *festschrift* in honor of Silvia de Groot, noted specialist on the Djuka, includes a number of articles by her colleagues on Surinamese Maroons (item **1135**); and, as already noted, several others have published on Bush Negro religious activities. During this report period, only a scattering of publications have appeared on Amerindians in Guyana or on East Indians (items **1023a, 1035, 1088, 1095,** and **1126**). This may well be due to difficult research conditions in present-day Guyana.

Other topics of numerically smaller representation but of lasting interest to Caribbeanists include social stratification, socioeconomic behavior, sociocultural change, problems of identity, effects of migration on the sending societies, applied studies on language and health, and folklore and aesthetics. Given the recent upsurge in women's studies, this genre of research has made a significant appearance on the list. The organized impetus for women's studies in the region has come principally from a multidisciplinary project entitled "Women in the Caribbean" sponsored by the Institute of Social and Economic Research (Eastern Caribbean) of the Univ. of the West Indies. To date, this group has produced a number of research monographs on such themes as perceptions and stereotypes of Caribbean women (item **1023**), women and politics in Barbados (item **1050**), women, work, and development (item **1058**), the demographics of employed women in Barbados (item **1084**), women and education (item **1148**), and women and the family (item **1149**). Other publications in this rubric although not part of the project publication series deal with female household heads (item **1085**), female status, the family, and male dominance (item **1093**), and the role of women in the Caribbean (item **1106**). The development of women's studies is both promising and welcome.

Not already covered and deserving special mention are a number of books and monographs, among them, Roger Abrahams's collection on the role of the verbal performer (item **1005**), Diane Austin's study of culture and class ideology in two Kingston neighborhoods (item **1011**), Lawrence Fisher's exploration of "madness" and the Barbadian social order (item **1054**), Paget Henry's study of peripheral capitalism in Antigua (item **1071**), Michel Laguerre's study of a Haitian urban community (item **1079**), Paulette Pierce's analysis of the struggle to nationalize the Guyanese sugar industry (item **1103**), Richard Price's collection of Saramaka oral history (item **1107**), Sally Price's account of Saramaka social and artistic life (item **1109**), the first English translation of Price-Mars's classic *Ainsi parla l'oncle* (item **1112**), and M.G. Smith's long essay on the literature on culture, race, and class in the Caribbean and pluralism in theoretical and territorial context (item **1127**).

The death in Feb. 1985 of Dr. Vera Rubin is sadly noted. Founder and longtime Director of the Research Institute for the Study of Man, an institution devoted to Caribbean social science, her contributions to the advancement of our knowledge of Caribbean culture and society and to our understanding of the human dimensions of West Indian life were profound. She will be missed.

I am indebted to Dr. Ansley Hamid for his valuable contribution to the preparation of this section.

1005 Abrahams, Roger D. The man-of-words in the West Indies: performance and the emergence of Creole culture. Baltimore, Md.: The Johns Hopkins Univ. Press, 1983. 203 p.: bibl., ill., tables.

Collection of 11 excellent articles by the author on the role of verbal performer in Nevis, St. Kitts, Tobago, and St. Vincent. Ob-jective of the volume is to establish the presence and importance of a performance complex in the English-speaking Caribbean, a set of traits which articulates expressive relationships.

1006 After Africa: extracts from British travel accounts and journals of the seventeenth, eighteenth and nineteenth centuries concerning the slaves, their manners, and customs in the British West Indies. Edited by Roger D. Abrahams and John F. Szwed. New Haven, Conn.: Yale Univ. Press, 1983. 444 p.: bibl., ill.

Objective of editors was "to seek out in the oldest documents available the encounter of Africans and Europeans in the New World, toward the discovery of what was and is distinctly Afro-American in the cultures of the Americas." Collection divided into: The Slave Accounts in Context; Ways of Speaking; Anancy Tales; Religion and Magic; Festivals, Carnivals, Holidays, and JonKanoo; Music, Dance, and Games; and, Miscellaneous. Substantial, insightful introduction included.

1007 Albuquerque, Klaus de and **Jerome L. McElroy.** Race and ethnicity in the United States Virgin Islands (Ethnic Groups [Gordon & Breach Science Publishers, New York] 6 : 2/3, 1985, p. 125–153, bibl., tables)

Emphasizing the effects of the American presence, migration, and recent affluence, major Virgin Islands ethnic groups (native islanders, French, Puerto Rican, white and black US mainlanders, and Commonwealth West Indians) are considered. "Census data and other evidence suggest some assimilation and a gradual shift from a plural, more 'flexible' West Indian model of social segmentation to a simpler, more 'rigid' (but no less complex) black-white dichotomy."

1008 Alexander, Jack. Love, race, slavery, and sexuality in Jamaican images of the family (in Kinship, ideology and practice in Latin America [see item 259] p. 147–180, bibl.)

Following the method and theory of David Schneider and R.T. Smith, author describes and analyzes the conceptions that 11 middle-class Jamaicans have about kinship and how these articulate with their beliefs about race, class, and status. "The analysis assumes that culture consists of a pure level of domains, such as kinship and age, which consist of a set of collective representations that cohere, and that pure domains combine on a conglomerate level to create domains— such as the family—that are guides for action."

1009 Ashton, Guy T. Migration and the Puerto Rican support system (RRI, 12 : 2, Summer/Verano 1982, p. 228–242, bibl.)

Puerto Rican migration and especially the "brain-drain" of third- and fourth-year college students at Inter-American Univ. in P.R., is related to historical and contemporary aspects of the Puerto Rican extended family.

1010 Austin, Diane J. Culture and ideology in the English-speaking Caribbean: a view from Jamaica (AES/AE, 10 : 2, May 1983, p. 223–240, bibl.)

The historical ambiguity presented by Caribbean societies, of a stability comprising radical social inequalities, is reflected in two types of Caribbean anthropology, one stressing opposition, the other domination. Here, both themes are incorporated in a single analytical perspective, which stresses the role of the Jamaican middle class as brokers between the working man and metropolitan sources of power.

1011 ———. Urban life in Kingston, Jamaica: the culture and class ideology of two neighborhoods. New York: Gordon & Breach Science Publishers, 1984. 282 p.: bibl., tables (Caribbean studies; 3)

Study of two neighborhoods, one composed primarily of manual workers and the other of individuals holding clerical and professional positions. Author details the cultures and ideologies that prevail in these two settings, and of one ideology which she claims is dominant—"an ideology about education grounded in middle class culture which acts to redefine the values and institutions of working class life." In addition to describing daily life in the neighborhoods, substantial material is offered on politics and power, religion, sport and leisure, conflict and dispute, and ideology and hegemony. Volume concludes with two case studies, one on the middle class position and the other on the working class position.

1012 Ayensu, Edward S. Medicinal plants of the West Indies. Algonac, Mich.: Reference Publications, 1981. 282 p.: bibl., ill., indexes.

List of 632 species in 114 families of plants includes standard scientific binomials. Also indicates local names of plants as well as purported medicinal use. Of value to field researchers.

1013 Baber, Willie L. Social change and the peasant community: Horowitz's

Morne-Paysan reinterpreted (UP/E, 21:3, July 1982, p. 227–241, bibl., ill., tables)

Restudy of Martinican community indicates to author that Horowitz overemphasized its egalitarian nature, de-emphasized class divisions, dissociated it from "the vicissitudes of a plantation economy," and, consequently, failed to take into account the Caribbean historical experience. Offers alternative interpretation based on processes linked to plantation economy and class relations structured through a plantation system.

1014 Barrow, Christine. Guidelines for the conduct of social surveys in the Caribbean: the experience of a five island interdisciplinary questionnaire survey. Cave Hill, Barbados: Institute of Social and Economic Research, Eastern Caribbean, Univ. of the West Indies, 1983. 86 p.: bibl., ill., maps, tables (Occasional papers; 17)

Cautionary tale on the administration of social surveys in the Caribbean; a report of the UNESCO Man and Biosphere Project in the Eastern Caribbean.

1015 Berleant-Schiller, Riva. Grazing and gardens in Barbuda (in The Keeping of animals: adaptation and social relations in livestock producing communities. Edited by Riva Berleant-Schiller and Eugenia Shanklin. Totowa, N.J.: Allanheld, Osum & Co., 1983, p. 73–91, bibl., tables)

Demonstrates the delicate association of land use (open grazing of semiferal livestock and small provision gardens) with physical environment, a customary land tenure which allows all Barbudans equal rights to undivided lands outside the single settlement, and political dependency. Land-use balance shifts over long dry-and-wet cycles but land use and tenure have preserved Barbuda from drought and domination. However, if all factors are interdependent, a substantial change in one would affect the others. Such a change has come with political independence of Antigua-Barbuda in 1981 which is eroding traditional patterns of land tenure.

1016 Besson, Jean. Family land and Caribbean society: toward an ethnography of Afro-Caribbean peasantries (in Perspectives on Caribbean regional identity. Edited by Elizabeth M. Thomas-Hope. Liverpool, England: Centre for Latin American Studies, Univ. of Liverpool, 1984, p. 57–83, tables)

Discounting the traditional explanation of the origin and persistence of the institution of family land in rural Jamaica and in the Caribbean generally—that it is an African or European cultural remnant—the argument here relates it first to the circumstances of plantation slavery, and then to the continuing monopoly of plantations in the contemporary Caribbean. Thus, family land is viewed as a bastion of resistance and freedom, a means by which these are passed on, and the rallying ground for new, distinctively Afro-Caribbean, cultural initiatives.

1017 A Bibliography of Caribbean migration and Caribbean immigrant communities. Edited by Rosemary Brana-Shute. Gainesville: Reference and Bibliographic Dept., Univ. of Florida Libraries: in cooperation with Center for Latin American Studies, Univ. of Florida, 1983. 339 p.: appendices (Bibliographic series; 9)

Collection of 2585 citations of literature on the movement of Caribbean peoples including materials on in-migration, acculturation of new peoples and their impact on receiving Caribbean societies, rural-urban phenomena, intra-regional migration, out-migration, and Caribbean peoples in metropolitan countries. Appendices include data bases searched, journals cited, second authors, origins of migrants, destination of migrants, and a topical index. For bibliographer's comment, see item **22.**

1018 Bilby, Kenneth M. Black thought from the Caribbean: ideology at home and abroad (NWIG, 57:3/4, 1983, p. 201–214, bibl.)

Review essay dealing with books on Rastafarians by Joseph Owens, Sebastian Clarke, John Plummer, Ernest Cashmore, and Dick Hebdige.

1019 ———. How the "older heads" talk: a Jamaican Maroon spirit possession language and its relationship to the creoles of Suriname and Sierra Leone (NWIG, 57:1/2, 1983, p. 37–88, bibl.)

Diacritical features of the "deep language" (Kromanti) used by participants possessed by spirits in Maroon ceremonies distinguish it from the Jamaican Creole used in ordinary life, but are similar to the creoles of Surinam and Sierra Leone. These data support decreolization theory. Includes glossary.

1020 Brathwaite, Edward Kamau. Kumina: the spirit of African survival in Jamaica (IJ/JJ, 42, 1978, p. 44–63, plates)

Utilizing text of an interview with a Kumina priestess and commentary provided by Congolese anthropologist Bunseki-Lumanisa on Mukongo background to text, author presents interestingly organized study of Jamaican Kumina.

1021 Brathwaite, Farley. Unemployment and social life: a sociological study of the unemployed in Trinidad. Bridgetown: Antilles Publications, 1983. 165 p.: bibl., tables.

Consequences of unemployment, rather than its determinants, are the subject of this study which finds little evidence of "social breakdown" among the Trinidadian unemployed. The importance of illicit strategies for survival is consistently underreported.

1022 Brockmann, C. Thomas. Ethnic participation in Orange Walk economic development (Ethnic Groups [Gordon & Breach Science Publishers, New York] 6:2/3, 1985, p. 187–207, bibl., tables)

Rapid economic development took place in Orange Walk, Belize, which led to increased ethnic heterogeneity and socioeconomic differentiation. The degree to which ethnic groups were involved in these economic changes and the nature of their participation varied by the socioeconomic-political history of each group and the individual's "place of origin on the center-satellite continuum."

1023 Brodber, Erna. Perceptions of Caribbean women: towards a documentation of stereotypes. Cave Hill, Barbados: Institute of Social and Economic Research, Eastern Caribbean, Univ. of the West Indies, 1982. 62 p.: bibl. (Women in the Caribbean project; 4)

Vol. 4 in research series on the role of women in the English-speaking Caribbean. Author examines images of Caribbean women drawn from the press and from church documents of Barbados, Jamaica, and Trinidad: the everyday performance of female roles during three time periods; the extent to which images developed into stereotypes; and, the relationship between images, stereotypes and female potential over time.

1023a Butt Colson, Audrey. El desarrollo nacional y los Akawaio y Pemon del Alto Mazaruni (III/AI, 43, julio/sept. 1983, p. 445–502, bibl., map)

Relationship, from a historical perspective, of the state-nation and the Upper Mazaruni Akawaio and Pemon communities of Guyana. Lengthy descriptions and analyses of several important events or processes in Amerindian-state relations. After an assessment of state impact on local culture and resource control, she concludes that from the Amerindian perspective, western civilization has led to a condition of permanent imbalance.

1024 Callam, Neville G. Invitation to docility: defusing the Rastafarian challenge (Caribbean Journal of Religious Studies [The United Theological College of the West Indies, Kingston] 3:2, Sept. 1980, p. 28–44)

Stress given by Rastafarians to a particular aspect of their social ethic (withdrawal heroism, or "naturism") in response to contextual exigencies permits the movement to continue as a protest group. Author reviews accomodations of dominant society to the movement and concludes that while it will survive in some form it may well be absorbed by society into its routine thereby reestablishing a normative order.

1025 Cashmore, E.E. The Rastafarians. London: Minority Rights Group, 1984. 11 p.: appendices, bibl. (Minority Rights Group report; 64)

History of Rastafarians and account of their major beliefs. Study fails to mention the tremendous role of ganja trafficking in the maintenance and growth of the movement.

1026 Cato, John D. The People's Temple: a socio-religious analysis (Caribbean Journal of Religious Studies [The United Theological College of the West Indies, Kingston] 2:2, Sept. 1979, p. 1–7, bibl.)

Discounting psychological aberration as a major category for interpreting the Jonestown tragedy, author argues that the People's Temple can better be viewed as a social movement responding to the religious, social, and ideological needs of a diverse collectivity ("true believers," the elderly, white ideologues, and the "alienated, frustrated and angry").

1027 Chase, Julia. Emigration and changing racial ratios in Saba, N.A. (RRI, 11:4, Winter 1981/1982, p. 501–506)

"As the percentage of black population increases the nature of race relations which have always been rather good on Saba, is also changing."

1028 Chevannes, Barry. Some notes on African religious survivals in the Caribbean (Caribbean Journal of Religious Studies [The United Theological College of the West Indies, Kingston] 5:2, Sept. 1983, p. 18–28)

Remnants of African religions continue to persist in the Caribbean because they are expressions of a world view—involving spirits, man and nature—which remain widespread. This world view is either fatalistic or revolutionary in different social contexts.

1029 Clarke, Colin G. Caribbean consciousness (in Perspectives on Caribbean regional identity. Edited by Elizabeth M. Thomas-Hope. Liverpool, England: Centre for Latin American Studies, Univ. of Liverpool, 1984, p. 122–134)

Fragmented by insularity, which smallness emphasizes, and permeated by colonialism, West Indian consciousness is a restricted and rare phenomenon. Only the French, British Commonwealth, and Dutch Islanders—and the Cubans—have an awareness of the West Indies, but the possibilities for cooperation are limited by linguistic and political barriers and increasingly by ideological differences. Despite counter-currents to insular fragmentation in the post-colonial period—such as the creation of CARIFTA, or through the regional Black Power and Rastafarian movements—West Indian identity, both regional and insular, remains unavoidably plural, perhaps perpetually so.

1030 Clarke, Sebastian. Jah music: the evolution of the popular Jamaican song. London: Heinemann Educational Books, 1980. 216 p.: plates.

Popular account of the historical origins of Jamaican music and the development of Reggae. Informative chapter on Bob Marley, Peter Tosh, and Bunny Wailer.

1032 Coreil, Jeannine. Allocation of family resources for health care in rural Haiti (Social Science and Medicine [Pergamon Press, New York] 17:11, 1983, p. 709–719, ill., tables)

Based on a household survey of 230 episodes of infant and child illness, author finds that allocation of family resources for health care is heavily influenced by cultural and ecological variables as well as medical and economic factors.

1033 Cosminsky, Sheila and Emory Whipple. Ethnicity and mating patterns in Punta Gorda, Belize (in Black Caribs: a case study in biocultural adaptation. Edited by Michael H. Crawford. New York: Plenum Press, 1984, p. 115–132, bibl., tables)

While endogamy is the ideal as well as the predominant practice of all ethnic groups (Garifuna, Creoles, Spaniards, East Indians, Chinese, Mayans, and others), inter-ethnic mating occurs according to rules and patterns. Ideal of endogamy and prevailing ethnic stereotypes help maintain ethnic boundaries and identity but inter-ethnic mating is facilitated by desire for children, acceptance of outside children, value placed on light skin, color-class hierarchy, increasing economic competition, migration, and excess of females.

1034 Craig, Dennis R. Language identity and the West Indian child (in Perspectives on Caribbean regional identity. Edited by Elizabeth M. Thomas-Hope. Liverpool, England: Centre for Latin American Studies, Univ. of Liverpool, 1984, p. 84–96)

Although it is important for children who speak Creole to be perfectly secure in the rich indigenous culture of which Creole is an aspect, educators are ill-advised in designing learning programs which increase that security while decreasing proficiency in the international, officially recognized European language through which freedom and socioeconomic advancement are vouchsafed. In the case of officially English-speaking West Indian territories, where a Mesolect is used, special methodological procedures are suggested which enhance both increased familiarity with the indigenous culture and proficiency in the officially recognized language.

1035 Cross, Malcolm. The East Indians of Guyana and Trinidad. London: Minority Rights Group, 1980. 18 p. (MRG report; no. 13)

Descriptive account of the indenture,

and of current East Indian-African relations in Guyana and Trinidad.

1036 Cultura y folklore de Samaná. Compilado por Dagoberto Tejeda Ortiz. Santo Domingo: Lotería Nacional, Depto. de Bienestar Social, 1984. 279 p.: tables.

Useful collection of eight already published but difficult to locate articles and other materials on the culture and folklore of the black "Americans" of Samaná, Dominican Republic. Of particular interest is H. Hoetink's historico-sociological study and Martha Ellen Davis's two essays on religion and on religious musical culture.

1037 Cultural patrimony and the tourism product: towards a mutually beneficial relationship. Final report, OAS/CTRC Regional Seminar, Hastings, Barbados, July 18–22, 1983. Washington: International Trade and Tourism Division, Dept. of Economic Affairs, OAS, 1983. 120 p.

Collection of papers presented at an oceanside seminar for scholars and tourist industry representatives: a willfully optimistic report on the mutually beneficial relationship between cultural resources and tourist industry initiatives.

1038 Dance, Daryl C. Folklore from contemporary Jamaicans. Knoxville: Univ. of Tennessee Press, 1985. 229 p.: bibl., maps, plates.

Collection of 298 Jamaican tales, games, riddles, songs, and rhymes organized into 11 chapters each with a short introduction: etiological tales, *anansesem*, duppy tales, big boy tales, tales about religion, tales about Rastafarians, miscellaneous tales, riddles, rhymes, songs, and children's games.

1039 Davidson, William V. The Garifuna in Central America: ethnohistorical and geographical foundations (*in* Black Caribs: a case study in biocultural adaptation. Edited by Michael H. Crawford. New York: Plenum Press, 1984, p. 13–35, bibl., ill., maps)

Succinct review of Garifuna origins, dispersal in Central America and patterns of settlement in time and place (Garifuna culture realm, trade area, village subsistence region, settlement proper, and family compound). Informative maps.

1040 Davis, E. Wade. The ethnobiology of the Haitian zombi (Journal of Ethnopharmacology [Elsevier Sequoia, Lausanne, Switzerland] 9:1, Nov. 1983, p. 85–104, bibl., plates, table)

The recent surfacing of three zombies has focused attention upon the claim that there is an ethnopharmacological basis for zombies. Poisons are suggested here whose consistent ingredients include tetrodotoxins, derived from various species of puffer fish. The symptomology of tetrodotoxication is compared with that of zombies; and preliminary laboratory tests are summarized. The role of zombies in voudou theology is described.

1041 Davis, Martha Ellen. Voces del purgatorio: estudio de la salve dominicana. Santo Domingo: Museo del Hombre Dominicano, 1981. 106 p.: bibl., map, music, plates (Investigaciones antropológicas; no. 15)

Description and analysis of *salve*, a class of Dominican religious and quasireligious music. Musical transcriptions provided.

1042 Développement rural en Haïti et dans la Caraïbe. Port-au-Prince: Dept. des sciences du développement, Faculté d'ethnologie, Univ. d'état d'Haïti, 1980. 424 p.: ill., maps, tables.

Proceedings of a colloquium on Haitian rural development, held in Port-au-Prince in 1979. Contributions are organized around the themes of literacy, community development, appropriate technology, rural health, religion, specific activities, regional organizations, and general approaches. Most participants appear to have been technicians or government officials.

1043 Dévieux, Liliane. Références ethniques dans les contes haïtiens (Anthropologie et Sociétés [Univ. Laval, Québec, Canada] 8:2, 1984, p. 139–159, bibl.)

Analysis of racial or ethnic references in Haitian folktales.

1044 Devonish, Hubert. Creole languages and the process of socioeconomic domination in the Caribbean: a historical review (*in* Aspects of Caribbean Creoles. Edited by Pauline Christie. Kingston: West Indian Assn. for Commonwealth Literature and Language Studies, 1983, p. 52–68, bibl. [Carib; 3])

Succinct historical review of Creole languages and development of patterns of social differentiation in the Caribbean. Consideration given to the language situation within plantation slave society, in late 18th-century Haiti, in the immediate pre-emancipation and post-emancipation periods in other parts of the Caribbean, and the contemporary situation. Concludes that the establishment of Creole as official language in any Caribbean country is a vital ingredient of any attempt to achieve political or socio-economic liberation.

1045 Diederich, Bernard. On the nature of zombie existence: the reality of a voudou ritual (FIU/CR, 12:3, Summer 1983, p. 14–17, 43–46)

Account of the appearance of three zombies and of the work of Haiti's leading psychiatrist and zombiologist.

1046 Dodd, David J. Rule-making and rule-enforcement in plantation society: the ideological development of criminal justice in Guyana (UWI/SES, 31:3, Sept. 1982, p. 1–35, bibl.)

In Guyana, there has never been a separation of powers and the criminal justice system, developing out of plantation "house rules" which protected dominant powers are now still indistinguishable from "house rules" which protect the interests of today's ruling party. The role of lower courts and the lawyers is explored in the context of the "inmate social system" of the "total institution" of plantation society.

1047 Douyon, Emerson. Crimes rituels et mort apparente en Haïti: vers une synthèse critique (Anthropologie et Sociétés [Univ. Laval, Québec, Canada] 8:2, 1984,. p. 87–120, bibl.)

Study of Haitian ritual crimes and deathlike comas in relation to parallel forms of justice. Author deals with ritual leaders and the making of zombies, the nature and personality of zombies, the perspectives of victims, the processes and stages of zombification, relevant ethnopharmological research, and social reaction.

1048 Dreher, Melanie C. Marihuana and work: cannabis smoking on a Jamaican sugar estate (SAA/HO, 42:1, Spring 1982, p. 1–8, tables)

Critical examination of the "amotivational syndrome," often cited as one of the deleterious effects of long-term marihuana use. Drawing on field data from three farms of one sugar estate, author evaluates work

performance in relation to marihuana use as well as the strategies employed by management to reinforce its own values as to use and productivity.

1049 Duany, Jorge. Ethnicity in the Spanish Caribbean: notes on the consolidation of creole identity in Cuba and Puerto Rico, 1762–1868 (Ethnic Groups [Gordon & Breach Science Publishers, New York] 6:2/3, 1985, p. 99–123, bibl.)

Comparison of incorporation of African and European immigrants after the expansion of sugar plantations in late 18th century. Argues that ethnicity must be viewed in relation to social class structure and that ethnic groups are conditioned by factors of production. This approach offers explanation of "the organization of cultural differences in Cuba and Puerto Rico during this period."

1050 Duncan, Neville and Kenneth O'Brien. Women and politics in Barbados, 1948–1981. Cave Hill, Barbados: Institute of Social and Economic Research, Eastern Caribbean, Univ. of the West Indies, 1983. 68 p.: bibl., tables (Women in the Caribbean project; 3)

Vol. 3 in research series on the role of women in the English-speaking Caribbean. Deals with Barbadian female participation in local politics and in formal legislative bodies; female membership on statutory boards, commissions, and public corporations; female partisan involvement; and women and electoral politics.

1051 Dunham, Katherine. Dances of Haiti. Los Angeles: Center for Afro-American Studies, Univ. of California, 1983. 78 p.: plates (CAAS special publication)

Revised English-language edition of earlier Spanish and English (1947) and French (1957) versions. Short but still valuable study that emphasizes material aspects of the dance, organization of dance groups, functions of dances, and interrelation of form and function. Includes Claude Lévi-Strauss's brief forward to the French edition and glossary.

1052 Durant-González, Victoria. The occupation of higglering (IJ/JJ, 16:3, Winter 1983, p. 2–12, bibl., plates)

Describes occupation of higglering in Jamaica: organization, skills, methods of recruitment, rewards and options it offers women. Article does not theorize as to the existence of such informal economic systems, and their occurrence alongside the corporate capitalist economy.

1053 Edwards, Melvin R. Jamaican higglers: their significance and potential. Swansea, Wales: Centre for Development Studies, Univ. College of Swansea, 1980. 58 p.: bibl.
Description of Jamaican higglers, or operators of the indigenous marketing system. The existence of informal economic systems, and of the unique cultural and social features in which they are imbedded, is not theorized.

1054 Fisher, Lawrence E. Colonial madness: mental health in the Barbadian social order. New Brunswick, N.J.: Rutgers Univ. Press, 1985. 275 p.: bibl., ill., plates.
". . . a comprehensive anthropological overview of Barbadian culture and a detailed ethnographic analysis of Barbadian views of 'madness' in the 1970s. It does so by moving backward and forward through time to bring the study of the madhouse within the context of everyday life, between the Barbadian Mental Hospital and the village. In addition, its unique—but not exclusive—objective is to explore the colonial realities of present-day Barbados through the orientations of madness of lower-class villagers and mental patients." A substantial contribution to the literature.

1055 Forsythe, Dennis. Rastafari, for the healing of the nation. Kingston: Zaika Publications, 1983. 236 p.: ill.
Report of the personal "discovery" of Rastafari by a Jamaican sociologist. Regards his experience "as a mystical journey and a modern manifestation of the ancient mystery Religious tradition." Interesting, idiosyncratic sections on Rastafari roots, concepts, the ganja controversy, Rastas and the Chakras, and West Indian culture through Rasta eyes.

1056 Gerber, Stanford N. and **Knud Rasmussen.** St. John, Virgin Islands: a note on immigration and "paradise lost" (RRI, 11:4, Winter 1981/1982, p. 477–501)
Class relations come to St. John, Virgin Islands, as a result of large-scale immigration.

1057 Gibson, Margaret A. Ethnicity and schooling: West Indian immigrants in the United States Virgin Islands (Ethnic Groups [Gordon & Breach Science Publishers, New York] 5:3, 1983, p. 173–197, bibl.)
Comparisons between native Cruzians and Down Islanders (immigrants from other islands to the Virgin Islands) suggest the dynamic relationship between ethnicity, schooling, sex role, economic opportunity and adult success, in a case where social class, race and cultural distinctions are minimal. Denied access to employment niches which birthplace and kinship offer to native Cruzians, Down Islanders, both boys and girls, performed better than their Cruzian classmates.

1058 Gill, Margaret and **Joycelin Massiah.** Women, work and development. Cave Hill, Barbados: Institute of Social and Economic Research, Univ. of the West Indies, 1984. 129 p.: bibl., ill., tables (Women in the Caribbean project; 6)
Vol. 6 in research series on the role of women in the English-speaking Caribbean. Two substantive papers are included: Margaret Gill's on women, work and development in Barbados, 1946–1970, in which economic structures and cultural patterns are explored; and Joycelin Massiah's on indicators of women in development which offers a model for assessing the well-being of women in Caribbean societies.

1059 Glazier, Stephen D. An annotated ethnographic bibliography of Trinidad (HRAF/BSR, 17:1/2, Spring/Summer 1982, p. 31–58, bibl.)
Slightly dated bibliography of articles, books, PhD dissertations, and Master's theses. For bibliographer's comment, see item 32.

1060 ———. Caribbean ethnicity revisited: editor's introduction (Ethnic Groups [Gordon & Breach Science Publishers, New York] 6:2/3, 1985, p. 85–97, bibl.)
Introduction to journal issue on Caribbean ethnicity in which editor stresses the complexity of the phenomenon and indicates that context and behavior as well as age, sex, wealth, and social mobility must be taken into account.

1061 ———. Marchin' the pilgrims home: leadership and decision-making in an Afro-Caribbean faith. Westport, Conn.: Greenwood Press, 1983. 165 p.: bibl., ill., plates, tables (Contributions to the study of religion; 10)

Ethnography of the Spiritual Baptists of Trinidad, which focuses on leadership decisions and how these play a critical role in "almost every aspect of church life." The belief system is described as are major church rituals, leadership roles as they relate to change, church organization and its dynamics, and leader's impact on church economics.

1062 Glick, Leonard B. Epilogue: the meanings of ethnicity in the Caribbean (Ethnic Groups [Gordon & Breach Science Publishers, New York] 6 : 2/3, 1985, p. 233–248, bibl.)

General statement on Caribbean ethnicity which concludes that the region is experiencing significant social change, "and that ethnicity, with its diverse potential meanings, may provide much of the foundation for Caribbean societies of the future."

1063 Goldberg, Richard S. The definition of household: a three-dimensional approach (Journal of Caribbean Studies [Assn. of Caribbean Studies, Coral Gables, Fla.] 4 : 1, Fall 1984, p. 29–36, bibl., ill., table)

In Grand Cayman, time, space, and social relations define the household.

1064 González, Nancie Loudon. Garifuna—Black Carib—social organization (*in* Black Caribs: a case study in biocultural adaptation. Edited by Michael H. Crawford. New York: Plenum Press, 1984, p. 51–65, bibl., tables)

Argues that Garifuna culture and society cannot be understood apart from the process of migration and that it "is largely responsible for shaping Garifuna social organization for some time." Migration has had "profound effects" on household and family structure as well as on religious, cultural, and political matters. Fiction persists that men are dominant but ethnographic reality is that women are strong, effective, and influential.

1065 ———. New evidence on the origin of the Black Carib: with thoughts on the meaning of tradition (NWIG, 57 : 3/4, 1983, p. 143–172, bibl., map, tables)

Historical data given on factors leading to the removal of Caribs from St. Vincent as well as on size of population landed on Roatan and on flight to and dispersal in Honduras, along with author's perspective on persistence and borrowing in relation to Black Carib cultural tradition. ". . . Black Carib culture is what it is today because some members . . . put down on Roatan were willing and able to make quick, opportunistic decisions without the burden of a traditional political and religious system which might have urged caution.

1066 ———. Rethinking the consanguineal household and matrifocality (UP/E, 23 : 1, Jan. 1984, p. 1–12, bibl.)

Rethinking the "type" of household structure the author has made influential in the literature, "the consanguineal household," she argues that it expresses rather marital and residential instability; and is an adaptive response to individualism, the assumption by women of male functions, and migratory wage labor.

1067 Grasmuck, Sherri. The impact of emigration on national development: three sending communities in the Dominican Republic. New York: Center for Latin American and Caribbean Studies, New York Univ., 1982. 28 p.: bibl., tables (New York Research Program in Interamerican Affairs. Occasional papers; 33)

Study of three communities in the Dominican Republic examines impact of emigration upon those conditions which provoked out-migration in the first place. Both agricultural stagnation and unemployment are exacerbated by emigration.

1068 Green, Vera. Migrants in Aruba and Curaçao: comparative adjustment patterns (RRI, 11 : 3, Fall 1981, p. 320–334, bibl.)

Economic and policy factors interrelate to determine the adjustment patterns of migrant oil refinery workers in Aruba and Curaçao.

1069 Gullick, C.J.M.R. The changing Vincentian Carib population (*in* Black Caribs: a case study in biocultural adaptation. Edited by Michael H. Crawford. New York: Plenum Press, 1984, p. 37–50, bibl., map)

Assessment of differing estimates of the Black and Yellow Carib population of St. Vincent for the pre-1797 period, the 19th century, the 20th century, and current condition. Useful short sections on population effects of cataclysms (hurricanes and volcanic eruptions) and consequent movement within St. Vincent.

1070 Harewood, Jack. White collar migrant labor: some observations on the case of Trinidad and Tobago in the last two decades (*in* White collar migrants in the Americas and the Caribbean. Edited by Arnaud F. Marks and Hebe M.C. Vessuri. Leiden, Netherlands: Dept. of Caribbean Studies, Royal Institute of Linguistics and Anthropology, 1983, p. 19–37)

Description and assessment of white-collar emigration from Trinidad since 1962. Economic and social changes in both sending and receiving countries which account for increased white-collar emigration in the period are discussed and the impact of this emigration on Trinidad and Tobago are explored.

1071 Henry, Paget. Peripheral capitalism and underdevelopment in Antigua. New Brunswick, N.J.: Transaction Books, 1985. 220 p.: tables.

Drawing on a theory of peripheral development within the broader context of dependency theory, author traces the postcolonial development of Antigua. Detailed accounts and analyses are given of colonial Antigua's peripheralization and the establishment of the economic, political, and cultural institutions; change and adjustment of these institutions over time, the international and local dimensions of the decolonization process; and the nature of the postcolonial economy, state, and cultural system of Antigua.

1072 Honychurch, Lennox. Our island culture. Roseau, Dominica: Dominica Cultural Council, 1983? 55 p.: ill., plates.

Affectionate guide to Dominica and Dominicans.

1073 Jenkins, Carol L. Ritual and resource flow: the Garifuna *dugu* (AES/AE, 10:3, Aug. 1983, p. 429–442, tables)

Among the Garifuna of Belize, *dugu* ceremonies, or ancestral feasts, have been increasing in size and frequency, in a context of malnutrition, declining subsistence activities and migration. The *dugu* is viewed here as a strategy for resource redistribution between wealthier migrants and their poorer kin. The role of *buyai* (Garifuna shamans) in effecting these redistributions is considered.

1074 Kerns, Virginia. Past and present evidence of interethnic mating (*in* Black Caribs: a case study in biocultural adaptation. Edited by Michael H. Crawford. New York: Plenum Press, 1984, p. 95–114, bibl., tables)

Contemporary interethnic mating has historic precedent—censuses and other accounts suggest "many exceptions to any normative rule of ethnic endogamy." Evidence is marshalled from 18th, 19th, and 20th centuries in support of position. Indication that rapid Black Carib population growth in Central America was due, in part, to reproduction with non-Caribs.

1075 Klass, Morton. Discussion: new ethnicity, new horizons (Ethnic Groups [Gordon & Breach Science Publishers, New York] 6:2/3, 1985, p. 223–232)

Discussion of articles on Caribbean ethnicity in two issues of *Ethnic Groups* (6:2 and 6:3).

1076 Knight, Franklin W. United States cultural influences on the English-speaking Caribbean during the twentieth century. San Germán: Centro de Investigaciones del Caribe y América Latina: Univ. Interamericana de Puerto Rico, 1983? 23 p.: tables (Documentos de trabajo; 11)

Although US expansion into the West Indies has been substantial, the "Americanization" of the region—fueled, in part, by West Indian migration to the US, tourism, the communications revolution, etc.—has been relatively limited given British traditions and different territorial levels of economic development.

1077 Knowles, Roberta. Socio-linguistic norms and linguistic diversity in a West Indian community (Caribbean Journal of Education [Univ. of the West Indies, Mona, Jamaica] 9:3, Sept. 1982, p. 213–228, bibl., table)

Selected Virgin Island adults are found to have communicative competencies which show sensitivity to sociolinguistic norms, regional variation, and abbreviation. Such features, at odds with the rules of classroom interaction, should be promoted "to open the lines of communication between the different elements we are made up of."

1078 Köbben, A.J.F. In vrijheid en gebondenheid: samenleving en cultuur van de Djoeka aan de Cottica. Utrecht, The Netherlands: Centrum voor Caraïbische

Studies, Instituut voor Culturele Antropologie, Rijksuniv. Utrecht, 1979. 191 p., 3 leaves of plates: bibl., ill., maps (Bronnen voor de studie van Bosneger samenlevingen; 4)

Study describes culture, kinship system, political organization, etc., of the Djuka tribe on the Cottica River, Surinam. Author concludes that Djuka social structure and the lack of external pressures for change account for their strong resistance to acculturation and ensure the continuity of Djuka culture. [N. Vicenti]

1079 Laguerre, Michel S. Urban life in the Caribbean: a study of a Haitian urban community. Cambridge, Mass.: Schenkman Publishing Co., 1982. 214 p.: bibl., ill., maps, plates.

Discusses the Haitian urban community as locus of frontiers between the capitalist and pre-capitalist ethic. In such a dependent economy, interlocking residential structures and kinship networks, mediated by the roles of the voodoo priest and Duvalier's tonton macoute, elaborate private and small-group strategies of survival.

1080 Larose, Serge and Frantz Voltaire.
Structure agraire et tenure foncière en Haïti (Anthropologie et Sociétés [Univ. Laval, Québec, Canada] 8:2, 1984, p. 65–85, bibl., tables)

Authors argue that the analysis of Haitian agrarian structure and land tenure should begin with an understanding of the social relations of production rather than on absolute size of holding. From this perspective, large and medium size properties of rural and urban proprietors should be sociologically differentiated as well as individual small holdings from "lineage property."

1081 Layng, Anthony. The Caribs of Dominica: prospects for structural assimilation of a territorial minority (Ethnic Groups [Gordon & Breach Science Publishers, New York] 6:2/3, 1985, p. 209–221, bibl., map)

While neither racially nor culturally different, the Caribs are a distinctive territorial minority group in Dominica, an ascriptive status directly linked to their life on a reservation. Future of this status is related to variable of structural pluralism; if reservation status changes, then there is a possibility of eventual structural assimilation into larger society.

1082 Lewis, Gordon K. The making of a Caribbeanist. San Germán: Centro de Investigaciones del Caribe y América Latina: Univ. Interamericana de Puerto Rico, 1983? 13 p. (Documentos de trabajo; 10)

Part autobiographical, part analytical essay which delineates the career pattern of the author and his intellectual roots and dissects several important issues and problems that confront Caribbean scholars including appropriate conceptual and technical approaches, the relationship between academic research and ideological belief, the North American monopoly of Caribbean studies, etc. Argues the need for interdisciplinary research for "fruitful" Caribbean studies.

1083 Lowenthal, David. "An island is a world:" the problem of Caribbean insularity (in Perspectives on Caribbean regional identity. Edited by Elizabeth M. Thomas-Hope. Liverpool, England: Centre for Latin American Studies, Univ. of Liverpool, 1984, p. 109–121)

Age-old West Indian parochialism, fostered by the islands' separate and exclusive relations with European mother countries, by the need to establish local hegemonies against imperial control and encouraged today by politicians protecting their sovereignties and separate fiefdoms, has not been eroded by frequent attempts at economic and political cooperation. Indeed, such cooperative efforts have succeeded only in allowing injustices to smaller states by larger ones, and in exacerbating dog-eat-dog rivalries among the larger states themselves. Regional unity and identity is more likely to be achieved through informal voluntary agencies and through extensions of the informal inter-island comings and goings which began during slavery and which have been increasing recently.

1083a Manning, Frank E. Carnival and the West Indian diaspora (The Round Table [Butterfield Scientific Ltd, Guildford, England] 286, 1983, p. 186–196, notes)

Views Toronto Carnival as a distillation of West Indian experience in urban Canada and as an ongoing dialectic between cultural expression and political processes. Author argues that the politics of these festivals illuminate how West Indian migrants are dealing with each other and how "they are coming to terms with Canadian society."

1084 Massiah, Joycelin. Employed women in Barbados: a demographic profile, 1946–1970. Cave Hill, Barbados: Institute of Social and Economic Research, Eastern Caribbean, Univ. of the West Indies, 1984. 131 p.: bibl., ill., tables (Occasional papers; no. 8)

Study of the Barbadian female work force based primarily on data drawn from the 1946, 1960, and 1970 censuses in order to identify the demographic factors related to female participation in economic life and the extent these factors have varied over time.

1085 ———. Women as heads of households in the Caribbean: family structure and feminine status. Paris: UNESCO, 1983. 69 p.: bibl., tables (Women in a world perspective)

Based on 1970 census data, author provides demographic profile of Commonwealth Caribbean female-headed households. Also includes sections on strategies for survival and principal sources of financial assistance available to female household heads in Barbados. Findings indicate that these heads are concentrated in low-paid, low-status occupations and are more disadvantaged than men in similar positions. Six, very short, case-studies of welfare recipients are appended.

1086 Maximilien, Louis. Le voudou haïtien: rite radas-canzo. Préface de Pierre Mabille. Port-au-Prince: Imprimerie H. Deschamps, 1982. 224 p., 55 p. of plates: bibl., ill.

Relatively detailed description of the basic elements and components of Haitian vodun.

1087 Mayer, Francine M.; Catherine Bonaiti; and Jean Benoist. Utilisation de l'approche généalogique pour l'étude génétique de l'hypoacousie dans un isolat de la Caraïbe (Anthropologie et Sociétés [Univ. Laval, Québec, Canada] 8 : 2, 1984, p. 161–177, ill., tables)

Preliminary results of a genealogical approach utilized to study the genetic aspects of hypoacusia among the residents of St. Barthelemy.

1088 Menezes, M. Noel. Amerindian life in Guyana. Georgetown: Ministry of Education, Social Development and Culture, 1982. 32 p.: map, plates.

Short, superficial descriptions of housing, transportation, occupations, children and Timehri paintings. Colorful photographs.

1089 Mikell, Gwendolyn. When horses talk: reflections on Zora Neale Hurston's Haitian anthropology (AU/P, 43 : 3, Sept. 1982, p. 218–230)

Informative essay on the anthropology of a black female anthropologist and writer. Author assesses Hurston's background and training, the influence of Boas and Benedict, and her use of insider-outsider perspectives in *Tell my horse* (1938) for understanding rural Jamaican and Haitian culture.

1090 Mills, Frank L. and S.B. Jones-Hendrickson. Christmas sports in St. Kitts-Nevis: our neglected cultural tradition. s.l.: s.n., 1984. 66 p.: plates.

Describes traditional Christmas sports, "a veritable bastion of Kittitian-Nevisian culture," and principal participants.

1091 Mintz, Sidney W. Reflections on Caribbean peasantries (NWIG, 57 : 1/2, 1983, p. 1–17, bibl.)

Caribbean peasantries are viewed as largely self-supporting, though involved in foreign markets also; in dialectical linkage with the plantations, in struggles for land, labor, and capital; and as representing "a mode of response to the plantation system and its connotations and a mode of resistance to externally imposed styles of life." In this view the significance of peasantries in Caribbean historical developments is accounted for.

1092 Morrish, Ivor. Obeah, Christ and rastaman: Jamaica and its religion. Greenwood, S.C.: Attic Press, 1982. 122 p.: bibl., maps, table.

Jamaican culture is presented as one in which "most of the religio-political movements of the world are to be found epitomized in some form." Rastafarianism is given special attention.

1093 Moses, Yolanda T. Female status, the family, and male dominance in a West Indian community (*in* Women and national development: the complexities of change. Edited by The Wellesley Editorial Committee. Chicago: Univ. of Chicago Press, 1977, p. 142–153, tables)

Substantial contributions to the household economy do not improve the status of women on Montserrat, where there is an ideology of male supremacy.

1094 Nagashima, Yoshiko S. Rastafarian music in contemporary Jamaica: a study of socioreligious music of the Rastafarian movement in Jamaica. Tokyo: Institute for the Study of Languages and Cultures of Asia and Africa, Tokyo Univ. of Foreign Studies, 1984. 227 p.: bibl., graphs, maps, tables (Symbolism and world view in Asia and Africa. Performance in culture; 3)

Concentrating on Nyabynghi or bynghi music, author deals with this genre in sociocultural context by describing the past and present nature of Rastafarianism; the ancestral heritage of the music as well as its local origins, growth and diversification; Rastafarian ritual and Nyabynghi musical performance; aspects of Rastafarian cosmology and faith through lyrics; internal and external influences on the music; and a comparison of bynghi music and reggae.

1095 Nevadomsky, Joseph. Developmental sequences of domestic groups in an East Indian community in rural Trinidad (UP/E, 24:1, Jan. 1985, p. 1–11, bibl., ill., tables)

Presents series of frequency distributions of various household forms according to age-decades of ever-married women. Shows the possibility of several developmental series, rather than a single unilinear model of domestic organization. Phases in any possible developmental patterns are temporary responses to various social and economic changes occurring among rural East Indians in Trinidad.

1096 ———. Explaining Caribbean family and household organization: a typology of the classics (Journal of Caribbean Studies [Assn. of Caribbean Studies, Coral Gables, Fla.] 4:1, Fall 1984, p. 38–46, bibl.)

Review of studies of lower-income families and domestic organization in the Greater Caribbean.

1097 ———. Social change and the East Indians in rural Trinidad: a critique of methodologies (UWI/SES, 31:1, March 1982, p. 90–126, bibl.)

Increasing political and economic involvement in the wider society by East Indians in rural Trinidad offer powerful arguments against the "plural society model" and the "retentionist model" perspectives which inform most studies of East Indians in the

Caribbean. By contrast, the systemic model, which describes the processes by which ethnic and cultural categories are gradually integrated into an overall stratification system, accounts for both increased participation as well as for cultural distinctiveness.

1098 Newton, Velma. The silver men: West Indian labour migration to Panama, 1850–1914. Mona, Jamaica: Institute of Social and Economic Research, Univ. of the West Indies, 1984. 218 p.: bibl., tables.

Thorough historical account of British West Indian emigration to Panama with emphasis on the role of West Indians in building the Panama Railroad and Canal. Useful data on emigration policies, the recruitment of labor, the demographics of the movement, effect on the sending colonies, and on the West Indian experience in Panama.

1099 Nicholls, David. Haiti in Caribbean context: ethnicity, economy and revolt. New York: St. Martin's Press, 1985. 282 p.: bibl.

Collection of author's reworked articles and new materials dealing with links between ethnic structures and economy in Haiti and how the particular manifestations of political domination and revolt in that country are to be understood in light of these links. Two articles, one on East Indians and black power in Trinidad and the other on the Arabs of the Antilles offer some comparative context. Volume is divided into three sections: 1) Ethnicity; 2) Economy; and 3) Domination and Revolt. Concludes that Haitian masses are basically conservative and that political strategies assuming existence of a revolutionary working class or peasantry will fail.

1100 Palacio, Joseph. Food and social relations in a Belizean Garifuna village (BISRA/BS, 12:3, 1984, p. 1–7)

Utilizing excerpts from his dissertation, author argues that community is divided into age categories, each with specific functions. "People in some age categories control the political structure and monopolize the food supply, bringing about strains in social relations and enhancing their position in the social hierarchy."

1101 ———. Food exchange systems (BISRA/BS, 12:3, 1984, p. 8–34, tables)

Utilizing excerpts from his dissertation, author demonstrates that food circulates in a Belizean Garifuna village through cash and non-cash exchange systems. The former involves both petty and large scale trading; the latter is based on participation in the subsistence economy and role obligation. Food exchange reflects rank in the local system.

1102 Pessar, Patricia R. Kinship relations of production in the migration process: the case of Dominican emigration to the United States. New York: Center for Latin American and Caribbean Studies, New York Univ., 1982. 41 p.: bibl. (New York Research Program in Inter-American Affairs. Occasional papers; 32)

Relations between husband and wife, and between parental and junior generations in Dominican international migrant households, are seen to be characterized by inequities, hierarchies of control, and struggle over rights and benefits which reflect the unequal system of exchange of commodities, capital and labor binding the US and the Dominican Republic together. The role of women's labor in particular is discussed.

1103 Pierce, Paulette. Noncapitalist development: the struggle to nationalize the Guyanese sugar industry. Totowa, N.J.: Rowman & Allanheld, 1984. 200 p.: bibl.

Author traces the sociopolitical development of Guyana "that culminated in the triumph of the Marxist-Leninist program to 'resist imperialism' and to place the profitable sugar industry firmly in the hands of 'the people.' The resulting national unity and euphoria were short-lived . . . and today the working class remains divided along racial lines." Arguments embedded in book about the compatibility of liberal democratic state forms with dependent relations and the compatibility of nationalization and Marxist-Leninist ideology with capitalism make this work of interest to students of Third World development and of the nature of Caribbean society.

1104 Pollak-Eltz, Angelina. Folklore y cultura en los pueblos negros de Yaracuy. Caracas: Editorial Arte, 1984. 105 p.: bibl.

Descriptions of folkloric practices and aspects of culture of the Afro-Venezuelan population of the Yaracuy River Valley including short sections on history, demography, agriculture, work, migration, education, life cycle, popular Catholicism, cults, fiestas, beliefs and superstitions, language, children's games, oral literature, etc.

1105 Pollard, Velma. The social history of Dread Talk (UWI/CQ, 28:4, Dec. 1982, p. 17–40, bibl.)

The impact of Rastafarianism upon Jamaican aesthetic life, in dance, music and speech forms, has been considerable, probably because Rastafarianism responds to "some of the deepest social forces that have shaped and still determine the discrepancies of Caribbean society." The case of Dread Talk, which has progressively "colonized" Jamaican Creole over the last few decades, is discussed.

1106 Powell, Dorian. The role of women in the Caribbean (UWI/SES, 33:2, June 1984, p. 97–122, bibl.)

Although in several societies there has been recently a visible shift in the roles of women from exclusive involvement in the family to increasing participation in the work force, Caribbean women have always had roles which span both the "private" and the "public" domains. Male-dominated research which assumes that women's familial role is paramount obscures this fact; while male-biased economic, political and educational institutions inhibit further participation by Caribbean women.

1107 Price, Richard. First-time: the historical vision of an Afro-American people. Baltimore, Md.: The Johns Hopkins Univ. Press, 1983. 189 p.: bibl., maps, music, plates (Johns Hopkins studies in Atlantic history and culture)

Collection of oral accounts told by contemporary Saramaka Maroons to author about key Saramaka historical events in the 17th and 18th centuries. These interesting materials are divided into three chronologically-ordered sections: 1) The Heroic years: 1685–1748; 2) Toward Freedom: 1749–1759; and 3) Free at Last: 1760–1762. Author provides extensive commentary for each account (see item **1108** for Dutch perspectives on many of these events and much of this period of time).

1108 ———. To slay the hydra: Dutch colonial perspectives on the Saramaka wars. Ann Arbor, Mich.: Karoma Publishers, 1983. 247 p.: bibl., ill., plates.

Collection of manuscript documents with an introduction by the author on the final years of a nearly century-old war of liberation by the Saramaka Maroons against the Dutch colonists in Surinam. Documents written by Dutch witnesses are organized in this volume around the following themes: The Abortive Peace of 1749; The Last Great Battle; The Djuka Connection; and, Free at Last.

1109 Price, Sally. Co-wives and calabashes. Ann Arbor: Univ. of Michigan Press, 1984. 224 p.: bibl., ill., plates (Women and culture series)

Account of Saramaka Maroon social and artistic life through an examination of the artistic expression (calabash decoration, textile arts, and popular songs) of women from the villages of the Pikilio. Since the institution of marriage brings together art and Saramaka social relations, the author, through an emphasis on women's conjugal experiences, "explores the ways in which cultural ideas about the sexes influence their artistic life and analyzes the complementary contributions that the most important artistic media make to their social life."

1110 ———. Sexism and the construction of reality: an Afro-American example (AES/AE, 10:3, Aug. 1983, p. 460–476, bibl., ill.)

The marked division of labor between men and women among the Saramaka of Surinam is reflected directly in their artistic work. Men's art borrows foreign motifs and materials, since masculinity requires men to migrate and to function well in "foreign" settings. Women, mostly confined to villages and horticultural camps, and compromised in terms of marital opportunity by an adverse male-female ratio, express parochialism and insecurity in their artistic efforts. The paper discusses misconceptions of women's art by ethnographers and by the Saramaka themselves.

1111 ———. Wives, husbands, and more wives: sexual opportunities among the Saramaka (FIU/CR, 12:2, Spring 1983, p. 26, 29, 54, 59, plates)

The joys and sorrows of polygamy along the Suriname River are recorded; sex-

ual banter, night-time riverine rendezvous, marriage, extramarital affairs and jealousy, husband-wife relations, and life among co-wives.

1112 Price-Mars, Jean. So spoke the uncle / Ainsi parla l'oncle. Translation and introduction by Magdaline W. Shannon. Washington: Three Continents Press, 1983. 252 p.: bibl., maps, plates.

Most welcome English translation of Haitian classic first published in 1928. Certainly the leading Haitian intellectual of his time, Price-Mars, in this work, attempted to restore "the value of Haitian folk-lore in the eyes of the people." Dealt directly with the impact of the African past on Haitian social structure and concentrated on the evolution of Voodoo, "emphasizing its religious nature throughout, from the animism of prehistoric Africa to a synthesis with Christianity in modern Haiti so as to demonstrate the strength of folkloric custom in the gradual development of the culture of a society." Interesting appendix on peasant marriage and family, local mores, and African survivals ca. 1922.

1113 Prince, Althea V. Anansi folk culture: an expression of Caribbean life (FIU/CR, 13:1, Winter 1984, p. 24–27, 49–51)

Drawing on examples of Anansi stories, calypso and reggae composition, author posits that, in a situation of conflicting ideologies, black folk culture is not "used as 'prescriptions' for survival, but are rather, expressions of the life condition of the black folk of the Caribbean."

1114 Quamina, Odida T. The social organization of Plantation Mackenzie: an account of life in the Guyana mining enterprises. Geneva: UN Research Institute for Social Development, 1981. 35 p., 5 leaves of plates: bibl., ill. (Participation occasional paper. Report; 81.4)

Insider's view of social relations, social organization, and change in Mackenzie, a bauxite company town. Role of Catholicism and other religions, education, company's impact on organization of the community, social significance of time and work schedules, and some aspects of the transition from company to popular control are dealt with.

1115 Quevedo, Raymond. Atilla's kaiso: a short history of Trinidad calypso. St. Augustine: Dept. of Extra Mural Studies, Univ. of the West Indies, 1983. 205 p.: bibl., music, plates.

History of Trinidad calypso by Atilla the Hun—whose real name is R. Quevedo—once himself a leading calypsonian.

1116 Rashford, John. The cotton tree and the spiritual realm in Jamaica (IJ/JJ, 18:1, Feb./April 1985, p. 49–57, bibl., plates)

The significance of Ceiba *pentandra* in the *myal* and *obeah* religions is described. The cotton tree is described as a shrine or sanctuary where communing with spirits can take place.

1117 Reckord, Verena. Reggae, Rastafarianism and cultural identity (IJ/JJ, 46, 1982, p. 70–79, bibl., plates)

Informal review of the development of Jamaican popular and Rastafari music (Mento, ska, big band jazz, Rock Steady, Reggae) and the function they play in the search for identity.

1118 Robotham, Don. Pluralism as an ideology (UWI/SES, 29:1, March 1980, p. 69–89, bibl.)

M.G. Smith's theory of the plural society (item **1127**) is understood as a theory of Jamaican society whose formulations owe much to Smith's alleged membership in the Jamaican nationalist middle class (for Smith's response, see item **1128**).

1119 Rosenberg, June C. El Gagá: religión y sociedad de un culto dominicano, un estudio comparativo. Santo Domingo: Univ. Autónoma de Santo Domingo, 1979. 233 p.: bibl., ill. (Publicaciones de la Universidad; 272. Colección Historia y sociedad; 37)

Rich description of a syncretic religious cult in the Dominican Republic with roots in 19th-century Dominican carnival and voodoo. Describes material culture, social organization, ceremonies and beliefs of one Gagá group and compares it with other Dominican Gagá groups. Notes differences with Haitian practices, examines some elements of Dominican voodoo, and gives examples of "primary" and "secondary" syncretic religious groups in the Caribbean.

1120 Rubenstein, Hymie. Caribbean family and household organization: some conceptual clarifications (Journal of Comparative Family Studies [Calgary, Canada] 14:3, Autumn 1983, p. 283–298, bibl., ill., table)

Utilizing St. Vincent data, author demonstrates a variable association between the elements of domestic organization which result in the independence or quasi-independence of the domestic group from family functions and their associated structural apparatuses. Consequently, "neither the domestic group nor the household is a bounded, closed, corporate group." This permits a fluid form of organization which maximizes the possibility for maneuverability in domestic life and allows for adjustments to be made.

1121 ———. Occupational complexity in an Afro-Caribbean village (Journal of Caribbean Studies [Assn. of Caribbean Studies, Coral Gables, Fla.] 4:1, Fall 1984, p. 111–140, bibl., tables)

Restrictions imposed by island's class stratification system and economic underdevelopment on life changes of St. Vincent villagers have produced village-level occupational complexity of which "occupational multiplicity" is one manifestation. Aspects of village socioeconomic organization are delineated as context for discussion and analysis of interrelation between own-account, wage-labor, full-time, and part-time work. Characterization of villagers as having "temporal orientation" would be incorrect and would lead to misguided social policies.

1122 ———. Remittances and rural underdevelopment in the English-speaking Caribbean (SAA/HO, 42:4, Winter 1983, p. 295–306, bibl.)

Against views which hold that remittances bestow several positive effects upon underdeveloped countries receiving them, this study concludes that remittances make no positive contribution to rural economic rejuvenation in the English-speaking Caribbean. The beneficiaries of migration continue to be the developed industrial-capitalist societies.

1123 Salgado, Antoine. Le phénomène des zombis dans la culture haïtienne. Port-au-Prince: Imprimerie des Antilles, 1982. 146 p.: bibl., ill.

General discussion on the phenomenon of zombies in Haitian culture.

1124 Searle, Chris. Words unchained: language and revolution in Grenada. London: Zed Books, 1984. 260 p.: plates.

Study records how increasing awareness of Grenadians' revolutionary potential, under Maurice Bishop's leadership, has affected their use of the English language.

1125 Shaw, Thomas A. To be or not to be Chinese: differential expressions of Chinese culture and solidarity in the British West Indies (Ethnic Groups [Gordon & Breach Science Publishers, New York] 6:2/3, 1985, p. 155–185, bibl., table)

Basing his argument on some of the very limited literature on the Chinese in the Caribbean, author views use of ethnicity among this population (particularly in Jamaica and British Guiana) as adaptive. In situations where Europeans were "overwhelmingly dominant," Chinese deemphasized ethnicity; in situations where economic and political power "were more shared or 'pluralistic,'" the Chinese exploited their ethnicity.

1126 Singaravélou. Les indiens de la Guadeloupe: étude de géographie humaine. Bourdeaux, France: Centre national de la recherche scientifique, 1975. 239 p.: bibl., ill., plates, tables.

Thorough detailed study of East Indians in Guadeloupe. Work divided into three principal sections: 1) the Indian peopling of the island (labor crisis, origins in India, recruitment patterns, arrival and installation); 2) the Indian population and its economic activities (distribution of population, population movement, Indians in agriculture, the scarcity of Indians in secondary and tertiary sectors; and 3) Indians in Guadeloupian society (creolization of the Indians, irreducible Indian culture traits, Indians in Antillean society).

1127 Smith, M.G. Culture, race and class in the Commonwealth Caribbean. Mona, Jamaica: Dept. of Extra-Mural Studies, Univ. of the West Indies, 1984. 163 p.: bibl.

". . . reviews various accounts of Anglo-Caribbean societies from 1945 to the present that discuss the parts that culture, race and class play in them. It seeks to assess the cumulative contributions of these studies and to clarify the critical issues and relations with which they deal. Following introductory outlines of the subject, of the literature and topic, and some clarifications of basic terms, attention is focused on . . . Grenada, Jamaica, Trinidad and Guyana, which have figured prominently in the debate so far and will probably continue to do so. Then, after evaluating several prominent 'models' or 'theories' that offer general 'explanations' of social structure in these Caribbean societies, it concludes with a brief statement of [the author's] views." Informative essay that places pluralism in theoretical and regional context.

1128 ———. Robotham's ideology and pluralism: a reply (UWI/SES, 32:2, June 1983, p. 103–139, bibl.)

Author responds to the "extraordinary mixture of prejudice, ignorance, dishonesty and presumption that motivated Robotham's essay (see item **1118**)." Detailed critique of Robotham's assertions that plural society theory as developed by M.G. Smith is a result of latter's class position and its attendant ideology.

1129 ———. Some future directions for social research in the Commonwealth Caribbean (UWI/SES, 33:2, June 1984, p. 123–155, bibl.)

Funded adequately so as to avoid its permanent conversion to a not-for-profit market research agency, the Institute for Social and Economic Research (ISER) is identified as the proper administrator of an integrated program of regional research which addresses the widest range of new relevant and appropriate data—some to be drawn from women's studies and from the ethnographic output from the Francophone Caribbean, Surinam, and Belize—to the solution of outstanding theoretical issues of race, culture, and class. The research program must identify needs and provisions for social assistance in the region and should describe the conditions, targets, and probabilities of effective regional and Third World cooperation, such as would increase the Third World's share of world production.

1130 ———. The study of needs and provisions for social assistance (UWI/SES, 31:3, Sept. 1982, p. 37–56)

Describes concepts, aims, design, and method used in a systematic study of needs and provisions for social assistance in Jamaica. Study reveals large gap between the volume of public need for social assistance and services and resources actually available to meet them. Means by which social service provisions may be rationalized are suggested.

1131 Smith, Raymond T. Family, social change and social policy in the West Indies (NWIG, 56:3/4, 1982, p. 111–142, bibl.)

By means of a critical review of T.S. Simey's *Welfare and planning in the West Indies*, author explores the premises on which social policy was based during the waning years of colonial rule. Then, with reference to selected research, he delineates a system of West Indian kinship, marriage, and family. Concludes with discussion of policy implications and argues "that a family system such as that of the West Indies arises in a particular kind of class society with particular kinds of sex roles, and it is unlikely to change until the pattern of class relations changes."

1132 The Social and economic impact of Carnival. Seminar held at the Univ. of the West Indies, St. Augustine, Trinidad, Nov. 24–26, 1983. St. Augustine, Trinidad: Institute of Social and Economic Research, Univ. of the West Indies, 1984. 244 p.

Collection of eight papers dealing with the arts and economics of Trinidad Carnival. The social impact of successive forms of Carnival is explored; this succession of forms is not related to broader developments in the global framework in which Trinidad may be viewed; nor are Carnivals theorized as economic enterprises in the global framework.

1133 Spalburg, Johan George. De Tapanahoni Djuka rond de eeuwwisseling: het dagboek van Spalburg: 1896–1900. Ingeleid door H.U.E. Thoden van Velzen en Chris de Beet. Utrecht, The Netherlands: Centrum voor Caraïbische Studies, Instituut voor Culturele Antropologie, Rijksuniv. Utrecht, 1979. 129 p., 2 leaves of plates: bibl., maps (Bronnen voor de studie van Bosneger samenlevingen; 5)

Teacher and missionary, Johan Spalburg's diary, written during his four-year stay with the Djukas of Surinam is one of the most important early documents on

Djuka society. It is especially valuable as the only eyewitness report based on an extended stay rather than on brief field trips. [N. Vicenti]

1134 Studies in Caribbean language. Edited by Lawrence D. Carrington. St. Augustine, Trinidad: Society for Caribbean Linguistics, 1983. 338 p.: bibl., tables.

Selection of 26 papers from the 3rd Biennial Conference of the Society for Caribbean Linguistics held in Aruba, 1980. Papers deal with: Caribbean linguistics, linguistic developments in the Caribbean disapora, social history and sociolinguistics, language and social identity, education in Creole settings, phonology, phonetics, and syntax.

1135 Suriname: slavernij, abolitie en nasleep, essays ter ere van Silvia W. de Groot (OSO [Surinaamse taalkunde, letterkunde en geschiedenis, Paramaribo] 2:2, Dec. 1983, p. 1–247, bibl.)

Issue of *OSO* journal in honor of Silvia de Groot, ethnohistorian of Maroon society and Caribbeanist, with slavery, abolition, and consequences in Surinam as its theme. In addition to a short statement of appreciation by R.A.J. van Lier and two articles by de Groot herself, substantive contributions are made by H. Hoetink, H.E. Lamur, P.C. Emmer, G. Oostindie and A. van Stipriaan, J.K. Brandsma, W.C.J. Koot, V.Th. Tjon-A-Ten and P. Uniken-Venema.

1136 Sutherland, Anne and Laurie Kroshus. A social history of Caye Caulker (BISRA/BS, 13:1, 1985, p. 1–27, maps)

Socioeconomic history of very small Belizean island located a mile from barrier reef. Although affected by tourism, a successful cooperative, motorized boats, mass communication, etc., island is still characterized by sense of individualism, autonomy, egalitarianism, reliance on fishing, and family as focus of individual loyalty. Nevertheless, "the days of isolation are over . . . ."

1137 Tanna, Laura. African retentions: Yoruba and Kikongo songs in Jamaica (IJ/JJ, 16:3, Aug. 1983, p. 47–52, bibl., music, plates)

Three Nago songs, collected in a Westmoreland community, are presented with translation and musical transcriptions. The songs demonstrate that African languages survive in the Jamaican oral tradition.

1138 ———. Anansi: Jamaica's trickster hero (IJ/JJ, 16:2, May 1983, p. 20–30, bibl., plates)

Analysis of the trickster and the trick; the potential for metaphor in the stories of Anansi, Jamaican folk hero and symbol.

1139 ———. Jamaican folk tales and oral histories. Kingston: Institute of Jamaica Publications, 1984. 143 p.: map, music, plates (Jamaica; 21. Anthology series; 1)

Collection of stories, songs, and riddles.

1139a Thoden van Velzen, H.U.E. and W. van Watering. Affluence, deprivation and the flowering of Bush Negro religious movements (KITLV/B, 139:1, Jan. 1983, p. 99–139, bibl.)

Detailed, carefully argued study of three important Bush Negro religious movements of the late 19th and early 20th centuries: *Gaan Gadu*, and the cults of Anake and Atjaimikule. Development of these movements is examined against historical backdrop of drastically changing relations of production, varying adaptations to new economic circumstances, and greatly differing ideational structures of the three. Conclusion is that new theological ideas that emerged cannot be viewed merely as a result of changing relations of production. Once the array of ideas is delineated, it becomes "fully clear how far consciousness has moved away from being, how little the intricacies of 'mind work' can be predicted from material forces."

1140 Thomas, J. Paul. The Caribs of St. Vincent: a study in imperial maladministration, 1763–73 (UWI/JCH, 18:2, 1983, p. 60–73)

Account of the expedition sent against Caribs of St. Vincent in 1772: how land-hungry, profiteering adventurers prevailed against an ignorant administration and a vulnerable native population.

1141 Thomas-Hope, Elizabeth. Off the Island: population mobility among the Caribbean middle class (*in* White collar migrants in the Americas and the Caribbean. Edited by Arnaud F. Marks and Hebe M.C. Vessuri. Leiden, The Netherlands: Dept. of Caribbean Studies, Royal Institute of Linguistics and Anthropology, 1983, p. 39–59)

Psychological dependence upon core countries becomes more entrenched as white-collar workers, attracted by high potential and opportunity, migrate.

1142 Thompson, Robert Farris. Flash of the spirit: African and Afro-American art and philosophy. New York: Random House, 1983. 317 p.: ill., plates.

Ambitious, richly illustrated volume on the visual and philosophic connections between Africa and Black America. Author deals with Yoruba art and culture and Kongo art and religion in the Americas; Vodun religion and art in Haiti; Mande-related art and architecture in the Americas; and, Ejagham art and writing in two worlds.

1143 Tobias, Peter M. The social context of Grenadian emigration (UWI/SES, 29:1, March 1980, p. 40–59, bibl.)

Emigration, a stimulus to Grenadian lower class males, is found in "manliness," a key value in lower-class men's informal associations. The international context in which emigration occurs is not explored.

1144 Trouillot, Michel-Rolph. Caribbean peasantries and world capitalism: an approach to micro-level studies (NWIG, 58:1/2, 1983, p. 37–59, bibl.)

Caribbean peasantries are thought to offer a privileged vantage point from which to study the relation between micro-level processes and over-arching world historical processes.

1145 Van Lier, R. Bonuman: een studie van zeven religieuze specialisten in Suriname. Leiden, The Netherlands: Institute of Cultural and Social Studies, Leiden Univ., s.d. 132 p. (YICA publication; 60)

Study of seven religious specialists in Surinam based on life history data.

1147 Wilk, Richard R. Rural settlement change in Belize, 1970–1980: the effects of roads (BISRA/BS, 12:4, 1984, p. 1–9, tables)

Based on 1980 census figures, author indicates that the growth of rural population is "highly dependent" on the quality of roads—the better the quality, the faster the growth.

1148 Women and education. Cave Hill, Barbados: Institute of Social and Economic Research, Eastern Caribbean, Univ. of the West Indies, 1982. 77 p.: bibl., tables (Women in the Caribbean project; 5)

Vol. 5 in research series on the role of women in the English-speaking Caribbean. Includes two substantive papers. Joyce Cole deals with official ideology and the education of Caribbean women, 1835–1945, with special reference to Barbados, and Patricia Mohammed details educational attainment of women in Trinidad and Tobago (1946–80).

1149 Women and the family. Cave Hill, Barbados: Institute of Social and Economic Research, Univ. of the West Indies, 1982. 162 p.: bibl., ill., tables (Women in the Caribbean project; 2)

Vol. 2 in a research series on the role of women in the English-speaking Caribbean. Includes the following articles: Hermione McKenzie "Women and Family in Caribbean Society;" Victoria Durant-González "The Realm of Female Familial Responsibility;" Jean Jackson "Stresses Affecting Women and Their Families;" Joycelin Massiah "Women Who Head Households;" and Dorian Powell "Network Analysis: a Suggested model for the Study of Women and the Family in the Caribbean."

ETHNOLOGY: South America, Lowlands

WAUD H. KRACKE, *Associate Professor of Anthropology, University of Illinois, Chicago Circle*

A MAJOR DEVELOPMENT OF THE LAST few years in Lowland South America has been the strengthening identity and growing self-awareness of indigenous peoples. One reflection of this is the appearance of writings on indigenous cultures by members of those cultures themselves, on the initiative of indigenous authors, with an anthropologist (if any) acting merely as a go-between or midwife. The outstanding work that exemplifies this trend is a set of Desana myths narrated by the old Desana priest Umúsin Panlõn Kumu, transcribed by his son, whose publication was arranged at their request by Berta Ribeiro (who worked with them to edit the translation under the title *Antes o mundo não existia*, item **1363**). Another example of such works is the introduction to Ye'cuana society written by a Ye'cuana villager through two spokesmen (item **1237**). Such writings clearly reflect important social developments underway as indigenous peoples take on a more active part in shaping their own future. It is hoped that this represents a trend within ethnography which will allow the indigenous thinker or self-ethnographer to speak directly to his or her public (item **1330**).

Two major new collections of articles constitute important advances in the comparison and synthesis of South American cultures. The volume on marriage practices in northern Lowland South America edited by Kenneth Kensinger (item **1294**) grew out of the first annual "Lowland South America" symposium held by the American Anthropological Association meetings (New Orleans, 1973). Its participants, finding themselves echoing a common theme, agreed that these works should be published together (items **1165, 1221, 1230, 1269, 1274, 1280, 1281, 1290, 1294, 1341, 1346,** and **1387**). Another major new collection, *Adaptive responses of native Amazonians* organized by Hames and Vickers (item **1153**), provides detailed empirical studies of the ecological adaptation of specific cultures to diverse ecological situations (items **1169, 1171, 1184, 1233, 1238, 1253, 1256, 1263, 1265, 1271, 1351, 1372, 1386,** and **1391**).

Another event to be noted is the posthumous collection of Pierre Clastres's essays (item **1202**) in which he develops the theme of tropical forest egalitarianism proposed in other works before his untimely death.

ETHNOGRAPHY BY AREA

This period is also marked by a proliferation of good ethnographic monographs, some of them outstanding. Two ethnographies of Gê/Bororo societies, while very different from each other, both emphasize the complexities of cosmological and social beliefs underlying ceremonial life in these cultures: J.C. Melatti's thorough and circumstantial portrayal of the Krahó ritual system (item **1303**) and J. Christopher Crocker's study of the symbolic structure of Bororo society and cosmos (item **1219**). Another interesting study focuses on a single Bororo ritual object (item **1232**). In addition, two classic monographs on Gê cultures have been translated into Portuguese (items **1289** and **1299**).

Another complementary pair of monographs has just been issued on societies of the Upper Xingú, on two of the original core Xingú societies. Both these cultures, Mehinaku and Kalapalo, have already been described in basic ethnographies (See *HLAS 37:1320* and *HLAS 41:1145*). The more current works delve into specific aspects of life in each culture. Gregor's *Anxious pleasures* (item **1246**) explores Mehinaku sexuality, with its attendant anxieties and fantasies; while Ellen Basso's *A Musical view of the universe* (item **1166**) analyzes communicative aspects of Kalapalo myth-telling, examining how the myths articulate feelings and problems in human relationships. One article (item **1167**) gives a regional view of Upper Xingú intertribal relationships.

In the Vaupes region, which has enjoyed considerable ethnographic attention in the last few years (See *HLAS 43*, p. 143 and *HLAS 45*, p. 129) work has reached the stage of comparative synthesis. The major new monograph on this region annotated below is Jean Jackson's *Fish people* (item **1268**) which starts from a description of one village and moves progressively outward to regional perspective on the Vaupes-Tucanoan societies. A brief but important and insightful contribution to the understanding of Vaupes social structure by Janet Chernela (item **1198**) adds these cultures to that group of Amazonian societies in which name transmission plays a crucial structural role as noted in *HLAS 45* (p. 130). Another brief article (item **1159**) compares the new Desana myths related by the above mentioned Umúsin to Reichel-Dolmatoff's controversial analysis of Desana cosmology (item **1188**). One article discusses relations between the hunting and gathering Maku and their Tucanoan neighbors (item **1309**), and several contributions finally address the still less explored Arawakan component of the Vaupes community of language groups (items **1245, 1262,** and **1263**).

Of four ethnographies on Amazonian Peru, two focus on economic relations between indigenous cultures and the dominant national and international economic structure: Michael Brown's on the Aguaruna (item **1176**) and Erwin Frank's on the Cashibo (item **1240**). Califano, writing on the various subgroups of the Mashco, elaborates on their material culture or "ergology". On the other hand, Chaumeil's new ethnography of the Yagua (item **1197**) focuses primarily on shamanism and curing.

Finally, with regard to the southern tip of the continent we have several ethnographies of the Selk'nam (Ona) and neighboring groups, of which the outstanding one is Anne Chapman's *Drama and power in a hunting society* (item **1196**). As the title suggests, this too centers on religious life, particularly shamanism and the

Hain initiation ritual which is a focus of religious and social life (see also item 1295).
Important regional syntheses have also been published. Of special note is vol. 2 of a three-volume handbook on indigenous Venezuelan cultures, *Los Aborígenes de Venezuela* (item 1150). There are also two overlapping synthetic surveys of Paraguayan cultures (item 1353) and of chaqueño cultures (item 1172). Several sweeping surveys of Colombian cultures are less noteworthy (item 1209).

INDIGENOUS MOVEMENTS AND THE DEFENSE OF INDIGENOUS CULTURES

The reality described by the above mentioned ethnographies is undergoing swift change as many of them acknowledge, some with a tinge of nostalgia (item 1219). Other works deal directly with the accelerating integration of these cultures into the world economic system (items 1176 and 1240). Does the ever-increasing deluge of ethnographies signify a sort of requiem for a heritage that will soon vanish in the ruthless course of development? Or will these cultures be permitted to survive, recoup their drastic loss of population (item 1371) and develop their own adaptations along traditional lines that could well point the way to a more balanced and less destructive exploitation of the full potential of the tropical forest environment (items 1322 and 1323, but see also item 1228 for a somewhat different view).

In the face of overwhelming national debts, the Amazonian nations are turning to the too easy (and ultimately self-defeating) solution of unchecked despoliation of the region's fragile resources. Colonization/agricultural development projects like Polonoroeste in Brazil (items 1297 and 1300), and in Peru, Palcazu (item 1345), and again in Brazil the massive Carajás mining/cattle/energy project associated with the Tucurui Dam (items 1199 and 1389) are formulated and implemented with minimal attention to their ecological effects and the devastation of the region's indigenous populations, whose lands are in some cases expropriated for these projects. Documentation of the destruction of indigenous cultures or threats to their lands and means of subsistence, constitutes a grim litany in the case of Brazil (see items 1162, 1185, 1186, 1205, 1227, 1250, 1254, 1286, 1306, 1330, 1336, and 1388); Ecuador (items 1170, 1240, and 1371); Peru (items 1170, 1216, 1240, and 1345); and Venezuela (items1163 and 1237). In Brazil, the invasion of Yanomami territory by hordes of prospectors, road-builders and others as well as failure of the government to establish a Yanomami park has been a focus of interest (items 1155, 1267, 1278, 1337, 1347, and 1390). Several publications denounce malfeasance in the establishment of inadequate reservations, or depredations of existing ones (see items 1155, 1186, 1227, 1243, 1261, 1325, 1327, 1336, 1343, 1344, and 1345). In Venezuela, there is much controversy over the effectiveness of its program to stimulate indigenous enterprises (items 1311 and 1366).

On the other hand, the past few years have witnessed the rapid development of an organized and self-conscious indigenous movement (item 1317). Although this has been especially dramatic in Brazil (items 1183, 1272, 1298, and 1306), movements continue to grow in Colombia (item 1248), Ecuador (items 1228, 1317, and 1355), Venezuela (items 1237 and 1317), and elsewhere (item 1317). Terence Turner (item 1359) stresses the active participation of indigenous peoples in such resistance to domination.

A major project in Brazil has begun to bear fruit with the appearance of the first two volumes of a set to be published by CEDI entitled *Povos indigenas no Brasil* (item **1324**). It is projected that this set of region-by-region surveys will eventually consist of 18 volumes. They are designed to fulfill the important goal of systematically documenting the situation of all Brazilian indigenous peoples. CEDI also issues a useful monthly bulletin of news clippings of events affecting such groups throughout Brazil (see item **1152**).

The increasing sophistication of the pro-indigenous movement in Brazil as well as in other Amazonian countries is reflected in an upsurge of interest in legal issues. Several conferences held on native populations and national legislation have published proceedings and documents on the topic (items **1173, 1206, 1211, 1235, 1338,** and **1352**). Likewise, a growing number of analyses of specific legal issues and cases concerning indigenous peoples have also appeared (items **1154, 1312, 1368,** and **1379**). Two contributions take a broad view, one from a systems perspective, of the impact of national and international economic structures on indigenous cultures (items **1240** and **1345**). Indigenous education is another topic that has emerged in recent years (item **1212**) and Bartolomeu Meliá raises important issues concerning bilingual education (item **1304**). The history of missionization, both Protestant and Catholic, are also the subject of several contributions (items **1170, 1207, 1235a, 1254, 1310, 1341,** and **1349**). A study of dreams portrays the psychological reaction of a people to contact (item **1247**). Another work examines the philosophical basis of the value of indigenous self-determination (item **1189**).

ETHNOHISTORY AND THE HISTORY OF INDIGENOUS PEOPLES

A field that has undergone a spectacular expansion of interest in recent years is the history of indigenous peoples, both ethnohistory as recorded in the memories and traditions of the people themselves (items **1256, 1287,** and **1330**), the part played by indigenous peoples in the history of the European invasion and conquest of South America (as is evident from the ethnohistory sections of *HLAS 44,* p. 95–121, and *HLAS 46,* p. 81–113) and the reconstruction of ancient indigenous cultures, especially the Coastal Tupi and Guarani cultures so richly described in early colonial writings. An especially stimulating and fertile contribution in this area is Hélène Clastres brilliant, and carefully documented study of messianic movements among the 16th-century Tupi and 19th-century Guarani (item **1201**) demonstrating that these movements grew out of internal historical dynamisms within Tupi societies and were not simply transitory reactions to conquest (on ancient Tupi religion, see also items **1308** and **1328**). Two articles deal with issues of Tupinambá cannibalism (items **1187** and **1239**). On a broader plane, Berta Ribeiro has written a readable and informative textbook for the general public on the part played by indigenous peoples in Brazilian history, from early Tupinambá contacts with the first colonists to selected cases of recent contact (item **1334**). Susñik also provides a similar survey of the role of indigenous peoples in the history of Paraguay (item **1354**).

The current rising interest in history among ethnographers—and interest in indigenous peoples among historians—undoubtedly reflects several different trends. One such trend is the recent rapprochement of anthropologists and historians spurred in the US by symbolic anthropology and in France by structural history; another is the indigenous peoples' own rising interest in their own pasts as they seek to redefine their identity (items **1214, 1237, 1330,** and **1363**). Brazil's concern with its early indigenous roots, especially Tupinambá, is also a reflection of a growing sense of national identity (items **1236, 1318,** and **1367**). There is also a demand for historical documentation for the verification of indigenous land claims (items **1243, 1325, 1326, 1327,** and **1330**). Many studies deal with indigenous policy (items **1235a** and **1357**) or with the impact of conquest, economic oppression and assimilation on indigenous cultures (items **1162, 1243, 1254, 1325, 1327, 1330** and **1350**). The history of missionization is another frequent topic (items **1194, 1207, 1235a, 1254,** and **1310**). An intriguing contribution is David Price's history of changes in names used to designate Mato Grosso tribes whereby he places such name shifts within each historical context (item **1326**).

Of great importance for the study of indigenous history is the publication or republication of a number of historical sources. Especially valuable in this regard is the ethnographic map of Kurt Nimuendajú, published with commentary and indexes (item **1242**). The Univ. of São Paulo is editing a series of classic sources for the history of Brazil, in Portuguese or translated into Portuguese, which includes many valuable historical accounts of indigenous peoples (items **1217, 1218, 1292,** and **1356**). Two sets of ethnographic notes by late 19th- and early 20th-century civil engineers (items **1277** and **11291**) are also worth noting. A number of other more recent classics on indigenous history have also been reissued and translated into Portuguese (items **1194, 1236, 1288, 1308,** and **1357**).

RELIGION, WORLD VIEW, AND ART

Interest in the traditional topics of cultural anthropology—ritual, shamanism, myth and cosmology—is also rising, though new models for their analysis are in the fore. An article on South American Indian religions is the centerpiece of Pierre Clastres's posthumous book of essays (item **1203**). Shamanism in particular "is in style these days" as Chaumeil remarks (item **1197**, p. 8), quoting Lot-Falck. Shamanism is the central theoretical focus of two new ethnographies (items **1197** and **1219**) as well as of Hélène Clastres's above mentioned historical study of Tupi messianic cults (item **1201**) and is featured in several other works (items **1178a, 1196, 1279, 1285, 1332,** and **1375**). A number of ethnographies and articles are organized around description and analysis of ritual (items **1196, 1220, 1262, 1303, 1370** and **1373**), and a comparative article discusses signal functions of ritual masks in different Brazilian culture areas (item **1365**).

Myth is another category of considerable interest (items **1166, 1188, 1245, 1289, 1363** and **1364**). Several of these works concentrate on semiotic questions of communication in mythic or ritual performance (items **1166, 1177, 1196, 1364,** and **1365**). Especially interesting is Michael Brown's discussion of the role of words in Aguaruna hunting magic (item **1177**), in which he challenges Tambiah's view of magical language as purely metaphorical.

Several articles discuss food taboos and couvade restrictions (items **1241, 1307,** and **1358**) and two touch on the use of hallucinogens (items **1181** and **1226**). Only two articles concern cosmology (items **1190** and **1339**), but others examine related aspects of the world view and concept of time (item **1293**), fundamental cognitive patterns underlying Gê thought (item **1222**) and cultural modes of classifying experience (items **1171, 1175, 1178a,** and **1321**).

Once again, death is a leading theme of many works (items **1200, 1201, 1203,**

1224, 1374 and 1375), four of them part of a collection on death in Brazilian cultures (see item 8393). Messianic movements are the subject of two major studies (items 1201, 1328, 1331, and 1335).

Insofar as the arts are concerned, four articles examine body painting and adornment among the Kayapó (items 1259, 1362, 1370 and 1373). Two articles discuss ceramics (items 1187 and 1207) and one major work analyzes Bororo feather headdresses (item 1232).

ETHNOMEDICINE AND ETHNOPSYCHOLOGY

Shamanism plays a curing role and is thus inextricably linked to ethnomedicine. Chaumeil's ethnography of Yagua shamanism devotes a chapter to the Yagua conceptualization and categorization of illnesses treated by shamans (item 1197). Other writings deal more extensively and specifically with the healing process (items 1178a, 1279, and 1313). Two articles, written from a Western medical perspective, deal with epidemics and disease in certain indigenous societies (items 1193 and 1275). With regard to the psychological aspects of indigenous life, a theme that has come in for some long-awaited treatment is sexuality. Several contributions devote attention to the topic, and three concentrate on aspects such as anxieties and fantasies associated with sex (item 1246 and 1166) as well as exchanges of sex and food (item 1340). Anxieties generated by contact are covered in two papers, one dealing with nightmares about the white man (item 1247) and another with suicide (item 1174). Although only two publications on dreams are annotated below (items 1175 and 1247), proceedings from a conference on cross-cultural approaches to dreams, held by the School for American Research, will be published by the Cambridge Univ. Press. This work will include three papers on dream beliefs in Lowland South American societies and one on dream omens in an Andean society. Surprisingly, only one article focuses on the once popular topic of the construction of the person in an indigenous society (item 1373).

SOCIAL ORGANIZATION

In addition to the articles on marriage practices in the above mentioned volume edited by Kenneth Kensinger (item 1294), studies of social structure are few but include some stimulating and innovative formulations. Especially interesting are two contributions on Northwest Amazonian societies by Janet Chernela (item 1198) and Jonathan Hill (item 1262), and Alcida Ramos's article on the problem of uxorilocal residence in patrilineal societies (item 1329). Ramos suggests three different modes for reconciling the two social patterns exemplified by three different lowland societies and discusses conditions under which institutionalized patrilineages may be formed in such societies (for other works on kinship and marriage, see items 1156, 1165, 1230, and 1342).

The model of egalitarian lowland societies put forward by Pierre Clastres is elaborated in his posthumous essays (item 1202). This theme is also referred to by Werner in his sociometric studies of Kayapó leadership (items 1382, 1383, and 1384). Hill (item 1262) suggests that both hierarchical and egalitarian modes of organization may coexist in a society, a more complex view that disposes of the old monolithic concepts of social structure (see also *HLAS 45:1301*).

The nature of territorial groupings in so-called "band" societies is questioned by Arcand in the case of the Cuiva band (item **1161**). An interesting book co-authored by several Brazilian anthropologists compares housing architecture in various Brazilian indigenous societies, noting how architecture is related to cultural concepts of space and social organization (item **1179**).

Dual organization is highlighted in several reprints of classics such as the retrospective compilation of Cardoso de Oliveira on Terena and Ticuna societies (item **1182**), and in the translation of David Maybury-Lewis's classic ethnography (item **1299**) which includes a new introduction on his concept of dual organization. Dual organization is also a leading theme in a collection of ethnographic papers on Brazilian indigenous societies (item **1284**). However, only three recent contributions highlight dualism and moieties (items **1274**, **1281**, and **1360**).

ECOLOGY

Colchester (item **1208**) stresses the importance of distinguishing "cultural ecology," the study of man as a part of his ecosystem, from "ethnoecology" which concerns cultural *concepts* of nature and of the ecosystem. Both of these distinct but related fields are growing. A very large number of studies annotated below are strictly concerned with ecological questions, the vast majority being detailed, quantitative studies of specific problems about hunting or gardening in particular societies (items **1169**, **1171**, **1184**, **1231**, **1233**, **1238**, **1240**, **1253**, **1255**, **1256**, **1262**, **1263**, **1265**, **1271**, **1273**, **1309**, **1351**, **1372**, **1386**, and **1391**). Two thirds of these are articles in the above mentioned Hames and Vickers collection (item **1153**). Of five articles addressing more ideological questions and which continue the lengthy ecological determinism argument, three appeared in a special issue of *Amazonia Peruana* (Vol. 3, No. 6) devoted to the topic and two were translations of earlier articles (see items **1168**, **1249**, **1251**, **1347** and **1348**).

Because the systematic understanding of native categories is a challenging and taxing enterprise, the number of studies of ethnoecology is smaller (item **1321**) but of high quality (items **1171**, **1208**, **1321**, **1322**, **1323**, and **1332**). Moreover, most of these works bridge the gap between ethnoecology and cultural ecology, in interesting and sometimes ingenious ways.

ANTHROPOLOGY IN SOUTH AMERICA

National traditions of anthropology in South America are growing in vigor, at a time when North American (US) anthropology is experiencing an identity crisis. In Argentina, we have witnessed the virtual rebirth of a national anthropology that was stifled under the military regime, a rebirth marked by the successful meeting of the First Argentine Congress of Anthropology (item **1164**). The growing strength of Brazilian anthropology is reflected in the continued existence of newly established periodicals (e.g. items **1158**, **1159**, and **1160**) and in the wide popularity of Roberto Da Matta's anthropology textbook (item **1296**) with its distinctively Brazilian perspective. The growing significance of Brazilian anthropology is also evident in the recent appearance of compilations of works by outstanding figures and founding fathers of Brazilian anthropology (items **1182**, **1236**, **1244**, **1313**, **1316**, and **1335**) as well as by a recently published reader of articles on Brazil's indigenous cultures (item **1284**). Several recent works trace the history of Brazilian anthropology and/or comment on its current direction. Perhaps the most outstanding and influential of these studies is Marisa Peirano's doctoral dissertation, *The Anthropology of anthropology: the Brazilian case* (Harvard Univ., 1980) which argues that a truly national Brazilian anthropology with an interest in the integration and identity of the national society has developed in recent years (see excerpt published in *Anuario Antropológico*, item **1318**). Julio Melatti also reviewed the history of Brazilian anthropology in two excellent bibliographic articles (items **1301** and **1302**). Thekla Hartmann continues Herbert Baldus's monumental *Bibliografía crítica da antropologia brasileira* with vol. 3, which brings it up to 1984 (item **1260**). An article by Otavio Velho comments on the present course of Brazilian ethnography (item **1367**), and Renate Viertler discusses recent concepts in religious ethnography (item **1376**).

In Venezuela, the annual bibliographies by Erika Wagner and Walter Coppens continue to appear (item **1380**). And finally, a welcome reissue is Patricia Lyons's reader, *Native South Americans* (item **1314**).

I would like to thank Kathryn Lee Hall for reading and annotating several articles in Spanish which are attributed to K.L. Hall in the ensuing bibliography.

1150 Los Aborígenes de Venezuela. v. 1, Etnologia antigua. v. 2, Etnología contemporánea. Editores, Walter Coppens *et al.* Caracas: Fundación La Salle de Ciencias Naturales, Instituto Caribe de Antropología y Sociología, 1983. 2 v.: bibl., ill., indexes, maps (Monografía; 26)

Vol. 2 of up-to-date handbook on Venezuelan Indians. Includes ethnographic articles on eight indigenous cultures by anthropologists familiar with them (first of two volumes on ethnography, preceding one was devoted to historical reconstruction: *Etnología antiga*). Articles in this volume are: Johannes Wilbert "Añu (Paraujano);" Kenneth Ruddle and Johannes Wilbert "Yukpa;" Donald J. Metzger and Robert V. Morey "Hiwi (Guahibo);" Paul Henley "Wanai (Mapoyo);" Walter Coppens "Hoti;" David John Thomas "Pemón;" Walter Coppens "Sapé" and "Uruak (Arutani)." Includes three indexes by subject, names (tribal and individual together), and geographic.

1151 Acciones indigenistas en el Paraguay: acontecimientos y perspectivas. Asunción: Banco Paraguayo de Datos (BPD): United Nations Assn., International Service (UNAIS), 1980. 66 p.: bibl., maps (Documentos especiales BPD)

Typed document briefly summarizes programs on behalf of Paraguayan indigenes sponsored by both government agencies and independent support groups.

1152 Aconteceu: povos indígenas no Brasil, 1981. São Paulo: Centro Ecumênico de Documentação e Informação (CEDI), 1983. 1 v.: maps, plates.

Compilation of articles on Brazilian indigenous groups that have appeared throughout 1981 in weekly *Aconteceu* bulletins, culled from major newspapers. Articles are organized by tribe within each geographic region of Brazil, and those on tribes are arranged chronologically. This valuable CEDI publication permits quick access to major news stories about any indigenous group in Brazil.

1153 Adaptive responses of native Amazonians. Edited by Raymond B. Hames and William T. Vickers. New York: Academic Press, 1983. 516 p.: bibl., ill., index, map (Studies in anthropology)

Major collection of empirical "microecological" studies, focusing on detailed, concrete studies of specific subsistence activities in indigenous communities rather than on sweeping theories. Introduction discusses geographical and theoretical background. Several articles use "optimal foraging theory" to draw comparisons with data on hunting and to explain divergences. Articles grouped by topic and annotated separately according to item number: "Cultivation" (see items **1184, 1263,** and **1271**); "Hunting and Fishing" (see items **1169, 1171, 1265, 1351, 1386,** and **1391**); "Nutrition" (see items **1233** and **1238**); and "Settlement Pattern" (see items **1253, 1256,** and **1372**).

1154 Agostinho, Pedro. Imputabilidade do índio nos casos de violência em situação interétnica (USP/RA, 21:1, 1978, p. 27–32, bibl.)

Discusses imputability of Indians for legal infractions under Brazilian law which equates them, with the usual justifications, with minors, the mentally ill, etc. Author attributes their lack of imputability to inter-ethnic contact which leaves the Indian "insecure and vulnerable, caught between the alternatives of submitting and being oppressed, or reacting and suffering the consequences."

1155 Albert, Bruce. Yanomani-kaingang: la question des terre indiennes au Brésil (*in* Indianité, ethnocide, indigenisme en Amérique latine. GRAL, Centre inter-disciplinaire d'études latino-americaines, Toulouse-le Mirail. Paris: Centre national de la recherche scientifique, 1982, p. 135–154, bibl., tables [Amérique latine. Pays ibériques])

Discusses Indian land guarantees in two instances: threats to the Yanomami and the movement for a "Yanomami indigenous park" (see also items **1278** and **1347**); and the invasion and destruction of Kaingang reservations, which resulted in conflicts with and assassinations of Kaingang leaders (see also item **1344**). Concludes with discussion of need for land reform and growing ethnic identity among Indians (see also item **1388**).

1156 Amadio, Massimo and **Lucia d'Emilio.** La alianza entre los candoshi-murato del Alto Amazonas (CAAAP/AP, 5 : 9, julio 1983, p. 23–36, bibl., map, tables)

Brief study of marriage alliances focuses on analysis of six cases of exchange between two or more Candoshi-Murato lineages. Appendix draws comparison with neighboring Jivaroan Aguaruna of Northern Amazon, Peru.

1157 Antropologia no Brasil (Anuário Antropológico [Edições Tempo Brasileiro, Rio de Janeiro] 82, 1984, p. 225–277)

Symposium provides history and reminiscences on the development of anthropology in Brazil: Luiz de Castro Faria "A Antropologia no Brasil: Depoimento sem Compromissos de um Militante em Recesso;" Egon Schaden "Os Primeiros Tempos da Antropologia em São Paulo;" and Thales de Azevedo "Primeiros Mestres de Antropologia nas Faculdades de Filosofia." Presentation by Julio Cesar Melatti.

1158 Anuário Antropológica. Edições Tempo Brasileiro. No. 80, 1982– . Rio de Janeiro.

Issue of this now firmly established new Brazilian annual on anthropology contains two articles on indigenous topics: Ramos on dysharmonic residence systems (item **1329**) and Melatti's survey of recent anthropology with Brazilian indigenous societies (item **1302**) as well as provocative review articles on recent publications concerned with indigenous societies and indigenism.

1159 ———. ———. No. 81, 1983– . Rio de Janeiro.

Contains five articles on indigenous societies: Bastos on Xingúan societies (item **1167**); Chernela (item **1198**) and Gorosito-Kramer on Uaupés societies; Posey on Kayapó ethnoentomology (item **1321**); and Viveiros de Castro on self-determination as a value (item **1189**).

1160 ———. ———. No. 82, 1984– . Rio de Janeiro.

Contains articles by Mariza Peirano (item **1318**), Thomas Gregor (item **1247**), Dennis Werner (item **1385**), Alcida Ramos (item **1329a**), and two symposia, one on "Construction of Identity in Indigenous Societies" (item **1214**), and another on "Anthropology in Brazil" (item **1157**).

1161 Arcand, Bernard. The Cuiva band (*in* Challenging anthropology: a critical introduction to social and cultural anthropology. Edited by David H. Turner and Gavin A. Smith. Toronto: McGraw-Hill Ryerson, 1979, p. 214–227, bibl.)

Article based on extensive residence with Cuiva of Colombia, challenges the concept of "band" as a political unit. Argues that the Cuiva band is a loose collection of local groups that occasionally gather for social occasion (for another article by same author, see item **1340**).

1162 Arnaud, Expedito. Os índios Mirânia e a expansão luso-brasileira: médio Solimões-Japurá, Amazonas. Belém, Brazil: Conselho Nacional de Desenvolvimento Científico e Tecnológico, Instituto Nacional de Pesquisas da Amazônia, 1981. 48 p., 2 leaves of plates: bibl., ill. (Boletim do Museu Paraense Emilio Goeldi. Nova série, Antropologia; 81)

Historical reconstruction of the movements of the Mirânia society and of their contact with the expanding Brazilian frontier, and description of their thorough integration into regional society by 1974.

1163 Arvelo-Jiménez, Nelly. The political struggle on the Guayana region's indigenous peoples (CU/JIA, 36:1, Spring/Summer 1982, p. 43–54, maps)

Author groups cultures of Venezuela's Guayana region (entire area southeast of Orinoco River) into five subregions depending on length and type of contact. Notes four examples of effects of contact (rubber gathering and missionization) on different cultures, and outlines colonial antecedents of current Indian policy. Explores hidden economic motives of current government policies and their ethnocidal tendencies.

1164 Bartolomé, Leopoldo J. Social anthropology in Argentina: First Congress (UC/CA, 25:2, April 1984, p. 213–214)

Commemoratory notice on the First Argentine Congress of Social Anthropology (Misiones, Aug. 30-Sept. 2, 1983) marking the revival of Argentine anthropology after years of repression.

1165 Basso, Ellen Becker. A husband for his daughter, a wife for her son: strategies for selecting a set of in-laws among the Kalapalo (in Marriage practices in Lowland South America [see item 1294] p. 33–44, bibl., charts, index)

Histories of attempted marriage arrangements for two young Kalapalo Indians (Xingú Carib speakers), illustrate factors influencing spouse choice, including the maximization of relationships of mutual support (ifútisu).

1166 ———. A musical view of the universe: Kalapalo myth and ritual performances. Philadelphia: Univ. of Pennsylvania Press, 1985. 343 p.: bibl., index, plates, tables.

Discusses the place of myth and music in Kalapalo (Xingú Carib) life. Two thirds of text consist of 18 myths translated at length in poetic form that reproduce the style of a narrative performance. Author stresses essential relevance of performance style and context for meaning of myth, and argues that myth expresses, explains, and makes meaningful a range of problematic human emotions, motives and psychological situations, especially grief and sexuality. Detailed analysis of vocal stylistic devices brings out communicative strategies through which such meaning is conveyed. Contrasts myth as explanatory modality with music as mode of achieving unity with others and with higher beings (see also item 1246). Includes 18 photos and index of myths.

1167 Bastos, Rafael José de Menezes. Sistemas políticos, de comunicação e articulação social no Alto-Xingú (Anuário Antropológico [Edições Tempo Brasileiro, Rio de Janeiro] 81, 1983, p. 43–58, bibl., graph)

Research proposal challenges images of "Xinguan Paradise," and proposes an interethnic model of upper Xingú society.

1168 Beckerman, Stephen. La abundancia de proteínas en la Amazonía: una respuesta a Gross (CAAAP/AP, 3:6, marzo 1982, p. 91–126, bibl., graphs)

Translation of HLAS 43:1076.

1169 ———. Carpe diem: an optimal foraging approach to Bari fishing and hunting (in Adaptive responses to native Amazonians [see item 1153] p. 269–299, graphs, tables)

Uses quantative data and ethnographic observations to discuss and explain seasonal distribution of time between hunting and fishing among the Bari (Motilones) of northern Colombia.

1170 Bellier, Irene. Mai Juna: los orejones, identidad cultural y proceso de aculturación (CAAAP/AP, 5:9, julio 1983, p. 37–61, bibl., maps, plates)

Analysis of the process of acculturation in this missionized Western Tucanoan society of the Peruvian montaña, and its disorganizing effects on the group's political and economic organization and cultural world. [K.L. Hall]

1171 Berlin, Brent and Elois Ann Berlin. Adaptation and ethnozoological classification: theoretical implications of animal resources and diet of the Aguaruna and Huambisa (in Adaptive responses of native Amazonians [see item 1153] p. 301–325, maps, tables)

Aguaruna and Huambisa, two Jivaroan groups in northern Peru, have detailed classifications of most of the animal species in their region. However, only a few species contribute significantly to their diet, because they are both available and easy to capture. Neither utilitarian nor symbolic importance explains why certain species are thoroughly classified, merely observation of nature.

1172 Braunstein, José A. and **Amalia Sanguinetti de Bórmida.** Algunos rasgos de la organización social de los indígenas del Gran Chaco. Buenos Aires: Univ. de Buenos Aires, Facultad de Filosofía y Letras, Instituto de Ciencias Antropológicas, 1983. 173 p.: appendices, bibl., ill. (Publicación; 2. Trabajos de etnología)

Survey of social structures of all indigenous Chaco societies. Compares form of residential groups, descent, marriage and kin terminology. Appendices provide lists of kin terms for 13 Chaco languages of five families.

1173 Brazilian Indians and the law. Translated by Bjorn Maybury-Lewis. Introduction by David Maybury-Lewis. Cambridge, Mass.: Cultural Survival, 1981. 14 p.: appendix (Occasional paper; 5)

Consists of documents approved at meeting held (Federal Univ. of Santa Catarina, Oct. 1980) by lawyers and anthropologists to discuss legal issues affecting indigenous Brazilians. Includes statements on Indian lands, FUNAI's "guardianship" of Indians, dams, national parks and Indian parks, and role of anthropologists in relation to FUNAI. Appendix lists participants.

1174 Brown, Michael F. La cara oscura del progreso: el suicidio entre los aguaruna del Alto Mayo (*in* Relaciones interétnicas y adaptación cultural. Edited by Michael F. Brown. Quito: Ediciones Mundo Shuar, 1984, p. 76–88, appendix, bibl.)

Discusses alarming rate of suicide among the Aguaruna, a Shuar people of Peru's northern Amazon region. Author collected case histories, four of which presented in appendix, while researching this group. Concludes by stressing impact of culture change.

1175 ———. Individual experience, dreams and the identification of magical stones in an Amazonian society (*in* Directions in cognitive anthropology. Edited by Janet W.D. Dougherty. Urbana: Univ., of Illinois Press, 1985, p. 373–387, bibl.)

Describes types of magical stones used in Aguaruna hunting, gardening and warfare, and the role of dreams or omens in finding

them and verifying their authenticity. Discusses issues of classification raised by such "subjective" criteria.

1176 ———. Una paz incierta: historia y cultura de las comunidades aguarunas frente al impacto de la Carretera Marginal. Traducción de Francisca Bartra Gross. Magdalena, Perú: Centro Amazónico de Antropología y Aplicación Práctica (CAAAP), 1984. 270 p.: graphs, ill., maps, photos, tables.

Important and balanced ethnography of the Aguaruna, Shuar people of northern Peru. Despite mention of highway in title, emphasizes traditional culture, covering domestic groups, kinship, subsistence, traditional concepts of health and illness, and religion. Chapters on community, illness and conclusions deal with existing problems and strategies for resolving them. Includes 10 photographs.

1177 ———. The role of words in Aguaruna hunting magic (AES/AE, 11, 1984, p. 545–558, bibl.)

Author argues that "magical" spells are not merely "expressive," but intended to act "instrumentally" on their object. Analyzes series of Aguaruna magical hunting songs (*anen*), showing how the poetic invocation of affect-laden images is structured as if to attract game in a manner analogous to that of erotic relationships.

1178 Buer, Wilhelm P. Curare-Pfeilgiftbereitung-heute (MVW/AV, 35, 1981, p. 15–30, bibl., graphs, ill., maps, tables)

Reports on chemical analysis of curare on arrowheads from Ecuador and southern Venezuela in Vienna's Museum für Völkerkunde. Attributes slight difference between composition of recent curare samples and those of 100 years ago to continous tradition in its preparation.

1178a Butt Colson, Audrey. Binary oppositions and the treatment of sickness among the Akawaio (*in* Social anthropology and medicine. Edited by J.B. Loudon. New York: Academic Press, 1976, p. 422–499, bibl.)

Detailed account of curing among the Akawaio, Carib-speakers of Guyana. Covers food avoidances and blowing as shamanic technique, and Akawaio conceptualizations of illness and curing: cold/sweet category, spirits, and concepts of balance and harmony and "the mediate state."

1179 Caiuby Novaes, Sylvia *et al.* Habitações indígenas. São Paulo: Livraria Nobel: Editora da Univ. de São Paulo, 1983. 196 p.: bibl., ill.

Seven chapters describe the houses of nine Indian societies of Brazil, relating house shapes to social structure and, in some cases, conceptualization of space. Chapters on Timbira (Ladeira), Shavante (Lopes da Silva), Bororo (Caiuby Novaes), Kaiapó and Parakanã (Vidal), Yawalapití, Karajá and Shavante (Sá), Waiãpi, and Wayana (Hussak van Velthem). See also *HLAS 45:1316*.

1180 Califano, Mario. Etnografía de los Mashco de la Amazonia Sud Occidental del Perú. Prólogo de Marcelo Bórmida. Buenos Aires: Fundación para la Educación, la Ciencia y la Cultura, 1982. 315 p.: bibl., ill.

General descriptive ethnography of this Arawakan-speaking people of the Peruvian Amazon, based on fieldwork with three of five component tribes: Huachipaire, Amaracaire and Zapiteri. Last half, "Ergologia," provides brief descriptions of 111 items of material culture, many with illustrations, and noting mythical reference per item. Marcelo Bórmida's prologue discusses author's theoretical orientation.

1181 ———. and **Alicia Fernández Distel.** The use of a hallucinogenous plant among the Mascho: Southwestern Amazonia, Peru (DGV/ZE, 107:1, 1982,p. 129–143, bibl., map, plates)

Describes drug derived from a *Brugmansia* shrub by the Huachipaire Mashco, their cultivation, pharmacology, preparation, and administration of it as well as associated beliefs and rituals. Authors describe their own subjective experiences while taking drug.

1182 Cardoso de Oliveira, Roberto. Enigmas e soluções: exercícios de etnologia e de crítica. Rio de Janeiro: Edições Tempo Brasileiro, 1983. 208 p.: bibl., graphs, tables (Bibliotéca tempo universitário; 68)

Consists of 11 essays reprinted here in three groups, spanning two of the major interests of Cardoso's thought to date: four classic papers on Terena and Tükuna societies from a structural perspective, and two on ethnic identity (see *HLAS 45:1231*). The introduction and the third section, critical

essays, hint at his current interest in scientific epistemology.

1183 ———. Movimientos indígenas e indigenismo en Brasil (III/AI, 3:41, julio/sept. 1981, p. 399–405)

Describes growth of Indian movement in Brazil and formation of UNI or UNIND (União das Nações Indígenas). Credits CIMI (Conselho Indigenista Missionário) with assistance in initial mobilization of Indians to pressure FUNAI.

1184 Carneiro, Robert L. The cultivation of manioc among the Kuikuru of the Upper Xingú (*in* Adaptive responses of native Amazonians [see item 1153] p. 65–111, bibl., chart, ill.)

Descriptive study of manioc cultivation by this Carib-speaking Xingú group. Concludes with calculation that the Kuikuru produce much more manioc than they consume.

1185 Carvalho, Edgard de Assis. As alternativas dos vencidos: índios Terena no Estado de São Paulo. Rio de Janeiro: Editora Paz e Terra, 1979. 1 v.: bibl, charts, maps, tables.

History of the subjugation of the Terena Indians and some statistics on their trade and employment on the Araribá reservation. Stresses detrimental effects of their shift from a subsistence to a commercial economy.

1186 Carvalho, José Porfirio F. de. Waimiri Atroari: a historia que ainda não foi contada. Brasília: s.n., 1982. 120, 34 p.: ill., ports.

Vivid history of contacts with Waimiri Atroari, Brazilian Indians north of Manaus, from first contact in 1884. Focuses especially on tragic events of 1974, in which author participated. Manaus-Boa Vista road was prematurely pushed through, over objections of sertanista Gilberto Pinto Figueredo Costa. Author recounts Costa's dismissal by FUNAI, his mysterious assassination on a road construction site, and the subsequent decimation of groups (not yet contacted) through measles epidemic brought about by the road as well as the reduction and eventual downgrading of their reservation.

1187 Carvalho, Sílvia Maria S. de. A cerâmica e os rituais antropofágicos (USP/RA, 26, 1983, p. 39–52, bibl.)

Proposes that individual in charge of performing the sacrifice in Tupinambá ritual prisoner execution is identified with victim. Cites as evidence design appearing on both their faces and on ceramic vessel for cooking victim's flesh. Elaborates on implications for Tupinambá cosmology (see item **1201** and **1239**).

1188 ———. Jurupari: estudos de mitologia brasileira. São Paulo: Editora Atica, 1979. 388 p.: bibl. (Ensaios; 62)

Wide-ranging analysis based on published sources, of selected myths from different Tucanoan and Arawakan societies of the Uaupés. Revision based on doctoral dissertation stimulated by Lévi-Strauss's neglect of the area. Author emulates Lévi-Strauss in wide geographic range of comparisons, and is particularly fascinated by possible Andean influences.

1189 Castro, Eduardo Viveiros de. A autodeterminação indígena como valor (Anuário Antropológico [Edições Tempo Brasileiro, Rio de Janeiro] 81, 1983, p. 233–242)

Discusses definition and ambiguities of concept of "indigenous self determination," in relation to issues of Brazilian indigenous policy, particularly guardianship and the growing indigenous movement.

1190 ———. Notas sobre a cosmologia Yawalapití (Religião e Sociedade [Rio de Janeiro] 3, 1978, p. 163–174, bibl.)

Discusses the place of spiritual beings in Yawalapití life, myth, and ritual. Creator spirits are sometimes mortal; immortal created spirits are essences of wordly beings (see item **1219**). Myth provides positive and negative models for social behavior, but ritual celebrates impossibility of repeating mythical archetypes.

1191 Censo y estudio de la población indígena del Paraguay, 1981. Asunción: Instituto Paraguayo del Indígena, 1982. 729 p., 3 folded leaves of plates: bibl., ill.

Population data, by region and tribe, and data on landholdings of Paraguay's indigenous groups in 1981.

1192 Chagnon, Napoleon A. Yanomamö: the fierce people. 3rd ed. New York: Holt, Rinehart & Winston, 1983. 224 p.: bibl., ill., index (Case studies in cultural anthropology)

Extensively revised new ed. of Chagnon's popular ethnography. Thoroughly reworked first chapter ("Doing Fieldwork") loses much of the original version's honest immediacy. Material taken from *Studying the Yanomamö* does not fit well here, but should be reprinted in original form. Other revisions contextualize ethnography more extensively in theoretical context, bring in results of recent research, and enhance image of ferocity which has shaped popular image of South American Indians.

1193 ——— and **Thomas F. Melancon.** Epidemics in a tribal population (*in* The Impact of contact: two Yanomamo case studies [see item **1267**] p. 53–78, bibl., charts, maps, tables)

Reports on a 1973 flu epidemic and its effects on three isolated Yanomamo villages on the Mavaca River, Venezuela. Using the epidemic's statistics on population and mortality, authors calculate its long-term effects on population and discuss cultural factors that increase mortality as well as impact on social organization.

1194 Chaim, Marivone Matos. Aldeiamentos indígenas: Goiás, 1749–1811. 2d. ed. rev. São Paulo: Nobel; Brasília: Instituto Nacional do Livro: Fundação Nacional Pró-Memória, 1983. 1 v.: appendix, bibl., charts, maps, tables.

Detailed and thorough study of indigenous cultures in the Brazilian state of Goiás in the 18th century, of Pombal's colonial Indian policy, and of Jesuit and other reductions and their failure in Goiás.

1195 Chapelle, Richard. Os índios Cintas-Largas. Translated by David Jardim Júnior. Belo Horizonte: Edições Itataia; São Paulo: Edições Univ. de São Paulo, 1983. 138 p.: maps (Series Reconquista do Brasil; v. 73) Translation of *HLAS 43:1087*.

1196 Chapman, Anne. Drama and power in a hunting society: the Selk'nam of Tierra del Fuego. Cambridge, England: Cambridge Univ. Press, 1982. 201 p.: bibl., graphs, ill., plates, tables.

Interesting new ethnography of these tragically decimated Tierra del Fuego hunters. Focuses primarily on a thorough discussion of the Hain initiation ceremony which is central to religious life. Study based on intensive field work with eight surviving

Selk'nam and Hauk, including one woman shaman as well as synthesis and discussion of early written descriptions. Corrects misconceptions of Gusinde and others, and deepens our understanding of male-female relationships and the role of the Hain in this complex hunting society (see also item 1295).

1197 Chaumeil, Jean-Pierre. Voir, savoir, pouvoir: le chamanisme chez les Yagua du nord-est péruvien. Paris: Editions de l'Ecole des hautes études en sciences sociales, 1983. 352 p., 8 p. of plates: bibl., ill., indexes (Recherches d'histoire et de sciences sociales, 0249–5619. Studies in history and the social sciences; 8)

Detailed description and analysis of shamanism in Yagua society. Stresses Yagua conceptions of shamanism. Describes initiation and shamanic practices and related beliefs, placing them in Yagua society's cosmological, political, economic, and ritual context. Final chapter details Yagua etiology of illness.

1198 Chernela, Janet. Estrutura social do Uaupés (Anuario Antropológico [Edições Tempo Brasileiro, Rio de Janeiro] 81, 1983, p. 59–69, bibl., table)

Succinct and innovative summary of Brazilian Uaupés Tucanoan social structure, based on fieldwork with the Uanano. Advances proposition that intra-sib status is transmitted in sibling-order ranked names which are passed on from grandparent sibling set to grandchildren. Status is also expressed in three ranked endogamous "generation groups," "grandchildren" being highest (for other articles by this author, see item 1340).

1199 CIMI: o Projeto Carajás e as suas consequências para as populações indígenas. São Luís: Conselho Indigenista Missionario, Maranhão-Goiás e Norte, 1983. 38 p.: bibl., maps, tables.

Pamphlet outlines financial plans for massive Carajás mining and ranching development project. Plans ignore disastrous consequences project would have on 11 indigenous nations whose reserves are in project area. Effects it would have on specific indigenous groups are detailed (see item 1389).

1200 Cipolletti, Maria Susana. Jenseitsvorstellungen bei den Indianern

Südamerikas. Berlin, FRG: D. Reimer, 1983. 368 p.: bibl., ill., maps.

Survey of religious beliefs about death ("Other-side representations") of both Lowland and Highland South American Indians. Reasonably up-to-date and well selected bibliography includes important recent contributions of Carneiro da Cunha (see *HLAS 43 : 1098*), De Civrieux (*HLAS 45 : 1240*), and H. Clastres and Lizot (*HLAS 43 : 1153*), though there is lack of references to many recent works on Bororo eschatology (e.g., items **1219** and **1375**, and *HLAS 43 : 1094*, *HLAS 43 : 1149*, and *HLAS 43 : 1214*). Includes 15 maps plotting distribution of various themes in death-beliefs (see also item **1203**).

1201 Clastres, Hélène. Terra sem mal: o profetismo Tupíguaraní. Tradução de Renato Janine Ribeiro. São Paulo: Editora Brasiliense, 1978. 124 p.

This brilliant and scholarly historical comparison of 16th-century Tupi religion with 19th-century Guarani migrations argues that the search for the "Land Without Evil," guided by "prophets", was not a response to colonization but wholly rooted in traditional religious beliefs. Concluding chapters examine the content of the beliefs espoused by the prophets, and the significance of the prophetic word.

1202 Clastres, Pierre. Arqueologia da violência: ensaios de antropologia política. Tradução de Carlos Eugênio Marcondes de Moura and Bento Prado Júnior. Preface by Bento Prado Júnior. São Paulo: Editora Brasiliense, 1982. 300 p.

Consists of 12 essays, posthumously published, that elaborate Clastres's thesis (see *HLAS 41 : 1126*) that (contrary to evolutionists) stateless societies have achieved structural means to preserve liberty from oppressive political domination. This thesis is developed in terms of religion in chap. 5 (see item **1203**), the economy in chap. 8 and war as a condition of liberty/group autonomy in chap. 11–12. These last two chapters, which provide book's title, were to be part of a longer work.

1203 ———. Mitos e ritos dos índios da América do Sul (*in* Clastres, Pierre. Arqueologia da violência: ensaios de antropologia política [see item **1202**] p. 53–104, bibl.)

Encyclopedia article written for forth-coming *Dictionnaire des mythologies et des religions* (to be published in Paris by Flammarion). Distinguishes Andean religions, with ancestor worship and agricultural deities, from Amazonian religions which lack gods and distance their dead, contrasting them as religions of stratified and unstratified societies, respectively. Interprets Tupi prophetism as protest against rising hierarchy in these bellicose coastal societies (see item **1201**).

1204 Coelho, Vera Penteado. Some aspects of the pottery of the Waurá Indians (DGV/ZE, 108:2, 1982, p. 235–254, bibl., ill., plates)

Engaging article on ceramics presents origin myths of clay and of pottery painting to introduce discussion of the motifs and iconography of Waurá pottery design. Concludes with consideration of the nature and conventional rules of representation in Waurá culture. Intriguing references as to the relationship of pottery and music are not developed. Original Portuguese version appears in item **1215**.

1205 Coelho dos Santos, Sílvio. Indígenas sobreviventes no sul no Brasil: perspectivas para seu destino (*in* Simpósio Nacional de Estudos Missioneiros, 2nd, Santa Rosa, Brazil, 1977. Anais. Santa Rosa, Brazil: Faculdade de Filosofia, Ciências e Letras Dom Bosco, 1978, p. 118–138, bibl.)

Discusses problems of the Kaingang, Kokleng (Xokleng) Guaraní and Xetá (Hetá) Indians in three southern states of Brazil, and criticizes inadequacy of FUNAI's programs for them.

1206 ———. O índio perante o direito. Florianópolis, Brazil: Editora da Univ. Federal de Santa Catarina, 1982. 1 v.

Work presented at conference of anthropologists and lawyers convened to discuss the situation of the Indian before Brazilian law (Oct. 1980). For other discussions of indigenous legal issues, see items **1211**, **1235**, **1338**, and **1352**).

1207 Colbacchini, Antônio. *Uké-wagúu:* em comemoração aos 80 anos da Missão Salesiana de Mato Grosso. Cuiabá, Brazil: Imprensa da Univ. Federal de Mato Grosso, 1983. 83 p., 18 leaves of plates: ports.

Reissue of highly lyrical 1937 account of 1902 establishment of Salesian Mission for Bororo Indians on its 80th anniversary. "Chief" Uké-wagúu's dream played important part in early conversions (see also item **1219**).

1208 Colchester, Marcus. Ecological modelling and indigenous systems of resource use: some examples from the Amazon of south Venezuela (FSCN/A, 55, 1981, p. 51–72, bibl., graph, table)

Distinguishes ecological anthropologists who focus on Indians' adaptation to resources from those who see Indian beliefs as intentionally regulating resource exploitation. Dubs these approaches as "'etic' and 'emic' biofunctionalists," thus perpetuating Harris's misuse of this once useful dichotomy. Argues that Amazonian Indians make subsistence choices not on basis of ideology of resource conservation, but on principle of conservation of effort. Concludes that effective ecological anthropology must take into account both cultural values and actual resource use (see item **1153** and *HLAS 45:1269*).

1209 Colombia indígena = Colombia's native peoples. Textos y diagramación, Julián Narváez Hernández. Fotografías, Gustavo Neito Roa et al. Traducción, Alvaro Wheeler. Bogotá: Ministerio de Gobierno, 1982. 229 p.: bibl., ill., table (Col. Legislación, doctrina y jurisprudencia; 3)

Government-sponsored book of photographs of 11 Colombian indigenous groups, with very brief Spanish/English text on each. Considerable misinformation (e.g., all Amazonian groups are classed as "hunting and fishing" cultures). Includes table of indigenous groups by region, lists language, population and economic (mis)classification, and text of government Indian Bill of 1983. To be used with caution.

1211 Comissão Pró-Indio, *São Paulo.* O índio e a cidadania. Edição de Lux Vidal. São Paulo: Editora Brasiliense, 1983. 100 p.: bibl.

Includes two sets of papers: pt. 1, "Indio: Cidadão?," contains those presented at the ABA's (Associação Brasileira de Antropologia) round table (April 1982) by: Eunice Durham, Maria Célia P. Machado Paoli, Maria Tereza Sadek R. de Souza, Carlos Federico Marés de Souza Filho, and Dalma de

Abreu Ballarí. Pt. 2, "Pataxó Hä Hã Hãi of Southern Bahia," includes historical sketch by Aracy Lopes da Silva, transcript of FUNAI hearing with Pataxó leaders, José Lázaro Alfredo Guimarães's legal decision, and Maria Manuela Caneiro da Cunha's brief on ethnic identity criteria.

1212 ———. A questão da educação indígena. São Paulo: Editora Brasiliense, 1981. 222 p.: bibls., graphs, ill., plates, tables.

Consists of 15 papers from Brazilian conference on indigenous education that describe specific experiences in the North (Acre and Rondônia), West Central and South regions of Brazil, and four discuss general philosophical and pedagogical issues. Concludes with two bibliographies, one of works on the topic in *América Indígena* since 1969, with abstracts of each, and one on indigenous education in Brazil (see also item **1304**).

1213 As Comunidades indígenas de Pernambuco. Recife: Governo do Estado de Pernambuco, Secretaria de Planejamento, Instituto de Desenvolvimento de Pernambuco, CONDEPE, 1981. 98 leaves: bibl., ill.

Pernambuco state official publication provides tribe-by-tribe description of population and social and economic conditions of six indigenous groups in Pernambuco. Proposes that the state develop assistance programs in cooperation with FUNAI.

1214 A Construição da identidade nas sociedades indígenas (Anuário Antropológico [Edições Tempo Brasileiro, Rio de Janeiro] 82, 1984, p. 167–224, bibl.)

Symposium on the problem of "tribal" identity among indigenous groups at various levels of contact. Includes introduction by Alcida Ramos questioning notion of "tribe" as an artifact of the contact situation (see item **1326**) and defining conference as a discussion of indigenous concepts of ethnic identity. Articles: Maria Rosario G. de Carvalho "A Identidade dos Povos do Nordeste;" Julio Cesar Melatti "Questões sobre a Identidade Krahó;" Anthony Seeger "Identidade Suyá;" Aracy Lopes da Silva "A Expressão Mítica da Vivência: Tempo e Espaço na Construição da Identidade Savante;" and Leonardo H.G. Fígoli "A Emergência de uma Identidade Regional no Campo das Relações Interetnicas."

1215 Contribuições à antropologia em homenagem ao Professor Egon Schaden. São Paulo: Univ. de São Paulo, Fundo de Pesquisas do Museu Paulista, 1981. 362 p.: bibl., ill. (Col. Museu Paulista. Série Ensaios; 4)

Articles on Lowland South Amerindians include: Hans Becher on "Mongolian spot" in newborn Yanomamö; Vera Coelho on Waurá ceramics (item **1204**); Waltraud Grohs-Paul on problems of minority education (e.g., Venezuela's Warao); K. and A. Hahn on masks of the Bolivian Chimanes; Ulf Lind on Lengua shamans (item **1285**); Bartolomé Meliá on Christian-Guaraní relations in 16th-century Paraguay (item **1305**); Adalberto Holanda Pereira on a Pareci myth; Antonio Porro on the 17th-century Omagua population (item **1320**); Rauschert-Alenani on ethnohistory of the Aparaí-Wayana (item **1330**); Reichel-Dolmatoff on Desana "shamanistic geography (item **1332**); Lux Vidal on Kayapó body painting and self representation (item **1373**); Renate Viertler on choice of terms in religious ethnography (item **1376**); and Otto Zerries in implements used by shamans throughout Lowland South America.

1216 Costales, Piedad and Alfredo Costales. Amazonia: Ecuador, Peru, Bolivia. s.l.: Mundo Shuar, 1983. 331 p., 4 leaves of plates: bibl., ill. (some col.)

Highly useful survey of indigenous groups of western Amazonia (lowland Ecuador, Peru, and Bolivia) covers linguistic affiliation and current situation of past and present groups. One chart lists 138 groups, since 1534, and indicates their survival status (surviving, in assimilation, in process of extinction, extinct). Also discusses natural resources, social legislation, mechanisms of domination, and landholding. Useful inventory of ethnolinguistic families and bibliography.

1217 Coudreau, Henri. Viagem ao Tapajós. Translated from the French by Eugênio Amado. Preface by Mário Guimarães Ferri. São Paulo: Editora da Univ. de São Paulo, 1977. 162 p.: ill, tables (Reconquista do Brasil series; 44)

Translation into Portuguese of classic account of 1895 Tapajós River expedition. Includes observations on Maué, Apiacá, Mundurucú and Tapanhuna Indians, census of whites and Mundurucú, meteorological record of voyage, and word lists of Maué, Apiacá and Mundurucú.

1218 ———. Viagem ao Xingú. Translated from the French by Eugênio Amado. Preface by Mário Guimarães Ferri. São Paulo: Editora da Univ. de São Paulo, 1977. 165 p.: appendices, ill., tables (Reconquista do Brasil series; 49)

Welcome translation into Portuguese of classic account of 1896 Xingú River expedition. Includes observations on Juruna and Arara Indians, appendices with word lists in Juruna and Arara, census of river, and metereological records (June-Oct. 1896). Illustrated with engravings and line drawings.

1219 Crocker, Jon Christopher. Vital souls: Bororo cosmology, natural symbolism, and shamanism. Foreword by David Maybury-Lewis. Tucson: Univ. of Arizona Press, 1985. 380 p.: bibl., ill., index, maps, plates, tables.

Unusual ethnography provides overview of Bororo conceptions of life and cosmos, organized around the dialectic between *aroe* (spirit essence inherent in names and in clan emblems) and *bope* (multiple spirits responsible for change and affliction), and the corresponding two types of shaman, *aroe etawa-are* (now defunct) and *bari*. Based on extensive fieldwork and close work with one knowledgeable elder, this ethnography provides deep insight into Bororo cosmology (see also items **1179, 1232, 1236, 1313,** and **1375**).

1220 Crocker, William H. Canela initiation festivals: "helping hands" through life (*in* Celebration: studies in festivity and ritual. Edited by Victor Turner. Washington: Smithsonian Institution Press, 1982, p. 147–169, plates)

Account of initiation ceremonies among the Gê-speaking Canela of central Brazil, presented as festivals of socialization into adult values, especially that of mutual help among ceremonial friends.

1221 ———. Canela marriage: factors in change (*in* Marriage practices in Lowland South America [see item **1294**] p. 63–98, bibl., index)

Account of marriage process among the Ramkókamekra Canela (Eastern Timbira group). Stresses the two-stage nature of marriage (solidified at childbirth) and recent changes in affinal and authority relationships, due to men's commercial employment and acculturation pressures. Also discusses parallel transmission of statuses and concepts of kin relationship.

1222 ———. Ultimate reality and meaning for the Ramkókamekra Canela, Eastern Timbira, Brazil: a triadic dualistic cognitive pattern (*in* Ultimate reality and meaning: interdisciplinary studies in the philosophy of understanding. Toronto: Univ. of Toronto Press, 1983, p. 84–111, bibl.)

Proposes underlying cognitive pattern of Canela (Gê) thought, wherein diadic oppositions are mediated by third element which is conceived to be in "parallel pairing" with each opposing element. Illustrates pattern with examples from Canela social life and conceptualization of social and natural processes, and uses examples to propose a relativistic view of ultimate reality and meaning.

1223 Cultural Survival Quarterly. Cultural Survival Inc. Vol. 8, Nos. 1/4, 1984– . Cambridge, Mass.

All four issues of vol. 8 contain articles on threats to indigenous cultures and movements in South America. *No. 1, Spring 1984*: Robin Wright and Stephen Sewartzman sum up 1983 events in Brazil, seriously detrimental administrative acts, significant changes in FUNAI, and assassination of 17 indigenous leaders (p. 75–81); T. Moore describes officially sanctioned invasion of Peru's Manu National Park for oil exploration and other development projects (p. 82–83). *No. 3, Fall 1984*: Jason Clay traces extinction of the Yahgan and Ona (p. 5–12); Richard Reed discusses threats to Mataco of Argentina's Chaco; Anthony Stocks describes displacement of Peruvian Candoshi Indians by highland migrants, and brief article covers situation of Aché in Paraguay with bibliography. *No. 4, Winter 1984*, entitled "Organizing to Survive," is annotated separately (item **1317**).

1224 Cunha, Manuela Carneiro da. Escatologia entre os Krahó: refleção, fabulação (*in* A Morte e os mortos na sociedade brasileira. [see item **8393**], p. 323–339, bibl.)

Portuguese version of *HLAS 45:1243*.

1226 Del Papa, Paolo. Un gruppo dell'Amazzonia peruviana: i Machiguengas dell'Urubamba (IGM/U, 62:6, nov./dic. 1982, p. 1123–1144, bibl., map, photos)
Ethnographic sketch of the Arawakan-speaking Machiguenga of S. Amazonian Peru. Concludes with description of psychic effects of ayahuasca which is taken by a ceremonial "ayahuasca society."

1227 Demarquet, Sonia de Almeida. Os Xokleng de Ibirama: uma comunidade indígena de Santa Catarina (Boletim do Museu do Indio [Rio de Janeiro] 3, dez. 1983, p. 1–64, appendices, bibl.)
Sketches history of Shokleng conflicts and pacification (1914–67) and current problems of FUNAI Post PI Ibirama in education, health care and subsistence as background for discussion of Oct. 1980 petition for "emancipation" (termination of FUNAI tutelage) by Ibirama Shokleng. Concludes that petition was not well advised, but was a protest against FUNAI program's inadequacies.

1228 Descola, Philippe. Ethnicité et développement économique: le cas de la Fédération des centre shuar (in Indianité, ethnocide, indigenisme en Amérique latine. GRAL, Centre interdisciplinaire d'études latino-américaines, Toulouse-le Mirail. Paris: Centre national de la recherche scientifique, 1982, p. 221–237 [Amérique latine. Pays ibériques])
Political and historical analysis of Shuar Federation's adoption of cattle-raising economy, following lead of early Salesian missionaries. Author points out destruction of ecosystem and of earlier egalitarian subsistence economic organization, and characterizes such destruction as insidious form of ethnocide. Adoption of highland term *minga* for collective labor signals new centralized orientation to authority.

1229 Dole, Gertrude E. Amahuaca women in social change (in Sex roles in changing cultures. Edited by Ann McElroy and Carolyn Matthiasson. Buffalo: SUNY, Dept. of Anthropology, 1979, p. 111–121, bibl. [Occasional papers in anthropology; 1])
Sketches traditional sex roles and division of labor among Amahuaca, Panoan-speakers of southeastern Amazonian Peru, and disruption of balance by male employ-

ment in lumbering. Also refers to problems of women moving to cities.

1230 ———. The structure of Kuikuru marriage (in Marriage practices in Lowland South America [see item **1294**] p. 45–63, bibl., index)
Denies any consistent pattern of marriage exchange or alliance among the Kuikuru, Carib-speaking Indians of the Xingú. Partners are now selected for distance, although author concedes that a now rarely used term for cross-cousin suggests past cross-cousin marriage and a discarded alliance structure.

1231 ———. The use of manioc among the Kuikuru: some interpretations (in The nature and status of ethnobotany. Edited by Richard I. Ford. Ann Arbor: Univ. of Michigan Press, 1978, p. 217–247, bibl., chart, ill. [Museum of Anthropology anthropological papers])
Describes preparation of *farinha* and other products from manioc roots among Carib-speaking Kuikuru of the Upper Xingú. Corrects widespread misconceptions about manioc and its preparation with clear account of chemical processes involved and variations in its preparation among Amazonian societies (see also items **1153, 1184** and **1322**).

1232 Dorta, Sonia Ferraro. Paríkó: etnografia de um artefato plumário. São Paulo: Fundo de Pesquisas do Museu Paulista da Univ. de São Paulo, 1981. 269 p.: ill. (some col.) (Col. Museu Paulista. Etnologia; 4)
Meticulously detailed study of Bororo headdresses and their construction examines designs created by plumage combinations, and nomenclature, iconography and clan associations of these designs. Based on field observation and interviews with the artists, as well as museum study. Introduction has good review of literature on material culture of Brazilian indigenous groups.

1233 Dufour, Darna L. Nutrition in the northwest Amazon: household dietary intake and time-energy expenditure (in Adaptive responses of native Amazonians [see item **1153**] p. 329–355, charts, map, photos, tables)
Quantitative study of food intake among the Tatuyo, a Tucanoan group on the

Colombian Vaupés, demonstrates generally adequate dietary protein and energy intakes.

1234 Ehrenreich, Jeffrey. Isolation, retreat and secrecy: dissembling behavior among the Coaiquer Indians of Ecuador (*in* Political anthropology of Ecuador [see item **1319**] p. 25–57, bibl., maps)

Describes how secretiveness and dissembling about traditional practices, as well as physical retreat to isolated area, serve as modes of defense against domination.

1235 En defensa de los pueblos indígenas. Lima: Comisión Evangélica Latinoamericana de Educación Cristiana, 1980. 190 p.: appendix.

Spanish language version of collection of documents put together by Paulo Suess of CIMI (item **1352**), with added preface by CELADEC (Comisión Evangélica Latinamericana de Educación Cristiana). Appendix includes final resolution of the First Pastoral Meeting of Amazonian Missions (Primer Encuentro Pastoral de Misiones en el Amazonas).

1235a Encuentro Latinoamericano de CEHILA, *9th, Manaus, Brazil, 1981.* Das reduções latino-americanas às lutas indigenas atuais. Organização de Eduardo Hoornaert. São Paulo: Edições Paulinas, 1982. 255 p.: bibl., ill. (Col. Estudos e debates latino-americanos; 3)

Symposium devoted to reducciones in various regions of Portuguese and Spanish America. Papers concerning Amazonian Indians include: M.M. Marral on Amazonian Peru; F.H. Fragoso on Franciscans in Grão Pará; E. Hornaert on Carmelites in Amazonian Brazil; J.R. de Carvalho on Carmelites in Solimões and Rio Negro; A. Menacho on Mojos and Chiquitos in Bolivia; and B. Meliá on the Guarani.

1236 Fernandes, Florestan. Investigação etnológica no Brasil, e outros ensaios. Petrópolis, Brazil: Editora Vozes, 1975. 298 p.: bibl., tables (Col. Sociologia Brasileira; 2)

Brings together five essays, originally published 1946–64, and grouped in two sections: 1) ethnohistorical ("The 'World of the Indians' and Its Crisis"); and 2) methodological ("The Ethnological Knowing of Reality"). Three deal wth the Tupinambá—their reaction to conquest, upbringing, and a bibli-

ographic essay on sources for the study of warfare—and one on a "marginal Bororo," educated to become a teacher.

1237 Fernandes Mireya, Rafael *et al.* Nos cuentan los makiritares (VMJ/BIV, 20:17, 1981, p. 23–41, ill., maps)

General introduction to history, environment, tribal organization and subsistence economy of the Ye'cuana (Makiritare) Indians of the Venezuelan Amazon Territory, narrated by Ye'cuana. First person account provides unique perspective on their world view and beliefs. Conclusion describes objectives of the "Unión Makiritare del Alto Ventuari" to protect rights and aid development efforts of the indigenous people. [K.L. Hall]

1238 Flowers, Nancy M. Seasonal factors in subsistence, nutrition, and child growth in a central Brazilian Indian community (*in* Adaptive responses of native Amazonians [see item **1153**] p. 357–390, charts, plates, tables)

Describes subsistence activities of Shavante village, and reports on a range of quantitative works, from time allocation studies of subsistence activities and records of success of individual hunting expeditions to a study of children's nutrition and growth. Concludes that shift to increased dependence on agriculture is not nutritionally beneficial.

1239 Forsyth, Donald W. Three cheers for Hans Staden: the case for Brazilian cannibalism (ASE/E, 32:1, 1985, p. 17–36)

Defends veracity and reliability of Hans Staden's account of Tupinambá cannibalism, questioned by William Arens.

1240 Frank, Erwin H. Ein Leben am Rande des Welkmarkts: Ökologie und Ökonomie der Comunidad nativa de Santa Martha. Bonn: Seminar für Völkerkunde, Univ. Bonn, 1983. 246 p., 18 p. of plates: bibl., ill., maps (Bonner amerikanistische Studien; 10)

Important ethnographic study of the Uni (Cashibo), a Panoan group of southern Amazonian Peru, focuses exclusively on the economy and ecology of this culture, "on the edge of the world market," detailing both traditional gardening, hunting and fishing, and also commercial production of gold, wood and a medicinal tree latex.

1241 ———. *Mecece*: la función sicológica social y económica de un complejo ritual de los Uni—Cashibo—de la Amazonía peruana (CAAAP/AP, 5:9, julio 1983, p. 63–78, bibl.)

Describes Uni (Cashibo) practice of *mecece*, a self-discipline ritual that includes avoidance of sex or of certain types of food practiced by men of this Peruvian Amazon society in cases of illness or death as well as for successful hunting, warfare or initiation rites. Author speculates on simple psychological and social functions and suggests ecological advantages.

1242 Fundação Instituto Brasileiro de Geografia e Estatística. Divisão de Atlas e Apoio Técnico. Mapa etno-histórico do Brasil e regiões adjacentes: adaptado do *Mapa de Curt Nimuendajú, 1944*. Rio de Janeiro: A Fundação, 1980. 97 p.: bibl., indexes, 1 map: col.; 103 cm., folded in cover 26 x 21 cm. Scale 1:5,000,000 (W° 75—W 35°/N 10°—S 35°)

Nimuendajú's map of tribal locations constitutes an invaluable resource for South American ethnography, especially for Brazil and adjacent regions. Map covers Amazon and Orinoco basins extending west to the Ucayali and Paraguay-Paraná to Río de la Plata. Accompanying booklet provides Nimuendajú's observations on the map, his index of tribes with language affiliations and numerical bibliographic references, list (unalphabetized) and index of bibliographic references. Also includes appreciations of Nimuendajú by Virgilio Corrêa Filho and Luís de Castro Faria, discussions of cartography and orthography by Rodolpho Pinto Barbosa and Charlotte Emmerich and Yonne Leite, and discussion of publication problems by George Zarur.

1243 Gallois, Dominique. Os Waiãpi e seu território. Belém, Brazil: Conselho Nacional de Desenvolvimento Científico e Tecnológico, Instituto Nacional de Pesquisas da Amazônia, 1981. 38 p., 1 leaf of plates: ill. (Boletim do Museu Paraense Emílio Goeldi. Nova série, Antropologia; 80)

Brief ethnographic sketch of the Tupi-speaking Waiampí of northern Brazil (Amapá), pacified in 1973. Includes table of current population and notes on successive demarcation proposals (for another article by this author, see item **1179.**

1244 Galvão, Eduardo. Encontro de sociedades: índios e brancos no Brasil. Prefácio de Darcy Ribeiro. Rio de Janeiro: Editora Paz e Terra, 1979. 300 p.: bibl., charts, ill., maps, tables (Col. Estudos Brasileiros; 29)

Posthumous collection of essays reprinted here without indicating sources. Despite title, only five of the 13 essays are on "the encounter of tribal and national society" in the Amazon, two of these focusing on the Río Negro region. Another is an important article on *panema* (Indian-derived Amazonian peasant belief), the rest are ethnographic notes on Xingú tribes (especially Kamayurá and Juruna), and general articles on Amazonian horticulture, culture areas and arts.

1245 González Ñáñez, Omar. Mitología guarequeña. Caracas: Monte Avila Editores, 1980. 286 p.: appendices, bibl., ill., photos (Col. Estudios)

Pt. 1 is erudite discussion of Warekena religion, based on fieldwork with this beleaguered northwest Amazon Arawakan groups in Venezuela, with wide references to anthropological literature. Pt. 2 consists of 19 annotated myths, in Spanish translation. Appendices include translation of article by Wilhelm Saake on Baniwa myths and reproductions of petroglyphs in line drawings and photographs.

1246 Gregor, Thomas. Anxious pleasures: the sexual lives of an Amazonian people. Chicago: Univ. of Chicago Press, 1985. 1 v.: ill., index, map, photos.

Pioneering ethnography of sexuality among Arawakan Mehinaku of the Xingú traces sexual anxieties in myths, dreams, and social life. Author stresses presence of universal sexual fantasy themes and anxieties, especially as elaborated in myths. Emphasizes female identification in men as source of sexual anxieties (see also item **1166**). Includes 30 photos and reproductions of native drawings.

1247 ———. Dark dreams about the white man (AMNH/NH, 92:1, Jan. 1983, p. 8–14, ill.)

Mehinaku anxieties about white men are reflected in nightmares about them. Article surveys menacing themes in such dreams as told to author, and explicates them in terms of Mehinaku experience. For Portuguese version, see *Anuario Antropológico* (Rio de Janeiro: Edições Tempo Brasileiro, 82, 1984, p. 53–68, bibl., tables).

1248 Gros, Christian. Une organisation indienne en lutte pour la terre: le Conseil regional indigène du Cauca (*in* Indianité, ethnocide, indigenisme en Amérique latine. GRAL, Centre interdisciplinaire d'études latino-américaines, Toulouse-le Mirail. Paris: Centre national de la recherche scientifique, 1982, p. 167–186, bibl., map, tables [Amérique latine. Pays ibériques])

History of CRIC (Consejo Regional Indígena del Cauca) and repression directed against it. Author describes lack of land among Cauca Indians, and half-century of violent confrontations that led to formation of CRIC by Páez and other Cauca groups (see also *HLAS 43:1132*).

1249 Gross, Daniel R. Consumo proteínico y desarrollo cultural en la Cuenca amazónica (CAAAP/AP, 3:6, marzo 1982, p. 59–90, bibl., tables)

Translation of *HLAS 39:1331*.

1250 ———. The Indians and the Brazilian frontier (CU/JIA, 36:1, Spring/Summer 1982, p. 1–14)

Brief survey of recent threats to Brazilian indigenes by Amazonian development projects, and critique of Brazil's indigenous policy. Emphasis on recent developments makes it a useful update of Shelton Davis's book on the topic (see *HLAS 43:1099*). For more on this topic, see items **1155, 1306,** and **1388.**

1251 ———. Proteína y cultura en la Amazonía: una segunda revisión (CAAAP/AP, 3:6, marzo 1982, p. 127–144, bibl., tables)

Author reiterates his protein limitation hypothesis and responds to critics (see item **1249,** *HLAS 43:1086* and *HLAS 43:1204*) by calling for more studies. Published together with translations of his original article and Beckerman's critique of it.

1252 ———. A shattered peace (Geo [Greener and Gahr, New York] 3:1, April 1981, p. 26–34, map, photos)

Describes confrontations between Txukarramãe as well as Kayapó Indians and workers who invaded their territory. Sketches FUNAI's broken promises to Indians.

1253 ———. Village movement in relation to resources in Amazonia (*in* Adaptive responses of native Amazonians [see item **1153**] p. 429–449, charts, maps, tables)

Presents data from comparative study of three Gê societies (Mekranoti Kayapó, Shavante and Canela) and a Bororo village to explain village movement. Though informants assigned other reasons for village moves (e.g., enemy attacks, disputes, commercial markets) an important factor, according to data, was garden soil depletion.

1254 Hahn, Robert A. Misioneros y colonos como agentes del cambio social: Brasil (III/AI, 41:3, julio/sept. 1981, p. 463–500, ill., tables)

Account of pacification and missionization (1950–75) of the Rikbaktsá (Canoeiros) Indians of Upper Tapajós, Brazil, where author conducted fieldwork.

1255 Hames, Raymond B. Comparison of the efficiencies of the shotgun and the bow in neotropical forest hunting (Human Ecology [Plenum, N.Y.] 7:3, Fall 1979, p. 219–252, bibl., tables)

Controlled field experiment among Ye'cuana and Yanomami demonstrates the shotgun's superior efficiency in hunting over the bow. Examines impact of shotgun use on animal populations, as well as impact of need for cash crop to purchase hunting technology.

1256 ———. The settlement pattern of a Yanomamö population bloc: a behavioral ecological interpretation (*in* Adaptive responses of native Amazonians [see item **1153**] p. 393–427, map, tables)

After discussing issues concerning causation of village movement in Amazonia, author details history of village movements, locations and fissioning among villages derived from ancestral Yanomamö village. Chief motives for frequent village moves were soil depletion and enemy raids. Alliance patterns influenced location choices. Author argues against game scarcity as determining factor.

1257 Harner, Michael J. The Jívaro, people of the sacred waterfalls. 2nd ed. Berkeley: Univ. of California Press, 1984. 233 p.: bibl., ill.

Reissue of classic ethnography of the Untsuri Shuar (see *HLAS 35:1272*) with new preface by author. Provides thorough bibliography of recent ethnographic literature on the Shuar, and discussion of recent developments in the Shuar Federation as well as part played by this book.

1258 Hartmann, Günter von. Bei den Mēkubenokré-Kayapo, Brasilien: aus den Tagebuchblättern Wilhelm Kissenberths (DGV/ZE, 107:1, 1982, p. 153–162, ill., maps, plates)

Account of two month-long visits to various Kayapó villages, in 1909, based on Wilhelm Kissenberth's notebooks.

1259 ———. Körperbemalungen der pau d'arco-kayapo, zentral-brasilien (DGV/ZE, 108:2, 1983, p. 255–270, ill., plates)

Describes Wilhelm Kissenberth's 1909 observations of Pau d'arco Kayapó body painting, with sparse comments on context in which specific designs occur. Includes some interpretations of designs (e.g., "snake") but not whether they are based on native exegesis or conjecture (see item **1373**).

1260 Hartmann, Thekla. Bibliografia crítica da etnologia brasileira. v. 3. Berlin, FRG: Dietrich Reiner Verlag, 1984. 729 p.: indexes, photos (Völkerkundliche Abhandlungen; Band 9. Publikationsreihe der Völkerkunde Abtailung des Niedersachsischen Landesmuseums und der Etnologischen Gesellschaft Hannover E.V. Herausgegeben von Hans Becher)

Very thorough annotated bibliography of publications on Brazilian indigenous peoples since 1968 continues vols. 1–2 of Herbert Baldus's compilation (see *HLAS 31:2051*). All 1883 entries are thoroughly annotated and provide references to book reviews. Includes indexes on author, subject and geographic headings, and tribal names as well as photos of noted ethnographers and their informants.

1261 Heck, Egon Dionísio and Wilmar D'Angelo. Os Guaranis no Brasil hoje (*in* Simpósio Nacional de Estudos Missioneiros, 2nd, Santa Rosa, Brazil, 1977. Anais. Santa Rosa, Brazil: Faculdade de Filosofia, Ciências e Letras Dom Bosco, 1978, p. 139–149)

Surveys locations and population of Guaraní groups in Brazil, status of their land, and type of work or subsistence they engage in. Briefly sketches their relations with

FUNAI, missionaries, and support group ANAI.

1262 Hill, Jonathan D. Social equality and ritual hierarchy: the Arawakan Wakuénai of Venezuela (AES/AE, 11:3, Aug. 1984, p. 528–544, map, tables)

Discusses social structure of Northwest Amazon Arawakan group from perspective of "structural ethnoecology." Argues that two distinct "modes of structuring behavior" permit alternating adaptations to seasonal fluctuations of fish availability. Egalitarian "natural-social mode," climaxing in exchange ceremonies between affines, predominates during abundance of dry season. During scarcity of rainy season, this mode gives way to a "ritual-hierarchical," one typified by initiation ceremonies, stressing lineage ranking and generational authority relationships.

1263 ——— **and Emilio F. Moran.** Adaptive strategies of Wakuénai people to the oligotrophic rain forest of the Río Negro basin (*in* Adaptive responses of native Amazonians [see item **1153**] p. 113–135, charts, maps, tables)

Compares social change in two Wakuénai villages of Arawakan-speakers on Venezuela's Upper Río Negro. Emphasizes role of region's poor, sandy soils. Notes that growing tendency to reside with wife's father serves different adaptive strategies in each village (see item **1329**).

1264 Hill, Kim. Los aché del Paraguay oriental: condiciones actuales e historia reciente (UCNSA/SA, 18:1, junio 1983, p. 149–177, bibl.)

Anthropologist who worked with Aché (Guayaki) Indians of Paraguay presents what he asserts to be their own version of the much-discussed events of their first contacts, in early 1970s. Criticizes works by Mark Münzel and Richard Arens (see *HLAS 37:1370* and *HLAS 39:1279*) which exaggerate or misrepresent the conflict between the Aché and Paraguayans.

1265 ——— **and Kristen Hawkes.** Neotropical hunting among the Aché of eastern Paraguay (*in* Adaptive responses of native Amazonians [see item **1153**] p. 139–188, charts, maps, tables)

Author describes territory, prey and techniques of hunting among Guaraní-speaking Aché (Guayaquí). Detailed quantitative data gathered by Hill on hunting time and prey bagged are analyzed to elucidate selection of prey and the effect of the hunter's age and size of hunting group.

1266 Hudelson, John E. The lowland Quichua as "tribe" (*in* Political anthropology of Ecuador: perspectives from indigenous cultures [see item **1319**] p. 59–79, bibl., maps)

Discusses formation of lowland Quichua as a social group, and its relationship with other indigenous groups of the Peruvian upper Amazon region.

1267 The Impact of contact: two Yanomamö case studies. Cambridge, Mass.: Cultural Survival; Bennington, Vt.: Bennington College, 1983. 78 p.: charts, indexes, maps, photos (Cultural Survival occasional paper; 11. Working papers on South American Indians; 6)

Two studies of devastating effects of Brazil's perimetral highway on Yanomamö society (see item **1337**), including epidemics introduced by contact (item **1193**).

1268 Jackson, Jean E. The fish people: linguistic exogamy and Tucanoan identity in Northwest Amazonia. Cambridge, England: Cambridge Univ. Press, 1983. 287 p.: bibl., charts, index, maps, tables.

Major summation of Tucanoan societies in Colombia/Brazil's Vaupés region which grew out of author's fieldwork on the Bará longhouse and expanded the common social structure of eastern Tucanoan societies and marriage network that links them to neighboring Makú. (Arawakan groups, also part of the regional community, are conspicuously absent). Specific details of social and daily lives and surroundings complement more abstract English-language monographs on ritual (see *HLAS 43:1130*), cosmology (see item **1363** and *HLAS 43:1180–1182*) and structural principles (see *HLAS 43:1129* and *HLAS 45:1213*). Concluding chapters focus on Tucanoan identity (see items **1159, 1332** and **1346**).

1269 ———. Vaupés marriage practices (*in* Marriage practices in Lowland South America [see item **1294**] p. 156–179, bibl., charts, tables)

Formulates principles governing marriage choice among Tucanoan groups on Vaupés River: direct exchange (ideally brother-sister exchange); genealogically close but geographically distant cross cousin; language-group exogamy; and continuation of marriage alliances between groups (see also item **1346**).

1270 Jeremías, Luis. Los Warao: un reportage fotográfico (VMJ/BIV, 20:17, 1981, p. 61–103, photos)

Collection of photographs with brief comments depicts rituals and daily life of Venezuela's Warao Indians. Emphasizes material culture (e.g., weaving of hammocks and baskets) and ritual implements and scenes, but also includes modern influences (e.g., school, medicine, sewing machine).

1271 Johnson, Allen. Machiguenga gardens (*in* Adaptive responses of native Amazonians [see item **1153**] p. 29–63, charts, tables)

Descriptive study of gardening among the Arawakan-speaking Machiguenga of Peru, taking into account both cultural categories and values and quantitative measurement of work costs of major tasks and garden yields.

1272 Juruna, Mário; Antônio Hohlfeldt; and Assis Hoffman. O gravador do Juruna. Porto Alegre: Mercado Aberto, 1982. 293 p. (Série Depoimentos; 2)

Journalist Hohlfeldt presents Juruna's political ideas on indigenous questions supplemented by transcripts of tapes of meetings and conversation held with government officials, recorded by Juruna on his ever-present tape recorder. Title refers to journalist as "Juruna's tape recorder" for transmitting Juruna's ideas to reading public. Chapters cover FUNAI's and Church's roles; question of Indian land and integration; Russell Tribunal and indigenous struggle; and Juruna's own candidacy and leadership role.

1273 Kaplan, Hillard and **Kim Hill.** Food sharing among Aché foragers: tests of explanatory hypotheses (UC/CA, 26:2, April 1985, p. 223–246, bibl., graphs, tables)

Quantitative data on food acquisition and sharing are used to test three different models derived from evolutionary ecology: "kin-selection hypothesis," "tit-for-tat reciprocity," and "cooperative acquisition." Includes comments by seven discussants and reply.

1274 Kaplan, Joanna Overing. Dualism as an expression of difference and danger: marriage exchange and reciprocity among the Piaroa of Venezuela (*in* Marriage practices in Lowland South America [see item **1294**] p. 127–155, bibl., charts, index)

Piaroa (Venezuela) marriages are moiety and clan exogamous, but, theoretically, endogamous within communal house. Spouses from outside become kindred retrospectively through children (e.g., by teknonymy), thus blurring kin/affine distinctions and overcoming insider/outsider contrast. Mythic dualism emphasizes dangers of affinal relationship.

1275 Kaplan, Jonathan E.; James W. Larrick; and James A. Yost. Workup on the Waorani (AMNH/NH, 93:9, Sept. 1984, p. 68–74, map, photos)

Medical study of Waorani of Ecuadorian montaña revealed high levels of immunoglobin protecting them from high levels of intestinal worm (*helminth*) infestations. Measles, polio and other epidemic diseases were introduced recently, and rubella after 1976. Syphilis and malaria are also recent, confirming that they were not endemic in precolumbian times.

1276 Kelekna, Pita. Achuara trade: counterpoise and complement to war (*in* Political anthropology of Ecuador [see item **1319**] p. 217–256, bibl., chart)

Describes central role of the trader as mediator of alliances and marriages in this society otherwise composed of highly competitive and mutually antagonistic warriors/shamans.

1277 Keller, Franz. A contribução de Franz Keller à etnografia de Paraná: noções sobre os indígenas da província do Paraná. Edited and with introduction and commentary by Lêda Aparecida Lovato. Rio de Janeiro: Fundação Nacional do Indio, Ministério do Interior, 1974. 1 v.: bibl. (Boletim do Museu do Indio. Antropologia; 1)

Publication of 1867 manuscript in 1974 (not previously annotated in *HLAS*). Contains ethnographic notes on Kaingang and various Guarani groups, made by engineer on his travels exploring for minerals. Lovato's introduction sketches history of contact with Paraná Indians, and her notes identify tribes mentioned in manuscript and discuss Keller's ethnocentrism.

1278 Kellman, Shelly. The Yanomamis: their battle for survival (CU/JIA, 36:1, Spring/Summer 1982, p. 15–42)

Interesting and readable article offers balanced view of Yanomami culture and traces struggle for protection of Brazil's Yanomami groups and for establishment of a continuous Yanomami Park. Based on published writings and on interviews with anthropologists and *indigenistas* directly involved in events (see also items **1155, 1193, 1337** and **1347**).

1279 Kempf, Judith. The politics of curing among the Coaiquer Indians (*in* Political anthropology of Ecuador [see item **1319**] p. 107–128, bibl., tables)

Describes shamanic curing ceremony among coastal lowland Coiaquer society, suggesting that curative aspects lie in the reordering of social relationships and in sanctioning the acting out of controlled impulses.

1280 Kensinger, Kenneth M. An emic model of Cashinahua marriage (*in* Marriage practices in Lowland South America [see item **1294**] p. 221–251, bibl., graphs, tables)

Describes marriage process of the Cashinahua (Panoan group in southeastern Peru) and complex rules for selecting a spouse, including four section moiety system. Classifies marriages as "real" or not according to three native polarities: ideal, personally relative, and pragmatic. Constructs "emic" clasification of marriages and discusses criteria for an etic (cross-culturally valid) definition of marriage (see also item **1341**).

1281 Kracke, Waud H. Kagwahiv moieties: form without function? (*in* Marriage practices in Lowland South America [see item **1294**] p. 99–124, bibl., charts, index)

Discusses rules for marriage choice in Central Tupi society such as moiety exogamy and its systematic violation, shortcycle marriage exchange system as an alternative rule, and ways of breaking rules. Also considers pre-contact changes in marriage system.

1282 Langdon, E. Jean. Power and authority in Siona political process: the rise and demise of the shaman (*in* Political anthropology of Ecuador [see item **1319**] p. 129–156, bibl.)

Describes central role attained by shamans in the history of resistance to Spanish control.

1283 Laurini, Osvaldo. Los últimos achuar primitivos: aborígenes de la Amazonia ecuatoriana. S.l.: O. Laurini, 1982. 205 p.: photos (some col.)

Travels among the Achuar by Argentine adventurer, fully illustrated with photos of people, travel scenes and material culture examples from author's collection.

1284 Leituras de etnologia brasileira. Coligidas por Egon Schaden. São Paulo: Companhia Editora Nacional, 1976. 534 p.: bibl., ill., tables.

Compilation not previously annotated in *HLAS*. Consists of reprints of 33 articles on Brazilian indigenous cultures by Brazilian and foreign authors, nine of which are translated into Portuguese. Opens with survey by Schaden on current research. Includes many classic articles (by Baldus, J.C. Crocker, W. Crocker, Da Matta, Lévi-Strauss, Melatti, Nimuendajú, Ribeiro, Cardoso de Oliveira, etc.). Section on social organization highlights dual organization. Among lesser known pieces of interest is Buarque de Holanda's "Lingua Geral in São Paulo."

1285 Lind, Ulf. Espiritos auxiliares dos xamãs Lengua no Paraguai (*in* Contribuções à antropologia em homenagen a Egon Schaden [see item **1215**] p. 129–134, bibl.)

On apprenticeship of Lengua (Maskoi) shamans of the Paraguayan Chaco and their acquisition of auxiliary spirits.

1286 Lisboa, Thomaz de Aquino. Os Enauenê-nauê, primeiros contatos, Amazônia matogrossense, 1974: os primeiros contatos com um povo verdadeiro e a sua luta pela terra. São Paulo: Edições Loyola, 1985. 111 p.: maps, plates, tables.

Account of first contact with Enauenê-nauê, on Rio Juruena in northern Mato Grosso, and struggle for delimitation of reservation to guarantee their land. Includes 24 transcribed documents and map of territory currently identified as theirs which is to be interdicted.

1287 Lizot, Jacques. Histoire, organisation et évolution du pueplement yanomami (EPHE/H, 24:2, avril/juin 1984, p. 5–40, bibl., map, tables)

Brief discussion of theories of Yanomamö origins and early history and reconstruction of population explosion during last half century. Traces movements of three ancestral villages of about 1880, and their successive fissioning into about 44 villages today. Argues that, despite demographic crisis, culture remained stable through gradual expansion into neighboring territory.

1288 Lugon, Clovis. A república "comunista" cristã dos Guaranís, 1610–1768. 3a. ed. Translated from the French by Alvaro Cabral. Rio de Janeiro: Editora Paz e Terra, 1977. 1 v.: bibl., maps.

Reissue (not previously annotated in *HLAS*) of glowing account of 17th- and 18th-century utopian Jesuit republic of reductions in Paraguay. Presented as historical study as well as model of liberation theology advocates.

1289 Lukesch, Anton. Mito e vida dos índios Caiapós. Translated from the German by Trude Arneitz von Laschan Solstein. Edited by Renate Brigitte Viertler. Photographs by Karl Lukesch. São Paulo: Livraria Pioneira: Editora da Univ. de São Paulo, s.d. 1 v.: bibl., ill., plates.

Discusses Kaiapó mythology in relation to group's life and religion, on the basis of fieldwork conducted in two Kaiapó villages (translation of *HLAS 33:1590*).

1290 Lyon, Patricia J. Change in Wachipaeri marriage patterns (*in* Marriage practices in Lowland South America [see item **1294**] p. 252–263, bibl.)

Describes disruption of marriage patterns among Wachipaeri Indians of southeastern Peruvian montaña caused by epidemic which reduced population to 71. Difficulties in finding appropriate partners threaten tribe with extinction.

1291 Mabilde, Pierre François Alphonse Booth. Apontamentos sobre os indígenas selvagens da Nação Coroados dos Matos da província do Rio Grande do Sul, 1836–1866. Coordenação de May Mabilde Lague. Revisão de Eivlys Mabilde Grant. São Paulo: IBRASA: em convênio com o Instituto Nacional do Livro, Fundação Nacional Pró-Memória, 1983. 232 p., 1 leaf of plates: port. (Biblioteca Estudos brasileiros; 14)

Newly edited publication of notes (1836–60s) by young Belgian civil engineer

on his intermittent observations of the
Kaingang (Coroadas) Indians of Rio Grande
do Sul, Brazil. Valuable ethnohistorical
document.

1292 Magalhães, José Vieira Couto de.
O selvagem. Edição comemorativa do
centenário da primeira edição. Prefácio de
Vivaldi Moreira. Belo Horizonte: Editora
Itataia, 1975. 1 v.: appendix (Reconquista do
Brasil series; 16)
  This 1975 reissue of a 1875 description
(not previously annotated in *HLAS*) of Tupi
Indians by a Brazilian general, is most valu-
able for its grammar of the Tupi "Lingua
Geral," a Brazilian national dialect still
spoken at the time in Santarem as well as on
the Rio Negro. Appendix facsimile of 1875
ed. reproduces "Course of the Lingua Geral."
Edited text of book's first half includes only
ethnographic descriptive material.

1293 Manelis Klein, Harriet E. El futuro
precede al pasado: la concepción toba
del tiempo (Maldoro [Arca Editorial, Mon-
tevideo] 16, nov. 1981, p. 58–62, ill.)
  Discusses concepts of time and space
implicit in the Toba language (Chaco). In it,
time is an endless cycle in which the future
precedes the past. Author explains how Toba
beliefs in life and death, kinship and cosmology reflect this basic understanding of
the universe. [K.L. Hall]

**1294 Marriage practices in Lowland South
America.** Edited by Kenneth M.
Kensinger. Urbana: Univ. of Illinois Press,
1984. 297 p.: bibl., ill., index (Illinios studies
in anthropology; 14)
  Consists of 11 articles on marriage in
cultures of the Amazon and Orinoco basins,
which are annotated separately (see items
**1155, 1221, 1230, 1269, 1274, 1280, 1281,
1290, 1346 and 1387**). A common theme is
flexibility of determinants in marriage
choice. Dualism and linguistic exogamy are
other points of interest. Several articles stress
change in marriage systems. Others discuss
definition of marriage, stressing its pro-
cessual nature. Excellent introduction by
Judith Shapiro (see item **1341**).

1295 Massone M., Mauricio. Cultura
selknam—ona. Santiago: Depto. de
Extensión Cultural del Ministerio de Educación, 1982. 101 p.: bibl., ill. (some col.) (Serie

El Patrimonio cultural chileno. Col. Culturas
aborígenes; 4)
  Profusely illustrated popular ethnography of the Selk'nam (Ona) of Tierra del
Fuego. Balanced, informative presentation
closes with account of their brutal extinction
(see also item **1196**).

1296 Matta, Roberto da. Relativizando: uma
introdução à antropologia social. 3a ed.
Petrópolis: Editora Vozes, 1981. 246 p.: bibl.,
charts.
  Popular introduction to anthropology
by leading Brazilian anthropologist puts forward theoretical statement of one point of
view within Brazilian anthropology. In epilogue (67 p.) author describes his studies of
Gaviões and Apinajé Indians and their relevance to certain anthropological issues.

1297 Maurer, Harry. The Amazon: development or destruction? (NACLA, 13:3,
May/June 1979, p. 26–37, maps, plates)
  Describes Brazilian policies of development of the Amazon and the actual process,
including land speculation by *grileiros*, and
its effects on indigenous peoples. Focuses on
the Yanomamö case and the Polamazonia
program.

1298 Maybury-Lewis, David. The Shavante
struggle for their lands: Brazilian Indians find their voice; election, an arm or a
trap for the Indian? (Cultural Survival Quarterly [Cambridge, Mass.] 7:1, Spring 1983,
p. 54–60, map, photos)
  Describes confrontations between
Shavante and FUNAI concerning demarcation and guarantees of Indian lands. Reports
on Mario Juruna's election to Congress. Concludes with transcript of round table discussion on Indian participation in elections, and
notes on Bahia's indigenous peoples.

1299 ———. A sociedade Xavante. Translated by Aracy Lopes da Silva. Rio de
Janeiro: Livraria Francisco Alves Editora,
1984. 400 p.: bibl., charts, maps, tables (Col.
Etnologia brasileira)
  Translation of classic ethnography of
the Shavante (see *HLAS 29:1641*) with new
preface in which author debates book's com-
mentators, particularly on the subject of dual
organization.

1300 ——— *et al.* In the path of Polonoroeste: endangered peoples of west-

ern Brazil. Cambridge, Mass.: Cultural Survival, 1981. 66 p.: appendix, bibl., ill. (Occasional paper; 6)

Consists of 10 articles on the World Bank's "Polonoroeste Project" to colonize Rondônia and western Mato Grosso, and its effect on dozens of tribes in those areas: Jason Clay on the project itself; David Price on the Nambiquara, Parecí, and southern Rondônia Indians; Denny Moore on the Gavião, Zoró, and Arara; Betty M. Lafer on the Suruí; Carmen Junqueira on the Cinta Larga. David Maybury-Lewis wrote the introduction. Appendix provides population data on 22 tribes in the project area.

1301 Melatti, Julio Cezar. A antropologia no Brasil: um roteiro. Brasília: s.n., 1983. 106 p.: bibl. (Trabalhos em ciências sociais. Série Antropologia; 38)

Guide to Brazilian anthropology, originally designed for introductory anthropology courses. Useful overview provides history of Brazilian anthropology, including research and interpretations of Brazilian national society, ethnic groups and folklore as well as indigenous groups, from 17th- and 18th-century chroniclers to present. Also covers linguistics, archaeology and physical anthropology. Author provides references to bibliographies and review articles on particular areas to expand his general coverage and to discuss outstanding works of particular periods and specific topics.

1302 ———. A etnologia das populações indígenas do Brasil nas duas últimas décadas (Anuário Antropológico [Edições Tempo Brasileiro, Rio de Janeiro] 80, 1982, p. 253–275)

Thorough review of ethnographic monographs on indigenous Brazilian societies (ca. 1960–80) classified by the topic of their principal focus. Key bibliographic work.

1303 ———. Ritos de uma tribo Timbira. São Paulo: Editora Atica, 1978. 364 p.: bibl., ill., map (Col. Ensaios; 53)

Careful and thorough descriptions of Krahó (eastern Timbira) rituals, with some social and mythological exegesis. Rituals are classified by function: life cycle, seasonal, initiation, and those involving consanguine-affine relations. Preceded by substantial overview of Krahó social organization.

1304 Meliá, Bartolomé. Educação indígena e alfabetização. São Paulo: Edições Loyola, 1979. 93 p.: bibl., charts, ill., tables.

Chap. 1, "Educação Indígena," describes various systems for educating or socializing an indigenous society. Rest of book discusses how to provide Western education to indigenous peoples. Author favors a model of bilingual education that relies on indigenous language to study indigenous "social science" topics rather than phasing out indigenous languages as some programs do (see also item **1212**).

1305 ———. La entrada en el Paraguay de los otros karaí (in Contribuições à antropologia em homenagem ao Professor Egon Schaden [see item **1215**] p. 157–167, bibl.)

Study of shifting relations between "Christians" and Guaraní in 16th/17th-century Paraguay, reflected in changing usages of term karaí (i.e., "charismatic shaman," "Christian," "Spanish overlord").

1306 Menget, Patrick. Reflexions sur le droit et l'existence des communautés indigènes au Brésil (in Indianité, ethnocide, indigenisme en Amérique latine. GRAL, Centre interdisciplinaire d'études latino-américaines, Toulouse-le Mirail. Paris: Centre national de la recherche scientifique, 1982, p. 123–133, bibl. [Amérique latine. Pays ibériques])

Stressing that there is wide variety among indigenous groups in Brazil, author criticizes persistent government policy of "emancipating" Indians from their special status. Describes "alternative indigenist policy" provided by CIMI and other pro-Indian groups (see also items **1189, 1223, 1250, 1352** and **1388**).

1307 ———. Time of birth, time of being (in Between belief and transgression: structuralist essays in religion, history and myth. Edited by Michael Izard and Pierre Smith. Translated by John Leavitt. With an introduction by James Boone. Chicago: Univ. of Chicago Press, 1982, p. 193–209, bibl.)

Translation of HLAS 43:1164 (for a more recent article by this author, see item **1340**.

1308 Metraux, Alfred. A religião dos Tupinambás e suas relações com a das demais tribos tupi-guaranis. Prefácio, tradução e notas de Estêvão Pinto. Apresentação de Egon Schaden. 2a. ed. São Paulo: Companhia Editora Nacional: Editora da Univ. de São Paulo, 1979. 225 p.: bibl., ill. (Brasiliana; v. 267)

Reissue of 1950 translation, with author's revisions, of 1928 French classic on ancient Tupinambá religion.

1309 Milton, Katharine. Protein and carbohydrate resources of the Maku Indians of northwestern Amazonia (AAA/AA, 86:1, March 1984, p. 7–27, bibl., graph, map, tables)

Ecological analyis of two northwest Amazon societies stresses intertribal relationships, demonstrates symbiotic relationship between riverine Cubeo and interfluvial Maku on Brazil's Uaupés River. Nutritional imbalances due to seasonal shortages and blackwater river conditions uncommon in the Amazon Basin, are alleviated through exchange of Maku protein and labor for Cubeo manioc.

1310 Monnier, Alain. Evangélisation structurale: l'exemple des Mashco du sudest péruvien (SSA/B, 46, 1982, p. 31–35, ill.)

Analyzes practice of "anthropological pastorialism" by Dominicans working with Mashko (Karákmbut), a recent doctrine that uses structuralist idiom to justify missionization in the face of the present *crise de conscience.*

1311 Morales, F. and Nelly Arvelo Jiménez. Hacia un modelo de estructura social caribe (III/AI, 41:4, 1981, p. 613–626, bibl., ill., maps)

Brief comparison of three Venezuelan Carib-speaking tribes—Pemon, Ye'cuana and ancient Kari'ña—introduces a critique of the assumptions of Venezuela's "Indigenous Enterprise" program. Conclusions challenge image of primitive communities as isolated, economically precarious and communitarian (see item **1366,** *HLAS 45:1180,* and *HLAS 45:1182).*

1312 Moreno, Miguel Ramón Legal. Análisis de un caso concreto de proceso judicial a un indígena (UCNSA/SA, 17:2, dic. 1982, p. 167–195)

Article focuses on the case of a Guarani Indian, Angel Santacruz, in an analysis of the

scope of jurisdiction of Paraguayan laws over the Guaraní people. Legal and philosophical arguments address the problem of conflict between indigenous value systems and federal law (see also item **1379).** [K.L. Hall]

1313 Mussolini, Gioconda. Ensaios de antropologia indígena e Caiçara. Organização de Edgard Carone. Prefácio de Antônio Cândido. São Paulo: Paz e Terra, 1980. 290 p.: bibl. (Col. Estudos brasileiros; 38)

Major essays on ethnomedicine of Bororo and Kaingang Indians (originally published 1944–53), plus four brief essays on coastal São Paulo fishing cultures, Caiçara (mestiço) and Japanese.

1314 Native South Americans: ethnology of the least known continent. Edited by Patricia J. Lyon. Prospect Heights, Ill.: Waveland Press, 1984. 433 p.: bibl., maps, photos.

Reissue of valuable reader of articles on Lowland South American Indians. Includes translations of some important studies by South American and European anthropologists, not otherwise available in English.

1315 Newton, Dolores. The individual in ethnographic collections (*in* Annals of the New York Academy of Sciences, 376, 31 Dec. 1981, p. 267–288, charts, ill., plates, tables)

Detailed study of the weave of burden baskets among the Eastern Timbira groups Krĩkati and Pukobye, stressing individual use of specific basket designs as a clue to historical origins of pattern distribution. Closes with a plea for documenting individual artists in museum collections.

1316 Nimuendajú, Curt. Textos indigenistas. Introdução de Carlos Moreira Netto. Edição com a prefácio de Paulo Suess. São Paulo: Edições Loyola, 1982. 1 v.

Collection of SPI (Serviço de Proteção aos Indios, now FUNAI) reports and letters by this Brazilian indigenist and anthropologist concerning tribes he contacted between 1910–45. Includes two classic articles on the Parintintin and Upper Madeira tribes, a biographical introduction by Carlos Moreira, and an appreciation and list of Nimuendajú's accomplishments by Herbert Baldus.

1317 Organizing to survive (Cultural Survival Quarterly [Cambridge, Mass.] 8 : 4, Dec. 1984, p. 1–92, ill., maps, photos) Issue devoted to organizations of indigenous peoples throughout the world, but especially South America (p. 18–32). Articles: "CONFENIAE: an Indian Confederation in Eastern Ecuador;" David Maybury-Lewis "Indian and Pro-Indian Organizations in Brazil;" John Freccione "The Ye'cuana of South Venezuela;" Yesid Campos Zornosa "Colombian Indian Organizations;" and Richard Chase Smith "Amazonian Indians Participate at UN." Issues include pull-out "Directory of Indigenous/Indigenist Organizations" by region which lists 31 South American entities (p. 45–58). Also includes articles by Stephen Schwartzmann and Linda Greenbaum on the World Bank's Polonoroeste Project.

1318 Peirano, Mariza G.S. A antropologia esquecida de Florestan Fernandes: os Tupinambá (Anuário Antropológico [Edições Tempo Brasileiro, Rio de Janeiro] 82, 1984, p. 15–49, bibl.)
Chapter from author's Harvard PhD dissertation, *The anthropology of anthropology: the Brazilian case.* Discusses Fernandes's early sociological/historical work on the Tupinambá, especially his masterpiece of the period, *A função social da guerra na sociedade Tupinambá.*

1319 Political anthropology of Ecuador: perspectives from indigenous cultures. Edited and with an introduction by Jeffrey Ehrenreich. Foreword by John H. Bodley. Albany, N.Y.: Society for Latin American Anthropology (SLAA): SUNY, Center for Caribbean and Latin America (CCLA), 1985. 256 p.
Consists of nine articles on strategies and cultural responses of highland and lowland indigenous societies to domination by Ecuador's national society. Organized into three parts: 1) Strategies and Responses to Encroachment: the Politics of Contact" contains articles by Luisa Stark on women in highland peasant uprisings, Jeffrey Ehrenreich on isolation, retreat, and secrecy among the Pacific lowland Coiaquier (item **1234**), and John Hudelson on the lowland Quichua (item **1266**); 2) "Political Process: the Politics of Shamanism and Curing" includes Frank Salomon on a colonial Andean shaman, Judith Kemp on the politics of curing among the Coaiquer (item **1279**), and E.J. Langdon on the rise and fall of the shaman in *montaña* Siona politics (item **1282**); and 3) "Economy and Ideology: the Politics of the Internal Order" contains Leo Chávez on commercial weavers, Barbara Butler on an Otavalo community's internal politics, and Pita Kelekna on the Achuara trader's political role (item **1276**).

1320 Porro, Antônio. Os Omagua do Alto Amazonas: demografia e padrões de povoamento no século XVII (*in* Contribuições à antropologia em homenagem ao Professor Egon Schaden [see item **1215**] p. 207–231, bibl., maps, tables)
After carefully comparing 16th- and 17th-century descriptions, reconstructs area occupied by early Omagua Tupi-speakers, locations of their villages along the Upper Amazon (Solimões), their settlement pattern and their population.

1321 Posey, Darrell A. O conhecimento entomológico Kayapó: etnometodologia e sistema cultural (Anuário Antropológico [Edições Tempo Brasileiro, Rio de Janeiro] 81, 1983, p. 109–124, bibl., charts, tables)
Describes study of Kayapó insect classification, stressing methodology of study and mythic-ritual significance of entomological knowledge among Kayapó.

1322 ———. Indigenous ecological knowledge and development of the Amazon (*in* The Dilemma of Amazonian development. Edited by Emílio Moran. Boulder, Colo.: Westview Press, 1983, p. 225–257, bibl., charts, maps, tables)
Describes Kayapó knowledge of their ecology, and suggests ways in which such knowledge could be used for the ecologically sound development of the Amazon region.

1323 ——— et al. Ethnoecology as applied anthropology in Amazonian development (SAA/HO, 43 : 2, Summer 1984, p. 95–107, bibl., map, tables)
Authors draw on indigenous ecological knowledge (ethnoecology) to suggest new strategies for the ecologically sound development of Amazonia.

1324 Povos indígenas no Brasil. v. 3, Amapá: norte do Pará. v. 5, Javarí. Apresentação de Carlos A. Ricardo. São Paulo:

Centro Ecumênico de Documentação e Informação, 1983. 2 v. (270, 154 p.): ill., maps, plates, ports.

First two volumes of important series which will document culture, contact history and present conditions of every indigenous nation in Brazil. Articles are written by specialists familiar with each culture. Vol. 3 covers the Palicur, Galibi, Karipuna, and Uaçá reservation that includes them as well as the Wiãpa, Wayana-Aparaí, Tiriyó, Kaxuyana and Carib-speakers of the Nhamunda and Mapuera Rivers. Vol. 5 has excellent historical introduction and articles on the Marubo, Mayoruna, Matís, Kulina, Kanamarí, and indeterminate groups on the Ituií/Itacoaí, Quixito and Jandiatuba Rivers.

1325 Price, David. Overtures to the Nambiquara (AMNH/NH, 93:10, Oct. 1984, p. 33–48, ill., maps)

Historical account of the pacification of Nambiquara Indians of western Mato Grosso, Brazil. Includes written and oral descriptions of events by both Nambiquara and SPI (Serviço de Proteção aos Indios) participants, reproduced verbatim. Events are intimately relatd to SPI's early history as well as to the participation of Col. Mariano da Silva Rondôn. For slightly revised Spanish translation for scholars that includes bibliography, see *América Indígena* (México, 43:3, julio/sept. 1983, p. 601–628, bibl.)

1326 ———. Pareci, Cabixi, Nambiquara: a case study in the Western classification of native peoples (SA/J, 69:1, 1983, p. 129–148, bibl., maps, table)

Historical study of names applied to tribal groups in western Mato Grosso, Brazil, describes how usages according to changing exploitative interests (for author's article on Nambiquara social structure, see item **1342**).

1327 ———. A reservation for the Nambiquara (*in* Involuntary migration and resettlement: the problems and responses of dislocated people. Edited by Art Hansen and Anthony Oliver-Smith. Boulder, Colo.: Westview Press, 1982, bibl., ill. maps)

Discusses considerations involved in the design of reservations for indigenous groups. Includes sketches of Nambiquara social organization and legal status of Brazilian Indians. Describes unsuccessful attempts to move and consolidate Nambiquara villages in a reduced reservation area.

1328 Queiroz, Maria Isaura Pereira de. O messianismo no Brasil e no mundo. 2a ed. rev. Prefácio de Roger Bastide. São Paulo: Alfa-Omega, 1977. 441 p.: appendix, bibl.

Major and important treatise (not previously annotated in *HLAS*) on world messianic movements devotes second half to their manifestation in Brazil, one third of it to indigenous Brazilian religious movements (see also items **1201** and **1331**).

1329 Ramos, Alcida Rita. Entre pais e esposas: a propósito de regime desarmônico e sua conseqüências (Anuário Antropológico [Edições Tempo Brasileiro, Rio de Janeiro] 80, 1982, p. 63–76, bibl.)

Compares three Brazilian indigenous societies (i.e., Mundurucú, Shavante, and Sanumá) to show how patrilineal descent may be reconciled with uxorilocal residence (with wife's parents) at marriage. Under favorable conditions (village endogamy), patrilineages may form around "agnatic aggregates" of co-residing fellow clansmen.

1329a ———. O Brasil no movimento indígena americano (Anuário Antropológico [Edições Tempo Brasileiro, Rio de Janeiro] 82, 1984, p. 281–286)

Sketches legal and social position of Brazilian Indians and contrasts growth of indigenous movement in Brazil with others in South America.

1330 Rauschert-Alenani, Manfred I. A história dos índios Aparaí e Wayana segundo suas próprias tradições (*in* Contribuções à antropologia em homenagem ao Professor Egon Schaden [see item **1215**] p. 233–253, bibl.)

Reconstructs, from their own opinions and traditions, the ethnohistory of two Carib-speaking groups of northern Pará, now united. The Aparaí recount absorbing several more primitive groups during their wanderings. Last pages describe contact with Brazilian society and subjugation.

1331 Regan, Jaime. Hacia la tierra sin mal: estudio sobre la religiosidad del pueblo en la Amazonía. Iquitos, Perú: CETA, 1983. 2 v.: appendix, bibl., ill., maps.

Extensive pastoral/anthropological study of popular religious beliefs in Amazonian Peru conducted by Jesuit priest. Documents both Catholic and indigenous beliefs, shamanistic practices and ritual, and describes a syncretic millenarian movement. Quotes extensive interviews conducted with more than 60 communities by local "pastoral agents." Appendix reproduces interview schedule.

1332 Reichel-Domatoff, Gerardo. Algunos conceptos de geografía chamanística de los indios desana de Colombia (*in* Contribuições à antropologia em homenagem ao Professor Egon Schaden [see item **1215**] p. 255–270, bibl.)

Describes mythological, religious and symbolic concepts whereby Desana organize geographic space (e.g., segments of an ancestral snake, rivers as hallucinogenic vines, hexagonal crystalline shapes).

1333 Ribeiro, Berta G. Araweté: a india vestida (USP/RA, 26, 1983, p. 1–38, ill., maps)

Ethnographic notes on the Araweté, a mid-Xingú Tupi-speaking group contacted in 1973, highlighting skirts traditionally worn by women. Appended lists summarize material culture, division of labor, and terms for wasps. Culture is being studied by E. Viveiros de Castro.

1334 ———. O índio na história do Brasil. São Paulo: Global Editora, 1983. 125 p.: bibl., ill., maps, table (História popular series; 13)

Didactic overview of role of indigenous peoples in Brazilian history, especially during 16th through 18th centuries, contributes to scholarship on this recent topic. Closes with chapter on indigenous contributions to Brazilian culture, and comments on the indigenous question and Indian policy.

1335 Ribeiro, Darcy. Uirá sai à procura de Deus: ensaios de etnologia e indigenismo. 3a ed. Rio de Janeiro: Paz e Terra, 1980. 173 p.: bibl., charts, ill., music, table (Col. Estudos brasileiros; 2)

Small collection gathers four ethnographic articles on Urubu-Ka'apor (Tupi), Kaduveo (Guaicuruan), and Ofaie-"Xavante" social organization, including two short papers on Rondôn, with bibliographies of his works and studies of his life. Title essay describes attempts by an Urubú Indian to reunite with Maïra across the sea (see items **1201, 1203, 1308** and **1328**).

1336 Rubinger, Marcos Magalhães; Maria Stella de Amorim; and Sonia de

Almeida Marcato. Indios Maxakali: resistência ou morte. Prefácio de Roberto Cardoso de Oliveira. Belo Horizonte: Interlivros, 1980. 199 p.: ill., ports.

Consists of three articles, one by each author, on conditions of the Maxakali Indians, living in a Minas Gerais reservation, history of their contacts and conflicts with surrounding cattle herders, *posseiros*, FUNAI and its predecessor SPI (Serviço de Proteção aos Indios).

1337 Saffirio, John and Raymond Hames. The forest and the highway (*in* The Impact of contact: two Yanomamö case studies [see item **1267**] p. 1–52, bibl., charts, plates, tables)

Documents effects of Brazil's Perimetrical Highway on Yanomamö social structure, hunting and sharing patterns. Concludes by recommending a "demarcated and appropriately protected Indian Park."

1338 Sampaio, Alvaro *et al.* O índio e o direito. Rio de Janeiro: Ordem dos Advogados do Brasil (OAB), 1982. 98 p. (Série OAB/RJ debate; 1)

Proceedings of conference of Indians, lawyers, anthropologists and indigenists held to discuss legal problems of Brazilian Indians. Vol. 1 in series on legal issues sponsored by Rio de Janeiro's OAB chapter.

1339 Schaden, Egon. O índio e a sua imagem do mundo: subsídios para um estudo de antropologia simbólica (USP/RA, 21:1, 1978, p. 33–44, bibl.)

Compares cosmologies of three Amazonian cultures, two Northwest Amazon (Desana and Maku) and one Xingú-Tupían (Kamayurá), in order to address the "symbolic integration of cultures." Concludes by stressing their uniqueness. Attributes problems of comparison to the use of different perspectives in ethnographic description.

1340 Sexual ideologies in Lowland South America. Edited by Kenneth M. Kensinger. Bennington, Vt.: Bennington College, 1984. 36 p.: bibl. (Working papers on South American Indians; 5)

Six essays that deal with sex, food, and other reciprocities of male-female relationships. Kensinger writes on sex and food in Cashinahua society; Menget on "Delights and Dangers" among the Xingú Tchicão; Arcand on the Cuiva's "sexed time;" Langdon on sex and power in Siona society; Gregor on a Mehinaku myth of matriarchy; and Chernela on sexual politics in the Northwest Amazon.

1341 Shapiro, Judith. Marriage rules, marriage exchange and the definition of marriage in Lowland South American societies (*in* Marriage practices in Lowland South America [see item **1294**] p. 1–30, bibl., index)

Introduction to volume on Lowland South American marriage practices. Article makes insightful theoretical contributions on conceptualization of marriage, exchange, and the relation between marriageable and prohibited categories of relatives.

1342 The Sibling relationship in Lowland South America. Compiled by Judith Shapiro. Edited by Kenneth M. Kensinger. Bennington, Vt.: Bennington College, 1985. 1 v. (Working papers on South American Indians; 7)

Issue in the Working Papers series dedicated to Charles Wagley, contains Judith Shapiro's introduction and the following papers: Donald K. Pollock "Looking for a Sister: Culina Siblingship and Affinity;" David Price "Nambiquara Brothers;" Kenneth Kensinger "Cashinahua Siblingship;" Jonathan Hill "Agnatic Sibling Relations and Rank in Northern Awarakan Myth and Social Life; Janet Chernela "The Sibling Relationship among the Uanano of the Northwest Amazon: the Case of Nicho;" and discussions by Raymond C. Kelly and Ellen Basso pointing out psychological aspects of sibling order.

1343 Simonion, Lígia T.L. Arquivo Kaingang/Guaraní e Xetá. Ijuí, Brazil: FIDENE, 1981. 101 p. (Cadernos do Museu Antropológico Diretor Pestana; 10)

Catalog of documentary and film collections on the Kaingang, Guaraní and Xetá, in archives of the Museu Antropológico Diretor Pestana. Includes separate listing under each culture of: legal documents (decrees, laws, and briefs); other documents (letters, reports, etc.); photos; maps; and published or unpublished texts (books, articles, newspaper articles). Constitutes valuable bibliography on these three tribes, as well as catalog of museum's collection.

1344 ———. Visualização: estado expropia e domina povo Guaraní e Kaingang. Ijuí, Brazil: FIDENE, 1980. 50 p.: maps, plates

(Cadernos do Museu Antropológico Diretor Pestana; 9)

Documents invasion, despoliation and/or reduction in size of 11 Kaingang and Guaraní reservations in Rio Grande do Sul. Contains 12 maps of original demarcated reserves, with commentary describing how they were reduced by expropriation, invaded or destroyed by official misuse. Includes two plans of shacks (i.e., official housing) planned for Indians in two reservations and five excellent photos by author.

Skidmore, Thomas E. Race and class in Brazil: historical perspectives. See *HLAS* 46:3680.

1345 Smith, Richard Chase. The dialectics of domination in Peru: native communities and the myth of the vast Amazonian emptiness. Cambridge, Mass.: Cultural Survival, 1982. 132 p.: appendices, bibl., maps, plates, tables (Occasional paper; 8)

Reports on intensive study of land use as well as on carrying capacity and social relations between Amuesha Indians and colonists in the Palcazu Valley of northern Peruvian montaña. Introduction demonstrates infeasibility of President Belaunde Terry's development project for this valley. Includes account of political events leading to Peruvian President's proposal, and of campaign in defense of indigenous lands in the area.

1346 Sorensen, Arthur P., Jr. Linguistic exogamy and personal choice in the Northwest Amazon (*in* Marriage practices in Lowland South America [see item **1294**] p. 180–193, bibl., index)

Account of relationships both sexual and personal among the Vaupés Tucanoan including how boys seek and court wives. Offers refreshingly personal view of marriage arrangement process. Stresses freedom of choice and consideration given to emotional preference in choice of spouse; language relationships tend to favor matrilateral cross-cousin marriage, but such marriages are not strictly prescribed (see also items **1268** and **1269**).

1347 Sponsel, Leslie E. La situación de los yanomama y de la civilización: una lección de ecología cultural desde el Amazonas (VMJ/BIV, 20:17, 1981, p. 105–116, bibl.)

General discussion of how failure of Amazonian tropical forest development projects is often due to ignorance of region's ecology. Includes brief discussion of need for Yanomami Park and bases appeal on ecological factors (see also items **1155** and **1278**).

1348 ———. Yanomama warfare, protein capture, and cultural ecology: a critical analysis of the arguments of the opponents (AI/I, 8:4, July/Aug. 1983, p. 204–210, ill.)

Criticizes Chagnon and Hames (see *HLAS 45:1237*) for equating cultural ecology with "protein limitation school" but defends hypothesis of limited protein availability but without adding new data.

1349 Stahl, Wilmar. Escenario indígena chaqueño: pasado y presente. Dibujos por Regina Stahl. Filadelfia, Paraguay: Asociación de Servicios de Cooperación Indígena-Mennonita, 1982. 144 p. bibl., ill. (some col.)

Mennonite missionary publication on the Nivaklé of the Paraguayan Chaco features Indian narratives of their life histories. Comments on traditional culture and followed by testimonials of conversion and history of Mennonite missionary work.

1350 Stearman, Allyn MacLean. The Yuquí connection: another look at Sirionó deculturation (AAA/AA, 86:3, Sept. 1984, p. 629–650, bibl., map, tables)

Notes on history of the Yuquí, a recently contacted branch of the Sirionó, both Guaraní-speaking groups of the Bolivian Chaco. Clarifies process of deculturation that occurred in the ancestral Chiriguano group through successive displacements and depopulation.

1351 Stocks, Anthony. Cocamilla fishing: patch modification and environmental buffering in the Amazon *várzea* (*in* Adaptive responses of native Amazonians [see item **1153**] p. 239–267, charts, maps, tables)

Describes exploitation of a floodplain lake where the Cocamilla live in Amazonian Peru. Uses quantitative data to argue that lake's area which is closest to the settlement and enriched by garbage, is reserved by the Cocamilla for intense exploitation during the high water season of scarcity.

1352 Suess, Paulo. Em defesa dos povos indígenas: documentos e legislação. São Paulo: Edições Loyola, 1980. 159 p.

Pt. 1, "Documentos," consists of final resolutions of conventions held to address problems of indigenous peoples and includes the Declarations of Barbados I and II. Pt. 2, "Legislação," reproduces the Brazilian constitutional article on rights of indigenous peoples, and law and decrees establishing FUNAI.

1353 Susñik, Branislava. Los aborígenes del Paraguay. v. 4, Cultura material. Asunción: Museo Etnográfico Andrés Barbero, 1983. 237 p.: bibl., maps, plates.

Broad survey, arranged by topics, covers subsistence, bodily adornment, tools and artisanship of Paraguay's cultures. Well illustrated with 96 photos. For ethnohistorian's comment, see *HLAS 46:1728*.

1354 ———. El rol de los indígenas en la formación y en la vivencia del Paraguay. Asunción: Instituto Paraguayo de Estudios Nacionales, 1983. 2 v.: maps.

Transcription of series of lectures in social anthropology organized by the Paraguayan Institute for National Studies (IPEN), on the role of indigenous peoples (especially Guaraní) in Paraguay's history. Description of original inhabitants, Guaraní and Chaco residents, and enumeration of Guaraní subgroups, is followed by account of Spanish conquest, encomiendas, major mestizo groups, and reductions ("the spiritual conquest").

1355 Taylor, Anne-Christine. Relations inter-ethniques et formes de resistance culturelle chez les Achuar de l'Equateur (*in* Indianité, ethnocide, indigenisme en Amérique latine. GRAL, Centre interdisciplinaire d'études latino-américaines, Toulouse-le Mirail. Paris: Centre national de la recherche scientifique, 1982, p. 239–251, bibl. [Amérique latine. Pays ibériques])

History of acculturation of the Achuar, a Shuar-speaking group of the Ecuadorian montaña. Stresses role of missionization and the ambiguous but more insidious acculturating effect of *Quichuization*. Emphasizes Achuar perceptions of acculturating groups and processes.

1356 Thevet, André. As singularidades da frança antártica. Translated from the French by Eugênio Amado. Belo Horizonte: Editora Itatiaia; São Paulo: Editora da Univ. de São Paulo, 1978. 271 p. (Reconquista do Brasil series; 45)

Welcome new ed. of classic French source on the 16th-century coastal Tupinambá around Rio de Janeiro, as well as other Indian groups of the Caribbean and North America. Now made available in a new Portuguese translation.

1357 Thomas, Georg. Política indigenista dos Portugueses no Brasil, 1500–1640. Translated from the German by Jesús Hortal. São Paulo: Edições Loyol, 1981. 256 p.: appendices, bibl.

Translation of 1968 historical study of Portuguese colonial policy toward, and treatment of, Brazilian Indians in the first one and a half centuries of colonial rule.

1358 Tomasini, Alfredo. El concepto de *tsamtáx* entre los Nivaklé del Chaco Boreal (DGV/ZE, 107:1, 145–152, bibl.)

Outlines Nivaklé concept of transformation of a person's soul into a cannibalistic monster-spirit, provoked by taboo violations. Largely based on exegesis in Spanish by Nivaklé informants.

1359 Turner, Terence. Anthropology and the politics of indigenous peoples' struggles (Cambridge Anthropology [s.n., s.l.] Spring 1979, p. 1–42, bibl.)

Critique of anthropological literature on the struggles of indigenous peoples. Author emphasizes that indigenous peoples have always taken a more active role in resisting encroachment and shaping their adaptation than anthropologists generally give them credit for.

1360 ———. Dual opposition, hierarchy and value: moiety structure and symbolic polarity in Central Brazil and elsewhere (*in* Différences, valeurs, hiérarchie: textes offertes à Louis Dumont. Compiled and edited by Jean-Claude Galey. Paris: Editions de l'Ecole des hautes études en sciences sociales, 1984, p. 335–370, bibl.)

Article cites central Brazilian moiety systems (especially eastern Timbira and Kayapó) to address and modify Louis Dumont's argument that binary oppositions in societies are hierarchical, with one pole including the other.

1361 ———. The Kayapó of Central Brazil (*in* Face values. Edited by Anne Sutherland. London: British Broadcasting Corp., 1978, p. 245–277, bibl., ill., plates)

Clear account, for the lay reader, of

Turner's analysis of Kayapó social and political organization. Stresses the age-set organization as a program for the reproduction of society (see *HLAS 43:1210*).

1362 ———. The social skin: bodily adornment, social meaning and personal identity (*in* Not work alone. Edited by Jeremy Cherfes and Roger Lewin. London: Temple Smith, 1980, p. 112–140, bibl., plate, tables)

Discusses social values represented by lip plugs, body painting, and other aspects of personal decor in Kayapó society, stressing that bodily adornment is a medium for the construction of a social self (see also items **1259, 1370** and **1373**).

1363 Umúsin Panlõn Kumu and **Tolamãn Kenhíri.** Antes o mundo não existia: a mitologia heroica dos índios Desana. Introdução de Berta Ribeiro. Illustrated by Tolamãn Kenhíri. S.l.: s.n., s.d. 239 p.: ill.

Desana myth cycle of creation, recounted by the *kumu* (priest) Umúsin (Portuguese name: Firmiano Arantes Lana) to his son Tolamãn Kenhíri (Portuguese name: Luiz Gomes Lana) who transcribed them in Desana and translated them into Portuguese. Berta Ribeiro, who arranged their publication, provides introductory sketch of Desana society and account of circumstances under which this unusual book was written.

1364 Urban, Greg. Speech about speech in speech about action (AFS/JAF, 97:385, 1984, p. 310–328, bibl., chart)

Presents a Shokleng (Southern Gê) myth in which a man's disobedience of instructions leads to his brother's death. Analysis holds that myth both: 1) encodes a vision of relationship between speech and social action; and 2) prescribes that relationship normatively (enjoins obedience).

1365 ——— and Janet Wall Hendricks. Signal functions of masking in Amerindian Brazil (Semiotica [Association Internationale de Sémiotique, The Hague] 47:1/4, 1983, p. 181–216, bibl., map, plates)

Surveys three principal areas of ceremonial mask use in Brazil: northwest Amazon, Upper Xingú, and Central Brazil (including Gê, Bororo, Tapirapé and Karajá). Stresses variation in four semiotic (communicative) functions of masks: representational, emotive, indexical (i.e., who wears masks), and disguise.

1366 Valdez, Alberto. Autogestión indígena. Prólogo de Nemesio Montiel Fernández. Caracas: Fondo Editorial Común, 1982. 154 p.: bibl., ill. (some col.) (Serie Autogestión y propiedad comunitaria)

Collection of articles by indigenist active in the promotion of indigenous commercial enterprises along the Orinoco. Covers indigenous enterprises, history of Indian policy in Venezuela, "platform for an indigenous policy in Venezuela," and other indigenist topics. For critical view, see item **1311.**

1367 Velho, Otávio Guilherme. Through althusserian spectacles: recent social anthropology in Brazil (SEM/E, 47:1/2, 1982, p. 133–149)

Interesting article on recent Brazilian anthropology comments on its broadening scope, academic structure, and Althusser's ideological influence (see also items **1260** and **1301**).

1368 Venturini, Ali José. Las comunidades indígenas en el derecho agrario venezolano: ensayo aproximativo (ACPS/B, 38:84, abril/junio 1981, p. 57–76)

Discusses status of Venezuela's indigenous population within its legal system. Considers "fundamental questions" (e.g., celluric linkage" of indigenous community to land it exploits, and criteria for ethnic determination), "primary characteristics" of Indian, and legal "types of communities." Analyzes legal issues in historical, anthropological, and functional contexts.

1369 A Verdade sobre o índio brasileiro. Edited by Gustavo de Faria. Rio de Janeiro: Guavira Editors, 1983. 64 p.: col. ill., map.

FUNAI official publication, profusely illustrated with color photographs, provides useful factual information about Brazil's indigenous population and FUNAI's history. Includes lists of missionary organizations working with Indians, recently contacted groups, population and land statistics on reservations (e.g., location, status, maps, corresponding tribal groups).

1370 Verswijver, Gustaaf. Les femmes peintes: une cérémonie d'imposition de noms chez les Kayapó-Mẽkrãgnoti du Brésil central (SSA/B, 46, 1982, p. 41–59, bibl., ill.)

Describes in detail one type of Kayapó name transmission ceremony. Comments on participating social groups and role relationships in the ceremony. Includes sketches of female body paint designs (see also items **1259, 1362** and **1373**).

1371 Vickers, William T. Development and Amazonian Indians: the Aguarico case and some general principles (in The Dilemma of Amazonian development. Edited by Emilio Moran. Boulder, Colo.: Westview Press, 1983, p. 25–50, bibl.)

Analyzes three "component systems" in the frontier development process of the Aguarico River basin, Ecuadorian Oriente, which exemplifies development of the Amazonian tropical forest. Describes: 1) traditional subsistence systems of Cofan and west Tucanoan Siona-Secoya; 2) major forms of corporate exploitation in Amazonia; and 3) colonization structure. Identifies major Indian problems in health, population loss, legal identity, tourism, and displacement of domestic by market production. Calls for rational and integrated planning among all Amazonian nations to guarantee native land rights.

1372 ——. The territorial dimensions of Siona-Secoya and Encabellado adaptation (in Adaptive responses of native Amazonians [see item **1153**] p. 451–478, maps, plate)

Study of territoriality and garden lands among Siona/Secoya, western Tucanoans of Ecuador. Determines present and 18th-century hunting territories. History of warfare and settlement relocations, together with data on extensive cultivable lands, suggests competition for hunting territories as major motive of warfare.

1373 Vidal, Lux. Contribution to the concept of person and self in Lowland South American societies: body painting among the Kayapó-Xikrin (in Contribuções à antropologia em homenagem ao Professor Egon Schaden [see item **1215**] p. 291–303, bibl., charts, ill.)

By outlining use or non-use of body painting, color and designs applied at different junctures in Xikrin-Kayapó rituals, author determines ritual and social meaning of body paint and of specific designs, as expressions of personhood in Kayapó society (for more on Kayapó body painting, see items **1259, 1362,** and **1370**).

1374 ————. A morte entre os índios Kayapó (*in* A Morte e os mortos na sociedade brasileira. Organização de José de Souza Martins. São Paulo: Editora HUCITEC, 1983, p. 315–322, bibl.)

On Kayapó attitudes toward death and beliefs about it, and their funeral practices.

1375 Viertler, Renate Brigitte. Implicações adaptivas do funeral ao processo de mudança social entre os Bororo de Mato Grosso (*in* A Morte e os mortos na sociedade brasileira [see item **8393**], p. 291–302)

Notes how importance and structure of Bororo funeral ceremonies are adaptive to high mortality and social conflicts resulting from contact, as well as to precontact *cerrado* environment.

1376 ————. Implicações de alguns conceitos utilizados no estudo da religião e da magia de tribos brasileiras (*in* Contribuções à antropologia em homenagem ao Professor Egon Schaden [see item **1215**] p. 305–317, bibl.)

Discusses various terms used by ethnographers to designate religious functionaries (e.g., "shaman," "priest") and theoretical implications of each choice.

1377 Villas Boas, Orlando. A vida de Orlando Villas Boas, depoimento: entrevista a Cesário Marques. Rio de Janeiro: Editora Rio Cultura, 1983. 97 p.: ports (Gente de sucesso)

Eldest of the two Villas Boas brothers tells his life story to interviewer Cesário Marques, principally recounting experiences in exploring and establishing the Parque Indígena do Xingú.

1378 Vivar A., Judith E. Los huarayo de Madre de Dios: algunos caracteres relevantes sobre su demografía (SGL/B, 98, enero/dic. 1979, p. 25–36, ill., tables)

Population statistics on this Tacanan-speaking group of southeastern Peru, bordering on Bolivia.

1379 Vysokolán, Oleg. Panorama del indigenismo, en 1982, en la República del Paraguay (UCNSA/SA, 18:1, junio 1983, p. 31–43)

Brief overview of social conditions and current legal status of Paraguay's indigenous community. Stresses legal and philosophical dimensions of increasing pressures on indigenous population to integrate into national society. Concludes with protest at government's failure to implement Statute of Indigenous Communities since its passage.

1380 Wagner, Erika and Walter Coppens. Novena bibliografía antropológica reciente sobre Venezuela (FSCN/A, 55, 1981, p. 73–84)

No. 9 installment covering 1981 publications of excellent annual bibliography of research on indigenous Venezuelans and on cultures in bordering countries also represented in Venezuela. Nos. 7–8 appeared in preceding issues of *Antropológica* (Caracas) and were inadvertently omitted from *HLAS* 45.

1381 Werner, Dennis. Amazon journey: an anthropologist's year among Brazil's Mēkranoti Indians. New York: Simon and Schuster, 1984. 296 p.: bibl., index, plates.

Engaging narrative account of author's field experiences provides glimpses into Kayapó culture at appropriate points in the narrative. Intended as undergraduate text, book is one more well written addition to growing body of personal accounts of fieldwork. Includes list of personal names, glossary of Kayapó terms, and useful bibliography of works on Kayapó culture which nevertheless lacks works by major Kayapó ethnographer Terrence Turner (see *HLAS 43:1210*).

1382 ————. Are some people more equal than others?: status inequality among the Mēkranoti Indians of Central Brazil (UNM/JAR, 37:4, 1981, p. 360–373, bibl., tables)

Initial report on quantitative study of leadership among the Mēkranoti Kayapó of Central Brazil. Describes principal leadership roles among Kayapó and argues that, though power is slight, access to power roles is unequally distributed. Confirms frequent observations of Amazonian leaders being poorer, not wealthier, than others.

1383 ————. Gerontocracy among the Mēkranoti of Central Brazil (CUA/AQ, 54:1, Winter 1981, p. 15–27, bibl., graphs, tables)

Sociometric study among Mēkranoti Kayapó, Gê-speakers, concludes that power of Kayapó elderly is best explained by their knowledge, especially of ceremonies. Suggests that understanding the functional importance of ceremonies (e.g., trekking as mechanism to alleviate intra-group conflicts) enables elders to manipulate ceremonies for political ends (see also items 1370, 1373 and 1374).

1384 ———. Leadership inheritance and acculturation among the Mēkranoti of Central Brazil (SAA/HO, 41:4, Winter 1982, p. 342–345, bibl., tables)
Tendency to father-son inheritance of leadership among Mēkranoti Kayapó is enhanced by contact with Brazilian society. Correlation of questionnaire results showed that inherited reputation for ambition, intelligence and knowledge of civilized ways were important factors explaining leadership inheritance.

1385 ———. Mulheres solteiras entre os Mēkranoti-Kayapó (Anuário Antropológico [Edições Tempo Brasileiro, Rio de Janeiro] 82, 1984, p. 69–81, bibl., tables)
Discusses factors which influenced a Kayapó girl's decision to become a "wanton." Statistical analysis of wanton cases reveals that important factors are early loss of mother and lack of ceremonial name.

1386 ———. Why do the Mēkranoti trek?
(in Adaptive responses of native Amazonians [see item 1153] p. 225–238, tables)
Author dismisses social and cultural explanations for the Gê pattern of periodic collective treks. Explains trekking rather as "primarily a way to optimize diet" by increasing protein consumption.

1387 Whitten, Norman E. and Dorothea S. Whitten. The structure of kinship and marriage among the Canelos Quechua of East-Central Ecuador (in Marriage practices in Lowland South America [see item 1294] p. 194–220, bibl., charts)
Canelos Quechua marriages are often cross-generational, designed to pass on soul substance inherited from grandparental generation. Author describes kinship system, alternative ways of arranging marriage, and process of forming marriage. Also discusses ayllu, time and transmission of shamanic power.

1388 Williams, Suzanne. Land rights and the manipulation of identity: official Indian policy in Brazil (JLAS, 15:1, May 1983, p. 137–161, bibl.)
Wide ranging critique of Brazilian Indian policy, beginning with the spurious 1981 "criteria of Indian identity" and the contradictions of the 1973 Indian Statute. Examines Tupinikin eviction from their lands by the Aracruz cellulose industry, and abusive policies of FUNAI at its nadir under Nobre da Veiga.

1389 Wright, Robin M. The great Carajás: Brazil's mega-program for the '80s (The Global Reporter [A journal of people, resources and the world, Anthropology Resource Center, Boston, Mass.] 1:1, March 1983, p. 3–6, maps, plates, tables)
Brief description of Brazil's massive World Bank-funded development project for the lower Tocantins River and its disorganizing effect on 12,562 Indians in more than 20 reserves within the project area (see item 1199).

1390 Yanomami (Interior [Ministério do Interior, Brasília] 8:43, março/abril 1982, p. 15–30, ill., plates)
Description of "interdiction" of Yanomami territory, for their protection in official publication, introduces sketch of Yanomami culture (as of mid 1985, a "Yanomamö Park" had not yet been approved, and their territory was being invaded by prospectors). Article is illustrated with beautiful photos by Claudia Andujar, and accompanying poetic translation of creation myth with drawings by three Yanomami.

1391 Yost, James A. and Patricia M. Kelley. Shotguns, blowguns and spears: the analysis of technological efficiency (in Adaptive responses of native Amazonians [see item 1153] p. 189–224, charts, plates, tables)
Uses quantitative data on hunting among the Waorani of northern Peruvian Amazon region to compare the efficiency of three weapons. Analyzes the effectiveness of each in bagging certain game. Comparisons are also made with Hames's study which compares shotgun with bow and arrow (item 1255).

ETHNOLOGY: South America, Highlands

ROGER RASNAKE, Assistant Professor of Anthropology, Goucher College

THE ANDEAN HIGHLANDS continue in this biennium to be a fertile area for anthropological research and publishing. New field investigations are now carried out as often by specialists residing and even trained in the Andean republics themselves as they are by anthropologists from the "developed" countries to the north. In the articles and books reviewed in this section, for example, over 60 percent were written by Latin American scholars. At the same time that more and more students in the Andean countries have gained professional experience in research and teaching (and this is especially true in the case of Peru), the number of new graduate students in the US with an interest in the Andes—which acts as an indicator of the future growth of the field—seems to be declining from a peak reached in the mid to late 1970s.

This shift towards "national" anthropologies has certain implications for the scholarly work produced. The monograph in both English and Spanish is considerably rarer than it was in the last decade. Indeed, no new major monograph on highland peoples in English published in this biennium has come to the attention of the editor; one exception, Norman Whitten's *Sicuanga Runa* (item **1463**) deals with a group on the eastern slopes of the Ecuadorian Andes who are more closely tied to lowland societies. Economic conditions in the Andean countries also dictate that the book-length study will be less often the mode of presentation of research results, although translations of works originally in English continue to be made (item **1488**).

Yet the absence of monographs is balanced by the vigorous production of articles, both in North and South America. As always, these have had two primary means of presentation. First, a major outlet for recent articles has been a number of edited collections; these will be described in a moment in the context of the discussion of specific topics. Secondly, one of the most exciting developments of the last few years has been the creation of several new journals. A very successful example of this is the *Revista Andina*, published by the Centro Bartolomé de las Casas in Cuzco. The *Revista*, now in its third volume, has already established a high editorial standard for articles and reviews, and provides an "academic" counterpart to the Centro's populist *Sur*, published for southern Peruvian peasants. The Univ. Católica of Lima has also published one number of a wide-ranging *Revista Antropológica*; it apparently replaces the *Debates en Antropología* published at la Católica through 1982. *Allpanchis Phuturinqa* of the Instituto de Pastoral Andina, which has published steadily since 1970, also continues to provide a voice for new research. Of interest to anthropologists working in Bolivia is the journal *Historia Boliviana*, published in Cochabamba and now in its fourth year; and *Historia y Cultura* of La Paz. The latter has recently found a new publisher and has undergone a facelift; it will no doubt appear more regularly than it has in the past.

Several research topics have received special attention in this biennium. Cultural ecology, the social concomitants of economic relationships, and the functioning of the Andean vertical economy is one such focus of interest. Perhaps the most important work to appear in this context is Lehmann's *Ecology and exchange in the Andes* (item **1400**, with individual articles cited by author). Lehmann has brought together a number of specialists with varied experience in the area, each of whom considers the organization of peasant economies and their relative degree of independence and integration in the nations that incorporate them. A brief mention of several of the articles serves to illustrate the issue addressed: Platt (item **1440**), for example, analyzes the *ayllu* of the Norte de Potosí in Bolivia in relation to its past involvement in the market economy and its ability to ensure access to lands in a context of communal tenure and petty commodity production; Harris (item **1430**) describes the vertical economy of the Laymi ethnic group, also in the Norte de Potosí, and their efforts to maintain the circulation of products and labor between the main ecological zones; Figueroa (item **1478**) compares a number of communities in southern Peru to demonstrate their increasing participation in a national economy; and Brady (item **1468**) analyzes the vertical economy of communities in Huancavelica and distinguishes between "vertical control" and the creation of exchange relationships among altitudinal zones.

Two other collections focusing on the Andean vertical economy were both the result of collaboration between Peruvian and Japanese scholars. Masuda and his students carried out careful ethnographic studies on verticality and related topics in a number of communities (item **1493**), while Millones and Tomoeda broaden the focus to include archaeological and ethnohistorical, as well as ethnological, concerns (item **1486**). Camino (item **1471**), Fujii and Tomoeda (item **1483**), Inamura (item **1487**), and Yamamoto (items **1515** and **1516**) provide especially good analyses from these two sources. A fourth collection which addresses issues of the peasant economy does so in the context of Bolivia. A work of variable quality, *Cambios en el agro y el campesinado boliviano* (issued by the Museo Nacional de Etnografía y Folklore in La Paz) nevertheless offers a range of significant research findings by Bolivian scholars (item **1424**). Other articles which deal with important issues relating to the Andean ecology and economy are those by Brush (items **1396** and **1469**), Collins (item **1474**), Fonseca (item **1482**), and Guillet (item **1404**).

Another focus of research and writing in the past two years has been that of migration, both to colonization areas and to the cities. Albó, Greaves, and Sandoval have published three volumes of their study of Aymara life in La Paz (item **1417**). Blanes (items **1421** and **1422**) examines the typical movements in recent years of migrants into the coca-growing areas of Bolivia. Lobo (item **1489**) has studied the urban neighborhoods to which rural migrants arrive when they come to the city. Both Flores (item **1427**) and Martínez (item **1492**) provide general overviews and annotated bibliographies of recent work in the field.

Finally, ritual and symbolism continue to be of interest to students of Andean societies. Rappaport (item **1456**) examines Páez conceptions of myth in the sacred definition of their territory. Allen (item **1465**) analyzes ideas surrounding death in Sonqo, Peru. Muratorio (item **1460**) assesses the impact of missionization on rural peoples in Ecuador. Platt (item **1438**) compares the symbolic world of Bolivian miners with that of Andean peasants. And Whitten, in a study of the Canelos Quichua of eastern Ecuador (item **1463**) demonstrates the continuing power of an indigenous symbolic world even as it is confronted with economic development.

GENERAL

1392 Amerlinck de Bontempo, Marijose.
¿Cultura?, ¿sociedad?, ¿economía?, o de cómo la antropología descubrió a los campesinos (UNAM/AA, 19, 1982, p. 33–58, bibl.)

Review article on the development of peasant studies within anthropology that would be useful for those unfamiliar with the field. Focuses especially on the conceptualization of the relation of the peasant economy to the incorporating State.

1393 Bastien, Joseph. Los Aymaras: notas bibliográficas (Revista Andina [Centro Bartolomé de las Casas, Cusco, Perú] 1:2, 1983, p. 545–578)

Useful review and annotated bibliography of some 70 books and articles on the Aymara in Bolivia and Peru.

1394 Bittmann, Bente; William E. Carter; and Karl-Georg Scheffer. On "Coca Chewing and High-Altitude Stress:" reply to Warwick Bray and Colin Dollery (UC/CA, 24:4, Aug./Oct. 1983, p. 527–529, bibl.)

In separate comments, each author responds to Bray and Dollery's argument that coca leaf use is not an adaptation to altitude (see item 1395). All agree that coca leaf is used in a wide range of ecologies, although Carter reiterates his conclusion that it nevertheless can be beneficial for conditions of stress encountered at high altitude. All also call for further research.

1395 Bray, Warwick and Colin Dollery. Coca chewing and high-altitude stress: a spurious correlation (UC/CA, 24:3, June 1983, p. 269–282, bibl.)

Contrary to the belief that the use of coca leaf is a response to the stresses of high altitude, coca leaf has never been restricted to the highlands either in the geographic dispersion of related species or in its traditional use. Bray and Dollery argue that coca leaf chewing is related to indigenous cultural identity and serves largely as a mild stimulant wherever it is found. Valuable summary article. For a reply to authors' thesis, see item 1394.

1396 Brush, Stephen. Traditional hillside farming systems (Culture and Agriculture [Anthropological Study Group on Agrarian Systems, s.l.] 18, Winter 1983, p. 9–16)

Looking at indigenous farming systems in mountainous regions all over tropical America, Brush examines such technological and social forms as communal land control, sectoral fallowing, water management, and slope modification as means to improving agricultural production and reducing the risks of crop failure. Interesting summary article.

1397 Cipolletti, María S. En torno a un relato andino: el *ukumari* (IPA/A, 19:22, 1982, p. 145–160)

Cipolletti argues that the widespread Andean *ukumari* stories, in which a bear

kidnaps and mates with a woman, have their origin in a European tale introduced in the 16th century.

1398 Congreso de Pueblos y Organizaciones Indias de Sud América, 2nd, *La Paz, 1983.* Conclusiones y documentos. La Paz: Consejo Indio de Sudamérica: Editorial Acuario, 1983. 56 p.: ill.

Proceedings of 2nd Congress of the Consejo Indio de Sudamérica, a grouping which attempts to unite indigenous peoples from throughout the continent. Drawing on an *indianidad* perspective, articles and documents brought together here are a useful introduction to the thought of those who believe a revitalization of indigenous cultures is a possible alternative to assimilation.

Cultural Survival Quarterly. See item 1223.

1399 Dillon, Paul H. Sobre la antropología totalizadora (Anthropologica [Pontificia Univ. Católica del Perú, Lima] 1:1, 1983, p. 159–207)

By means of a critique of the work of Rodrigo Montoya, Dillon develops an approach to ideology based on Pierre Bourdieu's theory of praxis. A coherent presentation of Bourdieu's thinking.

1400 Ecology and exchange in the Andes. Edited by David Lehmann. Cambridge, England: Cambridge Univ. Press, 1982. 245 p. (Cambridge studies in social anthropology; 41)

Stimulating collection of eight articles on Andean peoples and their economic arrangements; some address historic cases, other examine contemporary ones. Articles are of varying quality, with those by Platt, Harris, and Brady making the greatest contributions. For their individual annotations, see items 1430, 1440, and 1468.

1401 Esteva-Fabregat, Claudio. El campesino andino como terminal estructural (IGFO/RI, 42:169/170, julio/dic. 1982, p. 371–392)

Discussion of Andean rural peoples employing concepts from the peasant literature. Reiterates definitional questions on the nature of Andean society formulated by earlier students, yet ignores recent work carried out by others. The focus on State- "community" relations is useful; but the essay seems peculiarly distant from its subject.

1402 Estudios etnográficos del Perú meridional. Edited by Shozo Masuda. Tokyo: Univ. of Tokyo, 1981. 229 p.: bibl., ill.

Collection of seven essays which, like Millones and Tomoeda (item **1486**), largely focus on the vertical economy developed by Andean rural peoples. The tone of the essays is relentlessly ethnographic, emphasizing contemporary household-level production systems. Although not extremely innovative in approach or in theoretical perspective, this is a useful contribution.

1403 Flores Ochoa, Jorge A. Pastoreo de llamas y alpacas en los Andes: balance bibliográfico (Revista Andina [Centro Bartolomé de las Casas, Cusco, Perú] 1 : 1, 1983, p. 175–218)

Citing archaeological, ethnohistorical, and contemporary ethnological sources, Flores reviews a wide range of research on pastoralism and Andean camelids. Includes outstanding bibliography.

1404 Guillet, David. Toward a cultural ecology of mountains: the Central Andes and the Himalayas compared (UC/CA, 24 : 5, Dec. 1983, p. 561–574, bibl.)

Adopting a production-based mode of analysis, Guillet argues that the control of multiple zones in mountain ecologies is a strategy which reduces risks, provides a more adequate diet, and uses labor efficiently. Yet transformations may occur as the market provides new opportunities or as population increases. While slighting sociocultural factors, it is nevertheless a useful elaboration of the verticality concept.

Kroeger, Axel. South American Indians between traditional and modern health services in rural Ecuador. See item **1835**.

1405 Llanque, Domingo et al. Acerca de la historia y universo aymara. Lima: Centro de Información, Estudios y Documentación, 1981. 149 p.

Collection of short articles on Aymara culture and history. Several authors favor an impressionistic approach, rather than one based on fieldwork and systematic research. Of interest to ethnologists: Domingo Llanque "La Historia del Pueblo Aymara;" Gabriel Martínez "Los Aymaras Chilenos;" Héctor Martínez "Migración y Economía en Puno;" Inés Pozzi "La Educación Bilingüe en el Marco Legal de la Reforma Educativa Peruana;" and José Ayala "Desaventuras en el Universo Aymara."

1406 Parentesco y matrimonio en los Andes. Papers from the Symposium on Andean Kinship and Marriage, held in Toronto, Ont., in 1972. Edited by Enrique Mayer and Ralph Bolton. Lima: Pontificia Univ. Católica del Perú, Fondo Editorial, 1980. 722 p., 2 folded leaves of plates: bibl., ill.

Important collection of articles on kinship and marriage practices throughout the Andes, a number of which were previously published in an English ed. (see *HLAS 41 : 1221*). Only those articles not reviewed in earlier *HLAS* volumes are annotated here (items **1470, 1477, 1481, 1491, 1496,** and **1509**).

1407 Parkerson, Phillip T. The Inca coca monopoly: fact or legal fiction? (APS/P, 127 : 2, April 1983, p. 107–123)

In an ethnohistorical treatise with important contemporary implications, Parkerson argues convincingly that the supposed monopoly of the Incas on coca leaf production was a "legal fiction;" the Incas could never have rigidly controlled coca leaf use, "an important aspect of pan-Andean culture much older than the Inca Empire." It is clear that the belief that the widespread use of coca leaf is a late colonial or republican development is incorrect. For ethnohistorian's comment, see *HLAS 46 : 1687*.

1408 Romano, Ruggiero. Alrededor de dos falsas ecuaciones: coca buena, cocaína buena, cocaína mala, coca mala (IPA/A, 16 : 19, 1982, p. 237–252)

Romano recounts origins of the incorrect identification of coca leaf with one of 14 alkaloids found in the leaf, cocaine. Pointing to the central role of coca leaf in nutrition, natural medicine, ritual, and interzonal commerce, he argues that the destruction of the coca-leaf complex by the West contributes to the ethnocide of Andean peoples.

Ryn, Zdzisław. Los Andes y la medicina. See item **1846**.

1409 Sánchez, Rodrigo. La teoría de "lo andino" y el campesinado de hoy (IPA/A, 20, 1982, p. 255–281)

Sánchez argues that the focus on the "Andean" implied in such terms as verticality, reciprocity, and communal redistribution leads to a romanticized mystification of relations based on the market and on economic self-interest. The analysis of social classes and of the control of resources will yield, so the author believes, more valid results.

1410 Suess, Paulo. Culturas indígenas y evangelización. Lima: Centro de Estudios y Publicaciones, 1983. 104 p.

Brazilian theologian Suess argues that "indigenist" political action in the Andes and Amazonian Lowlands takes various routes—nationalist, populist, racist, "classist"—but that the true "liberating option" is that proposed by liberation theology. Useful work for those interested in missionization.

1411 Urbano, Henrique. Representaciones colectivas y arqueología mental en los Andes (IPA/A, 17:20, 1982, p. 33–84, bibl.)

Review article of research on Andean myth and religion. Urbano, who is extremely harsh in his assessments, focuses largely on ethnohistorical work but also examines some contemporary studies. A very useful bibliography accompanies the text. For ethnohistorian's comment, see *HLAS 46:1733*.

ARGENTINA

1412 Bartolomé, Leopoldo J. Panorama y perspectivas de la antropología social en la Argentina (IDES/DE, 22:87, oct./dic. 1982, p. 411–420, tables)

Throughout the 1970s, anthropology in Argentina remained chained to the theoretically outmoded Austrian diffusionist schoool long after that approach was abandoned elsewhere. Damaged by political struggles before 1976, anthropology, like other social sciences, became the target of official persecution thereafter. Academic reform is urgently needed to train a new generation of professionals.

1413 Cipolletti, María Susana. Llamas y mulas, trueque y venta: el testimonio de un arriero puneño (Revista Andina [Centro Bartolomé de las Casas, Cusco, Perú] 2:2, 1984, p. 513–538)

Key informant Calixto Llampa helps Cipolletti reconstruct the movements of muleteers from Jujuy as they traded throughout northern Argentina, southern Bolivia, and Chile. Disorganized and very descriptive.

1414 Cultura mapuche en la Argentina: en recuerdo de Susana Chertudi, septiembre 1981-marzo 1982. Catalog of an exhibition held at the Museo Nacional del Hombre, Buenos Aires. Buenos Aires: Ministerio de Cultura y Educación, Subsecretaría de Estado de Cultura, Instituto Nacional de Antropología, 1981. 92 p.: bibl., ill.

Catalog of an Argentine Mapuche exposition which inaugurated the new Museo Nacional del Hombre in Buenos Aires. Includes brief, superficial essay on Mapuche culture but has most useful bibliography. Great majority of items on exhibit are described, not portrayed.

1415 Waag, Else María. Tres entidades *wekufü* en la cultura mapuche. Buenos Aires: Editorial Universitaria de Buenos Aires, 1982. 246 p.: bibl. (Col. Argentina)

Study of Argentine Mapuche concepts of evil and ill fortune focuses on three supernatural beings: the flying head, walking skeleton, and child-goblin. There is little attempt to view Mapuche society in analytic terms. Appendix provides verbatim transcripts of informants' tales.

BOLIVIA

1416 Albó, Xavier. ¡Bodas de plata?: o, Requiem por una reforma agraria. Comentarios de Fernando Calderón, Carlos Quiroga and Alfonso Camacho. La Paz: Centro de Investigación y Promoción del Campesinado (CIPCA), 1979. 105 p.: bibl., ill. (Cuaderno de investigación CIPCA; 17)

Short but provocative study of the impact of the 1953 Agrarian Reform and of problems it both created and ignored. After reviewing demographic and social trends and examining developments in colonization and the law's application, Albó concludes with several proposals for reforming the Reform.

1417 ———; **Tomás Greaves;** and **Godofredo Sandoval.** Chukiyawu: la cara aymara de La Paz. v. 1, El paso a la ciudad. v. 2, Una odisea: buscar "pega." v. 3, Cabalgando entre dos mundos. La Paz: Centro de Investigación y Promoción del Campesinado (CIPCA), 1981–1983. 3 v. (150, 204, 196 p.): bibl., maps (Cuadernos de investigación CIPCA; 20, 22, 24)

Vol. 1–3 of major study of rural-urban migration to the city of La Paz which draws on interviews with some 1400 "ex-peasants." Vol. 1 focuses on continuing links between city and country and details motives for migration, urban settlement patterns, and problems migrants confront as they move to the city. Vol. 2 focuses on process by which countryside migrants join urban work force: by becoming artisans, petty traders, or construction workers; or, for women, domestic servants. Amply supported by census and interview data. Vol. 3 examines the "subjective" (i.e., conceptual and symbolic) aspects of informants' responses. More noticeably constrained by its quantitative methods than the earlier volumes, it is still able to point to strong continuities between rural and urban meaning-worlds and ritual practices; the future of the Aymara language also seems surprisingly bright. Important work.

1418 El Arte textil en Bolivia. Exposición realizada con la colaboración de Academia Nacional de Ciencias, Instituto Nacional de Fomento Lanero. Texto, Teresa Gisbert et al. La Paz: Univ. Mayor de San Andrés, Instituto de Estudios Bolivianos, 1982. 39 p., 8 p. of plates: bibl., ill.
Exhibition guide and catalog which briefly attempts to outline stylistic techniques and remaining zones of Andean textile production in Bolivia. Useful only as basic introduction.

1419 Arze, José Roberto. Algunos antecedentes ideológicos de la cuestión agraria (in Cambios en el agro y el campesinado boliviano [see item 1424] p. 135–140)
Arze examines the evolution of the terms *indio* and *campesino* and delineates what he sees as the two main intellectual approaches to the indigenous population, the "racist" and the "socialist-nationalist." A provocative analysis of the Bolivian elite's views of Andean peoples.

1420 Benton, Jane. Development on the Lake Titicaca shore (GM, 55:2, Feb. 1983, p. 86–91, map, plates)
Popular account of Aymara settlements on Lake Titicaca. Filled with inaccuracies in its discussion of the past, article emphasizes recent changes in the communities due to growing contact with the cities and tourism. Photographs are welcome.

Berg, Hans van den. Material bibliográfico para el estudio de los aymaras, callawayas, chipayas, urus. See item **11.**

1421 Blanes, José. De los valles al Chapare: estrategias familiares en un contexto de cambio. La Paz: Centro de Estudios de la Realidad Económica y Social (CERES), 1983. 191 p.: charts, maps.
Perceptive research report on household labor strategies among migrants to the tropical Chapare. The migrants are Quechua-speaking highland peasants who establish themselves as petty commercial farmers in their new home. Especially interesting since the Chapare is a major zone for the production of coca leaf.

1422 ———. Un intento teórico metodológico para el estudio de las migracions internas: el caso boliviano (in Cambios en el agro y el campesinado boliviano [see item **1424**] p. 65–77)
Internal migration reflects the deterioration and consequent "pauperization" of the peasant household economy due to the fragmentation of lands after the 1953 Agrarian Reform. Lowland colonization, the choice of only a minority of migrant households, still clearly reveals the growing tendency towards peasant submission to the demands of the market, leading to greater social stratification. Unfortunately, this simple message drowns in a sea of social science jargon.

1423 Calderón, Fernando and Jorge Dandler. Los movimientos campesinos y la etnicidad en el contexto de los procesos de participación popular en Bolivia (in Cambios en el agro y el campesinado boliviano [see item **1424**] p. 109–133)
Peasant movements in Bolivia are analyzed in terms of social class, ethnicity, and in relation to the nation-state. The authors give a brief history of Bolivian peasant activism and conclude with suggested priorities for research. Useful base-line article.

1424 Cambios en el agro y el campesinado boliviano. Papers presented at the Seminario sobre Cambios en el Agro y el Campesinado, sponsored by the Museo Nacional de Etnografía y Folklore, May 10–15, 1982. La Paz: Museo Nacional de Etnografía y Folklore, 1982. 183 p.: ill. (Advances de investigación; 2)
Collection of 15 papers, many of

which are annotated separately (see items
**1419, 1422, 1423, 1426, 1428, 1431, 1433,
1434, 1435, 1436, 1442, 1444,** and **1449**).
The essays are organized into three themes:
1) Agrarian Structures and Policies; 2) Mobility and Differentiation in the Peasant Work
Force; and 3) Ideology and Peasant Movements. Although of varying quality, the papers represent the many directions Bolivian
anthropologists and sociologists are following in ongoing research.

1425 Centellas G., José María. La verdad
sobre la coca y la cocaína. La Paz: Instituto Boliviano de Estudios de Comunicación Social, 1981. 39 p.: bibl.
Thoroughly superficial study of coca
leaf and cocaine in the form of an apology for
the recent Bolivian military regime's ineffectiveness in drug control. A very minor footnote in the study of the indigenous use of
coca leaf.

1426 Escobar Durán, Javier. La fuerza de trabajo en el área rural de Santa Cruz (in
Cambios en el agro y el campesinado boliviano [see item **1424**] p. 99–105)
The rapid growth of commercial agriculture in sugarcane and cotton in Santa
Cruz led to a crisis when both products became overly dependent on world markets.
Declines in production and mechanization
have led to a decrease in the need for permanent labor and a greater dependence on seasonal migration.

1427 Flores, Gonzalo. Migraciones en
Bolivia: bibliografía reciente (Revista
Andina [Centro Bartolomé de las Casas,
Cusco, Perú] 1:1, 1983, p. 143–150)
Flores offers a resumé of a limited
number of works which examine internal migration to the cities, to colonization zones,
and to areas of temporary wage labor in commercial agriculture. Useful review.

1428 ———. Rebeliones campesinas en el
período liberal: 1900–1920 (in Cambios en el agro y el campesinado boliviano
[see item **1424**] p. 141–148)
Flores recounts various means that
Bolivian peasants used in order to maintain
control of their lands in the face of growth of
the hacienda, and gives a summary of the
larger peasant mobilizations in the first two
decades of this century. Useful note on peasant movements.

1429 Harman, Inge Maria. Women and cooperative labor (Cultural Survival
Quarterly [Cambrige, Mass.] 8:2, 1984,
p. 38–40)
Among the Yuras of southern Bolivia,
women play major role in agricultural production and in ritual life; their contribution
in public cooperative tasks equals that of
men. The lack of socioeconomic stratification within the ayllu and the value of
women's work in the public domain promote
relative equality between the sexes.

1430 Harris, Olivia. Labour and produce in
an ethnic economy, Northern Potosí,
Bolivia (in Ecology and exchange in the
Andes [see item **1400**] p. 70–96)
Households of the Laymi ethnic group
manage social ties in order to have access to
the two ends of the Andean vertical ecology—highland *suni* and temperate *likina*.
Complex relationships, including marriage,
labor prestations, and various types of product exchanges maintain the interdependence
of the zones; even cash circulation is restricted to traditional patterns of exchange.
Valuable article.

1431 Ibarnegaray Ponce, Roxana. El desarrollo agrario en Santa Cruz: 1900–
1952 (in Cambios en el agro y el campesinado boliviano [see item **1424**] p. 17–30)
Development of commercial agriculture in lowland Santa Cruz preceded by some
decades the 1952 Bolivian Revolution; but
subsequent MNR economic policies strongly
supported ideology of large-scale landholders
there while championing the peasant cultivator in the highlands of the west. Interesting
historical note on the area.

1431 Mahnke, Lothar. Zur indianischen
landwirtschaft im siedlungsgebiet der
Kallawayas: Bolivien (UBGI/E, 4:36, Dez.
1983, p. 247–254, facsim., map, plates,
tables)
Description of verticality in the agriculture of the Kallawayas. Through such
technological developments as terraces, irrigation, crop rotation, and conservation, the
Kallawayas are well adapted to their Andean
ecosystem.

1433 Mendoza, Ignacio. Hipótesis sobre descampesinación y cholificación (in
Cambios en el agro y el campesinado boliviano [see item **1424**] p. 149–156)

Suggesting that "depeasantization" is inevitable for most Andean peoples, Mendoza attempts to withdraw the term *cholo* from the social science dustbin, where it most likely should remain. Author shows no familiarity with recent thinking on ethnicity.

1434 Moore, Winston. Política y visión en los Andes bolivianos (*in* Cambios en el agro y el campesinado boliviano [see item **1424**] p. 157–172)

Andean symbol systems have provided Quechua-speaking peasants a means to synthesize conceptually the oppressive impositions of dominant elites with their own social forms and their relations with the natural world. This is evident, for example, in their reinterpretation of Bolivian presidents as "Incas." Fascinating analysis.

1435 Núñez del Prado, José. Economía y migración en el Altiplano Norte (*in* Cambios en el agro y el campesinado boliviano [see item **1424**] p. 91–97)

Claiming to report on a survey of rural economy in five provinces of La Paz Dept., Núñez del Prado creates such a historical materialist fog around the data that they become obscured. His point is no surprise: that labor migration, population growth, and social differentiation are related to the growth of capitalist production, and that the peasant population forms a potential "reserve army" for that production.

1436 Paz Ballivián, Danilo. Estructura agraria boliviana (*in* Cambios en el agro y el campesinado boliviano [see item **1424**] p. 31–36)

Resumé of item **1437**, Paz applies a Marxist tool-kit to Bolivian agricultural forms, and is especially interested in characterizing types of haciendas and Andean communities both before and after the 1952 Revolution. Paz argues (and who would disagree?) that capitalist development and market conditions now largely shape agrarian realities in Bolivia.

1437 ———. Estructura agraria boliviana. La Paz: Librería Editorial Popular, 1983. 167 p.: bibl., charts.

Paz surveys the structural forms of Bolivian agrarian society prior to the 1952 Revolution, then describes changes (especially the process of "depeasantization") resulting from the Agrarian Reform, the

growth of large-scale commercial agriculture, and colonization. Author's use of "feudalism" and "precapitalist economic formations" seem unnecessarily rigid.

1438 Platt, Tristan. Conciencia andina y conciencia proletaria: Qhuyaruna y ayullu en el norte de Potosí (HISLA, 2, 1983, p. 47–73)

Platt shows that the symbolic world of Bolivian miners, both in small and large mines, represents a "transformational continuity" of an overarching Andean cultural framework shared with rural agriculturalists. Nor is there a major inconsistency betweeen the miners' cult to the *Tío* (or "Devil") and their renowned political activism. Significant contribution.

1439 ———. Liberalism and ethnocide in the southern Andes (History Workshop [A journal of socialist and feminist historians, Routledge & Kegan Paul, London] 17, Spring 1984, p. 3–18, ill.)

Andean peasants resisted 19th-century liberal reforms in land ownership and tribute of the Bolivian *criollo* elites because, from the Andean perspective, they betrayed the mutual pact which guaranteed group access to land in exchange for tribute and labor service. Thus, late 1800s rebellions became inevitable. Fascinating article.

1440 ———. The role of the Andean ayllu in the reproduction of the petty commodity regime in Northern Potosí (*in* Ecology and exchange in the Andes [see item **1400**] p. 27–69)

The Andean ayllu plays an important role in the reproduction of the regime of petty commodity production among peasant agropastoralists in the vertical economy of northern Potosí. Given the region's past involvement in the market, Platt argues that the nature of contemporary small-scale production and its limited market integration are primarily a result of state policies, not of peasant "traditionalism." Important analysis.

1441 Rivera Cusicanqui, Silvia. "Oprimidos pero no vencidos:" luchas del campesinado aymara y qhechwa, 1900–1980. La Paz: Confederación Sindical Unica de Trabajadores Campesinos de Bolivia (CSUTCB), 1984. 203 p.: map.

Fascinating history of peasant activism in the 20th century. Rivera argues that while the landmark 1952 Revolution remains a central focus for the legitimation of the peasant movement in today's Bolivia, a centuries-long view of resistance to elite domination embodied in such culture heroes as Tupaq Katari also forms part of the intellectual context of indigenous political participation. Includes the CSUTCB 1983 *Tesis política.*

1442 Romero Bedregal, Hugo. Planeamiento andino: práctica y teoría a partir del proceso de desarrollo histórico de los pueblos americanos (*in* Cambios en el agro y el campesinado boliviano [see item **1424**] p. 37–52)

Romero creates a cabalistic framework of cells and microregions to suggest a development process he sees as reflecting Andean concepts of "socioeconomic space." His program of "Andean planning," which rightly urges that rural peoples be the source and end of future development projects, will, one hopes, not be the source upon which such projects are based.

1443 Saignes, Thierry. ¿Quiénes son los kallawaya? (Revista Andina [Centro Bartolomé de las Casas, Cusco, Perú] 1 : 2, 1983, p. 357–384)

Saignes argues that the mysterious Kallawaya—renowned as ambulatory curers—were organized as a chiefdom when the Inkas settled *mitmaqkuna* among them. This multi-ethnic base may account for the broad medical knowledge they only later began to offer to those outside their territory. Fascinating synthesis of history and ethnology. For ethnohistorian's comment, see *HLAS 46:1710.*

1444 Sánchez, Carmen. Economía campesina y economía minera: caso del cantón Araca (*in* Cambios en el agro y el campesinado boliviano [see item **1424**] p. 79–90)

Situated in Loayza prov., the Araca tin mines have relied on peasants for their labor needs. Sánchez examines commercial and labor exchanges asd well as kin ties between peasants and miners in order to describe how the mining enterprise is able to control surplus value. Promising preliminary report.

1445 School, Wolfgang. Güteraustausch und regionale mobilität im Kallawaya-Tal: Bolivien (UBGI/E, 4:36, Dez. 1982, p. 254–266, maps, plates, tables)

Describes vertical ecological adaptations and economic exchanges in the Charazani area of Bolivia. Examines links outside the home valley, both in terms of the traveling Kallawaya curers and due to labor migration.

1447 Tendler, Judith; Kevin Healy; and Carol Michaels O'Laughlin. What to think about cooperatives: a guide from Bolivia. Rosslyn, Va.: Inter-American Foundation, 1983. 59, 272 p.: bibl.

Tendler examines four peasant cooperatives in Bolivia in terms of growth, leadership, marketing, credit, and capital investment. All such co-ops, she argues, face the danger of becoming the tools of the most economically powerful segment of their memberships. Informative and enlightening study.

1448 Urquidi, Arturo. Las comunidades indígenas en Bolivia. 2a ed. La Paz: Librería Editorial Juventud, 1982. 257 p., 12 leaves of plates: bibl., ill.

Urquidi, adopting narrow orthodox Marxist framework, repeats the same stereotypical views on native communities that he held in work's first ed. His understanding of the Andean ayllu, and of the Inka state, are particularly unenlightening. Book ignores all research carried out in the Andes during the last two decades, relying on hearsay and inappropriate generalizations.

1449 Velarde, Jorge. Desarrollo y campos de competencia de la política agraria boliviana (*in* Cambios en el agro y el campesinado boliviano [see item **1424**] p. 53–62)

Velarde locates the crisis in Bolivian agricultural policy in the focus on the distribution of production, rather than in production itself. In the absence of a coherent agrarian policy, the control of marketing has passed from the haciendas to a multitude of small-scale intermediary marketers. The peasant producer, Velarde concludes, is more exploited by the market than ever.

CHILE AND COLOMBIA

1450 Aspillaga Fontaine, Eugenio A. Algunas consideraciones de orden antropológico en torno a la proposición de creación de una nueva región en el sur de Chile

(SCHG/R, 150, 1982, p. 168–184, bibl., tables)

General description of the natural history, archaeology, and contemporary situation of the southernmost region of Chile, area inhabited by remnants of the foraging Alacaluf. Author suggests an active importation of population to the area. Very superficial treatment.

1451 Calvo, Mayo. Secretos y tradiciones mapuches. 2a ed. ampliada de *Leyendas del Calafquén.* Santiago: Editores Impresos Offset, 1980. 235 p.: bibl., ill.

Second ed. of Calvo's 1968 *Leyendas del Calafquén* (not previously annotated in *HLAS*), which brings together some 30 "traditions" of Mapuche culture. The result is entertaining, but makes no claims to analysis. Given the current repression of the Mapuche in Chile, this is perhaps all we can expect.

1452 Congreso Indígena Nacional, *1st, Bosa, Colombia, 1982.* Conclusiones y documentos. Bosa?: Organización Nacional Indígena de Colombia, 1982. 95 p.: ill.

Proposals and reports resulting from the Primer Congreso Indígena Nacional, held in 1982. Documents, dealing with lands, legislation, health, culture and religion, education, and political alternatives, provide informative resumé of Colombia's growing indigenous movement.

1453 Guy, Jim. The case of the Mapuche and Chile's "Bad" Law 2568 (DEA/IP, 5, Sept./Oct. 1981, p. 14–16)

Guy describes the destructive impact of a recent law promulgated by the Pinochet regime which eliminates communal land tenure in Mapuche communities. Guy feels that only international pressure may protect Mapuche culture from extinction; if the law is applied, it becomes "a euphemism for cultural genocide."

1454 Lagos Carrizo, Reinaldo; Emilio Mendoza Cruz; and Nolberto Ampuero S. La noche de los abuelos en Santiago de Río Grande (Chungara [Univ. de Tarapacá, Depto. de Antropología] 9, agosto 1982, p. 247–274, bibl., maps)

Authors describe in great detail the offerings made to Earth Mother, water spirits, and ancestors the night before irrigation canals are cleaned in a small community in the highlands of northern Chile. Little analysis

or contextualization is attempted of what is a rich symbolic event.

1455 Montupil Inaipil, Fernando. Inche tati, el pueblo mapuche: tradición indómita en Chile. Managua: Centro de Investigaciones y Estudios de la Reforma Agraria, Centro de Publicaciones, 1982. 205 p.: bibl., ill. (Col. Lautaro)

Impassioned defense of the Mapuche which is, unfortunately, a peculiar mixture of anecdote, discredited theory, and social scientific vocabulary. Most useful are sections referring to the Allende and present periods. Interesting as a document expressing Mapuche ethnic consciousness.

1456 Rappaport, Joanne. History, myth and the dynamics of territorial maintenance in Tierradentro, Colombia (AES/AE, 12:1, 1985, p. 27–45)

Páez strategies for maintaining control of their lands vary in different historical periods and in varying social contexts, but are all closely linked to their conception of the past, embodied in myths. The symbolic analysis of these ideologies of social space must take real political and historical events into account. Important study.

1457 Sotomayor Cantero, Sonia and Conrado Pérez Rebolledo. Elementos de la educación familiar mapuche transferibles a la escuela (CPES/RPS, 14:39/40, mayo/dic. 1977, p. 31–55, bibl.)

Somewhat anecdotal description of childhood learning within the Mapuche family. The Mapuches' positive affirmation of the child, seen in assigning responsibilities and demonstrating affection, leads to early development of cognitive and motor skills and to warm social ties. The school, with its focus on abstract knowledge, is largely irrelevant to Mapuche needs and serves as an agent for cultural disruption.

ECUADOR

1458 Cueva Jaramillo, Juan. Etnocentrismo en la cultural ecuatoriana en 150 años de vida republicana (*in* Arte y cultura: Ecuador, 1830–1980. Fernando Tinajero Villamar *et al.* Quito: Corporación Editora Nacional, 1980, p. 45–67, bibl. [Libro del sesquicentenario; 2])

Cueva challenges the "Eurocentric" view of European conquest and colonization advanced by the national elites, and pleads for a view of history and society "from the bottom up," from the point of view of the native peoples. While there is little new here, it is a coherent statement of the *indigenista* perspective.

1459 Fock, Niels and Eva Krener. Informe sobre *El viaje de investigación etnográfica danesa 1973–1974 a los indios cañari de Ecuador* (CCE/RA, 7, nov. 1981, p. 9–26)

Ethnography in the old style; Cañar could be in the South Seas. Fock and Krener provide an impressionistic field report with little that is new. The publications on the Cañari by L.A. Brownrigg (former *HLAS* contributing editor for this section) are much more useful.

1460 Muratorio, Blanca. Etnicidad, evangelización y protesta en el Ecuador: una perspectiva antropológica. Quito: Centro de Investigaciones y Estudios Socio-Económicos, 1982. 109 p.: bibl. (Banco Central del Ecuador. Col. Imágenes; 2)

Fascinating collection of three diverse articles on ethnicity and class consciousness in rural Ecuador. The impact of missionization on indigenous symbolic worlds as a preparation for incorporation into the capitalist mode of production is a major theme. Important contribution.

1461 Polo, Antonio. ¿Escolarizar al indígena?: influjo de la escuela sobre el nivel intelectual y la conformación de la personalidad en los niños de algunas comunidades de Bolívar. Traducción del original italiano de Javier Miera. Ilustraciones de Tonino Clemente. Fotos de Felipe Mayordomo. Quito: Ediciones Indoamérica, 1981. 144 p.: bibl., ill. (Col. Mundo andino; 1)

Polo uses dated sources for a pedestrian description of the Andean past, then goes on to repeat stereotypical ideas about Andean psychological characteristics. Comparing "white" and "Indian" children, he comes to the astonishing conclusion that common primary schooling reduces intellectual differences between them.

Rodríguez, Juan Evangelista. Historia de Cochasquí. See *HLAS 46:1703.*

1462 Walter, Lynn. Ethnicity, economy and the State in Ecuador. Aalborg, Denmark: Aalborg Univ. Press, 1981. 44 p.: bibl. (Development research series; 3)

Brief, somewhat superficial essay on ethnicity as a political and economic factor in national life. While correct in arguing that "Indian" is an imposed category, Walters seems convinced that Andean folk retain their localized ethnic group identities only due to isolation and exploitation. Useful as reference on the history of "Indian" legislation.

1463 Whitten, Norman. Sicuanga Runa: the other side of development in Amazonian Ecuador. Urbana: Univ. of Illinois Press, 1985. 314 p.: bibl., ill., index, maps.

Major study of the Canelos Quichua symbolic world, understood especially through artistic motifs in ceramics and via the experience of hallucinogenic drugs. Whitten deftly analyzes the contrasting worlds of power in which the Canelos participate—on the one hand, their increasing subjection to the nation-state, while on the other, their continuing control and intimate knowledge of the forest world. Very important work.

PARAGUAY

1464 Hack, H. Land problems in the Paraguayan Chaco (CEDLA/B, 34, junio 1983, p. 99–115, bibl., ill., map, tables)

Using a transactional model, Hack traces conflicts arising as the native Lengua population lost their lands to Mennonite colonies in the Chaco. Only in the 1970s, with the help of the Mennonite Church and international agencies, have the Lengua been able to expand their land resources. The Lengua are depicted inadequately.

PERU

1465 Allen, Catherine J. Body and soul in Quechua thought (UCLA/JLAL, 8:2, 1982, p. 179–196)

The human dead—ancestors, *chullpas,* and demons—continue, like dried potatoes, to have an ongoing spiritual power and identity. Force-feeding of coca, alcohol and food in ritual contexts is a means to communicate with these spiritual entities. Although not the comparative study implied by the title, a perceptive symbolic analysis.

1466 Altamirano, Teófilo. Migración y estrategias de supervivencia de origen rural entre los campesinos de la ciudad (Anthropologica [Pontificia Univ. Católica del Perú, Lima] 1:1, 1983, p. 127–158)

Altamirano sketches the way that poor rural migrants to Lima have adapted such strategies from their rural backgrounds as interfamilial cooperation, marriage arrangements, ongoing migration between town and country, and traditional curing practices to life in the city. Interesting article.

1467 Ansión, Juan. Verdad y engaño en mitos ayacuchanos (IPA/A, 17:20, 1982, p. 237–252)

Reviewing a series of tales about flying heads, mountains that punish liars, and sexual sirens, Ansión reflects on the nature of narration in Quechua culture and on the power of *engaño*, "deceit" or "fraud." Interesting discussion of oral texts and how they are best to be recorded and analyzed.

1468 Bradby, Barbara. "Resistance to capitalism" in the Peruvian Andes (*in* Ecology and exchange in the Andes [see item **1400**] p. 97–122)

Comparing two Huancavelica communities that were related through vertical ties, Bradby argues that neither is "resistant" to capitalism as such. She maintains that commodity relations have not, in either case, penetrated production, and that economic power comes from the ability to manipulate exchange ties with the outside world.

1469 Brush, Stephen; Heath J. Carney; and Zósimo Huamán. Dynamics of Andean potato production (Economic Botany [New York Botanical Gardens] 35:1, 1981, p. 70–88)

Report on research on indigenous potato farming in Peru's Mantaro Valley. Authors analyze Andean farmers' categorization of classes and types of potato, both wild and domestic, and describe the indigenous logic in selecting and intermixing varieties. Major concerns are inroads of commercial seed and danger of the loss of native germ plasm.

1470 Burchard, Roderick. Exogamia como estrategia de acceso a recursos interzonales: un caso de los Andes centrales del Perú (*in* Parentesco y matrimonio en los Andes [see item **1406**] p. 593–616)

Burchard examines the high incidence of male exogamy in one village of the central Peruvian Andes, a practice which contrasts with widespread endogamy in Andean communities. Author links exogamy to a regional effort to secure access to the various microenvironments of the vertical ecology. Interesting analysis of production and exchange practices.

1471 Camino, Alejandro. Tiempo y espacio en la estrategia de subsistencia andina: un caso en las vertientes sudperuanas (*in* El Hombre y su ambiente en los Andes centrales [see item **1486**] p. 11–38)

Camino describes subsistence patterns of four peasant communities in Cuyo-Cuyo, Puno, all of which maintain "traditional" systems of vertical control. He characterizes each of six ecological zones, then argues that vertical control as an "ideal" is simply "la búsqueda de diversificación de la base de subsistencia en un medio ambiente impredecible e inestable."

1472 Camino, Lupe. Los que vencieron al tiempo: Simbilá, Costa Norte, perfil etnográfico de un centro alfarero. Fotos interiores, Saia Bacal. Dibujos, Lupe Camino. Arte Final, Carmen Fragela. Piaura, Perú: Centro de Investigación y Promoción del Campesino, 1982. 139 p., 3 p. of plates: ill.

An "ethnography of work" of traditional potters in the coastal community of Simbilá. Useful for the description of technical and design aspects of Simbilá ceramics, author gives, in a disjointed presentation, a romanticized and superficial view of community life.

1473 Chirapo Cantuta, Escolástico. Origen y cambios en la producción y consumo en la nacionalidad aymara: los yanaques. Puno, Perú: Instituto de Investigaciones para el Desarrollo Social del Altiplano, 1982. 52 p., 16 leaves of plates: ill. (Serie Teoría y metodología; 2)

Description of the Aymara community of Yanaque in Puno, written by one of its residents. While not an analytic study, it is a valuable document in its own right designed to "difundir entre las nuevas generaciones los valores . . . de la etnia y nacionalidad aymara."

1474 Collins, Jane. The maintenance of peasant coffee production in a Peruvian valley (AES/AE, 11:3, Aug. 1984, p. 413–438)

Aymara subsistence farmers and herders in Huancané have migrated seasonally for decades to lowland valleys to supplement household income through coffee cultivation. Government policies, especially pricing practices and mandatory cooperative membership, lead to a continuing reliance on highland subsistence farming and to destructive cultivation practices in the lowlands. Important article.

1475 Deústua, José. Sobre movimientos campesinos e historia regional en el Perú moderno: un comentario bibliográfico (Revista Andina [Centro Bartolomé de las Casas, Cusco, Perú] 1:1, 1983, p. 219–240)

"Subjective" review article on recent work by historians and anthropologists on peasant movements in Perú. Useful, though rather idiosyncratic in approach.

1477 Escobar, Gabriel. Análisis preliminar del parentesco y la familia de clase media de la ciudad de Cuzco (in Parentesco y matrimonio en los Andes [see item **1406**] p. 681–691)

Focusing on the large kindreds found among the urban middle class of Cusco, Escobar describes the extended family, the developmental cycle of the household, marriage ties, and ritual kinship. Impressionistic but informative article.

1478 Figueroa, Adolfo. Production and market exchange in peasant economies: the case of southern highlands in Peru (in Ecology and exchange in the Andes [see item **1400**] p. 123–156, tables)

Data on the subsistence economies of eight peasant communities in southern Peru demonstrate integration of even the most isolated settlements into the national economy. While seemingly confusing household and community levels, Figueroa employs innovative analysis and survey techniques to argue a trend away from household production towards wage labor and internal migration.

1479 Fioravanti-Molinié, Antoinette. Multilevelled Andean society and market exchange: the case of Yucay, Peru (in Ecology and exchange in the Andes [see item **1400**] p. 211–230)

Author aplies Murra's model of verticality to the case of Yucay, paying special attention to land tenure. She examines the various levels of settlement and the links— social, economic, and symbolic—among them. Good descriptive article.

1480 Flores Ochoa, Jorge A. Causas que originaron la actual distribución espacial de la alpacas y llamas (in El Hombre y su ambiente en los Andes centrales [see item **1486**] p. 62–92)

Although documentation is sparse, Flores argues convincingly that the prehispanic territorial distribution of Andean camelids was much greater than it was early in this century. In recent years, the herds have suffered even greater destruction. The replacement of llamas and alpacas with European animals reflects "la marginalidad a la que se ha sometido a las poblaciones andinas que los pastorean." For ethnohistorian's comment, see *HLAS 46:1635.*

1481 —— and **Yemira D. Nájar Vizcarra.** Un aspecto del parentesco de los pastores de la puna alta (in Parentesco y matrimonio en los Andes [see item **1406**] p. 481–492)

Among Canchis pastoralists, the kin term *qusay* ("husband") is applied to a wide range of relationships when requests are made. Authors argue that this inversion of statuses serves to mobilize labor by including others within the metaphor of mutual assistance exhibited by husband and wife. Interesting tidbit.

1482 Fonseca M., César. El control comunal del agua en la cuenca del Río Cañete (IPA/A, 19:22, 1983, p. 61–73)

Fonseca surveys irrigation systems and canal maintenance societies in the Cañete Basin. In this zone of elaborate prehispanic terracing, Fonseca finds strong organizational and technical continuities. Useful description on a scarcely researched topic.

1482a Fuenzalida, Fernando *et al.* El Desafío de Huayopampa: comuneros y empresarios. 2a ed., rev. y aum. Lima: Instituto de

Estudios Peruanos, 1982. 449 p.: bibl., ill. (Estudios etnológicos en el Valle de Chancay; 6)

Augmented second ed. of important study first published 1968 (see *HLAS 35:1401*) when Huayopampa, near Lima, was fully involved in the market while retaining communal forms of organization. Fifteen years later, market production, technological innovation, and social stratification have all increased, but communal organization is still strong.

1483 Fujii, Tatsuhiko and Hiroyasu Tomoeda. Chacra, laime y auquénidos: explotación ambiental de una comunidad andina (*in* Estudios etnográficos del Perú meridional [see item **1402**] p. 33–63)

Descriptive ethnographic sketch of Caraybamba, Apurímac, a village which maintains an elaborate system of terraces and control of a range of ecological floors. Interestingly, the Caraybambinos hold some terraces in common for the benefit of festival sponsors; the authors also assert that the high unirrigated potato fields are communally held.

1484 García, José María. Con las comunidades andinas del Ausangate. Lima: Centro de Proyección Cristiana, 1983. 120 p.

Personal diary of a Jesuit priest, serving in rural communities in southern Peru, reflects some five years of experience with Quechua-speaking peasants. Though not an analytical work, this is a fascinating journal of discovery and a growing understanding of Andean life.

1485 Golte, Juergen and Marisol de la Cadena. La codeterminación de la organización social andina (IPA/A, 19:22, 1983, p. 7–34)

Spheres of exchange and circuits of reproduction between ecological levels in Tantaqocha vary with the altitudinal levels of the settlements. Authors examine the typical conversions between labor and product in the zone.

1486 El Hombre y su ambiente en los Andes centrales: ponencias presentadas en el Cuarto Simposio Internacional, Museo Nacional de Etnología, Osaka, diciembre 1980. Editado por Luis Millones y Hiroyasu Tomoeda. Suita, Japan: National Museum of Ethnology, 1982. 307 p., 1 folded leaf of

plates: bibl., ill., maps (Senri ethnological studies, no. 10)

Collection of articles by ethnologists, archaeologists, and ethnohistorians focusing on the applicability of Murra's concept of "vertical control" to the Central Andes. Ethnological articles are annotated separately (see items **1471, 1480, 1494, 1510,** and **1515**). Important contribution to the ongoing debate about Andean cultural ecology.

Hudelson, John E. The lowland Quichua as "tribe." See item **1266**.

1487 Inamura, Tetsuya. Adaptación ambiental de los pastores altoandinos en el sur del Perú (*in* Estudios etnográficos del Perú meridional [see item **1402**] p. 65–84)

Pastoralists in the puna of the district of Puica, Arequipa, herd their alpacas, llamas, and sheep between 4000 and 5000 m above sea level. Inamura describes well their herding practices, their economic and marriage exchanges with lowlanders, and their ritual and festive life. Author argues that they have established a long-term "stable symbiosis" with agriculturalists.

1488 Kleymeyer, Charles D. Poder y dependencia entre quechuas y criollos: dominación y defensa en la sierra sur del Perú. Lima: Centro de Investigaciones Socioeconómicas, Depto. de Ciencias Humanas, Univ. Nacional Agraria, 1982. 307 p.: bibl. (Col. Kuntur)

In an unrevised translation of his 1972 doctoral thesis, Kleymeyer examines the ironic mutual self-definitions of dominating urban-oriented "criollos" and dominated Quechua peasants. Weak on history and silent on recent work in ethnicity, it is nevertheless a valuable outline of rural society, stressing continuities in ethnic power relations even after the Velasco Alvarado revolution.

1489 Lobo, Susan B. Tengo casa propia. Lima: Instituto de Estudios Peruanos, 1984. 285 p.: bibl., ill., map.

Spanish version of Lobo's well received study of urbanization in Lima, *A house of my own.* Lobo looks at two cases, a government-sponsored neighborhood and a self-initiated barriada, over a period of 10 years. Important work and a very nice ed.

1490 Lozano Alvarado, Saniel E. Ande e indigenismo: identidad y conflicto. Prólogo, Antonio Cornejo Polar. Cajamarca, Perú: Univ. Nacional de Cajamarca, Dirección de Investigación y Proyección Social, 1982. 135 p.: bibl. (El Indigenismo en el Perú; 1)

Claiming to be a commentary on the *indigenista* movement in Peru, this essay is a curious blend of social science citations, unsupported assumptions, and fragments of romantic poetry and literature about rural Andean peoples. It is discouraging to see that the same old stereotypes of *indios*, *cholos*, and *mestizos* can still find their way into print.

1491 Malengreau, Jacques. Parientes, compadres, y comuneros en Cusipata, Perú (*in* Parentesco y matrimonio en los Andes [see item **1406**] p. 493–536)

Stimulating examination of social relations in a Quechua-speaking peasant community. Stressing the importance of a nuclear family's corporate obligations, Malengreau contrasts well the egalitarian ties among compadres and affines with the hierarchic links between comunarios and their mestizo padrinos.

1492 Martínez, Héctor. Migraciones internas en el Perú: aproximación crítica y bibliografía. Lima: Instituto de Estudios Peruanos, 1980. 193 p.: bibl.

After an introductory essay summarizing the results of his research, Martínez offers an annotated bibliography of nearly 700 entries on population movements from rural areas to the cities, from the mountains to the coast and to the eastern lowlands, and to mining centers. Invaluable reference.

1493 Masuda, Shozo. Cochayuyo, macha, camarón e higos charqueados (*in* Estudios etnográficos del Perú meridional [see item **1402**] p. 173–192)

Cochayuyo, a marine algae that is a prized addition to the diet of highlanders in southern Peru, is only one product of the sea that motivates rural Andean folk to move continually between the sierra and the coast. Masuda argues that ocean resources have been ignored in recent ethnographic studies of the vertical economy.

1494 ———. Dinamismo inter-regional en los Andes centrales (*in* El Hombre y su ambiente en los Andes centrales [see item **1486**] p. 93–106)

Inter-regional trade exists today between all ecological zones and even increases as the money economy and the market penetrate more deeply into rural areas. Masuda argues that beyond such monetary exchanges there are also modern manifestations of very ancient patterns. Little that is new here.

1495 Mayer, Enrique. On social anthropology in Peru (UC/CA, 24:4, Aug./Oct. 1983, p. 526)

Mayer argues that Osterling and Martínez (see item **1502**) overly emphasized sociocultural anthropology as an academic discipline, slighting both the importance of archaeology and the role of the field in policy-making. Valuable clarification.

1496 ———. Repensando "Más Allá de la Familia Nuclear" (*in* Parentesco y matrimonio en los Andes [see item **1406**] p. 427–462)

Revision of earlier article (see *HLAS 41:1309*). Mayer describes forms of the kindred, of reciprocal labor exchange, and of behavior among in-laws to show how nuclear family-centered networks are mobilized and maintained in a peasant village in northern Peru. Valuable contribution to kinship studies.

1497 Onuki, Yoshio. Aprovechamiento del medio ambiente en la vertiente occidental de los Andes en la región meridional del Perú (*in* Estudios etnográficos del Perú meridional [see item **1402**] p. 1–32)

Adopting rather pedantically Pulgar Vidal's six life zones, Onuki surveys a number of areas in the western slopes and valleys of the southern Peruvian Andes for human use of ecological resources at different altitudinal levels. In each zone, an active vertical economy is found. Very descriptive and impressionistic.

1498 Orlove, Benjamin S. *Tomar la bandera*: politics and punch in southern Peru (SEM/E, 47:3/4, 1982, p. 249–261, bibl.)

In Sicuani, Puno, a ritual whereby people "drink the flag" is celebrated using colored fruit punches made from specific products which are economically significant to the region. Orlove argues that, in addition to the wide range of meanings the Peruvian flag normally carries, this rite emphasizes Sicuani's role as a node in interregional trade. Imaginative analysis.

1499 Ortiz, Alejandro. Moya: espacio, tiempo y sexo en un pueblo andino (IPA/A, 17:20, 1982, p. 189–208)

Ortiz examines the semantics of place names and organizational terms in the town of Moya, relating myth and lexicon to the asymmetric relations among the three ayllus. A ritual calendar and an analysis of the Moyas' "sexualized vision of the world" conclude this somewhat disjointed discussion.

1500 Ossio A., Juan M. Cultural continuity, structure, and context: some peculiarities of the Andean compadrazgo (in Kinship, ideology and practice in Latin America. Edited by Raymond T. Smith. Chapel Hill: Univ. of North Carolina Press, 1984, p. 118–146, bibl., graph, table)

Compadrazgo in Andamarca is seen to link both individuals and kindreds, in the former case through asymmetric exchange while in the latter symmetrically. Ossio argues that compadrazgo reinforces the affinal ties established between kindreds, and, with a possible prehispanic antecedent, is an Andean reformulation of a foreign institution.

1501 ———. La propiedad en las comunidades andinas (IPA/A, 19:22, 1983, p. 35–60)

Reviewing concepts of property in Andean communities, Ossio argues that property rights, which take a wide range of forms, are never absolute but are always defined by the social group. Useful summary article.

1502 Osterling, Jorge P. and Héctor Martínez. Notes for a history of Peruvian social anthropology, 1940–1980 (UC/CA, 24:3, June 1983, p. 343–360, bibl.)

Authors provide descriptive account of the professionalization of anthropology in Peru, focusing on institutional developments—projects, university departments, and research institutes. Accompanied by several comments by others and a lengthy reply, the article is a useful, if unanalytical, chronology of the development of sociocultural anthropology in Peru.

1503 Oyakawa, Ofelia. Pastores y alpacas de altas punas: hablan los pastores alpaqueros de Puno, informe preliminar. Lima: ILLA, 1983? 196 p.: bibl.

Preliminary report on alpaca herding and wool marketing in Puno, stressing the shortage of suitable pasturelands, the poor commercial possibilities, and the inadequate technical inputs available to the 400,000 people who rely on alpaca herds for their livelihood. Includes recommendations to improve the situation.

1503a Posern-Zielínski, Aleksander. Inkarrí: szkice etnologiczne o Peru (The land of Incarrí: ethnological essays on Peru). Wrocław, Poland: Zakład Narodowy im. Ossolińskich, 1985. 304 p.: bibl., map.

Personal account by ethnologist of 1978 Polish Scientific Expedition to the Andes on the life of the Huaura Valley highlanders. [K. Complak]

1504 Proyecto piel de alpaca: convenio NUFFIC-UNTA. Instituto de Investigaciones para el Desarrollo Social del Altiplano. Puno, Perú: Univ. Nacional Técnica del Altiplano, Dirección Universitaria de Investigación, 1982. 73 p.: bibl., ill. (Publicación; 1)

Five research reports relating to the alpaca, three of which describe pastoralism and wool marketing in a rural community in Puno. Useful only to specialists.

1505 Quispe, Ulpiano. La *chupa*: rito ganadero andino (Revista Andina [Centro Bartolomé de las Casas, Cusco, Perú] 2:2, 1984, p. 607–628)

In Huancasancos, the sheep-herding *cofradía* mark the flocks in an elaborate annual ceremony in which the tails are offered to the gods of the mountain peaks. Very detailed description but an unconvincing analysis.

1506 Sallnow, M.J. A trinity of Christs: cultic processes in Andean Catholicism (AES/AE, 9:4, Nov. 1982, p. 730–749, bibl., map, table)

By examining three Christ shrines in rural Cuzco, Sallnow analyzes the political and ethnic concomitants of the syncretism and symbolic manipulation that result from the successive impositions on Andean peasants of "official" state-supported religions. Important contribution.

1507 Sánchez, Rodrigo. The Andean economic system and capitalism (in Ecology and exchange in the Andes [see item **1400**] p. 157–190, map, tables)

Attempting to reveal the penetration of capitalist relations into rural communities, Sánchez argues that the cultural mechanism of Andean reciprocity is, at base, merely a disguise for exploitative relations. While households are clearly involved in the sale of labor and products, the author apparently believes that this fragmented, impoverished area is representative of all Andean communities.

1508 Sato, Nobuyuki. El concepto de ayllu, y *qata/q'achun*: un estudio de la familia, el parentesco y el ayllu (*in* Estudios etnográficos del Perú meridional [see item **1402**] p. 139–171)

Marcapata, the rural economy of which was described in items **1515** and **1516**, is subdivided into four "communities" which rotate in political and ritual roles. Sato describes consanguineal and affinal kin terms, documents a high rate of marital endogamy, and concludes with a discussion of the ayllu concept. Well researched.

1509 Stein, William W. Familia y desarrollo educacional en Vicos, Perú (*in* Parentesco y matrimonio en los Andes [see item **1406**] p. 657–680)

Stein examines the impact of broad processes of social change on the ex-hacienda of Vicos, especially on the redefinition of gender roles and the impact of schooling. The dilemma of peasant faith in education vs. the exploitative nature of the schools and the contradictory new definitions of self that accompany secondary education is a major issue.

1510 Tomoeda, Hiroyasu. Folklore andino y mitología amazónica: las plantas cultivadas y la muerte en el pensamiento andino (*in* El Hombre y su ambiente en los Andes centrales [see item **1486**] p. 275–306)

Tomoeda compares Andean *atuq Antonio* and *chiwaku mentiroso* stories, a children's game, and the festival "tree-cutting" of northern Peru with certain myths and rites recorded in the Upper Amazon. Underlying them all is the common theme of "disjunction and dispersion;" in the Amazon, death is related to the cultural products of agriculture. Imaginative, if not wholly convincing, analysis.

1511 Urrutia, Jaime. De las rutas, ferias, y circuitos en Huamanga (IPA/A, 18:21, 1983, p. 47–64)

Very descriptive article detailing the routes used until recent years by drovers leaving Huamanga. Article becomes something of a laundry list of directions and places with little historical context and no analysis.

1512 Urton, Gary. Chuta: el espacio de la práctica social en Pacariqtambo, Perú (Revista Andina [Centro Bartolomé de las Casas, Cusco, Perú] 2:1, 1984, p. 7–56)

After examining Inkan conceptions of space in the *ceque* system and in the idea of *suyu*, Urton analyzes the concept of *chuta*, a contemporary measure of space in Pacariqtambo. The division and sharing of space in ritual contexts—and the debates that surround such sharing—reveal, according to Urton, important sociopolitical principles of the past and present. Interesting article.

1513 Valderrama F., Ricardo and **Carmen Escalante.** Arrieros, traperos, y llameros en Huancavelica (IPA/A, 18:21, 1983, p. 65–88, maps)

Drovers from the mining center of Huancavelica were organized through elaborate mechanisms of credit and exchange and were drawn from all social classes depending on the products they traded. Authors provide a meticulously—even an overly—detailed description of routes followed and products traded during the first half of this century.

1514 Wilson, Fiona. Marriage, property, and the position of women in the Peruvian Central Andes (*in* Kinship, ideology and practice in Latin America. Edited by Raymond T. Smith. Chapel Hill: Univ. of North Carolina, 1984, p. 297–325, bibl.)

Archival documents show that women in 19th-century Tarma inherited property but were strictly controlled in their use of it by fathers, brothers, and husbands in order to ensure the "purity" and status of the family and to bear and socialize the next generation. Interesting contribution to the study of local elites. For sociologist's comment, see item **8298.**

1515 Yamamoto, Norio. A food production system in the southern Central Andes (*in* El Hombre y su ambiente en los Andes centrales [see item **1486**] p. 39–62)

Through an examination of peasant use of the full range of ecological floors in Marcapata, Cuzco, Yamamoto meticulously presents a household-level production system which, he argues, is self-sufficient and does not rely on reciprocity and redistribution. Yamamoto proposes that such agropastoral systems are ancients adaptations among those groups occupying the slopes, but not the high plateaux, of the Andes.

1516 ———. Investigación preliminar sobre las actividades agropastoriles en el Distrito de Marcapata, Departamento del Cusco, Perú (in Estudios etnográficos del Perú meridional [see item 1402] p. 85–138)

First descriptive sketch of the vertical ecology of Marcapata, to which the author returns in item 1515. Carefully detailing agropastoral practices, Yamamoto provides good information on the altitudinal ranges of some 35 crops and a useful agricultural calendar. The treatment may well be, however, overly meticulous for all but the die-hard ecologists.

ANTHROLINGUISTICS

LYLE CAMPBELL, Associate Professor of Anthropology, Latin American Studies, and Linguistics, State University of New York Albany
ERNESTO C. MIGLIAZZA, Consultant in Anthrolinguistics, Washington, D.C.

MEXICAN AND CENTRAL AMERICAN INDIAN LANGUAGES

THE THEME COMMANDING THE MOST attention in the last biennium has been bilingualism and Indian education. While interest in this phenomenon encompasses all of Latin America, the greatest attention has been devoted to bilingual education in Mexico as exemplified by the works of Aguirre Beltrán et al. (item 1518), Donnadieu and Calvo (item 1527), Hamel and Muñoz Cruz (item 1530), Hernández Hernández (item 1537), Mayer (item 1552), Muñoz Cruz et al. (item 1533), Nahmad Sittón (item 1558), Rendón (item 1566), Ros Romero (item 1569), and Valiñas (item 1576).

Likewise, the number of works devoted to Mayan hieroglyphic writing attests to the recent growth of glyphic studies and the excitement they are generating (see items 1525, 1531, 1560, 1563, 1564, 1580, and 1670). Moreover, glyphic research has become truly international in scope as is evident in the contributions of scholars from France, Germany, Mexico, the Soviet Union, and the US.

Proof that linguistic study of native literatures has received more attention in recent years can be found in studies by the following authors: Anderson (item 1519), Benfeldt Rojas (item 1522), Carmack and Morales Santos (item 1561), León Portilla (item 1545), Watanabe (item 1578), and Yershova (item 1580). As in the past, most of these deal with either Nahuatl or Mayan examples.

Research in the various language families continues and has been most prolific in Chibchan languages (items 1520, 1529, 1534, and 1546). A welcome upsurge of interest in the study of Otomanguean languages should also be noted (items 1524, 1540, 1541, 1555, 1556, 1559, 1566, 1572, 1574, and 1581). In spite of the difficult political situation in Guatemala, numerous studies of the Mayan languages have appeared (items 1532, 1535, 1538, 1542, 1551, 1560, 1564, 1565, 1567, 1568, 1572, 1577, and 1578). Studies of Uto-Aztecan are represented by Langacker (item 1573), Lindenfeld (item 1547), and Willet (item 1579), and by several works on Nahuatl (items 1519, 1521, 1536–1539, 1543, 1544, 1549, etc.). [LC]

SOUTH AMERICAN INDIAN LANGUAGES

During the last two years there has been a proliferation of native texts, narratives and myths. Unfortunately many (not annotated in this section) are either in Spanish or Portuguese and thus of little interest to the linguist. The following recent publications constitute basic linguistic reference works: *Setenta mitos shuar* (item 1627); texts in Kamentza preceded by a short phonology (item 1615); Urioste's oral tradition of Waru Chiri in two volumes (item 1605). A few examples of folkloric interest include Wilbert and Simoneau's 111 narratives of the Bororo in English (item 1600); the traditional stories of the Catio in Spanish (item 1638); and four Huitoto myths in Spanish (item 1636).

Published descriptive works have decreased in comparison to previous years. Good examples of such recent studies are: Klumpp and Burquest on relative clauses in Piapoco (item 1608); a collection of excellent papers compiled by Cerrón-Palomino including descriptive papers by Adelaar, Cole, Weber, Landerman (item 1586); five good descriptive papers on Peruvian Amazonian languages edited by Wise and Boonstra (item 1594); descriptive studies of Aymara and Guarani in the collection edited by Pottier (item 1583). Other studies can be found in articles that examine the following languages: Chorote (item 1602); Yanomami (item 1612); and Quechua (item 1598). Two publications deal with discourse analysis of Ese-Ejja (item 1628), Andoke and Muinane (item 1599) and include texts. Pedagogical grammars have been published for Guarani (item 1609); Quechua of Ancash Huaylas (item 1595); Quichua (item 1606); and Nambikuara (item 1610).

Vocabularies of different lengths, some with grammatical notes include: Vaquero's 16th-century word list of five languages of Venezuela (item 1637); Mosonyi's review of unpublished vocabularies and grammars (item 1617); Adelaar's lexicon of Quechua spoke in Pacaraos (item 1582); Tosanto's word lists in Panare (item 1635); Charette's vocabulary of Warao of Guyana (item 1629); Beyersdorff's lexicon of Quechua agricultural and farming terms (item 1588); Cuesta's vocabulary of Aguaruna (item 1613); Dooley's vocabulary of Mbua Guarani (item 1596); Pérez's vocabulary of Guaiquer (item 1621); and finally, instructions on how to compile a vocabulary in indigenous languages (item 1619).

Their need notwithstanding, historical comparative studies are still lacking, with one notable exception: Büttner's comparison of Central Andean languages (item 1591). Additional publications are a short dialect comparison of varieties of Asurini (item 1618), a diglossia of two varieties of Hindi spoken in Guyana (item 1601), and Borja's etymology of a few Quechua lexical items (item 1611).

Numerous and excellent publications in sociolinguistics have appeared on language variation, multilingualism and bilingual education as well as language acquisition. Notable are the articles compiled by Cerrón-Palomino (item 1586) and Pottier (item 1583); Mosonyi's list of greetings in Carina, Guajiro, and Guahibo (item 1616); Vogt's and Fry's study of Cafundo Creole (item 1640); Carpenter's sociological variations of Quechua dialects (item 1592); Taylor's report on the Quechua spoken in the Lima area (item 1634); Corbera's edited compilation of six articles on languages of the Peruvian Amazon (item 1597); Robertson's Dutch lexical loans in Amerindian languages (item 1626); Cerrón-Palomino's study of multilingualism and language planning in South America (item 1593); Armatto de Velti's examination of influence of Spanish on Toba and vice-versa (item 1585); Larson's and Davis's work on bilingual education (item 1589); papers from a symposium on linguistic barriers to science (item **1630**); and Plaza's and Carvajal's study of consonant and vowel acquisition among children of La Paz (item **1622**).

The status of South America's many indigenous languages, conjectural for long, is being addressed and established at long last. Credible and current studies of the state of particular languages, including history, sociolinguistics and genetic relationships in specific areas of South America, have appeared in *América Indígena*. Good examples are: Stark's work on languages spoken in Ecuador (item **1633**); Wise's on languages of Peruvian Amazon (item **1641**); Kensinger's on Panoan languages (item **1607**); Sorensen on languages of Vaupes region (item **1632**); Migliazza's on 33 languages between the Amazon and Orinoco basins (item **1614**); Key's on languages of the Bolivian lowlands (item **1625**); and finally, a good overview of Colombian languages provided by Roselli (item **1620**).

Difficult to distinguish from sociolinguistics, ethnolinguistic studies are also gaining momentum in South America, as is clear from excellent studies such as Sorensen's examination of marriage in a linguistically based exogamy (item **1631**); Gifford's work on the ecological effect on speech (item **1604**); Brown's on the role of words in magical hunting songs (item **1590**); Sifonte's on the application of ethnoscience to Pemon oral literature (item **1587**); Verswijver's on the ethnography of name-giving in Kayapo (item **1639**). [EM]

OBITUARIES

We regret to report the death of a colleague and one of the best Latin American linguists, Jorge Suárez of the Univ. Nacional Autónoma de México, who died in Mexico on February 24, 1985. His extensive scholarly work included South American as well as Mesoamerican languages. Most notable is his recent publication: *The Mesoamerican Indian languages* (see item **1575**), a survey of all the languages of Central America and Mexico.

MEXICAN AND CENTRAL AMERICAN INDIAN LANGUAGES

1517 Aguirre Beltrán, Gonzalo. Franz Boas: la antropología profesional y la lingüística antropológica de México (UNAM/AA, 19, 1982, p. 9–31)

Boas's role is discussed through a description of his background, life, work in Mexico, and contributions to anthropology and linguistics.

1518 ———. Lenguas vernáculas: su uso y desuso en la enseñanza: la experiencia de México. México: Centro de Investigaciones y Estudios Superiores en Antropología Social, 1982. 3 v. (685 p.) (Cuadernos de la Casa Chata; 66–68)

Extensive and penetrating description and analysis of history and current status of language policy in Mexico with respect to the use of native languages in education. Three vols. cover not only use and disuse of vernacular languages in teaching, but provide extensive history of individuals and currents in linguistics and anthropology as practiced in Mexico.

1519 Anderson, Arthur J.O. Aztec hymns of life and love (UCSD/NS, 8, 1982, p. 1–74, ill.)

Translations of Nahuatl hymns of Sahagún's *Primeros memoriales* (Book II of the *Florentine Codex*), with extensive commentary and clarification of translations, together with much general information about their ethnographic content, meter, and secular and religious functions.

1520 Arosemena, Melquíades A. and **Frances C. de Arosemena.** Estudios sobre el discurso en guaymí. Panamá: Instituto Nacional de Cultura, Dirección del Patrimonio Histórico: Instituto Lingüístico de Verano, Panamá, 1980. 82 p.: bibl. (Lenguas de Panamá; 8)

Melquíades and Frances Arosemena present three studies of Guaymí narrative in the model of discourse analysis often employed by members of the Summer Institute of Linguistics: 1) text linguistics applied to Guaymí narrative; 2) analytical observations on a Guaymí text; and 3) the participants in a Guaymí narrative. Guaymí texts with Spanish translations include "the fisherman and the boa," "the proud fisherman," and "the sea monster."

1521 Barbosa Cano, Manlio. Atlas lingüístico del Estado de Puebla. México: SEP, INAH, Delegación Puebla, 1980. 103 p.: bibl. (Col. científica; 88. Antropología social)

Covers Indian languages of the state of Puebla, based on 1970 census. Discusses methodology and census limitations, historical panorama from mid 16th-century to present of Indian languages and their speakers. Two chapters describe distribution of languages in 1970; analyzes arrival of Indians from other Mexican states together with social consequences. Last chapters treats demographic traits of Indian immigrants. Appendix, published under separate cover, contains 22 large maps of approximately 42 x 60 cm. showing number and percentage of Indian language speakers in various municipalities.

1522 Bendfeldt Rojas, Lourdes. El *Popol Vuh*: por el mundo de su bibliografía (Cultura de Guatemala [Univ. Rafael Landívar, Guatemala] 1:3, nov./dic. 1980, p. 45–128, bibl.)

Extensive and valuable bibl. of 622 references of the *Popol Vuh*, the single most important book of Mayan literature. Covers complete translations, fragments, commentaries, lesser references, investigations, theses, and bibliographic commentaries.

1523 Bilingualism and language contact: Spanish, English, and native American languages. Edited by Florence Barkin, Elizabeth A. Brandt, and Jacob Ornstein-Galicia. New York: Teachers College, 1982. 320 p.: bibl., ill., index (Bilingual education series)

Papers for conference on borderland languages make up vol. intended as reference work on language contact, diversity, bilingualism, and need for socially grounded studies of linguistic phenomena. Divided into five sections: 1) "Perspectives;" 2) "Native American Languages in Contact;" 3) "Spanish in the Borderlands;" 4) Teaching and Learning;" and 5) "Language Maintenance, Language Shift, and Language Use."

1524 Bradley, C. Henry and J. Kathryn Josserand. El protomixteco y sus descendientes (UNAM/AA, 19, 1982, p. 279–343, charts)

Reconstructs Proto-Mixtec using data from 20 towns representing different varieties of Mixtec. Proposes Proto-Mixtec phonological system and rules to account for historical developments in the modern varieties. Includes cognate lists and proposed Proto-Mixtec forms for 45 items and 17 isogloss maps.

1525 Bricker, Victoria R. Directional glyphs in Maya inscriptions and codices (SAA/AA, 48:2, April 1983, p. 347–353, ill.)

Offers phonetic and semantic interpretation of Mayan directional glyphs in which the signs formerly thought to be *north* and *south* are identified as *zenith* and *nadir*, respectively, with *east* and *west* referring to the rising and setting sun. Supports suggestion that Mayan directional symbolism was related to the path of the sun across the sky and through the underworld.

1526 Bright, William. American Indian linguistics and literature. Berlin, FRG: Mouton, 1984. 159 p.

Papers, some published for the first time, center on language contact and oral literature. Divided into two parts: 1) American Indian linguistics (e.g., "The Classification of North American and Mesoamerican Indian Languages" which affirms Bright's adherence to the "Boasian position" and "Notes on Hispanisms," most important article to date on Spanish loans in Indian languages); and 2) studies of American Indian oral literature.

1527 Calvo, Beatriz; Laura Donnadieu; and María Elena Acosta. Un magisterio bilingüe y bicultural: el caso de la capacitación diferencial de los maestros indígenas del Estado de México. México: Centro de Investigaciones y Estudios Superiores en Antropología Social, 1983. 84 p.: bibl. (Cuadernos de la Casa Chata; 73)

Uses ethnographic research to analyze the process of formal training of Indian teachers in Mazahua area in the state of Mexico. Goal is to evaluate the difference between the intended formal and actual aspects of bilingual and bicultural teacher-training.

1528 Campbell, Lyle and David Oltrogge.
Proto-tol: Jicaque (IU/IJAL, 46:3, July
1980, p. 205–223, tables)
Reconstructs Proto-Tol, usually called
Jicaque, using material published in 1897 by
Membreño on now-extinct Jicaque of El
Palmar (called Western Jicaque) and authors'
own work on Eastern Jicaque (La Montaña
de la Flor). Analyzes Membreño's materials
philologically, presents Proto-Jicaque phonology together with changes in daughter
languages, and provides 241 lexical reconstructions with supporting cognates. Lists 27
loans into Jicaque from other Indian languages and notes potential cognates with preliminary sound correspondences between
Jicaque and Tequistlatec (Chontal of Oaxaca).

Campos, Julieta. La herencia obstinada: análisis de cuentos nahuas. See item **901.**

**1529 Clasificación de los idiomas indígenas
de Panamá con un vocabulario comparativo de los mismos.** Redactado por
Robert D. Gunn. Panamá: Instituto Nacional
de Cultura, Dirección del Patrimonio Histórico: Instituto Lingüístico de Verano, 1980.
49 p.: bibl., ill., tables (Lenguas de Panamá;
t. 7)
In two parts: 1) brief study by Michael
Kopesec of classification of Panama's native
languages, including family trees of Carib
and Chibchan families; and 2) comparative
vocabulary of 200 words in each language,
which should prove useful to Chibchan as
well as to Carib studies.

**1530 El Conflicto lingüístico en una zona
bilingüe de México.** Edición de Rainer
Enrique Hamel y Héctor Muñoz Cruz. México: Centro de Investigaciones y Estudios
Superiores en Antropología Social, 1982.
177 p.: ill. (Cuadernos de la Casa Chata; 65)
Eight papers are result of a sociolinguistics and pragmatics course at UNAM.
Central concern is the controversial relation
between language and bilingual education,
particularly in the Otomí area.

1531 Davoust, Michel. Etudes des glyphes
locatifs dans l'épigraphie maya (CEM/
ECM, 13, 1981, p. 165–185, bibl., ill.)
Study of locatives and emblem glyphs
seeks to find if locatives existed in Mayan
epigraphy. Concludes that only at Tikal and
Naranjo can a locative glyph substitute for an
emblem glyph; elsewhere they are always
preceded by the ruler's name glyph.

1532 England, Nora C. A grammar of Mam,
a Mayan language. Austin: Univ. of
Texas Press, 1983. 353 p.: ill. (Texas linguistics series)
Mam is perhaps the most complicated
of the Mayan languages, and England's grammar of it is excellent. Its broad coverage includes phonology, morphophonemics, roots
and words, stem formation, the noun phrase,
the verb phrase, sentence formation, complex
sentences, and a text with analysis and inter-
linear translation. It will prove a very useful
basic reference and will no doubt be much
cited both in Mayan studies and in general
linguistics.

1533 La Escuela otomí: entre la castella-
nización y el bilingüismo. v. 1, Materiales. Edición de Héctor Muñoz Cruz, Paula
Gómez López y Rainer Enrique Hamel. México: Centro de Investigaciones y Estudios
Superiores en Antropología Social, 1983. 1 v.:
bibl., ill. (Cuadernos de la Casa Chata; 78)
Vol. 1 of set on bilingual education in
Otomí schools in the Mezquital Valley. Includes transcriptions of classroom verbal
interaction that may prove useful to those interested in sociolinguistic or educational
aspects of verbal classroom interaction between teachers and students, as well as
distribution of Spanish and Otomí, their
function in the classroom, and glimpses of
acquisition of Spanish by Otomí children.
Linguists may find the Otomí portions of the
transcriptions interesting (presented with
Spanish translations).

1534 Estudios de lingüística chibcha. v. 1,
Estudios varios sobre las lenguas
chibchas de Costa Rica. v. 2, Estudios de lin-
güística chibcha. v. 3, Estudios de lingüística
chibcha. San José: Univ. de Costa Rica,
Depto. de Lingüística, Programa de Investiga-
ción, 1982–1984. 3 v. (91, 80, 197 p.): bibl.,
(Serie A)
Three vols. on Chibchan languages
represent a very significant advance. Vol. 1:
Adolfo Constenla U. "Algunos Aspectos de la
Etnografía del Habla de los Indios Guatusos;"
Enrique Margery P. "Descripción del Sistema
Fonológico de un Dialecto del Cabécar de
Ujarrás;" Thomas E. Payne "Subject in
Guaymí;" and Raymond A. Schlabach and
Stephen H. Levinsohn "Some Aspects of
the Bribri Verb." Vol. 2: Mafalda Bertoglia
Richards "Les Clasificadores Numerales
en los Dialectos Cabécares de Ujarrás y

Chirripo;" Adolfo Constenla Umaña "Desarrollo del Estudio Diacrónico de las Lenguas Chibchas, 1888–1980;" and Enrique Margery Peña "Sobre el Adjetivo Cabécar." Vol. 3: Enrique Margery P. "Etnoornitología del Cabécar de Ujarrás;" Adolfo Constenla U. "Los Fonemas del Muisca;" Margaret Dickerman D. "Split Ergativity and Subject in Bribri;" Arnulfo Prestán "Taxonomía Fonológica del Guatuso;" Víctor Sánachez C. "Análisis Fonológico del Guatuso;" and Jack L. Wilson "Relative Clauses in Bribri."

1535 Flores, J. Salvador and **Edilberto Ucan Ek.** Nombres usados por los mayas para designar a la vegetación. Xalapa, México: Instituto Nacional de Investigaciones sobre Recursos Bióticos, 1983. 30 p.: bibl., ill. (Cuadernos de divulgación; 10)

Pamphlet contains results of an ethnobotanical study of Yucatec Maya done in the Proyecto Flora Yucatanense del Instituto Nacional de Investigaciones sobre Recursos Bióticos. It provides the Yucatec Maya nomenclature of plants and their parts with several photos and illustrations.

1536 Gardner, Brant. A structural and semantic analysis of classical Nahuatl kinship terminology (UNAM/ECN, 15, 1982, p. 89–124, bibl.)

Paper's goal is to clarify the Nahuatl kinship system by applying linguistic methods. Examines terminology as a system using componential analysis and of terms in context employing methods from the ethnography of speaking.

1537 Hernández Hernández, Severo. Planteamientos básicos para una educación indígena bilingüe y bicultural en México (III/AI, 42:2, abril/junio 1982, p. 281–288)

Analyzes critically official policies with respect to Indian education in Mexico and urges acceptance of the proposals of the Alianza Nacional de Profesionales Indígenas Bilingües, Asociación Civil (Civil Association of the National Alliance of Bilingual Indian Professionals) for bilingual and bicultural Indian education, based on Indian culture and world view. In these proposals, "the pluricultural and plurilingual nature of the country would be recognized, as well as the inalienable right of ethnic groups to an education which respects cultural differences.

1538 Herrera, Guillermina. El fenómeno de ergatividad en la lengua mam (Cultura de Guatemala [Univ. Rafael Landívar, Guatemala] 2:1, enero/abril 1981, p. 23–40, bibl.)

Beginning with general description of ergativity and its traits in Mayan languages, Herrera analyzes ergativity in the Mam of Comitancillo. Shows that Mam deviates in some constructions from expected ergative patterns due to other syntactic causes.

1539 Hill, Jane H. and **Kenneth C. Hill.** Regularities in vocabulary replacement in modern Nahuatl (IU/IJAL, 47:3, July 1981, p. 215–226, tables)

Lexicostatistic 100-word lists were elicited from 75 speakers in 10 Nahuatl-speaking towns in Tlaxcala and Puebla. It was found that: 1) for items unremembered or replaced by hispanisms by some speakers, others will hesitate; 2) items which speakers miss, hispanize, or hesitate on are missing or hispanized in other Nahuatl dialects and other Mesoamerican languages for which 100-word lists are available; and 3) counter to proposals, individual different items of the lexicostatistic lists do not evidence different frequencies of replacement across languages.

1540 Jaeger, Jeri J. and **Robert D. Van Valin, Jr.** Initial consonant clusters in Yateé Zapotec (IU/IJAL, 48:2, April 1982, p. 125–138, bibl., tables)

Discusses Yateé Zapotec consonant clusters and the fortis/lenis contrast and uses Zapotec data to show that several proposed universals involving consonant clusters are inaccurate.

1541 Jamieson, Carole Ann. Conflated subsystems marking person and aspect in Chiquihuitlán Mazatec verbs (IU/IJAL, 48:2, April 1982, p. 139–167, bibl., tables)

Describes in detail, with phonological rules and many sample paradigms, Chiquihuitlán Mazatec (Otomanguean) personal verbs and the system that marks person and aspect.

1542 *Journal of Mayan Linguistics.* Louisiana State Univ., Dept. of Geography and Anthropology. Vol. 4, No. 2, 1984– . Baton Rouge.

Issue contains three articles: 1) Susan M. Knowles "Chontal Mayan Positionals;" Charles A. Hofling "On Proto-Yucatecan Word Order;" and M. Jill Brody "Cleft in

Tojolabal Maya: Structure and Discourse Function.

Karttunen, Frances. Nahuatl literacy. See *HLAS 46:1545.*

1543 Lastra de Suárez, Yolanda. El náhuatl de Tetzcoco en la actualidad. México: UNAM, 1980. 177 p.: bibl. (Serie antropológica; 22. Lingüística)

Goal of this modern treatment of the Nahuatl of San Jerónimo Amanalco, Tetzcoco, is to compare it with the first description of Nahuatl, by Olmos in 1547, partly based on same Tetzcoco area. The language has changed only slightly. The grammar follows Olmos' order of presentation to facilitate comparison (34 p.) Provides 13 short texts with translations. Includes valuable, substantial word list (p. 118–174) with frequent comparison to classical Nahuatl equivalents.

1544 León-Portilla, Miguel. Los nombres de lugar en náhuatl: su morfología, sintaxis y representación glífica (UNAM/ECN, 15, 1982, p. 37–72, bibl., ill.)

Nahuatl place names are situated in a broader framework of locatives in general; their morphology and derivational properties are described. Particular attention is given to locative suffixes. Body-part terms are found in the composition of many toponyms; the glyphic representations of these are analyzed and illustrated. For ethnohistorian's comment, see *HLAS 46:1551.*

1545 ———. Translating the Amerindian texts (UP/LAIL, 7:2, Fall 1983, p. 101–122)

Discusses translation broadly as it involves Indian languages. Considers lessons from three 16th-century examples (Sahagún with Nahuatl, Alcalá with Tarascan, and Molina with Quechua). Discusses translation principles and problems facing translators with respect to structural, semantic, and cultural differences.

1546 Leyendas y tradiciones Borucas. Narrated by Espíritu Santo Maroto. Grammatical introduction, commentary, notes, translation and setting of the text by Adolfo Constenla Umaña. San José: Editorial Univ. de Costa Rica, 1979. 164 p.: appendix, bibl., ill., maps, plates.

Handsome book in five pts.: 1) a very welcome sketch of Boruca (Chibchan) pho-

nology and grammar; 2) historical and cultural introduction to the themes of the Boruca texts; 3) texts with both literal and free translations; 4) very welcome Boruca vocabulary; and 5) appendix of texts in Spanish.

1547 Lindenfeld, Jacqueline. Langues en contact: le yaqui face a l'espagnol (La Linguistique [Presses universitaires de France, Paris] 18:1, 1982, p. 111–127, bibl.)

Documents Spanish influence on Yaqui (Uto-Aztecan) with examples from phonology, morphology, syntax (including coordination, relativization, nominalization, subordination, and comparison), and the lexicon. Shows that in any study of languages in contact, it is essential to take sociocultural facts into account along with linguistic facts themselves.

1548 Linguistics. Munro S. Edmonson, vol. editor. With the assistance of Patricia A. Andrews. Austin: Univ. of Texas Press, 1984. 146 p.: bibl. (Supplement to the *Handbook of Middle American Indians*; 2)

This vol. supplements vol. 5 of the *Handbook of Middle American Indians* with five grammatical sketches of different Middle American Indian languages: Searle Hoogshagen "Coatlán Mixe;" Yolanda Lastra de Suárez "Chichimeco Jonaz;" John Fought "Choltí Maya: a Sketch;" Paul Friedrich "Tarascan: from Meaning to Sound;" and Norman A. McQuown "A Sketch of San Luis Potosí Huastec." Each sketch is informative, though employing quite diverse organizations of material and linguistic orientations. Friedrich's Tarascan begins with meaning and works back to phonology. McQuown's Huastec is particularly useful in that it compares the modern language with the colonial material of Tapia Zenteno. Given their brevity, these sketches contain fewer linguistic examples than one would wish. None addresses the issues of concern to current formal theories, but they may be the more accessible for it.

1549 Macazaga Ordoño, César. Diccionario de zoología náhuatl. Introducción, iconografía, diccionario y vocabulario español-náhuatl, del autor. México: Editorial Innovación, 182. 169 p.: bibl., ill. (Col. Diccionarios monográficos de la cultura náhuatl)

Contains introduction (31 p.) which considers names and roles of animals in preconquest Nahuatl, a Nahuatl-Spanish zoological dictionary (158 p.), and a Spanish-to-Nahuatl list of animal parts and names (10 p.).

1550 Manrique Castañeda, Leonardo. Fray Andrés de Olmos: notas críticas sobre su obra lingüística (UNAM/ECN, 15, 1982, p. 27–35)

Describes and evaluates life and linguistic work of Andrés de Olmos (1490–1571), Franciscan missionary famous for his linguistic ability and known to have written extensively on several Mexican Indian languages. For ethnohistorian's comment, see *HLAS 46:1557*.

1551 Manuscrito de Chan Cah. Contains a photocopy of original ms. (in Historia) accompanied by transcription of Mayan text with parallel Spanish translation. México: Grupo Dzíbil: Compañía Editorial Impresora y Distribuidora, 1982. 128 p.: ill.

Reproduction and translation of early colonial Yucatec Maya document will prove very valuable for the study of the history of that language, and its contents will be very useful to anthropologists, historians, linguistics, and others. Photographed original is most valuable, since it preserved the integrity of the text with no loss of information that might be introduced had only the paleography been presented.

1552 Mayer, Enrique. Los alcances de una política de educación bicultural y bilingüe (III/AI, 42:2, abril/junio 1982, p. 269–280)

Mayer examines official educational policies and their destructive effects on Indian communities, explaining the limits of these projects and the prejudices they cause within Indian communities. He proposes an intercultural education which would respect the cultural traditions and ethnic identities of Indian groups.

1553 Mayers, Marvin. Dobletes y tripletes en el discurso de los mayas pocomchíes de Guatemala (Mesoamérica [Revista del Centro de Investigaciones Regionales de Mesoamérica, Antigua, Guatemala] 3:4, dic. 1982, p. 414–420)

Mayers proposes that Pokomchí (Mayan) world view is expressed in linguistic terms, where "dichotomy" and "trichotomy" are integral elements of this cognitive orientation and are reflected in Pokomchí dis-

course by doublets and triplets. Doublets are used to transmit primary information, with doublets and triplets for secondary formation, established by grammatical means. This has far-reaching implications for the nonverbal culture. Illustrated with samples of Pokomchí discourse and these literary devices.

1554 Miram, Helga-Maria. Numeral classifiers im Yukatekischen Maya. Hannover, FRG: Verlag für Ethnologie, 1983. 318 p.: bibl., plates, tables.

Through a combination of methods from ethnoscience and the "black-box" (input-output relations), Miram hits upon what she calls a "grey-box" method by which she presents a rather complete analysis and description of the Yucatec Maya system of numeral classifiers, richly illustrated with abundant photographs. The classifiers fall in three functional categories: qualifying, quantifying, and modifying.

1555 Mock, Carol C. Los casos morfosintácticos del chocho (UNAM/AA, 19, 1982, p. 345–378, bibl.)

Data on both "syntactic" and "morphological" cases in Chocho (Otomanguean) are presented showing it to be an "active" case language, arguing that in the typology of case the category active-inactive needs to be treated as independent from both ergative-absolutive and nominative-accusative types.

1556 ———. Tone sandhi in Isthmus Zapotec: an autosegmental account (Linguistic Analysis [Elsevier Science Publishing Co., New York] 12:2, 1983, p. 91–137)

Using autosegmental phonology, Mock shows how stress, pitch accents, and intonational boundaries fit together in Isthmus Zapotec (Otomanguean). She demonstrates how the process of tone sandhi arises from a four-way opposition among morpheme-level pitch accents. Phonemic tones are derived from underlying pitch accents via the rules: 1) lexical tone specification; 2) tone sandhi; and 3) tonal neutralization.

1557 Montoya Briones, José de Jesús and **María Cristina Morales V.** Un vocabulario náhuatl contemporáneo y algunos documentos antiguos sobre la Sierra de Hidalgo. México: Depto. de Etnología y Antropología Social, INAH, SEP, 1981. 39

leaves, 1 leaf of plates: maps (Cuadernos de trabajo; 28)

Contains three "working papers:" 1) modest Nahuatl vocabulary ordered by semantic domains from the Sierra de Hidalgo by José de Jesús Montoya; and 2–3) María Cristina Morales V. on historical documents from Tlanchinol, Calnali, and Lolotla (Hidalgo).

Musgrave-Portilla, L. Marie. The *nahualli* or transforming wizard in pre- and postconquest Mesoamerica. See item **962.**

1558 Nahmad Sittón, Salomón. La educación bilingüe y bicultural para las regiones interculturales de México (III/AI, 42:2, abril/junio 1982, p. 203–220)

Nahmad, Director of the Dept. of Indian Education in Mexico, surveys Mexican Indian policies and describes training of bilingual teachers and their role in educational programs. Evaluates achievements in literacy programs, teaching of Spanish, and elementary education.

1559 Nellis, Donald G. and Barbara E. Hollenbach. Fortis versus lenis in Cajonos Zapotec phonology (IU/IJAL, 46:2, April 1980, p. 92–105)

Describes nature of Cajonos Zapotec (Otomanguean) fortis and lenis consonants. Of particular interest is word-final devoicing (including sonorants) and the number of consonants pronounced as fricatives in at least some environments.

1560 Neuenswander, Helen. Vestiges of early Maya time concepts in a contemporary Maya community: implications for epigraphy (CEM/ECM, 13, 1981, p. 125–163, bibl., tables)

Describes Achi (Mayan) cognitive structure of time in detail together with certain hieroglyphic structures in support of the hypothesis that the Mayan layman has retained from earliest times a high level of proficiency in the art of telling time and that the unit upon which calculations are based is now (and then) the lunar cycle.

1561 Nuevas perspectivas sobre el *Popol Vuh.* Edición de Robert M. Carmack and Francisco Morales Santos. Guatemala: Editorial Piedra Santa, 1983. 428 p.

Vol. contains 29 papers (conference held Santa Cruz del Quiché, 1979) on the *Popol Vuh,* most famous book of Mayan

literature. Covers history, linguistics, symbolism, archaeology, ethnography, and papers by native Quiché speakers. Linguistic papers discuss loan words in the *Popol Vuh* by Lyle Campbell; modern and ancient Quiché literary styles by James Mondloch; grammatical parallelism in Quiché ritual language by William Norman; forms of Quiché verse by Dennis Tedlock; and the *Popol Vuh* compared with oral tradition of San Juan Chamula, Chiapas by Gary Gossen. These papers represent the best work on Mayan oral literature and style. Extremely important contribution.

1562 Parodi, Claudia. La investigación lingüística en México, 1970–1980. México, UNAM, 1981. 205 p.: bibl. (Cuadernos del Instituto de Investigaciones Filológicas)

Excellent resource for information on recent and on-going linguistic work in Mexico. Surveys and describes linguistic projects and institutions, and provides a detailed bibl. of work done by Mexicans or published by Mexican institutions (1970–80). Especially extensive on Indian languages and Hispanic linguistics.

1563 Perry, Steven S. The glyphic texts at Aguateca (CEM/ECM, 13, 1981, p. 187–190, bibl., ill.)

Describes glyphic texts of five stelae from Aguacateca, with particular attention to event glyphs ("verbs"). Includes reproductions of drawings of the stelae.

1564 Phoneticism in Mayan hieroglyphic writing. Edited by John S. Justeson and Lyle Campbell. Albany: SUNY, Institute for Mesoamerican Studies, 1984. 389 p.: appendices (Publication; 9)

Includes articles by field's most active scholars who employ linguistic methods and data in the decipherment of Mayan hieroglyphic writing: Lyle Campbell "The Implications of Mayan Historical Linguistics for Glyphic Research;" James Fox and John Justeson "Polyvalence in Mayan Hieroglyphic Writing;" Terrence Kaufman and William Norman "An Outline of Proto-Cholan Phonology, Morphology, and Vocabulary;" Floyd Lounsbury "Glyphic Substitutions: Homophonic and Synonymic;" Peter Mathews and John Justeson "Patterns of Sign Substitution in Mayan Hieroglyphic Writings: and 'Affix Cluster';" Barbara MacLeod "Cholan and Yucatec Verb Morphology and Glyphic Verbal

Affixes in the Inscriptions;" Berthold Riese "Hel Hieroglyphs;" Linda Schele "Some Suggested Readings of the Event and Office of Heir-Designate at Palenque;" and David Stuart "A Note on the 'Hand-Scattering' Glyph." Appendices contain very valuable basic reference material: Peter Mathews "A Maya Hieroglyphic Syllabary;" John Justeson "Interpretations of Mayan Hieroglyphs;" James Fox and John Justeson "Conventions for the Transliteration of Mayan Hieroglyphics;" and Lyle Campbell "Linguistic Orthographies." It is expected that this book will become major contribution to the field of Mayan writing.

1565 Pye, Clifton. Mayan telegraphese: intonational determinants of inflectional development in Quiché Mayan (LSA/L, 59:3, Sept. 1983, p. 583–604, bibl., tables)

Language acquisition data from Quiché (Mayan) suggest that considerable differences may exist across languages in the form of children's first words. Quiché verbs take a 'termination' which does not encode a simple semantic or syntactic meaning, but the children used it correctly in 86 percent of their first verbs. The syllable structure and stress rules promote the early acquisition of terminations, suggesting articulatory development interacts with intonation in morphological development.

1566 Rendón, Juan José. Alfabetización y estudios de afinidades entre variantes de la lengua zapoteca de la Sierra de Juárez, Oax. (UNAM/AA, 18, 1981, p. 239–278, bibl., tables)

Explores conditions necessary to develop a program to teach reading and writing and describes the one initiated in Yalalag in the Sierra de Juárez, Oaxaca. Examines great linguistic diversity among region's varieties of Zapotec and how they would affect developing such programs. Includes useful map, chart calculating divergence (with as much as 11 centuries separation), short word list from 19 dialects, and phonological correspondence chart.

1567 Robertson, John S. From symbol to icon: the evolution of the pronominal system from Common Mayan to Modern Yucatecan (LSA/L, 59:3, Sept. 1983, p. 529–540, bibl., tables)

Modern Yucatecan pronominal system is highly restructured from that of Common

Mayan, involving the regularization of the paradigm for formerly non-existent grammatical categories. Robertson's explanation involves Peircian symbols in 'logical fields.'

1568 ———. The history of the absolutive second-person pronoun from Common Mayan to Modern Tzotzil (IU/IJAL, 48:4, Oct. 1982, p. 436–443, bibl.)

Kuryłowicz's laws of analogy are used to explain the restructuring of the absolutive second-person pronoun from Common Mayan to Modern Tzotzil.

1569 Ros Romero, María del Consuelo. Bilingüismo y educación: un estudio en Michoacán. México: Instituto Nacional Indigenista, 1981. 259 p.: bibl., ill. (Col. INI; 63. Serie de antropología social; 63)

Attempt to understand functioning of formal education (in Tarascan school) and to see how it relates to informal education (in the family). Defines bilingualism and discusses issues in mother tongue instruction. Describes school's social context (ethnographic setting), linguistic situation and means of language acquisition (of both Spanish and Tarascan). Examines school's history and its language policy. Evaluates goals of literacy and Spanish instruction. When lack of materials, physical hardships, and apathetic attitudes converge, inefficiency prevails.

1570 Schele, Linda and Jeffrey H. Miller. The mirror, the rabbit, and the bundle: "accession" expressions from the Classic Maya inscriptions. Washington: Dumbarton Oaks, Trustees for Harvard Univ., 9183. 99 p.: bibl., ill. (Studies in pre-Columbian art & archaeology; 25)

Presents interpretations of Mayan glyphs related to "accession" based on linguistic and iconographic arguments. The glyph T617a is read as "mirror," *nen*, and is associated with rulers and priests. T757 was erroneously interpreted as "rabbit," *umul*, now known to depict a gopher, *bah*, having the phonetic value *ba*. Contributes considerably to phonetic readings and to historical content of Mayan glyphic texts. Offers excellent method for correlating variant iconographic representations with linguistic material from various Mayan languages. Actual linguistic arguments, however, are at times flawed, lacking rigor in the comparisons and changes suggested among Mayan languages.

1571 Sherzer, Joel. Kuna ways of speaking: an ethnographic perspective. Austin: Univ. of Texas Press, 1983. 1 v.: bibl. (Texas linguistics series)

Ethnography of speaking approach applied to Cuna (language of Panama). Describes relationship between language and culture and society. Different patterns of speech and styles in metaphor and chanted language are used for different social activities (e.g., politics, magic, rituals). Description of Cuna verbal art raises important questions and theoretical issues on role and nature and dimensions of language use. For ethnologist's comment, see item **986.** [E. Migliazza]

1572 Studies in Mesoamerican linguistics. Edited by Alice Schlichter, Wallace L. Chafe, and Leanne Hinton. Berkeley: Univ. of California, Linguistics Dept., 1983. 331 p.: bibl. (Reports from the survey of California and other Indian languages; 4)

Contains three articles on Mayan and three on Mixtec: 1) Jon P. Dayley "Voice and Ergativity in Mayan Languages;" 2) Tomas W. Larsen "Aguacatec Syntax from a Functional Perspective;" 3) Martha J. Macri "Maya Writing: Linguistic Evidence for Eastern Mayan Influence" (concludes there is none); 4) Claudia Brugman "The Use of Body-Part Terms as Locatives in Chalcatongo Mixtec;" 5) Martha J. Macri "Two Noun Class Systems in Mixtec;" and 6) Nicholas Faraclas "Preliminaries to Tonemic and Tonomechanical Analysis for the Chalcatongo Dialect of Mixtec."

1573 Studies in Uto-Aztecan grammar. v. 4, Southern Uto-Aztecan grammatical sketches. Edited by Ronald W. Langacker. Arlington, Texas: Summer Institute of Linguistics: Univ. of Texas at Arlington, 1984. 459 p.: bibl. (Publications in linguistics; 56)

Contains sketches of Tarahumara (by Don Burgess, p. 1–149) and Cora (by Eugene H. Casad, p. 151–459) following the organization of Langacker's overview of Uto-Aztecan (vol. 1 of series). These two grammatical descriptions provide relatively comprehensive basic information and are a significant contribution to the study of Uto-Aztecan and Mexican-Indian languages.

1574 Suárez, Jorge A. La lengua tlapaneca de Malinaltepec. México: UNAM, 1983. 641 p.: bibl. (Cuadernos del Instituto de Investigaciones Filológicas)

Rather comprehensive grammar, in the structuralist linguistic mold, of the Tlapanec language, now demonstrably of the Otomanguean family. Also contains ample Tlapanec-Spanish and Spanish-Tlapanec vocabulary. Very valuable basic reference on this little known language.

1575 ———. The Mesoamerican Indian languages. New York: Cambridge Univ. Press, 1983. 206 p.: bibl., ill., index, maps (Cambridge language surveys)

Aims to provide overview of Mesoamerican Indian languages. Begins with spotty history of linguistic study, followed by chapter on dialects and language classification. Quite traditional in its structuralist orientation to phonology, morphology, and syntax (two chapters each). Chapters on preconquest literature and prehistory of Mesoamerican languages are of questionable value, but final chapter on postconquest languages contains excellent material.

1576 Valiñas C., Leopoldo. Alfabeto o alfalfa-a-beto (UNAM/AA, 19, 1982, p. 267–278, bibl.)

Considers informally problems and advantages of official literacy and writing programs where many Mexican institutions seem to forget the relationship among alphabet, language, and culture, and between Spanish and Indian languages.

1577 Vogt, Evon Z. The genetic model revisited: on the origins and development of the Maya (UNAM/AA, 19, 1982, p. 73–98, bibl., graphs, tables)

After his first presentation of the "genetic model and Maya cultural development" 20 years ago, Vogt returns to clarify what was meant and to assess findings on the Mayan family. The method involves controlled comparisons in cultural, linguistic, geographic, and historical contexts, utilizing all branches of anthropology. Genetic units are defined by physical type, language, and systemic patterns (e.g., subsistence). Steps in the analysis include the distribution of related languages, glottochronological calculations of timedepths, location of the dispersal area (linguistic homeland), reconstruction of the proto language, archaeological correlations, physical anthropology, ethnohistory, and ethnographic data.

1578 Watanabe, John M. In the world of the sun: a cognitive model of Mayan cosmology (RAI/M, 18:4, Dec. 1983, p. 710–728, bibl., graph, map, tables)

Mam (Mayan) linguistic data are employed to construct a cognitive model of Mayan cosmology. Terms for directions, verb paradigms, and time periods show a conception of time and space in which directionality, motion, and time are linked to the movement of the sun. Comparison of this cognitive model with ethnographic and archaeological evidence suggests a similar structure underlies all Mayan cosmologies. For ethnologist's comment, see item **1002**.

1579 Willett, Elizabeth. Reduplication and accent in southeastern Tepehuan (IU/IJAL, 48:2, April 1982, p. 168–184, tables)

Contrary to previous thinking, shows that vowel length in southeastern Tepehuan (Uto-Aztecan) is underlying and that accent and reduplication patterns can be predicted by phonological rules.

1580 Yershova, Galina. Lírica maya de la antigüedad (URSS/AL, 7:67, julio 1983, p. 39–62, facsim., ill., plates)

Examines in detail *Cantares de los Mayas* (Maya songs), ancient Yucatec Maya document written in the Latin alphabet, discovered, translated, and published by Barrera Vázquez. Considers Maya poetics, proposes modifications in the translation, and shows relation between text and both Mayan wedding rituals and hieroglyphs on preconquest polychrome pots.

1581 Zúñiga, Rosa María. Toponimias zapotecas: desarrollo de una metodología. México: INAH, Depto. de Lingüística, 1982. 156 p.: bibl., maps (Col. científica; 117)

Work intends to develop a methodology for the study of place names and apply it to Zapotec names for toponyms of 58 municipalities in six districts of Oaxaca. Presents 355 names in both normalized and phonetic spellings of Zapotec, together with their Spanish translations and their official names.

SOUTH AMERICAN INDIAN LANGUAGES

1582 Adelaar, Willem F.H. Léxico del quechua de Pacaraos. Lima: Univ. Nacional Mayor de San Marcos, Centro de Investigación de Lingüística Aplicada, 1982. 107 leaves: bibl. (Documento de trabajo; no. 45)

Lexicon of a variety of Quechua spoken in Pacaraos (prov. of Huaral, Lima). Preceded by sociolinguistic information and short phonology.

Albó, Xavier and **Félix Layo.** Ludovico Bertonio, 1557–1625: fuente única al mundo aymara temprano. See *HLAS 46:1579*.

1583 América Latina en sus lenguas indígenas. Coordinación, presentación, y documentación de Bernard Pottier. Caracas: Monte Avila Editores, 1983. 476 p.: ill. (Col. Especial temas venezolanos)

Collection of articles (by different authors) in some Central and South American languages preceded by general historical perspective on Latin America. Topics: multilingualism; language situation of specific areas; descriptive studies of Nahuatl, Aymara, Guaraní; and sociolinguistics. Language index and classification follows Greenberg's traditional taxonomy.

1584 Andrade, Julieta de. Cultura creoula e lanc-patuá no norte do Brasil = Culture créole et langue patúa au nord du Brésil. Tradução, Marcel Jules Thiéblot. São Paulo: Escola de Folclore, 1984. 310 p. (Col. Pesquisa; 7)

Ethnographic description of some cultural aspects of Creole group in Amapá, North Brazil. Short traditional grammar of their language called "Lanc-patua" and a vocabulary plus 29 documents written in Lanc-patua. Book is written in two languages: Portuguese and English.

1585 Armatto de Welti, Zulema Inés. Introducción al estudio de las interferencias de la lengua aborigen toba en el español de los hablantes bilingües: interferencias fonológicas (UCNSA/SA, 18:1, junio 1983, p. 87–105, bibl.)

Study concerning interference of phonological system of Toba (primary language) to Spanish (secondary language). Also notes influence of Spanish (mostly syntactic) on Toba bilingual speakers.

1586 Aula quechua. Compilado por Rodolfo Cerrón-Palomino. Lima: Ediciones SIGNO, 1982. 277 p.: bibl., ill. (SIGNO universitario; 2)

Collection of excellent papers published on the occasion of the 400 years since the establishment of a Dept. of Quechua Language Studies at the Univ. of San Marcos. Contains papers on structural linguistics, sociolinguistics, historical and language teaching. Of theoretical interest is Cole *et al.* "Cláusulas Relativas Acéfalas: Evidencia del Quechua" and also Landerman "Las Sibilantes Castellanas, Quechua y Aymaras en el Siglo XVI: en Enigma Tridimensional."

1587 Barceló Sifontes, Lyll. Pemontón wanamarí: to maimú, to eseruk, to patasék = El espejo de los pemontón: su palabra, sus costumbres, su mundo. Caracas: Monte Avila Editors, 1982. 416 p.: bibl., ill. (Col. Temas venezolanos)

Extensive study of Pemon (Carib-Venezuela) oral literature, from anthropological viewpoint. Applies ethnoscience of the 1960s to diversified oral literature of the Pemon (collected by Armellada) resulting in an explicit Pemon cultural knowledge and world view.

1588 Beyersdorff, Margot. Léxico agropecuario quechua. Cusco, Perú: Centro de Estudios Rurales Andinos Bartolomé de las Casas, 1984. 129 p.: bibl.

Specialized lexicon of Quechua (Cusco variety, Peru) dealing with terms related to agriculture. Shows large domain of agriculture and farming in lexical items, and serves as guide to many Quechua lexical entries which do not have single and easy translation into Spanish.

1589 Bilingual education: an experience in Peruvian Amazonia. Edited by Mildred L. Larson and Patricia M. Davis. Washington: Center for Applied Linguistics; Dallas, Tx.: Summer Institute of Linguistics, 1981. 417 p.: bibl., ill., index.

Revised translation of *Educación bilingüe* (see *HLAS 43:4539*). Articles cover 25 years of bilingual education among Indians of Peru, by the Summer Institute of Linguistics (e.g., historical perspective, program's aspects, result of experiment, preparation of material and training of natives).

Black, Francis L. *et al.* Failure of linguistic relationships to predict genetic distances between the Waiãpi and other tribes of lower Amazonia. See item **1681.**

Braunstein, José A. and **Amalia Sanguinetti de Bórmida.** Algunos rasgos de la organización social de los indígenas del Gran Chaco. See item **1172.**

1590 Brown, Michael F. The role of words in Aguaruna hunting magic (AES/AE, 11:3, Aug. 1984, p. 545–558)

Ethnographic description of magical hunting songs of the Aguaruna (Jivaroan language) of Peru. In general, they consist of series of images expressed by esoteric lexicon and figurative language. They are regarded as efficacious for hunting purposes.

1591 Büttner, Thomas Th. Las lenguas de los Andes centrales: estudios sobre la clasificación genética, areal y tipológica. Traducción del manuscrito alemán por Sandra Luz Franco. Madrid: Ediciones Cultura Hispánica del Instituto de Cooperación Iberoamericana, 1983. 269 p.: bibl., ill. (Col. Amerindia)

Historical and typological comparative investigation about the languages spoken in the central Andes: Quechua, Aymara, Haguerau, Callahuaya, Chipaya. Attempts to clarify relationships among these languages and clearly states current problems.

1592 Carpentier, L.K. Aspects of Quichua dialectology. Bloomington: Indiana Univ., Center for Latin American and Caribbean Studies, 1984. 27 p.: bibl., maps (Andean studies occasional papers; 1)

Geographical and sociological variations of Ecuadorian Quichua dialects. Uses few phonological and morphological features to illustrate geographic division of six dialects. Use some lexical items to illustrate social dialects.

1593 Cerrón-Palomino, Rodolfo. Multilingüismo y planificación lingüística: el futuro de las lenguas oprimidas de América (CPES/RPS, 20:5, mayo/agosto 1983, p. 37–73, bibl.)

Sociolinguistic discussion of nature of multilingualism and language planning in South America. For the survival of indigenous languages author offers suggestions such as the publication of texts and more literature and periodicals in native languages.

Cipolletti, Maria S. En torno a un relato andino: el *ukumari*. See item **1397**.

1594 Conjunciones y otros nexos en tres idiomas amazónicos. Edición de Mary Ruth Wise y Harry Boonstra. Pucallpa, Perú: Ministerio de Educación, Instituto Lingüístico de Verano, 1982. 222 p. (Serie Lingüística peruana; 19)

Collection of five excellent descriptive papers basically written in 1974, and revised for this compilation. Four articles concern languages of Peru's Amazonian region: Sheila Tuggy "Las Secuencias Temporales y Lógicas en Candoshi: Jibaroan;" Harriet Kneeland "El 'Ser Como' y el "No Ser Como' de la Comparación en Matses (Panoan);" Harold Shaver "Relaciones entre Proposiciones en Nomatsiguenga" (Arawak-PreAndine) and "Funciones de la Partícula *Cara* en Nomatsiguenga." Includes introductory article by Mary Ruth Wise "Sobre Proposiciones y Oraciones."

1595 Córdova Guimaray, Jacinto. Gramática básica del quechua ancashino. Trujillo, Perú: Univ. Nacional de Trujillo, Dirección Universitaria de Proyección Social, 1982. 117 p.: bibl., ill.

Description of sentence types and phrase structure of Quechua (Ancash-Huaylas variety, Peru). Purpose is more didactic than descriptive, yet it is a linguistic contribution to our knowledge of Quechua morphosyntax. Includes good description with examples of postpositions and suffixes of nouns and verb phrases.

Costales, Piedad and **Alfredo Costales.** Amazonia: Ecuador, Peru, Bolivia. See item **1216**.

1596 Dooley, Robert A. Vocabulário do guarani: vocabulário básico do guarani contemporâneo: dialeto mbüá do Brasil. Brasília: Summer Institute of Linguistics, 1982. 322 p.

Vocabulary of 2500 entries of the Mbua variety of Guarani, spoken in south Brazil. Compiled for the purpose of helping Portuguese-speakers who want to learn Guarani. Vocabulary preceded by short phonology, orthography, and grammatical notes.

1597 Educación y lingüística en la Amazonía peruana. Compilador, Angel Corbera. Lima: Centro Amazónico de Antropología y Aplicación Práctica, 1983. 149 p.: bibl., ill. (Serie Lingüística)

Six ethnolinguistic articles on languages of Peru's Amazon region cover: bilingual education, orthography, names and kinship, descriptive notes and multilingualism.

1598 Espinoza Galarza, Max. El sufijo *macc* en la lengua quechua (SGL/B, 98, enero/dic. 1979, p. 37)

Brief note stating the three meanings of the suffix *mak* (*macc*) in Quechua.

Espinoza Soriano, Waldemar. Los fundamentos lingüísticos de la etnohistoria andina y comentarios en torno al anónimo de Charcas de 1604. See *HLAS 46:1629*.

1599 Estudios en andoke y muinane. Dirección General de Integración y Desarrollo de la Comunidad, División Operativa de Asuntos Indígenas, Instituto Lingüístico de Verano. Lomalinda, Colombia: Editorial Townsend, 1981. 215 p.: bibl. (Serie sintáctica; 13)

Contains two articles on discourse analysis by Summer Institute of Linguistic field researchers. Paul Witte describes main discourse features of Andoke (unclassified language of Colombia) presenting hierarchical levels of sentence, paragraph, and discourse and their connections. James Walton describes referential system of discourse participant which is strictly related to case markers as well as introducers of clauses and paragraphs in Muinane (Bora language of Colombia). Claims that in Muinane the clause is a significant level but the sentence is not. Includes analyzed texts in both Andoke and Muinane.

1600 Folk literature of the Bororo Indians. Edited by Johannes Wilbert and Karin Simoneau. Contributing editors, César Albisetti, Antonio Colbacchini, Angelo Jayme Venturelli. Los Angeles: UCLA Latin American Center Publications, 1983. 339 p.: bibl., ill., index (Folk literature of South American Indians. UCLA Latin American studies; v. 57)

Includes 111 narratives from the Bororo (Mato Grosso, Brazil) transcribed through the years by Don Bosco missionaries. Text is not in Bororo, only in English, thus useful for students of folklore and myth.

1601 Gambhir, Surendra K. Diglossia in dying languages: a case study of Guyanese Bhojpuri and standard Hindi (IU/AL, 25:1, Spring 1983, p. 28–37, tables)

Comparison of Guyanese Bhojpuri and standard Hindi, two languages (in complementary distribution) in a diglossia situation with Guyanese Creole. Guyanese Bhojpuri is used by the older generation in folk songs and in a limited way at home. Standard Hindi is used in books, rituals and movies. Guyanese Creole is increasingly replacing them in most of the domains.

1602 Gerzenstein, Ana. Lengua chorote. v. 2, Variedad 2: estudio descriptivo-comparativo y vocabulario. Buenos Aires: Univ. de Buenos Aires, Facultad de Filosofía y Letras, Instituto de Lingüística, 1978–1983. 2 v. (Archivo de lenguas precolombinas; 3–4)

Short phonemic, morphonemic and morphology description of Chorote (two varieties spoken in Argentina and Paraguay). Includes comparison between two varieties of Chorote and two-way Chorote-Spanish vocabulary. When sufficient data are available, attempts to reconstruct some forms of proto-Chorote.

1603 Gibson, Kean. Inherent variation or language change?: a study of two verbs in Guyanese Creole (LINGUA, 60:4, Aug. 1983, p. 341–349)

Analysis of two verbs in Guyanese Creole indicates language inherent variability rather than language change. Counter example to Bickerton's claim that linguistic variation is the synchronic aspect of linguistic change, and linguistic change is the diachronic aspect of language variation.

1604 Gifford, Douglas J. Dos notas de ecología andina (in International Congress of Hispanists, 4th, Salamanca, Spain, 1971. Actas. Dirección de Eugenio de Bustos Tovar. Salamanca, Spain: Asociación Internacional de Hispanistas, 1982, v. 1, p. 649–657)

Attempts to show ecological effects on speech with only two examples: influence of high altitude on consonants, and effect of bilingualism on Quechua speakers.

1605 Hijos de Pariya Qaqa: la tradición oral de Waru Chiri: mitología, ritual y costumbres. Edición, traducción y notas por George L. Urioste. Syracuse, N.Y.: Maxwell School of Citizenship and Public Affairs, 1983. 2 v. (332 p.): bibl., index (Latin American series; 6)

Republication of old and extensive Quechua manuscript on Waru Chiri's oral tradition, a description of the Andean man's world view. Since its 1939 first publication, other eds. followed in other languages. This two-vol. ed. has Quechua and Spanish versions on opposite pages.

1606 Jara J., Fausto. Morfología quichua. Quito?: Mundo Andino, s.d. 66 p.: ill.

Short morphology of Ecuador's Quechua written as a text to be used in schools and as handbook for those learning to speak Quechua.

1607 Kensinger, Kenneth M. Investigación lingüística, folklórica y etnográfica pano: retrospección y perspectiva (III/AI, 43:4, 1983, p. 849–875, bibl., tables)

Bibliographic review of recent ethnographic and linguistic literature on 11 Panoan languages of Brazil, Peru, and Bolivia.

1608 Klumpp, James and **Donald A. Burquest.** Relative clauses in Piapoco (IU/IJAL, 49:4, Oct. 1983, p. 388–399)

Description of some relative clauses in Piapoco. Basic characterization of relative clauses; absence of noun phrase and relative clause marker on the verb. Relativization follows Maxwell "Word Order Strategy" and is of the Postnominal Word Order type.

1609 Krivoshein de Canese, Natalia. Gramática de la lengua guaraní. Based on unpublished lectures of Dr. Reinaldo Decoud Larrosa presented at the Instituto de Lingüística Guaraní del Paraguay and the Facultad de Filosofía, Univ. Nacional de Asunción. Asunción: The Author, 1983. 179 p.: bibl. (Col. Nemitỹ)

A phonology, morphology and syntax of Guarani as spoken in Paraguay. Essentially it is a brief grammar presented in traditional style and based on recent description of Guarani by Decoud Larrosa. The purpose is pedagogical.

1610 Kroeker, Barbara. Aspectos da língua nambikuára. Brasília: Summer Institute of Linguistics, 1982. 166 p.

Good didactive grammar of Nambikuara to help non-Nambikuara to learn and study the language. There are plenty of exercises and examples in the phonology (pt. 1) and grammar (pt. 2). Small basic vocabulary at end.

1611 Larrea Borja, Piedad. /Agonía y resurrección del quichua? (in Arte y cultura: Ecuador, 1830–1980. Fernando Tinajero

Villamar *et al.* Quito: Corporación Editora Nacional, 1980, p. 265–284 [Libro del sesquicentenario; 2])

Etymology of some Quechua (Ecuador) lexical items and brief history and prospect of survival of Quechua in modern times.

1612 Lizot, Jacques and **Marie Claude Mattei-Muller.** El sistema fonológico yanomami central (VMJ/BIV, 20:17, 1981, p. 117–143, tables)

Criticizes Yanomami phonology in Migliazza's dissertation on the Yanomama languages. A non-trivial difference from Migliazza's phonological system is their interpretation of nasalization. Lizot's counter examples suffer from over differentiation and miss a valid generalization of the language. Moreover, his counter examples (p. 133) are polysyllabic, bimorphemic lexical items most of them with nasal consonants. Sound spectographic analysis of these examples shows all vowels in some degree nasalized. Thus, their postulation of two sets of vowels, nasal and oral, results in more complex description missing a language valid generalization.

Manelis Klein, Harriet E. El futuro precede al pasado: la concepción toba del tiempo. See item **1293.**

1613 Martín Cuesta, José. El aguaruna, la lengua del Cóndor. Lima: Librería Studium, 1982. 88 p.

Grammatical notes and small vocabulary of Aguaruna (Jivaroan-Peru) the author wrote 30 years for his personal use.

Meliá, Bartolomé. La entrada en el Paraguay de los otros karaí. See item **1305.**

1614 Migliazza, Ernesto C. Lenguas de la región del Orinoco-Amazonas: estado actual (III/AI, 43:4, 1983, p. 703–784, bibl., maps)

Current status of 33 languages still spoken between the Amazon and Orinoco basin. Covers denomination, number of speakers, ethnolinguistic situation, type of contact with the national society, published linguistic work and hints to the possibility of survival for each language. Similar article appeared in *Antropológica* (Caracas).

1615 Monguí Sánchez, José Raúl. La lengua kamentzá: fonética, fonología, textos. Prólogo de Antonio Tovar. Bogotá: Instituto

Caro y Cuervo, 1981. 228 p.: bibl., map, plates (Publicaciones; 59)

Consists mainly of texts in Kamentza (Sibundoy) with both literal and free translation in Spanish. Short phonology precedes actual texts and makes them more useful to linguist.

1616 Mosonyi, Jorge. Fenómenos de cortesía en comunidades indígenas (VMJ/BIV, 20:17, 1981, p. 187–201)

List of greetings in Carina, Guajiro and Guahibo (languages spoken in Venezuela). Social context in which they occur is limited to visitation, casual encounter and introductions.

1617 ———. La obra lingüística inédita de Lisandro Alvarado (VMJ/BIV, 20:17, 1981, p. 203–207)

Review of unpublished manuscripts dealing with various indigenous languages of Venezuela. Linguistic material (small vocabularies and grammars) was not collected by Alvarado himself but based on published material available at his time.

1618 Nicholson, Velda. Breve estudo da língua asuriní do Xingu. Brasília: Summer Institute of Linguistics, 1982. 85 p. (Ensaios lingüísticos; 5)

Short comparative study of Asurini; Xingu dialect and Trocara dialect. Compares consonants and vowels, some grammatical aspects, and small vocabulary organized as Voegelin's *Hopi domains.*

1619 Obregón, Hugo and **Jorge Díaz.** La elaboración de diccionarios de lenguas indígenas venezolanas: un modelo de cuestionaro (VMJ/BIV, 20:17, 1981, p. 145–186, tables)

Sample questionnaire with instructions to serve as tool for the compilation of an indigenous language dictionary. Consists of word lists organized according to food, housing, vegetation, animals, body parts, color terms, grammatical categories, etc. Designed for use during initial stages of fieldwork among Venezuelan Indians.

Ortiz, Alejandro. Moya: espacio, tiempo y sexo en un pueblo andino. See item **1499.**

1620 Patiño Roselli, Carlos. Sobre la lingüística de la Amazonia colombiana. Primer Seminario de Antropología Amazónica Colombiana. Bogotá: Comité de Publicaciones de ORAM, 1982. 43 p.: bibl., map, plate.

Overview of studies concerning languages of Colombia's Amazon region. Includes inventory of region's languages, historical-comparative studies of these languages, descriptive work published up to 1980, and good bibliography.

1621 Pérez T., Aquiles R. El idioma cuayker. Quito: Casa de la Cultura Ecuatoriana, 1980. 23 p.: bibl.

Small vocabulary of Cuaiker (a Macro-Chibchan language of Ecuador) compared with small word lists collected by André (1875), Hidalgo (1894), Triana (1907), Gutiérrez (1920), and Pankeri (1922).

1622 Plaza Martínez, Pedro and **Juan Carvajal.** Adquisición del lenguaje por niños monolingües castellano y aymara hablantes (N&N Ling/Notas y Noticias Lingüísticas [Instituto Boliviano de Cultura, Instituto Nacional de Antropología, La Paz] 7:1, enero/marzo 1984, p. 1–38, graphs, tables)

Experimental study of degrees of consonant and vowel acquisition by children in La Paz Dept., Bolivia. Two groups were selected: 48 Spanish monolingual and 45 Aymara monolingual children under six yrs.

1623 Price, David. The Nambiquara linguistic family (IU/AL, 20:1, Jan. 1978, p. 14–37, bibl., map, tables)

Contributes to a systematic classification of Nambiquara languages by comparing their phonology in three groups. Condensed version to appear as "Nambiquara Languages: Linguistic and Geographic Distances between Nambiquara Speech Communities" in *South American Indian languages: retrospect and prospect* edited by Harriet Klein and Louisa Stark (Univ. of Texas Press).

Rabinowitz, Joel. La lengua pescadora: the lost dialect of Chimú fishermen. See *HLAS 46:1697.*

1624 Reinhard, Johan. The Chonos of the Chilean archipelago (ICUAER/B, 23, 1981, p. 89–98, bibl.)

Comments on small catechism in Chono (extinct language of south Chile) collected by Jesuits and deposited in the National Library of Rome (dated 1767). No translation of catechism is available.

1625 Ritchie Key, Mary. Lenguas de las tierras bajas de Bolivia (III/AI, 43:4, 1983, p. 877–892, bibl., map)

Summary of current status of Bolivia's indigenous languages. Useful map shows their location, and list groups 32 languages in 12 families and six as unclassified.

1626 Robertson, Ian E. The Dutch linguistic legacy and the Guyana/Venezuela border question (CEDLA/B, 34, junio 1983, p. 75–97, map, tables)

Description of British linguistic arguments (1899) in their territorial dispute with Venezuela. Evidence includes: Dutch lexical loans in Amerindian languages, use of Dutch Creole, and nature of Creole Dutch.

Sacha Pacha: el mundo de selva: relatos bilingües. See *HLAS 46:1086.*

1627 Setenta mitos shuar. Edición de Marco Vinicio Rueda. Texto recogido magnetofónicamente por Ricardo Tankamash'. Traducción del shuar al castellano por Ricardo Tankamash' y Ampán Karákas. Quito: Mundo Shuar, 1983. 289 p.: ill.

Collection of 70 myths in Shuar language (Ecuador) transcribed and translated by two bilingual Shuar individuals. Notes on myth's structural analysis precede texts.

1628 Shoemaker, Jack; Nola Shoemaker; and Mildred L. Larson. Relaciones comunicacionales en la gramática ese-ejja. Traducción de Pedro Plaza Martínez. La Paz: Instituto Nacional de Estudios Lingüísticos, 1983. 107 p.: bibl.

Discourse analysis of Ese-Ejja (Tacanan language of Bolivia). Describes the communication relationship (relators and relations) and the structure of the paragraph. Includes useful examples.

1629 A Short dictionary of the Warau language of Guyana. Edited by Walter F. Edwards. Graduate researcher, Elizabeth Charette. Georgetown: Amerindian Languages Project, Univ. of Guyana, 1980. 167 p.: bibl.

Two-way vocabulary (Warau-English and English-Warau) preceded by linguistic introduction. Concerns Warau language version spoken in Guyana.

1630 Simposio Internacional sobre las Barreras Lingüísticas en el Desarrollo de las Ciencias y de la Tecnología en los

Países del Convenio Andrés Bello, 1st, *Trujillo, Perú,* 1979. Actas. Trujillo: Univ. Nacional de Trujillo, Depto. de Idiomas y Lingüística; Lima: Asociación de Profesores de Idiomas del Perú, 1979. 181 p.: bibl., ill.

Consists of 22 symposium papers on linguistic barriers to the development of science and technology (Peru). Some put forward models to facilitate studies of linguistic barriers to development within bilingual or multilingual situations. In general, emphasizes need and importance of studying and teaching indigenous as well as foreign languages.

1631 Sorensen, Arthur P., Jr. Linguistic exogamy and personal choice in the northwest Amazon (*in* Marriage practices in Lowland South America [see item **1294**] p. 180–193)

Excellent paper on the ethnography of marriage in a society which prescribes linguistic exogamy, preferential cross-cousin marriage and preference for sister exchange.

1632 ———. El surgimiento de un regionalismo tukano: presiones políticas (III/AI, 43:4, 1983, p. 785–795)

Examines linguistic exogamy of Vaupes River region both in Brazil and in Colombia in connection with recent developments and different linguistic patterns. Taking into account dynamics of national expansion, local missionary schools and native multilingualism, concludes by predicting survival of numerous indigenous languages while national languages (e.g., Spanish and Portuguese) will be used only as lingua francas.

1633 Stark, Louisa R. Las lenguas indígenas de las tierras bajas de Ecuador: historia y condiciones actuales (III/AI, 43:4, 1983, p. 797–821, bibl., map)

Provides brief history and sociolinguistic situation for each indigenous language of Ecuador. Map shows location of Quechua, Zaparo, Auca, Cofara, Barbacoa (Colorado and Cayapa), Tucano (Siona, Seoya, and Tetete), Jíbaro (Shuar and Achuar).

Szemiński, Jan. Acerca del significado de algunos de los términos empleados en los documentos relativos a la revolución tupacamarista: 1780–1783. See *HLAS 46:2729.*

1634 Taylor, Gerald. Lengua general y lenguas particulares en la antigua provincia de Yauyos, Perú (IGFO/RI, 43:171, enero/junio 1983, p. 265–291)

Commentary on 17th-century Quechua of Huarochiri text. Contains information on a variety of Quechua spoken at that time in Lima.

1635 Tosantos, Gonzalo. Apuntes sobre el idioma panare. Cumaná, Venezuela: Editorial Universitaria de Oriente, 1977. 80 p., 5 leaves of plates: ill.

Consists of word lists with Spanish translation, arranged by topics and some grammatical categories with examples written mainly for Panare Indians who desire to learn Spanish.

Urban, Greg. Speech about speech in speech about action. See item **1364.**

1636 Urbina Rangel, Fernando. Mitología amazónica: cuatro mitos de los Murui-Muinanes. Bogotá: Comité de Publicaciones de ORAM, 1982. 51 p., 2 leaves of plates: ill.

Contains four myths (translated into Spanish) of the Murui-Muinane (sometime referred to as Huitoto) of Colombia. Introduction discusses the nature of myths in general.

1637 Vaquero de Ramírez, María T. Fray Pedro de Aguado: lengua y etnografía. Caracas: Academia Nacional de la Historia, 1981. 355 p. (Biblioteca de la Academia; 148. Fuentes para la historia colonial de Venezuela)

Publication of Aguado's 16th-century writings. Includes ethnographic observations on Venezuelan life in his times, and word lists for five indigenous languages.

1638 Vélez Vélez, Luis Fernando. Relatos tradicionales de la cultura catía. Medellín, Colombia: Depto. de Antioquia, Secretaría de Desarrollo de la Comunidad, División de Acción Comunal, Sección de Asuntos Indígenas, 1982. 294 p.: bibl., map.

By the name Catio (Páez language of Colombia), author concludes acculturated, mostly bilingual Indians of Colombia's Antioquia Dept., also known as Chamies, Embena, and Embera. Book is large collection of traditional stories and myths in Spanish, more useful for the folklore scholar than the linguist.

1639 Verswijver, Gustaaf. Les femmes peintes: une cérémonie d'imposition de noms chez les Kayapó-Mẽkrãgnoti du

Brésil central (SSA/B, 46, 1982, p. 41–59, bibl., ill.)

Ethnographical description of name-giving ceremony of the Kayapo (Gê) of Brazil. Includes categories of names, their importance in the society, a detailed description of the ceremony in the village of Mekragnoti, its spatial organization, and meaning of body painting. For ethnologist's review see item 1370.

1640 Vogt, Carlos and Peter Fry. Ditos e feitos da falange africana do cafundó e da calunga de patrocínio—ou de como fazer falando (USP/RA, 26, 1983, p. 65–92, bibl.)

Social field study of attitudes toward Cafundo Creole, locally called "African language." In fact, Cafundo is not an African but a Portuguese-base Creole language used for ritual and to maintain unity and identity among subgroups of Brazil's black population.

Waag, Else María. Tres entidades *wekufü* en la cultura mapuche. See item **1415.**

1641 Wise, Mary Ruth. Lenguas indígenas de la Amazonía peruana: historia y estado presente (III/AI, 43:4, 1983, p. 823–848, bibl., maps, tables)

Reviews historical factors responsible for survival and/or extinction of indigenous languages. Examines problems related to genetic relationship of certain languages and lists 63 Peruvian languages (12 families) with maps showing their location. Excludes Quechua and Aymara languages.

Zuidema, Reiner Tom. El primer *Nueva crónica y buen gobierno.* See *HLAS 46:1749.*

HUMAN BIOLOGY

ROBERT M. MALINA, *Professor, Department of Anthropology, and Associate Director, Institute of Latin American Studies, University of Texas, Austin*

THE BIOLOGY OF HUMAN POPULATIONS of the past and present is the central theme of physical anthropology or biological anthropology. Nevertheless, the more appropriate label is human biology which aims to understand human biological variation, its nature, distribution and significance within the context of evolutionary theory and of course the cultural context. Human biology thus operates in a biocultural framework. This is especially evident in numerous studies of human adaptability and variation in Latin American populations.

The literature dealing with biological aspects of Latin American populations is diverse. This is due in part to the inclusion of a variety of biologically-related topics which do not ordinarily fall in the context of traditional physical anthropology or in the domain of human biology. The net result gives a relatively broad base to the human biology of Latin American populations.

This overview considers materials published through 1983 and 1984. Earlier materials are occasionally included, given inevitable delays in publication and the mail. The overview is divided into seven sections: 1) General; 2) Earlier Populations; 3) Demographic Considerations; 4) Population Genetics; 5) Human Adaptability; 6) Nutritional Anthropology; and 7) Biomedical Anthropology.

EARLIER POPULATIONS

Reports dealing with skeletal and dental characteristics of precolumbian populations appear to have decreased in number, but include several on skeletal features (item **1651**), demographic reconstruction (item **1647**), and microevolution (item **1650**). More specific analyses of earlier populations include a description of a new dental wear pattern in a Brazilian archaic population (item **1652**), analysis of fecal parasites in Peruvian and Chilean mummies (item **1648**), analysis of syphilis in mummies (item **1644**), and the use of electron spin resonance to date human bones (item **1649**). The nutritional status of earlier populations is a primary focus, and the volume by Antúnez de Mayolo (item **1645**) offers a reasonably comprehensive account of the diet and nutritional status of prehispanic Peruvians. The volume by van Beek (item **1646**), though not dealing with Latin America, provides an excellent field guide to dental morphology.

DEMOGRAPHY

Studies of demographic parameters are prominent and include most Latin American countries. Given population growth in Latin America, reproductive performance, fertility control, and related factors are more or less regularly monitored. Latin American populations also have high mortality rates, especially in the preschool ages. Hence, mortality statistics serve as an index of the health status of populations. Relationships between morbidity and mortality, between fertility and mortality, and between these indicators and various cultural and biological factors is complex. They highlight the need for the biocultural approach in human biology.

Reviews by Kano and Yamaguchi (item **1665**) and McGlashan (item **1666**) offer statistical summaries of mortality data for Latin American countries and for English-speaking countries and territories of the Caribbean respectively, while Ehrlich (item **1654**) considers demographic and several specific health problems for the Americas.

A number of country or region specific surveys of mortality and fertility have been published over the past few years and are included in this section. Several consider infant mortality and live births (items **1658** and **1663**), intrauterine mortality (item **1669**), the relationship between morbidity and mortality in Mexico (item **1674**), and determinants of childhood mortality in Nicaragua (item **1677**). Other mortality-related reports include analyses for Guatemala during 1950–81 (item **1653**); for Argentina, 1914–70 (item **1657**); for Mendoza, Argentina, 1979–82 (item **1667**) and Pernambuco, Brazil, 1930–78 (item **1664**); for Chile in the 1960s and 1970s (item **1668**); for Uruguay in the mid-1970s with comparative data for the 1960s and early 20th century (item **1673**); and for Cuba in a historical perspective (*HLAS 45 : 1667*) and in the 1970s (item **1670**).

Fertility-related reports, including analyses of relationships with a variety of factors such as education, area of residence, maternal characteristics, and so on, deal with Mexico (items **1655, 1660,** and **1662**); the Dominican Republic (item **1661**); Haiti (item **1676**); Costa Rica (item **1672**); Colombia (*HLAS 45 : 1676*); Venezuela (item **1656**); and the Mekranoti of central Brazil (item **1675**).

In related matters, Rosenwaike and Preston (item **1671**) consider age overestimation relative to Puerto Rican longevity, while Gage *et al.* (item **1659**) present a method of fitting a model life table.

POPULATION GENETICS

Research dealing with genetic aspects of Latin American populations continues to expand. Crawford (item **1683**) presents a comprehensive overview of genetic variation and population structure of the Black Caribs. A significant portion of the genetic research deals with documenting many genetic polymorphisms (item **1685**), population admixture and divergence (item **1684**), comparisons of tribal populations (item **1691**), and associations with cultural traits (item **1681**). As such research efforts continue, new genetic variants (item **1698**) and occasional clinical conditions (item **1686**) are identified. Emphasis continues on abnormal hemoglobins (items **1693** and **1699**) and sickle cell anemia (items **1688** and **1697**), while the use of surnames in genetic research appears to have increased (items **1679** and **1689**). Several studies of anthropometric dimensions are also included in the genetics section (item **1692**) and the question of balancing selection (item **1687**). Studies of Brazilian populations are more common in genetic research than in other Latin American groups.

HUMAN ADAPTABILITY

The area of human biology labeled human adaptability is perhaps the most diverse, commonly including studies of Man under different climatic, ecological, disease, and nutritional circumstances. Two edited volumes provide comprehensive, interdisciplinary views of specific populations, the Black Caribs (item **1713**) and native Amazonians (item **1700**). Other reports focus on more specific problems. For the sake of convenience, this section will concentrate on selected aspects of human adaptability research, while data related to nutritional and biomedical aspects are considered in separate sections.

The study of altitude stress in Latin American populations continues as a significant focus, particularly in Bolivia, and includes studies of growth (item **1719** and **1743**), responses of children, youth, and adults to submaximal and maximal exercise stress (items **1720**, **1722**, **1723**, and **1724**), hemoglobin concentration and iron nutriture (items **1708**, **1721**, and **1734**), diet and energy needs (items **1728** and **1733**), and red blood cell variation (items **1706** and **1711**).

Studies of responses to exercise stress (working capacity) and related tests (e.g., lung functions, anaerobic capacity) have increased considerably for Latin American groups, and include data for high altitude (see above), trained and untrained youth (items **1704**, **1718**, **1730**, **1739**, and **1747**), and nutritional stress (see item **1740** for a comprehensive review). Angeleli *et al.* (item **1703**) and Desai *et al.* (item **1714**) report on the work performance of migrant adolescent boys and adults in southern Brazil; Spurr and colleagues (items **1707**, **1741**, and **1742**) report their research on working capacity of marginally malnourished Colombian boys; while Torun *et al.* (item **1744**) present data on the energy costs of several physical activities in preschool Guatemalan children.

Growth studies comprise a significant portion of human adaptability research. Data on healthy, well nourished children can serve as reference data, while surveys of children in several segments of a population or country provide an indication of the overall health and nutritional status. Comparative studies of growth and maturity status of Latin American children and youth include samples from Mexico (items **1705**, **1710**, **1716**, **1735**, **1736**, **1737**, and **1746**); Guatemala (items **1709** and **1725**); Cuba (items **1702** and **1715**); Haiti (item **1701**); Venezuela (items **1729** and **1738**); and Chile (item **1745**). Many of these studies include a nutritional component, height reflecting nuritional history, weight reflecting current nutritional status and skinfolds reflecting subcutaneous fatness, and clearly illustrate the impact of socioeconomic differentials on the growth and maturity of Latin American children and youth.

The secular trend refers to the tendency of contemporary children and youth to be larger in size and mature earlier, and of adults to be taller than samples from several generations ago. The presence or absence of this developmental phenomenon continues to be examined in a number of Latin American populations (items **1717**, **1731**, and **1732**).

NUTRITIONAL ANTHROPOLOGY

Given the significant percentage of the Latin American population which lives under marginal or suboptimal nutritional circumstances, and given the role of nutritional stress in human adaptability research, a separate section on nutrition-related research is included. The nutritional literature for Latin America is vast and comprises a broad spectrum. Two edited volumes present comprehensive, interdisciplinary considerations of two nutritionally-related problems, malnutrition and behavior (item 1793) and energy intake and activity (item 1760). Although Latin America is not the primary focus of those two volumes, many of the contributors work in Latin America and examples from many Latin American samples are incorporated into the discussions.

By and large, the majority of the nutritional literature is of the survey type, including national surveys of Bolivia (item 1767), Uruguay (item 1759), and Venezuela (item 1753), general reviews of the nutritional situation of Cuba (item 1778) and the Dominican Republic (item 1806), and a variety of nutritionally-related studies of rather small indigenous communities (items 1756, 1758, 1781, 1785, 1787, 1790, 1802, and 1809).

More specific studies focus on nutritional status, especially of preschool children and pregnant/lactating women, dietary intake, familial circumstances such as household income, access to land, and various cultural practices as factors influencing nutritional status and malnutrition (items 1749, 1750, 1755, 1765, 1788, 1792, 1797, 1805, 1807, 1808, and 1819). Valverde et al. (item 1813) review the evidence of seasonal variation in nutritional status and growth, including several Latin American examples.

Age, height, weight, arm circumference and the triceps skinfold are rather widely used in the assessment of nutritional status (items 1772, 1775, and 1810), and the Latin American literature includes reference data for Argentine children (item 1789), an evaluation of the validity of arm circumference as an indicator of nutritional status (item 1764), and an energy/protein index using arm circumference and the triceps skinfold (item 1812). However, adult knowledge of weight for age charts is generally unsatisfactory in St. Lucia (item 1796).

Additional specific foci of nutritional research in Latin America include supplementation (items 1761 and 1763; see also item 1818 for a review of five non-Latin American supplementation trials) and balance studies (items 1757 and 1814); lactation, breastfeeding and infant growth (items 1752, 1754, 1766, 1771, 1786, 1791, 1795, 1798, 1803, and 1816); the care of malnourished children (item 1777); levels of specific nutrients such as zinc and copper (items 1768, 1769, and 1801), iron (item 1774), calcium (item 1820), and vitamin A (items 1773 and 1804); lead concentrations (items 1794 and 1817); the interaction of nutritional status and infectious disease (items 1751 and 1811); and intestinal parasites and nutritional status (items 1762, 1770, 1779, 1784, and 1800).

In contrast to the earlier survey of nutritional anthropology in Latin America, there is increasing awareness of obesity and fatness as a nutritional problem (items 1748, 1776, 1782, 1783, 1799, and 1807), and some awareness of the nutritional status of elderly individuals (item 1780).

BIOMEDICAL CONSIDERATIONS

Infectious disease has been and is a significant agent in the adaptive process. One of the major areas of interest in biomedical aspects of human biology is ethnomedicine, with emphasis on traditional medicine and its interface with modern, western medicine. Ryn (item **1846**) presents a general account of medical anthropology in the Andes, while Ortega-Pérez (item **1841**) reviews the heat-cold dichotomy in an Andean community. Many of the other biomedical works are rather specific in focus (e.g., diseases of the Peruvian Amazon, item **1838**), use of health services in rural Ecuador (item **1835**), the relationship between breastfeeding and use of health services (item **1821**), medical beliefs of the Garifuna (item **1825**), and health status and concerns of migrants (item **1828** and **1834**).

A number of reports dealing with specific diseases attest to the significance of infectious disease in Latin American populations (e.g., Chagas's disease, item **1836**, **1843**, and **1845**; diarrheal diseases, items **1827**, **1844a**, and **1850**; malaria, item **1822** and tuberculosis, item **1833**). Concern for the so-called "diseases of civilization" in Latin America is beginning to appear more regularly in the literature (e.g., hypertension, items **1832** and **1844**; serum cholesterol levels, item **1847**; smoking and lung disease, item **1824**; and, see also obesity in the section on nutritional anthropology, items **1782** and **1783**). Weiss and colleagues (item **1849**) present a review of evidence suggesting a New World Syndrome, characterized by obesity, adult onset diabetes, gallstones and gallbladder cancer in Amerindian peoples. Although not a disease, teen-age pregnancy, its biological consequences and related factors, appears to be an issue of increasing concern in the biomedical literature on Latin America (items **1823**, **1829**, and **1830**).

RECENT DOCTORAL DISSERTATIONS

The following deal with aspects of human biology and related issues in Latin America (1982–84), and are based on listings reported in the *Guide to Departments of Anthropology* published by the American Anthropological Association.

Demarest, William J. Left handedness and right handedness in Guatemalan populations: a cross-cultural examination of Marian Annett's single gene/right shift theory. Stanford Univ., 1983.

Garro, Linda. Variation and consistency in a Mexican folk illness belief system. Univ. of California at Irvine, 1983.

Garvin, Gloria Evelyn. Mental illness among the Cuna Indians of Panama. Univ. of California at Los Angeles, 1983.

Hess, Salinda. Domestic medicine and indigenous medical systems in Haiti: culture and political economy of health in a disemic society. McGill Univ., 1983.

Hill, Kim. Adult male subsistence strategies among Ache hunter-gatherers of Paraguay. Univ. of Utah, 1983.

Hutchinson, Janice Faye. A biocultural analysis of blood pressure variation among Black Caribs and Creoles of St. Vincent, West Indies. Univ. of Kansas, 1984.

Kaplan, Hillard. The evolution of food sharing among adult conspecifics: research with Ache hunter-gatherers of Paraguay. Univ. of Utah, 1983.

Kempf, Judith. The dynamics of culture and health: disease and curing among the Ecuadorian Coaiquer Indians under the impact of acculturation. SUNY at Albany, 1982.

Little, Bertis B. Sibling similarity in growth status and rate among school children in a rural Zapotec community in the Valley of Oaxaca, Mexico. Univ. of Texas at Austin, 1983.

GENERAL

1642 Coloquio de Antropología Física Juan Comas, *lst, México, 1980.* Estudios de antropología biológica. María Villanueva y Carlos Serrano, compiladores. México: UNAM, Instituto de Investigaciones Antropológicas, 1982. 572 p.: ill. (Serie antropológica; 51. Antropología física)

Proceedings of the 1st Juan Comas Colloquium on Physical Anthropology. Papers cover diverse areas of biological anthropology, including a history of physical anthropology in Mexico, genetics, dermatoglyphics, skeletal biology, growth and maturation, and traditional anthropometry.

1643 Coloquio de Antropología Física Juan Comas, 2nd, *México, 1982.* Estudios de antropología biológica. Rafael Ramos Galván y Rosa María Ramos Rodríguez, editores. México, UNAM, Instituto de Investigaciones Antropológicas, 1984. 588 p.: graphs, ill., maps, tables.

Proceedings of 2nd Juan Comas Colloquium on Physical Anthropology consists of 37 papers on virtually all areas: eight on skeletal biology of early populations, nine on growth and adaptability, six on genetics, two each on anthropometry and dermatoglyphics, and one on primate behavior. Several contributions are from Europe.

EARLIER POPULATIONS

1644 Allison, Marvin J. et al. La sífilis: ¿una enfermedad americana? (Chungara [Univ. de Tarapacá, Depto. de Antropología, Arica, Chile] 9, agosto 1982, p. 275–283, bibl., ill., tables)

Syphilis as a disease of American origin is discussed and 11 possible cases out of 3000 mummies examined are presented.

1645 Antúnez de Mayolo R., Santiago Erik. La nutrición en el antiguo Perú. Lima: Banco Central de Reserva del Perú, Oficina Numismática, 1981. 189 p.: bibl.

Reasonably comprehensive attempt at reconstructing the nutritional status and diet of prehispanic Peru, including brief consideration of nutritional status in contemporary Peru relative to the past.

1646 Beek, Coeffrey C. van. Dental morphology: an illustrated guide. 2nd ed. Bristol, England: John Wright and Sons, 1983. 135 p.: ill., tables.

Although this book does not deal with Latin America, it provides an excellent, illustrated field guide of dental morphology which would be useful in studies of earlier populations.

1647 Benfer, Robert A. The challenges and rewards of sedentism: the preceramic village of Paloma, Peru (in Paleopathology at the origins of agriculture. Edited by M.N. Cohen and G.J. Armelagos. New York: Academic Press, 1984, p. 531–558, bibl., graphs, tables)

Demographic and preliminary skeletal data are presented for this preceramic, Archaic site for the period 4500 to 8000 BP.

1648 Fouant, Monique M.; Marvin J. Allison; Enrique Gerszten; and **Guillermo Focacci A.** Parásitos intestinales entre los indígenas precolombinos (Chungara [Univ. de Tarapacá, Depto. de Antropología, Arica, Chile] 9, agosto 1982, p. 285–299, bibl., photo, tables)

Presence of fecal parasites in 63 adults and 25 juvenile mummies from Peru and Chile was examined. Majority of the mummies were Chilean (80 of 88) and 10 percent of them tested positively for parasites. Of the eight Peruvian mummies, 37 percent tested positively. There did not appear to be any significant adult/juvenile differences.

Handler, Jerome S. and **Robert S. Corruccini.** Plantation slave life in Barbados: a physical anthropological analysis. See *HLAS 46:2463.*

Kiple, Kenneth F. and **Virginia H. Kiple.** Deficiency diseases in the Caribbean. See *HLAS 46:2502.*

1649 Mascarenhas, S.; O. Baffa Filho; and **M. Ikeya.** Electron spin resonance dating of human bones from Brazilian shellmounds, *sambaquis* (AJPA, 59, 1982, p. 413–417, bibl., ill., tables)

Application of electron spin resonance to human bones yielded ages between 2000 and 5000 BP.

1650 Rothhammer, Francisco; Silvia Quevedo; José A. Cocilovo; and **Elena Llop.** Microevolution in prehistoric Andean populations: chronologic nonmetrical cranial variation in northern Chile (AJPA, 65, 1984, p. 157–162, bibl., tables)

Multivariate distance statistics based on 14 nonmetric cranial variables among five prehistoric samples indicate that about 70 percent of the variation can be explained by chronologic distance covering a period of 6500 yrs.

1651 Serra, Mari Carmen; Magalí Civera; and Arturo Romano P. Entierros en un sitio: formativo del sur de la Cuenca de México: Terremote-Tlaltenco, D.F. (UNAM/AA, 19, 1982, p. 55–91, bibl., ill., tables)

Descriptive osteometric and craniometric data are reported for the remains from 12 tombs.

1652 Turner, Christy G. and Lilia M. Cheuiche Machado. A new dental wear pattern and evidence for high carbohydrate consumption in a Brazilian Archaic skeletal population (AJPA, 61, 1983, p. 125–130, ill., tables)

Lingual surface attrition of the maxillary anterior teeth, a new dental wear pattern, was found in 85 percent of 46 adult crania from an Archaic site, 3000 to 4200 BP, near the Atlantic Ocean coast. The wear pattern is associated with a high caries rate.

DEMOGRAPHY

1653 Arias de Blois, Jorge. La mortalidad en Guatemala, 1950–1981. Guatemala: Secretaría General del Consejo Nacional de Planificación Económica, Dirección de Planificación Global, Depto. de Población y Empleo, 1983. 390 p.: bibl., ill., plates (Serie Resultados; 4)

Comprehensive analysis and summary of mortality for the country as a whole, for specific political and geographic subdivisions, etc. Variation by age, sex, urban/rural, ethnic group, civil status, occupation, and maternal characteristics (for infant mortality).

Coreil, Jeannine. Allocation of family resources for health care in rural Haiti. See item **1032.**

1654 Ehrlich, S. Paul, Jr. Selected health conditions in the Americas: a guide for health research policy (PAHO/B, 17:2, 1983, p. 111–125, bibl., tables)

Considers general data for the Americas on demography, life expectancy and several specific health problems (e.g., preschool mortality, cardiovascular disease, malaria) relative to health research and planning.

1655 Encuesta mexicana de fecundidad: 3 áreas metropolitanas. México: Secretaría de Programación y Presupuesto, Coordi-

nación General del Sistema Nacional de Información, 1979. 1 v.: ill., tables.

Comprehensive analysis of fertility in the metropolitan areas of Mexico City, Guadalajara, and Monterrey.

1656 Encuesta nacional de fecundidad, Venezuela, 1977: apéndice estadístico. Caracas: Presidencia de la República, Oficina Central de Estadística e Informática, 1980. 799 p.: tables.

Statistical summary of the national fecundity survey of Venezuela, including data on marital status, fecundity, child preference, knowledge and use of contraceptives.

1657 Estadísticas demográficas. v. 1, Años 1914–1943. v. 2, Años 1944–1970. Buenos Aires: Ministerio de Salud Pública y Medio Ambiente, Subsecretaría Técnica y de Coordinación Administrativa, Sistema de Información de Salud, Estadísticas de Salud, 1982–1983. 2 v.: tables (Estadísticas vitales y de salud. Serie 5, Serie histórica; 21–22)

Demographic statistics for the periods 1914–43 and 1944–70 are presented in each vol. Data are reported for the total country and for political subdivisions. Of historical use are the statistics for general mortality, infant mortality, and neonatal and postneonatal mortality, as indicators of general health conditions in the country over time.

1658 Estimación de los nacimientos ocurridos durante el período, 1950–1975. México: Secretaría de Programación y Presupuesto, Coordinación General de los Servicios Nacionales de Estadística, Geografía e Informática, 1980. 95 p.: bibl., ill., tables.

Number of live births in Mexico is estimated from several sources for 1950–75 time period: census and vital statistics information; estimates considering the omission of infant mortality; and estimates based on the Mexican Fertility Survey 1970–75.

1659 Gage, T.B.; B. Dyke; and P.G. Rivière. Estimating mortality from two censuses: an application to the Trio of Surinam (WSU/HB, 56:3, 1984, p. 489–501, bibl., ill., tables)

Describes method of fitting a model life table which requires data from two censuses taken some years apart.

1660 Garza-Chapa, R.; M.S. Escobar; R. Cerda; and C.H. Leal-Garza. Factors related to the frequency of twinning in the state of Nuevo León, Mexico during 1977 and 1978 (WSU/HB, 56:2, 1984, p. 277–290, bibl., tables)

Birth certificates indicated 2.7 monozygotic and 4.3 dizygotic twins per 1000 maternities. These rates are intermediate between those for Spaniards and Indians.

1661 Hobcraft, John and Germán Rodríguez. The analysis of repeat fertility surveys: examples from the Dominican Republic. Voorburg, The Netherlands: International Statistical Institute, 1982. 29 p.: bibl. (Scientific reports. World fertility survey; 29)

Analyzes changes in fertility and its three most important proximate determinants: nuptiality, breastfeeding and contraception. Also includes estimates of infant and child mortality from 1950–54 through 1975–78.

1662 Holian, John. Fertility differentials in Mexico: an individual level analysis (SECOLAS/A, 14, March 1983, p. 47–60, tables)

Uses one percent sample of 1970 Mexican census, limited to native born women in legal or consensual union aged 15–49 yrs. who have completed their education (n=65,355), to evaluate effects on fertility of residence (urban, semi-urban, rural) and level of education.

1663 Incidencia de la mortalidad infantil en los Estados Unidos Mexicanos, 1940–1975. México: Secretaría de Programación y Presupuesto, Coordinación General de los Servicios Nacionales de Estadística, Geografía e Informática, 1981. 265 p.: ill.

Tabular summary of infant mortality by five-yr. intervals, 1940–75. Reports data on all of Mexico, for each state and specific localities of Federal District. Also summarizes causes of infant mortality for each period and political subdivision.

1664 Informações demográficas de Pernambuco. v. 1, Evolução da mortalidade. v. 2, Evolução da população economicamente ativa, 1950–1978. v. 7, Distribuição espacial da população pernambucana, 1940–1980. v. 8, Cenário prospectivo da população pernambucana, 1981–1986. v. 9, Recife, os óbitos evitáveis. Recife: Governo de Pernambuco, Secretaria de Planejamento, Fundação de Informações para o Desenvolvimento de Pernambuco, 1980–1983. 5 v. in 2: bibl., ill., tables.

Reports estimates of life expectancy at birth, probability of dying between 10 and 60 years, infant mortality and crude death rates for five periods: 1930–40, 1940–50, 1950–60, 1960–70, 1968–78. Also considers sex differences and regional variation.

1665 Kano, Katsumi and Seiya Yamaguchi. A study of mortality patterns in Latin American countries using a statistical and epidemiological approach (Latin American Studies [Univ. of Tsukuba, Special Research Project on Latin America, Sakura-Mura, Japan] 7, 1983, p. 121–141, bibl., graph, tables)

Analysis of mortality patterns in Latin American countries chiefly based on *Demographic Yearbook* (1978) data. Analysis also includes data from geographic areas other than Latin America.

1666 McGlashan, N.D. Causes of death in ten English-speaking Caribbean countries and territories (PAHO/B, 16:3, 1982, p. 212–223, bibl., ill., tables)

Presents comparisons of mortality data from 10 island countries and territories.

1667 Martín de Rover, Matilde. Mortalidad en la Provincia de Mendoza, 1979–1980. Mendoza, Argentina: Dirección de Estadísticas e Investigaciones Económicas, Ministerio de Economía, 1982. 94 p.: ill., tables (Publicaciones estadísticas. Serie Estudios sociales; 130)

Reports age specific mortality and principal causes of mortality for following age groups, 1979–80: infancy, 1–4 yrs., 5–14, 15–24, 25–44, 45–59, 60 plus yrs.

1668 Medina L., Ernesto and Ana M. Kaempffer R. An analysis of health progress in Chile (PAHO/B, 17:3, 1983, p. 221–232, bibl., ill., tables)

Although overall mortality in Chile decreased by 20 percent in 1960s and 29 percent in 1970s, the most marked reductions occurred in infant (60 percent) and preschool (i.e., 1–4 yrs. or 67 percent mortality in 1970s).

1669 Mier y Terán, Marta and Cecilia Andrea Rabell. La mortalidad intrauterina en México. México: UNAM, Instituto de Investigaciones Sociales, 1982. 77 p.: ill., tables (Cuadernos de investigación social; 7)

Using data from the 1976–77 Mexican

fertility survey, provides tables of intra-uterine mortality. Also considers maternal factors related to the order of the pregnancy, age of the mother, multiple pregnancies, and result of the preceding pregnancy.

1670 Riveron Corteguera, Raúl; Francisco Valdés Lazo; and Roberto Rodríguez Castro. Análisis de la salud materno-infantil en Cuba, en la década 1970–1979 (Revista Cubana de Pediatría [La Habana] 54:2, 1982, p. 149–177, bibl., ill., tables)
Reviews maternal and child health statistics for Cuba. The decade saw a reduction in infant mortality of 50 percent and in mortality due to acute diarrhea diseases of 82 percent.

1671 Rosenwaike, Ira and Samuel H. Preston. Age overstatement and Puerto Rican longevity (WSU/HB, 56:3, 1984, p. 503–525, bibl., ill., tables)
Uses various demographic techniques to investigate accuracy of longevity. Findings suggest strong evidence of widespread overstatement of age at the older ages; hence, current life tables need to be modified.

1672 Rosero Bixby, Luis; Miguel Gómez; and Virginia Rodríguez. Determinantes de la fecundidad en Costa Rica: análisis longitudinal de tres encuestas. San José: Dirección General de Estadísticas y Censos, 1980–1982. 107 p.: bibl., ill.
Analysis of fertility trends includes socioeconomic differentials, attitudes towards population growth, ideal and desired numbers of children, and regulation of fertility.

1673 Tablas de mortalidad. Montevideo: Presidencia de la República Oriental del Uruguay, Secretaria de Planemiento, Coordinación y Difusión, Dirección General de Estadística y Censos, 1979. 50 p.: ill., tables.
Includes mortality tables for Uruguay for 1974–76, with comparative tables for earlier periods (e.g., 1963–64 and 1908–00).

1674 Vida y muerte del mexicano. Editor, Federico Ortiz Quesada. México: Folios Ediciones, 1982. 2 v.: bibl., ill. (Col. El Hombre y su salud; HS 1–2)
Vol. 1 contains basic data on morbidity and mortality in Mexico, nutritional status, infectious diseases, mental health, drug use, etc. Vol. 2 is more historical and general with little quantitative data.

1675 Werner, Dennis. Fertility and pacification among the Mekranoti of Central Brazil (Human Ecology [Plenum, New York] 11:2, 1983, p. 227–245, bibl., ill., tables)
Data from pregnancy histories (73 women) and genealogies indicate that changes in health status, contraceptive use, lactation periods and post-partum sexual abstinence are not as important in accounting for lower fertility as is warfare (high male mortality).

1676 Williams, Stephen J. Population dynamics and health in Haiti (UWI/SES, 30:2, June 1981, p. 140–156, bibl., tables)
Overview of population growth (1950–74), age-specific fertility, mortality and migration patterns. The evidence suggests high fertility and rapid population growth which exceeds the ability of the economy to provide a subsistence level standard of living.

1677 Wolfe, Barbara L. and Jere R. Behrman. Determinants of child mortality, health, and nutrition in a developing country (Journal of Developmental Economics [North Holland Publishing Co., Amsterdam] 11, 1982, p. 163–193, bibl., tables)
Examines determinants of child mortality and health and nutritional status in Nicaragua. Determinants vary in different regions of the country, are inversely related with the number of siblings, and are positively related with calorie intake, schooling, availability of refrigeration and quality of sewage systems.

POPULATION GENETICS

1678 Azevedo, Elaine S. Populações da Bahia: genética e história (Universitas [Revista de cultura da Univ. Federal da Bahia, Brazil] 29, jan./abril 1982, p. 3–13, bibl., maps)
Cultural characteristics of surnames were examined in 29,755 school children from 60 localities. Significant associations were apparent between surnames of religious connotation and black phenotypic characteristics, surnames of animal/plant reference and Indian phenotypic characteristics, surnames in an "other" category and white ancestry.

1679 ———; Theomario Pinto da Costa; Maria Christina B.O. Silva; and Lucia Regina Ribeiro. The use of surnames for interpreting gene frequency distribution and past racial admixture (WSU/HB, 55:2, 1983, p. 235–242, tables)

Uses surnames to assess black and Indian admixture in Manaus (state of Amazon) and for racial classification in Lencois (Bahia). Applies results to study of gene frequency in the former and to historical reconstruction of racial admixture in the latter.

1680 Bernal, J.E.; G. Ortega; and A. Umana. The contribution of genetic disease to pediatric mortality in a university hospital in Bogotá (Journal of Biosocial Science [Oxford, England] 15, 1983, p. 465–471, bibl., tables)

Out of 1463 pediatric necropsies, 26 percent had either a congenital defect or a disease considered genetic to some extent. Simple Mendelian diseases and chromosomal disorders accounted for more than five percent of total deaths.

1681 Black, Francis L. *et al.* Failure of linguistic relationships to predict genetic distances between the Waiãpi and other tribes of lower Amazonia (AJPA, 60, 1983, p. 327–335, bibl., map, tables)

Presents data on blood group, serum protein, erythrocyte enzyme and HLA traits for Tupi-speaking tribe of Brazil and French Guiana. Comparisons with other tribes indicate that intertribal genetic distances do not correlate with linguistic affinity.

1682 Castilla E., Eduardo and Leda María Orioli. El estudio colaborativo latinoamericano de malformaciones congenitas: ECLAMC/MONITOR (AI/I, 8:5, Sept./Oct. 1983, p. 271–278, bibl., tables)

Provides results of collaborative study of malformations in 1967–69 and 1980–81.

1683 Crawford, M.H. The anthropological genetics of the Black Caribs— Garifuna—of Central America and the Caribbean (Yearbook of Physical Anthropology [Alan R. Liss Inc., New York] 26, 1983, p. 161–192, bibl., ill., maps, tables)

Review of observed genetic variation and population structure of Black Caribs.

1684 Culpi, L. and F.M. Salzano. Migration, genetic markers and race admixture in Curitiba, Brazil (Journal of Biosocial Science [Oxford, England] 16, 1984, p. 127–135, bibl., map, tables)

Data (ABO, RH, hemoglobins) from 1000 blacks and 1001 whites indicates significant admixture (e.g., persons classified as white may have from three to 19 percent African ancestry). Carriers of abnormal hemoglobins have about the same degree of mobility as those with normal types.

1685 Dykes, Dale D.; M.H. Crawford; and H.F. Polesky. Population distribution in North and Central America of PGM and Gc subtypes as determined by isoelectric focusing, IEF (AJPA, 62, 1983, p. 137–145, bibl., ill., tables)

Analyzes Gc subtypes of 20 North and Central American populations and PCM subtypes in 11 populations to identity interpopulation variation.

1686 Fischer, Rivo R.; Waldir V. Pereira; Dalnei V. Pereira; and Israel Roisenberg. Inherited factor V deficiency: study of a Brazilian family (HH, 34, 1984, p. 226–230, bibl., ill., tables)

Genealogical and laboratory evidence for this very rare coagulopathy suggest an autosomal recessive pattern of inheritance.

1687 Goldstein, Marcus S. and Eugene Kobyliansky. Anthropometric traits, balanced selection and fertility (WSU/HB, 56:1, 1984, p. 35–46, bibl., tables)

Considers question of balancing selection in anthropometric traits in relation to fertility in a sample of Mexican families. Although differences are not significant, the evidence suggests several trends of balanced and directional selection.

1688 Hutz, Mara H.; F.M. Salzano; and J. Adams. Hb F levels, longevity of homozygotes and clinical course of sickle cell anemia in Brazil (American Journal of Medical Genetics [Alan R. Liss Inc., New York] 14, 1983, p. 669–176, bibl., ill., table)

Reports 13 relationships between Hb F levels and morbidity and mortality of 354 individuals with sickle cell anemia. Those with high Hb F levels are less anemic and have a more benign course of sickle cell anemia.

1689 James, Alice V. Isonymy and mate choice on St. Bart, French West Indies: computer simulations of random and total isonymy (WSU/HB, 55:2, 1983, p. 297–303, tables)

Results of this study indicate that the

Crow-Mange method of estimating random isonymy is not accurate for an isolate in the French West Indies because demographic aspects of the population are not taken into account. Uses computer simulations to improve the estimates.

1690 Lanchbury, J.S.; J.E. Bernal; and S.S. Papiha. Genetic polymorphism of glutamate-pyruvate transaminase and glyoxalase I in Colombia (HH, 34, 1984, p. 222–225, bibl., map, tables)

Describes genetic polymorphism of these two red cell enzymes in five Andean villages. Both systems show a slight excess of homozygotes.

1691 Long, Jeffrey C. and Peter E. Smouse. Intertribal gene flow between the Ye'cuana and Yanomama: genetic analysis of an admixed village (AJPA, 61, 1983, p. 411–422, bibl., ill., tables)

Single allele estimates of ancestral proportions obtained from either Di^a and ACP^a are unrealistic and suggest that admixture is not a good explanation for genetic variation in the Yanomama village of Borabuk.

1692 Malina, Robert M. *et al.* Assortative mating for phenotypic characteristics in a Zapotec community in Oaxaca, Mexico (Journal of Biosocial Science [Oxford, England] 15, 1983, p. 273–280, bibl., tables)

Examines spouse similarity in 68–70 pairs for several anthropometric characteristics and indices. Only correlations for age, height and grip strength were significant.

Mayer, Francine M; Catherine Bonaiti; and Jean Benoist. Utilisation de l'approche généalogique pour l'étude génétique de l'hypoacousie dans un isolat de la Caraïbe. See item **1087.**

1693 Naoum, Paulo Cesar; Luis Carlos de Mattos; and Paulo Roberto Curi. Prevalence and geographic distribution of abnormal hemoglobins in the state of São Paulo, Brazil (PAHO/B, 18:2, 1984, p. 127–138, bibl., maps, plates, tables)

In a sample of 17,439 subjects attending health facilities in 19 cities, 452 abnormal hemoglobins were detected, including 370 specific molecular variants, 45 thalassemias, seven metahemoglobin variants, and two fetal hemoglobin variants, in addition to several rare hemoglobins.

1694 Salzano, F.M. *et al.* New studies on the Macushi Indians of Northern Brazil (Annals of Human Biology [Taylor and Francis, London] 11:4, 1984, p. 337–350, bibl., map, tables)

Reports demographic and genetic data for three populations of Macushi Indians. Gene frequencies in 13 of 29 systems are in the middle third of the range observed among South American Indians. A private genetic polymorphism of esterase A was encountered in one of the villages.

1695 Santos, S.E.B.; F.M. Salzano; M. Helena L.P. Franco; and Maria J. de Melo e Freitas. Mobility, genetic markers, susceptibility to malaria and race mixture in Manaus, Brazil (Journal of Human Evolution [Academic Press, New York] 12, 1983, p. 373–381, bibl., ill., maps, tables)

Using seven genetic systems in 519 individuals with malaria and 435 matched controls, the estimated racial composition of this trihybrid population is 61 percent white, 27 percent Indian, and 12 percent black. Combined frequency of B and AB blood groups was higher in the malaria sample.

1696 Smouse, Peter E.; James V. Neel; and Wanda Liu. Multiple-locus departures from panmictic equilibrium within and between village gene pools of Amerindian tribes at different stages of agglomeration (Genetics [Genetics Society of America, s.l.] 104, 1983, p. 133–153, bibl., ill., tables)

Provides comparative analysis of departures from multiple-locus Hardy-Weinberg equilibrium for the Yanomama, Makiritare, Wapishana, and Ticuna from the lowlands of South America.

1697 Sousa, Maria das Gracias de Freitas and Eliane S. Azevedo. Multivariate study of birth weight and maternal heterozygosity for sickle cell anemia in Bahia, Brazil (HH, 34, 1984, p. 40–45, bibl., ill., tables)

In a series of 1008 newborns, maternal heterozygosity for sickle cell anemia had no measurable effect on birth weight.

1698 Weimer, T.A.; L. Schüler; E. Beutler; and F.M. Salzano. Gd(+) Laguna, a new rare glucose-6-phosphate dehydrogenase variant from Brazil (Human Genetics [Springer Verlag, Hamburg, FRG] 65, 1984, p. 402–404, bibl., ill., table)

Describes new, rare glucose-6-

phosphate dehydrogenase variant in a nine-year old boy of Portuguese ancestry suffering from an iron-refractory anemia.

1699 Zago, Marco A.; Fernando F. Costa; Luis G. Tone; and Cássio Bottura. Hereditary hemoglobin disorders in a Brazilian population (HH, 33, 1983, p. 125–129, bibl., tables)

A survey in a mixed population of the northeast São Paulo state indicated 5.3 percent incidence of abnormal phenotypes among 400 school children, 4.5 percent among 602 mothers, and 2.8 percent among 606 newborns. In a second survey of a hematological clinic sample, 471 of 1023 patients showed hemoglobinopaties.

HUMAN ADAPTABILITY

Adaptive responses of native Amazonians. See item **1153.**

1701 Allman, James. Age at menarche and fertility in Haiti (SAA/HO, 41:4, Winter 1982, p. 350–355, bibl., tables)

Age at menarche (retrospective method) in a rural sample (1974) was delayed (15.0 yrs.) compared to that in a sample (936) from Port-au-Prince (14.3 yrs.). The relatively high percentage of young women (15–24 yrs.) not in union is likely the major factor in the relatively low age-specific fertility rates and an important depressant of completed fertility.

1702 Alvarez, Laura; Sonia Oliver López; and José Jordán Rodríguez. Algunos aspectos del desarrollo: los adolescentes: estudio preliminar en el Sector 6 de Pediatría del Policlínico Docento Reina (Revista Cubana de Pediatría [La Habana] 54, 1982, p. 697–708, bibl., graphs, tables)

Describes height, weight, sexual development and skeletal age in 50 boys and 50 girls 10–15 yrs. of age.

1703 Angeleli, W.A. et al. Dietary supplementation and improvement in physical work performance of agricultural migrant workers of southern Brazil (SLN/ALN, 33:1, 1983, p. 158–169, bibl., graphs, tables)

After three months of dietary supplementation, the body weight and physical work performance of 14 agricultural migrant workers (19–37 yrs.) improved significantly.

1704 Arbesu Ruiz, Nelson and José Yáñez Ordaz. Posibilidades energéticas anaerobias en escolares de Ciudad de La Habana (Revista Cubana de Pediatría [La Habana] 54, 1982, p. 21–29, bibl., graphs, tables)

Describes anaerobic capacity, including alactacid and lactacids fractions of maximum oxygen debt for 120 boys and girls, 11–14 yrs. of age.

1705 Aréchiga, Julieta and Carlos Serrano. Parámetros antropométricos de crecimiento en un grupo indígena mayance, Tojolabal (CEM/ECM, 13, 1981, p. 307–337, graphs, ill.)

Results of an anthropometric survey of 287 and 267 girls 6–15 yrs. of age, including weight, height, sitting height, head circumference, arm circumference, triceps skinfold and estimated mid-arm muscle circumference, and comparative data for other areas of Mexico.

1706 Arnaud, J. and N. Gutiérrez. Human red cell glycolysis in high altitude chronic hypoxia (AJPA, 63, 1984, p. 307–314, bibl., ill., tables)

Evidence from 108 adult Quechua residents in La Paz indicates changes in enzyme activities and levels of various metabolic intermediates related to red cell glycolysis under hypoxic conditions.

1707 Barac-Nieto, M. et al. Marginal malnutrition in school-aged Colombian boys: body composition and maximal O_2 consumption (American Journal of Clinical Nutrition [Society for Clinical Nutrition, New York] 39, 1984, p. 830–839, bibl., ill., tables)

Boys, 6–16 yrs. of age, with significant weight for age or weight for height deficits, had greater maximal oxygen uptakes per unit body weight than boys with no growth deficits. Evidence suggests that nutritional compromise apparently influences the cellular mass rather than the support tissues of the body.

1708 Beard, John; Jere Hass; and Luis Hurtado Gómez. The relationship of nutritional status to oxygen transport and growth in highland Bolivian children (WSU/HB, 55:1, 1983, p. 151–164, bibl., tables)

Considers effects of nutritional adequacy on growth and oxygen transport in 41 preschool native highland Bolivian children

(3700 m). Iron nutriture was related to weight-for-height. Results have implications for the definition of anemia in young highland children.

1709 Bogin, Barry and Robert B. MacVean. Growth status of non-agrarian, semiurban living Indians in Guatemala (WSU/ HB, 56:3, 1984, p. 527–538, bibl., ill., tables)

Concerns growth status of 753 children from the Cakchiquel language group, 5–14 yrs. of age, for height, weight, arm circumference and two skinfolds. Draws comparisons with other Guatemalan samples and with rural Zapotec children from Oaxaca.

1710 Buschang, Peter H. and Robert M. Malina. Growth in height and weight of mild-to-moderately undernourished Zapotec school children (WSU/HB, 55:3, 1983, p. 587–597, bibl., ill., tables)

Compares mixed longitudinal data for height and weight for 165 school children, 6–13 yrs., with those of better nourished North and Mesoamerican children. Growth deficits in the Zapotec children are more indicative of environmental insults experienced during the preschool ages.

1711 Chakraborty, R. et al. Genetic components of variations of red cell glycolytic intermediates at two altitudes among the South American Aymara (Annals of Human Biology [Taylor & Francis Publishers, London] 10:2, 1983, p. 173–184, bibl., maps, tables)

Reports on red cell hemoglobin, hematocrit, 2,3-diphosphoglycerate and adenosine triphosphatase levels, for 876 individuals from six villages at two altitude levels (altiplano and coast) in the Arica Dept., northern Chile. Uses data for various pairs of relatives to estimate genetic component of variation in each trait.

1712 Champin, J.; J. Pinto-Cisternas; A. Rodríguez; and G. Muller. Some variables of the craniofacial complex in a Venezuelan population of Negroid ancestry (AJPA, 59:9, 1982, p. 9–19, bibl., ill., map, tables)

Describes age and sex associated variation in craniofacial features for 226 individuals, 8–60 yrs. of age, from La Sabana, a Venezuelan Negroid isolate.

1713 Current developments in anthropological genetics. v. 3, Black Caribs: a case study in biocultural adaptation. Edited by Michael H. Crawford. New York: Plenum Press, 1984. 395 p.: bibl., graphs, ill., plates, tables.

Interdisciplinary case study of the Black Caribs, consists of 20 chapters that consider ethnohistoric, sociocultural, and demographic data; nutritional, morphological, dermatoglyphic, and physiological observations; and comprehensive genetic studies.

1714 Desai, I.D. et al. Marginal malnutrition and reduced physical work capacity of migrant adolescent boys in southern Brazil (American Journal of Clinical Nutrition [American Society for Clinical Nutrition, New York] 40, 1984, p. 135–145, bibl., ill., tables)

Describes relationships between marginal nutritional status, anthropometric characteristics and physical work capacity (PWC 170) for samples of migrant (n=66 and 34) and well-off (n=55 and 30) boys 12 yrs. of age.

1715 Esquivel, Mercedes and Jorge Vassallo. Grasa subcutánea y estado nutricional: pts. 1/2 (Revista Cubana de Pediatría [La Habana] 53, 1981, p. 274–282, bibl., ill., tables; 54, 1982, p. 672–681, bibl., ill., tables)

Pt. 1 compares triceps, subscapular, and suprailiac skinfolds of 475 preschool children of both sexes to weight and weight for height. Pt. 2 describes relationships between the triceps, subscapular and suprailiac skinfolds, and body weight and a weight/ height index in a sample of 470 preschool children.

1716 Faulhaber, Johanna. La predicción de la estatura adulta según varios métodos en niños mexicanos (UNAM/AA, 19, 1982, p. 93–120, bibl., ill., tables)

Applies several adult stature prediction equations to 18 boys and 20 girls followed longitudinally from 1–2 months to 12–13 yrs. of age and measured again at 17+ (girls) or 18+ (boys) yrs. of age. Predictions based on samples of European ancestry over-predict the adult statures of Mexican mestizos.

1717 González, Gustavo F. et al. Secular change in growth of native children and adolescents at high altitude Huancayo, Peru—3,280 meters (AJPA, 64, 1984, p. 47–51, bibl., tables)

Comparison of body measurements of children, adolescent, and adults in 1978–82 with those of 1937 indicates a secular increase in this high altitude area.

1718 González Revuelta, María Elena and **Carlos Alberto Rodríguez Alonso.** Desarrollo físico y capacidad funcional: estudio en varones no entrenados de 11 y 12 años (Revista Cubana de Pedriatría [La Habana] 54, 1982, p. 38–48, bibl., ill., tables)

Describes growth, fatness, and physical work capacity in sample of 137 boys, 11 and 12 yrs of age. Excessive fatness had a negative effect on working capacity.

1719 Greksa, Lawrence P. *et al.* The physical growth of urban children at high altitude (AJPA, 65, 1984, p. 315–322, bibl., ill., tables)

Compares growth status of urban Aymara children, 10–19 yrs., resident in La Paz to Amerindian children resident at low and high altitudes.

1720 ———— *et al.* Work performance of high-altitude Aymara males (Annals of Human Biology [Taylor & Francis, London] 11:3, 1984, p. 227–233, bibl., tables)

Considers variety of work parameters in 28 rural males, 15–43 yrs. of age. All were native of high altitude and were presently working as porters in La Paz. Maximal and submaximal oxygen consumption were negatively related to age, maximal work output was positively related to age, while relative work intensity did not change with age.

1721 Haas, Jere D.; Daniel Small; John L. Beard; and **Luis Hurtado Goméz.** Variación en hemoglobina materna y peso al nacer en la altura (Anuario del Instituto Boliviano de Biología de la Altura [La Paz] 1983/1984, p. 97–104, bibl., ill., tables)

Although indigenous Quechua and Aymara women (n=39) in La Paz have lower values for hemoglobin and transferrin saturation, and are shorter than non-indigenous women (n=28), they give birth to larger infants. Evidence suggests a more efficient state of adaptation among the indigenous women.

1722 ———— *et al.* Capacidad máxima de trabajo de niños en la altura (Anuario del Instituto Boliviano de Biología de la Altura [La Paz] 1983/1984, p. 105–109, bibl., tables)

Compares maximal exercise performance in 34 high-altitude born and 33 low-

altitude born boys of European ancestry, 8–13 yrs. of age, resident in La Paz. Maximum work performance and maximum aerobic power did not differ between the two groups, but high-altitude born boys had higher maximal work output.

1723 ———— *et al.* Esfuerzo submáximo de niños en la altura (Anuario del Instituto Boliviano de Biología de la Altura [La Paz] 1983/1984, p. 111–114, bibl., tables)

Considers submaximal exercise performance of 29 high-altitude born (mean age 10.9 yrs.) and 26 low-altitude born (mean age 10.5 yrs.) boys of European ancestry resident in La Paz. Former appear to be better adapted to hypobaric hypoxia.

1724 ———— *et al.* Submaximal work performance of native and migrant preadolescent boys at high altitude (WSU/HB, 55:2, 1983, p. 517–527, bibl., ill., tables)

Describes and compares submaximal work performance of 29 high-altitude born and 26 low-altitude born boys of European ancestry resident in La Paz. Results suggest that the high-altitude born boys are better adapted to hypobaric hypoxia.

1725 Johnston, Francis E; Barry Bogin; Robert B. MacVean; and **Bruce C. Newman.** A comparison of international standards versus local reference data for the triceps of subscapular skinfolds of Guatemalan children and youth (WSU/HB, 56:1, 1984, p. 157–171, bibl., ill., tables)

Smoothed percentile distributions for the triceps and subscapular skinfolds are presented for a healthy, well-nourished sample of high socioeconomic status children, 5–18 yrs. of age. Makes comparisons with US reference data.

1726 Kieser, J.A.; H.T. Groeneveld; and **C.B. Preston.** Patterns of dental wear in the Lengua Indians of Paraguay (AJPA, 66, 1985, p. 21–29, bibl., ill., tables)

Describes wear patterns evident on dental casts of 202 individuals, 18–60 yrs. of age. There were no significant sexually dimorphic differences in wear patterns.

1727 Leatherman, T.L.; R. Brooke Thomas; Lawrence P. Greksa; and **J.D. Haas.** Anthropometric survey of high-altitude Bolivian porters (Annals of Human Biology [Taylor & Francis, London] 11:3, 1984, p. 253–256, bibl., tables)

Descriptive study of anthropometric characteristics of 138 rural, Aymaran, high-altitude males working as porters in La Paz. Includes comparisons with other samples.

1728 Leslie, Paul W.; James R. Bindon; and Paul T. Baker. Caloric requirements of human populations: a model (Human Ecology [Plenum, New York] 12:2, 1984, p. 137–343, bibl., ill., tables)
Describes and tests model for predicting human caloric requirements on four populations including the Andean community of Nunoa, Peru.

1729 López Contreras de Blanco, Mercedes; Maritza Landaeta de Jiménez; and Hernán Méndez Castellano. Evaluación nutricional antropométrica: combinación de tres indicatores (SVPP/A, 46:3/4, 1983, p. 98–105, bibl., ill., tables)
Describes and compares heights and weights of 221 boys and 174 girls, 2–7 yrs. of age, from the upper social strata of Caracas to international reference data.

1730 López Galarraga, Aldo *et al.* Relación de la edad biológica con indicadores morfológicos y funcionales en niños de 11–12 años (Revista Cubana de Pediatría [La Habana] 54, 1982, p. 49–64, bibl., ill., tables)
Describes relationships between skeletal age and submaximal oxygen consumption and physical working capacity and several anthropometric characteristics in a sample of trained (37) and untrained (69) school children, 11 and 12 yrs. of age.

1731 McCullough, John M. and Christine S. McCullough. Age-specific variation in the secular trend for stature: a comparison of samples from industrialized and non-industrialized regions (AJPA, 65, 1984, p. 169–180, bibl., ill., tables)
Regards fluctuating environmental conditions as underlying age-specific variation in secular changes in several school-age samples including Yucatecan Maya, Oaxaca Zapotec, Aruba and Mexican-Americans.

1732 Malina, Robert M. *et al.* Adult stature and age at menarche in Zapotec-speaking communities in the Valley of Oaxaca, Mexico, in a secular perspective (AJPA, 60, 1983, p. 437–449, bibl., tables)
Adult stature and age of menarche indicate no evidence for secular change since the turn of the century. Mean ages at menarche are 14.53 for adult women (retrospective) and 14.70 for school girls (status quo).

1733 Moreno-Black, Geraldine. Dietary status and dietary diversity of native highland Bolivian children (Ecology of Food and Nutrition [Gordon & Breach, London] 13, 1983, p. 149–156, bibl., tables)
Examines dietary intake, diversity, and adequacy of 117 boys, 7–11 yrs. of age, from La Paz. Associates increased diversity and quality positively with family income and maternal education, and negatively to maternal employment status.

1734 —— *et al.* The distribution of haemoglobin concentration in a sample of native high-altitude women (Annals of Human Biology [Taylor & Francis, London] 11:4, 1984, p. 317–325, bibl., ill., tables)
Considers hemoglobin, transferrin saturation, hematocrit, and total iron-binding capacity in 222 indigenous women living in La Paz. Prevalence of anemia and polycythemia in the population was low and not regarded as public health problem. Iron deficiency occurred in 11 percent.

1735 Parra, Adalberto *et al.* Plasma gonadotrophins profile in relation to body composition in underprivileged boys (Acta Endocrinológica [Copenhagen] 99, 1982, p. 326–333, bibl., ill., tables)
Compares plasma concentrations of LH and FSH, height, weight, estimated body composition (predicted height and weight) and stage of sexual development in 250 underprivileged and 357 clinically healthy boys, 9–16 yrs. of age, from Mexico City. The former were delayed in the overt signs of puberty by about two yrs. and had a mild degree of malnutrition.

1736 —— *et al.* The relationship of plasma gonadotrophins and androgen concentrations to body growth in boys (Acta Endocrinológica [Copenhagen] 98, 1981, p. 137–147, bibl., ill., tables)
Examines relationships between plasma concentrations of LH, FSH, 17 alpha-hydroxyprogesterone, androstenedione and testosterone, and height, weight, estimated body composition (predicted from height and weight), and stage of sexual development in 543 healthy boys, 6–16 yrs. of age, from Mexico City.

1737 ——— *et al.* The relationship of plasma gonadotrophins and steroid concentrations to body growth in girls (Acta Endrocrinológica [Copenhagen] 98, 1981, p. 161–170, bibl., ill., tables)

Describes relationships between plasma concentrations of LH, FSH, 17 alphahydroxyprogesterone, estradiol and progesterone, and height, weight, estimated body composition (predicted from height and weight) and stage of sexual development in 352 healthy girls, 6–16 yrs. of age, from Mexico City.

1738 Pereira Colls, Yvonne; Miriam González de Mendoza; and María Ramírez de Fernández. Desarrollo puberal en escolares de Mérida (AVAC / ACV, 33 : 2, 1982, p. 161–164, bibl., ill., tables)

Describes pubertal development of Mérida school children. Of the sample of 1946 children and youth, 7–20 yrs. of age, 342 males and 535 females showed some degree of sexual maturation. Estimated mean age at menarche was 12.55 yrs.

1739 Rodríguez Amores, Dulce María; Pilar Castellanos Delgado; and Graciela Nicot Balon. Importancia de la práctica deportiva para el mejoramiento de la función pulmonar (Revista Cubana de Pediatría [La Habana] 54, 1982, p. 30–38, bibl., ill., table)

Includes comparisons of vital capacity, forced expiratory volume and maximum expiratory flow rate for trained (25) and untrained (162) boys, 11 and 12 yrs. of age.

1740 Spurr, G.B. Nutritional status and physical work capacity (Yearbook of Physical Anthropology [Alan R. Liss Inc., New York] 26, 1983, p. 1–35, bibl., ill., tables)

Review of the functional consequences of nutritional status on maximal oxygen consumption, physical work capacity, heart rate response to exercise, work productivity, and endurance at submaximal workload. Includes many Latin American examples.

1741 ———; J.C. Reina; H.W. Dahners; and M. Barac-Nieto. Marginal malnutrition in school-aged Colombian boys: functional consequences in maximum exercise (American Journal of Clinical Nutrition [American Society for Clinical Nutrition, New York] 37, 1983, p. 834–847, bibl., ill., tables)

Reports maximum treadmill oxygen consumption for 1013 boys, 6–16 yrs. of age, classified as nutritionally normal, low weight for age and low weight for height. Marginally malnourished boys had significantly depressed exercise performance.

1742 ———; M. Barac-Nieto; J.C. Reina; and Romelia Ramírez. Marginal malnutrition in school-aged Colombian boys: efficiency of treadmill walking in submaximal exercise (American Journal of Clinical Nutrition [American Society for Clinical Nutrition, New York] 39, 1984, p. 452–459, bibl., ill., tables)

Finds marginal malnutrition had no significant effect on the efficiency of submaximal work during treadmill walking in sample of 658 boys, 6–16 yrs. of age.

1743 Stinson, Sara. Socioeconomic status and child growth in rural Bolivia (Ecology of Food and Nutrition [Gordon & Breach, London] 13, 1983, p. 179–187, bibl., ill., tables)

Describes effects of socioeconomic status on the growth of highland Aymara children and youth (sexes combined), 6–22 yrs. of age. Effects of growth status varied with indicator used.

1744 Torún, Benjamín; Francisco Chew; and Rubén D. Mendoza. Energy costs of activities of preschool children (Nutrition Research [Pergamon Press, New York] 3, 1983, p. 401–406, bibl, ill., tables)

Reports energy expenditures estimated via indirect calorimetry for 47 presently adequately nourished but previously malnourished Guatemalan children, 17–45 months of age, during several tasks (resting, sitting, walking leisurely, climbing stairs).

1745 Valenzuela, Carlos Y. Pubertal origin of the larger sex dimorphism for adult stature of a Chilean population (AJPA, 60, 1983, p. 53–60, bibl., ill., tables)

Data for a sample of children and youth, 6–20 yrs. of age from Santiago, indicates earlier puberty and earlier cessation of growth in females, but a similar timing of maturation in males compared to European reference data.

1746 Villanueva, María and Mercedes Mejía. Estatura, peso y desarrollo dental en un grupo de niños mestizos de Las Margaritas, Chiapas (UNAM / AA, 19, 1982, p. 121–131, bibl., graphs, tables)

Considers stature, weight, and eruption of permanent dentition in 92 boys and 72 girls, 9–12 yrs. of age, relative to other samples of Mexican children.

1747 Yáñez Ordaz, José and Nelson Arbesu Ruiz. Desarrollo de las posibilidades energéticas aerobias en un grupo de escolares cubanos (Revista Cubana de Pediatría [La Habana] 54, 1982, p. 9–20, bibl., tables)

Compares body size, grip strength, and aerobic capacity in trained (182) and untrained (175) school boys, 10–16 yrs. of age. The trained youth had higher values in all variables.

NUTRITIONAL ANTHROPOLOGY

1748 Alcázar, María Luisa; Jorge Alvear; and Santiago Muzzo. Influencia de la nutrición en el desarrollo óseo del niño (SLN/ALN, 34:2, 1984, p. 298–307, bibl., graphs, tables)

Reports Greulich-Pyle skeletal ages for obese (14), well nourished (8), and undernourished (38) Chilean children, 4–29 months of age. The obese were advanced while the undernourished were delayed in bone age, with greater delays in the more severely undernourished.

1749 Alvarez, María de la Luz; Ana Calfa; and Santiago Muzzo. Nivel socioeconómico de puerperas del Gran Santiago y algunos factores que influencian el peso de sus recién nacidos (SLN/ALN, 32:4, 1982, p. 882–891, bibl., tables)

Study of a representative sample of 400 mothers and their newborns indicated little influence of socioeconomic level (0.56 percent) on birth weight.

1750 Amorozo, Maria Christina de Mello and Roger Shrimpton. The effect of income and length of urban residence on food patterns, food intake, and nutrient adequacy in an Amazonian peri-urban slum population (Ecology and Food Nutrition [Gordon & Breach, London] 14, 1984, p. 307–323, bibl., graphs, tables)

Describes influence of income and length of urban residence upon food intake and dietary adequacies for 100 households in a slum suburb of Manaus.

1751 Atalah S., Eduardo; Patricia Bustos M.; and Elena Gómez A. Desnutrición infantil: costo social por patología respiratoria y digestiva (SLN/ALN, 33:2, 1983, p. 395–408, bibl., graphs, tables)

Hospital records for 1660 children admitted under 2 yrs. of age were analyzed for the effect of malnutrition on admission rate and duration of stay for diarrhea and respiratory infections. Mildly malnourished children had higher admission rates and longer hospital stays than children with normal weight for age.

1752 ——— *et al.* Efecto de la lactancia sobre el peso y composición corporal de la nodriza (SLN/ALN, 33, 1983, p. 649–663, bibl., graphs, tables)

Examines over six months impact of lactation on the nutritional status and body composition of 134 women (95 breast-feeding and 39 bottle-feeding) from Santiago, Chile.

1753 Atlas de nutrición. Caracas: Instituto Nacional de Nutrición. 316 p., 2 leaves of plates (1 folded): ill., tables.

Reasonably comprehensive atlas of nutritional status in Venezuela. Includes indicators of fertility and natality, morbidity, age-specific mortality, malnutrition related mortality, educational, social and economic aspects, consumption of foods and nutrients, and classification of the population under 15 yrs. of age on the basis of weight and height for age.

1754 Báez Martínez, José Manuel; María T. Abreu García; and Aníbal Arias. Patrones comparativos de la lactancia materna de una comunidad miskita en la costa atlántica de Nicaragua y una comunida malenké, en la República de Guinea, Africa (Revista Cubana de Pediatría [La Habana] 54, 1982, p. 724–732, bibl., graphs, tables)

Patterns of breast-feeding are compared in Malenke (407) and Miskito (110) mothers. Late weaning is more common among Malenke mothers.

1755 Batista Filho, Malaquias and Marco Antônio de Almeida Torres. Acesso à terra e situação nutricional em populações do semi-árido nordestino (Revista Pernambucana de Desenvolvimento [Instituto de Desenvolvimento de Pernambuco, Recife] 9:1, jan./junho 1982, p. 101–118, bibl., tables)

Reports nutritional status of preschool

and school-age children relative to family access to land and socioeconomic status for 532 families. Criteria include Gómez classification, Seoane-Latham criteria, hemoglobin levels and retinol levels.

1756 Berlin, Eloise Ann and **Edward K. Markell.** Parásitos y nutrición: dinámica de la salud entre los aguaruna-jívaro (CAAAP/AP, 3 : 6, marzo 1982, p. 51–58, tables)
Provides general evaluation of the health and nutritional status (clinical observations, heights and weights of adults, estimated food intake of five families) of an Aguaruna community of about 175 individuals.

1757 Bourges, Héctor and **Blanca Rosa López-Castro.** Protein requirements of young adult men fed a Mexican rural diet (SLN/ALN, 32 : 3, 1982, p. 630–649, bibl., graphs, tables)
Results of a multiple level nitrogen balance study of eight subjects suggest that the amount of protein needed to cover the requirements of 97.5 percent of the population was 136 mg N/kg body weight for the rural diet and 122 mg N/kg for a milk diet.

1758 Caillavet, Chantal. La nourriture dans les projets de développement: le cas d'un village indien en Equateur (IFEA/B, 11 : 1/2, 1982, p. 1–9, tables)
General discussion of cultural importance of food and patterns of food consumption of Indian communities and of a specific Ecuadorian village.

1759 Casal, Pedro M. Alimentación en el Uruguay. Montevideo: Palacio Legislativo, Biblioteca, 1980. 2 v. (973 p.): bibl., ill., index (Serie de temas nacionales; 9)
Very comprehensive analysis of general nutrition including food composition and nutritional processes, as well as nutritional status in Uruguay, food habits, attitudes and beliefs, and the nutrient composition and nutritional value of many local foods and plants.

1760 Current topics in nutrition and disease. v. 11, Energy intake and activity. Edited by Ernesto Pollitt and Peggy Amante. New York: Alan R. Liss, 1984. 418 p.: bibl., graphs, tables.
Includes 18 papers, many dealing specifically with Latin American populations

and topics such as: energy balance in populations; methodology for assessing energy balance and physical activity in children and adults; field studies of activity; production and metabolism, and consequences of activity; energy deficiency; and so on.

1761 Delgado, Hernán L.; Reynaldo Martorell; Elena Brineman; and **Robert E. Klein.** Nutrition and the length of gestation (Nutrition Research [Pergamon Press, New York] 1, 1982, p. 117–126, bibl., graphs, tables)
In a sample of 830 Guatemalan women, those who consumed more of a protein-energy or energy supplement had significantly longer gestational lengths.

1762 ———; Víctor E. Valverde; José M. Belizan; and **———.** Diarrheal diseases, nutritional status and health care: analysis of their interrelationships (Ecology of Food and Nutrition [Gordon & Breach] 12, 1983, p. 229–234, bibl., ill., tables)
Interrelationships among nutritional status, health care, and diarrheal diseases are evaluated in Guatemalan children birth to two yrs. of age. Chronic malnutrition is positively related to the incidence and duration of gastrointestinal disorders.

1763 ———; ———; Reynaldo Martorell; and **———.** Relationship of maternal and infant nutrition in infant growth (Early Human Development [Elsevier Biomedical Press, Amsterdam] 6, 1982, p. 273–286, bibl., graphs, tables)
Data from the INCAP four village study indicate that infant calorie supplementation before three months of age is significantly and negatively associated with infant growth, but after three months of age supplemental calories are significantly and positively related to infant weight and length gains.

1764 ———; ———; and **Robert E. Klein.** Análisis crítico de la validez del perímetro del brazo como indicador del estado nutricional proteínico-energético en niños pre-escolares (SLN/ALN, 33 : 1, 1983, p. 170–188, bibl., ill., tables)
Evaluates validity of arm circumference as an indicator of nutritional status in sample of 3699 Guatemalan children under five yrs. of age. The measurement is valid for detecting general malnutrition but

limited when used to detect acute or chronic protein energy malnutrition.

1765 Dewey, Kathryn G. Nutrition survey in Tabasco, Mexico: nutritional status of preschool children (American Journal of Clinical Nutrition [American Society for Clinical Nutrition, New York] 37, 1983, p. 1010–1019, bibl., tables)

Nutritional status of 149 children, 2–4 yrs. of age, was evaluated by anthropomorphic, biochemical and dietary methods. Intestinal parasites were evaluated in stool samples from 111 children: 68 percent were below third percentile for height for age, but only 15 percent were below the tenth percentile for weight for height. Average dietary intake was less than two-thirds of that recommended for Mexico. Parasites were detected in 75 percent of the stool samples.

1766 ———. Nutrition survey in Tabasco: patterns of infant feeding (American Journal of Clinical Nutrition [American Society for Clinical Nutrition, New York] 38, 1983, p. 133–138, bibl., tables)

Describes patterns of infant feeding for 149 mothers and 744 children born over a 25-year period in area which has undergone rapid economic development.

1767 Diagnóstico alimentario-nutricional de la población del Departamento de Pando. La Paz: Instituto Nacional de Alimentación y Nutrición (INAN), 1980. 60, 10, 55 p.: bibl., map.

General survey of nutritional status including calorie and nutrient consumption, foods consumed, food habits, nutritional status based on arm circumference, and prevalence of endemic goiter.

1768 Donangelo, Carmen Marino. Zinc status of nursing mothers and weight adequacy of their newborn babies (Nutrition Reports International [Los Altos, Calif.] 30:5, 1984, p. 1157–1163, bibl., tables)

Describes effect of zinc status of nursing mothers on the weight for age and urinary zinc/creatinine excretion of their infants in the first months of life of 16 full-term exclusively breast-fed Brazilian infants. Infants with less than 90 percent weight for age tended to have lower excretion rates.

1769 ——— and Carlos Eduardo Azevedo. Zinco sérico em crianças brasileiras de

famílias de baixa renda (SLN/ALN, 34:2, 1984, p. 290–297, bibl., graphs, tables)

Reports serum zinc levels for 103 low socioeconomic status children, three months to six yrs. of age. Serum levels decreased with the degree of malnutrition (i.e., lowest in the chronically malnourished).

1770 Dorea, José G; Ivonette S. Almeida; Eduardo F.O. Queiroz; and Mary Ruth Horner. Nutritional status and zinc nutriture in infants and children in a poor urban community of Brazil (Ecology of Food and Nutrition [Gordon & Breach, London] 12, 1982, p. 1–6, bibl., graphs, tables)

In a sample of 146 children, 1–12 yrs. of age, 27 had moderate or severe malnutrition, 92 percent were positive for one or more intestinal parasites, and five percent had low hair zinc levels.

1771 ———; M.R. Horner; V.L.V.A Bezerra; and M.L. Campanate. Longitudinal study of major milk constituents from two different socioeconomic groups of mothers in Brazil (Nutrition Reports International [Los Altos, Calif.] 29:3, 1984, p. 699–709, bibl., graphs)

The composition of milk was compared in women from high and low socioeconomic groups before and after nursing during 4 months of lactation. There were no socioeconomic differences.

1772 Dugdale, A.E. Nomograms for monitoring nutritional status (Ecology of Food and Nutrition [Gordon & Breach, London] 14, 1984, p. 59–62, bibl., graphs)

Presents nomograms for weight for age, height for age, and weight for height based on US reference data.

1773 Ferroni, Marco A. Food habits and the apparent nature and extent of dietary nutritional deficiencies in the Peruvian Andes (SLN/ALN, 32:4, 1982, p. 850–866, bibl., tables)

Compares food patterns and energy and nutrient intake in 1958 among urban and rural family units from the central and southern sierra. With the exception of vitamin A deficiency, there was little nutrient deficiency where calorie requirements were met. Nevertheless, about one-half of the population suffered some degree of calorie deficiency.

1774 Franzetti, Silvia; Luis A. Mejía; Fernando E. Viteri; and Edmundo Alvarez. Body iron reserves of rural and urban Guatemalan women of reproductive age (SLN/ALN, 34:1, 1984, p. 69–82, bibl., graphs, tables)

Describes body iron reserves (serum ferritin) of rural coastal (33), rural highland (32) and urban (104) women, 14–29 yrs. of age. Iron deficiency was evident in 45, 25, and 12 percent of women in each group.

1775 Galler, Janina R.; Frank Ramsey; Giorgio Solimano; and Kathleen J. Propert. Sex differences in the growth of Barbadian school children with early malnutrition (Nutrition Reports International [Los Altos, Calif.] 27:3, 1983, p. 503–517, bibl., graphs, tables)

Compares height, weight, weight for height and arm circumference of 129 children, 5–11 yrs. of age, who had histories of moderate to severe protein-energy malnutrition in the first year of life, to matched cases with no such history.

1776 Garn, Stanley M.; Karen R. Rosenberg; and Arnold E. Schaefer. Relationship between fatness level and size attainment in Central America (Ecology of Food and Nutrition [Gordon & Breach, London] 13, 1983, 157–165, bibl., graphs, tables)

In a sample of 15,085 individuals of both sexes, 8–80+ yrs., from six countries, level of fatness (triceps skinfold) was related to stature during growth and in adulthood. Fatter individuals also had higher levels of red cell, serum and urinary indicators of nutritional status.

1777 Gómez A., Elena; Eduardo Atalah S.; and Bernardo Salinas S. Costo-efecto social de dos sistemas de tratamiento del niño desnutrido, en Chile (SLN/ALN, 33:4, 1983, p. 770–784, bibl., graphs, tables)

Evaluates two approaches to the care of malnourished children: a group of 745 children under an ambulatory nutritional rehabilitation program and a group of 420 children attending day care centers.

1778 Gordon, Antonio M., Jr. The nutriture of Cubans: historical perspective and nutritional analysis (UP/CSES, 13:2, 1983, p. 1–39, bibl., tables)

Discusses nutriture of the Cuban population in rather general terms, including estimated dietary intake, land use, agricultural production, effects of rationing, and selected comparisons with other countries in the Caribbean (e.g., nutritional status of children via the Gómez classification). Includes "Comment" by Howard Handelman.

1779 Gupta, Mahesh C. and Juan José Urrutia. Efecto del tratamiento quimioterapéutico periódico de parásitos intestinales en el crecimiento de niños preescolares (SLN/ALN, 32:4, 1982, p. 825–849, bibl., graphs, tables)

Sample of 159 Guatemalan children 24–61 months of age was divided into a placebo and three treatment groups for intestinal parasites. Group receiving metronidazole gained significantly more weight and height than the other groups.

1780 Havlir, Diane V. *et al.* Nutritional status of the elderly in Palmares, Costa Rica (SLN/ALN, 33:2, 1983, p. 409–422, bibl., graphs, table)

Nutritional status of men and women 65+ yrs. of age from a small community northwest of San José, was assessed anthropometrically (n=191), clinically (n=38), and in terms of dietary adequacy (n=20). No severe nutritional problems were evident.

1781 Hill, Kim; Kristen Hawkes; Magdalena Hurtado; and Hillard Kaplan. Seasonal variance in the diet of Ache hunter-gatherers in Eastern Paraguay (Human Ecology [Plenum, New York] 12:2, 1984, p. 101–135, bibl., graphs, map, tables)

Seasonal variation in the diet is related primarily to variation in daily consumption of honey. Meat and vegetable consumption varied little across seasons; there was, however, high variance in vegetable species consumed across seasons.

1782 Immink, Maarten D.C.; Diva Sanjur; and María Burgos. Nutritional consequences of US migration patterns among Puerto Rican women (Ecology of Food and Nutrition [Gordon & Breach, London] 13, 1983, p. 139–148, bibl,. ill., tables)

Considers dietary intake and adequacy of non-migrant (253), return migrants (73), and forward migrants (189). After controlling for socioeconomic variables, forward migrants had more adequate energy and macronutrient intakes. Prevalence of obesity was lower in forward than among non- and return migrants.

1783 Jiménez Rodríguez, José Antonio; Fernando González Seivane; Leopoldo Peña Alonso; and Lidia Rivera Benítez. Factores de riesgo en la obesidad infantil [Revista Cubana de Pediatría [La Habana] 54, 1982, p. 538–554, bibl., graphs, tables]
Evaluates risk factors for obesity in 168 obese boys and girls. Poor food habits and sedentary lifestyle are implicated as main risk factors. In addition, 71 percent of the parents were also overweight.

1784 Johnson, Allan A.; Michael C. Lathan; and Daphne A. Roe. Nutritional anemias among preschool children in Guyana [Ecology of Food and Nutrition [Gordon & Breach, London] 13, 1983, p. 9–14, bibl., tables]
Measures anthropometric, hematological, and serological parameters in addition to stool analysis for parasites in 196 children, 1–5 yrs. of age. Results indicated anemia in 44 percent, iron deficiency in 16 percent, low serum folacin in 73 percent, low serum vitamin B_{12} in 29 percent, and parasites in 27 percent.

1785 Johnson, Allen and Clifford A. Behrens. Nutritional criteria in Machiguenga food production decisions: a linear-programming analysis [Human Ecology [Plenum, New York] 10:2, 1982, p. 167–189, bibl., graphs, tables]
Applies linear programming model utilizing parameters of the local economy to diet of the Machiguenga Indians of the Peruvian Amazon. Compares resulting solutions to observed food production.

1786 Juez, Gabriela *et al.* Growth pattern of selected urban Chilean infants during exclusive breast-feeding [American Journal of Clinical Nutrition [American Society for Clinical Nutrition, New York] 38, 1983, p. 462–468, bibl., graphs, tables]
Reports growth patterns for weight and length of 242 exclusively breast-fed healthy low middle and low socioeconomic level infants over the first year.

1787 King, Steve and Alice Levey. Observaciones de la dieta de los Angotero-Secoya del norte del Perú [CAAAP/AP, 3:6, marzo 1982, p. 27–38, bibl., tables]
Reports foods consumed and estimated nutrient intakes in terms of foods of animal and vegetable origin and beverages.

1788 Landman, J. and J. St.E. Hall. The dietary habits and knowledge of folklore of pregnant Jamaican women [Ecology of Food and Nutrition [Gordon & Breach, London] 12, 1983, p. 203–210, bibl., graphs, tables]
Examines dietary habits and beliefs of 125 pregnant Jamaican women of mixed parity and socioeconomic status.

1789 Lejarraga, H.; L. Markevich; F. Sanchirico; and M. Cusminisky. Tablas de referencia del perímetro del brazo desde el nacimiento hasta los doce años, para niñas y niños argentinos [SLN/ALN, 33:1, 1983, p. 139–157, bibl., ill., tables]
Presents sex-specific reference data for arm circumference for Argentine children birth to 12 yrs. of age.

1790 Levin, Suzanne. Food production and population size in the Lesser Antilles [Human Ecology [Plenum, New York] 11:3, 1983, p. 321–338, bibl., map, tables]
Estimates of cultivable land and productivity indicate that calories obtained from manioc are not likely to have limited population size. Animal protein is more likely to have been the limiting factor.

1791 López Bravo, Ilse *et al.* Breast-feeding, weight gains, diarrhea and malnutrition in the first year of life [PAHO/B, 18:2, 1984, p. 151–163, bibl., ill., tables]
In a sample of 207 infants, exclusively breast-fed infants made greater weight gains, had a lower frequency of diarrhea episodes, and had a lower occurrence of malnutrition.

1792 McLeod, Joan C. and Omawale. Food consumption and poverty in rural Jamaica [Ecology of Food and Nutrition [Gordon & Breach, London] 14, 1984, p. 297–306, bibl., graphs, tables]
Describes household food consumption and socioeconomic data for 110 households grouped by landholdings. Energy intake was low in one-third of the households, but protein-energy ratios were generally adequate.

1793 Malnutrition and behavior: critical assessment of key issues. Edited by Josef Brozek and Beat Schurch. Laussane, Switzerland: Nestle Foundation, 1984. 656 p.: bibl., graphs, tables.
Comprises proceedings of "symposium at a distance" (i.e., by correspondence, in-

cluding variety of papers dealing with the forms and assessment of energy-protein malnutrition, assessment of function— electrophysiological, psychometric, motor— mechanisms—social, environmental inter- actions—issues in design and analysis, and interventions). Uses variety of Latin Ameri- can examples throughout.

1794 Molina-Ballesteros, Gilberto *et al.* Lead concentration in the blood of children from pottery-making families ex- posed to lead salts in a Mexican village (PAHO/B, 17:1, 1983, p. 35–41, bibl., graphs, tables)

Describes blood lead levels and other indicators of lead intoxication in 153 chil- dren, 5–15 yrs. of age, whose families made pottery in home workshops. Compared to 80 control children, these children had higher levels of lead and zinc protoporphyrin in the blood and delta-aminolevulinic acid in the urine, suggesting considerable lead exposure.

1795 Novotny, Rachel and Leonardo J. Mata. Breast milk consumption in rural Costa Rica (SLN/ALN, 33:2, 1983, p. 377– 386, bibl., graphs, tables)

Measures breast milk consumption in 20 breast-feeding infants two days to six months of age. Mean consumption for 10 full breast-feeders (no supplementation) was 639 ml per day at a mean age of 42 days, while that of partial breast-feeders (supple- mented) was 396 ml per day at a mean age of 95 days.

1796 Owen, M.R. and P.J. Owen. Adult knowledge of childhood immunization and weight-for-age graphs in St. Lucia (West Indian Medical Journal [Univ. of the West In- dies, Mona, Jamaica] 32, 1983, p. 172–176, bibl., tables)

Knowledge of weight for age curves in children among adults was generally un- satisfactory and was determined largely by the clinic nurse. Knowledge of immuniza- tion, on the other hand, was satisfactory.

1797 Palacio, Joseph. Food and social rela- tions in a Belizean Garifuna village (BISRA/BS, 12:3, 1984, p. 1–35, tables)

Examines food and social relations in the context of the local value system, food exchange system, and food consumption patterns.

1798 Pigott, Jeralyn and Kathryn Kolasa. In- fant feeding practices and beliefs in one community in the Sierra of rural Ec- uador: a prevalence study (SLN/ALN, 33:1, 1983, p. 126–138, bibl.)

Describes infant feeding practices and beliefs of 54 women from a rural community. Sex differences in weaning and dietary sup- plementation were apparent.

1799 Piñeiro, Regino; Francisco Carvajal; and Julio González. Maduración ósea en el niño obeso (Revista Cubano de Pediatría [La Habana] 53, 1981, p. 17–22, bibl., tables)

Describes height, weight, and Greulich-Pyle skeletal ages for 152 obese children, 5–14 yrs. of age. In contrast to most other data, only 20 percent of the obese children were advanced in skeletal age.

1800 Rawlins, S.C. Changing patterns in the prevalence of intestinal parasites at the University Hospital of the West Indies: 1964–1981 (West Indian Medical Journal [Univ. of the West Indies, Mona, Jamaica] 31, 1982, p. 111–120, bibl., graphs, tables)

Changing prevalence of intestinal para- sites is described (e.g., hookworm, 8.7 per- cent in 1964 and 1.0 percent in 1978; tri- churiasis, 9.6 percent in 1964, 24.1 percent in 1973, and 11.1 percent in 1979). The 1–5 yr. old age group generally had the highest prevalences.

1801 Rodríguez, Aldo *et al.* Niveles de zinc y cobre en lactantes chilenos (SLN/ ALN, 34:1, 1984, p. 27–34, bibl., tables)

Presents zinc and copper levels in the plasma and hair of 81 well nourished chil- dren, 2–36 months of age.

1802 Romanoff, Steven. Women as hunters among the Matses of the Peruvian Amazon (Human Ecology [Plenum, New York] 11:3, 1983, p. 339–343, bibl., tables)

Discusses women's role as hunters, evidence indicating that couples bring back more meat than men alone.

1803 Ruz, Manuel *et al.* Composición química de leche materna: influencia del estado nutricional de la nodriza (SLN/ ALN, 32:3, 1982, p. 697–712, bibl., graphs, tables)

Chemical composition of milk from 16 underweight and 25 control subjects at 4, 8, and 12 weeks of lactation showed no meaningful differences in protein, lactose, energy, calcium, iron and copper contents.

1804 Santos, Leonor M.P.; Jean M. Dricot; Luiza S. Asciutti; and Christiane Dricot-d'Ans. Xeropthalmia in the state of Paraiba, northeast of Brazil: clinical findings (American Journal of Clinical Nutrition [American Society for Clinical Nutrition, New York] 38, 1983, p. 139–144, bibl., graphs, tables)

Results of survey of 10,922 clinical examinations of children, birth to 12 yrs. of age from six localities, indicate the highest occurrence of clinical signs of xerophthalmia in the semiarid Sertão region.

1805 Sellers, Stephen G. Diet patterns and nutritional intake in a Costa Rican community (Ecology of Food and Nutrition [Gordon and Breach, London] 14, 1984, p. 205–218, bibl., map, tables)

Considers energy and nutrient components of the diet, and budget and farming strategies for 26 family farm households in a municipal district to the east of Costa Rica's central plateau.

1806 La Situación de la infancia en la República Dominicana. Santo Domingo: Gobierno de Concentración Nacional, Secretariado Técnico de la Presidencia, Oficina Nacional de Planificación, 1983. 475 p.: ill.

Middle two sections of volume provide interesting data on child health and nutrition, including morbidity and mortality statistics for a variety of diseases (1973–81), infant mortality, estimated per capita nutrient consumption, and distribution of malnutrition of preschool children throughout the country.

1807 Smith, Meredith F.; Blas Santos; and Martha Fernández. Nutrition and public health in the Dominican Republic (SLN/ALN, 32:4, 1982, p. 867–881, bibl., graphs, tables)

Results of a nutrition survey of 295 mothers and 448 of their children under five yrs. of age from a mountainous region southwest of Santiago indicated incidence of moderate and severe undernutrition less than expected. Interestingly, 6.5 percent of the children were greater than 110 percent of the weight for age reference data.

1808 ———; Steven K. Paulsen; William Fougere; and J.S. Ritchey. Socioeconomic, education and health factors influencing growth of rural Haitian children (Ecology of Food and Nutrition [Gordon & Breach, London] 13, 1983, p. 99–108, bibl., graphs, tables)

In a survey of 160 women and their child closest to weaning age, amount of food or money available for food had the greatest impact on the child's current nutritional state (weight for age), while education variables had the greatest impact on long-term nutritional status (height for age).

1809 Soto, Julio. Ecología de la salud en comunidades nativas de la Amazonía Peruana (CAAAP/AP, 3:6, marzo 1982, p. 13–26, tables)

Reports health status of 377 Ashaninka and 121 Machinguenga on the basis of nutritional deficiencies, hemoglobin levels, hematocrit, serum proteins, prevalence of toxoplasmosis, and childhood morbidity.

1810 Stevens, M; J. Landman; R. Hayes; and G.R. Serjeant. Skinfold thickness and nutritional status of young Jamaican children (West Indian Medical Journal [Univ. of the West Indies, Mona, Jamaica] 32, 1983, p. 161–167, bibl., graphs, tables)

Describes height, weight, arm circumference and four skinfolds (triceps, biceps, subscapular, and suprailiac) for sample of 60 boys and 61 girls, 4–6 yrs. of age, of predominantly African ancestry.

1811 Uriburu, Graciela *et al.* Impacto nutricional de la alimentación complementaria en relación con la duración y gravedad de los episodios infecciosos (SLN/ALN, 33:4, 1983, p. 785–801, bibl., graphs, tables)

Nutritional impact of three different programs of supplementary feeding on 200 children, 6–24 months of age, from a periurban slum of San José, Costa Rica, is considered relative to the duration and severity of infectious disease.

1812 Valle, Alejandro and Manuel Amador. Indice energía/proteína en lactantes (Revista Cubana de Pediatría [La Habana] 53, 1981, p. 209–219, bibl., graphs, tables)

Describes energy/protein index based on triceps skinfold and arm circumference for 670 infants 3–11 months of age, 110 marasmic infants, and 118 overweight infants.

1813 Valverde, Víctor *et al.* Seasonality and nutritional status (SLN/ALN, 32:3, 1982, p. 521–540, bibl.)
Provides review of seasonal variation in growth and nutritional status. Effects on weight and height gain are apparent.

1814 Vargas, Emilio *et al.* Efecto de la suplementación de proteína animal y energía en la calidad proteínica de dietas a base de arroz y frijol en hombres adultos (SLN/ALN, 34:1, 1984, p. 48–68, bibl., graphs, tables)
Describes results of four brief nitrogen balance studies involving diets based on rice and beans, and animal protein and/or energy supplementation in Guatemalan adults.

1815 Veloso-Naves, M.M.; J.E. dos Santos; and J.E. Dutra de Oliveira. Diet and physical activity of obese schoolchildren of different socioeconomic levels (SLN/ALN, 30:5, 1984, p. 1197–1207, bibl., graphs, tables)
Compares calorie and nutrient intake, feeding habits and pattern of physical activity in 16 obese children, 7–12 yrs. of age, from upper and lower socioeconomic strata.

1816 Victora, Cesar G.; J. Patrick Vaughan; José Carlos Martines; and Lucio B. Barcelos. Is prolonged breast-feeding associated with malnutrition? (American Journal of Clinical Nutrition [American Society for Clinical Nutrition, New York] 39, 1984, p. 307–314, bibl., ill., tables)
Considers association between duration of breast-feeding and nutritional status (weight and length for age, weight for length) in 802 children, 12–36 months of age, from southern Brazil.

1817 Weber, Charles W.; George W. Nelson; M.V. de Vaquera; and P.B. Pearson. Lead concentration in hair of male pottery workers (Nutrition Reports International [Los Altos, Calif.] 30:5, 1984, p. 1009–1018, bibl., tables)
Lead and vanadium concentrations in the hair of 180 pottery workers were higher than in controls. Lead levels ranged from 3 to 601 ppm in the former and 1 to 40 ppm in the latter.

1819 Wong, Pablo; Inocencio Higuera; and Mauro E. Valencia. Relación entre ingreso familiar, gasto y consumo de alimentos en zonas urbanus marginadas de Sonora,

México (SLN/ALN, 34:2, 1984, p. 391–403, bibl., graphs, tables)
Considers relationships among household income, food expenditures and food consumption for 300 families from the marginal urban areas of Hermosillo.

1820 Zeni, Susana; María Luz P.M. de Portela; María del Carmen Morasso; and María Esther Río. Calcio/creatinina en orina basal en relación a la ingesta de calcio y al estado nutricional, en menores de tres años (SLN/ALN, 34:1, 1984, p. 35–45, bibl., graphs, tables)
Evaluates calcium/creatinine ratio as an indicator of calcium nutritional status in basal urine from 24 Argentine children 3–36 months of age over a 60 day period. Results suggest that the ratio does not reflect calcium intake; rather, it depends on bone calcium turnover.

BIOMEDICAL CONSIDERATIONS

Alcorn, Janis B. Huastec Mayan ethnobotany. See item 890.

1821 Anderson, John E.; Walter Rodrigues; and Antônio Marcio Tavares Thome. Breast-feeding and use of the health care system in Bahia, Brazil: three multivariate analyses (Studies in Family Planning [The Population Council, New York] 15:3, 1984, p. 127–135, bibl., tables)
Uses three multivariate methods to evaluate inverse relationships between breastfeeding and use of the health care system. In all three methods, education and place of last live birth had a net effect on breastfeeding.

1822 Banguero, Harold. Socioeconomic factors associated with malaria in Colombia (Social Science in Medicine [Pergamon Press, London] 19:10, 1984, p. 1099–1104, bibl., graphs, tables)
Describes methodology used to analyze social, economic, and health determinants of malaria incidence and applies the model to data for one of the most malaria affected areas in the country.

1823 Bermúdez Méndez, Vera; Carlos Raabe Cercone; and Laura Ortiz Malavassi. Embarazo entre las adolescentes: resultados de una encuesta realizada en la ciudad de

Limón, 1980. San José: Asociación Demográfica Costarricense, 1982. 94 p.: bibl., ill.

Analysis of characteristics of pregnant teen-agers and control group who were never pregnant includes family conditions, knowledge and use of contraception, care during pregnancy, impact of pregnancy, and general sex education concerning issues of pregnancy.

Browner, C.H. Criteria for selecting herbal remedies. See item **897.**

Butt Colson, Audrey. Binary oppositions and the treatment of sickness among the Akawaio. See item **1178a.**

1824 Chaieb, J.A. *et al.* An epidemiologic survey of smoking patterns and chronic obstructive bronchopulmonary disease in Porto Alegre, Brazil (PAHO/B, 18:1, 1984, p. 26–42, bibl., graphs, map, tables)

Reports results of a survey of smoking habits, obstructive lung disease and lung function in adult men and women.

1825 Cihen, Milton. The ethnomedicine of the Garifuna, Black Caribs, of Río Tinto, Honduras (CUA/AQ, 57:1, Jan. 1984, p. 16–27, bibl.)

Describes results of survey of medical beliefs and practices, both traditional and modern. For ethnologist's comment, see item **904.**

Cominsky, Sheila. Medical pluralism in Mesoamerica. See item **910.**

1827 Escobar, Gabriel J.; Eduardo Salazar; and **Mario Chuy.** Beliefs regarding the etiology and treatment of infantile diarrhea in Lima, Peru (Social Science in Medicine [Pergamon Press, London] 17, 1983, p. 1257–1269, bibl.)

In three samples of women, results of interviews indicate that diarrhea is not viewed as an infectious disease; rather, it is viewed within the hot-cold dichotomy.

Foster, George M. How to stay well in Tzintzuntzan. See item **922.**

1828 Foxman, Betsy; Ralph R. Frerichs; and **James N. Becht.** Health status of migrants (WSU/HB, 56:1, 1984, p. 129–141, bibl., ill., tables)

Compares morbidity, mortality, and fertility patterns of Quechua-speakers in lowland Bolivia to those of Spanish-speaking inhabitants of the region. Former had higher fertility and infant mortality rates.

1829 Frisancho, A. Roberto; Jorge Matos; and **Laura A. Bollettino.** Role of gynecological age and growth maturity status in fetal maturation and prenatal growth of infants born to young still-growing adolescent mothers (WSU/HB, 56:3, 1984, p. 583–593, bibl., tables)

Gynecological age of 412 adolescent mothers 13–15 yrs. of age from Lima, Peru, was not related to newborn maturity and size; rather, low gynecological age in combination with incomplete maternal growth resulted in lower birth weight.

1830 ———; ———; and **Pam Flegel.** Maternal nutritional status and adolescent pregnancy outcome (American Journal of Clinical Nutrition [American Society for Clinical Nutrition, New York] 38, 1983, p. 739–746, bibl., graphs, tables)

Results of a survey of 1256 adolescent mothers from Lima suggest that nutritional requirements of pregnancy may be greater among them than in older women, and these increased requirements may compete with those of the fetus.

García Ruiz, Jesús. El defensor y el defendido: dialéctica de la agresión entre los mochós. See item **924.**

1831 Halberstein, Robert A. The use of medicinal plants to control high blood pressure in the Caribbean (Florida Anthropologist [Florida Anthropological Society, Gainesville] 36:3/4, 1983, p. 167–176, bibl., table)

Critical discussion of medicinal plants used to control high blood pressure in the Caribbean.

1832 ——— and **John E. Davies.** Biosocial aspects of high blood pressure in people of the Bahamas (WSU/HB, 56:2, 1984, p. 317–328, bibl., map, tables)

Data from a variety of biocultural sources, including blood pressure readings for 167 adults, indicates hypertension in about one-third of the sample. These adults were older and heavier. Discusses cultural factors related to hypertension.

1833 Hunter, John M. and **Sonia Arbona.** Disease rate as an artifact of the health care system: tuberculosis in Puerto Rico (Social Science in Medicine [Pergamon Press, London] 19:9, 1984, p. 997-1008, bibl., graphs, maps, tables)

Distribution of tuberculosis is essentially a measurable artifact of the health care system rather than a reflection of true geographic prevalence.

1834 Inamura, Hiroshi and Hitoshi Araki. The adaptation states of temporary Japanese residents in Latin America (Latin American Studies [Univ. of Tsukuba, Special Project on Latin America, Sakura-Mura, Japan] 7, 1983, p. 143–170, tables)

Surveys personal and social concerns of Japanese adults and their children temporarily residing in São Paulo, Rio de Janeiro, Buenos Aires, Santiago, Lima, and Mexico City. Main concerns were safety, language, education, and illness.

Kaplan, Jonathan E.; James W. Larrick; and James A. Yost. Workup on the Waorani. See item **1275.**

1835 Kroeger, Axel. South American Indians between traditional and modern health services in rural Ecuador (PAHO/B, 16:3, 1982, p. 242–254, bibl., graphs, maps, tables)

Survey of 727 heads of households from four Indian groups indicated a marked preference for modern health services and self-care over traditional healers and drug sellers. Those living near modern services had higher esteem for traditional healers, while those dependent on traditional healers had higher esteem of modern services.

Logan, Kathleen. The role of pharmacists and over the counter medications in the health care system of a Mexican city. See item **951.**

1836 Lopes, Edison Reis et al. Morte súbita e doença de Chagas: análise dos fatores predisponentes do óbito súbito do chagásico crônico (IOC/M, 77:3, julho/set. 1982, p. 255–262, bibl., charts)

Examines sudden death in 116 cases of Chagas's disease more common in males. Emotional factors, physical effort, and season of the year do not play key roles in sudden death.

1837 Lozoya L., Xavier and Mariana Lozoya. Flora medicinal de México. v. 1, Plantas indígenas. México: Instituto Mexicano del Seguro Social, 1982. 1 v.: bibl., indexes.

Reasonably comprehensive listing of indigenous medicinal plants, including botanical description, distribution, ecology, popular synonyms, historical antecedents and bibliography, and chemical and pharmacological information for each plant.

1838 Lumbreras, Hugo. Vista panorámica sobre la patología tropical peruana y especial referencia a aquellas enfermedades que requieren estudio (CAAAP/AP, 3:6, marzo 1982, p. 7–12)

Brief overview of diseases of the Peruvian Amazon related to viruses, bacteria, rickettsiae, spirochetes, fungi, parasites, and poisonous animals.

Menéndez, Eduardo L. Poder, estratificación y salud: análisis de las condiciones sociales y económicas de la enfermedad en Yucatán. See item **954.**

1839 Montes Giraldo, José Joaquín. Medicina popular en Colombia: vegetales y otras sustancias usadas como remedios. Bogotá: Instituto Caro y Cuervo, 1981. 295 p.: bibl., index, maps (Publicaciones; 58)

Alphabetical listing of various ailments and the plants and other substances used as remedies.

1840 Morais, P.V.; W.F. Clarke; R.J. Hayes; and G.R. Serjeant. Heart size and chest shape in homozygous sickle cell disease (West Indian Medical Journal [Univ. of the West Indies, Mona, Jamaica] 32, 1983, p. 157–160, bibl., graphs, tables)

Compares chest diameters and cardiac volume in 6–8 yr. old normal children and children with sickle cell disease. Cardiac volume and anterior-posterior chest diameter are larger in children with sickle cell disease.

1841 Ortega Pérez, Fernando. La dicotomía caliente/frío en la medicina andina: el caso de San Pedro de Casta (PUCP/DA, 5, julio 1980, p. 115–139, tables)

Discusses in detail the heat-cold dichotomy in an Andean campesino community. Lists classification of medicinal herbs, foods, and illnesses.

1842 Ouensanga, Christian. Plantes medicinales et remèdes créoles. t. 1, Plantes médicinales. Fort de France: Editions Désormeaux, 1983. 1 v.: bibl., ill., index.

Systematic listing, including illustrations, of medicinal plants and their use in local remedies.

1843 Pereira, Maurício Gomes. Characteristics of urban mortality from Chagas's

disease in Brazil's federal district (PAHO/B, 18:1, 1984, p. 1–9, bibl., graphs, tables)
Chagas's disease accounted for 4.3 percent of all deaths in the district in 1977–78. It had a greater impact on adult mortality than on infant and early childhood mortality.

1844 Pina Coba, Bertha; José M. Cartaya; Roberto Martínez; and Juan Mendilahaxon. Cifras tensionales en el adolescente de 12–14 años: algunos aspectos clínico-epidemiológicos (Revista Cubana de Pediatría [La Habana] 54, 1982, p. 682–696, bibl., tables)
Hypertension is evaluated in 699 girls and 755 boys, 12–14 yrs. of age, relative to height, weight, sexual development and sport activity.

Plath, Oreste. Folklore médico chileno: antropología y salud. See *HLAS 46:1078.*

1844a Riveron Corteguera, Raúl and José A. Gutiérrez Muñiz. Las enfermedades diarreicas agudas en América Latina en el decenio 1970–1979: la situación de Cuba (Revista Cubana de Pediatría [La Habana] 53, 1981, p. 351–364, bibl., tables)
Reviews acute diarrheal diseases in several Latin American countries and compares them to Cuban data.

1845 Rojas de Arias, Antonieta *et al.* A seroepidemiologic survey of Chagas's disease in two Paraguayan villages (PAHO/B, 18:2, 1984, p. 164–171, bibl., map, tables)
Results of a survey of two randomly selected and widely separated villages, styles of home construction, climatic conditions, poor hygiene, lack of health education, and ignorance of the connection between the triatomids and Chagas's disease all tended to encourage proliferation of the triatomids and transmission of Trypanosoma cruzi.

Rubel, Arthur J.; Carl W. O'Nell; and Rolando Collado-Ardon. Susto: a folk illness. See item **979.**

1846 Ryn, Zdzisław. Los Andes y la medicina. La Paz: Instituto Boliviano de Cultura, Instituto Nacional de Antropología, Centro de Documentación Antropológica, 1981. 122 p., 8 leaves of plates: bibl., ill. (Serie Fuentes para la investigación y documentación andina; 4)
General account of medical anthropology in the Andes, including precolumbian

considerations, mountain sickness, biological anthropological studies of Andean natives, infirmities of the indigenous population, alcoholism, and migration to the lowlands.

1847 Schauer, I. *et al.* Colesterol total plasmático y niveles de HDL-colesterol en niños cubanos entre dos y quince años de edad (Revista Cubana de Pediatría [La Habana] 53, 1981, p. 29–35, bibl., graphs, tables)
Describes total plasma cholesterol and HDL-cholesterol in a sample of 1218 boys and girls, 2–15 yrs. of age.

Trotter, Robert T., II and Juan Antonio Chavira. Curanderismo. See *HLAS 46:1124.*

1848 Vélez Salas, Francisco. Plantas medicinales de Venezuela. 2a ed. Caracas: Inagro, 1982. 444 p., 5 leaves of plates: bibl., ill., index.
Consists of four parts: 1) history of the school of pharmacy; 2) botanical aspects of specific plants; 3) medicinal plants; and 4) political aspects of medicinal plants.

Villa Rojas, Alfonso. Breves consideraciones sobre la creencia del mal de ojo. See item **999.**

1849 Weiss, Kenneth; Robert E. Ferrell; and Craig L. Hines. A new world syndrome of metabolic diseases with a genetic and evolutionary basis (Yearbook of Physical Anthropology [Alan R. Liss, London] 27, 1984, p. 153–178, bibl., graphs, tables)
Review of a syndrome which includes tendency towards obesity at early adult age, adult onset diabetes mellitus, the formation of cholesterol gallstones and gallbladder cancer in many Amerindian peoples.

Weller, Susan C. New data on intracultural variability: the hot-cold concept of medicine and illness. See item **1003.**

1850 Wise, Robert P. The persistence of poor health in Guatemala: a preventive medical perspective: pt. 1 (Journal of Latin Community Health [Boston] 1:1, 1982, p. 71–79, bibl., tables)
Discusses variety of health indicators (e.g., mortality and life expectancy, mortality from measles and diarrhea, malnutrition).

JOURNAL ABBREVIATIONS
ANTHROPOLOGY

AAA/AA American Anthropologist. American Anthropological Association. Washington.

AAAS/S Science. American Association for the Advancement of Science. Washington.

ACPS/B Boletín de la Academia de Ciencias Políticas y Sociales. Caracas.

AES/AE American Ethnologist. American Ethnological Society. Washington.

AFA/JFA Journal of Field Archaeology. Boston Univ. *for the* Assn. for Field Archaeology. Boston.

AFS/JAF Journal of American Folklore. American Folklore Society. Austin, Tex.

AGS/GR The Geographical Review. American Geographical Society. New York.

AI/I Interciencia. Asociación Interciencia. Caracas.

AIA/A Archaeology. Archaeological Institute of America. New York.

AJPA American Journal of Physical Anthropology. American Association of Physical Anthropologists [and] the Wistar Institute of Anatomy and Biology. Philadelphia.

AMNH/NH Natural History. American Museum of Natural History. New York.

APS/P Proceedings of the American Philosophical Society. Philadelphia.

ASE/E Ethnohistory. Journal of the American Society for Ethnohistory. Buffalo, N.Y.

AT/A Antiquity. A quarterly review of archaeology. Antiquity Trust. Cambridge, England.

AU/P Phylon. Atlanta Univ. Atlanta.

AVAC/ACV Acta Científica Venezolana. Asociación Venezolana para la Avance de la Ciencia. Caracas.

BISRA/BS Belizean Studies. Belizean Institute of Social Research and Action [and] St. John's College. Belize City.

CAAAP/AP Amazonía Peruana. Centro Amazónico de Antropología y Aplicación Práctica, Depto. de Documentación y Publicaciones. Lima.

CCE/RA Revista de Antropología. Casa de la Cultura Ecuatoriana, Núcleo del Azuay. Cuenca, Ecuador.

CEDLA/B Boletín de Estudios Latinoamericanos. Centro de Estudios y Documentación Latinoamericanos. Amsterdam.

CEM/ECM Estudios de Cultura Maya. UNAM, Centro de Estudios Mayas. México.

CPES/RPS Revista Paraguaya de Sociología. Centro Paraguayo de Estudios Sociológicos. Asunción.

CU/JIA Journal of International Affairs. Columbia Univ., School of International Affairs. New York.

CUA/AQ Anthropological Quarterly. Catholic Univ. of America, Catholic Anthropological Conference. Washington.

DEA/IP International Perspectives: the Canadian Journal on World Affairs. Dept. of External Affairs. Ottawa.

DGV/ZE Zeitschrift für Ethnologie. Deutsche Gesellschaft für Völkerkunde. Braunschweig, FRG.

EANH/B Boletín de la Academia Nacional de Historia. Quito.

EEHA/AEA Anuario de Estudios Americanos. Consejo Superior de Investigaciones Científicas [and] Univ. de Sevilla, Escuela de Estudios Hispano-Americanos. Sevilla.

EM/A Arstryck. Etnografiska Museum. Göteborg, Sweden.

EPHE/H L'Homme. Revue française d'anthropologie. La Sorbonne, L'Ecole pratique des haute études. Paris.

FAS/FA The Florida Anthropologist. Florida Anthropological Society. Gainesville.

FIU/CR Caribbean Review. Florida International Univ., Office of Academic Affairs. Miami.

FSCN/A Antropológica. Fundación La Salle de Ciencias Naturales, Instituto Caribe de Antropología y Sociología. Caracas.

GM The Geographical Magazine. London.

HH   Human Heredity. Basel, Switzerland.

HICLR   Hastings International and Comparative Law Review. Univ. of California, Hastings College of the Law. San Francisco.

HISLA   HISLA. Revista latinoamericana de historia económica y social. Lima.

HRAF/BSR   Behavior Science Research. HRAF Journal of comparative studies. Human Relations Area Files. New Haven, Conn.

IAI/I   Indiana. Beiträge zur Völker-und Sprachenkunde, Archäologie und Anthropologie des Indianischen Amerika. Ibero-Amerikanisches Institut. Berlin, FRG.

IAP/P   Pesquisas. Anuário do Instituto Anchietano de Pesquisas. Pôrto Alegre.

ICP/R   Revista del Instituto de Cultura Puertorriqueña. San Juan.

ICUAER/B   Bulletin of the International Committee on Urgent Anthropological and Ethnological Research. Vienna.

IDES/DE   Desarrollo Económico. Instituto de Desarrollo Económico y Social. Buenos Aires.

IFEA/B   Bulletin de l'Institut français d'études andines. Lima.

IGFO/RI   Revista de Indias. Instituto Gonzalo Fernández de Oviedo [and] Consejo Superior de Investigaciones Científicas. Madrid.

IIE/A   Anales del Instituto de Investigaciones Estéticas. UNAM. México.

III/AI   América Indígena. Instituto Indigenista Interamericano. México.

IJ/JJ   Jamaica Journal. Institute of Jamaica. Kingston.

IOC/M   Memórias do Instituto Oswaldo Cruz. Rio de Janeiro.

IPA/A   Allpanchis. Instituto de Pastoral Andina. Cuzco, Perú.

IU/AL   Anthropological Linguistics. A publication of the Archives of the Languages of the World. Indiana Univ., Anthropology Dept. Bloomington.

IU/IJAL   International Journal of American Linguistics. Indiana Univ. *under the auspices*

of the Linguistic Society of America, American Anthropological Assn., *with the cooperation of the* Joint Committee on American Native Languages. Bloomington.

JLAS   Journal of Latin American Studies. Centers or institutes of Latin American studies at the univs. of Cambridge, Glasgow, Liverpool, London and Oxford. Cambridge Univ. Press. London.

JPS   The Journal of Peasant Studies. Frank Cass & Co. London.

KITLV/B   Bijdragen tot de Taal-, Land- en Volkenkunde. Koninklijk Instituut voor Taal-, Land- en Volkenkunde. Leiden, The Netherlands.

LINGUA   Lingua. North-Holland Pub. Co. Amsterdam.

LNB   Lotería. Lotería Nacional de Beneficiencia. Panamá.

LSA/L   Language. Journal of the Linguistic Society of America. Waverly Press. Baltimore, Md.

MHD/B   Boletín del Museo del Hombre Dominicano. Santo Domingo.

MLV/T   Tribus. Veröffentlichungen des Linden-Museums. Museum für Länder- und Völkerkunde. Stuttgart, FRG.

MNCR/V   Vínculos. Revista de antropología. Museo Nacional de Costa Rica. San José.

MV/BA   Baessler-Archiv. Museen für Völkerkunde. Berlin.

MVW/AV   Archiv für Völkerkunde. Museum für Völkerkunde in Wien und von Verein Freunde der Völkerkunde. Wien.

NACLA   NACLA: Report on the Americas. North American Congress on Latin America. New York.

NWIG   Nieuwe West-Indische Gids. Martinus Nijhoff. The Hague.

PAHO/B   Bulletin of the Pan American Health Organization. Washington.

PEMN/R   Revista del Museo Nacional. Casa de la Cultura del Perú, Museo Nacional de la Cultura Peruana. Lima.

PMK   Paideuma. Mitteilungen zur Kulturkunde. Deutsche Gesellschaft für kulturmorphologie von Frobenius Institut

aus der Johann Wolfgang Goethe—
Universität. Wiesbaden, FRG.

PUCP/DA   Debates en Anthropología.
Pontificia Univ. Católica del Perú, Depto. de
Ciencias Sociales. Lima.

RAI/M   Man. A monthly record of
anthropological science. The Royal
Anthropological Institute. London.

RRI   Revista/Review Interamericana. Univ.
Interamericana. San Germán, P.R.

SA   Scientific American. Published
monthly by Scientific American Inc.
New York.

SA/J   Journal de la Société des
américanistes. Paris.

SAA/AA   American Antiquity. Society for
American Archaeology. Menasha, Wis.

SAA/HO   Human Organization. Society for
Applied Anthropology. New York.

SAA/R   Relaciones de la Sociedad
Argentina de Antropología. Buenos Aires.

SCHG/R   Revista Chilena de Historia y
Geográfia. Sociedad Chilena de Historia y
Geografía. Santiago.

SEB/EB   Economic Botany. New York
Botanical Garden *for the* Society for
Economic Botany. New York.

SECOLAS/A   Annals of the Southeastern
Conference on Latin American Studies.

SEM/E   Ethnos. Statens Etnografiska
Museum. Stockholm.

SGL/B   Boletín de la Sociedad Geográfica
de Lima.

SLN/ALN   Archivos Latinoamericanos de
Nutrición. Organo oficial de la Sociedad
Latinoamericano de Nutrición. Caracas.

SOCIOL   Sociologus. Zeitschrift für
empirische Soziologie, sozialpsychologische
und ethnologische Forschung. Berlin, FRG.

SSA/B   Bulletin. Société suisse des
américanistes. Geneva.

SVPP/A   Archivos Venezolanas de
Puericultura y Pediatria. Sociedad Venezolana
de Puericultura y Pediatria. Caracas.

UA   Urban Anthropology. State Univ. of
New York, Dept. of Anthropology. Brockport.

UBGI/E   Erdkunde. Archiv für
Wissenschaftliche Geographie. Univ. Bonn,
Geographisches Institut. Bonn, FRG.

UC/BPC   Boletín de Prehistoria de Chile.
Univ. de Chile, Facultad de Filosofía,
Humanidades y Educación, Depto. de
Ciencias Sociológicas y Antropológicas.
Santiago.

UC/CA   Current Anthropology. Univ. of
Chicago.

UCLA/JLAL   Journal of Latin American
Lore. UCLA, Latin American Center. Los
Angeles.

UCNSA/SA   Suplemento Antropológico.
Univ. Católica de Nuestra Señora de la
Asunción, Centro de Estudios
Antropológicos. Asunción.

UCR/RCS   Revista de Ciencias Sociales.
Univ. de Costa Rica. San José.

UCSB/NS   New Scholar. Univ. of
California, Committee of Hispanic
Civilization [and] Center for Chicano
Studies. Santa Barbara.

UFP/EB   Estudos Brasileiros. Univ. Federal
do Paraná, Setor de Ciências Humanas,
Centro de Estudos Brasileiros. Curitiba.

UN/C   Chungará. Univ. del Norte, Depto.
de Antropología. Arica, Chile.

UNAM/AA   Anales de Antropología.
UNAM, Instituto de Investigaciones
Históricas. México.

UNAM/ECN   Estudios de Cultura Náhuatl.
UNAM, Instituto de Historia, Seminario de
Cultura Náhuatl. México.

UNLPM/R   Revista del Museo de la Plata.
Univ. Nacional de la Plata, Facultad de
Ciencias Naturales y Museo. La Plata,
Argentina.

UNM/JAR   Journal of Anthropological
Research. Univ. of New Mexico, Dept. of
Anthropology. Albuquerque.

UP/CSEC   Cuban Studies/Estudos
Cubanos. Univ. of Pittsburgh, Center for
International Studies, Center for Latin
American Studies. Pittsburgh, Pa.

UP/E   Ethnology. Univ. of Pittsburgh.
Pittsburgh, Pa.

UP/LAIL Latin American Indian Literatures. Univ. of Pittsburgh, Dept. of Hispanic Languages and Literatures. Pittsburgh, Pa.

URSS/AL América Latina. Academia de Ciencias de la URSS. Moscú.

USP/RA Revista de Antropologia. Univ. de São Paulo, Faculdade de Filosofia, Letras e Ciências Humanas [and] Associação de Antropologia. São Paulo.

UWI/CQ Caribbean Quarterly. Univ. of the West Indies. Mona, Jamaica.

UWI/JCH The Journal of Caribbean History. Univ. of the West Indies, Dept. of History [and] Caribbean Universities Press. St. Lawrence, Barbados.

UWI/SES Social and Economic Studies. Univ. of the West Indies, Institute of Social and Economic Research. Mona, Jamaica.

VMJ/BIV Boletín Indigenista Venezolano. Organo de la Comisión Indigenista. Ministerio de Justicia. Caracas.

WSU/HB Human Biology. Official pub. of the Human Biology Council. Wayne State Univ., School of Medicine. Detroit, Mich.

YAXKIN Yaxkin. Instituto Hondureño de Antropología e Historia. Tegucigalpa.

ECONOMICS

GENERAL

JOHN M. HUNTER, *Director Emeritus, Latin American Studies Center, Michigan State University*

THE OVERWHELMING CHARACTERISTIC of general economic literature regarding Latin America is its increase—increase in quantity, quality, indigenous origin, and its scope. This biennium is no exception; rather it reinforces earlier impressions.

In the past, I have decried the lack of serious literature with Latin American content in the "applied" fields of economics, particularly "labor" and "agricultural" economics (the "scope" referred to above). Remedying these lacunae may well be the most important publishing developments in recent years. See particularly publications issued by ILO's Regional Employment Program for Latin America and the Caribbean (PREALC) such as *Economía campesina y empleo* (item **2839**) and *Empleo y salarios* (item **2840**), as well as those issued by the UN's ECLA, *Medición del empleo y de los ingresos rurales* (item **2925**). The work of ECIEL, especially in its attention to comparative costs, has contributed substantially to *empirical* understanding of labor markets. Norberto García examines "conventional wisdom" in his *Industria manufacturera y empleo: América Latina, 1950–1980* (item **2870**). Among several substantial pieces on agriculture (e.g., Jacques Chonchol, items **2805** and **2806**) is an excellent "reader" selected by Antonio García, *Desarrollo agrario y la América Latina* (item **2828**)—some 900 p.

It is no surprise that the debt "crisis" occupies considerable space. Among the better pieces (and there is a wide range) are those by: Michael E. Conroy (item **2814**), Carlos F. Díaz Alejandro (item **2833**), David Dod (item **2834**), Javier Fernández Riva (item **2846**), Albert Fishlow (item **2850**), Stephen Rousseas (item **2975**), and Richard S. Weinert (item **3025**). This by no means exhausts the list, and these articles cover various facets of the "problem."

At least one anniversary of importance occurred in the biennium. *El Trimestre Económico* celebrated its 50th year! Any careful perusal of its contents over the decades would reveal the increasing importance of the "domestic" Latin American economics industry through the period. Early years presented considerable translation of "gringos" and others on Latin American and other topics. Current issues are largely original and high quality works by Latin American authors. This celebration includes several retrospective articles. One is particularly noteworthy: Felipe Pazos writes "Cincuenta Años de Pensamiento Económico en la América Latina" (item **2950**), remarkable because he did the same sort of review for *El Trimestre's* 20th anniversary! It is also a fine synthesis. Among other "perspective" articles are: Víctor L. Urquidi on development (item **3017**); Raúl Prebisch on the evolution of his thinking (item **2964**); Aníbal Pinto on ECLA's evolution (item

2954); Francisco de Oliveira on Celso Furtado (item **2943**); and Carmelo Mesa-Lago on economic systems and development (item **2927**).

A very useful reference work that also appeared was issued by SALALM (Seminar on the Acquisition of Latin American Library Materials) and consists of a volume stemming from its 1981 meeting on *Latin American economic issues: information needs and sources* (item **2988**). I will not try here to describe its contents but simply suggest that the probabilities are great that it would be useful to all those involved in serious research on Latin American economic issues.

2751 Aguirre, Carlos *et al.* El desafío tecnológico de los países andinos (SP, 24, dic. 1983, p. 67–83)

Looks at probable technical changes in industrial countries in years ahead and, against Andean Group background, suggests how the challenge may be met.

2752 Alemann, Roberto T. La función del estado en la economía exterior y la política fiscal (BPC/RE, 36, marzo 1983, p. 33–48)

Role of the State through its Central Bank and through fiscal policy.

2753 Altinir, Oscar and **Sebastián Piñera.** Análisis de descomposición de las desigualdades de ingresos en la América Latina (FCE/TE, 49[4]:196, oct./dic. 1982, p. 813–860, bibl., tables)

Seeks empirically to determine causes of inequality and importance of each in nine Latin American countries.

2754 Alvarez García, Marcos and **Antonio J.A. Martins.** De l'ALALC a l'ALADI: continuité ou changement? (IIDC/C, 32:1, 1982, p. 67–93, graphs, tables)

Finds ALADI too restricted and not a great improvement over LAFTA.

2755 Alzamora Traverso, Carlos and **Enrique V. Iglesias.** Bases for a Latin American response to the international economic crisis. New York: UN Economic and Social Council, 1983. 67 p. (E/CEPAL/G.1246)

Description of crisis; analysis of present means of adjustment; priority guidelines for regional and international activities to overcome the crisis.

2756 América Latina en el umbral de los años 80. New York: CEPAL, Naciones Unidas, 1979. 203 p.: bibl., ill. (E/CEPAL/G.1106)

Although published in 1979, serious and comprehensive review of Latin America. Pt. 1 treats elements of long-term evolution,

poverty and the distribution of income, structural changes in society. Pt. 2 treats seven topics in external relations.

2757 Análisis de algunas estrategias de apoyo financiero a las pequeñas unidades productivas en América Latina. New York: Naciones Unidas, Consejo Económico y Social, CEPAL, 1982. 53 p.

Concludes with policy recommendations for support of small business.

2758 Análisis de políticas poblacionales en América Latina. Quito: Instituto de Investigaciones, Facultad de Ciencias Económicas, Univ. Central del Ecuador, 1983. 225 p.: bibl.

Product of a seminar in Ecuador, largely of Ecuadorians. Most presentations are general; four are cases: Mexico, Cuba, Colombia, Ecuador.

2759 Análisis del comercio andino, 1969–1980: Bolivia, Colombia, Ecuador, Perú, Venezuela. Lima: Junta del Acuerdo de Cartagena, 1982? 68 p.: bibl., ill.

Official publication of considerable interest. Data terminating in 1980 is severe limitation. Paints broad picture only; much greater detail (than very broad categories of traded goods) is required for most purposes.

2760 Análisis del intercambio comercial entre la Comunidad Económica Europea y los países de América Latina, 1965–1980. Roma: Instituto Italo Latino Americano, 1982. 458 p.: ill.

Profiles of Latin American countries' trade with the EEC (plus Spain, Portugal), products imported and exported, trends. Data.

2761 El Análisis estructural en economía: ensayo de América Latina y España. Selección de José Molero. México: Fondo de Cultura Económica; Madrid: Instituto de Cooperación Iberoamericana, 1981. 388 p.: ill., indexes (*El Trimestre Económico.* Lecturas; 40)

Most pieces have appeared elsewhere but those pertaining to Spain, especially, are not readily available. Useful collection though lacking in focus.

2762 Andrieu, Pedro Enrique. Desarrollo regional e integración latinoamericana (IIAS/IRAS, 48:3/4, 1982, p. 350–362)
Reviews historical background, present situation and some aspects of future.

2763 Araníbar, Ernesto and Pedro Palma. Deuda externa: ¿negociaciones bilaterales ó club de deudores? (NSO, 66, mayo/junio 1983, p. 20–25, plates)
Debate on the issue.

2764 Arellano, José Pablo. La deuda externa latinoamericana: urge una solución (Contribuciones [Konrad-Adenauer-Stiftung A.C. Centro Interdisciplinario de Estudios sobre el Desarrollo Latinoamericano, Buenos Aires] 2, abril/junio 1984, p. 39–47)
Solution: greater availability of loan funds and better conditions. Creditor nations will exercise a key role.

2765 ———. ¿Se agrava el desempleo urbano al aumentar los puestos de trabajo en el sector moderno? Santiago: Corporación de Investigaciones Económicas para Latinoamérica, 181. 21 leaves: bibl., ill. (Notas técnicas; 45)
Reviews studies of the relation between migration and increasing employment opportunities. Period of adjustment and specification of migration function explain differences in results.

2766 Arndt, Hans W. The New International Economic Order: a retrospect (UNESCO/IRE, 28:4, 1982, p. 431–434)
Short statement of background, principal areas of concern, and assessment of gradual decline in intellectual and political legitimacy.

2767 Arriazu, Ricardo H. Policy interdependence from a Latin American perspective (IMF/SP, 30:1, March 1983, p. 113–163, tables)
Offers model of small semi-open economy subject to specific external shocks. Traces effects. More sophisticated elements are added (e.g., indexing, lags).

2768 Arroyo, Gonzalo. Modelos de acumulación, clases sociales y agricultura

(CSUCA/ESC, 8:22, enero/abril 1979, p. 15–37)
Sees basically two means of rural investment: 1) agro-business dominated by foreign capital dedicated to producing profits for fewer and fewer; and 2) agro-business along socialist model dedicated to welfare of the group and in harmony with industrial growth.

2769 Asociación de Economistas del Tercer Mundo, 2nd, La Habana, 1981. Memoirs. La Habana: Editorial de Ciencias Sociales, 1982. 171 p.
Dated. Product of five-day meeting in Havana (1981) of some 600 economists, sociologists, politicians. Central theme: international economic crisis and its effects on the Third World.

2770 Assael, Héctor. El pensamiento de la CEPAL: un intento de evaluar algunas críticas a sus ideas principales (FCE/TE, 51:203, julio/sept. 1984, p. 545–558)
Seven negative criticisms are examined and evaluated. Interesting piece.

2771 Avetisián, Artur. Colaboración en el campo de la energética (URSS/AL, 4, abril 1983, p. 56–63, ill.)
Cites USSR as world leader in hydroelectric energy generation. Recounts assistance to Cuba (largely thermoelectric), Argentina, etc.

2772 Bacha, Edmar L. A critique of Southern Cone monetarism (UN/ISSJ, 35:3, 1983, p. 413–422, bibl., ill.)
Conclusion: "nothing fails like failure."

2773 Báez, René. La integración latinoamericana: ilusiones y realidades (IPGH/RHI, 3, 1982, p. 203–227)
Reviews Latin American integration efforts. Concludes with various arguments: such efforts are part of the capitalist plot.

2774 Balassa, Bela. Disequilibrium analysis in developing economies: an overview (WD, 10:12, Dec. 1982, p. 1027–1038, bibl., tables)
Techniques are developed to analyze product and factor market disequilibria. Empirical evidence measuring costs of imposed disequilibria is examined.

2775 El Banco Mundial: un caso de "progresismo conservador." Edición de Hugo Assmann. San José: Depto. Ecuménico de Investigaciones, 1980. 245 p.: bibl., ill.

Unsympathetic analysis of World Bank policies, particularly as they have related to Central America (note date).

2776 Baró Herrera, Silvio. El Nuevo Orden Económico Internacional: antecedentes, problemas actuales y perspectivas. La Habana: Editorial de Ciencias Sociales, 1980. 400 p.: bibl., ill. (Economía)

Particularly interesting for its source. Somewhat dated. Four sections: issues from which arises need for a NIEO, crises of capitalism which gave rise to the New Order, its contents, problems of implementation.

2777 Barriga López, Leonardo. El Grupo Andino y las transnacionales. Bogotá: Editorial Temis Librería, 1980. 218 p.: bibl., indexes.

Pt. 1 is background on development and on integration and review of Latin American integration steps (p. 46–106 summarizes Andean Group). Pt. 2 analyzes specific problems of transnationals in Latin America and in Andean Group.

2778 Baumer, Jean Max *et al.* Transnational corporations in Latin America: interactions between nation states and transnational corporations: the case of German and Swiss firms operating in Colombia, Brazil, and Mexico. Diessenhofen, FRG: Rüegger, 1982. 175 p.: bibl., tables (Buchreihe. Institut für Lateinamerikaforschung und Entwicklungszusammenarbeit an der Hochschule St. Gallen für Wirtschafts- und Sozialwissenschaften; 25)

Interactions between state and transnational firms (considerably less broad than title suggests). The empirical section deals with Colombia, Mexico, Brazil, and with Swiss and German firms.

2779 Belaúnde Terry, Fernando *et al.* Dependencia y desarrollo en debate: diario de un simposio. Lima: Instituto Libertad y Democracia, 1983. 595 p.

Comprehensive discussion at 1981 symposium including a number of well known participants (e.g., Milton Friedman, Elliot Richardson, Larry Sjaastad, Mario Vargas Llosa). Serious discussion.

2780 Bernabé, Franco. Politiche industriali e industrializzazione: il caso dell'industria automobilistica (GEE/NA, 5, 1982, p. 369–397, tables)

General characteristics of the industry especially in Latin America; the Brazilian experience; the Argentine experience; conclusions.

2781 Berríos, Rubén. La experiencia del Pacto Andino en regular la inversión extranjera y los flujos de tecnología: un paso adelante, dos atrás (PAN/ES, 8, 1981, p. 117–128)

Decision 24 was a step in an "independence" direction. The fall of the governments of Torres, Allende, Velasco weakened the nationalistic movement, and the conditions of underdevelopment and dependency are alive and well.

2782 Berry, Albert. Predicting income distribution in Latin America during the 1980s (*in* Latin American prospects for the 1980s: equity, democratization, and development. Edited by Archibald R.M. Ritter and David H. Pollock. New York: Praeger, 1983, p. 57–84, tables)

Applies current knowledge to predicting inequality. Two plausible hopes for greater equality: tightening of unskilled labor market and better use of human capital through education. The latter, particularly, is subject to public policy manipulation.

2783 Die Beziehungen zwischen der Europäischen Gemeinschaft und Lateinamerika: Bestandsaufnahme und Perspektiven. Edited by Hans J. Petersen. Baden-Baden, FRG: Nomos, 1983. 274 p. (Schriftenreihe des Arbeitskreises Europäische Integration; 16)

Essays discuss Latin American integration and how it would affect trade with the Common Market. Worthwhile contributions by José Antonio Alonso and Vicente Donoso examine Spain's integration into the Common Market and its effect on her trade with Latin America. [G.M. Dorn]

2784 Bibliografía económica de los países miembros. v. 1, Bolivia, Colombia, Ecuador. v. 2, Perú, Venezuela, Subregión Andina. Lima: Junta del Acuerdo de Cartagena, Biblioteca, 1979–1980. 2 v.: indexes.

Vol. 1 not examined. Vol. 2 contents: list of persons and organizations; works listed by topics. Not annotated.

2785 Bird, Graham; Tony Killick; Jennifer Sharpley; and Mary Sutton. IMF policies in developing countries: the case for change (The Banker [Financial Times Business Publishing, London] 134:698, April 1984, p. 31–36)

Summarizes: *The quest for economic stabilisation: the IMF and the Third World* and *The IMF and stabilisation: developing country experience* (two vols.; London: Heineman Educational Books; New York: St. Martin's Press: in association with Overseas Development Institute, 1983?). Same authors?

2786 Blejér, Mario I. Liberalization and stabilization policies in the Southern Cone countries: an introduction (SAGE/JIAS, 25:4, Nov. 1983, p. 431–444, bibl.)

Although an introduction to three country studies (Argentina, Chile, Uruguay), there is some "meat" of its own: 1) discusses relationship between monetary forces and balance of payments; and 2) nature of the money supply under fixed exchange rates.

2787 ——— *et al.* Ensayos sobre el enfoque monetario de la balanza de pagos. México: Centro de Estudios Monetarios Latinoamericanos, 1982. 119 p.: bibl. (Estudios)

Theoretical pieces which appeared in English in various standard and obscure journals, 1978–79. Useful to bring them together and to present in Spanish.

2788 Blitzer, Silvia; Jorge E. Hardoy; and David Satterthwaite. Vivienda para la población de bajos ingresos: necesidades y respuestas gubernamentales en el Tercer Mundo (FCE/TE, 49[2]:194, abril/junio 1982, p. 423–449)

Reports on study in 17 countries in four regions of the world (includes Bolivia, Brazil, Colombia, Mexico). What is being done, an evaluation, recommendations. See also Jorge Hardoy's and David Satterthwaite's *Shelter: needs and responses* (New York: John Wiley & Sons, 1981).

2788a Brodersohn, Víctor; Agustín Cafferata; and Gustavo Tesoriero. Mano de obra rural y formas de explotación agropecuaria: una nota metodológica (CPES/RPS, 16:44, enero/abril 1979, p. 185–189)

Criticizes definition of labor used by CIDA studies of land tenure in Latin America. Recommends more quantitative and qualitative detail to more precisely define types of farms. Interesting methodological note, not specific to any country. [S.M. Smith]

2789 Brunella, Daniel A. Recursos energéticos de Latinoamérica (BPC/RE, 34, sept. 1982, p. 88–94)

Brief survey of energy resources and conclusion that Latin America is better off than some, worse off than others, with an urgent need to expand power resources.

2790 Buira, Ariel. La programación financiera y la condicionalidad del FMI (FCE/TE, 50[1]:197, enero/marzo 1983, p. 117–149, bibl.)

Thorough discussion of "conditionality" aspect of IMF and means IMF employs to determine conditions. Finds they are generally adequate but need greater review and flexibility, especially in cases of structural disequilibria.

2791 *Business Yearbook of Brazil, Mexico & Venezuela.* Graham & Trotman Ltd. 1981– . London.

Better than usual run of "guides and introductions" for businessmen. Gives backgrounds on economics, business regulation, city maps, useful addresses, etc.

2792 Cáceres, Luis René and Frederick José Jiménez. Estructuralismo, monetarismo e inflación en Latinoamérica (FCE/TE, 50[1]:197, enero/marzo 1983, p. 151–168, tables)

Discusses monetarist model and then develops "discrimination analysis" between inflationary and non-inflationary Latin American countries. Variable studies demonstrate that their behavior: 1) determines degrees of inflation and price stability, and 2) supports structuralist explanation.

2793 Calcagno, Alfredo Eric and Jean-Michel Jakobowicz. El monólogo Norte-Sur y la explotación de los países subdesarrollados. México: Siglo XXI Editores, 1981. 208 p.: tables.

Solid analysis of world economic condition and changes occurring therein particularly in and among the "North," seeking meaning and policy implications for the "South."

2794 ———; José A. Deheza; and Benjamín Hopenhayn. El colonialismo invisible. Buenos Aires: Ediciones Cuenca del Plata, 1982. 300 p.: bibl.

A good two-thirds reprints CEPAL's *Cuaderno* No. 33 by Alfredo Eric Calcagno (1980): "Inversiones Directas Extranjeras en

América Latina." This is preceded by short essay relating borrowing abroad to dependence, followed by an even shorter essay on how to "handle" the debt.

2795 Cardoso, Eliana A. Políticas de estabilização na América Latina: modelos de uso corrente e suas experiências fracassadas (IPEA/PPE, 13:2, agosto 1983, p. 465–487, bibl., tables)

Presents five models (mathematically) and touches on their efficiency.

2796 Carraud, Michel. L'intégration des pays andins. Paris: Economica, 1981. 232 p.: bibl.

Comprehensive, serious analysis of Andean Group in three parts: 1) juridical system; 2) new development strategy; and 3) Group's external relations.

2797 Carroll, T. Owen; Romis Chatterjee; and Vinod Mubayi. Energy planning in Latin America: a brief review of selected countries (LARR, 17:3, 1982, p. 148–172, tables)

Studies of Brazil, Costa Rica, Peru, Colombia, Jamaica as "representative" countries. Concludes with comments on regional organizations, requirements for integrated planning.

2798 Casas González, Antonio. El potencial de las fuentes convencionales en el abastecimiento energético de la América Latina (FCE/TE, 50:200, oct./dic. 1983, p. 1995–2016)

Energy planning; current use of conventional resources; policies and strategies.

2799 Castells, Juan Manuel. La crisis de alimentos en América Latina: investigación presentada a la Asociación Latinoamericana de Industriales y Cámaras de la Alimentación. Montevideo: Asociación Latinoamericana de Integración (ALICA), 1982. 78 p.: bibl.

Agriculture is subject of the myth that it is "natural," "traditional," "resource-based," "what-we-do-best." This has led to crucial neglect in favor of manufacturing at the cost of a threatened food supply.

Castillo, Heberto and Jacinto Viquera. Los energéticos, el petróleo—y nuestro futuro? See item **3083.**

2800 Catálogo de instituciones de desarrollo sin fines de lucro en América Latina, 1981. Santo Domingo: SOLIDARIOS,

Consejo de Fundaciones Americanas de Desarrollo, 1981. 407 p.

Country-by-country list of non-profit development agencies including, for each, officers, directors, objectives, funding, address, etc.

2801 Certificación de las calificaciones ocupacionales de los trabajadores de América Latina y el Caribe: informe final, proyecto 128. Montevideo: CINTERFOR, 1980. 124 p. (Informes; 99)

Report on undertaking to provide occupational "certification" which could contribute to regional integration. Short country reports on what the project has accomplished.

2802 Chaloult, Norma Beatriz and Yves Chaloult. The internal colonialism concept: methodological considerations (UWI/SES, 28:4, Dec. 1979, p. 85–99, bibl., tables)

More Latin American content than title suggests. Finds model weak, lacking coherence and consistency among its proponents and users. Suggests requirements for improving it.

2803 Cherol, Rachelle L. and José Núñez del Arco. Andean multilateral enterprises: a new approach to multinational investment in the Andean Group. Washington: IDB, 1982. 22 p.: bibl., tables.

Explains and analyzes Decision 169, an effort to encourage multinational firms within the Group (except for firms in Bolivia and Ecuador, Andean Multinational Enterprises must have 80 percent intra-Group capital). Adds to the set of much analyzed rules on foreign investment.

2804 Chilcote, Ronald H. Theories of development and underdevelopment. Boulder, Colo.: Westview Press, 1984. 178 p.: bibl., index.

"A critical review and assessment of the literature on development and underdevelopment." Starts with classical writers: Marx, Lenin, Trotsky. Very heavy emphasis on Latin American thought.

2805 Chonchol, Jacques. Agricultura, alimentación y energía: desarrollo de los países del Tercer Mundo (FCE/TE, 50[1]:197, enero/marzo 1983, p. 189–206)

Examines implications of the symbiotic relations between food, agriculture, energy in the economic process.

2806 ———. La reforma agraria y el desarrollo rural como estrategia de un Nuevo Orden Económico Internacional (FCE/TE, 49[2]:194, abril/junio 1982, p. 253–263)

The NIEO prescribes self-reliant styled development oriented towards *basic needs*. Latin America is moving away from both rather than toward. A fundamental reform of the agricultural economy is necessary to reverse these trends.

2807 Clairmonte, Frederick F. La dinámica del oligopolio mundial del tabaco (BNCE/CE, 33:6, junio 1983, p. 530–540, tables)

Oligopoly elements: automized technology; complex marketing wth heavy advertising; capital requirements and product diversification; growth of transnational conglomerate. Company-by-company analysis. Conclusions.

2808 Clinton, Richard L. América Latina: la región que nunca se desarrollará (UP/A, 13, 1983, p. 59–67, tables)

Less than happy with usual notions of development. Explores, then, the demographic situation and its consequences. Thoughts on solutions.

2809 Colaiácovo, Juan Luis and **Antonio A. Assefh.** Proyectos de exportación y estrategias de marketing internacional: textos y casos sobre agroindustria, servicios y artesanía. Rosario, Argentina: Ediciones del Río, 1983. 622 p.: ill.

Text built around the "case" method. Surely a helpful addition to the literature.

2810 Compendio de estadísticas de América Latina. La Habana: Comité Estatal de Estadísticas, 1982. 272 p.: tables.

Wide range of data by country in the first section and by topics (e.g., "health") in the second. Data are from standard UN sources (e.g., ILO, FAO, UNESCO, WHO).

2811 Conesa, Eduardo R. La integración financiera de América Latina (INTAL/IL, 7:74, nov. 1982, p. 15–20)

Outlines advantages offered by regional financial integration.

2812 Conferencia de Ministros y Jefes de Planificación de América Latina y el Caribe, 3rd, Guatemala, 1980. El estado actual de la planificación en América Latina y el Caribe: documento. Santiago: Instituto

Latinoamericano de Planificación Económica y Social, 1982. 278 p.: bibl. (Cuadernos del ILPES; 28. E/CEPAL/ILPES/G.15)

Thorough examination of planning in the 1970s—and proposals for the 1980s. A fundamental work for those interested in planning.

2813 Conferencia Regional Americana de la AISS, 1st, Ottawa, 1979. Primera Conferencia Regional Americana de la AISS [i.e. Asociación Internacional de la Seguridad Social]. Buenos Aires: Secretaría General de la AISS, 1980. 269 p. (Documentos de la seguridad social americana; 1980, no. 1)

Not atypical conference report. Themes: present state of retirement allowances, medical services for retirees, social services for retirees. Will be of greater interest if additional conferences follow.

2814 Conroy, Michael E. Global crisis and the Latin American backlash: implications for U.S. business (Texas Business Review [Bureau of Business Research, Univ. of Texas, Austin] 57:3, May/June 1983, p. 126–130)

Describes crisis (worst since 1930s). There is little likelihood of immediate recovery. Probable implications in Latin America: protectionism, default, nationalization, public sector growth, insurrection, anti-US sentiment.

Contreras, Victoria. Mercado de trabajo en cifras: 1950–1980. See item **3524.**

2815 Contreras Q., Carlos. Transferencia de tecnología a países en desarrollo. Caracas: Instituto Latinoamericano de Investigaciones Sociales, 1979. 262 p.: bibl., ill.

Note date. Pt. 1 describes various means of technology transfer and associated problems; pt. 2 describes national and international efforts to provide for and to regulate technological transfer.

2816 Cooperación hemisférica y desarrollo integral: informe para la Secretaría General de la OEA. Coordinación de Felipe Herrera. Washington: CIES, Secretaría de la OEA, 1982. 125 p.: bibl., ill.

Report prepared (1980) by group experts (Felipe Herrera, chairman) for OAS. Problems given particular attention: food, natural resources, energy, education, urbanization, technology, small countries. Also available in English: *Hemispheric cooperation and integral development* (1982).

2817 Cordero, Fernando. Importaciones y exportaciones de armas livianas en Argentina, Brasil, Colombia, Costa Rica, Chile, República Dominicana, Perú, México y Venezuela: 1970–1979. Stockholm: Institute of Latin American Studies, 1981. 26 p.: bibl., ill. (Occasional papers)

Straightforward account of trade in small arms; description of data; origins, destinations; the industry and foreign participation.

2819 La Crisis del capitalismo y los países subdesarrollados. Selection of papers presented at the 2nd Congress of the Asociación de Economistas del Tercer Mundo, Havana, 1981. México: Editorial Nuestro Tiempo, 1982. 215 p.: bibl. (Col. Desarrollo)

"Ponencias" (plus opening statement by Fidel Castro) to the 2nd Congress (La Habana, 1981) presented to the First Commission charged with analysis of the "crisis" and its impact on the Third World (see item 2769).

2820 La Crisis energética: testimonios. Edición de Raúl Cremoux. México: Terra Nova, 1981. 173 p. (Col. Crónicas de nuestro tiempo)

Interesting approach: editor interviews wide (international) range of politicians, scientists, journalists, researchers, industrialists, internationalists, literary notables on various aspects of the energy crisis. Most responses are of paragraph length.

2821 The Crisis of social security and health care: Latin American experiences and lessons. Carmelo Mesa-Lago, ed. Pittsburgh, Pa.: Center for Latin American Studies, Univ. Center for International Studies, Univ. of Pittsburgh, 1985. 1 v. (Latin American monograph and document series; 9)

Title is descriptive. Ten papers by scholars with comments by international technicians represent two years of collaborative research. Vol. is thus considerably more than usual collection of papers. Cases: Argentina, Brazil, Chile, Costa Rica, Cuba, Ecuador, Honduras, Mexico, Panama, Venezuela.

2822 ¿Crisis sin salida?: la economía mundial y América Latina. Sergio Aranda y Dorothea Mezger, comps. Caracas: Instituto Latinoamericano de Investigaciones Sociales: Centro de Estudio del Desarrollo, Univ. Central de Venezuela, 1982. 533 p.: bibl., ill.

Papers from 1981 seminar in Venezuela. Concentrates on two world crises: financial and energy. Mostly "crisis;" little "solution." Higher quality than usual *obras "crisistas."*

2823 Criterios económicos para evaluar políticas contra la pobreza. Preparado por el Proyecto Interinstitucional de Pobreza Crítica. Santiago: Naciones Unidas, Consejo Económico y Social, 1982. 57 p.: bibl., ill. (E/CEPAL/L.272)

Effort to specify social costs and benefits to anti-poverty measures to aid in choosing among them.

2824 Las Cuentas nacionales en América Latina y el Caribe. Santiago: Naciones Unidas, 1983. 109 p. (Cuadernos de la CEPAL, ISSN 0252–2195; 45)

Review of the status of national accounts and critiques of current practices. Does *not* present national accounts.

2825 Cuentas nacionales y producto material en América Latina: comparabilidad de ambos sistemas. Santiago: CEPAL, 1982. 129 p.: bibl. (Estudios e informes de la CEPAL; 17. E/CEPAL/G.1218)

Interesting (technical) effort to compare and reconcile National Accounts (GNP, etc.) with the system of "Material Product" used by centrally planned economies, notably Cuba.

2826 Dahlman, Carl and Larry Westphal. The transfer of technology (Finance and Development [International Monetary Fund, Washington] 20:4, Dec. 1983, p. 6–9)

Discusses issues, the nature of technological change, and how it occurs. Useful, general article.

2827 Delgado Ribas, Josep María. La integración de Hispanoamérica en el mercado mundial: 1797–1814 (UB/BA, 23:31, 1981, p. 41–52, tables)

Thorough study of trade in this interesting epoch.

2828 Desarrollo agrario y la América Latina. Selección de Antonio García. México: Fondo de Cultura Económica, 1981. 918 p.: bibl., ill. (El Trimestre Económico. Lecturas; 41)

Outstanding "reader" covering wide range of topics and pieces from early 1960s to late 1970s. Much attention to agrarian reform (case studies) and the role of agriculture and peasants in capitalistic development.

2829 El Desarrollo de las cuentas nacionales en América Latina y el Caribe: documento. Preparado por la División de Estadística y Análisis Cuantitativo de la CEPAL. Santiago: Naciones Unidas, Consejo Económico y Social, CEPAL, 1981. 70, 24 p.: bibl. (E/CEPAL/SEM.2/L.1)

Review of the techniques employed in preparing national account estimates and evaluation of improvement possibilities.

2830 El Desarrollo rural humanista en América: una perspectiva desde el IICA. Edición de José Emilio G. Araujo. San José: Instituto Interamericano de Ciencias Agrícolas, Dirección General, Dirección de Información Pública, 1980. 541 p. (Serie Desarrollo institucional; 5)

Accounting by IICA's Director General for the decade, 1970–80. Themes: future of IICA, state of agriculture and the rural sector.

2831 Diálogo sindical Norte-Sur: bases para la cooperación. Introducción y selección de textos por Julio Godio. Caracas: Instituto Latinoamericano de Investigaciones Sociales, 1982. 471 p.

Interesting collection (not as extensive as pagination suggests due to format) which explores possible activities for North-South labor cooperation (e.g., a countervailling power to MNCs).

2832 Díaz Alejandro, Carlos F. Os anos 40 na América Latina (IPEA/PPE, 12:3, dez. 1982, p. 719–756, bibl., tables)

Study of reaction to external shocks, globally and sectorally, with particular attention to income distribution and social welfare. This decade also provided conditioning background for policies which followed.

2833 ———. International markets in the 1980s (CU/JIA, 38:1, Summer 1984, p. 11–20)

Crisis of 1980s proximately caused by debt structure too great to be managed with slumping commodity trade. Some new international mechanism is required to deal with the latter.

2834 Dod, David. Restricción del crédito de la banca comercial en situaciones de crisis de la deuda internacional (CEMLA/M, 6:2, abril/junio 1983, p. 155–180, tables)

Examines 12 crises (1977–81) and terms of readjustments, speed with which agreement was reached, severity of restriction on new credit.

2835 Donald, Gordon. Agricultural pricing policies (Development Digest [Washington] 21:1, July 1983, p. 2–9)

General discussion of rationale, means, development agency views, review of research.

2836 Dornbusch, Rudiger. Políticas de estabilización en los países en desarrollo: ¿qué es lo que hemos aprendido? (IDES/DE, 22:86, julio/sept. 1982, p. 187–201, bibl., graphs)

Compares old scheme concerned with fiscal discipline and an "adequate" exchange rate with the new: a monetary focus and emphasis on purchasing power parity. Neither are fully satisfactory. Better scheme involves: monetary rules, exchange rate guidelines, interest rate policy.

2837 Durán de la Fuente, Hernán. Estilos de desarrollo de la industria manufacturera y medio ambiente en América Latina. Santiago: Naciones Unidas, 1982. 184 p.: ill. (Estudios e informes de la CEPAL; 11)

Review of manufacturing and its environmental impact. Last data are 1976, so latest decennial data are for 1970.

2838 Ebstein, Max. Aspectos financieros de una posible cooperación científica y técnica en el desarrollo agrario de Iberoamérica (IEAS/R, 32:122, enero/marzo 1983, p. 139–149, bibl.)

Projects agriculture's financial needs and then considers how Spanish finances might help meet those needs.

2839 Economía campesina y empleo. Santiago: Oficina Internacional del Trabajo, Programa Regional del Empleo para América Latina y el Caribe (PREALC), 1981. 326 p.: bibl., ill.

Essays on important and neglected topic presented at 1980 meeting. Four principal topics: background and theory, capitalism and labor market dynamics, mobility and labor supply, class formation. Several case studies of countries or regions.

2840 Empleo y salarios. Santiago: Oficina Internacional del Trabajo, Programa Regional del Empleo para América Latina y el Caribe (PREALC), 1983. 126 p.: bibl., ill.

Careful study of effects on prices and wages of a deteriorating external demand and of adjustments to that decline taking equity considerations into account.

2841 Las Empresas estatales en América Latina. Caracas: Centro Latinoamericano de Administración para el Desarrollo (CLAD), 1979. 308 p.: bibl., ill.

Important if dated study of the management of a crucial sort of enterprise. Three pts.: 1) nature of states and state enterprises; 2) relationships between them; and 3) overall view of the functioning of systems of state enterprises.

2842 Estudo comparativo da indústria de alimentos: administração e política de tecnologia na América Latina. Estudo patrocinado pelo International Development Research Center (IDRC), Canadá. Henrique Rattner, coordenação. São Paulo: Editora E. Blücher, 1983. 143 p.: bibl., ill.

Study of Brazil, Colombia, Mexico, Peru with special attention to the food industry. Considerable bibliography.

2843 Fajnzylber, Fernando. Intervención, autodeterminación e industrialización en la América Latina (FCE/TE, 50[1]:197, enero/marzo 1983, p. 307–328)

Interesting discussion of sociological requirements for industrialization based on self-sufficiency as opposed to that externally initiated and controlled.

2844 Feder, Ernest. Capital monopolista y empleo agrícola en el Tercer Mundo (CEESTM/TM, 1:2, enero/abril 1982, p. 275–329, bibl., table)

Sees agricultural operation expanding with foreign capital. This is inevitably capital-intensive which will lead to more rural *and* urban poverty.

2845 Felix, David. Income distribution and the quality of life in Latin America: patterns, trends, and policy implications (LARR, 18:2, 1983, p. 3–33, tables)

Well written and documented. Finds no *stable* tradeoff between growth and equity because: 1) fast growth sows seeds for own demise; and 2) growth leads to shifts to more egalitarian, but growth-retarding, policies.

2846 Fernández Riva, Javier. Rescheduling of the foreign debt with commercial banks and the flow of new credit. Austin: Univ. of Texas, Institute of Latin American

Studies, 1984. 34 p.: appendix, bibl. (ILAS special publication)

Rigorous (mathematical) examination of alternatives to rescheduling debt service at high cost from both banks' and borrowers' points of view.

2847 Ferrer, Aldo. Reflexiones sobre las industrializaciones sustitutivas y exportadoras: Corea y la América Latina (FCE/TE, 50[2]:198, abril/junio 1983, p. 629–640)

Analysis of Korean economy as example of export-oriented development. Contrasts that model with Latin American experience.

2848 Ferris, Elizabeth G. National support for the Andean Pact (JDA, 16:2, Jan. 1982, p. 249–270, tables)

Tests a number of hypotheses concerning the likelihood of a country to support integration (e.g., support varies directly with emphasis on increased exports). Perception of equity in distribution of benefits is key.

2849 Ffrench-Davis, Ricardo. Una estrategia de apertura externa selectiva (FCE/TE, 51:203, julio/sept. 1984, p. 485–526, bibl., tables)

Careful work largely oriented to the Chilean experience. Against hypothetical external scenario, outlines policies in five fields: 1) comparative advantage and tariffs; 2) exchange; 3) external debt and investment; 4) external shocks and instability; and 5) international cooperation.

2850 Fishlow, Albert. Latin America's debt: problem or solution (CJWB, 17:1, Spring 1982, p. 35–45, tables)

How debt came about; burden now and future; national experiences; prospects for the debt which eased adjustments in the 1970s becoming a problem of the 1980s. Principal danger is that international finance will be insufficient to maintain growth.

2851 Flit, Isaías. Integración tecnológica en América Latina y el Caribe: un plan de acción (SP, 15, sept. 1983, p. 105–116)

Most Latin American countries have "technological institutes" to "create a national technology." There is great heterogeneity but these common characteristics: 1) lack of human resource policy; 2) separation from planning process; and 3) separation from similar institutions. Many suggestions for remedy.

2852 ———. ¿Tecnologías apropriadas o su manejo apropiado? (SP, 8, sept. 1979, p. 75–82)

Thorough discussion of "appropriate" technology and policy implications of accepting a definition.

2853 Flores, Gustavo. La tecnología en los procesos de integración de América Latina (SP, 10, mayo 1980, p. 63–74, tables)

Outlines some problems of technological transfer and suggests a need to develop regional policy to serve as a means to reduce dependence.

2854 Flores Díaz, Max et al. La industrialización y desarrollo en América Latina. Caracas: Univ. Central de Venezuela, Facultad de Ciencias Económicas y Sociales, Instituto de Investigaciones Económicas y Sociales, 1981. 111 p.: bibl.

Critical review of post-World War II approach to development of Latin America. Concludes with application of Marx and Marxists to the analysis.

2855 Foreign debt and Latin American economic development. Edited by Antonio Jorge, Jorge Salazar-Carrillo, and René P. Higonnet. New York: Pergamon Press, 1983. 183 p.: bibl.

Proceedings of 1982 conference sponsored by lively group at Florida International Univ. Several general articles as well as country-specific ones on Jamaica, Dominican Republic, Central America, Brazil, Mexico, Haiti, Venezuela, Costa Rica.

2856 Fortín, Carlos. Latin America in the 1980s: issues, trends and prospects (CEDLA/B, 34, junio 1983, p. 3–15)

Thoughtful article on the failures of the *desarrollo* model (1960s), integrationist model (1970s), and the military model (especially in the Malvinas affair). Opens process to popular participation but also provides for uncertainty, instability.

Foxley, Alejandro. Latin American experiments in neoconservative economics. See item **3538.**

2857 ——— and **Oscar Muñoz.** Políticas de empleo en economías heterogéneas (CPES/RPS, 14:38, enero/abril 1977, p. 81–100, bibl.)

Theory has had poor explanatory value as well as poor prescriptive value. Discusses characteristics of labor markets and some ob-

served effects (e.g., industrialization). Suggests new approaches.

2858 Frankman, Myron J. Employment and the unperceived advantages of being a latecomer (*in* Latin American prospects for the 1980s: equity, democratization, and development. Edited by Archibald R.M. Ritter and David H. Pollock. New York: Praeger, 1983, p. 135–146, tables)

Desiderata are enjoyment of life and reduction of toil which mean that: 1) emphasis on labor-intensive industry, and 2) employment through industry are misplaced emphases. The "right" service industries are key.

2859 Fratianni, Michele. International debt crisis: policy issues (The Banker [Financial Times Business Publishing, London] 133:690, Aug. 1983, p. 37–42)

Viable strategy will involve contributions of debtors, creditors, national governments, and international organizations. Descriptive.

2860 Frenkel, Jacob A. Panel discussion on the Southern Cone (IMF/SP, 30:1, March 1983, p. 164–184)

Not Southern Cone-specific. Discusses two issues: 1) the proper sequencing of liberalization measures; and 2) gradualism vs. drastic measures during stabilization. Discussants do concentrate on the Southern Cone.

2861 Furtado, Celso. Obras escogidas. Prólogo de José Consuegra. Bogotá: Plaza y Janes, 1982. 340 p. (Antología del pensamiento económico y social de América Latina; 5. Sociales)

Convenient collection. Main themes: theory, critique, policy.

2862 ———. O quadro internacional (ECB, 29[8]:11, 1982, p. 196–207)

Chapter from *O Brasil pós-milagre* (see *HLAS 45:3628*) discusses principal strands of international scene since World War II.

2863 Galbis, Vicente. Ministate economics (Finance and Development [IMF, Washington] 21:2, June 1984, p. 36–38)

Reports research on 33 such states (less than one million population). Deals mostly with constraints on exchange rate and monetary policies. Findings: those which do best have stable effective exchange rates and supporting monetary policy.

2864 Galván, Césare G. El proceso capitalista de producción y reproducción de las disparidades tecnológicas (FCE/TE, 49[3]:195, julio/sept. 1982, p. 535–562)

Marxist examination of capitalistic production especially as related to technology and oligopoly—international inequalities cause rivalries between nations and groups of nations. General, not area-specific.

2865 Gambrill, Mónica-Calire. La nueva división internacional del trabajo: industrialización vía maquilladoras (CEESTM/TM, 1:2, enero/abril 1982, p. 331–344)

Takes a dim view both in theory and practice. But without alternatives, they may have to be accepted from time to time.

2866 The Gap between rich and poor: contending perspectives on the political economy of development. Edited by Mitchell A. Seligson. Boulder, Colo.: Westview Press, 1984. 418 p.: bibl., ill., index.

A "reader" with considerable range. Principal topics: definition, explanations, empirical evidence, case studies and conclusions. Not Latin American-specific, but case materials are.

2867 García, Antonio. Bases de economía política. 2a ed. Bogotá: Tiempo Americano Editores, 1981. 283 p.: bibl. (Antología del pensamiento económico y social de América Latina: 4:1)

Of history-of-thought interest is this republication of *Bases de la economía contemporánea* (1948) by prolific Marxist author who frequently deals with agriculture.

2868 García, Marcelo. Energía y Nuevo Orden Económico Internacional (CEESTM/TM, 1:1, sept./dic. 1981, p. 73–85)

Reviews petroleum (in particular) situation. Concludes world-wide planning of some sort is required to ascertain that Third World is not short-changed.

2869 ———. La transición energética y el Tercer Mundo: una comunicación (CEESTM/TM, 1:2, enero/abril 1982, p. 345–352)

Explains petroleum crisis in Marxist terms as extension of more general capitalistic crisis. Proposes a "democratic" strategy for the Third World.

2870 García, Norberto E. Industria manufacturera y empleo: América Latina, 1950–1980 (FEC/TE, 50:200, oct./dic. 1983, p. 2077–2122, tables)

Concludes that conventional wisdom is not substantiated as to poor employment generating capacity of Latin American industry. It is only partially correct with respect to the presumption that industry is unable to expand employment as the labor force expands.

2871 Garg, Ramesh G. Latin American and the Caribbean external debt: problems and prospects (IEI/EI, 35:3/4, agosto/nov. 1982, p. 445–457, bibl., tables)

Immensely general, but a good introduction.

2872 Garrido, Alberto. Alimentos, nuevo poder de las transnationales. Presentación, Pedro Rincón Gutiérrez. Mérida, Venezuela: Corpoandes, Librería Universitaria: FUNDACIPOL, 1982. 158 p.: bibl.

Adequately descriptive title except that the transnationals are exclusively US and PL 480 is also a culprit.

2872a Giordani, Jorge. La planificación como proceso social. Valencia, Venezuela: Vadell Hermanos Editores, 1980. 299 p.: bibl., ill., tables.

Examines why by the mid-1950s, it became well known that the planning process in Latin America was a failure, that such plans were merely documents used to obtain US or World Bank assistance. Considers planning not a technical service for the government but as a social process. Analyzes planning process in socialism (USSR), advanced capitalism (US), dependent capitalism (Latin America), and in Venezuela. [M.Hassan]

2873 Glade, William. The Levantines in Latin America (AEA/AER, 73:2, May 1983, p. 118–122, bibl.)

The experiences of Levantine immigrants demonstrate how historical circumstances provided them a comparative advantage in the supply of entrepreneurial resources. Considers both demand (pull) and supply (push) factors.

2874 Goede, Wolfgang C. Lateinamerika im Griff der deutschen Wirtschaft; eine entwicklungspolitische Bilanz der 70er Jahre. München, FRG: Verlag Holler, 1984. 329 p.

Argues that mass consumption will be

attained in Latin America only if the needy are integrated into the economic system, otherwise foresees unrest and revolution. In order to reach the masses and counter power of elites, proposes that private agencies such as churches and political foundations rather than federal government administer development funds. Points out how Common Market rules impede West German trade with Latin America. [G.M. Dorn]

2875 Gómez Campos, Víctor Manuel. Relaciones entre educación y estructura económica: dos grandes marcos de interpretación (FCE/TE, 49[4]:196, oct./dic. 1982, p. 939–973, bibl.)

Thorough review of relations between education and growth. Finds traditional approaches—1) correlation between expenditures for education and growth, and 2) individuals' education correlated with income—unsatisfactory. Proposes alternative.

2876 Gómez Sabaini, Juan and Hugo González Cano. Manual de finanzas públicas y política tributaria. Santo Domingo: Instituto de Capacitación Tributaria de la Secretaría de Estado de Finanzas, 1982. 179 p.: bibl., ill. (Col. Manuales de finanzas públicas; 15)

Examines aspects of government spending, its objectives, application through taxation, interest rates and effects, along with past and present experiences of taxation in Latin America. [R. Moncarz]

2877 González, Heliodoro. Can foreign aid continue as a growth industry for the bureaucracy?: Latin American cooperation at the United Nations (IAMEA, 37:1, 1983, p. 53–60, tables)

Discussion of the aid-and-behavior relationship at the UN. No relation. Should there be?

2878 Grabendorff, Wolf. Latin America un Westeuropa: neue Entwicklungsungen unde Akteure im interregionalen Beziehungsnetz (OLI/ZLW, 22, 1984, p. 40–56)

Traces new era of Latin American trade interests during last 25 yrs., when several Latin American nations began looking for new outlets (e.g., Mediterranean, Middle East, Eastern block nations). Theorizes that subsystem of Latin America and Western Europe may prove enduring phenomenon of 1980s international economics with increasing bilateral agreements. [G. M. Dorn]

2879 Green, Raúl H. Finances internationales et groupes nationaux en Amérique latine: le système financier international et les groupes privés industriels et financiers nationaux en Amérique latine dans les années 70: les cas de l'Argentine, Brésil, Chile et Mexique. Traduit de l'espagnol par Fabienne Houillon. Paris: Institut national de la recherche agronomique, 1982. 62 p.: bibl. (Série Economie et sociologie rurales)

Study of the 1970s, especially compared to the 1960s. Less direct foreign investment, more debt abroad, increasing participation of national groups of investors (e.g., Chile, Argentina, Brazil, Mexico).

2880 Green, Rosario. Capital transnacional y política internacional: los bancos y la deuda externa del Tercer Mundo (CEESTM/TM, 1:1, sept./dic. 1981, p. 87–94)

Discusses external debt and has suggestions for improving the lending "structure."

2881 Grunwald, Joseph. Reconstrucción de la industria maquiladora (FCE/TE, 50:200, oct./dic. 1983, p. 2123–2152)

Reports studies of Mexican, Haitian, Colombian "assembly" industries and presents general conclusions from these cases.

2882 Guth, Wilfried. International debt crisis: the next phase (The Banker [Financial Times Business Publishing, London] 133:689, July 1983, p. 25–30)

Banks' resources are limited. Other contributors will have to come from international institutions, governments, and *direct* private investment—if there is to be future growth.

2883 Harrisson, Pierre. L'Empire Nestlé. Préface de Susan George. Illustrations et graphiques de Louis Badler. Lausanne, Switzerland: Editions P.M. Favre, 1983. 493 p.: bibl., ill. (Col. CETIM)

Assessment of Nestlé. Chapters on Mexico, Peru, Colombia, Brazil, Dominican Republic.

2884 Herrera, Beatriz. Grupo Andino & COMECON: crítica a la integración económica. Lima: Editorial Pensamiento Crítico, 1982. 146 p.: bibl., ill. (Integración económica. Serie Tesis universitaria)

Very interesting study of economic integration covers the Andean Group and European socialist countries, Council of Mutual Economic Assistance (COMECON). Description of how common problems (e.g., those of LDCs) are handled by both groups is useful. Not really a "comparative" study.

2885 Hesse, Helmut. External prerequisites for the success of Latin American free trade policies. Paper presented at the International Conference on the Free Trade Movement in Latin America, Hamburg, 1981. S.l.: s.n., 1981. 36 leaves: bibl.

Examines free trade consequences for Latin American development. Finds variance from model and currently appearing practices are likely to bring less than optimal outcome to Latin America. Serious study.

2886 Hicks, Norman and Anne Kubisch. Cutting government expenditures in LDCs (Finance and Development [IMF, Washington] 21:3, Sept. 1984, p. 37–39)

Summary of research on sectors of governmental expenditures and how they fare in real terms when "bad times led to budget reductions." Examines 37 cases in 32 countries.

2887 Hopenhayn, Benjamín. Algunas notas sobre el "capitalismo periférico" en Raúl Prebisch (IDES/DE, 22:86, julio/sept. 1982, p. 287–294)

Reflections of Prebisch's 1981 *Capitalismo periférico: crisis y transformación*.

2888 Hosono, Akio. Economic relationship between Japan and Latin America (Latin American Studies [Univ. of Tsukuba, Japan] 6, 1983, 75–101, tables)

Examines changes in last two decades and analyzes policy to promote further changes in desirable directions.

Howe, Robert. A bibliographic guide to Latin American and Caribbean government publications on foreign investment, 1965–1981. See *HLAS 46:24*.

2889 Hughes, William R. Un nuevo modelo de acumulación en América Latina (Economía Política [Univ. Nacional Autónoma de Honduras, Instituto de Investigaciones Económicas y Sociales, Tegucigalpa] 18, dic. 1979/agosto 1980, p. 30–107, tables)

Introduction of neo-Marxist model concerning the internationalization of capital which permits analysis of roles of agroindustry, international lending, behavior of international organization, etc., as part of the international bourgeois strategy.

2890 Iglesias, Enrique V. The Brandt Report and Latin American development in the 1980s (*in* Latin American prospects for the 1980s: equity, democratization, and development. Edited by Archibald R.M. Ritter and David H. Pollock. New York: Praeger, 1983, p. 22–39)

Much broader than title suggests; thorough discussion of Latin America (and sometimes Third World) situation and how different countries and groups of countries view the problems of *the* crisis and prospects to resolve them.

2891 Illanes, Luis and Leonel Díaz McArthur. El control de los impuestos en los países en desarrollo de América. Santo Domingo: Instituto de Capacitación Tributaria de la Secretaría de Estados de Finanzas, 1982. 4 v.: ill. (Col. Manuales de finanzas públicas; 11–13, 16)

Manual of tax administration, less of law than of process. Vol. 1 examines problem; vol. 2, data; vol. 3, compliance to obligation; and vol. 4, penalties for noncompliance. It is *not* a compendium of Latin American practice.

2892 Impact of energy costs on the transport sector in Latin America. Proceedings of a seminar sponsored by the Ministry of Public Works and Transportation of Colombia and the Inter-American Development Bank. Washington: IDB, Economic and Social Development Dept., Technical Cooperation Div., Industrial Economics and Infrastructure Section, 1982. 405 p.: bibl., ill.

Based on 1980 seminar. Pt. 1 summarizes meeting; pt. 2 consists of technical papers; pt. 3 covers four case studies: Colombia, Brazil, Argentina, Central America and the Caribbean. Serious work.

2893 Incontro sulle relazioni italo latinoamericane nel settore chimico farmaceutico, *2nd, São Paulo, 1981.* Secondo incontro sulle relazioni italo latinoamericane nel settore chimico farmaceutico. Roma: Instituto italo latino americano, 1982. 272 p. (Pubblicazione dell'Instituto italo latino americano)

Very specialized. Proceedings of conference on Italian-Latin American interrelations in the pharmaceutical-chemical sector.

2894 Ingeniería y consultoría en Brasil y el Grupo Andino: posibles áreas de cooperación. Santiago: Naciones Unidas: IPEA, 1982. 320 p.: ill. (Estudios e informes de la CEPAL; 15. E/CEPAL/G.1215, agosto de 1982)

Serious and comprehensive study of the possibilities of Brazilian engineering consultation in the Andean Group—another aspect of possible regional cooperation.

2895 Instituto para la Integración de América Latina (INTAL). Div. de Asistencia Técnica. El transporte internacional en América Latina (INTAL/IL, 7:67, abril 1982, p. 24–34)

Overview of transport industry with emphasis on its international aspects.

2896 Integración y cooperación en América Latina. Antonio Jorge y Jorge Salazar Carrillo, eds. Rio de Janeiro: Instituto Latino-Americano de Desenvolvimento Econômico e Social (ILDES), 1982. 358 p.: tables (Col. ILDES; 4)

Anthology seeking to provide serious evaluation of cooperation in Latin America. Designed, too, to provide convenient and appropriate text for courses devoted to international trade.

2897 Inter-American Development Bank. Economic and social progress in Latin America: annual report, 1984. Washington: IDB, 1984. 1 v.: ill., tables.

Continuing very useful publication. This year's "topic" is economic integration. Sec. 2 summarizes country experiences. Sec. 3 is a convenient statistical "abstract."

2898 ———. Socio-economic progress in Latin America: annual report, 1983. Washington: IDB, 1983. 1 v.: ill., tables.

In addition to the customary review of the Latin American economy and each country's economy, this year's feature is "natural resources" with chapters: overview, agricultural land, water, forestry, fishing, minerals. Consistently useful publication.

2899 International commodity trade: Latin America—EEC. Edited by C.W.M. den Boer, L.F. Hagedoorn, and J.H. Stroom. Amsterdam: CEDLA, 1981. 351 p.: bibl., ill. (CEDLA incidentele publicaties; 20)

Careful set of papers examining policy effects on Latin American exports to the EEC.

2900 International dimensions of land reform. Edited by John D. Montgomery. Boulder, Colo.: Westview Press, 1984. 239 p.: bibl. (A Westview special study)

Thorough examination of land reform as an international issue. Latin America is accorded considerable attention. Substantial contribution.

2901 Irizarry, Rafael L. Sobre educación y desempleo en los países en vías de desarrollo: las paradojas de la industrialización dependiente (UPR/RCS, 22:3/4, sept./dic. 1980, p. 275–298, bibl., ill.)

The structure of industry (e.g., absence of R&D) provides little demand for high level locals. At the same time, many seek credentials for employment in the bureaucracies. Draws heavily on Puerto Rican experience.

2902 Jiménez de Lucio, Alberto. Las transnacionales y el Nuevo Orden Económico Internacional: entrevista (SP, 3, mayo 1978, p. 45–54)

Lengthy and well done interview. Interviewee was second officer of the UN Center for Study of Transnational Firms.

2903 Jung, Winfried. Problemas económicos y problemas de la política económica en América Latina (Contribuciones [Konrad-Adenauer-Stiftung A.C., Centro Interdisciplinario de Estudios sobre el Desarrollo Latinoamericano (CIEDLA), Buenos Aires] 2, abril/junio 1984, p. 29–38)

Crisis is worst since 1930s. Socialism has not worked; nor has Chicago neo-Liberalism. No reason to think that "austerity" imposed by the IMF will be helpful.

2904 Karlsson, Weine. El papel de las instituciones financieras multilaterales en el financiamiento externo de América Latina (LI/IA, 8:1, 1983, p. 43–60, tables)

Historical review of loans and lending policies of IDB and World Bank.

2905 Khan, M.H. and J.A. Zerby. A comparative study of socioeconomic development in Latin America (UWI/SES, 31:3, 1982, p. 129–154)

Ranking of 24 Latin American countries based on 120 indicators. Complex, but gives indication of structural characteristics of development.

2906 Kosobchuk, Svetlana. Tendencias de la concentración del capital en la banca

(URSS/AL, 6:54, 1982, p. 68–81, plates, tables)

As production becomes more capitalistic and concentrated so does banking which is largely interested, not in national well-being but in profits, risk, speculation—which leads to lending to already solvent firms.

2907 —— and **Nikolái Jolodkov.** Etapa contemporánea de dependencia financiera (URSS/AL, 2, Feb. 1984, p. 40–47, ill., tables)

Analysis of external debt and problems associated with it.

2908 Kuznetsov, Viacheslav. Política de avasallamiento del Fondo Monetario International (URSS/AL, 2, Feb. 1984, p. 48–55)

Suggests inter-Latin American monetary pools to correct balance of payments deficits and thus to help break the "monopoly" of the IMF.

2909 Lambert, Denis Clair. Un piége des globalisations Nord-Sud: le plafonnement des échanges entre l'Europe et l'Amérique latine (FDD/NED [Problèmes d'Amérique latine, 64] 4663/4664, 9 avril 1982, p. 35–78, tables)

Examines possibilities for trade between Europe (particularly) and Latin America in view of expectations of NIEO. Views them without great optimism and suggests other trade possibilities to be explored by Latin America.

2910 Latin America in the world economy: new perspectives. Edited by Diane Tussie. New York: St. Martin's Press, 1983. 238 p.: bibl., index.

Well done proceedings on conference at London School (1981) which examines the development problems of Latin America particularly the role of the State. Among contributors: Díaz Alejandro, Peter B. Evans, Aldo Ferrer.

2911 *Latin American Integration.* IDB, INTAL. June 1982- . Buenos Aires. INTAL periodical whose principal function is to report on research and other matters related to regional integration. Usually in Spanish.

2912 Latin American Regional Meeting of the Econometric Society, 2nd, Rio de Janeiro, 1981. Abstracts. Rio de Janeiro: s.n., 1981. 132 p.

One-half to one-page summaries of roughly 130 papers presented. Most, but not all, deal with Latin American topics; many are single country studies. Arranged alphabetically by author.

2913 Latin American-U.S. economic relations, 1982–1983. Latin American Economic System. Boulder, Colo.: Westview Press, 1984. 119 p.: bibl., ill., index, tables.

Interesting report prepared by the secretariat of SELA. Analyzes particularly impacts of US monetary and trade policies on Latin America. Will be helpful if we get a whole series of biennial analyses. Translation of *Las relaciones económicas de América Latina con Estados Unidos, 1982–1983* (Mexico: Siglo Veintiuno, 1983).

2914 Leipziger, Danny M. The concessionality of foreign assistance (Finance and Development [IMF, Washington] 21:1, March 1984, p. 44–46)

A piece on the methodology and implication of computing the "concessional" costs and benefits of assistance. Important consideration in estimating optimal amounts of assistance.

2915 Leiva Lavalle, Patricio. El financiamiento de las exportaciones en América Latina: los sistemas promocionales de financiación y seguro de crédito a la exportación. Santiago: Naciones Unidas, 1983. 212 p.: bibl. (Estudios e informes de la CEPAL; 18. E/CEPAL/G.1236)

Increasing exportation of manufacturers causes (and is caused by) new export incentive devices. Study examines financial devices and especially credit insurance related to the lag between orders, shipments, and payments. These arrangements are as important in international trade as are the goods themselves.

2916 Lizano, Eduardo. Relaciones económicas externas de América Latina (CM/FI, 24:2, oct./dic. 1983, p. 233–247)

Discusses external relations to reach desiderata on policy: complementary, global, flexible, realistic—with explanations of their significances.

2917 Lord, Montague J. Commodity export prospects of Latin America. Washington: IDB, Economic and Social Development

Dept., International Economics Sec., 1984.
96 p.: tables.

Econometric projection of regional exports, their relationship to prices, and export earnings related to prospective debt servicing.

2918 Luddemann, Margarete K. Nuclear power in Latin America: an overview of its present status (SAGE/JIAS, 25 : 3, Aug. 1983, p. 377–415, tables)

Substantial pieces on Argentina, Brazil, Mexico; shorter ones on Cuba, Chile, Colombia, Venezuela.

2919 MacEwan, Arthur. El problema de la deuda externa en América Latina: ¿un callejón sin salida? (AR, 9 : 35, 1983, p. 5–9, facsim., plates)

General descriptive piece. Most interesting are comments on the Cuban debt.

2919a ——— et al. Crisis capitalista contemporánea, movimiento obrero y perspectivas del desarrollo latinoamericano. Chilpancingo, México: Maestría en Ciencias Sociales, Univ. Autónoma de Guerrero, 1981. 250 p., 4 p. of plates: bibl., ill.

Series of papers by US, French, Italian, Argentine, Mexican academics. Title suggests major topics.

2920 Malavé Vera, Carmen. La OPEP y la crisis mundial del petróleo. Caracas: Univ. Central de Venezuela, Ediciones de la Biblioteca, 1982. 223 p.: bibl., ill (Col. Ciencias económicas y sociales; 28)

Study of OPEC, its origins, practices, and evaluation of its chances of success.

2921 Malloy, James M. and Silvia Borzutzky. Politics, social welfare policy, and the population problem in Latin America. Pittsburgh, Pa.: Univ. of Pittsburgh, Center for International Studies, Center for Latin American Studies, 1983. 1 v.: tables (Latin American reprints series; 18)

Reprinted from International Journal of Health Services (12 : 1, 1982). Population problem is seen as politically induced stemming from impacts and negative consequences of consciously formulated public policies—including social security programs.

2922 Martino, Orlando. Mineral industries of Latin America. Washington: Bureau of Mines, US Dept. of the Interior, 1981. 116 p.: ill., maps (Mineral perspectives)

Summary review of the mineral industries of 34 countries and areas in Latin America. Lists companies, provides maps with mine locations and roads, pipe lines, ports, etc.

2923 Martner, Gonzalo. Introducción a las economías del Tercer Mundo: un estudio histórico-económico sobre el desarrollo de Africa, Asia y América Latina. México: Centro de Estudios Económicos y Sociales del Tercer Mundo: Editorial Nueva Imagen, 1983. 1 v.: bibl., tables.

Begins with historical background. Pt. 1 deals with evolution of the "Third World," its organization and involvement with other "worlds." Pt. 2 (one half) is country-by-country analysis of development in Latin America.

2924 Mata Mollejas, Luis. Vías al desarrollo. Caracas: Vinicio Romero Editor, 1981. 278 p.: bibl., ill.

Less a "map" of development than a competent review of thought about "development," broadly considered to include economic, political, sociological thought and development's environmental impacts.

2925 Medición del empleo y de los ingresos rurales. Santiago: Naciones Unidas, 1982. 173 p.: bibl., tables (Estudios e informes de la CEPAL; 19. E/CEPAL/G.1226)

Seeks to identify causes of universal dissatisfaction with measurements of rural employment (hence unemployment) and incomes. Solid work, important topic.

2926 Mesa-Lago, Carmelo. Seguridad social y pobreza. Pittsburgh, Pa.: Univ. of Pittsburgh, Center for International Studies, Center for Latin American Studies, 1983. 1 v.: tables (Latin American Reprint series; 19)

Social security (broadly defined) is found to have had little impact in reducing the critical level of poverty (via protecting the needy, redistributing income, contributing to development). Pt. 2 makes recommendations.

2927 ———. Tendencias en los sistemas económicos y estrategias del desarrollo en la América Latina (FCE/TE, 50[2]:198, abril/junio 1983, p. 861–871, tables)

Review of economic systems, development models, and problems for the present decade.

2928 Miagkov, Evgueni. Un nuevo factor: el mercado de euromonedas (URSS/AL, 2, Feb. 1984, p. 62–66, ill.)

Examines complexities added to Latin American debt problem by borrowing in the European money market—debt essentially denominated in dollars.

2929 Miranda, Aníbal. Las condicionantes del desarrollo en América Latina: revisión (CPES/RPS, 17:47, enero/abril 1980, p. 101–120, graphs, tables)

Development, as undertaken by local government and encouraged by "centrist" powers, has not served well: growth has not been equilibrated nor has it increased the welfare of the majority of the people.

2930 Los Mitos de Milton Friedman. Rosario Green, comp. México: CEESTM: Editorial Nueva Imagen, 1983. 242 p.: tables (Serie CEESTEM-Nueva Imagen)

Anthology of responses to Friedman's *Freedom to choose.* Eight authors each deal with different aspects. One each deals with monetarism in Argentina and Chile.

2931 Morales, Julio. Los PRI en Latinoamérica: un crecimiento apoyado en millonaria deuda externa (RAE, 7:3, 1982, p. 143–149, ill., plates, tables)

Mexico and Brazil are PRI's (i.e., "recently industrialized countries") and argues that growth in 1960s and 1970s was carried largely through foreign borrowing. Data.

2932 Morgan, Theodore H. Does the World Bank have a role in the oil and gas business? (CJWB, 17:1, Spring 1982, p. 47–52, tables)

Bank does lend for gas and oil exploration and development. Can be powerful force in helping solve energy problems of LDCs. This is not without its problems.

2933 ——— and Albert Davis. The concomitants of exchange-rate depression: less developed countries, 1981–1983 (UC/EDCC, 31:1, Oct. 1982, p. 101–129, graphs, tables)

Seventeen-country sample. Major problem: which exchange rates to study? Effects: balance of payments, price changes, money income, capital flows. Important article.

2934 Mower, Alfred Glenn. The European community and Latin America: a case study in global role expansion. Westport, Conn.: Greenwood Press, 1982. 180 p.: bibl., index (Contributions in economics and economic history; 46)

Examination of the role of a newcomer on the scene (the European Community) and how it has developed relations with Latin American countries, individually and collectively. Essentially a study of the ECC; its relationship to Latin America is pursued as an illustrative case.

2935 Mullen, Joseph W. Energy in Latin America: the historical record. Santiago: Naciones Unidas, 1978. 66 p.: bibl., tables (Cuadernos de la CEPAL)

Examines growth and change in energy industries in three decades. Provides background for later study of petroleum crisis.

2936 Nósova, Natalia. Expansión de los bancos transnacionales (URSS/AL, 2, fev. 1984, p. 56–61, tables)

Brief review of loans and lending policies of imperialistic countries' banks in Latin America.

2937 Nouvelles perspectives de l'intégration latino-américaine = Nuevas perspectivas de la integración latinoamericana. Louvain, Belgium: Univ. catholique de Louvain, Centre d'études européenes, 1980. 264 p.: bibl., tables.

Series of papers presented at a 1979(?) seminar. Considerable attention to legal aspects.

2938 Novak, Michael. Why Latin America is poor: cultural factors in the creation of Latin poverty (FIU/CR, 11:3, 1982, p. 18–50, ill.)

Makes case that Latin American historical stagnation is in part result of predominant Catholicism. Analyzes several Church pronouncements on development. Responds to Gustavo Gutiérrez's *A theology of liberation.*

2939 Nueva fase del capital financiero: elementos teóricos y experiencias en América Latina. Jaime Estévez y Samuel Lichtensztejn, comps. México: Editorial Nueva Imagen, 1981. 391 p.: bibl., ill.

Pt. 1 reviews the increasing role of international finance and its implications. Pt. 2 consists of case studies: Argentina, Brazil, Chile, Jamaica, Mexico, Venezuela.

2940 O'Brien, Patricia J. Population policy, economic development, and multinational corporations in Latin America: issues and impacts. East Lansing, Mich.: Women in International Development, Michigan State Univ., 1983. 30 p.: bibl., tables (Working papers; 32)

Broader than title suggests. Considerably less than full examination of nature and role of MNCs in complex process.

2941 Oferta de América Latina y demanda de los mayores mercados mundiales de los principales metales, 1970–1990: aluminio, cobre, hierro, níquel, plomo, zinc, estaño. Santiago: Naciones Unidas, Consejo Económico y Social, CEPAL, 1982. 104 p.: bibl., ill. (E/CEPAL, L.269)

The title is adequate description. Competent work.

2942 Oliveira, Amaury Porto de. Natureza política de preço do petróleo (IBRI/R, 22:85/88, 1979, p. 5–30)

Thorough discussion of the evolution and complexities of petroleum pricing policies.

2943 Oliveira, Francisco de. Un clásico de *El Trimestre Económico:* Celso Furtado y el paradigma del subdesarrollo (FCE/TE, 50[2]:198, abril/junio 1983, p. 1019–1042)

Immensely friendly, but not uncritical, and thoughtful discussion of the thought of Celso Furtado. A considerable *homenaje.*

2944 Oogaki, Chiaki. Citrus production in Latin America and its impact on worldwide citrus trade, from current statistics: pt. 1, Citrus industry of Latin America (Latin American Studies [Univ. of Tsukuba, Special Research Project on Latin America, Sakura-Mura, Japan] 7, 1983, p. 171–179, bibl., graphs, map, tables)

Brazil is the major producer; its plantings have grown at 7.4 percent annually for two decades. It is the world's largest exporter and second in production.

2945 Organización de la investigación agropecuaria en América Latina: reflexiones e instrumentos para su análisis. Edición de Fanny de la Torre y J. Escoto. San José: Dirección de Información Pública y Comunicaciones del Instituto Interamericano de Cooperación para la Agricultura, 1982. 537 p.: bibl., ill., tables (Serie Investigación y desarrollo; 2)

Based largely on case studies: ICA (Colombia), INTA (Argentina), La Univ. Agraria La Molina (Peru). Pays particular attention to technological transfer.

2946 La Organización sindical por rama de industria en América Latina. Introducción, textos y comentarios, Francisco Iturraspe. Caracas: Instituto Latinoamericano de Investigaciones Sociales, 1980. 209 p., 6 p. of plates: bibl., ill., tables (Democracia económica)

Survey of types of unionization in Latin America. Chapters pertain specifically to Mexico, Uruguay, Chile and Bolivia, Argentina, Venezuela.

2947 Orlandi, Alberto. América Latina y la economía mundial del café. Santiago: Naciones Unidas, CEPAL, 1982. 104 p.: ill., tables (Cuadernos de la CEPAL; 42. E/CEPAL/G.1194)

Competent study of the coffee market. Finds a burdened, traditional structure in Latin America facing international oligopsony. Suggests return to stronger producer associations.

2948 Ortiz Mena, Antonio. Development in Latin America, a view from the IDB: addresses and documents, 1976–80. S.l.: s.n., 1981? 570 p.: ill., index, tables.

Collected pronouncements over 15 years. Chronological arrangement and other-than-thematic titling reduces usefulness. Indexing does not really solve the problem.

2949 Osorio-Tafall, B.F. Comentarios sobre el desarrollo y el Nuevo Orden Económico Internacional (CEESTM/TM, 1:2, enero/abril 1982, p. 255–273)

Recognizes that the NIEO "ideal" is not realistic. Considerable attention to how Third World should consider development problems during the Reagan administration.

2950 Pazos, Felipe. Cincuenta años de pensamiento económico en la América Latina (FCE/TE, 50:200, oct./dic. 1983, p. 1915–1948)

Extremely interesting piece written in celebration of the journal's 50th year (author wrote similar article for its 20th anniversary!). Fine synthesis.

———. Política de desarrollo económico: colección de artículos, ponencias e informes, 1949–1984. See item **3490.**

2951 People's participation in development in Latin America. Prepared by the Social Development Div. of the Economic Commission for Latin America to be presented at the International Seminar on Popular Participation to be held in Ljubljana, Yugoslavia, 17–25 May 1982. Santiago: UN, ECLA, 1982. 47 p.: bibl., tables (E/CEPAL/L.264)

General discussion of popular participation in the development process in Latin America; attempts to include it in planning; and rural, urban, female youth participation.

2952 Petras, James F. and Morris H. Morley. The rise and fall of regional economic nationalism in the Andean countries, 1969–1977 (UWI/SES, 27:2, June 1978, p. 153–170)

Interesting account of the Andean Group—from its "independent" stage early on, with progressive deterioration of its independence as it became more a mechanism of the multinationals.

2953 Petroff, G. Utilización de los bosques tropicales para la fabricación de pulpa y papel (OAS/CI, 22:3/4, 1982, p. 42–50, bibl., tables)

Technology has changed to make possible tropical forest conversion to pulp. Discusses problems yet to be solved to make it practicable.

2953a Philip, George D.E. Oil and politics in Latin America: nationalist movements and state companies. New York: Cambridge Univ. Press, 1982. 577 p.: bibl., ill., index, tables (Cambridge Latin American studies; 40)

Discusses world oil scenario and nationalization and performance of state oil companies in Argentina, Bolivia, Brazil, Mexico, and Venezuela. Compares continous and growing state control with role of private capital. [R. Moncarz]

2954 Pinto, Aníbal. Centro-periferia e industrialización: vigencia y cambios en el pensamiento de la CEPAL (FCE/TE, 50[2]:198, abril/junio 1983, p. 1043–1076)

Thoughtful review of ECLA's current views on development and policy.

2955 Plaza, Salvador de la et al. Dependencia y subdesarrollo. Prólogo de D.F. Maza Zavala. Bogotá: Plaza & Janes, 1983.

358 p.: bibl. (Antología del pensamiento económico y social de América Latina; 7)

Original (two exceptions) essays on various aspects of development. Some emphasis on Venezuela.

2956 Pluta, Joseph E. The declining public sector thesis: an additional test and implications for developing regions (UWI/SES, 28:4, Dec. 1979, p. 69–84, bibl., tables)

Five of 13 countries in sample are Latin American. Inconclusive results in testing hypothesis that real public sector expenditures have peaked.

2957 Políticas de estabilización y empleo en América Latina. Santiago: OIT, PREALC, 1982. 68 p.: tables (Investigaciones sobre empleo; 22)

Analyzes employment and stabilization impacts of various policies followed. Very general.

2958 Politics and economics of external debt crisis: the Latin American experience. Edited by Miguel S. Wionczek in collaboration with Luciano Tommassini. Boulder, Colo.: Westview Press, 1985. 481 p.: bibl., index, tables (Westview special studies on Latin America and the Caribbean)

Important book. It is current having had its genesis in an informal 1983 meeting; it treats subject from debtor point of view, asserting most literature originates in the North and, consciously or not, is concerned with effects there. Nine general essays and cases on Argentina, Brazil, Mexico, Venezuela, Chile, Peru, Central America.

2959 Population growth and urbanization in Latin America: the rural-urban interface. Edited by John M. Hunter, Robert N. Thomas, and Scott Whiteford. Cambridge, Mass.: Schenkman, 1983. 310 p.: tables.

Compilation of 19 selected papers presented at 1979 MALAS meeting. Organized around: population growth and social change; development strategies and migration; urbanization; the rural-urban interface; perspective.

2960 Portilla, Belfor. Problemas y perspectivas del Nuevo Orden Alimentario Internacional (CEESTM/TM, 1:1, sept./dic. 1981, p. 27–35)

Proposals, present situation, and prospects.

2961 Posibilidades de cooperación y complementación industrial entre América Latina y Japón para la producción y comercialización del hierro y el acero. S.l.: Naciones Unidas, Consejo Económico y Social, CEPAL, 1982. 142 p.: ill. (E/CEPAL/L.265)
Solid study with projections to the year 2000.

2962 Prácticas restrictivas y discriminatorias en el comercio internacional. Edición de Raymundo Barros Charlín. Alejandro Jara Puga *et al.* Santiago: Instituto de Estudios Internacionales, Univ. de Chile, 1979. 180 p.: bibl., tables (Estudios internacionales)
Rather broad analysis of trade practices and efforts to regulate and police them. Treats, among others, GATT, LAFTA, EEC. Considerable attention to dumping.

2963 Prayer, Cheryl. Is there a better way?: development and the World Bank (MR, 34:4, Sept. 1982, p. 12–30)
Final chapter of *The World Bank: a critical analysis* (New York: Monthly Review Press, 1982). Answer to above: Yes, it starts with a social revolution as a precondition for a "different and more humane development policy" (without models)—but that is not enough. . . .

2964 Prebisch, Raúl. Cinco etapas de mi pensamiento sobre el desarrollo (FCE/TE, 50[2]:198, abril/junio 1983, p. 1077–1096)
Evolution of Prebischian thoughts—by their thinker. Warrants attention.

2965 ———. Contra el monetarismo. Buenos Aires: El Cid Editor, 1982. 180 p.: bibl., ill. (Col. Estudios interdisciplinarios)
Anthology of Prebischiana including analyses of Hayek, Friedman (source of title), various lectures, a press conference, comments on Prebisch's own *Capitalismo periférico: crisis y transformación.*

2966 ———. La obra de Prebisch en la CEPAL. Selección de Adolfo Gurrieri. México: Fondo de Cultura Económica, 1982. 516 p.: bibl., ill. (El Trimestre Económico. Lecturas; 46)
Useful compendium. One set of pieces from late 1940s, one from 1960s, one set current. Near 100-p. introduction provides useful synthesis.

2967 Primera lista de productos del Grupo Andino para promoción prioritaria en 1982. Junta del Acuerdo de Cartagena. Lima: Red Andina de Información Comercial, 1982. 100 p.: tables (Perfiles básicos del mercado andino; 012. RAIC; 016)
Technical Andean Group document giving basic data on items considered priority for 1982 trade development.

2968 Productos seleccionados de la oferta exportable de Colombia para la XII Feria Internacional del Pacífico. Lima: Red Andina de Información Comercial, 1981. 92 p.: bibl., tables (Perfiles básicos del mercado andino. RAIC; 010)
Example of Andean Group export promotion. Covers 14 products and gives data on their trade history within the Group and with the rest of the world.

2969 Prospects for adjustment in Argentina, Brazil, and Mexico: responding to the debt crisis. Edited by John Williamson. Washington: Institute for International Economics, 1983. 63 p.: bibl., ill., tables.
Three short pieces (one per country, one per author) with brief discussion pieces by still another. Tends toward superficiality and to be ephemeral in interest—i.e., topic is short-term adjustment which for most purposes is gone before printing ink is on the paper.

2970 Puyana, Alicia. Cooperación económica Sur-Sur (CEESTM/TM, 1:1, sept./dic. 1981, p. 125–151, tables)
Reviews trade patterns. Argues that trade should become more South-South and that institutions should develop to assist this.

2971 Ramírez Ocampo, Augusto. Incidencia del aspecto político en las negociaciones del NOEI (PUJ/U, 3:2, julio 1982, p. 102–113)
Cites cases of political determination of decisions or lack of same. Suggests variety of policy needs to advance goals of NIEO.

2972 Redclift, M.R. "Urban bias" and rural poverty: a Latin American perspective (JDS, 20:3, April 1984, p. 123–138, bibl., table)
Study of food and energy policies in Brazil and Mexico with a view to testing the hypothesis of "urban bias." Findings tend to weaken the case for urban bias.

2973 Relaciones financieras externas y su efecto en la economía latinoamericana. Selección de Ricardo Ffrench-Davis. México: Corporación de Investigaciones Económicas para Latinoamérica: Fondo de Cultura Económica, 1983. 430 p.: ill., tables (*El Trimestre Económico*. Lecturas; 47)

Structure and size, global debt management; viability of the form of deficit finance; emerging unified world capital market.

2973a Reunión de Expertos sobre Ciencia, Tecnología y Empleo en Areas Rurales, *Bogotá, 1980.* Documento de relatoria: informe final. Bogotá: Fondo Colombiano de Investigaciones Científicas y Proyectos Especiales Francisco José de Caldas; Montevideo: UNESCO, Oficina Regional de Ciencia y Tecnología para América Latina y el Caribe, 1981. 67 p.

UNESCO conference final report consists of works presented by well known Latin American experts on science, technology, and rural employment such as Getúlio Tirado, Jorge Lopera, etc. [J. Salazar Carrillo]

Reunión de Técnicos de Bancos Centrales del Continente Americano, *La Paz, 1983.* See item **3080.**

2974 Roel, Virgilio. El imperialismo hoy y su ideología. Lima: Editorial Prometeo, 1982. 44 p.: bibl., tables (Documentos de economía; 1:1)

Transnationals are the pillars of the new, stronger, global imperialism. A principal ideologue of such imperialism is Milton Friedman whose nonsense is supposed to be science but is contraband.

2975 Rousseas, Stephen. International debt crisis: borrowers, banks & the IMF (CRIA/W, 27:1, Jan. 1984, p. 14–16, table)

Outlines the problem and discusses Kenen's proposed solution (supernational buyer of debt from banks) as a bailout of banks. Suggests that such a bailout is in the offing and on banks' terms.

2976 Rouzier, Philippe. Echange et développement: cadre théorique pour une alternative. Ottawa: Editions de l'Univ. d'Ottawa, 1981. 117 p.: bibl., ill., table (Livres et monographies de l'Institut de développement international et de coopération; 3)

Dissatisfied with the pessimism of development theory for the periphery, author seeks a better understanding of exchange and development *in space* and formulates first steps in an alternative to current trade practices for raw material producers. Haiti is the background for the essay.

2977 Rovetta, Vicente. El capital extranjero en la explotación de la minería y los metales de América Latina (Desarrollo Indoamericano [Barranquilla, Colombia] 16:74, agosto 1982, p. 33–42, table)

Brief review of production, manufacturing, investment on a country-by-country basis.

2978 Ruttan, Vernon W. Integrated rural development programmes: a historical perspective (WD, 12:4, April 1984, p. 393–401, bibl., table)

We have progressed through "community development," "integrated rural development," and "basic human needs" programs. Compares these and provides general conclusions regarding rural development programs.

2979 Saieh, Alvaro. Un análisis sobre la posibilidad de evaluar la solvencia crediticia de los países en desarrollo. Santiago: CEPAL, 1980. 89 p.: bibl., tables (Cuadernos de la CEPAL; 36. E/CEPAL/G.1118)

Examines and evaluates various indices of solvency (Latin American countries). Presents many data. Has also appeared in CEMLA's journal, *Monetaria.*

2980 Salazar Carrillo, Jorge. Comparaciones de precios, paridades de poder adquisitivo y producto real en la América Latina (FCE/TE, 49[3]:195, julio/sept. 1982, p. 703–730, tables)

Covers 16 countries. Background, methodological considerations, calculations.

2981 ———. Real product and price comparisons for Latin America and other world countries (UC/EDCC, 31:4, July 1983, p. 757-773, tables)

Methodological. Compares 11 Latin American countries and nine others (1970). Gross domestic product, private and public consumption and investment. Very useful.

2982 Sánchez, Vicente; Branislav Gosovic; and Osvaldo Sunkel. Problemática medio-desarrollo: aspectos internacionales (SP, 19, 1982, p. 37–49)

Covers wide range of topics on environmental management as it is internationally undertaken.

2983 Sanders, Thomas G. Population and development in Latin America and the Caribbean. Hanover, N.H.: Univ. Field Staff International, 1983. 1 v. (UFSI reports; 1983/7)

Identifies principal population trends and problems of the region. UFSI reports are, in general, current and perceptive.

2984 Schloz, Rudolf. Nuevas perspectivas en la cooperación económica y técnica entre la República Federal de Alemania y América Latina (Contribuciones [Konrad-Adenauer Siftung A.C. Centro Interdisciplinario de Estudios Sobre el Desarrollo Latinoamericano (CIEDLA), Buenos Aires] 2, abril/junio 1984, p. 58–63)

Extremely general. Urges EEC to develop a coherent policy, consistent with developmental objectives, toward Latin America.

2985 Schmink, Marianne. Household economic strategies: review and research agenda (LARR, 19:3, 1984, p. 87–101, bibl.)

Comprehensive literature review of important topic and recommendations for further research.

2986 Schultz, Theodore W. On the economics and politics of agricultural incentives (Development Digest [Washington] 21:1, July 1983, p. 10–21)

Agriculture is systematically undervalued in development, and this extends to suppliers of agricultural capital and agricultural research. Hence the potential of agriculture is not realized.

2987 Schwartz, Hugh H. Bottlenecks to Latin American industrial development. Washington: IDB, 1983. 44 p.: tables.

Emphasis is given to coping with bottlenecks and how to take advantage of opportunities.

2988 Seminar on the Acquisition of Latin American Library Materials, *26th, Tulane University, 1981.* Latin American economic issues: information needs and sources. Madison: SALALM Secretariat, Univ. of Wisconsin; Los Angeles: UCLA Latin American Center Publications, 1984. 1 v.: bibl., index.

Publication of *immense* potential. Among contributions are (representative but not exclusive): "labor migration statistics," "capturing fugitive literature," "government publications in Latin American agriculture,"

"meta-bibliography on land tenure, agrarian reform," "directories of data bases in Latin America," "bank needs and sources of information," bibliographies. For bibliographer's comment, see item **63.**

2989 Seminario sobre Economía de los Océanos, *lst, Santiago, 1976.* Economía de los océanos. Santiago: Naciones Unidas, Consejo Económico y Social, CEPAL, 1978. 2 v. (369 p.): bibl., ill., graphs, tables (Documento. E/CEPAL/L.156/Rev.2-E/CEPAL/L.156/Rev.2/Add.1)

Series of 16 seminar papers built around: 1) Third UN Conference on the Law of the Sea; 2) exploitation of living maritime resources; 3) exploitation of mineral resources; 4) political and economic implications; and 5) solution of controversy.

2990 Seminário sobre Integração Latino Americana, *Brasília, 1980.* Textos das conferências. Brasília: Editora Univ. de Brasília, 1982. 204 p.: ill. (Cadernos da UnB)

Three principal papers (Felipe Herrera on "cultural aspects," Enrique Iglesias on "economic aspects," and Félix Peña on "political aspects") with prepared comments on them and discussion. Well done.

2991 Serrano, Agustín. Dinámica y crisis del sistema capitalista mundial. Buenos Aires: Ediciones Lihuel, 1982. 399 p.: bibl., ill.

Carefully done and documented analysis. Little in way of prescription.

2992 Serulle Ramia, José and Jacqueline Boin. FMI: capital financiero, crisis mundial. Santo Domingo: Gramil, 1983. 509 p.: bibl., ill., tables.

Systematic examination of the evolution of the IMF and particularly its role *vis-à-vis* Third World countries in recent decades. Considerable country-by-country analysis.

2993 Sheahan, John. The outside and the inside: trade, finance, and domestic conflicts (LARR, 19:1, 1984, p. 173–180)

Reviews eight vols. (1979–81) on topics suggested in title by well known authors. A wealth of ideas is touched upon.

2994 Los Sistemas de administración presupuestaria en América Latina: resultados de una investigación. México: Asociación Mexicana de Presupuesto Público, 1982. 319 p.: bibl., ill.

Study of budgetary practices of 14

countries. Countries are grouped (e.g., Central America) for evaluation. Measure: "ideal" less "realized" equals "to implement."

2995 Slater, David. Capitalismo y desarrollo regional: ensayos críticos sobre la organización del espacio en el Tercer Mundo. Amsterdam: CEDLA, 1982. 209 p.: bibl. (CEDLA incidentele publicaties; 22)

Carefully done. Considerable attention to geography and geographers. Major thesis: current regional thinking has been critical of traditional analysis but has not gone far to adapt Marxist thought to analysis of regional development.

2996 Speir, Melanie S. Latin America: the foreign investment climate. Menlo Park, Calif.: SRI International, Business Intelligence Program, 1981. 28 p.: ill., tables (Research report; 651)

Overall view of politics and economies of Latin America. Country reports on Argentina, Brazil, Colombia, Costa Rica, Mexico. Entry indicates availability of current information through such services as SRI.

2997 Steger, Hans-Albert. Die soziales Entwicklung Lateinamerikas in den achtziger Jahren (OLI/ZLW, 22, 1984, p. 7–20)

Succinct synopsis of cooperative regional economic developments in Latin America since 1960. Brief overview of the region's most pressing economic problems (e.g., staggering foreign debts, unfavorable balances of trade, collapse of regional trade groups). Hopeful that diversification, more sophisticated industrialization, and control of inflationary spirals may improve 1980s economic prospects. [G.M. Dorn]

2998 Stoehrel, Viola. The political relevance of Eric H. Jacoby's writings on transnational corporations: a Latin American perspective (SEM/E, 36:3/4, 1981, p. 152–159)

Indictment of economic power of World Bank, IMF, and especially transnational corporations. No testing of hypotheses.

2999 Streeten, Paul P. The New International Economic Order (UNESCO/IRE, 28:4, 1982, p. 407–429)

Background, reviews options, and explores avenues for furthering common interests and resolving conflicts. Essentially optimistic.

3000 Sunkel, Osvaldo. Pasado, presente y futuro de la crisis económica internacional (FCE/TE, 51:203, julio/sept. 1984, p. 429–470, tables)

Careful historical analysis of policies and experiences of this century, hypotheses concerning causes of the crisis and suggesting in most general terms approaches for adjusting to it.

3001 Sutton, Mary. The costs and benefits of stabilisation programmes: some Latin American experiences. London: Overseas Development Institute, 1981. 51 p.: bibl. (ODI working paper; 3)

Discusses conventional, monetarist, structuralist/populist program as applied, respectively: Peru (1976–78); Chile (1975–78); Chile (1970–75); and Argentina (1973–76).

3002 Tablas de insumo-producto en América Latina. Santiago: Naciones Unidas, 1983. 383 p.: bibl., tables (Cuadernos estadísticos de la CEPAL, 0251–9437; 7. Cuadernos de la CEPAL. E/CEPAL/G.1227)

Brief explanatory note and 182 tables of various input-output data related to 17 countries. Little information on sources and reliability.

3003 Tanner, Hans. Latin America's small oil producers (NZZ/SRWA, 33:1, April 1983, p. 10–11)

Reviews developments in Trinidad and Tobago, Ecuador, Peru, and touches on other small producers.

3004 Tanzi, Vito. Fiscal disequilibrium in developing countries (WD, 10:12, Dec. 1982, p. 1069–1082, bibl., tables)

Classifies causes of disequilibria: export boom, price-inelastic tax system; public enterprise performance; increased expenditure because of political expediency or administrative weakness; worsening of terms of trade. Examines frequency of occurrence.

3005 Teitel, Simón. Creación de tecnología en la América Latina (FCE/TE, 50:200, oct./dic. 1983, p. 2397–2417, tables)

There is more indigenous technological innovation than usually considered. Examines cases and factors important in them. Reaches some policy conclusions.

3006 ———— and Francisco Colman Sercovich. Latin America (WD, 12:5/6, May/June 1984, p. 645–660, bibl., tables)

Comprehensive review of Latin American exports of technologies. Based on studies of Mexico, Argentina, Brazil, and the Andean Group.

3007 Tesauro de términos de la integración subregional andina. 3a ed. Lima: Biblioteca de la Junta del Acuerdo de Cartagena, 1983. 267 p.
Specialized classification system. Important tool for a small group of researchers.

3008 Tomassini, Luciano. Las negociaciones Norte-Sur: algunas alternativas (FCE/TE, 49[2]:194, abril/junio 1982, p. 363–386)
Discusses reasons for North-South stalemate, changes in the global economic-political situation, and suggests how these may be utilized to open negotiations again.

3009 Trade, aid, and U.S. economic policy in Latin America. Edited by Howard J. Wiarda and Janine T. Perfit. Prologue by H.E. Alejandro Orfila. Washington: Center for Hemispheric Studies, American Enterprise Institute for Public Policy Research, 1983. 81 p. (Occasional papers series; 6)
Collection of papers, mainly from US officials, related to title topics. No discussion, summary, or conclusion.

3010 Trade, debt, and growth in Latin America. Edited by Antonio Jorge, Jorge Salazar Carrillo, and Enrique P. Sánchez. New York: Pergamon Press, 1984. 165 p.: bibl., ill., tables.
Companion to 1983 vol. and proceesings of 1983 conference. Subregion-specific pieces on Caribbean, Central America, Mexico, Venezuela, Colombia, Brazil, South Florida. Also more general topics. Discussion included.

3011 Trade, stability, technology, and equity in Latin America. Edited by Moshé Syrquin and Simón Teitel. New York: Academic Press, 1982. 492 p.: bibl., ill., index, tables.
The refined product of a 1980 symposium at the Bar-Ilan Univ., Israel. Examines, at a high level, short- and long-run interactions between external factors (trade and financial flows) and the domestic economy.

3012 Transnational corporation linkages in developing countries: the case of backward linkages via subcontracting: a technical paper. New York: UN Centre on Transnational Corporations. 75 p.: bibl.

Based on studies of automotive industry in Peru, India, Morocco. Serious but severely restricted. One of main benefits comes through technology transfer.

3013 Tulchin, Joseph S. Emerging patterns of research in the study of Latin America (LARR, 18:1, 983, p. 85–94)
Gleaned from eight yrs. experience as editor of *Latin American Research Review.* More than economics. Fruitful areas of continued research: empirical resolution of debates on dependency, modes of production, transnational enterprise, corporatism.

3014 The Two faces of Third World debt: a fragile financial environment and debt enslavement (MR, 35:8, Jan. 1984, p. 1–10, tables)
Review of debt structure. To blame are banks which are severely threatened. Only drastic measures can provide solution (e.g., nationalization of the banks).

3015 Undermining rural development with cheap credit. Edited by Dale W. Adams, Douglas H. Graham, and J.D. Von Pischke. Boulder, Colo.: Westview Press, 1984. 318 p.: bibl., ill., index, tables (Westview special studies in social, political, and economic development)
Examination of well meant agricultural credit policies and undesired and undesirable outcomes—especially for the rural poor. Considerable emphasis on Latin America.

3016 Urquidi, Víctor L. El cambio estructural y la política monetaria en América Latina: posibles lecciones para otros países en vía de desarrollo (CEMLA/M, 6:2, abril/junio 1983, p. 133–154, bibl.)
Considerably more on the evolution and problems of monetary policy in Latin America than elsewhere.

3017 ——. Cuestiones fundamentales en la perspectiva del desarrollo latinoamericano (FCE/TE, 50[2]:198, abril/junio 1983, p. 1097–1126)
Reflects on his 40 yrs. of concern over Latin American development. Covers wide range of topics. Most impressive to him: lack of *an* answer or general solution to problems.

3018 Usui, Mikoto. International transfer of industrial technology: an appraisal of the Japanese performances in Latin American NICS (Latin American Studies [Univ. of

Tsukuba, Japan] 6, 1983, p. 123–151, bibl., tables)

Very interesting article which, in part, examines differences in means of technology transfer by Japan and US. Case material adds interest.

3019 Vaitsos, Constantine V. The role of transnational enterprises in Latin American economic integration efforts: who integrated, and with whom, how, and for whose benefit? New York: United Nations, 1983. 32 p.

Examines role of transnational enterprises in Andean Group, CACM, LAFTA. TNEs "constituted a major force in the process . . . and were the main beneficiaries."

3020 Valle, Silvia del and Rebeca Salazar. Los acuerdos sobre productos básicos: logros y restricciones, los casos del café, cacao y azúcar (CEESTM/TM, 1:1, sept./dic. 1981, p. 37–67, tables)

Considers modern commodity agreements and urges producer nations to organize production vertically and the work together in producer associations for marketing purposes.

3021 Villarreal, René. La contrarrevolución monetaria en el centro y la periferia (FCE/TE, 50[1]:197, enero/marzo 1983, p. 429–471, graphs)

Pt. 1 discusses theory of classical orthodoxy, particularly in US and the UK. Pt. 2 discusses the counterrevolution in Latin America as example in the periphery. Solid piece, preview of book-to-be from Editorial Océano.

3022 Villaveces Pardo, Ricardo. Algunas consideraciones sobre la integración andina (PUJ/U, 3:2, julio 1982, p. 116–130)

Colombian viewpoint; treats specifically industrial and agricultural aspects.

3023 Vivó, Gastón Hugo. El crecimiento de las empresas en los Estados Unidos y en la América Latina: un estudio comparativo. Miami, Fla.: Ediciones Universal, 1982. 121 p.: bibl., ill.

Examines the processes of business administration and growth to point out the requisites of modernization in Latin American commerce and industry.

3024 Vries, Barend A. de. Industrial policy in small developing countries (Finance and Development [IMF, Washington] 21:2, June 1984, p. 39–41)

Industrialization is a different process than for larger countries. Provides several policy recommendations.

3025 Weinert, Richard S. Coping with LDC debt (CU/JIA, 38:1, Summer 1984, p. 1–10)

An imaginative scheme for "coping" and sharing the costs.

3026 White, Eduardo. Measures strengthening the negotiating capacity of governments in their relations with transnational corporations: joint ventures among firms in Latin America: a technical paper. New York: Center on Transnational Corporations, 1983. 97 p.: tables.

Deals entirely with Latin America: background, integration efforts and joint ventures; power relations.

3027 Wiesner Durán, Eduardo. Las políticas económicas nacionales y su relación con la crisis financiera internacional (Contribuciones [Konrad-Adenauer-Stiftung A.C. Centro Interdisciplinario de Estudios sobre el Desarrollo Latinoamericano (CIEDLA), Buenos Aires] 2, abril/junio 1984, p. 22–28, tables)

Focuses on domestic policies as causes for much of the Latin American crisis. Resources were abundantly available; policies were mistaken, particularly those which led to excessive public spending. Correcting those errors would help.

3028 Wionczek, Miguel S. La competencia entre los exportadores de armas de Occidente (CM/FI, 24:2, oct./dic. 1983, p. 260–267)

With reduced arms trade, competition is increasing. Not Latin America-specific.

3029 ———. Los energéticos y la seguridad internacional en los ochenta: ¿realidades o falsas percepciones? (CM/FI, 24:1, julio/sept. 1983, p. 50–62)

Finds energy problems becoming less severe in developed countries but increasingly severe (and a serious threat to security) in Third World countries without oil.

3030 Worrell, DeLisle. Exchange rate policy for less developed countries (UWI/SES, 29:2, June 1980, p. 134–164, bibl., graphs)

Examines "state of the art" of exchange rate management in LDCs. Most attention to determination of "desirable" rate and less to "how (if) to manage?" and "what currency to calculate desirable rate in."

3031 Zhuravliova, Olga. Las trasnacionales y el problema de los alimentos en los países latinoamericanos (URSS/AL, 7:67, julio 1983, p. 17–23, plate, tables)

Transnationals contribute to food insufficienty by orienting production away from domestic needs and toward exports.

MEXICO

RAUL MONCARZ, *Professor of Economics, Florida International University,*

THE PRESENT SOCIOECONOMIC structure of Mexico has evolved as a result of various changes from the time of the Mexican Revolution. The nation's economy is a mixed one with private and public ownership of the means of production and with increasing government participation in recent years under the political administration of the Partido Revolucionario Institucional. Works that address these issues are grouped under the following subheadings in the bibliography: "Historical Evolution of the Mexican Economy and Current Issues" (items **3032–3052**); "The Role of Government" (items **3053–3055**); "The Public Sector" (item **3056–3059**); and "Foreign Investment" (items **3109–3111**).

The recent debt crisis, bank nationalization and devaluation of the peso were the focus of much international concern because of Mexico's standing in the international market. The nation underwent considerable growth after the discovery and export of oil. Studies that examine these aspects of the Mexican economy are listed under "Financial Crisis" (items **3060–3068**), "Bank Nationalization" (items **3069–3075**), "Devaluation" (items **3076–3079**), "Inflation" (items **3080–3081**), and "The Oil Industry (items **3082–3094**).

Mexico's trade is especially linked to the US, its principal importer of oil and goods. The relationship, however, goes beyond trade since strong socioeconomic ties exist between both countries, particularly in cities along the Mexican/American border (see items **3095–3104**).

As a developing nation, Mexico faces many of the problems inherent in growth such as unequal income distribution, unemployment and underemployment, all of which present serious problems for policy makers (see items **3112–3130**).

The agricultural sector, in decline as a result of industrialization, faces additional problems when decreasing industrial sector activity prevents it from absorbing unemployed farm workers. Government efforts to revive the farming industry have often failed when certain areas are favored while others are neglected (see items **3131–3141**).

Works addressing topics not discussed in this essay are grouped under "Miscellaneous" (items **3142–3165**).

I am greatly indebted to Lazara Gordon for her assistance in the preparation and editing of this section.

HISTORICAL EVOLUTION OF THE MEXICAN ECONOMY AND CURRENT ISSUES

3032 Bodayla, Stephen D. Bankers versus diplomats: the debate over Mexican insolvency (SAGE/JIAS, 24:4, Nov. 1982, p. 461–482, bibl.)

Covers Mexico's political development since the Revolution, instability of economy during and after it and measures taken towards stabilization. Detailed discussion of D.W. Morrow's policies as US ambassador and advisor to the International Committee and the Mexican government until his death in 1931.

3033 Buzaglo, Jorge D. Planning alternative development strategies: experiments on the Mexican economy. Stockholm: Institute of Latin American Studies, 1982. 271 p.: bibl., ill. (Monographs; 7)

Qualitative study deals with effects of alternative development approaches to development policies (combination of public investment and income distribution policies).

3034 Calderón R., Miguel Angel. El impacto de la crisis de 1929 en México. México: Fondo de Cultura Económica, 1982. 244 p.: bibl. (SEP/80; 36)

Discusses impact of 1929 crisis and analyzes its effect on trade, banking, industrial and agricultural sectors. Justifies present government intervention as necessitated by said crisis.

3035 Caso-Raphael, Agustín and Jorge Miranda. Patrones de política monetaria y gasto público en México: el desarrollo estabilizador (FCE/TE, 51:203, julio/sept. 1984, p. 591–614, bibl., tables)

Purpose of study is to present empirical evidence on how monetary and fiscal policies are affected by changes in economic activity during a stable period.

3036 Coloquio sobre Economía Mexicana, *El Colegio de México, 1979.* Panorama y perspectivas de la economía mexicana: memoria. Nora Lustig, comp. México: El Colegio de México, 1980. 609 p.: bibl., ill. (Col. Centro de Estudios Económicos y Demográficos; 11)

Essay digest presented by the Centro de Estudios Económicos y Demográficos de El Colegio de México in its 1979 Conference of the Mexican Economy. Topics: economic policies, financial problems and transformation of the agricultural sector.

3037 García Alba Iduñate, Pascual. La evasión fiscal en México: un estudio comparativo del impuesto sobre ingresos mercantiles con el impuesto al valor agregado. Azcapotzalco, México: Univ. Autónoma Metropolitana, 1982. 210 p.: bibl., ill., tables (Ensayos; 4)

Compares and contrasts value added taxes (VAT) to other forms of taxation and comes out in favor of VAT. Also shows validity of studies of Mexico's financial system must be seriously questioned given scant attention to key variable: fiscal evasion. Includes detailed estimates.

3038 Gómez Oliver, Antonio. Política monetaria y fiscal de México: la experiencia desde la posguerra, 1946–1976. México: Fondo de Cultura Económica, 1981. 206 p.: bibl., ill., tables (Sección de obras de economía)

Covers postwar period (1946–76), subsequent economic disequilibrium, high rates of inflation and low growth rates along with three devaluations of the peso until 1976.

3039 Heyman, Timothy. Chronicle of a financial crisis: Mexico, 1976–1982 (FIU/CR, 12:1, Winter 1983, p. 8–11, 35–59, photos, table)

Chronological summary of major events of the Mexican economy (1976–82). Discusses events leading to peso's devaluation in Feb. 1982 and criticizes rationale of bank nationalization in Sept. 1982. Also outlines the IMF's package and conditions.

3040 Labre, Armando. Hacia una política económica para el desarrollo social (FCE/TE, 50[1]:197, enero/marzo 1983, p. 359–375, tables)

Proposes incorporating economic policies geared towards the increased well-being of the masses and away from present income disparity.

3041 López G., Julio. The Mexican economy: present situation, perspectives and alternatives (WD, 11:5, May 1983, p. 455–465, bibl.)

Sector-by-sector analysis of factors leading up to recent (1980) crisis of the Mexican economy. Formulates alternative strategies of "nationalist but with a populist orientation," calling for a restrictive period of readjustment.

3042 Madrid H., Miguel de la. Mexico: the new challenges (CFR/FA, 63:1, Fall 1984, p. 11–100)

Summary of past, present, and future perspectives of Mexico's political economy. Recognition that economic growth has brought with it structural imbalances which must be corrected while facing external pressures and conflicts in the region. Recognition of Mexico's ability to maintain political stability and an adequate functioning economy in the first two years of his administration.

3043 Manual de estudios y proyectos para desarrollos industriales. v. 1, Estudios de factibilidad. v. 2, Normas técnicas. Juan P. Antún, coordinador. México: Secretaría de Asentamientos Humanas y Obras Públicas, Dirección General de Obras de Mejoramiento Urbano, 1982. 2 v. in 4: bibl., ill.

Effort to attain some rationality in the objectives, policies, and ends resulting from planning and urban development for the population. The four vols. should help in selecting the localities that would generate a well balanced regional development according to national plan priorities.

3044 Méndez Morales, José Silvestre. 100 [i.e. Cien] preguntas y respuestas en torno a la economía mexicana. México: Ediciones Océano, 1983. 188 p.: bibl., ill.

Consists of 100 simplified answers to key economic questions relating to the Mexican economy.

3045 The Mexican economic crisis: policy implications for the United States: report. Prepared by the Congressional Research Service, Library of Congress. Sponsored workshop help for the Subcommittee on International Trade, Investment, and Monetary Policy of the Committee on Banking, Finance, and Urban Affairs and the Subcommittee on Western Hemisphere Affairs of the Committee on Foreign Affairs, House of Representatives, 98th Congress, 2nd session. Washington: GPO, 1984. 274 p.: ill., tables.

Papers and proceedings of workshop on the Mexican economic crisis. Divided into two sessions: 1) on the economic situation; and 2) the political situation. Edited proceedings and papers provide basic document of information and analysis covering wide spectrum of views.

3046 México. Poder Ejecutivo Federal. Plan nacional de desarrollo, 1983–1988. México: Secretaría de Programación y Presupuesto, 1983. 430 p.

Presents plan's objectives, means, and execution.

3048 México: estadística económica y social por entidad federativa. México: Secretaría de Programación y Presupuesto, Coordinación General de los Servicios Nacionales de Estadística, Geografía e Informática, 1981. 170 p.: ill. (some col.), plates.

Presents important statistical information by state for the purpose of gathering important economic and social variables to better plan at the federal, regional, and sectoral level. Presented in four chapters including demographic and social indicators, economic indicators, financial indicators, and infrastructure aspects of communication and transport.

3049 México: información sobre aspectos geográficos, sociales y económicos. v. 1, Aspectos geográficos. v. 2, Aspectos sociales. v. 3, Aspectos económicos. México: SPP, Coordinación General de los Servicios Nacionales de Estadística, Geografía e Informática, 1981–1983. 3 v.: bibl., ill. (some col.), col. maps.

Covers evolution and conditions under which different economic activities take place in Mexico. Presentation is both qualitative and quantitative. Overview of present conditions of different sectors of economic activity. For geographer's comment, see item **5105.**

3049a Mexico's economic crisis: challenges and opportunities. Donald L. Wyman, ed. La Jolla: Center for US-Mexican Studies, Univ. of California, San Diego, 1983. 126 p.: bibl. (Public education reports; 5th. Monograph series; 12)

Overview of Mexico's crisis, austerity program, and development strategy in 1980s. Also explores dimensions of the crisis, including US role, trade and investment policy, labor market, policies of organized labor, and political aspects of the austerity program. Descriptive of Mexico's current problems and key variables affecting its future.

3050 Peña, Sergio de la. Acumulación originaria y la nación capitalista en México: ensayo de interpretación (FCE/TE, 50[2]:198, abril/junio 1983, p. 713–732)

Study puts into historical perspective Mexico's emergence as a capitalist nation and traces changes that led to socialist ideologies/policies of the 1960s.

3051 Review of the Economic Situation of Mexico. Banco Nacional de México (Banamex). Vol. 58, No. 685, dic. 1982– . México.

Includes President Miguel de la Madrid's inaugural address on Mexico's future governmental policies: reduction of growth in public spending, protection of employment, continuation of works in progress with cancellation on unnecessarily expensive or low priority programs, efficiency and honesty of government, etc. Reports on the economy: current statistical data (1980–82) on financial sector, prices, agricultural sector, industrial production, trade and tourism.

3052 Simposio sobre empresarios en México. v. l, Empresarios españoles y alemanes: siglos XVIII y XIX [por] Gloria Artís et al. v. 2, Intermediación, fracciones étnicas de clase, contextualización regional [por] Guillermo Beato, Guillermo de la Peña, Roberto Salazar. v. 3, Empresarios mexicanos y norteamericanos, y la penetración de capital extranjero: siglo XX [por] Marisol Pérez et al. México: Centro de Investigaciones Superiores del INAH, 1979. 3 v.: bibl., ill. (Cuadernos de la casa chata; 21–23)

Study of entrepreneurial activity in Mexico during different time periods. Lack of previous studies makes this work an important contribution to topic. Six chapters cover local and foreign entrepreneurs along with foreign penetration from the times of Porfirio Díaz until latter 1970s.

THE ROLE OF GOVERNMENT

3053 Brannon, Jeffrey T. Mexico's development dilemma (SECOLAS/SELA, 26:3, Dec. 1982, p. 2–15)

Historical overview (from 1960s to early 1980s) of the Mexican economy's development, the role of government and dilemma between the different political parties with detailed evaluation of key political figures, their policies, etc.

Estudo comparativo da indústria de alimentos: administração e política de tecnologia na América Latina. See item **2842.**

3054 Marzukúlov, Valeri. Metodología de la programación económica (URSS/AL, 2:26, feb. 1983, p. 24–31)

Argues for need to increase central planning by the Mexican government. Discusses said planning as it relates to industries and also to alleviate regional disparities. Evaluates three phases of central planning: identification, objective determination, and realization. Concludes by attributing Mexico's increased independence of recent.years to increased central planning.

3055 Pazos, Luis. Futuro económico de México. México: Editorial Diana, 1977. 151 p.: graphs.

Worthwhile if dated study (not previously annotated in HLAS). Critical of government intervention and its effect on the Mexican economy, it states that the future of Mexico lies in government decision-making and in how the country can influence such decisions.

Redclift, M.R. "Urban bias" and rural poverty: a Latin American perspective. See item **2972.**

THE PUBLIC SECTOR

3056 Brannon, Jeffrey and **Eric N. Baklanoff.** Ambivalencia de metas de una empresa paraestatal semi-autónoma: el caso de CORDEMEX (UY/R, 140:24, marzo/abril 1982, p. 103–122)

Evaluation of Mexico's ventures in the public sector and controlled production policies, outlining difficulties encountered in conversion process.

3057 Bravo Ahuja Ruiz, Víctor E. La empresa pública industrial en México. México: Coordinación de Investigaciones INAP, Instituto Nacional de Administración Pública, 1982. 257 p.: bibl. (Estudios. Serie 2, Administración pública mexicana; 4)

Comparative analysis of private and public enterprises in Mexico, advantages and disadvantages of public vs. private and their different social objectives.

3058 El Papel del sector público en la economía mexicana: participación del Gobierno de México en el proyecto internacional de investigación, julio de 1980. México: SPP, Coordinación General de los Servicios Nacionales de Estadística, Geografía e Informática: Centro Internacional para las Empresas Públicas de los Países en Desarrollo, 1982. 128 p.: bibl., tables.

Part of international study of public sector's role in economy. Very thorough examination of public sector including quantitative and qualitative data such as evolution of the industry, objectives and strategies, along with public administration. Required reading for students of public enterprise.

3059 Ruiz Dueñas, Jorge. Eficacia y eficiencia de la empresa pública mexicana: análisis de una década. México: Editorial Trillas: Univ. Autónoma Metropolitana, 1982. 180 p.: bibl., index.

Detailed study of efficiency of public sector policies in Mexico in 1970s.

FINANCIAL CRISIS

3060 Amerlinck Assereto, Antonio. Perfil de las crisis recientes del sistema financiero mexicano (BNCE/CE, 34:10, oct. 1984, p. 953–969, tables)

Description of sequence of events and economic policy decisions that led to 1976–82 financial crisis. Financial interdiction is for slow growth given its need to use local resources since access to foreign funds will be minimal. Expansion of money supply is under stricter control than before. Stresses importance of initial savings for strengthening financial system.

3061 Brannon, Jeffrey T. and **David A. Schauer.** Country risk assessment and U.S. banks: the case of Mexico (Texas Business Review [Bureau of Business Research, Univ. of Texas at Austin] 57:4, July/Aug. 1983, p. 192–196, tables)

Describes assessment of country risk on international loans and its overly optimistic application in the case of Mexico. Suggests future monitoring and increased communication measures in the international financial system with regard to LDCs.

3062 Bueno, Gerardo M. Endeudamiento externo y estrategias de desarrollo en México, 1976–1982 (CM/FI, 24:1, julio/sept. 1983, p. 78–89)

Discusses Mexico's external debt, its causes, and implications. Concludes that this problem is not the sole culprit of the economy's present crisis, proposes adoption of more realistic comprehensive measures.

3063 Cline, William R. Mexico's crisis, the world's peril (FP, 49, Winter 1982/1983, p. 107–118)

Mexico's 1982 financial crisis and its effect on the world's banking system. Discusses PRI's and new banking director Carlos Tello's financial policies, his criticism of IMF and nationalization of banks. Also deals with international financial system's loss of confidence in newly industrialized countries.

3064 Looney, Robert E. and **Peter C. Frederiksen.** A programmed approach toward a regional expenditure policy for Mexico (JDA, 17:1, Oct. 1982, p. 1–12, tables)

Analyzes Mexico's income disparity and planning problems then puts forth empirical analysis of regional infrastructure investment. The latter should follow two different approaches to meet different needs of developed and underdeveloped regions. Emphasizes optimal centralization for decision-making to induce private sector investments.

3065 Mexican economy: creative financing to the rescue (NACLA, 17:1, Jan./Feb. 1983, p. 40–44, photos)

Discusses rescue operation put together by the IMF, Bank of International Settlements, and private institutions to aid Mexico's 1982 financial crisis. Outlines creative financing techniques such as: advance payments from US and Spain for oil deliveries, guaranteed loans to finance food exports, deferred principal payments to private banks and others.

3066 Newell G., Roberto and **Luis Rubio F.** Mexico's dilemma: the political origins of economic crisis. Boulder, Colo.: Westview Press, 1984. 1 v.: bibl., index, tables (Westview special studies on Latin America and the Caribbean)

Analysis of economic, social, and political factors that led to the 1982 crisis.

3067 Ortiz, Edgar. La banca privada en México: formación de capital y efectos de la inflación; devaluación y comercio exterior (BNCE/CE, 31:1, enero 1981, p. 27–38)

Capacity for capital absorption is a significant function of financial sector in its ability to gather monetary surpluses and transform them into real investments. Empirical analysis of financial flows of 14 banks points to need for cooperation between financial intermediaries and government to fight inflation and strengthen financial sector.

3068 Street, James H. Mexico's development dilemma (CUH, 82:488, Dec. 1983, p. 410–414, 434)

Discusses Mexico's dilemma as it confronts dichotomy between restrictive austerity policies that would correct its financial situation and long-term expansive policies thwarted by monetary and fiscal restraints. Examines programs such as: Global Development Program and its attempt to spread industrialization throughout country; rural assistance and educational programs.

BANK NATIONALIZATION

3069 Colmenares, David; Luis Angeles; and Carlos Ramírez. La nacionalización de la banca. México: Terra Nova, 1982. 263 p.: tables (Col. Crónicas de nuestro tiempo)

Digest of articles written on nationalization of Mexico's banking sector, downfall of private banks, process of nationalization and its effects.

3070 Islas, Héctor. Economic and social conditions in Mexico (BNCE/CE, 28:8, Aug. 1982, p. 259–266, table)

Discusses different political parties participating in 1982 elections. Also analyzes preparations leading to elections, restructuring of electoral rolls along with decrease in abstentionism.

3071 ———. Economic and social conditions in Mexico (BNCE/CE, 28:12, Dec. 1982, p. 417–425)

Descriptive and documented account of events leading to nationalization of private banking system and introduction of generalized exchange controls.

3072 López Portillo, José. Sixth State of the Nation Report (BNCE/CE, 28:9, Sept. 1982, p. 306–324)

Summary of López Portillo's last State of the Nation Report in which he nationalized Mexico's private banks and the establishment of exchange controls.

3073 Márquez, Javier. La banca en México, 1830–1983 (FCE/TE, 50:200, oct./dic. 1983, p. 1873–1914)

Outlines history of banking sector of Mexico since 1830 to present, discussing implementation of its nationalization in 1982.

3074 Pazos, Luis. La estatización de la banca: ¿hacia un capitalismo de estado? México: Editorial Diana, 1982. 120 p.: bibl., tables.

Critical commentary of Mexico's bank nationalization. Discusses events leading to nationalization and interprets them as "scapegoat" device used to detract attention from other problems. Author declares said nationalization unconstitutional and believes control merely shifted from private to public sector for same capitalistic ends.

3075 Tello, Carlos. La nacionalización de la banca en México. México: Siglo Veintiuno Editores, 1984. 222 p.: bibl., tables (Economía y demografía)

Former Minister explains nationalization process. Presents political and social arguments in favor of the nationalization.

DEVALUATION

3076 Colmenares, David; Luis Angeles; and Carlos Ramírez. La devaluación de 1982. México: Terra Nova, 1982. 172 p. (Col. Crónicas de nuestro tiempo)

Digest of articles by three authors on the 1982 Mexican devaluation, events leading to it, and ensuing consequences.

3077 Conchello, José Angel. Devaluación 82: el principio del fin. México: Editorial Grijalbo, 1982. 190 p.: ill., plates.

Controversial, critical view of Mexico's devaluation of the peso and resulting, subsequent inflation.

3078 Olloqui, José Juan de. Un enfoque bancario sobre la crisis mexicana de pagos en 1982 (FCE/TE, 51:203, julio/sept. 1984, p. 527–544, tables)

A look at Mexico's situation that examines ratios and indexes. The 1982–83 crisis constituted one of the principal restrictions to reactivate process of economic recovery. Discusses peso's devaluation in 1982 and its continuing slide. Sees balancing of budget and slowing of inflation as important contributions to Mexico's revival.

3079 Torres Gaytán, Ricardo. Un siglo de devaluaciones del peso mexicano.

2a ed. México: Siglo Veintiuno Editores, 1982. 427 p.: bibl., ill., tables (Economía y demografía)

Historical perspective of Mexican peso's devaluation from Spanish colony to mid 1970s.

INFLATION

3080 Reunión de Técnicos de Bancos Centrales del Continente Americano, *20th, La Paz, 1983.* XX [i.e. Vigésima] Reunión de Técnicos de Bancos Centrales del Continente Americano. In English, French, Portuguese, and Spanish. La Paz: Banco Central de Bolivia, 1983. 38 v.: bibl., ill., tables.

Vols. analyze relation between inflation and yield of stocks quoted in Mexican Stock Exchange (1972–79). Results show negative relation between expected inflation and market's average yield. In the short run (one-to-three months) relation is negative, but in one year plus, the relation is positive.

3081 Romero Kolbeck, Gustavo. La economía mexicana y sus perspectivas (FCE/TE, 50[1]:197, enero/marzo 1983, p. 419–427)

Outlines present problems of Mexican economy. Proposes checks in budget deficit and inflation as a means of uninterrupted growth.

THE OIL INDUSTRY

3082 Angeles, Luis. México: una perspectiva petrolera de corto plazo (Iztapalapa [Univ. Autónoma Metropolitana, Div. de Ciencias Sociales y Humanidades, Iztalapa, México] 2:3, julio/dic. 1980, p. 39–47, bibl., ill.)

Similarities and differences between Mexican oil economy and other oil producing nations. Pessimistic about Mexico's oil wealth significantly affecting unemployment and income redistribution.

3083 Castillo, Heberto and Jacinto Viquera. Los energéticos, el petróleo—y nuestro futuro? México: Representaciones y Servicios de Ingeniería, 1982. 156 p.: bibl., ill., index.

Stresses importance of energy resources in Latin American economies and its rational utilization in order to break away from their present interdependence with developed countries.

3084 Economic and social conditions in Mexico: foreign sector (BNCE/CE, 28:11, Nov. 1982, p. 381–387, tables)

Analysis of Mexican balance of payments (1977–81), trade policies, and increased importance of hydrocarbons' contribution to GDP. Includes statistical data.

3085 Grayson, George W. Oil and politics in Mexico (CUH, 82:488, Dec. 1983, p. 415–419, 435)

A look at Petróleos Mexicanos (Pemex), Mexico's state monopoly, its activities during 1978–83, development and interaction with OPEC, labor unions, corruption, and financing difficulties.

3086 ———. An overdose of corruption: the domestic politics of Mexican oil (FIU/CR, 13:3, April 1984, p. 23–24, 46–49, ill.)

Informative and picturesque account reports on Mexican corruption by concentrating on the oil industry and encompassing both highest management levels and rank-and-file workers. While their union is nominally just another labor organization, with its 29 locals, it boasts not only of an effective political machine but of business interests that often siphon off funds from the rank and file to enrich the union's big shots.

3087 ———. The politics of Mexican oil. Pittsburgh, Pa.: Univ. of Pittsburgh, 1980. 283 p.: bibl., index, tables (Pitt Latin American series; 7)

Consists of 10 chaps. that make up history of Mexican oil industry in the 20th century. History, politics, and economics are interwoven throughout the book. For political scientist's comment, see *HLAS 45:6058.*

3088 La Industria petrolera en México. México: Petróleos Mexicanos: Secretaría de Programación y Presupuesto, Coordinación General de los Servicios Nacionales de Estadísticas, Geografía e Informática, 1980. 560 p.: bibl., ill., tables.

Report on Mexico's oil industry. Consists of six chaps. encompassing industry's importance in main economic variables, product activities generated by it, etc. Includes complete statistical guide and industry's profile up to 1979.

3089 Mexico oil report: an upstream perspective: an assessment. Houston, Tx.: Petroleum Information International, 1984. 55 leaves: ill., tables.

Looks at importance of Mexican oil industry since 1979 and its significance for US. Mexico has become its largest supplier of oil (about two percent of imports). Also examines constraints limiting future expansion of production (e.g., lack of financial resources for further exploration and development).

3090 Pérez Gazga, Flavio. Mexico's energy policy (CJWB, 18:3, Fall 1983, p. 25–31, tables)

Delineates Mexico's most important energy policy features, role oil plays in the nation's economy and the need for stable international oil market in order to achieve policy goals. Tables show oil as percentage of exports, investments, consumption, etc.

3091 Petróleo y desarrollo en México y Venezuela. Marcos Kaplan, coordinador. México: UNAM: Editorial Nueva Imagen, 1981. 451 p.: bibl., ill., tables.

Describes oil's role in Mexican and Venezuelan development as well as nationalization and the industry's social and economic costs.

Philip, George D.E. Oil and politics in Latin America: nationalist movements and state companies. See item **2953a.**

3092 Sanders, Thomas Griffin. Oil and the Mexican economy. Hanover, N.H.: Universities Field Staff International, 1982. 12 p.: bibl., ill., tables (UFSI reports, 0743–9644; 1982/no.12. North America)

Discusses oil's role in the Mexican economy, its impact on GDP and its failure to solve economic problems despite its positive impact.

3093 Székely, Gabriel. La economía política del petróleo en México, 1976–82. México: Colegio de México, Centro de Estudios Internacionales, 1983. 205 p.: bibl., tables.

Study examines why the Mexican government decided to change a traditional oil policy focused on a domestic market to an international one in 1976. Most convincing arguments derive from evidence that previous efforts to establish growth rates did not result in significant changes in economic and social policies.

3094 Velasco, Jesús-Agustín. Impacts of Mexican oil policy on economic and political development. Lexington, Mass.: Lexington Books, 1983. 237 p.: bibl., index, tables.

Study based on thorough research in costs and benefits of Mexican oil revenues as well as possible dangers. Examines problems that threaten the nation's stability, economic aspects of energy development, and the international economic context.

US-MEXICAN RELATIONS

3095 The Border that joins: Mexican migrants and U.S. responsibility. Peter G. Brown and Henry Shue, eds. Totowa, N.J.: Rowman & Littlefield, 1983. 254 p.: bibl., index, tables (Maryland studies in public philosophy)

Eight essays discuss foreign workers, illegal entry, immigration, and conditions in Mexico as well as historical, philosophical aspects, and possible alternatives for the migration dilemma.

3096 Dillman, C. Daniel. Assembly industries in Mexico: contexts of development (SAGE/JIAS, 25:1, Feb. 1983, p. 31–58, bibl., tables)

Discusses development of the Border Industrialization Program (BIP) and the beneficial implications to both countries (Mexico and US). Concentrates on labor intensive production phase carried out by the relatively low wage labor force (e.g., electronic and apparel industries). For geographer's comment, see item **5088.**

3097 Hansen, Niles. Interdependence along the U.S.-Mexico border (Texas Business Review [Bureau of Business Research, Univ. of Texas at Austin] 57, Nov./Dec. 1983, p. 249–254, tables)

Discusses recent population growth and per capita personal income increase in Mexican-American border cities and contributing factors. Includes brief discussion of 1982 peso devaluation and *maquiladora* program effects. Concludes by suggesting transboundary cooperation among American and Mexican cities to minimize potential social, economic, and environmental problems.

3098 Lupsha, Peter A. and **Kip Schlegel.** The political economy of drug trafficking:

the Herrera organization, Mexico & the United States. Albuquerque: Latin American Institute, Univ. of New Mexico, 1980. 25 p.: bibl., ill., tables (Working paper; 2)

Discusses economic and political implications of drug trafficking and contraband along Mexican-US borderlands.

3099 Nuncio, Abraham. El Grupo Monterrey. México: Editorial Nueva Imagen, 1982. 329 p.: ill., plates, tables (Serie Testimonios)

Discusses influential power of "Monterrey Group" companies, their large capital concentration and economic ties with US.

3100 Ortiz Wadgymar, Arturo. Aspectos de la crisis de los EE.UU. y sus principales impactos en el sector externo de México (UNAM/RI, 8:29, abril/junio 1980, p. 5–22)

Discusses different aspects and impact of US economic crisis in 1970s and its effect on Mexico's economy. Emphasizes how Mexico's dependence on US is harmful to its economy and concludes by predicting the downfall of capitalism.

3101 Pellicer de Brody, Olga. The foreign trade policy of the United States government toward Mexico: are there reasons for expecting special treatment? Translated by Graciela Platero. La Jolla: Program in US-Mexican Studies, Univ. of California at San Diego, 1981. 24 leaves: tables (Working papers in US-Mexican studies; 9)

Discusses US trade policies toward Mexico and American careful handling of political issues to maintain a cordial atmosphere. Also covers privileged participation of US in Mexico's market as EEC's and Japan's participation increases.

3102 Riding, Alan. Distant neighbors: a portrait of the Mexicans. New York: Knopf, 1985. 385 p.: bibl., index, tables.

Well documented wide ranging effort to explain the socioeconomic gap between the US and Mexico. Discusses Mexico's economy, political system, agriculture, petroleum, corruption, and the love-hate relationship between both countries. Provides facts and figures along a journey of a few thousand yrs. history.

3103 Torres Ramírez, Olga Esther. La economía de frontera: el caso de la frontera norte de México. México: Impresiones Aries, 1979. 120 leaves: bibl., tables.

Covers economic development since 1940s of Mexico's northern cities along US border, economic interdependence of cities on both sides, and migratory processes and urbanization.

3104 U.S.-Mexico relations: economic and social aspects. Clark W. Reynolds and Carlos Tello, eds. Rev. ed. Stanford, Calif.: Stanford Univ. Press, 1983. 375 p.

Excellent overview of US-Mexico relations edited and written by two well known experts in the field. Presents unique binational perspective on both nations' economic and social interaction and how their relations can be of long-term interest. Topics include trade, energy, agriculture, employment, immigration, national security, and long-term policies.

TRADE

3105 Balassa, Bela A. Trade policy in Mexico (WD, 11:9, Sept. 1983, p. 795–811, bibl., tables)

Provides evaluation of Mexican trade policies applied in 1956–82. Mexican experience confirms sensitivity of exports/imports to exchange rates. Future growth requires increased investment, particularly in export activities which can be encouraged by incentives such as subsidies rather than protection. (Paper also available as part of World Bank Reprint series 0253–2131; no. 281).

3106 Economic and social conditions in Mexico (BNCE/CE, 28:9, Sept. 1982, p. 295–299, tables)

Outlines historical transformation of Banco Nacional de Comercio Exterior (Bancomex) from national credit institution concerned with export promotion to a full service bank.

3107 Rapacki, Ryszard. Polska-Meksyk: gospodarka: stosunki ekonomiczne = Poland-Mexico: economy, economic relations. Warszawa: Państwowe Wydawnictwo Ekonomiczne, 1983. 304 p.: tables.

Good basic survey by Polish economist of Mexican present-day economic conditions, their vulnerabilities and main thrust in foreign trade. Also examines extent of

Polish-Mexican relations and evaluates possibilities for expansion. It is regrettable that only 63 p. are devoted to such a worthwhile topic. Includes many tables and footnotes based mostly on newspapers. Lacks bibliography, lists or indexes. [K. Complak]

3108 Weintraub, Sidney. Free trade between Mexico and the United States? Washington: Brookings Institution, 1984. 205 p.: bibl., index, tables.

Economic and political analysis of the case for free trade. Advocates approaching topic in rational terms and uses and analyzes relevant data for this purpose.

FOREIGN INVESTMENT

3109 Barrera Graf, Jorge. La regulación jurídica de las inversiones extranjeras en México. México: UNAM, Instituto de Investigaciones Jurídicas, 1981. 208 p. (Serie G. Estudios doctrinales; 52)

Analyzes regulation of foreign investment in Mexico and shortcomings of its legislation (i.e., I.L.E or Ley para Promover la Inversión Mexicana y Regular la Inversión Extranjera).

3110 Blomström, Magnus and Håkan Persson. Foreign investment and spillover efficiency in an underdeveloped economy: evidence from the Mexican manufacturing industry (WD, 11:7, June 1983, p. 493–501, bibl., tables)

Proposes positive relationship (direct and indirect) of foreign investment in host economies. Formulates statistical model to this effect, one that guarantees benefits to domestic industry as a result of spillover (indirect) benefits from foreign-owned plants (e.g., increased competition, training of local work force, speeding up transfer of technology).

3111 Carmona de la Peña, Fernando. La política de inversión extranjera y la dependencia estructural de México (URSS/AL, 11:59, nov. 1982, p. 31–47)

Discusses importance and impact of foreign capital investment in Mexico and its regulations. Concludes that Mexico's monopolistic capital structure along with foreign investment is the principal factor in the exploitation of the working class.

INCOME DISTRIBUTION

3112 Brazil and Mexico: patterns in late development. Sylvia Ann Hewlett and Richard S. Weinert, eds. Philadelphia: Institute for the Study of Human Issues, 1982. 349 p.: bibl., ill., index, tables (Inter-American politics series; 3)

Concentrates on labor, foreign investment and dependency, government intervention in the economy, poverty and income distribution. Foreign capital and technology have brought about rapid growth but with increased inequality.

3113 Gollás, Manuel. La economía desigual: empleo y distribución en México. México: Consejo Nacional de Ciencia y Tecnología, 1982. 506 p.: tables.

Consists of 14 chaps. on employment and income distribution in Mexico. Examines reasons for unequal distribution of income among regions, factors of production and individuals. Offers recommendations to resolve these difficulties.

3114 Looney, Robert E. and Peter C. Frederiksen. Prospects for economic stability in Mexico (Texas Business Review [Bureau of Business Research, Univ. of Texas at Austin] 57:3, May/June 1983, p. 117–119, table)

Discusses possibilities for economic stabilization in Mexico, proposing a fiscal and monetary policy program which emphasizes tax reform to reduce external borrowing as solution to Mexico's financial problems and economic downturn.

3115 Macroeconomía de las necesidades esenciales en México: situación actual y perspectivas al año 2000. México: Siglo Veintiuno Editores, 1983. 224 p.: bibl., ill., tables (Economía y demografía)

Explores nature of income distribution and its relation to the country's productive structure and satisfaction of essential needs now and through the year 2000. Uses simulation model for macro calculations of productive structures, income distribution, balance of trade, etc. Presents possible scenario of outcome provided there is no political intervention that would counteract these economic trends.

3116 Montoya, Rodolfo. La distribución del ingreso personal en Monterrey: análisis de factores explicativos. Monterrey, México: Facultad de Economía, Centro de Investigaciones Económicas, 1980. 88 leaves: bibl., ill., tables.

Studies relation of income disparities to human capital differences in Monterrey (1979). Compares 1979 results to those of 1965 and 1977.

3117 Necesidades esenciales en México: situación actual y perspectivas al año 2000. v. 1, Alimentación. v. 2, Educación. v. 3, Vivienda. v. 4, Salud. v. 5, Geografía de la marginación. 2a ed. México: Siglo Veintiuno Editores, 1982–1983. 5 v.: bibl., ill., tables (Economía y demografía)

Five vols. cover food, education, health and housing, along with geography of the "marginación." Vol. 1 describes basic food needs providing extensive coverage of present and a projection of what is needed to close the gap by the year 2000.

3118 Padilla Aragón, Enrique. Pobreza para muchos, riqueza para pocos. México: El Día, 1982. 197 p.

Focuses on Mexico's great income disparity and unfair distribution. Analyzes current political measures to check such disparities and supports increased government intervention as a means to solve problem along with reduction of inflation and increased economic growth.

3119 Vera, Gabriel; Carlos Bazdresch; and Graciela Ruiz. Algunos hechos sobre distribución del ingreso en México (CM/D, 110, marzo/abril 1983, p. 34–41, graphs, ill., tables)

Well documented paper on the distribution of income in Mexico. Examines family size and income distribution and finds that smallest family unit is not the one that is better off, family size increases with income.

LABOR PROBLEMS

3120 Clavijo, Fernando and Susana Valdivieso. La creación de empleos mediante el comercio exterior: el caso de México (FCE/TE, 50[2]:198, abril/junio 1983, p. 873–916, bibl., tables)

Determines relationship between on the one hand Mexico's unemployment and underemployment and on the other, its export-trade market. Notes direct and indirect effects of imports and exports in the utilization of labor inputs, productivity and resource allocation. Contrasts study's results with Hufbauer's and Levy's. Concludes that solution to Mexico's unemployment and/or underemployment problems does not lie in the job-creating potential of exports.

3121 Estadística de la industria maquiladora de exportación, 1974–1982. México: SPP, Instituto Nacional de Estadística, Geografía e Informática, 1983. 42 p.: plates, tables.

Basic information at state and municipal levels on the following: employed personnel, their wages, man-hours worked, value of inputs, and general expenses. Additionally, reports data on variables classified by 12 products processed by the industry for 1979–82. Also includes questionnaire used in study.

3122 García, Francisco. Un modelo para estudiar el desempleo en el área metropolitana de Monterrey. Nuevo León, México: Univ. Autónoma de Nuevo León, Facultad de Economía, Centro de Investigaciones Económicas, 1980. 29 leaves: bibl., ill.

Explores reasons for unemployment in Monterrey. Uses econometric model to conclude that sex is the most important variable in determining unemployment level, more so than education.

3123 Indices de productividad laboral para algunas clases de actividad económica de la industria manufacturera. México: Centro Nacional de Información y Estadísticas del Trabajo, 1980. 184 leaves: bibl., ill., tables (Serie Documentos de trabajo. Información estadística; 2)

Offers index of product per man-hours worked for certain sectors of manufacturing industries. Represents first approximation of development project of productivity measures. These indexes can serve as guide for direct evaluation of industries studied and to formulate better productivity guidelines for them.

3124 Información básica sobre la estructura y características del empleo y el desempleo en las áreas metropolitanas de las ciudades de México, Guadalajara y Monterrey. México: SPP, Coordinación General del Sistema Nacional de Información, 1979. 225 p.: bibl., tables.

Concerns aspects of labor force and employment in three metropolitan areas:

Mexico City, Guadalajara, and Monterrey. Involves representative sample of population of people over 12 yrs. of age.

3126 Marco conceptual de referencia del fenómeno laboral. Juan José Cantú Gutiérrez, coordinador. México: Centro Nacional de Información y Estadísticas del Trabajo, 1982. 598 p.: bibl., ill. (Serie Metodología; 5)

Reference aid on labor statistics issued by Sistema de Información para la Administración de Trabajo (SIAT).

3127 Ocupación salarios en el área metropolitana de Monterrey, 1980. Monterrey, México: Facultad de Economía, Centro de Investigaciones Económicas, 1981. 101 p.: bibl., tables.

Statistical representation of Monterrey's population, broken down into demographic structure, occupational structure of employed and unemployed, educational background, and income distribution.

3128 Ramones, Jesús. La mujer en el mercado laboral de Monterrey. Monterrey, México: Univ. Autónoma de Nuevo León, Facultad de Economía, Centro de Investigaciones Económicas, 1980. 39 leaves: bibl.

Examines impact of women on Monterrey's work force, their increased participation in the growing service sector, their inferior salaries, and status relative to those of men. Attributes these disparities to cultural and educational biases.

3129 Riquelme, Marcial Antonio. Educación y empleo: una relación cuestionable (CPES/RPS, 19:53, enero/abril 1982, p. 85–104, bibl., tables)

Refutes notion of education's effect on employment and emphasizes underestimated importance of structural factors such as parents' occupation, rural and urban area differences, etc. Concludes that although there is a high positive correlation between education, employment and salaries, structural bottlenecks prevent advanced education from guaranteeing employment/higher income *per se.*

3130 Tovar Guzmán, Bernardo and **Efraín Zappi Molina.** Análisis de la productividad laboral en la industria de fertilizantes (MSTPS/R, 4, enero/marzo 1981, p. 33–56, bibl., graphs, tables)

Attempts to establish labor productiv-

ity measures for the fertilizer industry and to analyze variables such as labor and product. Study impaired by lack of statistics.

AGRICULTURE

3131 Carlos, Manuel L. State policies, state penetration and ecology: a comparative analysis of uneven development and underdevelopment in Mexico's micro agrarian regions. La Jolla: Program in US-Mexican Studies, Univ. of California, San Diego, 1981. 39 leaves: bibl., tables (Working papers in US-Mexican studies; 19)

Discusses uneven development of agrarian regions in Mexico and effects of government policies favoring certain regions over others.

Lamartine Yates, Paul. Mexico's agricultural dilemma. See *HLAS 46:2225.*

3134 Olmedo, Raúl. México, economía de la ficción. México: Editorial Grijalbo, 1983. 213 p.: bibl., tables.

Attempts to trace roots of Mexico's underdevelopment and its dependency problems. Addresses incompatibility of farming and industrial sectors, income inequalities and government's new role. Argues for decentralization as solution to current problems.

3135 Palerm Viqueira, Juan Vicente. Notas para la interpretación de la expansión del capitalismo en la agricultura (Iztapalapa [Univ. Autónoma Metropolitana, Iztapalapa, México] 1:1, julio/dic. 1979, p. 204–217)

Outlines stages of development of Mexican agricultural sector, its performance under capitalist and non-capitalist systems, and present problems.

3136 Redclift, Michael. Production programs for small farmers: Plan Puebla as myth and reality (UC/EDCC, 31:3, April 1983, p. 551–570, tables)

Discusses the Puebla Project and its attempt to introduce new maize technologies to small farmers. Evaluates program's application and limited success in certain areas as well as its usefulness as a learning experience.

3137 Salazar Peralta, Ana María. El programa económico del Estado mexicano y el sector agrario (UNAM/AA, 18, 1981, p. 127–137)

Examines projects and policies of Mexican government and its effects on agricultural sector by focusing on small coffee producers.

3138 Schumacher, August. Agricultural development and rural employment: a Mexican dilemma. La Jolla: Program in US-Mexican Studies, Univ. of California, San Diego, 1981. 37 leaves: bibl., tables (Working papers in US-Mexican studies; 21)

Discusses post-war agricultural development in rural areas of Mexico and shift in policies from "trickle down" to unimodal efforts. Emphasizes importance of long-term programs despite success of temporary rural job creation programs.

INDUSTRIALIZATION

3139 Beato, Guillermo and Domenico Sindico. The beginning of industrialization in Northeast Mexico (AAFH/TAM, 39:4, April 1983, p. 499–518, tables)

Historical analysis of development of industrialization in Monterrey, Nuevo León region, NE Mexico (1890–1902). Discusses importance of transportation, government support of industrial activities and existence of well established local merchants. Incorporates analysis to a Latin American context.

3140 Fischer, Bernhard; Egbert Gerken; and Ulrich Heimenz. Growth, employment, and trade in an industrializing economy: a quantitative analysis of Mexican development policies. Tübingen, FRG: J.C.B. Mohr, 1982. 238 p.: bibl., ill., tables (Kieler Studien, 0340–6989; 170)

Quantitative analysis of development policies in Mexico's industrial sector and its effect on other sectors of economy.

3141 Robles, Gonzalo. Ensayos sobre el desarrollo de México. México: Banco de México: Fondo de Cultura Económica, 1982. 409 p.: bibl., ill. (Vida y pensamiento de México)

Posthumous essays on industrialization written by Robles and published by Banco de México.

MISCELLANEOUS

3142 La Actividad pesquera durante los cinco años del Departamento de Pesca. México: Secretaría de Pesca, 1982. 172 p.: bibl., col. ill., tables.

Systematic and orderly presentation of information related to fishing sector for 1977–81. Provides descriptive and numerical data on objectives and results obtained during Dept. of Fisheries' first five yrs., critical ones for industry's future growth and development.

3143 Andréieva, Yulia. Problemas del desarrollo del país y la lucha del proletariado (URSS/AL, 2:62, feb. 1983, p. 4–15)

Discusses growing political participation of Mexico's working class, combined success of leftist parties, and its effect on Mexico's social, economic, domestic, and foreign policies.

Business Yearbook of Brazil, Mexico & Venezuela. See item **2791.**

3144 Compendium of Mexican data and statistics. México: Mexico City Chamber of Commerce, 1980. 138 p.: bibl., ill., tables.

Summary of data and statistics covering social, political, and economic aspects of Mexico for 1980.

3145 Dahlman, Carl J. and Mariluz Cortes. Mexico (WD, 12:5/6, May/June 1984, p. 601–624, bibl., tables)

Examines technology exports from Mexico from perspective of a developing country's whose exports may serve as bias for a study of how to develop local technological capability. Sectors exporting technology concern areas in which country has acquired local technological capability reflecting influence of public support and/or political resource endowments.

3146 X [i.e. Décimo] Censo Industrial 1976: datos de 1975, desglose de materias primas consumidas por clase de actividad. México: SPP, Coordinación General de los Servicios Nacionales de Estadística, Geografía e Informática, 1981. 290 p.: tables.

Detailed statistical information (on 1975–76 but published in 1981) on each one of raw materials consumed by largest establishments of extractive and transformation industries classifying them according to activity, excluding oil.

3147 Estadística del subsector pecuario en los Estados Unidos Mexicanos. México: Secretaría de Agricultura y Recursos Hidráulicos, Subsecretaría de Agricultura y Operación, Dirección General de Economía Agrícola, 1982? 1 v.: tables.

Concise data of animal industry covering the 1978–79 yrs. Study consists of five pts. covering population, production, worth of population by species, and a concluding chapter. Basic information in terms of growth and possible trends for animal industry.

3148 Gereffi, Gary. The pharmaceutical industry and dependency in the Third World. Princeton, N.J.: Princeton Univ. Press, 1983. 291 p.: bibl., index, tables.

Broad account of pharmaceutical industry in Mexico and Third World. Makes persuasive case that Mexico lost advantages it once had in industry as a result of multiple dependencies and error on the Mexican position.

Grunwald, Joseph. Reconstrución de la industria maquiladora. See item **2881.**

3149 Guía industrial del Estado de Jalisco. Depto. de Programación y Desarrollo [e] Instituto Jalisciense de Promoción y Estudios Económicos. Guadalajara, México: Gobierno de Jalisco, Secretaría General, Unidad Editorial, 1979. 345 p.: ill., tables (Col. Textos Jalisco. Serie Estudios e inversión; 1)

Business's guide to the state of Jalisco. Provides investors with information on characteristics, laws and regulations, including investment incentives in the region. Also includes names, addresses of industrial and business enterprises.

3150 Heath Constable, Hilario Joy. Lucha de clases: la industria textil en Tlaxcala. México: Ediciones El Caballito, 1982. 151 p.: bibl., tables (Col. Fragua mexicana; 41)

Covers historical development of textile industry in Tlaxcala. Describes absorption of farm workers and their unemployment/underemployment as industry diminished in importance relative to others.

3151 La Industria metalmecánica y de bienes de capital en México. México:

SPP, Coordinación General de los Servicios Nacionales de Estadística, Geografía e Informática: Nacional Financiera, S.A. (NAFINSA), 1982. 538 p.: tables.

Presents series of tables in statistical context relative to metallurgical industry and includes specific information on capital goods industry because of its importance in nation's industrial development. Most of the data drawn from *System of Nacional Accounts, Statistical Annual of Foreign Trade,* and *Industrial Census.*

3152 La Industria química en México. México: SPP, Coordinación General de los Servicios Nacionales de Estadística, Geografía e Informática, 1982. 236 p.: bibl., tables.

Qualitative and quantitative summary of Mexico's chemical industry divided into four chaps.: 1) its relative importance among economic aggregates; 2) structure of production; 3) commercialization process; and 4) international comparison or the industry in a global context.

3153 La Industria siderúrgica en México. México: SPP, Coordinación General de los Servicios Nacionales de Estadística, Geografía e Informática: Secretaría de Patrimonio y Fomento Industrial: CANACERO, 1981. 314 p.: bibl., tables.

Significant indicators of ferrous industry allow for analysis and evaluation of its economic development. Study consists of six chaps. which include comparisons of industry with significant macro variables, its place within industrial sector, different productive phases, commercialization, financial aspects, and international comparisons.

3154 Información financiera de empresas mexicanas, 1975–1980. 3a ed. México: SPP, Coordinación General de los Servicios Nacionales de Estadísticas, Geografía e Informática: Bolsa Mexicana de Valores, 1982. 233 p.: col. ill., tables.

Provides information on behavior of most relevant financial variables of enterprises during 1975–80, taking as a reference corporations that participate in the organized stock exchange. Includes accounting relations and financial results of 55 businesses representative of each sector of economic activity.

3155 Información sobre los ingresos gubernamentales, 1970–1980. 2a ed. México: SPP, Coordinación General de los Servicios Nacionales de Estadística, Geografía e Informática: Secretaría de Hacienda y Crédito Público, 1982. 192 p.: bibl., tables.

Compilation of most significant statistics on federal, state, and municipal revenues. Six chaps. show structure, level of taxation, and evolution of most important indicators of three levels of government. Uniform and orderly presentation.

3156 Lindley, Richard B. Haciendas and economic development: Guadalajara, Mexico at independence. Austin: Univ. of Texas Press, 1983. 156 p.: bibl., ill., index, tables (Latin American monographs; 58)

Examines entrepreneurial activities of elite families in Guadalajara between 1810–21. Innovative analysis of the hacienda in the broader context of diversified family enterprise. Also includes study of credit market and kinship alliances.

Mac Donald Escobedo, Eugenio. Turismo, una recapitulación. See *HLAS 46:2229.*

3157 Manual de estadísticas básicas: sector industrial, información de la estadística industrial anual. México: SPP, Coordinación General de los Servicios Nacionales de Estadística, Geografía e Informática, 1982. 545 p.: tables.

Provides industrial statistics generated since 1950, classified according to different indexes and categories. Presents information from censuses, survey data, and administrative registries. Acquaints user with development of the industrial sector and wth specific sectorial data.

3158 Manual de estadísticas básicas del sector comunicaciones y transportes. México: SPP, Coordinación General de los Servicios Nacionales de Estadística, Geografía e Informática, 1981. 743 p.: tables.

Reports relevant information on transportation and communication sectors. Consists of six chaps. on highway, railroad, maritime and air transportation, and postal and electronic communications. Includes statistical information according to its importance to each sector and in the form of historical tables.

3159 Minello, Nelson and **Arístides Rivera.** Siderúrgica Lázaro Cárdenas-Las Truchas: historia de una empresa. México: Centro de Estudios Sociológicos, Colegio de México, 1982. 317 p.: bibl., ill., tables.

Studies Mexico's iron and steel industry, pros and cons of private vs. public use of capital and administration along with internal and external financing and political implications of the Las Truchas Project.

3160 Moreno Moreno, Prudenciano. Desarrollo económico y acumulación de capital en México: 1940–1980. México: Editorial Trillas: Univ. Autónoma Metropolitana, 1982. 178 p.: bibl., ill., index, tables.

Detailed analysis of economic development and capital accumulation of productive sector of Mexican economy, Mexico's place in world economy, and interdependence with other nations.

¿Nueva o vieja división internacional del trabajo?: industrialización en Venezuela y México. See item **3487.**

3161 Rodríguez, Raymundo. Algunas implicaciones de la teoría de la modernización en relación al comportamiento reproductivo de la población. Monterrey, México: Univ. Autónoma de Nuevo León, Facultad de Economía, Centro de Investigaciones Económicas, 1980. 32 leaves: bibl., ill., tables.

Comparison between Mexico City and Buenos Aires on fertility for 1963–64. Levels show that the cities are quite dissimilar due to different levels of development.

3162 Sistema de cuentas nacionales de México. t. 1, Resumen general. t. 2, Cuentas de producción: actividades primarias. t. 3, Cuentas de producción: actividades secundarias. t. 4, Cuentas de producción: servicios. t. 5, Oferta y utilización de bienes y servicios. t. 6, Cuentas del gobierno general de bienes y servicios. t. 7, Matriz de insumo-producto, año de 1975. México: SPP, Coordinación General de los Servicios Nacionales de Estadística, Geografía e Informática, 1981. 7 v. in 8: bibl., tables.

National accounts statistics covering 1970–78. Presents theoretical framework under which national accounts were developed. Shows quantitative results of accounts and those related to the product accounts, supply tables, and utilization of goods and services employment and salaries according to principal economic sectors.

3163 Sistema de cuentas nacionales de México: producto interno bruto por entidad federativa, 1980. México: SPP, Coordinación General de los Servicios Nacionales de Estadística, Geografía e Informática, 1982. 37 p.: bibl., col. ill., tables.

Statistical data on Mexico's GDP in 1980 broken down into economic sectors (e.g., farming, manufacturing, mining, construction, etc.) and regions.

3164 Submatriz de consumo privado por objeto del gasto y rama de actividad económica de origen, año 1970. México: SPP, Coordinación General del Sistema Nacional de Información: Banco de México, Subdirección de Investigación Económica y Bancaria:

Programa de las Naciones Unidas para el Desarrollo, 1980. 100 leaves: tables.

Statistics on personal consumption data broken down into different economic sectors.

3165 Unger, Kurt. Transferencia tecnológica y organización industrial en México: el papel de las marcas (BNCE/CE, 34:12, dic. 1984, p. 1202–1206)

Shows importance of technology transfer in industrialization process. Notes significance of labeling in consumer goods market, especially non-durables. In capital goods and national companies, they tend to lose their importance in the middle and long-runs. In intermediate goods, they are not feasible.

CENTRAL AMERICA, PANAMA, THE CARIBBEAN, AND THE GUIANAS (except Cuba and Puerto Rico)

MANUEL J. CARVAJAL, *Professor of Economics, Florida International University*

PERHAPS THE MOST NOTABLE TREND in the region's literature during the last two years is the dichotomy in socioeconomic behavior, interests, and even philosophical outlooks of Central American versus insular writings. On the one hand, the political situation in the isthmus has deteriorated severely, leading to military confrontation within, and ideological polarization among nations that until recently were heralded as paragons of prosperity through integration. The "war economy" concept (items **3234** and **3235**) has become popular as analysts attempt to examine coping (i.e., surviving, economically and otherwise) by the private sector under conditions of declining foreign investment, flight of domestic capital, growing unemployment, and income and output contraction.

On the other hand, violence and political turmoil, so prevalent throughout the islands' history, seem to have abated. Except for the Grenada adventure, the deposition of Duvalier in Haiti, and an occasional flare of discontent elsewhere, the islands' atmosphere has remained calm, although, judging by prior occurrences, such equilibrium could be easily upset. This interlude of tranquility, added to Caribbean Development Initiative efforts, has enhanced the subregion's growing potential, which is evinced by the continued formation of a genuinely indigenous school of economic thinking (items **3301, 3306,** and **3316**).

The dichotomy in overall conditions between the mainland and the islands is further revealed by their respective recent integration experiences. The successive crises and readjustments of the Central American Common Market (CACM) have eroded the confidence of its members and other nations in the Market's ability to alleviate problems and improve economic conditions (items **3172, 3177, 3180, 3181, 3182, 3183, 3190,** and **3214**). Although it is true that in the beginning the CACM contributed to the expansion of the urban middle class by fostering industrial development, it never succeeded in reshaping the individual economies nor in reducing the chronic poverty that permeates the area. The issue of inequitable distribution of benefits, especially detrimental to Honduras and favorable to El Salvador and Guatemala, remains unresolved and has to be addressed if a reasonable compromise is to be achieved. But the ultimate survival test lies in the CACM's capability to reconcile the seemingly contradictory policy objectives of the various nations, to accommodate their conflicting economic development models, and to overcome their political distrust and nationalistic rivalry. In contrast to CACM, studies of CARICOM (items **3303, 3304,** and **3321**) highlight the positive, relevant impact of this common market on Commonwealth Caribbean economies, in spite of the usual constraints such as limited size of market, homogeneous production and exports, etc.

Trade continues to command a great deal of attention. Regardless of ideological preference, social structure, or economic model adopted by any nation in the area, commerce with other regions of the world constitutes such a vital function that it would be absurd to discuss Central American or Caribbean development outside the scope of international trade (items **3203, 3224, 3293a,** and **3322**). Under appropriate circumstances, exports can function as an engine of growth, generating investment and employment leading to sustained economic expansion (items **3176, 3297,** and **3311**) and providing foreign exchange to pay for imports (item **3268**). But it would be equally incongruous to rely exclusively on development strategies oriented toward external markets whose price and income elasticities of demand for primary products are traditionally low and whose dynamics are not only uncontrollable but also often unforseen by countries in the region. Such excessive reliance usually degenerates into conditions of neocolonialism and dependency, topics quite popular in the indigenous literature (items **3260, 3310, 3313, 3314, 3327,** and **3333**).

Intertwined with dependency are issues of foreign investment (items **3201, 3301a,** and **3330**), credit and fiscal incentives (items **3196, 3278, 3288,** and **3315**), and industrialization (items **3195, 3206, 3222, 3323,** and **3343**). Eager to diversify their economies via promotion of industrial growth under the ECLA tutelage, many countries in the 1950s and 1960s extended all sorts of incentives to foreign investors who concentrated their funds on capital intensive, import substitution and export industries. The outcome has been the subject of debate by writers across the ideological spectrum who attempt to ascertain how states lose their ability to influence allocation of national resources in the pursuit of economic development and self-reliance. In other words, both the optimal mix of resource-allocation priorities and the hegemony to implement them monopolize much of the research (items **3197, 3210, 3223, 3228, 3276, 3277, 3292, 3325,** and **3336**).

While industrialization strategies have been moderately successful in raising income levels of a relatively small proportion of the labor force, they have failed to alleviate the pressure of massive unemployment, another leading topic in the literature (items **3170, 3192, 3212, 3218, 3261, 3273, 3282,** and **3294**). In fact, the opposite has occurred; foreign capital inflow and construction of industrial plants fostered labor's expectations of better-paying jobs in the manufacturing sector, promoting migration from the countryside and crowding into rapidly expanding cities (items **3200, 3230,** and **3289**). This has led, in turn, to even higher levels of unemployment, especially of a structural nature, a critical situation demanding specific consideration of human resource development (items **3285, 3287, 3296,** and **3326**), labor market and worker conditions (items **3233, 3240, 3242, 3249, 3263,** and **3291**), and poverty (items **3236, 3264, 3267,** and **3293**).

Most writers are critical of repatriation of profits from local operations to stockholders abroad, as well as of long-term accumulation of domestic capital (items **3184, 3203,** and **3220**). Greater state ownership and control, it is sometimes argued, would yield a more equitable, and thus preferable, resource allocation mix. So the extent of optimal government intervention into private affairs and overall role of the state are the object of continuous discussion (items **3174, 3221, 3237, 3241,** and **3335**). Several recent experiences with various degrees of socialism can be cited—Surinam, since shortly after its independence; Guyana, who declared itself a cooperative republic in 1970 and expropriated most foreign enterprises; Manley's 1972–80 rule in Jamaica; and, since 1979, Sandinista rule in Nicaragua which has brought this country into conflict with its neighbors.

Whereas greater state ownership and control may serve political purposes by instilling feelings of nationalism and restoring sovereignty in resource allocation against the dictates of economic imperialism, state control has failed to insulate the domestic environment from adverse external events. The decline of the private sector has dried up foreign capital sources while domestic capital has fled seeking a safe haven abroad, conditions which inevitably lead to decapitalization and economic retrogression. Quite interestingly, some assessments of the socialist experience are very critical of such state control and personalities involved in it (items **3309** and **3339**), denouncing authoritarian rule as a corruption of socialist ideas and even suggesting that the new ruling class is attempting to perpetuate itself in power.

Of course, any leaning toward socialism is likely to preoccupy the US whose political and military influence is monitored in numerous works (items **3168, 3186, 3189, 3191, 3254,** and **3258**). The brunt of the US presence, however, is felt in the area of economics, either in the form of direct aid (items **3229, 3318, 3319,** and **3328**) or indirectly through powerful institutions such as the International Monetary Fund (items **3253, 3305,** and **3331**), perceived by some as serving primarily the interests of more industrialized nations rather than Third World needs. When Central American and Caribbean governments hesitate to impose harsh and consequently unpopular measures to correct balance-of-payments disequilibria and ease their external debt (items **3284** and **3334**), the IMF forces them to succumb to pressures of fiscal austerity, wage controls, and devaluation, all of which are bound to bruise nationalist pride. The resentment caused by this interference in domestic policies, considered justified by some but not by others, was expressed quite eloquently by Manley at the pinnacle of his term in office when he said: ". . . some of the people who could lend us money will apparently do so only on the condition that they should be able to tell us how to conduct our affairs. . . (We) will not accept anybody anywhere in the world telling us what to do in our country . . . ."

In other developments, the last two years have witnessed a shift in emphasis from basic to applied and policy oriented studies. The general development effort is periodically analyzed (items **3286, 3312,** and **3342**), along with more specific probing into the availability of natural resources (items **3166** and **3271**), economics of the public sector (items **3187, 3239, 3250,** and **3338**), production (items **3193** and **3211**), accessibility to information (items **3173** and **3188**), inflation and monetary issues (items **3238, 3256,** and **3324**), regional development (items **3208, 3252,** and **3269**), health care needs (item **3219**), housing (items **3232** and **3340**), tourism (items **3302** and **3320**), and market integration (items **3280** and **3307**). Studies of the agricultural sector continue to dominate much of the literature (items **3215, 3225, 3227, 3275,** and **3337**), particularly those dealing with credit (items **3198** and **3329**), small farmers (items **3274** and **3317**), and agrarian reform (items **3205, 3226, 3255,** and **3257**).

Finally, references to the "crisis" abound, both in economic and political contexts (items **3175, 3178, 3185, 3194, 3199, 3207, 3213, 3216, 3259, 3295,** and **3300**), the latter being especially the case in Central America, along with guidelines to achieve an economic revival (items **3169, 3204, 3217,** and **3247**). There seems to be an emerging consensus, however, that a minimum of stability and peaceful coexistence, among as well as within countries, is indispensable for the success of any such revival efforts. The Central American conflict is exacerbated not merely by ideological polarization but by its international scope or, in other words, by the presence of outside forces for whom Central American welfare is less important than the attainment of geopolitical goals.

The bibliography annotated below constitutes a representative collection of relevant writings about the region. In addition to the many books and articles already mentioned, there are various compilations of essays either by different authors or by one author throughout several years (items **3251, 3265, 3266,** and **3270**), a practice which is becoming fashionable; works by international (items **3248** and **3283**) and regional (item **3167**) organizations and works sponsored by USAID (items **3209** and **3262**); as well as public sector publications (items **3244, 3245,** and **3290**), some of them dealing with development plans (items **3231, 3298,** and **3308**). Along these lines it is worth mentioning that the Nicaraguan government has started to produce some objective studies (items **3246** and **3243**), unlike the ideological propaganda generated until a couple of years ago.

The references annotated here are classified into five groups: 1) *General* contains 31 regional publications; 2) *Central America and Panama* consists of 68 entries related to Costa Rica, El Salvador, Guatemala, Honduras, Nicaragua, and Panama; 3) *Hispaniola*, the island shared by the Dominican Republic and Haiti, comprises 31 items; 4) *Commonwealth Caribbean*, including noninsular Belize and Guyana, embraces 46 references; and 5) *Dutch Caribbean and Surinam* consists of two works. All 178 entries were published during 1981–84 and, in addition to meeting the *HLAS*'s permanent value criterion, have contributed or are expected to contribute to the formulation of public policies.

GENERAL

3166 Aguilera, Jesús Antonio. Geopolítica y petróleo en la Cuenca del Caribe (NSO, 58, enero/feb. 1982, p. 43–54, maps, tables)

Exposition of production, refining, and transportation of oil in the Caribbean and additional "strategic reserve" dimension which enhances region's importance.

3167 Banco Centroamericano de Integración Económica. Gerencia de Programación y Promoción. Programa global para la participación del BCIE en el financiamiento del sector agropecuario en Centroamérica.

Tegucigalpa: El Banco, 1983. 109 p.: appendices, graphs, tables.

Divided into three pts.: 1) analysis of the agricultural sector (physical resources, land use and tenure, population, income, nutrition, and role of public sector); 2) development strategies (structural problems, production organization, infrastructure, marketing, institutional adequacy, and agroindustry); and 3) characteristics of the program (goals and objectives, constraints, and instruments).

3168 Barca, Alessandro. EE.UU. y la Cuenca del Caribe (NSO, 64, enero/feb. 1983, p. 110–115)

Views the Caribbean Basin Initiative

as a futile attempt by the US to stop the revolutionary movements in the region.

3169 Bolin, William H. Central America: real economic help is workable now (CFR/FA, 62:5, Summer 1984, p. 1096–1106)
Provides recommendations of short- and medium-term nature. Identifies priority areas as working capital; repair, refurbishment, and replacement of equipment along with remobilization of work force to operate it; and expansion of infrastructure, especially transport, storage, power, health, and education.

3170 Brodersohn, Víctor. La problemática del empleo en Centroamérica (FCE/TE, 49[2]:194, abril/junio 1982, p. 387–421, tables)
Concludes that economic growth has not contributed to better utilization of human resources. Recommends creation of job opportunities for the underemployed and formulation of policies conducive to development of rural industries, handicrafts, and social infrastructure, all labor intensive activities.

3171 Bulmer-Thomas, V. Economic development over the long run: Central America since 1920 (JLAS, 15:2, Nov. 1983, p. 269–294, tables)
Focuses primarily on agricultural sector because of its dominance in terms of employment, foreign exchange earnings, and output. Argues that the price paid for the continuing control of the oligarchy based on its agricultural export interests is a breakdown of socioeconomic relations in rural areas.

3172 Centro América: condiciones para su integración. José Miguel Alfaro et al. Edición de Francisco Rojas Aravena. San José: Ediciones FLACSO, 1982. 166 p.: bibl., tables (Col. 25 aniversario)
Consists of 10 articles by different authors on different aspects of integration such as need for peace, Sandinista revolution and counterrevolution, and deleterious consequences of the international economic crisis.

3173 Conference of the Association of Caribbean University and Research Libraries (ACURIL), *13th, Caracas, 1982.* Información y desarrollo en el Caribe: documentos oficiales. Caracas: Asociación de Bibliotecas Universitarias, de Investigación e Institucionales del Caribe, 1983. 224 p.: bibl., ill.
Collection of papers dealing with human resource development for national information infrastructures and systems. Also focuses on social demands and regional integration of information.

3174 Coraggio, José Luis. Estado, política económica y transición en Centroamérica: notas para su investigación (CSUCA/ESC, 13:37, enero/abril 1984, p. 73–87)
Identifies research priorities such as determinants of agricultural rent differentials, economic dependence, excessive openness of society, contradictions of the bourgeoisie, and formulation of public policy, all manifestations of the transformation of the State which is taking place in the region.

3175 The Crisis in Central America: its origins, scope, and consequences. New York: UN, Economic and Social Council, ECLA, 1983. 52 p.: bibl., ill. (E/CEPAL/G.1261.E/CEPAL/MEX/1983/R.3/rev.1.)
Predicts that longstanding inequalities of Central American economies will aggravate. In addition to intense political upheaval, conditions appear to lead towards a breakdown of superimposed development before alternative development models can be tested.

Cultural patrimony and the tourism product: towards a mutually beneficial relationship. See item **1037.**

Devas, Edmond. A check list of Caribbean tourism studies. See item **26.**

3176 Fuerst Weigand, Edgar. Industrialización y exportaciones no tradicionales: opciones estratégicas para una nueva política industrial del Estado frente a la crisis económica en Centroamérica (CSUCA/ESC, 13:37, enero/abril 1984, p. 107–135, bibl., tables)
Views efforts toward agroindustry for export as giving rise to a new international division of labor which emphasizes meeting basic needs. Argues that juxtaposing import-substitution vs. export-promotion industrialization strategies as only two alternatives creates a false dichotomy.

3177 El Futuro del Mercado Común Centroamericano: alcances y perspectivas después de veinte años de funcionamiento.

Ed. limitada. Guatemala: INFORPRESS Centroamericana, 1983. 129 p.: bibl., ill., tables.

Analysis of developments and performance of the CACM with special reference to industrialization, foreign investment and aid, unequal development, and labor force characteristics.

3178 Geyer, Georgie Anne. Central America: reflections on a region (GU/WQ, 7:1, 1984, p. 138–144)

Maintains that, basically, the struggle is not an economic one, resulting from poverty, or a military one resulting from communist infiltration. Instead, the revolution is carried out by middle-class young people (i.e., a political phenomenon) who become radicalized when denied legitimate access to political power.

3179 IESCARIBE Research Summaries. Institutos de Investigación Económica y Social de la Cuenca del Caribe/Institutes of Economic and Social Research of the Caribbean Basin. Florida International Univ. No. 1, 1982? [and] No. 2, 1983?- . Miami, Fla.

New journal published by IESCARIBE and edited by Jorge Salazar Carrillo and Irma Tirado de Alonso. Consists of papers, written by well known and respected Latin American economists, and organized thematically per issue: No. 1 encompasses works that deal with Latin America's external debt and economic growth; No. 2 includes contributions related to trade, debt, and development of Caribbean Basin. [J. Salazar Carrillo]

3180 Lizano Fait, Eduardo. Escritos sobre integración económica. San José: Editorial Costa Rica, 1982. 375 p.: bibl., ill., index, tables.

Collection of seven articles dealing with general aspects of integration (distribution of benefits and costs, national disparities, impact on income and employment, etc.) and four others devoted specifically to Central America.

3181 ———. El Mercado Común Centroamericano en una época de turbulencia (FCE/TE, 50[3]:199, julio/sept. 1983, p. 1475–1506)

Discusses prospects for the integration movement. After analyzing determinants of change in the isthmus, recommends guidelines and priorities for action.

3182 Mariscal, Nicolás. Integración económica y poder político en Centroamérica: intentos de restructuración de 1969 a 1981. San Salvador: UCA Editores, 1983. 338 p.: bibl., ill., tables (Col. Estructuras y procesos; 10)

After reviewing various regional integration models, assesses attempts to revive CACM. Concludes that integration efforts are destined to fail due to lack of interest by area governments and opposition by industrialists and business minorities.

3183 ———. La prevención de las decisiones reestructuradoras de la integración regional centroamericana, 1969–1981 (UJSC/ECA, 419, sept. 1983, p. 743–758)

Assessment of why numerous efforts to revive the Common Market between 1969–81 failed. Formulates and tests an interesting systematic model. Attributes failure to governments' negative attitudes and reluctance of industrial and trade minorities to endorse integration activities.

3184 Molina Chocano, Guillermo. Estado y proceso de acumulación en Centroamérica (CSUCA/ESC, 13:37, enero/abril 1984, p. 91–106, tables)

Characterizes growth in the last few years as enjoying high rates of return in the international market which created a significant differential rent for a highly protected urban-industrial sector. Expansion also has been accompanied by unprecedented growth of the external public debt.

Moreno, Dilcia. La cooperación internacional de Venezuela y las imágenes de autodeterminación que permite el sistema financiero internacional actual. See item **3485.**

3185 Pérez Brignoli, Héctor and Yolanda Baires Martínez. Growth and crisis in the Central American economies, 1950/1980 (JLAS, 15:2, Nov. 1983, p. 365–398, tables)

Examines various aggregate indices in attempt to establish nature of structural change induced by both industrialization and integration. Emphasizes repercussions of growth on employment and quality of life.

3186 Quenan, Carlos. Crisis centroamericana e iniciativas de paz (NSO, 63, nov./dic. 1982, p. 75–85)

Traces US foreign policy toward Central America attempting to show that developments in the region respond solely to Washington's designs.

3187 Readings in Caribbean public sector economics. Edited by Fuat M. Andic and S.B. Jones-Hendrickson. Kingston: Institute of Social and Economic Research, Univ. of the West Indies, Mona, 1981. 290 p.: bibl., tables.

Collection of 19 papers previously published elsewhere. Although articles may be somewhat dated, they maintain their methodological and didactic value. Divided into six pts.: 1) surveys; 2) public sector and growth; 3) fiscal incentives and harmonization; 4) taxes, shares, and incidence; 5) public policy and planning; and 6) local finance and administration.

3188 Report on the Latin American information infrastructure for development, with special reference to the Caribbean. Santiago: Centro Latinoamericano de Documentación Económica y Social, CEPAL, 1981. 202 p.: ill. (E/CEPAL/CLADES/L.9)

Identifies and describes socioeconomic information units to support development. Also surveys national and regional information infrastructures within the "minimum threshold" methodology framework.

3189 Rosenberg, Mark B. Obstáculos en los Estados Unidos a la política de Reagan en Centroamérica (*in* Centroamérica: más allá de las crisis. Edited by Donald Castillo Rivas. México: Ediciones SIAP, 1983, p. 311–330, graphs, tables)

Examines formulation of US foreign policy toward Central America and possible ways in which the process could be influenced from abroad.

3190 Rosenthal, Gert. Central American economic integration (*in* Latin American prospects for the 1980s: equity, democratization, and development. Edited by Archibald R.M. Ritter and David H. Pollock. New York: Praeger, 1983, p. 147–157, tables)

Inquires whether, in light of governments that postulate different paths to development, the Common Market can be equally responsive to contradictory economic policy objectives. Also questions whether or not the market mechanism can continue allocating resources within it when at least one member pursues greater intervention to regulate economic activities.

3191 Sebastián, Luis de. Una crítica a los aspectos económicos del Informe Kissinger (UJSC/ECA, 432/433, oct./nov. 1984, p. 789–802, tables)

Alleges that the Kissinger report is contradictory insofar as it calls for redistribution of wealth in Central America, but endorses the market system, which is incapable of carrying out an effective reallocation of resources.

Seminar on Economic Integration in the Caribbean, *Bridgetown, Barbados, 1983.* Ten Years of CARICOM: papers presented at a seminar sponsored by the Inter-American Development Bank. See item **128.**

3192 Soto, Max Alberto; Carlos Alberto Sevilla; and Charles R. Frank, Jr. Integración económica y empleo en la industria centroamericana. San José: Editorial Universitaria Centroamericana, 1983. 188 p.: bibl., tables (Col. Integración)

Analyzes determinants of labor demand in CACM, with emphasis on the substitutability between labor and capital, economies of scale, and employment generation.

3193 Stone, Samuel. Production and politics in Central America's convulsions (JLAS, 15:2, Nov. 1983, p. 453–469)

Explores divergences among the five nations. Argues that there is a direct link between each country's political system and production complex on which it depends. Also contends that the Common Market cannot prosper as long as members produce the same items for sale within one area.

3194 Torres Rivas, Edelberto. Derrota oligárquica, crisis burguesa, revolución popular: notas sobre la crisis en Centroamérica (FCE/TE, 50[2]:198, abril/junio 1983, p. 991-1018, tables)

Argues that the political preceded the economic crisis. Both are so closely intertwined that their manifestations may be confusing but, in the final analysis, whereas the political problem is ideological, economic one is product of bourgeois contradictions.

3195 Valladares, J. Situación actual y perspectivas de desarrollo de la industria celulósica en Centroamérica (OAS/CI, 22:3/4, 1982, p. 32–34, tables)

Probes into likelihood of substituting cellulose imports with domestic output in an effort to break dependency of this product on more developed countries.

3196 Valle Prieto, María Eugenia del and **Carlos Melesio Nolasco.** Las zonas francas en Centroamérica (UNAM/AA, 19, 1982, p. 251–266, bibl., tables)

Argues that industrialization efforts led to the production of nondurable consumer goods destined for foreign markets. As fiscal incentives and import exemptions were granted, urban population grew at a faster rate than rural one.

CENTRAL AMERICA AND PANAMA

3197 Andic, Fuat M. What price equity?: a macroeconomic evaluation of government policies in Costa Rica. Río Piedras: Institute of Caribbean Studies Univ. of Puerto Rico, 1983. 70 p.: bibl., tables (Caribbean occasional series; 4)

After analyzing overall development of the economy during last two decades (output, employment and wages, sectoral development, foreign trade, public finance, money, and inflation), evaluates government efforts in trade, industrial, fiscal, credit, and investment policies. Concludes that economy suffers from serious inefficiencies which are now beginning to hamper development and eroding equity.

3198 Antología de crédito agrícola. Compilado y adaptado por Humberto Coto Varela y María del Milagro Mora Valverde. San José: Editorial Univ. Estatal a Distancia, 1982. 303 p.: bibl., tables.

Comprehensive view of agricultural credit in Costa Rica. Surveys various classifications (maturity, crop, etc.), interest rates, banking system and other institutional considerations, farm and farmer information that should be required, benefit-cost analysis, and technical assistance. Views credit as an instrument of integrated rural development.

3199 Aranciba, Juan. Problemática centroamericana: Honduras, crisis y desarrollo (UNAH/RCE, 10, enero/abril 1983, p. 59–80, tables)

Probes different manifestations of the current economic crisis, including disequilibrium in the balance of payments, fiscal deficit, flight of capital, rapid increase in foreign debt, and drop in per-capita income.

3200 Argüello Rodríguez, Manuel. Desarrollo urbano. San José: Editorial Univ. Estatal a Distancia, 1981. 114 p.

After brief survey of prototype ancient, feudal, colonial, and capitalist cities, focuses on intra-city population movements, regional organization, urban policy and social movements, living conditions of the population, and land use.

3201 Argueta, Mario. 1880–1980 [i.e. Mil ochocientos ochenta-mil novecientos ochenta]: cien años del enclave minero en Honduras (HUN/RU, 7:17/18, 1981, p. 59–68, tables)

Traces development of mining activities and their dependence on foreign investment. Concludes that the country has not benefited substantially from these activities.

3202 Benítez Bonilla, Alberto. El sector externo de la economía salvadoreña. San Salvador: Banco Central de Reserva de El Salvador, 1982. 21 p.: tables.

Identifies five manifestations of the current economic crisis: deterioration of balance of trade; external credit contraction; flight of domestic capital; decline in foreign investment; and scarcity of natural resources. Focuses on external dependency, foreign exchange, monetary and fiscal policies, prices and wages, and growth of public debt.

3203 Biderman, Jaime. The development of capitalism in Nicaragua: a political economic history (LAP, 10[1]:36, Winter 1983, p. 7–32)

Contends that stagnation before 1950 was associated more with the historically conditioned class structure than with surplus transfer and that rapid, if uneven, growth since 1950 has been associated with accelerated capitalist development and apparently high rates of surplus transfer as well. Highlights role of the State, functional dualism, and proletarianization process.

3204 Bran, Salvador Osvaldo. Algunos lineamientos para lograr la reactivación económica en El Salvador (UJSC/ECA, 410, dic. 1982, p. 1109–1115)

Argues that civil war must come to a stop before economic reconstruction can take place. Contains 14 specific recommendations for economic development.

3205 Browning, David. Agrarian reform in El Salvador (JLAS, 15:2, Nov. 1983, p. 399–426, maps, tables)

Concludes that, by itself, the 1980 agrarian reform is incapable of satisfying long-term development needs, although it constitutes a significant first step toward altering the current agrarian structure. Stresses need for agricultural growth through more intensive land use. For geographer's comment, see item **5059.**

3206 Carcanholo, Reinaldo. Desarrollo del capitalismo en Costa Rica. San José: Editorial Universitaria Centroamericana, 1981. 388 p.: bibl., ill., tables.

Systematic analysis of capitalist development focusing on value theory, accumulation, and income differentials. Attributes many economic crises experienced by country to traditional coffee supremacy and emergence of industry since 1950. These crises include growing foreign debt, scarcity of basic grains, and increasing incidence of poverty.

3207 Castro, Nils. Panamá: un foro para la concertación (NSO, 64, enero/feb. 1983, p. 122–126)

Views Panama as playing a most important role in the solution of the Central American crisis.

3208 Celis U., Rafael; Luis Fernando Herrera; and Alan Treffeissen. Modelo multiperiódico de programación lineal para la región atlántica: base estadística y metodología. San José: Instituto Investigaciones en Ciencias Económicas, Univ. de Costa Rica, 1981. 27 p.: ill., tables (Documentos de trabajo; 29)

Exposition of linear-programming model whose objective function is defined as the present value of net income flow for 1970–80. Applies model to Limón prov., in many respects Costa Rica's poorest.

3209 Céspedes, Víctor Hugo et al. Costa Rica, una economía en crisis. Elaborado por encargo y con financiamiento de la Agencia para el Desarrollo Internacional. San José: Editorial Studium, 1983. 168 p.: bibl., ill., tables.

Analysis of deteriorating conditions of the Costa Rican economy. Among other topics, it focuses on balance of payments and international trade, foreign exchange, public finance, inflation, unemployment, wages, and income distribution.

3210 Conte Porras, J. El Banco de la Nación y nuestra estrategia para el desarrollo (LNB/L, 312/313, marzo/abril 1982, p. 77–92, ill., tables)

Discusses priority programs for Panama such as employment generation in rural areas, provision of social services, and increase in agricultural production. Places special emphasis on credit availability for crops, livestock, commerce, industry, housing, personal consumption, and public investment.

3211 Contreras B., S. Alejandro; René Rolando Mena Klee; and Jorge Luis Huertas Recinos. Sinopsis de la actividad petrolera en Guatemala. Trabajo elaborado para el II Encuentro de Ingenieros de México y Guatemala. Guatemala: Dirección General de Minería e Hidrocarburos, 1981. 56 leaves: ill., plates, tables.

Survey of Guatemalan oil industry. After historical overview, analyzes extraction, refining, and marketing activities; potential for by-products; and determination of prices.

3212 Costa Rica: el empleo en la crisis ac- tual, 1980–1982. San José: Ministerio de Planificación Nacional y Política Económica, Div. de Planificación y Coordinación Sectorial, Depto. de Población: Fondo de las Naciones Unidas para Actividades de Población, 1983. 115 leaves: bibl., ill., tables (Proyecto COS/79/P01. MIDEPLAN/058/PS/07)

In-depth analysis of labor force and employment. Focuses on composition of the labor force, seasonality factors, and geographical and occupational distribution of unemployment. Also addresses conceptualization and measurement of underemployment.

3213 Costa Rica hoy: la crisis y sus perspectivas. Jorge Rovira Mas, comp. San José: Editorial Univ. Estatal a Distancia, 1983. 248 p.: bibl., tables.

Consists of 12 papers by different authors on Costa Rican socioeconomic crisis. Covers, among other topics, capitalist accumulation trends, foreign trade dynamics, political influences, alternative growth strategies, public debt, entrepreneurship, income distribution, and social consequences of economic deterioration.

3214 Dada Hirezi, Héctor. La economía de El Salvador y la integración centroamericana, 1954–1960. 2a ed. San José: Editorial Universitaria Centroamericana, 1983. 133 p.: bibl., tables (Col. Integración)

After analysis of the country from an economic and social dependency perspective, contends that expansion of export sector created the need for industrial development (of socially dependent nature) which ultimately led to regional integration.

3215 Dufumier, Marc. La question agraire au Nicaragua (UP/TM, 24:95, juillet/sept. 1983, p. 597–608, bibl., table)

Analysis of agrarian transformation undertaken during first three yrs. of the Sandinista government. According to author, more emphasis on subsistence agriculture is needed given hostile US policies.

3216 Edelman, Marc. Recent literature on Costa Rica's economic crisis (LARR, 18:2, 1983, p. 166–180)

Lengthy review of four books and one collection of articles intertwined with author's own perspectives on whether or not the Costa Rican crisis can be addressed within its current democratic institutional framework. Also probes into which social classes or economic interests will eventually assume the burden for resolving the crisis.

3217 El Salvador. Ministerio de Planificación y Coordinación del Desarrollo Económico y Social. Acciones sociales para la reactivación económica nacional, 1982–1983. San Salvador: Ministerio de Planificación y Coordinación del Desarrollo Económico y Social, 1982. 64 leaves: tables.

Focuses on social aspects of economic phenomena. Contains specific sections on education, health and nutrition, criminal justice, community development, unemployment, and provision of services to the population affected by war and natural disasters. Also discusses institutional coordination and international technical cooperation.

3218 Empleo y salarios en Nicaragua. Santiago: Organización Internacional del Trabajo, Programa Mundial del Empleo, PREALC, 1980. 195 p.: bibl., tables (Documento de trabajo; 194)

Assessment of employment situation leading toward formulation of a rational employment policy. Focuses on long-term strategic options, estimation of labor utilization in agriculture, urban occupational structure, and rural employment policies.

3219 Ferguson, Anne. Marketing medicines: pharmaceutical services in a Salvadoran community (LAP, 10[4]:39, Fall 1983, p. 40–58)

Examines effects of different marketing networks for pharmaceutical products on health-care services in Asunción. Suggests that services provided are more responsive to business needs of pharmacy owners and national and multinational pharmaceutical firms than to health needs of the population.

3220 Fernández, Mario E. Dinámica del capital, evolución de la estructura de la tenencia de la tierra y paisaje rural en Costa Rica (CSUCA/ESC, 12:36, sept./dic. 1983, p. 105–136, graphs)

Land-tenure analysis points to long-run concentration of land and disappearance of small farmers in Guanacaste and San Carlos. Focuses on production of coffee, sugarcane, and livestock.

3221 Fitzgerald, Valpy. Estado y política económica en la nueva Nicaragua (CSUCA/ESC, 13:37, enero/abril 1984, p. 259–268)

Points out that although class struggle did not disappear with the triumph of the Sandinista Revolution, it acquired a new dimension in last five yrs.

3222 Fuerst Weigand, Edgar. La crisis actual de la acumulación del capital en la industria costarricense (CSUCA/ESC, 12:35, mayo/agosto 1983, p. 51–94, bibl., tables)

Hypothesizes that current industrial crisis is due to excess capital accumulation. Suggests import substitution strategy to facilitate industrial expansion.

3223 Garnier, Leonardo. Industria, Estado y desarrollo en Costa Rica: perspectivas y propuestas (CSUCA/ESC, 13:37, enero/abril 1984, p. 163–185)

Assessment of import substitution policies and criticisms they have elicited from conservative elements.

3224 Girling, Robert Henriques. Nicaragua's commercial policy: building a socially responsive foreign trade (LAP, 10[1]:36, Winter 1983, p. 33–44, tables)

Focuses on implementation of state management of foreign trade in order to improve responsiveness of imports and exports to national economic priorities, including employment and net foreign exchange use.

3225 Gordon, Sara. La transformación agraria en El Salvador: un conflicto interburgués (CSUCA/ESC, 12:36, sept./dic. 1983, p. 13–37, tables)

Argues that government elite does not allow modernizing sector to become independent of traditional agrarian sector, since both rely on same activities for their subsistence: coffee production and export, finance, industry, and commerce.

3226 Gudmundson, Lowell. Peasant movements and the transition to agrarian capitalism: freeholding versus hacienda peasantries and agrarian reform in Guanacaste, Costa Rica, 1880–1935 (UU/PS, 10:3, Spring 1983, p. 145–162)

Hypothesizes that two historically and structurally distinct peasantries—mercantile, smallholder emigrants from the Central Valley established in Guanacaste and subsistence, hacienda peasants on lowland colonial estates—responded differently to agrarian capitalism. While smallholders rebelled and organized themselves for agrarian reform within emerging capitalist order, hacienda peasants rose up against any change in the *status quo.*

3227 Guess, George M. Pasture expansion, forestry, and development contradictions: the case of Costa Rica (RU/SCID, 14:1, Spring 1979, p. 42–55, tables)

Costa Rica should initiate a multilevel growing and processing industry with high return potential for small farmers and rural workers, such as forestry. Forest-based development could contribute to dispersion of industries from crowded urban centers and stimulate emigration of workers from San José metropolitan area.

3228 Hernández Chávez, Alcides. Política económica y pensamiento neoliberal: el caso de Honduras (CSUCA/ESC, 13:37, enero/abril 1984, p. 231–257, bibl., tables)

Assesses Suazo government's performance, concluding that the market system is incapable of solving underdevelopment challenges. Accuses Liberal Party of conspiring with international capitalism and domestic oligarchy against public interest.

3229 Hickey, John. Can foreign aid continue as a growth industry for the bureaucracy?, case study: the Guatemalan private sector development initiatives project (IAMEA, 37:1, Summer 1983, p. 21–30)

Author's answer is positive on grounds that there is neither serious prospect nor capacity on part of US Congress to provide effective scrutiny of programs' efficacy. Also argues that there is no hope of public comprehension of what is going on.

3230 Hoegen, Miguel von. Concentración geográfica de los recursos financieros en Guatemala (Cultura de Guatemala [Univ. Rafael Landívar, Guatemala] 2:1, enero/abril 1981, p. 41–71, tables)

Explores concentration of population, decision making, and provision of public services in Guatemala City metropolitan area. Also analyzes need for financial resources to increase production capacity and banking system's role in facilitating access to these resources.

3231 Honduras. Consejo Superior de Planificación Económica. Estrategia para el desarrollo, 1982–1986. Tegucigalpa: El Consejo, 1982. 3 v.: tables.

Three-vol. publication outlining guidelines of 1982–86 Development Plan. Vol. 1 deals with overall strategies; vol. 2 presents policies and instruments by sector; and vol. 3 focuses on macroeconomic analysis.

3232 ——. ——. Plan Nacional de Desarrollo: Plan de Vivienda, 1982–1986. Tegucigalpa: El Consejo, 1983. 49 p.: tables.

After brief sector assessment, examines policies and programs concerning stability, growth, and income distribution goals and objectives. Also explores housing institutional setting.

3233 Ibarra, David. Costa Rica: política, política económica y política salarial (CM/FI, 24:2, oct./dic. 1983, p. 117–130)

Suggests that after three consecutive yrs. of declining real wages and salaries, further deterioration in workers' purchasing power without a comprehensive emergency program may lead to disruption of country's democratic tradition.

3234 Ibisate, Francisco Javier. La empresa privada frente a los tres problemas nacionales: el plan norteamericano, las elecciones y la guerra (UJSC/ECA, 415/416, mayo/junio 1983, p. 493–500)

Argues that Smith's invisible hand is too visible in El Salvador in a US plan that responds to US interests. According to author, private sector has opted to "produce war," thus leaving few resources to pursue economic growth.

3235 Instituto de Investigaciones Económicas, *San Salvador.* Hacia una economía de guerra: El Salvador, 1982–1983 (UJSC/ECA, 415–416, mayo/junio 1983, p. 439–458, tables)

Examines manifestations and consequences of a "war economy" resulting from military confrontation. Analyzes reduction in output, income, investment, and credit.

3236 International Fund for Agricultural Development. Misión Especial de Programación a Nicaragua. Informe de la Misión Especial de Programación a Nicaragua. Roma: The Fund, 1980. 268 p.: bibl., ill., tables.

In-depth assessment of economic conditions. Concludes that more than half the population lives in extreme poverty. Food consumption is one-third below recommended international standards and health and infant mortality indices are among the worst in Latin America. Contains specific recommendations for improvement.

3237 Irvin, George W. L'état et l'accumulation: le cas du Nicaragua actuel (UP/TM, 24, 1983, p. 115–125, bibl.)

Analyzes State-controlled capital accumulation after the Revolution. Emphasizes distribution of revenues, exports, and investment plans.

3238 Kemmerer, Donald L. and Bruce R. Dalgaard. Inflation, intrigue, and monetary reform in Guatemala, 1919–1926 (PAT/TH, 46:1, Nov. 1983, p. 21–38, table)

Describes monetary reform efforts up to establishment of the quetzal as the national currency and provisions to stabilize it.

3239 El Modelo económico costarricense: un análisis. San José: Asociación Nacional de Fomento Económico, 1980. 187 p.

Criticizes Costa Rican import substitution model on the grounds that protectionism breeds inefficiency. Contains 12 specific free enterprise type recommendations that include tax reform, emphasis on research and technology, and reduction in the relative importance of the public sector.

3240 Montes, Mauricio. La crisis económica de Honduras y la situación de los trabajadores. Tegucigalpa: Ediciones Sitraunah, 1982. 151 p.: bibl., tables.

Argues that instead of progressing in orderly evolution, Honduras is experiencing increasingly devastating crises whose only solution can be found in a violent change of structures (i.e., revolution). Symptoms of these crises are inflation, decline in international monetary reserves, deterioration of the balance of payments, erosion of domestic currency's purchasing power, growth of foreign debt, rising fiscal deficits, greater evidence of poverty, and more unemployment.

3241 Mora, Jorge A. and Angela Arias. Estado, planificación y acumulación de capital en Costa Rica: 1974–82 (CSUCA/ESC, 13:37, enero/abril 1984, p. 187–209)

Examines nature and degree of intervention by the State in the nation's economic affairs. Assesses impact of national development plan on development accomplishments.

3242 Morales, Oscar Armando. Las demandas laborales de los trabajadores salvadoreños: enero-octubre de 1982 (UJSC/ECA, 409, nov. 1982, p. 992-1007, tables)

Study of labor demands presented through professional associations and collective bargaining units, having to do with firing practices and salary equity considerations. Examines social and economic consequences of current labor situation.

3243 Nicaragua. Ministerio de Desarrollo Agropecuario y de Reforma Agraria. Centro de Investigaciones y Estudios de la Reforma Agraria. Informe de Nicaragua a la FAO. Managua: El Centro, 1983. 109 p.: bibl., ill., maps, tables (Col. Cmdte. Germán Pomares Ordóñez)

States national goals, objectives, and priorities pertaining to agrarian reform and rural development. Discusses conservation of natural resources, population growth and migration, social infrastructure (health, housing, and education), economic conditions, accessibility to land and water, female participation, extension activities, and rural poverty.

3244 ——. ——. ——. Producción y organización del agro nicaragüense. Managua: El Centro, 1982. 111 p.: bibl., ill., tables (Col. Cmdte. Germán Pomares Ordóñez)

Describes major agricultural indicators such as distribution of GDP, exports, generation of foreign exchange, and size and composition of the labor force. Divides country into eight regions for planning purposes and compares economic and social conditions among them.

3245 ———. ———. ———. 3 [i.e. Tres] años de reforma agraria. Managua: El Ministerio, 1982. 55 p.: ill., tables.

Discusses economic policies within the revolutionary setting, relative importance of agricultural sector, and development of infrastructure (health, education, nutrition, and training). Also assesses progress of agrarian reform and activities projected for immediate future.

3246 ———. **Ministerio de Trabajo. Dirección General de Empleo y Salario.** Los colectivos estatales de producción en Nicaragua (*in* La autogestión en América Latina y el Caribe. Santiago Roca, comp. Lima: Consejo Latinoamericano y del Caribe para la Autogestión (CLA): Instituto Interamericano de Ciencias Agrícolas (IICA), 1981, p. 184–208)

Assessment of collective production centers. Looks into research and evaluation efforts, division of labor, alienation, productivity, salaries, and economic surplus.

3247 Nolff, Max. La vía crucis de la Revolución Sandinista (NSO, 63, nov./dic. 1982, p. 33–46, map, tables)

Discusses economic performance of Nicaragua in the post-revolutionary period. Focuses on nature of the reconstruction program, importance of the private sector, agricultural and industrial planning, foreign trade, education and health, external assistance, and popular participation.

3248 Notas para el estudio económico de América Latina, 1982: Nicaragua. Santiago: Naciones Unidas, Consejo Económico y Social, CEPAL, 1983. 39 p.: bibl., tables (E/CEPAL/MEX/1983/L.13)

Survey of economic conditions leading to two percent decline in GDP. Includes sections on relative performance of various sectors (e.g., employment, foreign trade, balance of payments, external debt, prices, and implemention of monetary and fiscal policies.)

3249 Panamá, segmentación del mercado de trabajo: información estadística básica. Santiago: Organización Internacional del Trabajo, PREALC, 1982. 208 p.: bibl., tables (Documento de trabajo; 216)

Reports household survey data gathered by Panamanian Census Bureau. Includes brief introduction and 31 sets of statistical tables on labor force participation, employment, wages, occupational distribution, and household head characteristics.

3250 Posas, Mario and **Rafael del Cid.** La construcción del sector público y del Estado nacional de Honduras, 1876–1979. San José: Editorial Universitaria Centroamericana, 1981. 254 p.: bibl., tables (Textos del Instituto Centroamericano de Administración Pública. Col. Rueda del tiempo)

Discusses three distinct periods: 1) Agrarian capitalism and foreign domination (1876–1948); 2) capitalist development and expansion of the role of the State (1949–72); and 3) militarization of public sector (1972–79). Emphasizes institutional transformation as reflected by public policy priorities.

3251 Los Problemas socio-políticos del desarrollo en Costa Rica. Coordinadores, Guillermo Paz Cárcamo and Enrique Gutiérrez Diermissen. Heredia, Costa Rica: Unidad Coordinadora de Investigación y Documentación, Facultad de Ciencias Sociales, Univ. Nacional; San José: Editorial Univ. Estatal a Distancia, 1981. 279 p.

Seven articles by different authors deal with socioeconomic and political aspects of development. They address the process of changing structures, components of participatory democracy, constraints on the media, and possible transition toward socialism.

3252 Quiroga, Eduardo R. La revolución verde en el contexto institucional de Latinoamérica: un caso de estudio en El Salvador (NS, 6:12, 1981, p. 53–62)

Case study of Zapotitán irrigation district. Contends that more often than not irrigation practices applied to minifundia are doomed to fail because the necessary institutional transformations are not concomitant to technological innovation.

3253 Rivera Urrutia, Eugenio. El Fondo Monetario Internacional y Costa Rica, 1978–1982: política económica y crisis. San José: Depto. Ecuménico de Investigaciones, 1982. 179 p.: bibl., tables (Col. Centroamérica)

Attributes economic crisis to emergence of industrial sector and inability of any other social group to compete with industrialists. Focuses on import substitution model, fiscal reform, and exchange rate deterioration. Also analyzes factors leading to failure of first two agreements with IMF.

3254 Rosenberg, Mark B. Honduras: bastion of stability or quagmire? (*in* Revolution and counterrevolution in Central America and the Caribbean. Edited by Donald E. Schulz and Douglas H. Graham. Boulder, Colo.: Westview Pres, 1984, p. 331–349, tables)

Argues that Washington's policy has been manipulated and molded to the particular needs of Honduran military and civilian elites. Both military and economic aid is out of proportion relative to what the country can reasonably absorb.

3255 Ruhl, J. Mark. La influencia de la estructura agraria en la estabilidad política de Honduras (CSUCA/ESC, 12:36, sept./dic. 1983, p. 39–72, bibl., tables)

Analyzes land tenure and agrarian reform in both Honduras and El Salvador, concluding that Honduras's relative stability (with respect to El Salvador) can be partly attributed to more equitable distribution of land and a more vigorous agrarian reform program.

3256 Sebastián, Luis de. Inflación, moneda y balanza de pagos en El Salvador. 2a ed. San Salvador: UCA Editores, 1983. 191 p.: bibl., ill., tables (Col. Estructuras y procesos; 10)

After brief survey of economic conditions, discusses assumptions, theoretical arguments, and empirical testing of a monetary-approach model to the balance of payments.

3257 Seligson, Mitchell A. Agrarian reform in Costa Rica: the impact of the Title Security Program (IAMEA, 35:4, Spring 1982, p. 32–56, graphs, tables)

Concludes that while the land titling program does not serve to redistribute land, it provides tenure security so that small holders may thereby obtain bank credit, improve farm productivity, and raise incomes. Calls for more emphasis on redistributive aspects of the agrarian reform.

3258 Shepherd, Philip L. The tragic course and consequences of US policy in Honduras (World Policy Journal [New York] Fall 1984, p. 109–154, table)

Maintains that the Reagan administration neither understands the social reality of Honduras nor cares about it except as a springboard for counterrevolution and US military intervention in the region. Predicts that current policies will undermine long-run US-Honduran relations and exacerbate an already volatile Central American situation.

3259 Sojo, Ana. Morfología de la política estatal en Costa Rica y crisis económica (CSUCA/ESC, 13:37, enero/abril 1984, p. 139–162)

Identifies three periods with different approaches to policy formulation in recent years: 1) Economic crisis and peak of Keynesianism (1974–78); 2) crisis of hegemony within the elite and emergence of uncertainty about Keynesian policies (1978–82); and 3) consolidation of a new bourgeois hegemony along with modification of Keynesian policies (1982-present).

3260 Solórzano, Mario. Liberalismo a desatiempo: el modelo económico guatemalteco, 1954–1982 (CSUCA/ESC, 12:35, mayo/agosto 1983, p. 13–49, tables)

Identifies three major components of this economic model: 1) capitalist development based on both minifundia and latifundia; 2) industrialization via regional integration; and 3) greater dependency. All three are intertwined in the elite's overall conceptualization of the socioeconomic order.

3261 Soto, Max Alberto; Carlos Alberto Sevilla; and Charles R. Frank, Jr. Guatemala: desempleo y subempleo. San José: Editorial Universitaria Centroamericana, 1982. 188 p.: bibl., ill., tables (Col. Integración)

Contends that rapid and sustained growth of the construction sector is the best policy for fighting both unemployment and underemployment. Thus, an assessment of housing and construction industry is provided.

3262 Strasma, John *et al.* Agrarian reform in El Salvador. Washington: Office of Development Information and Utilization, AID, 1983. 260 p.: bibl., ill., tables.

Recommendations include simplifying legal process for granting and registering land titles, completing evaluation and payment for expropriated farms and their assignment to beneficiaries, creating an insurance system for losses, paying promptly for export crops, and encouraging cooperatives to hire professional managers.

3263 Trejos París, María Eugenia. ¿Un sector de economía laboral en Costa Rica? (CSUCA/ESC, 13:37, enero/abril 1984, p. 211–230)

Probes capital accumulation and role of the State in the labor economy. Hypothesizes that economy's labor component is a form of public capital accumulation. Views Caribbean Basin Initiative as an attempt to strengthen private sector.

3264 Zúñiga M., Melba Luz; María Celina Kawas C.; and Michael E. Conroy. Ingreso, gasto, barrio y familia: estrategias de los pobladores de barrios de ingresos bajos en Tegucigalpa. Tegucigalpa: Asesores para el Desarrollo, 1982. 225 p.: bibl., tables.

USAID-financed study based on sample of 200 urban households interviewed twice a month during one year. Data gathered covers earnings level and composition, consumption patterns, household composition, education and skills, decision making, migration, social mobility, and neighborhood ties.

HISPANIOLA (Dominican Republic and Haiti)

3265 Alemán, José Luis. 27 [i.e. Veintisiete] ensayos sobre economía y sociedad dominicanas. Santiago: Univ. Católica Madre y Maestra (UCMM), 1982. 561 p.: bibl., ill. (Col. Estudios; 74)

Papers grouped under five headings: 1) Agricultural problems (land tenure, agrarian reform, and production trends); 2) investment, employment, technology, and industrial incentives; 3) regional analysis, with specific references to Santiago de los Caballeros and Monseñor Nouel; 4) population; and 5) social considerations (education, religion, and corruption).

3266 Alvarez Betancourt, Opinio *et al.* Las instituciones financieras y el mercado de valores en la República Dominicana. Santo Domingo: Centro de Estudios Monetarios y Bancarios, 182. 134 p.: tables (Serie Programas; 1)

Consists of six papers by different authors dealing with financial institutions, the stock market, and capital markets in the Dominican Republic and their impact on economic development.

3267 Antonin, Arnold. Haití en el Caribe (NSO, 63, nov./dic. 1982, p. 103–112, tables)

Stresses Haiti's geopolitical importance within a US domination context. Criticizes current government's economic model on the grounds that almost 70 percent of the population lives in poverty, and the incidence has been growing in recent years.

3268 Bolling, H. Christine. Dominican Republic: factors affecting its capacity to import food. Washington: US Dept. of Agriculture, Economic Research Service, 1983. 25 p.: bibl., tables (Foreign agricultural economic report; 183)

Estimates that during 1960–80 Dominican food imports from US (over two-thirds of total food imports) increased more than twentyfold. GDP per capita growth rates, above 10 percent, accounted for the rise in demand. Predicts that increased Dominican production will not displace future imports because of country's ability to export its crops.

3269 El Desarrollo regional de Bonao: realidad y futuro. Santiago: Univ. Católica Madre y Maestra (UCMM), 1981. 147 p.: bibl., ill., tables (Col. Estudios; 67)

In-depth regional analysis covering population characteristics, provision of services, resource availability, community development, economic growth, and potential for the future.

3270 Despradel, Carlos. Trayectoria de un pensamiento económico. Santo Domingo: Editora Corripio, 1981. 341 p.

Papers written during last 10 yrs. on foreign trade and balance of payments disequilibria, assessment of agricultural sector, inflation, monetary policy, foreign investment, and reliability of statistical data.

3271 Diagnóstico preliminar agropecuario de la Regional Central. Edición a cargo de Francisco T. Rodríguez y Raúl Pineda. Santo Domingo: Secretaría de Estado de Agricultura, Subsecretaría Técnica de Planificación Sectorial Agropecuaria, Dirección Regional Central, 1982. 2 v.: bibl., ill., maps, tables.

In-depth regional analysis. Vol. 1 deals with natural resources (soils, climate, etc.) and drainage, while vol. 2 addresses population and economic issues (rate of growth, density, employment, income, land tenure, and nutrition), education and training, health, rural organizations, housing, provision of public services, communications, and role of major agricultural institutions (e.g., SEA, IAD, OCD, IDECOOP, INDRHI, BAGRICOLA, and INESPRE).

3272 Dominican Republic. Compendio de la legislación de la República Dominicana en materia de comercio. Recopilación de Kaplan, Russin, Vecchi & Heredia Bonetti. Santo Domingo: IES: FCE, 1982. 582 p.: bibl.

In-depth probe into commerce laws and legislation. Contains 38 chaps. covering areas such as the Constitution, immigration, foreign investment, bankruptcy, contracts, sales, transportation, taxes, agriculture, mining, patents, negotiable instruments, insurance, mortgages, health, nuclear energy, and administration of justice.

3273 ———. Secretariado Técnico de la Presidencia. Oficina Nacional de Planificación. Oficina Nacional de Estadística. La situación del empleo en la zona urbana en junio de 1980: resultados de la encuesta nacional urbana de mano de obra. Santo Domingo: El Secretariado, 1982. 149 p.: bibl., ill., tables.

Urban employment assessment based on survey questionnaire administered to 13,096 persons in 3665 households through 45 municipalities. Contains ample information on employment correlation with sex, age, marital status, economic sector, occupation, formal education, skills, and means of subsistence. Devotes one chap. to income and another to characteristics of the unemployed.

3274 Dorsey, Jeff; Annis Sheldon; and Stephen Vetter. Credit to small farmers in the Dominican Republic: beyond revolving loan funds (Grassroots Development [Inter-American Foundation, Washington] 6:2/7:1, 1983, p. 19–26, ill.)

Describes evolution of Dominican Financiera, a cooperative, and dilemmas it must resolve if it is to survive in its dual role as a bank and social movement of poor farmers.

3275 Executive Workshop on Farmer/Agrobusiness Joint Ventures, Puerto Plata, Dominican Republic, 1982. Conference report. New York: Fund for Multinational Management Education, 1982. 72 p.: bibl., ill., tables.

Explores possible cooperation between private and public sectors in solving agricultural problems. After analyzing specific investment opportunities, examines viability of establishing a relationship with farmers of limited resources. Concludes that established market position, rather than production or demand, is key to agricultural development.

3276 Los Grandes problemas nacionales. Edición de Frank Moya Pons. Carlos Despradel et al. Santo Domingo: FORUM, 1982. 126 p. (FORUM; 5)

Proceedings of seminar/workshop dealing with economic development constraints and economic costs of social development.

3277 Guiliani Cury, Hugo. Temor-esperanza-acción: un enfoque de política-económica para la República Dominicana. Santo Domingo: Taller, 1982. 302 p.: bibl., ill.

Addresses diverse areas of public policy formulation, such as incentives for industrial development, possible integration of the Dominican Republic to the CACM, and expansion of foreign markets for sugar exports. Trade, agricultural, industrial, monetary, and fiscal policies are specifically treated.

3278 López Valdés, José Ml. Incentivos monetarios, cambiarios y fiscales en las exportaciones no tradicionales en la República Dominicana. Santo Domingo: Centro de Estudios Monetarios y Bancarios, 1982. 55 p.: bibl., tables (Serie Estudios; 3)

Describes current monetary, foreign exchange, and fiscal incentives to expand nontraditional exports. Analyzes legal infrastructure, rediscounting, special credit programs, and foreign debt regulation.

3279 Lundahl, Mats. Haitian underdevelopment in a historical perspective (JLAS, 14:2, Nov. 1982, p. 465–475)

Review of five books dealing with various instances of underdevelopment, their evolution in a historical perspective, and possible ways to attain a higher standard of living for majority of the population. For historian's comment, see HLAS 46:2470.

3280 ———. Price series correlations and market integration: some evidence from Haiti (LI/IA, 8:1, 61–75, bibl., maps, tables)

Uses price data to calculate monthly correlation coefficients between every pair of markets as a measure of market integration.

3281 Messina, Milton. Nacionalismo y desarrollo. Santo Domingo: s.n., 1982. 157 p.: plates.

Collection of 36 articles published in *Listín Diario* (1977–82). Topics: foreign exchange, unemployment, protectionism and industrial development, economic determinism, impact of moral suasion, and unemployment.

3282 Nordström, Claes and Joseph Ramos. Empleo en la zafra azucarera dominicana. Santo Domingo: Secretariado Técnico de la Presidencia, Oficina Nacional de Planificación, 1981. 75 p.: bibl., tables (Serie Plandes; 55)

Concludes that mechanization of sugarcane harvesting would increase cost per unit and decrease employment opportunities. Instead, recommends technical changes to increase efficiency of current system.

3283 Notas para el estudio económico de América Latina, 1982: Haití. Santiago: Naciones Unidas, Consejo Económico y Social, CEPAL, 1983. 35 p.: bibl., tables (E/CEPAL/MEX/1983/L.12)

Survey of economic conditions leading to a meager 0.3 percent growth in GDP, mostly due to overdependence on agriculture and virtual stagnation of primary sector. Both private and public investment declined substantially and open unemployment reached 12 percent.

3284 Pérez Castro, Ivelisse. El endeudamiento público externo y la absorción de capital: el caso dominicano (CEMLA/M, 6:2, abril/junio 1983, p. 215–245, bibl., tables)

Investigates whether external financing is conducive to economic development or to bottlenecks whose burden outweighs whatever benefits may be derived from it. Proposed answer lies in economy's capital absorption capacity. Contends that foreign debt interest payments account for a substantial and increasing proportion of new loans.

3285 Population, ressources humaines et développement. Séminaire organisé par l'Institut haïtien de statistique et d'informatique *en collaboration avec la* Battelle Memorial Institute de Washington. Port-au-Prince: L'Institut, 1983. 317 p.: bibl., ill., tables.

Collection of papers, presented at symposium, explores population, human resource, and development dynamics. They also deal with industrial structure and optimal utilization of labor, education, internal migration, health, and capability of agricultural sector to respond adequately to demographic pressures.

3287 Ramírez, Nelson; Antonio Tatis; and Diana Germán. Población y mano de obra en la República Dominicana: perspectivas de la fuerza de trabajo y del empleo-desempleo en el período 1980–1990. Santo Domingo: Instituto de Estudios de Población y Desarrollo, 1983. 104 p.: bibl., ill., tables (Estudio; 1)

Discusses 1960–80 size and growth of labor force; distribution of labor by sex, age, residence, occupation, and economic sector; employment and unemployment; and availability of skills. Also projects supply of labor for 1980–90 and demand created by expansion of agriculture, manufacturing, and commerce/service sectors.

3288 Régimen de incentivos en la economía dominicana. Santo Domingo: FORUM, 1983. 197 p.: bibl., ill., tables (FORUM: 7)

Collection of five papers discusses impact on fiscal incentives of income tax structure, legal infrastructure, public consumption and expenditures, tax evasion, and possible tax reform.

Rouzier, Philippe. Echange et développement: cadre théorique pour une alternative. See item **2976.**

3289 Santo Domingo 2000. Santo Domingo: Univ. Nacional Pedro Henríquez Ureña, Colegio Dominicano de Ingenieros, Arquitectos y Agrimensores, s.d. 108 p.: ill.

Proceedings of seminar focusing on projections for Santo Domingo toward end of the century. Seven papers deal with zoning and urban growth, housing, transportation, and ecological considerations.

3290 Seminario sobre Reforma Fiscal en la República Dominicana, Santo Domingo, 1981. Seminario sobre reforma fiscal en la República Dominicana: política y administración. Santo Domingo: Instituto de Capacitación Tributaria (INCAT), 1982. 469 p.: bibl., ill., tables (Col. Fortalecimiento institucional; 8)

Consists of 12 papers dealing with various aspects of Dominican public finance:

consumption, foreign trade, income, and estate tax structures; fiscal incentives; and composition of public expenditures.

3291 La Situación laboral en la República Dominicana. Santo Domingo: FORUM, 1983. 101 p. (FORUM; 8)

Consists of five articles on labor economics by five different authors, dealing with cost of living, employment, workers' organizations and unionism, labor laws, and employer-employee relations.

3292 Stratégie du développement national et dimension culturelle. Port-au-Prince: Univ. d'Etat d'Haïti, Dép. des sciences du développement, Faculté d'ethnologie, 1982. 133 p. (La Revue de la Faculté d'ethnologie et du CRESHS; 38. Le *Bulletin de l'Académie des sciences humaines et sociales*; 11)

Proceedings of symposium on alternative development strategies. Contains eight papers emphasizing economic impact of cultural characteristics.

3293 Tata, Robert J. Haiti, land of poverty. Washington: Univ. Press of America, 1982. 127 p.: bibl., index, maps.

Views Haiti's widespread poverty as malfunction of physical, social, economic, and political systems. Then proceeds to analyze structure and operation of such systems in order to assess their contribution to human welfare. Also evaluates future potential.

3293a Tejera, Eduardo *et al.* Los problemas del sector externo en la República Dominicana. Santo Domingo: FORUM, 1982. 215 p. (FORUM; 1)

Five articles discuss international trade subjects such as balance of payment disequilibria, import regulation, foreign exchange markets, impact of money supply expansion, and growth and composition of public debt.

3294 Thoumi, Francisco E. Social and political obstacles to economic development in Haiti (*in* The Newer Caribbean: decolonization, democracy, and development. Philadelphia: Institute for the Study of Human Issues, 1983, p. 205–218)

Concludes that the main obstacle to development lies in country's power structure which concentrates decision-making in a few power centers and individuals not accustomed to delegating authority and using price

mechanisms to allocate resources. Identifies promotion of employment as a priority course of action.

3295 Vicens, Lucas. Crisis económica, 1978–1982. Santo Domingo: Editora Alfa y Omega, 1982. 404 p.: ill.

Thorough analysis of Dominican economy and its structural problems such as inflation, exchange rate deterioration, budget deficit, external debt, unemployment, and diminished inflow of foreign investment. Conducted within a framework of undesirable domestic capital accumulation, growing hegemony of foreign interests, and subordination to the dictates of the IMF.

COMMONWEALTH CARIBBEAN, BELIZE, AND GUYANA

3296 Abdulah, Norma. The availability and utilization of skills in Guyana. St. Augustine, Trinidad: Institute of Social and Economic Research, Univ. of the West Indies, 1981. 105 p.: bibl., tables (Occasional papers. Human resources; 4)

After brief survey of educational system and available training and vocational opportunities, examines country's skill fund and level of training of unemployed. Also covers length of unemployment, status in household, and chief means of support.

3297 Arjoon, Prem *et al.* Export marketing in the Caribbean: Caribbean case studies. 2nd ed. Bridgetown: Caribbean Development Bank; Geneva: International Trade Centre, 1983. 158 p.: bibl., ill.

Consists of 11 case studies examining marketing problems faced by Caribbean enterprises.

3298 Barbados Industrial Development Corp. Development plan, 1978–82. Bridgetown: The Corporation, 1982? 39 p.

Specific objectives are to create at least 5,000 jobs in the manufacturing sector, increase exports of manufactured goods (excluding sugar and molasses) by 20 percent per annum, and increase output of manufactured goods by 19 percent per annum.

3300 Beckford, George L. Socioeconomic change and political continuity in the Anglophone Caribbean (RU/SCID, 15:1, 1980, p. 3–14, bibl., tables)

Predicts that, as the economic crisis deepens in capitalist metropoles, the Commonwealth Caribbean economy will suffer from inflation, commodity shortages, and unemployment. Also predicts that younger age-cohorts of the population are likely to make demand which the system will be unable to fulfill, thus creating some social upheaval.

3301 ———. The struggle for a relevant economics (UWI/SES, 33:1, March 1984, p. 47–57)

Historical survey of the Dept. of Economics at the Univ. of the West Indies, Mona, Jamaica, since its inception in 1960.

3301a ——— and **Michael Witter.** Small garden bitter weed: the political economy of struggle and change in Jamaica. 2nd, expanded ed. Morant Bay, Jamaica: Maroon Publishing House, 1982. 167 p.: bibl., ill.

In the authors' own words, purpose of this book is "to weed out the capitalist/imperialist bitter weed infesting our small garden—from the days of King Sugar to the present Multinational Corporations/Multinational Banks imperialist nexus with the 'fifth column' of national client capitalists."

3302 Bélisle, François J. Tourism and food imports: the case of Jamaica (UC/EDCC, 32:4, July 1984, p. 819–842, graph, map, tables)

Argues that food imports for tourist consumption constitutes both a loss of scarce foreign exchange and a loss of agricultural income and employment. Estimates nature and extent of locally produced and imported food used by hotels and identifies reasons why hotels use imported food.

3303 Bennett, Karl M. An evaluation of the contribution of CARICOM to intraregional Caribbean trade (UWI/SES, 31:1, March 1982, p. 74–88, bibl., tables)

Attempt to ascertain what proportion of CARICOM countries' export growth can be attributed to the existence of a regional preferential market and what proportion can be attributed to normal market expansion. Findings indicate that, except for Barbados, regional preference played an important role in growth of exports.

3304 ———. Trade and payments in the Caribbean Common Market. Mona, Jamaica: Institute of Social and Economic Research, Univ. of the West Indies, 1982. 114 p.: bibl.

Shows that growth in regional trade, associated with CARIFTA/CARICOM, has had a major impact on participating countries. After a review of 1969–75 trade patterns, assesses relationship between regional trading status of each country and its overall payment status.

3305 Bernal, Richard L. The IMF and class struggle in Jamaica, 1977–1980 (LAP, ll[3]:42, Summer 1984, p. 53–82, bibl., tables)

Examines conflict in Jamaica (1977–80) between, on the one hand, IMF programs which sought to reinforce integration into the world economy and to preserve dependent capitalism and, on the other, Manley government policies which sought a mixed economy with a leading State role and a reduction of economy's openness.

3306 ———; **Mark Figueroa;** and **Michael Witter.** Caribbean economic thought: the critical tradition (UWI/SES, 33:2, June 1984, p. 5–96, bibl.)

Surveys work of Lewis, Radical Caribbean School, and Marxist Political Economy of the Caribbean. Argues that in spite of their differences, these three paradigms share an inherently critical perspective on Caribbean social reality, all serving to enrich understanding of this reality.

3307 Bourne, Compton. Structure and performance of Jamaican rural financial markets (UWI/SES, 32:1, March 1983, p. 1–21, bibl., tables)

Concludes that both savings mobilization performance and credit performance are weak and seriously in need of reform. Also contends that price, exchange rate, and foreign trade reforms are necessary to improve rural financial markets.

3308 Cayman Islands government: economic & financial review. Georgetown: Financial Secretary, 1982. 115 p.: ill., index, map, tables.

Focuses on effect of fiscal policy on allocation, distribution, and utilization of resources. Surveys development plans, reserve and investment funds, public debt, taxation, British aid, capital projects, and the civil service.

3309 Chandisingh, Rajendra. The State, the economy, and the type of rule in

Guyana: an assessment of Guyana's "socialist revolution" (LAP, 10[4]:39, Fall 1983, p. 59–74, tables)

Argues that government's socialist rhetoric is used as ideological legitimation for its restructuring of the State to affect its authoritarian rule, which is a corruption and abuse of socialist ideals. Suggests that ruling class may attempt to perpetuate its rule through a bloody dictatorship.

3310 Dependency under challenge: the political economy of the Commonwealth Caribbean. Edited by Anthony Payne and Paul Sutton. Manchester, UK: Manchester Univ. Press, 1984. 295 p.: bibl., index, map.

Assesses Commonwealth Caribbean individual and collective efforts to reverse dependency. Deals with theory behind the various strategies, strategies themselves, and their outcomes. Also traces emergence of the Commonwealth Caribbean as a regional subsystem and significant entity in international affairs.

3311 Dominica. Ministry of Finance. Statistical Div. Analysis of domestic exports. Roseau: The Div.: 1982. 13 leaves.

Examines volume and composition of 1976–80 exports. Results indicate that manufactured products are experiencing a rising trend in relative importance.

3312 Economic development of small states with particular reference to Antigua: some papers presented by Antiguans at seminars sponsored by the U.W.I. Dept. of Extra-Mural Studies, Antigua, 1976–1981. S.l.: The Dept., 1981. 75 p.

Collection of five articles spanning allocation priorities, economic impact of political independence, manpower, capital formation and finance services, and utilization of tourism resources.

3313 Edie, Carlene J. Jamaican political processes: a system in search of a paradigm (JDS, 20:4, July 1984, p. 248–270, bibl.)

Maintains that Manley's failure to recognize that the Jamaican state was subordinate to economic elite and foreign capital sources caused him to make serious blunders in his negotiations with the IMF. Consequently, material rewards to the masses diminished, and they eventually rejected him.

3314 Farrell, Trevor M.A. Decolonization in the English-speaking Caribbean: myth

or reality? (in The Newer Caribbean: decolonization, democracy, and development. Philadelphia: Institute for the Study of Human Issues, 1983, p. 3–13)

Contends that the Commonwealth Caribbean remains essentially colonized. The form, mechanisms, and agents of colonization may have changed, but control over the dynamic and path of development has been retained abroad.

3315 González Cano, Hugo. Los incentivos crediticios a las exportaciones no tradicionales en países del CARICOM. Santo Domingo: Instituto de Capacitación Tributaria de la Secretaría de Estado de Finanzas, 1982. 137 p.: bibl. (Col. Manuales de finanzas públicas; 14)

Pt. 1 surveys various kinds of nontraditional export credit programs, including those related to technical assistance, marketing, production, and shipping. Pt. 2 analyzes specific export credit incentives of Jamaica, Barbados, and Guyana.

3316 Greene, J. Edward. Challenges and responses in social science research in the English-speaking Caribbean (UWI/SES, 33:1, March 1984, p. 9–46, bibl.)

Reflects on research conducted by the Univ. of the West Indies' Faculty of Social Sciences in the past 21 yrs. Identifies four major development schools that have engaged Caribbean scholars: Cultural Pluralism, Plantation, Dependency, and Marxism-Leninism. Contends that the need to address public policy issues contributed towards bridging rigid disciplinary boundaries and led to research that is strongly focused on the newly emerging development sciences.

3317 Heffernan, Peter J. and **Stephen K. Pollard.** The determinants of credit use among small farmers in Jamaica (UWI/SES, 32:1, March 1983, p. 23–41, bibl., tables)

Discriminant analysis identifies characteristics of farm households and lenders that influence participation in rural financial markets. Their main characteristics are farm size, farm revenue, access to extension services, and the enterprise mix.

3318 Hickey, John. The stabilization program of the United States in Jamaica (IAMEA, 37:2, Autumn 1983, p. 63–72, tables)

Maintains that Jamaica has been designated as a foreign aid showcase by USAID, which means that the US has not pressed for policy reforms.

3319 Ince, Basil A. Coping with oil wealth: the case of Trinidad/Tobago and the Commonwealth Caribbean (in Latin American prospects for the 1980s: equity, democratization, and development. Edited by Archibald R.M. Ritter and David H. Pollock. New York: Praeger, 1983, p. 111–133, tables)

Argues that Trinidad/Tobago's aid program was originally conceived as a means of disposing of unprecedented wealth which the domestic economy could not absorb. Tying aid to purchase of Trinidad/Tobago's exports broadens avenues for exporting and regional marketing of commodities.

3320 Jones-Hendrickson, S.B. Tourism investment and ownership: local versus foreign (Bulletin of Eastern Caribbean Affairs [Institute of Social & Economic Research, Eastern Caribbean, Univ. of the West Indies, Cave Hill, Barbados] 8:5, Nov./Dec. 1982, p. 31–36)

Contends that expansion of tourism services is an expensive venture which generates a dependence effect. The tourist multiplier is minimized, instead of maximized, when dependency syndrome is operational in international tourism.

3321 Lestrade, Swinburne. CARICOM's less developed countries: a review of the progress of the LDCs under the CARICOM arrangements. Cave Hill, Barbados: Institute of Social and Economic Research, Eastern Caribbean, Univ. of the West Indies, 1981. 85 p.: bibl., tables (Occasional paper; 16)

Probes into special problems confronted by CARICOM LDCs. Discusses Caribbean Investment Corp., private joint ventures, intraregional investment and loan capital flows, ECCM's industry allocation scheme, technical assistance, and health management training.

3322 Long, Frank. Aspects of external trade and the Barbadian economy during the 1939–45 war: some preliminary observations (BMHS/J, 37:1, 1983, p. 57–67, tables)

Argues that since Britain's involvement in World War II resulted in a decline in value of imports and exports affecting Barbados, Canada played an important role in absorbing the island's exports and supplying imports, thus emerging between 1939–45 as the country's leading trading partner.

3323 ———. Industrialization and the role of industrial development corporations in a Caribbean economy: a study of Barbados, 1960–80 (IAMEA, 37:3, Winter 1983, p. 33–56, graphs, tables)

Suggests amendments to development planning such as fitting export-oriented industrialization within an overall context, providing self-correcting remedies for employment, generation of inter-industry linkages, balance of payments equilibrium, and integration of agrarian sector into industrialization strategy.

3324 McClean, A. Wendell A. Some evidence on the demand for money in a small open economy: Barbados (UWI/SES, 31:3, 1982, p. 155–170, tables)

Confirms existence of a well defined money demand function and suggests that, in addition to conventional negative interest rate effect, there is a positive interest rate effect associated with cost of illiquidity. Also argues that constraining price elasticity to unity could be a source of specification bias, resulting in serial correlation.

3325 McIntyre, Alister. Adjustment of Caribbean economies to changing international economic relations: opening statement at sixteenth West Indian agricultural economics conference (Bulletin of Eastern Caribbean Affairs [Institute of Social & Economic Research, Eastern Caribbean, Univ. of the West Indies, Cave Hill, Barbados] 8:5, Nov./Dec. 1982, p. 1–12)

Maintains that Caribbean countries face an international environment that undermines, rather than supports, their development. Surveys production possibilities, policy priorities for the 1980s, need for a new effort in multilateralism, and pressing problem of unemployment.

3326 McKee, David L. Some specifics on the loss of professional personnel from the Commonwealth Caribbean (IAMEA, 37:3, Winter 1983, p. 57–76, tables)

Analysis of migration into the US based on a survey of 40 professionals listed in *American Men and Women of Science*. Survey covers personal, family, and educational matters related to socioeconomic achievement.

3327 Mandle, Jay R. Caribbean dependency and its alternatives (LAP, 11[3]:42, Summer 1984, p. 111–124, bibl., tables)

Contends that what is lacking, above all, in the West Indies is a vibrant capital goods and machine tools industry. Production of these industries is viewed as the means through which new technology can be introduced into the economy.

3328 Massing, Michael. The Jamaica experiment (The Atlantic [The Atlantic Monthly Co., Boston, Mass.] 252:3, Sept. 1983, p. 37–56, ill.)

Argues that the Reagan Administration has selected Jamaica as the site for a high-stakes experiment intended to demonstrate superiority of capitalism over socialism.

3329 Nyanin, Ohene Owusu. Lending costs, institutional viability and agricultural credit strategies in Jamaica (UWI/SES, 32:1, March 1983, p. 103–133, bibl., tables)

Analysis of level, structure, and determinants of lending costs in a major agricultural program. Lending costs are shown to be debilitatingly high, with major components of costs being loan administration and risk.

3330 Palmer, Ransford W. Problems of development in beautiful countries: perspectives on the Caribbean. Lanham, Md.: North-South Pub. Co., 1984. 91 p.: bibl., ill.

Argues that a dependent industrialization strategy cannot be a substitute for an indigenous engine of growth if the Caribbean is to absorb its surplus labor into productive employment. After assessing impact of foreign capital inflow and emigration of labor to the US, discusses elements of appropriate technology for the region and fragility of Eastern Caribbean minieconomies.

3331 Paul, Alix-Hérard. The "destabilization" program of the IMF in Jamaica (IAMEA, 37:2, Autumn 1983, p. 45–61)

Jamaica is used as a case in point to illustrate difficulties faced by LDCs because of the dependent state of their economies, on the one hand, on the advanced capitalist countries and, on the other, on major international economic institutions when they attempt to implement socioeconomic development strategies. Argues that the IMF and other international institutions serve primarily the interests of advanced capitalist countries.

3332 Powell, Dorian. The role of women in the Caribbean (UWI/SES, 33:2, June 1984, p. 97–122, bibl.)

After a brief discussion of women's role and development, deals with family and work. Maintains that gross neglect of Caribbean women's work roles is unjustified, since women in the region have had a long history of work involvement, often functioning as primary workers. Also emphasizes women's education and political role.

3333 Quenan, Carlos. Belice: causas y perspectivas de una independencia tardía (NSO, 59, marzo/abril 1982, p. 77–85)

Exposition of political and economic structure of the new nation, where the colonial legacy is evident and manifest in the absence of universities, sewers, and television channels.

3334 Ramsaran, Ramesh. Financial constraints and economic development in the Commonwealth Caribbean: the recent experience. St. Augustine, Trinidad & Tobago: Institute of International Relations, 1983. 23 p.: bibl., tables (Occasional paper; 1)

Analysis restricted to Barbados, Guyana, Jamaica, and Trinidad and Tobago. Discusses recent development strategies of these countries and examines their aggregate savings-investment trends and growth of their public debt.

3335 Sandoval, José Miguel. State capitalism in a petroleum-based economy: the case of Trinidad and Tobago (in Crisis in the Caribbean. Edited by Fitzroy Ambursley and Robin Cohen. New York: Monthly Review Press, 1983, p. 247–268, bibl.)

Analyzes development of state capitalism and relates its evolution to capacity of the State to control and manage an enlarged economic surplus. Stresses that state intervention has in no way challenged the permanence of the capitalist system.

3336 Searle, Chris and **Don Rojas.** "To construct from morning:" making the people's budget in Grenada: interviews. St. George's, Grenada: Fedon Pubs., 1982. 168 p.: ill.

Although obsolete in some respects because of subsequent military developments, this document provides an interesting view in retrospect of resource-allocation priorities under the defunct Socialist government.

3337 Stone, Carl. Socialism and agricultural policies in Jamaica (IAMEA, 35:4, Spring 1982, p. 3–29, tables)

Explores relation between farmers' income flows and socioeconomic climate in nonagricultural areas and sectors. Concludes that positive gains in agriculture require a buoyant nonagricultural component.

3338 Studies in Caribbean public enterprise. v. 1, An overview of public enterprise in the Commonwealth Caribbean. v. 2, The legal framework of Commonwealth Caribbean public enterprise. Georgetown: Univ. of Guyana, Institute of Development Studies, 1983. 2 v.: bibl.

Contains five descriptive studies on the evolution of public enterprises in each country. Concludes that growth of the public sector and changing role of the State occurred because of failure of industrialization policies to foster employment and redistribute income, perceived weakness of the State in relation to major economic units, and inability of diversification efforts to reduce external dependence.

3339 Thomas, Clive Y. State capitalism in Guyana: an assessment of Burnham's co-operative socialist republic (*in* Crisis in the Caribbean. Edited by Fitzroy Ambursley and Robin Cohen. New York: Monthly Review Press, 1983, p. 27–48, bibl.)

Points out that the authoritarian state form that has accompanied the growth of state capitalism in Guyana is direct antithesis of socialism. State property of itself does not automatically ensure resource management by the people, which constitutes a fundamental condition of the socialist path of development.

3340 Underwood, John; Carson Charles; Trevor Sudama; and John Eckstein. Trip generation in Northern Trinidad. The Ombudsman's Office in Trinidad and Tobago: a preliminary report. Inflation in land and housing in Trinidad and Tobago. St. Augustine, Trinidad and Tobago: Institute of Social and Economic Research, Univ. of the West Indies, 1983. 92 p.: bibl., ill., tables (Occasional paper; 5)

Three papers: 1) part of wider study on transportation modeling systems pertinent to rapidly developing urban corridor of northern Trinidad; 2) identifies specific constraints inhibiting operative effectiveness of Ombudsman's Office; and 3) blames inflation in land and housing on excess demand, inability of housing sector to expand output, and rising cost of labor and building materials.

3341 Wong, David C. A review of Caribbean political economy (LAP, 11[3]:42, Summer 1984, p. 125–140, bibl.)

After examining colonization, slavery, rise of industrial capital, and emergence of working class, discusses transition from dependent development model into an activist government seeking partnerships with both foreign and local capitalists. Concludes that Caribbean prospects in the 1980s are not bright.

DUTCH CARIBBEAN AND SURINAM

3342 Caram, Anthony Richard. Geldanalyse en centrale bankpolitiek in Suriname: enige beschouwingen over de rol van het monetaire beleid bij de ekonomische ontwikkeling sedert 1957. s-Gravenhage: Pasmans, 1981. 270 p.: bibl., ill., tables.

Argues that because of small population, domestic income is insufficient to finance investments required by economic development. Spending power and savings are inadequate because of low income, thus keeping available resources from turning into productive assets, which in turn hampers creation of income. Recommends recourse to monetary financing as a way to break the circle.

3343 Scherm, Georg. Guyana und Surinam, wirtschaftsgeographische Probleme der Rohstoffabhängigkeit bauxitexportierender Entwicklungsländer. München, FRG: Florentz, 1982. 272 p.: bibl., ill., tables (Wirtschaftswissenschaftliche Forschung und Entwicklung; 79)

Analyzes both countries' disadvantages as raw material producers. Concludes that, because of smallness of economy, there is little potential for further industrialization and national self-sufficiency in agriculture. Attributes latter to low prestige in agricultural work and migration from rural areas.

CUBA

JORGE F. PEREZ LOPEZ, *Bureau of International Labor Affairs, United States Department of Labor*

IN MID 1982, THE CUBAN GOVERNMENT announced that severe short-term hard currency shortages would require a rescheduling of its hard currency foreign debt. The report of Cuba's National Bank—directed at Western creditors, explaining the reasons for the hard currency pinch and proposing an economic restructuring that would reverse the trend and permit a timely repayment of the debt (item **3345**)—is in itself a most revealing document. It provides, for the first time, data on Cuba's hard currency trade, balance of payments and debt and contains official estimates of the cost to the Cuban economy of US economic sanctions and of GNP for the period 1971–80.

The foreign debt problems have had an impact on the economic literature on Cuba. Several articles addressing aspects and prospects of the debt situation have appeared (items **3357, 3360, 3362,** and **3375**) and more can be anticipated. Also significant in this context is Fidel Castro's report to the Seventh Summit Conference of the Non-Aligned Countries (item **3351**) in which he presents his views on and solutions to the developing world's debt. Finally, as part of the debt rescheduling process, Cuba's creditors have demanded more up-to-date information on macroeconomic indicators and on developments in the external sector. As of Dec. 1983, Cuba began to comply with this requirement by publishing a very useful quarterly economic report (item **3356**).

Other studies annotated below and worthy of mention are two works written by Cuban economists, one concerns the sugar industry (item **3352**) and the other industrialization (item **3370**).

3344 Añé Aguiloche, Lia and **Norka Clerch Arza.** El comercio exterior de Cuba con América Latina y el Caribe en la etapa revolucionaria (Temas de Economía Mundial [La Habana] 9, 1984, p. 91–124)

Reviews Cuba's trade patterns with Latin American and Caribbean nations during the 1970s and 1980s.

3345 Banco Nacional de Cuba. Economic report. La Habana: El Banco, 1982. 64 p.: tables.

Basic document issued by the National Bank to justify Cuba's request to reschedule its hard currency foreign debt. For the first time, provides data on Cuban balance of payments, on value of services trade, on GNP, and on magnitude, maturity and other terms of the hard currency foreign debt. Also contains estimates of the cost to the Cuban economy of US economic sanctions and an economic restructuring plan proposed by the National Bank.

3346 Beauvais, Jean-Pierre. Achievements and contradictions of the Cuban workers' state (*in* Crisis in the Caribbean. Edited by Fitzroy Ambursley and Robin Cohen. New York: Monthly Review Press, 1983, p. 49–71, bibl.)

Argues that one of Cuba's main economic problems is very low economic consciousness of workers which results in very low worker productivity. Suggests that economic consciousness can only be raised through broader worker participation in decision making and day-to-day management of enterprises, two elements missing in Cuba.

3347 Blume, Helmut. Kuba: Die karibische "Zuckerinsel" (GR, 37:6, Juni 1985, p. 286–294, bibl., ill., maps, plates, tables)

Brief but far-ranging survey of Cuban sugar production and exports. Includes analysis of geographical, technological, and historical background of sugar in the Caribbean. Based on secondary sources. Shows renewed trends of concentration of sugar in total exports. That dependence is, however, somewhat mitigated, by the relatively high and stable prices paid by COMECON countries and other diversifying trends within the Cuban economy as a whole. While it is pointed out that privately run farms have been run more efficiently than large agro-industrial public enterprises, which now comprise 85 percent of sugar production, there is no indication as to whether this fact led to new approaches (i.e., reforming state enterprises or increasing the role of private farmers). [J. Peter Wogart]

3348 Brundenius, Claes. Revolutionary Cuba: the challenge of economic growth with equity. Boulder, Colo.: Westview Press, 1984. 224 p.: bibl., index, tables.

Slightly revised and updated version of earlier monograph (see *HLAS 45:3235*). Includes new section comparing Cuban economic performance and income distribution with other Latin American nations. Appendix 1 consists of author's article on the Cuban labor force (see item **3349**).

3349 ———. Some notes on the Cuban labor force, 1970–1980 (UP/CSEC, 13:2, Summer 1983, p. 65–77, tables)

Relying primarily on results of 1979 national demographic survey and 1970 census together some with estimates, author develops statistical profile of Cuban labor force in 1970s: size, employment and unemployment, distribution of employment by economic sector and between state and private enterprises. Where available, data on male/female differentials are also included.

3350 Cabrisas, Ricardo. El mercado internacional azucarero: situación actual (Cuba Socialista [La Habana] 10, marzo/mayo 1984, p. 57–91)

After discussing recent trends in the international sugar market, presents Cuba's objectives in the negotiation of a new International Sugar Agreement. Author is Cuba's Minister of Foreign Trade.

3351 Castro, Fidel. The world economic and social crisis. La Habana: Publishing Office of the Council of State, 1983. 224 p.: charts, tables.

Castro's report to the 7th Summit Conference of Non-Aligned Countries (New Delhi, March 1983). Characterizes condition of developing countries as one of crisis and paints a gloomy picture for the future. Makes several broad proposals to improve prospects; in particular, calls for reduction in defense spending by the superpowers, with a considerable part of these funds directed to the developing nations, elimination of barriers to exports from the developing nations and external debt relief, including cancellation of debt in some cases.

3352 Charadán López, Fernando. La industria azucarera en Cuba. La Habana: Editorial de Ciencias Sociales, 1982. 343 p.: bibl., charts, tables.

Valuable work presents broad analysis of Cuban sugar industry and its impact on the national economy through mid-1970s. Most important contribution (chap. 5) is a detailed analysis of the performance of each factor of production in the sugar industry during 1971–75 five-year period and impact of such performances on the sugar industry itself. Contains wealth of data from the Ministry of Sugar Industry heretofore not available.

3353 Cuba. Comité Estatal de Estadísticas. Anuario estadístico de Cuba: 1982. La Habana: El Comité, 1983? 591 p.: index, tables.

Comprehensive statistical yearbook structured in roughly the same manner as earlier vols. in the series (see *HLAS 45:3237*). Most series have been updated through 1982, including those for foreign trade. Includes for first time sections on investment and science and technology indicators. Also provides lengthy section on international data comparisons.

3354 ———. ———. La economía cubana: 1982. La Habana: El Comité, 1983? 20 p.: tables.

Brief overview of economic developments in 1982. Contains several useful statistical tables.

3355 ———. ———. **Dirección de Demografía.** Estadísticas de migraciones externas y turismo. La Habana: Editorial Orbe, 1982. 127 p.: tables.

Chap. 6 (p. 81–96) contains useful analysis of Cuba's experience with international tourism before and after the Revolution. Appendix tables 10 and 11 report annual data on number of arrivals of international tourists during 1950–59 and 1973–75.

3356 Cuba: Informe Económico Trimestral. Banco Nacional de Cuba, Comité Estatal de Estadísticas. No. 1, dic. 1982– . La Habana.

Quarterly analytical and statistical report prepared primarily for Cuba's Western creditors as part of debt rescheduling exercise. Emphasis is on macroeconomic indicators and on hard current foreign trade and balance of payments statistics. Also published in English under the title *Cuba: Quarterly Economic Report.*

3357 Cuba: recent economic trends (Economic Survey of Latin America and the Caribbean [UN, ECLA, Santiago] 1982, p. 243–269, tables)

Reviews Cuban economic developments in 1982 using same format of earlier studies (see *HLAS 45:3259*). Contains much statistical data drawn from statistical yearbooks and provided directly to ECLA by Cuban government. Deals in some detail with hard currency foreign debt situation. Review for 1981 is also available in *Economic Survey of Latin America and the Caribbean* (1981).

3358 Cuestiones de la ciencia y la tecnología en Cuba. Edición de Tirso Sáenz y Emilio García Capote. La Habana: Editorial Academia, 1981. 501 p.

Collection of papers dealing with different aspects of the relationship between science and technology policy and economic development in Cuba. Several were previously published in professional journals, especially *Economía y Desarrollo*. For education specialist's comment, see item **4417.**

3359 Edquist, Charles. Mechanization of sugarcane harvesting in Cuba (UP/CSEC, 13:2, Summer 1983, p. 41–64, tables)

Case study drawn from author's broader study of the impact of technical change on employment in sugarcane harvesting in Cuba and Jamaica. Contains very interesting chronology of the introduction of technology in Cuban sugarcane harvesting and attempts to estimate costs and benefits. Raises important questions regarding the trade-off between technology transfer and generating domestic technological capability.

3359a Gey, Peter. Kubas Wirtschaft & zwischen Ost und West: Binnen-und aussenwirtschaftliche Aspekte. Köln, FRG: Berichte des Bundesinstituts für Ostwissenschaftliche und Internationale Studien, 1983. 57 p.: tables.

Succinct survey of a quarter century of Cuban foreign trade. Includes special chapter on sugar and oil trade with the Soviet Union. Interesting chapter addresses Cuba's trade prospects in the 1980s. Contains excellent tables. [G.M. Dorn]

3360 González Rubí, Rafael. Cuba: avatares recientes de la economía (BNCE/CE, 34:1, enero 1984, p. 50–57)

Surveys economic developments in 1982–83. Provides useful discussion of external sector developments, including the hard currency balance of payments crisis of 1982 and Cuba's subsequent efforts to reschedule its hard currency foreign debt.

3361 González Vergara, Ramón and **Zoila González Maicas.** Sistema de estímulo a los fondos exportables en moneda nacional (UH/ED, 75, julio/agosto 1983, p. 74–87)

Describes regulations in place since 1981 designed to stimulate exports by permitting enterprises which produce exportables to capture part of the gains from international trade.

3362 Henry, Donald Putnam; Kip T. Fisher; and **Richard M. Rosenberg.** An analysis of Cuban debt. Santa Monica, Calif.: Rand Corp., 1984. 28 p. (R-3120-USDP)

Sketchy analysis of Cuban debt burden and of country's credit-worthiness. Takes into account both the outstanding debt of the Soviet Union and hard currency debt to Western creditors.

3363 Jorge, Antonio. How exportable is the Cuban model?: culture contact in a modern context (*in* The New Cuban presence in the Caribbean. Edited by Barry B. Levine. Boulder, Colo.: Westview Press, 1984, p. 211–233)

Concludes that Cuba's socioeconomic model, characterized by a high degree of centralization, high dependence on foreign aid (from the Soviet Union), and a high degree of personal control (Castro's) over economic decision making, is not likely to satisfy the real needs and objectives of most developing nations.

MacEwan, Arthur. El problema de la deuda externa en América Latina: ¿un callejón sin salida? See item **2919.**

3364 Marrero Artiles, Leví. Cuba: economía y sociedad. v. 9–11, Azúcar, Ilustración y conciencia: 1763–1868. Madrid: Editorial Playor, 1983–1984. 3 v. (319, 304, 237 p.): bibl., ill., index, maps, tables.

Three additional vols. of projected 16 on Cuban economic history began by author in 1972 (see *HLAS 43:3222* and *HLAS 45:3245*). These three vols. span reestablishment of Spanish rule after brief British occupation and beginning of independence war and cover following subjects: population, economic policies, land tenancy, agriculture, sugar production, tobacco and coffee industries, and developments in transportation.

3365 Pérez, Humberto. La plataforma programática y el desarrollo económico de Cuba (Cuba Socialista [La Habana] 3, junio 1982, p. 3–42)

Reviews results of the first five-year plan (1976–80) and objectives for the second (1981–85) in the context of guidelines for development adopted by the 1st Congress of the Cuban Communist Party.

3366 Radell, Willard W. Cuban-Soviet sugar trade, 1960–1976: how great was the subsidy? (JDA, 17:3, April 1983, p. 365–382)

Argues that conventional estimates of Soviet price subsidies to Cuba (e.g., those estimates made by the US CIA in item **3373**) concerning sugar trade are flawed and tend to overstate the extent of Soviet "generosity."

3367 Roca, Sergio. Economic policy and institutional change in socialist Cuba (Journal of Economic Issues [Assn. for Evolutionary Economics, Austin, Tx.] 17:2, June 1983, p. 405–413)

Evaluation of economic results of first five-yr. plan (1976–80). Speculates on prospects for the second five-yr. plan based on performance during the earlier period and developments in economic policy.

3368 ———. Rural public services in socialist Cuba (*in* Lonsdale, Richard E. and Gyorgy Enyedi. Rural public services: international comparisons. Boulder, Colo.: Westview Press, 1984, p. 225–244)

Explores urban/rural differentials in revolutionary Cuba with respect to delivery of public services. Shows that although elimination of urban/rural differentials has been an objective of the government, significant cleavages remain, particularly with regard to foodstuffs and consumer goods allocation and housing.

3369 Rodríguez, Carlos Rafael. Letra con filo. v. 2, Análisis y defensa de la economía. La Habana: Editorial de Ciencias Sociales, 1983. 570 p.

Useful collection of Rodríguez's economic writings and interviews with foreign media spanning 40 yrs. (1948–80). Essential for understanding the basis for revolutionary Cuba's development strategies.

3370 Rodríguez Mesa, Gonzalo M. El proceso de industrialización de la economía cubana. La Habana: Editorial de Ciencias Sociales, 1980. 324 p.: bibl., tables.

Important contribution. Describes Cuban industrialization strategy throughout mid-1970s and evaluates its effectiveness. According to author, Cuban industrialization model of this period stressed investments in the agricultural sector as a preliminary stage towards an accelerated industrialization that emphasized producer goods sector (along traditional socialist industrialization lines), beginning with the 1976–80 five-yr. plan.

3371 Rosa Castañeda, Héctor de la; Manuel Castro Tato; Vidal J. Rivero Pereira; and Carlos González Alvarez. Los criterios de eficiencia de inversiones. La Habana: Editorial de Ciencias Sociales, 1983. 187 p.

Collection of theoretical essays by a group of academic economists dealing with the role of investment in a centrally planned economy and with measures of investment efficiency. Cuban planners would do well to implement the cost-benefit analysis proposed in the volume as well as the methodology (in the Castro Tato and Rivero Pereira contribution) to analyze impact of industrial investment decisions on the balance of payments.

3372 Sánchez García-Calzadilla, María E. La participación de Cuba en la integración económica socialista (Revista Estadística [Instituto de Investigaciones Estadísticas (INSIE), La Habana] 5:9, dic. 1982, p. 59–87, bibl.)

Sketches Cuban economic relations with socialist countries. Emphasizes period prior to Cuba's formal entry into the Council for Mutual Economic Assistance (July 1982).

3373 United States. Central Intelligence Agency. Directorate of Intelligence. The Cuban economy: a statistical review.

Washington: CIA, 1984. 44 p.: tables (ALA 84–10052)

Useful compendium of economic statistics following the format of earlier issues (see *HLAS 45:3260*). Data originates primarily from Cuban official sources; exceptions are estimates of Cuban growth in GNP and of Soviet assistance to Cuba. Coverage focuses on 1970–82.

3374 Valdés, María Teresa. La evolución de la industria azucarera en Cuba y su papel en las relaciones económicas externas, 1959–1983 (Temas de Economía Mundial [La Habana] 10, 1984, p. 117–149)

Useful review of the performance of the sugar economy and exports during 1959–83.

3375 Valdés, Nelson P. Austeridad sin costo social: la deuda cubana (NSO, 68, sept./oct. 1983, p. 88–99)

Shallow analysis of the Cuban external debt situation and prospects. Fails to take into account large outstanding debt with the Soviet Union due in 1986 unless rolled over again. Contention that, unlike other debt-ridden nations, Cuba has been able to adjust its economy to meet debt obligations without incurring social costs is not supported by evidence presented. Diversion of public expenditures from productive to social activities, as is apparently the case in Cuba, is a short-sighted policy, costly in the medium and long term. Cuba's experience in managing an external debt is of little relevance from a policy standpoint because of the extent of its subsidization by the Soviet Union.

COLOMBIA AND ECUADOR

FRANCISCO E. THOUMI, *Chief, International Economics Section, Inter-American Development Bank*
CHARLOTTE JONES CARROLL, *Economist, The World Bank*
THOMAS F. CARROLL, *Professor of Economics, The George Washington University*

COLOMBIA

FEATURES OF THE LITERATURE on the Colombian economy that we discussed in *HLAS 45* (p. 295–296) have become more pronounced in publications issued in the last two years.

Works in English have declined markedly with only a minor book and a few articles annotated below. It would seem as if developments in Central America, Brazil, and the Southern Cone are not only monopolizing the attention of most English-speaking Latin Americanists, but that the traditional Colombian muddle deflects their interest or sparks no excitement among them.

Features of the economic literature on Colombia that have become more noticeable can be grouped under four categories. First, a heavy emphasis on empirical, sectoral and microeconomic policy issues. Remarkable in this respect is the scarcity of studies on fiscal, monetary, and exchange rate policies, while 20 percent of the books scanned deal with the agricultural sector. Secondly, more than one third of the monographs surveyed consists of collections of essays on specific topics or papers presented at seminars. This boom in compilations is concurrent with the survival struggle of new economic journals plagued by low subscription rates and poor sales. It would seem as if these collections of essays, that sell at a profit, fulfill the role that economic journals play in the US. Thirdly, a continuing trend is the scarcity of theoretical works. The few existing theoretical developments are found in leftist studies that interpret Colombian reality in Marxist terms, formulating economic theories that have no grounding on non-Marxist empirical studies. And fourthly, there is a notable increase in regional economics studies, especially in Antioquia, where the *Revista Antioqueña de Economía* is issued quarterly and where books on Antioquia's economic development and history have also been published.

That Colombian economic research is suffering because of a serious shortage of funds is evident in the decline in quality of some studies, and the heavy concentration in sectoral works which are easier to finance. Leading research institutions that developed in the 1970s are now suffering from erratic funding and precarious budgets while the most qualified researchers have relinquished either their field or their country. This problem is compounded by a significant decline in the enrollment of Colombian schools where economic research has traditionally been conducted. Clearly, such an environment is not conducive to intellectual debate, reflection or rigorous scholarship.

Given such circumstances it is not surprising that the quality of research is declining, a trend exemplified by the publication of large works without bibliographic references, barely revised, and poorly edited. One must conclude, regrettably, that in the last few years the level of scholarship of the economics profession in Colombia has retrogressed. [FT]

ECUADOR

As in the past years, there continues to be a scarcity of publications of quality on most economic issues in Ecuador. Works annotated below can be classified into: 1) general political-economic tracts; 2) economic development oriented project proposals, often region-specific and internationally sponsored; and 3) technical comments of a very narrow nature such as those on CEPE (item **3445**) and money supply (item **3447**). Many of the publications received by the Library of Congress are historical/sociological interpretations of Ecuadorian reality. The exceptions tend to be those studies sponsored in part by international aid agencies. One source of quality economic analysis mentioned in previous *HLAS* volumes—the local consultant firm, CONSULTEC—has, for the present at least, contributed most of its members to the Ecuadorian administration's cabinet. One document of note is the current country economic study of Ecuador by the World Bank (item **3436**).

With regard to pieces covering agrarian and rural questions, very few studies use original field data. A significant exception is the PRONAREG series (with French assistance), which provides regionalized descriptions of homogenous socioeconomic zones, which, combined with their previous work on land use classification is an extremely valuable basic information source (items **3440** and **3446**). Most of the sociologically-oriented research is the product of a network of Ecuadorian scholars in various academic and private consultant institutions such as FLACSO, PUCE, CIESE, and CEPLAES. These are frequently concerned with the consequences of land reform and consolidation of commercial agriculture on highland peasant communities. Coastal research material is rare.

Significant rural field research is still largely the domain of foreign scholars and, recently, foreign aid organizations. FAO has financed a study on rural poverty areas carried out by a local private organization, CESA, under the direction of a Belgian, Alain Dubly, AID, OAS, and the World Bank have financed studies on certain rural development project areas (in particular, Esmeraldas province, as in items **3440** and **3443**). AID has also funded studies on marketing, market town development, rural employment, and municipal development in intermediate population centers. Many of the resulting reports, however, are of limited circulation. Some scholarly works such as David Lehman's study of potato producers in Carchi will be published soon.

Since much recent work not based on field research drew on 1974 census data, one expects that a greater number of rural research studies will appear once the results of the 1982 census are fully available. [CJC and TFC]

COLOMBIA

3376 Acosta Medina, Amylkar. Glosas al contrato de El Cerrejón. Traducción de Francisco Justo Pérez. Medellín, Colombia: Editorial Lealón, 1981. 150 p.: appendices, bibl., ill.

Critical study of contract between Colombia and Exxon to exploit the coal mines of El Cerrejón. Argues that contract is detrimental to the country as it contains unjustifiable loopholes and other provisions that benefit Exxon.

3377 Ayala, Ulpiano. El empleo en las grandes ciudades colombianas. Bogotá: Centro de Estudios sobre Desarrollo Económico, Facultad de Economía, Univ. de los Andes, 1981. 3 v.: tables (Documento; 065)

Very detailed analysis of urban employment which discusses structure of employment, reproduction of the labor force and formation of social classes in Colombia.

3378 Bejarano, Jesús Antonio. La economía colombiana en la década del 70. Bogotá: Fondo Editorial CEREC, 1984. 161 p.: bibl., tables (Serie Textos; 2)

Collection of five essays in which author critically evaluates Colombian government policies during 1970s, particularly what he calls neoliberal theories applied by Pastrana, López, and Turbay administrations.

3379 ———. El régimen agrario: de la economía exportadora a la economía industrial. Bogotá: La Carreta, 1979. 370 p.: bibl., ill.

Small vol. uses Marxist capital accumulation framework to explain transition from an agricultural export-oriented economy to one which develops import substitution manufacturing. Focuses mainly on first four decades of this century.

3380 Berry, Albert R. and Ronald Soligo. Urban building and income distribution in Colombia: some relevant aspects (RU/SCID, 15:1, 1980, p. 39–60, bibl., graphs, tables)

Examines impact of construction boom promoted by Pastrana government. Concludes that employment of male, paid blue-collar workers increased significantly although impact on total employment was not that large and was merely temporary as López government changed strategies.

3381 Betancur, Belisario. Mensaje presidencial: informe al Congreso sobre la emergencia económica. Bogotá: Presidencia de la República, Secretaría de Información y Prensa, 1983. 142 p.

Small book made up by the report of President Belisario Betancur to the nation and congress. Spells out reasons why he determined that a "state of economic emergency" existed which, according to the constitution, allowed him to adopt several measures that by-passed congress.

3382 Botero Herrera, Fernando and Diego Sierra Botero. El mercado de fuerza de trabajo en la zona bananera de Urabá. Antioquia, Colombia: Univ. de Antioquia, Facultad de Ciencias Económicas, Centro de Investigaciones Económicas, 1981. 189 p.: ill.

Descriptive labor market study of Urabá, a banana growing area. Discusses in detail characteristics of labor demand and supply paying attention to technological aspects of production and to family relations of workers.

3383 Ciclo de Conferencias sobre la Política Económica y Social del Gobierno Nacional de Belisario Betancur, *Cali, Colombia, 1983.* La política económica y social del gobierno de Belisario Betancur. Vol. a cargo de Eduardo Lora. Cali: Corporación Editorial Universitaria de Colombia, 1983. 114 p.: bibl.

Compilation of essays on economic policies proposed by the Betancur government's development plan. Includes essays by high government officials and outside critics.

3384 Colombia. Depto. Nacional de Planeación. Cambio con equidad: Plan de Desarrollo, 1983–1986. Bogotá: El Depto., s.d. 1 v.

Betancur government's development plan. Sets guidelines to promote growth during world recession. Discusses sectoral growth, commercial policies, social policies, and plan's finances.

3385 ———. ———. Misión de Finanzas Intergubernamentales. Finanzas intergubernamentales en Colombia. Edición de Richard Bird. Bogotá: El Depto., 1981. 1 v.:

Most thorough report of government sector finances directed by Richard Bird. Provides main framework for tax and expenditure reforms proposed by the government at a later date.

3386 ———. ———. Plan de Integración Nacional, 1979–1982. Bogotá: El Depto., s.d. 1 v.

Turbay government's development plan. Emphasizes economic decentralization, mining and energy, and transport infrastructure development.

3387 Colombia 2000: estrategias de desarrollo para satisfacer las necesidas humanas esenciales en Colombia. Editor, Harold Banguero. Bogotá: Univ. de los Andes, Facultad de Economía, Centro de Estudios sobre Desarrollo Económico, 1982. 326 p.: bibl., ill., tables (Col. Debates-CEDE; 4)

Excellent study of policy and growth requirements that must be met to satisfy the basic needs of the Colombian population. Uses non-linear dynamic simulation model which projects demographic and economic variables trends for different social groups.

3388 Colombia en la economía mundial. Albrecht von Gleich, Diego Pizano Salazar, comps. Hamburg, FRG: Institut für Iberoamerika-Kunde, 1982. 288 p.: bibl., index, tables.

Collection of essays by top Colombian economists discuss country's relations with the Andean Group, European Economic Community, socialist countries, and nation's participation in the Tokyo Round, the international banana and coffee markets.

3389 Congreso Nacional de Comerciantes, 36th, Cúcuta, 1981. El empleo, el contrabando, las finanzas públicas y la integración fronteriza: cuatro grandes temas de interés nacional; documentos. Bogotá: Federación Nacional de Comerciantes, 1982. 212 p.: ill.

Compilation of papers presented at this congress discusses main economic issues affecting retail and wholesales in Colombia such as employment, contraband, border trade with Venezuela and Ecuador, and financial systems of local, departamental, and central governments.

3390 Controversia sobre el Plan de Vivienda sin Cuota Inicial. Fabio Giraldo Isaza, ed. Bogotá: Cámara Colombiana de la Construcción, 1983. 286 p.: ill.

Collection of essays about the controversial no-down-payment housing plan introduced by the Betancur government. Written a year after the program began, articles examine and evaluate several aspects. Authors are leading economists, politicians, and government officials that were involved in the program.

3391 Craig, Richard B. Domestic implications of illicit Colombian drug production and trafficking (SAGE/JIAS, 25:3, Aug. 1983, p. 325–350)

Argues that the government's drug eradication campaigns are inspired by the negative impact of the drug industry on Colombian society, and to a much lesser degree by US pressures on the Colombian government.

3392 Currie, Lauchlin Bernard. Moneda en Colombia: comportamiento y control. Bogotá: Fondo Cultural Cafetero, 1983. 171 p.: bibl., ill.

Discusses monetary policy in Colombia, its institutional limitations, and possible reforms. Emphasizes need for better and more frequent money supply information, if policies are to be improved.

Deas, Malcolm. The fiscal problem of nineteenth-century Colombia. See HLAS 46:2897.

3393 Decker, David R. and Ignacio Durán. The political, economic, and labor climate in Colombia. Philadelphia: Industrial Research Unit, Wharton School, Univ. of Pennsylvania, 1982. 129 p.: tables (Multinational industrial relations series, 0149–0818; 4. Latin American studies; 4e)

Concise country survey discusses Colombia's political system, main structural characteristics of its economy and pays special attention to labor law, relations, and organizations in the country.

3394 Déficit fiscal en Colombia: recopilación de las ponencias, comentarios y resúmenes referentes a los dos foros realizados en Medellín y Bogotá en septiembre 7 y 21 respectivamente. Presentación, Jesús A. Bejarano. Prólogo de Rodolfo González García. Comentaristas, Flor Angela Goméz et al. Bogotá: Fundación Fredrich Ebert de Colombia con patrocinio de la Contraloría General de la República, 1983. 144 p.: bibl., tables.

Leading Colombian economists and policy makers discuss growth of government's budget deficit in late 1970s and early 1980s. Several causes and explanations of such a deficit are offered.

3395 Drekonja-Kornat, Gerhard. Energieressourcen, Energiediskussion und Aussenpolitik (OLI/ZLW, 22, 1984, p. 57–73)

Anticipates improvement in Latin American energy resource planning by 1980s as countries such as Colombia strive to achieve "autonomía periférica." Also analyzes Colombian energy sources (e.g., coal, hydroelectric power, oil). Includes discussion of impact of energy planning on foreign policy formulation. [G.M. Dorn]

3396 Echavarría, Juan José and Alfredo L. Fuentes H. Relaciones económicas de Colombia con los países del Caribe insular. Bogotá: Banco de la República, 1981. 224 p.: bibl.

Very detailed study of Colombia's economic relations with CARICOM, Dutch Antilles, Puerto Rico, and the Dominican Republic. Explores ways to strengthen trade and financial flows in the region.

3397 —— and Guillermo Perry. Aranceles y subsidios a las exportaciones: análisis de su estructura sectorial y de su efecto en la apertura de la industria colombiana (FCE/TE, 50[1]:197, enero/marzo 1983, p. 269–306, bibl., tables)

Detailed study of protection and export subsidies which shows that in the 1967–74 period, the productive sectors receiving the highest subsidies were those in which social benefits exceeded private ones.

3398 Escobar, Christina. Trayectoria de la ANUC. Bogotá: CINEP, s.d. 177 p. (Colombia agraria; 6)

Chronological compilation of main events in the history of ANUC (Asociación Nacional de Usuarios Campesinos). Includes ANUC documents as well as reports on its activities and rural policies affecting them.

3399 El Estado y el desarrollo: ensayos sobre las formas de intervención, el poder económico, el sindicalismo y la empresa pública. Univ. de los Andes, Facultad de Economía, Centro de Estudios sobre Desarrollo Económico (CEDE). Bogotá: Editorial Dintel, 1982. 262 p.: bibl., ill. (Col. Debates-CEDE; 3)

Essays on types of government intervention, unions, public enterprises, and economic power in Colombia, Germany, and Chile. Of particular interest are works on the relation between the State and unions, social security policies and the State's role as regulator of economic power in Colombia.

3400 Estudio de la industria textil colombiana. Medellín, Colombia: Asociación Nacional de Industriales, 1983. 5 v. (1619 p.): ill.

Extremely detailed and comprehensive textile sector study describes the industry, its technology and equipment, markets, marketing problems, exports, imports, labor problems, finance, and labor productivity. In this context, also discusses cotton and wool separately as well as processes such as spinning, weaving, stamping/finishing, and knitting.

3401 Fajardo, D. et al. Campesinado y capitalismo en Colombia. Bogotá: Centro de Investigación y Educación Popular, 1981. 233 p.: bibl.

Compilation of six articles on rural policies and development. Three consist of historical analyses and three are empirical studies of tobacco in Boyacá, zizal in the country as a whole, and sugarcane in northern Cauca. Emphasis is on the welfare of employed peasants.

3402 Flórez, Luis B. and César González Muñoz. Industria, regiones y urbanización en Colombia. Bogotá: Editorial La Oveja Negra, 1983. 1 v.: tables.

Detailed study of manufacturing location, regional demand patterns, urban development, and regional development policies. Based on 1974 manufacturing data, but includes discussions of the dynamic aspects of regional and industrial growth.

3403 Forero Alvarez, Jaime and **Guillermo Rudas.** Producción y comercialización de perecederos agrícolas en zonas campesinas integradas al mercado de Bogotá: informe final del Componente Rural, Proyecto Mercadeo de Alimentos. Bogotá: Pontificia Univ. Javeriana, Facultad de Ciencias Económicas y Administrativas, Depto. de Investigación, 1983. 244 p.: bibl., ill., tables.

Very detailed study of production and marketing of fresh foods consumed in the Bogotá market. Discusses role of sharecropping, setting of prices, role of intermediaries and transportation. Concentrates on Bogotá highlands.

3404 Giraldo Samper, Diego and **Laureano Ladrón de Guevara C.** Desarrollo y colonización: el caso colombiano. Bogotá: Univ. Santo Tomás, Facultad de Sociología, 1981. 181 p.: bibl., ill.

Study of impact of the settlement process on the development of Colombian agriculture. Briefly covers history of settlements and emphasizes recent ones in Casanare, Urabá, Ariari-Guejar, and Caquetá.

3405 Gómez Arrubla, Fabio. Historia del Banco de la República: 60 años. Bogotá: El Banco, 1983. 323 p.: bibl. (Col. Banco de la República)

Very detailed history of Colombia's Central Bank covers events leading to its creation, ensuing evolution, financial systems, and finally, the bank's impact on Colombia's development.

Hernández G., María Magdalena. Bibliografía colombiana sobre pequeña y mediana industria, 1960–1980. See item **33.**

Hyland, Richard P. A fragile prosperity: credit and agrarian structure in the Cauca Valley, Colombia, 1851–87. See *HLAS 46:2901.*

3406 Lecturas sobre el sector externo de la economía colombiana: selección de documentos. Javier Ballesteros Mejía, ed. Bogotá: Facultad de Ciencias Económicas y Administrativas, Pontificia Univ. Javeriana, 1982. 189 p.: bibl., tables.

Compilation of presentations delivered at a 1982 seminar on Colombia's foreign sector. Although interesting, they lack empirical analysis, and, with one exception,

bibliographical references. Many authors are former Colombian policy makers.

3407 Lleras Restrepo, Carlos. La cuestión agraria, 1933–1971. Bogotá: Osprey Impresores, 1982. 375 p.: tables.

Collection of Lleras Restrepo's writings and speeches on rural sector issues (1933–71). Shows former President's ideas and their evolution.

3408 Mayer, Thomas. Export diversification as a counter to export instability: the example of Colombia. Kiel: Kiel Institute of World Economics, 1982. 21 leaves: bibl. (Kieler Arbeitspapiere; 145)

Examines income and allocation effects of an appropriate export diversification policy by using a computable general equilibrium model. Results show that an appropriate diversification of exports would raise income in the Colombian economy. [J. Salazar-Carrillo]

3409 Mendoza Morales, Alberto and **Angela Mendoza.** Retorno al campo. Bogotá: Editorial Orbs, 1981. 185 p.: bibl., ill., tables.

Study of rural sector covers topic from historical and regional angles. Proposes development strategy, based on rural development, which would make this sector the leading one in the country. Work won the Mario Ospina Pérez Prize in 1980.

3410 Navas Pinzón, Jorge. El salario de los pobres: ideas para desconcentrar el ingreso y la riqueza. Bogotá: Ediciones Tercer Mundo, 1983. 223 p.: bibl.

Policy proposal to the national convention of Colombia's Conservative Party. Argues that it is possible to raise salaries at the expense of rents and profits, without lowering employment. Some of its policy proposals such as an employment tax credit are interesting, but the economic analysis is fairly weak.

3411 Nuevas alternativas industriales para Colombia. Coordinador, Gabriel Poveda Ramos. Bogotá: Instituto de Fomento Industrial, 1982. 196 p.: bibl., ill., tables.

Sectoral study designed to identify manufacturing projects which are candidates for development during the 1980s. Financed by the Instituto de Fomento Industrial, this work was designed to promote a dialogue about country's industrial future, between the private and public sectors.

3412 Nutrición. Bogotá: Depto. Nacional de Planeación, 1979. 114 p.: bibl., ill., plates (DNP. PIA/PNAN. UNICEF)
Contains National Plan on Food and Nutrition of the López administration. Also includes good essays by leading experts on a few key nutritional issues particularly those affecting pregnant women and small children.

3413 Ocampo, José Antonio and Santiago Montenegro. Crisis mundial, protección e industrialización: ensayos de historia económica colombiana. Bogotá: Fondo Editorial CEREC, 1984. 400 p.: bibl., ill., tables (Serie Textos; 3)
Very good compilation of essays on the economic history of industrialization and protectionism. Emphasis is on industrial development as of 1900, especially 1900–50.

3414 Perry, Guillermo et al. Economía mundial y la economía colombiana. Bogotá: Univ. Nacional de Colombia, Facultad de Ciencias Económicas, Depto. de Economía, 1982. 100 p.: ill., tables.
Collection of essays by leading left-of-center Colombian economists on the world economy and Colombia's external sector that cover: world energy crisis, non-traditional exports, and the Colombian economy's further opening to international trade.

3415 Perry, Santiago. La crisis agraria en Colombia, 1950–1980. Bogotá: Ancora Editores, 1983. 202 p.: bibl., maps.
Marxist study of the rural sector. Discusses production systems and agricultural policies prevailing in Colombia and attributes sector's low rate of growth to structural characteristics of capitalist development and American imperialism.

3416 ¿Qué quedó de la emergencia económica? Coordinadora, Cecilia Acevedo de Molano. Bogotá: Biblioteca de la Cámara de Comercio, 1983. 272 p.
Under an "economic emergency" decree which allows the executive to by-pass congress, the government legislated the 1982 tax reform. Later, the Supreme Court denied its constitutionality. Provides chronology of these measures and includes Supreme Court opinions concerning them.

3417 Rey de Marulanda, Nohra. El trabajo de la mujer. Bogotá: Centro de Estudios sobre Desarrollo Económico, Facultad de Economía, Univ. de los Andes, 1981. 182 p.: bibl., tables (Documento; 063)
Very good study of women's employment in large Colombian cities. Provides characteristics of women in the labor force, their jobs, and changes in female employment during 1970s.

3418 Ridler, Neil B. Labour forces and land distributional effects of agricultural technology: a case study of coffee (WD, 11:7, July 1983, p. 593–599)
Examination of the implications of new coffee technologies on the Colombian coffee sector. Concludes that new technologies currently being applied will cause significant labor dislocations as they increase productivity in a sector with low international demand elasticities.

3419 Salama, Pierre et al. La problemática del empleo en América Latina y en Colombia. Medellín: Univ. de Antioquia, Facultad de Ciencias Económicas, Centro de Investigaciones Económicas, 1982. 363 p.: bibl., ill.
Compilation of articles by leading international and Colombian experts on employment issues. While the emphasis is on Colombia, they also deal with the energy crisis and employment as well as with technology and the employment of Colombians in New York and Venezuela.

3420 Sarkis, Bassam. El sistema de relaciones industriales en Colombia. Bogotá: Univ. de los Andes, Facultad de Administración, 1983. 286 p.: bibl., ill.
Designed to fulfill two objectives: 1) to analyze Colombian industrial relations emphasizing Labor Ministry's role, participation of unions, employers organizations, civil service, etc.; and 2) to provide a textbook. Author succeeds in achieving both goals.

3421 Sarmiento Palacio, Eduardo. Inflación, producción y comercio internacional. Bogotá: FEDESARROLLO, Procultura, 1982. 1 v.: tables.
Very good collection of Sarmiento's essays discuss the 1970s monetary experience, ensuing stabilization policies, the Turbay government's development plan, fiscal deficits, and industrialization problems that emerged. Excellent policy analysis by a most qualified policy maker.

3422 Silva Colmenares, Julio. Tras la máscara del subdesarrollo: dependencia y monopolios. Bogotá: C. Valencia Editores, 1983. 267 p.: bibl.

Marxist-Leninist study attributes Colombian underdevelopment to monopolist market structures that evolve under capitalism, and to Latin American dependency. Chapters on Colombia emphasize Colombian dependency and monopolies in the financial sector.

3423 Simposio Los Estudios Regionales en Colombia: el Caso de Antioquia, *Medellín, Colombia, 1979.* Memoria. Medellín: Fondo Rotatorio de Publicaciones FAES, 1982. 308 p.: bibl., ill., tables (Biblioteca colombiana de ciencias sociales; 5)

Excellent compilation by top economic historians who specialize in Colombia. Articles deal with aspects of Antioquia's economic history and development. Emphasis is on the role of manufacturing, mining, coffee, and entrepreneurship in Antioquia's growth.

3424 El Sistema colombiano de ahorro y vivienda. Servicios de Información Ltda. [and] Econometría Ltda. Bogotá: Banco Central Hipotecario, 1983. 173 p.: ill., tables.

Very good study of housing market includes econometric housing supply and demand functions, a simulation model and an analysis of housing finance systems in Colombia.

3425 Soler, Yezid and Fabio Prieto. Bonanza y crisis del oro blanco, 1960–1980. Bogotá: Editográficas, 1982. 192 p.: bibl., ill.

Detailed study of the development of cotton production, its boom from 1960 on, and its crisis in the late 1970s. Study is based on good data about costs, output, prices, cultivated areas, marketing, etc. Necessary reading for anyone doing further work on this topic.

3426 Udall, Alan. Urbanization and rural labor supply: a historical study of Bogotá, Colombia since 1920 (RU/SCID, 16:3, 1980, p. 70–83, bibl., graphs, tables)

Study of interrelationships between Bogotá's growth and the rural labor market in nearby areas. Concludes that modernization of the rural sector was a more important cause of labor migration to Bogotá than city's high wages.

3427 Vallejo Mejía, Hernán. Productos básicos, dependencia y subdesarrollo: el problema bananero. Bogotá: Ediciones Tercer Mundo, 1982. 295 p.

Study of the origins, developments and accomplishments of the Banana Exporting Countries Union and the Multinational Banana Marketing Organization. Provides excellent analysis of world banana markets which are discussed within a GATT/UNCTAD framework.

3428 Velásquez E., Marta Inés. Evaluación del régimen salarial y prestacional colombiano. Bogotá: ANIF-Fondo Editorial, 1982. 137 p.: bibl., ill. (Documentos ANIF)

Analysis of salary behavior patterns in Colombia during 1970s. Focuses on how such patterns affect other important economic variables (e.g., inflation, GNP, unemployment, productivity). [J. Salazar Carrillo]

ECUADOR

3429 Barsky, Osvaldo and Gustavo Cosse. Tecnología y cambio social: las haciendas lecheras del Ecuador. Quito: Facultad Latinoamericana de Ciencias Sociales, 1981. 199 p.: bibl., ill.

Well documented review of transformation of traditional highland haciendas into specialized dairy farms of high productivity during 1960s and 1970s. Discusses role of modernizing agrarian elites and official institutions in assisting process of technological change. Part of IICA-sponsored series on agricultural technology.

3430 ——— et al. Políticas agrarias, colonización y desarrollo rural en Ecuador: reflexiones sobre el proyecto de desarrollo rural integral Quininde-Malimpia-Nueva Jerusalem. Quito: Ediciones CEPLAES, 1982. 293 p.: bibl., maps.

Interesting case study on formulation of rural development project in Esmeraldas prov. subsequently financed by World Bank. First third provides general material on land reform and rural development in Ecuador. Three of authors were members of OAS advisory team. Emphasis is on participatory style of problem analysis and program definition, equity of benefits and bridge between traditional peasant and modern market systems.

3431 —— *et al.* El proceso de transformación de la producción lechera serrana y el aparato de generación transferencia en Ecuador. Quito: Facultad Latinoamericana de Ciencias Sociales (FLACSO), 1980. 557 p.: bibl., ill., tables (Documento PROTAAL; 40)

An IICA-FLACSO-SEDE Quito study of the highland dairy industry with particular attention to technology and the transfer of same. Presumably No. 40 in the monographic series PROTAAL devoted to agricultural technology in Latin America. [J.M. Hunter]

3432 Chiriboga, Manuel and **Renato Piccino.** La producción campesina cacaotera: problemas y perspectivas. Quito: Centro de Capacitación Campesina del Azuay: Centro de Arte y Acción Popular, 1982. 120 p.: ill., tables (Cuadernos de discusión popular; 6)

Political tract written on behalf of a coastal agricultural workers union (UROCAL) to sensitize members to issues in labor conflicts on cacao estates. Denounces national and international monopolies.

3433 —— *et al.* Ecuador agrario: ensayos de interpretación. Quito: El Conejo, 1984. 237 p.: tables.

Collection of six essays—typical of recent Ecuadorian interpretation of so-called "rural crisis"—representing twin problems of slow agricultural growth and unequal income distribution. Sociologist authors share neo-Marxist and nationalistic outlook. Only original contribution is Verdesoto's analysis of rural voting patterns 1978–80.

3434 Coyuntura económica: análisis y perspectiva de la economía ecuatoriana. Ernesto Arroba, ed. S.l.: Consultora para el Desarrollo Nacional (CONSULDENAC), 1982. 159 p.

Review of 1981 economic activities by sector, prepared by local consultant firm. Data in tables drawn from official sources. Presentation is descriptive and anecdotal, with little analysis.

3435 Economía, Ecuador, 1830–1980. Coordinación del proyecto, Enrique Ayala Mora. Coordinador del vol. 3, Alberto Acosta Espinosa. Supervisión editorial, Francisco Avila Paredes. Quito: Corporación Editora Nacional, 1983. 2 v.: bibl., ill., tables (Libro del sesquicentenario; 3)

Consists of 27 short essays on economic history of the Republic era by Ec-

uadorian economists, including businessmen, scholars and former government leaders (biographies provided). Covers general panorama, labor, agrarian and productive sectors. Repetitive. Format prevents treatment of subjects in depth but some useful information provided.

3436 Ecuador: an agenda for recovery and sustained growth. Washington: World Bank, 1984. 183 p.: ill. (some col.), plates (A World Bank country study)

Country economic study by key institution, with data through 1983 and projections to 1990. Covers agricultural, industrial, and petroleum sectors in addition to macroeconomic analyses. Generally widely sought source material for academics and those active in Ecuador studies.

3437 Ecuador, el mito del desarrollo. Coordinación, Sohel Riffka. Quito: Editorial El Conejo: Instituto Latinoamericano de Investigaciones Sociales (ILDIS), 1982. 237 p.: bibl., ill., tables (Col. Ecuador/hoy)

Collected conference papers analyze 1972–82 decade, in which social scientists reviewed transformation of country resulting from new petroleum income. Examines increased role of the State in agricultural and urban sectors. Concludes that decade's high growth was not equitable, owing to fundamental structural problems.

3438 Estructuras agrarias y reproducción campesina: lecturas sobre transformaciones capitalistas en el agro ecuatoriano. Selección de textos y comentario de Cristian Sepúlveda. Quito: Instituto de Investigaciones Económicas, Pontificia Univ. Católica del Ecuador, 1982. 294 p.: bibl., ill., tables (Publicaciones IIE-PUCE)

Collection of seven articles that review recent agrarian history and peasant problems in Central Highlands. Authors are from Quito's Catholic Univ. Economic Research Institute. Approach is sociological and neo-Marxist. Main themes: land reform impact limited to hastening break-up of haciendas into more intensive commercial estates (mostly dairy) with reduced labor demand; subsistence farming more vulnerable; social conflict on rise. Otavalo case study illustrates successful adjustment of one community.

Estudo comparativo da indústria de alimentos: administração e política de tecnologia na América Latina. See item **2482.**

3439 Farrell, Gilda. Mercado de trabajo urbano y movimiento sindical. Quito: Pontificia Univ. Católica del Ecuador (PUCE), Instituto de Investigaciones Económicas (IIE), 1982. 209 p.: bibl., ill., tables (Avance de investigación)

Compilation of labor-related information for period 1966–78 includes employment data for different industries, wage rates, employment conditions, trends in productivity and degrees of unionization. Part of social science monographic series issued by Ecuador's Catholic Univ.

3440 Flores Y., Marco. Gastos anuales por tamaño de unidad de producción agropecuaria. Quito: Programa Nacional de Regionalización Agraria, 1981. 75 leaves: tables (Diagnóstico socioeconómico del medio rural ecuatoriano)

Summarizes in table form results of 1975 survey of annual family expenditures by farm size (13 categories, seven farm sizes). Part of monographic series on socioeconomic conditions issued by Agriculture Ministry with French assistance.

3441 Friese, Thomas. Industriepolitik und Ausländische Direktinvestitionen in Ecuador. Freiburg i. Br., FRG: Univ. Freiburg, 1983. 183 p.: tables (Institut für Entwicklungspolitik Schriften; 10)

Examines industrialization and foreign investment in Ecuador and how these factors have contributed to country's modernization. Points out positive gains, as well as setbacks, the Central Bank's important role, and relevance of sound economic planning. [G.M. Dorn]

Grunwald, Joseph. Reconstrucción de la industria maquiladora. See item **2881**.

Ibarra, Hernán. Ecuador, bibliografía analítica agraria, 1900–1982. See *HLAS 46:25*.

3442 Instituto Ecuatoriano de Recursos Hidráulicos (INERHI). Plan de desarrollo, región I: Esmeraldas-Carchi-Imbabura. Quito: Secretaría General de la Organización de los Estados Americanos, 1980. 361 p.: ill., maps, tables.

River Basin Development Plan for northern region (Esmeraldas, Carchi, Imbabura, and Napo provs.) prepared by Ecuador's National Irrigation Institute and Planning Office with OAS assistance. Good recent data on existing infrastructure and production patterns with detailed proposals for development.

3443 Jaramillo, Marco. Diagnóstico socioeconómico de la Provincia de Esmeraldas. Otavalo, Ecuador: Instituto Otavaleño de Antropología, 1980. 2 v.: bibl., ill., maps, tables (Serie Antropología social; 10A. Col. Pendoneros; 37–38)

Review of Ecuador's first major local planning effort (in northwestern prov. of Esmeraldas), written by then head of rural development unit of National Planning Council. Rich in detail on proposed projects in agroindustry, forestry, new crops, livestock, tourism, health, education, transport, and rural development.

3444 Macías, W. Problemas socioeconómicos del Ecuador. Otavalo, Ecuador: Editorial Gallo Capitán, 1983. 332 p. (Ecuatextos; 1)

Intended as a secondary text, with mini-exams for each chap., it is worth noting as a representative example of an Ecuadorian neo-Marxist view of the country's history. Its description of origins of the country's structural problems (e.g., struggle between coastal agroexporters and highland landholders) reflects deeply imbedded regionalism that affects internal sociopolitical relations today. Includes exhaustive treatment of education system.

Orlandi, Alberto. América Latina y la economía mundial del café. See item **2947**.

3445 Pástor, Wilson; Xavier Lasso; and Oscar Garzón. CEPE y la apertura al capital externo: análisis crítico de las reformas a las Leyes de Hidrocarburos y Impuesto a la Renta y proposiciones alternas. Quito: Editorial El Conejo, 1981. 254 p. (Col. Ecuador/hoy)

Technical critique of reforms to hydrocarbons law and tax incentives proposed by Roldós Administration (1979–84) to attract foreign investors to the petroleum sector. Main objections are service contract concept and methodology of calculating income tax for foreign companies. Argument now overtaken by events.

3446 Ramos P., Manuel and Emanuel Faoroux. Las Zonas socio económicas actualmente homogéneas de la región amazónica ecuatoriana. Quito: Programa Nacional de Regionalización Agraria: Instituto

Latinoamericano de Investigaciones Sociales, 1980. 112 p.: ill., plates, tables (Diagnóstico socioecónomico del medio rural ecuatoriano; D)

Description of rural conditions in three Amazonian provs. Includes map breaking country into 57 homogeneous agrosocioeconomic zones. Data based on 1974 census, 1976–78 field observations and relevant historical reports. Useful reference produced by Agriculture Ministry with aid of French technical assistance.

3447 Reunión de Técnicos de Bancos Centrales del Continente Americano, *20th, La Paz, 1983.* XX [i.e. Vigésima] Reunión de Técnicos de Bancos Centrales del Continente Americano. v. 15. La Paz: Banco Central de Bolivia, 1983. 1 v.: ill., tables.

Vol. 15 of 38 (see item **3080**) is entitled *Money supply and its determinants in Ecuador: 1970–82.* Analyzes effects of income generated by oil and coffee booms on money supply, with data from Central Bank. Author uses only M1 (cash and checking accounts) as definition of money supply, rather than more sophisticated forms of financial intermediation. Concludes that by itself monetary policy is inadequate to achieve equitable growth in Ecuador's case.

3448 Roberts, Lois Crawford de. El Ecuador en la época cacaotera: respuestas locales al auge y colapso en el ciclo monoexportador. Traductores, Erika Silva y Rafael Quintero. Quito: Univ. Central del Ecuador, Editorial Universitaria, 1980. 276 p.: bibl., tables.

History, based on primary sources, of cocoa boom and bust era (1890–1925). Analyzes impact of unprecedented export earnings on Ecuadorian growth and coastal society and how country coped with collapse of cocoa market after World War I. Translation and first publication of PhD thesis written in 1960s.

3449 Sashin, G.Z. Ekvador. Moskva: Mysl, 1981. 150 p.: bibl., ill., tables (Sotsialno-ekonomicheskie problemy razvivaiushchikhsia stran)

Soviet survey of Ecuador's economic situation, foreign and domestic. Examines some social aspects and consequences. Major source appears to be *El Comercio.* [R.V. Allen]

3450 Vicuña Izquierdo, Leonardo. Economía ecuatoriana: algunos de sus problemas y la política económica reciente. Guayaquil, Ecuador: Imprenta de la Univ. de Guayaquil, 1982. 209 p.

Critique of Roldos Administration economic policies by well known academic (Univ. of Guayaquil) who represented universities on national planning board. Focus is on 1980–81 period. Highly repetitive collection of articles asserting that five-yr. plan sustains dependency of workers and campesinos, providing no channel for their participation.

VENEZUELA

JORGE SALAZAR-CARRILLO, *Chairman and Professor of Economics, Florida International University, Non-Resident Staff Member, Brookings Institution*
MOSTAFA HASSAN, *Visiting Professor of Economics, Florida International University*

IN THE LAST TWO YEARS, the economic literature on Venezuela has largely recovered from the decline we noted in *HLAS 45* (p. 303). Contrary to what was anticipated, the 1970s oil boom and the resulting beneficial trade gains have had negative effects on some sectors of the economy as well as on intellectual pursuits. Among the latter we include economic research which, ironically, blossomed after the oil bubble burst. It seems as if Venezuelans prefer to examine their problems in earnest only in troubled times. After the booming income, provided by a ten-fold oil price increase between 1973–82, failed to solve the nation's economic problems, Venezuelans began devoting their attention to them. Such concerns are evident in the growing number of works annotated for this *Handbook* volume.

Of all the works we have selected, the majority are official documents and/or government-sponsored studies. These are followed by academic publications or university-sponsored works. Third in importance are studies by private researchers. As expected, a large proportion of these publications concern the oil industry and related topics. Nevertheless, a surprisingly large number deal with non-petroleum aspects of the economy. Other subjects commanding attention are international economic relations, economic history, agrarian problems, technological developments, and income distribution.

Among writers whose contributions deserve special mention, we should note Tomás Enrique Carrillo-Batalla (items **3463** and **3464**). Especially worthwhile is his history of Venezuelan public finances and the changing ideologies that preceded and justified their modifications throughout the years (items **3465** and **3478**). Important contributions on Venezuelan industrialization are articles by Bitar and Troncoso (item **3460**) and Sonntag (item **3499**) as well monographs by Jongkind (item **3479**) and Karlsson (item **3480**). The last two works were published, respectively, in Amsterdam and Stockholm and attest to the interest generated by the Venezuelan experience among European economists. Indeed, most of the publications listed in the bibliography below are by Venezuelans with some European authors. North American contributions, however, are conspicuously lacking. In addition to the works noted above, studies that command attention are those resulting from government-sponsored projects and devoted to urban-regional economics. In brief, the literature on the Venezuelan economy generated during the last biennium demonstrates greater breadth and depth than in previous years.

Still, in terms of quality, much of Venezuela's economic literature continues to lag behind the best of the equivalent literature published in Brazil, Mexico and Argentina. One continues to expect the best from Venezuelan economists whose accomplishments are considerable indeed. Likewise, one expects of North American scholars a rekindling of interest in a leading nation of the Caribbean basin whose strategic importance and economic power should not be ignored.

3451 Acedo, Clemy Machado de *et al.*
Estado y grupos económicos en Venezuela: su análisis, a través de la tierra, construcción y banca. Caracas: Editorial Ateneo de Caracas, 1981. 296 p.: bibl., ill., tables (Col. Ensayo)
Analyzes effects of governmental policies on the country's socioeconomic structure. Focuses on 1944–59 period, and mainly on effects of public policy on real estate, construction, and banking industries.

3452 Alfonzo Ravard, Rafael. Cinco años de normalidad operativa: 1975–1980: discursos. Caracas: Petróleos de Venezuela, 1981. 370 p.: ill., tables.
Contains lectures delivered by President of Petróleos de Venezuela, entity responsible for nation's petroleum industry after its nationalization in 1975. Covers: formation and organization of Petróleos de Venezuela; institutional, professional, and administrative progress; importance of training and

technical development; future plans; and international perspectives on energy issues.

3453 Alvarez, Rubén. Pequeña y mediana industria en Venezuela. Caracas: Nueva Voz, 1979. 165 p.: bibl., ill., plates, tables (Col. Estudios)
Analyzes characteristics of small and middle industries and explains their role in the Venezuelan economy. Covers problems encountered and provides solutions concerning financing, production, distribution, human resources, and organization.

3454 Arellano Moreno, Antonio. Orígenes de la economía venezolana. 4a ed. corr. y aum. Caracas: Univ. Central de Venezuela, Ediciones de la Biblioteca, 1982. 400 p.: bibl., map (Col. Ciencias económicas; 4)
Essay on Venezuelan economic history. Describes country's socioeconomic structure between precolumbian times and 19th century. Focuses on international as well as na-

tional commercial relations and prevailing sociopolitical climate.

3455 Arocha Saturno, Norma and **Francisco Irureta.** Technological policies in the pharmaceutical sector in Venezuela: study. New York: UN Conference on Trade and Development, 1982. 31 p.: bibl. (UNCTAC/TT/25)

Focuses on main features of pharmaceutical industry in Venezuela. Describes in detail policies and institutional framework that govern procurement, import, registration, quality control, and price of pharmaceutical products.

3456 Atkinson, L. Jay and **Oswald R. Blaich.** Venezuela: a prospective market for grain and livestock products. Washington: US Dept. of Agriculture, Economic Research Service, 1983. 16 p.: tables (Foreign agricultural economic report; 189)

After examining agricultural production trends, food prices and policies, and grain-livestock prospects, concludes that Venezuela will continue to depend on agricultural imports to meet increasing domestic consumption needs, despite agricultural programs following oil revenue increase in mid 1970s. Covers production of livestock, rice, grain sorghum, and corn.

3457 Balestrini C., Cesar. Economía y política petrolera. Caracas: Librería La Lógica, 1984. 355 p.: ill.

Major study of oil industry: petroleum economics; mines and hydrocarbons legislation; US's and Venezuela's oil policies; Venezuela's energy situation; world oil production and reserves; oil history in Venezuela; nationalization; petroleum refining; financial aspects; OPEC; oil industry in Latin America and Mexico; natural gas and steel industries.

3459 Bilbao, Rafael R. To sow or not to sow: a historiographical essay on the Venezuelan agrarian question: 1973–1980 (PAIGH/H, 94, julio/dic. 1982, p. 133–150, bibl.)

Analyzes obstacles to agrarian development in Venezuela, reviews opinions and recommendations made by agricultural experts for improving the agricultural sector, and makes suggestions that would insure sustained agricultural growth.

3460 Bitar, Sergio and **Eduardo Troncoso.** La industrialización de Venezuela: 1950–

1980 (FCE/TE, 49[2]:194, abril/junio 1982, p. 265–294, tables)

Key article analyzes nature and characteristics of Venezuela's industrial sector. Draws comparisons with other Latin American economies. Believes industrial planning and policy are essential for the continuation of the notable industrial expansion begun in 1950.

3461 Burgos Villasmil, José R. Aspectos fundamentales de la sociedad anónima y del mercado de capitales. Caracas: Facultad de Ciencias Jurídicas y Políticas, Univ. Central de Venezuela, 1982. 255 p.: bibl.

Examines legal aspects of the corporation of Venezuela. Opens with general essay on it followed by 14 chaps. providing much detail on various aspects (e.g., business, partnership, regulations, capital, stocks, bonds, profits, Caracas stock market, etc.).

Business Yearbook of Brazil, Mexico & Venezuela. See item **2791.**

3462 Calderón Berti, Humberto. La coyuntura petrolera venezolana, 1982. Caracas: Ministerio de Energía y Minas, 1982. 46 p.: ill., tables (La Alquitrana; 9)

Collection of 1982 speeches by Minister of mining and hydrocarbons, Humberto Calderón Berti. Main topic: present and future health of Venezuela's petroleum industry in world context.

3463 Carrillo Batalla, Tomás Enrique. La distribución del ingreso en Venezuela: analísis crítico de una obra de la Dra. Lourdes de Ferrán (ACPS/B, 38:85/86, julio/dic 1981, p. 210–223, tables)

Critique of Ferrán's work based on analysis of income distribution in Venezuela. Points out main contributions and conclusions of her exhaustive study.

3464 ———. Historia crítica de la teoría de las fluctuaciones económicas y analísis del caso venezolano (ACPS/B, 38:85/86, julio/dic. 1981, p. 8–30)

Two-pt. essay on history of economic thought: 1) history of universal economic thought and different theories on economic fluctuations; and 2) results of empirical study of the Venezuelan economy.

3465 ———. Historia del pensamiento rector de las finanzas públicas nacionales: investigación analítica. Caracas: Academia de Ciencias Políticas y Sociales, 1983. 5 v.: bibl., ill., tables (Biblioteca de la Academia. Serie Clásicos de la finanzas públicas; 1–5)

Analysis of historical evolution of Venezuelan public finances. Compilation of actions taken up by Venezuela's Ministry of Finance (1830–1979).

3466 Consejo de Bienestar Rural, *Caracas.* Productos frutícolas y hortícolas: estudio integral del sector. Coordinador, Alonso Calatrava. Caracas: Banco Central de Venezuela, 1979. 532 p.: bibl., graphs (Col. Agricultura en Venezuela; 5)

Analysis of agricultural production in Venezuela. Emphasizes on main facets of production and distribution of fruits and vegetables. Includes statistics such as supply, prices, imports and exports for each product.

3467 La Cooperación internacional de Venezuela, lo realizado entre 1974–1981, las previsiones, 1981–1985: solidaridad en acción = The International cooperation of Venezuela, achievements between 1974–1981, provisions for 1981–1985: solidarity in action. Caracas: Ministerio de Información y Turismo, 1982. 96 p.: ill., tables.

Examines Venezuela's foreign economic policies in the Third World (e.g., financial assistance to Central American countries and Panama, establishment of Special Fund for the Caribbean, reciprocal credits, loans, credit lines, donations, scholarships, etc.)

3468 Country risk analysis, Venezuela: seminar report. Edited by Alice B. Lentz and Geoffrey S. Howard. New York: Fund for Multinational Management Education (FMME): Council of the Americas, 1981. 93 p.

Report that resulted from seminar organized by the Fund and the Council (New York, 1981). Focuses on socioeconomic and political climate in Venezuela and possibilities for change.

3469 Crazut, Rafael J. El Banco Central de Venezuela: notas sobre su historia y evolución, 1940–1980. 2a ed. Caracas: Banco Central de Venezuela, 1980. 334 p.: bibl. (Col. de estudios económicos; 7)

Encompasses history of Venezuela's Central Bank. Focuses on its conduction of monetary policy throughout the years and on its crucial role as "lender of last resort." Describes different instruments available for conducting such a monetary policy and their limitations.

3470 Crist, Raymond E. Westward thrusts the pioneers zone in Venezuela: a half century of economic development along the Llanos-Andes border (AJES, 42:4, Oct. 1983, p. 451–462)

Describes development that took place over last half century in Venezuela's Llanos-Andes border area. Summarizes factors that caused rapid thrust westward of pioneer zone along this border (e.g., public education, health, highway construction, government credit and subsidies, technologies).

3471 D'Ascoli, Carlos Alberto. Del mito del Dorado a la economía del café: esquema histórico económico de Venezuela. 2a ed. Caracas: Monte Avila Editores, 1980. 402 p.: bibl. (Col. Estudios)

Essay on Venezuelan economic history. Describes and analyzes evolution of nation's economy from Spanish colonization up to oil discovery. Previously published as *Esquema histórico-económico de Venezuela* (1970).

3472 Empleo y distribución del ingreso en Venezuela. Santiago: Organización Internacional del Trabajo, Programa Mundial del Empleo (PREALC), 1980. 92 p.: bibl., tables (Documento de trabajo; 193)

Complete analysis of employment and distribution of income in Venezuela divided into three sections: 1) labor's forces of supply and demand during last two decades and labor's main features; 2) effects of increasing oil revenues on inflation and income distribution; and 3) relationship between human capital and the national development process.

3473 Estadísticas de la Región Guayana. Caracas: Corporación Venezolana de Guayana, Div. de Estudio, Programación e Investigación, Sub-gerencia de Estadística, 1980. 312 p.: bibl., ill., tables.

Extensive statistical information on Guayana region for 1970–80. Includes information on population size, migration, family income, housing, price level, consumption, and other important socioeconomic characteristics and variables.

3474 Fundación para el Desarrollo de la Comunidad y Fomento Municipal. Bibliografía nacional comentada sobre desarrollo de la comunidad. Caracas: CEDISAM, 1981. 91 leaves: indexes.

Annotated bibliography of selected works by Venezuelan authors concerning economic development at the national and rural levels.

3475 Giménez Landínez, Víctor Manuel. Montaña Verde: un caso de reforma agraria. Caracas: Fondo de Crédito Agropecuario, 1982. 178 p.: bibl., ill., tables (Serie Desarrollo rural)

Discussion of legal, economic, and social aspects of "Montaña Verde," most debated case in Venezuela's agrarian reform since the law's creation. Presents contrasting arguments that arose and several social problems that resulted from it.

3476 ———. Reforma agraria y desarrollo rural integrado: marco conceptual e implicaciones jurídicas. 3a ed. Caracas: Fondo de Crédito Agropecuario, 1981. 275 p.: bibl., tables (Serie Desarrollo rural)

Concentrates on principal characteristics of modern agrarian reform. Explains various concepts of rural development and reform, and relates them to experience of several countries. Also deals with legal aspects of agrarian reform.

3477 Henao Jaramillo, Jaime. El café en Venezuela. Caracas: Univ. Central de Venezuela, Ediciones de la Biblioteca, 1982. 291 p.: bibl., ill. (some col.), tables (Col. Ciencias biológicas; 7)

Two factors have adversely affected Venezuela's agricultural sector: the petroleum industry by creating investment opportunities that produced higher returns than agriculture; and 2) depressed agricultural prices often lower than production costs. Coffee, however, produces the highest export value in agriculture and generates a relatively high percentage of employment. Also discusses various aspects of coffee as crop and product (e.g., history; production; varieties, types, and qualities of coffee; climate required; processing techniques; pests, chemicals, and fertilizers; etc.).

3478 Historia de las finanzas públicas en Venezuela. Compilación, ordenación y análisis por Tomás Enrique Carrillo Batalla. Con la cooperación de un grupo de investigación coordinado por Pedro Grases. Caracas: Cuatricentenario de la Ciudad de Caracas, 1982. 28 v.: bibl.

Massive historical set (28 vols.) on the

evolution and significance of public finances in Venezuela. For example, vols. 22–28 consist of a compilation and analysis of financial endeavors of public administrations during 1871–86. Divided into three sections: legislative, doctrinal, and statistical.

3479 Jongkind, Fred. Venezuelan industrialization, dependent or autonomous?: a survey of national and foreign participation in the industrial development of a Latin American OPEC country. Amsterdam: CEDLA, 1981. 229 p.: bibl., tables (CEDLA incidentele publicaties; 21)

Original very worthwhile research provides one of the most thorough tests of "dependency" theory, principally Osvaldo Sunkel's version of international interdependence, his most recent reformulation. Supported by substantial empirical data, this study represents most in-depth examination of various subsectors and executives of Venezuelan industry (e.g., transnationals, private, and domestic; immigrant firms; state corps.; etc.) For historian's comment see HLAS 46:2925.

3480 Karlsson, Weine. Evolución y localización de la industria manufacturera en Venezuela y América Latina. Stockholm: Institute of Latin American Studies, 1979. 26 p.: tables (Research paper series; 21)

Contrasts industrialization process in Venezuela and other Latin American nations. Discusses modern manufacturing artisanbased small industry as well as changing geographical concentration of manfacturing industry.

3481 Márquez, Jaime. Substitución de monedas, dualidad e indeterminación del tipo de cambio: análisis empírico de la experiencia venezolana (UCC/CE, 21:64, dic. 1984, p. 299–314, graphs)

Empirical study estimates elasticity of currency substitution for Venezuela. Author develops currency substitution model in order to explain the 400 percent depreciation experienced by Venezuelan bolívar in 1983.

3482 Mayobre, José Antonio. Obras escogidas. Caracas: Banco Central de Venezuela, 1982. 711 p.: bibl., plates (Col. de estudios económicos; 9)

Posthumous collection of essays, conferences and articles, spanning 40 yrs., written by Mayobre, former ECLA Secretary General. They concern economic problems in Latin America, specifically Venezuela, and potential solutions for them. Author also served in several Venezuelan cabinets during his brilliant career.

3483 Maza Zavala, D.F. Situación y perspectivas de la economía venezolana (ACPS/B, 38:85/86, julio/dic. 1981, p. 116–134)

Description of most recent changes undergone by Venezuela's economy. Emphasizes structural shifts and growth dynamics. Closing argument proposes a number of structural changes that would lead to the nation's economic development.

3484 Montiel Ortega, Leonardo. Petróleo y planificación: un enfoque actualizado de los problemas técnico-económicos del petróleo en Venezuela y el mundo. Caracas: Univ. Santa María, 1982. 385 p.: ill.

Discussion of technical and economic aspects of petroleum production in Venezuela. Points out importance of other natural abundant but yet unexploited energy sources in the country. Concludes by proposing reforms for the petroleum industry too conservatively administered over the years.

3485 Moreno, Dilcia. La cooperación internacional de Venezuela y las imágenes de autodeterminación que permite el sistema financiero internacional actual (Fragmentos [Centro de Estudios Latinoamericanos Rómulo Gallegos, Depto. de Investigaciones, Caracas] 12, enero/abril 1982, p. 54–95, tables)

Analysis of Venezuela's role in international financial cooperation, a system designed to assist developing countries in the achievement of socioeconomic goals. Focuses chiefly on Central America and the Caribbean.

3486 Moreno León, José Ignacio. Profundización de la nacionalización petrolera venezolana: aspectos económicos, administrativas y fiscales. Prólogo, Rafael Caldera. Caracas: Ediciones Centauro, 1981. 495 p.: bibl., ill., tables.

Complete description of structure underlying Venezuela's nationalized petroleum industry. Focuses on its administrative, economic, and fiscal aspects since nationalization. Emphasizes industry's importance in fiscal policy and in country's future development.

3487 ¿Nueva o vieja división internacional del trabajo?: industrialización en Venezuela y México. Edición de Graciela Gutman y Dorothea Mezger. Caracas: Editorial Ateneo de Caracas, 1982. 693 p.: bibl., ill., tables.

Collection of works presented at 1979 CENDES seminar in Caracas. They concern different models of industrialization in Venezuela and Mexico. Main focus is structural change of an economy engaged in foreign trade.

3488 Parra Luzardo, Gastón. El desafío del Cartel Petrolero. Maracaibo, Venezuela: Univ. de Zulia, Vicerectorado Académico, 1981. 293 p.: bibl., ill., tables.

Analysis of the international petroleum cartel's role in Third World social and economic conflicts. Chiefly a critique of capitalism as an economic system, work focuses on process of capital concentration and centralization in the so-called "Cartel Energético."

3489 ———. El despojo de Venezuela: los precios del petróleo. Maracaibo, Venezuela: Univ. de Zulia, Rectorado, 1979. 264 p.: bibl., tables.

Description of how, even after nationalization, Venezuela's petroleum industry was still controlled by multinational corporations. Attributes mismanagement of oil revenues and income disparities since industry's creation to the crucial role of capitalism.

3490 Pazos, Felipe. Política de desarrollo económico: colección de artículos, ponencias e informes, 1949–1984. Caracas: Banco Central de Venezuela, 1985. 579 p.: graphs, tables (Col. de estudios económicos)

Collection of works by distinguished Cuban economist resident in Venezuela. Consists of articles, reports, and essays published 1949-present. They address Latin American economic problems during the period and offer possible solutions.

Petróleo y desarrollo en México y Venezuela. See item **3091.**

Plaza, Salvador de la et al. Dependencia y subdesarrollo. See item **2955.**

3492 Reina Cordero, Reinaldo. Al final de la inflación: un estudio del fenómeno inflacionario venezolano en el contexto mundial. Barquisimeto, Venezuela: Ediciones de la Univ. Centro Occidental Lisandro Alvarado, s.d. 194 p.: ill.

Complete analysis of normative and postive aspects of the inflationary phenomenon in Venezuela. Describes structure of consumer price index, and how it can affect socioeconomic stability.

3493 Reunión de Técnicos de Bancos Centrales del Continente Americano, *20th, La Paz, 1983.* XX [i.e. Vigésima] Reunión de Técnicos de Bancos Centrales del Continente Americano. v. 9, Indicadores cíclicos de la economía venezolana. La Paz: Banco Central de Bolivia, 1983. 1 v.: bibl., tables.

Vol. 9 of 38-vol. proceedings of major conference (see item **3080**). Analyzes importance and characteristics of economic cycles indicators in Venezuela. Focuses on their importance in estimating economic activity levels and impact on nation's economic policy. Points out different types of indicators in Venezuela and their performance during 1970s and 1980s.

3494 Rico López, Darío. Análisis de estados financieros: empresas de seguros. Caracas: Univ. Central de Venezuela, Ediciones de la Biblioteca, 1982. 151 p.: bibl., ill. (Col. Ciencias económicas y sociales; 24)

Concerns analysis of financial statements of insurance companies. Divided into three sections: 1) general information on insurance business (e.g., mortality tables, cost, technical reserves); 2) specific information on financial statements of insurance companies (e.g., legislation, characteristics, income, assets, liabilities; and 3) methodology for analyzing and interpreting such financial statements, with respect to two specific Venezuelan insurance companies.

3495 Rodríguez Campos, Manuel. Venezuela, 1948–1958: el proceso económico y social de la dictadura. Caracas: Alianza Gráfica Editorial, 1983. 275 p.

Essay on Venezuelan economic history. Focuses on socioeconomic conditions during last dictatorship. Emphasizes structural changes undergone by the economy and public administration during the period.

3496 Salas, Guillermo José. Petróleo. 6a ed. Caracas: Monte Avila Editores, 1982. 241 p.: ill. (Col. Letra viva)

Covers history of petroleum in Venezuela as of 1863, including nationalization, establishment of OPEC (1960), geology, exploration, production, transportation, use of natural gas, the Orinoco area, and other sources of energy.

3497 Salas Capriles, Roberto. Se busca un industrial. Caracas: Cromotip, 1980. 334 p.: bibl., ill., tables.

Covers industrialization and industrial development in Venezuela. Explains importance of and obstacles to technology transfer, attitudes toward the Latin American integration process, international trade, prices, inflation and productivity. Also analyzes other industrial sectors and evaluates their status in early 1980s.

3498 Silva, Jesús. La división del trabajo en una moderna organización corporativa. Caracas: Univ. Central de Venezuela, Facultad de Ciencias Económicas y Sociales, Div. de Publicaciones, 1980. 176 p.: bibl. (Col. Libros)

Study addresses capitalist division of labor. Focuses on how workers are treated by a representative corporation and on how it conducts business. Basically, a critique of the capitalist system.

3499 Sonntag, Heinz R. and **Rafael de la Cruz.** Estado e industrialización en Venezuela (GEE/NA, 5, 1982, p. 331–367)

Written from a Marxist perspective, article emphasizes the State's support of the private sector in peripheral nations through industrial loans, subsidies, and other mechanisms of industrial planning and policy. Contends that such support can be traced back to 1930s when maintenance of the bourgeoisie and capitalism in Venezuela and other peripheral nations became part and parcel of government-supported industrialization.

3500 Torrealba Alvarez, Raúl. Petróleo en Venezuela: la nacionalización. Bogotá: Editorial Pluma, 1980. 577 p.: bibl., ill., tables.

Analyzes petroleum and economic conditions before and after industry's nationalization in Venezuela. Explains nationalization process as well as its impact in Venezuela. Also covers topics such as inflation and its relation to petroleum prices, energy crisis, and OPEC's creation.

3501 Uslar Pietri, Arturo. Venezuela en el petróleo. Caracas: Urbina & Fuentes, 1984. 256 p. (Col. Petróleo y política)

Critique of the administration of the

petroleum industry since its discovery as a resource. Focuses on public sector's inability to convert such an industry into an engine for growth and economic prosperity. Emphasizes misuse of petroleum revenues by Venezuelan governments.

3502 Valbuena, Jovito G. Etapas del crecimiento industrial venezolano (ULA/RG, 16/19, 1975/1978, p. 179–197, bibl., graphs)

Descriptive but informative article about the history of industrial development in Venezuela. Emphasizes such development throughout the country. Includes much empirical data.

3503 Venezuela. Fundación para el Desarrollo de la Región Centro Occidental de Venezuela (FUDECO). Evaluación de los servicios públicos. v. 1, Estado Yaracuy. v. 2, Estado Portuguesa. v. 3, Estado Lara. v. 4, Estado Falcón. Barquisimeto, Venezuela: FUDECO, 1982. 4 v.

Analyzes performance of telephone, water, electricity, health and sanitation services in major cities of all four states. Points out deficiencies and recommends solutions as well as institutions responsible for their implementation.

3503a ———. ———. Principales programas y proyectos para el Estado Falcón. Barquisimeto, Venezuela: FUDECO, 1982. 22 leaves: tables.

Consists chiefly of data on Falcón state programs and projects tabulated according to sectors and subsectors (e.g., agriculture, irrigation, industry, and mining). Tables also indicate programs' objectives, status, investment, financing, responsible organization.

3503b ———. ———. Principales programas y proyectos para el Estado Falcón. Barquisimeto, Venezuela: FUDECO, 1982. 22 leaves: tables.

Consists chiefly of data on Falcón state programs and projects tabulated according to sectors and subsectors (e.g., agriculture, irrigation, industry, and mining). Tables also indicate programs' objectives, status, investment, financing, responsible organization.

3504 ———. ———. Principales programas y proyectos para el Estado Lara. Barquisimeto, Venezuela: FUDECO, 1982. 12 leaves: tables.

Consists chiefly of data on Lara state programs and projects tabulated according to sectors and subsectors (e.g., agriculture, irrigation, industry, mining). Tables also indicate programs' objectives, status, investment, financing, responsible organization.

3505 ———. ———. VI [i.e. Sexto] Plan de la Nación, 1981–1985: Plan de Desarrollo de la Región Centro-Occidental. Barquisimeto, Venezuela: FUDECO, 1982. 157 p.: ill., plates, tables.

Concerns Venezuela's mid-western region. Explains its economic activities, their organization, unemployment, population, and finally general strategies, objectives and perspectives of region's economic and social development. For the complete version of the Sixth National Plan, see item **3506**; for a bilingual summary, see item **3507**.

3506 ———. **Oficina Central de Coordinación y Planificación.** VI [i.e. Sexto] Plan de la Nación: 1981–1985. v. 1, Desarrollo global. v. 2, Desarrollo sectorial. v. 3, Desarrollo regional. Caracas: CORDIPLAN, 1981. 3 v. in 4: ill., tables.

The Sixth National Plan upholds the continuity of Venezuelan development planning since 1959. Vol. 1 deals with general characteristics of the economy's global development. Vol. 2 covers development of each productive sector, development strategy for the infrastructure, and social and cultural development. Vol. 3 provides a national strategy for regional development. For the bilingual English/Spanish abridged version of the plan, see item **3507**.

3507 ———. ———. VI [i.e. Sexto] Plan de la Nación: 1981–1985, resumen = Sixth National Plan, 1981–1985, summary. Caracas: CORDIPLAN, 1981. 72 p.: ill. (some col.), plates, tables.

Summary of the Sixth National Plan (see item **3506**) in Spanish and English. Introduction outlines social and economic evolution of Venezuela in the past decade and identifies basic obstacles to economic development and social advancement. Includes several tables with data on goals, programs, investment, GNP, balance of payments, population, and employment.

3508 ———. **Oficina Central de Estadística e Informática.** XI [i.e. Onceavo] censo general de población y vivienda: 20 de octubre de 1981: censos 1950–1981: población total por entidades federales, distritos y municipios, sexo y grupos de edad. Caracas: La Oficina, 1983. 605 p.: tables.

Population and housing census (1981) divided into: 1) total population for the national, states, districts and counties, including comparative analysis of all censuses taken since 1950; and 2) information on housing and population.

3508a Venezuela: estadísticas de comercio exterior, 1980–1981. Montevideo: Asociación Latinoamericana de Integración (ALADI), 1981. 2 v.: tables.

Basic statistical information on international sectors of Venezuelan economy, especially export/import activities for 1980–81. Statistics are organized according to economic zones and countries, and by exports and imports of principal products. Information on Venezuelan exports concerns only non-traditional ones.

3509 La Vivienda multifamiliar: Caracas, 1940–1970. Caracas: Instituto de Arquitectura Urbana, s.d. 110 p.: ill.

Study of the evolution of architectural and housing patterns in Caracas, Venezuela. Emphasizes multi-family dwellings during 1940–70.

3510 Zanoni, José Rafael. El precio del petróleo. Caracas: Univ. Central de Venezuela, Facultad de Ciencias Económicas y Sociales, Div. de Publicaciones, 1981. 213 p.: bibl., ill., tables (Col. Libro)

Petroleum price study divided into two sections: 1) factors that affect petroleum prices; and 2) determination of such prices. Among factors affecting prices are petroleum reserves, cost of petroleum activity, other sources of energy such as nuclear and solar, etc. Section on the determination of prices deals with market structure (petroleum demand and supply), OPEC, the world market, etc. Concludes with analysis of what factors determine a coherent price structure.

CHILE AND PERU

MARKOS MAMALAKIS, *Professor of Economics, University of Wisconsin-Milwaukee*

CHILE

In 1985, the nation began experiencing a mild recovery. Unemployment was reduced, income began to rise, the industrial sector grew strongly in some areas and the balance of payments situation stabilized. Even the price of copper rose which generated significant additional export revenues. Foreign debt was still exorbitant but, at least, not increasing. The trade surplus continued to rise and compared favorably with the 1981–82 trade deficits. Compared with Argentina and Brazil, inflation was mild. After the financial panic of Jan. 1982, public confidence in the financial system was restored. President Augusto Pinochet remained in power even if Ministers of Finance and Economics changed as frequently as the seasons. The peso was gradually devalued and political activities were completely banned.

Economic publications annotated below include some outstanding technical works prepared under the auspices of the Catholic Univ., a number of polemical opposition documents published by CEPLAN, and numerous historical or descriptive studies. All of them contribute to our understanding of the historical evolution of the Chilean economy. Nevertheless, it is unfortunate that so few make either a general or major contribution to the discipline of economics or one of its subfields.

The following publications stand out in terms of their insights or lasting contributions to Chilean historiography: 1) the volume on Chilean economic policy

(item 3521) edited by Juan Carlos Méndez in 1979 reflecting the prevailing economic philosophy as well as the euphoria of 1976–79; 2) Alejandro Foxley *et al.*'s
Reconstrucción económica para la democracia (item 3539) which summarizes
the views of the small opposition group located at CEPLAN and tolerated by the
Pinochet regime; 3) Jorge Pinto Rodríguez's *Las minas de azogue de Punitaqui*
(item 3555), a study of mercury mines towards the end of the 18th century; and
4) the latest installment of the *Historical statistics of Chile* (see HLAS 45:3407,
HLAS 43:3473, and HLAS 41:3229), vol. 4, *Money, prices and credit services* (item
3550) which contains the most comprehensive collection and analysis of historical
statistics of money, prices, stocks and credits for all of Chile for more than 300
years (1630–1982).

PERU

Whereas in 1983 criticism of the Velasco Alvarado policies dominated much of the
literature, by 1985 it was criticism of the Belaúnde-Ulloa neo-liberal economic policies that began gaining momentum.

Much of the economic literature written in and about Peru continues as polarized in 1985 as it was during previous years, a polarization also afflicting Chile.
To those on the right end of the political spectrum, the so-called monetarist, neoliberal, Chicago-affiliated groups, all of Peru's economic, social and political ills are
caused by or attributed to agents such as excessive government intervention, Marxists errors, the dream world of Christian humanism, the narcissistic tenets or beliefs of dependency, center-periphery problems, a metropolis-colony relationship, or
structuralist theories. On the other hand, those on the left end of the political spectrum, the so-called "anti-exploitation" theorists whose philosophies range from
Christian humanism to the Mao variety of Marxism, blame the unfortunate predicament of Peru (and Chile as well) on American imperialism, the Chicago Boys, the
exploitative multinational corporations, the ills and evils of free markets, free
trade, financial liberalization and private ownership and initiative. Unfortunately,
such extreme economic ideologies often serve to conceal a fundamental lack of research as well as intellectual sterility. Given the little communication between the
two camps, there is no substantive debate that would serve to challenge, refine and
enrich opposing points of view. On the contrary, such debate in Peru is either strictly
polemical or for debate's sake rather than predicated upon a search for solutions to
what appear as intractable economic problems. Regrettably, polemics of this sort
are conducive to apathy and resignation rather than to the dynamism, initiative and
progress that result from legitimate intellectual exchange. The consequences are
that while governments and policies may change, change in the socioeconomic and
political conditions of the poor majority of the population is minimal.

However, we are fortunate in that an increasing number of studies in recent
years have been neither "right" nor "left." Instead, they focus on solving problems
such as urban and rural poverty and in a professional and rigorous manner. The following worthwhile Peruvian publications exemplify this trend: 1) Carlos Palacios
Moreyra's *La deuda anglo-peruana: 1882–1890* (item 3601) which reveals how the
same mistakes recurr disconcertingly throughout history; 2) Carlos Amat y León
Chávez's and Luis Bustamante Belaúnde's *Lecturas sobre regionalización* (item
3594) which emphasizes the important role played by decentralization; 3) Manuel
Ulloa's *Exposición del Ministro de Economía, Finanzas y Comercio* (item 3618)
which constitutes an important basic source on the philosophy of the second

Belaúnde presidency; 4) Bruno Revesz's *Estado, algodón y productores agrarios* (item **3609**) which is highly recommended because of its thoroughness, objectivity, quality and insights into economic history; and 5) Tom Alberts's study *Agrarian reform and rural poverty* (item **3569**) which provides an excellent review of agrarian changes since 1950.

CHILE

3511 Baklanoff, Eric N. Copper in Chile: the expropriation of a partially nationalized industry. Austin: Office for Public Sector Studies, Institute of Latin American Studies, Univ. of Texas at Austin, 1983. 15 p.: bibl., tables (Technical papers series; 38)

Careful examination of Chile's large scale copper sector between 1964–75.

3512 Bardón M., Alvaro. Estatismo y sub-desarrollo o la economía chilena en los setenta (*in* Hacia un nuevo diagnóstico de Chile. Andrés Sanfuentes, ed. Santiago: Editorial del Pacífico: Instituto de Estudios Políticos, 1973, p. 63–100)

Bardón played an important role in shaping economic policy in Chile up to 1980–81. This document is important because it describes Bardón's thinking about statism and the policies of President Salvador Allende.

3513 Barrera, Manuel. Worker participation in company management in Chile: a historical experience. Geneva: UN Research Institute for Social Development, Popular Participation Programme, 1981. 25 p.: bibl., tables (Participation occasional paper. Report; 81.3)

Excellent description and evaluation of worker participation in management during the Allende years.

3514 Briones, Guillermo. Mercado de trabajo, ocupación y educación universitaria en la economía neo-liberal: Chile, 1976–1981. Santiago: Programa Interdisciplinario de Investigaciones de Educación (PIIE), Academia de Humanismo Cristiano, 1982. 31 leaves (Serie Investigaciones)

Essay examines relationship between a university education and labor markets in a neo-liberal economy.

3515 Casos chilenos en comercialización. Jaime de la Fuente, ed. Santiago: Depto. de Administración, Facultad de Ciencias Económicas y Administrativas, Univ. de Chile, 1981. 1 v.: ill., tables.

Describes a variety of cases of product commercialization.

3516 Castillo Lea-Plaza, María Victoria. An examination of the determinants of the real interest rate in Chile, 1976–1980. Geneva: Institut universitaire de hautes études internationales, 1981. 47 leaves: bibl., ill., tables (Diplôme; 180)

According to this study, there exists a strong and positive relationship between inflation and the real interest rate on loans and a negative relationship between inflation and the real interest rate on deposits.

3517 Catastro frutícola. v. 1, V [i.e. Quinta] región: actualización 1981. v. 2, VI [i.e. Sexta] región: actualización 1982. v. 3, VII [i.e. Séptima] región: actualización 1981. Santiago: Corporación de Fomento de la Producción, Instituto Nacional de Investigación de Recursos Naturales, 1982. 3 v. in 4: tables (Publicación CIREN; 33–35)

Most comprehensive census statistics on fruit-growing in Chile.

3518 Chile. Presidencia de la República. Plan regional de desarrollo: 1982–1989. t. 3, Sectores de infraestructura y servicios. Coordinación: Oficina de Planificación Nacional, Secretaría Regional de Planificación y Coordinación. Santiago: Intendencia Regional de Magallanes y de la Antártica Chilena, 1982. 1 v.: ill., tables.

Increasing research has focused on regional development in recent years. Volume is a gold mine of information concerning regional development plans for region of Magallanes and Chilean Antarctica.

3519 Chile. Programa Socio-Económico, 1981–1989. Santiago: Ministerio del Interior, 1981. 54 p.

Document contains socioeconomic plan of Gen. Augusto Pinochet's government for 1981–89. Plan is inspired by the principle of a subsidiary role for the State.

3520 Chile: Series Estadísticas. Instituto Nacional de Estadísticas. 1981– . Santiago.

Ongoing serial publication consists of comprehensive collection that provides great variety of Chilean historical statistics.

3521 Chilean economic policy. Edited by Juan Carlos Méndez. Translated by Ann M. Gain de González. Santiago: Imprenta Calderón, 1979. 386 p.: bibl.

Volume was published in 1979 when some were still talking about the economic growth "miracle" of Chile. Indispensable document for anyone interested in Chilean intellectual history and the economic philosophy of 1973–79 era of Pinochet presidency. In addition to articles by Lorenzo Gotuzzo, Jorge Cauas, and Augusto Pinochet, includes valuable economic reports.

3522 Círculo económico. Santiago: L&A, 1981. 579 p.: ill. (some col.), index, tables.

Comprehensive statistical collection and description of Chilean economy during 1960–80, was prepared by New York Office of the Chilean Dept. Corp. (CORFO). Contains information of interest to almost any reader.

3523 Coeymans, Juan Eduardo. Migración ocupacional agrícola-no agrícola en Chile: período 1960–1979. Santiago: Pontificia Univ. Católica de Chile, Instituto de Economía, Oficina de Publicaciones, 1982. 54 leaves: bibl, tables (Documento de trabajo; 82)

Excellent study examines labor migration from agricultural to non-agricultural activities during 1960–79.

3524 Contreras, Victoria. Mercado de trabajo en cifras: 1950–1980. Santiago: OIT, PREALC, 1982. 180 p.: bibl., tables.

Excellent recopilation of statistics on and analysis of labor markets not only in Chile but throughout Latin America during 1950–80.

3525 Corbo, Vittorio. Chile: economic policy and international economic relations since 1970. Santiago: Pontificia Univ. Católica de Chile, Instituto de Economía, Oficina de Publicaciones, 1983. 64 p.: bibl., ill., tables (Documento de trabajo; 86)

Orthodox examination of economic events in Chile between 1970–82.

3526 ———. Dos ensayos sobre demanda por dinero en Chile. Santiago: Pontificia Univ. Católica de Chile, Instituto de Economía, Oficina de Publicaciones, 1981. 29 leaves: bibl., ill., tables (Documento de trabajo; 73)

According to this study, the demand for money in Chile was stable even during periods of important swings in the quarterly rate of inflation.

3527 Cortés Douglas, Hernán. Stabilization policies in Chile: inflation, unemployment and depression, 1975–1982. Santiago: Pontificia Univ. Católica de Chile, Instituto de Economía, Oficina de Publicaciones, 1983. 48 leaves: bibl., ill., tables (Documento de trabajo; 85)

In this study, Cortés argues that Chile's economic crisis in 1982 can be explained in terms of "a basic incompatibility between the full implementation of an economic doctrine of liberalism and the Chilean cultural tradition, . . ."

3528 Corvalán Vásquez, Oscar E. El aprendizaje en la industria: evaluación de una experiencia chilena. Montevideo: CINTERFOR, OIT, 1980. 191 p.: ill., tables (Estudios y monografías; 54)

Monograph contains a systematic analysis of apprenticeship program of Chile's INACAP (Instituto Nacional de Capacitación Profesional). Spanish version of PhD thesis accepted at the Univ. of Toronto. Concludes that benefits and returns from informal training can be as high as those divided from formal training.

3529 Cuentas nacionales de Chile, 1960–1982. Santiago: Dirección de Política Financiera, Banco Central de Chile, 1983. 134 p.: col. ill., tables.

Outstanding collection of Chile's official national accounts covering 1960–82.

3530 Cuentas nacionales trimestralizadas, 1980–1983. Santiago: Dirección de Política Financiera, Banco Central de Chile, 1983. 56 p.: ill. (some col.), plates.

First collection of quarterly national accounts of Chile for 1980–83.

3531 Destino de ingreso de capitales. Santiago: Presidencia de la República, Oficina de Planificación Nacional, 1983. 29 leaves: tables.

Provides detailed information on use or destination of Chile's foreign debt during 1973–82.

3532 Economía y organización de la investigación agropecuaria. Editores, Manuel Elgueta G. y Eduardo Venezian L. Santiago: Instituto de Investigaciones Agropecuarias, 1982. 297 p.: bibl., ill., tables.

Excellent collection of papers dealing with relation between research and agricultural development.

3533 Economic report of Chile. Edited by the Statistics and Publications Dept., Central Bank of Chile. Santiago: Central Bank of Chile, 1982. 174 p.: col. ill., tables.

Provides comprehensive picture of Chilean economic development during 1973–81. Includes much institutional information concerning economic change during 1973–81 Pinochet era.

3534 Las Empresas transnacionales en la economía de Chile, 1974–1980. Santiago: Naciones Unidas, 1983. 178 p.: bibl., ill., tables (Estudios e informes de la CEPAL; 22. E/CEPAL/G.1235)

Contains an excellent review of foreign companies and investment in Chile during 1974–80.

3535 Experiencias sobre bancos centrales: seminario. Santiago: Dirección de Política Financiera, Banco Central de Chile, 1983. 86 p.: bibl., tables (Estudios monetarios; 8)

Experiences of central banks are discussed by Kemmerer, Marshall, Vaubel, and Salin in this highly recommended collection.

3536 Ffrench-Davis M., Ricardo. Indice de precios externos para calcular el valor real del comercio internacional de Chile, 1952–80. Rev. ed. Santiago: Corporación de Investigaciones Económicas para Latinoamérica, 1981. 20 leaves: bibl, tables (Notas técnicas; 32)

Essay in which Ffrench-Davis develops a methodology for calculating an index of external prices that Chile will confront in its commercial relations abroad.

3537 ———. The monetarist experiment in Chile: a critical survey (WD, 11:11, Nov. 1983, p. 905–926, bibl., tables)

Critical survey of Chilean economic development during 1973–82, an experiment regarded as a failure by Ffrench-Davis.

3538 Foxley, Alejandro. Latin American experiments in neoconservative economics. Berkeley: Univ. of California Press, 1983. 213 p.: ill., tables.

In this lucidly written monograph, Foxley critically reviews what he calls "Latin American experiments in neoconservative economics." Concludes that "although neoconservative policies can exhibit some success in checking inflation and balance of payments problems, they have also generated a significant increase in inequalities within the economy and society . . ." "The main problem consists in restoring some degree of consensus about basic issues: growth and distribution, the role of the various economic agents (business, labor, government), rules of the economic game, and the political system that supports a civilized interaction among the members of society." Book's coverage ends in 1980–81 and includes some but not all major macroeconomic dimensions of these neoconservative experiments.

3539 ——— et al. Reconstrucción económica para la democracia. Santiago: Editorial Aconcagua: Corporación de Investigaciones Económicas para Latinoamérica (CIEPLAN), 1983. 348 p.: bibl., tables.

Important book because it contains the views of seven non-liberal and non-Marxist economists about what went wrong in Chile under Pinochet and how it can be corrected. While not providing a comprehensive blueprint for a development strategy, book does confront selected economic issues and their links to democracy. Essays are policy oriented, frequently polemic, and contain research carried out by CIEPLAN economists.

3540 Gaete J., Alden. Evolución espacio-temporal de la industria siderúrgica en Chile y en los Estados Unidos de Norteamérica (Revista de Geografía Norte Grande [Pontificia Univ. Católica de Chile, Santiago] 9, 1982, p. 11–20, bibl., maps, tables)

Quantitative study compares the spatial-temporal evolution of the steel industry in Chile and the US.

3541 Godoy Vera, Carlos. Antecedentes sobre la evolución de la industria automotriz. Santiago: Depto. de Informaciones Estadísticas y Publicaciones del Banco Central de Chile, 1982. 78 p.: bibl., ill., tables

(Serie de estudios económicos. Documentos de investigación; 12)
Review of Chile's automotive industry.

3542 Gómez, Sergio. Instituciones y procesos agrarios en Chile. Santiago: FLACSO: Consejo Latinoamericano de Ciencias Sociales, 1982? 167 p.: bibl., ill., tables.
Outstanding review and analysis of pivotal dimensions of agrarian and rural development in Chile.

3543 Goñi, José. La vía chilena al endeudamiento externo: un estudio del endeudamiento externo chileno, 1974–1982. Stockholm: Institute of Latin American Studies, 1983. 193 p.: bibl., ill., tables (Research paper series; 37)
Essay argues that "instead of becoming the mainstay of the economic model by providing the country with the financial resources needed, the foreign money undermined it, . . ."

3544 Gutiérrez Urrutia, Mario. Ahorro y crecimiento económico en Chile en el período 1960–81 (CEMLA/M, 6:2, abril/junio 1983, p. 181–214, bibl., tables)
Important empirical study examines the relationship between saving and economic growth in Chile during 1960–81.

3545 Indicadores económicos, 1960–1980. Santiago: Dirección de Política Financiera, Banco Central de Chile, 1981. 134 p.: tables.
Indispensable collection of extremely important economic time series.

3546 Indicadores económicos y sociales, 1960–1982. Santiago: Dirección de Política Financiera, Banco Central de Chile, 1983. 294 p.: col. ill., tables.
Most valuable collection of economic and social statistics.

3547 Kay, Cristóbal. Political economy, class alliances and agrarian change in Chile (JPS, 8:4, July 1981, p. 485–513)
Kay carefully and thoroughly examines major issues of agrarian change from a long-term historical perspective and within a dependency context.

3548 Larraín B., Felipe and **Gert Wagner H.** Previsión social: algunas consideraciones. Santiago: Pontificia Univ. Católica de Chile, Instituto de Economía, Oficina de Publicaciones, 1982. 82 p.: bibl., ill. (Documento de trabajo; 84)
Theoretical examination of certain aspects of social security.

3549 Le Fort V., Guillermo. Los desequilibrios monetarios y la balanza de pagos: Chile, 1950–1970. Santiago: Depto. de Economía, Univ. de Chile, 1980. 123 leaves: bibl., tables (Documento de investigación; 49)
Excellent study of Chile's balance of payments during 1950–70.

3550 Mamalakis, Markos. Historical statistics of Chile. v. 4, Money, prices, and credit services. Westport, Conn.: Greenwood Press, 1983. 510 p.: bibl.
Vol. 4 of major compilation contains comprehensive collection and analysis of historical statistics of money, prices, stocks, and credit during 1630–1982. Also provides detailed analysis of Chile's financial system during 1973–82. For previous volumes, see *HLAS 41:3229*, *HLAS 43:3473*, and *HLAS 45:3407*.

3551 Mathieson, Donald J. Estimating models of financial market behavior during periods of extensive structural reform: the experience of Chile (IMF/SP, 30:2, June 1983, p. 350–393, bibl., tables)
Outstanding work on financial reform in Chile.

Los Mitos de Milton Friedman. See item **2930.**

Monteón, Michael. Chile in the nitrate era: the evolution of economic dependence, 1880–1930. See *HLAS 46:3116.*

3552 El Movimiento cooperativo en Chile: análisis, período 1976–1982. Santiago: Confederación General de Cooperativas de Chile, 1983. 63 p.: bibl., ill., tables (Documento; 1)
Very worthwhile analysis of cooperative movement in Chile during 1976–82.

3553 Nuevas dimensiones del comercio internacional. Edición de Pilar Armanet Armanet y Raymundo Barros Charlín. Santiago: Instituto de Estudios Internacionales, Univ. de Chile, 1982. 121 p.: tables (Estudios internacionales)
Comprehensive exploration of the new dimensions of international trade.

Palma, J. Gabriel. Chile, 1914–1935: de economía exportadora a sustitutiva de importaciones. See *HLAS 46:3121.*

3554 Participación laboral: experiencias en Perú y Chile. Santiago: OIT, PREALC, 1982. 119 p.: bibl., ill., tables (Investigaciones sobre empleo; 21)

Examines three cases of labor participation in management: two designated as "Labor Community and Social Property" were initiated in Peru under Gen. Velasco; the third, referred to as "Social Property Area," was introduced in Chile by President Allende's Popular Unity government.

3555 Pinto Rodríguez, Jorge. Las minas de azogue de Punitaqui: estudio de una faena minera de fines del siglo XVIII. Coquimbo, Chile: Talleres Gráficos Univ. del Norte, 1981. 184 p.: bibl., ill.

Since the colonial period the mining sector has played a major role in Chilean economic development. Excellent examination of the mercury mines of Punitaqui at the end of the 18th century.

3556 Portales, Carlos and **Augusto Varas.**

The role of military expenditure in the development process: Chile, 1952, 1973, and 1973–1980; two contrasting cases (NOSALF/IA, 12:1/2, 1983, p. 21–50, tables)

Excellent study of role played by military expenditures in shaping Chilean economic development.

3557 Recent development of the securities market in Chile. Santiago: Superintendencia de Valores y Seguros, 1982. 68 p.: bibl., ill.

Short, accurate outline of Chilean securities market before financial panic of Jan. 1983.

3558 Reunión de Técnicos de Bancos Centrales del Continente Americano, *20th, La Paz, 1983.* XX [i.e. Vigésima] Reunión de Técnicos de Bancos Centrales del Continente Americano. v. 16. La Paz: Banco Central de Bolivia, 1983. 1 v.: bibl., ill., plates.

Vol. 16 of 38 (see item **3080**) in which authors Rosende and Toso explain Chile's high real interest rates during 1975–83. An upward adjustment in household permanent income resulted in indebtness and a supply of funds from abroad. They touch some critical points in a still wide open debate.

3559 Ropert, María Angélica. Sindicatos y salarios reales en la industria chilena, 1979–81. Santiago: OIT, PREALC, 1982. 61 p.: bibl., tables (Monografía sobre empleo; 25)

Study examines relationship between labor unions and real wages in Chilean industry during 1979–81.

3560 Ruiz-Tagle P., Jaime. La participación de los trabajadores en las empresas del área de propiedad social: Chile, 1970–1973. Santiago: Programa de Economía del Trabajo, Academia de Humanismo Cristiano, 1982. 46 p.: bibl.

Essay examines worker participation in social property enterprises during 1970–73.

3561 Sánchez González, Leonardo. Evolución histórica y aspectos normativos de la contabilidad pública en Chile. Edición de Leonardo Sánchez González. Santiago: s.n., 1983. 231 p.: bibl., ill., tables.

Comprehensive review of accounting in Chile.

Sater, William F. La agricultura chilena y la Guerra del Pacífico. See *HLAS 46:3138.*

3562 Scherman, Jorge. Estadísticas básicas del sector industrial externo chileno. Santiago: Corporación de Investigaciones Económicas para Latinoamerica, 1981. 24, 22, 7 leaves: bibl., tables (Nota técnica; 35)

Systematic description and evaluation of indices of industrial production prepared by the National Institute of Statistics and the Society for Industrial Development during 1969–80.

3563 Seminario sobre Análisis de Decisiones de Inversión y Tecnología en el Sector Industrial Pesquero, *Santiago, 1980.* El desarrollo de la industria pesquera. Santiago: Subsecretaría de Pesca: Fundación Chile, 1983. 154 p.: ill., plates.

Comprehensive examination of the fishing industry.

3564 Series de comercio exterior, 1970–1981. Edición de la Dirección de Política Financiera, Banco Central de Chile. Santiago: Depto. de Informaciones Estadísticas y Publicaciones, Banco Central de Chile, 1982. 96 p.: bibl., tables.

Excellent collection of Chilean foreign trade statistics for 1970–81.

Sjaastad, Larry A. Estabilización y tipo de cambio: el contraste entre Chile y Argentina. See item **3725**.

3565 Summary of the Chilean situation. New York: Business International Corp., 1979. 129 leaves: map, tables.
General economic survey of Chile (1973–79).

3566 Vargas, Verónica. Salarios agrícolas en Chile en el período 1975–1981: estudio de casos. Santiago: OIT, PREALC, 1982. 52 p.: ill., tables (Monografía; 24)
Contains selected studies of agricultural wages during 1975–81.

Villalobos R., Sergio. Los comienzos de la historiografía económica de Chile, 1862–1940. See *HLAS 46:3149.*

3567 Zahler, Roberto. Recent Southern Cone liberalization reforms and stabilization policies: the Chilean case, 1974–1982 (SAGE/JIAS, 25:4, Nov. 1983, p. 509–562, bibl., tables)
Systematic examination of Chile's stabilization and liberalization experiment during 1974–82.

PERU

3568 Agricultura y alimentación: bases de un nuevo enfoque. Manuel Lajo, Rolando Ames, Carlos Samaniego, eds. Carlos Amat y León Chávez *et al.* Lima: Pontificia Univ. Católica del Perú, Fondo Editorial, 1982. 536 p.: bibl., ill.
It is normally assumed that agriculture generates enough of a food surplus to feed the non-agricultural population. However, not in Peru where nutrition is inadequate and imports satisfy a major part of demand for food. Discusses Peru's food-nutritional crisis and strategy for increasing internal supply of food.

3569 Alberts, Tom. Agrarian reform and rural poverty: a case study of Peru. Boulder, Colo.: Westview Press, 1983. 1 v.: bibl. (Westview replica ed.)
Based on extensive data for land ownership, income distribution, and agricultural production, monograph assesses Peru's experience with development planning since 1950 and discusses efforts to improve standard of

living of rural population through changes in agrarian structure.

3570 Alva Castro, Luis. Endeudamiento externo en el Perú: bases para una posición conjunta en el contexto latinoamericano. Lima: Industrialgráfica, 1984. 111 p.: ill.
Careful examination of Peru's foreign debt between 1968–82.

3571 Amat y León Chávez, Carlos and **Héctor León.** Niveles de vida y grupos sociales en el Perú. Lima: Univ. del Pacífico, Centro de Investigación: Fundación Friedrich Ebert, 1983. 249 p.: bibl., ill.
Attempts to identify the relationship between levels of living and social groups in Peru.

3572 —— *et al.* El sistema tributario del Perú. Edición del Instituto de Desarrollo Económico (IDE), Escuela de Administración de Negocios para Graduados (ESAN). Lima: Mosca Azul Editores, 1983. 164 p.: ill.
Volume examines Peru's taxation system.

3573 Baba Nakao, Luis. Mercado de colocaciones y ahorro en el Perú. Lima: Centro de Investigación, Univ. del Pacífico, 1982. 239 p. (Cuadernos de coyuntura)
Excellent statistical examination of Peru's capital markets during 1976–80.

3574 Barreto, Emilio G. Crisis de la economía peruana, 1980–1983. Lima: Oficina de Copias e Impresiones del Jirón Moquequa. 215 p.
Critical review of Peru's economic policy during 1980–83. Highly recommended treatise covering an impressive number of topics.

3575 Basombrío Zender, Ignacio. Bancos: elementos para un debate. Lima: Centro de Investigación, Univ. del Pacífico, 1983. 150 p.
Essays on various aspects of Peruvian domestic banking policy particularly with respect to new banking law in early 1980s. One essay discusses Mexican nationalization of banking sector. [J.M. Hunter]

3576 ——. Exportación de manufacturas: un recuento histórico. Lima: Adex Biblioteca del exportador, 1980. 233 p.
Deals objectively with many important aspects of Peruvian manufacturing ex-

ports. Basombrío argues that Peru's true challenge is to increase such exports.

3577 Branch, Brian and **Jorge Borrani Williams.** Public enterprises in Peru: the perspectives for reform. Empresas públicas en el Perú. Austin: Office for Public Sector Studies, Institute of Latin American Studies, Univ. of Texas at Austin, 1982. 22 p.: bibl. (Technical papers series; 37)

Interesting points in these essays which examine evolution of Peruvian public enterprises from 1968–81.

3578 Cabieses, H. *et al.* Industrialization and regional development in Peru. Amsterdam: CEDLA, 1982. 171 p.: bibl. (CEDLA Incidentele publicaties; 23)

Examines Peru's decentralization policies, role of Trujillo and Arequipa as development poles, and function of the State in promoting industrialization.

3579 Cárdenas, Gerardo. El sector de economía social en el Perú: cooperativas y empresas autogestionarias. Lima: Centro de Estudios para el Desarrollo y la Participación, 1983. 453 p.: bibl., ill. (Serie Realidad nacional)

In political philosophy as well as in practice, cooperatives have played an important role in Peru. Major contribution to topic of "social economy" which has formed an integral part of Peruvian economic system.

3580 Censos nacionales, VIII de población, III de vivienda, 12 de julio de 1981: resultados de prioridad, nivel nacional. Lima: Instituto Nacional de Estadística, 1982. 2 v. (915 p., 4 p. of plates): ill., tables.

Extremely useful priority statistics of Peru's population census of July, 12, 1981.

3581 Chávez, Eliana *et al.* El Norte peruano: realidad poblacional. Papers presented at the Reunión Regional del Norte sobre Problemas de Población, Cajamarca, Nov. 20–25, 1981, organized by the Asociación Multidisciplinaria de Investigación y Docencia en Población. Lima: Ediciones AMIDEP, 1982. 182 p.: bibl., ill.

Collection of first rate articles examines employment, educational needs, internal migrations, role of women, demographic situation, and status of health in northern Peru.

3582 Chávez Achong, Julio. Introducción al problema agrario en el Perú. Lima:

Ideas, between 1981 and 1983. 171 p.: bibl., ill.

Informative, long-term, concise review of Peru's agrarian problem from a Marxist perspective.

3583 Conferencia Anual de Ejecutivos, *17th, Paracas, Perú, 1978.* Anales. Lima: Instituto Peruano de Administración de Empresas (IPAE), 1978. 287 p.: ill.

Leading members of Peru's business community outlook for 1980s.

3584 Cornejo Ramírez, Enrique. Diagnóstico de la situación económico-social del Perú. v. l, Marco internacional, el proceso geo-económico y su impacto en América Latina. v. 2, Marco nacional, la crisis económica y su impacto en el sector laboral y sindical. Consultor, Julián Licastro Giménez. Monterrico, Perú: INP, OCTI; Lima: Univ. de Lima, Centro de Investigaciones Económicas y Sociales (CIESUL), 1981. 2 v.: bibl. (Avances de investigación/CIESUL; 1–2)

Essays examine impact of economic crisis on selected aspects of Peru's labor markets.

3585 Dall'Orto, Augusto. Organización y desarrollo: reto peruano. Lima: A. Dall'Orto F., between 1978 and 1981. 189 p.

Theme is that without administrative reform economic development cannot be achieved in Peru.

Durand, Francisco. La industria en el Perú: bibliografía. See item **27.**

3586 Eguren López, Fernando; Jorge Fernández-Baca; and **Fabián Tume.** Producción algodonera e industria textil en el Perú. Lima: DESCO, Centro de Estudios y Promoción del Desarrollo, 1981. 323 p.: bibl., ill.

Examination of cotton and textile industries from a dependency perspective.

3587 Ehrhardt, Waltraud. Entwicklung durch Integration?: Peru im Andenpakt. Frankfurt, FRG: Peter Lang Verlag, 1982. 336 p.: bibl., ill., maps (Münchner studien zur internationalen Entwicklung 0721–3830; 4)

Discusses center-periphery concept in economic development while focusing on Peru and its role in the Andean Pact as a case study of a developing country. Succinctly analyzes spin-off effects, horizontal interactions, and multilateralization. [G.M. Dorn]

3588 Encinas del Pando, José A. The role of military expenditure in the development process: Perú: a case study, 1950/1980 (NOSALF/IA, 12:1/2, 1983, p. 51–114, tables)

Excellent study of role of military expenditures in Peru during 1950–80.

Estudo comparativo da indústria de alimentos: administração e política de tecnología na América Latina. See item **2842.**

3589 Fernández-Baca, Jorge; Carlos Parodi Zevallos; and Fabián Tume Torres. Agroindustria y transnacionales en el Perú. Lima: DESCO, Centro de Estudios y Promoción del Desarrollo, 1983. 260 p.: bibl., ill.

Examines relationship between transnational corporations and Peru's agroindustry. Systematic review of statistical information and suggests strategies for eliminating existing bottlenecks.

3590 Gonzales de Olarte, Efraín. Economías regionales del Perú. Lima: Instituto de Estudios Peruanos, 1982. 278 p.: bibl., ill., maps (Análisis económico; 6)

Peru's regional crisis and inequalities are explained in terms of "capitalist development." Only a change, a "redefinition in the mode of production could eliminate the sources of unequal regional development." Neither this nor other Marxist essays answer the question of why regional inequalities do not exist in advanced "private capitalist," while they are present in many "state capitalist" countries.

3591 González Roberto, Ernesto and Ronald Ruiz Chapilliquen. Planificación y centralismo. Lima: Promotores, Consultores y Asesores Andinos: Centro de Documentación e Información Andina, 1982? 160 p.: bibl., ill.

Concentration and centralization of the power of the State is, according to this treatise, primary cause of underdevelopment in Peru.

Gootenberg, Paul. The social origins of protectionism and free trade in nineteenth-century Lima. See *HLAS 46:2976.*

3592 Kennedy, Peter. Food and agricultural policy in Peru, 1960–1977. Austin: Office for Public Sector Studies, Institute of Latin American Studies, Univ. of Texas at Austin, 1983. 22 p.: bibl. (Technical papers series; 39)

Excellent analysis of Peru's agricultural sector during 1960–77. Concludes that military planners, like the precedessors, failed "in divising a coherent strategy to deal with the problems of ever-decreasing per-capital food production."

3593 Lajo Lazo, Manuel. Alternativa agraria y alimentaria: diagnóstico y propuesta para el Perú. Piura, Perú: Centro de Investigación y Promoción del Campesinado, 1983. 415 p.: bibl., ill.

Highly informative. Provides a diagnosis and advances a detailed strategy for curing Peru's agrarian nutrition problem. Although Lajo correctly blames the discrimination of agriculture as largely responsible for stagnation and malnutrition, some of his policies would continue past discrimination.

3594 Lecturas sobre regionalización. Edición de Carlos Amat y León Chávez y Luis Bustamante Belaúnde. Lima: Centro de Investigación, Univ. del Pacífico, 1981. 342 p., 1 folded leaf of plates: bibl., ill.

Collection of excellent articles deal with regional development in Peru. Decentralization is suggested as an instrument for strengthening democracy and cohesion of Peruvian society.

3595 Lima, una metrópoli: 7 debates. Abelardo Sánchez León, Luis Olivera C., eds. Julio Calderón *et al.* Lima: DESCO, 1983. 274 p.: bibl., ill.

Conference proceedings include seven articles and numerous comments. Detailed examination of major dimensions of what may be called the urban crisis of Lima.

Madueño, Víctor A. La Primera Guerra Mundial y el desarrollo industrial del Perú. See *HLAS 46:2988.*

3596 El Manejo presupuestal en el Perú: análisis de los presupuestos generales de la república para 1981 y 1982 y su financiamiento: enjuiciamiento del Partido Aprista Peruano. Lima: El Partido, 1982. 96, 19, 229 p., 7 folded leaves of plates: ill.

Contains critical evaluation of Peru's budgetary process during 1981 and 1982 by the Aprista opposition party.

3597 Manrique, Manuel. La Peruvian Corporation en el selva central del Perú.

Miraflores, Perú: Centro de Investigación y Promoción Amazónica, 1982? 93 p., 1 folded leaf of plates: bibl., ill., map (Documento; 3)
Excellent historical treatise of the Peruvian Corp.

3598 Nuevos ensayos sobre la economía peruana. Jorge González Izquierdo, ed. Fátima Aramburú *et al.* Lima: Centro de Investigación, Univ. del Pacífico, 1982. 150 p.: bibl., ill.
Comprehensive survey and analysis of foreign capital in Peru's industrial sector.

3599 Organization of American States. General Secretariat. Executive Secretariat for Economic and Social Affairs. Short-term economic reports. v. 7, Peru. 2nd ed. Washington: OAS, General Secretariat, 1981. 1 v.: bibl. (SG/Ser G.41.14)
Comprehensive survey of economic development in Peru, especially since 1973.

3600 ——. ——. ——. Programación del Desarrollo. Informes económicos de corto plaza. v. 7, Perú. Washington: La Programación, 1980? 1 v.
Comprehensive review of economic change in Peru during 1970–80.

3601 Palacios Moreyra, Carlos. La deuda anglo-peruana, 1822–1890. Lima: Librería Studium, 1983. 275 p.: bibl.
Excellent monograph traces rise and fall of Anglo-Peruvian foreign debt between 1822–1830. Of interest to historians as well as economists studying Latin America, Peru, and long term growth.

3602 Peru. Centro Nacional de Productividad. Dirección General de Investigación. Evolución de los niveles remunerativos en la industria y su impacto sobre la productividad del trabajo: caso textil: estudio. Lima: La Dirección, 1982. 156 leaves.
Excellent study of relationship between remunerations and labor productivity in the textile industry during 1975–79.

3603 ——. Instituto Nacional de Estadística. Dirección General de Cuentas Nacionales. Cuentas nacionales del Perú, 1950–1981. Lima: La Dirección, 1982. 96 p.: tables.
Complete set of Peruvian national accounts during 1950–81.

3604 ——. ——. ——. Producto bruto interno por departamentos, 1971–

1981. Lima: La Dirección, 1983. 158 p.: ill. (some col.)
Excellent document provides national account estimates by department during 1971–81.

3605 ——. ——. Dirección General de Indicadores Económicas y Sociales. Análisis del ingreso y gasto familiar de la encuesta nacional de propósitos múltiples y metodología empleada en el cálculo del índice de precios al consumidor de Lima metropolitana. Lima: El Instituto, 1981. 143 [i.e. 107] p.: ill.
Analysis of family income and expenditures of multiple purpose national survey and of methodology of calculating consumer price index for metropolitan Lima.

3606 Peru: background information. Prepared in collaboration with the Comisión Nacional de Inversiones y Tecnologías Extranjeras (CONITE) *and under the sponsorship* of Banco Central de Reserva del Perú, Banco de la Nación, Corporación Financiera de Desarrollo. S.l.: Merrill Lynch White Weld Capital Markets Group, 1982. 48 p.: ill.
Excellent general survey of major dimensions of Peruvian economy.

3607 El Proceso de liberalización de las importaciones: Perú, 1979–1982: documento. Lima: Banco Central de Reserva del Perú, 1983. 39, 19 p.: bibl.
Carefully examines impact of post-1979 trade liberalization on imports, tax revenues, and prices during 1980–82.

3608 La Producción y la productividad del grupo de empresas exportadoras de la rama textil: estudio. Lima: Centro Nacional de Productividad (CENIP), Dirección de Investigación, 1981. 215 leaves: bibl.
Excellent technical study of industrial sector's textile exporting segment during 1975–78.

3609 Revesz, Bruno. Estado, algodón y productores agrarios. Piura, Perú: Centro de Investigación y Promoción del Campesinado, 1982. 444 p.: ill.
Comprehensive as well as fascinating analysis of the relationship between the State, cotton and agricultural producers during 1935–79.

Revilla, Julio. Industrialización temprana y lucha ideológica en el Perú: 1890–1910. See *HLAS 46:3014.*

3610 Saberbein Chevalier, Gustavo. Acerca de la crisis. Lima: Centro de Investigación Económica para la Acción, 1982. 76 leaves.

Detailed criticism of neoliberal development strategy pursued under Belaúnde's second administration.

3611 Schuldt, Jürgen. Política económica y conflicto social. Lima: Univ. del Pacífico, Centro de Investigación, 1980. 130 p.: ill. (Serie Ensayos; 16)

Examines relationship between economic policy and social and sectoral conflict.

3612 El Sector externo y las reservas internacionales. Lima: Banco Central de Reserva del Perú, 1982. 139, 18 p.: ill.

Two short articles by Richard Webb, President of Peru's Central Bank, and five documents examine relationship between external sector and international reserves. Highly informative examination of 1960–81 period.

3613 Seminario sobre el Problema del Empleo en el Perú, 1st, Lima, 1980. El problema del empleo en el Perú. Narda Henríquez, Javier Iguíñiz, eds. Lima: Pontificia Univ. Católica del Perú, Fondo Editorial, 1983. 463 p.: bibl., ill.

Proceedings of a conference on employment problem in Peru. Careful examination of labor markets' major dimension in Peru and Latin America.

3614 Seminario sobre la Situación Actual y Tendencias del Problema Agrario en el Perú, Lima, 1981. Situación actual y perspectivas del problema agrario en el Perú. Fernando Eguren, ed. Masson Meiss et al. Lima: DESCO, 1982. 535 p.: bibl., ill.

Agrarian and nutritional problem only seems to get worse in Peru. Important dimensions of this agricultural crisis are examined.

3615 Simposio Internacional sobre el Perú frente a las Nuevas Tendencias del Comercio Internacional, Lima, 1983. El Perú frente a las nuevas tendencias del comercio internacional. Editada bajo la dirección de Eduardo Ferrero Costa. Lima: Centro Peruano de Estudios Internacionales, 1984. 328 p.: bibl., ill. (Serie Simposios y seminarios internacionales; 1)

Proceedings of a conference on international trade and Peru. Excellent collection of articles attempting to identify the problems and provide solutions. Ferrero Costa's introduction does a remarkable job of summarizing the articles and differing views.

3616 Social Science Planning Conference, 2nd, International Potato Center, Lima, 1981. Social science research at the International Potato Center. Lima: The Center, 1982. 196 p.: bibl., ill.

Numerous articles dealing with different aspects of the "social science of the potato." Examine potato culture, marketing, consumption, farmer adoption of new technologies, and greater utilization of the potatoe as a basic food.

Szlaifer, Henryk. Los enclaves de exportación y la agricultura alimenticia en el Perú de los años 1890–1920: a propósito de las tesis de R. Thorp y G. Bertram. See HLAS 46:3016.

3617 Torres Trujillo, Raúl and Carlos de la Torre Postigo. La información macroeconómico en el Perú. Lima: DESCO, Centro de Estudios y Promoción del Desarrollo, 1982. 192 p.

Outstanding survey of macrostatistics available in Peru.

3618 Ulloa Elías, Manuel. Exposición del Ministro de Economía, Finanzas y Comercio, Doctor Manuel Ulloa Elías, ante la Cámara de Senadores. Lima: s.n., 1981. 61 p.

Very important philosophical, political, and economic document for understanding Belaúnde's second presidency. Provides blueprint for Belaúnde's development strategy.

3619 ———. Mensaje a la Nación del Presidente del Consejo de Ministros y Ministro de Economía, Finanzas y Comercio, Doctor Manuel Ulloa Elías: versión de la exposición televisada, transmitida al país el 10 de enero. Lima: Ministerio de Economía, Finanzas y Comercio, Oficina de Comunicaciones, 1982. 32 p., 26 leaves of plates: col. ill.

Ulloa Elías's 1982 Message to the Nation. Gives view of the government concerning the 1981–82 global economic crisis and its impact on Peru.

3620 United States' investment in Peru: a study of the situation in 1980. Lima: Escuela de Administración de Negocios para Graduados (ESAN), Depto. de Investigación, 1982. 2 v.: ill.

Comprehensive review of US investment in Peru in 1980.

3621 Vásquez Bazán, César. Congreso Económico Nacional. Lima?: Ediciones Pueblo: Comisión Nacional de Plan de Gobierno del Partido Aprista Peruano, 198? 92 p.: ill.

Plan of Peruvian Aprista party. Very useful ideological reference volume.

3622 Vega Centeno, Máximo. Naturaleza y características del cambio técnico en un país sub-desarrollo: el caso de la industria manufacturera en el Perú. Louvain-la-Neuve, Belgium: Univ. catholique de Louvain, Faculté des sciences économiques, sociales et politiques, 1982. 294, ll p.: bibl. (Nouv. série; 150)

Examines nature of technological process in Peru's industrial sector.

3623 Wolfenson Ulanowski, Azi. El gran desafío. Lima: Intergráfica de Servicios, 1981. 366 p., 50 p. of plates: ill. (some col.)

Systematic analysis of electricity's role in Peruvian economic development.

3624 Yepes del Castillo, Ernesto. Perú, 1820–1920: ¿un siglo de desarrollo capitalista? 2a ed. Lima: Ediciones SIGNO, 1981. 331 p.: bibl. (SIGNO universitario; 1)

"Dependency" based analysis of Peruvian economic development between 1820 and 1920.

BOLIVIA, PARAGUAY, AND URUGUAY

STEPHEN M. SMITH, *Associate Professor of Agricultural Economics, The Pennsylvania State University*

THE PUBLICATIONS REVIEWED for this volume were, on the whole, more interesting than in recent years, from the point of view of topics covered and the depth and quality of analysis. There is much more critical work being done by scholars inside each country. This is an encouraging result of governments moving toward more open, democratic policies. The trend is most evident in Bolivia and Uruguay, but even in Paraguay there is a distinct difference. The emerging issues noted in *HLAS 45* (p. 321) such as foreign trade, foreign debt, recent economic policies, have become main concerns in the works annotated below. Specifically, the focus of much recent research is on: 1) the impacts of the national and international economic crises of the early 1980s; 2) critical analyses of the economic policies followed by governments in the 1970s and early 1980s; and 3) rural and small farm development issues.

BOLIVIA

The literature on Bolivia provides a comprehensive overview of the economic problems the country faces. The economy and policies are analyzed from several viewpoints, yielding a menu of solutions, although the most recent data used is 1980. The work on this topic that I recommend first is Ramiro V. Paz C. (item **3641**). There is also a good set of studies on peasant agriculture, primarily in the Cochabamba and southern regions, covering general development issues, specific projects and primary data research. The research projects from CERES are well done and interesting as for example Roberto Laserna's (item **3637**) and José Blanes Jiménez's and Gonzalo Flores Céspedes (item **3627**). And of particular value for research on rural development in Bolivia is the bibliography by Maruja Uribe and Margarita Hernández (item **3649**).

PARAGUAY

The context for much of the Paraguayan literature is the Itaipú hydroelectric development. This development is having, and promises to have, major impacts throughout the economy and society. A key concern is how to make the best use of the forthcoming large supply of energy, and the related development policies that should be followed. This puts Paraguay in a very different position from most developing countries, and leads to a set of interesting research issues, many of which are either central or partial foci in several of the studies reviewed here. Another major concern is the formulation of recent government economic policies, particularly the impact of export oriented agricultural growth based on foreign investment. A good study of this topic is *Crisis mundial y recesión doméstica: situación económica en 1982* (item **3653**). A third focus of research has been rural and agricultural development, particularly small farms. Analysis focuses on impacts of several forces—Itaipú, government economic policies, export agriculture. Very good works on these topics are Aníbal Miranda's (item **3661**) and Domingo M. Rivarola's (item **3662**). On the general topic of underdevelopment, the articles by Ricardo Rodríguez Silvero (item **3664**), its companion annotated in *HLAS 45:3510* and the comment on the latter by Antonio W. Hill (item **3657**) are interesting.

URUGUAY

As noted in previous volumes of *HLAS*, there is a preponderance of work on economic history, the livestock industry, and trade and trade statistics. Much of this is unimaginative. In recent literature, however, there is evidence of a major change in focus. There are several complementary (and overlapping) critical and analytical studies of the "neoliberal," free market economic policies, and their impact, followed by the military government from 1974 through the early 1980s. The set of works from CINVE constitute solid analysis, with Luis Macadar (item **3678**) being good basic reading. Daniel Olesker's study (item **3682**) comprehensively analyzes trade impacts of these policies. Another interesting theme is the small, family farm sector, covered in the set of studies from "Temas Nacionales" by CIEDUR. A good example is the overview by Danilo Astori *et al.* (item **3672**). See also *HLAS 45:3516* and *HLAS 45:3531* for other works in the CIEDUR monographic series "Colección Temas nacionales."

BOLIVIA

3625 Baptista Gumucio, Fernando. Estrategia nacional para el hierro y el acero: Mutún, Santa Cruz, Cochabamba. La Paz: Empresa Editora Khana Cruz, 1981. 139 p.: bibl., maps.

Thesis is that iron and steel industry is too important to Bolivian development goals to be judged on technical-economic basis. Proposes horizontal integration of regions with different roles in processing. Believes this also will lead to improved rail system, which will stimulate further development of these regions.

3626 Blanes, José. Desarrollo económico y sectores sociales en Bolivia: análisis de algunos aspectos estructurales. La Paz: Centro de Estudios de la Realidad Económica y Social, 1982. 143 p.: bibl., ill., tables (Serie Estudios políticos; 2)

Examines economic conditions (1900–52) underlying unequal development of dominated classes that came together for the 1952 Revolution, and their changes since 1952. Considers general societal conditions and particular conditions and changes within each distinct class. Good bibliography.

3627 ———— and Gonzalo Flores Céspedes. Campesino, migrante y "colonizador:" reproducción de la economía familiar en el Chapare tropical. La Paz: Ediciones CERES, 1982. 358 p.: bibl., plates, tables (Serie Estudios regionales; 3)

Very comprehensive, detailed and well done study of colonization in Chapare region. Analyses at macro-region and family levels. Based on 500 interviews and two case studies in 10 colonies, focusing particularly on economic and farming activities.

3628 Bolivia. Ministerio de Finanzas. Plan económico de emergencia. La Paz: El Ministerio, 1982. 105 p.: ill., tables.

Discusses economic and financial crises in early 1980s, and causes. Focuses on general economic problems, external debt, balance of payments, public spending. Proposes solutions and presents detailed government plan. Includes budget and economic statistics. Valuable for comparison with nongovernment studies of same topic.

3629 Campesinado y desarrollo agrícola en Bolivia. Santiago: Naciones Unidas, 1982. 175 p.: bibl., ill., tables (Estudios e informes de la CEPAL; 13. E/CEPAL/R205)

Analyzes 1950–77 changes in peasant agricultural economy. Examines changes in social and intersectoral relationships and economic behavior of peasant agriculture, against background of agrarian reform and changes in national and international economies. Primarily a review of the literature, but a valuable and interesting overview. Includes useful data.

3630 Canelas Orellana, Amado and Juan Carlos Canelas Zannier. Bolivia: coca cocaína, subdesarrollo y poder político. Cochabamba, Bolivia: Los Amigos del Libro, 1983. 526 p.: bibl., ill., tables.

Comprehensive discussion of current and historical role of coca leaf and cocaine in Bolivian culture, society, and economy. Considerable examination of institutions and solutions suggested to combat "the problem." Valuable for economists for treatment of programs for alternative crops for peasants. Very interesting and readable.

3631 Diez Canseco Alvarez, Manuel. El presupuesto como instrumento estabilizador en una economía primario-exportadora. Brasília: Ministério da Fazenda, Escola de Admnistração Fazendária, Centro de Pesquisa, 1982. 110 p.: bibl., tables (Col. Teses de mestrado; 4)

Applies "implicit deficit" and "cyclically neutral deficit" methods of fiscal budget analysis to evaluate fiscal policy in an underdeveloped, primary resource-exporting economy. Objectives are to determine usefulness of budget to smooth economic cycles, and if Bolivian government policies were stabilizing or not. Concludes policies were expansionist and destabilizing beginning in 1973.

3632 Eckstein, Susan and Frances Hagopian. The limits of industrialization in the less developed world: Bolivia (UC/EDCC, 32:1, Oct 1983, p. 63–95, tables)

Applies alternative explanations of industrialization (neoclassical, dependency, export sector ownership) to assess extent to which each explains patterns in Bolivia since 1952. Each explains certain aspects. Comparisons with other countries imply that general theoretical explanations are difficult. Provides review of problems and symptoms, but little real analysis of causes and solutions.

3633 Estudio de comercialización de productos agrícolas: Chuquisaca, Potosí, Tarija. Sucre, Bolivia: Acción Cultural Loyola (ACLO), 1980. 325 p.: bibl., ill., plates, tables.

Objective is to provide agricultural and marketing information for peasant cooperatives in Chuquisaca, Potosí, and Tarija. Based on 1979 producer and consumer surveys, covering demand and supply of agricultural products, marketing channels, information used, and storage infrastructure. Transportation, storage, and price information are main problems. Very valuable and interesting.

3634 Estudio de factibilidad para una cadena de silos intercomunales de papa: Chuquisaca-Potosí-Tarija. Sucre, Bolivia: Acción Cultural Loyola (ACLO), 1982. 178 p.: ill., plates, tables.

Feasibility studies (socioeconomic-technical) for each department for a chain of silos, based on peasant cooperatives. Part of project to study marketing system improvements to raise peasant incomes. This work examines recommendations of a previous study, and finds they are economically feasible under certain assumptions.

3635 García Ayaviri, Enrique. Planificación negociada y desarrollo regional. La Paz: Editorial Los Amigos del Libro, 1981. 210 p.: bibl., ill., tables.

Application of method allowing regional development plans and desires to be met within national development plans. Applied to a project in dept. of La Paz, 1973–81. Where regional and national goals do not coincide, they can be "negotiated," using traditional benefit-cost analysis, plus frameworks of social value and appropriate technology.

3636 International Fund for Agricultural Development. Misión Especial de Programación a Bolivia. Informe. La Paz: El Fondo, 1979. 1 v. (various pagings): bibl., ill., tables.

Description and analysis of current geographical distribution, incidence, and causes of rural poverty. Sketches a general strategy to eliminate it, and how to apply such strategy, with attention to IFAD's potential role. Includes review of general economic and agricultural situation through late 1970s. Complete bibliography.

3637 Laserna, Roberto. Constitución y desarrollo regional de Cochabamba. La Paz: Ediciones CERES, 1982. 86 p.: bibl., ill., plates, tables (Serie Estudios regionales; 5. Serie Documentos CERES)

Uses dependency framework to describe Cochabamba region: organization of its economic, social, and political space; historical development; economy; and regional / local agricultural market structure. Contains data and bibliography.

3638 ———. El "estado" boliviano, 1971–1978: economía y poder. 2a ed. Cochabamba, Bolivia: Univ. Mayor de San Simón, Instituto de Estudios Sociales y Económicos, 1980. 51 leaves: bibl. (Serie Estudios preliminares; 13)

Brief and interesting analysis of economic and political policies of the Banzer government. Divides period into two phases and discusses political and economic bases of each. Context is converging and diverging interests of various socioeconomic classes with needs of the military government.

3639 ——— and **Fernando Cosio.** La pobreza en Cochabamba: un análises socioeconómico en la periferia urbana, 1976–1977. 2a ed. Cochabamba, Bolivia: Univ. Mayor de San Simón, Instituto de Estudios Sociales y Económicos, 1978. 2 v.: bibl., ill., tables (Publicaciones IESE; 8–9)

Uses 1976–77 survey data from urban periphery of Cochabamba to relate occupa-

tion and education, as causal factors of poverty, to various socioeconomic variables. Contains ample descriptive and tabular data presentations, description of methodology, and good bibliography.

3640 Miller, Calvin J. and **Jerry R. Ladman.** Factors impeding credit use in small-farm households in Bolivia (JDS, 19:4, July 1983,p. 522–538, tables)

Uses discriminant analysis on farm household survey data from Chuquisaca, Potosí, and Tarija to determine reasons why small farmers do not use credit. Results reinforce knowledge that impediments are primarily non-economic (sociocultural) transactions costs. Valuable for policy-makers, though not surprising to those familiar with peasant farmers.

3641 Paz C., Ramiro V. Crisis económica: ¿sin solución? La Paz: Editorial Los Amigos del Libro, 1982. 112 p.: tables.

Good analysis of current economic problems and interrelationships of causal factors, also applicable to many developing countries dependent on natural resource exports. Proposes complete policy revisions, which not unrealistic but politically difficult, from reformist, neoclassical viewpoint. Clearly written and recommended background reading.

3642 Ramos Sánchez, Pablo. Temas de la economía boliviana. La Paz: Ediciones Puerta del Sol, 1983. 2 v.: tables.

Critical pieces on political economy and government economic policy in areas of industry and trade (vol. 1), and development, planning and economic crisis (vol. 2). Compendium of writings dating from early 1960s, showing development of author's ideas, now rector of major Bolivian university. Written from socialist dependency viewpoint.

3643 Recchini de Lattes, Zulma. Las mujeres en la actividad económica en Argentina, Bolivia y Paraguay (CPES/RPS, 17: 47, enero/abril 1980, p. 7–34, bibl., graphs, tables)

Another work in series by this author and collaborators (see *HLAS 45:3515*). Interesting literature review of relationship between women's labor market participation and national economic development stages. Uses "U-curve" relationship as context. Disaggregates data in order to explain more precisely divergencies from expectations.

3644 Resultados adelantados de la encuesta permanente de hogares, mayo-octubre de 1980. La Paz: Ministerio de Planeamiento y Coordinación, Instituto Nacional de Estadística, Depto. de Muestreo y Encuestas, 1981. 43 leaves: tables.

Presentation of data and methodology from 1980 socioeconomic survey of homes in La Paz and Santa Cruz. First of several planned publications drawn from survey of 10 cities.

3645 Rivera P., Alberto. Pachamama expensive: el contexto territorial urbano y la diferenciación social en la ciudad de La Paz, 1971–1976. La Paz: Centro de Estudios de la Realidad Económica y Social, 1981. 112 p.: bibl., ill., plates, tables (Serie Estudios urbanos; 1)

Uses supply, demand, and price of land and living space in La Paz, and income generated from it, to examine implications for structure of urban space and resulting quality of life for various classes. Analyzed within the hypothesis that system favors the privileged classes.

3646 Rondinelli, Dennis A. and **Hugh Evans.** Integrated regional development planning: linking urban centres and rural areas in Bolivia (WD, 11:1, Jan. 1983, p. 31–53, maps, tables)

Describes method applied in Dept. of Potosí to: 1) drawing profile of system of urban places and linkages between them; and 2) provide information for a program to develop linkages integrating rural population into national economy and society, and to facilitate providing services to the population.

3647 Sector formal de la ciudad de La Paz: los trabajadores y sus familias. La Paz: Ministerio de Trabajo y Desarrollo Laboral, Dirección General de Empleo, 1980. 77 leaves: tables.

Results of 1978 worker and family survey of employees in establishments of more than five employees. Contains presentation and discussion of data.

3648 Tendler, Judith; Kevin Healy; and **Carol Michaels O'Laughlin.** What to think about cooperatives: a guide from Bolivia. Rosslyn, Va.: Inter-American Foundation, 1983. 272 p.: bibl.

Study of four cooperatives within context of their history, functioning, problems

and successes, and their role (and of cooperatives in general) in development. Does not rely on traditional cooperativism principles to judge success/failure. This leads to interesting suggestions for evaluating cooperatives and other rural development projects. Good bibliography.

3649 Uribe, Maruja and **Margarita Hernández.** Bibliografía selectiva sobre desarrollo rural en Bolivia. Bogotá: Biblioteca IICA, 1980. 134 p.: index (Serie IICA, Documentación e información agrícola, 0301–438X; 92)

Over 1000 citations from period 1960–80, primarily Spanish language, grouped under several subject headings, including "Bibliography of Bibliographies," list of organizations related to rural development in Bolivia, index of authors. One of series of bibiographies, published or planned, on rural development in Andean countries. Very valuable.

PARAGUAY

3650 Cabonell de Masy, Rafael. El séctor agro-alimentario en Paraguay (IEAS/R, 32:122, enero/marzo 1983, p. 89–117)

Examines expansion of foreign investment in agribusiness in Paraguay, beginning in mid-1800s, including evolution of government policy toward foreign investment. Particular focus on current structure and recent development of agricultural production and processing sectors.

3651 Canese, Ricardo. Itaipú y la cuestión energética en el Paraguay. Asunción: Univ. Católica Nuestra Señora de la Asunción, 1983. 273 p.: ill. (Biblioteca de estudios paraguayos; 7)

Analyzes development perspectives and current policies in context of huge energy supplies forthcoming from Itaipú hydroelectric project. Examines sectors where electricity can be profitably used vis-à-vis other energy sources. Believes that in order to benefit from new energy, there must be changes in economic structures favoring foreign firms as well as in prevalence of luxury and speculative investment over productive national investment.

3652 ———. Las necesidades térmicas para las industrias y para la cocción de alimentos en el Paraguay (CPES/RPS, 19:54, mayo/agosto 1982, p. 35–65, bibl., graphs, tables)

Detailed technical-economic examination of qualities of energy sources vis-à-vis industrial needs, particularly food processing, to determine role of Itaipú hydropower in industrial and domestic needs. Concludes that electricity will be too expensive for several years, and that existing biomass energy sources should be developed. Abundant supporting data.

3653 Crisis mundial y recesión doméstica: situación económica en 1982. Asunción: Depto. de Estudios, Comité de Iglesias, 1983. 124 p.: bibl. (Serie Cuadernos de investigación; 9)

Examination of economic situation in early 1980s. Strong criticism of government economic policies and their results, especially those regarding foreign investment and export agriculture. Concludes that conditions were not created for further development, but the contrary, resulting in no domestic market for consumption or investment, and benefitting only a minority.

3654 Frutos, Juan Manuel. Con el hombre y la tierra hacia el bienestar rural. Asunción: Cuadernos Republicanos, 1982. 300 p.: bibl., ill., maps, plates, tables.

Describes policies, process, and results of agrarian reform and colonization in Paraguay from government's viewpoint. Considerable data by department and colony on population and land area, for different time periods.

3655 García, Antonio. El minifundismo en el proceso agrario del Paraguay: hacia un nuevo proyecto de desarrollo rural (CPES/RPS, 18:52, sept./dic. 1981, p. 109–143, bibl., tables)

Discusses past and recent processes of change in rural Paraguay, focusing on minifundia sector and its role in rural and national economy. Examines different characteristics and potentials of minifundia in old and newly colonized areas, proposing solutions to the "minifundia problem" in each area.

3656 Gillespie, Fran. Comprehending the slow pace of urbanization in Paraguay between 1950 and 1972 (UC/EDCC, 31:2, Jan. 1983, p. 355–375, tables)

Examines why Paraguayan urbanization is slower, although population growth rates are high. Regression analysis shows that new employment opportunities in agriculture (colonization in northeast) and in other industries in non-urban areas drew migrants. Concludes that creation of job opportunities in rural areas will have desired result of decreasing urban growth.

3657 Hill, Antonio W. En torno a la problemática del desarrollo paraguayo (CPES/RPS, 18:51, junio/sept. 1981, p. 129–147)

Discussion and elaboration of Rodríguez S.'s article (see *HLAS 45:3510*) on dependency structure of capitalist development in Paraguay. Criticizes him for descriptive affirmations and not causal explanations; tautologies; eclectic choice of factors instead of cohesive conceptual framework, thus leading to his erroneous conclusions on causes of Paraguayan underdevelopment.

3658 Instituto de Bienestar Rural. Memoria general del ejercicio, 1982. Asunción: El Instituto, s.d. 220 p.

Official report of Institute of Rural Welfare on agrarian reform and colonization activities. History of philosophy, policies, and programs since 1960s. Data by department and colony. Similar to Frutos's *Con el hombre y la tierra* (item **3654**).

3659 Masi, Fernando. Contribución al estudio de la evolución socioeconómica del Paraguay (CPES/RPS, 19:53, enero/abril 1982, p. 33–63, bibl.)

Analyzes forces underlying economic evolution, emphasizing continuing but varying influence of Argentina and Brazil. Describes period of economic stagnation; changes leading to rise of capitalist production after 1960; and then focuses on changes in 1970s, emphasizing Itaipú construction, regional Brazilian industrialization, and multinational investment in cotton and soybeans.

3660 Mauro, Luis Alberto. REPSA, el negociado del siglo! Asunción: El Foro, 1981. 484 p.: ill., tables (El Petróleo y sus manejos en el Paraguay; 1)

Traces history of REPSA, foreign-owned firm that obtained national oil refining concession in 1962. Analyzes why concession and resulting policies and practices were to Paraguay's disadvantage. Advocates government intervention in the company and prosecution of those involved.

3661 Miranda, Aníbal. Desarrollo y pobreza en Paraguay. Rosslyn, Va.: Inter-American Foundation; Asunción: Comité de Iglesias para Ayudas de Emergencia, 1982. 372 p.: bibl., ill., tables.

Explores relationship between development and poverty within context of a peripheral capitalist country experiencing rapid modernization and growth. Describes worsening poverty in Paraguay and its causes (from field studies and household surveys), and suggests policies based on abundant energy and natural resources. Frank criticism of 1970s development policies and their effects. Good data and bibliography. Valuable basic reading.

3662 Rivarola, Domingo M. Modernización agraria y diferenciación campesina (CPES/RPS, 18:52, set./dic. 1981, p. 145–178, tables)

Discusses recent forces affecting rural areas and peasants: Itaipú hydroelectric project; economic and migration relationships with Brazil and Argentina; internal agricultural policy of technical modernization and export focus. Concludes that modernization is only on new lands that are geared to exports and based on foreign investment, leading to sharpening of inequalities.

3663 Rivarola Paoli, Juan Bautista. Historia monetaria del Paraguay: monedas, bancos, crédito público. Asunción: Imprenta El Gráfico, 1982. 599 p.: appendix, bibl.

Comprehensive history from colonial times to present of national monetary, banking, budgetary, and public credit policies and internal and external forces influencing these policies. Analyzed within context of the development of various economic and financial institutions.

3664 Rodríguez Silvero, Ricardo. Paraguay: desigualdad estructural análisis de un típico síntoma de subdesarrollo (CPES/RPS, 19:54, mayo/agosto 1982, p. 117–182, bibl., graphs, tables)

Unequal economic structures are symptoms, not causes of underdevelopment. Causes are social structure, integration of periphery with international division of labor, and structural dependency. Not recognizing this distinction causes economic development failures in Third World. Uses Paraguayan economy from mid-1800s as example. Interesting, well done. Good companion to author's article (see *HLAS 45:3510*).

3665 ———. Paraguay: el endeudamiento externo (CPES/RPS, 18:50, enero/mayo 1981, p. 65–87, bibl., tables)

Examines role of foreign debt in a country with "structural deformities" (e.g., dependent country on capitalist periphery) to determine if debt plays a positive role, or simply aggravates deformities. Identifies general stages in process of Paraguay's becoming indebted, and relates them to a positive or negative role. Interesting approach that allows for generalizations.

3666 Schiefelbein, Ernesto and **José Miguel Pujol.** Integración de métodos económicos y demográficos para proyectar recursos humanos: el caso del Paraguay (CPES/RPS, 16:44, enero/abril 1979, p. 165–183, tables)

Theme is that economists and demographers must combine their knowledge and methods to project labor force demand and supply in order to more precisely meet prediction needs of society. Method applied to Paraguayan data. Discusses new data needs for such joint efforts.

3667 Seminario Estrategia de Desarrollo en Condiciones de Oferta Abundante de Energía Eléctrica, *Asunción, 1980.* Memoria. Asunción: Colegio de Graduados en Ciencias Económicas del Paraguay: Banco Interamericano de Desarrollo, 1980. 165 p.: bibl., ill., plates, tables.

Seminar proceedings focus on best use of electricity from Itaipú. Papers cover topics such as: physical and service infrastructure needs; socioeconomic basis for a growing energy demand and how to promote increased use; rate determination; substituting electricity for other energy sources; the bases for developing energy-intensive industries.

URUGUAY

3668 Alonso, José María. La problemática agraria uruguaya: una visión integral. Montevideo: Fundación de Cultura Universitaria: Centro Interdisciplinario de Estudios sobre el Desarrollo Uruguay, 1982. 47 p.: bibl., ill. (Col. Temas nacionales; 7)

Last in series (see *HLAS 45:3516, HLAS 45:3531*, and in this section, Indalecio Perdomo's work, item **3683**) discussing current agricultural situation and its historical basis. First part synthesizes previous volumes. Remainder discusses implications and possible future evolution under various policies.

3669 —— and **Carlos Pérez Arrarte.** Subordinación en el agro uruguayo: una caracterización contemporánea de los productores familiares. Montevideo: Fundación de Cultura Universitaria: Centro Interdisciplinario de Estudios sobre el Desarrollo/Uruguay, 1983. 199 p.: bibl., ill., tables (Col. Temas nacionales; 9)

Detailed description of family farm sector (defined by labor force characteristics), including main commodities produced, production methods, and destination of output. Useful statistics. Valuable publication.

3670 Astori, Danilo. Neoliberalismo y crisis en la agricultura familiar uruguaya. Montevideo: Fundación de Cultura Universitaria: Centro Interdisciplinario de Estudios sobre el Desarrollo/Uruguay, 1982. 168 p.: bibl. (Col. Temas nacionales; 10)

Detailed analysis of 1970s neoliberal economic policies and their impacts on family farm sector. Pt. 1 discusses policies' objectives, instruments, and results. Pt. 2 looks at reactions of family farm sector, based on examination of organizations of family farms and postures taken vis-à-vis such policies.

3671 ——. La tecnología ganadera uruguaya: un caso de estancamiento integral. Montevideo: Ediciones de la Banda Oriental, 1979. 55 p.: bibl., tables (Serie C. Resultados de investigación; 1)

Discusses long-term stagnation of livestock industry, its technological problems, and previous interpretations of causes. Proposes and applies alternative analytical framework—generation and diffusion of technology and producers' attitudes. Concludes that: 1) producers preferred government economic support to technological improvement; and 2) process of diffusion and adoption of technology also stagnated.

3672 —— *et al.* La Agricultura familiar uruguaya: orígenes y situación actual. Montevideo: Fundación de Cultura Universitaria: Centro Interdisciplinario de Estudios sobre el Desarrollo/Uruguay, 1982. 120 p.: bibl., tables (Col. Temas nacionales; 8)

Introduction to small/family farm sector and its historical evolution. Analyzes effects of 1970s neoliberal open market policies on this sector. Summary publication of research project on family farm sector in context of 1970s economic policies (see also items **3669** and **3670**). Interesting and valuable study.

3673 Castagnola, José Luis and **Martín Gargiulo Blanco.** Roles ocupacionales asalariados en la producción ganadera. Montevideo: Centro Latinoamericano de Economía Humana, 1981. 2 v. (220 p.): bibl., ill., tables (Serie Investigaciones; 20–21)

Primarily a sociological study of structure of salaried occupations in the livestock industry and their "social role." Theoretical and methodological discussions, with analysis based on primary field data from one case study and interviews with people who had held the various occupations. Detailed and interesting.

3674 Davrieux, Hugo. La industria del cuero: auge y declinación, 1968–1981. Montevideo: Centro de Investigaciones Económicas: Ediciones de la Banda Oriental, 1983. 217 p.: bibl., tables (Estudios CINVE; 4)

Describes and analyzes expansion and decline of hide processing industry, 1968–81. Influential factors examined are worldwide restructuring, State's role, and particularly response of entrepreneurs during period of State's favorable policies and good international market.

3675 Faroppa, Luis A. Políticas para una economía desequilibrada: Uruguay, 1958–1981. Montevideo: Ediciones de la Banda Oriental, 1982. 108 p.: bibl. (Temas del siglo XX; 5)

Interprets the economy since 1958, using earlier period as base to analyze 1970s free market policies. Breaks 1970s into phases. Purpose is to orient policy thinking toward more democratic future. Companion to Luis Macadar's work (see item **3678**), but directed at a broader audience.

Foxley, Alejandro. Latin American experiments in neoconservative economics. See item **3538.**

3676 Hanson, James and **Jaime de Melo.** The Uruguayan experience with liberalization and stabilization, 1974–1981 (SAGE/JIAS, 25:4, Nov. 1983, p. 477–507, bibl., graphs, tables)

Examines economic growth under 1974–81 liberalization program. Looks at financial market policies, commodity market regulations, trade reforms, monetary policy. Evaluates effects on exchange rates, interest rates, inflation, monetary reserves, and exports. Based on authors' World Bank project. Interesting companion to Uruguayan studies of same topic annotated in this section (items **3670, 3672, 3675, 3678, 3682, 3683,** and **3688**).

3677 Lacurcia, Hugo W. El modelo actual de programación monetaria en el Banco Central del Uruguay. Montevideo: Banco Central del Uruguay, 1982. 29 p.: tables (Selección de temas; 18)

Technical presentation of econometric model used to determine monetary policy from 1978–81. Brief comparison with previous models and summary of government policy.

3678 Macadar, Luis. Uruguay, 1974–1980: ¿un nuevo ensayo de reajuste económico? Montevideo: Centro de Investigaciones Económicas: Ediciones de la Banda Oriental, 1982. 318 p.: bibl., ill., tables (Estudios CINVE; 1)

Analyzes neoliberal, free market economic policy of 1970s, with historical analysis from 1950s as basis for political and economic conditions leading to new policy. Discusses new policies in context of: 1) adjustment to international economic changes; and 2) internal adjustments in light of future democratic government. Necessary reading.

3679 Martínez Bengochea, Pablo. El excedente financiero agropecuario del Uruguay. Montevideo: Centro Latinoamericano de Economía Humana, 1982. 2 v. (259 p.): bibl., ill., tables (Serie Investigaciones; 23–24)

Analyzes structure and evolution of financial asset flows between agricultural and non-agricultural economies from 1955–79. Focuses on relationship between these flows

and capital accumulation in agriculture, examining sources of surplus and reinvestment capital, destination of surpluses, and debt-financed fixed investment in agriculture. Good data source.

3680 Martorelli, Horacio; Agustín Canzani; Constanza Moreira; and **Daniel Olesker.** El cooperativismo en la situación socioeconómica del Uruguay actual: el caso de las cooperativas de producción de Montevideo. Montevideo: Centro Interdisciplinario de Estudios sobre el Desarrollo Uruguay, 1982. 2 v.: appendix, bibl., ill., tables.

General study of characteristics and roles of small business production cooperatives, based on surveys of all (20) such cooperatives in Montevideo in 1982. Examines current situation and perspectives in light of anti-coop attitudes of government policies.

3681 ——— and **Constanza Moreira.** Para desenmascarar la pobreza. Montevideo: Centro Latinoamericano de Economía Humana, 1983. 2 v. (281 p.): bibl., tables (Serie Investigaciones; 29–30)

General examination of nature and structure of poverty from 1962–81, broken into three phases corresponding to economic policies/conditions, and differentiating by urban-rural. Based on secondary data and previous studies. Ample data and bibliography.

3682 Olesker, Daniel. Comercio exportador, desenvolvimiento industrial y relaciones de dependencia. Montevideo: Centro Interdisciplinario de Estudios sobre el Desarrollo/Uruguay, 1982. 183 leaves: tables.

Detailed analysis of non-traditional exports from 1973–81, within context of critical examination of neoliberal, free market, export promotion policies. Concludes that: 1) exports grew in quantity and diversity, but because of marketing and not changes in production structure; and 2) dependency relationships sharpened, leaving country more at mercy of world economic events. Well written, interesting, with ample data.

3683 Perdomo, Indalecio. La política agraria uruguaya: una visión histórica. Montevideo: Fundación de Cultura Universitaria: Centro Interdisciplinario de Estudios sobre el Desarrollo/Uruguay, 1982. 53 p.: bibl. (Col. Temas nacionales; 6)

Historical review of phases of government agricultural policies, and social political and ideological bases. Covers periods 1930–50 (protectionist model); 1959–73 (attempts at liberalization); and 1973–81 (neoliberal market model).

3684 Prates, Suzana. Políticas públicas y primacía urbana en el Uruguay. Montevideo: Centro de Informaciones y Estudios del Uruguay, 1980. 106 p.: bibl., ill., maps, tables (Centro de Informaciones y Estudios del Uruguay; 28)

Analyzes population and industrial concentration in 20th century, within context of lack of specific government policies, although government was heavily involved in the economy. Attributes such concentration to lack of interest of regional power elites, especially large landowners/livestock producers.

3685 Rama, Martín. Protección y crecimiento industrial, 1975–1980. Montevideo: Centro de Investigaciones Económicas: Ediciones de la Banda Oriental, 1982. 127 p.: bibl., ill., tables (Estudios CINVE; 3)

Examines changes in trade barriers and export subsidies as explanations for nontraditional industrial and export growth in late 1970s. Regression analysis leads to tentative conclusion that these are not relevant variables during this period, and that credit, fiscal or administrative stimulants are perhaps more worthy of study.

3686 Rial, Juan. Población y desarrollo de un pequeño país: Uruguay, 1830–1930. Montevideo: Acali Editorial: Centro de Informaciones y Estudios del Uruguay, 1983. 187 p.: ill., tables (Economia & sociedad. Serie A; 4)

Describes changing socioeconomic population structure, using census data, during Uruguay's modernization period and demographic transition. Relates demographic variables to character of the economy and level of social development.

3687 Terra, Juan Pablo. Distribución social del ingreso en Uruguay: estratos de ingresos, categorías socio-profesionales y clases sociales alrededor de 1960. Montevideo: Centro Latinoamericano de Economía Humana, 1983. 203 p.: bibl., ill., tables (Serie Investigaciones; 31)

Largely previously unpublished survey data from 1955, 1962, and 1963. Describes income distribution nationally, in Montevideo, between urban and rural areas, and for socioeconomic classes. Useful as comparative reference.

3688 Wonsewer, Israel and Juan Young Casaravilla. Uruguay en la economía mundial. Montevideo: Fundación de Cultura Universitaria: Centro Latinoamericano de Economía Humana, 1981. 140 p.: bibl. (Economía y sociedad; 4)

Analyzes Uruguay's economy and policy and future perspectives in context of neoliberal open market policy followed since 1974. Discusses alternative models such as: 1) "delinking" the economy from international system; and 2) selective participation in world trade.

3689 Zubillaga, Carlos. El reto financiero: deuda externa y desarrollo en Uruguay, 1903–1933. Montevideo: ARCA/CLAEH, 1982. 297 p.: bibl., tables (Col. El Pasado inminente)

Examines "batllista" period, focusing on political-economic model, and dividing era into two periods: 1) when reforms were possible and attempted; and 2) when reforms were abandoned to desires to stay in power. Context is heavy foreign debt left from 19th century, attempted reforms to avoid reliance on debt, and later recurrence to debt.

ARGENTINA

MICHAEL B. ANDERSON, *Chief of the Economics Sector, Institute for the Integration of Latin America, Inter-American Development Bank, Buenos Aires*

FOR THOSE WHO HAVE FOLLOWED THE ECONOMIC situation in Argentina over the past five years or so, the number of articles criticizing or supporting the liberal policies of former Minister of Economy José Alfredo Martínez de Hoz will come as no surprise. The major criticisms by Sourrouille (item **3728**) and others are comprehensive, covering economic as well as political aspects of the liberal policies. Their arguments, it would be fair to say, constitute an attack on the conceptual basis of the program, or that the analysis of economic problems facing Argentina and of the roles to be played by the private and public sectors were wrong. Interestingly, many of these critics have become major participants in the democratic government that followed. Their own policies which could possibly be described as pragmatic Keynesian (giving private initiative its due but leaving to the State the right if not obligation to provide investment incentives as well as to orient their distribution by sector) is presented in a planning document which was circulated late in 1984.

Others including Wogart (item **3730**), Nogués (item **3714**), and de Pablo (item **3716**), attempt to explain the liberal experiment's failure as a consequence of its insufficiency and unreasonableness. The government set targets which were not realistic and incompatible with, for example, the growth in the money supply and fixed exchange interest rates at levels which could not be sustained over the medium run. From another perspective, Sjaastad (item **3726**) objects to the Martínez de Hoz's program arguing that the only liberal thing about it was its being more so than what preceded.

Another important theme among the current crop of works annotated below concerns changes in the industrial structure brought on by the liberal program. The study prepared by CEPAL (item **3718**) is particularly useful, given the mass of quantitative data it provides to document the havoc played on the sector by the liberal program. A broader view of the development of the sector is presented by Dorfman (item **3697**).

It is surprising, given the importance of inflation and the inability of any government to deal with it, that so few studies of the phenomenon were published, exceptions are the works by Frediani (item **3702**) and Faggella (item **3700**). The same can be said of the debt problem about which little has been written. Most authors do no more than attribute it to the liberal program without questioning why other countries in the region—without liberal regimes—were also affected.

Finally, one can find many good studies of what are classic Argentine themes: the cattle cycle, public finance, and economic relations with England. CEPAL/ECLA continues to publish its data series and studies derived from them (item **3696, 3698, 3709,** and **3728**).

3690 Abreu, Marcelo de Paiva. Argentina and Brazil during the 1930s: the impact of British and American international economic policies. Rio de Janeiro: Pontifícia Univ. Católica do Rio de Janeiro, Depto. de Economía, 1983. 33 leaves: bibl. (Texto para discussão; 57)

Discusses what author calls triangular relations among two Latin American countries (Argentina and Brazil) and England and the US. Reviews Argentina's relations particularly with England and the subordination of Argentine foreign policy to England's. Results on Argentina's trade balance and exchange earnings were negative and eventually affected country's ability to recover from the world Depression. Compares with England/ Brazil relations in which British leverage was weaker and US policy more benevolent. Greater emphasis on Brazil.

3691 Arnaudo, Aldo A. El crecimiento financiero argentino en los últimos cuarenta años (UNC/REE, 22/24:1/4, 1979/ 1981, p. 9–45, bibl., graphs, tables)

Describes evolution of financial assets over past four decades as well as more important institutional developments. Considers that Argentina is quite advanced in its financial development but that role of financial variables in the growth process has been ambiguous. Marks important distinction between monetary and non-monetary assets in an inflationary environment. Graphs.

3692 ———. Posibilidades de una política monetaria monetarista en una economía inflacionaria: Argentina, 1978–1981 (Económica [Facultad de Ciencias Económicas, Univ. Nacional de La Plata, Argentina] 29:1, enero/abril 1983, p. 3–25, bibl., graphs, tables)

Questions monetarist view of monetary policy when applied to an economy experiencing high rates of inflation. Distinguishes between active and passive policies and, on the basis of the post-1977 Argentine experience, argues that only the latter is possible in an inflationary environment. In Argentina even the application of a "deliberate" passive policy was impossible and led to policies that were reactions to extreme uncertainty. Finally, notes that size of fiscal deficit was major if implicit determinant in monetary policy, independent of inflation.

3693 Bertinotti de Petrei, Nelva M. Las migraciones en Argentina en el período 1970–1980 (UNC/REE, 22/24:1/4, 1979/1981, p. 83–92, graphs, tables)

One of few studies on population trends in Argentina, examines migration between provinces and external migration based on 1970 population censuses as well as other provincial sources. Draws comparison of trends with previous decade and concludes that overall migration patterns have been similar. Includes interesting and useful graphs and detailed data. Useful for closer examination of migration patterns "encouraged" by the recent military government.

3694 Boneo, Horacio. Regímenes políticos y empresas públicas: algunas cuestiones vinculadas al ámbito y dimensión del sector productivo estatal. Buenos Aires: Centro de Estudios de Estado y Sociedad, 1980. 35 p.: bibl., ill., tables (Estudios CEDES; 3:7)

Examines relation between government and public enterprise in Argentina between 1958 and 1979–80, with additional material for the last two years. Argues against traditional views of this relation or that public enterprise reflects, on the one hand, public policy goals and, on the other, is part of a nationalization-privatization dichotomy. Prefers to examine changes in relative prices as indicative of government's approach to public enterprises. Finds substantial contradictions between what governments say they will do and what happens in practice.

3695 Borda, Gabriel S. Comercio internacional argentino. Buenos Aires: Editorial Fraterna, 1982. 302 p.: bibl., tables.

Study describes Argentina's participation in international commerce and multinational organizations. Also examines commercial policies throughout history and their impact on country's growth.

3696 Cuccia, Luis. El ciclo ganadero y la economía argentina: indicadores y análisis de su evolución, 1953–1979. Santiago: Naciones Unidas, 1983. 168 p.: bibl., graphs, ill., tables (Cuadernos de la CEPAL; 43. E/CEPAL/G.1234)

Substantial contribution to what is a classic theme: causes of the cycle in Argentine meat prices and production. Study emphasizes reconciling data on stocks and slaughter and constructing indicators of the meat cycle. Based on these indicators, author describes short- and long-run cycles and influence of corresponding international cycle on prices and production in Argentina. Tables, graphs.

3697 Dorfman, Adolfo. Cincuenta años de industrialización en la Argentina, 1930–1980: desarrollo y perspectivas. Buenos Aires: Ediciones Solar, 1983. 618 p.: ill., tables (Biblioteca Dimensión argentina)

Based on 40-yrs. research, offers long view of industrialization, chronicling mistakes, lost opportunities and decline of Argentina's industrial sector and suggests proposals for reform. Interesting material on evolution of industrial structure as well as on particular industries.

3698 Empresas transnacionales en la industria de alimentos: el caso argentino: cereales y carne. Santiago: Naciones Unidas, CEPAL, 1983. 93 p.: bibl., graphs, ill., tables (Estudios e informes de la CEPAL; 29. E/CEPAL/G.1255)

Interesting and original study of transnational firms operating in Argentina. Study's motivation: possible conflict of interests between transnationals and the State, described in chapter 1. Thoroughly documents contribution of these firms to production including provision of inputs and marketing of meats and cereals as well as legislation affecting them. Includes tables, graphs but no conclusions.

3699 El Estado y la economía, 1930–1955: políticas económicas. Selección y prólogo, Graciela Malgesini y Norberto Alvarez. Buenos Aires: Centro Editor de América Latina, 1983. 2 v.: bibl., ill., tables (Historia testimonial argentina; 9, 12)

Fascinating collection of documents on the peronist era (vol. 2) and its antecedents (vol. 1) including famous Roca-Runciman Protocol and Pinedo Plan which Raúl Prebisch helped design. Provides economic summary of the period; for the non-specialist.

3700 Faggella, Oscar D. Inflación: experiencia argentina. Buenos Aires: Ediciones Fundación Forum, 1983. 123 leaves: graphs, ill., tables (Col. Monografías)

Attempts to distinguish between various causes of inflation (i.e., structural, demand-pull, cost-push). Argues that it is impossible to attribute inflation to any single cause and that stabilization policies to reduce inflation should be applied to its multiple causes. Good historical coverage, statistics and graphs.

Foxley, Alejandro. Latin American experiments in neoconservative economics. See item **3538.**

3701 Frediani, Ramón O. La demanda de carne vacuna en Argentina y en el mercado internacional (BPC/RE, 35, 1982, p. 118–129, bibl., tables)

Meat consumption in Argentina represents 25 percent of total consumption in the cost of living index. Per-capita levels have been as high as 104 kilos. Meat exports represent important if declining amount in overall exports. Attention devoted to estimating demand for meat is therefore not surprising. Author reviews previous works on subject and presents own estimates of both domestic and foreign prices and income elasticities of demand.

3702 ———. La relación déficit fiscal-inflación. Córdoba, Argentina: Instituto de Ciencias de la Administración, Univ. Católica de Córdoba, 1983. 64 leaves: tables (Cuadernos de administración pública)

Excellent review of Argentine public sector and causes and consequences of the fiscal deficit. Presents clear overview of how public sector accounts are constructed and uses both historical and actual data to examine whether the fiscal deficit is a cause or consequence of inflation. Also provides simple quantitative estimates of relation among the deficit, inflation, and other important macro variables.

3703 Gaba, Ernesto. La reforma financiera argentina (BCRA/EE, 19, sept. 1981, p. 1–52, graphs, tables)

Examines consequences of 1977 financial reform and effects that real positive interest rates had on the system's efficiency. Complete and detailed coverage. Tables, graphs.

3704 Guy, Donna J. La industria argentina: 1870–1940, legislación comercial, mercado de acciones y capitalización extranjera (IDES/DE, 22:87, oct./dic. 1982, p. 351–374)

Examines importance of commercial legislation and limitations of national capital market in industrialization and growing dominance of foreign, especially English, firms from 1870 to World War II. Only after major crises did official intervention gain importance and only as of 1930s was there significant government promotion of national industries. For historian's comment, see *HLAS 46:3262.*

3705 Guzmán, Oscar and Hugo Altomonte. Perspectivas energéticas y crecimiento económico en Argentina: un estudio global y sectorial de la demanda de energía. México: Colegio de México, 1982. 240 p.: ill., graphs, tables (Programa de energéticos)

Unusual study examines Argentina's energy sector within context of national economic development. Author's thesis that demand for energy is conditioned by overall development tendencies implies that simple linear projections of energy demand on GDP growth, as is commonly done in planning, are not sufficient for large investment in the sector. Comprehensive study. Tables, graphs.

3706 Herken Krauer, Juan Carlos. Determinantes de la tasa de inflación en la Argentina: un estudio econométrico de las teorías contendientes, 1946–1977 (FCE/TE, 51:202, abril/junio 1984, p. 313–340, bibl., graphs, tables)

Reviews monetary, cost-push, and structuralist approaches to explain Argentine inflation, based on regression models for 1946–77. After brief historical discussion and attempts to explain price movements, author presents equation for annual data. Combines elements from all approaches and applies various statistical and predictive power tests to determine adequacy of specification presented. Overall, prefers structural approach as superior. Unfortunately, article does not include original data.

3707 Heussen, Hejo. Weltmarkt und soziale Not: über die Unsicherheit sozialer Sicherheit in der Dritten Welt. Berlin: Sozialpolitischer Verlag, 1980. 408 p.: bibl., tables (AG SPAK Materialien; 44)

Historical overview of social security and health insurance in Latin America from late colonial period to post World War II. Examines infrastructure, labor relations, union organization, and their impact on demanding social services. Focuses on early role and contributions of cooperatives. Argentina is highlighted in this important contribution. [G.M. Dorn]

3708 Iglesias, Antonio. Política petrolera argentina. Buenos Aires: Distribuidores Librería del Plata, 1980. 273 p.: bibl., ill., tables.

While written from a private sector perspective, author presents reasonably argued and complete history up to early 1970s. Technical details will be of interest to specialists, but information on various governments' energy policies should be useful to others. Includes many statistics whose quality and accuracy are not easy to judge. No index.

3709 Itzcovich, Samuel and **Heber Carmelo.** La empresa pública en la economía: la experiencia argentina, estadísticas para el análisis económico y financiero. Santiago:

Naciones Unidas, CEPAL, 1983. 134 p.: tables (Estudios e informes de la CEPAL; 21. E/CEPAL/G.1232)

Comprehensive statistical description of public sector firms in Argentina. Authors attempt to provide sufficient information to determine which firms can be considered public (no easy task), sectors they belong to, their relation to the public sector and overall economy. Contains 1950–76 data with update through 1981.

Jenkins, Rhys. The rise and fall of the Argentine motor vehicle industry. See item **6519.**

3710 Jornadas de Finanzas Públicas, *14th,* *Córdoba, Argentina, 1981.* Trabajos de investigación. Organizadas por la Facultad de Ciencias Económicas, Univ. Nacional de Córdoba. Córdoba, Argentina: Comité Ejecutivo, Jornadas de Finanzas Públicas, 1982. 1 v. (various pagings): bibl., graphs, ill., tables.

Consists of 17 applied and theoretical studies on public finance. Former covers areas such as costs of public works, financing public deficit, industrial promotion, tax collection, and agricultural incentives. Tables, graphs.

Kuhl, Livio Guillermo; Horacio R. Rieznik; Rodolfo E. Biasca; and **Roberto Iglesias.** Una política industrial para la Argentina. See item **6521.**

3711 Mathieson, Donald J. Inflación, tipos de interés y balanza de pagos durante una reforma financiera: el caso Argentina (BCRA/EE, 22, junio 1982, p. 41–90, bibl., tables)

Examines effects of 1977 financial reform on financial sector, inflation, and balance of payments by means of small macro model. After presenting model and describing estimation procedures, discusses actual outcome, found to be reasonably consistent with model's projections. A dynamic simulation for 1980 is also carried out to further validate the model. Its implications are interesting and might have practical application for policy makers wishing to say something useful about their frequent reforms.

Los Mitos de Milton Friedman. See item **2930.**

3712 Nogués, Julio J. Política arancelaria y de promoción de exportaciones: elementos para su formulación (UNLP/E, 3, sept./dic. 1982, p. 211–243, bibl.)

Discusses economic consequences of 40-yrs. commercial policies typical of Argentina. Argues that benefits have accrued mostly to protected industries and probably caused substantial income loss. Consequences have been more demand for capital, more waste, distortion in industrial sector which includes an anti-export bias, declining competitiveness, and diseconomies of scale. Suggests that during transition towards a more open economy, as many resources should be devoted to retooling as were lost due to maintenance of antiquated industries. Also reviews commercial policies that would increase social welfare.

3713 ———. Substitución de importaciones versus promoción de exportaciones: impactos diferenciales sobre el empleo en el sector manufacturero argentino (IDES/DE, 22:86, julio/sept. 1982, p. 249–286, bibl., tables)

Are there differences in employment levels under policies of import substitution vs. export promotion? Answers that exporting industries in competition with imports are more labor intensive than those which do not compete. Industries exporting to developed countries are also more labor intensive than those exporting to less developed ones. Based on 1963–64 and 1973–74 census data. English version of article appeared in *World Development* (part of author's dissertation). Tables.

3714 ———. Tipo de cambio de paridad: algunas estimaciones para la economía Argentina (Ecónomica [Facultad de Ciencias Económicas, Univ. Nacional de La Plata, Argentina] 29:1, enero/abril 1983, p. 45–81, bibl., graphs, tables)

One of liberal program's central instruments, especially towards the end, was the pre-announced crawling peg. This is an important contribution to the growing debate as to its effects on the economy. Presents method for estimating a purchasing power parity exchange rate (PPA) and estimates difference between this PPA and the official exchange rate. Indicates that two major external sector crises in Argentina during 1970s occurred when this difference was greatest. Author's approach is compared to an equilibrium exchange rage estimate.

3715 ———. Tipo de cambio real e importaciones durante 1976–1981: una nota econométrica (BCRA/EE, 23, sept. 1982, p. 1–20, bibl., graphs, tables)

Estimates price elasticity of imports (1976–81) taking into account lack of foreign competition of domestic producers, changes in the tariff, etc. Also reviews period's major policies and how they affected the economy. Argues that, in context of high protection, a strong devaluation has short-run recessive effect on the economy. Results indicate significant price elasticity of demand for imports. Consequently, notes inadequacies of policies to reduce protection while simultaneously overvaluing the exchange rate.

O'Connell, Arturo. La Argentina en la Depresión: los problemas de una economía abierta. See *HLAS 46:3313.*

3716 Pablo, Juan Carlos de. El enfoque monetario de la balanza de pagos en la Argentina: análisis del programa del 20 de diciembre de 1978 (FCE/TE, 50[2]:198, abril/junio 1983, p. 641–669, bibl., tables)

Examines one of Martínez de Hoz's economic programs (1978) designed to reduce inflation and stimulate the economy. The pre-announced crawling peg was introduced and the nominal value of all government-controlled monetary variables were lagged to act as a break on overall prices. Tariff reforms were also introduced and inflation fell in 1979–80. But there was no supposed convergence between officially-controlled prices and the "market." Argues reason was rapid money expansion created by 1980 financial crisis. Tables.

3717 ———. Escritos seleccionados: 1968–1980. Buenos Aires: Ediciones Macchi, 1981. 465 p.: bibl., ill., tables.

The gadfly of Argentine economists, de Pablo presents a selection of his writings on Argentina, economics, and sometimes on both together. With good style and humor, de Pablo became an editorialist whose opinions made as much good sense as they did economic sense. He cannot be easily categorized and prefers to comment on the particular rather than the general, on events rather than whole administrations.

Pang, Eul-Soo. Buenos Aires and the Argentine economy in world perspective, 1776–1930. See *HLAS 46:2792.*

3718 El Proceso de industrialización en la Argentina en el período 1976–1983. Buenos Aires: Naciones Unidas, CEPAL, 1984. 1 v.: tables.

Study reviews process of industrialization (up to 1976) and desindustrialization (1976–83) based on detailed statistics drawn from ECLA/CEPAL's rich data base. Describes industrial policies emerging from the "Program of Recovery, Restructuring (i.e., Saneamiento) and Expansion" and their effects on growth and investment. Presents interesting new material on evolution of large and foreign firms. Final chapter examines actual situation and elements for industrial recovery. Tables.

Recchini de Lattes, Zulma. Las mujeres en la activad económica en Argentina, Bolivia y Paraguay. See item **3643.**

3719 Reunión Técnicos de Bancos Centrales del Continente Americano, *20th, La Paz, 1983.* XX [i.e. Vigésima] Reunión de Técnicos de Bancos Centrales del Continente Americano. v. 23, Estimación de un indicador de la producción mensual manufacturera. v. 24, La experiencia argentina: sentido y proyección de la Ley 22.529 sobre consolidación de entidades financieras. v. 36, La demanda de billetes y monedas en la Argentina: un análisis empírico. La Paz: Banco Central de Bolivia, 1983. 3 v. (42, 12, 32 leaves): bibl., tables.

Vols. 23, 24, and 36 of 38 (see item **3080**) are devoted to Argentina. Vol. 23 examines why given substantial month-to-month fluctuations in monetary variables, there is need to produce monthly estimate of real variables so as to confront problems arising from their interaction. Estimates production from limited data for economy's main industrial sectors or by use of seven variables with seasonal components removed. Well done statistical presentation, tables. Vol. 24 discusses the liberalization of the financial system in 1977. Rapid expansion of banking sector and general optimism in 1978–79 led, unfortunately, to failure of several banks in 1980, the beginning of the end of the Argentine miracle. Overexpansion and weakness of banking sector resulted in several Central Bank regulations cumulating in Law 22529 which attempted to consolidate and strengthen banks. Vol. 36 attempts to identify variables helpful in explaining money demand in Argentina.

What distinguishes this econometric study from others is the great care taken in defining variables utilized and attention paid to historical circumstances which in Argentina is no trivial matter. Regressions also have some unusual characteristics such as the inclusion of retail trade as a defining variable. Unfortunately, original data is not included.

3720 Rezk, Ernesto and Orlando Barra Ruatta. Algunas consideraciones sobre el efecto protección en la estructura arancelaria argentina (UNC/REE, 22/24: 1/4, 1979/1981, p. 97–129, tables)

Authors review elements to be taken into account in determining an effective rate of protection including effects of the exchange rate. While mostly conceptual, their application to the protection of a specific good under different tariff assumptions is interesting and may be useful to other researchers.

3721 Rofman, Alejandro B. La política económica y el desarrollo regional. Bogotá: Ediciones Universidad y Pueblo, 1981. 150 p.: bibl. (Col. Universidad y pueblo)

Case study of regional policy in Argentina: background, analysis of regional inequality, evaluation of regional policies, conclusions. Helpful for understanding economic history up to late 1970s. [J.M. Hunter]

3722 Schulthess, Walter Erwin. Los determinantes de la presión tributaria en la República Argentina. Córdoba, Argentina: Centro de Investigación y Perfeccionamiento en Ciencias Económicas y Administración Pública, Instituto de Ciencias de la Administración, Univ. Católica de Córdoba, 1982. 2 v.: bibl., ill., tables (Cuadernos de administración pública, 0326–0003; 26, 32)

Study of Argentina's tax system and particularly the tax burden (as percent of GNP) over past three decades. Pt. 1 attempts to determine principal determinants of change in tax burden shown to fluctuate considerably over time. Considers three clases of independent variables: economic, administrative, and institutional (type of government) and provides quantitative estimates of their influence. Pt. 2 runs regressions for same independent variables but the tax burden (dependent variable) is disaggregated into different clases and jurisdictions.

Schvarzer, Jorge. Martínez de Hoz: la lógica política de la política económica. See item **6537.**

——. Argentina, 1976–81: el endeudamiento externo como pivote de la especulación financiera. See item **6536.**

Sempat Assadourian, Carlos. El sector exportador de una economía regional del interior argentino, Córdoba, 1800–1860: esquema cuantitativo y formas de producción. See *HLAS 46:3350.*

3723 Sheahan, John. Early industrialization and violent reaction: Argentina and Brazil. Brighton, England: IDS, 1982. 36 p.: bibl., tables (Discussion paper, 0308–5864; DP 176)

While presenting no new material, author argues that the industrialization process, eventual conflicts, and reactions were similar in both Southern Cone countries. Believes that various interpretations (structuralist's, monetarist's, etc.) have some validity at different stages of industrialization. Concludes by addressing question of sustainable economic policies, need for consistency and fair distribution and inherent constraints to industrialization.

3724 Sidicaro, Ricardo. Estado intervencionista, grandes propietarios rurales y producción agropecuaria en Argentina: 1946–1976 (GEE/NA, 5, 1982, p. 399–432, tables)

Describes transformation of Argentine policy beginning with Perón in 1945 in support of import-substituting industrialization. Increasing State intervention was required to assure resources transfer from agricultural to industrial sector. Also, under the Radical Party, the State intervened to increase exportable surpluses to provide foreign exchange needed to import capital and intermediate goods for industrial production and growth. These policies were maintained throughout 1970s. Author mentions ability of agricultural sector to counter (invalidate) government measures causing an escalation of State controls. For historian's comment, see *HLAS 46:3351.*

3725 Sjaastad, Larry A. Estabilización y tipo de cambio: el contraste entre Chile y Argentina. Santiago: Centro de Estudios Públicos, 1981. 31 p.: bibl., tables (Documento de trabajo; 1)

Compares stabilization experiences of two major proponents of pre-announced crawling peg devaluations. Program's success in controlling inflation in Chile and its failure in Argentina are partly attributed by author to closeness in rates of devaluation and inflation in the former and their divergence in the latter. Also points out differences in policies on domestic rate of interest due to relative restrictions on flow of goods and capital between both countries.

3726 ——. O fracasso do liberalismo econômico no Cono Sul da América Latina (RBMC, 9:26, abril/junho 1983, p. 125–151, tables)

Liberal policies and their failure in Argentina, Chile, and Uruguay have become favorite topics of analysis in the monetarists-structuralist debate. Author argues that reforms carried out were neither liberal nor monetarist but merely more liberal and monetarist than before. Also argues that for such programs to be successful, they must be consistent and that both Argentina and, to lesser extent, Chile had serious internal inconsistencies. Helpful comparison between Argentina and Chile, weak on Uruguay.

3727 Soifer, Ricardo J. Argentina (WD, 12:5/6, May/June 1984, p. 625–644, table)

Using survey techniques, finds evidence of Argentine technology exports as well as direct investment abroad (mostly to other Latin American countries). Study's contribution is mainly taxonomic. Factors contributing to technology exports are not identified. Conclusions that such exports were significant is questionable in that firms surveyed do not provide representative sample nor is overall context of exports presented.

3728 Sourrouille, Juan V. and **Jorge Lucángeli.** Política económica y procesos de desarrollo: la experiencia argentina entre 1976 y 1981. Santiago: Naciones Unidas, CEPAL, 1983. 157 p.: graphs, tables (Estudios e informes de la CEPAL; 27. E/CEPAL/G.1233)

Excellent synthesis and criticism of the Martínez de Hoz period. Author (former Under-Secretary of Economics and Alfonsín's First Minister of Planning) argues that instead of transforming a State-dominated economy into a market system, government policies simply exposed inherent structural deficiencies in the economy glossed over by previous governments. Also criticizes program's inconsistencies and lack of flexibility in failure to look beyond monetary phenomena when confronted with recalcitrant problems such as high inflation. Tables, graphs.

3729 Vilariño, José. Incidencia del progreso tecnológico en el crecimiento del producto: Argentina, 1930–50. Mar del Plata, Argentina: Instituto de Investigaciones Económicas, Facultad de Ciencias Económicas y Sociales, Univ. Nacional de Mar del Plata: Secretaría de Planeamiento, Municipalidad del Partido de General Pueyrredón, 1982. 24 leaves: bibl., ill., tables (Serie de estudios; 5)

Given difficulties or lack of incentives for capital accumulation (1930–50) what factors were responsible for the observed 76 percent growth in output? Author investigates contribution of technological progress (tp) to this growth. Constructs an index of tp and his empirical results led to conclusion that almost four/fifths of increase in output per worker was due to tp. Useful table of parameters for other looking at post-1950 period.

3730 Wogart, Jan Peter. Combining price stabilization with trade and financial liberalization policies: the Argentine experience, 1976–1981 (SAGE/JIAS, 25:4, Nov. 1983, p. 445–476, bibl., tables)

Thorough quantitative review of impact of 1976–80 program on the economy. Presents his view of causes of the failure which include incomplete financial reform, distortions introduced with tariff reforms, deterioration of external accounts and rise of real wages during recession. Notes further that program's objectives shifted drastically from demand restraint stabilization to supply restructuring or to what has been called the industrialization of Argentina.

3731 ——— and José Silverio Marques. Trade liberalization, tariff redundancy and inflation: a methodological exploration applied to Argentina (CAUK/WA, 120:1, 1984, p. 18–39, bibl., graph, tables)

Authors present two simple measures of tariff redundancy and show extent to which such redundancy was reduced in various industrial subsectors (1977–79). They indicate that principal cause for this reduction was rapid rise in domestic prices during period and offer some evidence that reduction in redundancy restrained inflation towards end of 1979, although other factors contributed to resurgence in inflation early in 1980. With regard to output and productivity, overall impact of reduction in redundancy was to increase imports as local firms did not make the adjustments necessary to remain competitive.

BRAZIL

DONALD V. COES, *Associate Professor of Economics, University of Illinois at Urbana-Champaign*

WRITINGS ON THE BRAZILIAN ECONOMY in the past few years have been dominated by a sense of crisis, especially after the severity of the external debt problem became dramatically evident in late 1982. The economics literature has been affected by the *crise* in several ways, both positively and negatively.

As is usually the case in times of economic difficulty, economists find both a ready topic and an attentive audience. The balance of payments and external equilibrium consequently are the focus of much of the recent literature, and books and articles dealing with other topics frequently note their international economic aspects. The links between exchange rate policies and inflation, exports and agricultural development, capital flows and financial markets, or commercial policies and industrial structure, are examples of the attention devoted to Brazil's relations with the international economy.

The crisis has also exacted a toll from the Brazilian economics community, as well as from the public at large. Since there is no longer a shortage of academically trained economists as in the late 1960s and early 1970s, Brazilian economists' real wages have been affected by the same decline suffered by all Brazilians. In an attempt to maintain their real incomes, many Brazilian economists have sought extra work, adding to their teaching or consulting activities, or in some cases holding two or more jobs simultaneously. Others have been attracted to the financial sector, which has offered relatively better employment and income conditions in the past few years. Brazilian academic literature in economics has probably suffered, as economists' incentives and time for such activities decreased. In addition, a fall in the real level of public expenditure for universities and research in the social sciences, as well as real depreciation, have made it more difficult for Brazilian economists to continue their research, maintain contacts with the international economics community, keep up with the literature, or attend professional conferences.

Despite these adverse trends, it is probably more accurate to characterize the current situation as one of slow growth, rather than actual decline. Among the factors partially offsetting the economic squeeze is the continuing trend among Brazilian candidates for masters and doctoral degrees to publish their theses as books or articles. Such contributions form a substantial proportion of the publications noted below. Although a number of such theses were written for submission to foreign universities, the majority are from major Brazilian graduate institutions. As has been the case in the past, students and faculty from the Univ. de São Paulo (USP), the Fundação Getúlio Vargas (FGV), and Rio's Pontifícia Univ. Católica (PUC) dominate much of the academic literature on Brazilian economics.

A good sampling of the work of Brazilian economists affiliated with the principal graduate centers may be found in the *Anais* (item **3770**) of the 12th national meeting of ANPEC, the association of Brazilian centers in economics, and in the *Trabalhos apresentados* (item **3769**) at the accompanying meetings of the Sociedade Brasileira de Econometria (SBE).

Economists from a number of these institutions have been particularly active in discussions of Brazil's external economic problems. Among the works of note in this category are *Dívida externa, recessão e ajuste estructural* edited by PUC's Pérsio Arida (item **3766**), *Ensaios sobre o setor externo da economia brasileira* by FGV economists (item **3744**), and *Desenvolvimento capitalista no Brasil: ensaios sobre a crise* organized by Belluzo and Coutinho at the Univ. de Campinas (item **3762**).

A traditional theme in Brazilian economics is the Northeast. Works of note on its economic problems include studies by Univ. Federal de Pernambuco economists, *Desigualdades regionais no desenvolvimento brasileiro* (item **3763**) and *Emprego no Nordeste* (item **3768**), as well as the essays by Clóvis Cavalcanti *et al.*, *Nordeste brasileiro: um desenvolvimento conturbado* (item **3756**). In addition, the role of the *Revista Económica do Nordeste* in publishing many of the best articles on the Northeastern economy should be noted (e.g., items **3735, 3774,** and **3780**).

Several contributions noted below are not the work of academic economists. Melo Franco's and Pacheco's *História do Banco do Brasil* (item **3778**) is likely to become an important reference work for students of Brazilian financial development. Rosenn's monograph (item **3831**) on the regulation of foreign investment in Brazil is written from a legal viewpoint, and provides a wealth of institutional detail often ignored by economists.

Brazilian economic literature reflects both the difficulties of the current situation and earlier trends and traditions. The technical competence of Brazilian academic economists is reflected in the approach and level of many of the articles cited below. For all their mastery of the profession's tools, however, the literature reveals a strong commitment to local problems and policies, all of which will receive ample scrutiny with the return of democracy.

Abreu, Marcelo de Paiva. Argentina and Brazil during the 1930s: the impact of British and American international economic policies. See item **3690.**

3732 Albuquerque, Rui Henrique Pereira Leite de. Capital comercial, indústria têxtil e produção agrícola: as relações de produção na cotonicultura paulista, 1920–1950. São Paulo: Editora HUCITEC; Brasília: Conselho Nacional de Desenvolvimento Científico e Tecnológico, 1982. 268 p.: bibl., ill., tables (Economia & planejamento. Série Teses e pesquisas)

Based on Campinas master's thesis, study examines São Paulo's cotton sector (1920–50). Focuses on relationship between cotton growers and textile industry. Argues that contrary to widespread opinion, cotton culture was not a "democratic" sector in which small and independent producers predominated.

3733 Almeida, Fernando Lopes de. Política salarial, emprego e sindicalismo, 1964–1981. Petrópolis: Vozes, 1982. 113 p.: bibl., tables.

Rather summary treatment of Brazilian labor market since 1964. Alleges that compression of real wages after 1964 and increasing income inequality were consequences both of government policies intended to provide a market for sophisticated consumer durables and increase in capital-intensive production by multinational enterprises.

3734 Almeida, Julio Sergio G. de. Um estudo sobre as financeiras no Triênio 1965–67 (RBMC, 6:17, maio/agôsto 1980, p. 189–201, bibl., tables)

Analyzes rapid growth and development of financial enterprises in 1965–67 period, focusing on changes in financial institutions and market structure, as well as effects of government policies. Well documented review of financial markets in the period, based on Campinas master's thesis.

3735 Almeida, Manoel Bosco de. Taxas de retorno e preço do capital: uma medida alternativa do preço relativo do capital, o caso do Nordeste e Sudeste do Brasil, 1970

(BNB/REN, 13:3, julho/set. 1982, p. 633–656, tables)

Investigates differences between rates of return to capital in 21 Northeast and Southeast manufacturing sectors, using 1970 Industrial Census data. Shows that gross rates of return were higher in Southeast, despite higher capital-labor ratio, and partly attributes this difference to regional differences in economic efficiency.

3736 Aspectos da evolução da agropecuária brasileira, 1940–1980. Brasília: Secretaria de Planejamento da Presidência da República, IBGE, 1980. 73 p.: ill. (some col.), tables.

Summary of agricultural statistics from national census data (each decade plus 1975). Data includes producing areas by state and region, employment in agriculture, mechanization, and numbers of farms. Although these data could be obtained from individual censuses, their organization and presentation in a single source is helpful.

3737 Assis, José Carlos de. Os mandarins da República: anatomia dos escândalos na administração pública, 1968–84. Rio de Janeiro: Editora Paz e Terra, 1984. 231 p.: bibl. (Col. Estudos brasileiros; 75)

Muckraking, often polemical denunciation of financial mismanagement and corruption in public sector by a Folha de São Paulo journalist. Detailed and generally well documented examinations of seven cases, among them the "Capemi" scandal. Although not critical of public sector per se, Assis shows how the concentration of economic power may be abused in the absence of democratic safeguards.

3738 Assis, Milton Pereira de. Um modelo macroeconométrico de política a curto prazo para o Brasil. Rio de Janeiro: IPEA/INPES, 1981. 283 p.: bibl., ill., tables (Monografia; 32)

Specifies and estimates short-run Keynesian macroeconomic model for Brazil, using annual data for 1948–75 period. In addition to its detailed examination of the functioning of monetary, fiscal and exchange policy on macroeconomic activity, study is valuable source of macroeconomic time series. Based on author's Johns Hopkins doctoral dissertation.

3739 Avaliação do sistema de incentivos fiscais às exportações. São Paulo: Governo do Estado de São Paulo, Secretaria de Economia e Planejamento, 1979. 2 v.: bibl., ill., tables (Série Estudos e pesquisas; 27)

Government-sponsored study of characteristics and sources of Brazilian export growth, particularly in post-1968 period. Emphasizes role of export subsidies and related tax incentives, with particular emphasis on the BEFIEX (tax incentive special program for exports) established in 1972. Useful collection of statistical data for 1970s.

3740 Azevedo, Sérgio and Luis Aureliano Gama de Andrade. Habitação e poder: da Fundação da Casa Popular ao Banco Nacional da Habitação. Rio de Janeiro: Zahar Editores, 1982. 135 p.: bibl., ill., tables.

Analyzes history and politics of government financing for housing, focusing on Banco Nacional de Habitação (BNH). Although interpretive in approach, discussion is well documented and supported by detailed examination of financing procedures and by quantitative data.

3741 Bacha, Edmar. Vicissitudes of recent stabilization attempts in Brazil and the IMF alternative (*in* IMF conditionality. Edited by John Williamson. Washington: Institute for International Economics, 1983, p. 323–340, tables)

Review of Brazilian macroeconomic experience since 1968, leading to external payments crisis of early 1980s. Concludes with interesting analysis of costs and benefits Brazil might have faced had it gone to IMF at this time and committed itself to a stabilization program, as it was subsequently forced to do.

3742 Barros, José Roberto Mendonça de *et al.* Economia agrícola: ensaios. São Paulo: Instituto de Pesquisas Econômicas, Univ. de São Paulo (IPE-USP), 1982. 176 p.: bibl., ill., tables (Série Relatórios de pesquisa; 11)

Five essays on Brazilian agriculture by Univ. de São Paulo economists: De Barros discusses implications of large-scale bioenergy production; J. Pastore *et al.* analyze determinants of technical progress in six crops; F. Homem de Melo shows that integra-

tion of an agricultural sector into international markets tends to reduce price instability; C. Longo examines tax incidence in agriculture; and, in an concluding essay, J. Sayad addresses links between macroeconomic policies and agriculture.

3743 Batista Júnior, Paulo Nogueira. Mito e realidade na dívida externa brasileira. Rio de Janeiro: Editora Paz e Terra, 1983. 225 p.: bibl., tables (Col. Estudos brasileiros; 67)

Group of related essays on Brazilian balance of payments policies and prospects. Shows that worsening payments situation in recent years cannot be attributed to external shocks, and that domestic economic policy, particularly exchange policy, is largely to blame. Important contribution to discussion of one of Brazil's most pressing economic problems.

3744 ———; Antônio Carlos B. Lemgruber; Roberto de Rezende Rocha; and José Maria Gouveia Vieira. Ensaios sobre o setor externo da economia brasileira. Rio de Janeiro: FGV, Instituto Brasileiro de Economia, 1981. 212 p.: ill., tables (Estudos especiais IBRE; 2)

Nine essays by FGV economists on Brazilian balance of payments and exchange rate policies, five of them by Paulo Nogueira Batista Jr. Capital account and external debt are focus of several. Lemgruber's and Vieira's calculations of alternative effective or tradeweighted multilateral exchange rates are a useful contribution.

3745 Benevides, Moema Unis. Considerações sobre a política monetária brasileira: o caso do Banco no período 1945/1960 (RBMC, 8:23, maio/agôsto 1982, p. 101–117, tables)

Based on São Paulo master's thesis, article analyzes policy at Banco do Brasil from bank's 1946 return through Kubitschek development period. Argues that bank acted counter-cyclically, guaranteeing financing in periods of recession and tightening in expansionary periods. Includes several useful quarterly time series.

3746 Bonelli, Regis and Paulo Vieira da Cunha. Mudanças nas estruturas de produção, renda e consumo, e crescimento econômico no Brasil no período 1970–75 (IPEA/PPE, 12:3, dez. 1982, p. 807–850, bibl., tables)

Decomposes variations in real production into consumption, technology, income distribution, and final sectoral demand effects, using a multisector model with endogenous consumption. Although final demand and technology had positive effects, distributional effects were negative. Interesting methodology and extensive use of recent data.

3747 Branco, Marta Castello. Diferencial de juros e movimentos internacionais de capital: o caso brasileiro, 1943–1979 (IPE/EE, 12:3, dez. 1982, p. 41–50, bibl., tables)

Based on a PUC (Pontifícia Univ. Católica)/Rio de Janeiro master's thesis, work examines effect of interest rate differentials on international capital flows to Brazil. Shows that earlier conclusions of low interest-rate response may have resulted from failure to distinguish clearly between public and private borrowing. Latter does appear responsive to interest rates.

3748 Brangança, Luiz A. de. Análise de projetos: ênfase na avaliação da garantia governamental (RBMC, 8:23, maio/agôsto 1982, p. 135–142, bibl., tables)

Theoretical article deals with eminently real Brazilian phenomenon, the concession of government guarantees for risky projects without sufficient charge for assumption of risk. Uses Black and Scholes option-pricing approach to model government guarantees and examines incentives they create.

3749 Brasseul, Jacques. L'internationalisation de l'industrie brésilienne depuis 1964 (FDD/NED [Problèmes d'Amérique latine; 65] 4675/4676, 12 juillet 1982, p. 81–114, graphs, tables)

Reviews Brazilian economic strategy since 1964, which has resulted in greater openness to international trade and finance, without eliminating a high level of domestic protection. Criticizes distributional effects of Brazilian policies, which are compared to those of other developing nations.

3750 Brazil: an interim assessment of rural development programs for the Northeast. Washington: World Bank, 1983. 102 p.: bibl., ill., maps, plates, tables (A World Bank country study)

Summary of Brazilian federal government programs for rural development and

water use in the Northeast, based in part on Bank's extensive involvement in many of these projects. Frank and sometimes critical assessment of past experience, with recognition that regional poverty has social and political origins.

Brazil and Mexico: patterns in late development. See item **3112.**

3751 Brito, Ney Roberto Ottoni de et al. O mercado de capitais e a estrutura empresarial brasileira. Rio de Janeiro: Guanabara Dois, 1981. 292 p.: bibl., ill., index, tables.

Collection of related essays on Brazilian capital markets, the majority authored or co-authored by Brito. Contemporary portfolio, theory and efficient-markets hypotheses are combined with extensive empirical analysis to examine structure and characteristics of Brazil's financial system. The role of government intervention and subsidized credit receive particular attention.

Business Yearbook of Brazil, Mexico & Venezuela. See item **2791.**

3752 Cancian, Nadir Apparecida. Cafeicultura paranaense: 1900/1970. Curitiba: Grafipar: *em co-edição com a* Secretaria de Estado da Cultura e do Esporte do Paraná, 1981. 150 p.: bibl., ill., tables (Estudos paranaenses; 4)

Based on Univ. de São Paulo doctoral thesis, this study is well documented economic history of development of coffee cultivation in southern Paraná state. Argues that expansion of coffee sector was sensitive to relative prices, whose 1960s decline reduced coffee's role in state's economy.

3753 Cardoso, Eliana A. Imposto inflacionário, dívida pública e crédito subsidiado (IPEA/PPE, 12:3, dez. 1982, p. 707–718, bibl, chart)

Analyzes implications of recent monetary policy changes which reduce the money supply and increase the public debt, using a simple theoretical model. Shows that this policy will actually lead to an increase in the long-run inflation rate if the fiscal deficit is not simultaneously reduced.

3754 ———. Indexação e acomodação monetária: un teste do processo inflacionário brasileiro (IBE/RBE, 37:1, jan./março 1983, p. 3–11, bibl., graphs, tables)

Uses simple log-linear macroeconomic model to show that combination of monetary accommodation and indexation of wages and the exchange rate lead inflation rate to follow a random walk. Tests model with quarterly data for Brazil (1968–82) and concludes that random walk hypothesis cannot be rejected.

3755 Carvalheiro, Nelson. Crescimento e concentração de bancos comerciais no Brasil: o período 1964–1976 (RMBC, 9:26, abril/junho 1983, p. 153–175, bibl., tables)

Analyzes growth of commercial banks and concentraton in post-1964 period, which was characterized by rapid growth in banking sector. Using several measures of concentration, Carvalheiro shows that degree of concentration actually decreased slightly over the period. Private banks appear to have grown more rapidly than public ones.

3756 Cavalcanti, Clóvis de Vasconcelos *et al.* Nordeste do Brasil: um desenvolvimento conturbado. Recife: Editora Massangana, Fundação Joaquim Nabuco, 1981. 116 p.: ill., tables (Série Estudos pesquisas; 20)

Joint study by economists and sociologists of Northeast's position in Brazilian economy and attempt to explain its relative backwardness. Valuable both for its discussion of existing literature (chap. 1) and its macroeconomic analysis of the region (chap. 3–5). Among other interesting points, argues that Brazilian commercial policies often had regional effects unfavorable to the Northeast.

3757 Chahad, José Paulo Zeetano. Oferta de trabalho e composição ocupacional (IPE/EE, 12:2, agôsto/nov. 1982, p. 31–50, bibl., tables)

Based on Univ. of São Paulo doctoral dissertation, argues that conventional models of labor supply based on income-leisure choice which ignore occupation may be misleading and empirically questionable. Inclusion of occupation in labor supply estimates using data for laborers in Salvador helps explain changes in the slope of the labor supply function.

3758 ———. Oferta de trabalho e estrutura ocupacional. São Paulo: Univ. de São Paulo, Instituto de Pesquisas Econômicas (IPE-USP), 1981. 243 p.: bibl., ill., tables (Ensaios econômicos; 12)

Revision of Univ. of São Paulo doctoral dissertation, in which a theoretical model of labor supply is developed and tested econometrically with data from São Paulo. Author argues that labor supply cannot be treated as homogeneous, and that labor supply functions should not omit occupation as a potential explanatory variable.

3759 Changing dynamics of the Brazilian economy. Edited by Howard J. Wiarda and Janine T. Perfit. William G. Tyler, João Camilo de Oliveira Penna, and Dennis J. Mahar. Washington: American Enterprise Institute for Public Policy Research, Center for Hemisphere Studies, 1983. 55 p.: bibl., tables (Occasional papers series; 5)

Three essays by Tyler, Penna, and Mahar, respectively. Tyler examines Brazil's international economic relations, analyzing some future choices in commercial and financial policy faced by the government; Penna asks for greater understanding by Americans of Brazil's industrial and trade policies; and Mahar emphasizes continuing central role of the public sector in the Brazilian economy.

3760 Contador, Claudio R. Avaliação social de projetos. São Paulo: Atlas, 1981. 301 p.: bibl., ill., tables.

Textbook on analysis of social costs and benefits of projects by one of Brazil's leading economists. Although general and often theoretical in approach, it is inspired by typically Brazilian problems and often accompanied by empirical cases drawn from Brazil.

3761 Denslow, David, Jr. and William G. Tyler. Perspectives on poverty and income inequality in Brazil (WD, 12:10, Oct. 1984, p. 1019–1028, tables)

Uses preliminary tabulations of the 1980 census to analyze distribution of personal income in Brazil. Concludes that after worsening of the degree of relative inequality (1960–70), aggregate distribution remained stable in the following decade, due to offsetting effects of greater rural-urban equality and worsening inequality within agricultural sector.

3762 Desenvolvimento capitalista no Brasil: ensaios sobre a crise. Organizadores, Luiz Gonzaga de Mello Belluzzo e Renata Coutinho. São Paulo: Brasiliense, 1983. 2 v.: bibl., ill., tables.

Critical discussion of recent Brazilian

economic development by members of Economics Dept. of Univ. of Campinas. Essays' dominant theme is that external shocks which buffeted Brazilian economy in 1970s marked deeper internal problems arising from late industrialization and the form of capitalism developed in Brazil.

3763 Desigualdades regionais no desenvolvimento brasileiro. v. 1, Caracterização, evolução recente e fatores determinantes. v. 2, Políticas econômica setoriais e desigualdades regionais. v. 3, A política de desenvolvimento regional. v. 4, A expansão capitalista e o papel do Estado e o desenvolvimento regional no Brasil. Coordenador, Carlos Osorio. Recife: Ministério do Interior, SUDENE: Univ. Federal do Pernambuco, Instituto de Planejamento Econômico Social, 1984. 4 v. (300, 358, 584, 175 p.): graphs, maps, tables.

Four-vol. study of regional inequalities in development by Univ. of Pernambuco economists. Covers period since World War II, with emphasis on geographic effects of rapid growth beginning in late 1960s. Among topics considered are spatial effects of foreign trade policies, regional inequalities and migration, and role of the State in regional development. Abundance of tables, maps, and graphs add to study's usefulness.

3764 Dimensão da força de trabalho de nível superior no Brasil. Rio de Janeiro: FGV, Instituto de Recursos Humanos (IRH), 1982. 152 p.: bibl., ill., tables.

Survey of Brazilian labor force with university or equivalent education, based primarily on 1940–76 census, with increasing detail and discrimination for post-1970 period. Relates structure of highly educated labor force to economic structure and examines regional differences. Although descriptive and not analytical in approach, a useful contribution.

3765 Dimensões do desenvolvimento brasileiro. Coordenadores, Werner Baer, Pedro Pinchas Geiger, Paulo Roberto Haddad, com a colaboração de Michael Webb. Rio de Janeiro: Editora Campus, 1978. 396 p.: bibl., ill., plates, tables (Contribuições em economia; 3)

Collection of 12 original essays address regional disparity in Brazilian economic development such as concentration of benefits of growth in the Center-South and relative impoverishment of the Northeast, in the context of sectoral development strategies.

3766 Dívida externa, recessão e ajuste estrutural: o Brasil diante da crise. Organizador, Pérsio Arida. Rio de Janeiro: Paz e Terra, 1982. 206 p.: bibl., ill., tables (Col. Estudos brasileiros; 64)

Consists of 13 essays by members of PUC's Dept. of Economics in Rio, written in late 1982 following a marked worsening of Brazil's balance of payments and external debt. A common theme of the essays is their criticism of the Brazilian government's decision to resolve external crisis by a domestic recession. Informal and not analytical, collection is nevertheless a thoughtful contribution.

3767 Dowbor, Ladislau. La formation du capitalisme dépendant au Brésil. Paris: Anthropos, 1981. 263 p.: bibl., ill., tables.

Addresses the question why a relatively advanced degree of industrialization in Brazil has not led to more modern political and social structures. Argues that this is primarily due to the form of dependent capitalism which characterizes Brazilian development, marked by dominance of multinational enterprises and subordination to external centers of power.

3768 Emprego no Nordeste, 1950–1980: modernização e heterogeneidade. Organizador, Jorge Jatoba. José Ferreira Irmão et al. Recife: Ministério do Interior, SUDENE: Fundação Joaquim Nabuco, Editora Massangara, 1983. 535 p.: bibl., maps, tables (Série População e emprego; 15)

Group of studies by Federal Univ. of Pernambuco economists. José Feireirra Irmão and Yony Sampaio devote particular attention to regional variations in production and their effects on rural employment. Other major papers focus on evolution of urban employment in the Northeast and role of the public sector.

3769 Encontro Brasileiro de Econometria, 6th, São Paulo, 1984. Trabalhos apresentados. Organizador, Maurício Barata do Pinto. São Paulo: Sociedad Brasileira de Econometria (SBE), 1985. 525 p.: bibl., ill., tables.

Proceedings of SBE's meeting consist of 18 papers. Majority apply quantitative methods of analysis to economic problems, ranging in topic from monetary equilibria and indexation to interpretation of census and price data in Brazil. Papers' high quality and methodological sophistication constitute a valuable contribution to the discussion of Brazilian economic problems.

3770 Encontro Nacional de Economia, *12th, São Paulo, 1984.* Anais. v. 1–3. São Paulo: Univ. de São Paulo, Faculdade de Economia e Administração: Associação Nacional de Centros de Pós-Graduação em Economia (ANPEC), 1985? 3 v. (1778 p.): bibl., graphs, tables.

Proceedings of the Brazilian association of graduate centers in economics (ANPEC) meeting (São Paulo, Dec. 1984). Over 70 papers, ranging from economic demography to history of thought and macroeconomic analysis, many of them with an empirical focus on Brazilian problems. Although many papers appearing in earlier proceedings have appeared in revised form in other publications, majority of these papers are not published elsewhere.

3771 Estratos ocupacionais de baixa renda. Coordenador, Luiz Antônio Machado. Rio de Janeiro?: Comissão Nacional de Justiça e Paz, 1978. 223 p.: tables.

Study of economic situations of lower income groups in Recife, using an ethnographic approach based on non-structured interviews. Among the attitudes and experiences covered in the interviews were migration, participation in a formal labor market, and choice among unskilled occupations. Novel methodology and skillful editing provide a number of insights on this stratum of the labor force.

Estudo comparativo da indústria de alimentos: administração e política de tecnologia na América Latina. See item **2842.**

3772 O Exame de políticas econômicas setoriais. São Paulo: Governo do Estado de São Paulo, Secretaria de Economia e Planejamento, 1979. 237 p.: bibl., ill., tables (Série Estudos e pequisas; 33)

Government-sponsored study of major trends in Brazilian industrial policy and development since 1950s. Identifies a number of cycles of growth of specific sectors, linked both to internal policies and to international goods and financial market conditions. Ex-

tensive tables and quantitative data underlie much of the discussion.

3773 Ferreira, Carmosina N. Planejamento econômico e social no Brasil de 1930 à 1974: uma anàlise bibliográfica. Rio de Janeiro: Programa Nacional de Pesquisa Econômica, 1983. 3 v. (529 p.): indexes (Difusão e síntese. Suplemento; 1)

Extensive bibliography of more than 3000 primary and secondary sources on government economic plans and programs. Organized by sector and indexed by title and author, provides researchers with valuable catalog of material on Brazilian economic policy and development.

3774 Ferreira Alves, Francisco. Localização industrial Nordeste: análise de alguns indicadores, 1959-1970-1975-1980 (BNB/REN, 14:2, abril/junho 1983, p. 177–217, bibl., graphs, tables)

Uses several location-theory concepts developed by Walter Isard to analyze industrial location and specialization in the Northeast. Although largely descriptive, techniques provide an interesting picture of industrial development in the region between 1959 and 1980.

3775 Figueiredo, Vilma; Norma Beatriz Rancich Chaloult; and Heverton Peixoto. L'influence des cultures d'exportation dans un municipe du Rio Grande do Sul (FDD/NED [Problèmes d'Amérique latine; 65] 4675/4676, 12 juillet 1982, p. 147–158, bibl.)

In-depth examination of changes in agricultural production, land holding, and rural labor in the municipio of Cruzeiro do Sul. Growing importance of exportable crops, particularly soybeans, and decline of small farms is noted. Authors argue that policies, especially subsidized credit, have favored large-scale production.

3776 Filardo, Maria Lucia Rangel. Fontes de financiamento das empresas no Brasil. Rio de Janeiro: Ministério da Indústria e do Comércio, BNDE, 1980. 126 p.: bibl., ill., tabls.

Master's thesis which won 1980 BNDE Economics Prize. Analyzes sources of financing, both internal and external, for Brazilian non-bank firms, based on tax return samples (1972–75). Detailed comparison of financial indicators by sectors, concentrating on the choice by the firm of how much of its net profits should be retained for investment.

3777 Fox, M. Louise. Income distribution in post-1964 Brazil: new results (EHA/J, 43:1, March 1983, p. 261–271, bibl., tables) Based on Vanderbilt Univ. doctoral dissertation, article presents improved estimates of personal distribution of income in Brazil in 1960 and 1970. Shows that urban poverty increased over the decade. Careful review of earlier work and explanation of methodology. Also available as World Bank reprint (Series 0253–2131; no. 251).

3778 Franco, Afonso Arinos de Melo and **Cláudio Pacheco.** História do Banco do Brasil. v. 1, Primeira fase: 1808–1835. v. 2–5, História financiera do Brasil desde 1808 até 1951. Rio de Janeiro: Banco do Brasil, 1979. 5 v.: bibl., index, tables.
Five-vol. official history of Banco do Brasil and its predecessors, initiated by Melo Franco in 1942 and completed by Cláudio Pacheco in 1979, covering 1808–1951 period. Detailed account of monetary, exchange, and financial market policy making it in effect a financial history of Brazil. Invaluable reference for students of Brazilian economic history.

3779 Furtado, Celso. Não à recessão e ao desemprego. Rio de Janeiro: Paz e Terra, 1983. 107 p.: tables (Col. Estudos brasileiros; 69)
Collection of polemical essays by one of Brazil's best known economists, written in context of sharp deterioration of Brazil's external finances after mid-1982. Attributes inflation to economic and political disorganization and urges Brazil to terminate its agreement with the IMF and declare a unilateral moratorium in order to regain its freedom of action and national sovereignty.

3780 Galveas, Ernane. A política económico-financiera do Brasil (BNB/REN, 14:3, julho/set. 1983, p. 341–411, graphs, tables)
Text of presentation by the Finance Minister to the Escola Superior de Guerra in June 1983, examines Brazil's economic and financial situation. Unsurprisingly, emphasizes the two oil shocks and other external factors in causing Brazil's difficulties, and downplays internal policies. Abundant tables and graphs, primarily from the Banco Central and other government entities.

3781 Garófalo, Gílson de Lima. O mercado brasileiro de transporte aéreo regional. São Paulo: Univ. de São Paulo, Instituto de Pesquisas Econômicas (USP-IPE), 1982. 295 p.: bibl., ill., tables (Série Ensaios econômicos; 21)
Professorial thesis (livre docência) submitted to Univ. of São Paulo in 1981. Detailed analysis of demand for regional air transport in Brazil and role of government regulation and price-setting in this market. Considers role of regional airlines in future air transport and concludes with recommendations for several reforms.

3782 Gomes, Severo. Entre o passado e o futuro. São Paulo: Livraria Duas Cidades, 1982. 194 p.: bibl.
Collection of essays, most of them previously published in the national press, by former Minister of Commerce and Industry and subsequent critic of many government policies. Although not presented with documentation, and largely interpretative and subjective, they constitute a revealing sample of the thinking of a member of Brazil's political and economic establishment in early 1980s.

3783 Graziano da Silva, José F. and **Barbara A. Kohl.** Capitalist "modernization" and employment in Brazilian agriculture, 1960–1975: the case of the state of São Paulo (LAP, 11:1, Winter 1984, p. 117–136, bibl., tables)
Examines structural changes in agriculture in São Paulo state (1960–75), emphasizing alterations in labor relations, as temporary and wage labor partially replaced permanent labor. Comparisons with other regions and careful use of agricultural census make the study a useful contribution.

3784 Guimarães Neto, Leonardo. O emprego no Nordeste: sugestões de políticas (BNB/REN, 13:3, julho/set. 1982, p. 459–545, bibl., tables)
Wide-ranging examination of employment problems and policies in Northeast. Argues that technical and administrative solutions, such as directed colonization, support for small enterprises or technical assistance, all require political negotiation. Extensive references and informed discussion of policies.

3785 ———. A política de modernização das indústrias tradicionais no Nordeste: o caso da indústria têxtil (Revista Pernambucana de Desenvolvimento [Instituto de Desenvolvimento de Pernambuco, Recife] 9 : 1, jan./junho 1982, p. 67–99, bibl., tables)

Studies effects of modernization on employment in Northeast's textile industry, which declined both absolutely and relatively to the rest of Brazil (1939–70). Partly attributes reversal in the trend to government-sponsored technological development and investment in the sector.

3786 Heidemann, Dieter. Arbeitsteilung und regionale Mobilität an der Peripherie des Weltmarktes: zur Binnenwanderung in Nordostbrasilien. Mettingen, FRG: Brasilienkunde-Verlag, 1981. 335 p.: bibl., ill., maps, tables (Aspekte der Brasilienkunde / Aspetos de brasilologia; 2)

Detailed analysis of Northeast's economic and demographic structure by economic geographer. Examines effects of climate, land tenure and social organization, and available technology as partial determinants of population and labor force movement. Well documented, with numerous maps, tables, and extensive bibliography.

3787 Horta, Maria Helena T.T. Fontes de crescimento das exportações brasileiras na década de 70 (IPEA/PPE, 13:2, agôsto 1983, p. 507–542, bibl., tables)

Analyzes growth of Brazilian exports, particularly manufacturers, during 1970s, using a constant-market-shares approach. Attributes increase in competitiveness of Brazilian exports in first part of the decade to exchange rate policy and export subsidies, which helped offset unfavorable price trends after 1974.

3788 Hudson, Rexford A. The Brazilian way to technological independence: foreign joint ventures and the aircraft industry (IAMEA, 37:2, Autumn 1983, p. 23–43, table)

Examines Brazil's evolution from being an aircraft importer to an important exporter. Attributes much of Brazil's success to protection and to the establishment of joint ventures. Treatment is primarily descriptive, with little information on costs or relative efficiency.

3789 Humphrey, John. The growth of female employment in the Brazilian manufacturing industry in the 1970s (JDS, 20:4, July 1984, p. 224–247, bibl., tables)

Challenges the common view that industrial development marginalizes women by providing few job opportunities, forcing them into unemployment or low-wage service jobs. Analyzes rapid increase in female labor in the industrial sector during 1970s, which grew more rapidly than both male employment in industry and female labor in other sectors.

3790 Indústria da construção. Rio de Janeiro: IBGE: Secretaria de Planejamento da Presidência da República, 1982. 388 p.: plates, tables (Censos econômicos de 1975. Inquéritos especiais)

Special census of construction industry for 1975. Coverage includes firms in residential and non-residential building, transportation, sanitation, and other types of construction, organized by state. Provides data on total employment, wages, value of sales and of purchased inputs, and investment in material and equipment.

3791 Katzman, Martin T. The land and people of Northeast Brazil: is geography a useful guide to development policy? (UC/EDCC, 32:3, April 1984, p. 633–638)

Critical piece by American social scientist concerning Manuel Correia de Oliveira Andrade's The Land and people of Northeast Brazil (see HLAS 43:3703). Although sympathetic to Andrade's concern with equity and his mastery of Northeastern geography, Katzman criticizes many of book's conclusions. Argues that classical geography lacks a theoretical base and, therefore, is of limited usefulness in economic policy making.

3792 Kelly, Maria do Socorro de Barros; Edilberto X. de Albuquerque; Gilka Tavares Nobre; and Nara Pires Ferraz. Força de trabalho e emprego no Nordeste, 1968–1972. Recife: SUDENE, Depto. de Recursos Humanos, Divisão de Estudos Demográficos, 1978. 124 leaves: bibl., ill., tables (Série População e emprego; 4)

Quantitative examination of Northeastern labor force and employment, based primarily on IBGE data for the region. Analyzes distribution of labor force by age, sectors of economic activity and income groups. Also presents sexual differences in employment and labor force participation and draws some international comparisons. Primarily descriptive, study emphasizes importance of low-income, "informal" sector of Northeast's labor force.

3793 Langhammer, Rolf J. The importance of natural barriers to trade among developing countries: some evidence from the transport cost content in Brazilian imports (WD, 11:5, May 1983, p. 417–425, bibl., tables)

Tests hypothesis that "South-South" trade is at a cost disadvantage relative to "North-South" and historical patterns. Using cif/fob ratios for Brazilian imports at the eight-digit level, concludes that possible disadvantages are rather small, much less important as barriers to trade than are Brazilian tariffs.

3794 Laranjeira, Raymundo. Colonização e reforma agrária no Brasil. Rio de Janeiro: Civilização Brasileira, 1983. 203 p.: ill. (Col. Retratos do Brasil; 164)

Legal scholar's examination of origins and characteristics of agricultural land tenure in Brazil and legislation affecting its acquisition. Argues that actual system facilitates entrance and penetration of foreign groups, to the detriment of Brazilian sovereignty. Advocates greater emphasis on cooperatives and state farms.

3795 Levy, Maria Barbara and **Ana Maria Ribeiro de Andrade.** A gestão monetária na formação do Estado nacional (RBMC, 6:17, maio/agôsto 1980, p. 138–152, bibl.)

Examines Brazilian monetary development in early 19th century from installation of Portuguese court through independence. Emphasizes emergence of a credit system, parallel circulation of silver currency and inconvertible bank notes, and growth of financial links with the rest of the world.

3796 Lima, João Policarpo Rodrigues. Diferenciais de renda familiar na pequena produção agrícola: um estudo de caso (BNB/REN, 13:3, julho/set. 1982, p. 675–689, tables)

Studies income of small farmers in Caicó, Rio Grande do Norte, analyzing opportunity cost of farm labor and returns to different activities. Analyzes land tenure and production structure, and suggests that sharecroppers may actually have higher income than small proprietors who are more exposed to risk and competition of larger landowners.

3797 Lima, José Luiz; Iraci del Nero da Costa; and Francisco Vidal Luna. Estatísticas básicas do setor agrícola no Brasil. São Paulo: Univ. de São Paulo, Instituto de Pesquisas Econômicas (USP-IPE), 1983. 1 v.: ill., tables (Série Estatísticas básicas da economia brasileira; 2)

Useful collection of basic agricultural statistics, covering 1920–80. Among major series are export data for sugar, cotton, rubber, coffee, tobacco, soybeans, and oranges, as well as production data for rice, potatoes, beans, manioc, corn, and wheat. Sources are well documented and organizers have attempted to make the series temporarily consistent.

3798 Longo, Carlos A. Finanças governamentais num regime federativo: considerações sobre o caso brasileiro (IPEA/PPE, 12:3, dez. 1982, p. 851–892, bibl., tables)

Analyzes division of resources and responsibilities between federal, state, and local government public finances in Brazil since 1967 tax reforms. Argues that actual division is too highly centralized, depriving states and municipalities of autonomy, but questions whether they are prepared to accept the responsibilities of such autonomy.

3799 ——— and A.E. Müller. Impacto regional das finanças federais (BNB/REN, 13:3, julho/set. 1982, p. 657–673, tables)

Uses data from FGV to analyze net transfers of resource among regions through federal revenues and expenditures. Concludes that Southeast and South, especially São Paulo, transfer a large proportion of revenues collected there to rest of Brazil, the Northeast being an important beneficiary.

3800 Lopes, Francisco L. Inflação e nível de atividad no Brasil: um estudo econométrico (IPEA/PPE, 12:3, dez. 1982, p. 639–670, bibl., graphs, tables)

Econometric study of relation between inflation and level of economic activity, uses Brazilian data for 1969–81. Concludes that there is a very small, but statistically significant effect of the level of activity on rate of inflation.

3801 Lustosa, Ricardo Junqueira. Aversão ao risco e diversificação ótima de produção (RBMC, 8:23, maio/agôsto 1982, p. 143–152, graphs)

Develops theory of optimal choice of production activities in agriculture, using expected utility theory and Arrow-Pratt measure of absolute risk aversion. Shows that this model provides better explanation of observed behavior than does traditional model of profit maximization. Although applied to a sample of US farmers, article is one of first to introduce theoretical model to Brazil. Based on author's New York Univ. doctoral dissertation.

3802 Macedo, Roberto. Brazilian children and the economic crisis: evidence from the state of São Paulo (WD, 12:3, March 1984, p. 203–221, bibl., tables)

Slowdown in Brazilian economic growth in early 1980s may have asymmetrical effects on different classes and age groups. Article reviews macroeconmic trends and argues that a high degree of urbanization, government inattention to health and education, and concentration of effects of recession in urban industrial areas like São Paulo, make present crisis particularly severe for children in urban areas. Innovative use of indicators usually ignored by economists in Brazil.

3803 ———. Wage indexation and inflation: the recent Brazilian experience (*in* Inflation, debt and indexation. Edited by Rudiger Dornbusch and Mario Henrique Simonsen. Cambridge, Mass.: MIT Press, 1983, p. 133–159, tables)

Examines new wage indexation policy of semiannual adjustment adopted in 1979, from point of view of its effect on inflation. Concludes that new policy may have contributed slightly to rise in Brazil's inflation rate, but that it is not principal cause. Informative discussion of institutional framework of wage adjustment in Brazil.

3804 Machado, Marcos Fernandes. Rentabilidade dos ativos financeiros e inflação no Brasil: 1977–1981 (RBMC, 9:27, julho/set. 1983, p. 239–269, tables)

Estimates *ex post* real rates of return of major assets of Brazilian financial market, classified by maturity. Examines both fixed income assets (e.g., National Treasury Letters and Adjustable Obligations, savings deposits, certificates of deposit) and common stocks. None of them provided sufficient protection from inflation in 1977–81.

3805 ——— and Jane Maria Medeiros. Crédito subsidiado no Brasil, 1967– 1979 (RBMC, 6:17, maio/agôsto 1980, p. 172–188, appendix, bibl., tables)

Presents data on major programs of subsidized credit in Brazil since late 1960s.

Analyzes programs in terms of economic efficiency and sectoral distribution of credit. Authors argue that overall effect of programs has not promoted economic efficiency, and suggest a number of improvements. Detailed appendix is useful contribution in itself.

3806 Manual de estatísticas básicas do Nordeste. 4a ed. rev. e amp. Fortaleza: Banco do Nordeste do Brasil, Depto. de Estudos Econômicos do Nordeste, s.d. 433 p.: ill., tables.

Useful collection of statistical data on Northeast drawn from more than 50 government, academic, and institutional sources. Includes many economic time series for post-World War II period, ending in early 1970s. In addition to income and agricultural and industrial production data, statistics include demographic and social data for the region and its nine states.

3807 Mão de obra volante na agricultura. São Paulo: Conselho Nacional de Desenvolvimento Científico e Tecnológico: Univ. Estadual Paulista (UNESP), Faculdade de Ciências Agronômicas, Depto. de Economia Rural, 1982. 337 p.: bibl., ill., tables.

Collection of studies of migrant labor by agricultural economists. Questions addressed include sources of rural farm income, wage setting, time allocation, labor market segmentation, and sharecropping. Other essays deal with provision of public services to rural workers and availability of medical and legal assistance.

3808 Marques, Maria Silvia Bastos. Moeda e inflação: a questão da causalidade (IBE/RBE, 37:1, jan./março 1983, p. 13–38, bibl., tables)

Examines causal relationship between monetary variables (M 1 and monetary base) and inflation in Brazil in 1946–81, using Sims-Granger tests. Concludes that a feedback effect existed for the period as a whole, but that tests are inconclusive for various subperiods. Based on FGV Master's dissertation.

3809 Melo, Fernando Homem de. A política econômica e a pequena produção agrícola (IPE/EE, 12:3, dez. 1982, p. 67–85, tables)

Distributional effects of Brazilian agricultural policies favor larger producers, particularly those of exportable crops. Focuses on three areas of price stability, agricultural technology, and rural credit, arguing that government intervention in agriculture has been relatively unfavorable to small farmers.

3810 Miroux, Anne. Agriculture et balance des paiements au Brésil: nécéssité d'ajustement et redécouverte du secteur agricole (FDD/NED [Problèmes d'Amérique latine; 65] 4675/4676, 12 juillet 1982, p. 115–145, tables)

Reviews Brazilian agricultural policies in post-World War II period, emphasizing effects of external economic policies, including tariffs, export restrictions, and exchange rate overvaluation. Argues that balance of payments difficulties in 1970s have indirectly benefitted agricultural sector by increasing relative price of its output and by directing government attention to agriculture.

3811 Mueller, Charles C. Fronteira, frentes e a evolução recente da ocupação da força de trabalho rural no Centro-Oeste (IPEA/PPE, 13:2, agôsto 1983, p. 619–659, bibl., tables)

Examines rapid expansion of agriculture in Central-West region and its role in providing employment for excess labor from the Central-South. Concludes that form of agricultural expansion and development, which relied on large and intensive activities, did not favor rural employment.

3812 Munhoz, Dércio Garcia. Economia agrícola: agricultura: uma defesa dos subsídios. Petrópolis: Vozes, 1982. 107 p.: bibl., ill., tables.

Evaluation and defense of subsidized credit extended to agriculture in past decade. Argues that curtailment of these subsidies and rise in real interest rates would increase agricultural costs and rate of inflation faced by consumers.

3813 Muniz, Carlos José. Testes preliminares de eficiência do mercado de ações brasileiro (RBMC, jan./abril 1980, p. 80–94, bibl., tables)

Examines movements of daily rates of return on Brazilian stocks to verify whether or not they follow a random walk, implying market efficiency in a weak form. Concludes that random walk hypothesis may be accepted in the Brazilian case, based on analysis of 10 heavily traded stocks.

3814 Murtinho, Joaquim. Idéias econômicas de Joaquim Murtinho: cronologia, introdução, notas bibliográficas e textos sele-

cionados. Nícia Villela Luz, organizadora. Brasília: Senado Federal; Rio de Janeiro: Fundação Casa de Rui Barbosa, 1980. 534 p.: bibl., indexes (Ação e pensamento da república; 5)

Representative selection of speeches, essays, and reports by one of the leading economic policy-makers of Brazil's early republican period (1889–1911). Introductory essay by compiler Luz is an insightful exposition of economic ideologies and their influence on policy in late 19th-century Brazil.

3815 Nordeste: as pequenas cidades e o planejamento local. Coordenado por Brasilmar Ferreira Nunes. Fortaleza: Banco do Nordeste do Brasil, Depto. de Estudos Econômicos: Univ. Federal do Pernambuco, Mestrado de Desenvolvimento Urbano, 1981. 179 p.: bibl., ill., tables (Série Estudos econômicos e sociais; 12)

Study of urban planning problems and possibilities in a number of Northeast's smaller cities, sponsored by regional development bank. Emphasizes importance of local financial and technical capacities in planning process and advocates greater local control and involvement.

3816 Oliveira, Beauclair M. de. Evolução recente do sistema financiero e a questão dos conglomerados (RBMC, 6:18, set./dez. 1980, p. 305–314, bibl.)

Surveys major trends in post-World War II financial system, including concentration and reduction in number of banks (1946–64). Subsequent emergence of financial groups controlling variety of activities is then discussed. Useful introduction to Brazilian financial system and its development.

3817 Oliveira, Clonilo M. Sindeaux de. O sistema financiero regional e o desenvolvimento do Nordeste (BNB/REN, 14:3, julho/set. 1983, p. 443–457, bibl.)

Examines Northeast's financial system, using macroeconomic model with real and monetary sectors. Concludes that monetary policy multipliers are larger in Northeast than in rest of Brazil, so that changes in monetary policies are likely to have a greater impact.

3818 Oliveira, João do Carmo and Roberto Marcos da Silva Montezano. Os límites das fontes de financiamento à agricultura no Brasil (IPE/EE, 12:2, agôsto/nov. 1982, p. 139–159, bibl., tables)

Brazilian agricultural policy, based on subsidized credit, has been critized for both its distributive and its allocative effects. Authors argue that a third difficulty is that the evolution of financial markets has made agricultural credit instruments ineffective and obsolete. Helpful discussion of agricultural credit mechanisms.

Oogaki, Chiaki. Citrus production in Latin America and its impact on worldwide citrus trade, from current statistics: pt. 1, Citrus industry of Latin America. See item **2944.**

3819 Pechman, Clarice. O dólar paralelo no Brasil. Rio de Janeiro: Editora Paz e Terra, 1984. 156 p.: appendices, bibl. (Col. Estudos brasileiros; 79)

Based on FGV doctoral dissertation, analysis of illegal but openly-tolerated black market for dollars in Brazil. Well grounded in contemporary theory of assets markets, develops and tests model econometrically. Appendices list monthly parallel rates (1947–83).

3820 Pedrosa, Edilson Almeida. Programación monetaria: aspectos teóricos y el caso brasileño. México: Centro de Estudios Monetarios Latinoamericanos, 1982. 83 p.: bibl., ill., tables (Col. Investigaciones y ensayos; 48)

Prize-winning study of Brazilian monetary policy by Brazilian central bank economist. Reviews traditional models of money supply and then develops a model for Brazil, which is tested economically for 1970–79. Period is characterized by high degree of supply sensitivity to interest rates.

3821 Peláez, Carlos Manuel and **Wilson Suzigan.** História monetária do Brasil. 2a ed. rev. e amp. Brasília: Editora Univ. de Brasília, 1981. 432 p.: bibl., ill., tables (Col. Temas brasileiros; 15)

Second ed. of widely cited monetary history of Brazil, first published in 1976 and revised to include period following 1973 oil shock. Monetary theory is well integrated with statistical and institutional data in this interpretation of Brazilian monetary experience since 1808.

3822 Perdigão, Luís Antônio. Conglomerados financeiros: análise de seu desempenho do Brasil, no período 1978/1981 (RBMC, 9:27, julho/set. 1983, p. 183–237, bibl., tables)

Summary of FGV doctoral thesis. Analyzes principal forces behind growth of financial conglomerates in 1978–81. Presents both empirical data on financial market structure and theoretical model of conglomerate formation, which is then applied to Brazilian experience.

3823 Pereira, Luiz Carlos Bresser. Development and crisis in Brazil, 1930–1983. Translated from the Portuguese by Marcia Van Dyke and Nancy Voigt. Boulder, Colo.: Westview Press, 1984. 1 v.: bibl., index (Westview special studies on Latin America and the Caribbean)

Examines transformation of Brazilian economy from a primary export-oriented agrarian society to an industrialized nation with a high degree of both state intervention and private monopoly. Focuses on growth of a politically-conscious middle class, which author argues is now strong enough to challenge authoritarian "techno-bureaucracy" and democratize Brazilian society.

3824 Pereira, Reginaldo Ferreira and **Walter Lee Ness, Jr.** Características das empresas que utilizaram o mercado primário de ações (RBMC, 6:17, maio/agôsto 1980, p. 154–170, bibl., tables)

Tests hypothesis that firms which raise large share of capital through the stock market differ from other firms in terms of various economic and financial indicators. Using discriminant analysis of sample of Brazilian registered firms, finds that greater foreign control, higher profits, and firm debt reduce likelihood of firm's using domestic primary capital markets.

3825 Pinto, Maurício Barata de Paula. Exportações brasileiras de manufaturados: crescimento e mudança de estrutura. São Paulo: Instituto de Pesquisas Econômicas, Univ. de São Paulo (USP-IPE), 1983. 174 p.: bibl. (Série Ensaios econômicos; 24)

Revision of 1979 Johns Hopkins economics doctoral dissertation. Analyzes effects of different commercial policies on growth of Brazilian manufactured exports (1954–74). Presents both time series and cross-section econometric estimates. Argues that transition from import substitution to export promotion policies was not generally accompanied by marked improvement in efficiency.

3826 Prado, Eleutério F.S. Emprego e setor público no Brasil (IPE/EE, 12:2, agôsto/nov. 1982, p. 5–14, tables)

Uses 1975 input-output matrix, national accounts, family budget, and personal income tax data to evaluate role of public sector in providing employment. Concludes that when indirect effects of public sector's employment demand are added to direct ones, public sector accounts for about a fifth of total employment.

Redclift, M.R. "Urban bias" and rural poverty: a Latin American perspective. See item **2972.**

3827 Resende, André Lara. A política brasileira de estabilização: 1963–68 (IPEA/PPE, 12:3, dez. 1982, p. 757–806, bibl., graphs, tables)

Focuses on Economic Action Plan (PAEG) adopted in Nov. 1964, in effort to reduce inflation and improve balance of payments. Author attempts to estimate costs of stabilization and concludes with evaluation of degree of orthodoxy of the plan. Argues that it departed in many respects from traditional stabilization formulas.

3828 Rizzieri, Juarez Alexandre Baldini. Desenvolvimento econômico e urbanização: produtividade das cidades e custos de serviços públicos por ordem de tamanho urbano. São Paulo: Instituto de Pesquisas Econômicas, Univ. de São Paulo (USP-IPE), 1982. 219 p.: bibl., ill., tables (Série Ensaios econômicos; 18)

Study of spatial concentration of population in Brazil, with special emphasis on São Paulo, based on 1980 Univ. of São Paulo doctoral thesis. Well grounded in contemporary urban economic theory, study attempts to define optimum city size as a function of economies and diseconomies of scale. Concludes that a slight trend toward decentralization may be underway in Brazil.

3829 Rocha, Euzebio. Petróleo: do monopólio à entrega. São Paulo: Quilombo, 1982. 95 p. (Col. Cadernos do povo; 1)

Polemic in well established petroleum-and-national-sovereignty tradition. Attacks government's 1979 decision to allow foreign petroleum companies to search for oil in Brazil under risk contracts. Regards them as unconstitutional and inimical to the national interest. Although hardly objective, tract is a good statement of contemporary economic nationalism.

3830 Romão, Maurício. Características sócio-econômicas e desigualdades nas despesas familiares no Nordeste (BNB/REN, 14:1, jan./março 1983, p. 9–29, bibl., tables)

Based on Illinois doctoral dissertation, uses IBGE data on family expenditures in Northeast to estimate Gini coefficients for income distribution. Considers effects of age, education, family size, and occupational status. Concludes that larger families tend to be poorer, as do less educated ones, but that age is not closely related to income distribution.

3831 Rosenn, Keith S. Regulation of foreign investment in Brazil: a critical analysis. Washington: American Enterprise Institute for Public Policy Research, Center for Hemispheric Studies, 1983. 65 p.: bibl., tables (Occasional papers series; 8)

Well written and documented monograph on complex group of laws and administrative practices which regulate foreign investment in Brazil. Discusses profit remittance, regulation of direct investment and loans, technology transfer, income taxation and tax incentives. Excellent collection of information usually available in widely scattered sources.

3832 Rossi, José W. O menor da concentração da Gini aplicado a dados de distribuição de renda no Brasil (IPE/EE, 12:2, agôsto/nov. 1982, p. 111–115, tables)

Applies minor concentration ratio concept to analyze Brazilian distribution of personal income (1968–74). In combination with overall Gini index, measure suggests that worsening of income distribution in early 1970s occurred mainly at the expense of poorest sectors of the population.

3833 Rotstein, Jaime. Petróleo, a crise dos anos 80. Rio de Janeiro: Livraria F. Alves Editora, 1980. 150 p.

Written in aftermath of second oil shock, in late 1970s, this lengthy and often impassioned discussion of Brazil's energy problems and prospects argues that dangerous dependence on imported petroleum may be reduced and even eliminated by expansion of alcohol program. Approach is primarily impressionistic, with no economic analysis or documentation of statements.

3834 Salm, Claudio *et al.* Política de emprego. Rio de Janeiro: Instituto Euvaldo Lodi, 1982. 133 p.: bibl. (Col. Universidade & indústria. Monografias)

Six essays on contemporary Brazilian labor market by economists and labor market specialists. Authors discuss appropriate wage and salary policies to deal with recent worsening of labor market, as well as broader macroeconomic measures.

3835 Senna, José Júlio. A mão visível: problemas e controvérsias da política econômica brasileira. Rio de Janeiro: Instituto Brasileiro de Mercado de Capitais, 1983. 245 p.: bibl., ill., tables.

Wide-ranging consideration of Brazilian economy over past three decades, focuses on long-run effects of government intervention for short-term objectives. Suggests that government may have had a destabilizing role and that price controls, quantitative restrictions, and subsidies have not generally had socially beneficial effects.

3836 Sercovich, Francisco Colman. Brazil (WD, 12:5/6, May/June 1984, p. 575–599, bibl., tables)

Examination of Brazil's performance as a supplier of particular technologies. Development of technology in several sectors, among them sugar and alcohol, capital goods and equipment for steel production, have increased Brazilian exports, notably to other developing countries. Development of comparative advantage in some of these activities appears to be due both to natural resource bases and to policy emphasis.

3837 Setubal Filho, Laerte. A experiência cambial brasileira. São Paulo: Unipress Editorial, 1981. 112 p.: bibl., facsims.

Concise summary of Brazilian exchange rate policies since World War II, followed by compilation of newspaper articles documenting effects of multiple rate policies in early 1950s. Attributes many of Brazil's international payments problems to chronic overvaluation of the cruzeiro. Although descriptive and often anecdotal, book provides illuminating account of difficulties with exchange controls.

Sheahan, John. Early industrialization and violent reaction: Argentina and Brazil. See item **3723.**

3838 Silva, Adroaldo Moura da and **Decio K. Kadota.** Inflação e preços relativos: o caso brasileiro, 1970–1979 (IPE/EE, 12:1, jan./abril 1982, p. 5–30, bibl., graphs, tables)

Examines relationship between rate of inflation and dispersion of relative prices, showing that as inflation increased, so too did variation of relative prices. Careful use of extensive price data and attention to competing theories of inflation make this an important contribution.

3839 Silva, Paulo Fontenele e. Aspectos tecnológicos da estrutura industrial brasileira: uma análise de insumo-produto. Rio de Janeiro: BNDE, 1980. 114 p.: bibl.

Univ. of Brasília Master's thesis and recipient of BNDE 1980 award. Uses 1970 IBGE input-output matrix to study Brazilian interindustrial structure. Identifies a group of dynamic sectors and a traditional group with few linkages between the two. Shows that former is import-intensive and generates relatively less employment.

3840 Simonsen, Mário Henrique. Indexation: current theory and the Brazilian experience (*in* Inflation, debt and indexation. Edited by Rudiger Dornbusch and Mário Henrique Simonsen. Cambridge, Mass.: MIT Press, 1983, p. 99–132)

Develops theoretical macroeconomic model with imperfect indexation of labor contracts and applies it to Brazilian experience since 1965. Argues that indexation is not necessarily welfare-improving and that lagged wage indexation like Brazil's, accompanied by accomodating policies, may cause inflation rate to follow a random walk.

3841 Sinopse preliminar do censo industrial. Rio de Janeiro: IBGE, 1982. 354 p.: tables (IX [i.e. Noveno] recenseamento geral do Brasil; 3:1)

Summary of data from 1980 industrial census, prefaced by explanation of definitions and concepts used, coverage, and industrial classification. Tables by state give statistics on numbers of firms, employment, and value of production at a two-digit level, further classified by size of firms. A finer industrial classification is also given for numbers of firms and total 1980 production value, and 1975 and 1980 data are compared in other tables.

3842 Sousa, J. Colombo de. A Nordeste e a tecnocracia da revolução. Brasília: Horizonte Editora, 1981. 244 p. (Movimento cultural brasileiro)

Collection of essays on Northeast, written by Ceará lawyer and federal deputy with long involvement in region's policy making. Describes sporadic efforts to alleviate its drought-related problems before World War II and subsequent efforts by SUDENE. Argues that centralization of bureaucratic decisions in Brasília has worked against the Northeast.

3843 Souza, Aida Laura Ferreira de; Iêda Siqueira; and Regina Coeli de Siqueira Lana. Observações sobre a evolução da população rural e urbana no Brasil no período 1940 a 1980 (IBGE/RBE, 42:167, julho/set. 1981, p. 197–215, maps, tables)

Uses preliminary data from 1980 demographic census to state in thousands of words what a table or graph or two would show. Extensive discussion of trends in urban and rural population growth without ever defining an urban area. Article's redeeming features are tables and maps which collect information from five censuses.

3844 Szmrecsányi, Tamás. O planejamento da agroindústria canavieira do Brasil, 1930–1975. São Paulo: Editora HUCITEC: Univ. Estadual de Campinas, 1979. 540 p.: bibl., ill., tables (Economia & planejamento. Série Teses e pesquisas)

Based on Univ. of Campinas doctoral thesis, study examines government policy in sugarcane production and processing sector, focusing on special role of Sugar and Alcohol Institute (IAA). Concludes that overproduction in this sector may be reduced by greater alcohol production, and that this will require greater government intervention in sugar-growing industry.

3845 Tannuri, Luiz Antônio. O encilhamento. São Paulo: Editora HUCITEC: Fundação de Desenvolvimento da Unicamp, 1981. 140 p.: bibl., ill., tables (Economia & planejamento. Série Teses e pesquisas)

History and economic interpretation of speculative "bubble" of 1889–91 and ensuing readjustment of Old Republic's financial markets. One of few modern treatments of this episode, it emphasizes consequences of speculative boom for development of the Brazilian economy and financial instutitions.

3846 Thomas, Vinod. Pollution control in São Paulo, Brazil: costs, benefits, and effects on industrial location. Washington: World Bank, 1981. 127 p.: bibl., ill., plates, tables (World Bank staff working paper; 501)

World Bank-sponsored study of costs and benefits of different pollution control policies in metropolitan São Paulo, now one of world's most severely polluted cities. Focuses on industrial pollution and location of future industrial activities and considers alternative abatement policies, favoring some degree of spatial non-uniformity of policies.

3847 Trabalho volante na agricultura paulista. São Paulo: Governo do Estado de São Paulo, Secretaria de Economia e Planejamento, 1978. 428 p.: bibl., ill., plates (Série Estudos e pesquisas; 25)

Government-sponsored study of migrant labor in São Paulo state. Over past three decades non-resident migrant or salaried labor has replaced sharecropping in São Paulo agriculture. Examines trend at state and local levels and relates it to structural changes in agricultural economy.

3848 Tyler, William G. The anti-export bias in commercial policies and export performance: some evidence from the recent Brazilian experience (CAUK/WA, 119:1, 1983, p. 97–108, tables)

Analyzes decline in rate of export growth after 1974, arguing that it cannot be attributed entirely to demand-size factors. Suggests that Brazilian commercial policy, particularly import restrictions in response to oil shock, led to exchange overvaluation and an anti-export bias.

3849 ———. Incentivos às exportações e às vendas no mercado interno: análise da política comercial e da discriminação contra as exportações, 1980/81 (IPEA/PPE, 13:2, agôsto 1983, p. 543–573, bibl., tables)

Uses direct comparisons of internal and external prices to estimate implicit protection for various activities in Brazil. Concludes that the structure of protection tends to favor activities which use both human and physical capital relatively intensively, to detriment of more labor-intensive activities. Argues that structure also creates an anti-export bias.

3850 Vianna, Pedro Jorge Ramos. O setor externo nordestino (BNB/REN, 14:3, julho/set. 1983, p. 459–467)

Characterization of Northeast as a dependent and underdeveloped region, subordinated to economic interest of Brazil's Center-South. Estimates that combination of high protection, greater subsidization of manufactured exports from the South, and exchange rate overvaluation has resulted in an annual income transfer of about 45 billion 1982 cruzeiros from the Northeast to the rest of Brazil.

3851 Wells, John and **Andrés Drobny.** A distribuição da renda e o salário mínimo no Brasil: uma revisão crítica da literatura existente (IPEA/PPE, 12:3, dez. 1982, p. 893–914, bibl., graphs, tables)

Critical review of literature on minimum wage policies and personal distribution of income in Brazil. Argues that empirical work on link between minimum salary and worsening income distribution after 1960 is inconclusive, principally due to quality of data used to examine this issue. Useful bibliography and discussion of the literature.

JOURNAL ABBREVIATIONS ECONOMICS

AAFH/TAM The Americas. Academy of American Franciscan History. Washington.

ACPS/B Boletín de la Academia de Ciencias Políticas y Sociales. Caracas.

AEA/AER The American Economic Review. American Economic Association. Evanston, Ill.

AJES The American Journal of Economics and Sociology. Francis Neilson Fund [and] Robert Schalkenbach Foundation. New York.

AR Areíto. Areíto, Inc. New York.

BCRA/EE Ensayos Económicos. Banco Central de la República Argentina. Buenos Aires.

BMHS/J Journal of the Barbados Museum and Historical Society. Barbados, West Indies.

BNB/REN Revista Econômica do Nordeste. Banco do Nordeste do Brasil, Depto. de Estudos Econômicos do Nordeste. Fortaleza, Brazil.

BNCE/CE Comercio Exterior. Banco Nacional de Comercio Exterior. México.

BPC/RE Revista de Economía. Banco de la Provincia de Córdoba. Córdoba, Argentina.

CAUK/WA Weltwirtschaftliches Archiv. Zeitschrift des Instituts für Weltwirtschaft an der Christians-Albrechts-Univ. Kiel. Kiel, FRG.

CEDLA/B Boletín de Estudios Latinoamericanos. Centro de Estudios y Documentación Latinoamericanos. Amsterdam.

CEESTEM/TM Tercer Mundo y Economía Mundial. Centro de Estudios Económicos y Sociales del Tercer Mundo. México.

CEMLA/M Monetaria. Centro de Estudios Monetarios Latinoamericanos. México.

CFR/FA Foreign Affairs. Council on Foreign Relations. New York.

CJWB Columbia Journal of World Business. Columbia Univ. New York.

CM/D Diálogos. El Colegio de México. México.

CM/FI Foro Internacional. El Colegio de México. México.

CPES/RPS Revista Paraguaya de Sociología. Centro Paraguayo de Estudios Sociológicos. Asunción.

CRIA/W Worldview. Council on Religion and International Affairs. New York.

CSUCA/ESC Estudios Sociales Centroamericanos. Consejo Superior de Universidades Centroamericanas, Confederación Universitaria Centroamericana, Programa Centroamericano de Ciencias Sociales. San José.

CU/JIA Journal of International Affairs. Columbia Univ., School of International Affairs. New York.

CUH Current History. Philadelphia.

ECB Encontros com a Civilização Brasileira. Editora Civilização Brasileira. Rio de Janeiro.

EHA/J Journal of Economic History. New York Univ., Graduate School of Business Administration *for the* Economic History Assn. Rensselaer, N.Y.

FCE/TE El Trimestre Económico. Fondo de Cultura Económica. México.

FDD/NED Notes et Etudes documentaires. Direction de la documentation. Paris.

FIU/CR Caribbean Review. Florida International Univ., Office of Academic Affairs. Miami.

FP Foreign Policy. National Affairs Inc. [and] Carnegie Endowment for International Peace. New York.

GEE/NA Nova Americana. Giulio Einaudi Editore. Torino, Italy.

GIT/SCID Studies in Comparative International Development. Georgia Institute of Technology. Atlanta.

GR Geographische Rundschau. Zeitschrift für Schulgeographie. Georg Westermann Verlag. Braunschweig, Germany.

GU/WQ The Washington Quarterly. Georgetown Univ., Center for Strategic and International Studies. Washington.

HUN/RU Revista de la Universidad. Univ. Nacional Antónoma de Honduras. Tegucigalpa.

IAMEA Inter-American Economic Affairs. Washington.

IBE/RBE Revista Brasileira de Economia. Fundação Getúlio Vargas, Instituto Brasileiro de Economia. Rio de Janeiro.

IBGE/RBE Revista Brasileira de Estatística. Ministério do Planejamento e Coordenação Geral, Instituto Brasileiro de Geografia e Estatística. Rio de Janeiro.

IBRI/R Revista Brasileira de Política Internacional. Instituto Brasileiro de Relações Internacionais. Rio de Janeiro.

IDES/DE Desarrollo Económico. Instituto de Desarrollo Económico y Social. Buenos Aires.

IEAS/R Revista de Estudios Agro-Sociales. Instituto de Estudios Agro-Sociales. Madrid.

IEI/EI Economia Internazionale. Rivista dell'Istituto di Economia Internazionale. Genova, Italy.

IIAS/IRAS International Review of Administrative Sciences. International Institute of Administrative Sciences. Bruxelles.

IIDC/C Civilisations. International Institute of Differing Civilizations. Bruxelles.

IMF/SP Staff Papers. International Monetary Fund. Washington.

INTAL/IL Integración Latinoamericana. Instituto para la Integración de América Latina. Buenos Aires.

IPE/EE Estudos Econômicos. Univ. de São Paulo, Instituto de Pesquisas Econômicas. São Paulo.

IPEA/PPE Pesquisa e Planejamento Econômico. Instituto de Planejamento Econômico e Social. Rio de Janeiro.

IPGH/RHI Revista de Historia de las Ideas. Instituto Panamericano de Geografía e Historia [and] Editorial Casa de la Cultura Ecuatoriana. Quito.

JDA Journal of Developing Areas. Western Illinois Univ. Press. Macomb.

JDS Journal of Development Studies. London.

JLAS Journal of Latin American Studies. Centers or institutes of Latin American studies at the universities of Cambridge, Glasgow, Liverpool, London and Oxford. Cambridge Univ. Press. London.

JPS Journal of Peasant Studies. Frank Cass & Co. London.

LAP Latin American Perspectives. Univ. of California. Riverside.

LARR Latin American Research Review. Univ. of North Carolina Press *for the* Latin American Studies Association. Chapel Hill.

LI/IA *See* NOSALF/IA.

LNB/L Lotería. Lotería Nacional de Beneficencia. Panamá.

MR Monthly Review. New York.

MSTPS/R Revista Mexicana del Trabajo. Secretaría del Trabajo y Previsión Social. México.

NACLA NACLA: Report on the Americas. North American Congress on Latin America. New York.

NOSALF/IA Ibero Americana. Scandinavian Association for Research on Latin America (NOSALF). Stockholm.

NS NS NorthSouth NordSud NorteSur NorteSul. Canadian Assn. of Latin American Studies. Univ. of Ottawa.

NSO Nueva Sociedad. San José.

NZZ/SRWA Swiss Review of World Affairs. Neue Zürcher Zeitung. Zurich, Switzerland.

OAS/CI Ciencia Interamericana. Organization of American States, Dept. of Scientific Affairs. Washington.

OLI/ZLW Zeitschrift für Lateinamerika Wien. Osterreichisches Lateinamerika-Institut. Wien.

PAIGH/H Revista de Historia de América. Instituto Panamericano de Geografía e Historia, Comisión de Historia. México.

PAN/ES Estudios Latinoamericanos. Polska Akademia Nauk [Academia de Ciencias de Polonia], Instytut Historii [Instituto de Historia]. Warszawa.

PAT/TH The Historian. Phi Alpha Theta, National Honor Society in History. Univ. of Pennsylvania. University Park.

PUJ/U Universitas. Ciencias jurídicas y socioeconómicas. Pontificia Univ. Javeriana, Facultad de Derecho y Ciencias Socioeconómicas. Bogotá.

RAE Revista Antioqueña de Economía. Medellín, Colombia.

RBMC Revista Brasileira de Mercado de Capitais. Instituto Brasileiro de Mercado de Capitais. Rio de Janeiro.

RU/SCID *See* GIT/SCID.

SAGE/JIAS Journal of Inter-American Studies and World Affairs. Sage Publication *for the* Center for Advanced International Studies, Univ. of Miami. Coral Gables, Fla.

SECOLAS/SELA South Eastern Latin Americanist. Southeastern Conference on Latin American Studies. Clemson Univ. Clemson, S.C.

SEM/E Ethnos. Statens Etnografiska Museum. Stockholm.

SP Socialismo y Participación. Ediciones Socialismo y Participación. Lima.

UB/BA Boletín Americanista. Univ. de Barcelona, Facultad de Geografía e Historia, Depto. de Historia de América. Barcelona.

UC/EDCC Economic Development and Cultural Change. Univ. of Chicago, Research Center in Economic Development and Cultural Change. Chicago, Ill.

UH/ED Economía y Desarrollo. Univ. de La Habana, Instituto de Economía. La Habana.

UJSC/ECA ECA (Estudios Centroamericanos). Univ. Centroamericana José Simeón Cañas. San Salvador.

ULA/RG Revista Geográfica. Univ. de Los Andes. Mérida, Venezuela.

UNAH/RCE Revista Centroamericana de Economía. Univ. Nacional Autónoma de Honduras, Programa de Postgrado Centroamericano en Economía y Planificación. Tegucigalpa.

UNAM/AA Anales de Antropología. Univ. Nacional Autónoma de México, Instituto de Investigaciones Históricos. México.

UNAM/RI Relaciones Internacionales. Univ. Nacional Autónoma de México, Facultad de Ciencias Políticas y Sociales, Centro de Relaciones Internacionales. México.

UNC/REE Revista de Economía y Estadística. Univ. Nacional de Córdoba, Facultad de Ciencias Económicas. Córdoba, Argentina.

UNESCO/IRE International Review of Education. UN Educational, Scientific, and Cultural Organization, Institute for Education. Hamburg, FRG.

UNLP/E Económica. Univ. Nacional de La Plata, Facultad de Ciencias Económicas, Instituto de Investigaciones Económicas. La Plata, Argentina.

UP/A Apuntes. Univ. del Pacífico, Centro de Investigación. Lima.

UP/CSEC Cuban Studies/Estudios Cubanos. Univ. of Pittsburgh, Univ. Center for International Studies, Center for Latin American Studies. Pittsburgh, Pa.

UP/TM Tiers Monde. Univ. de Paris, Institut d'étude du développement économique et social. Paris.

UPR/RCS Revista de Ciencias Sociales. Univ. de Puerto Rico, Colegio de Ciencias Sociales. Río Piedras.

URSS/AL América Latina. Academia de Ciencias de la Unión de Repúblicas Soviéticas Socialistas. Moscú.

UU/PS   Peasant Studies. Univ. of Utah, Dept. of History. Salt Lake City.

UWI/SES   Social and Economic Studies. Univ. of the West Indies, Institute of Social and Economic Research. Mona, Jamaica.

UY/R   Revista de la Universidad de Yucatán. Mérida, México.

WD   World Development. Pergamon Press. Oxford, United Kingdom.

EDUCATION

LATIN AMERICA (except Brazil)

EVERETT EGGINTON, *Professor, School of Education, University of Louisville*

THE TASK OF REVIEWING TWO YEARS of literature on Latin American education is monumental. The abundance of research on education in this region published during the last two years is overwhelming; the task of selecting from among this crop those to include in this volume of the *Handbook* has been, at the very least, formidable. Evidence that this task has been accomplished may be gleaned from the annotations which follow. The serious student and scholar of Latin American education is forewarned, however, that the research below is not by any means exhaustive. There is an abundance of published research on Latin American education—some of it quite good—which, because of space limitations, I was not able to include. I do believe, however, that the annotations which follow constitute, at the very least, a good starting point toward understanding developments in Latin American education over the last two years.

Reviewing two years of published research and selecting the publications to include in the *Handbook* is but the first task. The second, to bring a sense of coherence to such a potpourri of published research is almost as difficult. For example, I could attempt to delineate the trends in educational research by looking at disciplinal contributions—those of economists, historians, sociologists, and anthropologists. Or I could do so by looking at the research by topical focus, such as elementary education, secondary education, higher education, non-formal education. In a similar vein, I could attempt to identify coherent trends by looking at country-specific research, by looking at interdisciplinary and symposia-inspired research, or by looking at issue-oriented research. After ruminating on these several possibilities, I have come to the conclusion that to superimpose these structures, or others, on a selection of publications as diverse in every respect as those reported below would be unwise. What follows then is little more than my own thoughts and feelings vis-à-vis the patterns and directions of research on Latin American education.

Educational research has once again been the focus of several publications. Chiappe and Myer's analysis of contemporary research potential in Colombia (item **4404**) highlights something of a consensus—an emerging trend: Published research on Latin American education is currently more plentiful and of higher quality than has been the case in the past; the degree to which it is utilized by policymakers in decisionmaking is, however, questionable. Bernales's examination of the proliferation of social science research in Peru and his suggestions on how to guide its future development (item **4489**) are consistent with this trend. Related to research utilization is, of course, dissemination, the focus of items **4467** and **4468**. The first looks at the way social scientists in Mexico disseminate their research; the second at the approach natural scientists take. Not everyone who has addressed the issue of educational research is in agreement on its improved quality. Bayce's critical assessment of both the value and quality of educational research in Latin America is a case in point (item **4307**) as is item **4515**, a conference report in which Venezuelan social scientists critically assess the quality of their country's research. Several items look specifically at trends in research in Latin America. Egginton's two articles focus on patterns in educational research (items **4318** and **4319**); Tulchin's contribution reflects on patterns of research on Latin America that he discerned during his eight years as editor of the *Latin American Research Review* (item **4370**).

Equal educational opportunity has once again received considerable attention. The literature, however, reflects little consensus or progress in this area. At one extreme is Jesús Giraldo's scathing indictment of the Colombian educational system (item **4405**), at the other, Sergio Martinić's educational needs assessment of a lower-class community in Santiago, Chile (item **4392**). Giraldo has absolutely no confidence in the formal educational system; Martinić has complete confidence. The rest of the literature on educational equity reflects the diversity of perspectives on the issue. Unfortunately, in this year's literature the pessimists clearly prevail. Banguero's analysis of school performance and nutrition does not augur well for educational equity among the poor (item **4402**). Solari and Franco's pessimistic assessment of educational opportunities in higher education, despite tremendous efforts, is disheartening (item **4507**). Riquelme's conclusion that parental socioeconomic status explains the relationship between years of education and occupational status is, at the very least, a direct challenge to the efficacy of schools to bring about social mobility (item **4356**). And finally, educational equity even in nonformal settings has been challenged. Item **4451** points out that educational opportunities among subgroups of Mexican workers has been unequal; those with the most power are the ones most likely to participate in these programs.

The literature on teachers and teaching and on curriculum is the focus of numerous publications. Argumedo's assessment of teacher training in Argentina shows in-service teacher training to be largely unrelated to teachers' classroom responsibilities (item **4375**). By contrast, Vera's survey of Argentine teachers demonstrates that they are favorably disposed to a more active and participatory role in their training (item **4386**), certainly a more optimistic conclusion. Grant's description of Jamaica's Project for Early Childhood Education—a training program for preschool teachers and paraprofessionals—fills a void in the teacher training literature (item **4437**).

The literature on the profession of teaching includes two items from Chile: the first looks at teachers' unions and the second, at the professionalization of primary and secondary school teachers (item **4394**). In analyzing the problems confronting university teachers throughout Latin America, Kliksberg concludes that their teaching methods are antiquated and inappropriate for the times; he calls for a "technology of pedagogy," that is, a total revision of the teaching process (item **4342**).

The literature on educational curricula is diverse. It includes, for example, Guerra's article which recommends using selected techniques of the mass media to develop students' critical thinking skills (item **4449**) and London's plea to US educators to be sensitive to and prepare for the continued influx of Caribbean students to their classrooms (item **4409**). In addition, the literature includes a call for a totally reorganized approach to postgraduate training in Cuba (item **4418**), a restructured curricula to meet rural students' needs in Honduras (item **4436**), and an experimental curricular package focusing on the history of the new world designed for Latin America's open universities (item **4335**).

The literature on science and technology is abundant. The current literature includes high quality material which both cuts across national boundaries and is country-specific. Among the general literature of note are: 1) Fernández-Collado and Baptista Fernández's article which points to inadequate communication among the region's scientists as well as to the dearth of effective science-oriented professional organizations as reasons behind Latin America's lack of progress in these areas (item **4327**); 2) Gurgulino de Souza's analysis of the problem, in which he concludes that governments need to establish national policy to support the development of science and technology and that government-supported research and technology centers are vital to a country's development (item **4334**); and 3) Hodara's article which argues that the greatest contribution international organizations can make toward developing the region's scientific and technological potential lies in their ability to sensitize governments to these development needs and to coordinate specific multinational science and technology projects (item **4336**). Among the country-specific pieces, Velasco's analysis of the detrimental effects of Pinochet's policies on science and technology is well worth reading (item **4397**) as is Antonorsi Blanco's discussion of the failure of Venezuela's planning process to achieve results of any consequence in these areas (item **4508**). While most of the literature points to a lack of progress in science and technology, there are exceptions. Most of the exceptions focus on Cuba. For example, items **4417** and **4421** point to the remarkable progress Cuba has made in these areas since the Revolution.

The literature which explores the relationship between education and development is intriguing and provides testimony to its complexity. On the one hand, there are those who see education as essential to development. For example, Adolfo Portela cites Argentina's failure to promote science in its educational system as a primary reason behind its failure to develop at a rate commensurate with the European countries with which it shares so much in common (item **4383**). And Tedesco looks at the evolution of industrial manpower in Argentina in the 1960s and explores its relationship to the educational system (item **4384**). On the other hand, there are those who see educational systems not so much in terms of a country's level of development but more as a reflection of its economic and social structure. Item **4314** contains two UNESCO-sponsored studies, the first of which constitutes a striking example of this latter point of view. Lavados Montes's study of regional higher education organizations adds a new dimension to our understanding of this already complex relationship, the emergence of international cooperation among the countries' universities (item **4343**). Miranda Pacheco's study confounds the education and development relationship even further by arguing that in addition to education, regional integration is essential to development (item **4348**). To this end, he proposes educational reforms that would reflect the common goals of the countries of the region.

The literature on educational policy, planning, and reform continues to be plentiful. Most striking is the growing number of contributions which discuss educational policy issues. A noteworthy contribution in this area is item **4382**, a general treatise on the development of educational policy in Argentina. Arizmende Rodríguez's collection of essays on educational planning in Mexico is a useful source for educational planners and policymakers (item **4439**). And Millares Reyes's analysis of the university reform movement in Latin America since 1918, with a specific focus on Ecuador, Peru, and Venezuela, is excellent (item **4347**). These three contributions to the policy, planning, and reform literature are but the surface of a particularly good crop.

The traditional themes are not neglected in this year's literature. Publications on the university and historical studies continue to be abundant. An emerging trend reflected in the higher education literature relates to university finance; Latin American governments are increasingly hard pressed to provide tuition-free higher education. Adrian's article describes the tuition dilemma in some detail (item **4301**). An excellent history among the contributions is Valcárcel's history of San Marcos Univ. (item **4495**). This is a well documented, well illustrated institutional history.

All in all, the education literature continues to be plentiful, although its quality is varied. New trends have emerged, as, for example, in the tuition dilemma in higher education; old trends have declined, as, for instance, the subject of nonformal education. Educational research in Latin America is by nature interdisciplinary, representing as it does many disciplines, many issues, many methodologies, and many nationalities. Two years ago in this space I was critical of the published research on Latin American education. At that time, I called for more research "grounded in theory and based on adherence to accepted methods." In retrospect, I do not think my criticism was justified; rather, it reflected my values superimposed on a research literature which by nature is eclectic. And its strength is its variety, its breadth, its scope—in short, its interdisciplinary richness.

GENERAL

4301 Adrian, William. The tuition dilemma in the Latin American university (UNESCO/IRE, 29:4, 1983, p. 449–464, bibl., tables)

Latin American governments are searching for funding alternatives to public subsidy for higher education. Tuition is viewed as a means to diversify support and reduce financial pressures on these governments. Describes rationale for and opposition to this approach.

4302 Alayón, Norberto. Las escuelas de trabajo social en América Latina. Buenos Aires: Editorial Humanitas, 1982. 126 p.: bibl., ill. (Col. Desarrollo social)

Summarizes principal activities, requirements, facilities, and finances of 46 schools of social work representing 13 countries of South and Central America (including Mexico) and the Caribbean. Based on a questionnaire survey which had been sent to almost 250 social work schools, the very low rate of return detracts from this otherwise useful source.

Almeida, Luciano Mendes de; Paul-Eugène Charbonneau; and Edenio Valle. A educação

na América Latina: continente em vias de desenvolvimento. See item **4519.**

4304 Antonorsi Blanco, Marcel. Tecnología suave: una interpretación crítica y otros ensayos. Caracas: Monte Avila Editores, 1980. 261 p.: bibl., ill. (Col. Estudios)

Author conceptually analyzes premise that any technology other than "soft" technology is ill-suited and dysfunctional for lesser developed societies. Discusses conditions under which soft technology would be preferable to hard technology and describes criteria for assessing its effectiveness.

4305 Aptekar, Lewis S. Suggestion for providing services to the handicapped in Latin America (WD, 11:11, Nov. 1983, p. 995-1004, bibl.)

Focusing on transferability of US models and programs for the handicapped to Latin America, argues that different needs in Latin America require different programs. Unfortunately, most Latin American countries base their programs for the handicapped on highly specialized US models. Among author's recommendations: community-based programs; low cost, low technology programs; service delivery by local residents.

4306 Ardila, Irenarco et al. Alternativas de educación para grupos culturalmente diferenciados: estudio de casos. Washington: Organización de los Estados Americanos, 1983. 197 p.: bibl., ill.

Very interesting case studies on minority education in Latin America. Originally presented at OAS-sponsored symposium on topic. Topics range from parent education in Chile, to education for street urchins in Colombia, multicultural education in Mexico, and bilingual education in Texas. Well worth reading.

4307 Bayce, Rafael. La investigación contemporánea en educación: una evaluación epistemológica de teoría y métodos. Montevideo: Centro de Informaciones y Estudios del Uruguay: Acali Editorial, 1983. 179 p.: bibl., ill. (Economía & sociedad. Serie A; 3)

Very critical assessment of the value and quality of educational research in Latin America (e.g., inappropriate, impractical, and therefore, misleading use of mathematical/statistical designs; educational research that does not lead to discovery of new and useful knowledge; and application of social research to education without vision).

4308 Bibliografía sobre educación para el trabajo. Santiago: UNESCO, OREALC, 1982. 14 p.: bibl. (OREALC/Biblos. e. técnica y prof.; 13)

Unannotated bibliography on vocational and technical education in Latin America and the Caribbean.

4309 Bibliografía sobre problemática universitaria. Dirigida y compilada por el Centro de Investigación de la Problemática Universitaria (CINPRU), Grupo de Univs. del Norte de Bogotá. Bogotá: Instituto Colombiano para el Fomento de la Educación Superior, Subdirección de Fomento, Div. de Recursos Bibliográficos, 1982. 299 p.: index.

Unannotated bibliography listing published materials on diverse aspects of higher education available in Bogotá libraries and research centers. Entries are listed alphabetically by topic.

4310 Bigott, Luis Antonio. Modelos de análisis de sistemas escolares. Caracas: Ediciones de la Facultad de Humanidades y Educación, Univ. Central de Venezuela, 1982. 1 v.: bibl., ill.

Comprehensive treatment of the theory and application of systems analysis to education. Describes in detail a variety of systems analysis models and applies them to different educational issues.

4311 Cariola S.J., Patricio. Educación y participación en América Latina: un paradigma emergente dentro del desarrollo educativo de América Latina (SP, 14, junio 1981, p. 129–158, bibl.)

Traditional model of educational development focuses on power of the State to institute change. Arguing that this conservative model inhibits development, author proposes a new kind of community as a necessary condition for educational development. Unfortunately, his description of such a community is nebulous. Includes useful annotated bibliography which focuses on community participation in formal and nonformal education.

4312 La Crisis y transformación de la universidad: vías posibles de colaboración entre universidades europeas y latinoamericanas. Editores, H.A. Steger, L. Scherz y A. Córdova. Nürnberg, FRG: Sección América Latina, Instituto Central, Univ. de Erlangen-Nürnberg, 1981. 152 p.: bibl.

Proceedings of conference of European and Latin American specialists on higher education, who met to explore avenues for potential collaboration in scientific research between both regions. Organized by the Collegium Humboldtianum of Bielefeld, FRG, and Univ. of Amsterdam's Center for Latin American Studies (Amsterdam, Oct. 1969), proceedings were finally published in 1981 by Erlangen Univ. (Nürnberg, FRG). Particularly noteworthy is the opening address by Hanns-Albert Steger, Univ. of Erlangen. In it, he describes significant differences among universities in Europe, US, and Latin America; analyzes potential problems and promises collaborative efforts in scientific research between European and Latin American university scientists.

4313 Los Déficits educativos en América Latina. Washington: Organización de Estados Americanos, Depto. de Asuntos Educativos, Unidad de Planeamiento, Investigación y Estudios de la Educación, 1979. 1 v.: ill. (Serie Atlas; 1. Col. de monografías y estudios de la educación)

Unanalyzed data on literacy and school access for all South and Central American countries (including Mexico) by state (or other appropriate political-geographic division within each country) and by age.

4314 El Desarrollo de América Latina y sus repercusiones en la educación: alfabetismo y escolaridad básica. Santiago: CEPAL, 1982. 254 p.: bibl. (Cuadernos de la CEPAL; 41. E/CEPAL/G.1193)

Two-pt. vol. contains two UNESCO-sponsored studies which focus on education and development in Latin America. Pt. 1 examines relationship between different countries' economic and social structures and their educational systems. Pt. 2, a country-by-country empirical study, looks at literacy and its relationship to basic education by different age cohorts.

4315 Diseño de evaluación de proyectos de innovación y reforma de la educación. Editor, E. Schiefelbein. Moisés Acuña *et al.* Santiago: Ministerio de Educación, Centro de Perfeccionamiento, Experimentación e Investigaciones Pedagógicas: Organización de los Estados Americanos, Programa de Desarrollo Educativo, 1982. 270 p.: bibl., ill. (OAS Doc. 21529)

Comprehensive evaluation strategy to assess efficacy of educational projects and innovations prepared by staff of Chilean Ministry of Public Education's Centro de Perfeccionamiento, Experimentación e Investigaciones Pedagógicas. Of uniformly high quality, strategy includes such elements as criteria for selecting projects, different assessment designs for different kinds of projects or innovations, sampling strategies, and supervision of experimental projects. Particularly noteworthy is N. McGinn and E. Schielfelbein's chap. on supervision and evaluation of experimental projects.

4316 Educación y formación profesional para grupos marginales urbanos. Montevideo: CINTERFOR/OIT, 1982. 52 p. (Informes; 111)

Complete proceedings of conference sponsored by Centro Interamericano de Investigación y Documentación sobre Formación Profesional (CINTERFOR) and Ecuador's Ministry of Education (Quito, March 1981). Book's title summarizes focus. Proceedings include complete summaries for each of six principal themes addressed: 1) professional training and social development; 2) professional education for marginal populations;

3) policy objectives in professional education for marginal populations; 4) strategies for teaching marginal populations; 5) planning and evaluating professional education programs for marginal populations; and 6) coordinating inter-institutional efforts in professional education for marginal populations.

4317 Education for international understanding, cooperation, and peace and education relative to human rights and fundamental liberties in Latin America and the Caribbean: final report. Santiago: UNESCO, Regional Office for Education in Latin America and the Caribbean, 1983. 50 p.

UNESCO's 18th General Conference (Paris, 1974) focuses on human rights. Series of recommendations on human rights were approved for member states to implement. In Nov. 1981, UNESCO's Regional Office for Education in Latin America and the Caribbean met to work out strategies for implementation. Monograph consists of final report for this regional meeting.

4319 Egginton, Everett and Sheree Koppel. Tendencias de la investigación educativa en América Latina (CEE/RL, 13:3, 1983, p. 117–147)

Analysis of contents of education sections of *HLAS* as of vol. 1 (1936) revealed numerous trends (e.g., changes in theme, regional focus, research methodologies). Article documents and describes these trends.

4320 Elissetche, Marcelo M. UPE in a Latin American perspective: strategies for action (UNESCO/IRE, 29:2, 1983, p. 155–158)

Brief assessment of progress made in Latin America during last 20 yrs. toward achieving educational goals set forth in the Charter of Punta del Este (1961). While acknowledging that considerable but uneven progress has been made, suggests new strategies for the future.

4321 Encuentro-Taller Subregional, *San José, 1983.* Producción de materiales de educación popular y estrategias para el conocimiento y difusión del proyecto principal de educación a nivel de las poblaciones de base. Santiago: UNESCO, OREALC, 1983. 32 p.

General conference report plus working papers on community-based adult education in Latin America.

4322 Ensayos sobre la educación de los adultos en América Latina. Coordinador, Carlos Alberto Torres. João Bosco Pinto *et al.* México: Centro de Estudios Educativos, 1982. 689 p.: bibl., ill. (Col. Estudios educativos; 6)

Very comprehensive collection of articles on adult and nonformal education in Latin America divided into four pts.: 1) social, economic, and political aspects of adult education; 2) pedagogical considerations in educating adults; 3) exceptional adult education programs; and 4) training of adult educators. Useful and comprehensive source. Contributors are a veritable who's who in adult education in Latin America.

4323 Escotet, Miguel A. La educación superior a distancia en Latinoamérica: mito y realidad en una innovación (UAG/D, 9:6, nov./dic. 1981, p. 27–40, bibl.)

Very pessimistic appraisal of Latin America's open university movement. Only a handful who begin there complete their studies in open universities; fully 70 percent of open university programs in Latin America have failed and been eliminated. Concludes that contrary to rhetoric of open university movement, it is, in fact, their total inflexibility to students' needs which is to blame for their demise.

4324 Estado de los tratados y convenciones interamericanos, revisado al 8 de mayo de 1980. Status of Inter-American treaties and conventions, revised to May 8, 1980. Washington: Secretaría General, Organización de los Estados Americanos, 1980. 53 p.: tables (Serie sobre tratados; 5)

Volume of tables summarizes country-by-country status of Inter-American treaties and conventions (revised to May 8, 1980). Several treaties and conventions focus on education. Useful source.

4325 Estudios e investigaciones sobre educación. Consejo de redacción, Josefina Aragoneses Alonso *et al.* Santiago: Pontificia Univ. Católica de Chile, 1980. 204 p.: bibl., ill. (*Anales de la Escuela de Educación*; 4:3)

Originally published as issue of *Anales de la Escuela de Educación* (Pontificia Univ. Católica de Chile), includes articles on children's literature, language development and learning, nonformal education, and participation in extracurricular activities and personal development.

4326 Evaluación del centro educativo. Editor, Rafael Herrera R. Santiago: Centro de Perfeccionamiento, Experimentación e Investigaciones Pedagógicas, 1983. 207 p.: ill. (Serie Ciencias de la educación; 5)

Material for this book was developed during OAS-sponsored Multinational Project on Educational Evaluation (1980–81) at Chile's teacher training and pedagogical research center (El Centro de Perfeccionamiento, Experimentación e Investigaciones Pedagógicas de Chile). Highly useful handbook consists of nine largely independent chaps.: 1–2 describe "centros educacionales" as social systems and as unique models; 3–5 focus on assessing educational needs, planning educational centers to meet needs, and developing evaluative criteria; and finally, 6–9 describe specific evaluation plans for different components of educational centers.

4327 Fernández-Collado, Carlos and Pilar Baptista Fernández. La universidad invisible: ideas sobre como instruir al estudiante latinoamericano para formar y mantener una comunidad científica (CPES/RPS, 17:47, enero/abril 1980, p. 69–77, bibl.)

Authors argue that scientific inquiry is a social phenomenon and that communication and collaboration among scientists are essential to its development. Development of science in Latin America has been severely hampered by poor communication among the region's scientists as well as by a dearth of effective science-oriented professional organizations. Reasons cited include inadequate financial resources and inflexible university bureaucracies.

4328 Fichas técnicas sobre equipos de bajo costo para la enseñanza de las ciencias. Editor, Carlos Jairo Díaz. Dibujos, Humberto Hincapié H. Santiago: UNESCO, OREALC, 1981. 36 p.: ill. (Boletín; 2)

Useful how-to manual on constructing low-cost equipment to be used in teaching science.

4329 Flores Olmedo, Luis. Diseños de investigación educativa. Quito: Editorial Siembra, 1982. 553 p.: bibl., ill. (SEIC; 2)

Comprehensive text describes purpose of different research designs and their application in educational settings.

4330 Foster, Mercedes S. Training biologists and resource managers in lesser developed countries (AI/I, 8:5, Sept./Oct. 1983, p. 289–293, bibl., ill.)

Little has been done to develop training programs in natural resources management among LDCs. Describes plan for such a program which grew from one developed by US Fish and Wildlife Service, Peace Corps, and Paraguay's National Forest Service.

4331 Gabaldón, Arnoldo. La enfermedad latinoamericana de la educación superior. Caracas: Programa de Publicaciones, Fondo Editorial para el Desarrollo de la Educación Superior, 1982. 337 p.: bibl., ill.

The disease the title refers to reflects, on the one hand, the inexorable growth of higher education enrollments in Latin American republics, and, on the other, a precipitous decline in the quality of higher education in these countries. The consequence, argues author, is disaster; the virtual demise of the Latin American university.

4332 Gadea, Jorge A. Los líderes se hacen, no nacen: manual práctico de entrenamiento de líderes. v. 1, Liderismo en acción. v. 2, Liderato por objetivos. v. 3, Interacción del grupo. v. 4, El grupo y la comunidad. v. 5, Organización y procedimientos. v. 6, Programas y actividades. v. 7, Liderato inspirador. 2a ed. Santo Domingo: J.A. Gadea & Asoc., 1983. 7 v.: ill.

Seven-vol. management training handbook designed to develop effective leaders for community service agencies in the Spanish-speaking world.

4333 García, Celina. Latin American traditions and perspectives (UNESCO/IRE, 29:3, 1983, p. 369–389, bibl., ill.)

Disjointed essay on relationship among traditional education, gender roles, and propensity toward violence in Latin American societies. Concludes that Latin American women ought to reject Western patterns of violence and actively seek alternatives to conflict resolution.

Gómez Campos, Víctor Manuel. Relaciones entre educación y estructura económica: dos grandes marcos de interpretación. See item **2875.**

4334 Gurgulino de Souza, Heitor. La investigación científica y tecnológica en América Latina (UAG/D, 9:6, nov./dic. 1981, p. 5–20, tables)

Compares and contrasts state of tech-

nology and scientific research among nations of Latin America. Among author's conclusions: governments need to establish national policy to support the development of research and technology; universities are integral to this development; government-supported research and technology centers are vital to a country's development.

4335 Hernández Sánchez-Barba, Mario. Historia de América. Madrid: Univ. Nacional de Educación a Distancia, Depto. de Historia, 1982. 500 p.: bibl.

Contains curriculum focusing on New World history designed for Latin America's open universities (universidades a distancia). Produced by History Dept. of Madrid's Univ. Complutense.

4336 Hodara, Joseph. Aportes, directrices y limitaciones de los organismos internacionales y regionales en las políticas latinoamericanas para la ciencia y la tecnología (AI/I, 8:4, julio/agosto 1983, p. 211–216)

Assessment of potential and accomplishments of selected regional and international organizations in promoting science and technology in Latin America. Referring specifically to OAS, ECLA, UNESCO, and UNCTAD, considers organizations' greatest contributions to be in their ability to sensitize governments to the potential of science and technology for development and in coordinating multinational science and technology projects.

4337 Indice acumulativo de documentos sobre educación, 1974–1980. Coordinadora, Ingrid Müller de Ceballos. Bogotá: Univ. Pedagógica Nacional, Div. de Biblioteca y Recursos Educativos, Centro de Documentación Educativa, 1981. 2 v. (768 p.)

Cumulative index, unannotated, of all documents received (1974–80) by the Documentation Center of Colombia's National Pedagogical Univ. Documents are listed in alphabetical order by their descriptors.

4338 ———: suplemento. Coordinadora, Ingrid Müller de Ceballos. Bogotá: Univ. Pedagógica Nacional, Div. de Biblioteca y Recursos Educativos, Centro de Documentación Educativa, 1982. 1 v.

Supplement to item **4337.** Lists material received by Centro de Documentación of the Univ. Pedagógica Nacional (Bogotá) during 1981–82.

4339 Infante, R. Evaluación de infraestructura física de educación básica a nivel comunal: observaciones y recomendaciones metodológicas (Revista de Geografía Norte Grande [Pontificia Univ. Católica de Chile, Instituto de Geografía, Santiago] 9, 1982, p. 49–57, bibl., ill., tables)

Community level planning model for "basic education." Useful for local level educational policy-makers.

4340 Informaciones estadísticas de la educación y análisis cuantitativo: contenido: políticas y programación socioeducativa en zonas urbanas marginales. Santiago: UNESCO, OREALC, 1984. 66 p. (OREALC/Estadísticas/30)

Report of UNESCO-sponsored workshop on education in economically depressed Latin American urban communities. Emphasizes need for school-community integration to achieve meaningful and effective education.

4341 Javier Palencia, Francisco. La universidad latinoamericana como conciencia. México: UNAM, Centro de Estudios sobre la Universidad, 1982. 123 p. (Col. Monografías. Serie de estudios sobre la universidad)

Explores extent to which Latin American university has fulfilled its role as conscience of society.

4342 Kliksberg, Naum. La crisis pedagógica en las universidades latinoamericanas: elementos para una reflexión crítica. Caracas: Univ. Central de Venezuela, Ediciones de la Biblioteca, 1983. 158 p.: bibl. (Col. Educación; 2)

Latin American universities face problems without precedent. For example, how to maintain academic standards in light of the "democratization" of higher education; how to maintain academic productivity in view of very limited resources; how to provide high-quality scientific and technological training necessary to meet regional needs. Argues that solution lies in the "technology of pedagogy" (i.e., teaching methods currently in use have always been used and are inappropriate for the times). Discusses recommended alternatives.

4343 Lavados Montes, Iván. Un nuevo enfoque de la cooperación internacional: la cooperación académica en América Latina (Contribuciones [Konrad-Adenauer-Stifung A.C. Centro Interdisciplinario de Estudios sobre el Desarrollo Latinoamericano (CIEDLA), Buenos Aires] 2, abril/junio 1984, p. 7–21, tables)

International cooperation is essential to development in Latin America; collaboration among the countries' universities through regional higher education organizations is an integral part of this process. Author is Executive Director of CINDA and expert on UN affairs.

4344 McKee, David L. Some specifics on the brain drain from the Andean region (ICEM/IM, 21:4, 1983, p. 488–499, tables)

Focuses on brain drain problems among Andean Pact countries. Cites US professional challenges and opportunities as most important reasons behind the exodus.

4345 The Major project in the field of education in the Latin American and Caribbean region: its objectives, characteristics, and methods of action. Santiago: UNESCO, Regional Office for Education in Latin America and the Caribbean, 1981. 20 p.

Comprehensive description of one of region's most significant educational development projects. Sponsored by ECLA, OAS, and UNESCO, pamphlet describes project's background, aims and objectives, plan of action, and time frame.

4346 Merani, Alberto L. La educación en Latinoamérica: mito y realidad. México: Editorial Grijalbo, 1983. 203 p.: bibl. (Col. pedagógica)

Educational systems in Latin America and beyond reflect technocratic and bureaucratic societies of which they are a part. Thus, educational systems, especially in LDCs which were at one time colonies, serve a very small elite very effectively; unfortunately, these systems do a disservice to everyone else.

4347 Millares Reyes, Edgar. La universidad y la reforma en América Latina. Sucre, Bolivia: Univ. Mayor, Real y Pontificia de San Francisco Xavier de Chuquisaca, 1980. 113 p.: bibl.

General treatment of Latin America's university reform movement since 1918. Noteworthy are author's original contributions to the theory of university reform (e.g., his discussion of the permanence of reform is thought provoking, or "If society is in a state of constant change, the university needs to change accordingly."). Also useful are his 10 conditions for successful university reform, discussed in some detail. These 10 conditions constitute a sort of modern day Córdoba Manifesto. Discussions of university reform in Ecuador, Peru, and Venezuela are well worth reading.

4348 Miranda Pacheco, Mario. Educación e integración latinoamericana (Revista de la Educación Superior [ANUIES, México] 11[41]:1, enero/marzo 1982, p. 44–53)

Analysis of relationship among education, development, and integration in Latin America. Argues that disparate social, economic, and political forces among different Latin American countries contribute to unique character of each. Proposes educational reforms to reflect common goals of region's countries.

4349 Morales, Víctor. Los estudios de postgrado en América Latina: visión panorámica (AI/I, 8:1, enero/feb. 1983, p. 23–30, ill., table)

While acknowledging significant growth among graduate programs throughout Latin America, bemoans their lack of coherence and planning which is explained, in part, by countries' unstable political structure and restraints on academic freedom. Interestingly highlights Cuba's graduate programs as the most coherent and most attuned to national needs.

4350 Oliveros Alonso, Angel. La educación secundaria en Iberoamérica. t. 1, Estudio comparativo. t. 2, Estudio por países. Madrid: Oficina de Educación Iberoamericana, 1981. 2 v.: bibl. (Serie XI, La Educación iberoamericana en sus documentos. Grupo A. Planes de estudio; 2)

Prepared by Office of Latin American Education (Iberoamericana) of Spain's Dept. of Information and Publications. Examines similarities and differences among systems of secondary education in Latin America.

4351 Ortiz Mena, Antonio. El financiamiento de la educación superior en América Latina: problemas y estrategias (Revista da Univ. Católica de Petrópolis [Brazil] 25–28 fev. 1980, p. 1–30, tables)

IDB President focuses on growth of higher education in Latin America and implications of such growth for curriculum and finance. Regarding curriculum, warns of need to address moral and ethical issues in so-

ciety; regarding finance, he posits alternatives to government subsidies which, he argues, are unrealistic in light of the inexorable growth of higher education in region.

4352 Osorio, Nelson T. El problema de los estudios interdisciplinarios sobre América Latina (CNC/A, 6, 1980–82, p. 75–78)

Discusses feasibility of interdisciplinary research in Latin America. Argues that two conditions must be met before such research is warranted: 1) disciplines involved should have attained high level of maturity with a well defined focus and methodology; and 2) an interdisciplinary approach should be used to address problems (i.e., they cannot be solved by applying techniques of a single discipline).

4353 Perfiles de proyectos: encuesta sobre proyectos innovadores de América Latina y el Caribe que usan tecnología educacional, 1980–1981. Washington: Secretaría General, Organización de los Estados Americanos, Programa Regional de Desarrollo Educativo, 1983. 564 p. (Serie Monografías y estudios de la educación; 7)

During 1980–81, the OAS surveyed its member states on innovative projects which use educational technology. This very useful report summarizes survey results. Includes total of 493 project profiles from all member states. Project profiles are indexed in five ways: 1) numerical order (oldest to newest); 2) country; 3) sponsoring institution; 4) project focus; and 5) key words. Indispensable source for those interested in educational technology in Latin America.

4355 Ribeiro, Darcy. La universidad necesaria. México: UNAM, Centro Universitario de Estudios Latinoamericanos de la Coordinación de Humanidades, 1982. 274 p.: ill. (Nuestra América; 5)

Thorough and comprehensive examination of higher education in Latin America. Six parts analyze: 1) factors which account for the "current crisis" in higher education in the region; 2) diverse models of higher education from disparate countries around the world; 3) traditional structure of higher education in Latin America; 4–5) forces behind and principles which guide modernization and change in higher education in Latin America; and 6) a new theoretical model of a Latin American university, based largely on the Univ. de Brasília where author was Rector. Well documented, thought-provoking analysis.

4356 Riquelme, Marcial Antonio. Educación y empleo: una relación cuestionable (CPES/RPS, 19:53, enero/abril 1982, p. 85–104, bibl., tables)

Analyzes relation among levels of education, occupational status, and socioeconomic factors in Latin America. Concludes that relation between education and occupation is explained by parents' socioeconomic status. In other words, high socioeconomic status is related to more years of formal education and to high occupational status. Author is in effect challenging the efficacy of schools to bring about social mobility.

4357 Roa Suárez, Hernando. Colombia: ciencia, investigación, universidad y pedagogía; consideraciones preliminares. Bogotá: Gráficas Ducal, 1982. 122 p.: bibl.

First analyzes meaning of each of four concepts (science, research, university, pedagogy) and then discusses relationships among them. Looking at them from historical and political perspectives, cautions against strict application of scientific principles and rigid research methodologies to the study of social problems and human behavior.

4358 Schiefelbein, Ernesto. Análisis del rol de la educación pre-escolar para reducir el fracaso escolar (CPES/RPS, 18:52, sept./dic. 1981, p. 7–32, graphs, tables)

Analysis of effects of preschool education on school readiness factors. Examines data from four countries—Argentina, Bolivia, Colombia, and Chile—to explore problem of school dropouts and grade repetition among primary students. Looks at characteristics which distinguish these students from those who neither repeat nor drop out; and finally, assesses effects—real and potential—of preschool education on this group.

4359 ———. Funciones de producción en educación: la experiencia de la América Latina. Washington: Secretaría General, Organización de los Estados Americanos, Programa Regional de Desarrollo Educativo, 1981. 70 p.: appendices, bibl., ill. (Serie Monografías y estudios de la educación; 3)

Summarizes principal studies which focus on relationship between production

functions and outcomes in education in Latin America. Includes two useful appendices which: 1) define and discuss educational production functions; and 2) summarize, in tables, relationship between different production functions and educational outcomes by different countries. Includes complete bibliography of studies cited.

4359a Seminario Internacional sobre Problemas de la Educación Contemporánea, *Caracas, 1980.* Problemas de la educación contemporánea. Caracas: Ediciones de la Facultad de Humanidades y Educación, Univ. Central de Venezuela, 1982. 360 p.: bibl.

Conference papers presented at International Seminar on Problems in Contemporary Education sponsored by Venezuela's Univ. Central's School of Education (Caracas, Nov. 1980). In three pts.: 1) theoretical and political problems which cut across national boundaries; 2) problems specific to individual Latin American countries (excluding Venezuela); and 3) problems in Venezuelan education.

4359b Seminario Regional sobre Estrategias Nacionales de Alfabetización, *Quito, 1981.* América Latina y el Proyecto Principal de Educación. México: CNTE: UNESCO, 1982. 305 p.: bibl., ill.

In Oct. 1981, UNESCO's Regional Office for Education and Ecuador's Ministry of Education and Culture sponsored the Regional Seminar on National Literacy Strategies. Seminar constitutes vital component of UNESCO's Principal Project for Education in Latin America and the Caribbean. Seventeen countries were represented. Contains working papers which focus on criteria for assessing national strategies (Luis Flores), descriptions of different national strategies (Julieta Costa Calazano), and post-literacy strategies (Calberto Brusa).

4360 Seminario Taller Multinacional de Documentación e Información Educacional, *1st, Lima, 1980.* Informe final. Lima: Centro Nacional de Documentación e Información Educacional, 1981. 177 p.: ill.

Complete seminar proceedings (Lima, Oct. 1980). Sponsored by OAS, Peru's National Institute for Research and Development of Education (INIDE), and National Center for Documentation and Educational Information (CENDIE). Contains final reports of different working groups, reports from member delegations (signatories of the

Convenio Andrés Bello), and conclusions and recommendations.

El SENAI [i.e., Serviço Nacional de Aprendizagem Industrial] y la cooperación técnica internacional. See item 4583.

4361 Sidel, Mark. Latin American studies in the People's Republic of China (LARR, 18:1, 1983, p. 143–153)

Based on author's personal observations and interviews during 18-month visit to People's Republic of China (1979–80). Documents growing interest in Latin American studies by China's scholars, teachers, and researchers. Describes state of the art of Latin American studies in that country as reflected in its universities, research centers, scholarly organizations, and research journals.

4362 Los Sistemas estadísticos nacionales de recolección de datos sobre actividades científicas y tecnológicas en los países latinoamericanos. t. 1, Venezuela, Colombia, México y Cuba. t. 2, Brasil y Perú. Paris: UNESCO, 1980. 2 v.: bibl., ill.

Brief description of organizations—government run or supported—which compile, store, and disseminate scientific and technological information. Prepared by UNESCO's Office of Statistics. Pt. 1 describes systems in Venezuela, Colombia, Mexico, and Cuba; pt. 2, in Brazil and Peru.

4363 Sizonenko, Alexandr. La latinoamericanística en las Repúblicas Federadas de la URSS (URSS/AL, 12:60, dic. 1982, p. 39–44)

Examines extent of Soviet scholars' interest in Latin America by era and by region. Concludes that vast majority of research was subsequent to World War II and that the Univ. of Kiev is currently the center of research on Latin America.

4364 Sociología de la educación: corrientes contemporáneas. Coordinadores, Guillermo González Rivera y Carlos Alberto Torres. Félix Cadena et al. México: Centro de Estudios Educativos, 1981. 458 p.: bibl., ill. (Col. Estudios educativos; 5)

Collection of papers presented at 1980 seminar on contemporary trends in sociology of education. Sponsored by Centro de Estudios Educativos (Mexico) and held in San Jerónimo (Mexico). Its states unifying theme was history of the sociology of education as an academic discipline in Latin America; a more realistic unifying theme would be a Marxist perspective on the sociology of education. Consists of 16 essays classified into four sections: 1) history of the sociology of education; 2) sociological theory; 3) contemporary authors in sociology; and 4) applied sociology (case studies). Important book.

4365 Sub-Regional Workshop on Innovations in the Pre and In-Service Training of Educators in Rural Areas, Turmero, Venezuela, 1982. Final report. Turmero: Centro de Capacitación Docente El Mácaro; Santiago: UNESCO, Regional Office for Education in Latin America and the Caribbean, 1982. 42 p.

Final report of UNESCO-sponsored workshop on innovations in pre-service and in-service training of teachers in rural areas. Participants from 13 Central American and Caribbean countries proffered recommendations on: role of rural educator, focus of rural curriculum, function of rural school in development, and role of "humanistic" technology in rural education.

4366 Tedesco, Juan Carlos. El problema de la enseñanza media en América Latina (CPES/RPS, 20:57, mayo/agosto 1983, p. 75–92, tables)

Secondary education in Latin America no longer can be considered elitist. Access to secondary education among children of region's lower and middle classes creates pressures for physical growth and curricular change which countries' school systems are hard pressed to accommodate.

4367 Teoría y praxis de la universidad a distancia. Edición de Luis M. Peñalver y Miguel A. Escotet. Caracas: Fondo Editorial para el Desarrollo de la Educación Superior, 1983. 2 v. (797 p.): bibl., ill.

Two-vol. set contains papers presented at two separate conferences on the open university (la universidad a distancia): 1) New Forms of Post-Secondary Education (Caracas, 1967); and 2) First Latin American Conference on Open Education (San José, 1981). Topics are objectives and achievements in the open university, evaluating personnel in open universities, and educational technology and the open university.

4368 Treviño, Esthela. ¿Una nueva educación en América Latina? México:

Consejo Nacional de Fomento Educativo (CONAFE), Dirección de Investigación y Desarrollo, 1982. 157 p.: bibl., ill.

The "new education" referred to in title has two focuses: education for liberation and lifelong education—concepts attributable to profound influence of Paulo Freire and Ivan Illich, respectively. This five-chap. monograph reports on institutional changes in education in rural Latin America stemming from an emphasis on the "new education." Specifically, looks at region's socioeconomic and political conditions which gave rise to the "new education;" at specific and significant programs; at new methods, materials, and resources; and at problems and obstacles which have confronted the "new education."

4369 Tünnermann Bernheim, Carlos. Estudios sobre la teoría de la universidad. San José: Editorial Universitaria Centroamericana, 1983. 534 p.: bibl., ill. (Col. Aula)

Author, Latin America's foremost authority on higher education and at the time Nicaragua's Minister of Education and Culture, now Ambassador to the US, facetiously posits in his introduction that since the university has been focus of so much research, its study ought to comprise a separate scholarly discipline—una ciencia de la universidad o "Universitología." Book is a distillation of a lifetime of study of higher education; summarizes author's vast knowledge of and insights about the university. In two pts.: 1) theoretical framework of the university— its mission, functions, structure, problems; and 2) the university from the perspective of Latin America. Outstanding book.

4370 Tulchin, Joseph S. Emerging patterns of research in the study of Latin America (LARR, 18:1, 1983, p. 85–94)

Author, former editor of the *Latin American Research Review*, reflects on patterns of research on Latin America discerned during eight yrs. as editor. Without attempting to be all-inclusive, identifies trends uniting many scholars, disciplines, and countries represented in nearly 2,000 articles, research notes, and essays published during those eight yrs.

4371 Universidad, clases sociales y poder. Compiladores, G.W. Rama *et al.* Caracas: CENDES, 1982. 309 p. (Col. Ensayo)

Papers originally presented at regional seminar on higher education sponsored by Comisión de Educación del Consejo Latinoamericano de Ciencias Sociales ("Situación Actual de las Universidades en América Latina," Sept. 1978, Bogotá). Papers reflect diversity of issues and different points of view related to the role of contemporary university in region's political, social, and economic life.

4372 Weinburg, Gregorio. Modelos educativos en el desarrollo histórico de América Latina (CPES/RPS, 14:39/40, mayo/dic. 1977, p. 59–123)

Essentially a history of Latin American education during 18th century in which author analyzes role education played in countries' development during this period.

4373 Zea, Leopoldo. Sentido de la difusión cultural latinoamericana, 1980. México: UNAM, Centro de Estudios sobre la Universidad, 1981. 122 p.: bibl. (Serie de estudios sobre la universidad)

Summarizes author's considerable experiences in cultural dissemination and diffusion throughout Latin America. Defining *cultura* at the outset in its very broadest sense—capacity to enrich oneself, to enjoy oneself, to be open to new experiences, to be open to everything life has to offer—he then distinguishes the Latin American culture from cultures of Europe, Asia, and Africa. Finally, discusses role of university in cultural diffusion. Includes conclusions and recommendations of two Latin American conferences which focused on cultural diffusion in the region.

4374 Zingaretti, Humberto E. Hacia una escuela de la esperanza. Buenos Aires: Editorial Humanitas, 1982. 183 p. (Educación hoy mañana; 9)

Consists of 45 brief essays on different but related aspects of education. Essays can be read in sequence or separately (e.g., first essay asks "Why educate at all?," answer: "It is a moral imperative;" second looks at goals of education; third considers means to achieve them). Whether read by student teacher, in-service teacher, or interested citizen, essays are thought-provoking and inspirational.

ARGENTINA

4375 Argumedo, Manuel. Perfeccionamiento y sistema educativo en Argentina (CPES/RPS, 17:47, enero/abril 1980,
p. 79–99)
Examines quality of in-service teacher
training in Argentina (1970–74). Well designed and comprehensive study emphasizes
need for reconceptualizing country's in-
service teacher training system. Among findings: in-service training is unrelated to teachers' classroom responsibilities; is conducted
infrequently and in a highly sporadic fashion;
consists of little more than series of unrelated short courses (i.e., not sequential); and
is not available to all teachers.

4376 Bravo, Héctor Félix. Educación popular. Buenos Aires: Centro Editor de
América Latina, 1983. 140 p.: bibl. (Biblioteca Política argentina; 42)
Equality of educational opportunity
provides, at the very least, possibility for
social mobility; in this way, education contributes to political stability. Argentina's governments, in failing to support education,
have unwittingly contributed to country's
political instability. This theme is echoed
throughout the 18 essays contained herein,
most of which are previously published journal articles or speeches.

4377 Fainholc, Beatriz. La educación rural
argentina. Buenos Aires: Librería del
Colegio, 1980. 158 p.: bibl., ill. (Biblioteca
Nueva pedagogía)
A traditional formal system of
education—designed to meet educational
needs in urban areas and based on educational models from developed countries—is
inappropriate for rural Argentina and by implication, for rural Latin America. Citing failure of rural education either to contribute to
country's development needs or to provide an
avenue for growth and mobility, calls for a
totally different kind of education for rural
Argentina. Her new model would be "economically autonomous" and totally free of
formal structure extant in country's traditional educational system.

4378 Fernández Berdaguer, María. Educación y empleo: resultados de una
encuesta (UNLP/E, 3, sept./dic. 1982,
p. 245–261, bibl., tables)

In looking at employment status of
students in economics at Univ. of Buenos
Aires, study reveals that most of them are
employed, that their responsibilities are
in areas related to their studies, and that
their level of employment depends largely
on their level of education.

4379 García de Vicens, Mónica. Medición
de la deserción escolar en la Argentina
(CPES/RPS, 16:45, mayo/agosto 1979,
p. 103–134, tables)
Examines relationship between school
desertion and other factors and shows that
high levels of repetition and absenteeism are
associated with high levels of desertion. Concludes that these factors can be used to predict desertion; its explanation, however, is
based on theory of social class and is thus far
more complex. Begs reader not to attribute
school desertion to a single cause.

4380 Herrera Figueroa, Miguel. Universidad
y educación triversitaria. Buenos
Aires: Plus Ultra, 1981. 162 p.: bibl.
After analyzing activities at Univ. Argentina John Fitzgerald Kennedy in Buenos
Aires, develops book's thesis: term *university*
is inaccurate in that it does not describe
what a university does, *triversity* would be
more accurate. For example, in serving the
community, a university strives to achieve
social, economic, and political goals; in
serving the education profession, its responsibilities are to students, teachers, and researchers; in organizing curricula, organizes
subject matter into hard sciences, humanities,
and technical sciences. Thesis seems somewhat contrived and its defense unconvincing.

4381 Miranda, Roberto Alfredo and **Osvaldo
Miguel Iazzetta.** Proyectos políticos y
escuela, 1890–1920. Prólogo de Ricardo
Bruera. Rosario, Argentina: Ediciones Maté-
tica, 1982. 598 p.: bibl., ill., index (Col. Política escolar)
Comprehensive documentary history
of Argentine education (1890–1920). Analysis focuses on evolution of country's educational policy (1890–1901 and 1916–20).
Examines effects of these policies on different components and levels of Argentina's
educational system.

4382 Ocerín, Reynaldo Carlos. Política educativa: bases para una reforma necesaria. Buenos Aires: Plus Ultra, 1981. 301 p.

General treatise on development of educational policy in Argentina. Includes discussion of its meaning in very general terms, role of individual and nation in its development, educational policy as it applies to lifelong education and to higher education, and educational policy in different jurisdictions.

4383 Portela, Adolfo *et al.* Ciencia, tecnología, industria y educación. Buenos Aires?: Editorial Fraterna, 1982. 159 p.: bibl., ill.

Argues that Argentina shares much more in common with industrialized, cultured, and developed countries of Europe than with the Latin American LDCs. Attributes country's failure to develop at rate commensurate with European countries to its failure to emphasize and promote science and technology either in its educational system or its industries.

4384 Tedesco, Juan Carlos. Educación e industrialización en la Argentina (CPES/RPS, 14:39/40, mayo/dic. 1977, p. 125–193, tables)

Examines evolution of industrial manpower in Argentina during 1960s and analyzes relationship between educational system and industrialization process. Toward these ends, notes country's formal and nonformal educational systems; considers industry's posture vis-à-vis employment of less privileged; and analyzes effects of educational inequalities on employment.

4385 ———. Educación y sociedad en la Argentina, 1880–1900. Buenos Aires: Centro Editor de América Latina, 1982. 169 p.: bibl., ill. (Capítulo. Biblioteca argentina fundamental; 157. Serie complementaria, Sociedad y cultura; 9)

Book's earlier version published in 1970. Analyzes late 19th-century conflicts between secular and Church-related groups vying for control over country's educational system and on how conflicts were resolved. Public and secular education won the day, but not without problems. Tedesco discusses these problems: educational inequalities, high rates of school desertion, and inadequate financial resources.

4386 Vera, Rodrigo. Perfeccionamiento e ideología del sector docente (CPES/RPS, 16:45, mayo/agosto 1979, p. 81–102)

Questionnaire study examines teach-ers' attitudes toward a more active and participatory role in teacher training rather than their traditional more passive role. Finds majority are comfortable with status quo but "favorably disposed" to change if conditions warrant.

BOLIVIA

4387 Estadística de educación, 1973–1976. La Paz: Instituto Nacional de Estadística, 1981. 80 leaves: ill., tables.

Comprehensive statistical summary of educational enrollments by level of education and by dept. for 1973–76.

CHILE

4388 Araya Rojas, Alberto A. Base de datos sobre la actividad científica y tecnológica nacional. Santiago: Comisión Nacional de Investigación Científica y Tecnológica (CONICYT), Dirección de Información y Documentación (DID), Depto. de Estadística del Sistema Científico Tecnológico, 1981. 107 p.: ill. (Serie Información y documentación; 22)

Chile's National Commission for Scientific and Technological Research (CONICYT) is responsible for developing science and technology. Describes one of CONICYT's main functions: collection and dissemination of data on science and technology.

4389 Avila M., Emilio *et al.* Medición de la redacción: experimentación de indicadores de la capacidad de usar el lenguaje escrito y su incorporación a la prueba de aptitud académica. Santiago: Univ. de Chile, Dirección de Servicios Estudiantiles, Servicio de Selección y Registro de Estudiantes, Div. Estudios, 1982. 55 p.: bibl. (Monografías; 15)

Detailed summary of the development of Chile's higher education admissions tests or "Prueba de Aptitud Académica." This comprehensive report chronicles entire process of developing a comprehensive measure of academic ability. Useful to other governments' education ministries contemplating an entrance examination requirement.

Briones, Guillermo. Mercado de trabajo, ocupación y educación universitaria en la economía neo-liberal: Chile, 1976–1981. See item **3514**.

Corvalán Vásquez, Oscar E. El aprendizaje en la industria: evaluación de una experiencia chilena. See item **3528**.

4390 Echeverría, Rafael. La política educacional del gobierno militar. Santiago: Programa Interdisciplinario de Investigaciones en Educación, Academia de Humanismo Cristiano, 1981. 25 leaves.

Brief analysis of changes in educational policy brought about by Augusto Pinochet's military government.

4391 González, Paulina and **Elizabeth Wicha.** Programas científicos cooperativos establecidos por CONICYT. Santiago: Comisión Nacional de Investigación Científica y Tecnológica (CONICYT), Dirección de Asistencia Técnica Internacional, 1981. 86 leaves (Serie Directorios; 11)

Handbook describes cooperative programs and agreements which focus on science and technology between Chile's National Commission for Scientific and Technological Research (CONICYT) and its counterpart organizations in Argentina, Brazil, Spain, US, England, and West Germany.

4392 Martinić, Sergio et al. Investigación en una comunidad urbana marginal del Gran Santiago, Chile: identificación de las necesidades educativas básicas. Santiago: UNESCO, OREALC, 1980. 73 p.: bibl., ill., plates.

Applying a unique "need assessment" methodology, study determines educational needs of a Santiago lower-class community. Methodology is potentially germane to marginal communities in rural and urban settings alike.

4393 Millas, Jorge. Idea y defensa de la universidad. Santiago: Editorial del Pacífico: Corporación de Promoción Universitaria, 1981. 154 p.

Collection of essays, articles, speeches by well known Chilean philosopher. Most essays reflect his concern over loss of university autonomy to forces antithetical to the meaning of a university. Argues that university needs to be defended against those special interests that would deny it autonomy to discharge its functions without restraint.

Chile's and Latin America's future depend on an autonomous university.

4394 Núñez P., Iván. El magisterio chileno. pt. 1, Sus primeras organizaciones gremiales. pt. 2, Las organizaciones del magisterio chileno y el estado de compromiso. pt. 3, Cambios en la situación del magisterio. Santiago: Programa Interdisciplinario de Investigaciones en Educación, Academia de Humanismo Cristiano, 1982. 3 v. (120, 142, 81 p.): bibl.

Three-pt. study. Pt. 1 reviews the teachers' union movement in Chile (1900–35). Focus is on primary and secondary school teachers, a group which constitutes the core of country's middle class. Pt. 2 reviews their union movement until the year in which Augusto Pinochet's military government assumed control (1936–73). Pt. 3 looks at educational changes in Chile resulting from economic, labor, and educational policies of this military government.

4395 ———. Tradición, reformas y alternativas educacionales en Chile, 1925–1973. Santiago: Vector, 1980? 50 p.: bibl. (Estudios Vector; 1)

In analyzing post-1925 educational reform in Chile, concludes that reformist efforts have largely failed. Attributes failure of educational reform largely to failure of country's "capitalist" model of development.

4396 Schiefelbein, Ernesto. Antecedentes para el análisis de la política educacional chilena en 1982. Santiago: Corporación de Promoción Universitaria, 1982. 353 p.: bibl., ill. (Serie Documentos de trabajo)

Interesting and useful summary of research published in Chile (1977–81) on a variety of education-related topics, including preschool, primary, and secondary education; adult, nonformal and informal education; and educational personnel and educational technology. By contrast to most publications which synthesize and summarize published research, Schiefelbein succeeds in integrating significant findings in aforementioned areas.

4397 Velasco, Ibelis. Some facts and many impressions on science and technology in Chile: pt. 1 (AI/I, 9:2, March/April 1984, p. 92–97, ill.)

Analysis of effects of Pinochet's policies on science and technology in Chile.

Cites two principal reasons for country's lack of progress in these areas: government repression and economic stagnation.

COLOMBIA

4399 Angulo Gómez, Guillermo. Informe al Congreso Nacional: mayo 1980-febrero 1981. Bogotá: Ministerio de Educación Nacional, 1981. 118 p.: ill. (some col.)

Minister of Education's constitutionally mandated report to the National Congress describes Ministry's accomplishments (May 1980-Feb. 1981). Particularly noteworthy are Minister's remarks on 1980 reform of country's system of higher education. His praise of reform is interesting in light of the fact that his predecessor was its principal architect.

4400 Arbab, Farzam and **Laurence D. Stifel.** University for rural development: an alternative approach in Colombia (JDA, 16:4, July 1982, p. 511–521)

Detailed description of unique and innovative experiment in rural higher education. This experimental university, located in an impoverished rural area in Norte del Cauca Dept., was begun in 1974 by several faculty members from Univ. del Valle in Cali. In describing the six-yr. curriculum which focuses on rural-based agrarian needs of the region, authors contend that this model could be transferred to other sections of country.

4401 Aubad López, Rafael and **Saúl Mesa Ochoa.** Cuatro ensayos a propósito del financiamiento de la educación superior. Antioquia, Colombia: Centro de Investigaciones Económicas: Asociación de Profesores, Univ. de Antioquia, 1982. 75 p.: bibl.

Four essays focus on: 1) FEDESARROLLOS's plan for financial higher education; 2) financing operations at Univ. de Antioquia; 3) options in financing higher education; and 4) student options on financing programs at Univ. de Antioquia.

4402 Banguero, Harold; Fabio Sabogal; and **José Alzate.** Nutrición y escolaridad: el caso colombiano; informe presentado al Programa de Estudios Conjuntos sobre Integración Económica Latinoamericana (ECIEL). Bogotá: Centro de Estudios sobre Desarrollo Económico, Facultad de Economía, Univ. de los Andes, 1979. 280 p.: ill. (Documento; 059)

Analysis of relationship between nutrition and school performance. Pt. 1 looks at determinants of malnutrition, analyzes extent of malnutrition in large sample (N = 4880) of school-age children from five of Colombia's largest cities, and establishes relationship between nutrition and physical growth and development of children. Pt. 2 looks specifically at relationship between extent of malnutrition and several indicators of school performance (e.g., academic achievement, repetition, dropout). Excellent study has few surprises: i.e., malnutrition is directly related to poverty.

4403 Betancur Mejía, Gabriel. ICETEX: la experiencia colombiana de crédito educativo (Revista da Universidade Católica de Petrópolis [Brazil] 25/28, fev. 1980, p. 39–82, tables)

Comprehensive summary of Instituto Colombiano de Especialización Tecnica en el Exterior (ICETEX) (i.e., history, services, administrative structure, funding sources). Prepared by ICETEX's founder and President for presentation at an international conference on financing education abroad. Clearly established ICETEX as most respected organization of its type in Latin America.

4404 Chiappe, Clemencia and **Robert Myers.** El fortalecimiento de la capacidad investigativa en educación en Colombia: 1960–1981 (UPN/RCE, 9:1, 1982, p. 77–108, bibl., tables)

Educational research potential in Colombia since 1960 leads authors to state that its considerable progress is largely due to favorable political climate. Unfortunately, this carefully documented and thorough study reveals a hiatus between research generated and research utilized, low demand for educational research, and lack of coordination and planning among educational researchers and organizations.

4405 Giraldo Giraldo, Jesús Helí. El niño colombiano frente a la crisis educativa. Bogotá: Ediciones Tercer Mundo, 1982. 73 p.

In this scathing indictment of Colombia's educational system, author focuses on its detrimental effect on the nation's children. Poignant and moving writing but simplistic and superficial analysis.

4406 Lloreda Caicedo, Rodrigo. Documentos sobre la reforma de la educación superior: discursos y reportajes del Ministro de Educación Nacional. Yerbabuena, Colombia: Imprenta Patriótica, Instituto Caro y Cuervo, 1980. 65 p.

Essentially a defense of Colombia's higher education reform law (Ley No. 8ª de 1979) by Minister of Education Lloreda Caicedo. Particularly interesting and somewhat controversial is his reasoning behind law's stipulation that university faculty are public servants.

4407 Zamora, Alonso de *et al.* Universidad Santo Tomás: 400 años. Bogotá: Univ. Santo Tomás, Centro de Enseñanza Desescolarizada, Sec. de Publicaciones, 1980. 314 p.

Comprehensive history of the Univ. of Santo Tomás, one of America's oldest and Colombia's first. Founded in Santafe de Bogotá in 1580, it operated until 1861. It reopened once again in 1965. This compilation of historical essays, many previously published, was released in 1980 in commemoration of the university's 400th anniversary. For historian's comment, see *HLAS 46:2671*.

COMMONWEALTH CARIBBEAN

4408 Alleyne, Michael. Education in the Caribbean: perspectives for the 80's, the function of the educational planner, and the role of the international agency (OAS/LE, 26:90, 1982, p. 17–25)

Examines difficulties inherent in educational planning in Commonwealth Caribbean in light of region's economic, social, and political uncertainties. Citing Trinidad-Tobago as an example, argues that traditional approaches to educational planning have neither reduced educational inequalities nor stimulated sustained and significant economic development.

Beckford, George L. The struggle for a relevant economics. See item **3301.**

4409 London, Clement B.G. Crucibles of Caribbean condition: factors of understanding for teaching and learning with Caribbean students in American educational settings (*in* Journal of Caribbean Studies [Assn. of Caribbean Studies, Coral Gables, Fla.] 2:2/3, Autumn/Winter 1981, p. 182–188)

In the last 25 yrs., more than three million people from the Caribbean have emigrated to US for economic, political, and social reasons; influx is expected to continue. In light of this and other factors which bind US and Caribbean interests, it is incumbent on US educators to be prepared for and sensitive to the needs of Caribbean students in their classrooms. Argues why US educators ought to plan accordingly and provides suggestions on how to prepare.

4410 Social sciences in Latin America and the Caribbean. Paris: UNESCO, 1982. 1 v.: bibl. (Reports and papers in the social sciences; 48)

In Jan. 1980, UNESCO sponsored a meeting on social science needs and priorities in English-speaking Caribbean and Surinam. Papers in this volume were inspired by and reflect the meeting's discussions. They provide information on the state of social sciences in the region and point out areas of mutual interest and concern to region's social scientists.

COSTA RICA

4411 Estadística de la educación superior, 1980. San José: Consejo Nacional de Rectores (CONARE), Oficina de Planificación de la Educación Superior (OPES), 1981. 226 p.: bibl., graphs, tables (OPES/18/8/81/v. 1. OPES-07/81)

Comprehensive statistical summary of higher education in Costa Rica broken down by its four universities: 1) Univ. de Costa Rica; 2) Instituto Tecnológico de Costa Rica; 3) Univ. Nacional; and 4) Univ. Estatal a Distancia. Includes summary tables on students, faculty, degrees and programs, scholarships, library holdings, administrative personnel, etc.

4412 Galvis Panqueva, Alvaro. Universidades a distancia en Latinoamérica: un análisis comparativo en lo metodológico. San José: Editorial Universidad Estatal a Distancia, 1982. 95 p.: bibl., ill., plates.

Compares pedagogical procedures employed in Latin America's two "open" universities (universidades a distancia): Univ. Estatal a Distancia (UNED) in Costa Rica and Univ. Nacional Abierta (UNA) in Venezuela. Examines their structure, organization, curriculum, technology, and faculty.

4413 Planes II: Plan Nacional de Educación Superior, 1981–1985: versión preliminar. San José: Consejo Nacional de Rectores (CONARE), Oficina de Planificación de la Educación Superior (OPES), 1981. 1 v. (various pagings): bibl., ill. (OPES/12/8o/v. 2. OPES-13/8o)

Costa Rica's five-yr. plan for higher education (1981–85). Prepared by Costa Rica's Office of Planning for Higher Education. Addresses (for each of country's four public universities) finance, faculty development, research, educational technology, extension services, student services, computing needs, libraries, administration, physical plant, and supplies and equipment.

4414 Rumble, Greville and **George A. Borden.** Meeting educational needs in Costa Rica: the role of the distance-teaching Universidad Estatal a Distancia (UNESCO/ IRE, 29:4, 1983, p. 427–448, bibl., tables)

In 1977, the Costa Rican government established the Univ. Estatal a Distancia (UNED). Created to alleviate pressures on three existing state-funded, campus-based universities, article assesses UNED's impact on student enrollment pressures, on access by disadvantaged students, and on country's need for trained manpower. Despite problems, authors conclude UNED is meeting its objectives.

4415 Seminario CINTERFOR/INA, *San José, 1983.* Apoyo logístico a la formación profesional. Montevideo: OIT, Centro Interamericano de Investigación y Documentación sobre Formación Profesional, 1983. 127 p.: bibl., ill., plates (Informe; 114)

Complete proceedings of seminar (San José, March 1983) on professional and technical (out-of-school) training sponsored by Centro Interamericano de Investigación y Documentación sobre Formación Profesional (CINTERFOR) and Costa Rica's Instituto Nacional de Aprendizaje (INA). Attended by representatives from six countries (all Central American plus Dominican Republic), seminar's conclusions and recommendations warrant consideration by those interested in technical and professional education.

CUBA

4416 Conferencia Internacional de la Educación, *38th, Geneva, 1981.* Cuba: organización de la educación, 1978–1980. La Habana: Ministerio de Educación, 1981. 166 p.: bibl.

Cuba's report to the UNESCO-sponsored 38th International Conference on Public Education (Geneva, 1981). In three languages (Spanish, English, French), this very informative and up-to-date report includes sections on country's educational goals, objectives, and priorities; on legal bases for its educational system; on administration, finance, and organization; and on recent legislation affecting education in country.

4417 Cuestiones de la ciencia y la tecnología en Cuba. Edición de Tirso W. Sáenz y Emilio García Capote. La Habana: Editorial Academia, 1981. 501 p.: bibl., ill.

Series of previously published book-length essays on science and technology in Cuba. Authors stress remarkable strides despite tremendous obstacles since the Revolution and compare these successes to lamentable consequences of country's pre-Revolutionary scientific and technological dependence. For economist's comment, see item 3358.

Human services in postrevolutionary Cuba: an annotated international bibliography. See item **34.**

4418 Novigrod, Daniel Stolik and **María Dolores Ortiz Díaz.** Algunas consideraciones sobre la educación de postgrado en Cuba (Revista Internacional de Países Socialistas [Ministerio de Educación, La Habana] 37:1, 1982, p. 113–118)

Less a description of postgraduate education in Cuba than it is a call for an entirely new and totally reorganized approach to Cuban postgraduate professional training.

4419 Pichardo, Hortensia. Biografía del Colegio de San Cristóbal de La Habana. La Habana: Editorial Academia, 1979. 292 p.: bibl., ill.

Comprehensive history of one of Cuba's oldest, and formerly most respected, schools. One of its unique features is its comprehensive nature, including a broad curriculum and an elementary and secondary division. Includes extensive documentation.

4420 Provenzo, Eugene F. and Concepción García. Exiled teachers and the Cuban Revolution (UP/CSEC, 13:1, Winter 1983, p. 1–15, table)

Analysis of experiences of 57 Cuban teachers exiled shortly after Castro's assumption of power in 1959 and currently living in Miami. Focus is on what happens when established educators are dispossessed of their traditional status and authority by a revolutionary government.

4421 Sáenz, Tirso W. and Emilio García Capote. Ernesto "Che" Guevara y el progreso científico-técnico en Cuba (AI/I, 8:1, Jan./Feb. 1983, p. 10–18, facsim.)

Role of "Che" Guevara in post-Revolutionary development of science and technology in Cuba.

4422 Tehume Alvarez, Juan and Jorge Rodríguez López. Algunos aspectos relacionados con la Organización Científica del Trabajo (OCT) del personal docente en la educación superior cubana (Revista Internacional de Países Socialistas [Ministerio de Educación, La Habana] 37:1, 1982, p. 45–56)

Ministry of Education policy on faculty accountability in higher education in process of development by OCT. Its purpose is to impose standards of performance among university faculty in light of University Reform Law of 1962 and the Ley de Categorías Docentes of 1975–76.

4423 Triana Benítez, Leonel. El control de la calidad de la preparación de los especialistas en los CES cubanos (Revista Internacional de los Países Socialistas [Ministerio de Educación, La Habana] 35:3, 1981, p. 171–173)

Describes system used by Cuba's Ministry of Education to monitor, evaluate, and control country's institutions of higher education.

DOMINICAN REPUBLIC

4424 Deláncer, Víctor Hugo. Planeamiento, educación y política: enfoques para una sociología de la educación dominicana. Santo Domingo: Taller, 1983. 145 p.: bibl.

Interesting examination of relation-

ship among education, educational planning, and politics from a functionalist perspective. After reviewing functionalist theories of renowned sociologists of functionalist school (Durkheim, Mannheim, Parson), author analyzes educational development in Dominican Republic from this perspective.

4425 IDEI: 10 años de educación a distancia, 1972–1982. Santo Domingo: Depto. Editorial del IDEI, 1982. 142 p.: ill., plates.

Dominican Republic's open university—Instituto Dominicano de Educación Integral (IDEI, Inc.)—was founded in April 1972 by members of Acción Pro-Educación y Cultura (APEC). Written to commemorate its 10th anniversary, book synthesizes school's philosophy, goals, objectives, organizational structure, results and experiences, as well as its vision of the future.

4426 Núñez Collado, Agripino. La UCMM: un nuevo estilo universitario en la República Dominicana. Santiago, Dominican Republic: Univ. Católica Madre y Maestra (UCMM), 1982. 2 v.: indexes (Col. Documentos; 29)

Two-vol. history of UCMM. Consists of compilation of articles and speeches reflecting university's origins, growth, and current status. Vol. 2 contains articles and speeches from 1977–82.

4427 Sánchez Hernández, Antonio. Problemática universitaria, 1977–1978. Santo Domingo: Editora de la Univ. Autónoma de Santo Domingo, 1980. 177 p.: ill., map (Publicaciones; 286. Col. Educación y sociedad; 14)

Compilation of newspaper reports focusing on variety of topics related to Univ. Autónoma de Santo Domingo (UASD). Articles reflect what author perceives as UASD's most significant issues during 1977–78 period.

ECUADOR

Macías, W. Problemas socioeconómicos del Ecuador. See item **3444.**

4428 Uzcátegui, Emilio. La educación ecuatoriana en el siglo del liberalismo. Quito: Editorial Voluntad, 1981. 346 p.: bibl. (Primer Premio Univ. Central; 1980)

One of country's foremost educators and renowned historians examines Ecuador's educational system since the late 19th-century Liberal Revolution. Comprehensive, well documented, up-to-date book (including thorough description of country's current educational system) earned author the prestigious Univ. Central Award for outstanding research for 1980.

4429 ――――. La educación en el Ecuador, 1830–1980 (*in* Arte y cultura, Ecuador, 1830–1980. Quito: Corporación Editora Nacional, 1980, p. 131–147)

Brief legislative history of education in Ecuador from 1830 (year in which it separated from Nueva Granada) to 1980 written by country's foremost educational historian. Good overview.

EL SALVADOR

4430 Escamilla, Manuel Luis. Reformas educativas: historia contemporánea de la educación formal en El Salvador. San Salvador: Ministerio de Educación, Dirección de Publicaciones, 1981. 287 p.: bibl., ill.

History of educational reform in El Salvador (1920–60). In addition to tracing history of country's educational system prior to first educational reform movement, analyzes major reforms of 1940, 1945, and 1968 in terms of history, policies, structure, goals, and level of success.

GUATEMALA

4431 Hoegen, Miguel von. Algunas características de los estudiantes de la Universidad Rafael Landívar en 1980, campus central (Cultura de Guatemala [Univ. Rafael Landívar, Guatemala] 1:3, nov./dic. 1980, p. 3–9, charts)

Demographic characteristics of students at private university of moderate size (5,000 students). Socioeconomic characteristics not unlike those of most universities throughout Latin America.

4432 ――――. La Universidad Rafael Landívar: un caso de demanda de estudios universitarios inelástica (Cultura de Guatemala [Univ. Rafael Landívar, Guatemala] 3:1, enero/abril 1982, p. 31–39, graphs, tables)

Examines elasticity of demand among different programs at Univ. Rafael Landívar. Concludes that, overall, demand for higher education, at least at this university, is inelastic (higher costs do not reduce demand porportionately); that least elastic programs are in economics, humanities, and agriculture; and that most elastic programs are in engineering, architecture, and law.

GUYANA

4433 Chandisingh, Ranji. Education in the revolution for socialist transformation and development. Georgetown: Guyana Printers, 1980. 36 p.

Address to 3rd Biennial Congress of the People's National Congress (Sophia, Aug. 1979) by Central Committee member of Guyana's Communist Party and Director of its Marxist education center (Cuffy Ideological Center). Lengthy discussion of achievements and goals related to education in Guyana. Assesses successes and failures in relation to Marxist ideology. Largely polemical and of limited utility.

HAITI

4434 Carrizo, Luis María and **Marcel Cauvin.** Population et scolarisation en Haïti: taux de scolarisation par département. Port-au-Prince: Département de l'éducation nationale, Direction de planification, Section des statistiques, 1981. 21 leaves: ill.

Education-related census data for 1970–80 period.

HONDURAS

4435 Almendarez, Juan. Lucha por la paz y la cultura. San José: Editorial Universitaria Centroamericana, 1982. 297 p.: bibl. (Col. Aula)

Collection of essays on higher education in Central America, with special emphasis on Honduras, by former rector of its National Autonomous Univ. Although specific focus varies, there is a common refrain throughout: the university *needs* to be the conscience of society.

4436 Chávez de Aguilar, María Alicia. Aplicación de un currículo flexible en un proyecto de Honduras. Santiago: UNESCO, OREALC, 1980. 26 p.: ill.

Qualitative case study of effects of a curricular innovation project on teachers, parents, and students in a marginal rural community in Honduras. Goals of project were to make education consistent with students' needs, interests, and problems; in short, to make education relevant to community. Study looked at effects of a curriculum restructured in light of students' needs, interests, and problems on students themselves, on teachers, and on parents. Effects are most positive on students and least positive on teachers; the reason, teachers fail to take a personal interest in the community and in most cases do not live in it.

JAMAICA

4437 Grant, D.R.B. Early childhood education: training teacher trainers and para-professional teachers. Kingston: Jamaica Publishing House: in cooperation with the Bernard van Leer Foundation, 1982. 173 p.: bibl., ill.

Describes Jamaica's Project for Early Childhood Education (PECE), a training program for pre-school, paraprofessional teachers which stresses clinical supervision and support and is based on a one-to-one relationship between teacher trainer and paraprofessional.

MEXICO

4438 Arizmendi Rodríguez, Roberto. Consideraciones sobre la planeación de la educación superior en México (Revista de la Educación Superior [ANUIES, México] 11[42]:2, abril/junio 1982, p. 5–43, bibl., tables)

Comprehensive description of planning process for higher education in Mexico. First describes history and development of higher education planning; then discusses contemporary planning process, focusing on National Plan for Higher Education (1981–91); and finally, unique considerations in planning at national, regional, state, and institutional levels.

4439 ———. Planeación y administración educativas. Toluca: Univ. Autónoma del Estado de México, 1982. 247 p.: bibl., ill. (Col. Ciencias y técnicas; 5)

Consists largely of author's previously published materials reflecting his extensive experiences in higher education administration and planning in Mexico. Topics: politics of educational planning, higher education administration, and planning at state and federal levels. Useful source for educational planners and policy-makers.

4440 Arredondo Alvarez, Víctor A. Maestrías en educación: sistema de créditos y modalidades de trabajo estudiantil (Revista de la Educación Superior [ANUIES, México] 11[42]:2, abril/junio 1982, p. 44–58)

Arguing for a need to coordinate programs among Mexico's universities and institutions of higher education, points out that a national system of "credit hours" would not be sufficient. Suggests, instead, measures which would result in a more unified system of higher education.

4441 Barojas, Jorge and Salvador Malo. Criterios de calidad y evaluación del posgrado: experiencia de un grupo de trabajo (Revista de la Educación Superior [ANUIES, México] 11[42]:2, abril/junio 1982, p. 59–72, ill.)

First presented at National Seminar on Postgraduate Studies in Mexico, article describes an approach to evaluating graduate-level programs in Mexico. Its evaluation design is not unique; rather, it integrates various approaches used in both summative and formative evaluations.

4442 Cámara, Gabriel. Impacto y relevancia de la educación básica: panorámica sobre el estado de la investigación. México: Centro de Estudios Educativos: Grupo de Estudios sobre el Financiamiento de la Educación, 1983. 100 p.

Documentary analysis of relevance and impact of basic education movement in Mexico. Describes genesis of movement and then looks at goals and objectives in light of country's manpower needs. Concludes basic education has failed to achieve its desired ends and attributes it to unrealistic breadth and diversity of its goals. Recommends steps to improve performance of basic education.

4443 Camp, Roderic A. The influence of European and North American ideas on students at Mexico's National Schools of Law and Economics (UCSB/NS, 8, 1982, p. 289–308)

Examines impact of university educational experiences—particularly experiences at UNAM's Schools of Law and Economics— on Mexican political leaders. These two schools were chosen because it is among their graduates that many of Mexico's most prominent political leaders have surfaced. Documents significance of educational socialization experiences on country's political leaders. Different experiences help to explain various policy emphasis from administration to administration.

4444 Carreras en el sistema de educación superior de México. México: ANUIES, 1981. 481 p. (Serie Consulta y documentación)

Complete directory includes very detailed information on each of nearly 2,000 academic and professional degree programs offered by Mexico's nearly 300 institutions of higher education. Very useful resource.

4445 Castrejón Díez, Jaime. El concepto de universidad. México: Ediciones Océano, 1982. 314 p.: bibl., ill.

General analysis of the meaning of the university, including history, relationship to society, curriculum, politics, organization and administration, and personnel (students, faculty, and staff). Focus is on concept of the university in its universal sense; particular attention is paid to the university in Mexico. Essential thesis reflects durability of the university, largely due to its very flexible nature, despite ever-changing nature of societies.

4446 Chávez, Ignacio. Ignacio Chávez, universitario nicolaíta: homenaje de la Facultad de Medicina Doctor Ignacio Chávez, Universidad Michoacana de San Nicolás de Hidalgo: sesquicentenario de su fundación, mayo 1980. Presentación, selección y notas de Enrique Arreguín Vélez. Morelia, México: Ediciones del Depto. de Difusión Cultural, Univ. Michoacana de San Nicolás de Hidalgo: Fondo Nacional para Actividades Sociales y Culturales de Michoacán, 1980. 174 p.: bibl. (Col. Testimonios culturales)

Homage to eminent cardiologist and professor of medicine; organizer, founder, and director of the National Institute of Cardiology; former rector of UNAM, to help commemorate 150th anniversary of the Facultad de Medicina Doctor Ignacio Chávez

of Univ. Michoacana de San Nicolás de Hidalgo. Personal recollections of a truly great human being, prepared by his closest friends and confidants, contribute significantly to his stature.

4447 Educación de adultos: nuevas dimensiones en el sector educativo. María Luisa de Anda, comp. México: Consejo Nacional Técnico de la Educación, 1983. 294 p.: bibl., ill.

Mexico's recently passed National Law on Adult Education, its newly created National Institute on Adult Education, and abundance of new didactic materials for adult learners are testimony to country's growing interest in and concern for adult education. Since 1980, the National Technical Council on Education (CNTE) has promoted and supported the study of adult education. Describes projects and evaluations sponsored by National Technical Council. Of particular interest is introduction which traces evolution of adult education in Mexico over last 40 yrs.

4448 Grousset, Bernardo A. and **Andrés Meissonnier.** La Salle en México. v. 1, Primera etapa: 1905–1921. v. 2, Segunda etapa: 1921–1947. México: Editora de Publicaciones de Enseñanza Objetiva, 1983. 2 v.: bibl., ill.

Two-vol. comprehensive history of "Lasallistas" in Mexico written to commemorate 300th anniversary of founding of the Instituto de los Hermanos de las Escuelas Cristianas in Rheims by S.J.B. de La Salle and order's 75th anniversary in Mexico. Lasallista history in Mexico reflects shifting distribution of power in country. Well illustrated and documented.

4449 Guerra, Georgina. El *comic* o la historieta en la enseñanza. México: Editorial Grijalbo, 1982. 82 p.: bibl., ill., plates (Col. pedagógica)

Suggests using selected mass media techniques, especially comics and *historietas*, to develop students' critical thinking skills.

4450 Guevara Niebla, Gilberto. Educación superior y desarrollismo en México (CP, 25, julio/sept. 1980, p. 54–70, table)

Examines post-Revolution developments in education, focusing on but not limited to higher education. Analysis reveals clear-cut linkage between education and disparate philosophies of country's different heads of state (e.g., under Lázaro Cárdenas, technical and popular education grew and prospered; under Manuel Avila Camacho, it suffered and declined). Reason: different philosophies regarding economic development. Cárdenas put his faith in education, Camacho in industry.

4451 Hermet, Gilles *et al.* Educación obrera y formación sindical en México. México: Secretaría del Trabajo y Previsión Social, Instituto Nacional de Estudios del Trabajo, 1980. 283 p.: bibl. (Cuadernos INET; 11)

Report on collaborative research effort initiated in 1975 between Mexico's Ministry of Labor and Social Welfare's National Institute of Labor Studies and Univ. of Paris's Social Science Institute of Labor. Results show that while workers' education in Mexico has progressed rapidly since 1962, only during last five yrs. has sufficient attention been paid to programs' quality and content. Also shows that educational opportunities among different subgroups of workers has been unequal (i.e., leaders, militants, those with most formal education, and those age 25–35 have been most likely to participate).

4452 Hernández, Natalio. Educación y realidad social indígena (UNAM/RMCPS, 103, enero/marzo 1981, p. 89–96)

Discussion of developments in bilingual education in Mexico. Regrettably, programs are still insufficient to meet national needs despite considerable strides during last 20 yrs.

4453 Hernández Luna, Juan. Ezequiel A. Chávez, impulsor de la educación mexicana. México: UNAM, Facultad de Filosofía y Letras, Colegio de Historia, 1981. 166 p.: bibl. (Col. Opúsculos. Serie Investigación)

Biography of well known late 19th- and early 20th-century Mexican educator Chávez. Perhaps best known as advisor and confidante to several of Mexico's Secretaries of Public Education (Joaquín Baranda, Justo Sierra, José Vasconcelos) his impact, while significant, has largely been behind the scenes.

4454 Hirsch, Esperanza. Maeva: una experiencia de evaluación institucional en la Facultad de Ingeniería de la UNAM (Revista de la Educación Superior [ANUIES, México] 11[42]:2, abril/junio 1982, p. 80–103, tables)

MAEVA (Modelo de Autoevaluación Administrativa) is an innovative model for self-assessment developed by UNAM's Engineering Faculty. Originally designed to evaluate its own faculty, this formative evaluation model could well be used by other institutions or programs for self-assessment. Model is based on organizational theory and on Management-by-Objectives to assess personnel performance.

4455 Historia de la educación de México en el siglo XX contada por sus protagonistas. Recogida en versión literaria por Víctor Hugo Bolaños. México: Editorial Educación, Ciencia y Cultura, 1982. 1 v.: ill. (Serie Educación dos mil)

Reflecting on educational developments during 20th century, seven of Mexico's most prominent educators describe their own professional experiences and their views. Very interesting contemporary history of country's educational system.

4456 Historia de la educación pública en México. Coordinadores, Fernando Solana, Raúl Cardiel Reyes y Raúl Bolaños. México: Fondo de Cultura Económica, 1982. 2 v. (642 p.): bibl. (SEP 80: 15)

Written to commemorate 60th anniversary of Mexico's Secretariat of Public Education, this two-vol. comprehensive history highlights education during the "Porfiriato" and during the Revolution; events surrounding creation of the Secretariat of Public Education in 1921; country's experiment with socialist education and its literacy campaigns; and education in contemporary Mexico.

4457 Información para la educación superior. 2a ed. México: SEP, Coordinación Nacional para la Planeación de la Educación Superior: ANUIES, 1982. 169 p.: bibl., ill., plates.

Complete proceedings of meeting sponsored by CONPES (Coordinación Nacional para la Educación Superior) on higher education planning (Guanajuato, 1980). Promulgated by country's Plan Nacional de Educación Superior and urgent necessity to coordinate information dissemination at national, regional, and state levels, conference was attended by representatives of Secretariat of Public Education (SEP), Asociación Nacional de Univs. e Institutos de Enseñanza Superior (ANUIES), and Sistema Nacional para la Planeación Permanente de la Educación Superior (SNPPES). Focus: "networking" as a means to information dissemination.

4458 Instituciones de educación superior: 1978–1979. México: ANUIES, 1979. 1 v. (Serie Consulta y documentación) Comprehensive directory of institutions of higher education in Mexico published by Asociación Nacional de Univs. e Institutos de Enseñanza Superior (ANUIES). Institutions are listed by state; unfortunately, information is minimal.

Levy, Daniel C. University and government in Mexico: autonomy in an authoritarian system. See *HLAS 46:2227.*

4459 Madrazo, Jorge. El sistema disciplinario de la Universidad Nacional Autónoma de México. México: UNAM, Instituto de Investigaciones Jurídicas, 1980. 192 p.: bibl. (Serie E. Varios; 7)

Concise judicial history of UNAM focuses essentially on legal bases for rights and responsibilities of its 297,000 students, 24,000 faculty, and 18,000 administrators.

4460 Marroquín, Emilio J. Algunas reflexiones sobre la matemática en el sistema de educación superior mexicano (Revista de la Educación Superior [ANUIES, México] 11[42]:2, abril/junio 1982, p. 73–79)

Brief description of different ways in which departments of mathematics are organized among Mexico's institutions of higher education.

4461 Mayer Celis, Leticia. Centros de poder en una facultad universitaria (CM/RE, 3:12, otoño 1982, p. 91–118, bibl., charts, ill.)

In examining locus of power and control within one UNAM faculty (Facultad de Medicina Veterinaria y Zootécnica), concludes it is informal groups and networks rather than more formal committees and departments which are most important in determining direction and policy.

4462 Muñoz Izquierdo, Carlos. Presente y futuro de la educación secundaria. México: Centro de Estudios Educativos: Grupo de Estudios sobre el Financiamiento de la Educación, 1983. 293 p.: bibl., ill.

In this comprehensive and important study of secondary education in Mexico, author shows that secondary educational opportunities are unequally distributed among socioeconomic classes; that teaching-learning process in secondary education is largely ineffectual; and that marketplace has yet to respond to increase in secondary school graduates. Proffers recommendations to diversify and modernize education at secondary level and to develop necessary infrastructure to plan effectively for educational change.

Nahmad Sittón, Salomón. La educación bilingüe y bicultural para las regiones interculturales de México. See item **1558.**

4463 Pasquel, Leonardo. Educadores veracruzanos. México: Editorial Citlaltépetl, 1983. 423 p.: ill., index (Col. Suma veracruzana. Serie Biografía)

Brief biographies of virtually all Veracruzanos who have made their mark on education in that Mexican state and beyond.

4464 Perissinotto, Giorgio. Educational reform in Mexico (CUH, 82:488, Dec. 1983, p. 425–428, 437, table)

Argues that Mexico's educational system is in a state of crisis and that despite rhetoric to the contrary, improvements are virtually nonexistent. Allowing that President Miguel de la Madrid recognizes grave problems confronting education in his country, its unfortunate economic situation precludes him from doing much about it.

4465 Plan Nacional de Educación Superior: lineamientos generales para el período 1981–1991. México: ANUIES: SEP, Coordinación Nacional para la Planeación de la Educación Superior, 1981. 240 p.

Mexico's 10-yr. Plan for Higher Education (1981–91). Approved in principle in Nov. 1978 by representatives from Mexico's Secretariat of Public Educacion and country's major institutions of higher education, this document, prepared by the national coordinating body for higher education (CONPES), constitutes the working plan. In four pts.: 1) summary of plan's principles approved at 1978 meeting; 2) analysis of Mexico's social, political, economic, and demographic characteristics; 3) higher education during this 10-yr. period in light of these national realities; and 4) institutional changes necessary to meet goals of the 10-yr. plan.

4466 Reunión Nacional de Coordinadores Universitarios de la Investigación y del Posgrado, *1st, San Luis Potosí, México, 1979.* Memorias. México: Univ. Autónoma de San Luis Potosí (UASLP): SEP, 1981. 222 p.: ill., plates.

Complete proceedings of this meeting, sponsored by Univ. Autónoma de San Luis Potosí and Secretariat of Public Education. In addition to representatives from the latter, National Council on Science and Technology, and state, regional and national universities, Venezuela's Institute for Scientific Research and the OAS were represented as well. Proceedings consist mostly of reports on state of research and postgraduate studies from among universities represented.

4467 Rodríguez Sala de Gomezgil, María Luisa and Aurora Tovar. El científico como productor y comunicador, el caso de México: ciencias exactas y ciencias de lo humano. México: UNAM, 1982. 159 p.

Analyzes means used by sociologists in particular and social scientists in general to communicate research findings with one another, with other scientists, and with society at large. Compares their productivity with counterparts in the natural sciences.

4468 ——— and ———. El científico en México: la comunicación y difusión de la actividad científica en México. v. 1, Ciencias exactas. México: UNAM, Instituto de Investigaciones Sociales, 1980. 1 v.: bibl., ill. (Cuadernos de investigación social; 2)

Authors examine ways in which scientists (physicists, mathematicians, natural scientists) disseminate their research. Conclude that scientists' social networks and age influence their mode of dissemination more than any other factors, that books and journals constitute their primary means of disseminating findings; and that geographical location in the country has little bearing.

4469 Rojas Rodríguez, Pedro Mario. La Ciudad Universitaria a la época de su construcción. México: UNAM, Centro de Estudios sobre la Universidad, 1979. 112 p.: ill., plates.

First describes UNAM's history from 1553 beginnings as Real y Pontificia Univ. de México to its transition to Univ. Nacional in 1910, and designation as "autonomous" in 1929. Focuses essentially on UNAM's recent past, i.e., the "Ciudad Universitaria," a project which did not begin until 1950s. Interest-

ing account of the development and its magnificent campus.

Ros Romero, María del Consuelo. Bilingüismo y educación: un estudio en Michoacán. See item **1569.**

4470 Sánchez García, Alfonso. Primer centenario del normalismo en el Estado de México: avance histórico. México: Biblioteca Enciclopédica del Estado de México: Secretaría de Educación, Cultura y Bienestar Social, Gobierno del Estado de México, 1982. 220 p.: bibl., ill. (Biblioteca enciclopédica del Estado de México; 114)

History of Mexico's normal school movement written in commemoration of its first 100 yrs. Thorough, well documented, and beautifully illustrated.

4471 Silos, Manuel. Los rendimientos de la escolaridad en el área metropolitana de Monterrey: un análisis de su comportamiento a través del tiempo. Monterrey, México: Facultad de Economía, Centro de Investigaciones Económicas, 1980. 21 leaves: bibl.

In analyzing effect of education on income (rate of return) in Monterrey, finds economic rate of return on the margin to be higher at upper income levels than at lower income levels. In comparing these results with those from similar studies in US, a consistent pattern emerges; during times of high employment, marginal rate of return on education is highest among upper income groups.

4472 *Solidaridad* y el sindicalismo universitario: 1972–1980. Recopilación, presentación e índices, José Woldenberg. México: Foro Universitario, STUNAM, 1982. 414 p.: index (Col. Documentos sobre la historia del sindicalismo universitario; 1)

Consists of reprints of every article related in any way to unions and syndicates in higher education which appeared in *Solidaridad* (1972–80), the official organ of the Mexican labor organization, Movimiento Sindical Revolucionario.

4473 Sucesión rectoral y crisis en la izquierda: la Universidad Autónoma de Puebla en 1981. t. 1, Enero, febrero, marzo. Prólogo, Daniel Cazes. Puebla, México: Editorial Univ. Autónoma de Puebla, 1983. 1 v. (Col. Universidad y sociedad; 2)

Case study containing many original documents of a turbulent year (1981) in the life of Univ. Autónoma de Puebla, a year during which elections were held for a new rector and a strike was called in relation to that election. Important contribution to contemporary history of higher education in Mexico.

4474 La Universidad amenazada. Selección y prólogo de Liberato Terán y Jorge Medina Viedas. Culiacán, México: Univ. Autónoma de Sinaloa, 1982. 2 v.: ill.

Two-vol. documentary analysis of events preceding the State takeover of Univ. Autónoma de Sinaloa (UAS) in Dec. 1980, of the year during which it was controlled by the State, and events leading up to its liberation a year later. Vol. 1 contains documents of students, parents, faculty, staff, Univ. Council, and other interested parties in the dispute; vol. 2 contains official pronouncements of the Univ.'s Rector and its Secretary General.

4475 Vaughan, Mary K. The State, education, and social class in Mexico, 1880–1928. DeKalb: Northern Illinois Univ. Press, 1982. 316 p.: bibl., index (The Origins of modern Mexico)

Analysis of educational policy formulation in Mexico during the Porfirian and Revolutionary periods (1880–1928). Looks specifically at relationship among a growing Mexican State, a dependent form of capitalism, and development of education. A revisionist interpretation of period that warrants serious scrutiny. Important book.

4476 Vázquez, Josefina Zoraida et al. Ensayos sobre historia de la educación en México. México: El Colegio de México, 1981. 234 p.: bibl., index.

Four historical essays about different epochs. Vázquez's essay analyzes influence of 16th-century Spanish thought on education in Nueva España; Tanck de Estrada looks at impact of 17th-century Bourbon reforms on education; Staples assesses education in post-Independence Mexico; and Arce Gurza examines effect of the Revolution on Mexican education.

NICARAGUA

4477 La Educación en tres años de revolución. Managua: Ministerio de Educación, 1982. 124 p.: ill., plates.

Concise summary of educational developments in Nicaragua since the Sandinista Revolution (July 1979). Prepared by country's Ministry of Education, this uncritical assessment of accomplishments is informative, useful and impressive. Still lacking among the literature on Nicaraguan education under the Sandinistas, however, is an unbiased and objective analysis of educational developments since the 1979 revolution.

4478 Gander, Catherine. Nicaragua: "Poor man's" adult education (NACLA, 17:5, Sept./Oct. 1983, p. 42–46, ill.)

Somewhat disjointed and uncritical description of Nicaragua's Literacy Campaign. Author, who worked in Nicaragua during campaign's two and a half yrs., most recently in the Vice-Ministry of Adult Education, stresses efforts of Popular Education Collectives (CEPs). Unfortunately, her treatment of campaign is similar to so many others, an entirely uncritical albeit interesting and informative view of adult education.

4479 Miller, Valerie Lee. Between struggle and hope: the Nicaraguan Literacy Crusade. Foreword by Carmen St. John Hunter. Boulder, Colo.: Westview Press, 1985. 258 p.: bibl., index (Westview special studies on Latin America and the Caribbean)

Examination of process of planning and implementing Nicaragua's National Literary Crusade. Describes struggles preceding the launching of campaign and evaluates its positive and negative results.

4480 Das Nicaragua der freien Menschen braucht unsere Hilfe: Projekt Indio Universität; Universidad Indígena, Nicaragua: Dokumentation. Tübingen, FRG: Der Förderkreis, 1982. 92 p.: ill.

Compilation of documents, newspaper articles and editorials, and personal letters which reflect current status of indigenous university in Nicaragua. An idea inspired by Nicaragua's Minister of Culture, Ernesto Cardenal, the indigenous university project has been supported (financially and personally) by the faculty of the Univ. of Tübingen (West Germany) who prepared this compilation.

4481 Nicaragua triunfa en la alfabetización: documentos y testimonios de la Cruzada Nacional de Alfabetización. Selección y coordinación, Hugo Assmann. Managua: Ministerio de Educación; San José: Depto. Ecuménico de Investigaciones, 1981. 672 p.: ill., plates.

Comprehensive description of Nicaragua's Literacy Campaign. Includes sections on campaign's goals and priorities, on preparation and implementation, and on outcomes and results. Largely composed of original documents (e.g., speeches, testimonies, reports). Excellent source.

PARAGUAY

4482 Cooney, Jerry W. Repression to reform: education in the Republic of Paraguay, 1811–1815 (History of Education Quarterly [New York] Winter 1983, p. 413–428)

In analyzing process of education in Paraguay during first 40 yrs. of independence, this historical study reveals importance of country's leaders to educational policy. Fernando de la Mora, an Enlightenment figure and prime mover of the Junta 1811–13, in his reforms of 1812 envisioned an enlightened citizenry and Paraguay's emergence as an important country. José Gaspar Rodríguez, country's first great dictator, considered higher education dangers if controlled by an elite. Carlos Antonio López, Paraguay's second great dictator, perceived revitalization of education as essential to country's modernization.

4483 Corvalán, Grazziella. Determinantes del primer empleo de los egresados de la educación técnica industrial. Asunción: Centro Paraguayo de Estudios Sociológicos, 1981. 67 p.: bibl., ill. (Col. REDUC-PAR; 2)

After examining occupational data on Paraguay's technical school graduates, argues that parents' socioeconomic status is primary determinant of graduates' place and level of initial employment. Secondary determinant: number of years of their formal schooling.

4484 Marecki, Sofía. Bibliografía sobre la educación en el Paraguay: período 1970/1981. Asunción: Centro Paraguayo de Estudios Sociológicos: Centro Paraguayo de Documentación Social, Red Latinoamericana de Información y Documentación en Educación, 1982. 98 p.: ill., index.

Annotated bibliography of education in Paraguay includes research published 1970–81. The 355 entries are in alphabetical order by author. Index references entries three ways: by author, institution, and theme. Very useful source.

Peters, Heinz. Das Paraguayische Erziehungswesen von 1811 bis 1865: Schule und Staat in einem Modell autozentrierter Entwicklung. See *HLAS 46:3397.*

4485 Rivarola, Domingo M. Educación y desarrollo en el Paraguay: la enseñanza básica (CPES/RPS, 14:39/40, mayo/dic. 1977, p. 245–350, tables)

Study analyzes relationship between socioeconomic development and education. In light of country's limited rate of economic expansion combined with its relatively high rate of educational development, especially at primary level, author warns of possible consequences from this imbalance; among them, increased emigration and instability.

4486 ———. Estado y educación superior: su evolución histórica (CPES/RPS, 16:46, sept./dic. 1979, p. 117–149)

Tracing development of Paraguay's two principal universities (la Católica y la Nacional) and focusing on problems common to both, concludes that reforms, in order to be effective, must come from within the institutions themselves.

4487 Situación lingüística y educación: estadísticas (CPES/RPS, 17:47, enero/abril 1980, p. 131–146, bibl., tables)

Data on language use (Spanish, Guaraní, other) by geographical location, sex, age, and (for school-age children) language of instruction.

PERU

4488 Barrantes, Emilio. La reforma educativa peruana: una nota polémica (SP, 14, junio 1981, p. 69–75)

Admirable defense of Peruvian Educational Reform Law of 1972, written in response to critical assessment previously published in same journal (Luis Piscoya's "La Reforma Peruana: ¿Teoría Inédita?" Author points out that the reform's most ardent advocates come from other countries; its most vocal critics, Peruvians themselves.

4489 Bernales B., Enrique. El desarrollo de las ciencias sociales en el Perú. Lima: Centro de Investigación de la Univ. del Pacífico, 1981. 126 p.: bibl.

Social sciences experienced unparalleled growth in Peru during 1970s. Bernales's study examines this proliferation, discusses its implications—both positive and negative—and sets goals to guide social science development in the future.

4490 Cruz, Antonio and Neptalí Carpio. Movimiento universitario en el Perú: 1909–1980. Lima?: Alma Matinal, 1981. 125 p.: bibl., ill., plates (Publicaciones de investigación universitaria)

Marxist interpretation of 20th-century history of higher education in Peru. According to authors, models of higher education imported from France and US and imposed on country by its ruling elite, have failed miserably. They allege the French model, based on a humanistic tradition and focused on training in law, philosophy, and theology, has failed because it is not oriented to change and transformation; the US model, based on narrow technological training for a capitalist state, has failed because it does not address educational needs of the people. Analysis is largely ideological and simplistic.

4491 Delgado, Kenneth. ¿Subsiste la reforma educativa? (SP, 7, junio 1979, p. 59–73, charts)

Provocative analysis of Peru's educational reform (la Ley General de Educación, 1972). After briefly describing organizational changes mandated by the law, concludes country's economic and political crises precluded significant growth and development.

4492 Fernández, Hernán. Empleo y educación en el Perú: notas para un debate (CPES/RPS, 18:51, junio/sept. 1981, p. 97–128, tables)

Detailed examination of relationship between education and employment. While concluding that educational level of country's economically active population has improved, especially among the young in urban areas, argues that it is country's economic crisis and not its educational system which is most responsible. In fact, author concludes that the perilous state of country's economy rendered the goals of its 1972 Educational Reform totally unrealistic; he draws this conclusion at the same time that he documents considerable growth in educational system at all levels.

4493 La Investigación educacional en el Perú: 1972–1980, estudio evaluativo. Lima: Ministerio de Educación, Instituto Nacional de Investigación y Desarrollo de la Educación (INIDE), Dirección de Investigaciones Educacionales, Proyecto Evaluación de la Reforma Educativa, 1981. 123 p.: bibl., ill.

Report to Peru's Ministry of Education prepared by an independent commission assessing a major goal set forth in Educational Reform Law of 1972: strengthening all aspects of educational research in the country. Systematically analyzes research focus, capability, and productivity of country's principal research organizations (Instituto Nacional de Planificación, Consejo Nacional de Investigación, Oficina Sectorial de Planificación Educativa) as well as by smaller and privately supported research organizations.

4494 Sánchez Lihón, Danilo. Diagnóstico de la documentación e información educacional en el área regional del oriente peruano. Lima: Centro Nacional de Documentación e Información Educacional, 1980. 96 p.: ill.

Comprehensive assessment of educational needs in eastern Peru, including Iquitos, Tarapoto, Contamana, and Pucallpa.

4495 Valcárcel, Carlos Daniel. Historia de la Universidad de San Marcos, 1551–1980. Caracas: Academia Nacional de la Historia, 1981. 159 p.: bibl., ill., plates (El Libro menor; 16)

Having operated without interruption since 1553, Univ. Nacional Mayor de San Marcos is the oldest in America. This brief but thorough history documents the proud heritage of this renowned center of learning. During its 40-plus years, it has had five separate locations in Lima. During its colonial history, it operated with five faculties (philosophy, theology, civil law, ecclesiastical law, and medicine); today it is a comprehensive university having added several new faculties (education, pharmacology, chemistry, dentistry, among others). Well documented, well illustrated, good bibliography.

PUERTO RICO

4496 Cao García, Ramón. Educación privada y desigualdad: un análisis económico (UPR/RCS, 23:1/2, marzo/junio 1981, p. 53–69, bibl., tables)

Explores motives behind Puerto Rican families' preference for private schools over public schools. Perceptions of higher quality, greater curricular choice, and increased employment opportunities are most often-cited reasons for selecting private over public schools. In this data-based study, author concludes that a vicious cycle exists—the wealthy choose private schools, an action which in turn contributes to greater economic inequality in Puerto Rico.

4497 Colón Rosado, Aníbal. Crisis de identidad de la educación católica en Puerto Rico. Santurce, P.R.: Cultural Puertorriqueña, 1981. 357 p.: bibl., ill.

Fascinating history of Catholic education from its earliest and prestigious beginning in 16th century to its somewhat ambiguous role in the Commonwealth today. Catholic education was prevalent until Oct. 18, 1898, the year in which sovereignty passed to US. Since then, author argues, Catholic educators have had to fight a long and arduous battle against formidable adversaries just to survive. Although still suffering from an identity crisis and still facing stiff opposition, the survival of Catholic education in Puerto Rico is no longer questioned.

4498 Virella, Federico E. Glosas universitarias. San Juan, P.R.: Biblioteca de Autores Puertorriqueños, 1982. 136 p.

Brief radio editorials focusing on the Puerto Rican university and aired on WVJP, Radio Caguas (June 1971-Sept. 1976). Themes vary considerably; examples include editorials on teaching quality, university finance, scholarships, function of the university in Puerto Rican society, campus violence, etc.

URUGUAY

4499 Arteaga, Juan José. Universidad y modelos universitarios (Estudios de Ciencias y Letras [Instituto de Filosofía, Montevideo] 6, 1983, p. 28–36)

Citing different and diverse national systems of higher education around the world, implores Uruguayans to accept a new Catholic university (Univ. Católica Dámaso Antonio Larrañaga) which differs significantly in many respects from the Univ. Mayor de la República.

4500 Barbé Pérez, Héctor. La función subsidiaria del Estado y la subvención a los institutos de enseñanza y subsidio escolar

a los alumnos (Estudios de Ciencias y Letras [Instituto de Filosofía, Montevideo] 7, 1984, p. 71–74)

Urges Uruguayan government to develop a new national plan for education which would recognize legitimacy of private as well as public education.

4501 Castellanos, Alfredo R. Proceso histórico de la neutralidad y el laicismo escolar en nuestro país (Estudio de Ciencias y Letras [Instituto de Filosofía, Montevideo] 7, 1984, p. 59–69)

Arguing that country's historical development falls into three disparate epochs—religious until 1877, secular until 1909, "irreligious" to present—author bemoans dearth of religious values and mores in contemporary education.

4502 Castillo, Luis del. Proyecto de estructura académica para una universidad diferente (Estudios de Ciencias y Letras [Instituto de Filosofía, Montevideo] 6, 1983, p. 16–21)

Yet another defense of proposed new Catholic university in Uruguay, La Univ. Católica Dámaso Antonio Larrañaga. This time focus is on differences between this proposed university and Univ. of the Republic. Since proposed new university will have different—yet essential—goals, concludes that the two institutions of higher education will be complementary.

Echenique, Carlos A. Las ideas pedagógicas del Dr. Fracisco A. Berra y su aporte al americanismo filosófico. See *HLAS 46:7667*.

4503 Etchegaray, Roger. La universidad católica en 1981–1982: una encrucijada para las hombres en busca de sentido (Estudios de Ciencias y Letras [Instituto de Filosofía, Montevideo] 7, 1984, p. 75–82)

Arguing that true scientific questions are more spiritual than technical, defends Catholic universities' focus on spiritual questions which reflect the meaning of life.

4504 Gutiérrez Semprún, Manuel. Universidad Dámaso Antonio Larrañaga: una universidad privada católica moderna (Estudios de Ciencias y Letras [Instituto de Filosofía, Montevideo] 6, 1983, p. 7–15)

Describes those features which distinguish the Univ. Católica Dámaso Antonio Larrañaga (UNDAL) from Uruguay's other institutions of higher education. Formerly Institute of Philosophy, Sciences, and Letters of Montevideo, this truly Catholic university was inspired by the patron after whom it is named—the Apostolic Delegate and head of country's Catholic Church during early part of 19th century.

4505 Rivero Iturralde, Gregorio. Iglesia y universidad en el Uruguay (Estudios de Ciencias y Letras [Instituto de Filosofía, Montevideo] 6, 1983, p. 37–42)

Although Monseñor Dámaso Antonio Larrañaga, Apostolic Delegate and head of the Catholic Church in Uruguay, provided inspiration behind country's national university (Univ. Mayor de la República, founded 1833), higher education in that country has been and remains largely secular. Describes genesis of Catholic Univ. Dámaso Antonio Larrañaga, formerly the Institute of Philosophy, Sciences and Letters of Montevideo, country's first truly Catholic university.

4506 ———. La universidad católica: una urgencia en la Iglesia desde el Vaticano II hasta nuestros días (Estudios de Ciencias y Letras [Instituto de Filosofía, Montevideo] 6, 1983, p. 22–27)

Citing Vatican II and Pope John Paul II's support for teaching of Christianity and Christian values in higher education in general and support of Catholic universities in particular, makes case for official recognition of Uruguay's new Catholic university—la Univ. Católica Dámaso Antonio Larrañaga.

4507 Solari, Aldo and Rolando Franco. Equality of opportunities and elitism in the Uruguayan university (NS, 6:11, 1981, p. 1–16)

Authors argue that despite public universities' open admissions policies, free tuition, flexible system of studies and examinations to meet needs of part-time working students, and a liberal system of grants, equal opportunities in higher education are still elusive. The reason, a rigid primary and secondary educational system which favors upper socioeconomic classes.

VENEZUELA

4508 Antonorsi Blanco, Marcel and Ignacio Avalos Gutiérrez. La planificación ilusoria: ensayo sobre la experiencia venezolana en política científica y tecnológica.

Caracas: Editorial Ateneo de Caracas, 1980. 204 p.: bibl.

Authors discuss failure of planning process in science and technology to achieve meaningful results and offer suggestions. Foremost among these: make planning process an integral part of political process; differentiate between science and technology and stress the latter (technology is oriented toward country's development; science is highly autonomous); imbue planners with power to implement their suggestions.

4509 Berbín, Lesbia Josefina. Consideraciones críticas sobre la lectura en los programas de educación primaria. Caracas: Ediciones de la Facultad de Humanidades y Educación, Univ. Central de Venezuela, 1982. 410 p.: ill.

In this published doctoral dissertation, author documents the abysmally low performance in all primary school subject areas—language arts, social studies, natural sciences, and mathematics—among elementary students in Ciudad Guayana. She then attempts to examine school-related causes behind their low performance. Description of problem is convincing, analysis is speculative, recommendations conjectural.

4510 Bracho Sierra, José Jesús. El problema de financiamiento de la educación universitaria en Venezuela. Caracas: Univ. Central de Venezuela, Facultad de Ciencias Económicas y Sociales, Div. de Publicaciones, 1980. 196 p.: bibl., ill. (Col. Libros)

Well-documented study depicting and explaining spiraling costs of education with specific focus on higher education. In view of the fact that current sources of income are insufficient to sustain projected growth of country's higher education, proposes intriguing and viable alternatives.

4511 Fernández Heres, Rafael. Educación en democracia: historia de la educación en Venezuela, 1958–1983. Caracas: Congreso de la República, 1983. 2 v.: bibl., ill.

Two-vol. history of education in Venezuela covering 25-yr. period (1958–83), during which country sustained uninterrupted democratic form of government. Most of material came from author's previously published book (see item **4512**), supplemented by recent material from 1981–82.

4512 ———. La instrucción de la generalidad: historia de la educación en Venezuela, 1830–1980. Caracas: Ediciones del Ministerio de Educación, 1981. 1 v.: bibl., ill., plates.

Vol. 2 of two-vol. history on Venezuelan education, covers 1936–80 period. Treatment is well documented; footnotes are voluminous.

4513 Peñalver, Luis Manuel. La universidad latinoamericana como factor de desarrollo científico-tecnológico (Revista da Universidade Católica de Petrópolis [Brazil] 25–28 fev. 1980, p. 106–116)

Comparing development of science and technology in Europe with Latin America, attributes Latin America's lack of development in these areas to failure of region's institutions of higher education to promote math and science. Describes what has been done in Venezuela to promote science and technology and recommends steps institutions of higher education could take to confront this problem.

4514 Regalado Linares, Inés. Contribución al estudio de la producción intelectual de los profesores egresados del Instituto Universitario Pedagógico de Caracas. Caracas: Univ. Central de Venezuela, Facultad de Humanidades y Educación, Escuela de Bibliotecología y Archivología, 1981. 2 v. (572 leaves): bibl., indexes.

Basically an unannotated bibliography in two vols. of published and unpublished research of the faculty of the Instituto Universitario Pedagógico de Caracas. Authors claim that it is necessary to know the level of productivity of Venezuelan scholars. The degree to which this "study" contributes to this end, however, is highly suspect.

4515 Seminario sobre Problemas de Investigación en Ciencias Sociales, 2nd, *Caracas, 1981.* Crítica de la investigación. Caracas: Ediciones Faces: Univ. Central de Venezuela (UCV), 1981. 284 p.: bibl.

Venezuelan social scientists examine current role of, as well as potential for, social science research in their country's development. Views are far-ranging, yet there is consensus on several points. To wit, public officials have not relied on research results in formulating development plans, relationship between public sector and universities has been strained, social science research lacks credibility largely because it has not been subjected to rigorous evaluation, and finally, quality of much of country's social science research is suspect.

4516 *Universidad Nuestra.* Asociación de Profesores de la Univ. Central de Venezuela (APUCV). 1982- . Caracas.

This issue contains 12 articles which reflect diverse perceptions regarding contemporary higher education and higher education in the future. Several articles focus on higher education in Venezuela; several others on higher education in general. Of particular interest is the contribution of Carlos Tünnermann Bernheim, Nicaragua's former Minister of Education, and one of Latin America's foremost authorities on higher education in the region. In his article, he analyzes significant issues in contemporary higher education in Latin America and reflects on innovative approaches to confront these issues.

4517 Valarino de Cemboraín, Elizabeth. Los subsistemas de bienestar a nivel superior en Venezuela: un modelo humanista para el asesoramiento a nivel universitario. Caracas: Univ. Central de Venezuela, Vicerrectorado Académico, 1980. 347 p: bibl., ill.

Originally a doctoral dissertation, book addresses a serious problem prevalent among Latin American universities—the dearth of student services. Documenting the deplorable state of student services and welfare at the Univ. Central de Venezuela, describes a methodology to develop, implement, and test efficacy of student welfare services from the perspective of the students.

BRAZIL

ROBERT E. VERHINE, *Faculdade de Educação, Universidade Federal da Bahia, Salvador, Brazil*
THOMAS J. LABELLE, *School of Education, University of Pittsburgh*

THE MATURITY OF DOCTORAL PROGRAMS, an increase in professional conferences and the existence of quality academic journals (i.e., *Revista Brasileira de Estudos Pedagógicos* and *Cadernos de Pesquisa*) in Brazil makes for a diverse, high volume, yet qualitatively uneven scholarly output on education. At the adult level, a major focus in the literature is consciousness raising and popular education. Fávero (item **4538**) brings together documents on such programs in the Northeast from the early 1960s. Wanderley (item **4587**) offers a detailed and favorable outlook at one such program, the Catholic radio-school (MEB), while Damasceno (item **4540**) finds the same program a means to propagate religious dogma. Freire's work in the Northeast is critically examined in Beiseigel (item **4525**) whereas Gerhardt (item **4556**) examines an early consciousness-raising experience in a small town and finds students treated unequally, a conclusion consistent with Damasceno's criticism of MEB. Bottom up popular education is the concern of Brandão (items **4527** and **4529**), and Bezerra and Garcia (item **4526**) with Brandão (item **4528**) describing four studies of rural life and learning, and Paiva (item **4572**) analyzing in-depth conversations with a peasant involved in civil rights and land reform movements. Paiva (item **4571**) is also concerned that an over emphasis on bottom up strategies may ultimately fragment the poor and facilitate their domination. Conversations with Freire are recorded in an edited volume by Vannuchi (item **4585**).

Turning to research on learning among school children, an insightful essay by Patto (item **4574**) indicates that there are marked differences in the results and interpretations of Piagetian inspired studies. Freitag (item **4551**) reveals that the school plays an important role in attenuating cognitive differences attributable to socioeconomic background whereas Carreher *et al.* (item **4535**) find that cognitive development is independent of class differences and attributable to schooling. Another study finds teacher quality the key determinant of primary level math achievement (item **4520**) and an exhaustive review of the literature by Brandão *et al.* (item **4530**) concludes that failure in school is a function of the school's inability to deal with poverty. Also relevant in this respect are Oliveira's research (item **4570**) documenting the class bias in intelligence testing and Farr's book (item **4545**) describing quality and procedural problems in public primary schools.

Associated with this emphasis on the contribution of in-school variables to achievement is the issue of teacher preparation and school reform at the primary level. In a call for alternative teacher education preparation models, Mello (item **4565**) offers an examination of how teachers contribute to social selection, and Novaes (item **4568**) offers an historical look at how, the author says, the profession has gone from teaching to child care. As to reform, Nunes's analysis (item **4569**) of the New School movement of the 1920s shows how well intentioned reformers fortified elite group hegemony. At the secondary level the effects of educational reform, specifically the Law of 1971 mandating an infusion of vocationalism, is a major concern. The *Anuário de Educação* (item **4521**) devotes most of an issue to evaluating the effects of this Law, and Bedran (item **4524**) reviews 187 studies on the subject. Both sources indicate that the Reform has done little to improve linkages between secondary education and the labor market. This position is supported by an empirical school/employment study by Vicentini (item **4586**) as well as a series of articles by Franco *et al* (item **4550**) who document the poor quality of secondary vocational programs in São Paulo. On a broader scale, Frigotto (item **4554**) builds on similar works (see e.g., *HLAS 45:4576*) by identifying both economically productive and non-productive schooling attributes. He also has published a recent study of SENAI (item **4553**) showing how this nationwide vocational apprenticeship program prepares workers in ways which serve monopoly capitalism. Other works in education/work relationships include anthologies edited by Gouveia (item **4557**), Levin *et al.* (item **4561**), and Souza and Silva (item **4542**).

Higher education receives the greatest attention from scholars. Among the contributions are two excellent historical studies: one by Cardoso (item **4534**) examining the establishment of the Univ. of São Paulo in the 1930s and the other by Cunha (item **4539**) who continues his earlier work (see *HLAS 45:4538*) by analyzing the politics of university expansion and modernization between 1945–64. The thinking that shaped university policies of the 1970s is revealed in the collected papers from 10 annual seminars sponsored by the Federal Council on Education (item **4582**). Papers from more recent conferences (items **4579** and **4537**) indicate that a decline in quality is associated with rapid higher education expansion. The issue of quality is also addressed by Whitaker (item **4588**) in his study of declining academic levels of university applicants. Works by Gatti (item **4555**) and the Univ. of Bahia (item **4560**) find that the nature and quality of research produced by graduate programs of education are inadequate. Finally, the university's lack of effective articulation with the labor market is dealt with in papers from a conference sponsored by the Instituto Euvaldo Lodi (item **4582a**) and in a study by Prandi (item **4577**).

Apart from research on levels of schooling is the literature on educational planning. Finger (item **4547**) outlines cultural and political constraints which explain why many Brazilian plans are never fully implemented, while Neves *et al.* (item **4567**) place educational planning in historical perspective, showing its role in the development of monopolistic capitalism in Brazil. Abib (item **4518**) examines planning and other administrative activities in Brazilian State Secretaries of Education, indicating that such processes are hampered by, among others, a tendency to consider only the technical side of what are essentially social phenomena. This same tendency, according to Mendonça (item **4566**), also applies to MOBRAL where sophisticated planning is said to have failed to produce satisfactory outcomes. Despite these weaknesses, planning remains an important function within Brazil's government bureaucracy, and some reports (e.g., item **4531**) are useful as indicators of national priorities.

The financing of education is another topic cutting across school levels. Brazil's educational expenditures as a percentage of GNP are shown by Melchoir (item **4564**) and Marques (item **4563**) to be lower than those of most other countries. They also review Brazil's complicated direct and indirect funding scheme, while Paro (item **4573**) offers a detailed analysis of direct schooling costs in the State of São Paulo. The issue of costs is also emphasized in recent evaluations of Brazilian experiments with educational technology. A book (item **4576**) discussing the organization and structure of Brazil's first educational TV project (implanted in Maranhão in 1969) notes that the program has been plagued by high costs and a lack of legitimacy. Santos's well written examination of the SACI project (item **4581**), an ambitious but never fully implemented satellite based teleducation program is more critical still, revealing how political forces combined with an unfounded faith in imported technology led to massive public expenditures.

Finally, in closing this essay, it is important to take note of several other examples of a growing diversity of educational studies that do not fit into the prior categories. These include a study of the role of rural cooperatives by Calazans *et al.* (item **4533**), an insightful analysis of programs developed by labor unions in São Paulo by Manfredi (item **4562**), a careful look at the role of preparatory courses for university entrance exams by Freitas (item **4552**), a detailed review of the origins and operations of primary night school efforts by Carvalho (item **4536**), and an evaluation of the effects of the professional certificate acquired via state administered vocational equivalency examinations by the Ministry of Education (item **4532**). Also of interest are quality studies dealing with the sexual education of adolescents (item **4523**), the production of culture for children (item **4578**), the educational situation of women (item **4580**), the content of history textbooks (item **4549**), and the status of special education (item **4544**).

We are grateful for the assistance rendered by Maria Thereza Reis Coutinho of the State Univ. of Bahia in the preparation of this section.

4518 Abib, Jorge José. As secretarias estaduais de educação e a administração dos sistemas de ensino. Brasília: Ministério da Educação e Cultura, Secretaria de Ensino de 1° e 2° Graus, 1980. 114 p.: bibl., ill.

Meticulous study of structure and operation of State Secretariats of Education in Brazil, based on analysis of legislation and official reports and documents. Identifies two principal problem areas: decision making (too slow) and human resources (inadequately trained and inappropriately utilized). Contends that various administrative reforms have had little effect because they consider only technical aspects of what is essentially a sociopolitical institution.

4519 Almeida, Luciano Mendes de; Paul-Eugène Charbonneau; and Edenio Valle. A educação na América Latina: continente em vias de desenvolvimento. São Paulo: ALMED Editora e Livraria, 1981. 381 p.: bibl. (Escola de Pais do Brasil; 3)

Anthology of 27 papers from continent-wide conference on education in Latin America, sponsored by what is apparently a Catholic religious group. Education is defined broadly and papers consider not only the school but also the family, community, Church, and mass media. Also includes pieces on education in specific countries, such as Bolivia, Uruguay, Chile, and Peru. Ambitious, informative effort although some articles are poor in quality, many have a religious bias, and Brazil per se is the focus of only three of the items.

4520 Análise de desempenho em matemática. Brasília: Depto. de Planejamento Educacional, Div. de Pesquisa, 1980. 169 p.: appendix, graphs, tables.

Study of determinants of math achievement in grades 1–8, based on a sample of 2500 students in Greater Brasília. Finds that achievement levels tail off markedly after the 4th grade and that chief determinants of score differentials are variables related to teacher quality. Competent work.

4521 Anuário de Educação. Edições Tempo Brasileiro [and] Edições Univ. Federal do Ceará. 1984- . Rio de Janeiro [and] Fortaleza.

Contains articles, research projects, and documents on current issues in Brazilian education. Includes five papers dealing with secondary level vocational education along with articles on the quality of educational research and on the financing of higher education. Some good background material.

4522 Barbosa, Ana Mae. Recorte e colagem: influências de John Dewey no ensino da arte no Brasil. São Paulo: Cortez Editora: Editora Autores Associados, 1982. 136 p.: ill. (Col. Educação contemporânea)

Historical study (originally Ph.D. dissertation) of influence of Dewey on Art education in Brazil. Although an admirer of Dewey, author believes that his thinking was incorrectly interpreted and applied in Brazil and thereby produced an Art education characterized by routinized busy work. Concludes that art teachers should seek to understand the local culture and the aesthetic proclivities of their students rather than rely on foreign instructional models.

4523 Barroso, Carmen and **Cristina Bruschini.** Educação sexual: debate aberto. Petrópolis: Vozes, 1982. 131 p.: bibl.

Report on sexual knowlege, values, and attitudes of adolescents from diverse social contexts, based on content analysis of debates with students from public and private secondary schools in São Paulo. Debates dealt with anatomy, birth control, and homosexuality. Outcomes suggest need for different sexual education strategies for different SES groups. Competent study of topical issue.

4524 Bedran, Maria Ignez Saad. Avaliação de estudos e pesquisas sobre a profissionalização do ensino de 2° grau no Brasil (INEP/RBEP, 65 : 149, jan./abril 1984, p. 22–37, tables)

Critical analysis of 187 studies on the vocationalization of secondary education in Brazil, as mandated by the Reform Law of 1971. Indicates that although much of literature is of dubious quality, it is nevertheless consistent in concluding that the Reform failed to link upper secondary schooling with labor market. Among the reasons most cited for this failure are: 1) impossibility of school/work integration in a capitalist society; and 2) the Law's incompatibility with prevailing social class interests. Useful overview, but does not contain bibliography of studies used.

4525 Beisiegel, Celso de Rui. Política e educação popular: a teoria e a prática de Paulo Freire no Brasil. São Paulo: Editora Atica, 1982. 304 p.: bibl. (Ensaios; 85)

Thorough, scholarly analysis of theory and practice of Paulo Freire's literacy work in early 1960s. Traces origins and evolution of Freire's thinking and discusses politics of implementing his ideas at local and national levels. Examines complex relationships between Freire's program, the Popular Culture Movement in Recife, Brazilian Ministry of Education, and Alliance for Progress and documents Freire's effect on other populist activity of the era. One of best works to date on the Freire phenomenon.

4526 Bezerra, Aída and **Pedro Benjamin Garcia.** Conversando com os agentes. Saber popular/educação popular. Petrópolis: Vozes; Rio de Janeiro: Nova, 1982. 62 p. (Cadernos de educação popular; 3)

Two articles on popular education, one which discusses backgrounds and methods of change agents in 1950s-60s movements and another which analyzes relationship between popular education and popular knowledge. Both works denounce elitist, authoritarian tendencies in programs for the masses and defend the need for the people themselves to define their educational projects.

4527 Brandão, Carlos Rodrigues. O ardil da ordem: caminhos e armadilhas da educação popular. Campinas: Papirus Livraria e Editora, 1983. 115 p.: bibl. (Col. Krisis)

Four essays by noted authority on popular education, dealing with: 1) dimensions of popular knowledge; 2) popular culture and the State; 3) participative methodologies for popular education; and 4) role of popular education within authoritarian society. Influential volume.

4528 ———. "Casa de escola:" cultura camponesa e educação rural. Campinas: Papirus, 1983. 248 p.: bibl., ill.

Contains four ethnographic studies of peasant culture and rural education in Brazil. Examines social reproduction of knowledge in rural society, considering both deliberate and non-deliberate educational processes. Suffers from lack of integrating concluding chapter but otherwise is high quality work by major Latin American anthropologist.

4529 ———. Educação popular. São Paulo: s.n., s.d. 86 p. (Primeiros voos; 22)

Reviews alternative interpretations of popular education and concludes that the concept should be used to refer to education which is generated by masses themselves, as part of their political activity, to produce their own unique body of knowledge. As such, popular education occurs independently of the professional educator, although latter may participate and assist in process. Provocative essay.

4530 Brandão, Zaia; Annamaria Bianchini Baeta; and **Any Dutra Coelho da Rocha.** Evasão e repetência no Brasil: a escola em questão. Rio de Janeiro: Achiamé, 1982. 104 p.: bibl., ill.

Analysis and critique of existing literature on causes of primary school failure. Reviews 80 studies (69 of Brazilian origins) and concludes that: 1) research to date is of insufficient quantity and quality; 2) findings for Brazil correspond to those reported for other countries; and 3) student failure derives primarily from manner that schools function in contexts of poverty. Informative and topical.

4531 Brazil. Congresso Nacional. Câmara dos Deputados. Comissão de Instrução Pública. Reforma de ensino primário e vários instituições complementares da instrução pública. Relator, Rui Barbosa. Rio de Janeiro: Fundação Casa de Rui Barbosa; Salvador: Fundação Cultura do Estado da Bahia, Conselho Estadual de Educação, 1981. 4 v.: bibl., ill., index (Obras completas de Rui Barbosa; 10)

Four-vol. publication of famous report on the reform of primary education in Brazil, mostly written by Rui Barbosa and presented to the Imperial Parliament in 1882. Calls for free and universal instruction and contains chapters on school finance and construction, educational organization and administration, learning contents and instructional methods, teacher preparation, etc. Well documented, with much statistical information on education in Brazil and in other countries at the time. Valuable historical reference.

4532 Brazil. Ministério da Educação e Cultura. Instituto Nacional de Estudos e Pesquisas Educacionais. Relações entre variáveis demográficas, econômicas e educacionais. Porto Alegre: Univ. Federal do Rio Grande do Sul, Faculdade de Educação, 1980. 104 p.: bibl., ill. (Série Estudos e pesquisas; 1)

Sophisticated quantitative analysis of census data pertaining to demographic, economic, and educational measures of development. Finds high correlation between the three variable groups, indicating that development is a global, uni-structured phenomenon. Concludes that social change efforts must involve integrated, multi-sector strategies and that education alone is likely to exert little impact.

4533 Calanzans, Maria Julieta Costa; Luis Felipe Meira de Castro; and Hélio R.S. Silva. Relevância da educação, do cooperativismo e da ação comunitária no meio rural brasileiro (INEP/RBEP, 64:147, maio/agôsto 1983, p. 9–26)

Describes a variety of educational programs related to rural community development and organization in Brazil. Gives particular attention to educational role of cooperatives, indicating—based on secondary data—educational level of cooperative members, nature of their participation in coopera-

tive affairs, and degree to which they benefit from cooperative services. Introductory overview.

4534 Cardoso, Irene de Arruda Ribeiro. A universidade da comunhão paulista: o projeto de criação da Universidad de São Paulo. São Paulo: Cortez Editora: Editora Autores Associados, 1982. 187 p.: bibl. (Col. Educação contemporânea. Série Memória da educação)

Historical study of the creation of Univ. of São Paulo, covering 1925–37 period. Reviews university's intellectual and political origins, revealing that, contrary to popular belief, the institution was founded by interests with authoritarian tendencies bent on forming modern elites and combatting communism. Good interpretive analysis helpful for comprehending Brazil's current system of higher education.

4535 Carreher, Terezinha N. and Analúcia D. Schiemann. Fracasso escolar: uma questão social (Cadernos de Pesquisa [Fundação Carlos Chagas, São Paulo] 45, maio 1983, p. 3–19, bibl., ill., tables)

Using Piagetian framework, compares low- and middle-class youth with regard to cognitive development and performance in mathematics. Finds that while school failure rates vary by social class, the same is not the case for levels of cognitive development and mathematical competence. Authors, therefore, reject cognitive deficit hypothesis as explanation for the poor's lack of school success. Important contribution to controversy over poverty/learning relationship.

4536 Carvalho, Celia Pezzolo de. Ensino noturno: realidade e ilusão. São Paulo: Cortez Editora: Editora Autores Associados, 1984. 112 p.: bibl. (Col. Polêmicas do nosso tempo; 12)

Reviews origins of primary-level night school in Brazil and reports results from study of night education in São Paulo. Describes school organization, teaching practices, curriculum content, and characteristics of teachers and students. Also records impressions of students concerning school and work. Argues that night school helps reproduce social structure by de-politicizing lower-class youth. Lacks polish, but is one of few works on important topic.

4537 Ciclo de Debates sobre Educação Brasileira Contemporânea, *Paraiba, Brazil, 1979.* Anais. Organizados por Alarico Correia Neto. João Pessoa: Univ. Federal da Paraiba, Editora Universitária, 1981. 333 p.: bibl.

Collection of papers, communications, and debates from conference sponsored by Univ. of Paraiba. Participants Darcy Ribeiro, Dermival Saviani, Newton Sucupira, and Luis Antônio Cunha address four themes: 1) contemporary education; 2) primary/secondary education; 3) higher education; and 4) popular education. Useful overview of current academic thinking, although work suffers from absence of introduction and conclusion.

4538 Cultura popular, educação popular: memória dos anos 60. Osmar Fávero, organizador. Rio de Janeiro: Graal, 1983. 283 p. (Biblioteca de educação; 3)

Compendium of historical documents (many never before published) produced during early 1960s by those involved in popular education movements of the time. These writings provided theoretical bases for a very creative era in Brazilian education, one in which notions of consciousness raising and liberation gained prominence. Important reference work.

4539 Cunha, Luiz Antônio Constant Rodrigues da. A universidade crítica: no ensino superior na república populista. Rio de Janeiro: F. Alves, 1983. 260 p. (Col. Educação em questão)

Historical study of Brazilian university during 1945–64 period. Analyzes politics of two processes—university expansion and university modernization—which marked the era. Sees university as "critical," both because it was in a state of crisis due to internal conflicts and because it was the center of an intensifying critique of the existing order. Provides basis for understanding post-1964 reforms and complements author's earlier work on the university before 1945 (see *HLAS 45:4538*).

4540 Damasceno, Maria Nobre. A prática educativa popular da Igreja e as dificuldades desta em lidar com a diferenciação econômica do campesinato (Educação & Sociedade [CEDES, São Paulo] 6:19, agôsto 1984, p. 112–134)

Highly critical evaluation of MEB

(Basic Education Movement), based on case study of peasant life in a Northeastern community. Analyzes nature of MEB and characteristics of peasant life and concludes that, rather than promoting revolution, MEB reinforces status quo by propagating an alienating religious dogma which views social change in micro terms and assumes that peasants are helpless. Derived from doctoral dissertation (UNICAMP).

Dimensão da força de trabalho de nível superior no Brasil. See item 3764.

4542 Educação: escola/trabalho. Edited by Paulo Nathanael P. de Souza and Eurides Brito da Silva. São Paulo: Pioneira, 1984. 274 p.: bibl., ill., tables (Biblioteca pioneira de ciências sociais)

Consists of nine papers written by leading Brazilian officials, including (in 1984) Minister of Education (Esther Ferraz), two Secretaries of Education (Eurides da Silva and Edivaldo Boanventura), Director of CENAFOR (Paulo de Souza), and head of Brazil's OAS office (Benno Sander). Authors deal with such topics as basic education, adult education, secondary schooling, educational administration, and popular education. Works offer insight into current policies and trends, but (contrary to what is implied by book's title) few deal directly with school/work relationships.

4543 Educação pré-escolar e antecipação da escolaridade: legislação básica. Compilação e organização, Leslie Maria José da Silva Rama e José Alvaro Pereira dos Santos. São Paulo: Secretaria de Estado da Educação, Coordenadoria de Estudos e Normas Pedagógicas, 1982. 341 p.: bibl.

Compilation of legislation relating to preschool education in Brazil. Includes federal-level documents as well as those specific to São Paulo state. Useful reference work.

4544 Encontro de Educação Especial, *1st, São Paulo, 1982.* Anais. São Paulo: Univ. de São Paulo, Faculdade de Educação, 1983. 256 p.: ill. (Série Estudos e documentos; 21)

Papers and round table discussions from 1982 conference on special education. Works relate to the teaching of those with mental and/or visual deficiencies. Valuable assessment of a field relatively neglected in Brazil.

4545 Farr, Regis. O fracasso do ensino. Rio de Janeiro: Editora Codecri, 1982. 118 p.: ill. (Col. Edições do Pasquim; 131)

Collection of newspaper articles vividly written by noted journalist who criticizes public first-level schooling in Rio de Janeiro. Contends that schools foster student passivity through routinized instruction administered by under qualified and poorly motivated teachers. Argues that authorities prefer quantity to quality, that the poor are discriminated against in the classroom, and that supplemental instruction for adults is merely a "dream factory." Author supports her case with both scholarly literature and her own interviews and observations.

4546 Feldmann, Marina Graziela. Estrutura do ensino de 1° grau: proposta e a realidade. Petrópolis: Vozes, 1983. 114 p.: bibl., ill.

Analysis of first-level schooling, as created by Reform Law of 1971, with emphasis on failure to effectively integrate what were formally the *primario* and *ginasio*. Sees problem related to historical division between mass and elite education and concludes that the Reform has not led to fundamental changes because the sociocultural dimensions of vertical integration have not been understood. Although there are many works critical of the Reform, this study's particular focus seems unique.

Fernandes, Antônia Régia Mendonça and Hilda de Sena Correa Wierderhecker. Catálogo coletivo dos periódicos brasileiros relacionados com educação. See *HLAS 46:49.*

4547 Finger, Almeri Paulo. Planejamento do ensino superior. Florianópolis: Editora da Univ. Federal de Santa Catarina (UFSC), 1983. 66 p.: bibl., ill. (Série didática)

Succinct overview of historical evolution and current status of academic and administrative structure of public higher education in Brazil, with particular emphasis on system-wide planning processes. Notes that due to cultural and political constraints, most plans have never been implemented. Useful as introduction to subject.

4548 Franco, Maria Aparecida Civatta.
Lidando pobremente com a pobreza: análisis de uma tendência no atendimento a crianças "carentes" de o a 6 anos de idade (Cadernos de Pesquisas [Fundação Carlos Chagas, São Paulo] 51, nov. 1984, p. 13–32, bibl., tables)

Examines alternative experience related to health care, feeding and education of lower class preschool children. Describes operations of six programs—in Brasília, Recife, and Fortaleza—and estimates economic costs involved. Shows advantages of integrating mothers and wider community in childcare process and argues that such programs should place greater emphasis on education.

4549 Franco, Maria Laura P. Barbosa. O livro didático de história no Brasil: a versão fabricada. São Paulo: Global, 1982. 105 p.: ill. (Teses; 9. Educação)

Content analysis of 15 Brazilian history textbooks, which concludes that most works offer elitist, paternalistic, and authoritarian view of social reality, resulting in a history which is abstract, partial, and alienating. Methodologically rigorous, although author's anti-establishment bias is evident.

4550 ——— and Maria Inês S. Durigan.
O aluno de cursos profissionalizantes o nivel de 2° grau: um retrato sem retoques (Cadernos de Pesquisa [Fundação Carlos Chaga, São Paulo] 48, fev. 1984, p. 47–56, bibl., tables)

Most recent of three articles reporting results from a study of secondary vocational schooling in São Paulo. Whereas earlier works (see *Cadernos de Pesquisa*, No. 47, and *Educação e Sociedade*, No. 14) revealed that vocational programs suffer from inadequate availability, inappropriate curriculum and poor quality, this last report paints a less pessimistic picture, indicating that students are generally satisfied with their vocational courses and that they intend to apply what they have learned in the labor market, rather than going on to college.

4551 Freitag, Barbara. Sociedade e consciência: um estudo piagetiano na favela e na escola. São Paulo: Cortez Editora: Editora Autores Associados, 1984. 239 p.: bibl., tables (Col. Educação contemporânea)

Well conceived study of development of cognitive structures among school children, based on Piaget's genetic psychology. Examines sample of 206 youths in São Paulo, ages 6–16, from three distinct social classes. Results indicate that: 1) performance differences attributable to SES disappear after eight yrs. of schooling; and 2) cognitive development promoted by the school is a function of informal social interaction rather than official curriculum. Author concludes that the school does not discriminate by social class, among those fortunate enough to enter and remain.

4552 Freitas, Renan Springer de. O oficial e o institucional: os "cursinhos" no sistema de ensino (INEP/RBEP, 65:151, set./ dez. 1984, p. 552–575, appendices, tables)

Study of important but little studied component of Brazilian education: the *cursinho* or preparatory course for university entrance exams. Application of statistical treatment to secondary data reveals prevalence of such courses and indicates that they do not improve the admission chances of students from academically weak schools. Concludes that the *cursinho* should be viewed as a level of the official educational system and that, like other levels, it reproduces social stratification.

4553 Frigotto, Gaudêncio. Fazendo pelas mãos a cabeça do trabalhador: o trabalho como elemento pedagógico na formação profissional (Cadernos de Pesquisa [Fundação Carlos Chagas, São Paulo] 47, nov. 1983, p. 38–45, ill.)

Critical, class-conflict based analysis of SENAI vocational training system. Examines SENAI's history and current instructional procedures and concludes that this nation-wide program serves dominant capitalist interests by preparing students to be submissive, malleable, and technically efficient workers. Argument not new, but some supporting material is.

4554 ———. A produtividade da escola improdutiva. São Paulo: Cortez Editores: Editora Autores Associados, 1984. 235 p.: bibl. (Col. Educação contemporânea)

Major addition to long line of Brazilian works which criticize the Theory of Human Capital. Author disagrees with both its proponents and detractors, contending that school/social structure relationships are more complex than either group recognizes. Argues that school has indirect rather than direct effect; it mediates social relations of production and, due to a host of internal and external contradictions, it has potential to serve either dominant or subordinate interests. Lucid analysis.

4555 Gatti, Bernadete A. Pós-graduação e pesquisa em educação no Brasil, 1978–1981 (Cadernos de Pesquisa [Fundação Carlos Chagas, São Paulo] 44, fev. 1983, p. 3–17, tables)

Detailed analysis of the status of graduate education programs in Brazil, with emphasis on 1978–81. Considers regional distribution of programs, nature of their faculties, and level and content of their scientific production. Notes that while expansion has been impressive, quality is uneven, inter-program communication limited, and incentives for research inadequate. Good overview.

4556 Gerhardt, Heinz Peter. Angicos, Rio Grande do Norte, 1962/63: a primeira experiência com o "Sistema Paulo Freire" (Educação & Sociedade [CEDES, São Paulo] 5:14, abril 1983, p. 5–34, bibl.)

Detailed description of first program to be based on Freire's method, developed in Rio Grande do Norte small town in early 1960s. Using documents produced then and interviews with those involved, reveals that while method advocates student-teacher equality, in practice the teachers become dominant. Useful contribution to Freire literature.

4557 Gouveia, Aparecida Joly. Democratização do ensino e oportunidades de emprego. São Paulo: Edições Loyola, 1981. 142 p.: bibl., ill. (Col. Educ-Ação; 4)

Collection of articles (many previously published) by noted Brazilian sociologist. Relying mainly on secondary data, makes inter-regional, inter-temporal, and inter-gender comparisons to indicate recent trends in schooling and employment. Suggests that educational expansion has been accompanied by a horizontal differentiation of courses which reinforces existing social disparities and limits meaningful mobility opportunities.

4558 Inter-American Community Education Workshop, 3rd, Belo Horizonte, Brazil, 1979. III [i.e. Terceira] Conferencia Interamericana de Educação Comunitária/Brasil = III Inter-American Community Education Workshop/Brazil. Equipe de redação, Regina Almeida et al. Equipe de tradução, Cleonice Carvalho Hermansen, Miriam Brandão e Carl E. Jensen. Washington: Partners of the Americas, 1980. 116 p.: ill. (some col.)

Papers and transcripts of international conference on community education, sponsored by Partners of the Americas. Defines theoretical/conceptual aspects of community education and presents eight case studies of Brazilian programs in operation. Although analyses and descriptions are generally superficial, presents useful starting point for anyone investigating the topic.

4559 Japiassu, Hilton. A pedagogia da incerteza e outros estudos. Rio de Janeiro: Imago Editora, 1983. 171 p. (Série Logoteca)

Six provocative essays by Brazilian philosopher-psychologist who is highly critical of the effects of modern science. Although some of papers, including those on Freud, Marx, and machismo, are only tangentially related to education, book's major theme concerns need for a pedagogy of uncertainty, free of dogmas and fixed dictates which hinder development of creative intelligence.

4560 Levantamento da pesquisa educacional no Nordeste. Salvador: Univ. Federal da Bahia, Centro de Estudios Interdisciplinares para o Setor Público, Mestrado em Educação, 1983. 172 p.: appendix, tables.

Study of the status of educational research in Northeastern Brazil, based on an eight-state survey of 31 research groups and 240 investigators. Indicates that scholarly output is of limited quantity and quality, tending to focus on micro rather than macro issues and favoring some topics (e.g., primary and university instruction) while neglecting others (e.g., secondary, preschool, and special education). Traces these problems to inadequacies in financing, infrastructure, and available time for research.

4561 Levin, Henry M. *et al.* Educação e desigualdade no Brasil. Petrópolis: Editora Vozes, 1984. 291 p.: appendices, bibl., ill., tables.

Collection of seven articles (five based on Stanford Ph.D. dissertations) which examine relationships between education and opportunities in Brazil, from an economic perspective. Includes studies of determinants of school achievement, effect of background on college entrance examination performance, participation of females in workforce, and contribution of schooling to income distribution. Quality scholarship.

4562 Manfredi, Silvia Maria. As entidades sindicais e a educação dos trabalhadores (Cadernos de Pesquisa [Fundação

Carlos Chagas, São Paulo] 47, nov. 1983, p. 65–78, ill., tables)

Historical study of educational programs developed by entities associated with urban labor unions in São Paulo (1960–78). Reveals that during 1960s labor union education was provided by government and offered to labor leaders for purposes of cooptation. After 1970, however, educational activities were increasingly promoted by unions themselves, as part of resistance to military regime. As unions have gained control over their educational efforts, instruction has become less school-like. Important work.

4563 Marques, Antônio Emílio. Despesas federais com educação, a loteria sem perdedores. Rio de Janeiro: Instituto de Planejamento Econômico e Social, Centro Nacional de Recursos Humanos (CNRH), 1984. 24 p.: bibl., ill. (Documento de trabalho; 10)

Indicates various sources of funds for public instruction in Brazil and estimates amounts allocated for education by federal government (1960–80). Reveals that federal government spends between four and 15 percent of its budget on education (depending on manner of calculation) and that, as a percentage of GNP, Brazil's educational expenditures are low compared to those of other nations.

4564 Melchior, José Carlos de Araújo. A política de vinculação de recursos públicos e o financiamento da educação no Brasil. São Paulo: Univ. de São Paulo, Faculdade de Educação, 1981. 118 p.: bibl., ill. (Estudos e documentos; 17)

Well documented analysis of the structure of public school financing in Brazil. Reviews historical bases for current arrangements. Argues for establishment of school tax to generate funds for education, but recognizes that this proposal runs counter to popular interpretation of notion of "free" education. Informative work, although some aspects are dated because derived from thesis written in 1972.

Meliá, Bartolomé. Educação indígena e alfabetização. See item **1304.**

4565 Mello, Guiomar Namo de. Magistério de 1° grau: da competência técnica ao compromisso político. São Paulo: Cortez Editora; Editora Autores Associados, 1982. 151 p.: bibl., tables (Col. Educação contemporânea)

Investigation of primary school teaching practices, focusing on teacher's role in promoting school failure among the poor. Using data from interviews with 564 São Paulo teachers, employs a deductive/inductive methodological approach which gives it both empirical and theoretical dimensions. Concludes that teachers are instrumental in social selection process and that their preparation—technical and political—is vital to student opportunity structures. Important, influential work.

4566 Mendonça, T. Nadia Jaime. MOBRAL: do discurso e realidade (INEP/RBEP, 65:151, set./dez. 1984, p. 576–593)

Evaluation of MOBRAL (The Brazilian Adult Literary Movement) based on classroom observation, achievement tests, and analysis of official documents and student textbooks. Indicates that despite technical sophistication, MOBRAL has not produced satisfactory outcomes and concludes that government would be better to invest its money in improving primary schooling for children.

4567 Neves, Lúcia Maria Wanderley; Maria das Gracas Corrêa Oliveira; Marileide de Carvalho Costa; and Edla de Araújo Lira Soares. Estado e planejamento educacional no Brasil: a formação do planejador (Cadernos de Pesquisa [Fundação Carlos Chagas, São Paulo] 51, nov. 1984, p. 55–63, bibl.)

Analyzes educational planning in Brazil from historical perspective, relating it to development of monopolistic capitalism in which, according to authors, it has been key to management of centralization/reproduction. Argues that with changing sociopolitical climate, task of preparing planners should be moved from governmental agencies to the university, where an emphasis can be placed on contextualization of education and use of planning for social transformation.

4568 Novaes, Maria Eliana. Professora primária: mestre ou tia? São Paulo: Cortez Editora: Editora Autores Associados, 1984. 143 p.: bibl., graphs, tables (Col. Educação contemporânea)

Study of primary school teaching profession, focusing on teacher's loss of prestige over past half century. Claims that teachers are victims of both a hierarchical division of labor inherent in capitalist bureaucratization and the fact that they are women, a sex whose inferior position within the family is replicated in the labor market. Reviews secondary data on teachers' pay, power and status, examines historical evolution of teacher training practices, and records opinions of a sample of teachers in Minas Gerais.

4569 Nunes, Clarice. A escola primária numa perspectiva histórica: 1922–1928 (INEP/RBEP, 65:151, set./dez. 1984, p. 538–551)

Historical study which evaluates practical applications of the New School movement, as manifested in Rio de Janeiro in 1920s. Examines changes in school enrollment age, teacher promotion structure, and primary school curriculum. Concludes that although many reformers during period felt they were serving popular interests, they were really contributing to strengthening dominant classes.

4570 Oliveira, Marta Kohl de. Inteligência e vida cotidiana: competência cognitivas de adultos de baixa renda (Cadernos de Pesquisa [Fundação Carlos Chagas, São Paulo] 44, fev. 1983, p. 45–54, tables)

Based on Stanford Ph.D. dissertation, reports on study of adults living in São Paulo squatter settlements. Compares their problem solving and reasoning processes with their performance on intelligence tests and in formal school situations. Finds that while test scores correlate with indicators of occupational and educational success, they do not adequately measure one's ability to handle everyday situations. Concludes that test scores must be interpreted in light of norms and needs of specific social groups.

4571 Paiva, Vanilda. Anotações para um estudo sobre populismo católico e educação no Brasil (INEP/RBEP, 65:151, set./dez. 1984, p. 595–622)

Analysis of relationship between populist pedagogical movement—as manifested on both university and grass roots levels—and Catholic thinking in Brazil during past two decades. Examines: 1) relationship between Brazilian Catholic thought and 19th-century Russian populism; 2) effect of populist tendencies on Brazilian intellectuals in early 1960s; and 3) radicalization of these tendencies in late 1970s. Work is followed by responses from three "populist radicals" who disagree with author's interpretations. Thought-provoking essay.

4572 ———. Pedagogia e luta social no campo paraibano (Educação & Sociedade [CEDES, São Paulo] 6:18, agôsto 1984, p. 5–56)

Analyzes two in-depth interviews with a single peasant who experienced first hand 20 yrs. of class-based social turmoil in the interior of Paraiba state. Author argues that within social conflict lies an educational process which must be understood before popular education efforts can succeed. Insightful, with interesting methodological approach.

4573 Paro, Vitor Henrique. O custo do ensino público no estado de São Paulo: estudo de custo/aluno na rede estadual de primeiro e segundo graus (Cadernos de Pesquisa [Fundação Carlos Chagas, São Paulo] 43, nov. 1982, p. 3–29, tables)

Estimates student/year direct costs, based on data from 66 elementary and secondary public schools in São Paulo state. Results are broken down by type and size of school, family income and deprivation level, region, and relative development of community. Competent analysis addressing a once popular but now neglected topic.

4574 Patto, Maria Helena Souza. A criança marginalizada para os piagetianos brasileiros: deficiente ou não? (Cadernos de Pesquisa [Fundação Carlos Chagas, São Paulo] 51, nov. 1984, p. 3–11, bibl.)

There are two major research groups in Brazil which are investigating lower-class school failure utililizing a Piagetian perspective. Interestingly, the two groups have produced conflicting interpretations, with one (São Paulo) suggesting that poor children lack cognitive development due to cultural deprivation and the other (Pernambuco) arguing that cognitive competence is independent of class origins and that source of school failure is school itself. This timely article provides an excellent summary and critique of this major academic debate.

4575 Pesquisa: influência da habilitação profissional obtida através dos exames de suplência profissionalizante na autovalorização do indivíduo. Brasília: Ministério da Educação e Cultura, Secretaria de Ensino de 1° e 2° Graus, 1980. 217 p.: ill. (some col.)

Evaluation of effects of professional certificate acquired via state administered vocational equivalency exams. Based on 2-yr. follow-up in Brasília, finds that exam graduates fair better than non-certificated and those with regular school diplomas on a number of occupational success indicators, including job fixidity, salary level, promotability, and self concept. Valuable because of paucity of works on this topic.

4576 Pontifícia Univ. Católica, *Rio de Janeiro.* **Depto. de Educação.** A proposta pedagógica da Fundação Maranhense de Televisão Educativa. Rio de Janeiro: Associação Brasileira de Tecnologia Educacional, 1981. 62 p.: bibl., ill. (Estudo e pesquisas; 19)

Concise review of origins, structure, and pedagogy of Brazil's first educational TV project (initiated in Maranhão state in 1969). Relying on pre-existing evaluations, concludes that the project has successfully expanded first-level instructional opportunities but suffers from high costs, lack of legitimacy, and poor articulation with traditional system. Booklet is pt. 1 of more extensive report on educational technology in Brazil, produced by Rio's Catholic Univ. (PUC-RJ).

4577 Prandi, J. Reginaldo. Os favoritos degradados: ensino superior e profissões de nível universitário no Brasil hoje. São Paulo: Edições Loyola, 1982. 135 p.: bibl. (Col. Educ-Ação; 6)

Analysis of relationship between higher education and labor market in Brazil, based on both secondary data and two surveys of university students in São Paulo. Argues that due to impact of international capitalism, both the quality of university life and conditions of college graduate in the workplace have declined in recent years. Notes that students are increasingly frustrated by their dwindling opportunities, although few understand the historical processes responsible for their predicament. Thoughtful (albeit somewhat rigid) Marxian interpretation.

4578 A Produção cultural para a criança. Organização Regina Zilberman. Edmir Perrotti et al. Porto Alegre: Mercado Aberto, 1982. 181 p.: bibl., ill., plates (Série Novas perspectivas; 3)

Contains eight articles on production of culture for children, focusing on the positive and negative aspects of theater, cinema, TV, comic books, literature, poetry, and plastic arts. While some essays treat topic in universal fashion, others (e.g., on theater, potery, and plastic arts) analyze cultural efforts which are uniquely Brazilian.

4579 A Propósito da qualidade do ensino superior no Brasil: anais de dois encontros. Brasília: Ministério da Educação e Cultura, Conselho Federal de Educação, 1982. 241 p.: bibl., ill.

Transcripts of two seminars on quality of higher education in Brazil, promoted by the Federal Council of Education. Includes formal presentations and accompanying debates, dealing with such issues as administrative organization, faculty selection and evaluation, stimulation of research and role of graduate studies. Participants generally agree that quality of Brazilian higher education is declining.

4580 Rosemberg, Fúlvia; Regina P. Pinto; and Esmeralda V. Negrão. A educação da mulher no Brasil. São Paulo: Global Editora, 1982. 112 p.: bibl. (Teses; 8)

In-depth study of educational situation of women in Brazil in 1970s, based on census and other secondary data. Discusses distribution of women by level and type of instruction, effect of adult literary programs on women, degree and nature of female participation in the labor market, and extent to which mothers in Brazil are served by preschool and childcare programs. Suggests that despite some progress, Brazilian women continue to suffer from sexist socialization and occupational segregation.

4581 Santos, Laymert Garcia dos. Desregulagens, educação, planejamento e tecnologia como ferramenta social. São Paulo: Brasiliense, 1981. 238 p.: bibl., ill.

Detailed, well written study of SACI Project, an ambitious satellite-based teleducation program which, despite heavy investment, was never fully implemented. Uses SACI experience to denounce imported mystique concerning infallibility of technical rationality-systematization. Provides useful historical account of evolution of educational technology in Brazil and offers insight into politics surrounding large-scale projects of this nature.

4582 Seminário de Assuntos Universitários: dez anos de reflexão e debate. Brasília: Ministério da Educação e Cultura, Conselho Federal de Educação, Depto. de Documentação e Divulgação, 1979. 507 p.: bibl., ill.

Papers from 10 seminars on higher education, promoted by Federal Council of Education (1966–77). Presentations are authored by Council members and thus depict evolution of official thinking on higher education during period of major change. They cover wide range of topics, including university reform and expansion, teacher preparation, graduate-level instruction, and system-wide financing. Valuable reference.

4582a Seminário Internacional sobre Educação e Trabalho, *Rio de Janeiro, 1981.* Educação e trabalho. Rio de Janeiro: Instituto Euvaldo Lodi, 1982. 416 p.: bibl., ill., tables (Col. Univ. & indústria. Monografias)

Collection of papers and debates from international conference on relationship between higher education and labor market. Includes contributions from most of Brazil's leading scholars and practitioners in field of education/work articulation. Presentations range from thought pieces to concrete case studies. Most are concerned with supply-demand disequilibrium for college graduates, resulting from government's policy of expanding university access to meet social demand. Good information source.

4583 El SENAI [i.e., Serviço Nacional de Aprendizagem Industrial] y la cooperación técnica internacional. Montevideo: CINTERFOR/OIT, 1982. 35 p.

Written to commemorate 40th anniversary of Brazil's national apprenticeship service, pamphlet describes SENAI's unique role in promoting similar efforts in other Latin American countries. [E. Egginton]

4584 III [i.e. Terceiro] PBDCT: III Basic Plan for Scientific and Technological Development: 1981/1985. Brasília: Secretaria de Planejamento, 1980? 76 p.

English version of government's plan for scientific and technological development (1980–85) which calls for, among other things, an increased emphasis on research devoted to primary and secondary school improvement. Useful reference, although few plans in Brazil are actually implemented as written.

4585 Vannucchi, Aldo. Paulo Freire ao vivo: gravação de conferências com debates realizadas na Faculdade de Filosofia, Ciências e Letras de Sorocaba, 1980–1981. São Paulo: Edições Loyola, 1983. 147 p.: bibl. (Col. Educação; 11)

Product of college workshop, contains two papers which summarize Freire's method and transcripts of four conferences in which the famous educator fielded audience questions. Very readable, with revealing glimpses into Freire's thinking at the time of his return to Brazil (1980) on such topics as revolution, Nicaragua, Marx, MOBRAL, Brazilian political parties, and current relevance of his approach.

4586 Vicentini, Maria Inês Fini Leite and Mucio Camargo de Assis. Terminalidade geral e continuidade de estudos de 2° grau: expectativas congruentes? (Cadernos de Pesquisa [Fundação Carlos Chagas, São Paulo] 45, maio 1983, p. 29–42, bibl., tables)

Study of secondary level terminality/continuity, using Getzel's model of school social system and based on over 3000 interviews with students, ex-students, teachers and employers. Reveals that: 1) students view secondary school as avenue to university; 2) teachers think that general education should be emphasized more than technical studies; and 3) employers do not value school as instrument for work preparation.

4587 Wanderley, Luiz Eduardo W. Educar para transformar: educação popular, Igreja Católica e política no Movimiento de Educação de Base. Petrópolis: Vozes, 1984. 524 p. (Publicaciones CID Sociologia religiosa; 7)

Ambitious study of MEB (Basic Education Movement), a Church-sponsored system of radio schools which in early 1960s sought to foster social change in Northeastern Brazil through adult literacy training and consciousness raising. Analyzes movement's origins, theory and practice, political relations with other groups and institutions, and impact on legal reality. Detailed and well documented, also includes lesson plans, classroom transcripts, a copy of the basic textbook, and results of evaluations conducted at the time. Important book.

4588 Whitaker, Dulce C.A. A seleção dos privilegiados: um estudo sobre a educação brasileira. São Paulo: Editora Semente, 1981. 132 p.: bibl. (Col. Revelações)

Seeks to determine, via an analysis of existing literature, why the quality of candidates for university admission has declined in recent years. Concludes that because of rapid industrialization and educational expansion in the country, many college aspirants today are products of traditional rural society and thus lack necessary "cultural capital." Includes useful documentation.

JOURNAL ABBREVIATIONS
EDUCATION

AI/I Interciencia. Asociación Interciencia. Caracas.

CEE/RL Revista Latinoamericana de Estudios Educativos. Centro de Estudios Educativos. México.

CES/CER Comparative Education Review. Comparative Education Society. New York.

CNC/A Actualidades. Consejo Nacional de la Cultura, Centro de Estudios Latinoamericanos Rómulo Gallegos. Caracas.

CP Cuadernos Políticos. Ediciones Era. México.

CPES/RPS Revista Paraguaya de Sociología. Centro Paraguayo de Estudios Sociológicos. Asunción.

CUH Current History. A monthly magazine of world affairs. Philadelphia.

ICEM/IM International Migration/Migrations Internationales/Migraciones Internacionales. Intergovernmental Committee for European Migration [and] the Research Group for European Migration Problems. Geneva.

INEP/RBEP Revista Brasileira de Estudos Pedagógicos. Instituto Nacional de Estudos Pedagógicos, Centro Brasileiro de Pesquisas Educacionais. Rio de Janeiro.

JDA Journal of Developing Areas. Western Illinois Univ. Press. Macomb.

LARR Latin American Research Review. Univ. of North Carolina Press *for the* Latin American Studies Association. Chapel Hill.

NACLA NACLA: Report on the Americas. North American Congress on Latin America. New York.

NS NS NorthSouth NordSud NorteSur NorteSul. Canadian Assn. of Latin American Studies. Univ. of Ottawa.

OAS/LE La Educación. OAS, Dept. of Educational Affairs. Washington.

SP Socialismo y Participación. Ediciones Socialismo y Participación. Lima.

UAG/D Docencia. Univ. Autónoma de Guadalajara. México.

UCSB/NS New Scholar. Univ. of California, Committee on Hispanic Civilization [and] Center for Chicano Studies. Santa Barbara.

UNAM/RMCPS Revista Mexicana de Ciencias Políticas y Sociales. Univ. Nacional Autónoma de México, Facultad de Ciencias Políticas y Sociales. México.

UNESCO/IRE International Review of Education. UN Educational, Scientific and Cultural Organization, Institute for Education. Hamburg, FRG.

UNLP/E Económica. Univ. Nacional de La Plata, Facultad de Ciencias Económicas, Instituto de Investigaciones Económicas. La Plata, Argentina.

UP/CSEC Cuban Studies/Estudios Cubanos. Univ. of Pittsburgh, Univ. Center for International Studies, Center for Latin American Studies. Pittsburgh, Pa.

UPN/RCE Revista Colombiana de Educación. Univ. Pedagógica Nacional, Centro de Investigaciones. Bogotá.

UPR/RCS Revista de Ciencias Sociales. Univ. de Puerto Rico, Colegio de Ciencias Sociales. Río Piedras.

URSS/AL América Latina. Academia de Ciencias de la URSS [Unión de Repúblicas Soviéticas Socialistas]. Moscú.

WD World Development. Pergamon Press. Oxford, UK.

GEOGRAPHY

GENERAL

CLINTON R. EDWARDS, *Professor of Geography, University of Wisconsin-Milwaukee*

FOOD SUPPLY, ENVIRONMENTAL deterioration, population increase, and socioeconomic problems associated with internal migration and development continue to loom large in the current geographical and related literature on Latin America. Over the past few years there has been a significant increase in the number of works on these subjects by Latin Americans. Not too many years ago, one heard from some Latin American academics and officials that, generally speaking, North American scientific investigators went to Latin America to do their research, and returned home and published the results in sources never seen by Latin American scholars. This has changed in two ways: foreign scholars are publishing more in Latin American journals, and Latin Americans themselves are participating increasingly in the research and publication on these themes. In addition, scholarly paraphernalia such as bibliographies, symposia, resource inventories, and other means of furthering research, provided by Latin American institutes and individuals, are becoming more numerous. New approaches and further development of theory concerning resource use and conservation are also appearing, for example through organizations like the Instituto de Geografía y Conservación de Recursos Naturales at the Univ. de los Andes in Venezuela (item **5001**).

Another development along these lines is the increasing interest in Spain concerning possibilities of Ibero-American cooperation in areas like economic development and forest conservation (items **5002** and **5015**).

The Conference of Latin Americanist Geographers (CLAG) continues its publication program with works on geographic education: *Guía para estudios postgraduados de geografía en los Estados Unidos de América* (1982); *New themes in instruction for Latin American geography* (1982); and further contributions to general research: *Contemporary Issues in Latin American Geography* (1983), the CLAG 1984 yearbook. CLAG also distributes a recent publication on development, *Geografía y desarrollo: métodos y casos de estudio* (1982).

5001 Andressen L., Rigoberto and **Ernesto Flores R.** Perspectivas de la investigación geográfica en el I.G.C.R.N. (ULA/RG, 20/21, 1979/1980, p. 29–45, bibl., table)

IGCRN is the Instituto de Geografía y Conservación de Recursos Naturales, founded in 1959, at Univ. de los Andes, Mérida, Venezuela. Describes theoretical, methodological, and practical approaches to study of resources and conservation in Latin America.

5002 Barrientos Fernández, Fernando. Plan de cooperación con Iberoamericana en el sector forestal y de conservación de la naturaleza (IEAS/R, 32:122, enero/marzo 1983, p. 57–76, table)

Outlines modes of cooperation between Spain and Latin American countries in areas of forest exploitation and conservation of forests and nature in general. Includes a plan for service by young graduates of technical programs and a series of colloquia and seminars. National programs of a number of countries are listed.

5003 Bassols Batalla, Angel. Relación entre subdesarrollo desequilibrio regional y contaminación del medio en México (URSS/AL, 8:56, agosto 1982, p. 75–83)

Emphasizes problems of regional imbalances and environmental deterioration in Mexico, but general principles and questions are relevant to other underdeveloped areas in Latin America.

5004 Casas Torres, José Manuel. Población, desarrollo y calidad de vida. v. 1, Curso de geografía de la población. Madrid: Rialp, 1982. 1 v.: bibl., ill., index, maps.

Text for a course on the geography of population, by the Director of the Institute of Applied Geography at the Univ. Complutense de Madrid. Not oriented to Latin America, but could be read with good effect by Latin American geographers to get a broader view of problems of population, development, and quality of life.

Caspar, Dale E. The urban development of Latin America: recent writings, 1977–1983. See item **25.**

5005 Congreso Latino-Americano de Zoología, *8th, Mérida, Venezuela, 1981.* Zoología neotropical: actas. Editor, Pedro J. Salinas. Mérida: Producciones Alfa, 1982. 2 v. (1531 p.): bibl., ill., index. Widely varied papers on virtually all aspects of zoological research in the Latin American tropics. Of special interest to geographers are sessions on ecology, economic zoology, zoogeography, and management and conservation of wild fauna.

5006 Contasti, Max. La capacidad epistémica como factor político y metodológico relevante en el proceso de planificación. Caracas: Sociedad Interamericana de Planificación: Sociedad Venezolana de Planificación, 1981. 75 p.: bibl.

Heretofore, planning, as a discipline, has not played an important role in social and other organization of human affairs. Brief sections on technology and development, and on myths and illusions, as well as scattered references to environmental planning are of interest to geographers.

5007 Conway, Dennis and Juanita Brown. Intraurban relocation and structure: low-income migrants in Latin America and the Caribbean (LARR, 15:3, 1980, p. 95–125, bibl., ill., maps, tables)

Investigates changing residential locations of rural-urban migrants from the time they arrive in the city until they find a "secure and stable dwelling environment." Identifies various zones occupied by migrants as they pass through various phases of "urbanization."

5008 Dourojeanni, Marc J. Recursos naturales y desarrollo en América Latina y el Caribe. Lima: Univ. de Lima, 1982. 437 p.: bibl., index.

Reviews population, economies, agricultural production, and food supply among Latin American and Caribbean countries. Uses of soil—for crops, livestock raising, forestry—depend on soil conservation, which has not characterized former use as demonstrated in a section on soil losses through erosion, desertification, salinization, and the like. Faunal resources and natural and man-made ecosystems are discussed by means of examples rather than an attempt at full coverage, as are various problems associated with mining and energy. Specific diseases are listed with brief comment on their relationships with environmental problems, and there is a short section on the situation and fate of native cultures.

5009 García, Antonio. Modelos operacionales de reforma agraria y desarrollo rural en América Latina. San José: Dirección de Información Pública y Comunicaciones, Instituto Interamericano de Cooperación para la Agricultura, 1982. 196 p.: bibl., ill. (Serie Investigación y desarrollo; 3)

Presents "operational models" based on agrarian structure, land reform, rural development, and modernization of agricultural technology. Scientific investigation of the mode of development, extension services and education for technological transfer, local financing, development of processing industries in agricultural regions, and support of international agencies are necessary for further development of Latin American food production.

5010 Hardoy, Jorge E. Urban cartography in Latin America during the colonial period (LARR, 19:3, 1983, p. 109–126, tables)

Points out that there is no history of Latin America's urban cartography, although much material, in the form of collections of city and regional plans, is available. Colonial material is especially rich in yielding insights into how various European powers proceeded with the establishment of urban centers, with interesting differences among them. Offers many suggestions as to sources and gives a preview of a projected atlas of about 250 city plans.

5011 Hughes, Carol and David Hughes.
Teeming life of a rain forest (NGS/ NGM, 163:1, Jan. 1983, p. 49–65, plates)

Brief and colorful glimpse at intricate ecology of rainforest environments of several of Costa Rica's wildlife sanctuaries.

5013 Lentnek, Barry. Regional development and urbanization in Latin America: the relationship of national policy to spatial strategies (in Internal migration systems in the developing world. Edited by Robert H. Thomas and John M. Hunter. Boston: G.K. Hall; Cambridge, Mass.: Schenkman, 1980, p. 82–113, table)

Examines growth of primate cities as the result of governmental policies concerning economic development. Problems in large cities stem from national policies and are thus difficult to deal with on local level.

5014 Maos, Jacob O. The spatial organization of new land settlement in Latin America. Boulder, Colo.: Westview Press, 1984. 179 p.: bibl., ill., maps, plans (Dellplain Latin American studies; 15)

Useful discussion of conceptual framework and spatial and social patterns of settlement in rural areas is followed by description of recent experiences in other parts of the world, with examples from Europe, Israel, Italy, and Spain. In the Latin American context, historical background, rural and urban population changes, and agrarian reform are illustrated by case studies from Venezuela, the Dominican Republic, Mexico, and Peru. Concludes with a "settlement model," elements including the family farm as basic unit.

5015 Maqueda, Angel María. Cooperación técnica con Iberoamerica para el desarrollo de la producción agropecuaria, áreas de colonización, regadíos y drenajes (IEAS/R, 32:122, enero/marzo 1983, p. 77–88)

Deals mainly with colonization, irrigation, and drainage as projects amenable to international cooperation in development of Latin American regions.

5016 Pan American Highway Congress, *13th, Caracas, 1979.* Final report. Washington: OAS, Executive Secretariat for Economic and Social Affairs, 1980. 116 p. (OEA/SerC./VI.l.13)

Reports and resolutions of the Congress, list of participants, and documents generated.

5017 Redistribución espacial de la población en América Latina. Editores, Joop Alberts y Miguel Villa. Santiago: Centro Latinoamericano de Demografía, 1980. 586 p.: bibl., ill., tables (Serie E; 28)

Readings by various authors on factors determining population distribution and role of population changes in planning for socioeconomic development. All articles, except one on internal migration in Brazil, deal with Latin America as a whole.

5018 Salas, Guillermo P. Estudio preliminar de los recursos minerales en Latino-América. México: Consejo de Recursos Minerales, 1980. 34 p.: bibl., col. maps (Publicación; 24-E)

Summary treatment with maps and tables of mineral sources based on standard reference works.

5019 Sánchez Marroquín, Alfredo. Potencialidad agroindustrial del amaranto. México: Centro de Estudios Económicos y Sociales del Tercer Mundo, 1980. 238 p.: bibl., ill., plates.

In addition to suggestions on modern potential of this ancient American grain, contains much interesting material on precolumbian importance and uses, wild and cultivated species, and cultivation methods.

5020 Schlenke, Ulrich and Reinhard Stewing. Endogener Tourismus als Gradmesser des industrialisierungsprozesses in Industrie-und Entwicklungsländern (UBGI/E, 37:2, Juni 1983, p. 137–145, bibl., tables)

Endogenous tourism is not suggested as an index to industrialization, but as a "model of the formation of industrial society, reflecting the character of its system." Not particularly relevant to Latin American countries, but represented in a table called "summary of national analysis" are Argentina, Mexico, Brazil, and Guatemala.

5021 Seminario Internacional sobre Producción Agropecuaria y Forestal en Zonas de Ladera de América Tropical, *Turrialba, Costa Rica, 1980.* Memoria. Editores, Andrés R. Novoa B. y Joshua L. Posner. Turrialba, Costa Rica: Centro Agronómico Tropical de Investigación y Enseñanza: Rockefeller Foundation, 1981. 357 p.: bibl., ill., maps, tables (Serie técnica. Informe técnico; 11)

Hilly and mountainous areas are often not differentiated from lowlands or plains in discussions of rural development strategies in Latin America. This seminar does so using historical analysis, ecology, and current land use studies in assessing current status and potential of these regions in agricultural production and other aspects of rural development.

5022 Simposio de Parques Nacionales y Reservas Biológicas, *1st, San José, 1980.* Primer Simposio de Parques Nacionales y Reservas Biológicas. San José: Univ. Estatal a Distancia, Programa de Educación Ambiental, 1982. 168 p.: bibl., ill., maps, tables (Serie Miscelánea; 5)

One of a series published under auspices of the "Program of Environmental Education" of the Univ. Estatal of Costa Rica. Papers concern present state and future of "natural areas" and national parks and preserves, emphasizing Costa Rica but with wider application in Latin America.

Slater, David. Capitalismo y desarrollo regional: ensayos críticos sobre la organización del espacio en el Tercer Mundo. See item **2995.**

5023 Szlajfer, Feliks. Rola plantacji w kształtowaniu przestrzeni społeczno-gospodarczej na przykładzie Ameryki Łacińskiej = The role of plantations in the socioeconomic space organization: the case of Latin America. Wrocław, Poland: Zakład Narodowy im. Ossolińskich, 1984. 102 p.: bibl., tables.

Polish geographer examines role of plantations in the organization of socioeconomic space in Latin America, Central America, and Costa Rica. Another contribution to dependency theory. [K. Complak]

5024 Villegas, Carmen and Laura Coto R. Bibliografía forestal de América tropical. Turrialba, Costa Rica: CIDIA, Biblioteca y Terminal de Servicios, 1979. 277 p.: indexes (Documentación e información agrícola, 0301–438X; 69)

Includes entries on Mexico and all Central and South American countries, as well as Cuba, Haiti, Jamaica, Puerto Rico, the Dominican Republic, and Trinidad & Tobago. Index of authors, species, and general subjects.

5025 Weischet, Wolfgang. Mucho verdor y pocos alimentos, el error de la feracidad de las regiones tropicales húmedas (Revista Norte Grande de Geografía [Pontificia Univ. Católica de Chile, Santiago] 7, 1980, p. 33–48, bibl., tables)

Humid tropics are poor because resources, especially soils, are generally poor. Other explanations, based on social criteria, are based more on public opinion than on results of investigation by specialists. Shifting field farming is probably optimum means of food production in humid tropics. There is indeed a "north-south gradient" of economic well-being, but it is based on environmental facts, not necessarily socioeconomic factors.

5026 Welch, Thomas L. and Myriam Figueras. Travel accounts and descriptions of Latin America and the Caribbean, 1800–1920: a selected bibliography. Foreword by Val T. McComie. Washington: OAS, Columbus Memorial Library, 1982. 293 p.: ill., index (Documentation and information series; 6. OEA/SG/o.1/IV/III.6)

Period covered "stretches from the heyday of European colonialism in the Western Hemisphere to the years following its demise." Arranged geographically, country by country, and alphabetized by author within countries. Entries dealing with more than one region are repeated in the pertinent section. All Latin American and Caribbean countries in the OAS are included, plus Belize, the Guianas, and Puerto Rico. Author index. Very useful for historical geographers who glean vignettes of past landscapes from travel accounts.

MIDDLE AMERICA
(Caribbean Islands, Central America, and Mexico)

TOM L. MARTINSON, *Professor of Geography, Ball State University*
GARY S. ELBOW, *Professor of Geography, Texas Tech University*

PUBLICATIONS ON MEXICO that have appeared since *HLAS 45* are highly varied. Topics range from a study of shifting agriculture in the Lacandon selva (item **5092**) to a report on the impact of building an oil refinery in a small town in Nuevo León (item **5107**).

The dominant theme to emerge from this varied collection is historical, with both the largest number of contributions and some of the most scholarly as well. Greenow has used relatively recently discovered loan records, *Libros de Hipotecas*, from Guadalajara to reconstruct rural-urban economic relations in the 18th century (item **5094**). Doolittle uncovered evidence to support early accounts of relatively advanced agriculture in northwestern Mexico (item **5090**). Swann examined changes in the population distribution of a part of the northern frontier of Mexico (item **5111**), while Watson presented a micro-study of population change during the colonial period in an Indian community in the state of Chiapas (item **5117**). Finally, in a work that might be considered more archaeological than historical, Turner has written on prehistoric agricultural terraces in the Río Bec area (item **5115**). Several articles come from the joint German-Mexican project in Puebla and Tlaxcala, most of them dealing with physical geography (items **5097, 5102, 5103, 5113,** and **5118**). Also worthy of note are an article on the relationship between Catholic or Protestant religious affiliation and adoption of new farming practices (item **5084**) and an impressive book on the natural history of lower Baja California (item **5119**).

The works on Guatemala have increased in number. They are dominated by three articles on the historical geography of the Cuchumatanes highlands by Lovell (items **5070** and **5071**). Aguilar Arrivillaga's well illustrated study of rural housing in Guatemala will please those with an interest in folk housing (item **5061**).

Works on the Caribbean and the remaining countries in Central America are not as numerous as those in the preceding regions, but some illustrate new emphases in geographical research. Blustain and LeFranc, for example, have collected a series of essays on strategies for the organization of small-farm agriculture in Jamaica that may presage greater emphasis on an aspect of agriculture that has long been ignored in Latin America (item **5041**).

Also welcome is another book of essays on environmental perception in the West Indies (item **5032**) that is one of the first attempts to employ techniques from geography's new perception and behavior paradigm in the analysis of Latin American problems.

A collection of works by noted Haitian geographer Georges Anglade (item **5038**) illustrates his breadth of geographical interest and his commitment to resource analysis in the Caribbean.

For biogeographers, there is a new field biology handbook of common plants and animals in Costa Rica (item **5052**) that is extensive and complete enough to be placed in general use.

Finally, the German geographers have contributed to our understanding of contemporary Central America in a fine series of articles in the journal *Geographische Rundschau* (items **5044, 5077,** and **5078**) on economic, agricultural, and political themes.

CARIBBEAN
GENERAL

5027 Brunet, Yves. Urbanisation circum-Caraïbeene: antécédent historique et tendances actuelles (ULIG/C, 23:60, déc. 1979, p. 399–417, bibl., maps, tables)

Classification of the Caribbean's city systems into extreme primate, moderate primate, and lognormal.

5028 Clarke, Colin. Colonialism and its social and cultural consequences in the Caribbean (JLAS, 15:2, Nov. 1983, p. 491–503)

Reviews the colonial experience, independence, and social and cultural inequality in the Caribbean in light of several recent social science texts.

5029 Corredor, Jorge Enrique. Identificación y análisis de ecosistemas del Caribe (AI/I, 9:3, May/June 1984, p. 145–151, bibl.)

Illustrates principal ecosystems of the Caribbean Sea in terms of functional ecology.

5030 Engelbrecht, Gerald A. Nos ambiente I: un enfoque efectivo y exitoso riba e problema di sushi solido na Aruba = an effective and successful approach to the solid waste problem on Aruba = un enfoque efectivo y exitoso al problema de inmundicias sólidas en Aruba. Orangestad, Aruba?: s.n., 1982. 135 p.: ill.

Introduces an ambitious plan to contain the solid wastes of Aruba.

5031 Innes, Frank C. Plantations as institutions under stress in the Caribbean today: a historical-geographic approach (NS, 6:12, 1981, p. 81–87)

Plantation study set in the context of renewable resources in the Caribbean.

5032 Perceptions of the environment: a selection of interpretative essays. Edited by Yves Renard. Bridgetown?: Caribbean Conservation Assn., s.d. 87 p.: ill. (Caribbean environment. Environmental studies; 1)

Highly perceptive essays illustrate use of phenomenological method in developing interrelationships between people and their environment.

5033 Sanguin, André-Louis. Saint-Martin, les mutations d'une île franco-néerlandaise des Antilles (SGB/COM, 35:138, avril/juin 1982, p. 123–140, maps)

St. Martin is a multicultural laboratory but exhibits a fragile political, economic, and ecologic organization that presages an uncertain future.

BARBADOS

5034 Hutt, Maurice Bateman. "Windows to the sea:" a report to CADEC on the establishment of coastal facilities along the south and west coasts of Barbados from the Grantley Adams Airport in Christ Church to Maycock's Bay in St. Lucy. Bridgetown: Cedar Press, 1980. 70 p.: ill.

Action plan for appropriate development of beachfront in Barbados.

5035 Nurse, Lionel L. Residential subdivisions of Barbados, 1965–1977. Cave Hill, Barbados: Institute of Social and Economic Research, Eastern Caribbean, Univ. of the West Indies, 1983. 119 p.: bibl., ill. (Occasional paper; 14)

Investigation of why process of subdivision of land for private housing in Barbados has been largely unsuccessful.

DOMINICAN REPUBLIC

5036 Ballista, Altagracia. La flora terrestre del litoral sur de la ciudad de Santo Domingo (in Contribuciones. Santo Domingo: Editora de la Univ. Autónoma de Santo Domingo, 1983, p. 31–40 [Publicaciones; 311. Col. Ciencia y tecnología; 15])

Inventory of plants in a littoral area south of Santo Domingo that has been declared a national park.

5037 Fito Maupoei, Pedro and José Carles Genoves. Posibilidades de aprovechamiento industrial de los subproductos de la elaboración de arroz de la República Dominicana. Santo Domingo: Instituto Dominicano de Tecnología Industrial; Valencia, Spain: Univ. Politécnica de Valencia, 1981. 100 p.: bibl., ill.

Examines distribution of rice production and offers suggestions for more efficient processing.

HAITI

5038 Anglade, Georges. Espace et liberté en Haïti. Montréal, Québec: ERCE: CRC, 1982. 143 p.: bibl., ill.

Collection of essays and interviews on geography and resources of contemporary Haiti written by distinguished geographer.

5039 Espace rural et société agraire en transformation: des jardins haïtiens aux marchés de Port-au-Prince. Port-au-Prince: Institut français d'Haïti, 1980. 232 p.: bibl., ill. (Recherches haïtiennes; 2)

Exceptionally detailed study of agricultural land use, crop production, and farm to market transportation in the Port-au-Prince area.

JAMAICA

5040 Felix, F. The effect of rainfall on sugar cane yields at Frome (UWI/SES, 30:3, Sept. 1981, p. 104–118, bibl., graphs, tables)

Rainfall is main factor influencing success of sugarcane crop at the Frome Estate, Jamaica.

5041 Strategies for organization and small-farm agriculture in Jamaica. Edited by Harvey Blustain and Elsie LeFranc. Arthur A. Goldsmith et al. Mona, Jamaica: Institute of Social and Economic Research, Univ. of the West Indies; Ithaca, N.Y.: Rural Development Committee, Center for International Studies, Cornell Univ., 1981? 217 p.: bibl., ill.

Report places long-overdue emphasis on development of small-scale agriculture in the Caribbean.

CENTRAL AMERICA
GENERAL

5042 Davis, L. Harlan. Implications of the food-energy situation in Central America (in Conference of Latin Americanist Geographers, 11th, Buffalo, N.Y., 1981. Contemporary issues in Latin American geography: proceedings. Edited by Barry Lentnek. Muncie, Ind.: Ball State Univ., 1983, v. 9, p. 129–137, bibl., tables)

Data on agricultural production from the 1970s show per capita food production

falling after a rise at mid-decade. Abrupt decreases in El Salvador and Nicaragua may be attributed to political problems, but other factors may also be of importance. Discusses implications of using high-cost energy supplies to increase productivity of marginal lands.

5043 Miller, Elbert E. Small farms in Central America (PAIGH/G, 96, julio/dic. 1982, p. 38–46, bibl., graphs)

Discussion of land tenure and agricultural production practices on small farms (0–4 hectares). Concludes that economic constraints make it difficult for small farmers to change farming practices to improve productivity.

5044 Nuhn, Helmut. Zentralamerika: Kleinstaatlichkeit, ökonomische Integration, politische Konflikte (GR, 35:10, Okt. 1983, p. 488–496, maps, plates, tables)

Elements of regional economic links in Central America, including useful maps of land use, population, distribution, and transportation.

5045 Park, Wayne et al. El desarrollo de la energía en América Central. t. 1, Diagnóstico regional. t. 2, Diagnóstico por países. McLean, Va.: Mitre Corp., Metrek Div., 1980. 2 v.: bibl., ill. (MTR; 80W6-01-02)

Survey of energy resources includes all forms and so is useful as background for economic planning.

BELIZE

5046 Calderón Quijano, José Antonio. Cartografía de Belice y Yucatán (EEHA/AEA, 32, 1975, p. 599–637, maps, tables)

Describes 30 maps from the 1726–1867 period, showing Belize and parts of Yucatán. These maps, some of which are reproduced in the article, are part of evidence amassed by writer to support Mexican claims to Belize.

5047 Everitt, John C. Belmopan, dream and reality: a study of the other planned capital in Latin America (PAIGH/G, 99, enero/junio 1984, p. 135–144, maps)

Describes Belmopan's growth during its first decade, discusses extent to which the planned capital has met objectives set out for it, and predicts future impact of the new capital on country.

5048 ———. Mennonites in Belize (Journal of Cultural Geography [Bowling Green State Univ., Ohio] 3 : 2, Spring/Summer 1983, p. 82–93, bibl., maps, table)

Description of Mennonite colonization in lowland tropics focuses on internal migration and secondary colonization within Belize. Mennonite immigrants have come to Belize to escape pressure for change in previous homes. Subsequent migrants in Belize are for similar reasons.

5049 Pearce, Douglas G. Planning for tourism in Belize (AGS/GR, 74 : 3, July 1984, p. 291–303, ill., maps, tables)

Findings of tourism research conducted under contract with Belizean government suggest that, despite limited facilities for tourism, warm climate and access to ocean recreation sites and Mayan ruins are attractions that can be developed. Nevertheless, tourist potential is limited in comparison with established areas in Mexico and the Caribbean.

5050 Sánchez, I.E. The flying potato (BISRA/BS, 11 : 3, 1983, p. 8–11)

Tips on cultivation of this plant (sp. *Dioseorea*), a vine producing a crop similar to the potato but whose fruits are developed above ground.

COSTA RICA

5051 Beaudet, Gaston; Pierre Gabert; and **Jean-Pierre Bergoeing.** Le Costa Rica: formes héritées (AGF/B, 59 : 487/488, mai/juillet 1982, p. 183–197, bibl., ill., map)

Paleoclimatic events have shaped geomorphology of central Costa Rica.

5052 Costa Rican natural history. Edited by Daniel H. Janzen. Chicago: Univ. of Chicago Pres, 1983. 816 p.: bibl., ill., index.

Field biologist's handbook extensively and competently reviews the state of knowledge of common plants and animals in Costa Rica.

5053 Fournier Origgi, Luis. Recursos naturales. San José: Editorial Univ. Estatal a Distancia, 1982. 216 p.: bibl., ill.

Textbook with a systems approach to environment and ecological contamination problems.

Hernández-Alarcón, Eduardo. Urbanization and modernization in Costa Rica during the 1880s. See *HLAS 46:2400.*

5054 Ortuño Medina, Francisco. Estudio y actualización de la política forestal de Costa Rica. San José: Univ. Estatal a Distancia, Programa de Educación Ambiental, 1981. 102 p.: ill. (Serie Miscelánea; 2. Proyecto DGF/PNUD/FAO/COS/72/013. Documento de trabajo; 8)

Recommendations on effective uses of Costa Rica's forest lands.

5055 Regiones periféricas y ciudades intermedias en Costa Rica. Editores, Miguel Morales y Gerhard Sandner. San José: Univ. Nacional de Costa Rica, Escuela de Ciencias Geográficas, 1982. 322 p.: bibl., ill.

Joint German-Costa Rican research team investigation concentrates primarily on population and agriculture.

5056 Sylvander, Robert B. Los bosques del país y su distribución por provincias. San José: Univ. Estatal a Distancia, Programa de Educación Ambiental, 1981. 121 p.: bibl., ill., map (Serie Miscelánea; 3)

General introduction to forest lands accompanied by good distribution map.

5057 Thelen, Kyran and **Arne Dalfelt.** Políticas para el manejo de áreas silvestres. San José: Editorial Univ. Estatal a Distancia, 1979. 107 p.: bibl. (Serie Educación ambiental; 1)

Outlines importance of natural areas and suggests appropriate methods for preservation.

5058 Villalobos Solé, Carlos. Animales y plantas comunes de las costas de Costa Rica. San José: Editorial Univ. Estatal a Distancia, 1982. 147 p.: bibl., ill. (some col.) (Serie Educación ambiental; 6)

Photographic record of plants and animals Costa Rica's rocky coasts, mangrove swamps, sandy beaches, and coral reefs.

EL SALVADOR

5059 Browning, David. Agrarian reform in El Salvador (JLAS, 15 : 2, Nov. 1983, p. 399–426, maps, tables)

Review of El Salvador's experience with agrarian reform since 1980, concludes that current attempts represent a profound change in country's agrarian structure.

GUATEMALA

5060 Aguilar, José María. Catálogo de árboles de Guatemala. Guatemala: Editorial Universitaria, 1982. 1 v.: ill. (Col. Mario Dary Rivera; 1)

Listing of common names with scientific equivalents. Illustrations of leaf morphology for some common trees may be an aid in identification.

5061 Aguilar Arrivillaga, Eduardo. Estudio de la vivienda rural en Guatemala. Guatemala: Editorial Universitaria, 1980. 211 p.: bibl., ill. (Col. Aula; 22)

There is much in this book that will interest cultural geographers, anthropologists, and others with an interest in folk housing in Guatemala. The many drawings of houses, floor plans, and details of construction are especially valuable. Includes some examples from Belize.

5062 Brockett, Charles D. Malnutrition, public policy, and agrarian change in Guatemala (SAGE/JIAS, 26:4, Nov. 1984, p. 477–497, bibl., tables)

Concentration of land ownership associated with commercialization of agriculture has led to a decline in standard of living of rural population, despite increased agricultural production and economic growth. A radical shift in government will be necessary to bring peace and social justice to Guatemala.

5063 Driever, Steven L. and Don R. Hoy. Población potencial de los mayas durante el período clásico (PAIGH/G, 96, julio/dic. 1982, p. 25–37, maps, tables)

Test of new method for estimating population based on ecological density. This method yields higher estimates of population potential than those of earlier researchers.

5064 Guerra-Borges, Alfredo. Compendio de geografía económica y humana de Guatemala. Guatemala: Instituto de Investigaciones Económicos y Sociales, Facultad de Ciencias Económicas, Univ. de San Carlos, 1981. 2 v. (349 p.): ill., maps.

Compendium of Guatemala's geography. Few maps are included and there is little regionalization of data. Much of the data comes from outdated sources and will be of little value for determining current status of social conditions in Guatemala.

5065 Hoegen, Miguel von. Concentración geográfica de los recursos financieros en Guatemala (Cultura de Guatemala [Univ. Rafael Landívar, Guatemala] 2:1, enero/abril 1981, p. 41–71, tables)

Study based on data for distribution by department of loans and discounts given by four types of financial institution for 1977–79. Between 75 and 80 percent of both the number and total value of loans were in Guatemala dept. Concentration of financial resources in central part of Guatemala increased during the period of study.

5066 Hoy, Don R. and François J. Belisle. Environmental protection and economic development in Guatemala's western highlands (JDA, 16:2, Jan. 1984, p. 161–176, bibl., graphs, map)

Environmental problems include deforestation, soil erosion, water contamination, industrial pollution, pesticide misuse, and biotic habitat destruction. Authors urge more consideration of potential environmental problems in selection and execution of development projects and advocate application of labor intensive alternate strategies for development.

5067 Hunter, John M. and Renate De Kleine. Geophagy in Central America (AGS/GR, 74:2, April 1984, p. 157–169, ill., maps, tables)

Precolumbian practice of eating earth continues today as part of the cult of Black Christ of Esquipulas. Clay tables made in Guatemala are consumed in many parts of Central America, including Belize, where they provide a large share of mineral supplements for pregnant Black Carib women.

5068 Jones, John Paul. The periodic and daily Indian market system of Southwest Guatemala (PAIGH/G, 96, julio/dic. 1982, p. 47–53, bibl., maps, tables)

Data from McBryde's classic study are used to examine how well the ca. 1940 market system of Southwest Guatemala fits a central place typology. Markets in densely populated areas tend to fit central place model, while isolated markets develop from a dominant growth center.

5069 Koechert, Andreas. Die guatemaltekische *comunidad indígena* (GR, 36:1, Jan. 1984, p. 14–19, bibl., graphs, ill., maps, tables)

Sketch of life in San Juan Sacatepéquez, with focus on factors causing seasonal migration to work on coastal plantations and discussion of role of Acción Católica, community development oriented Catholic organization, on the traditional *cofradía*-oriented political-religious community organization.

5070 Lovell, W. George. Landholding in Spanish Central America: patterns of ownership and activity in the Cuchumatán Highlands of Guatemala, 1563–1821 (IBG/T, 8:2, 1983, p. 214–230, maps, tables)

Indian lands in this remote part of Guatemala were not claimed by Spaniards until 17th century. Even after large haciendas came into being, Indians still managed to retain many of their ancestral lands. Valuable contribution to understanding of this distinctive part of Guatemala.

5071 ———. Settlement change in Spanish America: the dynamics of *congregación* in the Cuchumatán Highlands of Guatemala, 1541–1821 (CAG/CG, 27:2, Summer 1983, p. 163–174, ill., maps)

By 1550, Spanish colonists in Guatemala were consolidating dispersed Indian settlements into nucleated settlements (i.e., *congregaciones*). In the Cuchumatán Highlands, as elsewhere in Latin America, Spanish control gradually weakened and Indians reestablished dispersed settlement patterns in a process of *decongregación*. The imprint of *congregación* and *decongregación* persists in present-day settlement patterns.

5072 ———. To submit and to serve: forced native labor in the Cuchumatán Highlands of Guatemala, 1525–1821 (Journal of Historical Geography [Academic Press, London] 9:2, April 1983, p. 127–144, ill., maps, tables)

Account of the impact of *encomienda*, tribute, and *repartimiento* in exploitation of Indians of the Cuchumatán Highlands. Excellent explanations of colonial Spanish forced labor institutions and their impact on an Indian population.

HONDURAS

5073 Beetstra, T. Honduras. Amsterdam: Koninklijk Instituut voor de Tropen; Zutphen, The Netherlands: Terra, 1983. 80 p.: bibl., ill., maps, plates (Landendocumentatie; 5)

Country handbook by social geographer with the UNDP in Honduras. Describes country's history, political and social conditions and development, population, and economy. Documented with maps. [N. Vicenti]

5074 Hirth, Kenneth G. *et al.* Patrones regionales de asentamiento en la región de El Cajón: departamentos de Comayagua y Yoro, Honduras (YAXKIN, 4:1, junio 1981, p. 33–56, ill., map, plates)

Archaeological survey of area to be flooded by new dam reveals several important prehistoric sites.

5075 Informe técnico: uso actual de la tierra: valles del Depto. de Francisco Morazán. Tegucigalpa: Consejo Superior de Planificación Económica, Dirección Ejecutiva del Catastro, Depto. de Recursos Naturales, 1982. 126, 12, 35 leaves: ill.

Land use on a sample of farms in seven Honduras valleys.

5076 Manual de uso potencial de la tierra. Tegucigalpa: Gobierno de Honduras, Programa de Catastro Nacional, Componente de Recursos Naturales, 1979. 110 leaves: ill. (Convenio AID-522-T-024-CONSUPLANE)

Project is designed to assist land valuation and agricultural planning.

NICARAGUA

5077 Sandner, Gerhard. Regionalprobleme und Regionalpolitik (GR, 35:10, Okt. 1983, p. 524–532, maps, plates, tables)

New patterns of regional spatial organization of agriculture have emerged since the overthrow of Somoza.

5078 Wünderich, Volker. Die Agrarreform (GR, 25:10, Okt. 1983, p. 516–521, plates, tables)

Explanation of the process of agrarian reform in post-Somoza Nicaragua.

PANAMA

5079 Colonización y destrucción de bosques en Panamá: ensayos sobre un grave problema ecológico. Edición de Stanley Heckadon Moreno y Alberto McKay. Panamá: Asociación Panameña de Antropología, 1982. 174 p.: bibl., ill., plates.

Distribution and extent of forest destruction in selected areas in Panama.

5080 Núñez, Aminta. Consideraciones generales sobre los aspectos históricos, sociales, económicos y políticos de la costa arriba de Colón (*in* Simposio Nacional de Antropología y Etnohistoria de Panama, 5th, Panamá, 1974. Actas. Panamá: Ediciones Instituto Nacional de Cultura, 1978, p. 197–220, bibl., maps)

Background information on Colón Prov., containing maps of some important towns.

5081 Sübdorf, Erich. Vom Nadelöhr der Weltschiffahrt zum internationalem Finanzzentrum: Internationalisierung unter dem Einfluss der USA (GR, 35:10, Okt. 1983, p. 498–503, maps, plates, tables)

New map of Canal Zone reflects changes in economic relationship between Panama and US.

MEXICO

5082 L'Agriculture, la pêche et l'artisanat au Yucatan: prolétarisation de la paysannerie mayan au Mexique. Direction de Yvan Breton et Marie-France Labrecque. Préface de Sidney W. Mintz. Québec: Presses de l'Univ. Laval, 1981. 384 p.: bibl., ill.

Survey of primary economic activities concentrates on their social consequences.

5083 Christopherson, Susan. Female labor force participation and urban structure: the case of Ciudad Juárez, Mexico (PAIGH/G, 97, enero/junio 1983, p. 83–85)

Summary of research. New electronics and apparel manufacturing plants that have located in Ciudad Juárez employ largely women in jobs that are sensitive to international economic shifts. Families become dependent on incomes earned by women in insecure jobs.

5084 Clawson, David L. Religious allegiance and economic development in rural Latin America (SAGE/JIAS, 26:4, Nov. 1984, p. 499–524, bibl., map, tables)

Research conducted in Nealtican, Mexico, compares Protestant and Catholic farmer receptivity to agricultural innovation. There is a statistically significant correlation between Protestant religious affiliation and adoption of new practices in farming. Protestant development of local leaders promotes agricultural change.

5085 Coll de Hurtado, Atlántida. La crise mexicaine: un essai d'explication historique et géographique (Anales de Géographie [Paris] 92:512, juillet/août 1983, p. 414–432, map, graphs, tables)

Analysis and critique of role of investment in Mexican economic development. Foreign investment, mainly from US, has tended to retard country's economic development rather than advancing it.

5086 Commons, Aurea. Desarrollo demográfico de la región central de México, 1519–1980 (PAIGH/G, 97, enero/junio 1983, p. 31–35, maps, table)

Population change from the immediate preconquest period to present. Emphasizes 1895–1980 period from which census data was available.

5087 Crosby, Harry. Last of the Californios. La Jolla, Calif.: Copley Books, 1981. 196 p.: ill., plates.

Popular history will be of interest to lay reader. Includes many useful illustrations and photographs.

5088 Dillman, C. Daniel. Assembly industries in Mexico: contexts of development (SAGE/JIAS, 25:1, Feb. 1983, p. 31–58, bibl., map, tables)

Update of earlier research on Mexico's Border Industries Program reveals recent growth of satellite assembly plants as a result of changed Mexican policies and devaluation of peso. Satellite assembly plants contribute little beyond payment of wages to Mexican economy. For economist's comment see item **3096.**

5089 Doolittle, William E. Agricultural expansion in a marginal area of Mexico (AGS/GR, 73:3, July 1983, p. 301–313, map, plates, tables)

Case study in Municipio of Baviácora,

Sonora, Mexico. Data collected in the field show that expansion of small farmer agriculture into marginal areas is a response to population pressure, decline in productivity of more desirable land, and development of highway access to markets.

5090 ———. Cabeza de Vaca's Land of Maize: an assessment of its agriculture (Journal of Historical Geography [London] 10:3, July 1984, p. 246–262, ill., maps)

Historic accounts of eastern Sonora, Mexico, dating from Cabeza de Vaca, tell of relatively dense populations and well developed agriculture. Research based on historical documents, archaeological remains, and ethnographic studies support accounts of early visitors to the region.

5091 Dufresne, Lucie Suzanne. Estudio de ciertos procesos demográficos en Yucatán, para 1970–1980 (PAIGH/G, 99, enero/junio 1984, p. 121–134, bibl., maps, tables)

Census data from Yucatán state are used to identify three zones of population growth. Population growth zones are related to economic activities.

5092 Gelbert, Michel. *Shifting cultivation in der Selva Lacandona: Mexiko* (GH, 38:1, Jan. 1983, p. 17–26, ill.)

Description of annual agricultural cycle of Lacandon Maya. Gives considerable information on agricultural techniques and cultivars utilized. Comments on impact of shifting cultivation on forest and recommends means of forest preservation.

5093 Greenow, Linda. City and region in the credit market of late colonial Guadalajara (Journal of Historical Geography [London] 10:3, July 1984, p. 263–278, graphs, maps, tables)

Data from *Libros de Hipotecas* for 1721–1820 reveal that credit sources in Guadalajara funded rural economy. Concludes that Guadalajara's urban area and rural hinterland had a mutually dependent economic relationship.

5094 ———. Credit and socioeconomic change in colonial Mexico: loans and mortgages in Guadalajara, 1720–1820. Boulder, Colo.: Westview Press, 1983. 249 p.: bibl., graphs, maps, tables (Dellplain Latin American studies; 12)

Uses 18th-century mortgage records

(i.e., *Libros de Hipotecas*) to reconstruct Guadalajara's credit market. Finds that religious institutions controlled Nueva Galicia's credit market for most of colonial period. Contrary to some writers' ideas, Guadalajara, the principal city of region, seems to have maintained a symbiotic rather than a parasitic relationship with rural hinterland.

5095 Gutiérrez, Phillip R. The channelizatin of Mexican nationals to the San Luis Valley of Colorado (*in* Conference of Latin Americanist Geographers, 11th, Buffalo, N.Y., 1981. Contemporary issues in Latin American geography: proceedings. Edited by Barry Lentnek. Muncie, Ind.: Ball State Univ., 1983, v. 9, p. 69–83, bibl., graphs, map, tables)

Migration stream to the San Luis Valley is distinct from those to Texas and California. The primary source area is Chiuhuahua state, followed by Durango state. These areas are not important as source regions for migrants to other parts of Southwest. Data based on interviews with undocumented residents of study area.

5096 Hartung, Horst. Alignments in architecture and sculpture of Maya centers: notas on Piedras Negras, Copán, and Chichén Itzá (IAA, 10:2, 1984, p. 223–240, bibl., ill., maps)

Another addition to large body of recent work on the astronomical alignment of buildings in Maya ceremonial centers. Concludes that concepts developed and applied in planning ceremonial centers are comparable in sophistication to Maya astronomy, calendrics, and mathematics.

5097 Heine, Klaus. Sintflutartige Niederschlage in Mexiko vor 12,000 Jahren (IAA, 7:1/2, 1981, p. 69–76, bibl., graphs)

Evidence is cited for high levels of precipitation in Central Mexico about 12,000 BP. A 200-yr. period of increased glaciation in alpine zones and of erosion and floods on lower slopes is associated with contemporaneous events elsewhere around the world.

5098 Jáuregui, Ernesto. Visibility trends in Mexico City (UBGI/E, 37:4, Dez. 1983, p. 296–299, graphs, tables)

Atmospheric visibility records between 1937–80 show a regular reduction in air transparency. A slight improvement in frequency of bad visibility was recorded between 1975–80, but the number of clear days has not increased.

5099 —— and **Dieter Klaus**. Stadtklimatische Effekte der raum-zeitlichen Niederschlagsverteilung aufgezeigt am Biespier von Mexiko-Stadt (UBGI/E 36:4, Dez. 1982, p. 278–286, map, tables)

Uses data covering a 40-yr. period to analyze effect over time of Mexico City's urban area on precipitation patterns. Precipitation amounts and frequency of heavy storms have increased over city but decreased both windward and leeward of prevailing easterly winds.

5100 Jones, Richard C. Recent patterns of undocumented migration from Mexico to South Texas (Conference of Latin Americanist Geographers, 11th, Buffalo, N.Y., 1981. Contemporary issues in Latin American geography: proceedings. Edited by Barry Lentnek. Muncie, Ind.: Ball State Univ., 1983, v. 9, p. 84–98, bibl., graphs, map)

Undocumented migrants from Mexico tend to come from northeastern Mexico and from small to medium sized towns. This pattern has changed during 1970s as more distant states and larger urban areas contribute a larger share of migrants. Data are from INS records of apprehended migrants. A small sample of unapprehended migrants shows different characteristics.

5101 ——. Using U.S. immigration data: undocumented migration from Mexico to South Texas (NCGE/J, 83:2, March/April 1984, p. 58–65, bibl., maps, tables)

INS data are used to identify an undocumented migrant source region in Mexico. Source region, centered on Monterrey, is expanding. Recent migrants remain longer in US and are increasingly young, single, and of urban orgin.

5102 Klaus, Dieter and **Wilhelm Lauer.** Zur thermischen Asummetrie der West- und Osthange der Sierra Nevada (IAA, 7:1/2, 1981, p. 55–67, bibl., graphs)

Thermal assymetris are plotted for stations on slopes of Mexican volcanoes Popocatépetl and Ixtaccíhuatl.

5103 Knoblich, Klaus. Genese und Losungsinhalt MIneralisierter Grundwässer im zentramexikanischen Hochland (IAA, 7:1/2, 1981, p. 33–44, bibl., graphs, tables)

Analysis of origin and chemical content of mineralized ground water in Tlaxacala-Puebla area. Minerals are primarily of volcanic origin.

Licate, Jack Anthony. Creation of a Mexican landscape: territorial organization and settlement in the eastern Puebla basin, 1520–1605. See *HLAS 46:1997.*

5104 Lisocka, Bogumiła. Meksyk: kultura a problemy ludnościowe (*in* Społeczne i kulturowe uwarankowania procesów ludnościowych w wybranych krajach pozaeuropejskich. Edited by Elzbieta Reklajtis. Wrocław, Poland: Zakład Narodowy im. Ossolińskich, 1984, p. 15–35)

Polish geographer's chapter entitled "Mexico: Culture and Problems of Demography" contains some challenging data on these topics, but its conclusions are not unorthodox. Provides insights into ongoing research. [K. Complak]

5105 México: información sobre aspectos geográficos, sociales y económicos. v. 1, Aspectos geográficos. v. 2, Aspectos sociales. v. 3, Aspectos económicos. México: Coordinación General de los Servicios Nacionales de Estadística, Geografía e Informática, 1983. 3 v.: bibl., ill. (some col.), col. maps.

Compendium of basic facts about Mexico. Vol. 1 on geography has very small scale maps of rock types, physiographic provinces, climate, temperature and precipitation, rivers and river basins, soil types, and vegetation. For economist's comment on vol. 3, see item **3049.**

5106 Müller, Bernhard. Fremdenverkehr, Dezentralisierung und regionale Partizipation in Mexiko (GR, 36:1, Jan. 1984, p. 20–24, bibl., graphs, ill., maps)

Discusses tourism's role as a decentralizing factor in Third World countries. Tourist sites on Mexico's central Pacific Coast provide a case for analysis. Concludes that development of peripheral areas will not have long lasting effects without major changes in hierarchical relationship of the center with the periphery.

5107 Revel-Mouroz, Jean. Pétrole et mutation d'un espace géographique: le cas de la raffinerie de Cadereyta (CDAL, 24, 1981, p.139–165, graphs, ill., maps, tables)

Account of impact of locating Mexico's

largest petroleum refinery in a small, rural community near Monterrey. Refinery's construction set off uncontrolled migration and growth that overwhelmed local residents and radically altered rural, farm-oriented economy.

5108 Rice, Robert A. Freshwater fishing in Mexico: some consequences of large-scale drainage problems (Human Ecology [Plenum, N.Y.] 12:3, Sept. 1984, p. 315–318, tables)

Land drainage associated with a large agricultural colonization project in Tabasco, Mexico, has reduced both number of species of aquatic fauna and number of fish in region. Local residents who were once able to catch nearly all fish they ate now consume less fish and buy nearly all they eat. Brief but useful article.

5109 Sánchez, R.A. Oil boom: a blessing for Mexico? (GeoJournal [Wiesbaden, FRG] 7:3, 1983, p. 229–246, graphs, maps)

Analyzes economic impact of Mexico's oil boom and its policy response, explaining why petroleum production did not forestall a financial crisis. Recommended reading for anyone interested in Mexico's economic problems.

5110 Siemens, Alfred H. Wetland agriculture in prehispanic Mesoamerica (AGS/GR, 73:2, April 1983, p. 166–181, ill., map)

Raised fields interspersed with drainage canal systems permitted precolumbian farmers in tropical lowlands of Campeche, Chiapas, and Veracruz states, Mexico, and northern Belize to carry out highly productive use of marginal environments.

5111 Swann, Michael M. *Tierra adentro*: settlement and society in colonial Durango. Boulder, Colo.: Westview Press, 1982. 444 p.: bibl., graphs, maps, tables (Dellplain Latin American studies; 10)

Study of population change in late colonial Nueva Vizcaya focuses on demographic aspects of its development. Detailed and careful study that sheds light on processes shaping growth of Durango and area under its control.

5112 Téliz Ortiz, Daniel. La vid en México: datos estadísticos. Chapingo, México: Colegio de Postgraduados, 1982. 321 p.: charts, ill.

Compendium of information on Mexican grape production. Includes maps of grape producing areas, statistics on production, climate conditions, distribution of grape diseases, and other information of interest to viticulturalists.

5113 Trautmann, Wolfgang. Catálogo histórico-crítico de los nombres de lugar relativos a Tlaxcala. Puebla, México: Fundación Alemana para la Investigación Científica, 1980. 74 p.: bibl. (Comunicaciones Proyecto Puebla-Tlaxcala; Suplemento 8)

Compendium of historic place names, many of which are no longer extant, will be of interest to historians, ethnohistorians, historical geographers, and archaeologists.

5114 Tricart, Jean. L'eruption du volcan El Chichón, Méxique: mars-avril 1982 (Annales de Géografie [Paris] 92:512, juillet/août 1983, p. 385–401, bibl., ill., map)

Description of 1982 eruption of a Mexican volcano and its effects on surrounding settled areas.

5115 Turner, Billie Lee, II. Once beneath the forest: prehistoric terracing in the Río Bec region of the Maya Lowlands. Boulder, Colo.: Westview Press, 1983. 209 p.: appendix, bibl., ill., maps, plates (Dellplain Latin American studies; 13)

B.L. Turner II, best known for his work on precolumbian raised field agriculture, turns his attention here to agricultural terracing. Adds to increasingly larger sum of evidence of Maya landscape modifications to increase agricultural production in tropical lowlands of Mesoamerica.

5116 Vollmer, Günter. *Hispaniae Novae vera descriptia, 1579*: zur wirklichkeitstreue einer Mexiko-Karte im *Atlas des Abraham Ortelius* (IAA, 7:1/2, 1981, p. 169–202, bibl., graphs, tables)

Comparison of random locations on a 16th-century map of Mexico with existing sites shows a high degree of accuracy. Map was probably compiled from lost sources and is a valuable source of information on early colonial Mexico.

5117 Watson, Rodney C. La dinámica espacial de los cambios de población en un pueblo colonial mexicano: Tila, Chiapas, 1595–1794 (CIRMA/M, 4:5, junio 1983, p. 87–108, ill., map, tables)

Reconstruction of population changes during colonial period in a small, isolated Indian community.

5118 Werner, Gerd. Verbreitung, Nutzung und Zwestörung von Böden unter randtropischen Bedingungen im zentralmexikanischen Hochland (IAA, 7:1/2, 1981, p. 3–32, bibl., ill., graphs, maps)

Review of soil resources, their use, and destruction in Tlaxcala-Puebla area. Mexico faces increasing demand for food, while productive potential of many soils is reduced through misuse or destroyed by erosion. Excellent illustrations of soil erosion.

Yamada, Mutsuo. Mexico City: development and urban problems after the Revolution, 1910–1970. See *HLAS 46:2299.*

———. Mexico City: development and urban problems before the Revolution. See *HLAS 46:2300.*

5119 Zwinger, Ann. A desert near the sea: a natural history of the Cape Region of Baja California. New York: Harper & Row, 1983. 399 p.: bibl., ill.

Nicely illustrated and well written account of land and people of a little known part of Mexico. Will be a necessity for travelers to Baja California.

SOUTH AMERICA (except Brazil)

ROBERT C. EIDT, *Professor of Geography, University of Wisconsin-Milwaukee*

ENTRIES FOR THIS *HANDBOOK* represent a total of about 100 books and articles which cover travel, urban, political, regional, physical, and settlement phenomena, in that order of importance. Planning, representative of economic, regional, and settlement phenomena, dropped in significance compared with the previous edition of this *Handbook* section. Entries for each country represent, in general, major characteristics of the economy, and political problems concerned.

Venezuela had the largest number of items (17 percent), followed by Peru and Chile (16 percent each), and Argentina (14 percent). Entries from these countries made up nearly half the total.

Once again, the contributions from foreign sources have dropped, but are represented by American, French, and German efforts as usual. They deal primarily with regional-economic topics.

GENERAL

5120 Amerika, I Uzhna i a Amerika. Edited by Viktor V. Volski *et al.* Moskva: Mysl', 1983. 284 p.: ill. (some col.), maps, photos (Strany i narody)

Descriptive Soviet text of South America, country by country, with many photographs and small scale political and economic maps. [C.R. Edwards]

5121 Coelho, Aristides Pinto. A Antártida: nos confins dos três mares. Rio de Janeiro: Letras em Marcha Editora: Federação das Faculdades Celso Lisboa, 1982? 246 p.: ill. (some col.)

Presents summary look at human activity in Antarctica. Covers scientific studies carried out there, origins of the glaciated continent, water-land life conditions, and Brazilian interests in region.

5122 Hardoy, Jorge Enrique; Diego Armus; María Elena Langdon; and Juan Rial. Desigualdades regionales en Chile, Uruguay y Argentina: vistas a través de sus redes urbanas, 1865–1920 (IGFO/RI, 42:169/170, julio/dic. 1982, p. 317–369, maps, tables)

Regional urbanization in the Southern Cone has evolved unequally for various reasons. Authors examine climate, transport, soil, and other factors.

5123 Kandell, Jonathan. Passage through El Dorado: traveling the world's last great wilderness. New York: W. Morrow, 1984. 312 p.; bibl., index, maps.

Well written account of journey through the South American interior by a modern journalist. Provides insights into colonization schemes, road developments, mining actitivies, etc.

5124 Koch-Grünberg, Theodor. Del Roraima al Orinoco. v. 1–3. Traducción del alemán de Federica de Ritter. Revisada por Argenis J. Gómez. Caracas: Ediciones del Banco Central de Venezuela, 1982. 3 v.: bibl., ill. (Col. histórico-económica)

Translation of original work in German by Theodor Koch-Grünberg who journeyed through northern Brazil, southern Venezuela, and southeast Colombia early in the century. Author was friend of well known geographer W.M. Sievers and taught in Giessen. His original work was published between 1917–28. Much of value for geographers, anthropologists, and linguists.

Ronan, Charles E. Francisco Javier Iturri, S.J. and Alcedos's *Diccionario geográfico*. See *HLAS 46:2629.*

5125 Sauer, Carl Ortwin. Andean reflections: letters from Carl O. Sauer while on a South American trip under a grant from the Rockefeller Foundation, 1942. Edited by Robert C. West. Boulder, Colo.: Westview Press, 1982. 139 p.: bibl., index, map (Dellplain Latin American studies; 11)

Letters with comments on human and physical geofactors as recorded during Sauer's only extended trip to South America in 1942. Summary statement deals with academic life in South American universities.

5126 The South American handbook: 1982. Edited by J.A. Hunter and H. Davies. Bath, England: Trade & Travel Publications, 1982. 1 v.: ill., maps.

Probably the most comprehensive guidebook for travel in South America. This 58th ed. includes numerous practical hints of value to any kind of tourist as well as scientific traveler.

5127 United Nations. Economic Comission for Latin America (ECLA). The natural disasters of 1982–1983 in Bolivia, Ecuador, and Peru. New York: ECLA, 1984. 223 p.: ill., maps.

Discussion of social and economic effects of floods and drought with maps of af-fected areas in the three countries investi-gated. Includes data on cost of disasters and information about rehabilitation projects.

ARGENTINA

5128 Balbachan, Eduardo Luis. Los igno-rados pasajes de Buenos Aires. Buenos Aires: Editorial Rodolfo Alonso, 1982. 142 p.: ill., maps, photos.

Detailed description of city of Buenos Aires *pasajes* (alleys). Provides photographs, accurate location by street intersections, cadastral maps, and history of each alley's name.

Bibliografía sobre las Islas Malvinas. See item 21.

5129 Camacho, Horacio H. *et al.* Biblio-grafía geológica de la Argentina: 1980–1981. Buenos Aires: Consejo Nacional de In-vestigaciones Científicas y Técnicas, Centro de Investigaciones en Recursos Geológicos (CIRGEO), 1984. 219 p. (Publicación; 1)

Useful bibliography of Argentine geo-logical studies organized according to author, topic, stratigraphic entities, and taxomomic considerations.

5130 Corte, Arturo E. and **Lydia E. Espizua.** Inventario de glaciares de la cuenca del Río Mendoza. Mendoza, Argentina: Consejo Nacional de Investigaciones Científicas y Técnicas, Instituto Argentino de Nivología y Glaciología, 1981. 64 p.: bibl., ill., maps (16 folded, some col.)

Analysis of Mendoza River Basin ice bodies larger than 0.02 km^2 reveals over 600 km^2 of covered and exposed ice surfaces which generate water for lower areas.

5131 Daus, Federico A. and **Raúl C. Rey Balmaceda.** Islas Malvinas. 2a. ed. Buenos Aires: OIKOS Asociación para la Pro-moción de los Estudios Territoriales y Am-bientales, 1982. 242 p.: bibl., ill.

New ed. of 1955 monograph on Falk-land Islands, originally written by Federico Daus (see *HLAS 20:2008*). Includes bibliogra-phy of materials primarily from 1960s-80s.

5132 Destéfani, Laurio Hedelvio. Síntesis de la geografía y la historia de las Islas Malvinas, Georgias y Sandwich del Sur. Buenos Aires: Ministerio de Educación,

Centro Nacional de Documentación e Información Educativa, 1982. 108 p.: bibl., ill., maps (Nueva serie divulgación; 23)

One of few résumés of history of discovery and occupation of Malvinas/ Falklands, Georgia, and Sandwich Islands. Includes comments on physical geography.

Difrieri, Horacio A. El Virreinato del Río de la Plata: ensayo de geografía histórica. See *HLAS 46:2766.*

5133 Laura, Guillermo Domingo. El cinturón ecológico. Buenos Aires: Ediciones CEAMSE, 1979. 142 p.: bibl., ill., plates (some col.) (Ediciones CEAMSE; 1)

Analysis of results to date of an accord (1977) made between city of Buenos Aires and prov. of Buenos Aires to create a reserve area on garbage-reclaimed land for airports, cemeteries, parks, model urbanism, etc., by modern, ecologically-actuated means.

5134 Payró, Roberto Jorge. La Australia argentina: excursión periodística a las costas patagónicas, Tierra del Fuego e Isla de los Estados. Carta-prólogo de Bartolomé Mitre. Buenos Aires: Centro Editor de América Latina, 1982. 2 v. (496 p.): ill. (Capítulo. Las Nuevas propuestas; 6–7)

Journalist, with flair for detail, describes natural and human conditions in Patagonia around the turn of this century.

5135 Sassone, Susana M. Azul, Olavarría, Tandil: un sistema urbano. Buenos Aires: OIKOS Asociación para la Promoción de los Estudios Territoriales y Ambientales, 1981. 147 p.: bibl., ill., plates (Estudios geográficos pampeanos; 4)

A "normal" assessment of urban development is hindered by transportation's complex evolution and communications' improvements. These growth phenomena also make planning difficult. In the case of the Pampa's urbanization, author argues in favor of studying what has happened in cities, rather than analyzing with a theoretical scheme which does not take into account these crucial growth factors.

5136 Simposio sobre Problemas Geológicos del Litoral Atlántico Bonaerense, *Mar del Plata, Argentina, 1980.* Resúmenes. La Plata, Argentina: Comisión de Investigaciones Científicas, 1982. 298 p.: bibl., ill., maps, photos.

Results of a systematic study of littoral dynamics of Mar del Plata coastline. Papers discuss geomorphological changes with maps and comparative photographs from different years for three beach areas.

5137 Toponimia de la República Argentina. v. 1, Territorio Nacional de la Tierra del Fuego, Antártida e Islas del Atlántic Sur: pt. 1, Tierra del Fuego. Buenos Aires: Ejército Argentino, Instituto Geográfico Militar, 1982. 1 v.: bibl., col. maps.

Pt. 1 of set on Argentine place names. Place names and locations by latitude and longitude, and information concerning maps and other publications are given.

5138 Vecchio, Ofelio. Mataderos, mi barrio. 2a ed. Buenos Aires: Editora Nueva Lugano, 1981. 350 p.: ill.

Neighborhood study of one of many barrios in Buenos Aires, with attention to street names, public buildings, historical and personal events.

5139 Vivies Azancot, Pedro V. Entre el esplendor y la decadencia: la población de Misiones, 1750–1759 (IGFO/RI, 42: 169/170, julio/dic. 1982, p. 469–543, graphs, maps, tables)

Well documented and thoughtful analysis of decline in mission population following 18th-century Jesuits' explusion from South America. Jesuit planning probably would have failed because of an expanding regional economy which did not permit growth of mission system. For historian's comment, see *HLAS 46:2813.*

BOLIVIA

Blanes Jiménez, José. Bibliografía referida al trópico cochabambino. See *HLAS 46:15.*

5140 Ecología y recursos naturales en Bolivia: trabajos presentados en el simposio del 3 al 8 de mayo de 1982. Cochabamba, Bolivia: Centro Pedagógico y Cultural de Portales; La Paz: Univ. Mayor de San Andrés, Instituto de Ecología, 1982. 314 p.: bibl., ill.

Results of investigations carried out for symposium (Bolivia, 1982) on ecology and natural resources. Discusses altiplano, valleys, lowlands, and nation's resources.

5141 Englegert, Victor. Reed people of Titicaca (AMNH/NH, 91:1, Jan. 1982, p. 34–37, ill.)

Field report on people who build *totora* rafts in Lake Titicaca region.

5142 Fifer, J. Valerie. The search for a series of small successes: frontiers of settlement in eastern Bolivia (JLAS, 14:2, Nov. 1982, p. 407–432, ill., tables)

Examines various types of rural settlement in eastern Bolivia. States that spontaneous colonization has been responsible for almost 80 percent of new agricultural land opening in Bolivia since 1953. Describes latest attempts at populating interior (150 km northeast of Santa Cruz). Notes that such colonies have succeeded more in economic terms than as "safety valves."

5143 Gonzáles Moscoso, René. Geografía física y humana de Bolivia. Sucre, Bolivia: Librería-Editorial Tupac Katari, 1982. 126 p.: ill.

Small book presents maps with local terminology which may be helpful to Bolivian experts.

5144 Hiraoka, Mario. Japanese agricultural settlement in the Bolivian Upper Amazon: a study in regional ecology. Sakuramura, Japan: Univ. of Tsukuba, Special Research Project on Latin America, 1980. 160 p.: maps, plates, tables (Latin American studies; 1)

Careful investigation of pioneer settlements in lowland eastern Bolivia sheds light on modern processes of agricultural settlement that lead from initial crop farming to grazing with low carrying capacity. Strong suggestion that scientific attempts to work out appropriate methods of settlement are routinely overwhelmed by flood of squatters who follow new roads and apply harmful methods to little understood landscapes.

5145 Método de evaluación de proyectos de producción agrícola. La Paz: Centro de Investigación y Promoción del Campesinado (CIPCA), 1980. 483 p.: ill.

Assesses production projects in Bolivia for small farmers. Organized into three pts.: 1) indexes covering technical-economic aspects, education, and change; 2) specific project reports for Cochabamba, Chuquisaca, La Paz, Potosí, Tarija, and Santa Cruz; and 3) conclusions.

5146 West, Terry L. Llama caravans of the Andes (AMNH/NH, 90:12, Dec. 1981, p. 62–73, ill., maps)

Field report of llama drive in Bolivia during drought period which reactivated llama traffic between regions where such activity has died out.

CHILE

5147 Ahumada Bermúdez, Ramón and **Lisandro Chuecas M.** Algunas características hidrográficas de la Bahía de Concepción, 36°40′S—73°02′W y áreas adyacentes, Chile. Concepción, Chile: Gayana, Instituto de Biología, Univ. de Concepción, 1979. 56 p.: ill. (Miscelánea; 8)

Dynamic meteorological, water mass, and coastline conditions account for most hydrographical changes in Chile's Bay of Concepción.

5148 El Ambiente natural y las poblaciones humanas de los Andes del Norte Grande de Chile: Arica, lat. 18°28′S. v. 1–2. Edited by Alberto Veloso M. and Eduardo Bustos-Obregón. Santiago: UNESCO: MAB, 1982. 2 v.: bibl., ill., index, plates (El Hombre y los ecosistemas de montaña. MAB-6-UNEP-UNESCO: 1105-77-01)

Valuable investigation in two vols. of effects of altiplano physical conditions (Arica to Bolivian border) on biota, vertebrates, and human beings (Aymara). Includes lengthy discussion of hypoxia and reproduction, and of Aymara communities. Helpful photographs and bibliographies.

5149 Bibliografía geológica del norte de Chile. Compiled by Silvia Zolezzi Velásquez. Antofagasta, Chile: Univ. del Norte, Vice-Rectoría Académica, Unidad de Biblioteca y Documentación, 1982. 1 v.: index (Repertorios; 15. Serie I, Repertorio bibliográfico; 11)

Bibliography for northern Chile contains 1960s information on geology, paleogeography, and geophysics.

5150 Censo forestal, 1980. Santiago: Instituto Forestal: Corporación Nacional Forestal, 1981. 121 p.: ill., tables (Serie Informática; N-2)

Statistical summary of forest productivity in different regions of Chile.

5151 Cepeda A., Alonso. Geología económica del Distrito Río Blanco disputada. Santiago: Instituto de Investigaciones Geológicas, 1981. 43 p.: ill., col. maps (Boletín; 36)

Geologic study of mining area 60 km northeast of Santiago, Chile, reveals presence of copper reserves.

Gaete J., Alden. Evolución espacio-temporal de la industria siderúrgica en Chile y en los Estados Unidos de Norteamérica. See item **3540**.

5152 Galleguillos Araya, Abel. Pukará. Santiago: Imprenta de Carabineros, 1981. 120 p.: plates (some col.)

Human geography of northern Chile.

5153 Geografía económica de Chile. Edited by Gemines, Sociedad de Estudios Profesionales. Santiago: Editorial A. Bello, 1982. 1083 p.: bibl., ill.

Encyclopaedic summary of modern Chilean economic factors for country as a whole as well as for 13 administrative divisions or regions. Extensive tables with 1970s-80s statistics.

5154 Grenier, Philippe. Chiloé et les chilotes: marginalité et dépendance en Patagonie chilienne, étude de géographie humaine. Aix-en-Provence, France: EDISUD, 1984. 593 p.: appendices, bibl., graphs, ill., indexes, plates, tables.

Regional geography of Chiloé devotes special attention to 1950–70s developmental failures. Exemplifies what regional geographical studies can contribute to assessment of problems and their solution when applied to a marginally populated and productive area. Deals with agriculture, forestry, fishing, and ranching and integrates these economic aspects with physical geographical factors which influence their success. Well illustrated; lengthy bibliography.

5155 Krumm Saavedra, Guillermo. Características geográficas generales de Ausen y sus aborígenes (SCHG/R, 150, 1982, p. 96–103)

Brief statement on major physical geographical features followed by historical and modern details about native peoples (e.g., the Chonos).

Martínez Lemoine, René. Desarrollo urbano de Santiago: 1541–1941. See *HLAS 46:3108*.

5156 La Minería en Chile. Santiago: Instituto de Ingenieros de Minas de Chile, 1980. 131 p.: ill.

Brief history of Chilean mining enterprises and detailed discussion of copper production, petroleum, iron, precious metals, and some non-metals, as well as methods of organization.

Muniziga Vigil, Gustavo. Notas para un estudio comparativo de la trama urbana Santiago de Chile. See *HLAS 46:3119*.

5157 Muñoz S., Mélica; Elizabeth Barrera M.; and Inés Meza P. El uso medicinal y alimenticio de plantas nativas y naturalizadas en Chile. Santiago: Museo Nacional de Historia Natural, 1981. 91 p.: bibl., indexes (Publicación ocasional; 33)

Notes on use of some 75 plants found in Chile. Indexes by vernacular names and scientific names.

5158 Olivares E., Alfredo and Juan Gasto C. *Atriplex repanda:* organización y manejo de ecosistemas con arbustos forrajeros. Santiago: Univ. de Chile, Facultad de Ciencias Agrarias, Veterinarias y Forestales, Depto. de Producción Animal, 1981. 300 p.: bibl., ill. (some col.) (Ciencias agrícolas; 7)

Assessment of development possibilities for grazing land ecosystems by means of planting *Atriplex repanda*, a native forage shrub from northern Chile.

5159 Perspectivas de desarrollo de los recursos de la Región Aisén del General Carlos Ibáñez del Campo. v. 1, Bibliografía. v. 2, Caracterización climática. Santiago: Corporación de Fomento de la Producción, Instituto Nacional de Investigación de Recursos Naturales; Coihaique: Intendencia Región Aisén, Secretaría Regional de Planificación y Coordinación de la Región Aisén, 1979. 2 v.: bibl., ill. (Publicación; 26)

One of a series of studies preliminary to assessing natural resources and planning changes in Aisén, Chile.

5160 Porteous, J. Douglas. The annexation of Easter Island: geopolitics and environmental perception (NS, 6:11, 1981, p. 67–80, maps)

Explains reasons for Chilean annexation of Easter Island as involving prestige, naval power, agricultural potential, and westward expansion. For historian's comment, see *HLAS 46:3124.3*

Ramón, Armando de. Santiago de Chile, 1850–1900: límites urbanos y segregación espacial según estratos. See *HLAS 46:3127*.

5161 Riffo A., Pedro Eduardo. El volcán Hudson Norte (SCHG/R, 148, 1980, p. 156–167, map, photos, tables)

Brief report on appearance and consequences of new volcano in Chile dating from 1971 and named the North Hudson (Aisén).

5162 Schweitzer Lopetegui, Angela *et al.* Recuperación de patrimonio turístico: Cerro Santo Domingo de Valparaíso. Valparaíso, Chile: Servicio Nacional de Turismo, Región de Valparaíso, 1982. 280 p.: ill., maps, photos (Estudios turísticos; 2)

Detailed architectural record of this Valparaíso neighborhood contains many maps, drawings, and photographs that might aid in reconstruction. [T.L. Martinson]

COLOMBIA

5163 Buses y busetas: una evaluación del transporte urbano de Bogotá. Editor, Miguel Urrutia. Jorge E. Acevedo V. *et al.* Bogotá: Fundación para la Educación Superior y el Desarrollo, 1981. 138 p.: bibl., ill. (some col.), plates.

After a city reaches a certain size, efficient use of transport energy argues for public buses and microbuses, rather than automobiles. Consideration must be given to family income, size of main streets, funding, minimization of petroleum needs, and time required for journey to work. Bogotá is now large enough (4,000,000 inhabitants) to require much planning of public transport.

5164 Galeano A., Héctor; Myriam T. Calderón S.; and Arnulfo Zapata T. Bibliografía nacional de suelos, 1930–1980. Bogotá: Ministerio de Hacienda y Crédito Público, Instituto Geográfico Agustín Codazzi, 1981. 376 p.: bibl., indexes.

Compilation of soils research results published between 1930–80. Includes author and subject indexes which make it a useful source for earth scientists.

5165 Hernández de Caldas, Angela. Organismo agrícolas, pecuarios y forestales colombianos y sus siglas: un directorio = Directory of agricultural and forestry organiza-

tions of Colombia. Prólogo, Carlos Garcés Orejuela. Bogotá: Fundación Mariano Ospina Pérez, 1981. 103 p.: bibl., indexes.

Directory of agricultural, forestry, and other institutional organizations consists of 249 entries for Colombia. Includes title and addresses (e.g., journals, official publications).

5166 Myers, Barbara. A commercial use for taro: a project of the Instituto Matia Mulumba in Colombia. Washington: A.T. International, 1982. 14 p. (Working paper)

Report of assistant project involving production of taro flour and swine feed by black natives on Colombia's Pacific coast. Leadership and technical problems have delayed its progress.

5167 Ordenamiento y administración del espacio urbano en Bogotá, 1981. Bogotá: Alcaldía Mayor de Bogotá, Depto. Administrativo de Planeación Distrital, 1981? 275 p.: ill. (some col.), plates.

Well written monograph explains aspects of 1979 *Acuerdo* which established zoning for Bogotá's Sabana. The *Acuerdo* was designed chiefly to save the Sabana's agricultural lands from further urban encroachment and to control use of such space. Devotes much attention to conservation techniques and rehabilitation of old areas.

5168 Puerto Leguízamo, La Tagua y Leticia: reseñas analíticas. Bogotá: Univ. Nacional de Colombia, Programa Orinoquia-Amazonia, Comisión Bibliográfica, 1980. 120 p.: indexes (Serie Bibliografía y documentación; 4)

Bibliography with abstracts of important research works dealing with development of Puerto Leguizamo-La Tagua-Puerto Leticia region of Colombia. Topics include mapping, colonization, communications, soils, etc.

5169 Villarreal Torres, Jaime. El olor de mi pueblo. Bogotá: Ministerio de Desarrollo Económico, Corporación Nacional de Turismo-Colombia, 1983. 87 p.

Historical, economic, and other comments on El Banco (Bajo Magdalena), Colombia.

5170 Zandstra, Hubert G. *et al.* Cáqueza: experiencias en desarrollo rural. Presentación, Josué Franco. Bogotá: Centro Internacional de Investigaciones para el

Desarrollo, Oficina Regional para América Latina y el Caribe, 1978. 386 p.: bibl., ill.

Interesting summary of 5-yr. study of 2-4-ha.-sized farms that covered planning improvements and technicians in attempt to assess and change agricultural practices in Colombia's Cáqueza region. Concludes with examination of non-technical aspects of such a change process and discussion of politics involved.

ECUADOR

5171 Benalcázar Rosales, César. Ecuador, país de primavera en la mitad del mundo. 2a ed., aum. y actualizada. Quito: Editorial Epoca, 1981. 302 p.: plates (some col.)

Popularized geography of Ecuador with numerous color photographs.

5172 Gould, Stephen Jay. Agassiz in the Galápagos (AMNH/NH, 90:12, Dec. 1981, p. 7–14, ill.)

Report of little known trip undertaken by Louis Agassiz to the Galápagos in connection with his dispute with Darwin's theory.

5173 Larrea Donoso, Galo. Patrimonio natural y cultural ecuatoriano. Quito: Banco Central del Ecuador, 1982. 456 p.: bibl., ill. (col.)

Comments on physical and cultural habitat of Ecuador. Over half the book consists of pertinent legislation which defines rules for protection of nation's natural and cultural resources.

5174 Mendoza, Luis Aníbal. Geo-economía del Ecuador. Nueva ed. aum. y corr. Guayaquil, Ecuador: García Avilés, 1981. 332 p.: bibl., ill.

Economic geography of Ecuador with chapters on regions, population, agriculture, mining, industry, transportation, and commerce.

Pichincha: monografía histórica de la región nuclear ecuatoriana. See *HLAS 46:2619.*

5175 Seminario Técnico de la Asociación Panamericana de Instituciones de Crédito Educativo, 9th, *Estación Charles Darwin, Ecuador, 1980.* IX [i.e. Noveno] Seminario Técnico. Guayaquil, Ecuador: La Asociación (APICE), 1981? 219 p.: ill.

Report on continuing activities by different groups of scientists interested in Galápagos Islands.

5176 Zeas S., Pedro and **Marco Flores E.** Hacia el conocimiento de la arquitectura rural andina: caso Alta Montaña Cañar. Cuenca, Ecuador: Depto. de Difusión Cultural, Univ. de Cuenca, 1982. 311 p.: bibl., ill., maps, plates.

Informative volume on Andean vernacular architecture. Describes materials used for building rural structures in an Ecuadorian zone (3,000 m. altitude). Includes numerous sketches, maps, and photographs.

PARAGUAY

5177 Boh, Luis Alberto and **Annie M. Granada.** Apuntes sobre evolución histórica y tipológica de la vivienda popular urbana en el Paraguay. Asunción: Banco Paraguayo de Datos, 1980? 64 p.: bibl., ill., plates.

Discusses problems of orientation and construction of rural and urban settlement structures. Few drawings.

5178 Fogel, Ramón. Colonización agraria y distribución espacial de la población: características del proceso (CPES/RPS, 16:44, enero/abril 1979, p. 109–164, bibl., tables)

Examines colonization from economic and political aspects of populating a country. Considers lack of national colonies one of the reasons for 1904 peasant revolt in Paraguay. Following 1918 National Homestead Law, 90 percent of farm lots distributed in the country had been parceled out. The Chaco and so-called Eje Este are two major areas of settlement in modern times. A large number of colonists stems from minifundio areas in central Paraguay. Replication of subsistence agriculture is common, and only better planning with ample infrastructure will change it.

5179 Palmieri, Juan and **Juan Carlos Velázquez.** Geología del Paraguay. Asunción: Ediciones NAPA, 1982. 65 p.: bibl., ill., maps, photos (Col. Apoyo a cátedra. Serie Ciencias naturales)

Survey depicts major geologic formations of Paraguay with maps, useful photographs, and bibliography.

5180 Velázquez, Rafael Eladio. Poblamiento en el Paraguay en el siglo XVIII: fundación de Villas y formación de los núcleos urbanos menores (CPES/RPS, 15:42/43, mayo/dic. 1978, p. 175–189, map)

Paraguay's 18th-century settlements continue until now. Describes and illustrates basis for their existence and persistence.

Vives Azancot, Pedro A. Asunción, 1775–1800: persistencias rurales en la revitalización de su estructura urbana. See *HLAS 46:2812.*

PERU

5181 Aramburú, Carlos E.; Eduardo Bedoya Garland; and Jorge Recharte Bullard. Colonización en la Amazonía. Lima: Centro de Investigación y Promoción Amazónica, 1982. 161 p.: bibl., ill., plates.

Formulation of the Treaty of Amazon Cooperation signed by eight Latin American countries in 1980 and reactivation of road building toward eastern Peru have signaled expansion of agricultural frontier since beginning of present decade. Includes statistics for 1980–81, comments on various projects, and discussion of communications and agriculture.

5182 Baca Tupayachi, Epifanio. Cusco, sistemas viales, articulación y desarrollo regional. Cusco, Perú: Centro de Estudios Rurales Andinas Bartolomé de las Casas, 1983. 68 p.: bibl., ill., plates (Cuadernos para el debate regional; 10)

Evolution of rail and road system in Cusco region.

5183 Brisseau Loaiza, Janine. La Cuzco dans sa région: étude de l'aire d'influence d'une ville andine. Bordeaux, France: Ministère des universités, Centre national de la recherche scientifique, Centre d'études de géographie tropicale; Lima: Institut français d'études andines, 1981. 571 p.: bibl., maps (Travaux de l'Institut; 16. Travaux et documents de géographie tropicale, 0336–5522; 44)

Monumental work on Cusco region deals with its geography (physical and human), sociology, and economics. Pt. 1 (three chaps.) presents physical and cultural setting with historical background data; pt. 2 (five chaps.) analyzes Cusco's influence on surrounding region; and pt. 3 conclusion (two chaps.) discusses problems of regional urbanization. Numerous excellent photographs illustrate the textual interpretations.

5184 Estudio semidetallado de suelos de la zona del Río Manití, Iquitos. Lima: Instituto Nacional de Planificación: Oficina Nacional de Evaluación de Recursos Naturales: Empresa para el Desarrollo y Explotación de la Palma Aceitera, 1982. 1 v.: ill. (some col.), maps.

Introductory soil survey of an area 40 km east of Iquitos presents details of N, P, K levels, CEC, and other chemical and physical traits (texture) which assist in planning land use. Uses system similar to that of US soil conservation manuals and soil classification terminology. Soil information as well as FAO taxonomy make this a useful monograph.

5185 Inventario y evaluación semidetallada de los recursos de suelos y forestales de la zona de Atalaya. Lima: Oficina Nacional de Evaluación de Recursos Naturales (ONERN), 1982. 177 p.: appendices, maps, plates.

Consists of detailed modern soil analysis with resulting classifications (US and FAO) and use categories along Carretera Marginal de la Selva from Satipo-Urubamba. Designed for planners so that settlement activities along Carretera can be rationally developed. Nicely emphasizes forest vegetation types in terms of uses and distribution.

5186 Kuczynski Godard, Pedro-Pablo. Memoria de Energía y Minas, 1980–1982. Lima: Ministerio de Energía y Minas, 1982. 2 v.: ill. (some col.)

Draws useful statistical comparison between Peru and other Latin American countries. Valuable summary monograph consists of general accounting of condition of mining, electric power, and petroleum production in Peru where overall productivity has declined in recent years.

5187 Monheim, Felix. Die Entwicklung der peruanischen Agrarreform 1969–1979 und ihre Durchführung im Departement Puno. Wiesbaden, FRG: Steiner, 1981. 37 p.: bibl. (Erdkundliches Wissen; 55)

Analysis of Peru's two agrarian reform movements (1964 and 1969), one of which was civilian, the other military. Lack of planning and contradictions found in both reform models make for dubious outcomes.

5188 Muñoz, David. Memorias sobre el Amazonas peruano. Edición de Miguel Angel Pinto. Introducción, Jaime Miasta. Lima: Univ. Nacional Mayor de San Marcos, Dirección de Proyección Social, Seminario de Historia Rural Andina, 1980. 104 p.: glossary.

Notes of scientific value made in 1897–1901 by Muñoz while traveling in eastern lowland Peru.

5189 Murphy, Dervla. Eight feet in the Andes. London: J. Murray, 1983. 274 p.: ill., index, plates.

Remarkable account of modern journey through Cajamarca-Cusco area by mule. Includes well written details about life in the Andes, social problems, failures and successes of different ways of life.

5190 Ortiz, Dionisio. La montaña de Ayacucho: etnografía, geografía, historia. Lima: Gráfica 30, 1981. 306 p.: bibl., ill.

Geography, ethnography, and history of religious colonization efforts in Montaña de Ayacucho. Includes text of *Ley de Comunidades Nativas* and *Ley de Promoción Agropecuaria de Regiones de Selva y Ceja de Selva* (Decreto Ley 20653).

5191 Pulgar Vidal, Javier. Geografía del Perú: las ocho regiones naturales del Perú. 8a ed. Lima: Editorial Universo, 1981. 313 p.: ill. (some col.)

Eighth ed. of well known geography of Peru. Maintains its subdivision of country into eight regions: 1) coast; 2) Yunga; 3) Quechua; 4) Suni; 5) Puna towards west side of main Andean peaks; 7) Selva Alta; and 8) Selva Baja on east side.

5192 Symposium sobre Desarrollo de la Acuicultura en el Perú, *2nd, La Molina, Perú, 1981.* Segundo Symposium sobre Desarrollo de la Acuicultura en el Perú. Editor, Leoncio Ruiz Ríos. La Molina: Univ. Nacional Agraria, Programa Académico e Pesquería; Lima: Ministerio de Pesquería, Oficina de Cooperación Técnica y Económica, 1981. 342 p.: bibl.

Results of 2nd *acuicultura* symposium sponsored by National Agrarian Univ. and Ministry of Fishing. Discusses in detail production problems associated with mollusks, crustaceans, trout, and tropical fish. Covers various regions of country.

5193 Wright, Ronald. Cut stones and crossroads: a journey in the two worlds of Peru. New York: Viking Press, 1984. 239 p.: bibl., ill., index, plates.

Interweaves travel experiences with Inca and Peruvian history in a type of book rarely seen these days. The feel of place pervades author's writing style.

URUGUAY

5194 Klaczko, Jaime and Juan Rial Roade. Uruguay, el país urbano. Montevideo: CLASCO, Comisión de Desarrollo Urbano y Regional: Ediciones de la Banda Oriental, 1981. 144 p.: bibl., ill., maps.

Consists of an analysis of the growth of an Uruguayan urban network, by means of synthesizing historical forces and technological changes. Also discusses effects of a livestock-raising economy. This small but refreshing work explains the paradox of a nation whose productivity is mostly rural, while its population is 77 percent urban.

5195 Rial Roade, Juan; Angel Mario Cocchi; and Jaime Klaczko. Proceso de asentamientos urbanos en el Uruguay: siglos XVIII y XIX (CPES/RPS, 15:42/43, mayo/dic. 1978, p. 91–114, tables)

Explanation of the growth of urban network in Uruguay from colonial times. Stresses "apartness" of Montevideo.

VENEZUELA

5196 Briceño Monzillo, José Manuel. Nuestras fronteras con Colombia: reseña histórica. Mérida, Venezuela: Asociación de Profesores de la Univ. de los Andes, 1982. 149 p.: bibl., ill., maps, plates (Acción profesoral; 1)

Attempt to alert Venezuelans to historical shrinkage of their national territory after border negotiations with other countries. Suggests holding the line in Gulf of Venezuela and other places still under discussion.

5197 Carías Sisco, Germán. Fronteras en la selva: frente a Guyana, Colombia y Brasil. Caracas: Editorial Ateneo de Caracas, 1982. 285 p.: bibl., ill. (Col. Testimonios)

Description of conditions on Venezuela's frontiers by journalist who feels strongly that his nation should be populating and protecting these outposts.

Crist, Raymond E. Westward thrusts the pioneers zone in Venezuela: a half century of economic development along the Llanos-Andes border. See item **3470.**

5198 Drenikoff, Iván. Breve historia de la cartografía de Venezuela. Caracas: Academia Nacional de la Historia, 1982. 142 p.: ill. (El Libro menor; 32)

Useful and well documented review of maps and map-making concerning Venezuela, from the 15th century to present.

5199 Gacetilla de nombres geográficos. Caracas: Ministerio del Ambiente y de los Recursos Naturales Renovables, Dirección de Cartografía Nacional, Div. de Mapas, 1981. 645 p.: ill., plates (Publicaciones de la Dirección de Cartografía Nacional)

List of place names for states of Venezuela. Provides latitude and longitude.

5200 Gascón Sancho, Jesús. El mapa, su contenido y su lectura. Caracas: Ediciones de la Fundación de Educación Ambiental, 1982. 89 p.: ill., plates.

Purpose is to provide instruction in use and reading of maps, apparently at university level, with examples drawn from mapping of Venezuela. [C.R. Edwards]

5201 Hoyos, Jesús. Los árboles de Caracas. 2a ed. Caracas: Sociedad de Ciencias Naturales La Salle, 1979. 381 p.: bibl., ill., indexes, plates (Monografía; 24)

Consists of more than 1200 color photos of vegetation in city of Caracas with descriptive material. Useful references for entire region adjacent to the capital.

5202 Mago Leccia, Francisco. Los peces de agua dulce de Venezuela. Caracas: Depto. de Relaciones Públicas de Lagoven, 1978. 35 p.: bibl., ill. (Ecología. Cuadernos Lagoven)

Describes fresh water fishes of Venezuela with some attention to distributional features.

5203 Mendoza de Armas, Cesar. La agroclimatología, su importancia en el desarrollo agrícola. Caracas: Ministerio de Agricultura y Cría, Dirección General de Desarrollo Agrícola, 1981. 250 p.: bibl., ill., map (Comunicaciones agrícolas)

Summary of climatic classification efforts and use of these (primarily Thornthwaite) for defining Venezuela's livestock and cotton regions. Clearly written with useful map and bibliography.

5204 Morales Paul, Isidro. La delimitación de áreas marinas y sub-marinas al norte de Venezuela. Caracas: Academia de Ciencias Políticas y Sociales, 1983. 315 p.: bibl., ill., index (Biblioteca de la Academia. Serie Estudios; 9)

Study of the determination of maritime space in the Caribbean with special reference to Venezuela's coastal waters.

5205 Perna, Claudio. Evolución de la geografía urbana de Caracas. Caracas: Facultad de Humanidades y Educación, Univ. Central de Venezuela, 1981. 191 p.: bibl., ill.

Explains growth of Caracas historically by geographical methods. Principal changes, mostly distinguished by lack of planning, began during present century when petroleum became important in the Venezuelan economy.

5206 Petróleo y ecodesarrollo en Venezuela. Dorothea Mezger, comp. Georgias Garriga et al. Caracas: Instituto Latinoamericano de Investigaciones Sociales: Editorial Ateneo de Caracas, 1981. 445 p.: bibl., ill., maps.

Political-economic geography of natural resources in Venezuela with distribution maps of coal deposits, petroleum, uranium, etc.

5207 Santo Tomé de Guayana, Angostura o Ciudad Bolívar. Compilación y comentarios de Rafael Pineda. Ciudad Bolívar, Venezuela?: Asamblea Legislativa del Estado Bolívar, 1980. 2 v.: bibl., ill.

Reprints of major portions of monographs or articles dealing with city of Guayana (Ciudad Bolívar) from earliest literature through geographical writings (Vila) to ca. 1978.

5208 Schael, Guillermo José. Caracas, la ciudad que no vuelve. 3a ed., ampliada. Caracas: Gráficas Armitano, 1980. 224 p.: plates (some col.)

Book of b/w and color photographs depicting aspects of life in Caracas during first half of 20th century.

5209 Documento preliminar para la elaboración del Plan Nacional de Conservación, Defensa y Mejoramiento del Ambiente. Elaborado por Oficina del Plan Nacional del Ambiente. Caracas: Ministerio del Ambiente y de los Recursos Naturales Renovables, Dirección General de Planificación y Ordenación del Ambiente, 1980. 3 v. (585 p.): bibl., ill., maps (Serie de planes; DGSPOA/PL/24)

Valuable spatial investigation with maps illustrating distribution of numerous physical and human geographical phenomena for Venezuela. Planners' recommendations stress integrating government agencies with other institutions interested in development.

5210 Zinck, Alfred. Valles de Venezuela. Caracas: Lagoven, 1980? 150 p.: bibl., ill., plates (some col.) (Cuadernos Lagoven. El Hombre y su ambiente)

Views Venezuela through its numerous valleys with various groupings and taxonomic explanations. Includes useful air photos and colored block diagrams. Analyzes human use of different valley types. Geographers and geologists will appreciate non-encyclopedic approach to Venezuelan physical phenomena.

BRAZIL

MARIO HIRAOKA, *Professor of Geography, Millersville University of Pennsylvania*

AS IN PREVIOUS VOLUMES OF *HLAS*, the task of selecting studies that accurately reflect current issues poses a major problem. The fact that Brazilian geography encompasses such a wide range of topics as well as such regional diversity in addition to space restrictions imposed by *HLAS* and this contributing editor's particular interests, all combine to exacerbate the problem of providing a balanced view of the literature. What follows, then, is not an ideally comprehensive or balanced presentation of geographical sources on Brazil but rather, a partial selection resulting from the above constraints and preferences.

Areal comparisons of works annotated below show marked differences among regions. Topics related to Amazonia and the Northeast dominate the list. Unlike a decade ago, Amazonian studies no longer consist of mere descriptions of activities and events. Recent publication of research based on long-term observations and evaluations will facilitate the formulation of ecological and socioeconomic interpretations (see, for example, items **5246, 5307, 5311,** and **5318**). The continued inflow of farmers into Rondônia and accelerated mining developments in Carajás have prompted responses by specialists, environmentalists in particular. (items **5263, 5277, 5295,** and **5320**). The five-year drought, 1979–84, that caused much economic and human disruptions in the Northeast has exacerbated the already complex problems of the region. Many still view climate as the main culprit for its underdevelopment (items **5212, 5257,** and **5284**). Others attribute the region's social and economic difficulties to institutional and structural inefficiencies. A number of valuable contributions based on field inquiries have appeared (items **5241, 5252,** and **5308**). Brooks's essay (item **5221**) and the reports contained in the *Géographie et écologie de la Paraíba* (item **5254**) improve our understanding of difficulties encountered by rural inhabitants of the Northeast. In contrast to the northern regions, publications on the southern and central western portions are limited. Socioeconomic inequalities resulting from the modernization and capitalization of farming in São Paulo and Paraná are beginning to command attention (item **5261**), while research on ethnic communities, ecological changes and regional surveys continues as before (item **5233, 5234, 5276,** and **5302**). Dickenson's (item **5237**) text serves as a good introduction and synthesis of the variety of changes currently underway in the country.

There are few methodological and theoretical works among those annotated below. Katzman's (item **5268**) review of Manuel Correia de Andrade's seminal work on Northeast Brazil as well as his comments on the role geography plays in the formulation of economic development policy and evaluation, illuminate our assessment of the discipline. Critical evaluations of geographic theories and concepts as well as new directions in the field are offered by Santos (items **5309**). Ideas and methods developed in other areas and subjects as well as their potential for adaptation are discussed in works by Incao (item **5261**), Azevedo (item **5216**), and Takahashi and Yoshikae (item **5319**).

The topical coverage of Brazil is so varied that a representative selection is difficult. Fields which command much attention, such as demographic change, continue to lead in number of publications. They are exemplified by analyses treating the regional, rural-urban, and rural-rural population shifts, based on the 1980 census (items **5231, 5262, 5281,** and **5317**). Demography will continue to be of interest to a variety of specialists, a fact that reflects the eclectic nature of migration and growth phenomena (item **5211a**). The rapid population concentration and ensuing expansion of metropolitan regions with their problematic consequences and attempts at solving them continue to be analyzed from many perspectives (items **5224** and **5301**). Among urban areas, São Paulo, projected to be the world's second largest city within the next decade, has received the greatest attention (items **5260, 5300, 5324,** and **5329**). Brazilian efforts toward attaining energy independence have resulted in the creation of a rich data base. Individuals interested in energy-related topics (e.g., ethanol program, petroleum production, hydroelectric power generation) will be highly rewarded by Brazilian works as in, for example, items **5226, 5303, 5304,** and **5314**. The historical interpretation of Brazilian landscapes is aided by the continued publication of accounts by naturalists such as Adalbert (item **5211**), Avé-Lallemant (item **5215**), Burmeister (item **5223**), Debret (item **5235**), Freyreiss (item **5251**), Leal (item **5271**), Saint-Hilaire (item **5306**). Essays in historical geography worthy of mention are those by Dean (item **5333** and **5334**), Camargo (item **5224**), and Sales (item **5308**), explaining the metamorphosis of São Paulo state landscapes. Monographs on *municípios*, a source often overlooked, may be of potential value for spatial reconstructions. Pernambuco has begun to publish a monographic series on its municipalities, some of which are annotated below (items **5256, 5290, 5322,** and **5328**). Major disruptions of Brazil's environmental balance brought about by large-scale agricultural, mining, and power projects in the tropical rain forests, savannas, and coastal areas, have led to further investigations of tropical ecosystems and their inhabitants. The results of such research are beginning to appear in a variety of journals as well as books and are exemplified by the following authors: Bandeira (item **5217**); Hecht (item **5259**); Jordan and Russell (item **5266**); Leopoldo, Franken, and Matsui (item **5272**); Pebayle (item **5293**); Salati *et al.* (item **5307**); Silveira (item **5313**); Smith (item **5315**); and Uhl (item **5327**).

5211 Adalbert, Prinz von Preussen. Brasil, Amazonas, Xingú. Tradução de Eduardo Lima Castro. Apresentação e notas de Mário Guimarães Ferri. São Paulo: Editora da Univ. de São Paulo; Belo Horizonte: Livraria Itatiaia Editora, 1977. 243 p.: bibl. (Col. Reconquista do Brasil; 34)

Descriptions of mid-19th century Rio de Janeiro and lower Amazon valley.

5211a Aldunate, Adolpho *et al.* Estudos de população; estudo de caso: dinâmica populacional, transformações sócio-econômicas, atuação das instituições. v. 1, São José dos Campos. v. 4, Sertãozinho. v. 5,

Cachoeira de Itapemirim. v. 6, Santa Cruz do Sul. v. 7, Recife. v. 8, Instituições e reprodução. São Paulo: CEBRAP, 1976?-1982. 6 v.: bibl., ill., tables.

Consists of demographic case studies of distinctive parts of Brazil. Each vol. is organized around following topics: population dynamics, socioeconomic characteristics, and institutional roles in demographic parameters.

5212 Alves, Joaquim. História das secas: séculos XVII a XIX; homenagem ao primeiro centenário da abolição mossoroense. 2a ed. Natal: Assembléia Legislativa do Rio Grande do Norte; Mossoró: Fundação Guimarães Duque: Escola Superior de Agricultura de Mossoró, 1982. 242 p. (Col. Mossoroense; 225)

Attempt to portray drought and its consequences in Northeast during colonial period. Divided into three pts.: 1) 17th- and 18th-century droughts; 2) droughts according to 19th-century travelers and naturalists; and 3) 19th-century planners' and government's perception of and reaction to droughts.

5213 Andrade, Gilberto Osório de and **Rachel Caldas Lins.** João Pais, do Cabo: o patriarca, seus filhos, seus engenhos. Com estudo geneológico por Silvio Pais Barreto. Recife: Editôra Massangana: Fundação Joaquim Nabuco, 1982. 1 v.

Historical sketches of colonial sugar cane plantations in Pirapama drainage basin of northeast Pernambuco.

5214 Austin, Daniel F. and **Paulo B. Cavalcante.** Convolvuláceas da Amazônia. Belém: Conselho Nacional de Desenvolvimento Científico e Tecnológico, Instituto Nacional de Pesquisas da Amazônia, Museu Paraense Emílio Goeldi, 1982. 134 p.: bibl., ill. (Publicações avulsas; 36)

Contribution toward bridging the lacuna on the *Convolvulaceae* family. Discusses 132 taxa, including 125 species and seven varieties and subspecies.

5215 Avé-Lallemant, Robert. No Rio Amazonas, 1859. Tradução, Eduardo de Lima Castro. Belo Horizonte: Editora Itatiaia; São Paulo: Editôra da Univ. de São Paulo, 1980. 283 p. (Col. Reconquista do Brasil. Nova série; 20)

Traveler's account of Brazilian coast from Recife to Belém, and Amazon and

Solimões rivers to Peruvian border. Interesting glimpses of mid-19th century people and environment.

5216 Azevedo, Eliane S. Sobrenomes no Nordeste e suas relações com a heterogeneidade étnica (IPE/EE, 13:1, 1983, p. 103–116, bibl., graphs, table)

Attempts to correlate last names and ethnic backgrounds from sample surveys in Bahia. Contends that religious names are associated with blacks, while plant-animal names indicate aboriginal ancestry. Chronological changes in the distribution of last names serve as indices for investigating migrations and racial mixtures.

5217 Bandeira, Adelmar Gomes and **Paulo Celso S. Souza.** Influência do Pinheiro, *Pinus Caribaea*, sobra a fauna do solo na Amazônia. Belém: Conselho Nacional de Desenvolvimento Científico e Tecnológico, Instituto Nacional de Pesquisas da Amazônia, Museu Paraense Emílio Goeldi, 1982. 13 p.: bibl., plate, tables (Nova série zoologia; 114)

Study of soil faunae in areas planted with exotic trees and pastures show considerable differences from those of native species. Suggests that in timber and pasture projects, greater emphasis should be given to raising native species which are better adapted to local ecological conditions.

5218 Becker, Bertha K. Geopolítica da Amazônia: a nova fronteira de recursos. Prefácio de Orlando Valverde. Rio de Janeiro: Zahar Editores, 1982. 233 p.: bibl., ill., maps (A Terra e o homem)

Collection of articles on Amazonia, based on field research, offers significant insights on aspects of Amazonian development, including urban network changes, government planning and population movements, land use changes, and resource allocation and the State's role.

5219 Brazilian geographical studies. Organizers, Bertha K. Becker and Pedro Pinchas Geiger. Belo Horizonte: Comissão Nacional da União Geográfica Internacional, 1978. 397 p.: ill.

Collection of 20 articles on various aspects of Brazil, seen from a number of theoretical perspectives. Topics include geomorphology, geographical education, demography, regional development, and manufacturing geography.

5220 Brito, Maristella de Azevedo and **Olindina Vianna Mesquita.** Expansão espacial e modernização da agricultura brasileira no período 1970–75 (IBGE/R, 44:1, jan./março 1982, p. 3–49, maps, tables)
Uses census data to review agrarian changes that occurred 1970–75, especially increases in farming areas, production units, and agricultural input industries.

5221 Brooks, Reuben H. The adversity of Brazilian drought (Geojournal [Wiesbaden, FRG] 6:2, 1982, p. 121–128)
Examines differential adjustments to drought among residents of four ecological zones within Ceará state. Adaptive responses differed according to variables like ecological zones, farming scale, and age of head of household.

5222 Bunker, Stephen G. The cost of modernity: inappropriate bureaucracy, inequality, and development program failure in the Brazilian Amazon (JDA, 16:4, July 1982, p. 573–596, tables)
Evaluates politically imposed institutions in Amazonian colonization areas. These new government institutions, instead of hastening rural development as they were intended to, have aggravated socioeconomic inequalities and led toward project failures.

5223 Burmeister, Hermann. Viagem ao Brasil: através das províncias do Rio de Janeiro e Minas Gerais: visando especialmente a história natural dos distritos auri-diamantíferos. Tradução de Manoel Salvaterra e Hubert Schoenfeldt. Nota bio-bibliográfica, Augusto Meyer. Belo Horizonte: Editora Itatiaia; São Paulo: Editora da Univ. de São Paulo, 1980. 372 p.: bibl., ill. (Col. Reconquista do Brasil. Nova série; 23)
Consists of naturalist's observations, based on 5-month stay in Brazil, of region between Rio de Janeiro and Minas Gerais.

5224 Camargo, José Francisco de. Crescimento da população no Estado de São Paulo e seus aspectos econômicos. São Paulo: Instituto de Pesquisas Econômicas, 1981. 3 v. in 2: bibl., ill., col. maps, tables (Ensaios econômicos; 14–14a)
Study of relationship between population and economic growth in São Paulo state. Believes that demographic and economic growth prior to early 20th century were closely associated with expansion of coffee plantations. Distribution and migration of people also were influenced by changing locations of coffee regions. Sedentariness or settlement of population begins in the wake of land use changes in former coffee lands and establishment of manufacturing industries. Describes role of foreign immigrants in state's economic development.

5225 Cascudo, Luís da Câmara. História da alimentação no Brasil. v. 1, Cardápio indígena, dieta africana, ementa portuguêsa. v. 2, Cozinha brasileira. 2a ed. Belo Horizonte: Editora Itatiaia; São Paulo: Editôra da Univ. de São Paulo, 1983. 2 v. (926 p.): bibl., ill. (Col. Reconquista do Brasil. Nova série; 79–80)
Encyclopedia and chronology of Brazilian cuisine, its origins and folklore. Useful and interesting guide to Brazilian food.

5226 Caufield, Catherine. Dam the Amazon full stream ahead (AMNH/NH, 92:7, July 1983, p. 60–67, ill.)
From an ecological perspective, comments on hydroelectric projects underway in Amazonia. Author's preconceived views about dams and reservoirs in the region provide a gloomy picture of the future.

5227 Cavalcante, Paulo B. Frutas comestíveis da Amazônia. v. 3. Belém: Conselho Nacional de Desenvolvimento Científico e Tecnológico, Instituto Nacional de Pesquisas da Amazônia, Museu Paraense Emílio Goeldi, 1979. 61 p.: bibl., ill., plates, tables (Publicações avulsas; 33)
Vol. 3 of set, a catalog of native fruits of Amazonia, will be of interest to those studying traditional farming in the region.

5228 Cavalcanti, Clóvis de Vasconcelos *et al.* Nordeste do Brasil: um desenvolvimento conturbado. Recife: Editora Massangana: Fundação Joaquim Nabuco, 1981. 116 p.: ill. (Série Estudos pesquisas; 20)
Synthesis of economic development attempts in Northeast. Discusses variety of topics, including economy, environment, and demographic changes. For economist's comment see item **3756.**

5229 Christofoletti, Antônio. Geomorfologia fluvial. São Paulo: Editora E. Blücher, 1981. 1 v.: bibl., ill., indexes.
Intended as a textbook on fluvial geomorphology, present vol. attempts to explain processes and mechanisms observed in river channels. Chaps. 1–2 outline notions of

fluvial flow and sediment transport, while chap. 3 analyzes geometric characteristics of river channels. Last two secs. are intended to explain longitudinal profiles and typology of channels. Illustrated with numerous Brazilian examples.

Coelho, Aristides Pinto. A Antártida: nos confins dos três mares. See item **5121**.

5230 Conceição, Antônio José da. A mandioca. Cruz das Almas: Univ. Federal da Bahia, Escola de Agronomia, 1979. 382 p.: bibl., ill.
Provides summary of physical properties, cultivation techniques, diseases, and by-products of manioc.

5231 Costa, Célia Diogo Alves da; Maria Beatriz Afonso Lopes; Aida L.F. de Souza; and Iêda Siqueira. Primeiros comentários aos resultados do censo demográfico de 1980 (IBGE/RBE, 42:167, julho/set. 1981, p. 167–196, maps, tables)
Describes two aspects of 1970–80 demographic changes, regional and metropolitan. Report based on preliminary results of 1980 demographic census.

5232 Costa, Francisco Augusto Pereira da. Arredores do Recife. Com artigo sobre o bairro de Capunga de José Antônio Gonsalves de Mello. Prefácio, Leonardo Dantas Silva. Recife: Prefeitura da Cidade do Recife, Secretaria de Educação e Cultura, Fundação de Cultura Cidade do Recife, 1981. 161 p.: ill., plates (Col. Recife; 10)
Interesting vignettes of late 19th-century life around Recife.

5233 Dean, Warren. Deforestation in southeastern Brazil (in Global deforestation and the nineteenth-century world economy. Edited by Richard P. Tucker and J.F. Richards. Durham, N.C.: Duke Univ. Press, 1983, p. 50–67 [Duke Press policy studies])
Most of the once exuberant subtropical Atlantic coastal forest that stretched across Espírito Santo-Minas Gerais-São Paulo has vanished. Provides chronological account of processes that led to this change in flora.

5234 ———. Ecological and economic relationships in frontier history: São Paulo, Brazil (in Essays on frontiers in world history. Arlington: Univ. of Texas: Texas A&M Univ. Press, 1983, p. 71–100, maps)
Provides historical geography of São

Paulo state from a human ecological viewpoint. Describes ecological changes undergone by the flora, fauna, and aboriginal inhabitants, from precolumbian to modern times.

Debes, Célio. O surto ferroviário paulista: a importância de Rio Claro. See *HLAS* 46:3561.

5235 Debret, Jean Baptiste. Viagem pitoresca e histórica ao Brasil. Apresentação, Mário G. Ferri. Tradução e notas, Sérgio Milliet. São Paulo: Editôra da Univ. de São Paulo; Belo Horizonte: Livraria Itatiaia Editora, 1978. 3 v. in 2: bibl., ill., plates (Col. Reconquista do Brasil; 56–57)
Readers will gain insights into early 19th-century Brazilian society from author's account. Debret was one of French artists responsible for establishment of Rio's Academy of Fine Arts. Books are especially useful because of drawings that offer visual images of landscapes and cultural phenomena of the period.

5236 Denis, Ferdinand. Brasil. Prefácio, Mário Guimarães Ferri. Belo Horizonte: Livraria Itatiaia Editôra; São Paulo: Editôra da Univ. de São Paulo, 1980. 434 p.: bibl., ill., index (Col. Reconquista do Brasil; 46)
Superficial vignettes of Brazilian history and society from 16th to early 19th centuries.

5237 Dickenson, John P. Brazil. Foreword by J.M. Houston. New York: Longman, 1982. 219 p.: bibl., ill., index (World's landscapes)
Description and interpretation of Brazilian landscapes from a genetic viewpoint. Multiple landscapes are explained by a number of differing approaches. Book can serve as good introductory text on Brazilian geography.

5238 The Dilemma of Amazonian development. Edited by Emilio F. Moran. Boulder, Colo.: Westview Press, 1983. 347 p.: bibl., ill. (Westview special studies on Latin America and the Caribbean)
Potpourri of articles devoted to development of Amazonia is divided into three pts.: 1) human dimensions of Amazonian development; 2) assessments of current production system; and 3) methodological issues and future research directions. Topics range from fishing activities and agricultural sys-

tems to evaluation of present developments in the region.

5239 Eglin, Jean and Hervé Théry. La pillage de l'Amazonie. Présentation de René Dumont. Postface d'Alain Ruellan. Paris: F. Maspero, 1982. 200 p.: bibl., ill. (Petite collection Maspero; 266)

Informative and valuable background information on current developments in Amazonia. Numerous topics encompass multinational investments, peasant exploitation, and organized attempts to counteract such excesses.

5240 Estudo das potencialidades dos municípios da região geoeconômica de Brasília. v. 1, Cristalina, Go. v. 2, Formosa, Go. v. 3, Luziânia, Go. v. 4, Unaí, M.G. v. 6, Alexânia, Go. v. 7, Abadiânia, Go. v. 8, Pirenópolis, Go. v. 10, Cabeceiras, Go. v. 11, São João d'Aliança, Go. v. 12, Planaltina de Goiás, Go. Brasília: Companhia do Desenvolvimento do Planalto Central (CODEPLAN), 1981. 10 v.: bibls., ill., maps.

Consists of 10 surveys of municípios bordering Brasília. Each vol. follows a standard format that includes demography, economy, infrastructures, and socioeconomic growth potentials.

5241 Estudo de uso do solo e transportes para a região metropolitana de Salvador. v. 1, Cenário sócio-econômico. v. 2, Sistemas urbanos. v. 3, Gerçao de planos alternativos. v. 4, Avaliação das alternativas e estratégia indicada. v. 5, Sistemas de transportes. Salvador: Secretaria do Planejamento, Ciência e Tecnologia, Companhia de Desenvolvimento da Região Metropolitana de Salvador, 1979. 5 v.: bibl., ill., maps.

Multi-vol. set is a quantitative regional analysis of Salvador region designed for land use and transportation planning. [T.L. Martinson]

5243 Estudos de problemas brasileiros: conferências. Fortaleza: Univ. Federal do Ceará (UFC), Pró-Reitoria de Graduação, Coordenação Geral de Estudos de Problemas Brasileiros, 1980. 123 p.: bibl.

Synthesis of socioeconomic problems of Northeast Brazil.

5244 Faber, Gustav. Brasilien: Weltmacht von morgen. 4., neubearb. und erg. Aufl. Tübingen, FRG: Erdmann, 1981. 428 p.:

bibl., ill. (some col.), index (Buchreihe Ländermonographien; 2)

Introduction to the Brazilian people, landscapes, and culture.

5245 Fearnside, Philip M. Brazil's Amazon settlement schemes (Habitat International [Pergamon Press, Oxford, England] 8 : 1, 1984, p. 45–61)

Examines Brazilian government's purposes for developing the Amazon. Attributes limited results of development programs to such factors as conflicting objectives and absence of carrying capacity estimates, among others.

5246 ———. Development alternatives in the Brazilian Amazon: an ecological evaluation (AI/I, 8 : 2, March/April 1983, p. 65–78, ill., table)

Provides list of 14 development options including a short evaluation for each. Believes that developments should benefit local people over an extended period. Moreover, development alternatives should include a variety of options.

5247 ———. Land-use trends in the Brazilian Amazon region as factors in accelerating deforestation (Environmental Conservation [Elsevier Sequoia *for the* Foundation for Environmental Conservation, Lausanne, Switzerland] 10 : 2, Summer 1983, p. 141–148, plates)

Regards continued expansion of cattle ranching activities and pressures to exploit timber resources in Amazonia as main causes of accelerated rainforest deforestation.

5248 ——— and **Judy M. Rankin.** The new Jari: risks and prospects of a major Amazonian development (AI/I, 7 : 6, Nov./Dec. 1982, p. 329–339, tables)

Reports on present status of much publicized Jarí Project. Describes economic and ecologic viabilities of various forestry and agricultural activities under new management.

5249 Ferrarini, Sebastião Antônio. Lábrea, 1881 ontem-hoje 1981. Manaus: Comissão Permanente de Defesa do Patrimônio Histórico e Artístico, Estado do Amazonas, 1981. 192 p.: bibl., ill.

Socioeconomic and historical information about Lábrea, a município of Amazonia.

5250 Frey, Peter *et al.* Amazonien. Zürich, Switzerland: Orell Füssli, 1983. 251 p.: bibl., col. ill., maps, plates.

Pictorial book on contemporary Amazonia. The concise but well balanced account of current activities in the river basin is enhanced by superb photographs.

5251 Freyreiss, Georg Wilhelm. Viagem ao interior do Brasil. Tradução, A. Löfgren. Revisão e notas, Mário Guimarães Ferri. Belo Horizonte: Editora Itatiaia, 1982. 138 p.: bibl., ill. (Col. Reconquista do Brasil. Nova série; 57)

Consists of a naturalist's interpretation of early 19th-century Minas Gerais. Notes strong sociocultural contrasts between coastal and interior Brazil.

5252 García Júnior, Afrânio. Terra de trabalho: trabalho familiar de pequenos produtores. Rio de Janeiro: Paz e Terra, 1983. 1 v.: bibl., ill. (Col. Estudos sobre o Nordeste; 8)

Describes changing socioeconomic conditions among small family farmers in Pernambuco's southern *zona da mata*.

5253 Garlipp, Rubens Cristiano Damas; Ricardo Berger; and José Elidney Pinto Júnior. Recursos florestais brasileiros (OAS/CI, 22:3/4, 1982, p. 13–17, bibl., map, tables)

Evaluation of commercial forestry resources in Brazil, including afforested tracts. Reviews timber potentials of each of the five major regions.

5254 Géographie et écologie de la Paraíba, Brésil. v. 2. Bordeaux, France: Ministère des universités, Centre national de la recherche scientifique, Centre d'études de géographie tropicale, 1984. 1 v.: bibl., ill., maps (some col.) (Travaux et documents de géographie tropicale, 0336–5522; 50)

Contemporary geographic interpretation of Paraíba that consists of 15 essays analyzing socioeconomic, spatial, and ecological transformations in eastern half of state. Chiefly based on fieldwork, studies provide accurate insights into rural and urban changes in the *agreste* and *zona da mata*.

5255 A Grande São Paulo hoje. São Paulo: Empresa Metropolitana de Planejamento da Grande São Paulo (EMPLASA), 1982. 105 p.: bibl., ill., maps (some col.)

Synopsis of Greater São Paulo includes historical sketch, demographic characteristics, and socioeconomic changes as well as good illustrations and brief but useful bibliography.

5256 Gravatá. Recife: Governo de Pernambuco, Secretaria de Planejamento, 1982. 64 p.: ill. (Série Monografias municipais)

Socioeconomic synopsis of a município in ecologically transitional zone between *mata* and *agreste* in Pernambuco state.

Greenfield, Sidney M. Barbadians in the Brazilian Amazon. See *HLAS 46:3584.*

5257 Guerra, Paulo de Brito. A civilização da seca: o Nordeste é uma história mal contada. Fortaleza: Ministério do Interior, Depto. Nacional de Obras Contra as Secas, 1981. 324 p.: bibl., ill. (some col.)

Informative book on drought-prone Brazilian Northeast. Three topics are reviewed: 1) official strategies to lessen impact of droughts; 2) people and environment; and 3) proposals for region's agricultural development.

5258 Guerreiro, Manoel Gabriel. Desenvolvimento e perspectiva do setor mineral na Amazônia: perigo estratégico da desnacionalização (A Amazônia Brasileira em Foco [Rio de Janeiro] 14, 1981/1982, p. 51–82, tables)

Summary of mining activities in Amazonia warns about increasing participation of foreign enterprises in exploitation of region's minerals.

5259 Hecht, Susanna B. Agroforestry in the Amazon basin: practice, theory and limits of a promising land use (*in* Amazonia: agriculture and land use research. Cali, Colombia: Centro Internacional de Agricultura Tropical, 1982, p. 331–371)

Reports on advantages of employing agroforestry techniques for agricultural developments in the Amazon basin.

Heidemann, Dieter. Arbeitsteilung und regionale Mobilität an der Peripherie des Weltmarktes: zur Binnenwanderung in Nordostbrasilien. See item **3786.**

5260 Homem, Maria Cecília Naclério. Higienópolis: grandeza e decadência de um bairro paulistano. São Paulo: Prefeitura do Município de São Paulo, Secretaria Municipal de Cultura, Depto. de Patrimônio Histórico, Div. do Arquivo Histórico, 1980? 231 p.: bibl., facsims., ill. (part folded), maps, plans (Série História dos bairros de São Paulo; 17)

Dynamics of urban changes unleashed by the coffee boom can be observed in Higienópolis, a São Paulo's exclusive residential district. Traces origin and evolution of the *bairro* and notes current changes.

5261 Incao, Maria da Conceição d'. O *bóia-fria*: acumulação e miséria. 9a ed. Petrópolis: Editôra Vozes, 1983. 1 v.: bibl.

Study examines rural wage earners or *bóias frias* in southern Brazil. Uses as case study the evolution of laborer-employer relationship and deteriorating living conditions among *bóias frias* of western São Paulo.

5262 Informações demográficas de Pernambuco: movimentos migratórios, 1950–80. Recife: Fundação de Informações para o Desenvolvimento de Pernambuco (FIDEPE), 1981. 59 p.: bibl., maps.

Reviews migratory changes in Pernambuco (1950–80). Rural-urban migrations are still underway, with Recife as principal destination. Inter-state movements are declining in favor of intrastate moves. Within the state, largest flows occur from best agrometeorological areas.

5263 Instituto Brasileiro de Análises Sociais e Econômicas (IBASE). Carajás: o Brasil hipoteca seu futuro. Rio de Janeiro: Achiamé, 1983. 157 p.: bibl., ill.

Reviews Great Carajás Program, underway in eastern Amazonia. Describes project's environmental and economical impacts and then outlines ecologically and financially viable alternatives.

5264 International Geographical Union. Brazil National Commission. Latin American regional conference. v. 1, Brazilian geographical studies. v. 2, Simpósio e mesas redondas. Rio de Janeiro: IBGE, 1982. 2 v.: bibl.

Consists of proceedings of the Union's Latin American Regional Conference. Vol. 1 contains 19 articles on Brazilian geography and geographers, mostly devoted to spatial organization and biased toward urban topics. Vol. 2 consists of miscellaneous subjects discussed at symposia and round tables.

5265 Itapuã, análise preliminar do espaço geográfico. Pôrto Alegre: Univ. Federal do Rio Grande do Sul, Pró-Reitoria de Extensão, Depto. de Geografia, 1982. 203 p.: bibl., ill., plates (Texto para discussão; 7)

Describes demographic and economic changes of Itapuã, which lies in the periphery of Pôrto Alegre's metropolitan region.

5266 Jordan, Carl F. and Charles E. Russell. Jari: Productivity of plantations and loss of nutrients due to slash and burn (AI/I, 8 : 5, Sept./Oct. 1983, p. 294–297, bibl., ill.)

On the basis of experiments conducted in Amazonian Jarí forest, summarizes nutrient dynamics from primary forest to plantation. For a short period, high pulp production is possible at expense of nutrients accumulated by primary forest. However, as the afforested species do not have adequate time to restore lost minerals, nutrient contents in subsequent plantings decline.

5267 Jost, Stéphane. Nordeste brésilien: à nouveau la famine (CJN, 258, fév. 1984, p. 15–16, map, plate, table)

Brief note on 1979–84 drought and its effects on Brazilian Northeast.

5268 Katzman, Martin T. *The land and people of Northeast Brazil:* is geography a useful guide to development policy? (UC/EDCC, 32 : 3, April 1984, p. 633–638)

Review essay on Manuel Correia de Andrade's *The land and people of Northeast Brazil* serves as reference point for evaluating current status of geography in influencing economic development policies. Recognizes value of geography for area studies but believes that the atheoretical nature of the discipline is ill-suited for policy formulations and for evaluating propositions on development and underdevelopment. For economist's comment, see item **3791**.

5269 Klammer, Gerhard. Die Paläowüste des Pantanal von Matto Grosso und die pleistozäne Klimageschichte der brasilianischen Randtropen (ZG, 26 : 4, Dez. 1982, p. 393–416, bibl., graphs, maps, tables)

Explains unintegrated drainage and unusual relief features of the Pantanal by using SLAR images. Region's morphological and drainage characteristics were formed in a period of drier climate, as evidenced by sand flats, dunes, and coalesced alluvial cones.

5270 Koller, Osvino Leonardo *et al.* Aspectos sócio-econômicos da citricultura em Santa Catarina. Florianópolis: Empresa Catarinense de Pesquisa Agropecuária, 1982. 120 p.: ill.

Brazil has become one of the major producers of citrus. However, little is known about its producers, areas of cultivation, and marketing channels. Present synopsis offers some ideas about the citrus industry in Santa Catarina.

5271 Leal, Oscar. Viagem ás terras goyanas: Brazil central. Apresentação de Atico Vilas Boas da Mota. Ed. em fac-simile. Goiânia: Univ. Federal de Goiás (UFG), 1980. 255 p.: ill., plates (Col. Documentos goianos; 4. Publicação; 11)

Travel account of southern Goiás and portions of Mato Grosso. Although author's descriptions are not as complete as those of Saint Hilaire, Gardner, Castelnau, Kidder, Condreau, Pohl, Aires do Casal, or Vilhena, they nevertheless add substantive information on late 19th-century people and society.

5272 Leopoldo, Paulo Rodolfo; W. Franken; and E. Matsui. Hydrological aspects of the tropical rain forest in central Amazon (AI/I, 9:3, May/June 1984, p. 125-131, bibl., maps, tables)

Examines rainforest's role on the hydrologic cycle through an analysis of measurements taken from two upland rainforest sites near Manaus. In the present ecosystem, high amount of water returned to atmosphere as water vapor is a key element in maintenance of water balance. Deforestation will cause an imbalance in present cycling mechanism.

5273 Linhares, Maria Yedda Leite and Francisco Carlos Teixeira Silva. História da agricultura brasileira: combates e controvérsias. Prefácio, Francisco Iglésias. São Paulo: Brasiliense, 1981. 170 p.: bibl.

Attempts to deal with issues related to three topics: 1) ideas and ideologies that permeate interpretation of agriculture; b) methods and source materials employed in understanding Brazilian agriculture; and 3) food production in a colonial society.

5274 Lopes Neto, Alfredo. Algumas informações sobre jojoba: *Simmondsia chinensis*. Fortaleza: Fundação Instituto de Planejamento do Ceará, 1982. 102 p.: col. ill.

Discusses agronomic characteristics of *jojoba* plant (*Simmondsia chinensis*) for the semi-arid Northeast.

5275 Loewenstein, Pedro *et al.* Bibliografia e índice da geologia da Amazônia legal brasileira, 1965-1975. Belém: Conselho Nacional de Desenvolvimento Científico e Tecnológico, Instituto Nacional de Pesquisas da Amazônia, Museu Paraense Emílio Goeldi, 1980. 176 p.: indexes (Publicações avulsas; 35)

Geological bibliography of Brazilian Amazon covers 1965-75. Contains 1,247 references and is subdivided into 17 sections. Of value to geographers is a section on surface geology, including geomorphology and the Quaternary. For bibliographer's comment, see *HLAS 46:29.*

5276 Luyten, Sonia Maria Bibe. Comunicação e aculturação: a colonização holandesa no Paraná. São Paulo: Edições Loyola, 1981. 151 p.: bibl., ill., maps (Série Comunicação; 22)

Study of cultural changes at Carambeí, a Dutch immigrant community in Paraná state. Evaluates acculturation processes from an interethnic communication perspective. Perceives influence of various means of communication with the national society (e.g., the Church, economic relations, educational system, transportation networks) as acculturating agents.

5277 Madeira, Luiz Carlos Lopes *et al.* Salvar Carajás. Prefácio de Pinheiro Machado Netto. Porto Alegre: L&PM Editores, 1982. 103 p.

Debate concerning multinational involvement in mining at the Great Carajás Project.

5278 Madeiras da Amazônia: características e utilização = Amazonian timbers: characteristics and utilization. v. 1, Floresta Nacional do Tapajós. Brasília: Instituto Brasileiro de Desenvolvimento Florestal (IBDF): Conselho Nacional de Desenvolvimento Científico e Tecnológico, 1981? 1 v.: col. ill., index.

Catalog of 53 tree species from the Tapajós National Forest notes potential uses by lumber industry. Also describes trees' physical and mechanical properties, selected according to their prevalence and volume.

5279 **Maia, Tom** and **Thereza Regina de Camargo Maia.** O folclore das tropas, tropeiros e cargueiros no Vale do Paraíba. Rio de Janeiro: Ministério da Educação e Cultura, Secretaria da Cultura, Fundação Nacional de Arte, Instituto Nacional do Folclore, 1981. 125 p.: bibl., ill., map.

Account of mule trains, muleteers, and their folklore in Middle Paraíba Valley, São Paulo state. Provides interesting glimpses of traditional means of transportation in mountainous portions of region.

5280 **Maio, Celeste Rodrigues.** Projeto RADAM: análise e interpretação das folhas geológicas; Bacia Maranhão, Piauí (IBGE/R, 44:1, jan./março 1982, p. 147–161, bibl., graphs, photos)

Radar images from Projeto Radam offer numerous resource evaluation and planning possibilities. In the study, geological sheets of the Maranhão-Piauí basin are used to formulate a geomorphological interpretation.

5281 **Martine, George.** Expansão e retração do emprêgo na fronteira agrícola (Revista de Economía Política [Editôra Brasiliense, São Paulo] 2/3, julho/set. 1982, p. 53–76)

The traditional Brazilian solution to increase agricultural production and to ameliorate problem of excess rural labor has been to expand agricultural frontier into formerly unoccupied terrain. Article provides some reflections on potentials of agricultural frontier to generate employments through an examination of demographic changes in Paraná, Central West, and Amazônia (1970–80).

5282 **Matsuda, Noriyuki.** Spatial configurations of the Brazilian states with respect to human migration (Latin American Studies [Univ. of Tsukuba, Sakura-Mura, Japan] 5, 1983, p. 39–56, ill., tables)

Applies multidimensional scaling techniques to 1970 migration data to determine nation's functional regionalization. Identifies Minas Gerais, Rio de Janeiro, São Paulo, and Mato Grosso as core states, and Bahia, Paraná, and Federal District as semi-core states. Together, they form so-called central region.

5283 **Meggiolaro, Amélia Maria** et al. Baixa renda, um problema habitacional em Petrópolis. Rio de Janeiro: Livraria Editora Cátedra: *em convênio com a* Fundação Nacional de Arte, Secretaria de Assuntos Culturais, Ministério da Educação e Cultura, 1980. 151 p.: bibl., ill.

Study of low-income neighborhood in Petrópolis, a Rio de Janeiro metropolitan *município.* Attempts to offer solutions to problems of economically deprived groups generated by urban expansion.

5284 **Melões na caatinga?** (Interior [Ministério do Interior, Brasília] 9:50, maio/junho 1983, p. 20–36, graphs, maps, photos, tables)

Informative article outlines plans of Comissão de Estudos para o Aproveitamento Integrado dos Recursos Hídricos para o Semi-Arido Nordestino to irrigate Northeast's drought-prone areas with waters drawn from São Francisco River.

5285 **Moraes, Luciano Jacques de.** Serras e montanhas do Nordeste. Estudos petrográficos por Djalma Guimarães. 2a ed. Mossoró: Escola Superior de Agricultura de Mossoró, 1977. 2 v.: bibl., ill. (Col. mossoroense. Série C livros; 35)

Physiographic and petrographic investigation of highlands in Northeast Brazil. Originally published in 1924, these vols. place heavy emphasis on geology of Paraíba and Rio Grande do Norte states.

5286 **Moreira, Raimundo.** O Nordeste brasileiro: uma política regional de industrialização. Rio de Janeiro: Paz e Terra, 1979. 173 p.: bibl.

Review of industrial development policies in Northeast and their regional outcomes.

5287 **Nishizawa, Toshie** and **José Arnaldo Sales.** The urban temperature in Rio de Janeiro, Brazil (Latin American Studies [Univ. of Tsukuba, Sakura-Mura, Japan] 5, 1983, p. 29–38, bibl., graphs, ill., map)

Authors combine their data on Rio de Janeiro's maximum and minimum temperature with those collected by the Instituto Nacional de Meteorologia. The combined data are used to explain spatial differences in urban temperature.

Nordeste: as pequenas cidades e o planejamento local. See item **3815.**

5288 **Novos rumos da geografia brasileira.** Organizador, Milton Santos. São

Paulo: Editora HUCITEC, 1982. 219 p.: bibl., ill. (Geografia. Teoria e realidade)
Presents some of the purported theoretical views of Brazilian geography.

5289 A Organização do espaço na faixa da Transamazônica. v. 1, Introdução, sudoeste amazônico, Rondônia e regiões vizinhas. Rio de Janeiro: IBGE, 1979. 1 v.: bibl., ill., maps.
Reports on changing spatial organization in southwest Amazon as result of agricultural and mining activities that began with highway construction projects in late 1960s. Concentrates primarily on colonization activities in Rondônia territory.

5290 Ouricuri. Recife: Fundação de Informações para o Desenvolvimento de Pernambuco (FIDEPE), 1982. 65 p.: bibl., ill. (Série Monografias municipais; 7)
Outlines biophysical and socioeconomic features of western Pernambuco *município*. Part of monographic series to disseminate geographic information on lesser known municipalities of this state.

5291 Ouro. Edited by Adalberto Ferreira Pinto. Belo Horizonte: Metais de Minas Gerais (METAMIG), 1981. 222 p.: bibl., ill. (some col.)
Well illustrated book on gold (e.g., geologic aspects, history of exploitation, economic role).

5292 Pandolfo, Clara Martins. Ecologia e desenvolvimento da Amazônia = Ecology and development of the Amazon. Belém: Ministério do Interior, Superintendência do Desenvolvimento da Amazônia, Depto. de Recursos Naturais, 1982. 33 p.: ill.
Presents government's arguments to counteract erroneous notions about ecological changes in Amazonia. Disputes deforestation and savannization rates as reported by others.

5293 Pebayle, Raymond. Mangrove et ethologie humaine au Brésil (AGF/B, 60:496, juin/oct. 1983, p. 231–246, map)
Brief comments on the ecology of mangroves and their uses by local inhabitants. Describes negative effects of mangrove stands by increasing urbanization and industrialization along coastal zone.

5294 Pinto, Aloizio de Arruda. Trópicos úmidos: resumos informativos, bibliografia. Colaboração técnica de Neusa

Catarina Pinheiro Garcia, Nazira Leite Nassar, Divina Aparecida Silva. Brasília: Empresa Brasileira de Pesquisa Agropecuária (EMBRAPA), Depto. de Informação e Documentação, 1978. 2 v.: indexes.
Useful annotated bibliography on Amazonia. Vol. 2 of this set includes 670 annotations of interest to natural scientists and geographers.

5295 Pinto, Lucio Flávio. Carajás: o ataque ao coração da Amazônia. Rio de Janeiro: Editôra Marco Zero: Studio Alfa Fotoletra e Editôra, 1982. 112 p. (Col. Nossos dias; 2)
Journalist voices his apprehensions about viability of the Great Carajás Program. Includes description of projects undertaken and their economic and ecologic consequences.

5296 Potencial de produção de oleaginosas, mamona e dendê. Salvador: Governo do Estado da Bahia, Secretaria do Planejamento, Ciência e Tecnología, Centro de Planejamento e Estudos, 1981. 160 p.: bibl., ill. (Relatórios de pesquisa; 3)
Reports on agricultural and economic possibilities of oil palm and castor bean cultivation in Bahia. Considered as parts of the PROOLEO program, these plants are being evaluated as alternative sources of energy and lubricants.

5297 Prance, Ghillean T. A terminologia dos tipos de florestas amazônicas sujeitas a inundação (Acta Amazônica [Manuas, Brazil] 10:3, 1980, p. 495–504)
Attempt to classify main types of Amazonian floodplain forests. Since there is considerable confusion in the literature, author attempts to offer a new classification. Presents seven types of floodplain forests.

5298 A Questão do aluminio: o presente e o futuro da indústria do aluminio no Brasil (A Amazônia Brasileira em Foco [Rio de Janeiro] 14, 1981/1982, p. 9–49, tables)
Overview of Brazil's aluminum industry. Includes information on uses, ore distribution, processing industries, and industrial policies.

5299 Questões de organização do espaço regional. Gilda Collet Bruna, organizadora. Lauro Bastos Birkholz *et al*. São Paulo: Livraria Nobel: Editôra da Univ. de São Paulo, 1983. 273 p.: bibl., ill.

Collection of articles on spatial organization in Brazil. Covers topics such as metropolitan growth, recreational planning in river basin, and regional development.

5300 Reconstituição da memória estatística da Grande São Paulo. São Paulo: Empresa Metropolitana de Planejamento da Grande São Paulo (EMPLASA), 1980. 256 p.: bibl., ill. (some folded), maps.

Valuable source for understanding metropolitan São Paulo's historical geography. Although limited on descriptive materials, volume's cartographic, photographic, and statistic materials should prove to be of value to those interested in urban history.

5301 Rivière d'Arc, Hélène and Graciela Schneier. Activites informelles et espace: le cas de villes nouvelles de Ciudad Guayana, Venezuela, et Camaçarí, Brésil (UP/TM, 24:95, juillet/sept. 1983, p. 653–667, bibl., maps)

Examines origins of informal sector and spatial characteristics of two new industrial cities: Ciudad Guayana and Camaçarí. Points out differences in their informal sectors from those of old, established, multifaceted cities.

5302 Rönick, Volker. Das nordöstliche Rio Grande do Sul, Brasilien: naturräumliche Gliederung und wirtschaftliche Bewertung. Paderborn, FRG: Schöningh, 1981. 150 p.: bibl., ill. (Münstersche geographische Arbeiten; 13)

Regional study of northeast Rio Grande do Sul describes its four major physiographic regions as well as principal economic zones and distinctive man-environment relations of each. Final sec. covers problems and prospects of each subunit for economic development purposes.

5303 Rothman, Harry; Rod Greenshields; and Francisco Rosillo Callé. The alcohol economy: fuel ethanol and the Brazilian experience. London: F. Pinter, 1983. 188 p.: bibl., ill., plates.

Comprehensive survey of Brazilian ethanol economy. Explores antecedents of National Alcohol Program (PNA), production, technology, environmental effects of large scale alcohol production, and economical and technological feasibilities of ethanol manufacturing in Third World.

5304 Rotstein, Jaime. Soberania e política energética. Rio de Janeiro: F. Alves, 1983. 220 p.: ill.

Proposals for energy independence in Brazil. Argues for an increased use of ethanol and for development of an alcohol engine technology to substitute diesel engines. Believes reliance on ethanol based energy will lessen two of nation's major hardships: foreign indebtedness and petroleum dependence.

5305 Saes, Flávio Azevedo marques de. As ferrovias de São Paulo, 1870–1940. São Paulo: Editôra HUCITEC; Brasília: em convênio com o Instituto Nacional do Livro, Ministério da Educação e Cultura, 1981. 199 p.: bibl., ill. (Col. Estudos históricos)

Discusses rise and fall of São Paulo state railroads. Examines in detail influence of coffee plantations on railroad network, rail transport and development of São Paulo's economy, and economic efficiency of rail lines.

5306 Saint-Hilaire, Auguste de. Viagem a Curitiba e Província de Santa Catarina. Prefácio, Mário G. Ferri. Tradução, Regina Regis Junqueira. São Paulo: Editôra da Univ. de São Paulo; Belo Horizonte: Livraria Itatiaia Editôra, 1978. 209 p.: bibl. (Col. Reconquista do Brasil; 9)

Originally published in French (1851), provides detailed descriptions of customs, land, and people of Paraná and Santa Catarina during early 19th century.

5307 Salati, Eneas; Herbert Otto Roger Shubart; Wolfgang Junk; and Adélia Engrácia de Oliveira. Amazônia: desenvolvimento, integração e ecologia. São Paulo: Editôra Brasiliense, 1983. 327 p.: ill.

Consists of four chaps. of which the first three explain fine interdependency of biophysical elements in Amazonia and how human activities may change this delicate ecological balance. Final chap. offers an overview of human occupation in Brazilian Amazon.

5308 Sales, Teresa. Agreste, agrestes: transformações recentes na agricultura nordestina. Rio de Janeiro: Paz e Terra; São Paulo: CEBRAP, 1982. 196 p.: bibl. (Série Cadernos CEBRAP; 36)

Land reform attempts, new rural legislation, and capitalization and modernization of Brazilian agriculture are unequivocally changing rural landscapes and affecting inhabitants, especially landless and family farmers. Analyzes effects of changing land uses, labor legislation, and fiscal incentives in Northeast, especially the *zona da mata* and *agreste*.

5309 Santos, Mílton. Economia espacial: críticas e alternativas. Tradução de Maria Irene de Q.F. Szmrecsányi. São Paulo: Editôra HUCITEC, 1979. 167 p.: bibl. (Economia & planejamento. Série Teses e pesquisas)

Consists of critical evaluation of various geographical concepts about economic development in LDCs. Reviews various theories including center-periphery, central place theory, and development poles and offers alternatives.

5310 Sarcinella, Luigi. O gigante brasileiro. São Paulo: R. Kempf Editores, 1982. 977 p.: bibl., ill.

Delightful vignettes illustrate the various Brazilian landscapes, peoples, and culture.

5311 Schmink, Marianne. Land conflicts in Amazonia (AES/AE, 9:4, 1982, p. 341–357)

Examination of land disputes between small and large landholders in Amazonia. From a colonization area in southeast Pará, examines evolution and polarization of ideological viewpoints and how they are related to material status and political viewpoints.

5312 Segre, Anna. La localizzazione dell'industria automobilistica in America Latina: il casi di Belo Horizonte, Brasile, e Córdoba, Argentina (SSG/RGI, 90, 1983, p. 251–272)

Brief essay on development of automobile industries in Belo Horizonte and Córdoba emphasizes their social and economic impact on their respective urban areas and regions.

5312a Seminário de Estudos Urbanos, Rio de Janeiro, 1981. Solo urbano: tópicos sobre o uso da terra. Organizador, L.A. Machado da Silva. Luiz Cesar de Queiroz Ribeiro et al. Rio de Janeiro: Zahar Editores, 1982. 95 p.: bibl., ill. (Série Debates urbanos; 1)

Examines question of land uses in urban areas from three angles: 1) effects of land tenure on dwelling construction in a capitalist society; 2) influence of circular causa-

tion theory on a city's internal structure; and 3) effects of legal/institutional mechanisms on social use and ownership of urban land, and their influences on spatial organization.

5313 Silveira, Isolda Maciel da. Quatipuru: agricultores, pescadores e coletores em uma vila amazônica. Belém: Conselho Nacional de Desenvolvimento Científico e Tecnológico, Instituto Nacional de Pesquisas da Amazônia, Museu Paraense Emílio Goeldi, 1979. 82 p.: ill., plates (Publicações avulsas; 34)

Cultural ecological study of rural village in northeast Pará. Contends that its economic system, based on swidden and supplemented by fishing and gathering activities, is able to support a dense population, as well as generate produce for urban markets.

5314 Simpósio sobre Alcool, São Paulo, 1982. Anais: desde a plantação da cana-de-açúcar até o consumo do álcool. São Paulo: Secretaria da Indústria, Comércio, Ciência e Tecnologia, Academia de Ciência do Estado de São Paulo, 1982. 342 p.: ill. (some col.), plates (Publicação ACIESP; 27)

Consists of papers presented at Symposium on Alcohol (São Paulo, 1982). They cover a wide range of topics associated with production, processing, and consumption of ethanol.

5315 Smith, Nigel J.H. Caimans, capybaras, otters, manatees, and man in Amazonia (Biological Conservation [Elsevier Publishing Co., Essex, England] 19:3, 1981, p. 177–187)

Wildlife in riaprian Amazonia has been exploited commercially since colonial times. Focuses on results of aquatic animal harvests, especially for international markets.

5317 Souza, Aida Laura Ferreira de; Iêda Siqueira; and Regina Coeli de Siqueira Lana. Observações sobre a evolução da população rural e urbana no Brasil no período 1940 a 1980 (IBGE/RBE, 42:167, julho/set. 1981, p. 197–215, maps, tables)

Interpretation of rural-urban population changes (1940–80) based on Preliminary Synopsis of 1980 Demographic Census.

5318 Sternberg, Hilgard O'Reilly. Frontières contemporaines en Amazonie brésilienne: quelques conséquences sur l'environnement. Paris: Centre de recherche et documentation sur l'Amérique latine, 1981. 29 p.: bibl., ill., maps.

Brief essay on current agricultural developments in the Brazilian Amazon and their ecological consequences.

5319 Takahashi, Nobuo and Nelson Massatake Yoshikae. Structure de l'espace financier au Brésil (Latin American Studies [Univ. of Tsukuba, Sakura-Mura, Japan] 7, 1983, p. 77–102, bibl., maps)

Spatial structure of Brazilian financial activities is depicted cartographically. Shows causes for concentration of financial activities in Rio de Janeiro-São Paulo-Belo Horizonte axis and uses case studies to explain dynamics of banking networks.

5320 Théry, Hervé. Routes transamazoniennes et réorganization de l'espace: le cas de Rondônia (SGB/COM, 34:133, 1981, p. 5–22)

Explains spatial rearrangement underway in Federal Territory of Rondônia, as a result of recent colonization and highway construction activities.

5321 Thivent, Agnès. En Amazonie orientale, place aux multinationales! (CJN, 248, mars 1983, p. 29–33, map, photos)

Covers eviction of rural squatters as a result of land alienation to mining and agricultural projects operating in areas under the sway of the Carajás project.

Thomas, Vinod. Pollution control in São Paulo, Brazil: costs, benefits, and effects on industrial location. See item **3846.**

5322 Timbaúba. Recife: Fundação de Informações para o Desenvolvimento de Pernambuco (FIDEPE): Fundação de Desenvolvimento Municipal do Interior de Pernambuco (FIAM), 1982. 75 p.: bibl., ill. (Série Monografias municipais; 10)

Socioeconomic and historic synopsis of a northeast Pernambuco município in the *zona da mata*. Vol. is part of monographic series on Pernambuco municipalities.

5223 Tocantins, Leandro. Amazônia, natureza, homem e tempo: uma planificação ecológica. 2a ed., rev. e aum. Rio de Janeiro: Civilização Brasileira, 1982. 177 p.: bibl. (Col. Retratos do Brasil; 165)

Introduction to historical interpretation of Amazonia. Offers interesting glimpses of region, largely based on personal experiences.

5324 Townroe, Peter M. Spatial policy and metropolitan economic growth in São Paulo, Brazil (Geoforum [Pergamon Press, Oxford, England] 15:2, 1984, p. 143–165)

Given the continued rapid growth of São Paulo's metropolitan area and in order to check excessive concentration of its economy and population, government authorities have begun to consider decentralizing by relocating manufacturing industries in the interior. Study based on industrial survey carried out by World Bank (1980–82) in São Paulo. Author offers an alternative planning policy.

5325 Trabalho e condições de vida no Nordeste brasileiro. Inaiá Maria Moreira de Carvalho, Teresa Maria Frota Haguette, organizadoras. São Paulo: Editôra HUCITEC; Brasília: CNPq, 1984. 293 p.: bibl., map (Estudos brasileiros)

Collection of 11 articles on socioeconomic characteristics of Northeastern low-income groups. Articles can be organized according to three topics: livelihood strategies, regional labor structure, and solutions to area's poverty.

5326 Tricart, Jean. El pantanal: un ejemplo del impacto geomorfológico sobre el ambiente (UC/IG, 29, dic. 1982, p. 81–97, bibl., ill.)

Attempts to explain origins of Pantanal landforms. During dry periods of the Quaternary, flood fans were excavated by wind creating numerous lakes and swamps. The Pantanal's varied life forms have established an equilibrium with the landforms. Major changes, such as those on its margins, will create major ecosystemic imbalances.

5327 Uhl, Christopher. You *can* keep a good forest down (AMNH/NH, 92:4, April 1983, p. 70–79, ill.)

Explains rainforest recovery rates according to size of disturbance on forest floor. States that tropical forest destruction in the Amazon may be minimized by altering portions of shifting cultivation systems and adopting them for agricultural developments.

5328 Vitória de Santo Antão. Recife: Fundação de Informações para o Desenvolvimento de Pernambuco (FIDEPE): Fundação de Desenvolvimento Municipal do Interior de Pernambuco (FIAM), 1981. 88 p.: bibl., ill. (Série Monografias municipais; 3)

Brief description of biophysical and socioeconomic characteristics of a Pernambuco *município* on western border of *zona da mata*. Part of monographic series on Pernambuco municipalities.

Weinstein, Barbara. The Amazon rubber boom: 1850–1920. See *HLAS 46:3694.*

5329 Wilheim, Jorge. Projeto São Paulo: propostas para a melhoria da vida urbana. Rio de Janeiro: Paz e Terra, 1982. 241 p.: bibl., ill. (Col. Estudos brasileiros; 62)

Brazilian architect presents interesting ideas on redevelopment of São Paulo. Describes current urban problems (e.g., hous-

ing, health, education) and offers possible solutions.

5330 Zacca, Eliana França dos Santos and **Joaquina Barata Teixeira.** Diagnóstico de recursos humanos da região amazônica. v. 1, Os recursos humanos na economia regional. Belém: Ministério do Interior, Superintendência do Desenvolvimento da Amazônia, Depto. de Recursos Humanos, Div. de Estudos e Avaliação de Recursos Humanos, 1977. 1 v.: bibl.

Vol. 1 of three provides survey of demographic and economic characteristics of northern region (Amazonia).

CARTOGRAPHY

ANDREW M. MODELSKI, *Geography and Map Division, The Library of Congress*

THE MOST SIGNIFICANT DEVELOPMENT in the cartography of Latin America, as reflected in the selected material, is the very large increase in the availability of regional and thematic atlases. Of 32 geographic regions covered in this issue of the *Handbook*, 18 are represented by atlases, many by multiple issues. Argentina (11), Brazil (41), Chile (9), and Colombia (6) accounted for 67 of the 71 recorded volumes, or 35 percent of the 200 maps listed. In previous editions, only some 5 percent of the entries were atlases.

As in previous listings the majority of entries include maps and atlases received and cataloged in the Geography and Map Division of the Library of Congress within the last two years. This record provides an adequate sampling of some 2,000 available reference map and atlases processed for the Latin American region.

The subjects covered in this bibliography reflect the scope of the mapping activities for the region. They depict physical geography, transportation, and most of the other aspects of the socioeconomic and cultural environment. The most prolific are Argentina, Brazil, Chile, Colombia, Mexico, and Peru. Regrettably, map coverage for several countries only includes maps made by outside interests, because no maps were received from the countries themselves. Most of the stimulus for mapping activities in Latin America is provided by individual government agencies and the Pan American Institute of Geography and History, Commission on Cartography which sponsors the production of the region's unified hemispheric map series published at the scale of 1:250,000.

An important *Atlas of Central America and the Caribbean*, scheduled for publication towards the end of 1985, will be annotated in *HLAS 49*. This atlas encompasses subjects that range from natural resources to military strength, population to foreign policy. More than 200 two-color maps and diagrams and text depict the region as a whole and in detail. It was compiled by the London based "Diagram Group."

We also wish to note a most useful and comprehensive Brazilian bibliography on maps and atlases, published by Fundação Instituto Brasileiro de Geografia e Estatística (IBGE), Biblioteca Central, entitled *Mapas e outros materiais cartográficas na Biblioteca Central do IBGE.*

In conclusion, we caution the reader that the items annotated below represent only a very selective sample drawn from recent acquisitions at the Library of Congress. For a more detailed study of the large collection of thousands of maps and atlases of Latin American countries, we invite the reader to visit the Library and examine the maps first hand, or to write for such information directly to: Geography and Map Division, Library of Congress, Washington, D.C. 20540.

CARIBBEAN
GENERAL

5331 Atlas of the Caribbean Basin. 2nd ed. Washington: Dept. of State, Bureau of Public Affairs, 1984. 1 atlas (16 p.): col. ill.; 22 x 28 cm. (Dept. of State publication; 9398)
For sale by: Superintendent of Documents, US Government Printing Office, Washington, D.C. 20402.

5332 Petroconsultants S.A. Haiti and Dominican Republic: synopsis 1979, including current activity. Geneva: Petroconsultants, 1982. 1 map: photocopy; 54 x 83 cm.
Oil and gas leases. Depths shown by contours. At head of title: Foreign Scouting Service. Includes "List of Rightholders," table of "Summary of Activity during 1982," and location map.

5333 Société nouvelle pétrole et affrètements. Caribbean area. Paris: La Société, 1982. 1 map: col.; 55 x 62 cm.
Shows petroleum shipping terminals and capacities of terminals. "Not to be used for navigation." Includes note, distance lists, and inset of Maracaibo Lake.

BAHAMAS

5335 Bahamas flight planning chart. Nassau: Bahamas Tourist Office, 1983. 1 map; on sheet 46 x 61 cm., folded to 23 x 16 cm.
Bahamas flight planning chart includes island aeronautical profiles of Grand Bahama, New Providence, Bimini, Abaco, Andros, Long Island, Eleuthera, Exuma, Berry, Cat Island.

5336 Knowles, Aaron H. Pathfinder maps, Freeport, Grand Bahamas. Freeport, Bahamas: Island Publications Co., 1983. 2 maps on 1 sheet: index; 46 x 63 cm.

Covers Freeport and Lucaya, Bahamas, and Grand Bahama Island, Bahamas. Includes telephone directory, indexed ancillary maps of "International Bazaar" and "Downtown," location map, and advertisements.

5337 Petroconsultants S.A. Bahama Islands with southern Florida, synopsis 1983, including current activity. Geneva: Petroconsultants, 1983. 1 map: photocopy; 43 x 60 cm.
Depths shown by contours. At head of title: Foreign Scouting Service. "April 1980." Includes location map, "Key to Wildcat Wells," statistical data, table of "Summary of Activity during 1979," and inset of "Southern Florida" with "Key to Wildcat Wells."

BARBADOS

5338 Great Britain. Directorate of Overseas Surveys. Barbados 1 : 20,000: geology of the Scotland Area. Ed 1/ D.O.S. 1982. Scale 1:20,000. Tolworth, England: Government of U.K., The Directorate for the Government of Barbados; St. Michael, Barbados: Energy and Natural Resource Div., Ministry of Finance and Planning, 1982. 1 map: col.; 75 x 85 cm. (D.O.S.; 1228)
Relief shown by contours and land form drawings. Includes three cross sections and index to 1 : 10,000 geology DOS 1227 sheets showing location of 1 : 20,000 geology DOS 1228.

5339 Petroconsultants S.A. Barbados, synopsis 1979, including current activity. Geneva: Petroconsultants, 1983. 1 map: photocopy; 54 x 40 cm.
"April 1983." Includes "List of Rightholders," table of "Summary of Activity during 1979," statistical data, and location map.

5340 Stevenson Hardtke Associates. Expansion and improvement of the port of

Bridgetown, contract D, onshore facilities: extent of 1975 port expansion. Revision no. 2, area B-reclamation area rev., 4/13/77. Scale 1:2,400. 1" = 200'. S.l.: s.n., 1981? 1 map; 60 x 95 cm.

Covers Bridgetown, Barbados. At head of title: Government of Barbados, Prime Minister's Office, Port Management Division. Oriented with north toward upper left.

5341 United States. Central Intelligence—Agency. Barbados. Scale ca. 1:175,000. Washington: CIA, 1980. 1 map: col.; 20 x 17 cm.

Shows parish boundaries. Relief shown by shading.

CUBA

5342 Atlas histórico-biográfico José Martí. Scales differ. La Habana: Instituto Cubano de Geodesia y Cartografía: Centro de Estudios Martianos, 1983. 1 atlas (120 p.): bibl., ill. (some col.), indexes, col. maps, ports; 34 cm.

Contents: Ambito histórico; Los primeros años; Raíces del latinoamericanismo martiano; Guerras independentistas; El Partido Revolucionario Cubano; Desembarco y caída en combate; Vigencia y presencia martianas.

5343 Empresa de Cartografía, La Habana. Mapa turístico de Cuba. La Habana: Empresa de Cartografía del ICGC, 1983. 1 map: col.; on sheet 55 x 93 cm.

"Editado en 1983 'Año del XXX Aniversario del Moncada.'" Alternate title: Mapa turístico nacional. Includes location map, distance chart, index to points of interest, inset showing airways from Cuba, and col. ill.

5344 Fresquet, Matilde Roig de. Mapa de Cuba. Design and art work by Matilde Roig de Fresquet. Coral Gables, Fla.: Moderna Poesia, 1980. 2 maps on 1 sheet: col.; 67 x 95 cm.

Contents: Física; División política a partir de 1975.

5345 Instituto Cubano de Geodesia y Cartografía. Miniatlas de Cuba. Redactor principal Jorge Carasa Pereira. Scale 1:7,000,000. La Habana: El Instituto, 1983? 1 atlas (60 p.): col. ill., col. maps; 19 cm.

Cover title. Shows latest statistics of 1975.

5346 Soto, F. Mapa monumental de La Habana presentado en la primera Feria Nacional de los Municipios de Cuba en el Exilio del 6–20 de abril del 1983, Orange Bowl-Miami. Miami, Fla.: The Author, 1983. 1 map; 43 x 71 cm., folded to 23 x 10 cm.

Shows monuments in Havana, Cuba, pictorially.

5347 United States. Central Intelligence Agency. Cuba. Scale 1:2,450,000. Washington: CIA, 1983. 1 map; 22 x 52 cm.

Relief shown by shading and spot heights. Includes comparative area map, location map with radial distances, and subject maps of "Economic activity," "Sugar," "Population," and "Land utilization."

DOMINICAN REPUBLIC

5348 Batista, César. Carta de la República Dominicana, división territorial, 26 provincias, 1 Distrito Nacional. Scale 1:600,000. Santo Domingo: Dirección General Aeronáutico Civil, 1982. 1 map; 47 x 71 cm.

Shows administrative divisions and locations of international airports, domestic airports, military airports, agricultural tracks, and private agricultural tracks in Dominican Republic. "6-9-81." Reproduced from manuscript original.

5349 Cotes, Cesar. República Dominicana, síntesis geográfica. Santo Domingo: Secretaría de Estado de Educación, Bellas Artes y Cultos, 1983? 1 map: col.; 36 x 52 cm.

Relief shown by shading. "Este mapa constituye un material del apoyo del manual de aprendizaje del programa Especial de Educación Ciudadana." Statistical data and lists of islands, rivers, bays, lakes, principal elevations, and provs. with municipios and districts on verso.

5350 Dominican Republic. Dirección General del Catastro Nacional. Plano de la ciudad de Santo Domingo: inventario nacional de inmuebles urbanos 1981. Revisado por Rafael Antonio Urbaez B. Santo Domingo: La Dirección, 1981. 1 map; 105 x 240 cm.

5351 ———. Subdirección General de Mantenimiento de Carreteras. Mapa red vial nacional. La red vial fue actualizada de acuerdo al último inventario de carreteras,

realizado en 1980, por la Subdirección; Programa Mantenimiento de Carreteras; Roy Jorgensen Associates, Inc., Sept. 1980. S.l.: s.n., 1981. 1 map; 107 x 164 cm.
Shows roads in Dominican Republic.

5352 Turismo Dominicano. The Dominican Republic, tourist map and colonial zone. Santo Domingo: Turismo Dominicano, 1981. 2 maps on 1 sheet: col.; 46 x 60 cm.
Relief shown by shading and spot heights. Includes text, distance chart, descriptive index to points of interest, location map, col. ill., and ancillary maps of "Monte Cristi," "Puerto Plata, tourist port," "Samana, tourist port," "Barahona," "La Romana," and "Higuey."

5353 United States. Central Intelligence Agency. Dominican Republic. Washington: CIA, 1983. 1 map; 34 x 49 cm. Scale 1:1,000,000.
Relief shown by shading and spot heights. In lower right margin: 11A. Includes subject maps of "Population," "Land utilization," and "Economic activity."

5354 Univ. Autónoma de Santo Domingo. Instituto Geográfico Universitario. Mapa de la República Dominicana. Scale 1:600,000. Santo Domingo: El Instituto, 1983. 1 map: col.; 47 x 71 cm.
Also shows administrative divisions. "División territorial vigente a energo 1983." "Corrección de nombres 1-1-83." Relief shown by spot heights. Stamped on: Universidad Autónoma de Santo Domingo, Instituto Geográfico Universitario, Santo Domingo. Includes inset of "Carreteras de concreto."

HAITI

5355 Anglade, Georges. Atlas critique d'Haïti. Montréal, Canada: Groupe d'études et de recherches critiques d'espace, Dépt. de géographie, Univ. du Québec à Montreal: Centre de recherches caraïbes de l'Univ. de Montréal, 1982. 1 atlas (79 p.): bibl., col. maps; 25 x 35 cm. Scales differ.

5356 Petroconsultants S.A. Haiti and Dominican Republic, synopsis 1982. Scale 1:1,000,000. Geneva: Petroconsultants, 1983. 1 map; 54 x 82 cm.
"April 1983." Depths shown by contours. At head of title: Foreign Scouting Ser-

vice. Includes "List of Rightholders," table of "Summary of Activity during 1982," and location map.

5357 United States. Central Intelligence Agency. Haiti. Scale 1:1,000,000. Washington: CIA, 1983. 1 map; 35 x 40 cm.
Relief shown by shading and spot heights. Includes location map with radial distances, comparative area map, and subject maps of "Population," "Vegetation and land use," and "Economic activity."

JAMAICA

5358 Chang, Laurence. A true & exact map of the island nation of Jamaica: showing various monuments & historical points. Jamaica: Bolivar Press, 1980. 1 map: col.; 34 x 54 cm.
Also shows administrative divisions. Selected points of interest shown pictorially.

5359 Petroconsultants S.A. Jamaica, synopsis first half 1982. Geneva: Petroconsultants, 1982. 1 map; 53 x 109 cm.
"August 1982." Depths shown by contours. At head of title: Foreign Scouting Service. Includes "Geological sketch map," tables of "Summary of Activity during First Half 1982" and "Wildcat Drilling," "Generalized Stratigraphic Table," notes, "List of Rightholders," statistical data, and location map.

PUERTO RICO

5360 ———. Puerto Rico, synopsis 1982. Geneva: Petroconsultants, 1983. 1 map; 39 x 109 cm.
"January 1983." Depths shown by contours. At head of title: Foreign Scouting Service. Includes "List of Rightholders," notes, "Geological Sketch Map," and location map.

5361 Puerto Rico. Autoridad de las Fuentes Fluviales. Distribución geográfica estimada de bloques de carga para interrupciones distribuidas, bloques 1–25: Puerto Rico. Enterese con anticipación de las interrupciones eléctricas: área metropolitan de San Juan. San Juan: La Autoridad, 1981. 2 maps on 1 sheet; 32 x 92 cm.
Shows electrical service interruptions

in Puerto Rico and San Juan metropolitan area, Puerto Rico. "Programa experimental y tentativo." "Suplemento especial para: El Mundo, El Nuevo Día, El Vocero, The San Juan Star, La Semana, El Oriental, Bayamon." Includes text, schedule of "Programa de interrupciones distribuídas," and two insets.

5362 Toro Sugrañes, José A. Nuevo atlas de Puerto Rico. Río Piedras: Editorial Edil, 1982. 1 atlas (182 p.): maps; 23 cm. Includes glossary.

5363 United States. Dept. of the Interior. Monumentos Históricos Nacionales de San Juan, Puerto Rico = San Juan National Historic Sites, Puerto Rico. Washington: The Dept., 1982. 1 map: col. 46 x 39 cm.
Pictorial map. Alternate title: *El viejo San Juan.* Includes text and ill. Text, map of "Ruta de la flota y galeones Españoles," and col. ill. on verso.

TRINIDAD AND TOBAGO

5364 Petroconsultants S.A. Trinidad offshore, synopsis first half 1982. Geneva: Petroconsultants, 1982. 1 map; 54 x 61 cm.
Covers Trinidad and Tobago. "October 1982." Depths shown by contours. At head of title: Foreign Scouting Service. Includes "List of Rightholders," table of "Summary of Activity during First Half of 1982," statistical data, and location map.

5365 Trinidad and Tobago. Lands and Surveys Div. Port of Spain. 3rd ed. Scale 1:10,000. Port of Spain: The Div., 1981. 1 map: col.; 56 x 74 cm.
Covers Port of Spain, Trinidad and Tobago. Indexed. Map of "Town of Puerta de España as in 1757" on verso.

5366 ———. Water and Sewerage Authority. Map of Trinidad showing trunk & distribution mains. Valsayn, St. Joseph. Revision, 'B' Picton #3, Mt. Hope, Mallick, Calefornia [sic] & San Fernando Reservoirs included, 19-2-81. S.l.: s.n., 1982. 1 map; 65 x 98 cm.
Shows water distribution and storages in Trinidad and western portion of Tobago. Includes inset of "Chaguaramas showing reservoirs."

5367 United States. Central Intelligence Agency. Trinidad and Tobago. Washington: CIA, 1983. 1 map; 38 x 36 cm.
Relief shown by shading and spot heights. Includes subject maps of "Population," "Economic activity," "Land utilization," and location map with radial distances.

VIRGIN ISLANDS

5368 Flowers-Molard, C. City of Charlotte Amalie, St. Thomas, U.S. Virgin Islands. Charlotte Amalie, Virgin Islands: The Author, 1980. 1 map; 62 x 86 cm.
"Base map: Government of the Virgin Islands Public Works Department." "Map of Charlotte Amalie, St. Thomas, V.I." Includes inset of "St. Thomas, U.S.V.I.," index to points of interest, and ill.

5369 Great Britain. Directorate of Overseas Surveys. British Virgin Islands. Ed. 1-DOS 1982. Tolworth, England: The Directorate; Road Town, British Virgin Islands: Survey Dept., 1982. 1 map: col.; 82 x 103 cm (DOS; 446)
Relief shown by shading, gradient tints, and spot heights. Includes text, location map, and indexed inset of Road Town.

5370 Lang, Kurt. Shaded relief road map of St. Thomas & U.S.V.I.; Street map of Charlotte Amalie. Birmingham, Ala.: Carto-Craft Corp.; St. Thomas, US Virgin Islands, 1981. 2 maps on 1 sheet: col., indexes; 64 x 97 cm.
Relief shown by shading and spot heights. "Map compiled from U.S. Geodetic Survey maps and maps of the Public Works Department of the Government of the Virgin Islands." Includes text, inset, and advertisements.

5371 Official Publications (firm). The map of maps with new route signs: facts about St. Thomas, U.S. Virgin Islands: facts about St. John, U.S. Virgin Islands. St. Thomas, US Virgin Islands: Official Publications, 1983. 2 maps on 1 sheet: col., indexes; 57 x 82 cm.
Includes text, two location maps, telephone directories, insets of airport, Havensight Mall, downtown Charlotte Amalie, Cruz Bay, and Frenchtown, col. ill., and advertisements.

5372 Schneider, Philip A. The United States Virgin Islands, a full color shaded relief map: the complete reference map of the islands. Champaign: Dept. of Geography, Univ. of Illinois, 1983. 2 maps on 1 sheet: col., indexes; 47 x 71 cm.

Includes indexed insets of Christiansted and Charlotte Amalie. Indexes on verso.

5373 **United States. Central Intelligence Agency.** Saint Christopher and Nevis. Washington: CIA, 1983. 1 map: col.; 21 x 17 cm.

Relief shown by shading and spot heights. Includes location map and index to parishes.

CENTRAL AMERICA
GENERAL

5374 **Aerospace Center,** *US.* Central America. Prepared by DMAAC. Scale 1:8,858,000. St. Louis: DMAAC, 1981. 1 map: col.; 44 x 56 cm. (JPC; 39)

Covers Central America, West Indies, northern South America, eastern Mexico, and southern US. "July 1980." Plotting charts. Central America.

BELIZE

5375 **Cubola** (firm). Belize, Central America, tourist map. Produced by Cubola for Belize Tourist Board. Belize City: The Board, 1982. 1 map: col.; 51 x 76 cm.

Belize facilities map and guide for visitors. Includes text and 11 ancillary maps. Text and eight maps on verso.

5376 **Great Britain. Directorate of Overseas Surveys.** Belize. Ed. 1-DOS 1980. Scale 1:250,000. Tolworth, England: The Directorate; Belmopan, Belize: Land and Surveys Dept., Ministry of Natural Resources, 1980. 2 maps: col.; 59 x 82 cm. (DOS; 649/1)

Relief shown by contours, hypsometric tints, and spot heights. Includes location map and two insets of administrative boundaries.

5377 **Petroconsultants S.A.** Belize, synopsis 1982, including current activity. Geneva: Petroconsultants, 1983. 1 map; 63 x 67 cm.

"March 1983." Depths shown by contours. At head of title: Foreign Scouting Ser-

vice. Includes "Geological Sketch Map of Belize," "List of Rightholders," table of "Summary of Activity during 1982," statistical data, and location map.

COSTA RICA

5378 **Bergoeing G., Jean Pierre.** Carta geomorfológica del Valle Central de Costa Rica = Carte geomorphologique de la Vallée centrale de Costa Rica = Geomorphological map of the Central Valley of Costa Rica. Ed. 1–1981. Scale 1:50,000. San José: Convenio Univ. de Costa Rica, Depto. de Geografía: M.O.P.T., Instituto Geográfico Nacional, 1981. 9 maps: bibl., col.; 53 x 59 cm.

Relief shown by contours, hachures, and spot heights. Accompanied by: Geomorfología del Valle Central de Costa Rica (explicación de la carta geomorfológica 1:50.000), 1982. (49 p.: ill., maps, profiles; 21 cm.). Base map: Costa Rica 1:50,000. Some sheets include index map.

5379 **Colorcroquis de Costa Rica.** San José: Lehmann Editores, 1979. 1 atlas (42 leaves): chiefly ill.; 21 x 27 cm. (Col. Escolar Lehmann)

5380 **Francisco Mas y Asociados.** Proyecto fronterizo Costa Rica-Panamá. Scale 1:50,000. San José: Ministerio de Agricultura y Ganadería, 1981. 3 maps on 6 sheets: col.; 59 x 87 cm.

Relief shown by contours and spot heights. Depths shown by contours and soundings. "Fondo de preinversión— OFIPLAN." Contents: Clasificación de suelos; Capacidad del uso de la tierra; Ubicación de observaciones.

5381 **Instituto Costarricense de Acueductos y Alcantarillados. Depto. de Estudios Básicos.** Mapa de ubicación general de cuencas: inventario nacional de cuencas hidrográficas: Costa Rica. Dibujo, R. Montero Caballero. San José: El Instituto, 1980. 1 map; 48 x 52 cm.

Accompanied by: Inventario nacional de cuencas potencialmente utilizables para abastecimiento de agua.

5382 ———. ———. Mapa geomorfológico de la cuenca del Río Potrero, Nicoya, Guanacaste. Dibujo, Guiselle Mora Q. Scale

1 : 25,000. San José: El Instituto, 1981. 1 map; 40 x 56 cm.
Geomorphology. Potrero River Watershed (Nicoya).

5383 Instituto Geográfico Nacional, *Costa Rica.* Ciudad de San José. Servicio Geodésico Interamericano. San José: El Instituto, 1982? 1 map: col.; 21 x 50 cm.

5384 Instituto Nacional de Vivienda y Urbanismo. Depto. de Urbanismo. Gran área metropolitana: San José. Colaboradores, equipo técnico de OPAM. Scale 1 : 50,000. San José: INVU, 1981. 4 maps; 104 x 165 cm.
Relief shown by contours and spot heights. Base map: Costa Rica 1 : 50,000. IGNCR. Contents: Infraestructura primaria; Uso del suelo propuesto; Intensidad de uso; Areas de restricción y de mejoramiento.

5385 Madrigal, Rodolfo and Elena Rojas. Mapa geomorfológico de Costa Rica. Scale 1 : 200,000. San José: Oficina de Planificación, Sectorial Agropecuaria, 1980. 9 maps: col.; 53 x 69 cm.
Relief shown by contours and spot heights. Depths shown by contours. Base map: Costa Rica 1 : 200,000. Ed. 2-IGNCR. Accompanied by: Manual descriptivo del *Mapa geomorfológico de Costa Rica* (escala 1 : 200.000, 79 p.; 25 cm.). Includes index map.

5386 Mapa geológico de Costa Rica. Scale 1 : 200,000. San José: Ministerio de Industria, Energía y Minas, Dirección de Geología, Minas y Petróleo, 1982. 9 maps: col.; 46 x 69 cm. and 54 x 69 cm.
Relief and depths shown by contours. Includes index map.

EL SALVADOR

5387 Instituto Geográfico Nacional Ingeniero Pablo Arnoldo Guzmán. Carta magnetométrica lecturas de intensidad total, sin correcciones: El Salvador. Scale 1 : 300,000. San Salvador: El Instituto, 1981. 1 map: col.; 52 x 96 cm.
Relief shown by contours.

5388 ———. Planos Urbanos, departamentos: Ahuachapán, Santa Ana, Sonsonate. San Salvador: El Instituto, 1984. 1 atlas (43 leaves): all maps; 27 x 33 cm.

5389 Petroconsultants S.A. El Salvador, synopsis 1982. Geneva: Petroconsultants, 1983. 1 map; 60 x 81 cm.
Depths shown by contours. At head of title: Foreign Scouting Service. Includes text, statistical data, "Designation of Blocks and Sub-blocks," and location map.

5390 United States. Central Intelligence Agency. El Salvador. Washington: CIA, 1983. 1 map; 27 x 42 cm.
Relief shown by shading and spot heights. Includes comparative area map, location map with radial distances, and subject maps of "Economic activity," "Population," and "Vegetation and land utilization."

GUATEMALA

5391 Arevalo Fong, Guillermo Antonio. Análisis cartográfico de la ciudad de Guatemala de 1776 a 1976: 200 años de urbanismo. Guatemala: Univ. de San Carlos de Guatemala, Facultad de Arquitectura, 1979. 84 leaves, 40 leaves of plates: ill.; 22 x 28 cm.

5392 Guatemala. Depto. de Acueductos y Alcantarillados. Dirección de Obras Públicas. República de Guatemala: amplicación de acueducto a El Progreso; Depto. El Progreso, densidad de población. Levantó, A.E. Scobedo, abril 79. Scale 1 : 2,000. Guatemala: La Dirección, 1982. 1 map; 68 x 92 cm.
Oriented with north toward the lower right.

5393 ———. Ministerio de Energía y Minas. Dirección General de Hidrocarburos. Mapa de pozos petróleros. Calcado, ploteo y dibujo, Edmond Hernández. Revisó, Franz Burmester. Guatemala: La Dirección, 1984. 1 map; 62 x 54 cm.
"Pozo no., 71 . . . junio 4 / 84 . . ."

5394 ———. Secretaría de Minería, Hidrocarburos y Energía Nuclear. Dirección General de Minería e Hidrocarburos. Mapa general de actividades petroleras, escala 1 : 1,000,000: Guatemala. Dibujo, Edgar Ardón. Revisó, Edwin Valenzuela. Guatemala: La Dirección, 1982. 1 map; 61 x 54 cm.
Includes two tables of "Areas de contrato de exploración y explotación petrolera."

5395 Instituto Geográfico Nacional Ingeniero Alfredo Obiols Gómez. Ciudad

de Mazatenango. Guatemala: El Instituto, 1982. 1 map: col.; 40 x 44 cm.
Relief shown by contours and spot heights. Alternate title: Ciudad de Mazatenango. Indexed.

5396 Instituto Geográfico Nacional, *Guatemala.* Mapa escolar de la República de Guatemala. Guatemala: El Instituto, 1982. 1 map on 4 sheets: col.; 111 x 108 cm.
Relief shown by shading. "La información básica de este mapa fue tomado del mapa oficial preliminar de la República de Guatemala (hipsométrico) a escala 1 : 500,000 publicado por el IGN en 1965." Includes table of "Municipios de la República de Guatemala," text, col. ill., inset of "Ejemplos de accidentes geográficos en perspectiva," and chart of "Principales volcanes de Guatemala."

5397 Instituto Nacional de Sismología, Vulcanología, Meteorología e Hidrología, *Guatemala.* Informe final, estudio de aguas subterráneas en el Valle de la Ciudad de Guatemala: mapas: proyecto Estudio de aguas subterráneas en Guatemala. Instituto Geográfico Nacional, Programa de las Naciones Unidas para el Desarrollo, INSIVUMEH. Guatemala: El Instituto, 1980. 1 atlas (22 leaves [some folded]): ill., col. maps; 68 x 58 cm.
Cover title. Date on *presentación*: 1980. To accompany: *Informe final del estudio de aguas subterráneas en el Valle de la Ciudad de Guatemala, 1978.*

5398 Niederheitmann, Alfredo. Carta de rutas y aeródromos para Guatemala y El Salvador. S.l.: s.n., 1980. 1 map; 61 x 52 cm.
"Para actualizaciones de esta carta a partir de enero de 1980 . . ."

5399 Petroconsultants S.A. Guatemala, synopsis first half 1982, including current activity. Geneva: Petroconsultants, 1982. 1 map; 74 x 60 cm.
Depths shown by contours. At head of title: Foreign Scouting Service. Includes table of "Summary of Activity during First Half 1982," "List of Rightholders," and location map.

5400 Plan urbano del Puerto Santo Tomás de Castilla. Scales differ. Guatemala: Empresa Portuaria Nacional Santo Tomás de Castilla, 1980. 1 atlas (159 p.): bibl., maps (some col.); 32 x 43 cm.
On most maps and plans: Dirección General de Obras Públicas; Empresa Portuaria Sto. Tomás de Castilla.

5401 United States. Central Intelligence Agency. Guatemala. Washington: CIA, 1983. 1 map: col.; 50 x 78 cm.
Relief shown by shading and spot heights. Includes ancillary subject maps of "Population," "Internal migration," "Indian population" and "Industry and agriculture," comparative area map, location map with radial distances, and graphs of "Principal trade commodities" and "Labor force by sector."

HONDURAS

5402 Berganza D., J. Alfonso. Honduras y su división político-territorial: historia de la creación de los departamentos. Tegucigalpa: Ministerio de Educación Pública, Depto. de Recursos de Aprendizaje, Sección de Producción Materiales Educativos, Medios Audiovisuales, Programación, 1982. 1 atlas (20 p.): col. ill.; 14 x 22 cm.

5403 Castellanos García, J. Efraín. Atlas geográfico de Honduras. 2a ed. Scales differ. Tegucigalpa: Corporación Editora Nacional de Servicopiax Editores, 1980. 1 atlas (158 p.): ill. (some col.) maps (some col.); 21 x 28 cm.

5403a Editorial Kapelusz. Honduras: mapa físico-político. Scale 1 : 1,600,000. Tegucigalpa: Editorial Kapelusz, 1983. 1 map; 31 x 44 cm.
Relief shown by gradient tints and spot heights. Includes ancillary map of "Islas Santanilla o de El Cisne."

5403b ———. Honduras: mapa político. Scale 1 : 1,600,000. Tegucigalpa: Editorial Kapelusz, 1983. 1 map; 30 x 44 cm.
Relief shown by spot heights. Includes insets of "Islas Santanilla o de El Cisne" and Central America.

5404 Honduras. Ministerio de Comunicaciones, Obras Públicas y Transporte. Dirección General de Caminos. Depto. de Estudios y Proyectos. República de Honduras: mapa general de la red vial. Tegucigalpa: La Dirección, 1982. 1 map; 86 x 140 cm.
Alternate title: Mapa "provisional." Includes table listing principal roads and island inset.

5405 ———. **Servicio Autónomo Nacional de Acueductos y Alcantarillados. Unidad de Catastro.** Plano general del distrito metropolitano: Tegucigalpa. Dibujo, Poly Humberto Rivas y Moisés Ricardo Ochoa. Scale 1 : 10,000. Tegucigalpa: El Servicio, 1983. 1 map on 2 sheets; 136 x 62 cm.

5406 **Land Resources Development Centre,** *Great Britain.* Honduras 1 : 500,000. La Mosquitia. Tolworth Tower, England: The Centre, 1981. 6 maps; 85 x 60 cm.

Spanish and English. "This map accompanies Project Report 110, La Mosquitia, Honduras: resources and development potential, and together with the report, is published by the Land Resources Development Centre . . ."

5407 **Michigan State Univ. Comprehensive Resource Inventory and Evaluation System.** Map of natural resources in Choluteca Department, Honduras. In cooperation with AID/Honduras and the Honduran Government. Lansing, Mich.: The System, 1983. 7 maps; on sheets 71 x 56 cm.

Contents: Choluteca Holdridge life zones; Choluteca land use/cover; Choluteca agro-ecological zones; Choluteca annual temperature; Choluteca annual precipitation; Choluteca elevations; Choluteca soil units.

5408 **United States. Central Intelligence Agency.** Honduras. Washington: CIA, 1983. 1 map: col.; 41 x 61 cm.

Relief shown by shading and spot heights. Depths shown by contours. Includes location map with radial distance, comparative area map, subject maps of "Population," "Land utilization" and "Economic activity," and graphs of "Population," "Educational levels," "Population growth 1925–75," "Land use," "Occupation," "Principal trade commodities 1980" and "Per capita gross domestic product 1945–80."

NICARAGUA

5409 **Instituto Geográfico Nacional** [and] Instituto Nicaragüense de Turismo, *Managua.* Mapa guía de la ciudad de Managua. Scale not given. Managua: El Instituto Nicaragüense de Turismo, 1982. 2 maps: col.; 55 x 68 cm.

Relief shown by gradient tints and spot heights. Includes text, indexes to points of interest for city, distance chart, location map, inset, and ill.

5410 **Petroconsultants S.A.** Nicaragua, synopsis 1982, including current activity. Scale 1 : 1,000,000. Geneva: Petroconsultants, 1983. 1 map; 53 x 97 cm.

Depths shown by contours. At head of title: Foreign Scouting Service. Includes table of "Summary of Activity during 1982," statistical data, and location map.

5411 **United States. Central Intelligence Agency.** Nicaragua. Washington: CIA, 1983. 1 map; 39 x 41 cm.

Relief shown by shading and spot heights. Includes comparative area map, location map with radial distances, and subject maps of "Population," "Economic activity," and "Land utilization."

PANAMA

5412 **Panama. Ministerio de Obras Públicas.** Mapa general de carreteras: República de Panamá. Panamá: El Ministerio, 1981. 1 map: 47 x 114 cm.

5413 **Petroconsultants S.A.** Panama, synopsis 1982. Geneva: Petroconsultants, 1983. 1 map; 54 x 82 cm.

Depths shown by contours. At head of title: Foreign Scouting Service. Incudes "List of Rightholders," "Geological Sketch Map of Panama," table of "Summary of Activity during 1982," location map, and statistical data.

5414 **United States. Central Intelligence Agency.** Panama. Washington: CIA, 1983. 1 map; 51 x 61 cm.

Relief shown by shading and spot heights. Includes comparative area map, location map with radial distances, ancillary maps of "Proposed canal routes" and "Canal Zone (U.S. administration)," and subject maps of "Population," "Vegetation," and "Economic Activity."

MEXICO

5415 **Asociación Nacional Automovilística,** *México.* Carta geográfica de México. 11a ed. México: La Asociación, 1981. 1 map: col.; 84 x 116 cm.

Relief shown by spot heights. Accompanied by: Carta geográfica de México: indice general de poblaciones y pueblos (64 p.; 17 cm.). Includes inset of Mexico City region. Distance chart in accompanying index.

5416 ———. Guíamarilla de la Ciudad de México = Mexico City guide. 9a ed. Scale ca. 1:24,000. México: La Asociación, 1983. 1 atlas (31, 15 p.): indexes, col. maps; 23 cm.
Cover title. "Copyright Carlos Encinas González y Carlos Encinas Ferrer." Cover. Issued folded as pocket atlas 23 x 13 cm; opens flat to 23 x 24 cm.

5417 Ayre, Linda. Grupo étnico-zapoteco, distribución etno-lingüística zapoteca en el distrito de Villa Alta, Oaxaca. Scale ca. 1:220,000. Elaboró, L. Ayre. Dibujo, L. Ayre y Angel Ramírez. Oaxaca, México: C. Regional, INAH, 1981? 1 map; 42 x 28 cm.
Includes two location maps.

5418 Centro SAHOP Yucatán, *México.* Estado de Yucatán. Elaborado por el Centro SAHOP no. 30. Dibujo, C.A. Rivero L. Mérida, México: El Centro, 1983. 1 map; 47 x 54 cm.
Includes distance lists and inset of "Ciudad de Mérida."

5420 Chávez, Agustín Velázquez. 5 [i.e. Cinco] planos del siglo XVI. México: Fernando Loera-Cháves y Peniche, 1984. 1 atlas (32 p., 5 leaves of plates): ill.; 51 cm.

5421 Cubola (firm). Atlas of Belize. 7th ed., June 1982. Belize: Cubola Productions, 1982. 1 atlas (36 p.): col. ill., col. maps; 28 cm.

5422 García de León G., Carlos. Carta general del Estado de Colima. Elaborada en el Instituto de Geografía de la UNAM en colaboración con Unificación, Progreso y Alianza Cívica, Asociación Política Nacional. Scale 1:200,000. México: El Instituto, 1982. 1 map: col.; 56 x 69 cm.
Relief shown by contours. "Carta . . . basada en quince hojas de la Carta topográfica de la República Mexicana, publicada en 1973 por CETENAL . . ."

5423 García de Miranda, Enriqueta and **Zaida Falcón de Gyves.** Atlas: nuevo atlas Porrúa de la República Mexicana. 6a ed. México: Editorial Porrúa, 1984. 1 atlas (219 p.): col. ill.; 34 cm.

5424 General Drafting Co., Inc. Mexico. Prepared for Exxon. Convent Station, N.J.: The Company, 1982. 1 map: col.; 60 x 84 cm.
Relief shown by spot heights. Legend in English and Spanish. Includes text, distance chart, index, and ancillary maps of "Relief map of Mexico" and "Mexico, D.F. and vicinity." Text, chart of road signs, and indexed maps of "Downtown Monterrey" and "Mexico, D.F. (central area)" on verso.

5425 Guía Roji, S.A. México: atlas de carreteras = road atlas. Scale 1:2,000,000. 1 cm. = 20 km. México: Guía Roji, 1982. 1 atlas (32 p.): col. ill., col. maps; 26 cm.

5426 Guías urbanas: directorio de planos: Mexicali, Tijuana, Ensenada, Tecate, San Felipe, San Luis, Calexico. Ed. especial. Scale not given. S.l.: Ediciones Corona, 1984. 1 atlas (537 p., 6 folded p. of plates): maps (some col.); 21 cm.
Spine title: Guías urbanas, Baja California.

5427 H.M. Gousha Co. Mexico, tourist map 1983: the amigo country. Prepared for Secretaría de Turismo, Consejo Nacional de Turismo. San José, Calif.: The Company, 1983. 1 map: col.; 39 x 67 cm.
Relief shown by spot heights. Includes text, index, distance chart, and ancillary "Enlarged Map of Central Mexico." General information, chart of road signs, and indexed maps of "Central Mexico City" and "Metropolitan Mexico City" on verso.

5428 Kistler Graphics, Inc. Mexico in 3-D. Denver, Colo.: Kistler Graphics, 1981. 1 model: col., plastic; 36 x 49 x 2 cm.
Relief also shown by shading and gradient tints. Legend in English and Spanish. "Base map [copyright] 1957 Jeppesen & Co." "Cultural overlay [copyright] the H.M. Gousha Company."

5429 Kokusai Kyōryoku Jigyōdan. Report on geological survey of the Pachuca, Zimapán area, central Mexico. Phase I, photogeological interpretation, geological survey. Scale 1:50,000. México: Japan International Cooperation Agency: Metal Mining Agency of Japan: Consejo de Recursos Minerales de México, 1980. 1 atlas (4, 14 folded leaves of plates): all maps; 32 cm.
Title from case. Title on plates: Geological survey of the Pachuca, Zimapán area. Phase I. "MJ, MI, AC, JA."

5430 Libromaya (firm). Plano actualizado de la ciudad de Mérida, Yucatán. Los textos y traducciones de los elementos que integran este hoja fueron realizados por Nicolás Vallado Díaz. Mérida, México: The Firm, 1983. 1 map; on sheet 56 x 43 cm. Includes ancillary map of "Municipios aledaños a la ciudad de Mérida." Text and map of central city with index to points of interest in Spanish and English on verso.

5432 Mexico. Coordinación General de los Servicios Nacionales de Estadística, Geografía e Informática. Síntesis geográfica de Coahuila. Nomenclátor del Estado de Coahuila. México: Secretaría de Programación y Presupuesto, Instituto Nacional de Estadística, Geografía e Informática, 1983. 1 atlas (3 v.): col. ill., col. maps; 28–41 cm.
Portfolio: Anexo cartográfica. Scale 1 : 1,000,000 (13 folded leaves of plates: all col. maps; 40 cm.). Includes index and gazetteer. Contents: División municipal y principales localidades; Vías de comunicación; Climatología; Geología; Hidrología; Regiones fisiográficas del estado.

5433 ———. Secretaría de Agricultura y Recursos Hidráulicos. Dirección General de Estudios. Subdirección de Agrología. Mapa general de la República Mexicana. México: La Subdirección, 1980. 1 map: bibl., col.; 102 x 152 cm.
Relief shown by gradient tints. Accompanied by: Memoria técnica del mapa general de la República Mexicana (1981, 36 p.: ill., map; 28 cm.). Includes island inset.

5434 ———. Secretaría de Comunicaciones y Transportes. Dirección de Análisis de Inversiones. Depto. de Cartografía y Representación. México, mapa de carreteras. México: La Secretaría, 1983. 1 map: col.; 67 x 93 cm.

5435 ———. Secretaría de Patromonio y Fomento Industrial. Subsecretaría de Minas y Energia. Dirección General de Minas. Plantas de beneficio instaladas en la República Mexicana. Ed. sept. de 1981. México: La Dirección, 1981. 1 map: col.; 30 x 44 cm.
Shows locations of minerals and capacity of mines. Accompanied by list of concessions (2 p.; 47 x 35 cm.). Recopilación estadística de la producción mínera mexicana (toneladas métricas). List of concessions on verso.

5436 ———. ———. ———. ———. Principales centros mineros productores de carbón, azufre, fierro, fluorita, barita y manganeso con datos de producción de 1980: México. México: La Dirección, 1981. 1 map: col.; 30 x 44 cm.
Accompanied by statistical data: Producción por municipios durante los años 1979–80 en toneladas (2 p.; 34 x 47 cm.)

5437 National Geographic Society, US. Cartographic Div. Mexico; Central America. John B. Garver, chief cartographer. Richard J. Darley, senior associate chief. John F. Shupe, associate chief. Scale 1 : 3,803,000. 1 cm = 1 in. = 60 miles. Washington: The Society, 1982. 2 maps on 1 sheet: both sides, col.; 55 x 83 cm.
Relief shown by shading and spot heights. Depths shown by gradient tints and soundings. Includes index to "National Parks of Mexico," geographical equivalents, and abbreviations.

5438 Petroconsultants S.A. Mexico, synopsis first half 1982. Geneva: Petroconsultants, 1982. 1 map; 29 x 85 cm.
Depths shown by contours. At head of title: Foreign Scouting Service. Includes table of "Summary of Activity during First Half 1982," location map, "List of Rightholders," and statistical data.

5439 Sanz Crespo, Julio. Guía ilustrada de la ciudad de México. Cortesía de Petróleos Mexicanos. Investigación, proyecto y dirección, Martine Chomel de Coelho. Diseño, dibujos y realización, Norma Delbosco y Alberto Gasson. México: s.n., 1983. 1 map: col.; 83 x 59 cm.
Includes descriptive index to points of interest and ill. Text and map of "Delegaciones del Distrito Federal" on verso.

5440 Velarde Bonnin, José Juan. Pto. Peñasco, Son.: plano de catastro portuario. Scale 1 : 2,000. México: Subsecretaría de Puertos y Marina Mercante, Dirección General de Obras Marítimas, Subdirección de Estudios y Proyectos, 1980. 1 map on 2 sheets; 73 x 102 cm.
Relief shown by formlines. Includes two insets and location map.

5440a Winlund, Ed et al. ChartGuide Mexico west: navigation charts, current plus discontinued, all updated from last chart dates, with major added information: all islands, harbors and shoreline from San Diego to Guatemala, including Sea of Cortez detail. Anaheim, Calif.: ChartGuide, 1983. 1 atlas (74 p.): ill., maps; 36 x 52 cm.

5441 Zwick, Peter C. Cozumel, Mexico, historical chart, shipwreck & Maya ruin sites, coral reef diving data. Scale 1:55,000. S.l.: s.n., 1983. 1 map; on sheet 89 x 59 cm. Includes text.

SOUTH AMERICA
GENERAL

5442 Aiello, José L. *et al.* Atlas eólico preliminar de América Latina y el Caribe. Quito: Organización Latinoamericana de Energía, Programa Latinoamericano de Cooperación Energética, 1983. 6 v.: col. ill; 28 cm. (Serie Documentos D-PLACE; 8)

5443 Lombardi, Cathryn L.; John V. Lombardi; and K. Lynn Stoner. Latin American history, a teaching atlas. Scales differ. Madison: Univ. of Wisconsin Press *for the* Conference on Latin American History (CLAH), 1983. 1 atlas (104, 40 p.): bibl., index, maps; 29 cm.

Contents: The Latin American environment; The Iberian background; the Ameridian background; Discovery and conquest; The colonial governments; Trade, resources, and competition; The independence of Spanish America; Latin American boundaries; Latin American international relations.

5444 Vázquez de Acuña, Isidoro. Don Juan de la Cruz, su mapa de América Meridional, 1775, y las fronteras del Reino de Chile. Santiago: Instituto de Investigaciones del Patrimonio Territorial de Chile, Univ. de Santiago, 1984. 1 atlas (159 p., 1 folded leaf of plates): ill.; 27 cm. (Col. Terra nostra; 3)

ARGENTINA

5445 Argentina. Servicio de Hidrografía Naval. Croquis de los ríos. Pt. 2, Río Paraguay Confluencia: km. 1236. Asunción: km. 1632.5, i.e., km. 1215–1243. S.l: s.n., s.d. 1 atlas.

5446 Automóvil Club Argentino. Area de Cartografía Vial y Turística. República Argentina: red caminera principal. Dibujo,

Juan C. Corso. Buenos Aires: El Club, 1984. 1 map: col.; 96 x 57 cm.

Relief shown by shading. Depths shown by gradient tints. Includes three insets. Text, index, map of "Esquema de distancias," map showing distances from Buenos Aires, col. ill., and directories of Automóvil Club Argentino's lodgings, recreational facilities, and automobile service stations on verso.

5447 Carvallo, Casiano Néstor. Historia cartográfica de Misiones. Posadas, Argentina: Ediciones Montoya, 1983. 1 atlas (64 p.): ill.; 23 cm.

5448 Centro Cartográfico Buenos Aires. Atlas geográfico de la República Argentina. Buenos Aires: El Centro, s.d. 1 atlas (20 p.): col. ill.; 40 x 29 cm.

5449 Centro Editor de América Latina. Atlas de la actividad económica de la República Argentina. Scales differ. Buenos Aires: El Centro, 1983. 1 atlas (1 v.): col. ill., col. maps; 33 cm.

Contents: v. 1, Los recursos.

5450 ———. Atlas total de la República Argentina. Dirección, Elena Chiozza y Ricardo Figueira. Scale differ. Buenos Aires: El Centro, 1983. 1 atlas (4 v.): bibl., col. ill., index, col. maps; 33 cm.

Contents: Atlas físico v. 1; Atlas político; Atlas demográfico; Atlas económico v. 1.

5451 Difrieri, Horacio A. Atlas de Buenos Aires. Buenos Aires: Municipalidad de la Ciudad de Buenos Aires, Secretaría de Cultura, 1981. 2 v.: ill. (some col.); 33 cm.

5452 Editorial Filcar. Guía Filcar, capital federal y suburbanos. Ed. combinada 2 en 1. 33a ed. Buenos Aires: Editorial Filcar, 1981. 1 atlas (103, 239): col. maps; 29 cm.

Rev. ed. of: *Guía de planos, ciudad de Buenos Aires y suburbanos* (2 en 1, (1979). Includes indexes.

5453 Editorial Guí-Pla. Guí-Pla: libro de esquemas gráficos para la ubicación práctica de calles, lugares y parajes: Mar del Plata, comercios industrias. 15a ed. Buenos Aires: Guí-Pla, 1984. 1 atlas (82, 126 p.): ill. (some col.); 32 cm.

5454 Kleiner, Alberto. Atlas de los territorios de la Jewish Colonization Association en Argentina y Brasil, 1913–1941. Buenos Aires: Libreros y Editores del Polígono, 1983. 1 atlas (65 leaves): ill.; 34 cm.

5455 Otero, Héctor O. *et al.* Atlas de los recursos pesqueros demersales del Mar Argentino. Mar del Plata, Argentina: Ministerio de Economía, Secretaría de Intereses Marítimo, Subsecretaría de Pesca, Instituto Nacional de Investigación y Desarrollo Pesquero (INIDEP), 1982. 1 atlas (248 p.): chiefly maps; 28 cm. (Serie Contribuciones; 423)

5456 Petroconsultants S.A. Argentina, synopsis first half 1982, including current activity. Geneva: Petroconsultants, 1982. 1 map; 186 x 81 cm.
Depths shown by contours. At head of title: Foreign Scouting Service. Includes "List of Rightholders," table of "Summary of Activity during First Half 1982," "Key to Main Sedimentary Basins," "Tectonic Sketch Map," location map, statistical data, and notes.

5457 Promotora Argentina. Atlas argentino y universal. Buenos Aires: Promotora Argentina, 1981. 1 atlas (64 p.): col. ill., col. maps; 28 cm.
Cover: Datos último censo.

5458 United States. Central Intelligence Agency. Argentina. Washington: CIA, 1983. 1 map; 56 x 34 cm.
Relief shown by shading and spot heights. Includes comparative area map, location map with radial distances, and subject maps of "Population," "Economic activity," and "Vegetation."

BOLIVIA

5459 Bolivia. Ministerio de Transportes y Comunicaciones. Servicio Nacional de Caminos. Depto. de Planificación. Bolivia, red vial 1982. La Paz: El Servicio, 1982. 1 map: col.; 62 x 58 cm.
Road map of Bolivia.

5460 Instituto Nacional de Estadística, *Bolivia.* Atlas censal de Bolivia. La Paz: El Instituto, 1982. 1 atlas (294 p.): ill. (some col.); 33 cm.

5461 Petroconsultants S.A. Bolivia, synopsis first half 1982, including current activity. Geneva: Petroconsultants, 1982. 1 map; 81 x 113 cm.
At head of title: Foreign Scouting Service. Includes inset, "Tectonic Sketch Map," table of "Summary of Activity during the First Half 1981," "List of Rightholders," statistical data, and location map.

5462 United States. Central Intelligence Agency. Bolivia. Washington: CIA, 1983? 1 map; 49 x 44 cm.
Relief shown by shading and spot heights. Includes location map with radial distances, comparative area map, and subject maps of "Population and administrative divisions," "Vegetation," and "Economic activity."

BRAZIL

5463 Alteração da cobertura vegetal natural do eixó Tocantins-Araguaia: Belém, 1981. Brasília: Ministério da Agricultura, Instituto Brasileiro de Desenvolvimento Florestal, Depto. de Economia Florestal, Programa de Monitoramento da Cobertura Florestal do Brasil, 1981. 62 leaves: ill.; 30 cm. (Relatorio; 1)

5464 A.P.M. (organization). **Setor de Engenharia.** Porto de Manaus: áreas portuárias e de expansão. Scale 1:1,000. S.l.: PORTOBRAS: A.P.M., O Setor, 1983? 1 map; on sheet 62 x 132 cm.
Cadastral map.

5465 Atlas climatológico do Estado de Minas Gerais. Scale 1:3,300,000. Belo Horizonte: Secretaria de Estado da Agricultura, Sistema Operacional da Agricultura, Empresa de Pesquisa Agropecuária de Minas Gerais (EPAMIG): Ministério de Agricultura, Instituto Nacional de Meteorologia (INEMET), 50 Distrito de Meteorologia (50 DISME): Ministério da Educação e Cultura, Univ. Federal de Viçosa (UFV), 1982. 1 atlas (ca. 100 leaves): col. maps; 32 × 41 cm.

5466 Bahia, *Brazil* (state). **Centro de Planejamento e Estudos. Coordenação de Recursos Naturais.** Município de Itaberaba, Estado da Bahia. Elaborado pela equípe técnica de cartografia da Coordenação de Recursos Naturais do Centro de Planejamento e Estudos (SEPLANTEC), 1981. Salvador: O Centro, 1981. 1 map; 62 x 89 cm.

Relief shown by contours and spot heights. "Projeto 'Mapas municipais da Bahia'." Includes location map.

5467 ———. **Secretaria das Minas e Energia. Diretoria de Distribuição. Depto. de Engenharia de Distribuição.** Mapa do sistema elétrico do Estado da Bahia, 1981–1988: escala 1:1.000.000. Compilação temática, Div. de Cartografia e Cadastro do Sistema de Distribuição. Planejamento cartográfico-temático e preparo para impressão por Aerofoto Cruzeiro S.A. Salvador: A Secretaria: Companhia de Electricidade do Estado da Bahia, 1981. 1 map: col.; 111 x 102 cm.

Includes location map, statistical data, and four insets.

5468 ———. **Secretaria de Indústria e Comércio. Depto. de Indústria e Comércio.** Cartografia básica do CIA. Scale 1:5,000; Universal transverse Mercator proj. Salvador: O Depto., 1983. 1 atlas (166 leaves): col. maps; 31 × 44 cm.

5469 Brazil. Conselho Interministerial do Programa Grande Carajás. Programa Grande Carajas: aspectos físicos, demográficos e fundiários = Carajás program: physical, demographic, and tenure aspects. Scale 1:2,500,000. Rio de Janeiro: República Federativa do Brasil, O Conselho, 1981. 1 atlas (45 leaves): col. maps; 55 × 54 cm.

English and Portuguese. Includes text of Decree-law no. 1,813 and no. 85,387. Contents: Geology and mineral resources; Geomorphology; Soils; Vegetation cover; Climate; Agricultural suitability; Agricultural zoning; Land settlement; Population.

5470 ———. **Depto. Nacional de Estradas de Rodagem. Div. de Planos e Programas.** Album cartográfico rodoviário. Rio de Janerio: A Div., 1982. 1 atlas (4, 31 folded leaves): 31 col. maps; 72 cm.

Folded col. map in pocket.

5471 ———. **Diretoria do Serviço Geográfico do Exército.** Mapa índice no. 14: cartas do Brasil. Brasília: A Diretoria, 1983. 1 map: col.; on sheet 86 x 94 cm.

"Cartas publicadas por: DSG, FIBGE, outras organizações." Includes inset of "Mapa índice reduzido (MIR)." Text on verso.

5472 ———. **Ministério das Minas e Energia. Depto. Nacional da Produção Mineral.** Mapa geológico do Brasil e da área oceânica adjacente incluindo depósitos mine-

rais: escala 1:2,500,000 = Geologic map of Brazil and adjoining ocean floor including mineral deposits: scale 1:2,500,000. Coordenador geral, Carlos Schobbenhaus. Brasília: O Depto., 1981. 1 map on 4 sheets: col.; 197 × 206 cm.

Depths shown by contours. Includes two insets and one ancillary map.

5473 ———. **Ministério do Exercito. Depto. de Engenharia e Comunicações. Diretoria de Serviço Geográfico do Exército.** Regiões militares. Brasília: A Diretoria, 1982. 1 map: col.; 33 × 38 cm.

Includes inset of "Exército e comandos militares" and 1982 calendar. On verso: Comando e distritos navais; Areas de atuação das DL; Comandos aéreos regionais.

5474 ———. **Ministério do Interior. Superintendência do Desenvolvimento da Região Centro-Oeste.** Mapa geopolítico da área de atuação da SUDECO: região centro-oeste do Brasil. Planejamento cartográfico-temático, compilação, preparo para impressão e execução do relevo por Aerofoto Cruzeiro S.A., Rio de Janeiro. Scale 1:2,000,000. Brasília: A Superintendência, 1981. 1 map: col.; 106 × 120 cm.

Relief shown by shading. Includes table of geographic data and six insets with text of "Programas da desenvolvimento coordenados pela SUDECO." Text on verso.

5475 ———. **Ministério dos Transportes. Depto. Nacional de Estradas de Rodagem. Diretoria de Planejamento. Grupo de Projetos Cartográficos.** Plano nacional de viação, sistema rodoviário do PNV. Scale 1:5,000,000. Brasília: O Depto., 1983. 1 map: col.; on sheet 88 x 95 cm.

Includes table of "Relação descritiva das rodovias do sistema rodoviário federal" and three insets.

5476 Cardoso, Jayme Antonio and Cecília Maria Westphalen. Atlas histórico do Paraná. Curitiba: Indústria Gráfica Projeto, 1981. 1 atlas (78 p.): ill.; 33 cm.

5477 Castro, Therezinha de. Atlas-texto de geopolítica do Brasil. Rio de Janeiro: Capemi Editora, 1982. 1 atlas (58 p.): col. maps; 21 x 28 cm.

5478 Centro de Planejamento da Bahia. Mapa geomorfológico, Estado da Bahia, escala 1:1.000.000. Coordenação geral, Marcílio Franco Monteiro. Concepção e organização, Tereza Cardoso da Silva. Elaboração, Dário Maria Cardoso Nascimento. Planejamento cartográfico, Nair Bessa Diniz Gonçalves. Salvador: Secretaria do Planejamento, Ciência e Tecnologia, O Centro, 1980. 1 map: col.; 111 x 102 cm. (Recursos naturais; 3).

Depths shown by contours. "Base geográfica, compilada do Mapa político do Estado da Bahia, da Secretaria do Planejamento Ciência e Tecnologia, na escala 1 : 1.000.000-1978." Includes location map.

5479 ———. Mapa hidrogeológico, Estado da Bahia, escala 1 : 1.000.000. Coordenação geral, Marcílio Franco Monteiro. Concepção e organização, Aldo da Cunha Rebouças. Elaboração, Maria da Conceição de Oliveira Cunha e George Thadeu Marques de Souza. Colaboração, Diva Vinhas Nascimento Barbosa. Planejamento cartográfico, Nair Bessa Diniz Gonçalves. Bahia: O Centro, 1980. 1 map: col.; 111 x 102 cm. (Recursos naturais; 2)

Depths shown by contours. "Base geográfica, compilada do Mapa político do Estado da Bahia, da Secretaria do Planejamento, Ciência e Tecnologia, na escala de 1 : 100.000-1978." Includes inset of "Pluviosidade anual e balanço hídrico" and location map.

5480 ———. Superintendência de Recursos Naturais. Nucleo de Cartografia. Mapa do sistema de transportes, Estado da Bahia, escala 1 : 1.000.000. Salvador: Secretaria dos Transportes e Comunicações, 1981. 1 map: col.; 111 x 102 cm., folded in cover 27 x 22 cm.

Relief shown by contours and spot heights. Depths shown by contours. "Tendo por base o Mapa do Estado da Bahia, escala 1 : 1.000.000 (IBGE) . . ."

5481 Companhia do Desenvolvimento de Planalto Central. Estudo das potencialidades dos municípios da região geoeconômica de Brasília. Scales differ. Brasília: CODEPLAN, 1983. 1 atlas (4 v.): col. maps; 30–60 x 42–43 cm.

Subtitle on some vols.: *Aspectos físicos e sócio-econômicos.*

5482 Dantas, José Robinson Alcoforado. Mapa geológico do Estado de Pernambuco, escala 1 : 500.000. Planejamento cartográfico, Gilberto Ruy Derze. Colaboração, Adejardo F. da Silva *et al.* Desenho, Silvio

Barreto Peixoto Filho. Cartografia por Triservice Ltda. Recife: Ministério das Minas e Energia, Depto. Nacional da Produção Mineral, 4° Distrito Regional, 1980. 1 map on 2 sheets: bibl., col.; sheets 67 x 156 cm. (Série Mapas e cartas de síntese; 1. Seção geologia; 1)

Published jointly with Govêrno do Estado de Pernambuco, Secretaria da Indústria Comércio e Minas, Minérios de Pernambuco S.A. Accompanied by: *Mapa geológico do Estado de Pernambuco; texto explicativo* (112 p.: maps; 28 cm.); and by Luiz Augusto Andrade Krauss *et al., Bibliografía comentada de geologia de Pernambuco: 1924–1980* (Recife: Minérios de Pernambuco, 1981, 156 p.: 22 cm.); José Francisco Borges, *Como ganhar dinheiro com minérios em Pernambuco* (Recife: Minérios de Pernambuco, 1981, 8 p.; 16 cm.) and *Núcleos regionales de artesanato mineral en Pernambuco* (Recife: Minéiros de Pernambuco, 1981?, 2 p.; 22 x 30 cm., folded to 22 x 10 cm.). Also includes location map and ancillary map of "Principais trabalhos utilizados."

5483 ———; José Antônio Lopes Caúla; and Haroldo Robson da Silva. Mapa geológico do Estado da Paraíba, escala 1 : 500.000. Recursos minerais, Ioman Leite Pedrosa. Planejamento cartográfico, Gilberto Ruy Derze. Colaboração especial, B. Bley de Brito Neves, Cleosmar Ribeiro Santos. Campina Grande: Secretaria de Energia e Recursos Minerais, Companhia de Desenvolvimento de Recursos Minerais da Paraíba, 1982. 1 map: col.; 78 x 108 cm.

Accompanied by: *Mapa geológico do Estado da Paraíba: texto explicativo* (133 p.: maps; 28 cm.). Includes location maps, "Mapa-índice dos trabalhos utilizados," and inset of "Compartimentação geotectônica, Provinca Borborema." Bibliography in accompanying text.

5484 Editôra Abril. Mapa do Brasil 1984: Guia Quatro Rodas: rodovias e ferrovais. Preparado para Realmatic do Banco Real. São Paulo: Editôra Abril, 1984. 1 map: col.; 79 x 90 cm.

"Suplemento especial do Guia Quatro Rodas." "Não pode ser vendido separadamente." "Amazônia, escala aprox. 1 : 12.300.000" and "Foz do Iguaçú; Asunción; Buenos Aires; Montevideo," and one other ancillary map.

5485 ———. Mapa do sul: Guia Quatro Rodas: rodovias e ferrovias 1984: Brasil. Preparado para Realmatic do Banco Real. Scale ca. 1 : 1,300,000. São Paulo: Editôra Abril, 1984. 1 map: both sides, col.; 108 x 95 cm. on sheet 59 x 96 cm. Also shows Uruguay. "Suplemento especial do Guia Quatro Rodas do sul." "Não pode ser vendido separadamente." Includes ancillary map showing eastern São Paulo region and index.

5486 EMBRATEL, *Brazil* (agency). Assessoria de Comunicação Social. Sistemas de telecomunicações: Brasil. Scale 1 : 10,000,000. Brasília: EMBRATEL, 1984. 1 map: col.; on sheet 44 x 62 cm.

5487 FLUMITUR, *Rio de Janeiro* (agency). FLUMITUR Guia de folclore: Estado do Rio de Janeiro. Apôio, BANERJ. Rio de Janeiro: Secretaria de Estado de Indústria, Comércio e Turismo, Cia. de Turismo de Estado do Rio de Janeiro, FLUMITUR, 1982. 3 maps on 1 sheet: both sides, col.; 80 x 60 cm. "Imprensa oficial. RJ 82." Portuguese and English. Includes index to touristic regions, text, and directories of BANERJ. Contents: Arte e artesanato = Handicraft; Danças e folguedos = Dances and popular celebrations; Mapa de acesso rodoviário = Road access map.

5488 Fundação Instituto Brasileiro de Geografia e Estatística. Atlas de Roraima. Scale 1 : 5,000,000. Rio de Janeiro: Presidência da República, Secretaria de Planejamento, IBGE, 1981. 1 atlas (44 p.): col. maps; 34 x 43 cm. Cover title. "Edição em convênio com o Governo do Território de Roraima" (pt. 1). Bibliography (p. 44).

5488a ———. Brasil: divisão política e social. Rio de Janeiro: Presidência da República, Secretaria de Planejamento, IBGE, 1983. 1 map: col.; 32 x 36 cm. Alternate title: *República Federativo do Brasil.* Includes inset of "Divisão regional."

5489 ———. Div. de Atlas e Apoio Técnico. Mapa etno-histórico do Brasil e regiões adjacentes. Adaptado do mapa de Curt Nimuendaju, 1944. Coordenação de documentação, MEC SPHAN Pró-Memória. Scale 1 : 5,000,000. Rio de Janeiro, 1980. Rio de Janeiro: IBGE, 1981. 97 p.: bibl., port ; 26 cm.

5490 Fundação Instituto de Desenvolvimento do R.G. do Norte. Mapa físico: Estado do Rio Grande do Norte. Scale 1 : 500,000. Natal: Estado do Rio Grande do Norte, Secretaria do Planejamento, A Fundação, 1982. 1 map: col.; 66 x 96 cm. Relief shown by contours and spot heights. Depths shown by contours. Includes inset of Natal.

5491 Fundação Nacional do Indio, *Brasília.* Mapa etnográfico do Brasil. SA-ASPLAN, Coordenação de Engenharia. Scale 1 : 5,000,000. Brasília: A Fundação, 1980. 1 map; 45 x 42 cm. Indexed.

5492 Geomapas (firm). Brasil, mapa rodoviário e político. Scale 1 : 5,000,000. São Paulo: Geomapas, 1983. 1 map: col.; 94 x 89 cm., folded in cover 23 x 16 cm. Includes inset, table of statistical data, and distance chart.

5493 ———. Mapa turístico do novo Rio. São Paulo: Geomapas, 1983. 2 maps on 1 sheet: col.; 60 x 90 cm. Relief shown by shading, formlines, and spot heights. Cover title. Includes text and indexes.

5494 ———. Planta da cidade de Curitiba, escala 1 : 20.000. Ed. 1983. Curitiba: 1983. 1 map: col.; 105 x 80 cm. Includes inset.

5495 Iconografia de Pernambuco: cartas, fortificações, aspectos urbanos: edição comemorativa da instalação do Museu da Cidade do Recife. Patrocínio da Prefeitura da Cidade do Recife, Secretaria de Planejamento e Urbanismo com o apoio da Secretaria de Planejamento da Presidência de República. Coordenação editorial de Edson Nery da Fonseca e Marco Aurélio de Alcântara. Recife: Pool Editorial, 1982. 1 atlas (151 p.): ill., maps; 51 x 37 cm. Accompanying text: *Notícia da apresentação em Madrid e Lisboa do álbum iconografia de Pernambuco, Recife* (Pool Editorial, 1982, 31 p.)

5496 Ide, Bernardo Yasuhiro *et al.* Zoneamento agroclimático do Estado de Santa Catarina, 2a etapa. Scale 1 : 1,600,000. Florianópolis: Empresa Catarinense de Pesquisa Agropecuária, 1980. 1 atlas (106 p., 10 leaves of plates): maps (1 col.); 32 x 46 cm. Cover title: Zoneamento agroclimático, Estado de Santa Catarina. "Convênio, Ministério da Agricultura/ Subsecretaria de Planejamento e Orçamento (SUPLAN), Secretaria da Agricultura e do Abastecimento/Comissão Estadual e Planejamento Agrícola (CEPA-SC) e Empresa Catarinense de Pesquisa Agropecuária S.A. (EMPASC)" (p. 3). Bibliography: p. 103–106.

5497 Instituto de Terras do Amazonas. Estado do Amazonas. Manuas: ITERAM, 1982. 1 map: col.; 61 x 104 cm.

Also shows administrative divisions. Includes text, statistical data, location map, ancillary map of "Zona Franca de Manaus," and sheet index.

5498 Livraria do Globo. Guia das ruas de Pôrto Alegre. Compilado por Hans A. Thofehrn *et al.* Pôrto Alegre: A Livraria, 1983. 1 atlas (181 p.): index, col. maps; 20 cm.

5499 Mapa geológico do Estado de São Paulo, escala 1 : 500.000. Elaboração, Carlos Alberto Bistrichi *et al.* Asessoria, Yociteru Hasui, Fernando Flávio Marques de Almeida. Colaboração, José Augusto Mioto *et al.* Cartografia, Maria do Carmo Soares Rodrigues dos Santos. Desenho, Mirna Mangini Ferracini. Apôio técnico, Waldomiro de Oliveira, Júlio Sinkus. São Paulo: Instituto de Pesquisas Tecnológicas do Estado de São Paulo, 1981. 1 map on 2 sheets: col.; 124 x 188 cm., sheets 130 x 100 cm.; 21 cm. (Monografias; 6)

Accompanied by: *Mapa geológico do Estado de São Paulo, escala 1:500.000: v. 1.* Nota explicativa por Fernando Flávio Marques de Almeida *et al.* (São Paulo: Div. de Minas e Geologia Aplicada, Instituto de Pesquisas Tecnológicas do Estado de São Paulo, 1981, 126 p.: maps; 30 cm.).

5500 MAPLAN, *Manaus, Brazil* (firm). Planta da cidade de Manaus, escala 1.20.000. Ed. 1983. Manaus: MAPLAN, 1983. 1 map: col.; 76 x 90 cm.

Includes indexes and inset of city center.

5501 Mapograf Editôra. Brasil, rodoviário. São Paulo: Mapograf Editôra, 1981. 1 map: 46 x 102 cm.

Legend in Portuguese and English. Includes insets of "Amazônia" and "Território de Federnando de Noronha," two distance charts, and index.

5502 Martin, Louis *et al.* Mapa geológico do quaternário costeiro do Estado da Bahia, escala 1 : 250.000. Cartografia e desenho, Josephina Tamacoldi. Colaboração, Fernando Fontes Taboada. Salvador: Estado da Bahia, Secretaria das Minas e Energia, Coordenação da Produção Mineral, Coordenação da Produção Mineral, Programa Cartográfico, 1980. 4 maps on 2 sheets: bibl.; col.; 89 x 68 cm. or smaller, sheets 102 x 72 cm. (Série Cartografia temática especial)

Depths shown by contours. Legend in Portuguese and French. Accompanied by: *Mapa geológico do quaternário costeiro do Estado da Bahia, escala 1:250.000: texto explicativo* (56 p.: maps; 27 cm.). Includes location map, index map, ancillary map, and diagram.

5503 Mato Grosso, *Brazil* (state). **Secretaria de Indústria, Comércio e Turismo.** Diagnóstico de oportunidades industriais do Estado de Mato Grosso. Cuiabá: A Secretaria, 1980? 1 atlas (67 leaves): col. maps; 46 x 66 cm.

5504 Minas Gerais, *Brazil.* **Instituto de Geociências Aplicadas.** Atlas índice de levantamentos relativos às geociências e recursos naturais do Estado de Minas Gerais. Belo Horizonte: O Instituto, 1982. 1 atlas (135 p.): col. maps; 39 x 47 cm.

5505 ———. Secretaria de Estado da Agricultura. Zoneamento agroclimático do Estado de Minas Gerais. Scale 1 : 3,000,000. Belo Horizonte: A Secretaria, 1980. 1 atlas (114 p.): bibl., col. maps; 36 x 45 cm. "Trabalho elaborado pela Secretária de Estado da Agricultura por determinação do Governador Francelino Pereira dos Santos."

5506 Movimento Brasileiro de Alfabetização. Centro Cultural. Mapa cultural: artesanato, folclore, patrimônio ecológico, patrimônio histórico. Rio de Janeiro: MOBRAL, 1980. 1 atlas (2 v. [1043 p.]): bibl., ill., maps; 22 x 30 cm.

Includes glossary.

5507 Petroconsultants S.A. Brazil, synopsis first half 1982, including current activity. Geneva: Petroconsultants, 1982. 1 map; 97 x 109 cm.

Depths shown by contours. At head of title: Foreign Scouting Service. Includes "List of Rightholders," table of "Summary of Activity during the First Half of 1982," chart of

"Crude Oil Production 1982–1982," and statistical data.

5508 Polimapas Editôra. Estado do Rio Grande do Norte, mapa rodoviário, turístico, escolar, polivisual; escala 1 : 500.000. Equipe técnica, José Nönoya Filho *et al.* São Paulo: A Editôra, 1982. 1 map: col.; 60 x 92 cm.

Also shows administrative divisions. Includes inset of "Novo divisão territorial do Brasil," indexes to cities and regions, and col. ill. of state flag.

5509 ——. Mapa polivisual do Brasil, político, turístico, escolar, regional, rodoviário. Equipe técnica, José Nönoya Filho, Natanael Alves da Silva, Manuel Salvador da Silva. 21a ed., 1983. Scale 1 : 6,000,000. São Paulo: A Editôra, 1983. 1 map: col.; 76 x 93 cm.

Includes list of "Municípios brasileiros com mais de 25 mil habitantes C.E.P. e distância em km por rodovia a partir de São Paulo," statistical data, distance chart, text, and col. ill. of national and state flags. Insets: Brasil, físico; Brasil, grandes organismo de desenvolvimento.

5510 ——. Novo mapa polivisual da região da Grande São Paulo e arredores, escala 1 : 150.000. Desenho de José Nönoya Filho, Natanael Alves da Silva, Manoel Salvador da Silva. Ed. 1983. São Paulo: A Editôra, 1983. 1 map: col.; 83 x 104 cm.

Includes inset of "Estado de São Paulo, divisão regional e política."

5511 Rio Grande do Norte, *Brazil.* **Fundação Estadual de Planejamento Agrícola do Rio Grande do Norte.** Zoneamento edafoclimático: Rio Grande do Norte. Natal: Fundação Instituto de Desenvolvimento do Rio Grande do Norte (IDEC), 1981. 55 leaves: maps (some col.); 43 x 58 cm.

5512 Sá, Eudoro Luiz Tude de *et al.* Mapa dos recursos minerais do Estado da Bahia: escala 1 : 1.500.000: 1980. Desenho cartográfico por Josephina Tamacoldi. Compilação de dados, Francisco da Costa Araujo Filho e Glaudemiro Ferreira da Cruz Neto. Salvador: Secretaria das Minas e Energia, Coordenação da Produção Mineral, Programa Cartográfico, 1981. 1 map: bibl., col.; 74 x 123 cm. (Série Cartografia temática especial)

"Base cartográfica obtida por redução da base do Mapa geológico do Estado da Bahia 1 : 1.000.000 SME/1978." Accompanied by: *Mapa dos recursos minerais do Estado da Bahia: escala 1 : 1.500.000: 1980: text o explicativo* (70 p.: maps; 27 cm.). Includes location map, 11 insets, 22 graphs, two tables of statistical data, and indexed lists of "Localidades minerais do Estado da Bahia por microrregiões homegênes" and "Areas minerais em desenvolvimento."

5513 ——. Mapa metalogenético do Estado da Bahia, escala 1 : 1.000.000. Desenho cartográfico, Josephina Tamacoldi. Salvador: Secretaria das Minas e Energia, Coordenação da Produção Mineral, 1982. 1 map: col.; 116 x 112 cm.

Includes location map, compilation diagram, and inset of "Domínios geotectônicos / geocronológicos."

5514 Salvia, Flávia la. Mapa da vegetação original, vegetação atual e ação antrópica do Estado do Rio Grande do Sul. Scale 1 : 1,000,000. Pôrto Alegre: Secretaria da Agricultura, Depto. de Comandos Mecanizados, Div. de Geografia e Cartografia, 1983. 1 map: col.; 84 x 78 cm.

Phytogeography: Brazil.

5515 São Paulo, *Brazil* (state). **Secretaria de Estado dos Negócios do Interior. Coordenadoria de Ação Regional. Instituto Geográfico e Cartográfico.** Hipsometria do Estado de São Paulo, 1982: plano cartográfico do Estado de São Paulo. Scale 1 : 1,000,000. São Paulo: O Instituto, 1982. 1 map: col.; 75 x 92 cm.

Relief shown by contours, shading, gradient tints, and spot heights. Depths shown by contours and gradient tints. Includes ancillary maps of "Estrutura e geologia" and "Divisão geomorfológica."

5516 ——. Secretaria da Indústria, Comércio, Ciência e Tecnologia. Programa de Desenvolvimento de Recursos Minerais. Inventário cartográfico do Estado de São Paulo. São Paulo: O Programa, 1981. 1 atlas (339 p.): bibl., col. map; 30 x 42 cm.

5517 ——. ——. ——. Mapa de jazidas e ocorrências minerais do Estado de São Paulo: escala 1 : 500.000. São Paulo: A Secretaria, 1981. 1 map on 2 sheets: col.; 124 x 188 cm.

Issued as vol. 3. Abstract in English in vol. 1. Accompanied by text (2 v., 758 p.:

map; 30 cm.). Includes location map and compilation diagram.

5518 Schaeffer, Juan E. Guia Schaeffer Rio de Janeiro, RJ. 15a ed. Scale 1 : 27,000. Rio de Janeiro: Editôra Presidente: Editôra Geográfica Paulini, 1982. 1 map: col., index; 78 x 109 cm.
Alternate title: Rio, cidade do Rio de Janeiro, Estado do Rio de Janeiro. "Guia Schaeffer de bolso." Index on verso.

5519 Telecomunicações de São Paulo S.A. Configuração do sistema de transmissão, existente dez. 87, com base nos eventos do plano de trabalho 1981/1985, da Diretoria Técnica, Estado do São Paulo. Scale 1 : 1,000,000. São Paulo: Telecomunicações de São Paulo, 1984. 1 map: col.; 62 x 91 cm.
Includes inset of "Area secundária de São Paulo."

5520 United States. Central Intelligence Agency. Brazil. Washington: CIA, 1983. 1 map: 39 x 44 cm.
Relief shown by shading and spot heights. Includes comparative area map, location map with radial distances, and subject maps of "Population, administrative divisions, and economic regions," "Natural vegetation," "Land use," "Temperature and precipitation," and "Economic activity."

CHILE

5522 Chile. Depto. de Geología General. Mapa geológico de Chile. Santiago: Servicio Nacional de Geología y Minería, 1982. 1 map on 6 sheets: col.; 78 x 72 cm.
Depths shown by contours and gradient tints.

5523 ———. **Dirección de Vialidad.** Mapa vial II Región. Scale 1 : 500,000. S.l.: s.n., 1984? 1 map on 2 sheets; 122 x 93 cm.
Road map of region of Antofagasta, Chile. Includes location map.

5524 ———. **Fuerza Aérea. Servicio Aerofotogramétrico.** Carta de navegación, jet: escala 1 : 2.000.000. 2a ed., 1981. Santiago: El Servicio, 1981. 3 maps: col.; on sheets 86 x 49 cm. and 88 x 49 cm.
Relief shown by contours, shading, gradient tints, and spot heights. Includes index map.

5525 COPEC (firm). Rutas camineras: Chile. Preparado para Mobil. Santiago: COPEC, 1983. 4 maps: col.; 72 x 26 cm.
Includes location map, insets, and ancillary map of Territorio Chileno Antártico. Distance chart and city maps on verso.

5526 Geoplán Ingenieros. Atlas de Chile: regionalizado. Cartografía y diagramación, Rony Vergara E. y Jorge Antognini G. Scale 1 : 2,000,000. Santiago: Editorial Lord Cochrane, 1981? 1 atlas (61 [i.e. 63] p.): bibl., col. ill., col. maps; 21 x 28 cm.
Cover title: Atlas de Chile, superior. Rev. ed. of: *Atlas de Chile 78* by Léon Rivera G. (1978?).

5527 ———. Mapa turístico de Chile. Santiago: Editorial Lord Cochrane, 1980. Maps: col.; on sheets 50 x 38 cm.
"Autorizada su circulación por resolución no 33 del 24 de enero de 1980 . . ." Geographic coverage complete in 13 sheets. Each sheet covers one region. Relief shown by spot heights. Includes location map. Some sheets include insets. Text and descriptive list of points of interest in Spanish and English and directories on verso.

5528 Instituto de Investigaciones Geológicas, *Chile.* Carta magnética de Chile, 1 : 100.000. Dibujado por Gabriel Silva M. Santiago: El Instituto, 1980. Maps: col.; 56 x 84 cm.
Relief shown by contours and spot heights. Alternate title: Carta magnética de Chile. Includes location map and index to adjoining sheets.

5529 Instituto Geográfico Militar, *Chile.* Atlas cartográfico del Reino de Chile, siglos XVII–XIX. Santiago: El Instituto, 1981. 1 atlas (266 p.): maps (some col.); 41 x 60 cm.

5530 ———. Atlas de la República de Chile. 2a ed. Santiago: El Instituto, 1983. 1 atlas (349 p.): bibl., col. ill., index, col. maps; 42 cm.
Contents: Antecedentes general; Mapa físico de Chile, escala 1 : 1,000,000; Mapas temáticos nacionales; Mapa temáticos regionales.

5531 ———. Atlas regionalizado de Chile. 2a ed., reimpresión, actualizada. Scale 1 : 1,500,000. Santiago: El Instituto, 1981. 1 atlas (64 p.): bibl., col. ill., col. maps; 34 cm.
Rev. ed. of: *Atlas escolar de Chile con*

la regionalización actualizada (El Instituto, 1980).

5532 Instituto Hidrográfico de la Armada, *Chile.* Atlas hidrográfico de Chile. 2a ed. Valparaíso, Chile: El Instituto, 1980. 1 atlas (38, 258 p.): ill. (some col.), maps (some col.); 33 x 45 cm.

5533 Instituto Nacional de Estadísticas, *Chile.* **Depto. de Geografía y Censos. Subdepto. de Cartografía.** Región Metropolitana de Santiago. Dibujante, José Tortella Latorre. Scale 1 : 500,000. S.l.: s.n., 1984. 1 map; 41 x 67 cm.

Covers Metropolitana, Chile. Includes indexed inset of "Provincia de Santiago (Capital Santiago), mapa esquemático con la división político administrativa" and index to provinces.

5534 INUPAL (firm). Gran mapa caminero de Chile, geográfico y turístico, 1982–1983. Santiago: INUPAL, 1982. 5 maps on 2 sheets: col.; 72 x 23 cm.

Relief shown by spot heights.

5535 ———. Mapas tiket INUPAL para todo Chile: turismo y servicios = INUPAL tiket maps for all Chile: tourism and services. 2nd international ed. Santiago: INUPAL, 1980? 1 atlas (6, 21, 5 p. [some folded]): col. ill., col. maps; 27 cm.

5536 Petroconsultants S.A. Chile, synopsis first half 1982. Geneva: Petroconsultants, 1982. 1 map; 87 x 81 cm.

Depths shown by contours. At head of title: Foreign Scouting Service. Includes "List of Rightholders," table of "Summary of Activity during First Half 1982," inset, statistical data, and location map.

5537 Producciones R.P.M. Descubriendo Chile: rutas y planos de norte a sur. Scale ca. 1 : 2,000,000. Santiago: Producciones R.P.M., 1981? 1 atlas (12 p.): col. maps; 26 cm.

5538 Santiago, Chile: XII Asamblea General del IPGH y Reuniones de Consulta Conexas, Santiago, marzo, 1982. Santiago: s.n., 1982. 1 map: col.; 16 x 17 cm.

Alternate title: Centro de Santiago: bienvenidos a Chile. Includes text. Text and col. ill. on verso.

5539 Silva Calderón, José *et al.* Atlas caminero de Chile, 1982. Santiago:

Silva & Silva, 1981? 1 atlas (30 folded p.): col. map; 24 cm.

At head of title: S&S Cartografía. On most maps: Arte Cartográfico Ltda.

5540 Silva G., Osvaldo. Atlas de historia de Chile. Santiago: Editorial Universitaria, 1983. 1 atlas (110 p.): col. ill.; 27 cm. (Col. Imagen de Chile)

5541 Silva & Silva. Plano de Santiago y mini atlas caminero de Chile, 1983. Santiago: Silva & Silva, 1983. 7 maps on 1 sheet: col.; 55 x 77 cm.

Relief shown by shading and spot heights on map of Santiago. At head of cover title: S&S Cartografía. Accompanied by index (40 p.; 18 cm.). Includes ancillary maps of Valparaíso, Viña del Mar, Talcahuano, and Concepción. Contents: Plano de Santiago: 1) Arica-Antofagasta; 2) Antofagasta, La Serena; 3) La Serena-Rengo 4) Rengo-Temuco; 5) Temuco-Castro; 6) Osorno-Polo Sur.

5542 United States. Central Intelligence Agency. Chile. Washington: CIA, 1983. 1 map: 55 x 30 cm.

Relief shown by shading and spot heights. Includes inset of "Easter Island (Isla de Pascua)" and "Isla Sala y Goméz," location maps with radial distances, comparative area map, and subject maps of "Population and admnistrative divisions," "Vegetation," and "Economic activity."

5543 Univ. de Chile. Depto. de Geografía. Mapa geomorfológico de Mincha, escala 1 : 50.000. Santiago: El Depto., 1983? 1 map: col.; 37 x 32 cm.

Relief shown by contours and spot heights. "Base cartográfica: Hoja Mincha 1 : 50.000 Instituto Geográfico Militar . . ." Includes graph and compilation diagram.

COLOMBIA

5544 Arango Cálad, Jorge Luis and **Alvaro Ponce Muriel.** Mapa geológico generalizado del Depto. de Nariño, escala 1 : 400.000. Bogotá: Ministerio de Minas y Energía, Instituto Nacional de Investigaciones Geológico-Mineras, 1982. 1 map: bibl., col.; 70 x 62 cm.

Cover title of accompanying text: *Mapa geológico del Departamento de Nariño, escala 1 : 400.000: memoria explica-*

tiva. Accompanied by: *Reseña explicativa del Mapa geológico del Departamento de Nariño: informe no. 1818* (1980, 40 p.: ill., maps; 24 cm.). Includes compilation diagram and index map of published geological maps in Colombia.

5545 Cartur (firm). Depto. de Cundinamarca. Scale 1 : 500,000. Bogotá: Cartur, 1982. 1 map: col.; 48 x 42 cm.
Shows climate by colors. Relief shown by contours. Includes location map, coat of arms, text, statistical data, ancillary map of "Bogotá," indexed ancillary map of "Regiones naturales," and list of "Municipios."

5546 Colombia. Ministerio de Desarrollo Económico. Corporación Nacional de Turismo de Colombia. Colombia, mapa vial y turístico. Bogotá: La Corporación, 1981. 1 map: col.; on sheet 88 x 63 cm., folded to 22 x 11 cm.
Alternate title: Colombia, mapa turístico de carreteras. Indexed maps of Cartagena, Barranquilla, Cali, Medellín, and Bogotá on verso.

5547 Cundinamarca, *Colombia.* **Depto. Administrativo de Planeación.** Conozca Cundinamarca atlas. Dirección científica, Manuel Felipe Olivera A. *et al.* Scale 1 : 500,000. Bogotá: El Depto., 1982. 1 atlas (66 p.): col. maps; 59 cm.
Contents: Determinantes de los paisajes naturales; Determinantes de actividades productivas; Redes que permiten la movilización de personas, los bienes y los servicios; Malla urbana y servicios; Actividades.

5548 Flórez, Luis. Manual del atlas lingüístico-etnográfico de Colombia. Bogotá: Instituto Caro y Cuervo, 1983. 307 p., 1 folded leaf of plates: bibl., ill.; 24 cm.
Cover title: Manual del ALEC.

5549 Instituto Geográfico Agustín Codazzi. Atlas regional Orinoquia-Amazonia. Bogotá: Ministerio de Hacienda y Crédito Público, El Instituto, 1983. 1 atlas (162 p.): bibl., ill. (some col.), col. maps; 50 cm.
Contents: División político-administrativa; El medio natural; Aspectos sociales; Infraestructura y servicios; Aspectos económicos; Organización espacial.

5550 ———. Atlas regional Pacífico. Scale 1 : 3,000.000. Bogotá: Ministerio de Hacienda y Crédito Público, El Instituto,

1983. 1 atlas (96 p.): ill. (some col.), col. maps; 49 cm.
Contents: El medio natural; Geografía de la población; Aspectos económicos; Comunicaciones y servicios; Elementos de organización regional.

5551 ———. Circunscripciones electorales y división político administrativa de Colombia. Bogotá: Registraduría Nacional del Estado Civil, 1983. 1 atlas (457 p.): col. ill.; 34 cm.

5552 ———. **Sección de Geofísica.** Mapa gravimétrico anomalías simples de Bouguer. Con la colaboración del Servicio Geodésico Interamericano. 2a ed. Scale 1 : 1,500,000. Bogotá: Ministerio de Hacienda y Crédito Público, El Instituto, 1983.

5553 ———. **Subdirección Cartográfica.** Departamento de Cundinamarca. 4a ed. Scale 1 : 250,000. Bogotá: Ministerio de Hacienda y Crédito Público, El Instituto, La Subdirección, 1983. 1 map: col.; 98 × 84 cm.
Relief shown by contours and gradient tints. Includes compilation diagram, inset of "Plano de la ciudad de Bogotá D.E.," table of "Coordenadas y altitud en metros de los puntos geodésico," location map, and index map to 1 : 100,000 sheets. Representative example of dept. maps published by this authority.

5554 ———. ———. Departamento del Meta. Scale 1 : 500,000. Bogotá: Ministerio de Hacienda y Crédito Público, El Instituto, La Subdirección, 1982. 1 map: col.; 77 x 88 cm.
Relief shown by contours and gradient tints. Includes inset of "Plano ciudad de Villavicencio, escala 1 : 30.000," compilation diagram, location map, index map to 1 : 100,00 sheets, and table of coordinates. Representative example of dept. maps published by this authority.

5555 ———. ———. Departamento del Tolima, mapa físico para uso escolar, 1983: escala 1 : 400.000. Bogotá: Ministerio de Hacienda y Crédito Público, El Instituto, La Subdirección, 1983. 1 map: col.; 80 x 56 cm.
Relief shown by contours and gradient tints. Includes two location maps showing Tolima in Colombia and Colombia in America. Representative example of dept. maps published by this authority.

5556 ———. ———. Plano de la ciudad de
Cali. 2a ed. Scale 1 : 25,000. Bogotá:
Ministerio de Hacienda y Crédito Público, El
Instituto, 1983. 1 map: col.; 50 x 80 cm.,
folded to 27 x 11 cm.
Relief shown by contours. Panel title:
Cali, la Sultana del Valle. Oriented with
north to the right. Indexes, text, maps of city
center and city region, and col. ill. on verso.
Representative example of dept. maps pub-
lished by this authority.

5557 ———. ———. República de Colombia,
división política-uso escolar. Bogotá:
Ministerio de Hacienda y Crédito Público, El
Instituto, 1980. 1 map: col.; 95 × 68 cm.
Includes three island insets, statistical
data, and location map.

5558 Llaves de Colombia Ltda. Directorio
del tránsito y transportes de Bogotá,
D.E. Bogotá: Editécnicos, 1982. 1 atlas (various pagings): ill. col. maps; 21 cm.
Cover title: Llaves de Bogotá.

5559 Petroconsultants S.A. Colombia, synopsis first half 1982. Geneva: Petroconsultants, 1982. 1 map; 109 x 60 cm.
Depths shown by contours. At head of
title: Foreign Scouting Service. Includes "List
of rightholders," table of "Summary of Activity during First Half 1982," charts of
"Crude Oil Production 1981–1982" and
"Natural Gas Production 1981–1982," "Tectonic Sketch Map," and location map.

5560 United States. Central Intelligence
Agency. Colombia. Washington: CIA,
1983. 1 map; 50 x 39 cm.
Relief shown by shading and spot
heights. Includes three island insets, location
map with radial distances, comparative area
map, and subject maps of "Population,"
"Land use," and "Economic activity."

ECUADOR

5561 Atlas del Ecuador. Dirección, Anne
Collin Delavaud. Patrocinio, Georges
Laclavère. Participación, Juan Cueva
Jaramillo. Colaboración, Rodrigo Cabezas et
al y del Instituto Geográfico Militar. Scales
differ. Paris: Les Editions J.A.; Quito: Banco
Central del Ecuador, 1982. 1 atlas (80 p.): col.
maps; 30 cm. (Atlas del mundo)
Includes glossary and index.

5562 Dávila, Violeta Jaramilla de. Atlas
geográfico del Ecuador. 2a ed., actualizada. Quito: Atlas Geográfico del Instituto
Geográfico Militar: Atlas Histórico Geográfico de Morales y Eloy, 1983. 1 atlas (80 p.):
col. ill.; 22 x 28 cm.

5563 Ecuador. Ministerio de Recursos Naturales y Energéticos. Dirección General
de Geología y Minas. Mapa geológico nacional de la República del Ecuador: este mapa
representa solo una parte del territorio nacional. Coordinador, Rafael Longo. Cooperación tecnica, Gobierno Británico, Institute of
Geological Sciences (NEC), London. Coordinador, John Baldock. Scale 1 : 1,000,000.
Quito: La Dirección, 1982. 1 map: col.;
107 x 77 cm.
Relief shown by contours. Includes
inset of "Provincia de Galápagos, escala
1 : 2,000,000," "Mapa índice de los datos
geológicos," two cross sections, and coat
of arms.

5564 Instituto Geográfico Militar, Ecuador.
Ciudad de Quito, plano de nomencla-
tura-sectorización y distritos: escala
1 : 15.000. Quito: El Instituto, 1983. 1 map
on 2 sheets: col.; 46 x 179 cm.
"Publicado por el I.G.M. en base a la
ordenanza municipal . . . Quito Abril . . .
1983." Relief shown by contours. Oriented
with north toward upper right. Includes indexes and coats of arms.

5565 ———. La región sur del Ecuador:
Programa Regional para el Desarrollo
del Sur (PREDESUR). Scale 1 : 250,000.
Quito: PREDESUR, 1982. 1 map: col.;
90 x 122 cm.
Covers El Oro, Loja, and Zamora provs.
Relief shown by contours and spot heights.
Includes statistical data and compilation
diagram.

5566 ———. República del Ecuador, mapa
político. Scale 1 : 1,000,000. Quito: El
Instituto, 1982. 1 map: col.; 84 x 111 cm.
"Este mapa contiene información actualizada al 31 de marzo de 1.981." "Separa-
ción de colores . . . 1982." Stamped on:
Edición provisional. Sujeto a correcciones.
Includes ancillary map of "Provincia de
Galápagos, Archipiélago de Colón, territorio
insular," inset of "Situación del Archipiélago
de Galápagos con relación al territorio continental," note, statistical data, list of administrative divs., and coat of arms.

5567 Petroconsultants S.A. Ecuador, synopsis first half 1982, including current activity. Geneva: Petroconsultants, 1982. 1 map; 92 x 79 cm.
Depths shown by contours. At head of title: Foreign Scouting Service. Includes "List of Rightholders," list of "Wildcat Wells in Sta Elena area," statistical data, table of "Summary of Activity during First Half 1982," and location map.

5568 United States. Central Intelligence Agency. Ecuador. Washington: CIA, 1983. 1 map; 32 x 30 cm.
Relief shown by shading and spot heights. Includes inset of "Galápagos Islands (Archipiélago de Colón)," location map with radial distances, comparative area map, and subject maps of "Population," "Economic activity," and "Vegetation."

FRENCH GUIANA

5569 Martin, Bernard. Map of Cayenne. Cayenne: Artec publicité, 1984. 1 map: col.; 20 x 28 cm.

5570 ———. Plans Cayenne, Kourou, St. Laurent, Paramaribo, reseaux routier = roads maps. Cayenne: Editions Artec, 1982. 7 maps on 1 sheet: col. sheet 51 x 71 cm.
Includes text, directories, indexes to cities, and distance list.

5571 United States. Central Intelligence Agency. French Guiana. Washington: CIA, 1983. 1 map; 24 x 17 cm.
Relief shown by shading and spot heights. Includes location map with radial distances, comparative area map, and subject map of "Economic activity" and "Vegetation."

GUYANA

5572 Petroconsultants S.A. Guyana, synopsis first half 1982. Geneva: Petroconsultants, 1982. 1 map; 76 x 81 cm.
Depths shown by contours. At head of title: Foreign Scouting Service. Includes "List of Rightholders," table of "Summary of Activity during First Half 1982," "Guyana Geological Index Map," statistical data, and location map.

5573 United States. Central Intelligence Agency. Guyana. Washington: CIA, 1983. 1 map; 37 x 31 cm.
Relief shown by shading and spot heights. Includes location map with radial distances, comparative area map, and subject maps of "Economic activity," "Vegetation," "Population," and "Ethnic groups."

PARAGUAY

5574 Guía General de Asunción e Interior del Paraguay (firm). Plano de la ciudad de Asunción, zona del centro. Asunción: Dirección General del Turismo, 1982? 1 map; 17 x 25 cm.
Oriented with north toward upper left. Indexed for points of interest. Descriptive index to points of interest on verso.

5575 Paraguay. Dirección del Servicio Geográfico Militar. Paraguay. 2a ed., año 1.982. Asunción: La Dirección, 1982. 1 map: col.; 62 x 53 cm.
Relief shown by shading. Includes location map and col. portraits.

5576 Petroconsultants S.A. Paraguay, synopsis 1982. Geneva: Petroconsultants, 1982. 1 map; 53 x 65 cm.
At head of title: Foreign Scouting Service. Includes "List of rightholders," statistical data, location map, table of "Summary of Activity during 1982," and inset of "Structural Sketch."

5577 United States. Central Intelligence Agency. Paraguay. Washington: CIA, 1983. 1 map; 37 x 54 cm.
Relief shown by shading and spot heights. Includes location map with radial distances, comparative map, and subject maps of "Population," "Vegetation," and "Economic activity."

PERU

5578 Cartográfica Nacional, S.A. Carreteras del Perú, guía turística. Lima: Cartográfica Nacional, 1982. 3 maps on 1 sheet: col.; 27 x 22 cm.
"Mapa del Perú, "Plano de la ciudad de Lima y alrrededores [sic]," and indexed "Plano de centro de Lima" on verso.

5579 Dymond, Jack and John B. Corliss.
Chemical composition of Nazca plate surface sediments. Scale ca. 1:42,000,000. Boulder, Colo.: Geological Society of America, 1980. 11 maps on 1 sheet: col.; sheet 56 x 46 cm. (Map and chart series; MC–34:2)
Issued with: *Bathymetry of the Peru-Chile trench and continental margin*, compiled by R.A. Prince (see item **5586**). Accompanied by text.

5580 Góngora Perea, Amadeo. Mapa político del Perú: escala 1:2.500.000. Lima: Cartográfica Nacional, 1982. 1 map: col.; 85 x 58 cm.
Cover title: Perú, mapa político, caminero turístico. Includes location map.

5581 Instituto Geográfico Nacional, Peru.
Departamento de Ucayali, mapa físico político. Lima: El Instituto, 1984. 1 map: col.; 55 x 77 cm.

5582 ———. Mapa físico político del Perú, 1982: escala 1.000.000. 2a ed. Lima: El Instituto, 1982. 1 map on 4 sheets: col.; 208 x 147 cm; sheets 112 x 78 cm.
Relief shown by gradient tints and spot heights. Depths shown by contours and gradient tints. At head of title: Ministerio de Guerra. Includes location map, statistical data, and compilation diagram.

5583 Multiservicios E.I.R.L. Guía y planos de calles de Lima y Callao. Scale 1:20,000. Lima: Multiservicios para Planiguías, 1983. 1 atlas (286 p., 2, 46 folded leaves of plates): col. maps; 22 cm.
Cover title: Guía de calles, Lima, Callao, Bainearios. Includes indexes.

5584 Peru. Oficina Nacional de Evaluación de Recursos Naturales. Mapa de capacidad de uso mayor de las tierras del Perú, 1981, escala 1:1.000.000. Lima: La Oficina, 1981. 1 map on 8 sheets: col.; 208 x 147 cm., sheets 62 x 77 cm.
Includes graph and location map.

5585 Petróleos del Perú. Depto. Contratos de Operaciones. Div. Catastro. Mapa de áreas de contratos de operaciones petrolíferas y áreas operadas directamente por Petróleos del Perú Lima: Petróleos del Perú, 1981. 1 map: 53 x 37 cm.
Depths shown by contours. Includes location map.

5586 Prince, R.A. Bathymetry of the Peru-Chile trench and continental margin. Boulder, Colo.: Geological Society of America, 1980. 9 maps: bibl., col.; 61 x 41 cm. or smaller (Map and chart series; MC–34:1)
Depths shown by contours and gradient tints. Contoured by author and others. Accompanied by text. Includes index map.

5587 Ravines, Roggers. Mapa arqueológico del Valle del Jequetepeque. Lima: Instituto Nacional de Cultura, Proyecto Especial de Irrigación Jequetepeque-Zaña, 1981. 1 portfolio (atlas): ill. (some col.); 29 cm. (Materiales para la arqueología del Perú; 1)

5588 ——— and A. Matos. Inventario de monumentos arqueológicos del Perú: Zona Norte, primera aproximación. Scale 1:200,000. Lima: Instituto Nacional de Cultura, 1983. 1 atlas (162 p.): col. maps; 30 x 37 cm.

5589 United States. Central Intelligence Agency. Peru. Washington: CIA, 1981. 1 map; 52 x 37 cm.
Relief shown by shading and spot heights. Includes location map with radial distances, comparative area map, and subject maps of "Population," "Vegetation," and "Economic activity."

SURINAM

5590 Dahlberg, H.N. Map of the Republic of Suriname. Gegevans van het Centraal Bureau Luchtkaartering. Scale 1:1,000,000. Paramaribo: C. Kersten & Co., 1982. 1 map: col.; 68 x 52 cm.
Relief shown by shading, gradient tints, and spot heights. Cover title. Alternate title: Suriname. Includes location map, explanatory notes, and col. ill.

5591 Petroconsultants S.A. Surinam & French Guiana, synopsis 1982. Geneva: Petroconsultants, 1983. 1 map; 62 x 81 cm.
Depths shown by contours. At head of title: Foreign Scouting Service. Includes location map, table of "Summary of Activity during 1982," List of Rightholders," and statistical data.

5592 United States. Central Intelligence Agency. Surinam. Washington: CIA, 1983. 1 map; 41 x 32 cm.

Relief shown by shading and spot heights. Includes location map with radial distances, comparative area map, and subject maps of "Population," "Vegetation," and "Economic activity."

URUGUAY

5593 Daroczi, Isabel; Elena García; and **Miguel Liguera.** Atlas para la República Oriental del Uruguay. Dibujantes, Ana María Laurido y los autores. S.l.: Ediciones Raschetti; Montevideo: Ediciones de Montevideo, 1983. 1 atlas (124 p.): col. ill., col. maps; 31 cm.

5594 Impresora Visión S.C. Mapa carretero de la República Oriental del Uruguay. Fotomecánica, Vassallo. Dibujos cartográficos, Jorge Elía. Montevideo: Automovil Club del Uruguay, 1983. 1 map: col.; 62 x 56 cm.

Alternate title: Mapa rutero de la República Oriental del Uruguay. Includes inset of Montevideo metropolitan area, distance chart, and ancillary maps of Montevideo-Maldonado region and "Rutas de salida." Includes 18 local route maps with telephone directories on verso.

5595 Petroconsultants S.A. Uruguay, synopsis 1982. Geneva: Petroconsultants, 1983. 1 map; 54 x 40 cm.

Depths shown by contours. At head of title: Foreign Scouting Service. Includes "List of Rightholders," table of "Summary of Activity during 1982," statistical data, and location map.

5596 SEGRAB (firm). Mapa MONTPLAN de la República Oriental del Uruguay. Montevideo: Meldix, 1981. 1 map: col.; 70 x 63 cm.

Includes statistical data, ancillary map of "Mapa de Montevideo-Canelones (parcial), red de carreteras, caminos y avenidas de acceso," distance chart, and chart of road signs.

5597 United States. Central Intelligence Agency. Uruguay. Washington: CIA, 1983. 1 map; 41 x 36 cm.

Relief shown by shading and spot heights. In lower right margin: 31A. Includes location map with radial distances, comparative area map, and subject maps of "Population and administrative divisions," "Vegetation," and "Economic activity."

5598 Uruguay. Dirección Nacional de Turismo. Uruguay, mapa turístico. Montevideo: La Dirección, 1983. 1 map: col.; on sheet 65 x 58 cm., folded to 22 x 20 cm.

Includes flight time chart. Text, descriptive points of interest, map of "Zonas turísticas," location map, and col. ill. on verso.

5599 ———. Servicio Geográfico Militar. Carta regional de la República Oriental del Uruguay. Scale 1 : 1,000,000. Montevideo: El Servicio, 1981. 1 map: col.; 67 x 97 cm.

"Compilacion correspondiente al área territorial nacional en base a información planimétrica obtenida en hojas 1 : 100.000 del plan cartográfico nacional, 1981." Relief shown by gradient tints. Includes ancillary map of "Límite territorial marítimo de la República Oriental del Uruguay," and glossary.

5600 ———. ———. República Oriental del Uruguay, carta geográfica. Scale 1 : 500,000. Montevideo: El Servicio, 1982. 1 map on 2 sheets: col.; 145 x 108 cm.

Relief and depths shown by contours. Includes insets of Montevideo region and "Superficie territorial de la República Oriental del Uruguay," location map, statistical data, and sheet index.

VENEZUELA

5601 Alvarez Bernal, Fernando. Atlas climatológico de Venezuela, 1951/70. Caracas: Univ. Central de Venezuela, 1983. 1 atlas (132 p.): ill.; 22 cm.

5602 Atlas de Venezuela. Caracas: Discolar, 1983. 1 atlas (320 p.): ill. (some col.), indexes, col. maps; 28 cm.

Contents: Temas históricos; Temas físicos; Temas económicos; Los estados.

Drenikoff, Iván. Breve historia de la cartografía en Venezuela. See item **5198.**

5603 Electricidad de Caracas. Dependencia de Servicios Técnicos. Div. de Dibujo. Plano de Caracas con guía de calles y avenidas. 5a ed., rev. y aumentada. Scale 1 : 10,000. Caracas: La Div., 1983. 1 atlas (165 p.): index, col. maps; 20 cm.

One folded col. map in pocket.

5604 Petroconsultants S.A. Venezuela, synopsis first half 1982. Geneva: Petro-

consultants, 1982. 2 maps; 81 x 83 cm. and 81 x 80 cm.
Depths shown by contours. At head of title: Foreign Scouting Service. Includes table of "Summary of Activity during First Half 1982," index map, table of "Venezuela, Crude Oil Production 1981–1982," "List of Rightholders," and indexes list of "South Lake Maracaibo Service Contract Area."

5605 United States. Central Intelligence Agency. Venezuela. Washington: CIA, 1983. 1 map; 41 x 51 cm.
Relief shown by shading and spot heights. Includes location map with radial distances, comparative area map, and subject maps of "Population," "Vegetation," "Economic activity," and "Petroleum."

5606 Venezuela. Ministerio del Ambiente y de los Recursos Naturales Renovables. Dirección General de Información e Investigación del Ambiente. Dirección de Cartografía Nacional. Venezuela en mapas. Caracas: Dirección de Cartografía Nacional, 1983. 1 atlas (48 p.): col. ill.; 45 cm.

JOURNAL ABBREVIATIONS
GEOGRAPHY

AES/AE American Ethnologist. American Ethnological Society. Washington.

AGF/B Bulletin de l'Association de géographes français. Paris.

AGS/GR The Geographical Review. American Geographical Society. New York.

AI/I Interciencia. Asociación Interciencia. Caracas.

AMNH/NH Natural History. American Museum of Natural History. New York.

BISRA/BS Belizean Studies. Belizean Institute of Social Research and Action [and] St. John's College. Belize City.

CAG/CG Canadian Geographer/Le Géographe canadien. Canadian Assn. of Geographers. Toronto, Canada.

CDAL Cahiers des Amériques latines. Paris.

CIRMA/M Mesoamérica. Centro de Investigaciones Regionales de Mesoamérica. Antigua, Guatemala.

CJN Croissance des jeunes nations. Paris.

CPES/RPS Revista Paraguaya de Sociología. Centro Paraguayo de Estudios Sociológicos. Asunción.

EEHA/AEA Anuario de Estudios Americanos. Consejo Superior de Investigaciones Científicas [and] Univ. de Sevilla, Escuela de Estudios Hispano-Americanos. Sevilla.

GH Geographica Helvetica. Schweizerische Zeitschrift für Länder- und Völkerkunde. Kümmerly & Frey, Geographischer Verlag. Bern.

GR Geographische Rundschau. Zeitschrift für Schulgeographie. Georg Westermann Verlag. Braunschweig, FRG.

IAA Ibero-Amerikanisches Archiv. Ibero-Amerikanisches Institut. Berlin, FRG.

IBG/T Transactions. Institute of British Geographers. London.

IBGE/R Revista Brasileira de Geografia. Conselho Nacional de Geografia, Instituto Brasileiro de Geografia e Estatística. Rio de Janeiro.

IBGE/RBE Revista Brasileira de Estatística. Ministério do Planejamento e Coordenação Geral, Instituto Brasileiro de Geografia e Estatística. Rio de Janeiro.

IEAS/R Revista de Estudios Agro-Sociales. Instituto de Estudios Agro-Sociales. Madrid.

IGFO/RI Revista de Indias. Instituto Gonzalo Fernández de Oviedo [and] Consejo Superior de Investigaciones Científicas. Madrid.

IPE/EE Estudos Econômicos. Univ. de São Paulo, Instituto de Pesquisas Econômicas. São Paulo.

JDA Journal of Developing Areas. Western Illinois Univ. Press. Macomb.

JLAS Journal of Latin American Studies. Centers or institutes of Latin American studies at the universities of Cambridge, Glasgow, Liverpool, London and Oxford. Cambridge Univ. Press. London.

LARR Latin American Research Review. Univ. of North Carolina Press *for the* Latin American Studies Association. Chapel Hill.

NCGE/J Journal of Geography. National

Council of Geographic Education. Menasha, Wis.

NGS/NGM National Geographic Magazine. National Geographic Society. Washington.

NS NS NorthSouth NordSud NorteSur NorteSul. Canadian Assn. of Latin American Studies. Univ. of Ottawa. Ottawa.

OAS/CI Ciencia Interamericana. Organization of American States, Dept. of Scientific Affairs. Washington.

PAIGH/G Revista Geográfica. Instituto Panamericano de Geografía e Historia, Comisión de Geografía. México.

SAGE/JIAS Journal of Inter-American Studies and World Affairs. Sage Publication *for the* Center for Advanced International Studies, Univ. of Miami. Coral Gables, Fla.

SCHG/R Revista Chilena de Historia y Geografía. Sociedad Chilena de Historia y Geografía. Santiago.

SGB/COM Les Cahiers d'outre-mer. Institut de géographie de la Faculté des lettres de Bordeaux, Institut de la France d'outre-mer [and] Société de géographie de Bordeaux *avec le concours* du Centre national de la recherche scientifique [and] VI Section de l'Ecole pratique des hautes études. Bordeaux, France.

SSG/RGI Rivista Geografica Italiana. Società di Studi Geografici e Coloniali. Firenze, Italy.

UBGI/E Erdkunde. Archiv für Wissenschaftliche Geographie. Univ. Bonn, Geographisches Institut. Bonn, FRG.

UC/EDCC Economic Development and Cultural Change. Univ. of Chicago, Research Center in Economic Development and Cultural Change. Chicago.

UC/IG Informaciones Geográficas. Univ. de Chile, Depto. de Geografía. Santiago.

ULA/RG Revista Geográfica. Univ. de Los Andes. Mérida, Venezuela.

ULIG/C Cahiers de géographie de Québec. Univ. Laval, Institut de géographie. Québec, Canada.

UP/TM Tiers monde. Univ. de Paris, Institut d'Étude du développement économique et social. Paris.

URSS/AL América Latina. Academia de Ciencias de la Unión de Repúblicas Soviéticas Socialistas. Moscú.

UWI/SES Social and Economic Studies. Univ. of the West Indies, Institute of Social and Economic Research. Mona, Jamaica.

YAXKIN Yaxkin. Instituto Hondureño de Antropología e Historia. Tegucigalpa.

ZG Zeitschrift für Geomorphologie. Gebrüder Borntraeger. Berlin, FRG.

GOVERNMENT AND POLITICS

GENERAL

6001 Alexander, Robert J. Latin America: human rights and democracy (Freedom at Issue [Freedom House, New York] 76, Jan./ Feb. 1984, p. 25–28, map)

Brief review of human rights and political democracy picture in Latin America for 1983. The most spectacular advance was made in Argentina with the replacement of a repressive military apparatus with a civilian regime. Economic crises in a large number of other countries may endanger both secure democracies (Colombia, Costa Rica, and the Dominican Republic) and established dictatorships (Chile, Paraguay, and Guatemala). Finds human rights situation in Nicaragua in 1983 "equivocal." [D.W. Dent]

6002 Angulo Novoa, Alejandro *et al.* Debate político. Bogotá: Centro de Investigación y Educación Popular, 1983. 151 p.: bibl. (Serie Controversia; 112)

Role of Papal Encyclicals and Catholic social thought applied to problem of human rights abuses in Central America and Caribbean. Also notes numerous military interventions of US in the area all contrary to international and inter-American law as well as current position of the Church. [W.R. Garner]

6004 Autoritarismo y alternativas populares en América Latina. Edición, Francisco Rojas Aravena. Daniel Camacho *et al.* San José: Ediciones FLACSO, 1982. 217 p.: bibl., ill. (Col. 25 aniversario)

One of the most active groups of academics in Latin America, centered in Chile's FLACSO, have collected their views on authoritarian and other forms of political systems. For the most part, however, they deal with broad philosophical issues and less with concrete Latin American cases. [R.A. Camp]

6005 Berryman, Phillip. Basic Christian communities and the future of Latin America (MR, 36:3, July/Aug. 1984, p. 27–40)

Phillip Berryman, who has written extensively on the "New Church" in Latin America, traces development of the "Basic Communities" movement throughout the region during the past decade. In a rather realistic assessment, points out that it remains a minority movement within the Church but warns against considering its relatively small number among parishes proportional to its political and religious influence which is increasing rapidly. [G.W. Wynia]

6006 Carranza, Mario. Military coups and militarization in Latin America (JPR, 20:4, 1983, p. 367–375, bibl.)

Review essay of Alain Rouquié's book *L'Etat militaire en Amérique latine* (1982) which uses a historical-comparative perspective in order to examine civil-military relations. Reviewer disagrees with Rouquié on degree of permanence of military governments. [D.W. Dent]

6007 Corrales, Andrés. Soziale und politische Implikationen der Öffnung der katholischen Kirche Lateinamerikas (OLI/ZLW, 22, 1984, p. 21–39)

Succinct analysis of profound political and social impact of radical changes in the Catholic Church in Latin America, such as growing acceptance of liberation theology and proliferation of base communities. Examines struggle between conservative and progressive sectors of the Catholic hierarchy in several countries. Concludes that changes which have taken place are irreversible and their impact will be felt in other parts of the world. [G.M. Dorn]

6008 Los Derechos humanos: sus fundamentos en la enseñanza de la Iglesia. Bogotá: Consejo Episcopal Latinoamericano (CELAM), Equipo de Reflexión Teológico-Pastoral, 1982. 175 p.: bibl. (Documentos CELAM; 57)

Descriptive history of the evolution of human rights policy and advocacy of the

Catholic Church in Latin America. Emphasizes doctrine. [R.A. Camp]

6009 Duff, Ernest A. Leader and party in Latin America. Boulder, Colo.: Westview Press, 1985. 177 p.: bibl., index (A Westview special study)

Important work that examines relationship between eight political leaders and party development in Latin America (1920s-30s). Uses comparative case-study approach to analyze factors associated with success and failure of long-lasting political institutions. His findings corroborate conclusions of others on relationship between institutionalized political parties and relative absence of political repression. Moreover, institution builders and not caudillos or charismatic leaders are the sine-qua-non for political peace and prosperity in the long run. [D.W. Dent]

6010 El Ensayo político latinoamericano en la formación nacional. Introducción, compilación y notas de Raymundo Ramos. Investigación histórico, Frida Varina. México: Instituto de Capacitación Política, 1981. 558 p.: bibl. (Serie Antologías)

Interesting compilation of essays by leading Latin American statesmen and intellectuals (1806–1979) dealing with topic of political and cultural nationalism. Excellent selections include brief biography of each contributor. [R.A. Camp]

6011 González Casanova, Pablo. La crisis del Estado y la lucha por la democracia en América Latina (SP, 10, mayo 1980, p. 117–124)

Study designed to classify a State apparatus in terms of its ability to generate democracy. Variously defines and also classifies latter concept according to patterns of elites and/or other groups involved in the struggle for democracy. Also describes State patterns according to types of services performed. That is, the "State" is *substantively* defined and, unfortunately, far from the more useful procedural definitions of the concept. Here lies the significance and weakness of this article by a distinguished Mexican political scientist. [W.R. Garner]

6012 Guerra García, Francisco. Identidad nacional y democracia en América Latina (SP, 17, marzo 1982, p. 1–8)

Isolates facets of national identity that combine to make for a colonial or neo-colonial State culture and that ultimately produce major demand for change towards democratic socialist political forms. Political culture and democracy, as is so often the case, are defined *substantively*. As Guerra states without qualm, "for us social scientists who do not aspire to neutrality [in the discussion], our job is to translate theoretical problems into actual political discourse [leading to change.]" [W.R. Garner]

6013 ———. Reflexiones en torno a la organización de la práctica política (SP, 19, sept. 1982, p. 51–60)

Think-piece stresses psychological bases of political behavior that leads to adoption of socialist public policy. Traces various Latin American movements that appear to have been the result of mentalities he defines and identifies as those that have been more (or less) successful in establishing democratic socialism in their respective countries. [W.R. Garner]

6014 Kuznetsova, Emma. Modernización neocapitalista de las relaciones sociales (URSS/AL, 8:56, agosto 1982, p. 84–91)

Brief analysis of the theory and practice of "modernization" of social relations in Latin America. Argues that under conditions of "State monopoly capitalism" the goal of elites in Chile, Mexico, and Brazil is to modify strategy and tactics of development in order to modernize capitalism rather than alter class structure. [D.W. Dent]

6015 Lateinamerika: Herrschaft, Gewalt und internationale Abhängigkeit. Edited by Klaus Lindberg. Wolfgang König *et al.* Bonn: Verlag Neue Gesellschaft, 1982. 358 p.: bibl.

Several major West German Latin Americanists examine questions of power, violence, and international politics in Latin America. Wolfgang König speculates adroitly on the possibilities of economic integration at a regional level. Dieter Nohlen addresses question of democratization of authoritarian regimes. Peter Waldmann analyzes impact of guerrilla activities in Argentina, Uruguay, Guatemala, and Nicaragua. Wolf Grabendorff, among others, studies Latin America-US relations. Valuable, thoughtful collection of essays which reflect West German scholarship on Latin America. [G.M. Dorn]

Latin American politics: a historical bibliography. See item 37.

Martins, Antonio J. Etat et société en Amérique latine: éléments de bibliographie. See item 39.

6017 Nef, Jorge. Political democracy in Latin America: an exploration into the nature of two political projects (in Latin American prospects for the 1980s: equity, democratization, and development. Edited by Archibald R.M. Ritter and David H. Pollock. New York: Praeger, 1981, p. 161–181)

Despite the passage of several US presidential administrations and multiple changes in our perception of Latin America, there remain two constant assumptions held by political and academic elites: 1) emphasis on ideological continuity as seen in the concern for developmentalism and stability; and 2) a close relationship between Latin American studies and US policy. Posits that emphasis on developmentalism produces "dependency" economics and the stress on order breeds a "moralistic" preoccupation with "anti-Communism and authoritarian regime support" on the part of US. Cites Reagan administration as prime example but also notes elements of phenomenon in presidencies of Carter, Kennedy, and Nixon. Interesting analysis. [W.R. Garner]

Nunn, Frederick M. Yesterday's soldiers: European military professionalism in South America, 1890–1940. See HLAS 46: 1911.

6018 Pérez Sáinz, Juan Pablo et al. El Estado del capitalismo periférico. Bogotá: Centro de Investigación y Educación Popular, 1982. 160 p.: bibl. (Col. Teoría y sociedad; 6)

Marxist critique of societies of the periphery employing capitalist principles to solve problem of underdevelopment. Standard dependency themes and analysis with case studies from Brazil and Colombia. [D.W. Dent]

6019 Philip, George D.E. Military-authoritarianism in South America: Brazil, Chile, Uruguay, and Argentina (PSA/PS, 32:1, March 1984, p. 1–20)

In this brief but provocative piece of inquiry, Philip objects to most of the existing interpretations of military-authoritarianism's origins, most particularly those offered by Samuel Huntington, Guillermo O'Donnell, and Juan Linz in their respective works. In place of structuralism, political moderniza-

tion theory, and authoritarian theory, he offers, albeit tentatively, a "two track" explanation that stresses conditions within the military organization and its ability to control its opposition as most essential to explaining its behavior. Much more will have to be done, however, to make his theory any more convincing than former ones. [G.W. Wynia]

——. Oil and politics in Latin America: nationalist movements and state companies. See item 2953a.

6020 Quintanilla Obregón, Lourdes. Lombardismo y sindicatos en América Latina. México: Ediciones Nueva Sociología, 1982. 358 p.: bibl. (Col. Metodología y técnicas de investigación social)

Historical overview of the Latin American Federation of Labor and its impact on the evolution of Latin American labor movements from 1930s to present. [R.A. Camp]

Rangel, Carlos. La inestable Latinoamérica. See HLAS 46: 1786.

6021 Rendón Vásquez, Jorge. La administración pública del trabajo: concepto, principios, organización y evolución. Lima: Centro Interamericano de Administración del Trabajo, 1980. 405 p.: ill.

Peruvian prof.'s lectures to Venezuelan graduate students on governmental administration in area of organized labor. Solid example of Latin American public administration text. [W.R. Garner]

6022 Rey, Juan Carlos. Problemas sociopolíticos de América Latina. Caracas: Editorial Ateneo de Caracas: Editorial Jurídica Venezolana, 1980. 338 p.: bibl.

Venezuelan political scientists offer several theoretical models for the study of political underdevelopment in Latin America including bureaucratic authoritarianism, the national security State, and populist models of development. Excellent analysis by Latin American scholars. [D.W. Dent]

6023 Santos, Theotonio dos et al. América Latina en el mundo actual. México: Ediciones El Caballito, 1979. 303 p.: bibl., ill.

Wide-ranging anthology with many authors. Four major pts.: 1) capitalist crisis and imperialist strategy: 2) Latin America and new tendencies in central capitalist countries; 3) dependent Latin American militarism; and 4) action capabilities for Latin America in a changing world order. [J.M. Hunter]

6024 Scheina, Robert L. Latin American navies (Proceedings [US Naval Institute, Annapolis] 110:973, March 1984, p. 30–35, ill., map)

Naval historian briefly assesses economic and political climate from Mexico to Argentina noting changes in armed forces with emphasis on strength of current naval power. The emphasis on "exciting naval news" including which country is buying what kind of weapons is more valuable than geopolitical analysis. [D.W. Dent]

6025 Seminario Internacional: Los Derechos Humanos en América Latina, Quito, 1979. Derechos humanos en América Latina. Organizadores, Asociación Latinoamericana de Derechos Humanos (ALDHU) e Instituto Latinoamericano de Investigaciones Sociales (ILDIS). Bogotá: Ediciones Internacionales, 1981. 324 p.: bibl., ill. (some col.)

Compilation of papers and documents of an international seminar on human rights (Quito, 1979) and the constitutive assembly of the Latin American Assn. of Human Rights. Useful collection of views. [R.A. Camp]

6026 Seminario Internacional: Políticas Económicas y Perspectivas Democráticas en América Latina en los Años 80, Quito, 1982. Los modelos de la crisis. Compilación, Sohel Riffka. Quito: Editorial El Conejo, 1983. 344 p.: ill. (Col. Ecuador hoy)

How adequate have theories of political economy been for understanding "crises" that have plagued Latin American economies in the 1980s? Answers are provided by economists, lawyers, and politicians at a seminar (Quito, 1982). Capitalist theories come under heavy attack while variations of socialism point the way toward Latin America's future. [D.W. Dent]

6026a Sociedad, política e integración en América Latina. Edición de Manfred Wilhelmy. Gonzalo Fernández et al. Santiago: Ediciones CINDE, 1981? 210 p.: bibl. (Biblioteca Ediciones CINDE)

Study of national (Chile, Brazil, Mexico, Venezuela, Peru) politics (generally, democracy and authoritarianism) and policies with respect to integration on a regional or subregional basis. Seeks to generalize. [J.M. Hunter]

6027 Tagle Martínez, Hugo. Visión de la doctrina política de la Iglesia Católica. S.l.: Instituto de Estudios Generales, 1981. 115 p.

General analysis of Church-State relations, but not directly concerned with Latin America. [R.A. Camp]

6027a Vargas Llosa, Mario. Latin America: a media stereotype (The Atlantic [The Atlantic Monthly Co., Boston] 253:2, Feb. 1984, p. 20–24)

Peruvian novelist's critique of German counterpart, Günther Grass, who sees only the Cuban model as "relevant" to required socioeconomic-political change in Latin America. Vargas Llosa asks why the "German model" applies to Western Europe (and to Germany in particular) but not to Nicaragua? States that Grass is possessed by "subconscious doubt" about capacity of Latin Americans to achieve liberty and respect for human rights as enjoyed by other Western democracies and that this reveals "unconscious prejudice, an inchoate sentiment, a sort of visceral racism." One might well ask whether Grass's cultural relativism is any more relevant to Latin America than is Vargas Llosa's hypersensitivity. Otherwise, a novel and necessary confrontation. [W.R. Garner]

6028 Wesson, Robert. Populism and military coups (in New military politics in Latin America. Edited by Robert Wesson. New York: Praeger, 1982, p. 17–34)

The link between populism as a response to modernization and military coups is examined by looking at politics of development in Brazil, Chile, Argentina, Guatemala, Uruguay, and Peru. Reveals a paradox in Latin American modernization whereby efforts to solve problem of highly unequal societies leads to governments by force rather than governments by consensus. More interesting for its treatment of populism within Latin American context than politics of military intervention. [D.W. Dent]

6029 Wolpin, Miles D. Sociopolitical radicalism and military professionalism in the Third World (CUNY/CP, 15:2, Jan. 1983, p. 203–220)

Third World military officers should support socially radical and economically nationalistic civilian political movements in order to fulfill their professional aspirations rather than seize the governmental apparatus. Interesting thesis that definitely needs further testing and elaboration. [D.W. Dent]

MEXICO

RODERIC A. CAMP, *Professor of Political Science, Central College, Pella, Iowa*

THERE IS MUCH TO commend in the field of Mexican politics since the publication of *HLAS 45*. While major deficiencies continue as in, for example, the lack of general overviews and political biographies, other useful trends are becoming more established.

Among the most notable gaps in Mexican political history since 1929, has been the omission of a serious analysis of Mexico's official party and its antecedents. Therefore, the work by Luis Javier Garrido, a political historian, fills a significant void (item **6065**). This outstanding volume, meticulously researched, will serve as a benchmark for any future study, and is to be followed by a second volume, continuing the party's history as of 1945.

Whereas the influx of regional and local studies has overwhelmed recent historical analysis of Mexico, political scientists have been slow to respond to this interest. There have been a few exceptions, encouraged by a group from UNAM, the national univeristy, among them Irma Teresa Corrales, whose article on the state of Hidalgo (item **6054**) provides an excellent picture of Mexican state-national relations.

In Mexican political studies primarily by Mexicans, a subject that continues to monopolize the attention is organized labor. Although most of the contributions are of article length, the Mexican Institute of Social Security has put together an imaginative collection of occupational risks (item **6090**). But for a more traditional political-historical analysis, Barry Carr's book on the labor movement, 1910–29, provides a basis for understanding the peculiar relationship between the government and organized labor in the post-revolutionary era (item **6049**). One of the best case studies of the importance of the rank and file to the relationship between the Mexican Federation of Labor and the government is Ian Roxborough's analysis of the motor vehicle industry (item **6093**). Finally, Kenneth Coleman and Charles Davis have applied survey analysis to identify the degree of worker satisfaction in the 1970s (item **6052**).

In public administration, Mexicans have generated the bulwark of the literature, most of which has taken a very traditional approach. A major contribution, from an unlikely source, is an outstanding reference work published by the Secretaría de la Presidencia, similar to US government organization manuals (item **6078**). Because of the numerous changes in Mexican public administration since 1977, the article by Mark Rorem (item **6092**) will help scholars wade through the myriad legal implications of these changes.

Although other interest groups, such as the Church and the military, are still neglected, there is some evidence of rising-interest in organizations or elites representing the private sector. Among these are Dale Story's original analysis of the attitudes of representatives of major industrial chambers (item **6097**), and Carlos

Arriola's characterization, in a descriptive vein, of Mexican entrepreneurial groups (item **6042**).

Since the political reforms of 1977, there is an an even greater need of serious studies of opposition leaders and groups in Mexico. An exception to this scanty literature and one that uses empirical sources, is an analysis by Charles L. Davis and Kenneth Coleman of the support commanded by both PRI and its leading opposition party, PAN, up to 1973 (item **6057**). Hopefully, future studies will bring their analysis up through the 1980s.

6040 Aguilar Mora, Manuel. El bonapartismo mexicano. v. 1, Auge y decadencia. v. 2, Crisis y petróleo. México: J. Pablos Editor, 1982. 2 v.: bibl.

This two-vol. work is a serious analysis, in a Marxist framework, of Mexican political process. Although beginning with 1920s, essentially focuses on post-1968 period and on crises of José López Portillo period.

6041 Alvarado, Salvador. La reconstrucción de México. Precedida de un discurso de Miguel de la Madrid H. Comentario histórico preliminar de Antonio Pompa y Pompa. México: Partido Revolucionario Institucional, 1982. 3 v.: bibl., ill. (Biblioteca fundamental de historia de México; 5–7)

This three-vol. work is a service to 20th-century historians since it collects together ideas of a major activist and pragmatic ideologue of the Mexican Revolution of 1910.

Alvarez, Mayda. Los jóvenes y el sistema político mexicano: elementos para una proposición. See *HLAS 46:2170.*

6042 Arriola, Carlos. Las organizaciones empresariales y el estado. México: Fondo de Cultura Económica, 1981. 213 p.: bibl. (SEP/80; 3)

In a field where so little has been written on the Mexican case, this book provides some useful characteristics of relations between the State and major business organizations.

6043 Ayala Anguiano, Armando. México en crisis: el fin del sistema. México: Ediciones Océano, 1982. 166 p.

Imaginative account of bureaucratic corruption in Mexican politics and what might happen, fictionally that is, if the official bureaucracy was renovated.

6044 Aziz Nassif, Alberto. Historia y coyuntura de la reforma política en México, 1977–1981. México: Centro de Investiga-

ciones y Estudios Superiores en Antropología Social, 1982. 259 p.: bibl. (Cuadernos de la Casa Chata; 47)

Helpful collection of responses by official sources and opposition party leaders which helps to document their views of political reforms introduced after 1977.

6045 Bailey, John J. and **Donna H. Roberts.** Mexican agricultural policy (CUH, 82:488, Dec. 1983, p. 420–424, 436)

Provides a helpful, concise description and analysis of Mexican Food System (SAM), and suggests agricultural policies to be followed by the de la Madrid administration in 1983.

6046 Bastian, Jean-Pierre. Protestantismo y política en México (UNAM/RMS, 43:43, 1981, p. 1947–1966)

On some very thin evidence from 1930s, for the most part, claims that protestantism has been and is an ideological apparatus of the dependent capitalist State.

6047 Bonilla Machorro, Carlos. Ejercicio de guerrillero. 2a ed. México: Grupo Editorial Gaceta, 1983. 299 p.: ill.

Very personal account, with some interesting documentation, of Lucio Cabañas and his guerrilla movement in Guerrero in 1970s.

6048 Cabral, João Batista Pinheiro. O Partido Liberal Mexicano e a greve de Cananea. Brasília: Editôra Univ. de Brasília, 1981. 96 p.: ill. (Cadernos de UnB)

Brief interpretation of Mexican Liberal Party's role and Cananea mining strike before outbreak of 1910 Revolution.

Cardiel Reyes, Raúl. La filosofía política del México actual. See *HLAS 46:7542.*

Carr, Barry. Marxism and anarchism in the formation of the Mexican Communist Party: 1910–1919. See *HLAS 46:7543.*

6049 ———. El movimiento obrero y la política en México, 1910–1929. Traducción de Roberto Gómez Ciriza. 1a ed. corr y ampliada de la ed. original. México: Ediciones Era, 1981. 282 p.: bibl. (Col. Problemas de México)

Thoroughly researched history of the evolution of organized labor during revolutionary and immediate post-revolutionary periods which documents relationship between Mexican government and organized labor, conflicts within movement and impact on the larger environment.

6050 Casillas H., Roberto. La decisión presidencial. México: Aconcagua Ediciones y Publicaciones, 1983. 104 p.

Theoretical interpretation of presidential power by a former presidential appointments secretary.

6051 Castro, Simón Hipólito. Guerrero: amnistía y represión. México: Editorial Grijalbo, 1982. 170 p.: ill., plates.

Provides biographical information on important guerrilla leader, Lucio Cabañas, causes for his movement, his kidnapping of Rubén Figueroa, and general problem of political prisoners in Mexico.

6052 Coleman, Kenneth M. and **Charles L. Davis.** Preemptive reform and the Mexican working class (LARR, 18:1, 1983, p. 3–31, bibl.)

These two authors, who have been among the leaders in using survey data to analyze beliefs of large groups of Mexicans, conclude that Mexico's industrial workers in 1970s were not aware of changes indicating their lives had improved, suggesting a more difficult road for the government in satisfying worker demands in 1980s.

6053 Coll, Tatiana et al. Lucha obrera en México: la visión de sus líderes y conceptos fundamentales. México: Editorial Popular de los Trabajadores, 1983. 218 p. (Biblioteca del trabajador. Col. Memoria y organización)

Series of interviews, without any critical commentary, with six leading figures of Mexican labor movement, organized by question.

6054 Corrales, Irma Teresa. Heterogeneidad del Estado y conflictos regionales: desaparición de poderes en Hidalgo (UNAM/RMS, 44:1, enero/marzo 1982, p. 119–149)

Excellent analysis of relationship between national government and state govern-

ment of Hidalgo. Concludes that a degree of regional autonomy exists to allow displaced national politicians to act forcefully in state politics without national interference.

6055 Couffignal, Georges. Cuestiones a propósito del estudio del sindicalismo: el caso mexicano (Iztapalapa [Univ. Autónoma Metropolitana, Iztalapa, México] 2:3, julio/dic. 1980, p. 105–121, ill.)

Interesting and well researched theoretical piece on the complexity of present union movements in Mexico, which argues that the political system can be understood from an examination of unions and viceversa.

6056 Davis, Charles L. Political regimes and the socioeconomic resource model of political mobilization: some Venezuelan and Mexican data (SPSA/JP, 45:2, May 1983, p. 422–448, tables)

Author's conclusions stem from data he has developed for more than a decade on mobilization in Mexico. Believes that class consciousness leads to alienated politization in that country.

6057 ——— and **Kenneth M. Coleman.** Electoral change in the one-party dominant Mexican polity, 1958–1973: evidence from Mexico City (JDA, 16:4, July 1982, p. 511–521)

Excellent study through 1973 which concludes that PAN (Mexico's leading opposition National Action Party) has successfully recruited increased support from the nonaligned voter, and that recently, PRI has failed to do likewise.

6058 Dobrzycki, Wiesław. Myśl polityczna i praktyka Rewolucji Meksykańskiej = Political thought and practice of the Mexican Revolution. Warszawa: Centralny Ośrodek Metodyczny Studiów Nauk Politycznych, 1982. 432 p.: bibl.

Polish political scientist presents valuable reading of "political and nationalist revolution" in Mexico. Based on a variety of official sources and a great deal of secondary literature. Unfortunately, the monograph was published as a lecture in poorly mimeographed form and limited printings. [K. Complak]

6059 Estructura administrativa del estado de Chiapas. México: Instituto Nacional de Administración Pública (INAP): Instituto de Administración Pública del Estado de Chiapas, 1981. 745 p.: bibl., ill., plates (Estudios. Serie II, Administración pública mexicana; 1)

Incredibly detailed government organization manual for Chiapas state.

6060 Figueroa A., Rodulfo. Las prioridades nacionales y las políticas de reclutamiento de funcionarios públicos en los países en desarrollo. México: El Colegio de México, Centro de Estudios Internacionales, 1981. 143 p.: bibl. (Jornadas; 95)

Brief, theoretical analysis of some of recruitment problems inherent in Mexican public administration. Concluding sections offer some concrete alternatives applicable to Mexican case.

6061 Flores Magón, Ricardo. Artículos políticos 1910. México: Ediciones Antorcha, 1981. 3 v.

Useful collection of articles, essays, and comments (1910–12) by one of Mexico's pre-revolutionary intellectuals and anarcho-syndicalist leaders.

6062 Fuchigami, Takashi. The Mexican political elites: a survey of Secretaries of State (Latin American Studies [Univ. of Tsukuba, Sakura-Mura, Japan] 5, 1983, p. 135–169, bibl., graphs, tables)

Example of on-going state-of-the-art research on Mexico by Japanese. Attempts to describe trends in background characteristics of cabinet secretaries.

6063 García Cárdenas, Luis. Historia de la administración pública en México (IIAS/IRAS, 49:1, 1983, p. 17–38)

Essentially, a brief historical overview of the evolution of legislation affecting public administration in Mexico.

6064 García Salord, Susana. Interpretaciones del movimiento estudiantil popular del 68 (CP, 25, julio/sept. 1980, p. 71–84)

Useful analysis of major theoretical interpretations of 1968 student movement in Mexico. By providing a comparative framework, author makes it possible to assess strengths and weaknesses of each interpretation. Concludes that no single interpretation provides an accurate picture.

6065 Garrido, Luis Javier. El partido de la revolución institucionalizada; medio siglo de poder político en México: la forma-ción del nuevo estado, 1928–1945. México: Siglo Veintiuno Editores, 1982. 380 p.: bibl., ill., plates (Sociología y política)

Outstanding work, most thorough yet to date, of the history of official party's (PRI) evolution and its first two decades of operation in Mexico. Garrido's analysis is objective and detailed, and opens up a wealth of information to other scholars.

6066 Granados Chapa, Miguel Angel. Examen de la comunicación en México. México: Ediciones El Caballito, 1981. 224 p.: bibl. (Col. Fragua mexicana)

Series of essays and speeches by well known Mexican author on various means of communication in Mexico. A number of these contain hard-to-obtain information on radio and television, and he discusses critical question of relationships between political values and the media.

Grayson, George W. An overdose of corruption: the domestic politics of Mexican oil. See item **3086.**

6067 Grindle, Merilee Serrill. Official interpretations of rural underdevelopment: Mexico in the 1970s. La Jolla: Program in US-Mexican Studies, Univ. of California at San Diego, 1981. 49 leaves: bibl., ill. (Working papers in US-Mexican studies; 20)

Discusses Echeverría and José López Portillo administrations' interpretations of the causes of Mexican rural underdevelopment and what are the implications for reform of agrarian policies.

6068 Gutiérrez, Estela and **Fernando Talavera.** El sindicalismo universitario: las fuerzas de izquierda y el Estado (CP, 25, julio/sept. 1980, p. 29–53)

Analysis of efforts of university workers to organize within National Univ. and the relationship between the State and various groups hoping to represent these workers. Identifies achievements and failures of various representatives within workers movement and disparities in labor legislation and actual conditions in which Mexican labor must organize.

6069 Hellman, Judith Alder. The role of ideology in peasant politics: peasant mobilization and demobilization in the Laguna Region (SAGE/JIAS, 25:1, Feb. 1983, p. 3–30, bibl., chart)

Fascinating case study of the impact of

ideology on structure of peasant organizations, their leadership style, and links they form with national leaders in one of the most important agrarian regions.

6070 Las Ideas políticas y los partidos en México: historia documental. Selección de Daniel Moreno. México: Editorial Pax-México: Librería C. Césarman, 1982. 511 p.: bibl.

Work of considerable value for political historians who wish to examine evolution of political parties or organizations from independence through end of Porfiriato. Excellent collection of more than 50 essays, mostly by notable political figures.

6071 Instituto Político Nacional de Administradores Públicos (IPONAP) and Instituto de Estudios Políticos, Económicos y Sociales (IEPES). El desafío municipal. México: Instituto de Capacitación Política, 1982. 317 p.: bibl., ill. (Serie Administración pública. Breviarios ICAP)

Contains a number of useful essays with hard-to-obtain information about municipalities written by expert consultants during 1982 presidential campaign.

6072 Lajous, Alejandra. Los orígenes del partido único en México. 2a ed. México: UNAM, Instituto de Investigaciones Históricas, 1981. 268 p.: bibl. (Serie de historia moderna y contemporánea; 11)

Serious analysis of evolution of antecedents to PRI, but work by Javier Luis Garrido is a much more comprehensive account (see item **6065**).

6073 Lehr, Volker G. Der mexikanische Autoritarismus: Parteien, Wahlen, Herrschaftssicherung und Krisenpotential. München, FRG: Wilhelm Fink Verlag, 1981. 303 p.: appendices, tables (Lateinamerika Studien; 8)

Incisive study of Mexican authoritarianism using framework devised by Juan Linz. Traces authoritarian rule from Porfiriato to López Portillo, analyzing the corporate structure, voting patterns, elements of political stability/instability, as well as potential for crisis. Invaluable appendices presenting figures for many key elections, local as well as national, enhance this major contribution. [G.M. Dorn]

6074 Looney, Robert E. Mexican policy dilemmas during the de la Madrid presidency (IAMEA, 37:1, 1983, p. 31–52, tables)

Excellent summary of paradoxes between policy goals and policy alternatives faced by the de la Madrid presidency. Believes that government can implement an economic program which can overcome past problems, but it will depend on President's political will.

Maciel, David. Ignacio Ramírez, ideólogo del liberalismo social en México. See *HLAS 46:7548.*

6075 Madrid Hurtado, Miguel de la. Los grandes problemas nacionales de hoy: el reto del futuro. México: Editorial Diana, 1982. 335 p.

Contains essense of President Miguel de la Madrid's philosophy, as expressed during his presidential campaign, as he took office in 1982.

6076 ———. La modernización del Partido Revolucionario Institucional. México: PRI, 1982. 206 p.

President de la Madrid's personal view of reforms necessary to modernize the PRI as taken from his 1982 presidential campaign.

6077 Martínez Assad, Carlos R. El henriquismo, una piedra en el camino. México: Martín Casillas Editores, 1982. 66 p.: bibl., ill. (Col. Memoria y olvido. Imágenes de México; 20)

Brief, although interestingly illustrated account of opposition campaign of Gen. Miguel Henríquez Guzmán against official party candidate.

6078 Mexico. Coordinación General de Estudios Administrativos. Manual de organización del Gobierno Federal, 1982. México: Presidencia de la República, La Coordinación, 1982. 885 p.: ill., plates.

Manual is 1982 version of an erratic history of Mexican government organization manuals, in format and content, since 1947. Excellent reference for legal precedents of each administrative unit in executive branch, but contains no names of officeholders.

6079 Mols, Manfred. Der mexikanische Präsidentschaftswahlkampf, 1969–1970 (JGSWGL, 18, 1981, p. 329–386, graphs)

One of Germany's leading scholars on Mexico provides his interpretations of presidential campaign of 1969–70. Believes that problems which emerged during this campaign will be those facing Mexico in 1980s.

6080 ———. Was bleit von Mexikos politischer Stabilität in den achtziger Jahren? (IAA, 9:2, 1983, p. 177–196, bibl.)

One of West Germany's leading students of Mexican politics provides a general overview of political stability and impact of recent events on that characteristic.

Neymet, Marcela de. Cronología del Partido Comunista Mexicano. See *HLAS* 46:2249.

6081 Partido Socialista Unificado de México (PSUM). Grupo Parlamentario. Una voz del pueblo en la Cámara. v. 1, Colegio Electoral y primer período ordinario de sesiones, LI Legislatura, Cámara de Diputados, 1979. México: PSUM, 1982. 1 v.: bibl., index.

Collected speeches of representatives and party deputies of the Unified Socialist Party of Mexico before Federal Electoral Commission and 1979 legislative session. Useful source of leftist ideology in Mexico.

6082 Pérez Arce, Francisco. Los primeros años de la insurgencia, 1970 y 1971 (Historias [INAH, México] 1, julio/sept. 1982, p. 55–66)

Labor historians will find this a useful compilation of details for individual strikes taking place at Ayotla Textile factory in 1970–71.

6083 Pérez-Ayala, R. Política personal y vacío de poder: el presidencialismo mexicano. México: PAC & Editores, 1983. 209 p.: index.

Not a serious analysis of the power of Mexican presidency, especially concerning the designation of a successor, but contains many interesting anecdotes.

6084 Puga, Cristina. Dos proyectos de la burguesía mexicana (Iztapalapa [Univ. Autónoma Metropolitana, Iztapalapa, México] 1:1, julio/dic. 1979, p. 16–31)

Author describes historical foundation and general characteristics of what she believes to be two tendencies within Mexican private sector: modernism and conservatism.

6085 Las Razones y las obras: gobierno de Miguel de la Madrid; crónica del sexenio 1982–1988, primer año. México: Presidencia de la República, Unidad de la Crónica Presidencial, 1984. 325 p.: ill., plates, tables.

Rather than a propaganda piece from the government, this is a useful monthly chronology of the first year of de la Madrid's administration. Includes criticisms of various groups and parties about important issues of 1983.

6086 Redclift, M.R. Development policymaking in Mexico: the *Sistema Alimentario Mexicano* (SAM). La Jolla: Program in US-Mexican Studies, Univ. of California at San Diego, 1981. 26 leaves: bibl. (Working papers in US-Mexican studies; 24)

Brief, interesting analysis of Mexican Foodstuffs System, how it came about, basic elements for its success, and probable future in 1981.

6087 La Reforma política y la izquierda. México: Editorial Nuestro Tiempo, 1979. 141 p.: bibl. (Col. Encuestas y debates)

Presents results of an open-ended survey of Mexican leftist parties asking a dozen questions about the political reform. Results are presented in essays provided by representatives of each party.

6088 Rendón Corona, Armanso. Los directores del Gobierno Federal Mexicano: 1970–1977 (Iztapalapa [Univ. Autónoma Metropolitana, Iztapalapa, México] 2:3, julio/dic. 1980, p. 74–91, tables)

Interesting attempt to describe career patterns and trajectories of division heads within federal government agencies, an important mid-level post-prediction of patterns among higher level officeholders.

6089 Retchkiman K., Benjamín and **Gerardo Gil Valdivia.** El federalismo y la coordinación fiscal. México: UNAM, Instituto de Investigaciones Jurídicas, 1981. 102 p.: bibl. (Serie G. Estudios doctrinales; 50)

Collection of essays on general issues of and relationships among decentralization of political authority, unequal regional development, and unequal distribution of resources. Several participants are among Mexico's leading authorities on the subjects.

Riding, Alan. Distant neighbors: a portrait of the Mexicans. See item 3102.

6090 Riesgos de trabajo. México: Instituto Mexicano del Seguro Social, Secretaría General, Secretariado Técnico de Información y Documentación, Centro de Documentación, 1980. 325 p.: bibl., ill. (Lecturas en materia de seguridad social)

Brings together a number of excellent articles by Mexicans and non-Mexicans on worker-related subjects, including workers' compensation in Mexican social security law, occupational diseases, and on-the-job accidents.

6091 Rodríguez y Rodríguez, Jesús. La detención preventiva y los derechos humanos en derecho comparado. México: UNAM, Instituto de Investigaciones Jurídicas, 1981. 256 p.: appendices, bibl. (Serie B. Estudios comparativos. Estudios especiales; 19)

Standard legal text on preventive detention which places Mexico in comparative perspective. Contains numerous appendices of regional and international agreements on human rights.

6092 Rorem, Mark O. Mexico's organic law of federal public administration: a new structure for modern administration (HICLR, 1:2, Winter 1978, p. 367–388)

Very helpful interpretation of changes in administrative laws and their relationship to changes in the federal bureaucracy. Believes law breaks new ground by grouping together many quasi-governmental functions and establishing sound administrative controls to coordinate public administration.

6093 Roxborough, Ian. Labor in the Mexican motor vehicle industry (in Political economy of the Latin American motor vehicle industry. Edited by Richard Kronish and Kenneth S. Mericle. Cambridge, Mass.: MIT Press, 1984, p. 161–194, tables)

Excellent case study which demonstrates that powerful forces are working to make all official unions pay closer attention to rank and file and that overall, labor movement is in a state of flux, and that CTM will have to renegotiate its position with government.

———— and **Ilan Buzberg.** Union locals in Mexico: the "new unionism" in steel and automobiles. See *HLAS 46:2275.*

6094 Sanderson, Steven E. Political tensions in the Mexican party system (CUH, 82:488, Dec. 1983, p. 401–405, 436)

Brief, but insightful update on tensions which divide and characterize Mexico's PRI. Warns of future problems with which government may be unable to cope.

Schmidt, Henry C. The Mexican intellectual as political pundit, 1968–1976: the case of Daniel Cosío Villegas. See *HLAS 46:2282.*

6095 Segovia, Rafael. La situación mexicana: algunas perspectivas (in Iberoamérica en los años 80: perspectivas de cambio social y político. Enrique Baloyra Herp y Rafael López-Pintor, comps. Madrid: Centro de Investigaciones Sociológicas, 1982?, p. 119–129, tables)

General overview, by one of Mexico's leading political scientists, of political situation in 1980s.

6096 Spalding, Rose J. México en los ochenta: internacionalización económica, tecnificación del Estado y relegitimación (in Iberoamérica en los años 80: perspectivas de cambio social y político. Enrique Baloyra Herp y Rafael López-Pintor, comps. Madrid: Centro de Investigaciones Sociológicas, 1982?, p. 131–146, tables)

Brief exploration of some of the economic and political tendencies which characterize, and will ultimately impact on, Mexico in 1980s. Emphasizes economic dependency, increase of technical specialization among politicians and administrative structure, and political reform of mid-1970s.

6097 Story, Dale. Industrial elites in Mexico: political ideology and influence (SAGE/JIAS, 25:3, Aug. 1983, p. 351–375, tables)

Original analysis, based on interviews, of attitudes of members and leaders of several major industrial chambers in Mexico. Important addition to scanty literature on economic elites in Mexico. For historian's comment, see *HLAS 46:2287.*

6098 Tardanico, Richard. Revolutionary nationalism and State building in Mexico: 1917–1924 (ISU/PS, 10:1, 1980, p. 59–86)

Analyzes efforts of Mexico's revolutionary leadership to establish political structures helpful to attaining nationalist goals. Concludes that regimes of Carranza and Obregón were unable, because of Porfirian legacies, to create a State capable of implementing more nationalist goals. Concludes that Obregón did make several important advances.

Valadés, J.C. Precursores del socialismo antiautoritario en México. See *HLAS 46:7554*.

Varela, Roberto. Procesos políticos en Tlayacapan, Morelos. See item **997**.

CENTRAL AMERICA

STEVE C. ROPP, *Professor of Political Science, University of Wyoming*

THE LITERATURE ON CENTRAL AMERICA continues to expand at an exponential rate and a number of major research gaps have been filled during the past several years. Most notable has been the appearance of a number of country studies on Honduras and Costa Rica that help balance the earlier focus on Nicaragua and El Salvador. James A. Morris has provided us with a fine book on Honduran politics (item **6174**), the most important since William Stokes's 1950 volume (see *HLAS 16:1393*). Also valuable is the work of Mario Posas and Rafael del Cid, which analyzes the historical origins of the Honduran state (item **6176**). Costa Rican politics is well treated by Charles Ameringer (item **6128**) who offers a general overview of the democratic process and by José Luis Vega Carballo who provides valuable insights concerning the origins and contemporary character of the political system (item **6137**).

Equally noteworthy is the appearance of several excellent overviews of regional political developments. The best of these is Walter LaFeber's volume (item **6111**) which combines discussion of US policy with astute analyses of the internal political dynamics of each country. Another highly useful overview is that of Thomas Anderson (item **6099**) who provides an excellent synthesis of recent political developments in the region. Finally, there is a growing number of edited works which contain a substantial number of good individual articles. Of these edited volumes the six best are: *La Crisis centroamericana,* edited by Daniel Camacho and Manuel Rojas B. (Ciudad Universitaria Rodrigo Facio, Costa Rica: Editorial Universitaria Centroamericana, 1984, 444 p.: bibl., ill.); *Trouble in our backyard: Central America and the United States in the eighties,* edited by Martin Diskin (New York: Pantheon Books, 1984, 264 p. : bibl., index); *Political change in Central America: internal and external dimensions,* edited by Wolf Grabendorff et al. (Boulder, Colo.: Westview Press, 1984, 312 p.: bibl., index); *Central America: anatomy of a conflict* edited by Robert S. Leiken (item **6104a**); *Revolution and counterrevolution in Central America and the Caribbean,* edited by Donald E. Schulz and Douglas H. Graham (Boulder Colo: Westview Press, 1984, 555 p.: bibl., index); and *Rift and revolution: the Central American imbroglio,* edited by Howard J. Wiarda (Washington: American Enterprise Institute for Public Policy Research, 1984, 392 p.: bibl, index). There are a number of valuable contributions to these volumes which are annotated below: from the one edited by Camacho and Rojas, items **6168, 6199,** and **6201;** from the one by Diskin, items **6118, 6144,** and **6169;** by Grabendorff et al., items **6110, 6142,** and **6170;** by Leiken, items **6115** and **6186;** by Schulz and Graham, item **6122;** and by Wiarda, items **6107, 6108,** and **6153.** We should also note the volume edited by James A. Morris and Steve C. Ropp, *Central America: crisis and adaptation* (Albuquerque: Univ. of New Mexico, 1984, 311 p.: bibl., index), from which items **6129** and **6190** have been selected.

In spite of these positive trends in the literature, many problem areas still remain. There is a continued regional imbalance, with spectacular developments in Nicaragua and El Salvador being covered at the expense of developments elsewhere. Severe neglect is most obvious in the cases of Belize and Panama, perhaps because some scholars refuse to recognize that they really are Central American countries. The continuing propensity to focus on the dramatic and topical is of course understandable but has skewed the literature badly in the direction of analyses of revolutionary movements, terror, and violence. Studies of political actors other than guerrilla groups or revolutionary leaders are much needed but the current political climate impedes research on more "mundane" actors.

Cross-national trends do suggest that more attention is being focused on the political role of the Catholic Church and the armed forces since both have been recognized as critical protagonists in highly dynamic crisis contexts. There are now suggestive analyses of the behavior of the former by Phillip Berryman (item **6103**) and Tommie Sue Montgomery (item **6116**), and of the latter by Ronald McDonald (item **6113**) and Richard Millett (item **6115**). An outstanding sociological treatment of the rise of militarism in El Salvador has been provided by Rafael Guidos Véjar (item **6152**).

GENERAL

6099 Anderson, Thomas P. Politics in Central America: Guatemala, El Salvador, Honduras, and Nicaragua. New York: Praeger: Hoover Institution, 1982. 221 p.: bibl.

Sober and balanced presentation of recent social and political history of Guatemala, El Salvador, Honduras, and Nicaragua by noted authority on the region. Concludes that Central American politics most fundamentally is a struggle between various groups to control allocation of land resources.

6100 ——. The war of the dispossessed: Honduras and El Salvador, 1969. Lincoln: Univ. of Nebraska Press, 1981. 203 p.: bibl.

Deals with 1969 war between Honduras and El Salvador and sheds considerable light on some of the conditions underlying current regional crisis. Encroachment of agro-business enterprises on traditional peasant landholdings in El Salvador forced hundreds of thousands of peasants to emigrate to Honduras. Their return to El Salvador after the war further heightened class tensions there.

6101 Baloyra-Herp, Enrique A. Reactionary despotism in Central America (JLAS, 15:2, Nov. 1983, p. 295–319, bibl., tables)

Written by an astute academic observer of Central American politics, article applies label "reactionary despotism" to regimes in El Salvador and Guatemala. Reactionary despotism is seen as a "regime of exception" in which landed oligarchy chooses to share power with the military in order to prevent change in dominant economic system of export agriculture.

6102 Barry, Tom; Beth Wood; and Deb Preusch. Dollars and dictators: a guide to Central America. Albuquerque, N.M.: The Resource Center, 1982. 263 p.: bibl., ill., index.

Argues that industrialization and development of Central American that was spurred by US investment left the traditional oligarchy virtually untouched. Best single source of information concerning regional economic investments of US multinational corporations.

6103 Berryman, Phillip. The religious roots of rebellion: Christians in Central American revolutions. Maryknoll, N.Y.: Orbis Books, 1984. 452 p.: bibl., index.

Written by former pastoral worker and representative of American Friends Service Committee in Central America, book examines Christian involvement in regional crisis from an historical and ethical perspective. Particularly useful for an understanding of Theology of Liberation and of how Christian beliefs have been reconciled with revolutionary ethics.

6104 Buckley, Tom. Violent neighbors: El Salvador, Central America, and the United States. New York: Times Books, 1984. 358 p.: maps.

Lively journalistic account of author's travels in Central America during 1980–83. Contains series of valuable interviews with prominent political figures on both the right and left of political spectrum. Particularly insightful on El Salvador.

6104a Central America: anatomy of a conflict. Edited by Robert S. Leiken. New York: Pergamon Press, 1984. 351 p.: bibl., index.

Reader on US policy toward Central America which contains much useful information concerning domestic origins of regional crisis. Particularly worthwhile are chaps. on past US policy (Walter LaFeber), the Central American military (Richard Millett, item **6115**), and the Salvadoran Left (Robert Leiken).

6105 Centro América 1982: análisis económicos y políticos sobre la región. Guatemala: Inforpress Centroamericana, 1982. 340 p.: ill., tables.

Useful compendium of information concerning political and economic developments in region during the year. Compiled by a team of Central American journalists and researchers, contains a wealth of data not readily available in any other single source. Based on weekly reports that are synthesized annually.

6106 Cohen, Isaac and **Gert Rosenthal.** The dimensions of economic policy space in Central America (in The Future of Central America: policy choices for the US and Mexico. Edited by Richard R. Fagen and Olga Pellicer. Stanford, Calif.: Stanford Univ. Press, 1983, p. 15–34, tables)

Discusses "policy space" within which Central America's reformist politicians must maneuver. Such space is defined by level of external economic dependency, of social inequality, and of popular participation. Compares degree of policy space in various Central American countries, suggesting that it is most limited in El Salvador and Guatemala.

6107 Ebel, Roland H. The development and decline of the Central American city-state (in Rift and revolution: the Central American imbroglio. Edited by Howard J.

Wiarda. Washington: American Enterprise Institute for Public Policy Research, 1984, p. 70–104 [Studies in foreign policy. AEI studies; 394])

Provocative article built upon author's well known thesis that the dominant political unit in Central America has been the city-state. Argues that city-states are collapsing due to mass popular mobilization and reduced support from abroad. They will either survive as garrison states or be replaced by nation-states.

6108 Evans, Ernest. Revolutionary movements in Central America: the development of new strategy (in Rift and revolution: the Central American imbroglio. Edited by Howard J. Wiarda. Washington: American Enterprise Institute for Public Policy Research, 1984, p. 167–193 [Studies in foreign policy. AEI studies; 394])

Suggests that tactics used by revolutionary movements in El Salvador and Guatemala have been influenced by their own learning experiences combined with those of Nicaragua's victorious FSLN. Military caution is stressed along with the effort to build broad-based opposition coalitions. These movements now seek international support from a wide variety of nations and international organizations, not wishing to rely exclusively on Cuba.

Geyer, Georgie Anne. Central America: reflections on a region. See item **3178**.

Gordon, Sara. América Central: bibliografía. See *HLAS 46:23*.

6109 La Iglesia de los pobres en América Central. Edited by Pablo Richard and Guillermo Meléndez. San José: Depto. Ecuménico de Investigaciones, 1982. 345 p.: bibl.

Attempts to present a synthetic analysis of the experience of the Catholic Church since 1960 in every Central American country except Belize and Panama. Examines this experience with regard to Church relationships with dominant classes (through the State) and with the popular masses. Although not a synthetic treatment, individual country chaps. are informative.

6110 Krumwiede, Heinrich-W. Regimes and revolution in Central America (in Political change in Central America: internal and external dimensions. Edited by Wolf Grabendorff, Heinrich-W. Krumwiede, and

Jörg Todt. Boulder, Colo.: Westview Press *in association with the* Friedrich Ebert Foundation, 1984, 9–36, table [Westview special studies on Latin America and the Caribbean])

Interesting attempt to deal theoretically with question of conditions which encourage successful social-revolutionary movements in Central America. Concludes that chances of success are enhanced where a strong social-revolutionary movement faces a weak regime under favorable international conditions.

6111 LaFeber, Walter. Inevitable revolutions: the United States in Central America. New York: W.W. Norton & Co., 1983. 357 p.: bibl.

One of US best known diplomatic historians offers a careful analysis of the pattern of US-Central American relations and its implications for domestic political developments within the region. Decline in US hegemony is viewed as having major implications for stability of Central American regimes. Contains excellent bibliographical note.

6113 McDonald, Ronald H. Civil-military relations in Central America: the dilemmas of political institutionalization (*in* Rift and revolution: the Central American imbroglio. Edited by Howard J. Wiarda. Washington: American Enterprise Institute for Public Policy Research, 1984, p. 129–166, table [Studies in foreign policy. AEI studies; 394])

Thoughtful interpretation of historical evolution of civil-military relations in Central American societies. Sequential modernization, professionalization, and institutionalization of armed forces have altered political balance between civilian politicians and military officers. The military is now so influential in most countries that coalitions within armed forces are as important as civil-military ones.

6114 Millett, Richard. The Central American region (*in* Latin America: its problems and its promise: a multidisciplinary introduction. Edited by Jan Knippers Black. Boulder, Colo.: Westview Press, 1984, p. 299–328, bibl.)

Brief but solid account of Central America's history and current developments as they relate to the regional crisis. Attributes current crisis to four fundamental factors: 1) accumulated "burden of the past" due to failure of traditional oligarchies to adapt; 2) failure of increasingly professional armed forces to develop national allegiances; 3) uneven distribution of benefits of post-World War II economic growth; and 4) global economic crisis of 1970s.

6115 ———. Praetorians or patriots?: the Central American military (*in* Central America: anatomy of conflict [see item 6104a] p. 69–91)

Argues that Central American military institutions have played a significant role in regional violence. Although a product of regional history and social dynamics, they have also been heavily influenced by external powers. The regional crisis will only end when these military institutions begin to concern themselves with welfare of entire nation.

6116 Montgomery, Tommie Sue. Cross and rifle: revolution and the Church in El Salvador and Nicaragua (CU/JIA, 36:2, Fall/Winter 1982/1983, p. 209–221)

Carefully crafted interpretation of the role of both Catholics and Protestants in the Nicaraguan and Salvadoran revolutions. Discusses three types of Church leaders (traditional, reformist-Marxist, and reformist-populist) and maintains that personal relations among these leaders became polarized as class struggle increased in these two countries.

6117 ———. Liberation and revolution: Christianity as a subversive activity in Central America (*in* Trouble in our backyard: Central America and the United States in the eighties. Edited by Martin Diskin. Foreword by John Womack, Jr. Epilogue by Günter Grass. New York: Pantheon Books, 1984, p. 76–99)

Describes activities of Roman Catholic Church's Christian base communities in Central America and argues that they are transforming traditional societies. Insightful interpretation which suggests that the Church is playing a social role similar to one it played in an earlier transition period, the Reformation.

6119 Pearson, Neale J. Costa Rica, Honduras, and Panama (*in* Communism in Central America and the Caribbean. Edited by Robert Wesson. Stanford, Calif.: Hoover Institution Press, 1982, p. 94–116)

Fine comparative treatment of Marxist parties in Costa Rica, Honduras, and Panama by long-time observer of regional politics. States that these parties are well organized but have limited popular appeal. Because their leaders have tended to benefit from existing political systems and politics is not highly polarized, these parties will probably not challenge governments militarily.

6120 Revolution and intervention in Central America. Edited by Marlene Dixon and Susanne Jonas. San Francisco: Synthesis Publications, 1983. 344 p.: bibl., index (Contemporary Marxism series)

Part of monographic series on contemporary Marxism, book contains collected statements of many Central American guerrilla leaders and other political figures on the Left. Focus is on guerrilla movements in El Salvador and Guatemala, with Guerrilla Army of the Poor (EGP) being considered most important group in the latter country.

6121 Ropp, Steve C. En espera de un Cavour: la crisis actual y la unificación de Centroamérica (Revista Occidental [s.l.] 1 : 3, mayo/agosto 1984, p. 355–368)

Suggests that contemporary Central America is similar to early 19th-century Italy with regard to a number of fundamental elements of structure and process. These similarities may point to eventual unification of Central America as happened with Italian states in 1861. A likely source of military power to facilitate forced unification is El Salvador.

6122 Schulz, Donald E. Ten theories in search of Central American reality (in Revolution and counterrevolution in Central America and the Caribbean. Edited by Donald E. Schulz and Douglas H. Graham. Boulder, Colo.: Westview Press, 1984, p. 3–64, tables [Westview special studies on Latin America and the Caribbean])

A fine overview of the literature attempting to explain the Central American crisis. Theories discussed include competitive exclusion of peasants through agricultural modernization, demographic theory, psychoeconomic theories of relative deprivation, petrification of political institutions, and external destabilization (among others). Concludes that these theories collectively "provide a reasonably comprehensive, multi-

dimensional frame of reference" for understanding the crisis (p. 4).

6123 Simán, José Jorge. Consideraciones sobre desigualdad económica, ilegitimidad política y perspectivas de cambio en Centroamérica (in Iberoamérica en los años 80: perspectivas de cambio social y político. Enrique Baloyra-Herp y Rafael López-Pintor, comps. Madrid: Centro de Investigaciones Sociológicas, 1982?, p. 95–116, tables)

A too brief but serious attempt to examine roots of Central American crisis. States that these roots can be found in failure of Liberal agro-export model of development and in failure of industrialization to spark modernization. Author believes that El Salvador and Guatemala are experiencing the deepest structural transformations.

6124 Sobrino, Jon. Persecución a la Iglesia en Centroamérica (UJSC/ECA, 36 : 393, julio 1981, p. 645–664, ill.)

Analyzes the nature and extent of Church persecution by governments in El Salvador, Guatemala, and Honduras. Persecution in these three countries is viewed as increasingly systematic and aimed at dismantling Church pastoral structures. In Honduras, it takes a milder form and is largely preventative.

6125 Visita pastoral de Juan Pablo II a América Latina (RCPC, 38 : 178, enero/marzo 1983, p. 1–108, ill., plates)

Collection of speeches delivered by Pope John Paul II during his 1983 visit to Central America. An important primary document for those interested in impact of the Catholic Church as an institution on domestic political developments in the region.

6126 White, Richard Alan. The morass: United States intervention in Central America. New York: Harper & Row, 1984. 319 p.: bibl., index, map.

Polemical discussion of US counterinsurgency doctrine as applied to Central America and of its effects on domestic politics in the region. Argues that encouragement of military alliances among different kinds of regional governments has actually furthered process of internal social and political disintegration because militarization increasingly polarizes body politic.

BELIZE

6127 Thorndike, Tony. Belizean political parties: independence crisis and after (ICS/JCCP, 21:2, July 1983, p. 195–211, map)

Summary description of bases of support for Belize's two major political parties. The traditionally strong Peoples' United Party (PUP) draws its strength from rural mestizos, Mayans, and urban working class Creoles, and the United Democratic Party (UDP) from conservative middle class Creoles and ex-PUP mestizo dissidents. Also discusses post-independence political situation.

COSTA RICA

6128 Ameringer, Charles D. Democracy in Costa Rica. New York: Praeger: Hoover Institution, 1982. 138 p.: bibl.

Highly readable vol. examines historical origins and current health of Costa Rican democracy. Suggests that some of the keys to survival of this democratic system under conditions of increasing stress are open discussion of national problems in a free press and continued commitment to democratic mores.

6129 Booth, John A. Representative constitutional democracy in Costa Rica: adaptation to crisis in the turbulent 1980s (*in* Central America: crisis and adaptation. Edited by Steve C. Ropp and James A. Morris. Albuquerque: Univ. of New Mexico Press, 1984, p. 153–188, bibl.)

Argues that Costa Rica is experiencing a political crisis but one narrower in scope than most other Central American countries. Its crisis is essentially the product of economic difficulties that may at some point threaten existing political arrangements. But continued political stability is encouraged by low degree of social stratification, legitimacy of government institutions, and elite flexibility.

6130 Gudmundson, Lowell. Estratificación socio-racial y económica de Costa Rica, 1700–1850. San José: Editorial Univ. Estatal a Distancia, 1978. 178 p.: bibl., ill. (Serie Estudios sociopolíticos; 3)

Important book (not previously annotated in *HLAS*) which questions fundamental premise upon which most contemporary analysis of Costa Rican politics is based. Uses census data to suggest that colonial egalitarianism is partly a present-day myth and that Costa Rican society was considerably stratified prior to introduction of coffee in 19th century.

6131 Harrison, Lawrence E. Nicaraguan anguish and Costa Rican progress (This World [Institute for Educational Affairs, New York] 6, 1983, p. 29–50, tables)

Provocative essay speculates about fundamental differences between "peaceful" Costa Rica and strife-torn Nicaragua. After examining a number of arguments, concludes that Costa Rica's political culture evolved favorably because country did not remain in mainstream of Hispanic American culture. Remote, poverty-stricken and with a small Indian population, Costa Rica's colonial experience was "in some ways reminiscent of the New England colonies" (p. 48).

6132 La Palabra social de los Obispos costarricenses: selección de documentos de la Iglesia Católica Costarricense, 1893–1981. Edición de Miguel Picado. San José: Depto. Ecuménico de Investigaciones, 1982. 217 p.: bibl., index (Cuadernos DEI; 6)

Important collection of key social pronouncements and exchanges of view between Catholic Church leaders and lay authorities in Costa Rica over better part of a century. A large portion relate to activities of Víctor Sanabria, the San José Archbishop who aligned himself politically with labor and Communist Party in 1940s.

6133 Partido Liberación Nacional. Volvamos a la tierra: programa de gobierno: 1982–1986. San José: PLN, 1982. 137 p.

National Liberation Party goals for 1982–86 emphasize economic self-sufficiency through agricultural diversification. Party argues that "limits of growth" have been reached with regard to roles and scope of the State. Useful primary document for those interested in historical evolution of PLN ideology.

El Pensamiento contemporáneo costarricense. See *HLAS 46:7561*.

6134 Rosenberg, Mark. Las luchas por el seguro social en Costa Rica. San José: Editorial Costa Rica, 1980. 210 p.: bibl.

Broader in scope than its title would suggest, this thoroughly researched monograph uses Costa Rican social security policy to trace historical pattern of State-society relations. Prior to 1940s, an ideology of government non-intervention prevailed which was supported by patronal social relations and a liberal internationally dependent political economy.

6135 Sewastynowicz, James. Community power brokers and national political parties in rural Costa Rica (CUA/AQ, 56:3, July 1983, p. 107–115, bibl.)

Brief case study from an anthropological perspective of phenomenon of political power brokerage between peasants and national leaders. Concludes that local brokers have served to ensure that national development and prosperity had local consequences. Local district brokers are being rapidly replaced as agents of national institutions are increasingly represented at local level.

6136 Solís, Javier. La herencia de Sanabria: análisis político de la Iglesia costarricense. San José: Depto. Ecuménico de Investigaciones, 1983. 173 p. (Col. Centroamérica)

Deals with thoughts and activities during 1960s-70s of those priests within the Costa Rican Catholic Church who subscribed to the theology of liberation. While analysis of why the Church in this country remained essentially conservative is not strong, book does contain some useful primary documents.

6137 Vega Carballo, José Luis. Orden y progreso: la formación del Estado nacional en Costa Rica. San José: Instituto Centroamericano de Administración Pública, 1981. 338 p.: bibl.

Well researched and crafted exploration by one of Costa Rica's leading scholars of the development and evolution of the Costa Rican State since 19th century. Offers valuable insights concerning economic and ideological roots of State formation and is particularly useful in explaining limited role of the military.

6138 ———. Poder político y democracia en Costa Rica. San José: Editorial Porvenir, 1982. 168 p.: bibl. (Col. Debate)

Serious and provocative analysis of the origins of Costa Rican democracy. Contends that the democratic system can be explained by existence of a number of "constants:" egalitarianism, institutionalization of a democratic State, indirect methods of class domination, and a common bond of nationalism.

6139 Volio, Marina. Jorge Volio y el Partido Reformista. 4a ed. San José: Editorial Univ. Estatal a Distancia, 1983. 277 p.: bibl., ill., plates.

Authorized biography about an extremely important figure in Costa Rican political history; Volio founded the Reformist Party in 1920s which injected progressive Church social doctrine into politics. Not good analytical history but can serve as useful introduction to Volio's ideas.

EL SALVADOR

6140 Acerca de la situación militar en El Salvador (URSS/AL, 8:56, agosto 1982, p. 59–74)

Detailed evaluation by Farabundo Martí Front for National Liberation of the results of major guerrilla offensive conducted in early 1981. Analyzes strengths and weaknesses of both guerrilla and government military units. Important primary source for those interested in evolution of guerrilla military strategy.

6141 Arene, Alberto. La reforma agraria como estrategia político-militar de la contrarrevolución en El Salvador (UJSC/ECA, 35:384/385, oct./nov. 1980, p. 972–982)

Well documented discussion of origins and purposes of the Salvadoran agrarian reform program. Views it as part of a politico-military strategy developed by Christian Democrats and elements within armed forces to reverse revolutionary process. Perceives the US government as having played a major role in policy formulation and implementation.

6142 Arson, Cynthia. The Salvadoran military and regime transformation (in Political change in Central America: internal and external dimensions. Edited by Wolf Grabendorff, Heinrich-W. Krumwiede, and Jörg Todt. Boulder, Colo.: Westview Press: in association with the Friedrich Ebert Foundation, 1984, p. 97–113, [Westview special studies on Latin America and the Caribbean])

Well researched essay focusing on various factions within Salvadoran military and on civil-military relations. Three military groups are seen as having struggled for hegemony within armed forces after 1979 coup: conservatives opposed to all political and economic reform, reformist junior officers who believed instability was due to economic injustice, and modernizing hardliners.

6143 Baloyra, Enrique A. Political change in El Salvador (CUH, 83:490, Feb. 1984, p. 54–58, 85–86)

Describes the Pact of Apaneca concluded by El Salvador's major political parties prior to 1982 elections. Compares this agreement to ones subscribed to by political parties in countries such as Colombia and Spain, agreements which led to establishment of consociational democracy. Concludes that this will not happen in El Salvador because of exclusion of the Left and remaining disagreements among groups who supported the Pact.

6144 ———. Reactionary despotism in El Salvador: an impediment to democratic transition (*in* Trouble in our backyard: Central America and the United States in the eighties. Edited by Martin Diskin. Foreword by Jonh Womack, Jr. Epiloque by Günter Grass. New York: Pantheon Books, 1984, p. 102–123)

One of leading authorities on Salvadoran politics specifies a model of existing coalition there which he labels "reactionary despotism." Derived from earlier work of Spanish sociologist Salvador Giner, model suggests that this coalition and its associated mode of domination are typical of late developing capitalist countries. Core coalition members include large agricultural planters, merchants, suppliers of agricultural credit, and military officers.

6145 Bonner, Raymond. Weakness and deceit : US policy and El Salvador. New York: Time Books, 1984. 408 p.: bibl.

Although focused primarily on US policy, this book by a correspondent for the *New York Times* offers numerous insights concerning political developments in El Salvador. Bonner is particularly well versed on activities of the military, right-wing groups, and left-wing guerrillas. Somewhat ahistorical.

6146 Christian, Shirley. El Salvador's divided military (The Atlantic [The Atlantic Monthly Co., Boston] 251:6, June 1983, p. 50–60, plates)

Excellent synopsis of Salvadoran military history including the twin origins of armed forces in external defense missions and defense of domestic coffee producers. Contains a sophisticated discussion of factions within the military. One small flaw is that author treats internal "military democracy" of 1979–80 as an aberration rather than as a return to a form of internal governance that had been standard since 1948.

6147 Dunkerley, James. The Long War: dictatorship and revolution in El Salvador. London: Junction Books, 1983. 264 p., 8 p. of plates: bibl., ill., index, map.

Sympathetic account of revolutionary struggle in El Salvador which views this struggle as containing strands both of bourgeois democratic reformism and socialism. The strand of democratic reformism is seen as ultimately failing to establish itself due to lack of a deep social base, high levels of popular mobilization, and strength of radical left. Places conflict in broad international and historical perspective.

6148 El Salvador, elecciones, marzo 1982. San Salvador: Secretaría de Información de la Presidencia de la República, Consejo Central de Elecciones, 1982. 317 p.: ill. (some col.)

Critical document for those who wish to study 1982 Salvadoran elections. Contains all political party platforms and statutes, results of electoral surveys, information concerning electoral process and vote tallies. These were the most important Salvadoran elections in more than 50 yrs.

6149 El Salvador entre el terror y la esperanza: los sucesos de 1979 y su impacto en el drama salvadoreño de los años siguientes. Selección y prólogo de Rodolfo R. Campos. San Salvador: Univ. Centroamericana José Simeón Cañas, 1982. 788 p. (Col. Debate; 1)

An important primary source containing transcripts of news programs broadcast daily in El Salvador beginning in 1978 by YSAX. This radio station was established by reformist Archbishop Oscar Arnulfo Romero. An invaluable source of information concerning Church thinking on most national issues of the day.

6150 El Salvador, la larga marcha de un pueblo, 1932–82: selección de artículos y entrevistas extraídos de diversos revistas y documentos. Prólogo, Antonio Alvarez-Solís. Presentación, María López Vigil. La masacre del 22 de enero de 1980, José Luis Morales. Nuestro derecho a la vida, Marianella García Villas. Madrid: Editorial Revolución, 1982. 284 p.: ill., maps.

Excellent compendium of information on Salvadoran politics. Contains well selected excerpts from various articles and books that deal with Salvadoran political history and development of guerrilla movement. Particularly useful for maps of war zones and biographical notes on leaders of FDR-FMLN.

6151 Flores Macal, Mario. Origen, desarrollo y crisis de las formas de dominación en El Salvador. San José: Servicios Editoriales Centroamericanos, 1983. 137 p.: bibl.

Useful general introduction dealing with historical origins of system of political domination in El Salvador. Based entirely on secondary sources, presents the conventional wisdom that the oligarchy was formed in colonial times around economic base of indigo cultivation. This oligarchy then shifted to coffee, creating a system of political and economic domination that is now collapsing.

6152 Guidos Véjar, Rafael. El ascenso del militarismo en El Salvador. San José: Editorial Universitaria Centroamericana, 1982. 218 p.: bibl.

Astute suggestive sociological analysis of developments during 1920s which led to emergence of military dictatorship of Maximiliano Hernández Martínez by 1930s. British capital is replaced by US capital and new investment priorities in the public sector lead to the creation of new groups within the dominant class. When the Great Depression exacerbates these new upper-class divisions, the military enters politics.

6153 Jung, Harald. The civil war in El Salvador (*in* Political change in Central America: internal and external dimensions. Edited by Wolf Grabendorff, Heinrich-W. Krumwiede, and Jörg Todt. Boulder, Colo.:

Westview Press: *in association with the* Friedrich Ebert Foundation, 1984, p. 82–96 [Westview special studies on Latin America and the Caribbean])

Argues that the civil war in El Salvador during 1960s-70s pitted elements of lower class against each other. During 1960s, military regime began to favor permanently employed farm workers over seasonal workers. Such favoritism and cooptation were reinforced by ORDEN with members gaining preferential access to permanent farm employment and loans.

6154 López Vallacillos, Italo. Trayectoria y crisis del Estado salvadoreño: 1918–1981 (UJSC/ECA, 36:392, junio 1981, p. 499–528, ill., tables)

Brief but serious examination of "constants" in Salvadoran history that explain current crisis. One has been the division of dominant class into two factions: the traditional coffee oligarchy and the new agroindustrial sector. Attempts at reform have required a dialogue between these two factions with the former always setting limits of change. Reform cannot be achieved by such a dialogue and will occur only through application of a more revolutionary model. For historian's comment, see *HLAS 46:2413.*

6155 McColm, R. Bruce. El Salvador's guerrillas: structure, strategy, and . . . success? (Freedom at Issue [Freedom House, New York] 74, Sept./Oct. 1983, p. 3–16)

Written from a conservative perspective, this is a well stated assessment of different philosopies and points of tension among guerrilla groups operating in El Salvador. Contains fairly extensive biographical information on guerrilla leaders.

6156 Martín Baró, Ignacio. Aspiraciones del pequeño burgués salvadoreño (UJSC/ECA, 36:394, agosto 1981, p. 773–788, bibl., ill., tables)

Based on an attitudinal survey of lower-middle class groups in El Salvador, presents the not-so-startling but important conclusion that they have upper-middle class or upper-class aspirations. Concludes that these aspirations make them natural allies of oligarchy. Therefore, they need to be aware of the needs of impoverished masses and given attractive alternatives to materialist middle-class visions.

6157 Mons. [i.e. Monseñor] Oscar Arnulfo Romero, arzobispo y mártir: su muerte y reacciones. San Salvador: Arzobispado de San Salvador, 1982. 628 p.: bibl., ill., plates.

Narrowly focused but important vol. for those interested in impact that assassination of Archbishop Oscar Arnulfo Romero had on Salvadoran politics. Contains masses of newspaper clippings giving perspective on the assassination of virtually every domestic sector and interest group including guerrillas.

6158 The NACLA report: El Salvador, 1984 (NACLA, 18:2, March/April 1984, p. 13–47, ill.)

Fine summary of political developments in El Salvador (1980–84). Excellent on civilian coalitions, civil-military coalitions, and balance of forces within the dissident FDR-FMLN. This summary of events was compiled by the editorial board of *Estudios Centroamericanos*, a major publication of Jesuit-run Central American Univ.

6159 Ptacek, Kerry. Misconceptions about the role of the Church (*in* Crisis and opportunity: U.S. policy in Central America and the Caribbean. Edited by Mark Falcoff and Robert Royal. Washington: Ethics and Public Policy Center, 1984, p. 263–278)

Attempts to correct general impression that the Catholic Church opposes Salvadoran government and is sympathetic to the guerrillas. This impression is conveyed by the fact that unofficial Church groups use ecclesiastical authority without reference to actual views of the hierarchy. Suggests that the Church's true view is that both left- and right-wing violence are to be condemned.

6160 Schmidt, Steffen W. El Salvador: America's next Vietnam? Salisbury, N.C.: Documentary Publication, 1983. 217 p., 7 p. of plates: bibl., ill., index.

Explains and interprets Salvadoran crisis at three levels: 1) a personal level of compassion for suffering that is taking place; 2) the level of the nation State, that is the search for domestic origins of crisis; and finally 3) the international level which both left and right view as most important.

6161 Villalobos, Joaquín. Desarrollo militar y perspectiva insurreccional en El Salvador (URSS/AL, 11:59, nov. 1982, p. 63–79)

Head of Salvadoran People's Revolutionary Army (ERP) outlines military situation as of 1982. Includes considerable information concerning perceived strengths and weaknesses of government forces, and advice for improving guerrilla fighting capabilities. Suggests that masses will become principal actor in next strategic phase.

GUATEMALA

6162 Aguilera Peralta, Gabriel. Le processus de militarisation de l'Etat guatemalteque (NS, 8:15, 1983, p. 59–81, bibl., tables)

Broad overview of historical evolution of Guatemalan army and its relationship to civilian authority. Army is viewed as a "planters' army," originating not with independence from Spain but in late 19th century under tutelage of new coffee oligarchy. Today, the officer class is merely part of governing class.

6163 Black, George; Milton Jamail; and Norma Stoltz Chinchilla. Guatemala: the war is not over (NACLA, 17:2, March/April 1983, p. 2–38, bibl., tables)

Well documented survey of political and military situation in Guatemala during 1970s and early 1980s. Particular emphasis is placed on historical origins and activities of various guerrilla groups and on social and economic changes which took place in Indian highlands.

Brockett, Charles D. Malnutrition, public policy, and agrarian change in Guatemala. See item **5062.**

6164 Castellanos Cambranes, Julio. Orígenes de la crisis del actual orden establecido en Guatemala. Stockholm: Institute of Latin American Studies, 93 p.

Contends that roots of Guatemala's contemporary political problems can be found in the Spanish conquest. The conquest was the fundamental act of violence that created a system of racial stratification that has been perpetuated to this day. Class stratification resulted from racial stratification, and both were reinforced by the advent of coffee cultivation.

6165 Gliejeses, Piero. Guatemala: crisis and response (*in* The Future of Central America: policy choices for the U.S. and Mexico. Edited by Richard R. Fagen and Olga

Pellicer. Stanford, Calif.: Stanford Univ. Press, 1983, p. 187–212)

Careful analysis by a leading scholar of relationship between various social forces in Guatemala since early 1950s. The military is seen as having developed its own economic base and as having wrested political control from the hands of the national bourgeoisie. Political system is viewed as highly polarized for three decades.

6166 Guatemala in rebellion: unfinished history. Edited by Jonathan L. Fried *et al.* New York: Grove Press, 1983. 342 p.: bibl., ill., index.

Collection of short excerpts from a wide variety of sources which attempts to convey a sense of the roots of rebellion in contemporary Guatemala. Although quite choppy and propagandistic, it is a valuable source for documents which are not readily available elsewhere.

6167 Guatemala!: the horror and the hope. Edited by Rarihokwats for Four Arrows. York, Pa.: Four Arrows, 1982. 4 v. (287 p.): ill.

Published by a group which seeks to address problems of indigenous groups throughout the Western Hemisphere, this series of pamphlets covers a wide range of Guatemalan political issues. Although highly polemical and uneven, they contain some valuable information concerning human rights abuses and activities of government security forces.

6168 Poitevin, René. La crisis en Guatemala (*in* La Crisis centroamericana. Edited by Daniel Camacho and Manuel Rojas B. Ciudad Universitaria Rodrigo Facio, Costa Rica: Editorial Universitaria Centroamericana: Facultad Latinoamericana de Ciencias Sociales, 1984, p. 52–70 [Col. Seis])

States that central feature of Guatemalan crisis is structural heterogeneity of both governing and popular classes, a heterogeneity attributable to racial and religious differences. Such heterogeneity leads to weak government legitimacy which in turn results in high levels of military violence to maintain current political system.

6169 Schoultz, Lars. Guatemala: social change and political conflict (*in* Trouble in our backyard: Central America and the United States in the eighties. Edited

by Martin Diskin. Foreword by John Womack, Jr. Epilogue by Günter Grass. New York: Pantheon Books, 1984, p. 174–202, table)

Excellent objective analysis of the roots of conflict in contemporary Guatemala. Suggests that rapid socioeconomic change associated with large-scale introduction of commercial agriculture along Pacific coast and mineral development in north has disrupted Indian communities through population displacement and increasing demand for labor.

6170 Torres-Rivas, Edelberto. Problems of democracy and counterrevolution in Guatemala (*in* Political change in Central America: internal and external dimensions. Edited by Wolf Grabendorff, Heinrich-W. Krumwide, and Jörg Todt. Boulder, Colo.: Westview Press: *in association with the* Friedrich Ebert Foundation, 1984, p. 114– 126, tables [Westview special studies on Latin America and the Caribbean])

Brief analytical essay on contemporary structure of political power in Guatemala. This regime structure is called an *estado de excepción*, "a variation of a military dictatorship, emerging in response to a particular kind of political and economic crisis and characterized by its continous difficulty in maintaining order by legal means" (p. 117).

HONDURAS

6171 Honduras: a country study. Edited by James D. Rudolph. Washington: American Univ., 1984. 294 p.: bibl., maps.

Part of US Dept. of the Army's Area Handbook Series, vol. describes and analyzes political, social, and economic systems of Honduras. Particularly useful from a political perspective are the historical chap. by Richard L. Millett, description of the political system by James A. Morris, and description of the growing government role in the economy by J. Mark Ruhl.

6172 MacCameron, Robert. Bananas, labor and politics in Honduras, 1954–1963. Syracuse, N.Y.: Maxwell School of Citizenship and Public Affairs, 1983. 166 p.: bibl.

Astute observer of Honduran politics provides helpful analysis of the formation and evolution of the labor movement. Suggests that labor's gains since 1954 have been more illusory than real due to factors such as the underdeveloped state of Honduran economy, external dependency, and economic development policies of specific administrations.

6173 Meza, Víctor. Política y sociedad en Honduras: comentarios. Tegucigalpa: Editorial Guaymuras, 1981. 399 p. (Col. Códices)

Series of newspaper commentaries written 1975–81. Although strictly journalistic in nature, they yield considerable insight about the period of military reformism. Particularly good on changing civil-military coalitions and on labor matters.

6174 Morris, James A. Honduras: caudillo politics and military rulers. Boulder, Colo.: Westview Press, 1984. 156 p.: bibl., ill., index (Westview profiles. Nations of contemporary Latin America)

By far the best book about Honduran politics published since William S. Stokes's work of 1950. Argues that after World War II, armed forces filled political power vacuum left when traditional political parties could not deal with issues of national development. Excellent discussion of regional bases of support of National and Liberal parties.

6175 Posas, Mario. Conflictos agrarios y organización campesina: sobre los orígenes de las primeras organizaciones campesinas en Honduras. Tegucigalpa: Univ. Nacional Autónoma de Honduras, 1981. 91 p.: bibl. (Col. Realidad nacional; 1)

Short but serious monograph dealing with origins of peasant unions in Honduras. Argues that unions began to form in 1950s as a response not to expansion but rather contraction of large-scale capitalist agriculture. Using organizing skills they had learned on banana plantations, workers whose employment had been terminated took up not only subsistence farming but union organizing.

6176 ——— and **Rafael del Cid.** La construcción del sector público y del Estado nacional en Honduras: 1876–1979. San José: Editorial Universitaria Centroamericana, 1983. 372 p.: bibl.

Indispensable for understanding historical evolution of Honduran State. Concludes that expansion and functional differentiation of the State occurred largely during short pre-reformist and reformist periods.

After 1950, decision making was increasingly influenced by the military.

6177 Rosenberg, Mark B. Honduran scorecard: military and democrats in Central America (FIU/CR, 12:1, Winter 1983, p. 12–15, 39–42, map)

Brief, insightful discussion of bargaining between civilian politicians and military leaders which made possible the return to civilian rule in 1980. The armed forces, which heretofore had relied on the National Party for civilian support, now tilted toward the Liberal Party. Focuses on a critical transition in Honduran politics.

———. Honduras: bastion of stability or quagmire? See item **3254.**

6178 Ruhl, J. Mark. Agrarian structure and political stability in Honduras (SAGE/JIAS, 26:1, Feb. 1984, p. 33–68, tables)

Excellent research piece attempts to determine whether differences in political stability of Honduras and El Salvador can be attributed to differing land tenure patterns. Concludes that this is indeed the case with Honduran peasants having more access to land and to relatively well paying alternative employment on banana plantations.

6179 Salomón, Leticia. Militarismo y reformismo en Honduras. Tegucigalpa: Editorial Guaymuras, 1982. 246 p.: bibl., ill. (Col. Códices)

Case study of Honduran armed forces which indicates that they emerged during 1970s as a powerful political actor after establishing their relative autonomy from traditional power blocs. Their ability to establish this relative degree of autonomy was result of a decrease in cohesion of traditional political parties and an increase in political activities of historically dormant peasant population.

6180 Santos M., Benjamín. Datos para el estudio del movimiento social cristiano: Honduras, 1981. Tegucigalpa: Instituto de Investigaciones Socio-Económicas, 1981. 137 p.: bibl.

This modestly titled vol. gives a fine account of the evolution of the Social Christian movement in Honduras. The movement prospered in early 1970s but soon became overextended and out of touch with increasingly conservative governments. Formation of regional development councils controlled by military excluded grass roots religious organizations from development process.

6181 Slutsky, Daniel and **Esther Alonso.** Empresas transnacionales y agricultura: el caso del enclave bananero en Honduras. Tegucigalpa: Editorial Universitaria, 1982. 141 p.: bibl.

Authors develop provocative thesis that changes in Honduras's banana industry have altered ways in which this industry affects national decision making. Because banana companies have diversified their local economic holdings, they can now influence politics "from below" through local pressure groups. Unfortunately, thesis is not well documented.

NICARAGUA

6182 Bolaños Hunter, Miguel. Nicaragua: a view from within (*in* Crisis and opportunity: U.S. policy in Central America and the Caribbean. Edited by Mark Falcoff and Robert Royal. Washington: Ethics and Public Policy Center, 1984, p. 381–398)

Written by former Nicaraguan counter-intelligence officer, article purports to describe methods which Sandinistas have used to monitor and influence all major sectors of society. Suggests that these security activities are supported by large numbers of advisors from Soviet Union, Eastern-bloc, and Cuba.

Borge, Tomás. El arte como herejía. See *HLAS 46:5864.*

6183 ——— *et al.* Sandinistas speak. New York: Pathfinder Press, 1982. 160 p.: ill., index.

Contains key writings and speeches of Tomás Borge, Carlos Fonseca, Daniel Ortega, Humberto Ortega, and Jaime Wheelock. Particularly important are early theoretical formulations of Carlos Fonseca and Humberto Ortega's 1980 interview with Chilean journalist Marta Harnecker outlining Sandinista guerrilla strategy.

6184 Cabezas, Omar. La montaña es algo más que una inmensa estepa verde. La Habana: Casa de las Américas, 1982. 255 p. (Testimonio)

Autobiographical account of a university student's entry into the FSLN and his subsequent experiences as a guerrilla fighter. Excellent analysis of the psychology of the guerrilla, extreme sense of isolation and fear of dying. Neophyte guerrilla at first views mountains as a source of symbolic strength, later as a trap, and finally as a source of real inner strength.

6185 Colburn, Forrest. Theory and practice in Nicaragua: the economics of class dynamics (FIU/CR, 12:3, Summer 1983, p. 6–9, 40–42, ill.)

Argues that Sandinista leadership faces major structural constraints in attempting to improve economic conditions of the poor. Rural agricultural producers are forced to sell their goods at low prices to satisfy consumer demands of politically important urban sectors and to increase foreign exchange. This creates political problems for the regime in the countryside.

6186 Cruz Sequeira, Arturo. The origins of Sandinista foreign policy (*in* Central America: anatomy of conflict [see item **6104a**] p. 95–109)

Article's title is somewhat misleading. Deals primarily with origins and perpetuation of divisions among top leaders of Sandinista government. Particularly useful as an insider's view of these divisions and for perspective on Sandinista relations with the Soviet Union, Cuba and West European socialists.

6187 Dreifus, Claudia. The Sandinistas: *Playboy* interviews with Daniel Ortega, Tomás Borge, Ernesto Cardenal and Sergio Ramírez (Playboy [Chicago] 30:9, Sept. 1983, p. 57–68, 140, 188–200, ill.)

In depth interview with three of the most important members of Sandinista government (Borge, Ortega, and Ramírez). Contains important insights into backgrounds, personalities and perceptions of these individuals. Particularly valuable for assessing their view of Reagan administration and its policies.

6188 Fagen, Richard. The Nicaraguan crisis (MR, 34:6, Nov. 1982, p. 1–16)

Brief but imaginative account of strengths and weaknesses of Sandinista government. Rural support for revolution is viewed as being strong with political struggle between classes confined to major cities. Tension is caused by fact that Sandinistas dominate political "high ground" yet economic power remains in hands of bourgeoisie.

6189 Francou, François; Carlos Corsi; and María Cristina García de Corsi. La Iglesia de Nicaragua. S.l.: s.n., 1983. 58 p.: bibl.

Slim vol. discussing role of Catholic Church in Nicaraguan revolution with much reservation expressed as to where that role is leading. Argues that Sandinistas have attempted to make the Church an institutional vehicle for the propagation of Marxism. Highly critical of FSLN for these proselytizing activities.

6190 Gorman, Stephen M. Social change and political revolution: the case of Nicaragua (*in* Central America: crisis and adaptation. Edited by Steve C. Ropp and James A. Morris. Albuquerque: Univ. of New Mexico Press, 1984, p. 33–66)

Stresses certain unique historical features of Nicaraguan condition that contributed to collapse of Somoza dynasty and subsequent revolution. Early contact with British and US interests led to early emergence of a virulent anti-imperialism. Nicaraguan society became increasingly complex after World War II but political apparatus remained essentially unchanged.

6191 Gorostiaga, Xabier. Dilemmas of the Nicaraguan revolution (*in* The Future of Central America: policy choices for the US and Mexico. Edited by Richard R. Fagen and Olga Pellicer. Stanford, Calif.: Stanford Univ. Press, 1983, p. 47–66)

Informative essay sketching policy dilemmas confronting Nicaragua's Sandinista leaders. Can basic human needs be satisfied within framework of a capitalist economy? How can democracy be maintained in a mass populist context? Is real national independence possible within US geostrategic orbit? Claims that Sandinistas have addressed these dilemmas pragmatically.

6192 Hacia una política cultural de la Revolución Popular Sandinista. Managua: Ministerio de Cultura, 1982. 328 p.

Perhaps best subtitled *The Commanders pontificate on culture*, this collection of speeches does convey a sense of the importance that Sandinista leaders attach to cultural transformation. Culture is to be "massified" through cultural workshops to

be held in many organizations including the army.

6192a Nicaragua: a country study. Edited by James D. Rudolph. Washington: American Univ., 1984. 278 p.: bibl., maps.

Part of US Dept. of the Army's Area Handbook Series, vol. describes and analyzes political, social, and economic system of Nicaragua. Those interested in the contemporary political structure will find chaps. on Government and Politics (by Jan Knippers Black) and National Security (by Jack Child) of considerable utility.

6193 Nolan, David. The ideology of the Sandinistas and the Nicaraguan revolution. Coral Gables, Fla.: Institute of Inter-American Studies, 1984. 203 p.: appendices, bibl., index, maps.

Well articulated and provocative study of Sandinista ideology. Argues that Sandinismo stresses unity of theory and practice, anti-imperialism, vanguard elitism and collectivism. Particularly useful are appendices which include a detailed list of pre-revolutionary and post-revolutionary organizations, biographical sketches, and a chronology of events.

6194 Ortega Saavedra, Humberto. Sobre la insurrección. La Habana: Editorial de Ciencias Sociales, 1981. 104 p. (Ediciones especiales)

Nicaragua's Minister of Defense expounds upon guerrilla strategy developed by Tercerista faction of the FSLN. Temporary alignment with bourgeoisie is necessary to neutralize this class. Guerrillas alone cannot defeat enemy and must work with masses to being about a large-scale uprising.

6195 Report of the Latin American Studies Association Delegation to observe the Nicaraguan general election of November 4, 1984 (LASA Forum [LASA, Austin, Tx.] 15:4, Winter 1985, p. 9–43)

Report of a 15-member delegation from LASA who closely observed first general elections held in Nicaragua after the overthrow of Anastasio Somoza Debayle. Delegation concluded that Sandinistas received a strong popular mandate but that elections also established existence of a viable opposition.

6196 La Revolución de Nicaragua. v. 1, A partir de octubre de 1977. v. 2, Sucesos de enero de 1978. León: Univ. Nacional Autónoma de Nicaragua, 1980. 2 v.: bibl., ill. (Cuadernos universitarios; 2a ser., no. 26–27)

Two vols. of primary source material (newspaper clippings) dealing with public reaction to political developments in Nicaragua (1977–79). Vol. 1 contains accounts of reaction of various groups, including National Guard, to guerrilla activities of the FSLN. Vol. 2 concentrates on reaction to Pedro Joaquín Chamorro's assassination.

6197 Tirado, Manlio. La revolución sandinista. México: Editorial Nuestro Tiempo, 1983. 196 p.: bibl. (Col. La Lucha por el poder)

Uneven but nonetheless valuable account of Nicaraguan revolution by a Mexican journalist. Treatment of FSLN activities in 1960s is quite good, but author is weak in his accounts of 1978–79 period. The 1980 period analysis improves again with good descriptions of Sandinista policy changes and opposition they elicited.

6198 Wheelock, Jaime. Nicaragua: imperialismo y dictadura. La Habana: Editorial de Ciencias Sociales, 1980. 213 p.: bibl., ill. (Economía)

Written by Nicaragua's Minister of Agriculture, this is perhaps the most definitive work to date on the historical perspective that the Sandinista leadership brings to its revolution. Coffee cultivation serves as base in the 19th century for establishment of a dependent agro-export economy. This Liberal agro-export "project" weakens in 1970s, presaging ultimate victory of Sandinistas.

PANAMA

Conte-Porras, Jorge. Iconografía de Omar Torrijos H. See *HLAS 46:2388*.

———. La rebelión de Las Esfinges: historia del movimiento estudiantil panameño. See *HLAS 46:2389*.

6199 Gandásegui, Marco A. La crisis centroamericana y el Canal de Panamá (*in* La Crisis centroamericana. Edited by Daniel Camacho and Manuel Rojas B. Ciudad Universitaria Rodrigo Facio, Costa Rica: Editorial Universitaria Centroamericana: Facultad Latinoamericana de Ciencias Sociales, 1984, p. 197–235 [Col. Seis])

Ideologically biased but nonetheless serious attempt to examine Panamanian foreign policy toward Central America and the Caribbean during 1970s. Argues that foreign policy directions came almost exclusively from Gen. Omar Torrijos and had purpose of garnering support for new canal treaties. Panamanian leadership in "banana wars" with United Brands won early respect and friendship of governments in Costa Rica and Honduras.

6200 Greene, Graham. Getting to know the general: the story of an involvement. New York: Simon & Schuster, 1984. 249 p.

Short personal memoir which describes author's visits to Panama and discussions with Gen. Omar Torrijos during period of canal treaty debates (1976–78). Has value only insofar as it reveals Torrijos's extraordinary ability to charm and influence a wide variety of international figures.

6201 Leis, Raúl. Panamá: puente de riqueza ajena "bajo el paraguas del Pentágono" (*in* La Crisis centroamericana. Edited by Daniel Camacho and Manuel Rojas B. Cuidad Universitaria Rodrigo Facio, Costa Rica: Editorial Universitaria Centroamericana: Facultad Latinoamericana de Ciencias Sociales, 1984, p. 152–196)

Brief account from a leftist perspective of major political developments in Panama (1970–82). Stresses fact that recent economic crisis and death of Gen. Omar Torrijos in 1981 resulted in a return to political power of the "imperialist bourgeoisie."

6202 ———. Radiografía de los partidos. Panamá: Centro de Capacitación Social, 1984. 121 p.

Written by sociologist who edits *Diálogo Social*, this short book gives a capsule summary of history and recent activities of Panama's major political parties. Although not a balanced and objective treatment, contains valuable insights, particularly concerning behavior of these parties in period directly preceding 1984 presidential elections.

Martínez, Daniel. Panamá: 1821–1979. See *HLAS 46:2417*.

6203 Ropp, Steve C. Panama and the Canal (*in* Latin America: its problems and promises. Edited by Jan Knippers Black. Boulder, Colo.: Westview Press, 1984, p. 329–342, bibl.)

Suggests that Panama's gradual movement toward a more democratic political system during late 1970s and early 1980s was more the result of deteriorating economic conditions and of pressure from US than of fundamental attachment to democratic principles. The armed forces, traditionally a stable institution, may become more volatile due to generational change.

6204 Torres, Miguel. La construcción del sector público en Panamá: 1903–1955.

San José: Instituto Centroamericano de Administración Pública, 1982. 206 p.: bibl.

Part of larger project funded by Ford Foundation designed to investigate historical origins of public sector in various Central American countries. Based on primary sources and largely descriptive, discusses public sector growth during four periods in three subsectors (production, reproduction, and control).

THE CARIBBEAN AND THE GUIANAS

ANDRES SUAREZ, Professor Emeritus of Political Science, Center for Latin American Studies, University of Florida

AT LAST, THE PRESENT STATE of comparative politics in the Commonwealth Caribbean is subject to study in a valuable effort by Patrick Emmanuel (item **6207**), an attempt not undertaken since the 1974 article by J.E. Greene (see *HLAS 37:8201*). In contrast to Greene who, under the prevailing influences of the 1970s, emphasized methodology, Emmanuel focuses on more substantive questions. He discusses and then discards three paradigms: ethnocultural pluralism, Marxism, and plantation dependency theory. Instead, he proposes an interpretation that draws on social class analysis and dependency theory, a combination that is eclectic if not especially original given today's criticism of dependency theory. Nevertheless, Emmanuel's article does summarize most of the literature and pays due attention to size, a crucial factor in the Caribbean, often overlooked by students of the region.

A second and very different paper by Emmanuel (item **6210**), apparently prompted by the Grenadian experience, also deserves to be mentioned. This work discusses the "non-capitalist path of development," a Soviet concoction the real purposes of which are being disclosed of late by Soviet theoreticians who have substituted Emmanuel's terminology with the expression "countries with a socialist orientation." Since Emmanuel's article was written before the collapse of the Grenadian revolution, one should read his discussion of this event in conjunction with some very important documents (item **7232**) that are mentioned in the last paragraph of this introductory essay.

In 1975, the Organization of Popular Power in Cuba rekindled the enthusiasm of observers who perceived the new organs as symptomatic of the increasing democratization of the Cuban Revolution. Recent visitors to Cuba, however, raise doubts as to the accuracy of this forecast. Ritter (item **6232**), who witnessed the nomination meetings of Feb. 1979, found that "there were no adequate means for the public to participate either in leadership selection or policy making." Jørgensen (item **6225**) basically agrees. In the municipality of Nuevitas he noticed the "adaptation" of the citizenry to the constraints imposed by the central power, that is, the "maximum leader" and the Political Bureau of the Communist Party. Even at a local level, popular demands were articulated only if and when they were compatible with expectations transmitted *a priori* by party leaders.

A third contribution on Cuba conveys criticism of its regime from the point of view of the libertarian and anti-Stalinist left. Beauvais's study (item **6213**) notes that, as of the 1970s, there occurred a fundamental break with the "egalitarianism" proclaimed during the Revolution's early period. He clearly states the dilemma confronted in the 1980s: "Either democratic self-organization of the masses, or confiscation of the Revolution by bureaucratic layers." The recent introduction of Marxism-Leninism classes at every level of the educational system "following syllabuses 'imported' from the Soviet Union, is not very likely to improve the situation."

Among several problems that affect the formulation of US policies towards the Caribbean Basin, two very important ones are unsatisfactory information concerning the region's revolutionaries as well as lack of evidence regarding their real intentions. Hence the significance of the *Grenada Documents* (item **7232**) published by the Departments of State and Defense (Sept. 1984). For the first time, one is in a position to compare revolutionary rhetoric with political reality in the Caribbean. Unfortunately, the veracity of the region's revolutionaries leaves much to be desired. Behind their publicized proclamations of national sovereignty and popular democracy, there were definite plans to tie Grenada's future to Cuba and the Soviet Union. What remains as the puzzling element of this whole saga is the motivation of Grenada's leader, the so-called Bishop Enigma: Was he a true believer or merely another one of those "Caribbean politicians" who, according to Anthony P. Maingot (item **6253**), are exemplified by Michael Manley and Forbes Burnham—manipulators who, deciding to "play the Cuban card," are unaware of the consequences, the mortal danger of such irresponsible maneuverings?

GENERAL

6205 Ambursley, Fitzroy and **Robin Cohen.** Crisis in the Caribbean: internal transformations and external constraints (*in* Crisis in the Caribbean. Edited by Fitzroy Ambursley and Robin Cohen. New York: Monthly Review Press, 1983, p. 1–26, bibl.)

Brief discussion, from a far-left perspective, of topics such as culture, race and national identity, pitfalls of "the non-capitalist path," class alliances and revolutionary strategy, transition to socialism, and inability of "the sclerotic American far right" to face revolution.

6206 Ameringer, Charles D. The tradition of democracy in the Caribbean: Betancourt, Figueres, Muñoz and the democratic Left (FIU/CR, 11:2, Spring 1982, p. 28–31, 55–56, plate)

Well founded recognition of roles played by these three leaders in the politics of the Caribbean Basin, including their relations wth US liberals of 1950s and 1960s. Particularly timely observations now that there is so much emphasis on the authoritarian tradition in some quarters.

6207 Emmanuel, Patrick A.M. Approaches to the comparative study of Caribbean politics: some comments (UWI/SES, 30:3, Sept. 1981, p. 119–136, bibl.)

Preliminary reflections on three prevalent approaches: ethnocultural, pluralism, Marxism, and plantation-dependency theory. Tentative suggestions for future research.

6208 ———. Elections and parties in the Eastern Caribbean: a historical survey (FIU/CR, 10:2, Spring 1981, p. 14–17, ill., tables)

Analysis of main trends in Eastern Caribbean politics since 1950s, covers three stages: 1) dominance of labor movements; 2) emergence of alternative parties; and 3) formation of radical political organizations. Good summary.

6209 ———. General elections in the Eastern Caribbean: a handbook. Cave Hill, Barbados: Institute of Social and Economic Research, Eastern Caribbean, Univ. of the West Indies, 1979. 194 p.: appendix, bibl. (Occasional paper; 11)

Data on 57 general elections held in eight Eastern Caribbean countries (1951–79). Appendix includes names, affiliations, constituencies, and vote performance for all candidates.

6210 ———. Revolutionary theory and political reality in the Eastern Caribbean (SAGE/JIAS, 25:2, May 1983, p. 193–227, bibl.)

The "non-capitalist path of development" is a transitional model to socialism suggested by Soviets for Third World countries. Model's applicability to Eastern Caribbean is found wanting. Among factors overlooked by Soviet theoreticians are: nature of rural proletariat, level of resources endowment, and lack of socialist traditions. Article also includes section on Grenada written before publication of the *Grenada Documents* (see item **7232**).

6211 **Erskine, Noel Leo.** Decolonizing theology: a Caribbean perspective. Marynoll, N.Y.: Orbis Books, 1981. 130 p.: bibl., index.

After the theology of liberation, we have now black theology. Author is a Jamaican Prof. of Theology at Emory Univ.

6212 **Serbín, Andrés.** La evolución de la ideología de la izquierda caribeña (NSO, 61, julio/agosto 1982, p. 55–65, ill.)

Concerns the Commonwealth Caribbean as of the rise of region's Black Power Movement (1968–73). But as of 1980s, detects new trends that convey dilution of ethnic element and predominance of different varieties of Marxist and nationalist components.

CUBA

6213 **Beauvais, Jean-Pierre.** Achievements and contradictions of the Cuban workers' state (*in* Crisis in the Caribbean. Edited by Fitzroy Ambursley and Robin Cohen. New York: Monthly Review Press, 1983, p. 49–71, bibl.)

A critique of recent Cuban economic policies by a radical leftist—apparently trotskyist. The new "system of economic management and planning," the increasing role of the Soviet Union and the typical "paternalism" of Cuban leaders threatens with the confiscation of the revolution by the bureaucracy.

6214 **Castro, Fidel.** Problemas actuales de los países subdesarrollados: selección de discursos. La Habana: Oficina de Publicaciones del Consejo de Estado, 1979. 272 p.

Speeches, whole texts, and excerpts, delivered by Castro between 1973–79, dealing with underdevelopment.

6215 **Congreso del Partido Comunista de Cuba,** *1st, La Habana, 1975.* Memorias. La Habana: Partido Comunista de Cuba, Depto. de Orientación Revolucionaria, 1976. 3 v.: ill. (some col.)

Speeches, reports, resolutions of 1975 congress not previously annotated in *HLAS*.

6216 **Cuba, dictatorship or democracy?:** edition includes account of national experience of People's Power. Edited and with an introduction by Marta Harnecker. Translation into English by Patrick Greanville. 5th ed., rev. and expanded. Westport, Conn.: L. Hill, 1980. 239 p.: bibl.

Original ed. (1975, see *HLAS 41:7201*) has been substantially rewritten to include the experience of two yrs. of People's Power.

6217 **Del Aguila, Juan M.** Cuba, dilemmas of a revolution. Boulder, Colo.: Westview Press, 1984. 193 p.: bibl., ill., index (Westview profiles. Nations of contemporary Latin America)

Probably best short introduction to study of Cuban regime available. Summarizes historical background in 43 p. and devotes remainder to a discussion of revolutionary transformation as well as "Performance and Prospects." Final characterization that "a stable totalitarianism in which the charismatic factor is present but is no longer dominant," is, of course, questionable.

6218 **Domínguez, Jorge I.** Cuba in the 1980's (USIA/PC, 30:2, March/April 1981, p. 48–59, ill.)

The Cuban regime's perspectives for 1980s are assessed in this well grounded paper, especially supported by Cuban data. Perspectives appear bleak.

6219 ———. Revolutionary politics: the new demands for orderlines (*in* Cuba: internal and international affairs. Edited by Jorge I. Domínguez. Beverly Hills, Calif.: Sage Publications, 1982, p. 19–70)

Characterizes Cuba's regime as a "consultative oligarchy." Author's text, however, is not always congruous with this characterization and the main evidence—*Granma's* summaries of speeches at the Popular Assembly,—is rather weak. Nevertheless, a thoughtful paper.

6220 Eckstein, Susan. Structural and ideological bases of Cuba's overseas programs (Politics & Society [Los Altos, Calif.] 11:1, 1982, p. 95–121)

Overseas programs of civilian assistance generate foreign exchange needed by Cuba although in general, such activities are consistent with Soviet global interests. Material considerations are important factors that explain Cuba's foreign policy.

6221 Farber, Samuel. The Cuban communists in the early stages of the Cuban Revolution: revolutionaries or reformists? (LARR, 18:1, 1983, p. 59–83)

Recounts Communist assets (e.g., cadres, organizational autonomy, Soviet connection) in order to reevaluate Communists' role in early stages of the Revolution. Merely a historical exercise as the influence exercised later by the Old Communists was nil.

6222 Forster, Nancy. The revolutionary transformation of the Cuban countryside. Hanover, N.H.: Univ. Field Staff International, 1982. 18 p.: bibl. (UFSI reports, 0743–9644; 26. North America)

Author visited Cuba in 1980. The "revolutionary transformation" is based on secondary sources, all in English with one or two exceptions. The second pt. of paper contains some interesting observations in the field.

6223 Green, Gil. Cuba at 25: the continuing revolution. New York: International Publishers, 1983. 117 p.

US visitor who finds nothing to criticize in the island pleads for establishing normal diplomatic and trade relations with Cuba.

6224 Inter-American Commission on Human Rights. La situación de los derechos humanos en Cuba: séptimo informe. Washington: CIDH, 1983. 241 p.: bibl. (OEA/ser. L/V/II.61, doc. 29)

Title is self-explanatory.

6225 Jørgensen, Bård. The interrelationship between base and superstructure in Cuba (NOSALF/IA, 8:1, 1983, p. 27–41, bibl., maps, tables)

Specifically, this is a study on the municipality of Nuevitas. The Organ of People's Power in Nuevitas does not strengthen self-government but local administration. Notes that 70 percent of the delegates are members of Communist Party.

6226 *Lateinamerika.* Semesterbericht der Sektion Lateinamerikawissenschaften der Wilhelm-Pieck-Univ. Fall 1982– . Rostock, GDR.

Contributions by East Germans and Soviet scholars provide an assessment of "socialism in Cuba." All are written within a Marxist perspective and contain no citations for sources. [G.M. Dorn]

6227 LeoGrande, William M. The theory and practice of socialist democracy in Cuba: mechanisms of elite accountability (USC/SCC, 12:1, Spring 1979, p. 39–62)

Very sympathetic article on Organs of People's Power by one who thinks that Cuba is "explicitly a proletarian dictatorship." Author's footnotes suggest that he is unable to read Spanish, and that his knowledge of pre-Castro's Cuba is less than mediocre.

6228 Mencia, Mario. La prisión fecunda. La Habana: Editora Política, 1980. 292 p.: ill.

Fruitful prison is a collection of excerpts from letters and other documents written by Fidel Castro while in jail after the Moncada assault. They have been selected, twisted, and embellished in ways that display the exceptional qualifications of the leader and his foresight.

6229 Montaner, Carlos Alberto. Cuba, claves para una conciencia en crisis. Madrid: Playor, 1982. 154 p. (Biblioteca cubana contemporánea)

Collection of essays on some of the most vital issues in Cuba's past and present history. In general, criticizes Cuban grandiloquence and emphasizes the heavy constraints imposed on island's history by its geography and size.

6230 Perlmutter, Amos and William M. LeoGrande. The party in uniform: toward a theory of civil-military relations in communist political systems (APSA/R, 76:4, Dec. 1982, p. 778–789, bibl.)

Brief section on Cuba (less than one p.) is clearly insufficient in an effort to establish a comparative framework for study of civil-military relations in communist political systems. Insofar as the rest is concerned, article is thoughtful and deserves attention.

6231 Piñeiro, Manuel. La crisis actual del imperialismo y los procesos revolucionarios en la América Latina y el Caribe (CDLA, 139, julio/agosto 1983, p. 21–26)

Author is Chief of the American Dept., Central Committee, Cuban Communist Party. Article previously appeared in *Cuba Socialista* (4, sept./nov. 1982). Its main purpose is to summarize Cuban, Nicaraguan, and Grenadian experiences. They confirm that necessary conditions for revolutionary success are: unity, the masses, and arms. Military confrontation is unavoidable, and therefore, the need for adopting a politicomilitary strategy. Piñeiro's role in Cuban leadership suggests this is the Castro "line."

6232 Ritter, Archibald R.M. The authenticity of participatory democracy in Cuba (*in* Latin American prospects for the 1980s: equity, democratization, and development. Edited by Archibald R.M. Ritter and David H. Pollock. New York: Praeger, 1983, p. 182–213, tables)

Author visited Cuba (Feb. 1979) and his paper covers the experience of Organs of People's Power during its first four yrs. Concludes that there is no evidence of popular control over selection of leaders at national level, while at local level it "exists to some degree." Concerning formulation of policies, second indicator of democracy chosen by author, Party control persists. Good study of government mechanisms adopted as of 1976.

6233 Roca, Sergio. Cuba confronts the 1980s (CUH, 82:481, Feb. 1983, p. 74–78)

Good short analysis emphasizes economic trends.

6234 Thomas, Hugh. The Revolution off balance. Washington: Cuban-American National Foundation, 1983. 19 p. (Occasional paper; 5)

Expert in Cuban history looks at Castro regime after 25 yrs. and does not like what he sees. His arguments should not be overlooked.

6235 ———; Georges A. Fauriol; and Juan Carlos Weiss. The Cuban Revolution, 25 years later. Boulder, Colo.: Westview Press; Washington: Georgetown Univ., Cen-

ter for Strategic and International Studies, 1984. 69 p.: maps, plates (CSIS Significant issues series, 0736–7163; 6:11)

Proceedings of a conference in which some 20 experts on Cuban affairs discussed political control, economic management, culture, and social development of the Revolution.

DOMINICAN REPUBLIC

6236 Balaguer, Joaquín. Pedestales: discursos históricos. Barcelona: I.G. Manuel Pareja, 1979. 167 p.: ill. (Discursos; 6)

Ex-President of the Dominican Republic speaks about Latin American and Dominican figures of the past. His speeches shed more light on his own personality than on those he praises.

6237 Campillo Pérez, Julio G. Elecciones dominicanas: contribución a su estudio. 3a ed., rev. and updated. Santo Domingo: Relaciones Públicas, 1982. 550 p.: bibl. (Academia Dominicana de la Historia; 49)

Third ed. of book originally published in 1966 under the title *El Grillo y el ruiseñor*. Includes much information on 1982 election. No index. To be read with caution.

6238 Despradel, Fidelio *et al.* Debate sobre la Izquierda: análisis de la obra *Nuestra falsa izquierda*. Santo Domingo: Centro Dominicano de Estudios de la Educación (CELADEC), 1980. 505 p.

Members of atomized Dominican left devote 500 p. to their petty squabbles with quotes from Marx, Lenin, Stalin, Mao, and every other saint in Marxist pantheon. An extravagant display of intellectual alienation.

Franco, Franklin J. Historia de las ideas políticas en la República Dominicana: contribución a su estudio. See *HLAS 46:7564.*

6239 Guzmán Fernández, Silvestre Antonio. Discursos presidenciales. Santo Domingo: Oficina Nacional de Administración y Personal, 1982. 3 v.: ill. (Cols. Estudios políticos; 1. Col. ONAP)

Important source for study of Guzmán administration.

6240 Hermann, Hamlet. Caracoles, la guerrilla de Caamaño. 3a ed. Santo Domingo: Alfa y Omega, 1980. 258 p.: ill., plates.

Francisco Caamaño and eight more guerrillas landed in the Dominican Republic on Feb. 2, 1973. Author, one of two survivors, was captured at the end of March. No heroics, no glamour. Fascinating narrative of a guerrilla's daily life.

6241 Infante, Fernando A. *Aquelarre*: 4 años de política dominicana, 1978–1982. Santo Domingo: Editora Alfa y Omega, 1982. 212 p.: bibl.

Summary of political events based mainly on readings of domestic press. Useful material for understanding idiosyncracies of Dominican political life.

6242 Moreno Ceballos, Nelson. El Estado dominicano: origen, evolución y su forma actual, 1844–1982. 2a ed. Santo Domingo: Punto y Aparte Editores, 1983. 351 p.: ill.

Marxist synthesis based on secondary sources.

6243 Los Problemas de la institucionalización y preservación de la democracia en la República Dominicana. Santo Domingo: FORUM, 1982. 173 p. (FORUM; 2)

FORUM consists of a group of interested citizens who meet periodically to discuss contemporary national problems. The Executive Secretary is historian Frank Moya Pons in charge of publication. FORUM publishes papers and debates as a monographic series of which 15 worthwhile vols. have appeared. This installment (No. 2) is of same high quality. The series should be seriously considered by anyone with a professional interest in Dominican politics.

6244 Rodríguez, Adrián and Deborah Huntington. Inherit the wind (NACLA, 16:6, Nov./Dec. 1982, p. 2–35, bibl., ill.)

Examination of Guzmán administration in the Dominican Republic. Good reporting helps reader to overlook usual disparaging references to bourgeois politicians, multinationals, etc.

6245 Wiarda, Howard J. and Michael J. Kryzanek. The Dominican Republic, a Caribbean crucible. Boulder, Colo.: Westview Press, 1982. 153 p.: bibl., ill., index (Nations of contemporary Latin America)

Short, well balanced, competent introduction that furthers one's understanding of this troubled country. Covers essentials including foreign policy. Authors' conclusions are cautious, as they should be when dealing with such a poor nation facing appalling problems after such a turbulent past.

6246 Wipfler, William Louis. Poder, influencia e impotencia: la Iglesia como factor socio-político en República Dominicana. Traducción de Samuel E. James. Santo Domingo: Ediciones CEPAE, 1980. 314 p.: bibl.

Covers social and political role of the Church in Dominican history. Good beginning for a neglected topic.

FRENCH GUIANA

6247 Schwarzbeck, Frank. Recycling a forgotten colony: from green hell to outer space in French Guiana (FIU/CR, 13:2, Spring 1984, p. 22–24, 47–48, map, plates)

German political scientist is author of this informative paper covering history of French Guiana from departamentalization to present alternatives.

GRENADA

6148 Ambursley, Fitzroy. Grenada: the New Jewel revolution (*in* Crisis in the Caribbean. Edited by Fitzroy Ambursley and Robin Cohen. New York: Monthly Review Press, 1983, p. 191–222, bibl.)

Substantially enlarged and updated version of article originally published in *New Left Review*. Criticisms of Maurice Bishop have been eliminated. Author's Marxist approach does not hinder his analytical ability.

6249 Bishop, Maurice. Selected speeches, 1979–1981. La Habana: Casa de las Américas, 1982? 284 p.:

Valuable source for study of Bishop regime starting with his first Address to the Nation, the day of the successful coup.

Grenada Documents: an overview and selection. See item 7232.

6251 In the spirit of Butler: trade unionism in free Grenada. Rev. ed. St. Georges, Grenada: Fedon Publishers, 1982. 104 p.: ill.

Speeches and documents from Third Trade Union Conference for the Unity and

Solidarity of Caribbean Workers (1981). Includes one speech by Bishop.

6252 Jacobs, W. Richard and **Ian Jacobs.** Grenada, el camino hacia la revolución. La Habana: Casa de las Américas, 1981. 158 p. (Cuadernos Casa; 25)

Spanish translation of *Grenada, the route to revolution* (La Habana: Casa de las Américas, 1979).

6253 Maingot, Anthony P. Options for Grenada: the need to be cautious (FIU/CR, 12:4, Fall 1983, p. 24–28, plate, tables)

Early reaction to the invasion pointing out that fundamental question is how to return to democracy.

6254 Manley, Michael. Grenada in the context of history: between neo-colonialism and independence (FIU/CR, 12:4, Fall 1983, p. 6–9, 45–47, map, plates)

Jamaica's ex-Prime Minister recognizes that majority of nations in the region supported invasion. Nevertheless, he strongly criticizes it. Also contributes to mythicizing of Bishop and, of course, absolves Cuba of any responsibility.

Naipaul, V. S. An island betrayed: Grenada's revolution. See item **7246.**

6255 Payne, Anthony; Paul Sutton; and **Tony Thorndike.** Grenada: revolution and invasion. New York: St. Martin's Press, 1984. 233 p.: bibl., index, maps.

Post-mortem of so-called Grenada Revolution which, perhaps unconsciously, reflected Bishop's political legacy: war against US imperialism, friendship with Cuba, and promotion of socialist revolutions that are neither socialist nor revolutionary. Authors had available minutes of Central Committee of the New Jewel Movement.

6256 Ryan, Selwyn. The Grenada questions: a revolutionary balance sheet (FIU/CR, 13:3, April 1984, p. 6–9, 39–43)

Well conceived paper assesses performance of Bishop government and recognizes severe economic constraints that small size imposes on states such as Grenada. Although the intervention is not explicitly discussed, notes that "so far, the Americans have played all their cards right."

6257 Sánchez, Néstor D. What was uncovered in Grenada (FIU/CR, 12:4,

Fall 1983, p. 21–23, 59, plates)

Inventory of US Deputy Assistant Secretary of Defense for Inter-American Affairs of materials captured in Grenada.

Searle, Chris and **Don Rojas.** "To construct from morning:" making the people's budget in Grenada: interviews. See item **3336.**

GUYANA

6258 Avebury, Lord and **British Parliamentary Human Rights Group.** Guyana's 1980 elections: the politics of fraud (FIU/CR, 10:2, Spring 1981, p. 8–11, 44)

Data supports Human Rights Group's contention that elections in Guyana have been "rigged massively and flagrantly."

6259 Chandisingh, Rajendra. The State, the economy, and the type of rule in Guyana: an assessment of Guyanas Socialist Revolution (LAP, 10:4, 1983, p. 59–74, bibl.)

Sample of Marxist analysis discovers that the Guyanese State is under control of a consuming "petty-bourgeoisie ruling class." From workers' point of view, nationalization has changed nothing. Curiously, this kind of analysis is never applied to Cuba or any other "socialist" state. For economist's comment, see item **3309.**

Dodd, David J. Rule-making and rule-enforcement in plantation society: the ideological development of criminal justice in Guyana. See item **1046.**

6260 General Assembly, 2nd, Georgetown, *1977.* "Workers together with Christ:" report. Georgetown: Cedar Press, 1978. 102 p.: ill.

Contains much material from this Assembly: addresses, reports of work groups, resolutions, etc. (not previously annotated in *HLAS*).

6261 Greene, J. Edward. Cooperativism, militarism, party politics and democracy in Guyana (*in* The Newer Caribbean: decolonization, democracy, and development. Edited by Paget Henry and Carl Stone. Philadelphia: Institute for the Study of Human Issues, 1983, p. 257–180, tables [Inter-American politics series; 4])

Discussion of Guyanese politics in 1970s. Scenario has changed considerably since this article was written.

6262 Hintzen, Percy C. Bases of elite support for a regime: race, ideology, and clientelism as bases for leaders in Guyana and Trinidad (CPS, 16:3, Oct. 1983, p. 363–392, bibl., tables)

Based on interviews with well reputed leaders from both nations but does not provide specifics on how additional data was collected. Tries to ascertain "the relative importance of ideological, racial, and clientelistic support for the regime among the elite" of both nations, "given the choice of a socialist development strategy" in Guyana and a capitalist strategy in Trinidad.

6263 ——— and **Ralph R. Premdas.** Race, ideology, and power in Guyana (ICS/ JCCP, 21:2, July 1983, p. 175–194, table)

Burnham's control of the military and police plus popular support mobilized by ethnic appeals allowed him to switch from anti-communism in 1950s to cooperation with Socialist Bloc and Third World Radicals in 1970s. In 1980s, however, policies of moderation reflect interests of blacks entrenched in the army and bureaucracy.

6264 People's Progressive Party, Guyana. For socialism in Guyana: political programme of the People's Progressive Party. Prague: Orbis Press Agency, 1982. 75 p.

At present, the PPP holds that the struggle must be revolutionary democratic with a socialist orientation. Its program strongly criticizes Burnham, proposes a National Patriotic Front, and supports all forms of struggle: peaceful and nonpeaceful.

6265 A Report on the referendum held in Guyana: a question of human rights, July 10th 1978. Georgetown: Committee for Concerned Citizens, 1978? 66 p.: appendix, ill.

Background and results of referendum. Appendix compares returns as reported by the government and Committee.

6266 Serbín, Andrés. Nacionalismo, etnicidad y política en la República Cooperativa de Guyana. Caracas: Bruguera, 1982. 276 p.: bibl., ill. (Autores latinoamericanos)

Introduction to Guyana, written by an Argentine anthropologist, explores effects of ethnicity and politics on development of national consciousness.

6267 Spinner, Thomas J., Jr. Guyana update: political, economic, moral bankruptcy

(FIU/CR, 11:4, Fall 1982, p. 9–11, 30–32)

Recent trends, under Emperor Burnham, as seen by a historian.

6268 Thomas, Clive Y. State capitalism in Guyana: an assessment of Burnham's Cooperative Socialist Republic (in Crisis in the Caribbean. Edited by Fitzroy Ambursley and Robin Cohen. New York: Monthly Review Press, 1983, p. 27–48, bibl.)

In contrast to classical model, in the capitalist periphery today "political/state power is being used as an instrument for the consolidation of a new depending ruling class." State property has nothing to do with socialism. Insightful contribution, although author's perception that Guyana is going through a process of "fascistization" is questionable.

HAITI

6269 Bellegarde-Smith, Patrick. Class struggle in contemporary Haitian politics: an interpretative study of the campaign of 1957 (Journal of Caribbean Studies [Assn. of Caribbean Studies, Coral Gables, Fla.] 2:1, Spring 1981, p. 109–127)

Designed as "a contribution to the understanding of Caribbean class struggle and elite ideological structure." Generally speaking, attempts to apply European social structure concepts and terminology to Caribbean result in frustration. This article is no exception.

6270 Castor, Susy. Dictadura y resistencia en Haití: la instancia cultural (AR, 8:30, 1982, p. 18–23, plates)

Negritude and Vodu have been manipulated by François and Jean Claude Duvalier to reinforce their totalitarian control. In the last five yrs., author perceives emergence of a new culture of "urban resistance," but does not present evidence of it.

6271 Paley, William. Haiti's dynastic despotism: from father to son . . . (FIU/CR, 8:1, Winter 1984, p. 13–15, 45, ill.)

Perceptive analysis of relationship between class and color, importance of *classe intermediare,* and role of the State under Jean Claude.

6272 Weinstein, Brian and **Aaron Segal.** Haiti: political failures, cultural successes. New York: Praeger, 1984. 175 p.: bibl., index, map (Politics in Latin America)

Introduction to Haiti provides good retrospective of country's political history since the US occupation in 1915. [A. Pérotin-Dumon]

JAMAICA

6273 Ambursley, Fitzroy. Jamaica: from Michael Manley to Edward Seaga (*in* Crisis in the Caribbean. Edited by Fitzroy Ambursley and Robin Cohen. New York: Monthly Review Press, 1983, p. 72–104, bibl.)

Author's extreme radicalism leads him to a provocative suggestion: obsession with race among all classes in Jamaica is a symptom of the prevailing social conservatism. Well articulated critique of Manley's "democratic-socialism" by a proponent of socialist revolution now.

6274 Forbes, John D. Jamaica: managing political and economic change. Washington: American Enterprise Institute for Pubic Policy Research, 1985. 54 p.: bibl.

Undergraduates and general public will benefit from this short, competent, and well balanced introduction to Jamaican politics. Author correctly emphasizes huge problems faced by Seaga in 1984.

6275 Gonsalves, Ralph. The Rodney Affair and its aftermath (UWI/CQ, 25, 1979, p. 1–24, bibl.)

Recollection of the Rodney Affair by the President of the Guild of Undergraduates at the time. Purpose of exercise is to stress significance of these events for the history of "the democratic and revolutionary struggles of Caribbean peoples."

6276 Horne, Winston A. van. Jamaica: problems of Manley's *The Politics of change, 1972–1980* (Journal of Caribbean Studies [Assn. of Caribbean Studies, Coral Gables, Fla.] 2 : 2 / 3, Autumn / Winter 1981, p. 210–226)

Author believes key for understanding policies of Manley's government is in his work *The Politics of change: a Jamaican testament* (Washington: Howard Univ. Press, 1975). Very critical of these policies. Provides some data on their conspicuous failures.

6277 Johnson, Janis and **Robert A. Rankin.** Interviewing Michael Manley: the role of the opposton in Jamaica (FIU / CR, 11 : 3, 1982, p. 26–29, ill.)

Manley praises Sandinista pluralism but strongly criticizes both Seaga and Caribbean Basin Initiative. Says nothing about his own disastrous administration or his enduring friendship with Castro.

6278 LaGuerre, John Gaffar. The Moyne Commission and the Jamaican left (UWI / SES, 31 : 3, 1982, p. 59–94)

Identifies the left as intellectuals (univ. graduates, professionals, self-educated). Discusses reactions to the Commission among different groups on the left.

6279 Manley, Michael. Jamaica: struggle in the periphery. London: Third World Media: *in association with* Writers and Readers Publishing Cooperative Society, 1982. 259 p.: bibl., ill., index (Library of the Third World)

More useful for Manley's biographers than for students of his government's policies. To Manley, Khadaffy sounds "like a mystic" (p. 109); Castro's adventures in Africa remind him of "the days of Alexander the Great" (p. 112); and Jamaican middle classes—including Manley?—are nothing but "bastards," offsprings of slave-owners "who, with little work to do, had a lot of time to breed with the more attractive slave girls" (p. 27). Attributes his own political defeat mainly to "destabilization." There is even a "destabilization diary" on the "unprecedented levels" of violence and terrorism promoted—according to Manley—by the CIA.

6280 Munroe, Trevor. Unite against imperalism! Build the Workers Party! Kingston: Workers Party of Jamaica, 1979. 76 p.: ill.

Consists of the central address to the public session of the Party's 1st Congress. This is the pro-Soviet Communist Party of Jamaica, the 91st in the world, and Munroe is its Secretary General. The line: critical support for Manley.

6281 Payne, Anthony. The Rodney riots in Jamaica: the background and significance of the events of October 1968 (ICS / JCCP, 21 : 2, July 1983, p. 158–174)

Background, events, and their significance for Jamaican politics.

6282 People's National Party. Principles and objectives: People's National Party. Kingston: The Party, 1979. 68 p.: plates.

After two yrs. of internal discussion a document was adopted proclaiming that the party's main goal was its transformation into a democratic socialist party. Draws a distinction between democratic socialism and scientific socialism.

6283 Perspectives on Jamaica in the seventies. Edited by Carl Stone and Aggrey Brown. Kingston: Jamaica Publishing House, 1981. 486 p.: bibl., ill.

Compilation of papers organized into four pts.: 1) "Aspects of the Political Economy," with contributions by Carl A. Stone, Vaughan A. Lewis, Louis Lindsay, Edwin Jones, Claremont Kirton, and Mark Figueroa, and Dwight Venner; 2) "Elections and Voting," with papers by Carl Stone, Marion Miller, Dennis Green, and the PNP and JLP; 3) "The Media and the Transformation Process," with contributions by Aggrey Brown, UNESCO, and Sheila Nicholson; and 4) "Community Development and Social Trends," with papers by Barry Chevannes, Peter Philipps, Carl Stone, and Sheila Mitchell. For sociologist's comment, see item **8207.**

6284 Stephens, Evelyne Huber and **John D. Stephens.** Democratic socialism in dependent capitalism: an analysis of the Manley government in Jamaica (ISU/PS, 12:3, 1983, p. 373–411, tables)

Neither dependency theory nor the world system approach explain failure of democratic socialism in Jamaica. Domestic factors such as balance of class forces, a clientelistic party, and weak state capacity are more relevant. Sophisticated and insightful discussion of Manley government, although probably authors overestimate Manley's commitment to socialism.

6285 Stone, Carl. Democracy and clientelism in Jamaica. New Brunswick, N.J.: Transaction Books, 1980. 262 p.: bibl., ill., index, tables.

Book is end product of a long-time intimacy with and reflection on Jamaican politics. Intended as a contribution towards a better understanding of both Jamaican and Caribbean politics. Tables and figures enrich text. Remarkable accomplishment.

6286 ———. Democracy and socialism in Jamaica: 1972–1979 (in The Newer Caribbean: decolonization, democracy, and development. Edited by Paget Henry and Carl Stone. Philadelphia: Institute for the Study of Human Issues, 1983, p. 235–255, tables [Inter-American politics series; 4])

Government populist policies towards greater democratization overestimated extent of popular support. Increasing alignment with Cuba and anti-US postures strengthened opposition. Economic policies failed miserably. Sophisticated analysis of both Manley governments.

———. The Jamaican reaction: Grenada and the political stalemate. See item **7253.**

6288 ———. The political opinions of the Jamaican people, 1976–81. Kingston: Blackett Publishers, 1982. 78 p.: bibl.

Collection of most important polls conducted by author over past six yrs. His introduction deals with difficulties of polling Jamaican public opinion.

6289 ———. Seaga is in trouble: polling the Jamaican polity in mid-term (FIU/CR, 11:4, Fall 1982, p. 4–7, 28–29, table)

Trends in Jamaican public opinion (Oct. 1980-Oct. 1982). Attributes decline in JLP support mainly to economic deterioration.

6290 Witter, Michael and **George Beckford.** Small garden—bitter weed: the political economy of struggle and change in Jamaica. Ltd. student and electoral ed. Morant Bay, Jamaica: Maroon Publishing House, 1980. 128 p.: ill.

Jamaica is the garden. Colonialists and their lackeys are the weeds. As stated in its preface, book's purpose is "To sharpen our intellectual machetes." Authors' manifesto provides "a scenario for building a socialist society rooted in the cultural tradition of our people."

LESSER ANTILLES: BRITISH COMMONWEALTH

6291 Henry, Paget. Decolonization and the authoritarian context of democracy in Antigua (in The Newer Caribbean: decolonization, democracy, and development.

Edited by Paget Henry and Carl Stone. Philadelphia: Institute for the Study of Human Issues, 1983, p. 281–312 [Inter-American politics series; 4])

Attempt to clarify the relationship between democracy and peripheral capitalism. To this end, author applies a sort of structuralist approach which, on the one hand overlooks heavy constraints dictated by size, and on the other, overemphasizes one single international variable: the "quasicolonization" of the world under US-Soviet hegemony.

6292 Howard, Michael. Post-war public policy in Barbados, 1946–1979 (UWI/ SES, 31:3, 1982, p. 95–128, tables)

Concerns budgetary policies such as revenues and expenditures. Includes some interesting data but, as author himself recognizes, more research will be required.

6293 Michaels, Robert A. Changing the guard in Dominica: elections and a hostage crisis (FIU/CR, 10:2, Spring 181, p. 18–19, 48, ill.)

Informative, especially since there is not that much published on Dominica.

6294 Nanton, Philip. The changing pattern of State control in St. Vincent and Grenadines (in Crisis and the Caribbean. Edited by Fitzroy Ambursley and Robin Cohen. New York: Monthly Review Press, 1983, p. 223– 246, bibl.)

Imaginative article which discusses "the crisis of the State" in St. Vincent and Grenadines (384 km²). It augurs a return to repression.

6295 Richards, Vincent A. Decolonization in Antigua: its impact on agriculture and tourism (in The Newer Caribbean: decolonization, democracy, and development. Edited by Paget Henry and Carl Stone. Philadelphia: Institute for the Study of Human Issues, 1983, p. 15–35, tables [Inter-American politics series; 4])

Title is self-explanatory. Information provided is not easily available elsewhere.

6296 Vanguard Nationalist and Socialist Party of the Bahamas. The struggle for freedom in the Bahamas. Nassau: The Party, 1980? 73 p.: bibl.

Concerns The Ten Point Program for "Bahamian socialism." Designated as "scientific socialism," it is actually a blending of nationalism, socialism, and black power.

6297 Will, W. Marvin. Mass political party institutionalisation in Barbados: analysis of the issues and dynamics of the post-independence period (ICS/JCCP, 19:2, July 1981, p. 134–156, tables)

Briefly explores geographical, historical and political culture factors in order to explain greater party development and institutionalization of competitive politics in Barbados. The 1971 election receives extensive attention while the following one, 1976, is shortly dealt with in a Postscript.

LESSER ANTILLES: DUTCH

6298 Bergh, G. van Benthem van den et al. Aruba en onafhankelijkheid: achtergronden, modaliteiten en mogelijkheden: een rapport en eerste aanleg. Den Haag: Institute of Social Studies, 1978. 142 p.: bibl., tables.

Report of the Institute of Social Studies on background and underlying factors in Aruba's quest for independence and problems that could arise after its declaration. Report addresses public in both the Netherlands and Aruba as well as their respective governments. [N. Vicenti]

6299 Phalen, John H. and Ann Marie Powers. Ethnicity and independence: political ideologies and interethnic relations in the Netherlands Antilles (SOCIOL, 32:2, 1982, p. 140–160, bibl.)

Examines riots that erupted in Aruba in Aug. 1977 against possibility of forming a new independent state in association with Curaçao. Authors attribute island's reaction to its peculiar cultural traits and apply Clifford Geertz's concept of "ideology as a cultural system" to explain Aruba's resistance.

LESSER ANTILLES: FRENCH

6300 Bangou, Henri. Le Parti socialiste française face à la décolonisation: de Jules Guesde à François Mitterrand; le case de la Guadeloupe. Paris: L'Harmattan, 1985. 287 p.: bibl., index.

Essay by Guadeloupe communist leader. Useful as a source which documents

French Antillean politics in the "decolonization" era. [A. Pérotin-Dumon]

6301 Blerald, Philippe Alain. Guadeloupe-Martinique: a system of colonial domination in crisis (*in* Crisis in the Caribbean. Edited by Fiztroy Ambursley and Robin Cohen. New York: Monthly Review Press, 1983, p. 148–165, bibl.)

Article's intention is to present crisis's socioeconomic, ideological, cultural, and institutional dimensions. Result, however, is mostly Marxist rigmarole.

PUERTO RICO

6302 Berríos Martínez, Rubén. Dependent capitalism and the prospects for democracy in Puerto Rico and the Dominican Republic (*in* The Newer Caribbean: decolonization, democracy, and development. Edited by Paget Henry and Carl Stone. Philadelphia: Institute for the Study of Human Issues, 1983, p. 327–339 [Inter-American politics series; 4])

Democracy is something other than political rights. It includes "the enjoyment by workers of the product of their work and the existence of democratic economic enterprises." Dependent capitalism is incompatible not only with full democracy but with political democracy as well. Discussion of Puerto Rican and Dominican cases is too brief and superficial. Makes no attempt to delineate the road to socialist democratic model.

6303 Carr, Raymond. Puerto Rico, a colonial experiment. New York: Vintage Books, 1984. 477 p.: bibl., index (A Twentieth Century Fund study)

Scholarly book written by British historian who specializes in Spain. He does not break new ground but deals professionally with complexities of American-Puerto Rican relationship. Book's sophisticated approach can be conveyed by transcribing a section's title: "The Reluctant Imperialist."

6304 Córdova, Gonzalo F. Santiago Iglesias: creador del movimiento obrero de Puerto Rico. Traducción de Sara Irizarry Concepción. Río Piedras, P.R.: Editorial Universitaria, 1980. 231 p.: bibl., ill., plates.

Describes labor and political activities

of Socialist Party leader. Originally a Master's thesis.

6305 González Díaz, Emilio. La lucha de clases y la política en el Puerto Rico de la década 40: el ascenso del PPD (UPR/RCS, 22:1/2, marzo/junio 1980, p. 37–69, bibl., maps, plates, tables)

Although the PPD would appear to be a mass party, it is actually more representative of the middle class. Its members do not own means of production but wish to control the State apparatus in order to strengthen their economic role. After 1946, party leadership or middle classes as a whole—it is not clear which—forsook their popular commitments and allied themselves "to a sector of the North America imperialist bourgeoisie." Another contribution to Marxism's demise by so-called disciples of Marx.

6306 Picó, Fernando; Milton Pabón; and Roberto Alejandro. Río Piedras, P.R.: Ediciones Huracán, 1982. 236 p.: ill. (Col. La Nave y el puerto)

Jesuit professor and student leader discuss incidents of 1981 student strike from a leftist perspective.

6307 Quintero Rivera, Angel. Conflictos de clase y política en Puerto Rico. 2a ed. Río Piedras, P.R.: Ediciones Huracán, 1978. 158 p.: bibl., ill., plates (Cuaderno Cerep; 2)

Study uses Marxist approach and is supported by thorough familiarity with relevant sources.

6308 Taller de Formación, *Puerto Rico.* La cuestión nacional: el Partido Nacionalista y el movimiento obrero puertorriqueño: aspectos de las luchas económicas y políticas de la década de 1930–40. Río Piedras, P.R.: Ediciones Huracán, 1982. 207 p.: bibl. (Col. Semilla)

Pt. 1 is nothing but a rehash of Lenin's works on the national question. Only in pt. 2 do authors try to deal with topic of the title.

SURINAM

6309 Boom, Henk. Staatsgreep in Suriname. Utrecht: Veen, 1982. 192 p.: ill., plates.

Diary of a Dutch newspaper correspondent who witnessed beginning of Surinam's 1980 revolution. Describes political situation on eve of general election and roles played by Premier Henck Arron and opposition leader Jaggernath Lachmon. [N. Vicenti]

Dew, Edward. Did Suriname switch?: dialectics à la Dante. See item **7224.**

6311 ———. Suriname tar baby: the signature of terror (FIU/CR, 12:1, Winter 1983, p. 4–7, 34, map)

Recent events in Surinam under Papa Doc Bouterse.

6312 ———. The year of the sergeants: what happened in Surinam (FIU/CR, 9:2, Spring 1980, p. 5–7, 46–47, plates)

Describes crisis of Surinamese politics and sergeants' coup.

6313 Herrenberg, Henk. Suriname, the strategy. Translation, R. Bremer. Paramaribo: Dubois & Dubois, 1980. 120 p.

English translation of writings by Surinam leader of 1960s and 1970s who favored a multiracial political system. Documents process leading to nation's independence. [A. Pérotin-Dumon]

6314 Hira, Sandew. Balans van een coup: drie jaar 'Surinaamse revolutie'. Rotterdam, The Netherlands: Futile, 1983. 175 p.: bibl.

Examination of background and political climate in Surinam leading to Feb. 1980 coup d'état. Analyzes development of political situation in various publications over a period of three yrs. [N. Vicenti]

6315 ———. Class formation and class struggle in Surinam: the background and development of the coup d'état (in Crisis in the Caribbean. Edited by Fitzroy Ambursley and Robin Cohen. New York: Monthly Review Press, 1983, p. 166–190, bibl.)

Once reader works his way through intricacies of first section (i.e., development of the class structure), he comes across a discussion of a political party system in which there are not only Stalinists and Maoists but followers of Albania's Evenr Hoxha as well. Bewildering indeed.

6316 ———. De staatsgreep in Suriname: achtergronden en vooruitzichten. Amsterdam: Internationale Socialistiese Publikaties; Antwerpen: L. Lesoil, 1980. 69 p.: bibl., ill.

Discusses economic development, social structure, and political climate in Surinam before and after Feb. 1980 coup d'état. Also examines popularity of the military government. [N. Vicenti]

6317 Kroes, Rob. The small town coup: the NCO political intervention in Surinam (AFS, 9:1, Fall 1982, p. 115–134)

Welcome contribution sheds light on perplexing politics of this Caribbean state.

6318 Ooggetuige. De decembermoorden in Suriname: verslag van een ooggetuige. Met een nawoord van H. Chin A. Sen. 2e druk. Bussum, The Netherlands: Wereldvenster, 1983. 77 p.: ill.

Provides details on Dec. 1982 political murders in Surinam based on author's diary and interviews with Major Roy Horb who was found dead in his cell and officially declared a suicide. Author, who prefers to remain anonymous, offers a dissenting opinion about Horb's death. Describes political situation and other events related to Dec. 1982 murders. [N. Vicenti]

6319 Sedney, Jules. Kiezen en delen: kritische analyse van het kiesstelsel en inrichting van de staat: presentatie van een funktioneel alternatief. Paramaribo?: Sedney?, 1980. 192 p.

Critical analysis of Surinam's electoral system and the State's organization. Offers an equitable and functional alternative for election of political representatives at national as well as local levels. [N. Vicenti]

6320 Slagveer, Jozef. De nacht van de revolutie: de staatsgreep in Suriname op 25 februari 1980. Foto's, Lucien Chin A. Foeng. Paramaribo: Kersten, 1980. 208 p.: ill.

Eyewitness report of the night of the revolution (25 Feb. 1980) as recounted by Major Bouterse and other members of the National Military Council involved in the coup d'état. Includes *Abendanon Report* on unrest within the military prior to coup. [N. Vicenti]

6321 De Woelige dagen van maart 1982. Samenstelling, Lucien Pinas. Paramaribo: Apollo, 1983. 112 p.: ill.

Documentary compilation on attempted coup d'état in Surinam (March 1982) by Sergeant-Major Hawker and Lieutenant Rambucos. Includes communiqués by military leader D. Bouterse defending his actions in the execution of W. Hawker. [N. Vicenti]

TRINIDAD AND TOBAGO

6322 Jacobs, W. Richard. The politics of protest in Trinidad: the strikes and disturbances of 1973 (UPR/CS, 17:1/2, April/July 1977, p. 5–54, tables)

Very detailed and well documented study of these events. Its conclusion discusses questions of authoritarian mobilization and mass spontaneity.

6323 LaGuerre, John Gaffar. The general elections of 1981 in Trinidad and Tobago (ICS/JCCP, 21:2, July 1983, p. 133–157, map, tables)

Good piece is informative and analytical.

6324 ———. The politics of communalism: the ordeal of the left in Trinidad and Tobago, 1930–1955. St. Augustine, Trinidad: Dept. of Government, Univ. of the West Indies, 1979. 64 p.: bibl.

Examines adequacy of "pluralist" and "consensualist" models to explain Trinidadian politics during this period. Well researched.

6325 Okpaluba, Chuks and **W. Richard Jacobs.** Public sector disputes regulation: the Trinidad and Tobago model [by Chuks Okpaluba]. Patterns of political corruption in Caribbean society: a comparative study of Grenada, Jamaica, and Trinidad and Tobago [by W. Richard Jacobs]. St. Augustine, Trinidad: Institute of Social and Economic Research, Univ. of the West Indies, 1978. 91 p.: bibl. (Occasional papers)

Two papers. Second one by Jacobs suggests a remedy: the de-professionalization of political roles. "In this regard, Fidel Castro has made an important contribution" (p. 85).

6326 Parris, Carl D. Personalization of power in an elected government: Eric Williams and Trinidad and Tobago, 1973–1981 (SAGE/JIAS, 25:2, May 1983, p. 171–191, bibl.)

Perceives a process of *delegitimation* in Trinidad and studies Williams's strategies to arrest it. Rejects notion that there is an emerging oligarchy and emphasizes instead the system's increasing domination by the Prime Minister.

6327 ———. Resource ownership and the prospects for democracy: the case of Trinidad and Tobago (*in* The Newer Caribbean: decolonization, democracy, and development. Edited by Paget Henry and Carl Stone. Philadelphia: Institute for the Study of Human Issues, 1983, p. 313–326 [Inter-American politics series; 4])

Opposes modernization to development. Implementation of former model— characterized by "advanced" consumption behavior and subordination of the country— "will lead unavoidably to the emergence of" a strong regime. Includes statements by Prime Minister and other government officials to prove that Trinidad-Tobago is going through such a "modernizing" experience.

6328 ———. Trinidad and Tobago: September to December 1973 (UWI/SES, 30:3, Sept. 1981, p. 42–62, bibl.)

Describes Eric Williams's strategy to remain as Prime Minister and political leader.

6329 Ryan, Selwyn. The Church that Williams built: electoral possibilities in Trinidad and Tobago (FIU/CR, 10:2, Spring 1981, p. 12–13, 45–46, ill., tables)

Examines political party spectrum in Trinidad-Tobago after death of Eric Williams. Includes poll data.

6330 Sutton, Paul. Black power in Trinidad and Tobago: the "crisis" of 1970 (ICS/JCCP, 21:2, July 1973, p. 115–132)

Fair, well articulated, and insightful paper supported by an impressive number of footnotes.

COLOMBIA, VENEZUELA, AND ECUADOR

DAVID W. DENT, *Professor of Political Science, Senior Fellow, Center for Public Policy and International Affairs, Towson State University*

THIS REVIEW Of RECENT POLITICAL research on Venezuela, Colombia, and Ecuador reveals a number of important trends: 1) most of the research is focused on political parties, electoral behavior, and presidential leadership; 2) subjects such as Church-State issues, agrarian and rural topics, urban issues, and human rights are totally ignored; and 3) all three governments and political systems receive a healthy dose of criticism and some praise for the way in which they have maintained democratic structures and processes.

Most of the material on Venezuela deals with party politics, elections, and general assessments of the democratic system after celebrating 25 years of democracy. Three contributions focusing on different subjects are of particular note. Ellner (item **6371**) provides an excellent analysis of leftist political parties and the growth of the labor movement during the 1930s and 1940s in an effort to understand present-day party coalitions and ideologies. Rey (item **6022**) provides a valuable study of several theoretical models of political underdevelopment in Latin America. A valuable contribution to the study of civil-military relations is provided by Bigler (item **6366**) who argues that Venezuela's resilience stems from the widely accepted and flexible rules of the political game. Nevertheless, Martz (item **6380**) finds that the prospects for the Lusinchi government are not so rosy due to foreign debts ($35 million), business failures, unemployment, and distortions of the petroleum market.

The literature on Colombian politics is heavily influenced by Betancur's election including his maverick policies, revisionist works on Gaitán, and the politics of drug trafficking. Betancur's efforts to stabilize the countryside and legitimize his government are closely linked to his relations with the military, his amnesty initiative, and Colombia's role in the Contadora peace process. Blum (item **6334**) examines the links between Betancur's "peace settlement" and his foreign policies. Negative assessments of the amnesty can be found in Jimeno and Volk (item **6352**), Iten (item **6350**), and Lamberg (item **6354**). Two excellent studies that link both internal and external political problems are Craig's (item **6340**) and Premo's (item **6360**). Premo worries that the Colombian military's growing counter-insurgency mission and its efforts to eradicate illicit drug production have moved Colombia closer to "bureaucratic-authoritarian" rule. Craig, who has done numerous studies on the illicit drug situation, demonstrates how drug trafficking has fundamentally altered the way of life in Colombian cities and regions (particularly Antioquia, Atlántico, and the Guajira). The basic political implications center on a negative national image compounded by rampant corruption and growing political cynicism. Unfortunately, the internal forces of poverty, rural neglect, and maldistribution of income so prevalent in Colombia are likely to continue to exacerbate the problems.

The revisionist works on Gaitán can be found in Santa (item **6361**) who reexamines the events surrounding Gaitán's assassination in 1948. A more thoughtful and comprehensive anthology is provided by Moreno (itm **6345**) who covers the period 1924–48. The five-study review by Henderson (item **6349**) is valuable both in its efforts to understand Gaitán and in its assessment of various methods of social science research.

The political research on Ecuador is not impressive this time from the standpoint of scholarly research. The turmoil surrounding the untimely deaths of Roldós and Bucaram in 1981 generated some attention but they are only small pieces of what we need to know about leadership, Ecuadorian populism, and party politics in Ecuador. The election of Febres Cordero in 1984 may serve to spark some of these research topics.

The decade of the 1980s has brought a return to civilian rule in many parts of Latin America. What is likely to follow this pattern is a shift in topics including less attention to human rights, military rule, and bureaucratic-authoritarianism. Yet one area of research that needs attention is the theoretical and empirical understanding of the breakdown of military-authoritarian governments in Latin America. This should not detract from studies of political leaders and party development since they may offer major clues for understanding the operation of on-going democratic governments such as the ones in Venezuela and Colombia. The contributions of Duff (item **6009**) and Sarles (item **6626a**) offer valuable insights into parties and successful institutionalization. The above-mentioned study by Sarles of political control and mobilization in Brazil develops a theory of stages within the bureaucratic-authoritarian State. Wolpin (item **6029**) develops an interesting thesis in which he argues that Third World military officers should support socially radical and economically nationalistic civilian political movements in order to fulfill their professional aspirations instead of taking over the government. It would also help if more research attention were devoted to urban and rural political issues, education, and the role of women in politics. Has the rural sector disappeared from the political researchers agenda?

COLOMBIA

6331 Alvarez Restrepo, Antonio. Los golpes de estado en Colombia. Bogotá: Banco de la República, 1982. 236 p.: bibl.

History of coups d'état in Colombia from the first (Bolívar in 1828) to the eighth (Rojas Pinilla in 1953). Attempts to classify and explain relative absence of military takeovers within Colombian system.

6332 Betancur, Belisario. Colombia cara a cara. 7a ed., rev. Bogotá: Ediciones Tercer Mundo, 1981. 218 p.: bibl., ill.

Seventh ed. (rev.) of Betancur's assessment of Colombia's social, economic, and political problems and a prescription for what needs to be done. By 1986 we should be able to determine how far Betancur's Presidency has come to fulfilling these promises now that he has come "face to face" with realities of Colombian political life.

———. Mensaje presidencial: informe al Congreso sobre la emergencia económica. See item **3381**.

6333 ———. ¡Sí, se puede! 2a ed. Bogotá: Ediciones Tercer Mundo, 1982. 286 p.

Major policy statements by President Betancur before becoming president in 1982. Rhetoric is designed to be uplifting despite economic difficulties and deteriorating relations with US.

6334 Blum, Leonor. Colombia's peace offensive (CRIA/W, 26 :10, Oct. 1983, p. 14–15)

Brief treatment of maverick policies of President Betancur including important links between his peace settlement with domestic guerrillas and his foreign policies.

6335 Campos, Judith Talbot and **José Martín.** El comportamiento electoral en Cali, 1978. Cali, Colombia: Univ. del Valle, Centro de Investigaciones y Documentación Socio-Económica (CIDSE): Fundación Friedrich Naumann, 1980. 218 p.: bibl.

Regional study of voting behavior in Cali with special emphasis on voting abstention. Profile of voter who abstains in Colombia is a male, low educational levels employed in private sector, and only recently arrived from a smaller rural village.

Carbonell, Abel. Obras selectas. See *HLAS* 46:2896.

Carrizosa Argáez, Enrique. Linajes y bibliografías de nuestros gobernantes, 1830–1982. See item **79.**

6336 Ciclo de Conferencias sobre la Políticas Económica y Social del Gobierno Nacional de Belisario Betancur, *Cali, Colombia, 1983.* La política económica y social del gobierno de Belisario Betancur. Vol. a cargo de Eduardo Lora. Cali: Corporación Editorial Universitaria de Colombia, 1983. 114 p.: bibl.

Series of conference papers aimed at assessing economic and social policies of Betancur after one yr. as president. Monetary and fical policy are debated with considerable acumen. For economist's comment, see item **3383.**

6337 Collins, Charles David. La prensa y el poder político en Colombia: tres ensayos. Cali, Colombia: Univ. del Valle, Centro de Investigaciones y Documentación Socio-Económica (CIDSE), 1981. 157 p.: bibl., ill. (Serie Estudios socio-económicos del CIDSE; 2)

Three essays on role of the press in a capitalist state and a case study of political power and the press in Cali. Findings highlight strong association between political power and newspaper ownership.

6338 Colombia. Presidencia. Discursos y mensajes del Presidente de la República, Julio César Turbay Ayala. v. 1, Agosto de 1978 al mes de agosto de 1979. v. 2, Agosto de 1979 a agosto de 1980. v. 3, Agosto de 1980 a julio de 1981. v. 4, Agosto de 1981 a febrero de 1982. v. 5, Meses de marzo, abril, mayo y junio de 1982. Bogotá: Secretaría de Información y Prensa, Presidencia de la República, 1982. 5 v.: indexes.

Presidential speeches and essays (Aug. 1978–June 1982). Useful works for analyzing presidential rhetoric and Liberal ideology. Also offer insights into government-opposition struggles, nature of Colombia's elitist democracy, and economic policy making.

6339 Colombia: Turbay & M–19 view Betancur (NACLA, 17:1, Jan./Feb. 1983, p. 36–39, photos)

Interviews with former President Turbay and Alfonso Yaqui (member of Political Committee of the M–19 guerrillas) on topics such as Betancur's dialogue with guerrillas, role of Colombian military, and future of Colombian democracy.

6340 Craig, Richard B. Domestic implications of illicit Colombian drug production and trafficking (SAGE/JIAS, 25:3, Aug. 1983, p. 325–350)

Valuable study of the causes and consequences of Colombia's illicit drug production and trafficking. Economic implications are staggering in virtually all categories of trafficking. Political implications center on a negative national image compounded by increasing political cynicism and rampant corruption. Drug trafficking "has not only transformed the nation's political economy and compromised its judicial integrity, but has fundamentally altered the very life of particular cities and regions." Moreover, internal causes of poverty, rural neglect, and maldistribution of income cry out for political solutions. For economist's comment, see item **3391.**

6341 Crónica de gobierno: Belisario Betancur. v. 1, Agosto-noviembre 1982. Bogotá: Secretaría de Información y Prensa, Presidencia de la República, 1984. 1 v.

Brief history of first five months of Betancur Presidency emphasizing domestic and foreign policy proposals of the new administration.

Decker, David R. and Ignacio Durán. The political, economic, and labor climate in Colombia. See item **3393.**

6342 Discursos y mensajes de posesión presidencial. Recopilación de Hernán Valencia Benavides. Bogotá: Imprenta Nacional, 1983. 2 v.: bibl. (Col. Presidencia de la República. Administración Turbay Ayala; 7)

Inaugural speeches by Colombia's founding fathers and 19th-century presidents. Introductory material and interpretations should be of value to historians and political biographers.

6343 Echandía, Darío. Obras selectas. t. 4, El gobernante, el parlamentario. Bogotá: Banco de la República, 1981. 309 p.

Speeches and key writings of former President Echandía. Vol. is divided into secs. according to Echandía's political position: president, minister, ambassador to Vatican, governor, and member of Congress.

6344 Findley, Roger W.; Fernando Cepeda Ulloa; and Nicolas Gamboa Morales. Intervención presidencial en la economía y el estado de derecho en Colombia. Bogotá: Univ. de los Andes, CIDER, 1983. 177 p.: bibl.

Discusses evolution of legal presidential power over 100 yrs., by examining all constitutional amendments beginning in 1886, and including constitutional changes of 1979. [F. Thoumi]

6345 Gaitán, Jorge Eliécer. Trayectoria del pensamiento político de Gaitán. Comp., David Moreno. Bogotá: Centro Cultural Jorge Eliécer Gaitán, 1983. 91 p.: bibl., ill., index.

Historical and political anthology of Gaitán's political thought and movement he created. Book is divided into three stages: 1) 1924–32, Origins of the Movement; 2) 1933–35, UNIR, Revolutionary Alternative to the Bipartisan Regime; and 3) 1944–48, Gaitanist Popular Movement.

6346 Gallón Giraldo, Gustavo. La república de las armas: relaciones entre fuerzas armadas y Estado en Colombia, 1960–1980. Bogotá: Centro de Investigación y Educación Popular, 1983. 115 p.: bibl. (Serie Controversia; 109–110)

Critical analysis of civil-military relations (1960–80) in which author argues that Colombia's problem is not growing militarization but essential nature of a repressive State under conditions of democratic decline.

Gómez, Laureano. Obras selectas. See *HLAS* 46:2900.

6347 Gómez Gómez, Elsa *et al.* La elección presidencial de 1982 en Bogotá: dinámica de la opinión electoral. Bogotá: ANIF, Fondo Editorial, 1982. 106 p.: bibl., ill. (Documentos ANIF)

Panel study of voting behavior in Bogotá (March-May 1982) when electorate went to polls to select legislators and president. Further confirmation of importance of party label over ideology for determining voting turnout and candidate preference.

6348 Hartlyn, Jonathan. Colombia: old problems, new opportunities (CUH, 82:481, Feb. 1983, p. 62–65)

Perceptive assessment of emerging policies and opportunities of newly elected Betancur administration. Many of the policies of the Turbay yrs. (1978–82) are being abandoned in search for greater legitimacy through a more nationalistic and independent foreign policy. Yet at same time, argues that "turmoil, crises, and 'muddling through' will continue."

6349 Henderson, James D. Gaitán from without, or, no cheers for Liberalism (UCSB/NS, 8, 1982, p. 509–515, bibl.)

Review of recent (1970s) works on Gaitán, Gaitanismo, and Colombian political history. Reviewer uses these five studies under review to protest "over-reliance upon ahistorical paradigms" in social science writing that tends to "lock history into a cage of preconceptions." "Loose-knit, anecdotal study of Julio Ortiz" is preferred approach for getting a handle on this famous Colombian populist.

6350 Iten, Oswald. Colombia's difficult search for peace (NZZ/SRWA, 33:9, Dec. 1983, p. 18–20)

Brief analysis of President Betancur's efforts to find peace through a unique amnesty law offered to country's 5,000–6,000 guerrillas. Political efforts to stem violence and reach some accommodation with guerrillas does not seem to have worked: "The existence of the amnesty does not in itself make it easy for the rebels to return to civilian life."

6351 Itinerario de un gobierno democrático. Bogotá: Secretaría de Información y Prensa, Presidencia de la República, 1982. 4 v.

Four-vol. set of policy statements by President Turbay (Aug. 1978-Jan. 1981).

6352 Jimeno, Ramón and **Steven Volk.** Colombia: whose country is this, anyway? (NACLA, 17:3, May/June 1983, p. 2–35, bibl., charts, maps, photos)

Leftist account of Colombia's historical dependence on US and absence of civilian State control over vital sectors of economy and society. Assessment of insurgent movement and Betancur's amnesty should lay to rest claims that Cuba is source of violence, terrorism, and political instability in Colombia. Betancur is portrayed as a failed leader, having again fallen victim to military, right-wing forces, and US domination.

6353 Kline, Harvey F. Energy policy and the Colombian elite: a synthesis and interpretation. Washington: American Enterprise Institute for Public Policy Research, Center for Hemispheric Studies, 1982. 25 leaves: bibl. (Occasional papers series; 4)

Brief study of national energy policy and recent Colombian politics in which author finds that party elite factionalism and patrimonial politics have led to an energy policy that is fragmented, made by "exceptional actors" (high level ministers or multinational corps.), or a non-existent policy. Useful both for its understanding of Colombian national politics and Colombia's energy potential and problems.

6354 Lamberg, Robert F. Colombia: false premises for pacification (NZZ/SRWA, 33:1, April 1983, p. 12–13)

Betancur's failure to pacify a number of guerrilla groups is apparently based on several false premises including validity of Venezuelan model, guerrilla's interest in social reform, and their solely national basis of operation.

6355 Lovera, Virgilio. Tiempo de guerrilleros: prisionero en Bogotá. Bogotá: Ediciones Tercer Mundo, 1981. 151 p.

Venezuelan Ambassador to Colombia offers a narrative detail of his captivity by M–19 guerrillas in the Dominican embassy in Bogotá in 1980. Develops a certain degree of sympathy for his captors while he attempts to understand political socialization and ideology of the M–19 opposition.

6356 Lozada Lora, Rodrigo and **Eduardo Vélez Bustillo.** Identificación y participación política en Colombia. Bogotá: Fundación para la Educación Superior y el Desarrollo, 1982. 234 p.: ill., bibl.

Thorough examination of voting behavior and political participation based on 1,913 adults in five regions of country in 1981. Authors finds little difference between Liberals and Conservatives across a wide range of socioeconomic and attitudinal variables. Major finding is importance of the level of socioeconomic status on political participation (i.e., those at the bottom who need to use political leverage the most are in reality those who use it the least).

6357 Morales Benítez, Otto. Reflexiones sobre el periodismo colombiano. Bogotá: Fundación Univ. Central, 1982. 347 p.: bibl., index.

Analysis of Colombia's major newspaper and role of the press in Colombian politics. Most of the discussion focuses on Colombia but some attention is given to UNESCO debate over control and interpretation of news, both written and broadcast.

6358 Moreno Narváez, Fabio. La planeación educativa durante el Frente Nacional: aportes para su análisis y su historia. Bogotá: Univ. Pedagógica Nacional, Centro de Investigaciones, 1982. 166 p.: bibl., ill.

Brief history of education planning during the 16 yrs. of National Front. Useful for understanding structure and process of politics of education at all levels.

Palacios, Marco. La fragmentación regional de las clases dominantes en Colombia: una perspectiva histórica. See *HLAS 46:2905.*

6359 Pastrana Borrero, Misael. Reflexiones después del poder: antologías, Colombia política, política internacional. Medellín, Colombia: Fondo Editorial Rotatorio, Biblioteca Pública Piloto, Fundación Social y Cultural, Cámara de Comercio, 1981. 450 p. (Col. Fondo . . .; 7)

Collection of lectures and essays by former President Misael Pastrana after leaving office in 1974. Problems of economic development, Third World resources, planning, ecology, political economy, and nature of political change in Colombia are discussed.

6360 Premo, Daniel L. The Colombian armed forces in search of a mission (*in* New military politics in Latin America. Edited by Robert Wesson. New York: Praeger, 1982, p. 151–173)

Excellent historical treatment of civil-military relations emphasizing changing role of military's mission in Colombian society. Non-interventionist tradition is being threatened by its growing counter-insurgency mission against organized guerrilla activity, efforts to eradicate illicit drug production, and territorial disputes wth Nicaragua and Venezuela. Finds it "ironic that in recent years military's role in Colombian politics appears to be moving toward increased involvement at a time when military elsewhere in Latin America is moving away from 'bureaucratic-authoritarian' rule."

6361 Santa, Eduardo. ¿Qué pasó el 9 de abril?: itinerario de una revolución frustrada. Bogotá: Ediciones Tercer Mundo, 1982. 229 p.: bibl., ill.

Historian reexamines events surrounding assassination of Liberal leader Jorge E. Gaitán in 1948, from both the standpoint of participant-observer and "objective" analyst.

6362 Santana R., Pedro. Desarrollo regional y paros cívicos en Colombia. Bogotá: Centro de Investigación y Educación Popular, 1983. 207 p.: bibl. (Serie Controversia, 0120–4165; 107–108)

Critical study of political strikes and regional disparities in Colombian economic and social development. Further confirmation of Colombia's difficulty in translating its limited political democracy into economic democracy.

6363 Urrutia, Miguel. Gremios, política económica y democracia. Bogotá: Fondo Cultural Cafetero: FEDESARROLLO, 1983. 234 p.: bibl., ill.

Study, written on Ford Foundation grant, deals with nature and function of pressure groups in Colombian legislative politics. Admits that such groups might generally be thought of as "paper tigers," but notes that in Colombia their functions are important. [W.R. Garner]

6364 Wilde, Alexander. Conservaciones de caballeros: la quiebra de la democracia en Colombia. Bogotá: Ediciones Tercer Mundo, 1982. 132 p.: bibl.

Spanish translation of earlier title "Conversations among Gentlemen" that appeared as part of a study of the breakdown of democratic regimes in Latin America.

6365 Zelinsky, Ulrich. Los partidos políticos tradicionales de Colombia y su influencia sobre la administración pública: un estudio del clientelismo (IAA, 9/2, 1983, p. 155–175, bibl., tables)

Three-pt. article that examines relationship between Colombia's political party system and public administration. Puts considerable emphasis on spoils system and patronage as a Spanish political heritage that has carried over to present unitary-presidential system. Positive change can be seen in emergence of a new class of technocrats with achievement orientation, flexibility, and better qualifications than their predecessors.

VENEZUELA

Avendaño Lugo, José Ramón. El militarismo en Venezuela: la dictadura de Pérez Jiménez. See *HLAS 46:2912.*

6366 Bigler, Gene E. Professional soldiers and restrained politics in Venezuela (*in* New military politics in Latin America. Edited by Robert Wesson. New York: Praeger, 1982, p. 175–196)

Excellent three-part study of civil-military relations emphasizing: 1) maintenance of civilian control; 2) pattern of military professionalism and organization; and 3) new challenges to maintenance of democratic system. Threshold for military intervention is high and likely to remain so in the near future. Claims that a great deal of Venezuela's resilience stems from fact that "The rules of the game are flexible enough and widely enough accepted by elites and popular supporters of particular governments to permit a fairly broad range of reforms, challenges, and crises."

6367 Blanco Muñoz, Agustín. La lucha armada: hablan tres comandantes de la izquierda revolucionaria, Lino Martínez, Moisés Moleiro, Américo Martín. Caracas: Univ. Central de Venezuela, Facultad de Ciencias Económicas y Sociales, Div. de Publicaciones, 1982. 377 p. (Testimonios violentos; 6. Serie Coediciones)

Three founding leaders of MIR reflect on revolutionary strategy, tactics, and goals that reveal roots of current factional separation between MIR-Moleiro and MIR-Américo.

6368 Caldera, Rafael. Moldes para la fragua. 3a ed., rev. y aum. Caracas: Dimensiones, 1980. 431 p.: bibl., ports.

Using metaphor of "molds for the blacksmith's shop" ex-President Caldera offers his thought on 40 people who have had an impact on his life from Bolívar to Jesus of Nazareth.

6369 4 [i.e. Cuatro] presidentes: 40 años de acción democrática. t. 1, Rómulo Betancourt, Rómulo Gallegos. t. 2, Raúl Leoni, Carlos Andrés Pérez. Caracas: Ediciones de la Presidencia de la República, 1981. 2 v.: ill.

Major political addresses of four AD presidents: Gallegos, Betancourt, Leoni, and

Pérez. Useful two-vol. set for examining AD ideology, presidential rhetoric, and leadership style.

Davis, Charles L. Political regimes and the socioeconomic resource model of political mobilization: some Venezuelan and Mexican data. See item **6056.**

Documentos para la historia de Acción Democrática. See *HLAS 46:2917.*

6371 Ellner, Steve. Los partidos políticos y su disputa por el control del movimiento sindical en Venezuela, 1936–1948. Caracas: Univ. Católica Andrés Bello, 1980. 181 p.: bibl. (Col. Manoa; 27)

Account of interaction between major leftist political parties and fledgling labor movement (1936–48). Excellent analysis for understanding parties, coalitions, and political ideologies from Popular Front to present party coalitions and debates.

6372 English, Adrian. The Venezuelan Navy (Navy International [Maritime World Ltd., Surrey, England] 89:1, Jan. 1984, p. 22–25, plates)

Venezuela's Navy is a recent creation (1950s), yet today it is one of the best equipped and most efficient in Latin America with only 7,500 in all ranks including 4,000 marines.

6373 La Estadísticas evolutiva de los partidos políticos en Venezuela desde 1958 hasta 1979. 2a ed. Caracas: Consejo Supremo Electoral, Dirección de Estudios Especiales, Div. de Estadísticas, 1983. 48 p.: ill. (some col.), tables.

Valuable voting data (1958–79) prepared by Statistical Div. of Supreme Electoral Council. Analyzes vote by party, region, office, and turnout over this 21-yr. period.

6374 Fernández, Eduardo. COPEI: 37 años de vida política, Mensaje a la Nación pronunciado por el Dr. Eduardo Fernández (Informe ODCA [Organización Demócrata Cristiana de América, Secretaría General, Caracas] 104, 1983, p. 58–64)

General Secretary of COPEI reviews past 37 yrs. of Venezuelan democracy emphasizing what has been accomplished by COPEI and what needs to be done. Partisan pitch for COPEI platform and candidate (Rafael Caldera) in 1983 presidential election.

6375 Filippi, Alberto. La configuración histórica del Estado venezolano: 1830–1864 (GEE/NA, 5, 1982, p. 215–267)

Historical examination of State formation in early decades of independence in Latin America with particular emphasis on historical peculiarities of Hispano-American nation-state and impact of federalism and caudillism on the Venezuelan State.

Flórez, Carlos M. Gómez, patriarca del crimen: el terror y el trabajo forzado en Venezuela. See *HLAS 46:2919.*

6376 Foro Los Socialcristianos y Venezuela, *Caracas, 1982.* Los copeyanos. Víctor Manuel Giménez Landínez *et al.* Caracas: Ediciones Centauro, 1982. 186 p.: bibl., plates.

Brief examination of the history of COPEI through a series of conference papers presented in 1982.

6377 Herrera Campins, Luis. Hacia una nueva etapa del proceso democrático de Venezuela. Caracas: Ediciones de la Presidencia de la República, 1983. 13 p.: ill., plates.

Brief treatment of the process of philosophy of democracy in Venezuela in commemoration of 25th anniversary of the democratic system.

6378 Jornadas sobre la Democracia en Venezuela, *Caracas, 1978.* Sobre la democracia: ciclo de conferencias. Rafael Caldera *et al.* Prólogo, Hans Leu. Caracas: Editorial Ateneo de Caracas, 1979. 336 p. (Col. Teoría política)

Series of 10 papers presented at conference on democracy in 1978. Diversity of political views reflected in values of participants augurs well for Venezuelan pluralism despite fact that diagnosis of democratic health is not favorable.

6379 Lacava, Gloria. Venezuelan elections: Madison Avenue style (NACLA, 17:6, Nov./Dec. 1983, p. 36–39, ill.)

Pre-election analysis of 1983 presidential election emphasizes cost, strength of major candidates, and policies of each party. David Garth, New York media expert, ran Caldera's campaign Madison Avenue style but to no avail. Notes growth of legitimate electoral left.

6380 Martz, John D. The crisis of Venezuelan democracy (CUH, 83:490, Feb. 1984, p. 73–77, 89)

Prospects for Lusinchi's government are not rosy because of massive foreign debt ($35 billion), extensive business failures, rampant unemployment, and distortions of petroleum market. Internal political problems centering on differences over doctrinal and personal hegemony lead author to conclude that "it can no longer be assumed that democracy is stable in Venezuela."

6381 ———. Los peligros de la petrificación: el sistema de partidos venezolano y la década de los ochenta (*in* Iberoamérica en los años 80: perspectivas de cambio social y político. Enrique Baloyra Herp y Rafael López-Pintor, comps. Madrid: Centro de Investigaciones Sociológicas, 1982?, p. 149–165, bibl.)

Brief analysis of political party system since 1958 reveals a crisis of "petrification" for democratic system unless major parties revise their objectives and party doctrines such as social justice and development economics. Feels that both major parties have lost contact with the majority in urban and rural sectors.

6382 Myers, David J. and **Robert O'Connor.** The undecided respondent in mandatory voting settings: a Venezuelan exploration (UU/WPQ, 36:3, Sept. 1983, p. 420–433, bibl., tables)

Authors demonstrate how undecided respondents can be studied by using data from 1978 Venezuelan election where compulsory voting is part of electoral system. Conclusions reinforce importance of measuring magnitude of sympathy for party and regime combined with "discriminate function techniques" as a methodological tool.

6383 Peña, Alfredo. Conversaciones con Carlos Andrés Pérez. Caracas: Editorial Ateneo de Caracas, 1979. 2 v. (Col. Actualidad política).

Series of interviews with ex-president Pérez on key political events in Venezuelan history. Vol. 1 deals with: 1) Oct. 1948 revolution; 2) military takeover of 1948; 3) leftist insurrections of 1960s; and 4) Niehous kidnapping.

Pensamiento político venezolano del siglo XIX. See *HLAS 46:2930.*

6384 Pérez, Carlos Andrés. Discursos militares, 1974–1979. Caracas: Ministerio de la Defensa, 1979. 390 p.

In speeches and addresses (1974–79), ex-President Pérez reveals his thoughts about Venezuelan military and civil-military relations. Speeches indicate institutionalized relationship between executive branch and armed forces and importance of presidential praise of the military for survivial of the democratic system.

6385 Petkoff, Teodoro. Del socialismo existente al nuevo socialismo (SP 15, sept. 1983, p. 47–61)

Leader of MAS argues for a more authentic socialism (humanistic) to replace "false" socialism of authoritarian bureaucracies. This would include the elimination of bourgeois ownership of means of production followed by the socialization of means of production through democratic procedures.

6386 Stambouli, Andrés. La democracia venezolana: de los requisitos de estabilidad a las exigencias de eficacia (*in* Iberoamérica en los años 80: perspectivas de cambio social y político. Enrique Baloyra Herp y Rafael López-Pintor, comps. Madrid: Centro de Investigaciones Sociológicas, 1982?, p. 167–173)

Analysis of prerequisites of stability and pluralist democracy in Venezuela. Emphasizes social and economic paternalism of the State, availability of petroleum reserves, and organizational base of both major parties. A future of scarce resources does not augur well for stability and democracy in Venezuela.

6387 Torrealba Narváez, Luis. La reforma administrativa municipal de Venezuela (ACPS/B, 39:89, sept. 1982, p. 89–118)

Detailed study of need for reform in municipal administration emphasizes coordination of both centralized and decentralized models to achieve greater administrative efficiency.

6388 Venezuela en vísperas de elecciones (URSS/AL, 9, sept. 1983, p. 47–52, ill.)

Interesting series of interviews conducted by Soviet Latin Americanists with members of a delegation of municipal representatives (Venezuelan) in 1982. Questions that deal with Venezuelan-Soviet relations, alliances during Malvinas crisis, and ideological alliances with José Napoleón Durante are the most noteworthy.

ECUADOR

6389 Arellano Gallegos, Jorge. Identificación ideológica de los partidos políticos ecuatorianos. Cuenca: Libros Ecuatorianos, 1982. 51 p.

Brief guide to understanding political ideologies and party platforms for ecuadorian voters.

6390 Astudillo Romero, Jaime. Mito y realidad de la seguridad nacional en el Ecuador. Cuenca: Fondo de Cultura Ecuatoriana, 1981. 249 p.: bibl. (Col. Realidad nacional; 1)

Critical assessment of values and instruments implicit in the operation of national security state. Author would like to see more pluralist state apparatus in national development rather than one that stresses values of capitalism and anticommunism.

6391 Bucaram: historia de una lucha. Quito: Editorial El Conejo, 1981. 299 p. (Col. Ecuador/hoy)

Favorable biography of founder of CFP (Concentración de Fuerzas Populares) and one of Ecuador's populist caudillos who died in 1981. Treatment of Bucaram's career allows for treatment of the roots of populism in Ecuadorian politics.

6392 Cabezas, Rodrigo. Crónica de una política petrolera. S.l.: s.n., 1980? 183 p.: ill.

Brief treatment of petroleum policy (1960s-70s) with emphasis on trade patterns, legal structure, and relations with US as OPEC member.

Chiriboga, Manuel and **Renato Piccino.** La producción campesina cacaotera: problemas y perspectivas. See item **3432.**

6393 Galarza Zavala, Jaime. Quiénes mataron a Roldós. Quito?: Ediciones Solitierra, 1982. 232 p.

Implicates a wide range of national and international interests that would benefit from Roldós's death. Interesting bit of investigative reporting but case still seems far from closed.

6394 Jaime Roldós: ideario político del Presidente. Recopilación de Alba Chávez de Alvarado, Carlos Alvarado Loor. Guayaquil, Ecuador: Depto. de Investigación de la Comunciación Social, Facultad de Comunicación Social, Univ. de Guayaquil, 1982. 222 p.: ill.

Compilation of ideological positions on domestic and international politics, the economy, education, boundary and fishing rights problems, and miscellaneous topics gleaned from public documents, speeches, and lectures of former Ecuadorian President Jaime Roldós whose 21-month tenure as President ended with an Andean plane crash. Good reference on ideological position of Roldós administration. [W.R. Garner]

6395 Mendoza, Luis Aníbal. El costo político en el Ecuador: estudio crítico de la realidad económica, social y política de la República en esta última década. Guayaquil, Ecuador: Nueva Luz, 1983. 188 p.

Brief assessment of political and economic changes in national politics from the overthrow of Velasco to presidency of Osvaldo Hurtado. Ecuador's demon seems to be inability of political system to do much about problems of underdevelopment.

North, Liisa L. Problems of democratization in Peru and Ecuador. See item **6438.**

6396 Roldós Aguilera, Jaime *et al.* ¡Viva la patria! 3a ed. Quito: Editorial El Conejo, 1981. 247 p.: ill., plates.

Seven well known Ecuadorians pay homage to President Roldós and his administrative accomplishments during his 21 months in office. Although favorable in tone, it is possible to glean numerous gems from this political eulogy.

6397 Seminario Interno sobre Metodología de la Investigación Científica, *Quito, 1981.* La investigación socio-económica en el Ecuador: reflexiones acerca del método. Selección de textos e introducción, Fernando Rosero Garcés *et al.* Quito: Instituto de Investigaciones Económicas, Facultad de Economía, Pontificia Univ. Católica del Ecuador, 1982. 162 p.: bibl.

Seven short essays examine application of social science methodology to understanding social, economic, and political life in Ecuador. Authors seem to favor Marxist dialectical methods over empiricism and formal theory. Valuable in light of emphasis of methods of social science investigation.

6398 28 [i.e. Veintiocho] de mayo de 1944: documentos. Guayaquil, Ecuador: Depto. de Publicaciones, Facultad de Cien-

cias Económicas, Univ. de Guayaquil, 1983. 264 p.: ill., plates (Biblioteca ecuatoriana; 44)

Series of documents from early 1940s that shed light on political conditions that led to democratic reforms in 1940s and 1950s.

BOLIVIA, PERU, AND CHILE

WILLIAM R. GARNER, *Associate Professor of Political Science, Latin American Studies Advisory Committee, Southern Illinois University at Carbondale*

BOLIVIA

AS IS OFTEN THE CASE, the literature on Bolivia is somewhat uneven. One of the several significant exceptions is the Ladman compilation, *Modern-day Bolivia* (item **6405**) which contains analyses of certain largely ignored political factors occurring between the 1952–53 MNR period and the present Siles Suazo administration. Also worthy of note are *Encuentros, interviús* (item **6403**) and Gregorio Selser's *Bolivia: el cuartelazo de los cocadólares* (item **6408**). A good publication on human rights violations under military regimes of the 1970s is found in Quiroga Santa Cruz (item **6407**) and consists of testimony given before the US Senate under the sponsorship of the Washington Office on Latin America (WOLA). As for the military period preceding the Siles Suazo government—particularly the García Meza regime—note *Der Putsch in Bolivien* (item **6406**), Selser (item **6408**), and *Los Cien primeros días de una larga noche* (item **6400**). An excellent study by de la Cueva (item **6401**) meticulously documents the role both of private and public capital in contemporary Bolivian industry. One should also note Calderón G.'s "Conflicto y Políticas Urbanas en Bolivia en el Contexto de las Relaciones Clase-Estado, 1952–1976" (item **6399**), a novel contribution on the evolution of Bolivian political culture and its relation to urban conflict from the 1950s MNR period to the midpoint of the Banzer Suárez regime.

PERU

Among the number of impressive works published, one of the most significant is Lowenthal and McClintock's compilation *The Peruvian experiment reconsidered* (item **6444**) in which various Peruvianists critically assess the military *docenio* (1968–80). Werlich (item **6455**) presents a thorough and well written analysis of development through Dec. 1983, and Malloy (item **6434**) offers a solid corporatist interpretation of the troubled second Acción Popular Presidency of Belaúnde Terry. Valuable critique is also given in Alva Castro's Aprista-oriented *La Necesidad del cambio* (item **6409**), Nieto (item **6437**) who approaches the government from the standpoint of the Peruvian left, and the broadside attack on the Belaúnde administration by Pease García (item **6441**).

A sizeable portion of the present literature is still exclusively devoted to the impact of the Velasco-Morales Bermúdez period. Béjar (item **6414**) attacks the Velasco "First Phase" as "bourgeois." Caballero's *From Belaúnde to Belaúnde* (item **6416**) is one of the more trenchant analyses of both Velasco and Morales periods. Guerra García (item **6428**) sees nothing novel about the *docenio*, stating that it represented little more than a continuation of trends begun in the 1920s. Palmer (item **6440**) praises both accomplishments *and* failures of the military and Pilar Tello's two-volume set of interviews with top military functionaries under both Velasco and Morales Bermúdez is a lasting contribution to an understanding of the *docenio* (item **6445**). Stephens notes the unexpected strengthening of Peruvian labor and leftist political groups (item **6451**).

Cobas has written a work that examines foreign influences on the Peruvian military throughout history (item **6418**). An interesting study by Encinas del Pando (item **6422**) analyzes the dysfunctional relationship (during the 1950–80 period) between military expenditures and what he conceptualizes as "traditional Peruvian equilibrium" as the major contributing factor to Peru's current malaise. Langton, in collaboration with a Peruvian scholar (item **6432**), applies political socialization techniques—so functionally utilized in the US—to the Peruvian military period, reaffirming what are generally expected hypotheses concerning the military socialization experience for Peruvians, in general, and Andean miners in particular.

APRA continues to make a solid contribution through studies such as Casas Grieve's (item **6417**) on contemporary Peruvian political economy and Mercado Jarrín's theoretical analysis of the proper functions of military government (item **6435**). Aprista memorials to Haya de la Torre persist in works such as Flores Galindo's (item **6423**), García Toma's (item **6425**) and *Secretos electorales* (item **6450**).

A novel area of interest for this section is the Sendero Luminoso movement, and it has been well examined by a number of writers. Of particular note are studies by McClintock (item **6433**), Gaupp (item **6426**), and Harding (item **6429**). Possibly, one of the most important contributions, after McClintock, is that written by Peruvian novelist Mario Vargas Llosa who was appointed head of a presidential investigatory commission to study the circumstances of the murder of eight Peruvian journalist in Ayacucho dept. by Indians who mistook them for members of Sendero Luminoso (item **6454**).

In the area of electoral behavior analysis—most importantly, the 1980 elections—one should note a major government study, *Resultados de las elecciones políticas generales de 1980* (item **6448**) and another by Dietz (item **6420**). On the 1980 politicization role played by Peruvian television, see Oviedo Valenzuela's work (item **6439**).

Two important additions to the literature in political theory are noted here. One such work is North's comparative study of increased pressures on Ecuadorian and Peruvian democratic structures as a result of mass-based demands in their respective political cultures. The author notes that the frustration experienced by both South American nation-states and populations resembles that which now threatens Central American regimes (item **6438**). Another study, by DESCO, *¿Que significa hacer política?* (item **6488**), is valuable to the general concerns of political psychology.

CHILE

As in *HLAS 45*, general assessments of major questions now facing Chile are largely negative. Johnson (item **6478**) and Nef (item **6483**) provide important review essays on major studies of Chilean politics up to and including the UP/Allende period. Arriagada's small monograph (item **6457**) treats specific problem areas for the current collage of democratic opposition groups and the potential for any post-Pinochet return to democracy. Sigmund, in two excellent articles (items **6490** and **6491**), notes changes that have occurred within the armed forces and, more importantly, declining levels of democratic politicization both within various factions of the military and, most alarmingly, within the civilian population. The general decrease in democratic proclivities is echoed in works by Garretón Merino (items 6472, 6473, and 6474). It is clear that such emphasis on the loss of a democratic learning experience is one of the most significant topics in the literature annotated for this section. Volk (item 6497) gives good coverage to Pinochet's "second war" (i.e., his attempts to deal with the economy) and Arturo Valenzuela (item 6495) predicts waning support for the military among all sectors but is pessimistic about the democratic (and otherwise anti-Pinochet) opposition whose fragmentation will continue.

Studies of the opposition in Chile give only slightly brighter perceptions of party system vitality for any eventual return to democratic processes. Dinges (item 6469) notes with grim resignation that options may *possibly* exist for a return to representative institutions but infers that the question is moot at this point. Garretón M. (item 6472) provides a barely more optimistic prognosis. Nef (item 6482) observes that the Christian Democrats (PDC) are still quite fragmented but that the Chilean Catholic Church appears to be the institution with the most staying power as a united opposition force. According to the authors of *Temas socialistas* (item 6494) and Zemelman and Arrate (item 6498) the Socialist Party is presently making comprehensive plans and organizational arrangements as an underground so as to be in a position to return to power when the military period is over. Osiel and Willis (item 6485), however, see the Communist Party—among all opposition groups—as "most durable."

Negative criticism of the military abounds (mostly published outside Chile). Chavkin (item 6462) writes from his experience of interviewing hundreds of refugees from the early Pinochet years. Garretón M., in two works (items 6473 and 6474), is most angered by the near-disappearance of structures for democratic socialization resulting from 10 years of authoritarian rule and these sentiments are repeated in the Garretón M. and Moulian study (item 6475). In her important contribution on military policy dealing with labor organization, Hurtado-Beca (item 6477) observes the deliberate weakening of union structures. Nef (item 6482) notes an ingrained bias against democratic institutions within the military while Portales and Varas (item 6487) address the problem of budgetary impact of what have historically been considered essential public programs for Chile's population. Sigmund (item 6490) attributes economic failure to the Chicago Boys who promised an economic miracle. The sole pro-government study is Repetto Bertelson's (item 6459) who offers a fairly lame apologia based on what he perceives as increased political participation.

Fewer studies of the UP/Allende period are reviewed for this volume than in *HLAS 45*. Of note, however, is *Chile: convergencia socialista* (item 6463) which provides a relatively dispassionate autopsy of the groups that formed Unidad Popular (1970–73). Molina S. (item 6480) has written an intriguing study of the Christian Democratic period which he sees as having set the stage upon which the Allende experiment was acted out.

The subject of human rights is of even more import than it has been in past *Handbook* volumes. Reports from Americas Watch (item 6460), Amnesty International (item 6456), and two volumes published under the auspices of the Chilean Catholic hierarchy (items 6470 and 6492) are aimed at pressuring Pinochet's administration to end institutionalized repression.

The Chilean Church appears to be among the most potent and empirical sources of material for both academics and the general public at this time. Theoretical works such as *Hacia la civilización del amor: Chile 2000* (item **6476**) and that of Chaporro N., *Socialismos y socialismo democrático* (item **6461**) are particularly tight, non-polemical works. The influence of former-Cardinal Silva Henríquez is apparent in the 1981 publication, *Chile visto por Mensaje, 1971–1981* (item **6466**). Brian H. Smith's extremely important study of the evolution of the Chilean Church as a political force (item **6493**) cannot be praised too highly. Jorge Nef (item **6482**) and, amazingly, the Soviet publication, *América Latina*, (item **6465**), both point to the Chilean Church as the single most important influence in contemporary Chile and the only enduring organization capable of providing democratic direction for the country after Pinochet.

Political theory—with contemporary Chile as basis for various studies—has been advanced in several important works. The Church-sponsored ILADES publication, for example, *Del liberalismo al capitalismo autoritario* (item **6468**) draws a rare and significant distinction between governmental intervention as a *procedural* act with the *substance* of such intervention to be evaluated as a separate issue. A collection of the most salient ideological comments made by former President Eduardo Frei (item **6471**) is now available for Chilean and other readers. Meza Villalobos's article (item **6479**) on traditional emphases on the concept of "Rey" and, to a lesser extent, "Cortes"—as precursors of the post-colonial president and congress, respectively—is an important aid for understanding authoritarian dictatorship within Latin American political culture (and most significantly in present-day Chile). Moulian (item **6481**) offers an important negative critique of "inquisitional," fundamentalist Marxist-Leninism and its weakness as a result of these two qualities. He also observes that, in general, the so-called "bourgeois" ideologies are studied with far more scientific rigor than are either revisionist or classical Marxism. Ruiz (item **6489**) posits that Chilean political thought does not merit its "conventional interpretation," that is, as a continuous evolution of liberal-democratic philosophy. Finally, Augusto Pinochet (item **6486**), in a long-interview that makes up one volume, gives a frank rationale for military action in Sept. 1973 as well as for current government policy. In sum, these and the above-mentioned materials from the Chilean experience are rich and diverse in content.

BOLIVIA

6399 Calderón G., Fernando. Conflicto y políticas urbanas en Bolivia en el contexto de las relaciones clase-Estado, 1952–1976 (CPES/RPS, 18:51, junio/sept. 1981, p. 43–58)

Analyzes Bolivian urban politics over past 25 yrs. in relation to qualities that differentiate the nation from its neighbors: 1) a deeply significant precolumbian heritage; 2) self-sufficient Quechua culture; 3) a monocultural mining economy; and 4) existence of Bolivia as a conflict society with "middle groups" controlling urban politics. Novel, important contribution.

6400 Los Cien primeros días de un larga noche: la violación de los derechos humanos en Bolivia. Quito: Padi, 1981. 212 p.: ill.

Pub. in Ecuador, study is an indictment of the Presidency of Luis García Meza (July 1980-Aug. 1981). Tedious but well researched study of a very repressive period.

6401 Cueva, J.M. de la. Bolivia, imperialismo y oligarquía. La Paz: Ediciones Roalva, 1983. 370 p.: bibl., ill., tables.

Examines role of foreign capital (both private and public) in corporate life of contemporary Bolivia. While somewhat conspiratorial, it is still a worthwhile study. Includes detailed information on financial "penetration," quoted in dollars, of various international groups vis-à-vis Bolivian enterprises. Valuable reference.

6402 Dandler, Jorge. Dinámica de un movimiento campesino e incertidumbre populista: de la revolución de 1952 a la reforma agraria en Bolivia (PUCP/DA, 2, mayo 1978, p. 89–117, bibl.)

Marxist analysis of revolutionary process that assumes dominant role for peasant class (without major contributions by urban proletariat). Based on author's experience of over 15 months in Cochabamba Valley (1952–53). Attempts to explain dynamics of the 1952 MNR "revolution." Fairly tight Marxist case study.

6403 Encuentros, interviús: Roberto Arnez Villaroel, para que el pueblo de Bolivia no sufra una nueva frustración (URSS/AL, 2, Feb. 1984, p. 78–86, ill.)

Review of interviews with Villaroel pubished in Soviet journal. Discusses ideological orientation and component groups now characterizing Bolivian UDP, headed by Siles Suazo. Views military as only possible threat to Siles's ability to finish out presidential term in 1984.

6404 Kohl, James V. The Cliza and Ucureña war: syndical violence and national revolution in Bolivia (HAHR, 62:4, Nov. 1982, p. 607–628, map)

. In contrast to other studies, article stresses patronage system in Cochabamba Valley as a major factor in 1950s MNR "revolutionary" period. Case study reflects author's analysis of rural Cochabamban syndicalism in 1959–60 and its role in setting the stage for the militarism that has characterized Bolivian politics from 1960s to present. Should be read in conjunction with Dandler's article (item **6402**). For historian's comment, see *HLAS 46:3042*.

Lara, Jesús. Guerrillero Inti Peredo. See *HLAS 46:3043*.

Laserna, Roberto. El "Estado" boliviano, 1971–1978: economía y poder. See item **3638**.

6404a Lucho Espinal, testigo de nuestra América. Compilado por la Asamblea Permanente de los Derechos Humanos de Bolivia. Madrid: Iepala, 1982. 191 p.: ill.

Testament to the life of Lucho Espinal, Bolivian journalist (Spanish by birth) and human rights activist, who was assassinated in 1980. Includes Espinal's editorials on a variety of subjects and documents relating to his death. Compiled by the group he worked with, the Permanent Assembly of Human Rights. [Y. Ferguson]

6405 Modern-day Bolivia: legacy of the revolution and prospects for the future. Edited by Jerry R. Ladman. Tempe: Center for Latin American Studies, Arizona State Univ., 1982. 409 p.: bibl., index.

Collection of studies compiled as general overview of Bolivia's political and economic evolution since MNR "revolution" (1952). Ed. has sought successfully to close a gap in literature dealing with military regimes of 1960s and 1970s, particularly the Banzer Suárez administration. Papers were presented at conference on "Modern-Day Bolivia" (Arizona State Univ., March 1978). Excellent collection.

6406 Der Putsch in Bolivien = El Golpe militar en Bolivia. Hamburg, FRG: Institut für Iberoamerika-Kunde, 1980. 116 p.: ill. (Aktueller Informationsdienst Lateinamerika = Boletín de prensa latinoamericana, 0342–0388; 16/17–80)

World-wide compilation of photocopied articles drawn from numerous major newspapers on the García Meza coup and its immediate aftermath (July-Aug. 1980).

6407 Quiroga Santa Cruz, Marcelo. Los derechos de los bolivianos también son derechos humanos: intervención de Marcelo Quiroga Santa Cruz ante el Senado de los Estados Unidos (SP, 3, mayo 1978, p. 118–125)

Text of testimony given in Nov. 1977, at US Senate and sessions sponsored by WOLA (Washington Office on Latin America). Former Bolivian government minister places emphasis on continued US government support of Banzer administration and on the question "Why?"

6408 Selser, Gregorio. Bolivia, el cuartelazo de los cocadólares. México: Mex-Sur Editorial, 1982. 307 p.: bibl.

Argentine journalist charts development of Bolivian policy during period between the coup against Lidia Gueiler's government and establishment of Natusch Busch regime and the inauguration of President Hernán Siles Suazo. Good coverage of García Meza period. The three yrs. after

Gueiler are seen as period during which drug traffic became foundation for political ambition and violence (including massive human rights violation). Good study.

PERU

6409 Alva Castro, Luis. La necesidad del cambio. Prólogo de Luis Alberto Sánchez. Lima: APRA, s.d. 297 p.

Anti-AP/Belaúnde study of industrial development by an early follower of Haya de la Torre. Includes APRA's economic "blueprint" for 1980s. Also interesting as an example of Aprista views of Peru's international economy.

Aricó, José. Mariátegui y los orígenes del marxismo latinoamericano. See *HLAS 46:7588.*

6410 Barton, Carol. Peru: "dirty war" in Ayacucho (NACLA, 17:3, May/June 1983, p. 36–39, photos)

Account of Peruvian government counterinsurgency atrocities against those suspected of being followers of the Sendero Luminoso movement in the Andes.

6411 Bedoya Garland, Eduardo. Ocupaciones de tierras en el Fundo Saipai: antecedentes e historia del movimiento (PUCP/DA, 8, mayo 1982, p. 77–106, bibl., tables)

Attempts to explain interaction of Montaña *campesinos* and their *latifundista* counterpart on a large landholding called Saipai (or Pra Alto) during 1945–64 period. Case study is of interest from standpoint of current land tenure debate and state of agrarian reform *after* the military *docenio.* For historian's comment, see *HLAS 46:2956.*

6412 Béjar, Héctor. APRA-PC, 1930–1940: itinerario de un conflicto (SP, 9, feb. 1980, p. 13–40)

Traces political conflict between Peruvian Communist Party and APRA— traditional Mariátegui-Haya de la Torre ideological conflict—during 1930s with emphasis on military's posture during period. Excellent bibliographical source. For historian's comment, see *HLAS 46:2957.*

6413 ———. Izquierda peruana: hacia nuevos puntos de partida (SP, 10, mayo 1980, p. 11–20)

Paper presented at Feb. 1980 seminar on Latin American power structures and political alternatives. Suggests options open to the Peruvian left (see also item 6412). Good study of ideological currents and left political behavior up until 1980.

6414 ———. Velasco: ¿reformismo burgués? (SP, 5, dic. 1978, p. 73–86)

Velasco period of Peru's military *docenio* is viewed as a construct of the military, while the "Second Phase" or Morales-Bermúdez period is termed "bourgeois." Sees only Velasco administration as having been capable of operating effectively with the Peruvian left. Important contribution.

6415 Belaúnde Terry, Fernando. Discursos y declaraciones del Señor Presidente de la República Arquitecto Fernando Belaúnde Terry. Lima: Oficina Central de Información, Dirección de Información, Presidencia de la República, 1981. 8 v.

Multi-vol. compilation of official statements by the President dating from July 1980-Aug. 1981.

6416 Caballero, José María. From Belaúnde to Belaúnde: Peru's military experiment in third-roadism. Cambridge, England: Centre of Latin American Studies, Univ. of Cambridge, 1981. 49 p.: bibl. (Working papers, 0306–6290; 36)

Autopsy of military *docenio* which views the Agrarian Reform as its major contribution. Although virtually all of its policies in other areas of Peruvian life met with little success, the military *did* produce a new set of national configurations that will never allow Peru to be the same again—even in areas of perceived failure. Significant analysis that should be read by all interested in the military experiment from Velasco through Morales Bermúdez and elections of 1980.

6417 Casas Grieve, Luis Felipe de las. Neoliberalismo y aprismo: una recusación aprista al actual liberalismo. Lima: Comisión Nacional de Plan de Gobierno Partido Aprista, 1983. 140 p.: bibl.

Theoretical study of Peruvian political economy from an APRA viewpoint. Excellent piece that should be read by students of political theory and by policy specialists.

6418 Cobas, Efraín. Fuerza armada, misiones militares y dependencia en el Perú. Lima: Horizonte, 1982. 333 p.: ill., plates.

Emphasis is on foreign influence (particularly US and European) on Latin American military establishments and, in particular, that of Peru. Excellent foundation for future work by students of Latin American military elite behavior.

6419 Congreso Nacional Extraordinario del Partido Comunista del Perú, 8th, *Lima, 1982.* ¡Hacia un gobierno popular!: por el camino de la izquierda unida y de la acción de masas. Lima: Comisión Nacional de Propaganda del PCP, 1982. 55 p.: ill.

Strategy manifesto issued by the Peruvian Communist Party Congress (Lima, Jan. 1982).

6420 Dietz, Henry. Movilización, austeridad y votación en el Perú: las masas de Lima como objetivo, víctima y votante (SP, 18, junio 1982, p. 53–74, bibl., tables)

Assessing 1968–80 period, author observes its principal ideological foundations, increasing frustrations of military government who sought to institutionalize their principles. Also examines mass-base of limeño politics, especially the poor and their role both as recipient of novel forms of governmental services and as electoral and partisan counter-force against the Velasco/Morales-Bermúdez administrations. Excellent study.

6421 Documentos para la historia del Partido Comunista Peruano: etapa 1939–1948. Lima: El Militante, 1980. 141 p.

Compilation of Communist Party (PCP) documents dealing with Party's evolution during World War II and into that of East-West Cold War tensions.

6422 Encinas del Pando, José A. The role of military expenditure in the development process: Peru, a case study, 1950–1980 (NOSALF/IA, 12:1/2, 1983, p. 51–114, tables)

Addresses relationship between nationalism and MILEX (military expenditures) as they impact on TEP (traditional equilibrium of Peru). Given what author sees as a disintegration of TEP during the three decades under investigation—a time during which Peru was undergoing sustained economic growth even if with serious inflation problems—the constant threat of military intervention in the economic and political spheres is seen as chief cause of political decline and disintegration/disequilibrium in modern Peru. Intriguing study.

6423 Flores Galindo, Alberto. Un viejo debate: el poder (SP, 20, dic. 1982, p. 15–41)

Theoretical investigation of Haya de la Torre's views of political power and Marxism based largely on historic Haya-Mariátegui conflict and, more precisely, on Berlin correspondence of Eudocio Ravines during 1920s.

Franco, Carlos. Mariátegui-Haya: surgimiento de la izquierda nacional. See *HLAS 46:7598.*

6424 García-Sayán, Diego. Tomas de tierras en el Perú. Lima: Centro de Estudios y Promoción del Desarrollo (DESCO), 1982. 319 p.: bibl. (Serie Estudios)

Peruvian Revolutionary Communist Party (PCR) and "Patria Roja" faction of Communist Party give accounts of various land seizures during 1972–78 and processes of land development in each case.

6425 García Toma, Víctor. Las alianzas del APRA. Lima: Promociones Gráficas Imagen, 1982. 150 p.: bibl.

Flattering portrait of Haya de la Torre and his half-century leadership of APRA. Of value to the critical student of Aprismo.

6426 Gaupp, Peter. Peru: a "shining path" to darkness (NZZ/SRWA, 33:10, Jan. 1984, p. 28–31, ill.)

Emphasizes history and ideological orientation of the Sendero Luminoso movement as representative of "a highly schismatic brand of Marxism." Good analysis and fairly non-polemical.

6427 Guasti, Laura. Industrialización y revolución en el Perú: 1968–1976 (UP/EA, 9:17/18, 1981, p. 103–137)

Advises against using 1971–75 Peruvian economic model by more industrialized countries contemplating foreign investment in Peru (or other Third World nations). Likewise, Third World countries are urged to avoid as much as possible any foreign industrial enterprise penetration and to pursue autonomous internal industrial schemes. One can only assume that the writer is espousing questionable import substitution policies.

6428 Guerra García, Francisco. Velasco: del Estado oligárquico al capitalismo de Estado. Lima: Centro de Estudios para el

Desarrollo y la Participación, 1983. 119 p.
(Serie Realidad nacional)

Attempts to demonstrate that the Velasco *docenio* was simply a continuation of economic and political developments begun in 1920s and that (along with contributions of APRA and, in general, the Left) state capitalism finally evolved out of the traditionalist "oligarchic state."

6429 Harding, Colin. Reporting the war in Ayacucho (INDEX, 12:6, dec. 1983, p. 15–17)

Concerns the murder of eight Peruvian journalists (Jan. 1973) by Andean Indians who were later exonerated. Indians mistook journalists for members of Sendero Luminoso. Points to numerous acts of harrassment and repression by armed forces under Belaúnde Terry as "overkill" measures in their attempt to eradicate Sendero Luminoso from Ayacucho dept.

6430 Jaworsky, Helan. El futuro de Lima: problemas de administración y gobierno (SP, 4, sept. 1978, p. 43–70)

Good theoretical piece on public administration in large Latin American urban centers. Uses Lima as case study of "overnationalization" (centralization) of government services with resulting misgovernment and inefficiency.

6431 Kammann, Peter. Movimientos campesinos en el Perú, 1900–1968: análisis cuantitativo y cualitativo preliminar. Lima: Univ. Mayor de San Marcos, Seminario de Historia Rural Andina, 1982. 284 p.: bibl., ill.

Study by social scientists at the Univ. of San Marcos using sophisticated methodology in analysis of 104 peasant movements in eight Peruvian depts.

6432 Langton, Kenneth P. The influence of military service on social consciousness and protest behavior: a study of Peruvian mine workers (CPS, 16:4, Jan. 1984, p. 479–504, bibl., graphs, table)

Study of military influence on Peruvian miners. Suggests that while socialization under military regimes produces groups that can integrate more easily into hierarchical political structures, such experiences tend to dull social class consciousness and reduce levels of political participation. Also suggests that—as previously assumed—military authoritarianism tends to produce economic inequity.

6433 McClintock, Cynthia. Sendero Luminoso: Peru's Maoist guerrillas (USIA/PC, 32:5, Sept./Oct. 1983, p. 19–34, plates)

Probably best discussion of Sendero Luminoso movement published to date. Examines circumstances of its founding, influence of Mariátegui and five distinct stages of armed struggle as a major contribution to any discussion of revisionist Marxism. McClintock posits that Sendero followers are those who see no material betterment possible from past or present Peruvian leftist groups; hence Sendero is a frustration-based phenomenon. Compare with studies by Harding (item **6429**), Gaupp (item **6426**), and Barton (item **6410**).

6434 Malloy, James M. Peru's troubled return to democratic government. Hanover, N.H.: Universities Field Staff International, 1982. 11 p.: bibl. (UFSI reports, 0743–9644; 1982/no. 15. South America).

Posits that Peru's return to democracy during second Belaúnde Terry administration is, in the most obvious sense, a return to reliance on age-old Latin corporatist structures that strengthen position of the President. Second AP government, says Malloy, is another example of Peruvian tendency to seek corporate solutions in periods of sociopolitical crisis. Excellent study.

6435 Mercado Jarrín, Edgardo. Política y defensa nacional. Tomada de la versión magnetofónica de la conferencia. Lima: Partido Aprista Peruano, Comisión Nacional de Plan de Gobierno, 1982. 47 p.: ill. (Ediciones Pueblo)

Aprista statement resulting from conference held on relation between political processes and national defense policy. Includes secs. on: 1) goals and methods established by the armed forces; 2) practical meaning of the concept of "national defense"; and 3) whether Peru does need an efficient national defense apparatus. Important contribution.

6436 Morales Bermúdez Cerruti, Francisco. El proyecto nacional. Lima: Centro de Documentación e Información Andina, 1982? 200 p.: bibl.

Apologia for Morales Bermúdez's presidential term (second phase of *docenio*). Addresses problem of Andean integration, relation of armed forces to normal political processes, political thought of various luminaries in Peruvian politics, and, perhaps most dangerously from the standpoint of political theory, questions concerning proper role of the State in its quest for "social constitutionalism."

6437 Nieto, Jorge. Izquierda y democracia en el Perú, 1975–1980. Lima: Centro de Estudios y Promoción del Desarrollo (DESCO), 1983. 124 p.: bibl. (Praxis; 17)

DESCO study of 1975–82 period and attitudes of Peruvian left concerning the return to democracy (1980). Includes important discussion of built-in difficulties involved in left-Acción Popular interchange.

6438 North, Liisa L. Problems of democratization in Peru and Ecuador (*in* Latin American prospects for the 1980s: equity, democratization, and development. Edited by Archibald R.M. Ritter and David H. Pollock. New York: Praeger, 1983, p. 214–239, bibl., tables)

Comparative study of democratic development and "marginated sectors" under Presidents Roldós (Ecuador) and Belaúnde Terry (Peru). Key to author's analysis is perceived incapacity of democratic forms to meet mass-based expectations, an incapacity she attributes to lack of economic infrastructure. Sees similar problem in Central America where demands have reached level of mass-violence and massive governmental repression. Prognosis is that similar demands increasingly will impact on Peru, Ecuador, and Bolivia. Excellent study.

6439 Oviedo Valenzuela, Carlos. Manejos de la propaganda política. Lima: Promotores, Consultores y Asesores Andinos, Centro de Documentación e Información Andina, 1982. 200 p.: bibl.

Focuses on the role of television in Peruvian political process. Includes case studies of television use by all major political parties. Excellent study in political communications.

6440 Palmer, David Scott. Reformist military rule in Peru, 1968–80 (*in* New military politics in Latin America. Edited by Robert Wesson. New York: Praeger, 1982, p. 131–149)

Assessment of Peruvian military *docenio*, characterizing the military "revolution" as perhaps the most committed to reform of all military experiments in 20th-century Latin America. Regime failures are seen as result of inability of Peruvian bureaucracy to respond to commands coming from authoritarian military structures in typically unquestioning military fashion. Sees period's major contribution as an enlarged and dynamic state apparatus, heretofore not accomplished in Peru. Ends with optimistic speculation that governments of 1980s and 1990s will have an opportunity (and desire?) to continue to build on initiatives begun by Velasco and Morales Bermúdez. Important study.

6441 Pease García, Henry. Un perfil del proceso político peruano: a un año del segundo belaundismo. Lima: Centro de Estudios y Promoción del Desarrollo (DESCO), 1981. 115 p.: bibl. (Serie Publicaciones previas; 2)

Study by DESCO staff attacks policies of post-military Belaúnde regime as well as most other contemporary Peruvian party organizations. Blames immobility and powerlessness of present party structures (especially AP) for increasing level of violence now facing the nation (e.g., Sendero Luminoso).

6442 El Pensamiento comunista, 1917–1945. Selección, prólogo y bibliografía, Alberto Flores Galindo. Lima: Francisco Campodónico F.; San Isidro, Perú: Mosca Azul Editores, 1982. 228 p.: bibl. (Biblioteca del pensamiento peruano; 3)

Writings by Peruvian leftists (members of either the Communist Party or other Socialist movements) during 1917–45. Of particular value are those by José Mariátegui and Eudosio Ravines. Good reference.

6443 Peru: torture and extrajudicial executions: letter of Amnesty International to President Fernando Belaúnde Terry, August 1983. New York: Amnesty International USA, 1983. 49 p.: appendix.

Amnesty International's response to human rights abuses both by Sendero Luminoso and Peruvian government forces in their attempts to eradicate the former. Appendix contains valuable multi-case documentation which supports indictment of policies espoused by both Sendero and Belaúnde's administration (as stated in Amnesty's formal letter to President Belaúnde, also reprinted here).

6444 The Peruvian experiment reconsidered.
Edited by Cynthia McClintock and Abraham F. Lowenthal. Princeton, N.J.: Princeton Univ. Press, 1983. 442 p.: bibl., index.

Impressive group of Peruvianists contribute their views—some very optimistic, some quite negative—on the question of the military *docenio*'s "success." The regime's achievements were, in many instances, those least expected or welcomed by the military. Not only such perceived failures of the military leadership, but the "success" of their 12-yr. rule needs to be properly assessed. According to Lowenthal, an assessment not so much in terms of what the leadership's original goals were but rather in comparison with what other Latin American "revolutions" have accomplished. Major contribution.

6445 Pillar Tello, María del. ¿Golpe o revolución?: hablan los militares del 68; entrevistas. Lima: Ediciones SAGSA, 1983. 2 v.: appendices.

Two-vol. set of interviews by Lima journalist with various members of the military during 1968–80 *docenio*. Emphasis is on various areas of specific public policy. Appendices are of particular value as they identify legal bases for the military's "revolutionary" program during this period. Good collection of interviews and government documents.

6446 Prado, Jorge del. El P.C.P., su doctrina, su línea y su proyecto nacional expuestos ante la fuerza armada: un diálogo principista y respetuoso. Conferencia dictada en el CAEM por el Secretario General del PCP. Lima: Comisión Nacional de Propaganda del PCP, 1982. 23 p.: ill.

Statement (July 1982) of Peru's Communist Party concerns plans for first months of Belaúnde's presidency. From conference sponsored by CAEM, Peru's major military educational institution.

6447 Pulgar Vidal, Javier *et al.* Regionalización. Lima: Comisión Nacional de Plan de Gobierno del Partido Aprista Peruano, 1982. 153 p.: bibl., ill. (Ediciones Pueblo)

Aprista study of the unevenness in development among various Peruvian areas

stemming either from inaction by government structures during *docenio* or because of dysfunctional military policy.

6448 Resultados de las elecciones políticas generales de 1980. Lima: Jurado Nacional de Elecciones, 1980. 2 v.: tables.

Massive and thorough two-vol. statistical analysis by National Election Center of 1980 Peruvian general election returns. Major contribution.

6449 Rojas Samanez, Alvaro. Partidos políticos en el Perú: manual y registro. Lima: Centro de Documentación e Información Andina, 1982. 160 p.: appendix, bibl., ill.

Peruvian journalist, formerly of Arequipa's *El Pueblo* and later editor of Lima review, *Caritas*, presents good sketch of historical development and present configuration of Peru's major political parties. Includes interesting appendix on party electoral power during 1980 election.

6450 Secretos electorales del APRA: correspondencia y documentos de 1939. Thomas M. Davies, Jr. y Víctor Villanueva, comps. Lima: Editorial Horizonte, 1982. 156 p.

Compilation of Haya de la Torre correspondence dealing wth electoral policy of Apristas under military regime of Benavides. Excellent reference for those interested in late 1930s from standpoint of Haya's personality and political strategy.

6451 Stephens, Evelyne Huber. The Peruvian military government, labor mobilization, and the political strength of the left (LARR, 18:2, 1983, p. 57–93, bibl., tables)

Investigates reasons for unexpected strengthening of organized labor and the Peruvian left during the military period. Emphasizes the "non-exclusionary" nature of the first phase (Velasco) and administrative assistance provided by SINAMOS together with the structure of Comunidad Industrial concept whereby labor and management participated in profit sharing, ownership and management of their concerns. Probably one of the most important analyses of organized labor during the *docenio* to date.

6452 Sulmont, Denis. L'évolution récente du mouvement syndical au Pérou (Amérique latine [Centre de recherche sur l'Amérique latine et le Tiers monde, Paris] 7, automne 1981, p. 60–71, tables)

Traces rapid growth of Peruvian unionization from the Velasco period through the more traditional "second phase" of Morales Bermúdez. Under present Belaúnde administration, process appears to be slowing down owing to increasing influence of international capital in the Peruvian economy.

6453 Thorndike, Guillermo. Uchuraccay: testimonio de una masacre. Lima: The Author, 1983. 94 p.: ill. (Libro visión)

Photographic essay dealing with ongoing civil war in Ayacucho dept. Covers events and aftermath of massacre of Lima journalists in remote Andean village (see item **6454**).

6454 Vargas Llosa, Mario. Inquest in the Andes: a Latin American writer explores the political lessons of a Peruvian massacre (The New York Times Magazine, 31 July 1983, p. 18–23, 33, 36–37, 42, 48–51, 56, ill., map)

Peruvian novelist—named Chair of Belaúnde-appointed investigatory commission—gives account of circumstances surrounding the death of eight Peruvian journalists after they were mistakenly identified as members of Sendero Luminoso by Andean Indians in mountains near Ayacucho. See also the article by Harding (item **6429**). For Spanish original of this translation, see *HLAS 46:5430.*

6455 Werlich, David P. Peru: the shadow of the Shining Path (CUH, 83 : 490, Feb. 1984, p. 78–82, 90)

Describes devolution of Belaúnde's regime in face of multi-faceted crisis. The nation's economy is crippled by austerity programs to allow for servicing of massive foreign debt, plagued by persistent inflation and high unemployment. Notes growing criticism of human rights violations resulting from emergence of the most significant threat to domestic stability in 20th century: Sendero Luminoso. Economic disorientation in addition to Belaúnde's inability or unwillingness to control the nation's internal security forces have generated much insecurity for the second Acción Popular administration. Excellent summary of 1983.

CHILE

6456 Amnesty International. Chile, evidence of torture: an Amnesty International report. London: Amnesty International, 1983. 75 p.: ill.

Documentation of the function of torture as public policy in post-1973 period. Should be read in conjunction with Americas Watch report (item **6460**) which gives a broader discussion of human rights abuses in contemporary Chile.

6457 Arriagada Herrera, Genaro. 10 años: visión crítica. Santiago: Editorial Aconcagua, 1983. 247 p.

US-born, Chilean-educated political journalist (and editor of press publishing this vol.) has written articles on the most critical themes preoccupying Chileans since the Pinochet coup 10 yrs. earlier. Interesting that this vol. could have been published in Santiago. Excellent collection.

6458 Atria B., Raúl. Características y tendencias de la estructura de partidos en Chile (*in* Hacia un nuevo diagnóstico de Chile. Edición de Andrés Sanfuentes. Raúl Atria B. *et al.* Santiago: Editorial del Pacífico: Instituto de Estudios Políticos, 1983, p. 31–62, charts, graphs)

Written as critique of article by Joan Garcés on Chilean political dynamics during UP/Allende period. Rather than emphasizing "tripolarization" (Garcés), Atria stresses party structure, electoral trends, political mobilization and, ultimately, development of clientilist parties. These factors—especially their effect on the fate of Chilean Christian Democrats—prevented this party from staving off the tripolarization discussed by Garcés.

Barnard, Andrew. El Partido Comunista de Chile y las políticas del Tercer Período, 1931–1934. See *HLAS 46:3060.*

6459 Bertelsen Repetto, Raúl. Participación y representación en la nueva institucionalidad (Política [Instituto de Ciencia Política, Univ. de Chile, Santiago] 3, 1983, p. 169–179)

Seeks to explain increased political participation under Pinochet as based on the 1977 "apertura" and first report of the Study Group on the New Constitutionalism (Aug.

16, 1978). While Chileans from all sectors of society may now participate freely in the political process, the Chilean experience of 1970–73 was only of the "limited type" and thus inferior to Pinochet's. The verbiage used to repudiate the Allende period constitutes a tortuous exercise. Nevertheless, a valuable study in authoritarian apologia.

6460 Brown, C.G. Chile since the coup: ten years of repression. New York: Americas Watch, 1983. 137 p.: bibl. (An Americas Watch report)

Report by respected human rights organization addresses repression under the Pinochet regime in areas of political, individual, and cultural rights. Last chap. is devoted to detailed statement on US involvement in the fall of Allende's government. Compare with Amnesty International's report (item **6456**).

6461 Chaparro N., Patricio. Socialismos y socialismo democrático. Santiago: Instituto Latinoamericano de Doctrina y Estudios Sociales, 1981. 2 v.: bibl., ill.

Pt. 1 of this Church-sponsored study constitutes an analysis of social thought over past three centuries. Examines potential compatibility between socialist impulse and traditional Chilean democracy. Pt. 2 uses four typologies drawn from an empirical investigation of 50 nation-states to present an interesting discussion. The typologies are: 1) non-democratic Marxism; 2) democratic socialism; 3) democratic capitalism; and 4) non-democratic capitalism. Important study in that author *does* draw a distinction between democracy and authoritarianism as *political* forms and capitalism and socialism as *economic* systems. Hence, Marxist-Leninist socialism is as authoritarian as the authoritarian capitalism of Pinochet's regime.

6462 Chavkin, Samuel. The murder of Chile: eyewitness accounts of the coup, the terror, and the resistance today. New York: Everest House, 1982. 286 p.: ill., index.

Author's perceptions of contemporary Chile based on hundreds of interviews with Chilean exiles. Of importance to anyone desiring accurate personal accounts of what happened in earlier periods of Pinochet's regime.

6463 Chile: convergencia socialista (SP, 12, dic. 1980, p. 149–168)

Final document contains results of seminar on the "crisis of the left" in contemporary Chile. Fairly dispassionate essay/autopsy focuses on groups that made up Unidad Popular (1970–73).

6464 Chile, 1973–1983: diez años de realizaciones = Chile, 1973–1983: ten years of achievement. Santiago: Ministerio Secretaría General de Gobierno, 1979. 144 p.: ill. (some col.)

Expensive government publication presents military regime's assessment of Chilean achievements in the post-1973 period. Emphasizes rights of citizens.

6465 Chile vista por un periodista inglés: entrevista a Richard Gott (URSS/AL, 9, sept. 1983, p. 43–46)

Interview with former foreign correspondent for the *Manchester Guardian* (1960s) pub. by Soviet official organ on Latin America. Pinochet's Chile is viewed negatively, as one would expect, but, interestingly, Gott perceives Chilean Catholic Church—especially its univ. student organizations, as one of the most potent forces against current government.

6466 Chile visto por *Mensaje,* 1971–1981: selección de editoriales. Santiago: Editorial Aconcagua, 1981. 220 p. (Col. Mensaje)

Selected editorials and articles originally pub. in Chilean publication, *Mensaje.* Most (post-1973) inclusions are written within ideological viewpoint of former Archbishop Silva Henríquez. Stress is on a "Christian vision" of contemporary Chilean life.

6467 Cuevas Farren, Gustavo. Objetivos nacionales: una reflexión analítica (Política [Instituto de Ciencia Política, Univ. de Chile, Santiago] 3, 1983, p. 9–26)

Analysis of 20th-century communist bloc tensions based on what author sees as "forces of nationalism." However, the conceptualization of "nationalism" is drawn from the Spanish Falange under leadership of Primo de Rivera.

6468 Del Liberalismo al capitalismo autoritario: contribución de ILADES al "objectivo general" de las Orientaciones Pastorales 1982/85 de la Conferencia Episcopal de Chile. Santiago: Instituto Latino-americano de Doctrina y Estudios Sociales (ILADES), 1983. 192 p.

Chilean Catholic Church organization's study of modern liberalism from its 18th-century roots to neo-liberalism of the Pinochet period. Interesting and important distinction is drawn between the *essence* of State intervention—important for a definition of current "liberal" policy—and the *process* of intervention itself.

DeShazo, Peter. Urban workers and labor unions in Chile, 1902–1927. See *HLAS 46:3073.*

6469 Dinges, John. Chile: the rise of the opposition (NACLA, 17:5, Sept./Oct. 1983, p. 15–26, ill.)

Examination of post-1973 Chilean political forces: Christian Democrats, univ. students, the Church, labor and the increasingly fragmented left. Includes thorough discussion of potential opposition to Pinochet's government.

6470 ¿Donde están? v. 3–7. Santiago: Arzobispado de Santiago, Vicaría de la Solidaridad, 1979. 5 v.: ill.

Pub. by the Vicariate of Solidarity of the Catholic hierarchy, these five vols. contain information on hundreds of individuals whose disappearance since 1973 was reported to this organization. The Vicariate not only assists by receiving such information on missing persons but also represents a potent public opinion weapon against the military regime. For vols. 1–2, see *HLAS 45:6289.*

6471 Frei, Eduardo. El pensamiento de Eduardo Frei. Selección y notas, Oscar Pinochet de la Barra. Santiago: Editorial Aconcagua, 1982. 264 p. (Col. Lautaro)

Various significant philosophical and policy statements made by the late President compiled by a former student. Important reference source for Frei's political and social thought.

6472 Garretón Merino, Manuel Antonio. Chile: la transición política y el proceso de convergencia socialista (SP, 24, dic. 1983, p. 95–103)

Spokesman for Convergencia Socialista movement, a reorganized Socialist Party, calls for adoption of specific measures by Chilean Communist Party and factions of Christian Democrats in joint action to pro-

mote democratic institutions when Pinochet regime is no longer in power.

6473 ———. Modelo e projeto políticos do regime militar chileno (*in* A Ciencia política nos anos 80. Bolivar Lamounier, organizador. Brasília: Editora Univ. de Brasília, 1983, p. 55–75 [Col. Cadernos da UnB])

Former Socialist Party leader sees increasing institutionalization of the military government as a permanent setting for Chilean politics. Party fragmentation, a decade of military rule, lack of class cohesion do not bode well for a return to democratic institutions. Compare with author's article (item **6472**).

6474 ———. El proceso político chileno. Santiago: Facultad Latinoamericana de Ciencias Sociales (FLACSO), 1983. 206 p.: bibl.

FLACSO study pub. through auspices of York Univ. (Canada) and School of Advanced Studies (Paris). Attempts to oganize events of Christian Democratic and Allende periods into a logical, chronological whole through the Pinochet era. Compares all three periods and notes differences among them. Devotes final chap. to the potential for democracy pointing out major obstacles now firmly entrenched in the Chilean political process and body politic. Garretón is not optimistic. Important study.

6475 ——— and **Tomás Moulian.** La Unidad Popular y el conflicto político en Chile. Santiago: Ediciones Minga, 1983. 168 p.: bibl.

Thorough analysis of UP period and 10-yr. hiatus in democratic norms under Pinochet. Emphasizes break in democratic socialization and void in understanding, particularly among younger Chileans, of the nature of vanished democratic practice and, in particular, the nature of Allende's administration. Excellent study.

6476 Hacia la civilización del amor, Chile 2000. Coordinadores, Jaime Lavados, Bernardino Piñera y Sergio Silva. Santiago: Conferencia Episcopal de Chile, 1983. 171 p.: bibl.

Interesting work sponsored by Chilean Catholic hierarchy consists of an interdisciplinary study that transcends Chile and seeks to develop an eclectic model for a "just and Christian society" in the 21st century.

Emphasizes "signs of the times" with reference to theological, psychological, natural and social science developments. Its position is close to liberationist strain of contemporary Latin American-Roman Catholicism. Of importance is the study's publication in Pinochet's Chile.

6477 Hurtado-Beca, Cristina. Chile, 1973–1981: desarticulación reestructuración autoritaria del movimiento sindical (CEDLA/B, 31, dic. 1981, p. 91–117, tables)

Description of destitute conditions of Chilean labor movement and its restructuring by the military under organic-authoritarian lines (1973–81). Well researched statement emphasizes techniques of military regime through Pinochet's decree law powers. Paper presented at Amsterdam conference.

6478 Johnson, Dale L. Chile: before and during (SS, 46:4, Winter 1982/1983, p. 461–476, bibl.)

Review essay on studies by Boorstein, Caviedes, Gil, Loveman, Palacios, Sigmund, Smirnov, and Tapia Videla. Compare with Nef's article (item **6483**).

6479 Meza Villalobos, Néstor. Los orígenes de la cultura política de los chilenos (Política [Instituto de Ciencia Política, Univ. de Chile, Santiago] 3, 1983, p. 81–123, bibl.)

Discussion of Chilean political culture during colonial period with particular emphasis on symbols ("Rey," "Cortes"). Fundamental essay for understanding effect of the Spanish monarchy on Chile's development as a colony and as a nation-state.

6480 Molina S., Sergio. El diagnóstico en 1964 y los cambios producidos durante el gobierno de la Democracia Cristiana (in Hacia un nuevo diagnóstico de Chile. Edición de Andrés Sanfuentes. Santiago: Editorial del Pacífico: Instituto de Estudios Políticos, 1983, p. 11–30)

Looks at Christian Democratic Party (PDC) developments (1965–70) and infers that the Frei administration set stage for the Allende/UP experiment.

6481 Moulian, Tomás. Democracia y socialismo en Chile. Santiago: Facultad Latinoamericana de Ciencias Sociales (FLACSO), 1983. 232 p.: bibl.

Analysis of socialism (within the framework of democratic political institutions) in which most impressive contribution

lies in the negative critique of traditional Marxist-Leninist thought by the author. The sectarian, "inquisitional" form of fundamentalist Marxism and particularly its weakness in Latin American politics, is due primarily to fact that it has not been studied with the same rigor as bourgeois ideologies. Excellent contribution to the literature.

6482 Nef, Jorge. Economic liberalism and political repression in Chile (in Latin American prospects for the 1980s: equity, democratization, and development. Edited by Archibald R.M. Ritter and David H. Pollock. New York: Praeger, 1983, p. 304–329)

Discussion of internal and external forces that led to national security regime in 1973. Sees major internal force as military's ideological bias against 50 yrs. of civilian democratic tradition. In analysis of groups that oppose and support the Pinochet regime, Nef sees PDC as the *largest* but most fragmented and the Catholic Church as the most potent. External support groups include present US administration, Pentagon, and CIA. Probably one of the most thorough analyses to be produced in post-coup period. Written by political scientist now in Canadian exile.

6483 ———. The revolution that never was: perspectives on democracy, socialism, and reaction in Chile (LARR, 18:1, 1983, p. 228–245)

Review essay of major works on post-Allende period. Includes remarks on studies by Alexander, Sigmund, Palacios, Boorstein, Gil, Sideri, Valenzuela, Stallings, and Drake. Excellent overview of major analytical literature on Allende period. Compare with Johnson's article (item **6478**).

6484 O'Brien, Philip J. and **Jackie Roddick.** Chile, the Pinochet decade: the rise and fall of the Chicago Boys. London: Latin America Bureau, 1983. 118 p.: ill., tables.

Latin American Bureau, an interdominational organization of church groups (London), provides a valuable statistical study of socioeconomic and political conditions under the military government. Of particular interest is the treatment of political parties, all of which have been dissolved since the 1977 presidential decree. Includes interesting statement on Pinochet's political economy as "fusion of old fascism and new monetarism."

6485 Osiel, Mark J. and **Eliza Willis.** Is Chile headed for a showdown? (DIS, 31:2, Spring 1984, p. 207–214)

Interesting article from Chilean left assesses contemporary opposition to the military. Includes statements on fragmented leftist party organizations with Communist Party seen as most durable. Rightist parties are quickly dismissed. Provides scenarios for action by various groups in a post-Pinochet period.

6486 Pinochet Ugarte, Augusto. The crucial day, September 11, 1973. Translated by María Teresa Escobar. Santiago: Editorial Renacimiento, 1982. 271 p.: ill.

Presented as long interview with President who seeks to provide rationale for public policy of Chile's armed forces from 1973 until present. Pinochet's responses are based on East-West set of "anti-communist" assumptions. Interestingly enough, the President *does* distinguish between Marxism-Leninism as an all-encompassing socio-political philosophy and communism as an international political movement. This distinction plus Pinochet's frankness are the only positive aspects of the vol.

6487 Portales, Carlos and **Augusto Varas.** The role of military expenditure in the development process: Chile 1952, 1973, and 1973/1980; two contrasting cases (NOSALF/IA, 12:1/2, 1983, p. 21–50, tables)

Landmark study of public policy allocations with dependent variable being military expenditure. Major contribution. For economist's comment, see item **3556.**

6488 ¿Qué significa hacer política? Edited by Norbert Lechner. Regis de Castro Andrade *et al.* Lima: Centro de Estudios y Promoción del Desarrollo (DESCO), 1982. 251 p.: bibl.

Study in theory of "political action" with contributions on topics such as Marxism and the Chilean left, the individual in society, socialism, human response to dictatorship, relevant aspects of Max Weber's sociology, and "the democratic question." Valuable think-piece.

Remmer, Karen L. Party competition in Argentina and Chile: political recruitment and public policy, 1890–1930. See item **6533.**

6489 Ruiz, Carlos. Notes on authoritarian ideologies in Chile (NS, 6:11, 1981, p. 17–36)

Study of authoritarian currents in Chilean political thought from early 19th century to present. Attempts to refute "conventional interpretation" of Chilean thought that perceives 1810–1973 period as one of continuous development of liberal-democratic institutions. For philosopher's comment, see *HLAS 46:7617.*

6490 Sigmund, Paul E. Chile: ten years of Pinochet (CRIA/W, 26:12, Dec. 1983, p. 8–10, ill.)

Assessment of Pinochet's administration during 1973–81 which emphasizes the failure of its "economic miracle" (1981–83) and the dismissal of Friedman's "Chicago Boys." Notes a resocialization experience during the military period producing a Chilean mass-base more susceptible to future military governments.

6491 ———. The military in Chile (*in* New military politics in Latin America. Edited by Robert Wesson. New York: Praeger, 1982, p. 97–116)

Analysis of Chile's military, its evolution, past and current roles, and self-perceptions. The armed forces' intervention in 1973 was a result of lack of military self-confidence. Offers interesting observation that the military is still non-political as Pinochet relies almost exclusively on civilian advisors. In Sigmund's view, this assures that Pinochet, should he live, will be able to remain in office until his "constitutional" term is over in 1989. Good analysis of domestic civil-military dynamics.

6492 Simposium Internacional sobre Derechos Humanos, *Santiago, 1978.* La Iglesia y la dignidad del hombre: sus derechos y deberes en el mundo de hoy. Santiago: Arzobispado de Santiago, Vicaría de la Solidaridad, 1978. 106 p.: bibl., ill. (Estudios; 4)

Result of international conference held under auspices of Archdiocese of Santiago. Spokesmen include Arns from Brazil, Methodist Bishop Bonino (Uruguay), Executive Secretary of Commission on Human Rights of the OAS, William Thompson of the US National Council of Churches, and others. Indicates political force of the Chilean Church in international arena under Pinochet regime.

6493 Smith, Brian H. The Church and politics in Chile: challenges to modern Catholicism. Princeton, N.J.: Princeton Univ. Press, 1982. 383 p.: bibl., index.

Study of the Chilean Catholic Church and its atypical evolution, probably designed as a case study. Impressive as a meticulous, empirical analysis of a microcosm, the Church in a modern society. It is, however, also "universal" in its analysis of the Church in a Third World context. Smith's work constitutes a monumental contribution on the subject and should be read by all Latin Americanists and most certainly by students of Chile. Analysis with a clear perspective based on massive data.

6494 Temas socialistas. Edición de Eduardo Ortiz. Santiago: Vector, Centro de Estudios Económicos y Sociales, 1983. 190 p.: bibl., ill. (Serie Ediciones especiales)

Compilation of articles on the activities of the now moribund Chilean Socialist Party stresses its intellectual and political life under the military.

6495 Valenzuela, Arturo. Chile's political instability (CUH, 83:490, Feb. 1984, p. 68–72, 88)

Sees waning of support for Pinochet regime after decade of rule. Although opposition parties and groups face many difficulties, an opposition does survive. Both support for and opposition to regime depends on the military itself which remains dedicated to "order" but is not sufficiently politicized at this time. Implication is that a politicized military may very well spell problems for present government. Good treatment of Chilean dilemma through fall of 1984.

6496 Vergara, Pilar. Autoritarismo y cambios estructurales en Chile. Santiago: Facultad Latinoamericana de Ciencias Sociales (FLACSO), 1981. 63 p.: bibl. (Documento de trabajo; 132)

Analysis of economic change under Pinochet indicates that Chile's economy is in process of changing from an orthodox State-controlled capitalist mode to one more easily penetrated by world capitalism via a slow dismantling of State economic controls.

6497 Volk, Steven. The lessons and legacy of a dark decade (NACLA, 17:5, Sept./Oct. 1983, p. 2–14, ill.)

Study deals with Pinochet's "second war," one aimed at a radical restructuring of the economy, political system, and socioeconomic behavior of Chile's population. Cites US government as regime's major prop and deindustrialization as most important trend in new economic order.

6498 Zemelman, Hugo and **Jorge Arrate.** El Partido Socialista de Chile: ¿recuperación o renovación de su identidad? (NSO, 65, marzo/abril 1983, p. 18–26, plates)

On 50th anniversary of the founding of Chile's Socialist Party, author sees it as reformulating its ideas and mass-based organization to meet needs of a post-Pinochet society.

ARGENTINA, PARAGUAY, AND URUGUAY

GARY W. WYNIA, *Professor of Political Science, Carleton College*

THE PAUCITY OF SCHOLARLY works on the politics of the Southern Cone is finally coming to an end. This is especially true in Argentina where liberty was restored in 1983, allowing the publication of many works that had been kept off the presses during the military's rule. Equally impressive is the appearance of new publishers, among them the Editorial de Belgrano which began issuing social science monographs in earnest in 1982, and the Centro Editor de América Latina, a prolific little operation run by the people who directed the EUDEBA national university press in the early 1960s before they were expelled from it by Gen. Onganía in 1966. Their aim is the mass circulation of small volumes on Argentine history and contemporary politics written by scholars and journalists; in one series alone they have published over 70 books in just two years, all of them put on sale at newstands as well as in bookstores.

The subjects of inquiry during the past two years are quite diverse. Among them are new studies of the Peronist government in 1973–76 (items **6510, 6516,** and **6523**), and analyses of the military regime just ended, most of which concentrate on its economic rather than political failures including a couple of excellent studies of liberalization policies (items **6537** and **6542**). The Falkland/Malvinas War has also attracted attention, though more from journalists than scholars who are not yet permitted access to the files of those who directed the war from London and Buenos Aires. The best of the lot is a volume by three *Clarín* reporters (item **6508**) who chronicled the decisions made by the country's commanders in 1981 and 1982. Especially popular within Argentina are several volumes of tales told by soldiers involved in the combat (item **6520**). The war and the conflict with Chile over islands in the Beagle Channel renewed interest in foreign policy, and among recent works are new histories of postwar policy (item **7295**), critiques of the country's geopolitical obsessions (item **7283**), and concerns for its nuclear technology (item **6541**). For more on the Falkland/Malvinas War, see the International Relations section in this volume (p. 620–625).

Studies of the 1983 election which restored democracy to the country and catapulted Radical Raúl Alfonsín into the presidency are only beginning to be written (items **6499** and **6504**). In short, a new era has begun in Argentina, one in which interest in politics is heightened by its being practiced by civilian politicians again. If they are allowed to continue unmolested, a growing cadre of young scholars are certain to raise the quantity and quality of scholarship on the subject in the next few years.

With only a few exceptions, scholars continue to stay away from Stroessner's Paraguay, and the best that is available are updates on political events there (item **6545**), and introductory works for classroom use (item **6544**). Uruguay will undoubtedly attract more attention in the days ahead now that democracy is being restored there, starting with elections in 1985, the first held in over a decade. Meanwhile, study of the Tupamaros (item **6546**) and the military's take-over in the early 1970s (item **6550**) continue to be written.

What is conspicuously missing from recent scholarships on the Southern Cone are new theories on the region's politics or additional insights into old ones. For example, "dependency" attracts less attention now than it did a few years ago, especially among Argentines who seem more interested in studying the particulars of their country's politics than in theorizing about it on a grand scale as they did after "bureaucratic authoritarianism" was invented in 1966. Theorizing will never disappear, fortunately, but we should not expect much of it for a while. In the meantime, we stand to gain from intimate looks at politics by the scholars who are closest to it.

ARGENTINA

6499 Abos, Alvaro. Las organizaciones sindicales y el poder militar: 1976–1983. Buenos Aires: Centro Editor de América Latina, 1984. 150 p.

Another in the more than 60 books published by Centro Editor during 1983–84 on recent Argentine political history. In this one we learn how organized labor responded to its repression by the Videla regime after the peronist government was overthrown in 1976. Narrative relies heavily on summations of documents issued by authorities and labor leaders.

6500 Acuña, Marcelo Luis. De Frondizi a Alfonsín: la tradición política del Radicalismo. v. 1–2. Buenos Aires: Centro Editor de América Latina, 1984. 2 v. (281 p.): bibl. (Biblioteca Política argentina; 48–49)

Originally written as a doctoral dissertation at York Univ. in Canada, this is the most detailed history in print on the life of the Radical Party during past two decades. Timing of its publication could not have been better, for in the process of tracing party's decline and defeat by peronists in 1973 and its aftermath, it documents rise of Raúl Alfonsín and his dissident movement within the party and his defeat of the old guard prior to 1983 elections.

6501 Balbín, Ricardo. Discursos parlamentarios-políticos. Recopilación y selección efectuada por Carlos Alberto Giacobone. Buenos Aires: Ediciones Adelante, 1982. 171 p.

Ricardo Balbín, leader of largest wing of the Radical Party from 1950s until his death in 1981, was known less for his political profundity than his political dexterity. This is a collection of the speeches made during 1940s while serving as member of Congress when Perón was president. Obviously a useful source of information for students of that era and the Radical Party.

6502 Balbín, un caudillo, un ideal. Coordinador de la obra, Carlos Alberto Quirós. Ricardo Balbín et al. Buenos Aires: Editorial Abril, 1982. 224 p.: ill. (Suplemento no. 8 de la revista Siete Días)

After Radical Party leader Ricardo Balbín died in 1981, his colleagues published this vol. of his speeches and added essays written by other Radicals, peronist rivals, and journalists. A solid tribute and resource for students of recent Radical politics.

6503 Bittel, Deolindo F. Qué es el peronismo. Buenos Aires: Editorial Sudamericana, 1983. 264 p.: appendix, bibl., ill., plates (Col. de los partidos políticos nacionales)

As elections approached in late 1983, each political party was asked to prepare an explanation of its purpose and ideology. This is one of the series that resulted. Peronist Deolindo Bittel writes a brief history of the peronist movement and outlines a platform for the post-Perón era. Appendix includes a chronology of movement's history (35 p.).

6504 Borrini, Alberto. Como se hace un presidente. Buenos Aires: Ediciones El Cronista Comercial, 1984. 258 p.

Political campaigns are infrequent in Argentina and studies of them even rarer. None was more intriguing than the one conducted in 1983 that led to Radical Raúl Alfonsín's upset of peronist Italo Luder in the presidential race. Reasons for his triumph are many, but journalist Borrini suggests that one of the most important was the Radicals' sophisticated use of mass media. The study examines techniques and media expenses of all major parties in 1983 campaign.

Bray, Arturo. Armas y letras: memorias. See HLAS 46:3379.

6505 Buchanan, Paul. State corporatism in Argentina: labor administration under Perón and Onganía (LARR, 20:1, 1985, p. 61–95)

Examines means used by authorities to control organized labor and compares peronist (1945–66) and military (1966–79) governments. Evidence that methods were different in each case is not all that surprising, given their contrasting political objectives, but article is nevertheless informative because of data it offers on official Labor Ministry and its relations with labor movement's bureaucracy.

6506 Camps, Ramón Juan Alberto. Caso Timerman: punto final. Buenos Aires: Tribuna Abierta, 1982. 227 p.: ill.

Gen. Ramón J.A. Camps was Police Chief of Buenos Aires prov. when several thousand Argentines were arrested and killed in late 1970s. Here he attempts to justify kidnapping and torture of journalist Jacobo Timerman. Much of the work is composed of what he says are transcripts of Timerman's testimony and investigations of the financing of the Montonero movement by David Graiver, an acquaintance of Timerman.

6507 ———. El poder en la sombra: el Affaire Graiver. Buenos Aires: RO.CA. Producciones, 1983. 246 p., 8 p. of plates: ill.

The so-called "Graiver Affair" remains a source of controversy in Argentina. Military officers who conducted the anti-terrorist campaign of late 1970s claim that the wealthy Graiver brothers helped finance terrorist organizations like the Montoneros. Apparently, the military killed the Graivers as they did

9,000 others. Others deny the connection. In this vol., one of those officers, Ramón J.A. Camps, Police Chief of Buenos Aires prov., attempts to document his charges against the Graivers.

6508 Cardoso, Oscar R.; R. Kirschbaum; and E. van der Kooy. Malvinas: la trama secreta. Buenos Aires: Editorial Sudamericana: Planeta, 1983. 366 p.: ill. (Col. Espejo de la Argentina)

Three journalists from the Buenos Aires daily *Clarín* offer a fascinating account of the decisions that went into the planning and waging 1982 Falkland/Malvinas Islands War. Drawn from interviews with officials in Argentina, London, and Washington, narrative offers new insights into the behavior of officials in the Galtieri administration. An example of investigative journalism at its best, and Argentines' appreciation of it is evident in the sale of 14 separate printings during the first nine months after book's publication. Essential reading for students of the conflict.

6509 Carranza, Mario Esteban. The role of military expenditure in the development process: the Argentine case, 1946/1980 (NOSALF/IA, 12:1/2, 1983, p. 115–166, tables)

Were it not for the abundance of tables with data on military expenditures over a 35-yr. period, article would hardly be worth consulting. Analysis is weak and confined to describing basic data, but provides a valuable source of difficult-to-find information on military budgets in Argentina.

6510 Cavarozzi, Marcelo. Autoritarismo y democracia: 1955–1983. Buenos Aires: Centro Editor de América Latina, 1983. 143 p.: appendix, bibl. (Biblioteca Política argentina; 21)

Collection of presidential addresses, interviews, and other political documents from past two decades prefaced by an 80-p. essay on Argentine politics during 1955–83 period. Suggests that the dynamic of Argentine politics changed after 1966 when the military took it upon itself to rule the country after a decade of unsuccessful experiments with rigged democracies. Also points to Argentines' tolerance of autocratic government as one of its primary causes.

6511 Censo nacional de población y vivienda, 1980. Serie B., Características generales. v. 1–26. Buenos Aires: Ministerio de Economía, Hacienda y Finanzas, Subsecretaría de Programación Económica, Instituto Nacional de Estadística y Censos, Comité Ejecutivo Nacional del Centro, 1982. 26 v. in 27: maps, tables.

It is a shame that only demographers get excited by census data, for there is much in them that everyone should study. This Argentine 1980 census is a case in point. It tells us much about how Argentina changed during past two decades. As Argentine officials who have examined data are discovering, more Argentines are poor now than a decade ago, and fewer are as literate as was previously believed.

Ciria, Alberto. Flesh and fantasy: the many faces of Evita and Juan Perón. See *HLAS 46:3204.*

———. Política y cultura popular: la Argentina peronista, 1946–1955. See *HLAS 46:3205.*

6512 Clementi, Hebe. Juventud y política en la Argentina. Buenos Aires: Ediciones Siglo Veinte, 1982. 155 p.

Historian examines participation of youth movements in Argentine politics during first half of this century. In this largely narrative account, she examines univ. reforms of 1920s, nationalist, socialist and communist movements, and role young party dissidents played in the Radical Party during 1930s.

6513 ———. El radicalismo, nudos gordianos de la economía. Buenos Aires: Ediciones Siglo Veinte, 1982. 201 p.

Radicals Hipólito Yrigoyen and Marcelo de T. Alvear occupied Argentine presidency between 1916–30, but there remains substantial dispute over what they contributed to country's economic reform. Although Clementi does not resolve them, she does document Radical policies on the three most important issues of that time: railways, beef production, and petroleum development, demonstrating how Radical governments sustained a process already well underway with policies aimed at advancing growth in each of these three areas. Most important, includes copies of documents like the *Roca-Runciman Treaty* and legislation restructuring the financial system during 1930s.

6514 Compilación cronológica de los Presidentes, Vice-Presidentes de la Nación Argentina, Ministros de Hacienda, de Economía, Secretarios de Estado de Haciendo y/o Finanzas, Secretarios de Estado de Programación y Coordinación Económica y sus respectivos Subsecretarios, 1854–1978. v. 1–2. Buenos Aires: Ministerio de Economía, Hacienda y Finanzas, Depto. Biblioteca, 1981. 2 v.: facsims.

Valuable reference work for historians and other students of Argentine government if only because it lists in chronological order all of nation's finance and economics ministers and prominent decrees defining their authority from the constitutional republic's founding in 1854 until 1978. Strictly an official document which attempts no narrative on performance of these governments.

6515 Decker, David R. The political, economic, and labor climate in Argentina. Philadelphia: Industrial Research Unit, Wharton School, Univ. of Pennsylvania, 1983. 131 p.: bibl., ill., index, tables (Multinational industrial relations series, 0149–0818; 4. Latin American studies; 4f)

Handy little book that supplies basic information on structure of Argentine economy and data on labor law and union organizations. Though brief and superficial, an up-to-date reference work.

6516 Di Tella, Guido. Argentina under Perón, 1973–76: the nation's experience with a labour-based government. New York: St. Martin's Press, 1983. 246 p.: bibl., index.

Di Tella has written the most complete economic study of the last Peronist regime yet available. Examines regime chronologically and methodically, interpreting behavior of Juan Perón, Isabel, and their colleagues. Most important, traces economic policies from phase to phase, demonstrating how the government tried but failed to prevent deterioration into one of the nation's worst crises in 1976. Concludes that despite Peron's death and party's deterioration, peronism will remain prominent in national politics for some time to come.

Escude, Carlos. La Argentina: ¿paria internacional? See item **7283**.

6517 Frondizi, Arturo. Qué es el Movimiento de Integración y Desarrollo. Buenos Aires: Editorial Sudamericana, 1983. 279 p.

One in a series of vols. on and by Argentina's political parties written to inform electorate of their platforms before 1983 election. Here ex-President Frondizi discusses his MID Party, one that has always received more attention because of his leadership than it merits from its very small support in the electorate.

Gillespie, Richard. Armed struggle in Argentina. See *HLAS 46:3254*.

6518 El Interrogatorio: Galtieri, Anaya, Menéndez y Costa Méndez (Gente [Buenos Aires] 959, 8 dic. 1983, p. 4–34, 68–95, ill.)

Secrecy is the way of life of Argentine armed forces in peace as well as war, so we know little about what they really believe they are doing. Never more so than when they invaded the Falkland/Malvinas Islands and fought a losing battle to retain them. Investigations were undertaken within armed forces after the defeat and testimony from its perpetrators was taken. Thanks to *Gente* magazine, we can now read some of their self-defenses. President Leopoldo Galtieri tells why he thought his invasion would bring a diplomatic settlement rather than war, Foreign Minister Nicanor Costa Méndez blames British for failure to reach a peaceful settlement after invasion, and Gen. Mario Benjamín Menéndez, Commander of the Argentine Army of Occupation, laments the inadequate support he received from Galtieri when forced to fight a war. Many of the explanations given by Galtieri and his colleagues are unconvincing; nevertheless, their testimony offers a close look at military minds at work, revealing their simplicity as well as misplaced patriotism.

6519 Jenkins, Rhys. The rise and fall of the Argentine motor vehicle industry (*in* Political economy of the Latin American motor vehicle industry. Edited by Rich Kronish and Kenneth S. Mericle. Cambridge: MIT Press, 1984, p. 41–73, tables)

Many of Argentina's economic dilemmas and their adverse consequences are evident in the performance of its automobile industry as this excellent history demostrates. Examines industry's growth during 1960s and roles government promotion and foreign capital played in its development. Perhaps most revealing is a comparison with Brazil whose automobile industry was much like Argentina's for a time until greater concentration of capital, through the efforts of Volkswagen, raised productivity in Brazil while its decline in Argentina left industry there operating at low capacity and high cost.

6520 Kon, Daniel. Los Chicos de la guerra: hablan los soldados que estuvieron en Malvinas. Buenos Aires: Editorial Galerna, 1982. 222 p.

When troops returned from their defeat in the Malvinas Islands, Argentines were eager to learn about their travails, so enterprising journalists immediately went to work interviewing soldiers and officers. This is one of many books that resulted. Offers close look at what it was like to wait for and fight the British as they invaded the islands. Through the words of eight soldiers, we learn of their anxieties, heroism, and defeat.

6521 Kuhl, Livio Guillermo; Horacio R. Rieznik; Rodolfo E. Biasca; and Roberto Iglesias. Una política industrial para la Argentina. Buenos Aires: Editorial Club de Estudio, 1983. 951 p.: tables.

Team of economists previously associated with Industry Secretariat of the Ministry of Economy recently published this encyclopedic study of nation's economy. Filled with aggregate data on resources, production and trade, as well as comparisons of Argentina's industrial performance in recent times with those of countries like Mexico and Brazil, vol. is a valuable resource for anyone interested in understanding Argentine economy: past, present, and future. Data on nearly every aspect of economy is provided as are close examinations of particular industries.

Lanús, Juan Archibaldo. De Chapultepec al Beagle: política exterior argentina, 1945–1980. See item **7295**.

6522 López Saavedra, Emiliana. Apelación a la democracia. Entrevistas con Raúl Alfonsín et al. Buenos Aires: Editorial Redacción, 1983. 187 p.

Fifteen interviews completed before political party conventions in mid-1983 with party leaders, several of whom would become presidential nominees. Among them are Radicals Raúl Alfonsín, Ricardo Balbín, and Fernando de la Rúa, and peronists Italo Luder, Antonio Cafiero, and Miguel Angel Robledo. Valuable document for students of 1983 election.

6523 Maceyra, Horacio. Cámpora/Perón/ Isabel. Buenos Aires: Centro Editor de América Latina, 1983. 167 p.: bibl. (Biblioteca Política argentina; 25)

Already more is written about the economics of Perón's last government than its politics. This little book offers a narrative that helps right the balance. Essential, if elementary, history of this rather complicated three-yr. experience with peronist government.

6524 Moncalvillo, Mona. Reportajes de humor. Buenos Aires: Ediciones de la Urraca, 1983. 556 p.: ill.

Collection of rich, diverse, and frank interviews conducted by journalist Moncalvillo for the prominent *Humor* magazine (1982–83). Among those interviewed are Radicals Raúl Alfonsín and Arturo Illia, peronist politicians Italo Luder and Antonio Cafiero, novelists Ernesto Sábato and Mario Vargas Llosa, and human rights activist and Nobel Prize winner Adolfo Pérez Esquivel. Fascinating cross-section of prominent personalities.

6525 Mora y Araujo, Manuel. El ciclo político argentino (IDES/DE, 22:86, julio/sept. 1982, p. 203–230, bibl., chart, graph)

Essay in political theory that argues against the more deterministic, structural interpretations of Argentine politics. Stresses failures of political elites and armed forces to cope effectively with each other and with limited options before them when they govern. Author's argument is cumbersome and not drawn together in a conclusion, but each pt. is valuable in itself.

6526 O'Donnell, Guillermo. Notas para el estudio de procesos de democratización política a partir del Estado burocrático-autoritario (IDES/DE, 22:86, julio/sept. 1982, p. 231–248)

Written originally in 1978, essay offers

a host of speculations about how democracy might be restored after the termination of the then well established bureaucratic authoritarian regimes in Argentina and Brazil. Draws some lessons from Spanish, Greek and Turkish experiences, and in a postscript added in 1982, argues that democratic government will be most feasible way out of the bureaucratic-authoritarian regime since a more radical government would only provoke further military intervention.

6527 Oszlak, Oscar. La conquista del orden político y la formación histórica del Estado argentino. Buenos Aires: Centro de Estudios de Estado y Sociedad (CEDES), 1982. 72 p.: bibl. (Estudios CEDES; 4:2)

Contending that it was formation of the Argentine State in 19th century and its supervision of society during boom yrs. that made Argentina so bountiful, Argentine political scientist Oszlak documents growth of Argentine government, focusing on the development of its repressive capacity, its cooptation of prominent forces in society, and its economic penetration throughout the nation. By contemporary standards the Argentine State was actually quite weak, yet as author points out, the nation was held together in its early yrs. as much by its government as by its oligarchy.

6528 Pérez Esquivel, Adolfo. Christ in a poncho: testimonials of the non-violent struggles in Latin America. Edited by Charles Antoine. Translated from the French by Robert R. Barr. Maryknoll, N.Y.: Orbis Books, 1983. 139 p.: bibl.

Contains background information and talks by Argentine Nobel Peace Prize winner Adolfo Pérez Esquivel. Reader can obtain a fair representation of his philosophy and activities. [R.A. Camp]

6529 Perón, Juan Domingo. Doctrina peronista. Buenos Aires: Editora Volver, 1982. 365 p.

Before 1983 elections, the Peronist Party published collections of statements and speeches by Juan Perón from early 1940s until his death in 1974. One of many such vols. published.

6530 ———. Manual de adoctrinamiento peronista: materias fundamentales y básicas: apuntes doctrinarios para una historia del peronismo. 2a ed. Buenos Aires: Editora Volver, 1983. 398 p.

Most recent ed. of excerpts from Peronist Party documents that define its principal positions on matters such as capitalism and communism and on objectives of the movement as created by Juan Perón during his first presidency. Without intending to do so, its editors have documented many ambiguities and contradictions in party's ideology.

6531 Peronismo y dictadura. Recopilación de Deolindo F. Bittel. Buenos Aires: Editora del Movimiento Nacional Justicialista, 1983. 167 p.

Collection of statements and documents issued by peronist movement while armed forces governed Argentina (1976–83). Includes movement positions on human rights, economic liberalization, and the 1982 Falkland/Malvinas War.

6532 El Poder militar en la Argentina, 1976–1981: aspectos históricos y sociopolíticos. Peter Waldmann y Ernesto Garzón Valdés, comps. Dante Caputo et al. Frankfurt, FRG: Vervuert, 1982. 220 p.: bibl. (Editionen der Iberoamericana. Reihe III, Monographien und Aufsätze; 10)

Pub. in West Germany two yrs. before Argentine military allowed new democratic elections, this is a collection of very diverse papers delivered at conference (Univ. of Augsberg, 1981) by German, Argentine, and North American scholars. Topics range from immigration at the turn of the century to interpretations of military behavior in 1970s, and recent Argentine foreign policy. Among the authors is Dante Caputo, appointed Foreign Minister by President Raúl Alfonsín in 1983.

6533 Remmer, Karen L. Party competition in Argentina and Chile: political recruitment and public policy, 1890–1930. Lincoln: Univ. of Nebraska Press, 1984. 1 v.: bibl., index.

By focusing on the emergence of modern political parties in Chile and Argentina at end of 19th century, author attempts to demonstrate how party development affected power struggles in both countries. Substantial analysis of party governments and public policies during first three decades of this century reveal contrasts between patterns of party development in the two countries, most notably the suddenness of change in Argentina and its adverse effects on democratic government. An informative work, though the conclusion that the consolidation of democratic institutions depends on "their acceptability to the propertied and powerful" is no revelation.

6534 Riz, Liliana de. Retorno y derrumbe. México: Folios Ediciones, 1981. 151 p.: bibl., index (Col. América Latina; AL 1)

Brief but informative analysis of last peronist regime which attempts to demonstrate how conflicts among major social forces tore apart the populist regime after Perón's death in 1974.

Romero, José Luis. El drama de la democracia argentina. See *HLAS 46:3336.*

6535 Schoultz, Lars. The populist challange: Argentine electoral behavior in the postwar era. Chapel Hill: Univ. of North Carolina Press, 1983. 141 p.: bibl., ill., index (James Sprunt studies in history and political science; 58)

Using aggregate data, votes in Argentine elections (1946–73), and multivariate regression statistical techniques, Schoultz searches for sources of support for the peronist party. Not surprisingly, finds most of it among working class; at the same time, demonstrates that as much as one third of it comes from middle class as well, especially people in small businesses and government employees. Perhaps study's greatest value is its research design which illustrates what one can accomplish in the study of electoral behavior in countries like Argentina where substantial data is available.

6536 Schvarzer, Jorge. Argentina, 1976–81: el endeudamiento externo como pivote de la especulación financiera. Buenos Aires: Centro de Investigaciones Sociales sobre el Estado y la Administración, 1983. 61 p.: bibl., tables (Cuadernos del bimestre; 1)

Brief but perceptive essay examines causes of financial crisis that resulted from the military's economic liberalization measures in 1979 and 1980 and documents the indebtedness that resulted from it.

6537 ———. Martínez de Hoz: la lógica política de la política económica. Buenos Aires: Centro de Investigaciones Sociales sobre el Estado y la Administración, 1983. 157 p.: tables (Ensayos y tesis CISEA; 4)

Brief but informative monograph that dissects and criticizes economic program

followed in Argentina (1976–81). Stresses obstacles to economic liberalization and mismanagement of financial policies. Essential reading for anyone who wants to understand why military regimes seldom succeed in their efforts to discipline the Argentine economy using market mechanisms.

6538 Sebreli, Juan José. Los deseos imaginarios del peronismo: ensayo crítico. Buenos Aires: Editorial Legasa, 1983. 213 p.

Essayist Sebreli, known for his iconoclasism, tries hard in this vol. to supply evidence to support Marxist contention that when peronism began it was more bourgeois than proletarian and more fascist than populist. Data is too selective and self-serving to settle the matter, but he does renew concern about the true ideological and political nature of this ambiguous but powerful Argentine invention.

6539 Sindicalismo y regímenes militares en Argentina y Chile. Coordinación, Bernardo Gallitelli y Andrés A. Thompson. Amsterdam: CEDLA, 1982. 330 p.: bibl., ill. (CEDLA incidentele publicaties; 25)

Collection of papers given at the Center for Latin American Studies and Documentation (Amsterdam, 1981). They document repression of labor organizations by military governments in post-1973 Chile and post-1976 Argentina. Data is supplied on labor conflicts before and after the coups, trends in wage rates, and tactics used by military governments to weaken mass movements. Authors are English, Argentine, and Chilean.

6540 Sonntag, Gabriela. Eva Perón: books, articles, and other sources of study; an annotated bibliography. Madison, Wis.: SALALM, 1983. 54 p.: ill. (Bibl. series; 7)

Sonntag has put together a lengthy, annotated bibl. on Eva Perón, which describes 130 books and 232 articles. It is an excellent source of information for students of peronism and modern Argentine history.

6541 Spector, Leonard S. Nuclear proliferation today. New York: Vintage Books, 1984. 478 p.: bibl., index, maps.

In this study sponsored by the Carnegie Endowment, author brings us up to date on nuclear industries and weapons production capacities in several Third World nations. Of interest to students of Latin

America are lengthy chaps. on Argentina and Brazil that provide substantial detail on their respective nuclear technologies and plans for further development.

Winston, Colin M. Between Rosas and Sarmiento: notes on nationalism in peronist thought. See *HLAS 46:3374.*

6542 Wogart, Jan Peter. Combining price stabilization with trade and financial liberalization policies: the Argentine experience, 1976–1981 (SAGE/JIAS, 25:4, Nov. 1983, p. 445–476)

Economist at World Bank takes close look at so-called liberalization program pursued by Minister of Economy Martínez de Hoz under military goverment that ruled Argentina in late 1970s. Makes no effort to criticize program, but does provide an excellent summary of it and its effects, certainly the most informative available in English. Moreover, includes an abundance of data on performance of agriculture, industry, banking as well as foreign trade and borrowing. For economist's comment, see item 3730.

PARAGUAY

6543 Kharitonov, Vitali̇i Aleksandrovich. Paraguay, dictadura militar-policial y lucha de clases. Traducción, Zoila Victoria Carneado. La Habana: Editorial de Ciencias Sociales, 1980. 283 p.: bibl. (Política)

Polemical history of Paraguay written not only to condemn Stroessner dictatorship for its misdeeds but also to reeducate members of Paraguay's Communist Party whom Soviet author believes have a major role to play in liberating the country. More valuable as a history of Paraguay's Communist Party than of Paraguay itself.

6544 Lewis, Paul H. Socialism, liberalism, and dictatorship in Paraguay. New York: Praeger; Stanford, Calif.: Hoover Institution Press, 1982. 154 p.: bibl., index, map (Politics in Latin America)

Little book consists of an introduction to the country and its recent politics by Paraguay specialist Paul Lewis. Pt. of a monographic series of country studies sponsored by Hoover Institution.

Volta Gaona, Enrique. La revolución del 47. See *HLAS 46:3406.*

6545 Williams, John Hoyt. Stroessner's Paraguay (CUH, 82:481, Feb. 1983, p. 66–68)

Brings one up to date on events in Paraguay up to early 1983.

URUGUAY

6546 Actas tupamaras: una experiencia de guerrilla urbana. Madrid: Editorial Revolución, 1982. 254 p. (Revolución; 10)

Fascinating vol. has no single author. Pub. in Madrid, preface states that it was compiled from recollections of members of the Tupamaro urban guerrillas who fought and lost in Uruguay in early 1970s. Over a dozen of their operations (i.e., robberies, kidnappings, and attacks against government institutions) are recounted. Though each is quite brief, together they offer a valuable basic source for students of the movement and of guerrilla warfare.

6547 Araujo, Ana María. Tupamaras. Paris: Des Femmes, 1980. 280 p.: bibl. (Pour chacune; 31)

A unique commentary: a feminist critique of Uruguayan society that focuses on the Tupamaros and the women who were part of this guerrilla movement.

6548 Castellanos, Alfredo and **Romeo Pérez.** El pluralismo: examen de la experiencia uruguaya, 1830–1918. Montevideo: Centro Latinoamericano de Economía Humana (CLAEH), 1981. 2 v. (251 p.): bibl. (Serie Investigaciones; 14–15)

In this examination of Uruguayan political history during the 19th century, authors trace development of political parties and government institutions. Unfortunately, rather than interpreting events, authors list quotations from newspapers during relevant periods. Nevertheless, the paucity of material on the topic makes it a useful resource.

6549 González, Luis E. Uruguay, 1980–1981: an unexpected opening (LARR, 19:3, 1983, p. 63–76)

Here we have a much needed interpretation of the Uruguayan electorate's rejection of the ruling military's proposed constitution in a plebiscite in 1980. Article is brief and its findings hardly profound, but with the aid of Gallup poll data, supports contention that opposition to the military spread across all social and political sectors, as did the vote, except for absence of the extreme left from the latter.

Jacob, Raúl. Benito Nardone: el ruralismo hacia del poder, 1945–1958. See *HLAS* 46:3424.

6550 Jellinek, Sergio. Uruguay, a pilot study of transition from representative democracy to dictatorship. Stockholm: Institute of Latin American Studies, 1980. 85 p.: bibl., ill. (Occasional papers)

Well informed occasional paper in which author traces "breakdown" of democracy in Uruguay in early 1970s. Argues that it resulted from a series of political ruptures rather than from any sudden breakdown or convulsion. Argument is simplistic and underdeveloped.

6551 Prieto, Rubén Gerardo. Trabajadores rurales y proceso revolucionario: un ejemplo concreto, UTAA, Unión de Trabajadores Azucareros de Artigas, y el MNLT, Movimiento Nacional de Lucha por la Tierra: Uruguay, 1961–1972. Stockholm: Instituto de Estudios Latinoamericanos, 1979. 64 p.: bibl. (Occasional papers)

Another in a lengthy series of papers on contemporary Uruguayan politics issued by Stockholm's Institute of Latin American Studies. Author here offers a detailed analysis of rural labor movements during 1960s. Argues that even though a "revolutionary mentality" does not yet exist among most Uruguayan rural laborers, there exists a potential for revolutionary protest.

BRAZIL

MARGARET J. SARLES, *Research Associate, University of Maryland, College Park*

IS A NEW FORM OF DEMOCRACY arising in Brazil? While scholars ponder the "redemocratization" of regimes across the continent, the literature on Brazilian politics suggests that the country will never return to the pre-1964 form of democracy. In general, works annotated below can be divided into two groups. The first analyzes the past, particularly the political turmoil of *abertura*, and the possibilities—or lack of them—of developing a true political democracy. The second documents specific changes in the late 1970s and early 1980s. The former writings are often more scholarly and analytic, adopt a national perspective, and many focus on the post-1974 governments. The latter as a group are atheoretical, concentrate on local or sectoral activities, and are exemplified by case studies, state development plans, and national decentralization plans. However, they document cases of grassroots and state activity and show a system developing that is not "guided from above" by either the clientelist politics which traditionally characterized rural Brazil or the ideological and charismatic leadership that mobilized urban workers in the early 1960s. In both cases, edited volumes and collections of previously published works abound.

In the first category of national, largely retrospective studies, two of the best works are Helio Jaguaribe's article on populism, authoritarianism, and democracy (item **6564**), which presents a skeptical view of Brazil's ability to implant a democracy in an unequal social structure, and Simon Schwartzman's analysis of the roots of patrimonialism (item **6579**). Authoritarianism and statism are the objects of additional studies by Tavares (item **6582**), Martins (item **6572**), and Guimarães (item **6563**). On a less theoretical plane, Benevides's work on the democratic/authoritarian ambivalence in the UDN (item **6620**) and a study of Jânio Quadros (item **6622**) illustrate how these elements have played out in recent politics.

The single best overview of the post-1964 military period is a collection of articles which analyzes changes in political institutions and social forces over a 20-year period (item **6581**). The day-to-day political control exercised by the military has also been a focus of study. Several works analyze the restricted areas of press maneuverability: Chagas (item **6585**), Nunes (item **6587**), and *Os Debates* . . . (item **6586**). The National Union of Students (UNE), revived legally in 1979, has published interesting accounts by each UNE president of government repression (item **6589**). The "party fidelity" law (item **6621**) and the 1982 electoral "package" engineered by the government (item **6570**) illustrate the military's bargaining tactics in party and electoral politics. Two thoughtful attempts to summarize the entire range of mechanisms available to the government, as well as the limits of dissent, have been written by Moreira Alves (item **6553**) and Dale Krane (item **6566**). As a group, these works provide a fairly complete view of how the military government operated in its non-coercive aspects.

The literature focuses on the emergence of new political forces in the post-1974 governments. Perhaps the best is Krischke's edited volume (item **6556**) which compiles some of the most outstanding (already published) articles of the period by some of Brazil's most renowned political analysts. The articles in Trindade's edited volume (item **6557**) may be equally good; they are more closely focused on the choices to be made in supporting agriculture, labor, and other sectors. Kucinski's book is important as the only chronological overview of the entire *abertura* period (item **6567**), as is Tavares's essay linking Brazil's economic model to political change in this period (item **6582**). There are also many collections of newspaper columns, interviews, and published essays which concentrate on *abertura* (items **6560, 6561, 6570, 6574, 6575,** and **6577**) from a variety of ideological perspectives.

The second strain of literature on politics is new and exciting, characterized by case studies documenting the rise of pluralism among urban workers, agricultural workers, consumers, and other groups. The studies are of uneven quality, but overall provide compelling evidence of a strong and fundamental shift in the political system.

The literature on the labor movement, for example, argues without exception that unions are becoming more autonomous, and are now a far cry from the "directed unions" supervised by Ministers of Labor since the Vargas era. Interestingly, there is virtually nothing published here on labor's relationship with political parties—in spite of three national "labor parties" vying for labor support—nor on the relationship of unions to other elements of the political system. Rather, the literature is focused inward. José Alvaro Moíses, the most preeminent writer on unions today, has gone farthest in analyzing the participatory nature of the "new unionism" (items **6612, 6619, 6556,** and **6657**). From a more quantified and historical perspective, Maria Almeida has also written an excellent synthesis of changes in and increased mobilization of the labor force (item **6605**). Two well written books of case studies of strikes in the auto industry (items **6607** and **6611**) bolster Moises's basic thesis.

One of the most interesting facets of the increase in local political participation is that it is no longer confined to São Paulo auto factories, or even to urban labor in general. Three outstanding books of case studies document the rise of participatory democracy in rural and non-union settings. CONTAG, the Confederation of Agricultural Workers' Unions, has published detailed studies on protest movements, strikes, and land invasions, particularly among agricultural workers in the Northeast (item **6616**). The Catholic Church's organizational efforts in local communities also appears to be bearing fruit (item **6617**). Overall, the book that best illustrates the growing vitality of pluralism in Brazil today, however, is *Alternativas populares da democracia: Brasil, anos 80* (item **6619**). The case studies here consider not only unions and the Church, but examples from consumer activism and rural *município* democracy. Taken as a group, all of these works argue forcefully that in whatever direction Brazil may turn, it cannot revert back to traditional clientelism or directed mobilization.

From a different perspective, the literature on public administration further bolsters the argument that there is no turning back politically. Of chief importance are the publications from the Ministry of Debureaucratization and Minister Hélio Beltrão (items **6590, 6591,** and **6595**), particularly *Descentralização e liberdade,* in which Beltrão insistently argues that government centralization is incompatible with democracy. There are a spate of administrative plans published by the states (items **6592, 6596, 6597,** and **6598**) which, although poor reading, give a sense of change within state bureaucracies away from traditional bureaucratic patrimonialism towards more professional and participatory state governments.

It is disappointing that with the political party reforms of the 1970s, little has been published on the post-1979 parties, with the exception of the Partido Democrático Republicano (item **6624**). Electoral politics, during a period in which no national elections were held, are completely neglected. In contrast to a weak literature on parties, however, there are two excellent contributions in public policy. Foremost is Evaldo Vieira's *Estado e miséria social no Brasil* (item **6604**) which is the first analytic overview I have seen of changes in social policies. It covers a 30-year time span and relates administrative policies to the larger political system. Such a book has been badly needed. It is one of the best books reviewed here. The second work (item **6601**) focuses on urban policies and planning, with an excellent section on public investment in the context of Brazil's modernization.

As the literature on local participation continues to develop, syntheses are more and more necessary, relating individual changes to systemic ones. The combination of national decentralization on the one hand and local democracy on the other points out the lack of literature to date focusing on state governments. Comparative studies of changes at the state level would be especially useful.

NATIONAL POLITICS

Alimonda, Héctor A. "Paz y administración—"Ordem e Progresso:" notas para un estudio comparativo de los estados oligárquicos argentino y brasileño. See item **8321**.

6552 ———. Reassessing the literature on military intervention (LAP, 11:1, Winter 1984, p. 137–142, bibl.)

Based on 1964 Brazilian coup data, author addresses general problem of military intervention in Latin American political systems. Emphasizes pre-coup preparation and role of US political, diplomatic, and military decision-makers (as in "Operation Brother Sam"). Various "organic elites" within Brazil are included as coalition members with assistance groups representing US. In such cases, a military coup becomes not only inevitable

but successful. Interesting and important contribution. [W.R. Garner]

6553 Alves, Maria Helena Moreira. Mechanisms of social control of military governments in Brazil 1964–80 (*in* Latin American prospects for the 1980s: equity, democratization, and development. Edited by Archibald R.M. Ritter and David H. Pollock. New York: Praeger, 1983, p. 240–303, tables)

Analyzes with good factual detail major mechanisms used by Brazilian military to maintain social control in a "national security" state: laws, repressive apparatus, control of the judiciary, information, unions, and military. Useful study and good basis of comparison with other non-democratic regimes.

6554 Bastos, Eduardo Marcos Chaves; José Nilo Tavares; and Edgar de Godoi da

Mata-Machado. O modelo econômico e político brasileiro: crise e alternativas. Rio de Janeiro: Achiamé, 1983. 140 p.: bibl., ill.

Bastos's compact historical analysis of Brazil's economy, 1956–74, and Tavares thoughtful article linking the economic model to major characteristics of *abertura* are well worth reading. Book is also valuable as it prints the official party platforms of the PP, PDS, PDT, PMDB, PT, and PTB.

6555 Batista, Estanislau Fragoso. Cantata de um anistiado—para depois. São Paulo: Edições Loyola, 1981. 234 p.

Riveting diary of a sergeant innocently caught up in the military rebellions of 1963, imprisoned in 1964, and eventually expelled from armed forces.

6556 Brasil: do "milagre" à "abertura." Paulo J. Krischke, organizador. Paul J. Singer *et al.* São Paulo: Cortez Editora, 1982. 249 p.: bibl., ill.

Classic articles (most already pub.) by well known social scientists on 1972–77 period. Araújo's examination of changes in class structure (particularly in agriculture), Moisés on the labor movement, and Lamounier on São Paulo electoral behavior have excellent empirical data. Other essays are equally impressive. Recommended.

6557 Brasil em perspectiva: dilemas da abertura política. Hélgio Trindade, organizador. Pôrto Alegre: Editora Sulina, 1982. 133 p.: bibl., ill.

A number of distinguished social scientists analyze *abertura* in articles on inherent political dilemmas, alternative economic models, agrarian reform, new unionism, the role of business, 1982 elections. Together, they trace radical changes occurring across nearly all sectors in this period.

6558 Bunker, Stephen G. Policy implementation in an authoritarian State: a case from Brazil (LARR, 18:1, 1983, p. 33–58, bibl.)

Using a bureaucratic-authoritarian framework, Bunker critizes implementation of a major policy of colonization and rural development along the Transamazon Highway, suggesting that the B.-A. model needs to incorporate regional disparities and limited government capacities.

6559 Caminha, João Carlos Gonçalves. Delineamentos da estratégia. Ed. rev. e aum. Rio de Janeiro: Biblioteca do Exército Editora, 1982–1983. 3 v. (Publicação; 524. Col. General Benício; 205–207)

Developed from courses taught at the School of Naval Warfare, this is a revision of a 1974 work. Vol. 1 deals with linkage of war to international relations, vol. 2 with naval strategy and tactics.

6560 Cardoso, Fernando Henrique. Perspectivas: Fernando Henrique Cardoso: idéias e atuação política. Organização, Eduardo P. Graeff. Rio de Janeiro: Paz e Terra, 1983. 216 p.: bibl. (Col. Estudos brasileiros; 70)

Collection of principal newspaper articles by and interviews with Brazil's most celebrated academic/politician that range from his decision to enter electoral politics in 1978 until he became a Senator in 1983, documenting an era of dramatic political change.

6561 Chaves Neto, Elias. Sentido dinâmico de democracia. Apresentação Paulo Sérgio Pinheiro. São Paulo: Brasiliense, 1982. 225 p.: bibl. (Memória política)

Compilation of articles written (1955–64) by Chaves Neto for the *Revista Brasiliense* which he founded; posthumously selected and published. Analyzes Brazil's political turmoil of the period from his vantage point as leader of the Partido Comunista do Brasil.

6562 Figueiredo, Osmar Salles de. Brasil, passado e presente. São Paulo: Editôra Pedagógica e Universitária, 1979. 278 p.: bibl., col. ill. (Col. Kairós)

Undergraduate textbook for a course on "Brazilian Problems," book looks historically at geopolitics and demography, and discusses Brazil's national security doctrine in depth and sympathetically, as well as other social issues.

Gomes, Eduardo Rodrigues. Campo contra cidade: o ruralismo e a crise oligárquica no pensamento político brasileiro, 1910–1935. See *HLAS 46:7627.*

Graham, Richard. Obstacles to re-democratization in Brazil: a historical perspective. See *HLAS 46:3581.*

6563 Guimarães, J.C. de Macedo Soares. Realidade brasileira. Rio de Janeiro: Editôra Nova Fronteira, 1981. 271 p.: bibl.

Based on a well reasoned historical analysis of the political culture of statism in Brazil, Guimarães presents a comprehensive plan for total governmental reorganization: a federative system, district voting, a cabinet selected from the Congress, and radical bureaucratic changes in specific ministries and their policies. Interesting and provocative.

As Idéias políticas no Brasil. See *HLAS* 46:7630.

6564 Jaguaribe, Hélio. Populismo, autoritarismo e democracia, nas presentes condições brasileiras (ECB, 29[8]:11, 1982, p. 175–195)

Studying current "transition to democracy" phase of Brazilian politics, Jaguaribe argues that fundamental problem of democracy in Brazil lies in contradiction between a political culture which legitimizes democracy as the only acceptable form of government and a social structure based on privilege.

6565 John Paul II, *Pope.* Pronunciamentos do Papa no Brasil. Textos apresentados pela Conferência Nacional dos Bispos do Brasil (CNBB). Petrópolis: Vozes, 1980. 289 p.: index.

Carefully organized, with a detailed subject index, book includes all speeches given by Pope John Paul II in his 1980 trip to Brazil.

6566 Krane, Dale. Opposition strategy and survival in praetorian Brazil: 1964–79 (SPSA/JP, 45:1, Feb. 1983, p. 28–63, bibl., tables)

Tests Hirschman's framework of "exit, voice, and loyalty" by analyzing the limits of "safety zones" of vocal dissent and "interest articulation" in Brazil under the military, pointing out strengths and weaknesses of model's explanatory power.

6567 Kucinski, Bernardo. Abertura: a história de uma crise. São Paulo: Brasil Debates, 1982. 168 p.: ill., indexes (Brasil hoje; 5)

Political history of the *abertura* period (1974–80), illustrates its complexity and tentative, back-and-forth nature in presidential and administrative politics, and rise of opposition forces. Factual, well focused, and well written.

6568 Lamounier, Bolívar. 1970 [i.e. Mil neuf cents soixante dix] -1980: structures

sociales, élections et changements politique au Brésil (FDD/NED [Problèmes d'Amérique latine, 65] 4675/4676, 12 juillet 1982, p. 25–36, tables)

Development (through the 1970s) of Brazilian class structure and sociopolitical change is traced by French political scientist at the Univ. of São Paulo. Interesting study with tables that should be of interest for empirical research on the two variables addressed in the study. [W.R. Garner]

6569 Leite, Rogério C. de Cerqueira. Quem tem medo do nacionalismo? São Paulo: Brasiliense, 1983. 76 p.: bibl.

Polemical monograph decrying influence of foreign multinationals and North American consumerism, and arguing that true patriots must be more nationalistic.

6570 Leme, Nelson Paes. 1982 [i.e. Mil novecentos e oitenta e dois], a conquista da democracia. Prefácio de Alceu Amoroso Lima. Rio de Janeiro: Graal, 1982. 107 p. (Col. Tendências; 3)

Good selection of his 1982 political columns from *Tribuna de Imprensa*, focusing on 1982 electoral "package" and other governmental machinations to stay in power. Excellent details on roles of key players.

6571 McDonough, Peter. Repression and representation in Brazil (CUNY/CP, 15:1, Oct. 1982, p. 73–99, tables)

Based on survey data, analysis concludes that elites' support for popular participation in government varies widely but is often lukewarm, and that there is little elite agreement on what should be the characteristics of a Brazilian democratic state.

6572 Martins, Ives Gandra da Silva. O poder. Introdução de Ruy Mesquita. São Paulo: Editôra Saraiva, 1984. 94 p.

Essay on the powers of government (representative, productive, tributary, etc.), arguing the point made more succinctly in Mesquita's introduction: government's heavy intervention in the economy—"estatização"—is a danger to Brazil's democratic institutions.

6573 Nunes, Jorge Fischer. O riso dos torturados: anedotário da guerrilha urbana. Pôrto Alegre: Proletra, 1982. 202 p.: ill.

These memoirs recount Fischer's experience as an active guerrilla and add one more articulate voice to the testimony of tortures, imprisonments, and government-sponsored repression under the military. Well written and unique for its black humor and political cartoons.

Pereira, Luiz Carlos Bresser. Development and crisis in Brazil, 1930–1983. See item **3823.**

6574 Portocarrero, Nilza Pereira da Silva. Vida de uma repórter: fatos e depoimentos políticos. Brasília: s.n., 1981. 179 p.

Author is journalist covering national politics since 1950. Book is a compilation of her major political interviews with Congressional and Senate figures of Geisel and Figueiredo administrations. Topic is national politics.

6575 Prestes, Luis Carlos. Prestes hoje. Rio de Janeiro: Editora Codecri, 1983. 132 p.: ill. (Col. Vivendo política; 05)

Informal and wide-ranging reflections on national and international politics by Brazil's most famous communist. Interesting perceptions on PCB's relationship to Brizzola and other opposition groups, and two speeches on PCB policy.

6576 Ribeiro, Carlos Reinaldo Mendes. Você é socialista: ainda que não saiba. Pôrto Alegre: Mercado Aberto, 1982. 103 p.: ill. (Série Depoimentos; 3)

Comparison of the organization and effects of socialist and capitalist systems, clearly written and in a dogma-free style, is designed to attract readers to proposition that they are born socialists. Ends with a questionnaire which "should verify that we are all socialists."

6577 Santos, Wanderley Guilherme dos. Kantianas brasileiras: a dual-ética da razão política nacional. Rio de Janeiro: Paz e Terra, 1984. 93 p. (Col. Estudos brasileiros; 72)

Satirical articles on Brazilian democracy, constitutional principles, role of the State, national security, etc., add to a rich Brazilian vocabulary of political type-casting (e.g., estatofílicos, instantaneistas). Reprinted from Folha da São Paulo (1979–83).

6578 Schneider, Ronald M. The Brazilian military in politics (in New military politics in Latin America. Edited by Robert Wesson. New York: Praeger, 1982, p. 51–77)

Article is most interesting for its bibli-

ographic review of works by Brazilians on the Brazilian military and for its description of the end of military dependence on foreigners.

6579 Schwartzman, Simon. Bases do autoritarismo brasileiro. Rio de Janeiro: Editôra Campus, 1982. 163 p.: bibl., ill. (Contribuções em ciências sociais; 10)

Complete revision of Schwartzman's earlier São Paulo e o Estado nacional, and greatly improved. His analysis of Brazilian party groups along the dual continuum of restriction/mobilization and cooptation/representation is only one good example of an excellent synthesis of political theory and Brazilian history. Recommended.

6580 Seminário sobre Modelos Alternativos de Representação Política no Brasil, Univ. de Brasília, 1980. Modelos alternativos de representação política no Brasil e Regime eleitoral, 1821–1921. Afonso Arinos et al. Apresentação de José Francisco Paes Landim. Com um apêndice sobre Regime eleitoral, 1821–1921 de Augusto Tavares de Lyra. Brasília: Editôra Univ. de Brasília, 1981. 195 p. (Cadernos da UnB)

Five panels of national politicians and academics discuss, in theoretical framework, topics such as the relationship of political representation in Brazil to juridical theory, to parliamentary debate, to district representation, etc.

6581 Sociedade e política no Brasil pós-64. Organizadores, Bernardo Sorj e Maria Herminia Tavares de Almeida. Sebastião C. Velasco e Cruz et al. São Paulo: Brasiliense, 1983. 261 p.: bibl., ill.

Authors of these nine thoughtful articles have deliberately viewed post-1964 period from a 20-yr. perspective in analyses of parties, armed forces, urbanization, unionization and other major institutions. Soy/Wilkinson study is particularly welcome, given paucity of data and political analysis in agriculture.

6582 Tavares, José Antônio Giusti. A estrutura do autoritarismo brasileiro. Pôrto Alegre: Mercado Aberto, 1982. 181 p.: bibl., ill. (Série Novas perspectivas; 2)

In this revision of his published master's thesis, Tavares develops a political theory of the State, offering "Bismarkian" and "Bonapartist" models with which to interpret post-1945 regimes, and analyzing the democratic, populist, and authoritarian strains in Brazil's modern history.

6583 Teixeira, Luiz Gonzaga. Utopia: manual do militante. São Paulo: Instituição Brasileira de Difusão Cultural, 1983. 204 p.: bibl. (Biblioteca Sociologia e política; 40)

Explication, perhaps closer to a moral tract, of author's personal views of Utopian ideals and philosophy. Of interest primarily as an illustration of the wide variety of "community models" of change currently being published in Brazil.

6584 Wolfe, Alan et al. A Questão da democracia. São Paulo: Centro de Estudos de Cultura Contemporânea; Rio de Janeiro: Paz e Terra, 1980. 172 p.: bibl. (Col. CEDEC/Paz e Terra; 4)

Six articles from a leftist-radical perspective on democracy and capitalism, including provocative theoretical essays by Alan Wolfe and Teotônio dos Santos. Herbert de Souza's essay on Brazil posits a political opposition divided into two wings—liberal and democratic-populist—and analyzes potential conflicts between them with considerable insight.

PRESS AND STUDENT OPPOSITION

6585 Ciclo de Estudos sobre Problemas Brasileiros, 3rd, Pôrto Alegre, Brazil, 1981. 3° [i.e. Terceiro] Ciclo de Estudos sobre Problemas Brasileiros: íntegra dos trabalhos apresentados e debatidos. v. 1, A imprensa no processo democrático, por Carlos Chagas. Pôrto Alegre: Assembléia Legislativa, Estado do Rio Grande do Sul, Diretoria de Anais, 1981. 1 v.

Vol. 1 is primarily a long presentation by highly respected columnist Carlos Chagas who briefly reviews the treatment of the press under each military administration. Cursory, but there is little published on the subject. Vols. 2–6 were not available for review at press time.

6586 Os Debates dos jornalistas brasileiros, 1970–1982. Brasília: Federação Nacional dos Jornalistas Profissionais, 1983. 216 p.

Descriptive summary of official proposals approved by professional journalist organizations (1970–82). Secs. advocating legislative and internal reforms, on unionism and on censure present a startling picture of how heavily regulated this profession remains.

6587 Historia da UNE [i.e. União Nacional dos Estudantes]. v. 1, Depoimentos de ex-dirigentes. São Paulo: Editorial Livramento, 1980. 1 v. (Col. História presente; 4)

History of National Student Union (UNE), told in the wake of its legal resurrection in 1979. Each chap. is an analysis by an ex-UNE president recounting major events of his presidency (1961–70), emphasizing UNE's militancy, its struggles, and finally its losses against government repression.

6588 Nunes, Antônio Carlos Felix. Fora de pauta: histórias e história do jornalismo no Brasil. São Paulo: Proposta Editorial, 1981. 107 p.: ill.

Former columnist for Notícias Populares, Nunes offers a leftist perspective on press censorship (1969-late 70s), covering major journalism/regime struggles. Good on journalist-union linkages.

6589 Sá, Adísia. Biografia de um sindicato: Sindicato dos Jornalistas Profissionais do Ceará. Fortaleza: Edições Univ. Federal do Ceará (UFC), 1981. 146 p.: bibl.

History of professional unionized journalism in Ceará, interspersed with three-to-four p. biographies of major state journalists active during 1951–83.

PUBLIC ADMINISTRATION

6590 Beltrão, Hélio. Descentralização e liberdade. Rio de Janeiro: Editôra Record, 1984. 173 p.

In this collection of essays and interviews, Beltrão, a respected administrator appointed Special Minister for Debureaucratization, argues that bureaucratic centralization is most serious problem facing Brazil, that federalism, municipal autonomy, privatization, greater individual rights, must be encouraged.

6591 —— et al. Desburocratização: idéias fundamentais. Brasília: Presidência da República, Programa Nacional de Desburocratização, 1982. 114 p.

Speeches and articles by Special Minister of Debureaucratization and his aides, describing two-yr. old program and its relevance and importance for *abertura* and democracy, for the judicial system, business community, and the poor.

6592 Estratégia governamental: metodologia do Paraná. v. 1, Formação de uma estratégia governamental. Curitiba: Governo do Estado do Paraná, Secretaria da Administração: Editôra da Univ. Federal do Paraná, 1980. 1 v.: bibl., ill.

Public administration development plan and methodology for Paraná worked out for Ney Braga when he assumed the governorship in 1979. Of only specialized interest.

6593 Ferrari, Levi Bucalem. Burocratas & burocracias. São Paulo: Editôra Semente, 1981. 120 p.: bibl. (Col. Revelações)

Reinterpretation of 1977 attitudinal and background survey of São Paulo bureaucrats. Interesting comparisons of public and private sector attitudes.

6594 Instituto Brasileiro de Administração Municipal (IBAM). IBAM: 30 anos, 30 años, 30 years. Rio de Janeiro: IBAM, 1982. 110 p.: bibl., ill.

Self-laudatory history of IBAM over last 30 yrs., but with a good chap. on IBAM's success in encouraging political and economic decentralization; it is not optimistic about dramatic changes in the short run.

6595 Programa Nacional de Desburocratização, *Brazil.* Desburocratização: medidas adotadas. Brasília: O Programa, 1982. 44 p.: index.

Annotated list of 248 measures taken (1979–81) by National Program of Debureaucratization, set up by the President to simplify federal bureaucratic procedures.

6596 Rio de Janeiro, *Brazil* (state). **Superintendência de Modernização Administrativa.** Estrutura organizacional do Poder Executivo. Rio de Janeiro: Governadoria do Estado do Rio de Janeiro, Secretaria de Planejamento e Coordenação Geral, Superintendência de Modernização Administrativa, 1979. 142 p.: ill.

Organizational charts for Rio de Janeiro state government show all executive offices, state ministries, judicial system, autarchies, foundations, etc. Of interest to specialists.

6597 São Paulo, *Brazil* (state). **Grupo de Assessoria e Participação do Governador (GAP).** Democracia participativa: uma certa idéia. GAP, 1981: dois anos de realizações; democracia participativa, agora! São Paulo: Governo do Estado de São Paulo, Administração Paulo Maluf, Sistema de Assessoria e Participação, 1980–1981. 2 v. (372, 247 p.): ill.

These two vols. show Paulo Maluf's efforts as Governor of São Paulo in 1980 to encourage "participatory democracy" through "Advisory and Participatory Groups" or GAPS. Books outline areas of activity (e.g., agricultural productivity, transportation), evaluate progress, and laud the governor.

6598 Seminário sobre Treinamento de Recursos Humanos para o Setor Público, *Salvador, Brazil, 1979.* Anais. Salvador: Fundação Centro de Pesquisas e Estudos (CPE), 1979. 174 p.: bibl.

Specialized report focuses on recruitment, training, and evaluation of academic public administration training, nationally and in Bahia. Some interesting panel discussions on matching such training to Brazil's current development model.

6599 Siqueira, Jacy. O planejamento governamental em Goiás: experiência, críticas, sugestões. 2a ed. Goiânia: Oficinas da Unigraf, s.d. 224 p.: ill.

Summary of state administrative plans for Goiás, with references and data back to 1938. Of interest to specialists.

POLICY STUDIES

6600 Miranda, Maria Augusta Tibiriçá. O petróleo é nosso: a luta contra o "entreguismo," pelo monopólio estatal, 1947–1953, 1953–1981. Prefácio, Severo Gomes. Apresentação, Alfredo de Moraes Filho. Petrópolis: Vozes, 1983. 551 p.: bibl., ill., plates.

Detailed history of campaigns to create and maintain a State oil monopoly in Brazil, written from an insider's viewpoint. Good reference for information about conventions supporting monopoly, with names of participants.

6601 Schmidt, Benício Vieiro. O Estado e a política urbana no Brasil. Pôrto Alegre:

Editôra da Univ.: L&PM Editores, 1983. 213 p.: bibl., ill.

Excellent analysis of urban policy in Brazil. Describes patterns of urban growth, details conflicts and policies since 1930, and public investments in urban programs by geographic area and sector. Welcome addition to a thin literature.

6602 Simpósio de Agropecuária da Região Geoeconômica de Brasília, Brasília, 1976. Simpósio de Agropecuária da Região Geoeconômica de Brasília. Brasília: Câmara dos Deputados, Comissão de Agricultura e Política Rural, Centro de Documentação e Informação, Coordenação de Publicações, 1979. 314 p.

Similar to US Congressional hearings, in this symposium (March 1976) Federal Deputies quizzed executive branch representatives on the development of Brasília "geoeconomic" region (i.e., roads, mining, agriculture, construction). A rare opportunity for legislature to question directly the executive during this period, but of little substantive interest.

6603 Simpósio sobre Política Nacional de Saúde, 1st, Brasília, 1979. 1° [i.e. Primeiro] Simpósio sobre Política Nacional de Saúde. v. 1, Conferências. Brasília: Câmara dos Deputados, Comissão de Saúde, Centro de Documentação e Informação, Coordenação de Publicações, 1980. 1 v.

Proceedings of 1st Symposium on National Health Policy (Oct. 1979) include major presentations on its social and economic context; need for decentralization; public and private alternatives; and 50 yrs. of Brazilian experience. Considering lack of published debate on health care, a welcome publication.

Spector, Leonard S. Nuclear proliferation today. See item **6541.**

6604 Vieira, Evaldo Amaro./ Estado e miséria social no Brasil: de Getúlio a Geisel, 1951 a 1978. São Paulo: Cortez Editôra, 1983. 240 p.: bibl.

Author of *Authoritarianism and corporatism in Latin America* (Pittsburgh, Pa: Univ. of Pittsburgh, 1977) analyzes national social policies in education, health, housing, and social welfare by administration (1951–64), plus a chap. on policies (1964–74). Excellent research, with policies presented in

context of party politics and democracy. Recommended.

LABOR

6605 Almeida, Maria Herminia Tavares de. Le syndicalisme brésilien entre la continuité et le changement (FDD/NED [Problèmes d'Amérique latine; 65] 4675/ 4676, 12 juillet 1982, p. 37–56, tables)

Excellent analysis of changes in unionism based on good primary data, noting that the large post-1978 union growth cannot be explained by national mobilization efforts. One of the very few efforts to synthesize complex current nature of unionism. Recommended.

6606 Andrade, Pedro de. Encontros da classe trabalhadora de 1906 até a CONCLAT, 1981. São Paulo: Editôra Quilombo, 1981. 112 p.: bibl., ill.

Resolutions passed and themes of about 25 Brazilian workers' conferences (1906–81). Purpose is to show labor movement's coherence over time; also illustrates, especially in agriculture, chronic nature of labor problems.

6607 Brito, José Carlos Aguiar. A tomada da Ford: o nascimento de um sindicato livre. Petrópolis: Vozes, 1983. 139 p.: ill., plates.

Detailed, well written account of the six-day 1981 strike against Ford Motor Co. by a strike leader, with documents, organizational charts, and photographs.

6608 Cândido Filho, José. O movimiento operário: o sindicato, o partido. Petrópolis: Editôra Vozes, 1982. 203 p.: bibl.

Introductory history of workers' organizations in Western Europe and Brazil. Last 25 p. provide useful details on Brazilian union organization (i.e., numbers, location, financing, etc.).

6609 Fe e compromisso político. São Paulo: Edições Paulinas, 1982. 90 p.

Speeches delivered at the 2nd "Week of the Worker" in São Paulo, by practitioners of liberation theology, supporting political militancy of workers as a Christian duty.

6610 Humphrey, John. Control del trabajo en la industria automotriz brasileña

(CP, 24, abril/junio 1980, p. 67–77, bibl.)
Making interesting comparisons between conditions in US during early days of unionization and conditions in Brazil, argues that labor improvements in Brazil in late 1970s are caused by changes in industry structure, particularly lack of skilled labor, leading to frequent job rotation and job insecurity.

6611 Maroni, Amnéris. A estratégia da recusa: análise das greves de maio/78. São Paulo: Brasiliense, 1982. 135 p.: ill.

Master's thesis analyzes formation of "comissões de fábrica" (the beginnings of independent unions) in three São Paulo 1978 strikes. Examines strikes in Massey Ferguson do Brasil, Caterpiller do Brasil, and MWM Motores Diesel Ltda. Well researched.

6612 Moisés, José Alvaro. Lições de liberdade e de opressão: os trabalhadores e a luta pela democracia. Prefácio, Lula. Rio de Janeiro: Paz e Terra, 1982. 245 p.: bibl., ill. (Col. Estudos brasileiros; 56)

Labor movement and Partido dos Trabalhadores are fortunate to have this activist/prolific scholar as chronicler for the rise of "new unionism." This collection of his academic presentations and speeches is a rich source of information on labor changes in late 1970s and early 1980s.

LOCAL STUDIES

6614 Blay, Eva Alterman. As prefeitas: a participação política da mulher no Brasil. Rio de Janeiro: Avenir, 1981. 63 p.: bibl., ill.

Well researched study of the two percent of Brazilian mayors who are women: who they are, how they were elected, what kind of *município* supports them. Welcome addition to the literature.

Campello, Netto. História parlamentar de Pernambuco. See *HLAS 46:3544*.

6615 Carneiro, Bernice Pereira et al. Monografia municipal de Vila Bela da Santíssima Trindade. Cuiabá: Fundação de Pesquisas Cândido Rondon, 1981. 241 p.: ill. (part folded)

Vol. 3 of planned monographic series on all Mato Grosso *municípios*. Extremely detailed data on agricultural and industrial production, commercial development, and

other social and economic information. Series may serve as excellent source for municipal studies.

6616 Confederação Nacional dos Trabalhadores na Agricultura (CONTAG). As lutas camponesas no Brasil: 1980. Apresentação de José Francisco da Silva. Rio de Janeiro: Editôra Marco Zero, 1981. 112 p.: ill. (Col. Nossos dias; 1)

Essential background for scholars of rural organization and activism in Brazil. Region-by-region, strike-by-strike account of rural actions, illustrating new activism at local and national levels, through CONTAG, now with about 6.8 million members. Highly recommended.

6617 Cooperativismo e coletivização no campo: questões sobre a prática da "Igreja Popular" no Brasil. Organizado por Neide Esterci. Prefácio de José de Souza Martins. Rio de Janeiro: Editôra Marco Zero: Instituto de Estudos da Religião, 1984. 159 p. (Cadernos do ISER; 16)

Rich case studies of rural community action programs supported by the Catholic Church. Notable for documentation of the diversity of organizational forms which emerged from the Church's efforts. Particularly strong is Esterci's comparisons of these models. Recommended.

6618 Cuiabá na nova realidade sócio-política do Estado. Cuiabá: Governo do Estado de Mato Grosso, Gabinete de Planejamento e Coordenação: Prefeitura Municipal de Cuiabá, Secretaria Municipal de Planejamento e Coordenação, 1980. 262 p.: bibl., ill., map, plates.

Statistical look at the capital of Mato Grosso, with an overkill of information (e.g., map of bus routes), but a superb source of primary data on education, health, infrastruction, industry, and other sectors.

Juruna, Mário; Antônio Hohlfeldt; and Assis Hoffman. O gravador do Juruna. See item **1272.**

6619 Moisés, José Alvaro et al. Alternativas populares da democracia: Brasil, anos 80. Petrópolis: Vozes, 1982. 139 p.: ill. (Col. de estudos latino-americanos Nuestra América)

Excellent and important essays analyze case studies of the rise of grassroots, "horizontal" democracy in Brazil in 1980s.

Moises's discussion of the "new unionism," Souza Lima on CEB's (Catholic community organizations), Evers on urban "cost of living" movement, and Souza's study of a rural *município*'s move to democracy are graphic illustrations of fundamental changes in the character of local political organizations. Recommended.

PARTIES AND ELECTIONS

Bandecchi, Pedro Brasil. Liga Nacionalista. See *HLAS 46:3529.*

6620 Benevides, Maria Victoria de Mesquita. A UDN [i.e. União Democrática Nacional] e o udenismo: ambigüidades do liberalismo brasileiro, 1945–1965. Rio de Janeiro: Paz e Terra, 1981. 297 p.: bibl., index, plates (Col. Estudos brasileiros; 5)

Published PhD dissertation on major post-1945 opposition party UDN. Pt. 1 is a chronological party history; pt. 2 analyzes policies and organization. Stresses "ambivalences" of party as liberal, pro-military, pro-human rights. Welcome contribution.

6621 Britto, Luiz Navarro de. O mandato imperativo partidário (UMG/RBEP, 56, jan. 1983, p. 147–153, bibl.)

Concise analysis of the "law of party fidelity," one weapon in arsenal of legal strictures which controlled politicians during military rule.

6622 Carli, Gileno dé. Os tempos de Jânio Quadros. Recife: Oficinas Gráficas da Companhia Editôra de Pernambuco, 1982. 196 p.

Includes new eds. of *JQ: Brasília e a grande crise* and *Anatomia da renúncia*, both books on Quadros pub. in 1960s, and a long preface analyzing Quadros's contemporary political relationships. Of interest as his political star rapidly rises again in São Paulo politics.

6623 Felizardo, Joaquim José and **Mateus Schmidt.** Partidos políticos e eleições no Brasil. Pôrto Alegre: Escola Superior de Teologia São Lourenço de Brindes: Editôra Vozes, 1982. 64 p.: bibl. (Col. Periferia; 7)

Brief and superficial summary of elections (1947–78) with emphasis on results in Rio Grande do Sul.

Lima Júnior, Olavo Brasil de. Electoral participation in Brazil, 1945–1978. See *HLAS 46:3605.*

6624 Pedro Aleixo e sua obra política. Organização de Maurício Brandi Aleixo, Vítor Jorge Abdala Nósseis, José Carlos Brandi Aleixo. Belo Horizonte: Senado Federal, Centro Gráfico, 1982. 405 p.: bibl. (Obra do Instituto Brasileiro de Estudos Políticos Pedro Aleixo; 2)

Valuable compendium of primary source material on the formation of *Partido Democrático Republicano* in 1970s, the valient effort of Senator and Vice-President Pedro Aleixo. Includes biographical sketches of founders, key documents and writings.

6625 Picaluga, Izabel Fontenelle. Partidos políticos e classes sociais: a UDN na Guanabara. Petrópolis: Vozes, 1980. 218 p.: bibl., maps (Col. Sociologia brasileira; 12)

Examines national UDN history, emphasizing social bases of the parties and gradual party polarization in Guanabara. Includes secs. on UDN relationships with major political groups.

6626 Reis, Palhares Moreira. Realidade eleitoral brasileira. São Paulo: Editôra G.T.B., 1982. 240 p.: ill., maps.

Eight articles primarily on Pernambucan elections (1954–79), many reprinted from *Revista Brasileira de Estudos Políticos*. Approach is analytic and empirical, with excellent maps.

6626a Sarles, Margaret J. Maintaining political control through parties (CUNY/CP, 15:1, Oct. 1982, p. 41–72, tables)

Well conceived, empirical study of strategies of control and mobilization within the bureaucratic-authoritarian state. Using the *município* as a unit of analysis and 1974 Brazilian election results, author uncovers different mobilization strategies for government and non-opposition parties. ARENA was most successful in areas susceptible to controlled mobilization; the MDB was more successful using a strategy of mass mobilization where *municípios* were richer and more modern. Important study for understanding political institutionalization and stages of bureaucratic-authoritarian rule. [D. W. Dent]

Segatto, José Antônio. Breve história do PCB. See *HLAS 46:3677.*

OFFICIAL SPEECHES
AND BIOGRAPHIES

6627 Almeida, Nosser. Uma voz do Acre no Congresso Nacional. Brasília: Câmara dos Deputados, Centro de Documentação e Informação, Coordenação de Publicações, 1981. 3 v.: ill.
The PDS Federal Deputy from Acre has collected his speeches delivered to Chamber of Deputies in 1980, mostly on state themes.

6628 Alvares, Elcio. Mensagens ao povo. Vitória: Governo do Espírito Santo, Secretaria da Comunicação Social, 1981. 361 p.
Speeches by governor of Espírito Santo (1975–78), arranged chronologically. Local themes, largely non-political.

6629 Brazil. Congresso Nacional. Câmara dos Deputados. Diretoria Legislativa. Deputados brasileiros: repertório biográfico dos membros da Câmara dos Deputados, 46a. Legislatura, 1979–1983. Brasília: Centro de Documentação e Informação, Coordenação de Publicações, 1981. 641 p.: indexes.
Pub. for each new Congress, official biographies of federal deputies, with basic social and political history.

6630 Castelo, João. Mensagem aos maranhenses. São Luís: SIOGE, 1982. 197 p.
Speeches by PDS Governor of Maranhão, João Castelo (1981–82). The 34 speeches are summarized individually as well.

6631 Cerqueira, Marcello. Cadáver barato: um retrato do terrorismo. Prefácio, Antônio Houaiss. Rio de Janeiro: Pallas, 1982. 102 p.
Congressional speeches and articles by PMDB Federal Deputy opposing right-wing terrorism in Brazil, focusing on bombing of Riocentro in 1981.

6632 Chaves, Aloysio. Um ano de mandato. Brasília: Senado Federal, Centro Gráfico, 1982. 387 p.
Senator from Pará has included in this collection speeches and debates he gave in 1979 in the Senate and as a member of various committees, including Constitution and Justice, Social Legislation, Education and Culture, and various joint committees.

6633 Cioni, Lúcio. E justo lutar: discursos pronunciados. Brasília: Câmara dos Deputados, Centro de Documentação e Informação, Coordenação de Publicações, 1982. 115 p.
Speeches delivered to Chamber of Deputies in 1981, by a federal deputy from Paraná, who was first a member of ARENA, then PMDB.

6634 Dados biográficos dos Senadores, período 1946 a 1970: documento preliminar. Brasília: Projeto de Biografias dos Senadores do Império e da República, 1981. 271 p.: bibl., indexes.
Biographies of senators (1946–70) excluding those also serving after 1971, whose biographies are in later publications. Part of larger Senate research effort, much unpublished data are also apparently available. Basic data include family political connections.

6635 Freire, Marcos. Em defesa do homem e do meio. Brasília: Senado Federal, Centro Gráfico, 1980. 2 v.: ill.
Speeches delivered in 1979 by senator (and national opposition leader) from Pernambuco on police violence, agriculture and drought in the Northeast, unionism, and health and ecology issues.

6636 ———. Ultima palavra. Brasília: Senado Federal, Centro Gráfico, 1982. 261 p.
Speeches by senator and MDB leader from Pernambuco cover national themes of party transformation, amnesty, individual rights, and economic issues such as the energy crisis.

6637 Guedes, Geraldo. Mais um ano de mandato a serviço de Pernambuco: discursos pronunciados e projetos de lei apresentados pelo Deputado Geraldo Guedes, em 1979. Brasília: Câmara dos Deputados, Centro de Documentação e Informação, Coordenação de Publicações, 1980. 241 p.: plates.
Speeches and legislation introduced into Chamber of Deputies in 1979 by ARENA Federal Deputy from Pernambuco. Indexed by subject—primarily problems in Pernambuco.

6638 Jurema, Aderbal. Regionalismo & modernismo: discursos acadêmicos. Brasília: s.n., 1981. 77 p. (Col. Machado de Assis; 40)

Speeches by Pernambucan Congressman, mostly on Northeast and regional, cultural, and literary themes, in the old tradition of congressman/gentleman scholar.

6639 Maciel, Marco. Vocação e compromisso. Apresentação, Margarida Cantarelli. Rio de Janeiro: Livraria J. Olympio, 1982. 98 p.

Biographical information and 15 speeches by governor of Pernambuco (1979–82) on national and state issues.

6640 Müller, Gastão. Atuação no Senado nos primeiros quatro meses. Brasília: Senado Federal, Centro Gráfico, 1979. 171 p.

Speeches and debates of Senator Gastão Müller, Fourth Secretary of ARENA, from Rio Grande do Sul, in his first four months in office.

Salgado, Plínio. Discursos parlamentares. See *HLAS 46:3667.*

6641 Suruagy, Divaldo. Contemporâneos. Maceió: IGASA, 1981. 256 p.

Informal recollections (about one and half p. each) of 80 major national and Alagoan political figures by former governor and popular federal deputy from Alagoas. Highly personal and anectodal, so of limited scholarly used.

JOURNAL ABBREVIATIONS
GOVERNMENT AND POLITICS

ACPS/B Boletín de la Academia de Ciencias Políticas y Sociales. Caracas.

AFS Armed Forces and Society. Univ. of Chicago. Chicago.

APSA/R American Political Science Review. American Political Science Assn. Columbus, Ohio.

AR Areíto. Areíto, Inc. New York.

CDLA Casa de las Américas. Instituto Cubano del Libro. La Habana.

CEDLA/B Boletín de Estudios Latinoamericanos. Centro de Estudios y Documentación Latinoamericanos. Amsterdam.

CP Cuadernos Políticos. Ediciones Era. México.

CPES/RPS Revista Paraguaya de Sociología. Centro Paraguayo de Estudios Sociológicos. Asunción.

CPS Comparative Political Studies. Northwestern Univ., Evanston, Ill. and Sage Publications, Beverly Hills, Calif.

CRIA/W Worldview. Council on Religion and International Affairs. New York.

CU/JIA Journal of International Affairs. Columbia Univ., School of International Affairs. New York.

CUA/AQ Anthropological Quarterly. Catholic Univ. of America, Catholic Anthropological Conference. Washington.

CUH Current History. Current History, Inc. Philadelphia.

CUNY/CP Comparative Politics. City Univ. of New York, Political Science Program. New York.

DIS Dissent. Dissent Publishing Assn. New York.

ECB Encontros com a Civilização Brasileira. Editôra Civilização Brasileira. Rio de Janeiro.

FDD/NED Notes et études documentaires. France, Direction de la documentation. Paris.

FIU/CR Caribbean Review. Florida International Univ., Office of Academic Affairs. Miami.

GEE/NA Nova Americana. Giulio Einaudi Editore. Torino, Italy.

HAHR Hispanic American Historical Review. Duke Univ. Press *for the* Conference on Latin American History of the American Historical Assn. Durham, N.C.

HICLR Hastings International and Comparative Law Review. Univ. of California, Hastings College of Law. San Francisco.

IAA Ibero-Amerikanisches Archiv. Ibeo-Amerikanisches Institut. Berlin.

IAMEA Inter-American Economic Affairs. Washington.

ICS/JCCP Journal of Commonwealth & Comparative Politics. Univ. of London, Institute of Commonwealth Studies. London.

IDES/DE Desarrollo Económico. Instituto de Desarrollo Económico y Social. Buenos Aires.

IIAS/IRADS International Review of Administrative Sciences. International Institute of Administrative Sciences. Bruxelles.

INDEX Index on Censorship. Writers & Scholars International. London.

ISU/PS Politics & Society. Iowa State Univ. Ames.

JDA Journal of Developing Areas. Western Illinois Univ. Press. Macomb.

JGSWGL Jahrbuch für Geschichte von Staat, Wirtschaft und Gesellschaft Lateinamerikas. Köln, FRG.

JLAS Journal of Latin American Studies. Centers or institutes of Latin American studies at the universities of Cambridge, Glasgow, Liverpool, London, and Oxfod. Cambridge Univ. Press. London.

JPR Journal of Peace Research. Edited at the International Peace Research Institute. Universitetforlaget. Oslo.

LAP Latin American Perspectives. Univ. of California. Riverside.

LARR Latin American Research Review. Univ. of North Carolina Press *for the* Latin American Studies Assn. Chapel Hill.

MR Monthly Review. Monthly Review, Inc. New York.

NACLA NACLA: Report on the Americas. North American Congress on Latin America. New York.

NOSALF/IA Ibero Americana. Scandinavian Assn. for Research on Latin America (NOSALF). Stockholm.

NS NS NorthSouth NordSud NorteSur NorteSul. Canadian Assn. of Latin American Studies, Univ. of Ottawa.

NSO Nueva Sociedad. San José.

NZZ/SRWA Swiss Review of World Affairs. Neue Zürcher Zeitung. Zurich, Switzerland.

OLI/ZLW Zeitschrift für Lateinamerika Wien. Österreichisches Lateinamerika-Institut. Wien.

PSA/PS Political Studies. Political Studies Assn. of the UK. Oxford, England.

PUCP/DA Debates en Antropología. Pontificia Univ. Católica del Perú. Depto. de Ciencias Sociales. Lima.

RCPC Revista del Pensamiento Centroamericano. Centro de Investigaciones y Actividades Culturales. Managua.

SAGE/JIAS Journal of Inter-American Studies and World Affairs. Sage Publications *for the* Center for Advanced International Studies, Univ. of Miami. Coral Gables, Fla.

SOCIOL Sociologus. Berlin.

SP Socialismo y Participación. Ediciones Socialismo y Participación. Lima.

SPSA/JP Journal of Politics. Southern Political Science Assn. *in cooperation with the* Univ. of Florida. Gainesville.

SS Science and Society. New York.

UCSB/NS The New Scholar. Univ. of California, Committee on Hispanic Civilization and Center fo Chicano Studies. Santa Barbara.

UJSC/ECA ECA (Estudios Centroamericanos). Univ. Centroamericana José Simeón Cañas. San Salvador.

UNAM/RMS Revista Mexicana de Sociología. Univ. Nacional Autónoma de México, Instituto de Investigaciones Sociales. México.

UP/EA Estudios Andinos. Univ. of Pittsburgh, Latin American Studies Center. Pittsburgh, Pa.

UPR/CS Caribbean Studies. Univ. of Puerto Rico, Institute of Caribbean Studies. Río Piedras.

UPR/RCS Revista de Ciencias Sociales. Univ. de Puerto Rico, Colegio de Ciencias Sociales. Río Piedras.

URSS/AL América Latina. Academia de Ciencias de la Unión de Repúblicas Soviéticas Socialistas. Moscú.

USC/SCC Studies in Comparative Communism. Univ. of Southern California, School of International Relations, Von KleinSmid Institute of International Affairs. Los Angeles.

USIA/PC Problems of Communism. US Information Agency. Washington.

UU/WPQ Western Political Quarterly. Univ. of Utah, Institute of Government *for the* Western Political Science Assn.; Pacific Northwest Political Science Assn.; and Southern California Political Science Assn. Salt Lake City.

UWI/CQ Caribbean Quarterly. Univ. of the West Indies. Mona, Jamaica.

UWI/SES Social and Economic Studies. Univ. of the West Indies, Institute of Social and Economic Research. Mona, Jamaica.

INTERNATIONAL RELATIONS

GENERAL

YALE H. FERGUSON, *Professor of Political Science, Rutgers University-Newark*

THE GENERAL LITERATURE on the international relations of Latin America over the past two years has been noteworthy partly for what it has not contained. Almost entirely absent have been significant works on dependency, multinational corporations, the New International Economic Order, and other familiar "Third World" issues. In explaining the shift, one can only surmise that such factors as the grave recession that gripped much of the world in the last decade and the ongoing international debt crisis—not to mention the singular lack of sympathy in the Reagan administration for Third World problems of development (at least as usually conceived)—has led to a downplaying of Latin American demands, coupled with a willingness to settle for whatever benefits may be derived from foreign investment and trade on traditional terms. At the same time, the literature is replete with security issues that some years ago seemed to have been eclipsed by economic concerns.

By far the most significant historical work in the period under review is Bryce Wood's new book on *The Dismantling of the Good Neighbor Policy* (item **7110**), a sequel of sorts to his previous volumes on *The Making of the Good Neighbor Policy* (see *HLAS 24:3474*) and *The United States and Latin American wars, 1932–1942* (see *HLAS 30:1134*). Meticulously researched and using mainly primary sources, Wood argues that the 1954 US intervention in Guatemala signaled the effective death of the Good Neighbor. Washington intervened unilaterally, as it had promised not to do, and thereby "lost credibility and an honorable reputation in Latin America and elsewhere that it has not regained . . ." There is an interesting consonance between Wood's thesis and part of a major essay by Robert A. Friedlander (item **7031**), who maintains that the post-World War II policy of the US was a "major departure from the overall precedents of the past;" he sees in the Reagan administration's policy toward Central America a particularly condemnatory "return to . . . Monroeism." Another article by Constance Ashton Myers (item **7075**) sheds light on an obscure, although intriguing, international nongovernmental organization, the Inter-American Commission of Women, which was founded after the war mainly on Mrs. Roosevelt's inspiration and ultimately found its "effectiveness . . . smothered . . . and personnel pacified with titles and well-furnished offices."

Other works of a historical nature that merit special mention are, first, a book by Mexican author Manuel Fernández de Velasco (item **7029**) on the diplomacy involved in the US's acquisition of Florida, 1809–19, drawn primarily from the papers of the Spanish ambassador to the US who was involved in the negotiations. Another article, by UNAM scholar Lothar Knauth (item **7057**), traces the 19th century background of contemporary Japanese-Latin American relations. Demetrio Boersner has produced an unusually good short history of Latin America's international relations (item **7012**), stressing the growing power, significance, and autonomy of leading Latin American countries and the declining hegemony of the US. As we shall note below, the decline-of-hegemony theme is a common one in recent writings, as it is in Friedlander's essay mentioned previously: Friedlander states that, although the Reagan policies have been "a conscious attempt to break loose from the political quagmire created by the Vietnam War," "the United States in the decade of the 1980s . . . can no longer maintain the obligations of the Truman-Eisenhower-Kennedy era. If not a clay colossus, America is, nonetheless, a much-reduced image of its former self." Lastly, Robert Shaplen has written a splendid article-length history of the Non-Aligned Movement (item **7094**), emphazing its problems and suggesting that "if the . . . movement is to have any significance henceforth," it will have to stop internal bickering and "decide what sort of positive role it can really play in the world."

Those scholars interested in contemporary Latin American foreign policies had reason to rejoice in late 1984 with the almost simultaneous appearance of two excellent collections of essays on this subject: Jennie K. Lincoln and Elizabeth G. Ferris's *The Dynamics of Latin American foreign policies* (item **7025**) and Heraldo Muñoz and Joseph T. Tulchin's *Latin American nations in world politics* (item **7062**). The latter volume was the product of a 1982 conference involving scholars from the Univ. de Chile and the Univ. of North Carolina at Chapel Hill. The quality of individual selections is almost uniformly high, the principal countries (and many not-so-principal) countries of the region are covered, and the editors (and some of the authors) have made a real effort to explore theoretical implications. Results suggest, to this reviewer, both how much more we now know about the policies and the foreign policy making process even in relatively obscure (as far as the traditional literature has been concerned) places like Bolivia, and how relatively useless general international relations theory is for analyzing and explaining such phenomena. Alberto van Klaveren (item **7062**) comments that the many "disparate elements" available for comparative studies "have yet to be systematized and integrated into a coherent and comprehensive approach." Still another author of an essay not included in either of these two books, the Venezuelan Alberto Cisneros-Lavaller (item **7016**), similarly traces various approaches to the study of inter-American relations and complains of "the absence of elementary modeling or systematic data collections" and "the lack of innovative methodologies."

The complaint of Howard J. Wiarda (items **7107, 7108,** and **7109**) is of a different nature: that scholars and policy makers alike have been unduly ethnocentric in their views of the Third World. Wiarda would emphasize Latin America's "persistent corporatism and organic statism, its neomercantalist and state-capitalist economic structures, its personalism and kinship patterns, its Catholicism . . . its patrimonalism and unabashed patriarchialism, its patron-client networks now extended to the national level, its distinctive patterns and arenas of state-society relations, and its historic relations of dependency . . ." Nevertheless, Wiarda acknowledges that not all Latin Americans see themselves in these terms, preferring "to cast their lot" with the "Western model." The problem, as also expressed in several introductions to this section in previous *Handbook* volumes, is the gap between aspirations and accomplishments that is so often a source of instability in Latin America. Non-democratic regimes are unable to establish their legitimacy because of the widespread view that the only legitimate government is a democratic one, while democratic governments, attempting to cope with grave economic and social problems, often fall to the pull of what appears to be a dominant authoritarian tradition.

Wiarda's occasional paper is especially interesting because he reflects therein on the current applicability of his model, as well as on some of the "political" uses to which the model has been put. He regrets that some readers have condemned the model on the grounds that it justifies repressive regimes, and that some such regimes have, indeed, regarded it as justification of sorts. Noting that the corporatist model is increasingly out of favor in Iberian Europe as well as parts of Latin America, he reminds us that "ancient" corporatist "currents" lie just beneath the surface and "may again be restored to power." Yet, in his view, the future "is more likely to hold a pluralism and possible fragmentation." The lesson, as he sees it, is: "The very diversity and complexity of these nations and systems, both domestically and internationally, demands pragmatically that the models we use to interpret them reflect that diversity and complexity, rather than being tied too closely to any currently prevailing regime or intellectual orthodoxy." Amen to that, in this reviewer's opinion!

Heightened Cold War tensions in Latin America give added significance to several works focusing on Soviet policies in the region. By far the most important of these is a splendid book by Cole Blasier (item **7010**). The Soviet Union's increased "presence" in the Western Hemisphere—in terms of more diplomatic relations, trade, economic and military assistance, and ships at sea—is undeniable. (On Latin America's economic relations with COMECON countries through 1980, see the ECLA study, item **7088**.) The issues of course, are how this increased presence it to be interpreted and how the US and other countries should respond. Blasier stresses that the export of revolution to Latin America is not high on the list of Soviet priorities and that "normalization" of diplomatic and trade relations with regional governments of different ideological bents is actually encouraging. A USSR enmeshed in "proper" relations is less likely to jeopardize those ties by being too overtly subversive. Blasier also points out that trade relations are almost entirely in Latin America's favor, that the Soviets have given little actual aid to radical governments except Cuba, and that even the Cuban relationship has been a "political asset" but "economic liability" for Moscow. As for the US response, Blasier states: "The argument that in revolutionary situations the United States should counter Soviet interference by interference of its own is based on two false assumptions: first that Moscow can create and control revolutions, and second, that the United States has the power and knowhow to prevent them." Also, "U.S. interference has often served Soviet rather than U.S. causes. That is because interference by the United States in Latin America has often had the effect of uniting a wide spectrum of Latin Americans against the United States, creating anti-American political alignments on which the Soviet Union has been able to capitalize."

Several articles reinforce many of the arguments advanced by Blasier. Paul Sigmund looks specifically at Soviet relations with Cuba and Allende's Chile (item **7096**) and concludes: "it is . . . evident . . . that when Soviet national interests and those of other[s] are seen to conflict, the Soviet interest is immediately preferred." Castro was snubbed in the 1962 missile crisis, and Allende got only token economic aid. In Sigmund's assessment the pattern of the past has been "one of conservatism, caution, and preference for gradual change." W. Raymond Duncan (item **7023**) and Seth Singleton (items **7097** and **7098**) both suggest that whatever advances in influence the Soviets may appear to have made in recent years owe, in large part, to US indifference to Third World economic problems and demands. However, both observe that nationalism in Latin America continues to be a powerful deterrent to significant Soviet advances. Singleton writes: "The Soviet system . . . is generally regarded by progressive Marxists and non-Marxists alike as stultified, inefficient, oppressive, and undemocratic." Duncan reminds us that even Latin American communism "beats with a distinct national impulse." He recommends that the US "ride with nationalist movements" rather than oppose them by military means. "The essential point here is that nationalism . . . is a constant barrier to Soviet penetration . . . This point applies to Cuba as well as to Mexico or Nicaragua, and it teaches a lesson that bears far more attention from Washington than [has recently been the case]."

Blasier, in his book, does mention that the Soviets have recently become a little less dogmatic than they used to be about the "peaceful road" as the only road to power, accepting revolutionary victories whenever and however they can get them, without at the same time giving the resulting governments much practical help. Sigmund and Singleton both suggest that the Soviet perspective might be evolving, and Singleton goes so far as to predict a "Soviet foreign policy reappraisal" presumably tied to new leadership in the USSR. However, the scholarly consensus clearly supports Augusto Varas's view that the USSR has only a "fairly narrow margin for maneuver" in Latin America and its strategy must remain "essentially reactive, dependent above all on the hemispheric policies pursued by the United States."

The writings of Soviet scholars, unfortunately, shed little light on the USSR's official perspective on the Latin American region and the policies of the US and other outside powers. Aside from the usual polemics, there seems to be (for whatever reason) a slight increase in the number of items that evidence serious analysis. The dominant theme (see, for example Khachaturov in item 7056 and Gornov in item 7043) seems to be the declining hegemony of the US and the desire of even "bourgeois" and anticommunist governments to diversify dependency. Otherwise of note is a two-part series by Boris Martínov and Vladimir Súdarev (item 7070) on Latin American territorial conflicts. Their treatment of "colonial" conflicts like the Falklands is highly propagandistic, but their survey of other territorial problems (Beagle Channel, Marañón, and so forth) is incisive and largely objective. Artur Avetisián (item 7006) reviews in useful detail various Soviet-sponsored power projects in Cuba, Argentina, Brazil, Peru, and Nicaragua.

The Reagan administration policies in the region, of course, continue to generate substantial controversy all along the ideological spectrum. The torrent of right-wing publications advancing various prescriptions for policy and praise for the Reagan posture that greeted his electoral victory in 1980 has somewhat subsided. However, a few items under review fall distinctly in that category. For instance, the Editor of *Commentary*, Norman Podhoretz (item 7084), excoriates critics of the Reagan policies, accusing them of being closet pacifists, isolationists, appeasers, and/or pro-Marxist. As he sees it, "the United States must do whatever may be required, up to and including the dispatch of American troops, to stop and then reverse the totalitarian drift in Central America." Another example are several articles in the *Air University Review*: Neil Livingston (item 7063) maintains that the US must stand ready to fight any number of "dirty little conflicts" around the globe, in support of "any force" that is resisting the Soviets. Moreover, he asserts that the exclusion of the media in the Grenada invasion is a textbook case of needed information control and only regrets that there has been so much reportage, undermining US objectives, in the Central American arena. Robin Montgomery Navarro (item 7074) urges US intellectuals to stop criticizing their own government and start helping the US to fashion a psychological warfare strategy to counter Soviet/Cuban propaganda in Latin America. Montgomery Navarro, as well as Joseph Strodder (item 7100), recommend ever closer cooperation among the US and

Latin American military establishments through training, standardization of weapons, and so on.

The preponderence of opinion in the literature, however, is that the Reagan policies are sorely misguided. As Abraham F. Lowenthal observes (item **7065**), the administration initially appeared to be "coping with hegemony in decline" (on this theme, see also especially Gustavo Lagos's opinion in item **7060** and the editor's introduction to a collection of articles from *Foreign Policy*, item **7030**) by not being nearly as hard-line in actual policies as its campaign rhetoric might have suggested. Lowenthal, in fact, outlines a number of factors that tend to insure that fundamental changes in US policy toward Latin America, either in conservative or liberal direction, do not occur. Nevertheless, Lowenthal (item **7064**), after the stepped-up campaign against Nicaragua and other events, had to admit that, despite the very real constraints, Reagan appeared to be determined to "stay the course," in Central America and the Caribbbean. Lowenthal argued: "The Reagan administration appears intent on ignoring or denying Latin America's emergence. It has attempted to restore U.S. dominance with threats of force, security assistance, support for friendly governments, and covert intervention against anti-U.S. movements." In Lowenthal's view, such efforts have been "counterproductive, particularly in the large countries of the region," and have to some extent diverted US attention from other more pressing international economic problems.

Other authors have made similar criticisms: Carlos Astiz (item **7005**) observes that the US has built an "uneasy relationship" with those Latin American countries seeking to preserve the status quo and has made "deeply suspicious" those seeking "to modify Latin American society." R.J. Vincent (item **7104**) complains: "The Reagan Administration, by making [traditional US] values the servant of the contest with the Soviet Union rather than the master, and by making every issue in international relations subordinate to the contest with the Soviet Union, has stunningly reduced the range of American power." Theodore Draper (item **7021**) expresses his inability to find a rational explanation as to how the political character of El Salvador and Nicaragua is any serious "threat" to the US or Mexico; "countries," he insists, "are not dominoes." The second report of the Inter-American Dialogue (item **7003**) recommends downplaying the East-West factor in Central America, working for political settlements mainly through the Contadora process, and ending US aid to the *contras*. Howard J. Wiarda (item **7108**) rules out "gunboat diplomacy" and makes a case for "prudence" and "restraint." Meanwhile, much more strident and perennial critics of the US, like Gregorio Selser (item **7093**), have had a field day with the Reagan policies. Their faimilar charges about such things as CIA plots, US support for reactionary political forces, and so on currently appear to have rather more substance than some years in the past!

We should conclude this overview of the "general" category literature by mentioning a few miscellaneous items. ECLA has produced an extremely useful study (item **7101**) of Western Europe's trade with and investment in Latin America through 1980. Eric N. Baklanoff (item **7007**) has analyzed Spain's recent economic ties with Latin America, and he makes cautious forecasts about the likely future of that relationship. In a final item of interest, Brian Loveman and Thomas M. Davies (item **7047**) have supplemented an excellent collection of Che Guevara's writings on guerrilla warfare with a country-by-country survey of how guerrilla movements have fared.

7001 Africa y América Latina: perspectivas de cooperación interregional. Edición de la CEPAL y la Comisión Económica para Africa. Santiago: Naciones Unidas, 1983. 286 p.: bibl. (E/CEPAL/G.1198)

Wealth of information relating to African/Latin American economic relations. Book produced by ECLA and the Economic Commission for Africa. Good reference. [M.J. Francis]

7001a Alschuler, Lawrence R. The développement latino-américain et l'Ordre économique international: vers une formulation des lois du mouvement du capitalisme périphérique (NS, 6:11, 1981, p. 53–65, bibl.)

Ottawa political scientist reviews the proposal for a NIEO and dependency theory, insisting that too little emphasis has been given to the perspective of Wallerstein, Frank, et al.—that there is one worldwide capitalist system with both a center and periphery.

7002 América Latina: ¿clase media de las naciones? Obra editada bajo la dirección de Francisco Orrego Vicuña. Santiago: Instituto de Estudios Internacionales de la Univ. de Chile: Instituto Chileno de Estudios Humanísticos, 1979. 165 p.: bibl., ill. (Estudios internacionales)

Papers on various aspects of Latin America's role in international affairs from conference sponsored by FRG's Konrad Adenauer Foundation at the Univ. of Chile in 1978. Among contributors are former Foreign Minister of Chile Gabriel Valdés and well-known scholars Luciano Tomassini, Gustavo Lagos, Heraldo Muñoz, and Manfred Wilhelmy.

7003 The Americas in 1984: a year of decisions: report of the Inter-American Dialogue. Washington: Aspen Institute for Humanistic Studies, 1984. 82 p.: ill.

Second report of the Inter-American Dialogue (March 1984) convened under the auspices of Aspen Institute for Humanistic Studies and continued chairmanship of Sol Linowitz. Report offers a somewhat more "liberal" alternative to that of the Kissinger Commission, although the measured recommendations it contains bespeak its very "Establishment" origins. Would have been considerably more interesting, in this reviewer's opinion, had it included a few less current and former government officials and foundation heads and a greater representation from academe; yet perhaps under those circumstances, it might have carried less weight even than the minimal effect it had on Reagan administration policies. Perhaps report's most significant recommendations concern Central America: downplaying the East-

West factor, arguing for political settlements, opposing aid to Nicaraguan *contras*, and endorsing principal reliance on the Contadora process.

7004 Armstrong, Robert. By what right?: US foreign policy, 1945–83 (NACLA, 17:6, Nov./Dec. 1983, p. 2–35)

Short counterculture text-like survey of history and decision-making process behind US foreign policies. NACLA presents an irreverent view of the world, and the personalities, and bureaucracies, that have shaped US involvement. The tone, like so many of NACLA's efforts, is irritatingly "superior" and occasionally sophomoric, but the interpretation advanced is often right on target (pun intended).

7005 Astiz, Carlos A. U.S. policy in Latin America (CUH, 82:481, Feb. 1983, p. 49–51)

Two yrs. after Reagan administration came to power, Astiz observes, it had built an "uneasy relationship" with those Latin American countries seeking to preserve the status quo and had made "deeply suspicious" those attempting "to modify Latin American society." As Astiz sees it: "The energies of the Reagan administration are clearly misdirected," focused on "a domestic struggle for power in El Salvador" and "the bungling policies of a reformist regime in Nicaragua," rather than on much more serious continuing economic problems like the debt crisis.

7006 Avetisián, Artur. Colaboración en el campo de la energética (URSS/AL, 4, abril 1983, p. 56–63, ill.)

Reviews various Soviet-sponsored power projects in Cuba, Argentina, Brazil, Peru, and Nicaragua.

7007 Baklanoff, Eric N. Spain's emergence as a middle industrial power: the basis and structure of Spanish-Latin American economic interrelations. Washington: American Enterprise Institute for Public Policy Research, 1985. 60 p. (AEI Occasional papers; 11)

Careful analysis of Spain's economic relations with Latin America, with cautious forecasts about relationship's future. Notes that Spain's emergence as a middle industrial power with near-"miracle" economic growth rates in 1960s and 1970s, enabled it to play a more active international role. Baklanoff writes "Because of Spain's recently achieved economic strength, the *madre patria* has been able to substitute . . . 'practical' *Hispanismo* for 'lyrical' *Hispanismo*—to make good its quest for a special relationship with its former colonies." Although trade with Latin America has expanded, it appears to have stabilized at only nine to 11 percent of Spain's total trade and 2.5 to three percent of Latin America's. On the other hand, Spain's investment (as of 1982) was about half in Latin America (ca. $1 billion), and Spain has become a significant supplier of technology. The "medium term" overall prospect for expanded economic relations is "ambiguous and uncertain," depending in large part upon whether Spain can regain its economic momentum and become a viable participant in the European Economic Community—in which case, outlook is "promising."

Bartley, Russell H. Acerca de la historia de las corrientes ideológicas en la Latinoamericanística. See *HLAS 46:1902.*

7008 Barylski, Robert V. Civil-military relations in developing countries: the Soviet view: the armed forces in the political system (AFS, 10:3, Spring 1984, p. 464–469)

Review essay discusses collection by Soviet editor (V.E. Chirkin) on military and politics. Barylski quotes Chirkin to the effect that Soviet attitude toward military regimes has been becoming more positive, even as Western scholars have become increasingly critical. From Soviet perspective, radical military regimes are a distinct possibility in the Third World, inaugurating changes that push their countries down the road to socialist revolution. However, more common leftist view of rightist military regimes, that repression itself serves to build a social explosion and radical outcomes, is not discussed.

7009 Becker, David G. Development, democracy and dependency in Latin America: a post-imperialist view (TWF/TWQ, 6:2, April 1984, p. 411–431)

Asserts: "Far from being old liberal wine in new Marxian bottles, as diehard *dependencistas* are wont to charge, post-imperialism offers a more telling critique of late-capitalist class domination in developing countries than *dependencismo* could ever manage." "Development"—in the sense of improvements in the quality of life and some

movement in the direction of real democracy—is happening in Latin America.

Die Beziehungen zwischen Lateinamerika und der Bundesrepublik Deutschland = Las Relaciones América Latina—República Federal de Alemania. See *HLAS 46:12.*

7010 Blasier, Cole. The giant's rival: the USSR and Latin America. Pittsburgh, Pa.: Univ. of Pittsburgh Press, 1983. 213 p.: appendices, bibl., index (Pitt Latin American series)

Important, definitive study of Soviet policy in Latin America, which should be required reading for all US policy-makers and anyone seeking an objective analysis of this controversial subject. Discusses Soviet objectives and "presence" in Latin America, diplomatic, trade and party relations, Cuba, and US policies. Appendices include commentary on Soviet Latin Americanists, Soviet magazines and broadcasts, and Eastern European trade with Latin America. Stresses that the "normalization" of Soviet relations and trade with many Latin American countries is a healthy sign that the export of revolution is not high on USSR's list of priorities in the region. Buttressing this interpretation is the experience with Cuba, which Blasier sees as a "political asset" but "economic liability" for Soviets. Blasier writes: "The argument that in revolutionary situations the United States should counter Soviet interference by interference of its own is based on two false assumptions: first, that Moscow can create and control revolutions, and second, that the United States has the power and knowhow to prevent them." Moreover, "U.S. interference has often served Soviet rather than U.S. causes. That is because interference by the United States in Latin America has often had the effect of uniting a wide spectrum of Latin Americans against the United States, creating anti-American political alignments on which the Soviet Union has been able to capitalize."

7011 ——— and Aldo C. Vacs. América Latina frente a la Unión Soviética (CM/FI, 24:2, oct./dic. 1983, p. 199–232)

Short article summarizes increase of diplomatic and economic relationships between Soviet Union and many Latin American countries in recent yrs. Emphasizes extent to which both sides to the relationship benefit, rather than the often-alleged "threat" that an increased Soviet presence in the hemisphere supposedly poses.

7012 Boersner, Demetrio. Relaciones internacionales de América Latina: breve historia. Caracas: Nueva Sociedad; México: Editorial Nueva Imagen, 1982. 378 p.: bibl., tables.

Unusually well done short history of international relations in Latin America, with a thoughtful concluding chap. setting forth various overall themes (continuity and discontinuity, dependency, and so on). Some 10 chronological tables summarize principal dates and events. Author stresses growing power, significance, and autonomy of leading Latin American countries and declining hegemony of US. These trends, he believes, will ultimately overcome any effort by the conservative Reagan administration to reassert US control. Would some publisher like to do a paperback English version for classroom use?

7013 Brown, Chester L. Latin American arms: for war?: the experience of the period 1971–1980 (IAMEA, 37:1, 1983, p. 61–66, tables)

Expresses concern about growth of military expenditures in the region, despite his acknowledgement that: "Generalization is difficult, perhaps impossible."

7014 Butler, Judy. Toward a New Information Order (NACLA, 16:4, July/Aug. 1982, p. 2–35, bibl., ill.)

NACLA publication translated and adapted from Juan Somavia's introduction to Gregorio Selser and Rafael Roncagliolo's *Trampas de la información y neocolonialismo: las agencias de noticias frente a los países no alineados* (México: ILET, 1979). Authors decry supposedly systematically biased reporting of news media of industrialized Western countries and laud UNESCO's call for a New Information Order that would emanate from the non-aligned and developing countries. In author's view, an "alternative press" would be "part of a political project that seeks to transform society."

7015 Calvert, Peter. Boundary disputes in Latin America. London: Institute for the Study of Conflict, 1983. 28 p.: bibl., map (Conflict studies, 0069–8792; 146)

Short discussion of major Latin American boundary disputes. Gives historical background and recent developments. Excellent

source, but its brevity makes it necessarily superficial. [M.J. Francis]

7015a Calvet de Montes, Fay Dorys. Importancia geopolítica de la integración latinoamericana. Buenos Aires: Adrogué Gráfica Editora, 1982. 176 p.: bibl., ill.

Rambling pseudo-scientific study of background conditions favoring or hampering Latin American integration. Long on statisics like energy potential of dams but weak on political factors that have been central to the integration process to date.

7016 Cisneros-Lavaller, Alberto. Old wine in new bottles: an essay on the study of inter-American relations (UCSB/NS, 8, 1982, p. 267–288, bibl.)

Interesting essay by Venezuelan scholar traces various approaches to the study of inter-American relations that have appeared in the literature over the yrs. Especially useful with regard to Latin American "geopolitical" contributions, although there are also numerous works by North American writers cited and some of these are discussed insightfully. However, there are several key works omitted, and the analysis sometimes degenerates into little more than a list of authors and titles. Complains of "the absence of elementary modeling or systematic data collections" and "the lack of innovative methodologies."

7017 Corea, Gamani. North/South issues: the UNCTAD perspective (IRRI/SD, 36:1, 1983, p. 3–14)

Text of a speech made by Secretary General of UNCTAD to the Royal Institute for International Relations in late 1981. Thoughtfully assesses the significant, but limited, accomplishments of UNCTAD and says that he is struck by the less-than-suspicious conditions under which negotiations must continue in at least the short term (e.g., low growth rates in industrialized countries). Neverthless, insists that industrialized countries have an important economic and political stake in the growth and prosperity of developing countries.

7018 The Crisis in Latin America: strategic, economic, and political dimensions. Edited by Howard J. Wiarda. Foreword by Nancy Landon Kassebaum. Washington: American Enterprise Institute for Public Policy Research, 1984. 32 p.: bibl. (AEI studies in foreign policy)

Slim vol. emanating from Public Policy Week forum at AEI (Dec. 1982). Mark Falcoff, discussing "Latin America as a Strategic Theater" suggests that many Latin American governments are only publicly opposed to US attempts to counter regional security threats, that privately they have many of the same fears; moreover, that many governments do not share the perspective of many North American scholars about declining US hegemony. Joseph Grunwald offers an overview of Latin American economic problems, their roots, and likely future course. Wiarda presents some thoughtful observations on "new realities in Latin America and in US-Latin American relations" and prescriptions for policy. Arguing for a "prudence model" to guide the US, he states: "The United States cannot be a mere 'moral force' . . . Heavy-handed interventionism and cold war rhetoric, however, are not appropriate strategies either."

7019 Daza Valenzuela, Pedro. Visión de América Latina (Política [Instituto de Ciencia Política, Univ. de Chile, Santiago] 3, 1983, p. 147–158)

Chile's OAS ambassador speaks to the familiar rhetorical issue: What is Latin America? Focuses mainly on common problems of economic development, as well as contrasts in such matters as per capita income. Also notes that Latin Americans have always conceived of themselves as having a "democratic vocation," which nonetheless has encountered an obstacle or two on its road to fulfillment.

7020 Destler, I.M. and Eric R. Alterman. Congress and Reagan's foreign policy (GU/WQ, 7:1, 1984, p. 91–101)

Authors attempt to explain why Congress, even the Democrat-controlled House, appears so unable to mount an effective opposition to President Reagan's ideological foreign policy stances on matters like aid to the *contras*. In their view, it reflects the inherent inability of Congress, as an institution, to lead in the foreign policy process.

7020a Diniz, Artur José Almeida. A política e o Terceiro Mundo: contradições políticas e econômicas contemporâneas. Belo Horizonte: Editôra da *Revista Brasileira de*

Estudos Políticas, 1983. 223 p.: bibl. (Estudos sociais e políticas; 36)

Discussion of the lack of Third World development which faults mercantilist policies of developed countries and attributes uneven levels of development to cold war ideology and resulting alliance system. Highly ambitious work. [M.J. Francis]

7021 Draper, Theodore. Falling dominoes (The New York Review of Books, 30:16, Oct. 1983, p. 6, 10, 12, 14, 16, 18, 20, ills.)

Brilliant article by longstanding critic of US interventions. Observes that "every major [post-World War II] commitment [of the US] has been justified in the name of defending faraway dominoes." Turning his attention to Central America, he asks for (and cannot find) a rational explanation of exactly how the political character of El Salvador and Nicaragua—given disparities in population and military power—is a "threat" to Mexico and/or the US. Concludes that "countries are not dominoes."

7022 Dunbar Ortiz, Roxanne. The Fourth World and indigenism: politics of isolation and alternatives (The Journal of Ethnic Studies [Western Washington Univ., Bellingham] 12:1, Spring 1984, p. 79–105, bibl.)

Identifies and takes issue with two approaches to the "problem" of the Indians of America: assimilation and ethnic particularism (Pan-Indianism). In her view, despite such conflicts as that of the Sandinista government in Nicaragua with the Miskito population, best perspective is that of "anti-imperialist national liberation forces, which [make] clear that the political realities of the world also include the Indian struggle."

7023 Duncan, W. Raymond. Soviet power in Latin America: success or failure? (in The Soviet Union in the Third World: successes and failures. Edited by Robert H. Donaldson. Boulder, Colo.: Westview Press, 1981, p. 1–26)

In this leading analyst's opinion, the significance of increased Soviet diplomatic, economic, technical, and trade relations with Latin America should not be overestimated. Soviets "envision limited opportunities to erode U.S. and Western influence, but . . . the region remains of lower priority than Africa and Asia." The USSR is "a great power in quest of traditional great power concerns," including "at minimum the search for influence to guarantee territorial security in the long run, access to markets and resources . . . and a generally cautious and pragmatic assessment of opportunities." It is hard to determine how "successful" Soviets have been to date: Washington's apparently somewhat weakened position, Duncan suggests, may only reflect US failures to meet Latin American economic demands, while "Latin American communism . . . beats with a distinct national impulse." Recommends that US "ride with nationalist movements" rather than oppose them by military means: "The essential point here is that nationalism . . . is a constant barrier to Soviet penetration . . . This point applies to Cuba as well as to Mexico or Nicaragua, and it teaches a lesson that bears far more attention from Washington than has been the case during the recent era in U.S.-Latin American affairs."

7024 Dupras, Maurice. Canada and the OAS (DEA/IP, Jan./Feb. 1984, p. 15–17)
Liberal member of Canadian Parliament, Chairman of Subcommittee on Latin America and the Caribbean of Commons Committee on External Affairs and National Defense, argues that his country should increase its involvement in OAS from Permanent Observer to full membership.

7025 The Dynamics of Latin American foreign policies. Edited by Jennie K. Lincoln and Elizabeth G. Ferris. Boulder, Colo.: Westview Press, 1984. 325 p.: bibl., index (Westview special studies on Latin America and the Caribbean)
Excellent collection of essays which should be in the scholar's library as well as the classroom. Editors explore general issues involved in comparing Latin American foreign policies. Additional chaps. in pt. 1 focus on interstate conflict, regional integration, US-Latin American relations. Pt. 2 on South America has chaps. on Argentina, Brazil, Chile, Peru, Venezuela and Colombia, and Bolivia. Pt. 3 is on Central America as a subregion, with country chaps. on Mexico, Nicaragua, and Cuba's subregional role. Pt. 4 (Ferris) sets forth a proposed agenda for future research.

7025a Estrella Vintimilla, Pablo. América Latina: las razones de la ira. Cuenca, Ecuador: Univ. de Cuenca, Instituto de Investigaciones Sociales, 1983. 332 p.: bibl.
Impassioned assault on US imperialism with particular fury directed at Reagan administration. Nothing new in the analysis although Reagan's willingness to exercise power in the hemisphere (and talk about it in terms that Latin Americans have traditionally objected to) will certainly serve as "proof" of US intentions to dominate the area for those predisposed to believe this. [M.J. Francis]

7025b Estudios sobre la reestructuración de ALALC. Edición de Raymundo Barros Charlín y Pilar Armanet Armanet. Gonzalo Valdés Budge et al. Santiago: Instituto de Estudios Internacionales, Univ. de Chile, 1980. 104 p.: bibl. (Estudios internacionales)
Set of well done papers dealing with Latin American economic integration although tending to be rather legalistic and olympian in perspective. Almost no attention is paid to domestic political factors that have stalled integration. [M.J. Francis]

7026 Evers, Tilman Tönnies et al. US-Intervention und kapitalistische Gegenrevolution. Berlin: Olle & Wolter, 1982. 302 p.: bibl., ill. (Lateinamerika; 6)
Collection of several essays by Latin American Marxists like Gregorio Selser (translated into German) on theme of "U.S. Intervention and Capitalist Counterrevolution" in Latin America, followed by brief overviews of 13 Latin American countries written by German observers of similar ideological bent.

7027 Ezcurra, Ana María. La ofensiva neoconservadora: las iglesias de U.S.A. y la lucha ideológica hacia América Latina. Madrid: Instituto de Estudios Políticos para América Latina y Africa (IEPALA), 1982. 260 p.: bibl.
Old-style Latin American polemic on the "threat" of "neo-conservatism" in the US to Latin America, with particular attention to activities of a Cuban-exile Committee on Religion and Democracy in Cuba. Also mentioned, however, is opposition of numerous US church leaders and denominations to Reagan administration's Central American policies.

7028 Fagg, John Edwin. Pan Americanism. Malabar, Fla.: R.E. Krieger Publishing

Co., 1982. 218 p.: bibl., index (An Anvil original; 0570–1062)

Short paperback text by prominent US-Latin American historian. Traces history of Pan-American ideal and US policies from independence to present in 124 p. (less than half devoted to post-World War II era). Appended are 24 well choosen readings, including several primary sources. Useful for history courses on college level; perhaps less so for political science surveys of the subject because of limited coverage of recent events.

7029 Fernández de Velasco, Manuel. Relaciones España-Estados Unidos y multilaciones territoriales en Latinoamérica. México: UNAM, Facultad de Filosofía y Letras, 1982. 200 p.: bibl., ill., plates (Seminarios)

History of diplomacy surrounding US acquisition of Florida from Spain, mostly 1809–19 period. Draws mainly on papers of Spanish Ambassador to US, Luis de Onís.

7029a Ferrero Costa, Eduardo. El desarrollo del Nuevo Derecho del Mar y las 200 millas (SP, 12, dic. 1980, p. 123–138)

Informative discussion of the results of the Law of the Sea negotiations. Favors the new law. [M.J. Francis]

7030 Foreign policy on Latin America, 1970–1980. Edited by the staff of *Foreign Policy.* Boulder, Colo.: Westview Press; Washington: Carnegie Endowment, 1983. 184 p.: bibl., index.

As title suggests, an anthology of articles on Latin America pub. by *Foreign Policy* (1970–80). Quality is generally high and most have stood the test of time, at least as historical documents. Greatest number by single author is three by Abraham Lowenthal. Accurately, present editor remarks in his brief introduction that a "persistent theme" running through the articles "is the steady decline in U.S. control over the politics and economies of Latin America."

7031 Friedlander, Robert A. United States policy towards armed rebellion (LIWA/ YWA, 37, 1983, p. 39–62)

Notes that the Reagan policy was, in a sense, "a conscious attempt to break loose from the political quagmire created by the Vietnam War" and reassert traditional US power. However, he argues that post-World War II "policy toward armed rebellion during

the Cold War was, in truth, a major departure from the overall precedents of the past"— which he attempts to demonstrate by looking at US policy from Monroe to F.D.R. Good Neighbor Policy. El Salvador appears to Friedlander to represent a "return to the Monroeism of the past," yet "the United States in the decade of the 1980s no longer carries the burden, and can no longer maintain the obligations, of the Truman-Eisenhower-Kennedy era. If not a clay colossus. America is, nonetheless, a much-reduced image of its former self."

7032 Fructífero diálogo entre latinoamericanistas (URSS/AL, 7:67, julio 1983, p. 73–80)

Account of a special session of the Scientific Council of the Latin American Institute of the Academy of Sciences in USSR, convened to commemorate 60th anniversary of the Soviet Union and including leaders from various communist parties, workers organizations, and national liberation movements in Latin America.

7033 Fuentes, Carlos. 1983 [i.e. Nineteen hundred and eighty three] Commencement address (Harvard University Gazette [Cambridge, Mass.] June 1983, p. 11–13, ill.)

Fuentes's commencement address at Harvard in 1983. An impassioned and eloquent plea for the US to respect the principle of non-intervention and negotiate political solutions to problems in Central America and elsewhere with the aid of "friends" like the *Contadora* powers. Fuentes reminds us, with reference to Mexico: "We were the first domino."

7034 Gannon, Francis X. Will the OAS live to be 100?: does it deserve to? (FIU/CR, 13:4, 1984, p. 12–14, 42–43)

Long-time consultant to OAS Secretary General reviews history of the organization, as well as reasons for its current inertia, and answers question posed in the title in the affirmative. OAS survives because it is occasionally useful, and Gannon insists, if it lacks "teeth," the member states have only themselves to blame. Also makes several suggestions to improve organization's functioning, including efforts to incorporate English-speaking Caribbean states more effectively (Falkland/Malvinas issue opened up a serious rift).

7035 García Gómez, Alberto. Los derechos humanos y el derecho a la paz (UNL/H, 22, 1981, p. 281–288)

Makes the rather obvious, although no less significant, point that there is a relationship between human rights and peace: namely, that all "rights" that have been the subject of numerous treaties and protocols do not do the individual much good when that individual loses his/her fundamental "right to life" in war.

7035a García Robles, Alfonso. El Nuevo Orden Internacional y el desarme. México: Partido Revolucionario Institucional, 1982. 13 p. (Estudios de la política exterior; 7)

Document-filled discussion of disarmament and arms control issues as they link with the NIEO concept. Author is Mexico's Nobel Peace Prize winner. [M.J. Francis]

7036 Garza, Luis Alberto de la. Antecedentes históricos de las relaciones Japón-América Latina (UNAM/RI, 9 : 30, enero/marzo 1982, p. 69–73)

Suggests that one should see early Spanish connections with the Philippines, some of them via New Spain, as laying something of a groundwork for more recent links between Japan and Latin America. Underscores same theme (one of several) in companion essay by Lothar Knauth (item **7057**).

7037 Gay, Daniel. Les élites québécoises et l'Amérique latine. Montréal, Canada: Nouvelle optique, 1983. 341 p.: bibl. (Matériaux)

Sociologist at Laval Univ. in Quebec surveys images of Latin America and its problems as reflected in newspapers and other elite publications.

7038 Gil, Federico G. Evolución de la política latinoamericana de los Estados Unidos (*in* Iberoamérica en los años 80: perspectivas de cambio social y político. Compilado por Enrique Baloyra Herp y Rafael López-Pintor. Madrid: Centro de Investigaciones Sociológicas, 1982?, p. 177–190)

Textbook-style overview of US-Latin American policies, especially since World War II through about 1982. In discussing Reagan administration, emphasizes early confusion about its real policies that stemmed from seemingly somewhat contradictory pronouncements of various personalities like Haig and Enders.

7039 Golob, Ignac. Non-alignment and détente (Socialist Thought and Practice [Belgrade] 23 : 3, 1983, p. 72–77)

Yugoslav suggests that Non-Alignment Movement has conceived the only "true" vision of détente which superpowers should start subscribing to with all deliberate speed.

7040 Goncharova, Tatiana. Aspectos políticos e ideológicos del Movimiento del Países no Alineados (URSS/AL, 10 : 58, oct. 1982, p. 42–54)

Article by Soviet analyst examines some of the significant ideological differences within Non-Aligned Movement over the yrs., but concludes various unifying factors—resistance to imperialism, development problems, and so on—are likely to lead to Movement's eventual consolidation.

7041 González, Heliodoro. Can foreign aid continue as a growth industry for the bureaucracy?: Latin American cooperation at the United Nations (IAMEA, 37 : 1, 1983, p. 53–60, tables)

Regular contributor to this journal points favorably to former UN Ambassador Kirkpatrick's denunciation of "outrageous and unbalanced criticism of the United States" in the world organization and to expressed desire of House Appropriations Subcommittee on Foreign Assistance to tailor its policies to rewarding "friends" and punishing "enemies."

7042 Gordon, Sheldon E. The Canadian government and human rights abroad (DEA/IP, 6, Nov./Dec. 1983, p. 8–10)

Gordon, member of the editorial board of Toronto *Globe and Mail*, criticizes "short shrift" given by External Affairs to a report of a parliamentary subcommittee on Canada's relations with Latin America—with particular attention to human rights.

7043 Gornov, Mijail. América Latina: intensificación de la lucha contra el imperialismo y la oligarquía por la democracia y el progreso social (URSS/AL, 8 : 56, agosto 1982, p. 4–16)

In this Soviet author's view, 1980s mark a "new qualitative phase in the evolution of the battle of the peoples of Latin America against imperialism and reaction." His evidence, on the one hand, is what he sees as increasingly "independent" and influential role of Latin American countries on the world scene, the revolution in Nicaragua, and the steady democraticization of regimes elsewhere in the continent; and on the other hand, the Reagan administration's political and military pressure against changes that might threaten traditional US hegemony in the region.

7044 Governance in the Western Hemisphere. Edited by Viron P. Vaky. New York: Praeger: *with the* Aspen Institute for Humanistic Studies, 1983. 532 p.: bibl.

Well crafted collection of essays on "governance," a concept that embraces nongovernmental as well as official institutions and patterns of association and interchange. Thoughtful scholars present readable, analytic essays on topics as diverse as debt, human rights, and collective security. Unfortunately, the Aspen Institute chose not to index this important vol. [G.W. Grayson]

7045 Grass, Günter. Epilogue: America's backyard (*in* Trouble in our backyard: Central America and the United States in the eighties. Edited by Martin Diskin. Foreword by John Womack Jr. Epilogue by Günter Grass. New York: Pantheon Books, 1984, p. 245–253)

Famous German novelist has high praise for the Sandinista revolution. He writes: "Anyone who, like me, visited Poland last year and has just returned from Nicaragua, realizes how foolish the superpowers have been in trying to control their backyards. For this time they are faced by a new and unfamiliar kind of opposition—and it won't be crushed. Both movements are the same—socialist and Catholic . . ." For a riposte to Günter Grass's views on Latin American politics, see Mario Vargas Llosa's article (item **6027a**).

Grayson, George W. The joint oil facility: Mexican-Venezuelan cooperation in the Caribbean. See item **7137**.

7046 Grličkov, Aleksandar. The policy of non-alignment and socialism as a world process (Socialist Thought and Practice [Belgrade] 23:3, 1983, p. 37–47)

Yugoslav author sees Non-Aligned Movement's opposition to blocs and imperialism, as well as subscription to the concept of peaceful coexistence, as helping to create conditions under which a variety of socialist experiments can prosper on the world scene.

7047 Guevara, Ernesto. Guerrilla warfare. Introduction and case studies by Brian Loveman and Thomas M. Davies, Jr. Lincoln: Univ. of Nebraska Press, 1985. 440 p.: bibl., ill., index.

Extremely valuable book which reprints Guevara's writings on guerrilla warfare, comments generally on changing character of insurgencies in Latin America and shifting US response, and offers a relatively detailed account and chronology of experiences country-by-country. Editors observe: "In the short run, both U.S. policy makers and Che Guevara failed. Instead of either 'many Vietnams' or 'constructive democratic reform,' the U.S. and Latin American responses to Che Guevara's anti-imperialist struggle gave birth to military governments and terrorist regimes that frequently adopted as public policy institutionalized torture, repression, and antipolitics."

7048 Hacia un Nuevo Orden Económico Internacional: temas prioritarios para América Latina. Compilado por Ricardo Ffrench-Davis y Ernesto Tironi. México: Fondo de Cultura Económica, 1981. 305 p.: bibl. (Sec. de obras de economía)

Collection of essays and commentaries on international trade, finance, and technology transfer by a veritable who's who of international economists: Ricardo Ffrench Davis, Carlos Díaz Alejandro, Enrique Iglesias (ECLA Executive Secretary), William Cline, Albert Fishlow *et al.* Excludes only the Marxist perspective.

7049 Hosono, Akio. Economic relationship between Japan and Latin America (Latin American Studies [Univ. of Tsukuba, Japan] 6, 1983, p. 75–101, tables)

Summary of Japan's trade with and investment in Latin America since 1960s. Views future economic relations between the two areas as basically complementary in almost all sectors, albeit differentiated to some extent by country, size of enterprise, and other factors. Argues for more cooperation based on mutual understanding of economic policies and cultures of both parties to the relationship, commenting nevertheless that "cultural and academic interchange between Latin America and Japan remains in a backward state." For economist's comment, see item **2888**.

7050 Human rights and basic needs in the Americas. Edited by Margaret E. Crahan. Washington: Georgetown Univ. Press, 1982. 343 p.: bibl.

Collection of essays that is one of the products of a project initiated in 1977 by the Woodstock Theological Center (Washington). Pt. 1 (by Crahan) discusses the State in Latin America, evolution of the military in various Latin American countries, and impact on human rights of the ideology of national security. Pt. 2 concerns "basic needs," how these can be defined and the impact of capital flows and such things as IMF standby agreements thereon. Pt. 3 analyzes US policies and contains two of the best essays in the collection: Brian H. Smith's "U.S.-Latin American Military Relations since World War II" and Lars Schoultz's "The Carter Administration and Human Rights in Latin America."

7051 Human rights in the Americas: the struggle for consensus. Edited by Alfred Hennelly and John Langan. Washington: Georgetown Univ. Press, 1982. 291 p.: bibl.

First of two vols. from a project initiated in 1977 by the Woodstock Theological Center (Washington). This collection of essays is somewhat more theologically and theoretically oriented than its companion vol. (see item **7050**). Of particular interest to Latin Americanists is Alfred Hennelly's "Human Rights and Latin American Theology."

7052 Iglesias, Enrique. Latin America calls for new partnership arrangement (DEA/IP, 2, March/April 1981, p. 21–25, plate)

Sophisticated analysis of the contemporary international political economy by the Executive Secretary of ECLA. Among other things, makes a plea to revise traditional concept of dependence "to accomodate the tremendous dynamism of interdependence" and argues against any attempt by North to try to divide South by wooing newly industrializd countries—these, he stresses, still have significant pockets of "poverty, inequality, and injustice."

7053 Incontro sulla cooperazione dell'Europa allo sviluppo dell'America latina, Roma, 1980. Incontro sulla cooperazione dell'Europa allo sviluppo dell'America latina. Roma: Istituto italo-latino americano, 1981. 352 p.

Speeches and other documents from 1980 meeting held to strengthen European cooperation in the development efforts of Latin American and Caribbean countries. Meeting sponsored by the President of the Council of Ministers of the European Community, President of the Italian-Latin American Institute, and Secretary General of OAS.

7054 Inter-American Juridical Committee. Recomendaciones e informes del Comité Jurídico Interamericano, Rio de Janeiro. Washington: Secretaría General, Organización Estados Americanos, 1982. 675 p. (Documentos oficiales; 12)

Documents trace activities of the Inter-American Committee of Jurists (1978–80). CJI discussed such matters as general norms of private international law, torture as a potential international crime, territorial issues like Belize, and industrial property.

7055 Kaldor, Mary. Armamenti e Terzo mondo: indusrializzazione o sottosviluppo? (MULINO, 32:286, marzo/aprile 1983, p. 259–278)

Italian translation of a chap. in a 1982 British publication, *The Baroque arsenal*. Examines in some detail the growth of military spending and industrial development in many Third World countries (e.g., Argentina and Brazil). In her view, this is creating potentially explosive situations because a "huge military-industrial edifice" is being created on a "fragile social foundation."

7056 Khachaturov, K. Latin America and imperialist ideology (IA, 12, Dec. 1982, p. 92–100)

He writes: "Recent events—most notably the conflict between Britain and Argentina—have reminded the peoples of Latin America of the great significance imperialism attaches to strengthening its strategic, military, and economic positions in that region . . . Contrary to the laws of historical development and present-day realities, the USA is trying by all means available to continue its hegemonistic policy to the south of its own borders, clinging to the outdated notion that Latin American countries still remain its 'backyard.'" In Khachaturov's view, the "ruling circles" in Latin America are increasingly looking to diversify relationships, with the European countries, Japan, and Israel, as a means of decreasing dependency on the US. All of these countries share a "bourgeois ideology and a shared platform of direct as well as covert anticommunism," but they are attempting by word and deed—"Hispanism, Social Democracy, Socialist International, and so on—to distance themselves from their North American rival."

Klementeva, N.M. Razvitie sviazei mezhdu SSSR i riadom stran Latinskoi Ameriki v oblasti kultury, 1965–1975: bibliografi- cheskii ukazatel = Developments of relations between the USSR and a number of countries in Latin America in the sphere of culture, 1967–1975: bibliographic guide. See item **36.**

7057 Knauth, Lothar. Antecedentes históri- cos de las relaciones Japón-América Latina (UNAM/RI, 9 : 30, enero/marzo 1982, p. 9–20)

Interesting article by UNAM scholar traces "historical antecedents" of contempo- rary Japanese-Latin American relations.

7058 Komatina, Miljan. Policy and move- ment of non-alignment and the United Nations (Socialist Thought and Practice [Belgrade] 23 : 3, 1983, p. 60–71)

According to this Yugoslav analyst: "The non-aligned countries have become the basic factor of the democratization of the UN. By challenging the disposition of forces within the world Organization, they have re- duced the scope for great-Power and bloc domination . . ."

7059 Kownacki, Piotr. Sojusz dla Postępu: taktyka polityczna ozy program rozwoju gospodarczego, synteza polityki USA wobec krajów Ameryki Lacińskiej, 1961– 1974 = The Alliance for Progress: the politi- cal tactics or a program for economic devel- opment, an overview of USA's policy towards the Latin American countries, 1961–1974. Wrocław, Poland: Zakład Narodowy im. Ossolińskich, 1983. 164 p.: bibl.

Polish political scientist writes ac- count of the failures of the Alliance for Prog- ress, J.F. Kennedy's foreign policy initiative. Includes wide range of materials. [K. Complak]

7060 Lagos, Gustavo. Las relaciones entre Estados Unidos y América Latina (in Iberoamérica en los años 80: perspectivas de cambio social y político. Compilado por Enrique Baloyra Herp y Rafael López-Pintor. Madrid: Centro de Investigaciones Socio- lógicas, 1982?, p. 191–210)

Significant essay by leading Latin American scholar. Attempts to explain the relatively extreme shift from Carter's "lib- eral" policies to "conservative" ones of

Reagan. Does so by stressing that both have different approaches to essentially the same phenomenon, the declining hegemony of the US. While pushing human rights, Carter also opted for greater tolerance of ideological plu- ralism; Reagan, on the other hand, has made a concerted effort to reverse the decline in US influence. Neither approach has proved to be especially successful, not even in the Central American and Caribbean subregion where US hegemony has traditionally been strong. Ac- cording to Lagos, the world is increasingly multipolar, offering Latin American coun- tries "broad opportunities to . . . diversify de- pendence and gain more autonomy."

7061 LaRocque, Gene R. and Stephen D. Goose. Arming the Third World (CRIA/W, 25 : 10, Oct. 1982, p. 19–21)

Brief but incisive analysis of trends in Third World arms acquisitions and the sources of supply. LaRocque and Goose com- ment: "In the great debate over who is the number one arms merchant to the Third World, the U.S. and the USSR accuse each other, yet each seems to try hard to catch up."

7062 Latin American nations in world poli- tics. Edited by Heraldo Muñoz and Joseph S. Tulchin. Boulder, Colo.: Westview Press, 1984. 278 p.: bibl., index (Foreign rela- tions of the Third World; 3)

Splendid collection of essays stem- ming from a 1982 conference held in Chile, jointly sponsored by the US National Science Foundation and the Comisión Nacional de Investigación Científica y Tecnológica of Chile, and involving scholars mainly from the Instituto de Estudios Internacionales of the Univ. de Chile and the Institute of Latin American Studies of the Univ. of North Caro- lina at Chapel Hill. The purpose, as Tulchin describes it, was to test "the dominant para- digms of the field with a view to exploring their appropriateness for the analysis of Latin American international relations." Not all the essays are explicitly theoretical in con- tent, but nearly all are of high quality and provide useful information with theoretical implications. Case studies include the "Southern Cone," Argentina, Brazil, Chile, Peru, Venezuela, Colombia, Mexico, and Cuba. However, as Alberto van Klaveren comments in his thought-provoking lead es- say, the many "disparate elements" available for comparative studies "have yet to be systematized and integrated into a coherent and comprehensive approach."

7063 Livingstone, Neil C. Fighting terrorism and "dirty little wars" (AF/ AUR, 35:3, March/April 1984, p. 4–16, ill.)

Rather scary (at least to this reviewer) article, especially appearing in *Air University Review*, that attempts to make the case that "dirty little conflicts" "are critical to Western security." States that US should support literally "any force" around the globe that is resisting the Soviets, that the Grenada operation offers an example of how the media should be excluded from coverage of US operations, and that US involvement in Central America has been curtailed partly because there has been too much publicity, and so on in that vein.

7064 Lowenthal, Abraham F. Change the agenda (FP, 52, Fall 1983, p. 64–77)

Should be read in conjunction with another of Lowenthal's essays, written some months earlier (see item **7065**), part of the argument of which is incorporated in this item. Lowenthal observes that in late 1982 (when he had previously written), Reagan's approach to Latin America was apparently moderating much like Carter's (albeit for different starting positions); however, in 1983, Reagan appeared determined to "stay the [conservative ideological] course" that he had promised in the 1980 campaign. In so doing, argues Lowenthal: "The Reagan administration appears intent on ignoring or denying Latin America's emergence. It has attempted to restore U.S. dominance with threats of force, security assistance, support for friendly governments, and covert intervention against anti-U.S. movements. The administration's efforts have been counterproductive, particularly in the large countries of the region." Moreover, the Reagan policy has diverted attention and energies from other important hemispheric problems like the financial crisis, which "is a far greater threat to inter-American and global security than leftist revolutionaries in Central America."

7065 ———. Ronald Reagan and Latin America: coping with hegemony in decline (*in* Eagle defiant: United States foreign policy. Edited by Kenneth A. Oye, Robert J. Lieber, and Donald Rothchild. Boston: Little, Brown & Co., 1983, p. 311–335)

Begins by asking why it is that so many US administrations come into office pledging drastic changes in US policy toward Latin America and so often end up with those promises deferred. His answer is that a number of international and domestic factors, including the policy-making process itself, work to defeat new policy initiatives. His examples are the Carter administration and, writing in late 1982, the Reagan administration as well. At that time Reagan policies appeared to be much more moderate than campaign rhetoric had suggested; the hard line on Nicaragua (support for the *contras*, mining operations, and so on) came later. As Lowenthal himself subsequently acknowledged (item **7064**), he was to some extent wrong about Reagan. However, the factors he highlights are real enough and an interesting point of departure for trying to explain why the Reagan case has broken all the "rules." For Spanish version of this article, see *Foro Internacional* (México, 24:1, julio/sept. 1983, p. 21–49).

7066 Luckham, Robin. Militarisation and the new international anarchy (TWF/ TWQ, 6:2, April 1984, p. 351–373, graphs, table)

Maintains that the arms race has been a significant factor in deepening the global economic recession and has been a factor that "bears disportionately on the Third World." However, "neither the arms race nor the recession can be controlled without a major reordering of the present international anarchy," which seems to be an unrealistic goal. The fundamental problem, to Luckham, is: "Nationally-dominant classes may benefit from a sub-optimal allocation of resources or even from recession within a national economy, as perhaps in Reagan's United States, Thatcher's Britain, or Pinochet's Chile."

7067 Maira, Luis. América Latina y la crisis de hegemonía norteamericana. Lima: DESCO, 1982. 328 p.: bibl. (Estudios internacionales)

Effort by Chilean scholar (then with CIDE in Mexico) to explain to his readers the reasons for rise of New Right in US and Reagan administration's initial Latin American policies. Perceptive and balanced analysis.

7068 ———. Nota preliminar sobre la influencia—creciente—del pensamiento de la nueva derecha norteamericana en Amé-

rica Latina (UNAM/RMS, 43:43, 1981,
p. 1923–1943)

Attempt by a prominent Chilean analyst (then with Mexico's CIDE) to explain to a Latin American audience the political currents that brought Ronald Reagan to power in 1980 and some of the ideas emanating from the Reagan camp. Maira, writing in 1981, predicted that the Reagan victory would tend to strengthen conservative regimes and political factions in Latin America.

7069 Martin, Benjamin. Spain, the US, and Latin America (DIS, 30:4, Fall 1983, p. 416–419)

Notes that strengthening ties with Latin America has been high on the foreign policy agenda for Spain's new Socialist government, with Prime Minister Felipe González presiding over the Socialist international's regional activities in support of democratic development, human rights, and social justice. In author's view, González is in a unique position to champion the *Contadora* process, since the Reagan administration has little influence over Spain and, indeed, needs Spain's backing in such matters as the stationing of US missiles on European soil.

7070 Martínov, Boris and **Vladimir Súdarev.** Litigios territoriales en América Latina: pt. 1–2 (URSS/AL, set. 1982, p. 3–23, map; 10:58, oct. 1982, p. 21–41, maps)

Articles by two Soviet authors on Latin American territorial disputes. First article is somewhat more propagandistic than the second in that it stresses that most Latin American disputes have derived directly or indirectly from colonialism as in the Chaco War/Standard Oil, Arbenz Guatemala/CIA, etc. Second article presents more objective discussion of Beagle Channel dispute, Marañón controversy, Gulf of Venezuela problem, etc. Authors note that it has been the official USSR position that such disputes should be resolved through negotiations rather than force.

7071 Mates, Leo. Role of the founders of non-alignment (Socialist Thought and Practice [Belgrade] 23:3, 1983, p. 48–59)

Article by a Yugoslav surveys history of the Non-Aligned Movement, with emphasis upon the role of leaders like Tito, Nehru, and Nkrumah. Notes with pride that Tito's last appearance at the Havana conference resulted in a strong majority vote for his position, reemphasizing movement's original thrust, rather than thinly-disguised pro-Eastern bloc position of Castro's Cuba.

7072 Moncayo, Guillermo. Las relaciones políticas entre América Latina y la República Federal de Alemania (Contribuciones [Konrad-Adenauer-Stiftung, CIEDLA, Buenos Aires] 2, abril/junio 1984, p. 48–57)

Short discussion by Argentine of West Germany's relations with Latin America, which somehow manages to overlook some of the most interesting aspects thereof: controversies over supply of nuclear energy to Argentina and Brazil, Bonn's evolving positions on the continuing crisis in Central America, and so on.

7073 Montaner, Carlos Alberto. América Latina y USA (Linden Lane Magazine [Millburn, N.J.] 2:1, enero/marzo 1983, p. 20–22)

Intriguing and extremely perceptive reflections on the impact of North American culture on Latin America, what author terms "a profound process of transculturation."

7074 Montgomery, Robin Navarro. Psychological warfare and the Latin American crisis (AF/AUR, 36:5, July/Aug. 1982, p. 48–57)

Proposes that the US fashion a psychological warfare strategy of its own to counter the appeal to Castro, which "is derived to a large extent from his perceptual affinity with basic currents of intellectual thought in Latin America." US intellectuals, Montgomery insists, should stop always criticizing their own country and start showing what a failure the Castro model is both in terms of freedom and economic performance. Also, US should build on Reagan administration's efforts to foster ever-closer relations with Latin American military, including a vast increase in the number of Latin American officers trained in US.

7075 Myers, Constance Ashton. The United States and the Inter-American Commission on Women: first twenty-five years of the relationship (SECOLAS/A, 14, March 1983, p. 61–79)

Thoughtful, carefully researched, and well written article by historian, traces evolution of an obscure international nongovernmental organization devoted to the cause of women's rights. Will be of interest to students of international organizations, as well as of women's issues and of inter-American relations. Concludes: "no international organization, before, during, or following the years of [Mrs.] Roosevelt's influence succeeded in bringing about equal civil rights in fact. And almost inevitably, the IACW went the way of small change-oriented groupings. Once co-opted into the bureaucratic structures that are the building blocks of modern state and international systems, their effectiveness was smothered and their personnel pacified with titles and well furnished offices."

7076 Nakagawa, Fumio. Japanese-Latin American relations since the 1960s: an overview (Latin American Studies [Univ. of Tsukuba, Japan] 6, 1983, p. 63–74, ill., table)

Pt. 1 of multi-part article offers overview of Japanese-Latin American relations since 1960s, with some pertinent historical background such as the violence that erupted against Japanese residents of Peru in 1930s. Argues that, while most Japanese and Latin American elites have continued to see economic relations between the two areas of the world as inherently complementary, a certain segment of Latin American counter-elites has come to view Japanese presence and investment as merely an extension of capitalist imperialism. For their part, Japanese businessmen in Latin America have a feeling of superiority and react negatively to local elites, values, and institutions that reinforce economic underdevelopment.

7076a Navarro Dávila, Fabián. Apuntes sobre la derecho territorial americano (IGME/RG, 17, dic. 1982, p. 59–82)

Interesting historical/legal discussion of various territorial disputes that plague the Western Hemisphere. Good review of hemispheric international law. [M.J. Francis]

Nef, Jorge. Political democracy in Latin America: an exploration into the nature of two political projects. See item **6017.**

7077 Orozco Giraldo, Yolanda. El *Informe MacBride*: el tránsito de la microcomunicación a la macro-comunicación como problema (UPB, 36:127, mayo 1982, p. 125–149, plates)

Bolivian author complains that too little attention has been given by UN and elsewhere to the problem of assuring transfer of information technology to developing countries, the subject of a UNESCO report.

7078 Orrego Vicuña, Claudio. Latin America: a human rights perspective for the 1980s (*in* Latin American prospects for the 1980s: equity, democratization, and development. Edited by Archibald R.M. Ritter and David H. Pollock. New York: Praeger, 1983, p. 40–53)

Orrego Vicuña reflects on the prospects for human rights in Latin America. In his view, 1970s saw a great deal of progress in the development of a moral consciousness, legal norms, and some institutions supporting human rights, which he believes bodes well for the future as military regimes democratize.

7079 Pajómov, Iván. Algunos aspectos de las relaciones de España con los países de América Latina (URSS/AL, 8:56, agosto 1982, p. 92–106, ill., tables)

Factual survey by Soviet economics doctoral candidate of Spain's relations with Latin America over the yrs., with emphasis on post-Franco rapprochement. Includes trade statistics and country-by-country listing of development projects.

7080 Panikkar, Raimundo. Is the notion of human rights a Western concept? (ICPHS/D, 120, Winter 1982, p. 75–102)

Thought-provoking critique of Western concept of human rights from an (East) Indian perspective. Concludes that, although conceptions differ to a significant extent, the world should definitely not give up attempting to define and enforce human rights. The task is to try to reconcile different traditions as a means of enhancing a human condition that is no longer one of isolated cultures.

7081 Parkinson, F. Latin America: her newly industrialising countries and the New International Economic Order (JLAS, 16:1, May 1984, p. 127–141)

Insightful article, definitely worth reading, by longtime analyst of Latin America's international relations. Reviewing Prebisch's initial prescriptions for Latin American development and subsequent thinking about them in ECLA/UNCTAD and *dependencia* circles, Parkinson stresses that inadequate attention has been given to the contrasts between newly industrialized countries (NICs) and sub-NICs. In his view, large-scale economic integration will remain only a dream and schemes have to be devised to protect the sub-NICs from the worst effects of transnational corps.

7082 Patel, Surendra J. La era del Tercer Mundo (BNCE/CE, 33:6, junio 1983, p. 511–517)

Director of UNCTAD's Div. of Technology surveys technological changes of last several centuries and concludes that bringing benefits of technological change to Third World is *the* task for next era in human history.

7082a Peirano Basso, Jorge. Buenos oficios y mediación: la práctica internacional en el último cuarto de siglo. Montevideo: Ediciones Idea, 1983. 125 p.

Prof. of international law deals with uses of good offices and mediation in the settlement of disputes. Emphasizes period since World War II and UN's role. [M.J. Francis]

Pérez, Louis A., Jr. Armed struggle and guerrilla warfare in Latin America: a bibliography of Cuban sources, 1959–1979. See *HLAS 46:33.*

7083 Persaud, Wilberne H. Technology transfer: conceptual and development issues (UWI/SES, 30:2, June 1981, p. 18–44, bibl.)

Specialized, well documented description of the contributions of Latin American nations to the development of the Law of the Sea. While not afflicted by unanimity, these countries justify extensive claims over their coastal waters and resources on the grounds of "following suit," nationalism, conservation, economic advancement, and exploitation (sparking demands for "compensatory justice"). [G.W. Grayson]

7084 Podhoretz, Norman. Appeasement by any other name (AJC/C, 76:1, July 1983, p. 25–38)

Discussing two main issues, defense spending and Central America, the Editor of *Commentary* excoriates critics of the Reagan administration's policies. Accuses them of being closet pacifists, isolationists, appeasers, and/or pro-Marxist. In his view, "the United States must . . . do whatever may be required, up to and including the dispatch of American troops, to stop and then reverse the totalitarian drift in Central America."

7085 Posada R., Enrique. La Fundación Bariloche: una mirada optimista hacia el futuro (UPB, 36:127, mayo 1982, p. 99–107, plates)

Sets forth some of the basic recommendations in the world futures model advanced by the Bariloche Foundation of Buenos Aires. Notes that report is quite optimistic, if right decisions are made, about possibilities of creating a safe and just world within the limits of existing resources.

7086 Ramírez Ocampo, Augusto. Incidencia del aspecto político en las negociaciones del NOEI (PUJ/U, 3:2, julio 1982, p. 102–113)

Colombian author reviews disappointing progress toward proposed establishment of a NIEO and makes a number of suggestions that he feels will be helpful, perhaps the most earth-shaking of which is that the developing countries should establish a separate mechanism for direct negotiations with the socialist countries.

7087 Rangel, Carlos. El tercermundismo. Prólogo de Jean-François Revel. Caracas: Monte Avila Editores, 1982. 286 p.: bibl. (Col. Estudios)

Rangel addresses what he believes to be the essential nature of the Third World, its problems and political approaches best suited to overcoming them. Essentially a monograph on political theory. Argues for a humane and democratic socialism: socialism without Hobbes's Leviathan.

7088 Relaciones económicas de América Latina con los países miembros del Consejo de Asistencia Mutua Económica (CAME). Santiago: Naciones Unidas, 1982. 154 p.: bibl., ill. (Estudios e informes de la CEPAL; 12. E/CEPAL/G.1204)

ECLA-published study incorporating findings of a joint project (with UNCTAD *et al.*) that culminated in a conference (Mexico, 1980). Extraordinarily useful analysis (with supporting statistics and tables) of Latin America's bilateral and multilateral economic relations with countries in the Eastern-bloc Council of Mutual Economic Assistance. Final chap. focuses on Cuba, its only Latin American member.

Relaciones financieras externas y su efecto en la economía latinoamericana. See item 2973.

7089 Reunión Tripartita sobre Progreso Compartido en la Década de los 80, *Washington, 1981*. Memoria. Organizadores, Consejo Interamericano de Comercio y Producción (CICYP) *et al*. Washington: Organización de los Estados Americanos, 1982. 170 p.

Proceedings of a conference (July 1981) under united sponsorship of CICYP, OAS, IDB, ORIT. Idea apparently was to get representatives of business, labor, and governments together to discuss their respective viewpoints and concerns regarding common problems like the energy crisis, debt, and inflation.

7090 Riffe, Daniel and Eugene F. Shaw. Conflict and consonance: coverage of Third World in two US papers (AEJ/JQ, 60, Winter 1982, p. 617–626, tables)

Study of reporting on the Third World by *Chicago Tribune* and *New York Times*. Author's research suggests, rather surprisingly, that the Third World has not been slighted quantitatively; however, "published news items about the Third World were more likely to deal with conflict or upheaval than were published accounts from First and Second World nations." In author's opinion, the effect was to reinforce unfortunate stereotypes.

7091 Sandall, Roger. "Colonia" according to Naipaul (AJC/C, 76:6, Dec. 1983, p. 77–81)

Discussion by Australian anthropologist of the writings of Trinidadian V.S. Naipaul (see item 7246). Sandall finds a central theme in Naipaul's works to be the notion that "the most damaging consequence of colonialism" is "a legacy of destructive resentment." Particularly condemned is the attitude of "Westernized intellectuals" who are "sent home to countries where they no longer truly belong, whose bitterness is expressed in noisy public rejection of the West and all it stands for, combined with a private longing both for its amenities and for the prestige which only Western success and approval can bestow."

7091a Santos, Theotonio dos. Imperialismo y dependencia. 2a ed. México: Ediciones Era, 1980. 491 p.: bibl., index (El Hombre y su tiempo)

Very complete and strong statement of a particular vision of hemispheric relations: the dependency perspective. Probably as clear a statement as is available. Latin American thinking seems to be evolving away from being dominated by the dependency paradigm and this book now suffers from having been originally published in 1978 with only a minor revision in 1980. [M.J. Francis]

Scheina, Robert L. Latin American navies. See item **6023**.

7092 Selected literature on non-alignment (Socialist Thought and Practice [Belgrade] 23:3, 1983, p. 107–112)

Surprisingly lengthy list of Yugoslav publications on the subject of non-alignment.

7093 Selser, Gregorio. Reagan: de El Salvador a las Malvinas. México: Mex-Sur Editorial, 1982. 318 p.: bibl.

Perennial critic of US policies toward Latin America has a field day with those of the Reagan administration. Some of Selser's familiar charges about US support for reactionary political forces, CIA plots, and so on appear to have a little more substance nowadays.

7094 Shaplen, Robert. A reporter at large: the paradox of nonalignment (The New Yorker [New York] 14, May 1983, p. 82–102)

Splendid article on the Non-Aligned Movement, which discusses in a balanced and detailed fashion the movement's history—emphasis on major conferences of the last decade or so—and its principal problems. None the least of the problems, of course, has been the split between pro-Soviet members like Cuba and "moderates" like Yugoslavia and India. Shaplen writes: ". . . if the nonaligned movement is to have any significance henceforth it will have to move itself away from its present position of bickering dissent and denunciation, and decide what sort of positive role it can really play in the world."

7095 Shulgovski, Anatoli. URSS-América Latina: encuentro de dos mundos (URSS/AL, 12:60, dic. 1982, p. 8–23)

Prof. and chief of the sec. on political and social problems of the Latin American Institute of the Soviet Academy of Sciences, surveys the list of Latin American intellectuals and political figures like José Carlos Mariátegui of Peru, who over the yrs. have been inspired by one or more aspects of the Soviet example and/or whose policies, at least to some extent, paralleled those of the USSR.

7096 Sigmund, Paul E. The USSR, Cuba and the revolution in Chile (*in* The Soviet Union and the Third World: successes and failures. Edited by Robert H. Donaldson. Boulder, Colo.: Westview Press, 1981, p. 26–50)

Observes that Soviet ideology was "quite inadequate" as a guide to predicting "sudden turn to the left" in both the Cuban Revolution and Allende's Chile and that Soviets "were initially very cautious in the policies which they adopted toward them." With the advice of local parties, they eventually formed policies that "were confirmed by subsequent events:" the relative success of Castro's Cuba in advancing "Soviet strategic interests in the Western Hemisphere and Africa" and the collapse of Allende's experiment, the latter providing "grist for the Soviet propaganda and organizational mill for years to come." Yet, says Sigmund, "it is also evident from the two cases that when Soviet national interests and those of other[s] are seen to conflict, the Soviet interest is immediately preferred." Castro was snubbed in the 1962 missile crisis, other Latin American Communist parties received little real help, and Allende got only token economic aid. Although Sigmund leaves open the question of whether Soviet perspective is now shifting, he sums up pattern of the past as "one of conservatism, caution, and preference for gradual change."

7097 Singleton, Seth. Defense of the gains of socialism: Soviet Third World policy in the mid-1980s (GU/WQ, 7:1, 1984, p. 102–115)

Maintains: "Soviet policy now cloaks its imperialism as defense and seeks to pin the imperialist label on the United States. As long as Americans appear insensitive to Third World concerns, and make anti-Sovietism the sole basis of aid and collaboration, this Soviet effort may succeed. Military responses play into Soviet hands if they are not joined to positive initiatives to make the Third World and its hot spots a more just and prosperous place."

7098 ——. Soviet policy and socialist expansion in Asia and Africa (AFS, 6:3, Spring 1980, p. 339–369, tables)

Argues that, while "it is very important not to harbor illusions about what the Soviet leadership would like to do," it "is equally important not to exaggerate what they have achieved or are capable of doing." "Overestimation," he believes, "stems largely from the misperception that the only limit to Soviet expansion is American power;" in fact, other limitations derive from both Third World nationalism and Soviet internal problems. "The Soviet system . . . is generally regarded by progressive Marxists and non-Marxists alike as stultified, inefficient, oppressive, and undemocratic. Third World leaders may value tanks and Soviet-built factories if these can be had in time of need, but that sort of connection builds little long-term loyalty." Moreover, the USSR's commitments to Cuba, Afghanistan, and elsewhere are a "major drain on resources" for a country that has experienced an "apparently inexorable decline in the rate of economic growth." According to Singleton, the "1980s will probably see a Soviet foreign policy reappraisal," the outcome of which is by no means certain.

7099 La Solución pacífica de controversias. Obra editada bajo la dirección de Francisco Orrego Vicuña y Jeannette Irigoin Barrene. Santiago: Instituto de Estudios Internacionales, Univ. de Chile, 1981. 203 p.: bibl. (Perspectivas del derecho internacional contemporáneo; 2. Estudios internacionales)

Vol. 2 of papers presented at conference on international law organized by the Institute of International Studies, Univ. of Chile (Santiago, 1980). Not surprisingly, most of the contributions, including some by OAS functionaires, are highly legalistic in character: for example, an analysis (by the Executive Secretary of the Inter-American Commission on Human Rights) of the Inter-American Court of Human Rights pays zero attention to how it might deal with problems in the country where the conference was held.

The Spanish Civil War, 1936–39: American hemispheric perspectives. See *HLAS 46:1913.*

7100 Strodder, Joseph H. Commonality of military doctrine in the inter-American region (AF/AUR, 34:1, Nov./Dec. 1982, p. 70–75)

Proposes: "The recent increasing focus on political instability in Central America and the Caribbean area and the potential consequences for U.S. security interests in those regions makes especially timely a current proposal before the Inter-American Defense Board to examine the desirability of an interoperability plan for its member forces." Author is naive in his presumption that such a plan could, in fact, be adopted and (in this reviewer's opinion) even more remise in failing to consider, directly or indirectly, the political and moral consequences—not to mention the insubstantiality of the presumed "potential consequences for U.S. security interest."

7100a Tettamanti, Leopoldo H. Comunidad internacional e interés nacional: ¿poder o cooperación? (CRIT, 55 : 1888, sept. 1982, p. 478–486)

Latin American diplomat's attempt to suggest a world policy between legal niceties on the one side and power politics on the other. Feels that the international system is in a state of transition that may open door to positive developments if the great powers and others follow appropriate, farsighted policies. [M.J. Francis]

7100b Trindade, A.A. Cançado. The Inter-American Juridical Comittee: an overview (RIIA/WT, 38 : 11, Nov. 1982, p. 437–442)

Short, interesting piece on little known organ of the OAS: the Inter-American Juridical Committee. [M.J. Francis]

7101 United Nations. Economic Commission for Latin America (ECLA). International Trade and Development Div. The Economic relations of Latin America with Europe. Santiago: The Div., 1980. 156 p.: bibl., ill., tables (Cuadernos de la CEPAL. E/CEPAL/G.1116)

Useful analysis by ECLA staff of Europe's trade with and investment in Latin America, as well as additional financing extended to public and private sectors (as of 1980). Many helpful statistics and tables.

7101a Vaky, Viron P. Inter-American security: lessons from the South Atlantic (CRIA/W, 26 : 1, Jan. 1983, p. 17–20, ill.)

Brief, thoughtful overview of the inter-American system by a former US Assistant Secretary of State for Inter-American Affairs. Excellent piece although it ignores Central American situation. [M.J. Francis]

7102 Valdez Baquero, Rodrigo. Latinoamérica y el Derecho del Mar. Quito: Ministerio de Relaciones Exteriores, 1982. 29 p. (Col. Cuadernos ecuatorianos; 6)

Address of Ecuador's Deputy Foreign Minister to a conference organized to celebrate the 13th anniversary of the Declaration of Santiago, one of the initial Latin American salvos on the need for changes in the international Law of the Sea.

7103 Vasiliev, Yuri. Suecia y los países de América Latina: relaciones especiales (URSS/AL, 9, sept. 1983, p. 17–26)

Soviet author discusses in some detail Switzerland's economic and political relationships with Latin America, including Cuba. Notes that these relationships are somewhat "special," owing in part to Switzerland's traditional neutrality and lack of colonial past: the country is a "singular 'intermediary' agent in the capitalist world."

7104 Vincent, R.J. The Reagan administration and America's purpose in the world (LIWA/YWA, 37, 1983, p. 25–38)

Chides the administration for saying it is reasserting "America's" role in the world, while abandoning the very values that make for "Americanness." He writes: ". . . the United States should recognize how difficult it is to further the values for which it was established *and* . . . continue the attempt. The Reagan Administration, by making those values the servant of the contest with the Soviet Union rather than the master, and by making every issue in international relations subordinate to the contest with the Soviet Union, has stunningly reduced the range of American power. For those whose instinct it is that the United States can be a force for good in the world, the Reagan Administration's interpretation of its purpose is a profound disappointment."

7105 Vukadinovic, Radovan. Conflicts between non-aligned countries and possibilities of resolving them (Socialist Thought and Practice [Belgrade] 23 : 3, 1983, p. 78–91)

Urges that greater attention be given to Tito's proposal for an effective mechanism for the peaceful settlement of territorial disputes involving members of the Non-Aligned Movement.

7106 Wells, Samuel F., Jr. Limits on the use of American military power (WQ, 7 : 5, Winter 1983, p. 121–130, ill.)

Concerns US military capabilities generally; for instance, he expresses disappointment that the Reagan budget requests have focused so much on "big ticket" high-tech weaponry rather than a strengthening of US capacity to wage conventional war. Article is of relevance to Latin Americanists mainly for Well's comments about El Salvador, which he sees as not "another Vietnam:" In his view, guerrillas there are factionalized and lack both good leadership and sanctuaries in neighboring countries. Their "greatest asset" "has been the sloth, corruption, and factionalism of El Salvador's military leadership." Also observes that the Reagan administration has been largely unsuccessful in generating support for the campaign against Nicaragua and that US public awareness about both El Salvador and Nicaragua is minimal (but may well increase with US commitments in the subregion).

7107 Wiarda, Howard J. Ethnocentrism in foreign policy. Washington: American Enterprise Institute for Public Policy Research, 1985. 67 p. (AEI studies in foreign policy)

Important book that raises a significant intellectual issue with potentially major policy implications. Argues that scholars and policy-makers alike have been unduly ethnocentric in their views of the Third World, especially but not exclusively of non-Western societies. As for Latin America, Wiarda would emphasize region's "persistent corporatism and organic statism, its neomercantilist and state-capitalist economic structures, its personalism and kinship patterns, its Catholicism . . . its patrimonialism and unabashed patriarchialism, its patron-client networks now extended to the national level, its distinctive patterns and arenas of state-society relations, and its historic relations of dependency . . ." However, he admits, there are problems with this formulation, "not the least of which is that not all Latin Americans accept them or wish to accept them, still preferring to see themselves in terms of the Western model and still preferring to cast their lot with that model."

7108 ———. In search of policy: the United States and Latin America. Washington: American Enterprise Institute for Public Policy Research, 1984. 147 p.: bibl. (AEI studies; 396)

Insists that a fundamental ethno-centrism accounts for continuing inability of US to make effective policy for Latin America. Our views of the region are replete with myths and stereotypes, and are often condescending. Analyzing several aspects of US policies and the way policies are made, Wiarda makes a number of suggestions for improvement. He cautions, for example: "One should not expect pluralism to exist in Nicaragua to the same degree as it does in the United States, and certainly in the present revolutionary context . . . There remains some degree of pluralism in Nicaragua, more at the popular level than at the societal level, more at the societal level than at the level of state machinery—but not entirely absent even there." His concluding chap. points to "new realities" in Latin America and US-Latin American relations, outlines various unacceptable policy options (e.g., "gunboat diplomacy"), and makes the case for "prudence" and "restraint."

7109 ———. Interpreting Iberian-Latin American interrelations: paradigm consensus and conflict. Washington: American Enterprise Institute for Public Policy Research, 1985. 57 p. (Occasional papers series; 10)

Intriguing looking-backwards statement by one of the primary articulators of the "corporatist model" as a perspective on Latin American/Iberian politics. He writes: "Currently the corporatist paradigm, so long dominant in Iberia and Latin America, is both out of favor and out of power in Madrid, Lisbon, and some of the Latin American capitals. That has as much to do with the shifting and often fickle political winds that blow as it does with many more objective assessments of its utility as a conceptual model. We do know, however, that beneath the surface in Portugal, Spain, and these other countries are currents that are very ancient and not particularly socialistic or even democratic and that may again be restored to prominence if not to power . . . One suspects that the future in Iberia and Latin America is more likely to hold a pluralism and probably fragmentation . . . In that case there may be some regret that the issue became so intensely politicized and that the prevailing paradigms were so closely tied to political movements and particular regimes in power. The very diversity and complexity of these nations and systems, both domestically and internationally, demands pragmatically that the models we use to interpret them reflect that diversity and complexity, rather than being tied too closely to any currently prevailing regime or intellectual orthodoxy."

7110 Wood, Bryce. The dismantling of the Good Neighbor Policy. Austin: Univ. of Texas Pres, 1985. 290 p.: bibl., index.

The fly-leaf of this vol. quotes Cole Blasier to the effect that it "will surely be one of the half dozen classics in U.S. diplomatic history with Latin America," and this contributing editor enthusiastically agrees. Wood made his reputation as the leading authority on the Roosevelt Good Neighbor Policy, following a book specifically on that subject (see *HLAS 24:3474*) with another on *The United States and Latin American wars, 1932–1942* (see *HLAS 30:1134*). This book is the third in an informal series, which advances the melancholic thesis—supported by meticulous research into primary sources that is Wood's hallmark—that the US intervention in Guatemala tolled the death knell of the Good Neighbor. Diplomatic history this may be, but the conclusons that are as topical as tomorrow's headlines support Wood's own assessment that he really was a political scientist. "Beginning with Guatemala, the United States gradually dismantled the Good Neighbor Policy, and with it the political features of the OAS and the inter-American system. It avoided the crucial test of the policy by refusing to submit its judgment of the strength of a foreign threat—communism in Guatemala—to the formal consideration of the other members of this society that had been formed by its unilateral renunciation of intervention, and by the treaties of Rio de Janeiro and Bogotá. The warm, self-generated identification of our interest with that of Latin America that Simon G. Hanson had recalled in 1953 disappeared in the preoccupation with the interest of the United States alone. In the process

there were three losers: the United States government lost credibility and an honorable reputation in Latin America and elsewhere that it has not regained; the Guatemalan people lost the opportunity for a freer and fairer social and economic order (which they are still fighting for); the American states jointly lost a chance to face a Soviet threat and to forge a new political order in Latin America."

7111 Yálovlev, Piotr. La política exterior de paz de la Unión Soviética y América Latina (URSS/AL, 1:61, enero 1983, p. 4–16)

According to this Soviet analyst, the USSR, throughout its history, has followed a policy of advancing peace and combating fascism, racism, and imperialism—in contrast to the posture of US. Closes with a discussion of the XXVI USSR Communist Party Congress in 1981, which declared itself to be in favor of all good things.

7112 Zea, Leopoldo. La experiencia multinacional soviética y los problemas para la integración latinoamericana (URSS/AL, 12:60, dic. 1982, p. 24–38)

Famous Mexican scholar mentions at the outset Soviet's success in integrating disparate peoples into a single political entity (the USSR) and notes that this somewhat resembles the Bolivarian goal of a united Latin America. He then recapitulates much of the history he has recounted elsewhere about the continued triumph of "Monroeism" over "Bolivarism" in the evolution of the inter-American system. The OAS, he argues, has been particularly offensive in partially legitimizing repression of progressive forces in Guatemala, Cuba, the Dominican Republic—and now El Salvador and Nicaragua. In this connection, he applauds the united Latin American stance in opposition to the British/US position in the Falklands/Malvinas episode. In this, he asks "*la hora de Bolívar?*"

MEXICO, CENTRAL AMERICA, THE CARIBBEAN AND THE GUIANAS

GEORGE W. GRAYSON, *John Marshall Professor of Government, College of William and Mary*

THE CRISIS IN CENTRAL AMERICA and the Caribbean has spawned a new growth industry of books, most of them edited, on the troubled region. Unfortunately, many of these volumes suffer from overbreadth, superficiality, paucity of original research, lack of comparative studies among countries, the quest for instant topicality, and podium-pounding dogmatism that often substitutes sloganeering for analysis. Irrespective of their orientation, the preachiness of ideologues is the academic equivalent of fingernails scratching a blackboard. However, Latin America and the Caribbean produce a disproportionate share of Marxists who relentlessly (and simplistically) excoriate dependency, neocolonialism, and multinational firms—without recognizing either the domestic causes of underdevelopment (e.g., corruption, poor educational systems, weak entrepreneurial spirit, mismanagement) or the conspicuous progress achieved by Asian and European nations (e.g., Denmark, Cyprus, Malta, and Singapore) also subjected to external economic penetration. Aaron Segal, Prof. of Political Science at the Univ. of Texas at El Paso, points out these and other defects in a review essay whose elegant prose is only rivaled by its intellectual vitality (item **7252**).

Although not imposing a single analytic framework on their contributors to facilitate comparisons, Donald E. Schulz and Douglas H. Graham have assembled the sturdiest, most uniformly substantive collection of essays on the region—with sections devoted to the structural and institutional sources of stability, country studies, and the international dimensions of the crisis (item **7194**). Even broader in scope and more ambitious in objective is Juan Tokatlian and Klaus Schubert's *Relaciones internacionales en la Cuenca del Caribe . . .* (item **7250**), which combines a section on US policy toward the region with, generally innovative, chapters on international organizations and the Caribbean Basin, the basin "por dentro," and Colombia's role in the region. Invaluable is Abraham Lowenthal's essay that argues that the perceived threat to the US in the region is "psycho-political" not "strategic-military"—a telling point neglected by many observers who concentrate on ideology or resources in justifying or opposing Washington's demarches. Unfortunately, events have overtaken some of these 40 chapters, all of which were written in 1982 or earlier. The Atlantic Council's Working Group co-chaired by James R. Greene and Brent Scowcroft has fashioned an outstanding array of possible US policy options, embracing economic, social, political, energy, migration, and security issues (item **7211a**). Illustrative of the balance and steady judgment that suffuse these proposals is David Scott Palmer's articulate advocacy of Washington's pursuing a "collaborative" approach in the area rather than the "hegemonic" option preferred by hawks or the "damage limitation" alternative championed by many doves.

First-rate chapters on Soviet (by Jiri Valenta), Cuban (W. Ray Duncan), and Venezuelan (Martz) policies toward the region highlight an uneven volume edited by H. Michael Erisman and John D. Martz that attempts to focus—sometimes through a mist of purple prose—on the limitations under which Washington labors in pursuing often ill-defined goals toward Central America and the Caribbean (item **7221**). Increasingly, extra-hemispheric forces have interested themselves in a region once considered the backyard of the colossus of the North. Eusebio Mujal-León (item 7187) has written an exquisitely well researched and thoroughly documented account of how European Socialist parties have sought—with, at best, marginal success—to venture into the area.

As the most decisive US foreign action in recent memory, the dispatch of troops to Grenada has generated scores of books and articles. By far the best is V.S. Naipaul's "An Island Betrayed" (item 7246), which, in prose that fuses into poetry, demonstrates the New Jewel Movement's lack of legitimacy, making its revolution one of words spouted by a newly educated elite who disdained their own people. "But the words were mimicry. They were too big; they didn't fit; they remained words. The revolution blew away; and what was left in Grenada was a murder story." A dozen pages of Naipaul's insights on culture, race, and ethnicity tell us more about the world's most famous spice island than a library full of jargon-laden, class-based treatises. More academics concerned about the Caribbean should study both his analytic categories and felicitous language. The Depts. of State and Defense have disseminated a telephone book-sized selection of documents that reveal, beyond a shadow of a doubt, the Marxist-Leninist orientation of the New Jewel Movement (item 7232).

The intense interest lavished on Central America and the Caribbean diverted attention from Mexico, except as generally predictable descriptions of its policy toward the region appear in collected works. A notable exception is Douglas Bennett and Kenneth Shape's path-breaking examination of the nation's auto industry, stressing negotiations between multinational corporations and the Mexican government. Instead of emphasizing immutable power capabilities of the two parties, the authors underline the convergence of interests that existed on investment goals and the contextual character of influence, especially the structure of domestic and international relationships in which each actor is enmeshed. Their study is a splendid marriage of theory with data, the latter derived from personal interviews (item 7120).

Lewis L. Gould (item 7231) continues the rehabilitation of McKinley, begun in the 1960s. In his handling of the Spanish-American War and the subsequent emergence of an American empire in 1898–1900, the 25th President is portrayed as an effective leader, who, in fact, was the first modern US chief executive, foreshadowing the imperial presidency of the Johnson-Nixon era.

MEXICO

7113 Administración del desarrollo de la frontera norte. Compilado por Mario Ojeda. México: Colegio de México, 1982. 190 p.: bibl., map (Col. Frontera norte)

US-Mexican border provides a splendid theme for seven scholars who discuss regional history and culture, economic development strategies, migration questions, and federal-state-local relations (on both sides of the Rio Grande). Insipid bibl. and tedious essay on dependency compensated for by helpful tables and map of a *sui generis* zone.

7114 Applegate, Howard G. and C. Richard Bath. Hazardous and toxic substances in U.S.-Mexico relations (Texas Business Review [Univ. of Texas at Austin, Bureau of Business Research] 57:5, Sept./Oct. 1983, p. 229–234)

Illuminating overview of a critical bilateral issue. The framework for regulating toxic substances is even worse in Mexico than in the US where the proliferation of agencies, blurred state-federal lines of responsibility, and weak-kneed enforcement abound. "Neither country has a strong moral position . . . and both can be faulted for not taking into consideration effects of the public health of citizens in the other country."

7115 Argüello, Silvia and **Raúl Figueroa E.**
El intento de México por retener
Texas. México: Fondo de Cultura Económica,
1982. 291 p.: bibl. (SEP/80; 10)
Advances the beguiling thesis that, despite contention of most historians, Mexican politicians in 1837–44 period had not written off Texas. Indeed, the Mexican consul in New Orleans directed a herculean effort, which included an information network that sometimes relied on spies, to regain Texas for his country.

7116 Arroyo Pichardo, Graciela. La evolución de las relaciones entre México y Rumanía en el contexto internacional del siglo XX. México: UNAM, Facultad de Ciencias Políticas y Sociales, 1981. 273 p.: bibl.
More descriptive than analytic, this book is the definitive work on Mexican-Romanian relations. Deletion of commonly known facts about Mexico would have halved the size of, and thereby improved, the vol. which undoubtedly springs from a univ. thesis.

7117 Azurduy, Victoria et al. Petróleo y soberanía. Dibujos de Rogelio Naranjo. México: Proceso: TEDSA, 1981. 283 p.: ill.
Uneven collection of Proceso magazine articles that reflect the strident nationalism and anti-Yankee sentiment that key on Mexico's oil resources. Put briefly: it's a recent rendition of "the gringoes-are-after-our-black-gold" theme screechily sung by academics, politicians, and journalists.

7118 Bagley, Bruce Michael. Mexican foreign policy: the decline of a regional power? (CUH, 82:488, Dec. 1983, p. 406–409, 437)
Excellent essay emphasizing that Mexico's initiatives in Central America during 1979–82 oil boom offered "reasonable alternatives," not "frontal opposition" to US positions as Mexicans recognized Washington's strategic interests. Economic hardships at home coupled with increasing militarization in the region have limited the role that Mexico, through Contadora process, can play in Central America.

7119 Bell, Samuel E. and **James M. Smallwood.** The Zona Libre, 1858–1905: a problem in American diplomacy. El Paso: Texas Western Press, Univ. of Texas at El Paso, 1982. 88 p.: bibl. (Southwestern studies; 69)
Impeccably prepared monograph points out that long before the maquiladoras, a Mexican zona libre, in existence from 1858–1905, spurred commercial development of towns along the Rio Grande—with significant economic and political repercussions far beyond the border.

7120 Bennett, Douglas and **Kenneth Sharpe.**
Agenda setting and bargaining power: the Mexican State versus transnational automobile corporations (in Political economy of the Latin American motor vehicle industry. Edited by Rich Kronish and Kenneth S. Mericle. Cambridge: MIT Press, 1984, p. 195–229, tables)
Authors draw upon their encyclopedic knowledge of the auto industry to fashion a keenly persuasive theoretical framework that is invaluable in analyzing bargaining encounters in Mexico in particular and those involving transnational corps. and LDC host countries in general. Impressive symbiosis of theory and data.

7121 Castillo, Heberto. PEMEX sí, PEUSA no. México: Proceso, 1981. 372 p.: ill.
Muckraking look at Mexican oil industry. Sprinkled among highly emotional (and scantily documented) attacks on the CIA, US government, and American energy companies are hair-raising accounts of corruption within PEMEX, Mexico's state oil monopoly, and the Oil Workers Union who make Teamsters look like a bunch of Little Lord Fauntleroys.

7122 Cline, William R. Mexico's crisis, the world's peril (FP, 49, Winter 1982/1983, p. 107–118)
Preference for clichés over clear policy recommendations in the conclusion mars an otherwise well written article that places Mexico's Aug. 1982 crisis in the context of an extremely burdened international financial structure. For economist's comment, see item **3063.**

Coll de Hurtado, Atlántida. La crise mexicaine: un essai d'explication historique et géographique. See item **5085.**

7123 Cornelius, Wayne A. Immigration, Mexican development policy, and the future of U.S.-Mexican relations. La Jolla:

Program in US-Mexican Studies, Univ. of California at San Diego, 1981. 39 leaves: bibl. (Working papers in US-Mexican studies; 8)

Mordantly attacks those who believe an assertive border policy would encourage elites in oil-endowed Mexico to channel more resources into job creation. In labeling such a policy as "counter-productive," he argues that the Mexican government is unlikely to jettison its development strategy of "growth first, permanent (mainly industrial) jobs later." Tendency both to set up strawmen and overstate the commitment of Mexican leaders to adopt a long-term employment plan.

7124 ———. Legalizing the flow of temporary migrant workers from Mexico: a policy proposal. La Jolla: Program in US-Mexican Studies, Univ. of California at San Diego, 1981. 17 leaves: bibl. (Working papers in US-Mexican studies; 7)

Immigration specialist proposes legalizing the entry of undocumented temporary workers both to reduce their vulnerability to exploitation and enhance their access to medical care and union membership. This carefully elaborated plan will raise hackles of those concerned about the already large number of illegal workers in US and job competition and downward wage pressure that attends their presence.

7125 La Declaración Franco-Mexicana (UJSC/ECA, 36:395, sept. 1981, p. 916–946, tables)

Text of 1981 Franco-Mexican communiqué recognizing the Salvadoran left (FMLN and FDR) as a "representative political force." Supplementing this declaration is a score of related and relevant documents. Extremely useful primary material.

7126 Demicheli, Tulio H. Felipe González y las dos izquierdas (Vuelta [México] 7:80, julio 1983, p. 45–48)

President Felipe González proved a *"vistante incómodo"* to the Mexican left because he believes in democratic socialism, civil liberties, Sandinistas' pluralist goals, and defense of the West. A chasm separates Mexican and European lefts because latter is more mature, evinces govering experience, suffered consequences of Third Reich, and has first-hand knowledge of "communist paradises." Deft piece.

Durán, Esperanza. Revolution and international pressures: the Mexican experience, 1910–1920. See *HLAS 46:2193*.

7127 Ellacuría, Ignacio. La Declaración Conjunta Mexicano-Francesa sobre El Salvador (UJSC/ECA, 36:395, set. 1981, p. 845–866, ill.)

Extremely sympathetic, turgid account of Franco-Mexican Communiqué on EL Salvador that too often substitutes clichés for analysis. Still, one of the few articles available on an important, but overrated, diplomatic demarche.

7128 Fallows, James. Immigration: how it's affecting us (The Atlantic [The Atlantic Monthly Co., Boston] 252:2, Nov. 1983, p. 45–106, plates)

Well written analysis of why immigrants flock to US, including an examination of the impact of newcomers on this country. Simpson-Mazzoli reform bill is discussed along with obstacles to its passage. Despite its Statue of Liberty ethos, the "U.S. cannot provide a new home for all of the oppressed."

7129 Franco de León, Luis Enrique and José Gallardo Taboada. Reflexiones sobre la política exterior de México hacia la Comunidad Económica Europea (UNAM/RI, 8:29, abril/junio 1980, p. 23–38, bibl.)

Its 1975 commercial accord with the European Community was part of the new internationalism of Mexico, which—in the past—had pursued a foreign policy characterized by legalisms, passivity, and even isolation. Yet, this agreement neither improved Mexico's trade account with ECC members nor reduced its dependency on US. Hence the need for "policies more objective, realistic and efficient and, therefore, less rhetorical and demagogic."

7130 Freebairn, Donald K. Agricultural interaction between Mexico and the United States (SAGE/JIAS, 25:3, Aug. 1983, p. 275–298, tables)

Ambitious article that attempts: 1) an overview of Mexican and US agriculture; 2) a discussion of bilateral agricultural trade; and 3) an analysis of the forces that promote concentration in agriculture on both sides of Rio Grande. While a great deal is covered in 24 p., piece fails to examine critically the highly publiciced SAM program (since discontinued) and minimizes profound differences in agriculture in neighboring countries.

7131 Fushigami, Takashi. Japón y México desde 1970: una evaluación tentativa (Latin American Studies [Univ. of Tsukuba, Japan] 6, 1983, p. 103–122, appendix, tables)

Nine well conceived tables integrated into a thoughtfully prepared text make this the best brief overview of recent Japanese-Mexican affairs. Appendix chronicles evolution of bilateral ties from resumption of diplomatic relations in 1952 to a 160,000 barrel per day oil deal in late 1981.

7132 García, Mario T. History, culture and society of the Borderlands (UCSB/NS, 8, 1982, p. 467–472)

Concise review of Stanley R. Ross's edited vol. on US-Mexican border. While correctly noting and summarizing the ideas in its several excellent essays, García laments the ahistorical character of the book that focuses on culture, politics, economics, immigration, health, border psychology, and ecology.

7133 García y Griego, Manuel. The importation of Mexican contract laborers in the United States, 1942–1964: antecedents, operation, and legacy. La Jolla: Program in US-Mexican Studies, Univ. of California, San Diego, 1981. 59 leaves: bibl. (Working papers in US-Mexican studies; 11)

Sturdy overview of bracero program, leading to conclusion that the 22-yr.-long scheme fostered conflict rather than cooperation in US-Mexican relations. Little evidence supports contention that the present quest for an alternative to undocumented Mexican migration is leading US policymakers "back to another bracero program."

7134 Gordillo y Ortiz, Octavio. La Revolución y las relaciones internacionales de México. México: Biblioteca del Instituto Nacional de Estudios Históricos de la Revolución Mexicana, 1983. 187 p.: bibl. (Biblioteca . . .; 93)

Description of US-Mexican relations during the Revolution written by a strong nationalist who has relied heavily on Isidro Fabels's *Historia diplomática de la Revolución mexicana*. Failure to delve into US archival material is but partially offset by an informative 49-p. chronology of events (1910–20).

7135 Goulet, Denis. Mexico and the U.S.: discord among neighbors (CRIA/W, 27:1, Jan. 1984, p. 7–10, ill.)

Analysis is eclipsed by cant, this time from a liberal, in this attack on US Central American policy. Superficial comparison between interventions in Afghanistan and Grenada precede contention that: "Obsolete balance of power thinking blinds American strategies to a sound diagnosis of regional problems and . . . limits their ability to find solutions."

7136 Una Gran jornada de integración: memoria de la gira por Costa Rica, Panamá, Brasil, Venezuela, Cuba, Costa Rica y Nicaragua, julio-agosto de 1980. México: Coordinación General de Comunicación Social, 1981. 189 [i.e. 285] p.: ill.

Consists of 100 documents related to President José López Portillo's effort to project Mexico's influence as a regional leader during a mid-1980 visit to Costa Rica, Panama, Brazil, Venezuela, Cuba, and Nicaragua.

7137 Grayson, George W. The joint oil facility: Mexican-Venezuelan cooperation in the Caribbean (FIU/CR, 12:2, Spring 1983, p. 19–21, ill., table)

Examination of Mexican-Venezuelan joint facility that makes oil, on concessionary terms, available to 10 Central American and Caribbean nations. One of the best kept secrets in South-South cooperation, this aid mechanism provided $857 million to beneficiaries in 1980–82 period alone. Despite severe economic problems at home, donors have continued program to assist distressed economies of recipients and to project their own political influence.

Hansen, Niles. Interdependence along the U.S.-Mexican border. See item **3097.**

7138 India-México: diálogo Sur-Sur. México: Coordinación General de Comunicación Social, 1981. 111 p.

Interviews, speeches, and reports related to President López Portillo's Jan. 1981 "working trip" to Spain, Egypt, and India. Dominant theme is Mexico's aspirations for, and solidarity with, Third World.

7139 *Informe: Relaciones México-Estados Unidos.* Centro de Estudios del Tercer Mundo (CEESTEM), Programa de Estudios de las Relaciones México-Estados Unidos. Vol. 1, No. 3, julio/dic. 1982- . México.

Even thought shot through with ideological pap associated with ex-President Echeverría's Third World studies center CEESTEM (now extinct), this publication boasts a worthwhile piece, except for its conclusions, on Mexican-Guatemalan relations (p. 10–71), stressing tensions caused by influx into Chiapas state of Gautemalan refugees. Helpful, too, is summary of key treaties and accords between Mexico and Guatemala (p. 268–273).

7140 Lápshev, Evgueni. Fundamentos ideológicos de la política exterior (URSS/AL, 2:62, feb. 1983, p. 16–23)

Stresses USSR's enthusiasm from Mexican diplomacy tht promoted "latinoamericanismo," a concept that excluded the imperialist US. Still, author regrets Mexico's failure, in zeroing in on the "poor South" and "rich North," to distinguish within latter the aggressive, imperialist, capitalist states from those peace-loving socialist nations which are faithful friends and allies of developing countries.

7141 López Portillo, José. Discurso del Presidente de México al ser condecorado por el Gobierno de Nicaragua (RPC, 37:175, abril/junio 1982, p. 105–108)

Important speech in which López Portillo praises Sandinistas' revolutionary successes, while, tactfully, reminding them of their commitment to pluralism and democracy. Mexican leader opposes US military intervention in region, calls for disarming contras in return for Nicaraguan renunciation of weapons' purchases, and champions non-aggression pacts between Nicaragua and the US, as well as between Nicaragua and neighbor states.

7142 ———. En Costa Rica, Brasil y Cuba. México: SPP, Dirección General de Documentación y Análisis, 1980. 223 p.: bibl., index (Cuadernos de filosofía política; 37)

Compendium of official speeches, texts of press conferences, protocols signed, and such generated by Mexican President López Portillo on his July-Aug. 1980 state visits to Costa Rica, Brazil, and Cuba. [Y. Ferguson]

Lupsha, Peter A. and **Kip Schlegel.** The political economy of drug trafficking: the Herrera

organization, Mexico & the United States. See item **3098.**

7143 Madrid Hurtado, Miguel de la. Pronunciamientos de campaña. México: Partido Revolucionario Institucional, Comité Ejecutivo Nacional, Secretaría de Asuntos Internacionales, 1982. 132 p. (Documentos de la política exterior; 2)

Excerpts from de la Madrid's foreign policy speeches during 1982 presidential campaign that once again reveal official candidate's ability to offer platitudes, brigaded with revolutionary and nationalistic rhetoric, on virtually all subjects for virtually all audiences.

7144 Martínez Legorreta, Omar. El balance del poder y las tensiones en Asia y la Cuenca del Pacífico: el papel de las potencias intermedias; un punto de vista mexicano (CM/FI, 24:1, julio/sept. 1983, p. 63–77)

General summary of the entire geopolitical situation in the Pacific Basin with some emphasis on current and potential ole of Mexico in the region. Good illustration of the position of intermediate powers in contemporary world politics. [M.J. Francis]

Menéndez, Iván. En defensa propia: México contra la guerra. See *HLAS 46:2237.*

7145 México-Estados Unidos, 1982. Compilado por Lorenzo Meyer. Sergio Aguayo *et al.* México: Colegio de México, 1982. 164 p.: ill. (Col. México-Estados Unidos)

Heavily documented chaps. by five Mexican researchers on their country's relations with US. Nationalistically-motivated advocacy pierces veil of scholarly objectivity in a book that well illuminates defensive, critical attitude of academics toward Reagan administration in particular and US in general.

7146 Mexico-United States Interparliamentary Conference, 20th, *Washington and San Francisco, Calif., 1980.* Twentieth Mexico-United States Interparliamentary Conference: background materials for U.S. Delegation use only. *For the use of the* Committee on Foreign Affairs and Foreign Relations of the House of Representatives and the Senate. Washington: US GPO, 1980. 330 p.: bibl., ill.

Impressive collection of articles, speeches, memoranda, and documents to prepare US congressmen for annual parley with Mexican counterparts. That this event has the reputation as a junket is not the fault of staff members who amassed excellent materials on key bilateral issues.

7147 Niblo, Stephen R. British propaganda in Mexico during the Second World War: the development of cultural imperialism (LAP, 10:4, 1983, p. 114–126)

Persuasive account of how Great Britain, remembering Zimmerman Telegram of World War I, manipulated Mexican public opinion to gain support for Allies in World War II. Crucial to venture's success was placement of articles, particularly through British subsidized Havas News Service, in Mexican newpapers. Such cultural imperialism "did not end with the termination of hostilities." For historian's comment, see *HLAS 46:2250.*

Nuncio, Abraham. El Grupo Monterrey. See item **3099.**

Ortiz Wadgymar, Arturo. Aspectos de la crisis de los EE.UU. y sus principales impactos en el sector externo de México. See item **3100.**

Pellicer de Brody, Olga. The foreign trade policy for the United States government toward Mexico: are there reasons for expecting special treatment? See item **3101.**

7148 Perspectivas actuales de las relaciones entre México y Estados Unidos. Edición de Edmundo Hernández Vela S. México: UNAM, Coordinación de Humanidades, 1980. 124 p.: appendix, bibl.

Eight Mexican scholars provide commentaries and polemics about status of relations with US following President Carter's Feb. 1979 visit to Mexico. As valuable as any essay is an appendix prepared by Eduardo Roldán on presidential meetings, dating to the first, between Porfirio Díaz and William Howard Taft in 1909.

Powell, Thomas G. Mexico and the Spanish Civil War. See *HLAS 46:2260.*

7149 Purcell, John F.H. Trade conflicts and U.S.-Mexican relations. La Jolla: Program in US-Mexican Studies, Univ. of California at San Diego, 1982. 49 leaves: bibl. (Working papers in US-Mexican studies; 38)

Astute examination of bilateral commercial issues precedes three conclusions: 1) foreign policy and trade matters are central

to political debate in Mexico; 2) an ideological alternative to free trade exists in Mexico; and 3) protectionism, subsidies, and other acts of State economic intervention are deemed crucial to preserving social order. Mexico's dilemma is "how to maintain political stability while moving toward export-led growth without a radical restructuring of society."

7150 Ramírez López, Berenice. México y Centroamérica: relaciones establecidas situaciones y perspectivas (Iztapalapa [Univ. Autónoma Metropolitana, Div. de Ciencias Sociales y Humanidades, Iztalapa, México] 2:3, julio/dic. 1980, p. 122–133)

Marxist cant notwithstanding, article sheds light on Mexico's growing economic ties to Central America since mid-1960s. Its mounting economic role in region is seen, perhaps naively, as a Mexican contribution to forging a NIEO.

Rapacki, Ryszard. Polska-Meksyk: gospodarka, stosunski ekonomiczne = Poland-Mexico: economy, economic relations. See item **3107.**

Referencia en torno a la política de México hacia Centroamérica: 1923–1937. See *HLAS 46:2435.*

7151 Relaciones México-Estados Unidos: Bibliografía Anual. El Colegio de México. Vol. 1, julio 1980/junio 1981–. México.

Vol. 1 of serial consists of comprehensive bibliography of books, as well as articles appearing in 80 journals, magazines, and newspapers on bilateral relations pub. in English and Spanish. Eight secs. embrace: 1) general relations; 2) politics; 3) economics; 4) energy; 5) border questions; 6) migrant workers; 7) Mexican Americans; and 8) North American vision of Mexico. Indexed according to author.

7152 Reunión Internacional sobre Cooperación y Desarrollo, *Cancún, México, 1981.* Cancún: diálogo para la historia. México: Coordinación General de Comunicación Social, Presidencia de la República, 1981. 126 p.

Bland description of some of the themes and actors at 1981 Cancún conference. Cited only because of dearth of material on this North-South meeting whose realizations failed to match expectations of

Mexico's López Portillo administration, its host. For a good summary, see item **7153**.

7153 ———. Cancún 1981: antecedentes, debates y conclusiones. México: Secretaría de Relaciones Exteriores, 1982. 242 p.

Best summary available of background, debates, and conclusions of Oct. 1981 International Meeting on Cooperation and Development hosted by Mexico. Particularly revealing is how US assured exclusion of Castro, President pro-tem of the Non-Aligned Movement (p. 17–18).

Riding, Alan. Distant neighbors: a portrait of the Mexicans. See item **3102**.

7154 Ruiz García, Enrique. La estrategia mundial del petróleo: una teoría del poder, una teoría de la dependencia. México: Editorial Nueva Imagen, 1982. 230 p.: bibl. (Serie Testimonios)

UNAM Marxist scholar examines history of petroleum exploitation from earliest discoveries and production, through OPEC, and beyond. Sees in Mexico's current position only a repeat of traditional pattern: exploitation of non-renewable resources, with few exceptions, has led to a new form of dependency with most of the benefits accruing to privileged classes at home and abroad. [Y. Ferguson]

Saxe-Fernández, John. Petróleo y estrategia: México y Estados Unidos en el contexto de la política global. See *HLAS 46:2280*.

7155 Serrano Migallón, Fernando. Isidro Fabela y la diplomacia mexicana. México: Fondo de Cultura Económica, 1981. 293 p.: bibl. (SEP/80; 16)

Perspectives on career of a venerable Mexican diplomat who, serving his country from the Revolution to World War II, is best known for crystalizing the "Carranza Doctrine" that rejected the Monroe Doctrine, while emphasizing sovereignty, equality, and uniformity of laws of all nations.

Sovetsko-meksikanskie otnosheniia = Relaciones mexicano-soviéticas: 1917–1980: Sbornik dokumentov. See *HLAS 46:2286*.

7156 United States. Congress. House. Committee on Post Office and Civil Service. Subcommittee on Census and Population. The Hispanic population, a demographic and issue profile: hearings before the Subcommittee on Census and Population of the Committee on Post Office and Civil Service, House of Representatives, September 13–15, 1983. Washington: US GPO, 1983. 288 p.: bibl., ill. (98th Congress, 1st Session)

The rose in this thorny document is a Library of Congress report (p. 264–282) on demographic and socioeconomic characteristics of the heterogeneous US Hispanic population derived from a 1980 census. Included is a 3.5 to six million estimate of illegal immigrants in the US, approximately 70 percent having arrived from Mexico in 1970s.

U.S.-Mexican relations: economic and social aspects. See item **3104**.

7157 Verea, Mónica. Entre México y Estados Unidos: los indocumentados. México: Ediciones El Caballito, 1982. 189 p.: bibl.

Serves principally as a compendium of Mexican conventional wisdom on unlawful aliens—e.g., US public opinion has exercised strong pressure on its government; chicanos support a more restrictive US border policy (in fact: masses do, leaders don't), and illegals don't displace US workers.

CENTRAL AMERICA

Abel, Christopher. Documentary review. See item **7209**.

Anderson, Thomas P. The war of the dispossessed: Honduras and El Salvador, 1969. See item **6100**.

7158 Barnes, Michael et al. Can the U.S. live with Latin revolution?: the dilemmas of national security (Harper's Magazine [New York] 268:1609, June 1984, p. 35–48, map)

Potpourri of views on US involvement in Central America spiced by bon mots (e.g., Carlos Fuentes compares Mexican Revolution to a "fat lady who drives a Mercedes-Benz," while Christopher Dickey sees Honduras "being turned from a banana republic to a bivouac"). Amid glibness and generalizations, point it made—by Fred Ikle—that US has supported revolution-spawned regimes, as indicated in Portugal in 1974, but has misgivings about those that prefer militarism to pluralism.

7159 Beck, Rochell and **Nancy Anderson.** What children in the U.S. learn about

Central America (OAS/LE, 27:92, 1983, p. 48–65, bibl.)

Content analysis of textbooks and other materials used by American school children reveal a distorted picture of Central America; namely, 1) region's unimportance, except as it affects interests of US, generally depicted in a "helper" role; 2) racial and ethnic stereotyping of a people, often portrayed as peasants or guerrillas who are exotically different from North Americans; and 3) blatant errors of fact. Materials leave students "poorly prepared," "confused," and "alienated" from Central American people and their cultures."

7160 Berner, M.F.C. The Panama Canal and future United States hemisphere policy (LIWA/YWA, 34, 1980, p. 205–219)

Succinct account of events in Panama and the US preceding negotation of Panama Canal Treaties forms useful element in this essay, last half of which misreads or misinterprets many trends in US-Latin American relations. For instance, contrary to author's prediction, Latin American nations have not negotiated collectively with Washington on economic issues, tensions have not sharpened over nuclear technology, and human rights have not remained a sensitive issue.

7161 Britton, John. Carleton Beals and Central America after Sandino: struggle to publish (AEJ/JQ, 60:2, 1983, p. 240–310)

Fascinating look at the resistance of US editors, from World War II to Castro's victory, to publishing Carleton Beals's articles because the journalist indicted both imperialism and Somoza-type tyrants. ". . . journalists and scholars have become concerned with restrictions on the flow of information from the Third World nations into U.S.-based mass media, and . . . Beals's frustrations in covering Central America were an early reflection of this trend."

Castro, Nils. Panamá: un foro para la concertación. See item **3207.**

Central America: anatomy of a conflict. See item **6104a.**

7162 Centroamérica: más allá de la crisis. Coordinado y compilado por Donald Castillo Rivas. Contribuciones de Gabriel Aguilera Peralta et al. México: Ediciones SIAP, 1983. 423 p.: bibl., ill.

Wide-ranging collection of chaps. on

Central America concentrating on: 1) internal conditions of the five nations; 2) regional economic structures; and 3) international relations. Welcomed are individual essays on such seldom researched topics as Panamanian, Venezuelan, and Canadian policies toward area. One viewpoint—unabashed sympathy for "popular movements"—pervades this vol.

7163 Chace, James. Deeper into the mire (NYRB, 31:3, March 1984, p. 40–48, ill.)

Review article of recent works on Central America, including Kissinger Commission's *Report*, provides framework for penetrating critique of US policy in region. "By continuing a long history of relying on repressive local military forces to effect change . . . the Reagan administration does not appear to be planning for a future that will allow countries with fragile democracies to grow stronger and hardy democracies to flourish."

Cruz Sequeira, Arturo. The origins of Sandinista foreign policy. See item **6186.**

7164 Dissent paper on El Salvador and Central America (UCSB/NS, 8, 1982, p. 325–348)

Romantic appeal to abandon confrontation for negotiation in El Salvador, with attention riveted on possibility of pursuing "Zimbabwe option." Parallels between El Salvador and Zimbabwe are far less compelling than suggested. Moreover, Duarte's 1984 overtures to the opposition following his election has, in effect, brought about the recognition of the "FDR/DRU coalition . . . [as] a legitimate and representative political force in Salvadorean politics." Still, the struggle continues.

7165 Edelman, Marc. Costa Rica: see-saw diplomacy (NACLA, 17:6, Nov./Dec. 1983, p. 40–43, ill.)

Unsympathetic account of Costa Rican foreign policy that, under President Luis Alberto Monge, features coordinated efforts with US to isolate Nicaragua diplomatically in exchange for critically needed economic assistance. In expressing concern that such action will compromise Costa Rica's "quasi-Pacifist philosophy" (sic), author imputes all policy changes to San José, ignoring the Sandinistas' increasing disdain for their original goals.

Evans, Ernest. Revolutionary movements in Central America: the development of new strategy. See item **6108.**

7166 Falcoff, Mark. The *El Salvadoran White Paper* and its critics (AEI Foreign Policy and Defense Review [American Enterprise Institute for Public Policy Research, Washington] 4:2, 1982, p. 12–18)
Rehabilitates much-maligned 1981 State Dept. *White Paper* on outside communist involvement in El Salvador. Argues convincingly that critics of Reagan administration's Central American policy seized on three admitted errors in the report to misrepresent and attempt to discredit essentially accurate materials.

7167 Farer, Tom J. Manage the revolution? (FP, 52, Fall 1983, p. 96–117)
Cogently argues that Washington adopt the "Finland option" in Central America; namely, permitting diverse domestic systems and foreign policies, while standing ready to use force to prevent a "military relationship" between any country in the isthmus and an extrahemispheric power.

7168 Fursman, Noël. Belice: balance de los dos primeros años de vida independiente (CM/FI, 24:2, oct./dic. 1983, p. 131–154)
Well executed discussion of competing claims to Belizean territory provides insights into domestic politics of a newly independent nation linked by tradition to English-speaking Caribbean but by disputed geography to a Spanish-speaking isthmus. Centers on defense options, including possible roles of US, UK, and Mexico.

7169 The Future of Central America: policy choices for the U.S. and Mexico. Edited by Richard R. Fagen and Olga Pellicer. Contributors, Adolfo Aguilar Zinser *et al.* Stanford, Calif.: Stanford Univ. Press, 1983. 228 p.
A dozen Mexican and North American scholars examine, through a liberal optic: 1) nature of Central American crisis and its impact on domestic policies; 2) perception of, and policy related to, crisis; 3) Mexico's Central American policies and implications for Mexican-US relations; and 4) developments in Guatemala and Nicaragua. Editors reflect the theme of this policy-oriented vol.: "Decades of inequality, exploitation, and violence

have left wounds . . . all we can ask is that US policies cease being part of the problem of Central America and begin to be constructive elements.

Gandásegui, Marco A. La crisis centroamericana y el Canal de Panamá. See item **6199.**

7170 Gaupp, Peter. Guatemalan refugees in Mexico (NZZ/SRWA, 33:7, Oct. 1983, p. 26–28, ill., map)
Brief description of problems and prospects of Guatemalan refugees in Chiapas, Mexico's southernmost state. Atrocities witnessed by deracinated peasants make it unlikely—in the short run, at least—that they will return home despite appeals by Guatemalan officials.

7171 González, Gabriel A. Genocidio y guerra de exterminio en El Salvador (UJSC/ECA, 35:384/385, oct./nov. 1980, p. 983-1000, ill., tables)
Title captures tone of this diatribe against Salvadoran authorities. Of more interest than the purple prose are the five tables that purport to show the occupational and age breakdowns of assassination victims.

Grayson, George W. The joint oil facility: Mexican-Venezuelan cooperation in the Caribbean. See item **7137.**

7172 Guandásegui, Marco A. La conjoncture Centre-américaine et le Canal de Panama (NS, 8:15, 1983, p. 101–128)
Exceptionally well documented account of the assiduous—detractors would say Machiavellian—coalition-building accomplished by Torrijos both to gain diplomatic support of Panama Canal treaties and invest coherence in his nation's foreign policy.

7173 Hallin, Dan. The media go to war: from Vietnam to Central America (NACLA, 17:4, July/Aug. 1983, p. 2–11, ill., plates)
Perceptive comparison of US media coverage of Vietnam and Central American conflicts. While executive branch still enjoys continual coverage, often critical, of its viewpoint, media has become more asertive in post-Vietnam-Watergate era. For instance, journalists are more inclined to interview rebel leaders, label administration statements "propaganda," and report discrepancies between official version and the reality of an

event. Still, journalists' pursuit of balance too often means blandness.

7174 El Hambre en los países del Tercer Mundo. Managua: Centro de Investigaciones y Estudios de la Reforma Agraria, 1983. 76 p.: bibl., chart, ill., maps, tables (Col. Cmdte. Germán Pomares Ordóñez)

Condemnations of imperialism, dependency, and political aspects of food aid suffuse this data-laden document on hunger in the Third World in general and in Nicaragua in particular. Propaganda aside, contains useful information including maps, tables, and charts on an often neglected issue in Nicaragua. Embraces Sandinistas rhetorical commitment to food self-sufficiency in the short-run and grain exports in future yrs.

7175 Hayes, Margaret Daly. The stakes in Central America and the U.S. policy responses (AEI Foreign Policy and Defense Review [American Enterprise Institute for Public Policy Research, Washington] 4:2, 1982, p. 12–18)

Respected scholar/Senate staff member offers sensible advice on Washington's policy toward Central America—to wit: 1) support responsible, progressive reforms; 2) recognize that suspicion greets any US initiative; 3) aggressively implement quiet diplomacy rather than vice-versa; and 4) make a long-range commitment to advancing mobility and opportunity in region.

7176 Hersh, Kathy Barber. Sanctuary for Central Americans: a treat to INS policy? (FIU/CR, 12:1, Winter 1983, p. 16–19, 43, map, photos)

Sympathetic examination of how a growing number of churches in US are defying authorities by providing sanctuary and legal support—a modern-day "underground railroad"—to refugees from strife-torn El Salvador. Includes map of route followed by the uprooted from Central America to Rio Grande. INS refers to the US Immigration and Naturalization Service.

7177 Hicky, John. Can foreign aid continue as a growth industry for the bureaucracy?: Guatemala's private sector development initiatives project (IAMEA, 37:1, 1983, p. 21–30)

AID venture in Guatemala is subject of this coup d'oeil at US foreign assistance, a "growth industry" woefully neglected by scholars. Concludes that, for want of commitment or interest, neither Congress, the press, nor academics will scrutinize most programs, even the boondoggles. Conventional wisdom aside, foreign aid boasts an effective political constituency.

7178 Honduras/Nicaragua: war without winners (NACLA, 16:5, Sept./Oct. 1982, p. 2–12, ill, map)

Honduran and Nicaraguan armed forces have their strengths and weaknesses, but, overall, a balance of force exists in sophisticated arms. Increasing militarization of Honduras by the Pentagon imperils civilian government, while increasing changes of a war with Nicaragua that "could easily spark off a regional conflagration involving all the nations of Central America, and perhaps the US. and Mexico—on opposing sides." Valuable analysis precedes this questionable conclusion.

7179 Human Rights and United States policy in Central America: transcript of a symposium at Stanford University, January 13, 1983, and a summary of human rights conditions in 1982. Stanford, Calif.: Stanford Central America Action Network, 1983. 44 p.: ill.

Opinions of human rights activists dominate this spirited Stanford conference held on eve of US's biennial certification of human rights progress in El Salvador. Symposium's most interesting feature is the point-counterpoint between Father Robert Drinan ("suspend military aid") and Hoover Institution Fellow Robert Wesson ("U.S. can't walk away").

7180 Informe de un genocidio: los refugiados guatemaltecos. 2a ed. México: Ediciones de la Paz, 1983. 82 p.: ill.

Words and photos depict the anguish of thousands of Guatemalan Indians, systematically persecuted and deracinated by the Guatemalan Army, who have fled to Mexico. Although romanticizing the "progressive policy" of Mexico's government, book correctly praises supportive role of Mexican Church and—above all—the ineffable courage of the refugees.

LaFeber, Walter. Inevitable revolutions: the United States in Central America. See item **6111.**

Leonard, Thomas M. The 1977 Panama Canal treaties in historical perspective. See *HLAS 46:2412.*

7181 Leónov, Nikolái. Inquietures y esperanzas de Guatemala (URSS/AL, 8:56, agosto 1982, p. 29–39, ill.)

Soviet academic describes atrocities in Guatemala committed by alleged US satraps, discusses evolution of guerrilla organizations in the strife-convulsed country and accuses both Washington and Peking of aiding and abetting reactionaries in their unwinnable struggle against national liberation elements who act in concert with the dialectic movement in history.

7182 Libby, Ronald T. Listen to the Bishops (FP, 52, Fall 1983, p. 78–95)

Incisive discussion of the profound transformation of the Catholic Church in international affairs since Medellín (1968) and Puebla (1979) conferences. Illuminating description of new currents in the Salvadoran and Nicaraguan churches precedes an analysis of US Bishops' mounting influence on Washington's Central American policy, a phenomenon largely overlooked by scholars.

7183 Maintenance of peace and security in the Caribbean and Central America: report of the International Peace Academy workshop at Cancún, Quintana Roo, Mexico, 7–9 October 1983. Edited by Jack Child. New York: International Peace Academy, 1984. 93 p., tables (Report; 18)

Mixed bag of papers on security issues—with the best, contributed by the editor, applying peace-keeping techniques to Central American conflicts. Child defines peace-keeping, outlines its basic principles, and provides a typology of conflicts—all of which he relates to the Central American/Caribbean region since World War II. While agreeing on the inapplicability of previous OAS experiences in pursuing peace in El Salvador, some specialists will disagree that "the relevant precedent becomes Zimbabwe . . ."

México, Estados Unidos y la guerra constitucionalista de Nicaragua. See *HLAS 46:2419.*

7184 Millett, Richard. Central American cauldron (CUH, 82:481, Feb. 1983, p. 69–73)

Assigns the collapsing regional economy as a "major cause" of Central America's

political strife. The economic decline has coincided with surging political involvement, especially by young people pessimistic about future. Inflation, civil violence, and economic malaise have driven many members of middle class to an extremism reminiscent of Weimar Germany.

7185 Morin, Claude. La crise politique centre-américaine: des structures et un conjoncture (NS, 8:15, 1983, p. 5–32)

Canadian scholar's polemical condemnation not only of US's destructive, exploitative presence in Central America, but of a Canadian policy toward the region that is replete with "embarrassing contradictions." Accuses Ottawa of sacrificing noble principles in international affairs to ingratiate itself with its powerful neighbor for economic gain.

7186 Mühlemann, Christoph. Reagan's Central American tightrope act (NZZ/SRWA, 33:6, Sept. 1983, p. 6–7)

Rare editorial from a respected European publication that strongly backs President Reagan's Central American policy, pointing out that—between 1970 and 1981— the Soviet dispatched far more military aid ($4 billion) to the Latin American-Caribbean region than did the US ($1.5 billion).

7187 Mujal-León, Eusebio. El socialismo europeo y la crisis en Centroamérica (CM/FI, 24:2, oct./dic. 1983, p. 155–198)

Masterfully researched and meticulously documented study of mounting involvement of Spanish, French, and West German Socialist parties in the Central American conflict. Publicity and debate aside, their effectiveness in the region has been constrained by limited resources, their declining influence with the Socialist International, and essentially symbolic importance of Central America for European governments. Still Washington should expand dialogue with Europe's social democrats to nourish cooperation instead of conflict over Central America.

7188 Palmer, David Scott. Military governments and U.S. policy: general concerns and Central American cases (AEI Foreign Policy and Defense Review [American Enterprise Institute for Public Policy Research, Washington] 4:2, 1982, p. 24–29)

Persuasively contends that, except for

a handful of countries, there are palpable constraints on US influence over Latin American nations. Short-term security challenges in El Salvador and Nicaragua must not blind Washington to its primary self-interest; specifically, encouraging civilian rule throughout the hemisphere.

7189 Partido Conservador Demócrata de Nicaragua. La revolución nicaragüense y la OEA (RPC, 37:175, abril/junio 1982, p. 95–99)

Nicaraguan conservatives submit 12-item bill of particulars to demonstrate that Sandinistas have made a mockery of the June 1979 OAS resolution that called for promotion of pluralism, human rights, and prompt elections by post-Somoza government.

7190 Política estadounidense hacia El Salvador (UJSC/ECA, 36:393, julio 1981, p. 716–732)

Key documents by US diplomats, Salvadoran heads of government, agricultural and business organizations, and center-right political parties (PCN and MDS) on Salvadoran affairs, especially relations with US.

7191 ¿Por qué la Internacional Socialista apoya al FDR? (UJSC/ECA, 36:393, julio 1981, p. 695–697)

Socialist International's support for the FDR springs from "democratic conviction," "solidarity with a people often frustrated in rigged election," and a belief that Salvadoran society must be rebuilt on "new foundations and values." Pub. long before President Duarte launched his 1984 peace initiatives which have sparked intramural debate over the SI's proper policy.

Quenan, Carlos. Crisis centroamericana e iniciativas de paz. See item **3186.**

7192 El Reto democrático en Centro América: entre lo inédito y lo viable. Edición de Ricardo Sol. Colaboradores, Manuel Acosta Bonilla et al. San José: Depto. Ecuménico de Investigaciones (DEI), 1983. 379 p. (Col. Centroamérica)

Consists of 20 Central American and Panamanian figures' reflections on the meaning of, and prospects for, democracy in their region. Intellectual sparks fly over the legitimacy of electoral democracy vs. "popular democracy." Editor Sol does a first-rate job of categorizing the competing views in a so-

phisticated essay on political theory that concludes the vol.

7193 La Revolución es irreversible: plática con Carlos Carrión Cruz y el Padre Fernando Cardenal, miembros de la Asamblea Sandinista del FSLN (URSS/AL, 1:61, enero 1983, p. 44–57)

US military threats notwithstanding, Sandinista leaders declaim irreversibility of their revolution because of international support it enjoys, weakening of the counter-revolution, implementation of agrarian reform, educational advances, and other structural changes. Soviet journal audience is also informed of "great advances" in social relation, literacy, health care, housing, and cultural activities enjoyed by Miskito Indians, despite some of their leaders' "treasonous, pro-imperialist actions."

7194 Revolution and counterrevolution in Central America and the Caribbean. Edited by Donald E. Schulz and Douglas H. Graham. Boulder, Colo.: Westview Press, 1984. 555 p.: tables (Westview special studies on Latin America and the Caribbean)

The best recent, edited work in English on Central America, with secs. devoted to: 1) structural/institutional sources of instability; 2) country-by-country analyses; and 3) international dimensions of the regional crisis. Unlike most books of this genre, the editors present a variety of viewpoints. Of the many first-rate chaps., those on theory (Schulz), Jamaica (Carl Stone), and Mexico (Dennis Hanratty) stand out. Excellent content makes up for sad technical quality.

7195 Revolution and intervention in Central America. Edited by Marlene Dixon and Susanne Jonas. New rev. ed. San Francisco, Calif.: Synthesis Publications, 1983. 344 p.: bibl., index (Contemporary Marxism series)

Marxist author and organizer bring together, albeit from their perspective, an incomparable assortment of essays and documents, including interviews with rebel leaders on the revolutionary struggle in Central America. Particularly useful to students of these insurrections are materials on the relatively unknown Guerrilla Army of the Poor, Guatemala's principal rebel force.

Rosenberg, Mark B. Obstáculos en los Estados Unidos a la política de Reagan en Centroamérica. See item **3189.**

7196 Schifter, Jacobo. Costa Rica, 1948: análisis de documentos confidenciales del Departamento de Estado. San José: Editorial Universitaria Centroamericana, 1982. 249 p.: bibl. (Col. Seis)

Convincing explanation, buttressed by material from US Dept. of State archives, of why Washington maintained a "hands off" policy toward the left-leaning Picardo regime in post-World War II Costa Rica, but intervened to oust Guatemalan reformers in 1954.

7197 Schmidt, Steffen W. El Salvador: America's next Vietnam? Salisbury, N.C.: Documentary Publications, 1983. 217 p.: bibl, ill., index, plates.

The worth of this highly readable book lies less in its chatty, anecdote-filled discussion of El Salvador's political evolution, focusing on US policy toward the strife-ravaged country, than in an exceedingly valuable bibliography. The 13 succinct bibliographical essays provide an exceptional panorama of recent works on El Salvador and the region.

Sebastián, Luis de. Una crítica a los aspectos económicos del *Informe Kissinger.* See item **3191.**

7198 Serra, Luis. La política del gobierno de Reagan hacia Nicaragua (OCLAE, 8, 1982, p. 28–34, ill.)

Journalist's recitation of alleged political, military, economic, and ideological "aggressions" committed against Nicaragua. Several considerations militate against US military intervention (e.g., a prolonged guerrilla war, costly occupation, opposition from European allies, and possible loss of Mexican and Venezuelan oil supplies). Still, "the irrational factor" cannot be disregarded. A window on Nicaraguan thinking.

7199 Shenk, Janet. El Salvador: entering the quagmire (NACLA, 15:3, May/June 1981, p. 2–5, ill.)

Comparisons between El Salvador and Vietnam deemed "appropriate and even compelling." Parallels include concern over domino effect (Mexico has replaced Japan as ultimate target), reliance on counterinsurgency, and release of self-serving white papers that leading newspapers treat as gos-

pel. In elaborating this facile analogy, author overlooks several differences (e.g., early and widespread congressional skepticism about US involvement in Central America and moderate reformism of Duarte and Christian Democrats).

7200 ——. El Salvador: no easy victory (NACLA, 15:3, May/June 1981, p. 6–19, ill., map)

Polemical reiteration of belief that peace can only emerge from negotiations between Salvadoran government and FDR/FMLN. Contains sketches of the army's three key officers: Colonels Guillermo García, Gutiérrez, and Vides Casanova.

Shepherd, Philip L. The tragic cource and consequences of US policy in Honduras. See item **3258.**

7201 Studds, Gerry E. 86 razones para suspender la ayuda militar de EEUU a EL Salvador: en busca de una solución política negociada (UJSC/ECA, 36:393, julio 1981, p. 675–691, ill.)

Liberal US congressman, supported by 85 colleagues—one for each backer of House Resolution 1509—offers a laundry list of reasons for suspending military aid that only "sharpens" political problems confronting El Salvador. Predates Salvadoran constituent assembly and presidential elections.

7202 Torres-Rivas, Edelberto. Central America today: a study in regional dependency (*in* Trouble in our backyard: Central America and the United States in the eighties. Edited by Martin Diskin. Foreword by John Womack, Jr. Epilogue by Günter Grass. New York: Pantheon Books, 1984, p. 2–33, tables)

Infelicitously written Marxist analysis of the economic development of Central American nations concentrating on coffee industry. Most important contribution is description of a "four-story society" that author believes to exist in these countries, composed of a basement (fallen craftsmen and the permanently underemployed), second level (industrial and agricultural proletariat), third level (middle groups), and fourth level (economically dominant bourgeoisie).

7203 Ungo, Guillermo M. The people's struggle (FP, 52, Fall 1983, p. 51–63)

Passionate critique of both El Salvador's "oligarchic-military government" and Washington's support for "ruthless" anti-communism. Scoffs at US's alleged promotion of pluralism, for "[d]eath, jail, exile, or silence is the price of opposition to the government . . ." Written before Duarte's election as president, thus jeremiad offers no evidence to support contention that "the FDR and FMLN have a broad popular base."

7204 U.S. intelligence performance on Central America (NACLA, 16:5, Sept./Oct. 1982, p. 22–35)

Carefully prepared staff report for House Select Committee on Intelligence identifies greatest achievements of intelligence community in Central America as determining the Salvadoran guerrillas' organization, activities, and access to Cuban aid. Weaknesses include belated understanding of the character of the Salvadoran right and its links to the armed forces and terrorism.

7205 Un Viaje histórico: el Papa en una región de conflicto. Compilado por Héctor Ferllini S., Miguel Diáz S., Oscar Castillo R. San José: Uruk Editores, 1983. 194 p.

Scholars will feast on the rich contents of this pocketbook of interviews, papal messages, episcopal pronouncements, and presidential speeches related to Pope John Paul II's March 1983 visit to Central America, Belize, and Haiti.

7206 Volk, Steven. Honduras: on the border of war (in Trouble in our backyard: Central America and the United States in the eighties. Edited by Martin Diskin. Foreword by John Womack, Jr. Epilogue by Günter Grass. New York: Pantheon Books, 1984, p. 204–243)

Emphasizes exploitation of Honduras by US-based fruit companies, often linked to local oligarchs and generals. Revulsion against endemic corruption helped vault Roberto Sauzo Córdoba into the presidency; however, the Pentagon's pulling Honduras into the regional conflict has imperiled the fragile democracy.

7207 Vorozhéikina, Tatiana. Organizaciones revolucionarias de El Salvador y el movimiento popular (URSS/AL, 8:56, agosto 1982, p. 17–28, ill.)

Soviet researcher's description of groups constituting El Salvador's revolutionary front (FMLN). Special praise is lavished on the Communist Party whose "profound

and multifaced experience, historic age, and well-prepared cadres" have made it the movement's "principal cementing force."

White, Richard Alan. The morass: United States intervention in Central America. See item **6126.**

7208 Whitehead, Laurence. Explaining Washington's Central American policies (JLAS, 15:2, Nov. 1983, p. 321–363, tables)

Wide-ranging article that, simplistically, identifies but two possible motivations for US Central American policy (i.e., "'falling dominoes' or the reconstruction of a network of . . . allies linked to American global and regional military-corporate and financial interests"). A readiness to employ clichés weakens a piece that provides insights into US public opinion and congressional decision-making with respect to the region.

THE CARIBBEAN AND THE GUIANAS

7209 Abel, Christopher. Documentary review (JLAS, 15:2, Nov. 1983, p. 471–480)

Reviewer concludes that a House of Commons report on UK's relations with Caribbean and Central America reveals "a picture of confusion, lacunae and inconsistencies in British policy and of a large measure of subordination to U.S. policy that is a consequence of inertia as well as of conscious decision." Useful for students of legislative participation in policymaking who, heretofore, have concentrated on US Congress.

7210 Anderson, Thomas D. Geopolitics of the Caribbean: ministates in a wider world. New York: Praeger, 1984. 175 p.: bibl., index, maps (Politics in Latin America)

Though eclectic, this thin vol. demonstrates that the hugely important field of geography is still fecund, nourished by Anderson's perceptive knowledge of history and politics. Too few social scientists can define, much less explain the significance of, folded rock formations, sedimentary basins, trade winds, or surface currents and their relevance to geopolitics.

7211 Ashley, Paul W. The Commonwealth Caribbean and the contemporary world order: the cases of Jamaica and Trinidad (*in* The Newer Caribbean: decolonization, democracy, and development. Philadelphia, Pa.: Institute for the Study of Human Issues, 1983, p. 159–176)

A good idea—the comparison of Jamaican and Trinidadian development strategies and their responses to recent economic crises—founders on tired and unpersuasive excuses about how "penetration," external "influence," and "dependency" on multinational firms frustrate economic advancement. From this patronizing perspective, nationals of Trinidad and Jamaica have little or no avenues for effectively shaping their economic destiny . . .

7211a Atlantic Council's Working Group on the Caribbean Basin. Western interests and U.S. policy options in the Caribbean Basin: report of the Atlantic Council's . . . James R. Greene and Brent Scowcroft, cochairmen. Richard E. Feinberg, rapporteur. Robert Kennedy, corapporteur. Foreword by Kenneth Rush. Boston: Oelgeschlager, Gunn & Hain, 1984. 331 p.: bibl., index, map.

Trove of enlightened essays on US policy options in the Caribbean Basin. Especially compelling is David Scott Palmer's articulate advocacy of Washington's pursuing a "collaborative" approach in lieu of "hegemonic" or "damage limitation" alternatives in the region. The Wonder and Elliott chap. on energy issues is exceptionally well done.

Avetisian, Artur. Colaboración en el campo de la energética. See item **2771.**

Barca, Alessandro. EE.UU. y la Cuenca del Caribe. See item **3168.**

7212 Baloyra Herp, Enrique. Internationalism and the limits of autonomy: Cuba's foreign relations (*in* Latin American nations in world politics [see item 7062] p. 168–185, bibl.)

Sophisticated analysis of Cuban foreign policy between Dec. 1980 and Aug. 1982 by scholar sympathetic to, but not uncritical of, Castro's regime. International activism prevents isolation, enhances Cuba's Third World role, and counterbalances growing dependency on USSR. Castro can more easily engage in confrontation than conciliation with US, lest detente (and consumerist influences) prove unsettling.

7213 Bellegarde-Smith, Patrick. International relations/social theory in a small state: an analysis of the thought of Dantès Bellegarde (AAFH/TAM 49:2, Oct. 1982, p. 167–184)

Analysis of the ideas of "the most significant and influential diplomat produced by the Republic of Haiti in this century," as reflected in his writings (1898–1962 but mainly 1930s). Dantès Bellegard's diplomatic career was truly extraordinary: including the Paris legation, the Holy See, League of Nations, Permanent Court of Arbitration, various Pan-African and Pan-American conferences, Ambassador to both US and UN. His "unabashedly elitist positions and close association with Western thought and international politics failed to endear him to middle class politicians and social thinkers who succeeded him." Nevertheless, author concludes: "His was a small stage, but men and woman of quality could be born anywhere; indeed, they were a *necessity* for small states." [Y. Ferguson]

7214 Byron, Michael J. Fury from the sea: Marines in Grenada (Proceedings [US Naval Institute, Annapolis, Md.] 110:975, May 1984, p. 118–131, bibl., ill., map)

Marine officer's Sands-of-Iwo-Jima-style account of Grenada invasion, known as operation "Urgent Fury," which—above all—reaffirmed continuing utility of the mobility and tactical flexibility inherent in naval amphibious forces.

7215 Campbell, Frank A. The New International Information and Communication Order: a Caribbean perspective. Georgetown: Publications Div., Ministry of Information, 1980. 28 p.: ill.

Masks of fairness and accuracy are used to disguise the Guyanese Minister of Information's formula for Third World control of international communication, emphasizing a preference for "the right to communicate" over "mere freedom of the press." The throttling of Guyana's once professional and free-wheeling press speaks volumes for the "development journalism" espoused by author.

7216 Castro, Fidel. Fidel Castro speeches. v. 1, Cuba's internationalist foreign policy, 1975–80. v. 2, Our power is that of the working people. Edited by Michael Taber. New York: Pathfinder Press, 1983. 2 v.: bibl., index.

Vol. 1 consists of a collection of pronouncements by Cuba's leader on Angola, Ethiopia, Vietnam, the Non-Aligned Movement, Cuban Americans, policy toward US, and the Sandinista revolution. One of the few compilations in English of Castro's speeches. Vol. 2 was not available for review at press time.

7217 ———. La invasión a Grenada. México: Editorial Katún, 1983. 154 p.: appendix (Realidad social; 2)

Official Cuban reaction to US intervention in Grenada. Particularly interesting is Castro's 26 Oct. 1983 press conference in which he claims to have urged factions within the New Jewel Movement to resolve their differences peaceably. Includes 93-p. "appendix" with an interesting hodgepodge of press reports, diplomatic exchanges, and interviews.

7218 ———. On Grenada (MR, 35:8, Jan. 1984, p. 12–29)

Castro maligns the Coard faction within the New Jewel Movement as "extremists drunk on political theory," speculates that CIA masterminded Bishop's demise and contends that "there was no coordination whatsoever" between the Grenadian army and Cuban construction workers. He most tests reader's gullibility in insisting that Bishop never informed him of intramural dissensions afflicting NJM.

7219 ———. The world economic and social crisis, its impact on the underdeveloped countries, its somber prospects and the need to struggle if we are to survive: a report to the Seventh Summit Conference of Non-Aligned Countries. New Delhi: People's Publishing House, 1983. 224 p.: bibl.

Report from Non-Aligned Countries' Seventh Summit Conference (New Delhi, 1983) addressing world economic crisis, destructive role of transnational firms, escalating arms race, and steps for redistributing income from the impecunious South to affluent North to achieve a NIEO. The self-serving fixation on external exploitation—as opposed to domestic factors causing underdevelopment—weakens the credibility of the

"irrefutable" facts and realities cited. For economist's comment, see item **3351**.

7220 Castro and the narcotics connection: special report. Washington: Cuban American National Foundation, 1983. 88 p.: ill.

Cuban American National Foundation marshals impressive information that the Castro regime is financing terrorism by shipping narcotics to US. Most compelling is the Jamie Guillot-Lara case, involving Nov. 1982 indictment for drug smuggling of four Castro aides. Especially useful are a map of the alleged trafficking route and a collection of 21 media reports on the subject.

7221 Colossus challenged: the struggle for Caribbean influence. Edited by H. Michael Erisman and John D. Martz. Boulder, Colo.: Westview Press, 1982. 260 p.: bibl., index (Westview special studies on Latin America and the Caribbean)

First-rate chaps. on Soviet (Jiri Valenta), Cuban (W. Ray Duncan), and Venezuelan (Martz) policies toward the region highlight this uneven vol. that focuses—sometimes through a mist of purple prose—on limitations under which Washington labors in pursuing often ill-deined goals with respect to Central America and the Caribbean.

7222 Corrada Guerrero, Rafael. Orden y desorden en el Caribe (UPR/RCS, 22:3/4, sept./dic. 1980, p. 249–271, bibl., graphs, ill., tables)

Comparative study of economic strategies in Puerto Rico and Venezuela's Guayanese region that advocates optimum use of available productive capacity and an emphasis on social investment to reduce external dependency. In calling for greater import substitution and controls on foreign investment, author's "real Antillean alternative" will probably impede development, sharpen inefficiency, and spark disorder.

7223 Cuba: totalitarismo marxista; total violación de los derechos humanos (Informe ODCA [Organización Democrata Cristiana de América, Secretaría General, s.l] 104, 1983, p. 1–16, charts)

Scathing report of discrepancies between liberating goals of 1976 Cuban Constitution and oppression besetting large numbers of citizens. Data from Mariel exodus informs secs. dealing with divided families, religious persecution, impediments to education, and food shortages. Condemns both lack of means to defend one's rights and absence of an independent judiciary.

7224 Dew, Edward. Did Suriname switch?: dialectics à la Dante (FIU/CR, 12:4, Fall 1983, p. 29–30, plate)

Explores the "dialectic of repression/relaxation/unrest repression" in Surinamese politics, probing: 1) links between former Dutch colony and Grenada; 2) mercurial dictator Bouterse's squabbles with Cubans and homegrown political organizations; and 3) Surinam's improbable impact on US-Dutch defense questions. In sum, "It's a downward dialectic . . . more familiar to Dante than to Marx."

7225 Diederich, Bernard. The end of West Indian innocence: arming the police (FIU/CR, 13:2, Spring 1984, p. 10–12, plate)

Journalistic account of US training of security forces in the Eastern Caribbean in the wake of Grenada intervention. Suggests that this training will increase problems by raising level of domestic and regional violence.

7226 Domínquez, Jorge I. High noon: reflexiones sobre la política de la Administración Reagan hacia Cuba (AR, 9:35, 1983, p. 12–18, plate)

Convincing study of the "fracaso" of Reagan's "High Noon" Cuban policy because its fixation on ideological concerns has strengthened Cuban-Soviet ties to the detriment of US security interests. Frustration of the Reagan administration has found essential bilateral conflicts spilling over into relations with nations in Central America and southern Africa.

Eckstein, Susan. Structural and ideological bases of Cuba's overseas programs. See item 6220.

7227 Los Estados Unidos y Trujillo, año 1946: colección de documentos del Departamento de Estado y de las fuerzas armadas norteamericanas. Edición de Bernardo Vega. Santo Domingo: Fundación Cultural Dominicana, 1982. 2 v.: bibl., ill., indexes.

Research gem in form of official US documents, organized chronologically, relating to Trujillo regime in 1946—an important year because of: 1) sharp rise in an overt, unified opposition; 2) founding of Juventud Democrática and Partido Socialista Popular; 3) short-lived pact between the dictator and the communists; and 4) flareup of strikes in sugar industry. Commentaries, indexes, and photos add sparkle to this archival jewel.

7228 Falcoff, Mark. Thinking about Cuba: unscrambling Cuban messages (GU/WQ, 6:2, Spring 1983, p. 3–16)

No-nonsense critique of Wayne Smith and others who imply that Cuba's foreign policy goals are "due the same deference as those of the Soviet Union or China." Precipitous normalization of US-Cuban relations could: 1) promote a Cuba lobby in US; 2) create in the State Dept. vested interests for conciliation, even in the face of *Fidelista* adventurism; and 3) provide Castro with greater economic leverage within Soviet bloc. Resumption of diplomatic relations will occur some day. "But before that can happen, the Cubans themselves will have to rethink the meaning of their national experience, much as the Chinese have done."

7229 Fenton, Robert E. Caribbean Coast Guard: a regional approach (Naval War College Review [Newport, R.I.] 37[302]:2, March/April 1984, p. 26–40, map, tables)

Clear, nuts-and-bolts proposal for US, serving as "role model," to train a "Caribean Coast Guard," composed of existing coast guards, police forces, and/or navies. This multilateral unit would undertake search-and-rescue services, environmental and economic resource protection, and marine aids to navigation, and limited defense operations.

7230 Gallegos, Rómulo *et al.* 1948–1958, Cuba: patria del exilio venezolano y trinchera de combatientes. Prologo, Simón Alberto Consalvi. Caracas: Ediciones Centauro, 1982. 476 p. (Enero 23, 1958, XXV aniversario)

Exceptionally moving account, told through articles in *Bohemia*, of the fraternal asylum that Rómulo Gallegos and other Venezuelans fleeing the military dictatorship in 1948 enjoyed in then-democratic Cuba.

7231 Gould, Lewis L. The Spanish-American War and President McKinley. Lawrence: Univ. Press of Kansas, 1982. 164 p.: bibl., ill., index.

Continues trend begun by H. Wayne Moran (*William McKinley and his America*) in 1960s to portray McKinley as an effective chief executive, who, in fact, was first modern president, foreshadowing the imperial executives of six decades later. Discusses coming of Spanish-American War, the President's handling of war itself, and emergence of an American empire (1898–1900).

Grayson, George W. The joint oil facility: Mexican-Venezuelan cooperation in the Caribbean. See item **7137.**

Green, Gil. Cuba at 25: the continuing revolution. See item **6223.**

7232 Grenada Documents: an overview and selection. Washington: Dept. of State: Dept. of Defense, 1984. 1 v. (various pagings)

US government-pub. collection of captured documents provides overwhelming evidence of Marxist-Leninist orientation of Grenada's New Jewel Movement in both domestic and foreign affairs. Especially interesting is NJM's clumsy attempts—in concert with other leftist members in region—to influence policy of Socialist International. Essential reference work.

7233 Haley, Edward P. Cuba and United States strategy (AF/AUR, 35:1, Nov./ Dec. 1983, p. 82–93, tables)

Deftly challenges the "minimalist" position that only the establishment of a Soviet base justifies US military action in Central America. Inadequate conventional forces militate against such intervention. "The unavoidable conclusion is that . . . the United States has at best one Marine division with its air wing available for service in the Caribbean without disrupting assignment of other units to other theaters. In a word, Cuba has the military initiative in the region."

Henry, Paget. Decolonization and the authoritarian context of democracy in Antigua. See item **6291.**

7234 Hippolyte-Manigat, Mirlande. Haiti and the Caribbean Community: profile of an applicant and *problematique* of widening the integration movement. Translated by Keith Q. Warner. Kingston: Institute of Social and Economic Research, Univ. of the West Indies, 1980. 256 p.: bibl., index.

Erudite treatise on attempt by Haiti, deemed a pariah by its neighbors, to gain membership in—or, at least, some form of affiliation with—a reluctant CARICOM. Excellent chaps. on Haitian geography, society, culture, and economics furnish a backdrop to a fascinating diplomatic minuet.

7235 Horowitz, Irving Louis. Cuba and the Caribbean (CRIA/W, 26:12, Dec. 1983, p. 19–21)

Highly articulate, compelling appeal to include the Soviet Union in Caribbean peace discussions. "To bring the Russians into the negotiating process is to permit a serious policy discussion between the contending parties—making clear that the massive Soviet presence in Cuba is at least as much an agenda item as the modest U.S. presence in El Salvador." Also, points to three factors—its military alliance with Moscow, economic structure, and extreme authoritarianism—that militate against Cuba's integration into the region.

7235a Johns Hopkins University. Study Group on United States-Cuban Relations. Central American and Caribbean Program. Report on Cuba: findings of the Study Group . . . Boulder, Colo.: Westview Press; Washington: Foreign Policy Institute, School of Advanced International Studies, The Univ., 1984. 36 p. (SAIS papers in international affairs; 2)

Johns Hopkins study group sensibly concludes that US policy toward Cuba, which currently lacks long-range objectives, should focus on gradual engagement because the key to containing *Fidelista* influence lies not in US policy toward Cuba itself but in Washington's response to regional problems.

Johnson, Janis and **Robert A. Rankin.** Interviewing Michael Manley: the role of the opposition in Jamaica. See item **6277.**

7236 Lewis, Vaughan A. Caribbean state systems and the contemporary world order (*in* The Newer Caribbean: decolonization, democracy, and development. Philadelphia, Pa.: Institute for the Study of Human Issues, 1983, p. 123–139)

Trenchant examination of why the NIEO championed by Caribbean Basin states failed to materialize. Complements delineation of four "political parameters" characterizing US policy toward region: 1) ensuring order; 2) treating area as "exemplary;" 3) containing the negative effects of raw material dependency; and 4) crafting a trade and aid strategy.

Lowenthal, David. "An island is a world:" the problem of Caribbean insularity. See item **1083.**

7237 MacDonald, Scott B. and **Albert L. Gastmann.** Mitterrand's headache: the French Antilles in the 1980s (FIU/CR, 13:2, Spring 1984, p. 19–21, map, plate)

Brief analysis of obstacles that Mitterrand's radical and ideologically-minded advisers faced in attempting to "liberate" Martinique and Guadeloupe. Most local moderates and conservatives strongly oppose being "cast from the French fold," while communists fear that immediate independence would enhance US influence. "The French Antilles remain . . . little changed by the socialists and locked into status quo politics."

Maingot, Anthony P. Options for Grenada: the need to be cautious. See item **6253.**

7238 Maira, Luis. Caribbean state sysetms and middle-status powers: the cases of Mexico, Venezuela, and Cuba (in The Newer Caribbean: decolonization, democracy, and development. Philadelphia, Pa.: Institute for the Study of Human Issues, 1983, p. 177–204)

Diffuse essay on Mexican, Venezuelan, and Cuban policies vis-à-vis English-speaking Caribbean. Particularly worthwhile is explanation of misgivings Latin American nations evinced toward former European colonies of the area. In a sec. on joint initiatives, Maira lavished attention on SELA and OLADE (both paper organizations), but neglects to mention multi-million dollar San José oil facility.

7239 Manitzas, Nita Rous. Cuba and the contemporary world order (in The Newer Caribbean: decolonization, democracy, and development. Philadelphia, Pa.: Institute for the Study of Human Issues, 1983, p. 141–158)

Crisp, cleanly written, and balanced account of how one underdeveloped state, Cuba, fashioned a distinct development strategy in a complex and—at times—hostile international environment. This phenomenon is explained in terms of Cuba's economic relations to superpowers, its successful forging of a national community and the role of ideology—with "rational choice" serving as the catalytic agent in this complex mix.

Manley, Michael. Grenada in the context of history: between neocolonialism and independence. See item **6254.**

———. Jamaica: struggle in the periphery. See item **6279.**

7240 Marcella, Gabriel and **Daniel S. Papp.** The Soviet-Cuban relationship: symbiotic parastic? (in The Soviet Union in the Third World: successes and failures. Edited by Robert H. Donaldson. Boulder, Colo.: Westview Press, 1981, p. 51–68)

While providing no new facts or analysis, article outlines reasonably well the advantages and disadvantages of Soviet-Cuban cooperation from each partner's perspective. Authors conclude that bilateral ties will "remain intimate" in the near-term and probably in the long-run, absent a major change in US policy toward Castro regime.

7241 Massing, Michael. Grenada before and after (The Atlantic [The Atlantic Monthly Co., Boston] 253:2, Feb. 1984, p. 76–87, ill.)

Telling criticism of US government's exaggerated anxiety over Grenada's Port Salines airport, pierced by a 9,000-foot-long runway, highlights a piece that romanticizes regime of the New Jewel Movement, discounting both the deviance of revolutionary Grenada in English-speaking Caribbean and broader geopolitical issues that influenced US intervention.

7242 Miguez, Alberto. Cuba et le Mouvement des non-alignés (FDD/NED [Problèmes d'Amérique Latine; 64] 4336/4664, 9 avril 1982, p. 169–179)

Provides valuable journalistic cameos of Cuba's role at six Nonaligned Movement conferences from Belgrade (1961) to Havana (1979). Although Havana's diplomats claim last summit reduced from five to two the intramovement factions, polarization impelled by undisguised Cuban advocacy of Soviet goals weakened the organization and Castro's standing in it.

7243 Montaner, Carlos Alberto. The roots of anti-Americanism in Cuba: sovereignty in an age of world cultural homogeneity (FIU/CR, 13:2, Spring 1984, p. 13–16, 42–46, plate)

Argues the inevitability, once Spain was ousted, of strong US influence in Cuba because the "nation is wet and pliable clay" in the hands of its giant neighbor. The paradox is that, thanks to Cuban Americans, this influence will reappear—in an even more robust form—in the post-Castro period.

7244 Montero, Oscar. Grenada: el Señor Presidente y la imagen videogénica (AR, 9:35, 1983, p. 19–21, ill.)

This overwritten, highly emotional attack on TV coverage of the Grenada intervention contains more than a scintilla of truth about the tendency of evening news to neglect—or omit—historical, economic, and ideological context in which events take place. More important is the creation of images that "prevent the viewer's flicking off the set."

7245 Muñoz, María Elena. Historia de las relaciones internacionales de la República Dominicana. t. 1, El colonialismo europeo y las relaciones domínico-haitianas: 1844–1861. Santo Domingo: Editora Alfa y Omega, 1980. 1 v.: bibl. (Historia y sociedad; 38)

Dominican scholar traces her homeland's international relations from the colonial epoch to independence to the war with, and occupation by, Haiti to annexation by Spain in 1861. Despite inclusion of memorial images, author lacks an analytic framework, indulges in hyperbole (especially regarding Haitians), and fails to include an index.

7246 Naipaul, V.S. An island betrayed: Grenada's revolution never got beyond slogans and texts, amid the heat and torpor, language and intentions blurred (Harper's Magazine [New York] March 1984, p. 61–72, plates)

Insightful, elegant essay on Grenada crisis, stressing lack of legitimacy of, and grassroots support for, Maurice Bishop's New Jewel Movement whose members were the island's first educated generation. "The revolution was a revolution of words. The words had appeared as an illumination, a short-cut to dignity, to newly educated men who had nothing in the community to measure themselves against and who, finally, valued little in their own community . . . The revolution blew away; and what was left . . . wa a murder story."

7247 O'Shaughnessy, Hugh. Grenada: revolution, invasion, and aftermath. Lon-

don: H. Hamilton with the *Observer*, 1984. 258 p.: ill., plates.

One of Britain's most respected Latin American watchers has crafted a solid, journalistic account of the 1983 intervention.

Payne, Anthony; Paul Sutton; and Tony Thorndike. Grenada: revolution and invasion. See item **6255.**

7248 Petras, James. A military policy in search of an economic rationale: Reagan's Caribbean Basin aid program (BNCE/CE, 28:11, Nov. 1982, p. 400–402)

Excoriates Caribbean Basin Initiative as "a political shell" for advancing Washington's essentially military approach to region. Although not offering an alternative development strategy, author insists that inefficient bureaucracies of foreign bank accounts will swallow up new funds unless restructuring of land ownership, credit, and commerce take place.

Piñeiro, Manuel. La crisis actual del imperialismo y los procesos revolucionarios en la América Latina y el Caribe. See item **6231.**

7249 Ramsaran, Ramesh. The US Caribbean Basin Initiative (RIIA/WT, 38:11, Nov. 1982, p. 430–436)

Succinct explanation of Caribbean Basin Initiative is followed by criticism of the essentially bilateral venture as, among other things, a threat to Commonwealth Caribbean integration. Concludes US failed to learn from Alliance for Progress "whose benefits were largely confined to privileged groups unwilling to undertake . . . fundamental reforms . . ."

Rauls, Martina. Die Beziehungen des Karibischen Raumes zu Afrika = Las Relaciones entre el area del Caribe y Africa: introducción bibliográfica = Relations between the Caribbean area and Africa: introductory bibliography. See *HLAS 46:35.*

7250 Relaciones internacionales en la Cuenca del Caribe y la política de Colombia. Edición, Juan Tokatlian y Klaus Schubert. Bogotá: FESCOL: Cámara de Comercio y Bogotá, 1982. 591 p.: appendices, bibl. (Biblioteca de la Cámara; 2)

Best recent vol. on Caribbean Basin because of its distinguished contributors, comprehensive coverage, astute analyses, and excellent appendices and bibliography. (One only regrets the absence of an index). Typical of the excellence of most of the 40 essays is that of Abraham Lowenthal who emphasizes that the perceived threat to US in the region is "psycho-political" (*inseguridad nacional*) not "strategic-military" (*seguridad nacional*).

Revolution and counterrevolution in Central America and the Caribbean. See item **7194.**

7251 Rodríguez, Carlos Rafael. Sobre la cooperación de Cuba con la URSS y los países del CAME (URSS/AL, 1:61, enero 1983, p. 38–43)

Reveals Cuba's overwhelming dependence on Soviet Union, with attention to such key sectors as textiles, energy, transport, mining, and sugar. Laments North American "economic aggression" designed to curb sales of Cuban nickel and interfere with loans sought from international banks. Yet, he stresses importance of the 20 percent of island's economic relations conducted with capitalist countries.

Ryan, Selwyn. The Grenada questions: a revolutionary balance sheet. See item **6256.**

Sánchez, Néstor D. What was uncovered in Grenada. See item **6257.**

Sánchez García-Calzadilla, María E. La participación de Cuba en la integración económica socialista. See item **3372.**

7252 Segal, Aaron. Collecting the Caribbean: the not-so-hidden politics of explanation (FIU/CR, 13:2, Spring 1984, p. 29–31, 50, 51, ill., maps)

Articulately and compelling, author savages recently edited works on the Caribbean for failing to: 1) define geographic area studies; 2) provide non-Marxist viewpoints; 3) employ rigorous methodologies; and 4) employ empirical research. Segal reserves his severest criticism for the "one-sided, single school, deterministic analyses" that abound. Instead of "breast-beating about external dependency," researchers should examine countries such as Cyprus, Denmark, Malta, and Singapore—"all economically dependent small states, but each has created leverage and options not found in the Caribbean." Reading this five-p. review should enable scholars to avoid hours of slogging through jargon-suffused materials whose analytic

categories too often "life only in the contributors' brains."

Stone, Carl. Demoracy and socialism in Jamaica: 1972–1979. See item **6286.**

7253 Stone, Carl. The Jamaican reaction: Grenada and the political stalemate (FIU/CR, 12:4, Fall 1983, p. 31–32, 60, plate, table)

Survey research adorns this skillfully prepared essay on linkage of events in Jamaica and Grenada. US intervention in the latter following Bishop's demise "set the stage in Jamaica for a discrediting of socialism and communism and an emotional identification with the cause of anti-communism and the role of the U.S. as protector of democratic interests in the region."

7254 Trainor, John C. Naval option for the Caribbean: the US Coast Guard (Naval War College Review [Newport, R.I.] 36[296]:2, March/April 1983, p. 31–39, map)

Advocates greater reliance on a frequently overlooked service, the US Coast Guard, to accomplish training, search and rescue, anti-pollution, and safety missions in the Caribbean Basin.

7255 United States. Congress. House. Committee on Foreign Affairs. Subcommittee on International Economic Policy and Trade. Issues in United States-Cuban relations: hearing before the Subcommittees [sic] on International Economic Policy and Trade and the Subcommittee on Inter-American Affairs of the Committee on Foreign Affairs, House of Representatives, December 14, 1982. Washington: US GPO, 1983. 82 p. (97th Congress, 2nd Session)

Pros (Thomas O. Enders) and cons (Wayne S. Smith) of US policy toward Cuba are eclipsed by wrenching testimony of Cuban poet Armando Valladares Pérez, who spent 22 yrs. in Cuban political prisons before his 1982 French-procured release. If nations are judged by how they treat their poets, history will not absolve the *fidelista* regime.

7256 Windt Lavandier, César de. La Segunda Guerra Mundial y los submarinos alemanes en el Caribe. San Pedro de Macorís, República Dominicana: Univ. Central del Este, 1982. 362 p.: bibl., ill., maps, plates.

Photos, maps, and diagrams enhance

appeal of this awkwardly organized study of German submarine operations in the Caribbean. Detailed accounts of strategy, sinkings, life aboard vessels, and captains' backgrounds compensate for such hyperbole as the contention that Hitler lost World War II on 16 Feb. 1942, the day when submarine U-156 failed to knock out the Aruba oil refinery.

SOUTH AMERICA

MICHAEL J. FRANCIS, *Professor of Government, University of Notre Dame*

THE MAJOR TOPIC OF STUDY regarding the international relations of South America was, of course, the tragic struggle in the South Atlantic from April to June of 1982. Prior to that time one could joke that more ink than blood had been spilled in regard to the Malvinas/Falkland question—and certainly the topic had long been a pre-occupation of Argentine authors. But suddenly that bleak outcropping of rock in the South Atlantic became not only the focus of international attention but a place where many young men with much to live for died as a result of the miscalculations of their elders on both sides of the Atlantic (for documents, see item **7293**).

A certain type of publication on this conflict designed to justify the invasion emerged in Argentina. Some of these works were formulated along narrow legalistic lines, their argument based on Argentina's having inherited ownership at the time of independence of previously Spanish colonies that were unjustly taken over by the British in 1833. The more legalistic of these works stop short of encouraging an invasion (items **7281, 7285, 7303,** and **7308**). There is a pathetic and somewhat tragic cast to the more jingoistic of such writings (item **7306**) in support of the invasion published during the heat of the struggle, their authors making brave statements while raw recruits trying to save Galtieri's adventure shivered in their foxholes (item **7271**). For an account from the perspective of such an Argentine soldier, see items **6250** and **7314.**

Although the British make their own legal case for control of the islands, neither side has been anxious to trust the fate of their claims to a judicial decision. Partly, this is due to the stark difference of these legal claims. The British claim is based on the fact of 150 years of occupation and the population's composition (mostly controlled by London) and desire to remain British (items **7277** and **7282**). There is some disagreement between the claims as to historical events (who saw what when?), but chiefly it is a matter of two different legal idioms: the British speaking the language of the *status quo* and self-determination, while the Argentines speak of territorial integrity and anti-colonialism.

The military side of the struggle commanded much attention. The Argentine air force came in for a good deal of praise, some of it by officials of that service (items **7267** and **7280**). In particular, the effectiveness of the six French Exocet missiles were subject to scrutiny (item **7317**). Unfortunately, some of the Argentine literature praising one or another branch of the armed services should be read with caution more as part of the continuing intramural struggle between such Argentine services for prestige, influence and a larger share of the budget. A branch that certainly fared poorly in the South Atlantic was the Argentine army. Although a number of experts tried to determine the "lessons" of the Malvinas/Falkland conflict, there seemed to be a strong bias among these military observers that there was nothing new to be learned from this war, only old lessons that had been forgotten or ignored (item **7290, 7298, 7299a,** and **7307**).

If the jingoism was less blatant on the British side, it was there nevertheless (items **7320** and **7321**). Background events in Buenos Aires that led to the invasion apparently were so mysterious to British observers that they assumed the invasion was simply the result of Galtieri's stupidity and, therefore, a more interesting subject to focus on were military operations (items **7272** and **7289**). For example, the tenacity of the British foot soldier came in for much praise and the sinking of the *Belgrano* was perceived as an obvious maneuver during a state of war (item **7279**).

By far the best work on the Argentine side is *Malvinas, la trama secreta* (item **6508**), the result of a year's investigative effort on the part of three journalists. While the book virtually ignored the actual fighting, it offers a blow-by-blow account of how the decision to invade/occupy the islands was made and the ensuing diplomacy. These reporters apparently gained access to a number of transcripts of important diplomatic conversations. In particular, they thoroughly analyze the US role. Two other works that help us to understand the Argentine decision-making process are Moneta's (item **7302**) and Tulchin's (item **7312**). Viola's book (item **7319**), in turn, attempts to analyze Argentina's mistakes.

Another good work but by a British historian who specializes in Latin America, is Peter Calvert's *The Falkland crisis* (item **7276**). This work, however, was written immediately after the conflict and much new information has since come to light. For analysts who offer intelligent criticisms of London's policy in the South Atlantic one should consult Beck (item **7270**), Makin (item **7299**), and Smithers (item **7309**).

There have been two bibliographical essays. The longer one (item **7286**) is valuable although it is too pro-Argentine in tone to take some of the judgments seriously. The other is a thoughtful essay by an Englishman which is critical of all sides and makes a number of excellent points (item **7296**). For a short readable piece that gets beneath the superficialities, this is a good place to start.

Several writers discuss the struggle considering the long-term implications of Washington's support of the British—usually deciding that this was going to damage US influence by increasing the sense of Pan-Latin Americanism (items **7268, 7297,** and **7307**). Other accounts of the war written by Latin Americans from Chile (item **7284**), Brazil (item **7274**), and Ecuador (item **7304**) offer differing perspectives.

A less publicized and less bloody territorial conflict recently took place between Ecuador and Peru. Judging from the number of books published, the Ecuadorians feel a good deal more strongly about this conflict than the Peruvians. There were at least four descriptions of the struggle written by Ecuadorians and, although one must consider their one-sidedness, a valuable picture of what went on does emerge from their works (items **7339, 7341, 7342,** and **7343**).

Prior to the April 1982 move into the Falkland Islands, the boundary dispute that seemed most likely to lead to violence was the Beagle Channel controversy involving three islands located at the southern tip of the continent and claimed by Argentina and Chile (item **7318**). Recently, there was a sharp drop in the number of books on either side of that dispute although a related issue—Antarctica—has attracted a good deal of interest (items **7258, 7262,** and **7331**). The division of the continent is based on a settlement which will be due for renegotiation after 1991, and there is no doubt that such future negotiations to determine the region's new legal arrangement will be difficult and protracted. The conviction that the region has important resources is part of our world's belief system and the reason why countries want access to Antarctica. Whether such visions of riches is real or imaginary remains to be seen.

Bolivia is a country plagued by border disputes with virtually all its neighbors (items **7320** and **7321**), and this has spawned some patriotic/legalistic literature. The boundary question between Colombia and Venezuela has been exacerbated by the fact that there are important mineral resources in the Gulf of Venezuela. Complex legal/historical arguments have been advanced by both sides on this topic (items **7337, 7360** and **7361**). Several other studies examined boundary disputes in general (item **7076a**).

To an extent, many of the works discussed so far concern the development of international law throughout the hemisphere, always a popular topic in Latin America (items **7292** and **7082a**). A good source to start studying these concerns is the short introduction to boundary trouble spots in Latin America by Peter Calvert (item **7015**).

Another important issue that involves boundaries is the international Law of the Sea. The UN-sponsored Law of the Sea meetings eventually produced a document which largely accepts the 200-mile limit for certain activities. These talks have generated some commentaries (e.g., item **7029a**), including works from the Brazilian (item **7323**), Chilean (item **7332**), and Peruvian (items **7347** and **7357**) perspectives. Because the west coast South American countries have long advocated the 200-mile limit, its recognition in the Law of the Sea discussions represented a major victory for those states. For an excellent set of papers on the Law of the Sea which were produced before the talks started see Orrego's *Política oceánica* (item **7330a**).

Related to the Law of the Sea is the notion of a Pacific Basin, that is to say the Pacific area constituting an economic unit of sorts, a fashionable concept nowadays that is partly the result of the dynamism of the Japanese economy. Two Latin American works (items **7263** and **7144**) deal with this notion although Martínez uses the geopolitical approach to emphasize a potential Mexican role.

Among books received for review in this volume of the *Handbook*, there appears to be a slight decline in the number of South American works haranguing US imperialism in Latin America, a proposition that seems difficult to prove given the unpopularity of the Reagan administration's interventionist policies in Central America and elsewhere (items **7261** and **7025a**). One can only speculate as to the possible reasons for this drop. The much predicted decline of North American hegemony in the hemisphere may be one reason. Secondly, it is obvious that Argentina, Brazil, Venezuela (item **7358**) and other important South American countries are pursuing interests on the continent that appear to be at least as imperialist as those of the US. Thirdly, the dependency concept (item **7091a**) is no longer the analytical touchstone it once was to scholars in Latin American studies. To the extent that dependency has led to a neglect of factors such as internal barriers to development, it has fallen into disfavor. On the other hand, when used as an analytical tool, it has remained part of Latin Americans' perception of their situation. Overall, however, we may have entered a post-dependency period in terms of thinking about Latin America.

As an approach to understanding the international relations of South America, geopolitics continues to spawn numerous studies (items **7260, 7299b, 7331, 7338,** and **7346**). If understood as an antidote to thinking that ignores geographical and power realities, geopolitics can explain a good deal. However, in Latin America primarily it has been a favorite theory of military men or militarily-oriented scholars. In their view, military force serves as the principal means for the continuation of the nation state, therefore, one's thinking should move in the direction of analyzing potentially conflictual situations. Indeed, geopolitics is such an inexact science that it can be used to argue that any particular state is somehow pivotal. This ethnocentrism dominates geopolitical writing (much of which is repetitive) in that almost every book contains the implication that the country in which it was published is somehow particularly vital to western civilization.

This perception of geopolitical significance is related to the problem of arms buildup in Latin America. Although compared to other areas of the world one can argue that the presence of GNP spent on military expenditures is not so great, it nevertheless is an important budgetary consideration hampering development. Three works deal with this problem (items **7035a, 7257,** and **7291**) which undoubtedly will continue to attract interest. In this regard it is somewhat reassuring to read a study prepared for the US Congress which concludes that Argentine is not likely to move in the direction of building a nuclear weapon, even though there is the available technology to produce it (item **7315**).

The role of multinationals in hemispheric politics is not as popular a topic as in previous volumes of the *Handbook*. One work dealt with Argentina's attempts to control the transfer of technology (item **7273**), another concerned automobile manufacturing in Colombia (item **7336**), and one naive work on Paraguay was designed to attract foreign investment (item **7345**).

Analysis of the OAS or hemispheric organizations in general did not stimulate much scholarship. There was only a thoughtful prescriptive overview by a Venezuelan diplomat (item **7336**) and a short analysis of the Inter-American Juridical Committee (item **7100b**).

As usual there were various studies of the foreign policies of several individual countries: Venezuela (items **7355, 7357, 7359,** and **7362**); Colombia (item **7335**); Argentina (item **7305**); Chile (items **7328** and **7333**); and Peru (item **7348**).

The most interesting piece of writing on Latin American foreign policy was a series of methodologically and theoretically sophisticated pieces drawn from a single book, *Latin American nations in world politics*, edited by Heraldo Muñoz and Joseph Tulchin (item **7062**). One dealt with the formulation and implementation in what is believed to be the most modern South American foreign service or Brazil's (item **7322**). Another looked at the evolution of Colombia's foreign policy process (item **7335**). Tulchin analyzed the impact of authoritarianism on foreign policy using Argentine as an example (item **7312**). And Wilhelmy's work applied the bureaucratic politics model to the Chilean experience (item **7333**).

GENERAL

Abreu, Marcelo de Paiva. Argentina and Brazil during the 1930s: the impact of British and American international economic policies. See item **3690**.

7257 Agüero, Felipe. Armas y desarme en Sudamérica. Santiago: Facultad Latinoamericano de Ciencias Sociales (FLACSO), 1982. 95 p.: bibl. (Documento de trabajo; 141) Because there is so little scholarly analysis of the problem, this short but good introduction serves as a valuable source on the topic of South American arms buildup and the possibility of arms control in the region.

Carías Sisco, Germán. Fronteras en la selva: frente a Guyana, Colombia, y Brasil. See item **5197**.

7258 Milenky, Edward and **Steven Schwad.** Latin America and Antarctica (CUH, 82:481, Feb. 1983, p. 52–53, ill.)

Very brief but effective discussion of an issue that has received little attention in US. Good introduction to topic.

7259 Pérez del Castillo, Alvaro. Bolivia, Colombia, Chile y el Perú. La Paz: Editorial Los Amigos del Libro, 1980. 396 p., 4 p. of plates: ill.

Historical study of socioeconomic and political differences among four countries which have placed strains on the Andean Pact and of common factors which have strenghthened it. Emphasizes geographical and military developments which led to the Pact of Cartagena as an attempt "to prevent the Balkanization" of the four countries covered. Obviously a warning to Bolivia about her relations with Southern Cone. [W.R. Garner]

7260 Selcher, Wayne A. Recent strategic developments in South America's Southern Cone (*in* Latin American nations in world politics [see item **7062**] p. 101–118)

Concise summary of major geopolitical issues dividing Southern Cone countries. There are mountains of materials on this in Spanish but so little in English that this account is an important source.

7261 The Southern Cone: U.S. policy and the transition to democracy; the proceedings of a conference, "U.S. Policies to Accompany the Transition to Democracy in the Southern Cone." Co-sponsored by the Dept. of Government, Georgetown Univ. and the Washington Office on Latin America (WOLA). Washington: WOLA, 1983. 74 p.

Series of short papers on US policy toward Southern Cone countries. Although weighted in an anti-US administration direction, there are Dept. of State representatives and some exchange of views. More polemical than analytical in places but generally a good short collection of pieces.

7262 Symposium Internacional sobre el Desarrollo de la Antártica, *Punta Arenas, Chile, 1977.* Desarrollo de la Antártica. Edición bajo la dirección de Francisco Orrego Vicuña y Augusto Salinas Araya. Santiago: Editorial Universitaria, 1977. 374 p.: bibl., ill. (Estudios internacionales)

Series of papers from 1977 conference (not previously annotated in *HLAS*) sponsored by the Instituto de Estudios Internacionales, Univ. de Chile. As usually true of research connected with this Institute, these are serious works of scholarship and analysis. But as is probably inevitable at such meetings, Antarctica takes on an exaggerated significance.

7263 Trans-Pacific Seminar, *3rd, Viña del Mar, Chile, 1975.* Ciencia y tecnología en la Cuenca del Pacífico: estudios. Auspiciado por la Sociedad Australiana de Estudios Latinoamericanos, la Comisión Andina de Educación Superior y el Consejo de Rectores de las Univs. Chilenas. Organizado por el Instituto de Estudios Internacionales de la Univ. de Chile. Edición de Francisco Orrego Vicuña. Santiago: El Instituto, 1976. 336 p.: ill. (Col. Estudios internacionales)

The concept of the Pacific Basin became a fashionable one in mid-1970s as is exemplified by this conference (not previously annotated in *HLAS*). Its papers vary in quality and language (English and Spanish). Includes interesting material on specific problems of technology transfer. Dialogue occasionally futuristic when speaking of the Pacific Basin or technology.

7264 Varas, Augusto. Ideology and politics in Latin America-USSR relations (USIA/PC, 33:1, Jan./Feb. 1984, p. 35–47, ill.)

Balanced account (written by a prof. at FLACSO, Santiago, Chile) of USSR's regularization of diplomatic and economic ties with South American countries. Maintains that such regularization has been useful for both parties to the relationship. USSR has only a "fairly narrow margin for maneuver" in that part of the world and its strategy must remain "essentially reactive, dependent above all on the hemispheric policies pursued by the United States." [Y. Ferguson]

7265 ———. Relaciones hemisféricas e industria militar en América Latina (SP, 17, marzo 1982, p. 9–21)

Argues that the growth of arms manufacturers in certain countries has been associated with regimes (e.g., military regimes in Argentina and Brazil) that have been able and willing to divert scarce resources from the satisfaction of basic human needs. [Y. Ferguson]

7266 ———. The Soviet Union in the foreign relations of the Southern Cone (*in*

Latin American nations in world politics [see item **7062**] p. 243–259]

Knowledgeable, balanced account of the topic with emphasis on Allende government period in Chile, Argentina's wheat sales to Russia, and Brazil's effort to pressure the West by acting as if trade with Russia were an important economic alternative.

ARGENTINA

7267 Andrada, Benigno Héctor. Guerra aérea en las Malvinas. Buenos Aires: Emecé Editores, 1983. 239 p., 16 p. of plates: ill.

Glorifies role of the Argentine Air Force in Malvinas/Falklands War. Although focus is strictly military, book probably should be read also as a document in the continuing struggle for influence among the various Argentine military services. Author is Air Force officer.

7268 Arias Quincot, César. El conflicto de las Malvinas: contexto internacional, actores y enseñanzas (UP/A, 13, 1983, p. 69–80, table)

Although speculative, this is an excellent discussion of the world's reaction to Malvinas/Falkland conflict. Author is quite critical of Galtieri government but observes that the war may have helped strengthen a sense of Pan-Latin Americanism.

7269 Authors take sides on the Falklands: two questions on the Falklands conflict answered by more than a hundred mainly British authors. Edited by Cecil Woolf and Jean Moorcroft Wilson. London: C. Woolf Publishers, 1982. 144 p.: index.

Collection of comments by prominent English-speaking authors regarding the value of the British engagement in Malvinas/Falkland dispute. As one would guess, there is a great deal of diversity and a fundamental split between those who supported the British government and those who advocated a passive response.

7270 Beck, Peter J. Britain's Antarctic dimension (RIIA/IA, 59:3, Summer 1983, p. 429–444)

Places British efforts in Malvinas/Falkland conflict in the context of the Antarctic question. Quite good in explaining

how Thatcher's actions in the South Atlantic, prior to April 1982, gave impression that London was not concerned with the area.

7271 Berger, Martín. El rescate de las Malvinas. Buenos Aires: Bruguera, 1982. 208 p.: ill.

Written in the heat of the moment, this is a detailed account of the military and diplomatic saga of Malvinas/Falkland War strictly from an Argentine perspective. Book came out before Argentines realized what a debacle the situation had become. There are many brave words here that seem naive in retrospect.

7272 Bishop, Patrick Joseph and **John Witherow.** The winter war: the Falklands. London: Quartet Books, 1982. 152 p., 8 p. of plates: ill.

Two British journalists give a factual account of the military side of Malvinas/Falkland struggle from British point of view. Detailed but virtually no political analysis.

7273 Cabanellas, Guillermo. The Argentine transfer of technology law: an analysis and commentary (HICLR, 3:1, 1979, p. 29–103)

Long legal discussion of Argentina's 1971 law attempting to regulate transfer of technology. Very detailed but little about the politics of the law.

7274 Cabral, Antônio et al. Guerra santa nas Malvinas. Prefácio de Carlos Chagas. Apresentação de Hermano Alves. São Paulo: EMW Editores, 1983. 175 p.: bibl., ill. (Col. Testemunho)

Four journalists with differing types of expertise write secs. on Malvinas/Falkland War. Pub. in Brazil, and mostly written by Brazilians, book has a broader perspective than most Argentine accounts and one which is presented within a Latin American framework, something lacking from British versions.

7275 Calvert, Peter. Britain, Argentina and the Falklands (Contemporary Review [Contemporary Review Co., London] 244:1417, Feb. 1984, p. 62–67)

Very brief discussion of the implications of Alfonsín government for British foreign policy—tied, of course, to Malvinas/Falkland issue.

7276 ———. The Falklands crisis: the rights and the wrongs. New York: St. Martin's Press, 1982. 183 p.: bibl., index, map.

"Instant" account of Malvinas/ Falkland War by prominent British expert on Latin America. Well written and insightful narrative, especially on the question of what led to the war. Although Calvert's account is far better than most journalistic versions, final account of this struggle remains to be written.

7277 ———. Sovereignty and the Falklands crisis (RIIA/IA, 59:3, Summer 1983, p. 405–413)

Analysis, which supports London's position, of conflicting Argentine-British legal claims to Malvinas/Falkland archipelago.

Cardoso, Oscar R.; R. Kirschbaum; and E. van der Kooy. Malvinas: la trama secreta. See item **6508.**

7278 Carril, Bonifacio del. El futuro de las Malvinas. Buenos Aires: Emecé Editores, 1982. 82 p.: bibl.

Argentine diplomat is author of this 55-p. essay (plus documents) regarding the future of Malvinas/Falkland Islands. Written after Argentina's defeat, pamphlet emphasizes justness of Argentine cause and dilemmas the islands present London. Latter is good point for discussion.

7279 Childs, Nicholas. The *General Belgrano*: a peace initiative torpedoed? (Navy International [Maritime World Ltd., Haslemere, England] 89:4, April 1984, p. 238–240)

Intended to answer Labour MP Tom Dalyell's criticism of Thatcher's decision to sink the *General Belgrano*, article deals only with claim that the sinking was intended to stop Peruvian peace initiative. Defends the Prime Minister while evading other criticisms of the sinking.

7280 Colombo, Jorge Luis. *Super-Etendard* naval aircraft operations during the Malvinas War (Naval War College Review [Newport, R.I.] 37]303]:3, May/June 1984, p. 12–22, map)

Argentine Air Force officer's account of air-to-surface missiles procedures used against British Navy in Malvinas/Falkland conflict. The French unwillingness to pro-

vide technical assistance and the limited number of missiles caused severe problems, but article sees the success of the Exocets as a triumph of air force professionalism.

7281 Destéfani, Laurio Hedelvio. The Malvinas, the South Georgias, and the South Sandwich Islands: the conflict with Britain. Buenos Aires: Edipress, 1982. 143 p.: bibl., ill., index, maps.

Compilation of historical detail on Malvinas/Falkland Islands controversy— primarily in period before 1834. Purpose is to explain justness of Argentine claim and exemplary patience shown by Buenos Aires since British rule was consolidated on the islands. Publication of this monograph was underwritten by prominent Argentine corporations to help propagandize Argentine claim.

7282 Dunnett, Denzil. Self-determination and the Falklands (RIIA/IA, 59:3, Summer 1983, p. 415–428)

Good discussion of the self-determination issue as it applies to Malvinas/Falkland controversy. Author is British scholar and his approach largely legalistic.

7283 Escude, Carlos. La Argentina: ¿paria internacional? Buenos Aires: Editorial de Belgrano, 1984. 165 p.

Contains two provocative essays by young historian that are critical of Argentina's traditional approach to foreign policy. Argues that misconceptions of power that rely too much on the possession of territory and diplomatic defiance of other nations actually weaken Argentina's position internationally. We are told that Argentina could advance its interests more successfully by engaging the rest of the world in a more flexible and pragmatic manner. [G.W. Wynia]

7284 Espinosa Moraga, Oscar. La cuestión de las Islas Falkland, 1492–1982. Santiago: Estado Mayor General del Ejército, 1983. 208 p.: bibl., ill. (Biblioteca del oficial; 48)

Historical/legal account of Malvinas/ Falkland dispute to which has been attached an account of the war and a number of documents—including the lengthy British Ministry of Defense report "Lessons of the Falkland Campaign." Book's Chilean author gives account an interesting perspective.

7285 Estrada, Marcos de. Una verdad sobre las Malvinas. Buenos Aires: Secretaría de Cultura, Presidencia de la Nación, Ediciones Culturales Argentinas, 1982. 53 p.: bibl., ill.

Short, detailed historical account of Argentine claim to Malvinas/Falkland Islands. Pamphlet ends more than 150 yrs. ago.

7286 Etchepareborda, Roberto. La bibliografía reciente sobre la cuestión Malvinas: pts. 1/2 (RIB, 34:1, 1984, p. 1–52; 34:2, 1984, p. 227–288)

Although this two-pt. bibliographic essay is dogmatically pro-Argentine in its discussion of Malvinas/Falkland conflict, it is an extremely valuable source of citations and information. For bibliographer's comment, see *HLAS 46:72.*

7287 ———. Zeballos y la política exterior argentina. Buenos Aires: Editorial Pleamar, 1982. 121 p.: bibl. (Estrategía y política)

Short biography of Estanislao Severo Zeballos, prominent Argentine intellectual and diplomat who was Foreign Minister under three presidents towards end of 19th century. Concentrates on his thinking. Some material on the settlement of Río de la Plata waters question.

7289 Fox, Robert. Eyewitness Falklands: a personal account of the Falklands campaign. London: Methuen, 1982. 337 p., 16 p. of plates: ill., index.

Detailed memoir/account of Malvinas/Falkland military engagement by journalist who accompanied British forces. Long on detail but short on political analysis.

7290 Friedman, Norman. The Falklands War: lessons learned and mislearned (FPRI/O, 26:4, Winter 1983, p. 907–940)

Naval expert provides detailed discussion of the naval conflict in Malvinas/Falkland War. Deftly done although with a navy bias, tends to dismiss long-run importance of Exocet missiles.

7291 Goldblat, Jozef and **Víctor Millán.** The Falklands/Malvinas conflict: a spur to arms build-ups. Solna, Sweden: Stockholm International Peace Research Institute, 1983. 63 p.: bibl., ill.

Very brief, dispassionate analysis of Malvinas/Falklands War by the Stockholm International Peace Research Institute. Pamphlet covers mainly factual matters with an emphasis on the question of the implication of this conflict for future wars. Much information is crammed into a few pages.

7292 González Ramírez, Jorge A. La agresión: su concepto en los tratados y organismos internacionales. Buenos Aires: Círculo Militar 1983. 147 p., 1 leaf of plates: bibl., ill. (Biblioteca del oficial; 714)

Argentine colonel discusses legal side of what constitutes aggression—a difficult legal question. Much of the book consists of quotations from various documents. Very legalistic in approach.

7293 Guerra de las Malvinas y del Atlántico Sur: partes oficiales comparativos: Argentina, Gran Bretaña: partes oficiales publicados por *Latin American Newsletters.* Buenos Aires: Editora CATALOGOS, 1983. 167 p.

Interesting and useful collection of official Argentine and British statements regarding Malvinas/Falkland War from April 2, 1982 until the surrender.

7294 Hanrahan, Brian and **Robert Fox.** "I counted them all out and I counted them all back:" the Battle of the Falklands. London: British Broadcasting Corp., 1982. 139 p., 16 p. of plates: ill.

Transcripts of radio broadcasts of two BBC reporters who travelled with the British task force to Malvinas/Falkland area. Lots of "stiff-upper-lipism" in accounts of military activities. Some interesting materials on limitations placed on press coverage.

El Interrogatorio: Galtieri, Anaya, Menéndez y Costa Méndez. See item **6518.**

Kon, Daniel. Los Chicos de la guerra: hablan los soldados que estuvieron en Malvinas. See item **6520.**

7295 Lanús, Juan Archibaldo. De Chapultepec al Beagle: política exterior argentina, 1945–1980. Buenos Aires: Emecé, 1984. 571 p.

Lanús has written the most complete chronicle of recent Argentine foreign policy. It is organized topically and focuses on such issues as Argentina's place in East-West conflict, its voting record at UN, and events leading to conflicts with Chile over Beagle Channel Islands and with Britain over Malvinas. Does not examine Malvinas/Falkland War and its aftermath, however. [G.W. Wynia]

7296 Little, Walter. The Falklands affair: a review of the literature (PSA/PS, 32:2, June 1984, p. 296–310)

Perhaps most sensible, balanced piece to appear on Malvinas/Falkland conflict is this survey of some of the writing on the topic. Brings out some interesting criticisms of British foreign policy prior to Argentine occupation. Observes that insofar as legal aspects of the controversy are concerned, what happened was that territorial integrity and self-determination, principles that under normal circumstances are in agreement, came into conflict over this question. Author is certainly no apologist for London's policies.

7297 Lunin, Víctor. La crisis en el Atlántico Sur y sus consecuencias (URSS/AL, 11:59, nov. 1982, p. 4–26, ill.)

Left-wing account of Malvinas/ Falkland crisis that interprets it as a NATO vs. Latin America conflict. Tries to link Castro and Eastern bloc to anti-colonial interests of the Latin American countries.

7298 McGruther, Kenneth R. When deterrence fails: the nasty little war for the Falkland Islands (Naval War College Review [Newport, R.I.] 36[296]:2, March/April 1983, p. 47–56)

Naval officer attempts to find lessons of Malvinas/Falkland conflict. Not surprisingly, emphasizes naval power and argues that politicians should turn the conduct of war over to experts not insert diplomacy once military force is unleashed. Pre-Clausewitz.

7299 Makin, Guillermo A. Argentine approaches to the Falklands/Malvinas: was the resort to violence foreseeable? (RIIA/IA, 59:3, Summer 1983, p. 391–403)

Good article on the views of the various post-1945 governments in Buenos Aires on the subject of Malvinas/Falkland controversy. Sympathetic to Argentina's attempts to settle matter fairly, author argues that London had much warning as to the seriousness of Argentina's interest in the Islands.

7299a Marini, José Felipe. El conocimiento geopolítico. 2. ed. Tucumán: Univ. Nacional de Tucumán, 1982. 473 p.: bibl., ill. (Publicación; 1319)

Competent treatment of geopolitics concentrates on the world as a whole rather than Argentina. Valuable summary of the geopolitical approach.

7299b Maurer, John Henry *et al.* Forum: navies in foreign policy (FPRI/O, 26:3, Fall 1982, p. 569–583)

Primarily a set of observations regarding the naval side of Malvinas/Falkland experience. Pro-British and pro-navy in tone, discussion has very little about politics of the conflict.

7300 Meister, Jürg. Der Krieg um die Falkland-Inseln 1982: geschichtliche Hintergründe, Strategie und Taktik der Kriegsführung; politisch-wirtschaftliche Perspektiven. Osnabrück, FRG: Biblio Verlag, 1984. 302 p., 13 leaves of plates: appendices, ill., maps.

Exhaustive, well researched historical overview of Malvinas War. Provides historical background as well as factual documentation on international issues relating to South Atlantic region. Appendices include facts and figures on Malvinas and its dependencies, on Antarctic region, complete information on British and Argentine war support system and material, and a complete chronology of the war and its aftermath. Important contribution of interest to specialists in Southern Cone. [G.M. Dorn]

7301 Military lessons of the Falkland Islands war: views from the United States. Edited by Bruce W. Watson and Peter M. Dunn. Foreword by F. Clifton Berry, Jr. Boulder, Colo.: Westview Press; London: Arms & Armour Press, 1984. 181 p.: bibl., index (Westview special studies in military affairs)

Although the "military lessons" of Malvinas/Falkland conflict is the focus of this collection, "military" is defined broadly enough to include intelligence and diplomacy. General tone is that, in fact, there are no "new" lessons—only lessons that have been forgotten or ignored. Useful analytical book in parts.

7302 Moneta, Carlos J. The Malvinas conflict: analyzing the Argentine military regime's decision-making process (*in* Latin American nations in world politics [see item 7062] p. 119–132)

Useful discussion of Argentine's government motivations in occupying the Malvinas/Falkland Islands. Certainly should be read by anyone studying that conflict.

7303 Morzone, Luis Antonio. Soberanía territorial argentina. Prólogo de Eduardo

A. Pigretti. 2a ed., ampliada y actualizada. Buenos Aires: Ediciones Depalma, 1982. 582 p.: bibl., maps.

Second ed. of a book taking an international law approach to various aspects of Argentine sovereignty: boundary disputes, territorial waters, air space, etc. Straightforward and encyclopedic in approach, it consistently supports Argentine position on controversial topics. Uncritically Argentine account of Malvinas/Falkland conflict is tacked on. Because it was written after the invasion but prior to the defeat, it is badly dated.

7304 Ortiz, Gonzalo *et al.* Malvinas, la trampa del imperio. Quito: Editorial El Conejo, 1982. 135 p.: bibl., ill. (Col. Ecuador/hoy)

Ecuadorian writers expressing support for Argentine invasion of Malvinas/Falklands. Account was published prior to Argentina's defeat. Not a particularly useful book for understanding of the situation except to expose reader to some of the non-Argentine justifications for invasion.

7305 Pérez Llana, Carlos E. La reinserción de la Argentina en el mundo. Buenos Aires: Fundación para la Democracia en la Argentina, 1983. 117 p. (Col. Sin censura)

Intelligent, broad essay on the need for a more independent foreign policy for Argentina after Malvinas/Falkland debacle. Highly general but gives brief coverage to a large number of topics.

7306 Randle, Patricio H. La guerra inconclusa por el Atlántico Sur. Prólogo de Roberto M. Levingston. Buenos Aires: Oikos, 1982. 182 p.

Militant Argentine nationalist's account of Malvinas/Falkland conflict. Typical of nationalists, author believes the national will would triumph if only the leadership were better. At one point, he declares that "When one struggles for the homeland, to die isn't defeat, defeat is to surrender." Not a useful source in terms of analysis.

Rapaport, Mario. El factor político en las relaciones internacionales: política internacional vs. teoría de la dependencia, un comentario. See *HLAS 46:3330.*

7307 Reimann, Elisabeth. Las Malvinas, traición made in USA. México: Ediciones El Caballito, 1983. 142 p.

Book's stated objective is to reveal how US urged England forward in Malvinas/Falkland crisis and how US betrayed other countries in the hemisphere by not supporting Buenos Aires. Criticisms are from the ideological left.

7308 Segreti, Carlos S.A. Tres archipiélagos argentinos: Malvinas, Georgias, Sandwich; historia de un compromiso nacional. Córdoba, Argentina: TA.P.AS, 1983. 170 p.: bibl.

Very detailed and very Argentine account of legal claims to Malvinas/Falkland, Georgia, and Sandwich Islands.

7309 Smithers, Peter. Lessons of the Falklands episode (Contemporary Review [Contemporary Review Co., London] 242: 1408, May 1983, p. 242–247)

Good analysis which tries to understand Malvinas/Falkland crisis as a failure of British diplomacy to send proper signal to Buenos Aires. Makes a number of excellent points but mostly emphasizes British failures.

7310 *Sunday Express Magazine* Team. War in the Falklands: the campaign in pictures. London: Weidenfeld and Nicolson, 1982. 153 p.: ill. (some col.)

Good photographic account of Malvinas/Falkland conflict includes pictures from both sides (although mostly British and with a pro-British text). Not of much use to the scholar.

7311 Trask, Roger R. Spruille Braden versus George Messersmith: World War II, the Cold War, and Argentine policy, 1945–1947 (SAGE/JIAS, 26:1, Feb. 1984, p. 69–95, bibl.)

Solid account of struggle between two Dept. of State figures over post-World War II US policy towards Perón. Sees the division as one between an internationalist and Latin Americanist school of thought, although author recognizes that individuals' personalities played a role too.

7312 Tulchin, Joseph S. Authoritarian regimes and foreign policy: the case of Argentina (*in* Latin American nations in world politics [see item **7062**] p. 186–199)

In the process of trying to look at basic question of foreign policy decision-making in authoritarian regimes, author does much to explain context of the decision to occupy Malvinas/Falkland Islands. Good work that questions the conventional wisdom of foreign policy formulation.

7313 Turner, Frederick C. The aftermath of defeat in Argentina (CUH, 82: 481, Feb. 1983, p. 58–61)

Published prior to Alfonsín's election, article gives a valuable overview of the impact of Malvinas/Falkland defeat on Argentina's domestic politics.

7314 Túrolo, Carlos M., h. Así lucharon. Buenos Aires: Editorial Sudamericana, 1982. 327 p.

Recollections of 10 Argentine military men who participated in Malvinas/Falkland war. Gives one an excellent feel for the situation of the common soldier (see also item 6520).

7315 United States. Congress. Senate. Committee on Governmental Affairs. Subcommittee on Energy, Nuclear Proliferation, and Government Processes. U.S. policy on exports of helium-3 and other nuclear materials and technology: hearing before the Subcommittee on Energy, Nuclear Proliferation, and Government Processes of the Committee on Governmental Affairs, United States Senate. Washington: US GPO, 1982 [i.e. 1983]. 153 p.: bibl. (97th Congress, 2nd Session)

Two Congressional Research Service short reports on Argentina's nuclear program. They conclude that the ability to build a weapon is there but that Argentine policy indicates a lack of interest in the idea.

7316 Vignes, Alberto J. Dos años de política internacional argentina, 1973–1975. Buenos Aires: Editorial Pleamar, 1982. 195 p.

Extensive set of public statement relating to Argentine foreign policy during 1973–74 collected by Foreign Minister Alberto Vignes. Gives some insight into peronista foreign policy objectives of the period.

7317 Villarino, Emilio. Exocet. Buenos Aires: Editorial Abril, 1983. 310 p., 4 leaves of plates: ill. (some col.) (Revista siete días. Suplemento; 10)

Primarily of interest to military historians, this is a detailed account of the real and hypothesized impact of Argentina's use of the Exocet missiles in Malvinas/Falkland War. Although it may exaggerate Exocet's impact, experience of that war certainly suggests that this type of weapon has some important implications.

7318 Villegas, Osirio Guillermo. La propuesta pontificia y el espacio nacional comprometido. Buenos Aires: Editorial Pleamar, 1982. 140 p.

Mixture of geopolitics, international law, and Argentine patriotism characterizes this discussion of Beagle Channel dispute written by an Argentine general. Intended audience is the papal representative who was mediating the case at the time.

7319 Viola, Oscar Luis. La derrota diplomática y militar de la República Argentina en la guerra de las Islas Malvinas. 2a ed. Buenos Aires: Tinta Nueva, 1983. 251 p.: ill.

Although structure of chaps. is disconcerting and artificial, this is a solid Argentine account of the causes of the Malvinas/Falkland War and reasons for Argentina's defeat. Interlaced with quotations from Machiavelli, author criticizes all those involved in the debacle. Pro-Argentine account of the country's humiliation.

BOLIVIA

7320 Miranda Guzmán, Secundino. Avance al oeste: doctrina luso-brasilieña. La Paz: Hepta Producciones, 1982. 248 p., 15 p. of plates: ill.

Bolivian calls into question the accuracy of the survey of the Bolivian-Brazilian border conducted in late 1930s and early 1940s. Not surprisingly, he believes the error made favored Brazil.

7321 Política de fronteras: ciclo de conferencias y seminario desarrollado del 6 al 14 de septiembre de 1976. Dirección de Jorge Escobari Cusicanqui. Antonio de Sáinz Vila et al. La Paz: Instituto de Estudios Internacionales, Univ. Mayor de San Andrés, 1978. 127 p.

Series of papers on the various Bolivian frontiers. Much concern was expressed over problem at conference where papers were presented. Although hardly an unbiased source, book gives one a brief introduction to Bolivia's perceptions.

BRAZIL

7322 Barros, Alexandre de S.C. The formulation and implementation of Brazilian foreign policy: Itamaraty and the new actors (*in* Latin American nations in world politics [see item **7062**] p. 30–44)

Although author attacks view that Brazilian diplomatic service is purely professional and apolitical, he discusses the evolution of modern Brazilian foreign policy in terms of the relatively professional foreign service adjusting to a broadening international mandate (particularly in area of trade) generated in Brasília. Solid argument.

7323 Cabral, Milton. As novas fronteiras do mar. Brasília: Senado Federal, Centro Gráfico, 1980? 204 p.: bibl.

Brazilian Senator's account of UN Law of the Sea Conference with some commentary as to general importance of oceans.

7324 Hirst, Monica. Democratic transition and foreign policy: the experience of Brazil (*in* Latin American nations in world politics [see item **7062**] p. 216–229)

Competent discussion of Brazilian foreign policy utilizing well-nuanced theoretical approach of Fernando Henrique Cardoso.

7325 Rocha, Francisco Heitor Leão da. Estudos da política e das relações internacionais. S.l.: s.n., 198? 172 p.: ill.

Rather "textbookish" account of Brazil's role in international affairs. Broad coverage does not reflect a lot of scholarship. Ethnocentric and superficial but possibly a competent introduction to Brazil's role.

Smith, Joseph. American diplomacy and the Naval Mission to Brazil: 1917–1930. See *HLAS 46:3683.*

7326 ———. United States diplomacy toward political revolt in Brazil, 1889–1930 (IAMEA, 37:2, Autumn 1983, p. 3–21)

Hard to find much of a theme in this article except that the quality of US diplomatic reporting is weak. However, work does have some interesting specifics.

7327 Young, Jordan M. Brazil, emerging world power. Malabar, Fla.: R.E. Krieger Pub. Co., 1982. 242 p.: bibl., index (Anvil original)

Very basic introduction to Brazil's potential role as a world power. Vol.'s distracting format (half description and half readings) and design for use as textbook interferes with the narrative.

CHILE

7328 Muñoz, Heraldo. The international policy of the Socialist Party and foreign relations of Chile (*in* Latin American nations in world politics [see item **7062**] p. 150–167)

Well done discussion compares Chilean Socialist Party's foreign policy stance during World War II and during Allende administration. Although topic is somewhat narrow, author's expertise and balance are clear.

Nef, Jorge. Economic liberalism and political repression in Chile. See item **6482.**

7329 Petrus Putter, Andrés. La política marítima de Sudáfrica (Política [Instituto de Ciencia Política, Univ. de Chile, Santiago] 3, 1983, p. 159–168)

Article on "The Maritime Policy of South Africa" whose author is Admiral-in-Chief "Comandante en Jefe de la Armada de Sudáfrica." Of interest because of article's being featured in a Univ. of Chile publication.

7330 Pinochet Ugarte, Augusto. Introduction to geopolitics. Translation by Liselotte Schwarzenberg Matthei. Santiago: Editorial Andrés Bello, 1981. 261 p.: bibl., ill.

English translation of textbook by none other than the current President (dictator) of Chile. Writes that it was "developed from notes and analyses gathered in 15 years of teaching courses in military geography at different national and foreign military institutes." Pinochet accepts as the foundation of this "new science" of geopolitics the "organic conception of State—considered as a superperson, as the highest form of social evolution." [Y. Ferguson]

7330a Política oceánica. Edición de Francisco Orrego Vicuña. Santiago: Univ. de Chile, Instituto de Estudios Internacionales, 1977. 414 p.: bibl., ill. (Estudios internacionales)

Collection of well-researched papers presented at 1976 Univ. of Chile seminar. Although dated, the essays provide good background.

Porteous, J. Douglas. The annexation of Easter Island: geopolitics and environmental perception. See item **5160.**

7331 Riesco, Ricardo. Chile y sus perspectivas geográficas frente al Pacífico y la Antártica (Revista Norte Grande de Geografía [Pontificia Univ. Católica de Chile, Santiago] 7, 1980, p. 49–56, bibl., maps)

Brief geopolitical discussion of Chile's interest in the Pacific and Antarctica which is a good example of how geopolitics can be used to make any given country have some sort of pivotal international role.

7332 Santis Arenas, Hernán. La zona económica exclusiva, última frontera territorial (Política [Instituto de Ciencia Política, Univ. de Chile, Santiago] 3, 1983, p. 27–79, map)

Geopolitical approach to idea of economic zones in the New Law of the Sea arrangements. Most of emphasis is on Chile's situation. Much of the analysis is historical.

Segreti, Carlos S.A. Límites con Chile bajo Austrias y Borbones. See *HLAS 46:3347.*

Sigmund, Paul E. The USSR, Cuba and the revolution in Chile. See item **7096.**

7333 Wilhelmy, Manfred. Politics, bureaucracy, and foreign policy in Chile (*in* Latin American nations in world politics [see item **7062**] p. 45–62)

Astute and theoretically sensitive account of the interplay of bureaucratic politics and domestic politics in the making of Chilean foreign policy. Argues that overall bureaucratic-politics model of such scholars as Graham Allison is not applicable to LDCs. Excellent, if not path-breaking, piece.

COLOMBIA

7334 Asencio, Diego; Nancy Asencio; and Ron Tobias. Our man is inside. Boston: Little, Brown, 1983. 244 p.: facsim.

Detailed account of 1980 capture of Dominican Republic Embassy in Bogotá by terrorists. Author was US Ambassador to Colombia at the time and one of the hostages. His story is both fascinating and instructive as to the nature of terrorist groups. A much more balance and insightful vol. than one might have predicted.

Blum, Leonor. Colombia's peace offensive. See item **6334.**

Briceño Monzillo, José Manuel. Nuestras fronteras con Colombia: reseña histórica. See item **5196.**

Craig, Richard B. Domestic implications of illicit Colombian drug production and trafficking. See item **6340.**

7335 Drekonja-Kornat, Gerhard. Colombia: learning the foreign policy process (SAGE/JIAS, 25:2, May 1983, p. 229–250, bibl.)

Very useful essay that starts with idea that Colombia has power resources to play a larger role in international relations and then tries to explain why it apparently sought a low profile policy. Provocative and mature discussion.

7336 Fleet, Michael. Bargaining relations in the Colombian motor vehicle industry (*in* Political economy of the Latin American motor vehicle industry. Edited by Rich Kronish and Kenneth S. Mericle. Cambridge: MIT Press, 1984, p. 231–260, tables)

Clear, factual account of Colombian motor vehicle industry which provides some good evidence for debate over operations of MNCs in LDCs.

Relaciones internacionales en la Cuenca del Caribe y la política de Colombia. See item **7250.**

7337 Vázquez Carrizosa, Alfredo. Las relaciones de Colombia y Venezuela: la historia atormentada de dos naciones. Bogotá: Ediciones Tercer Mundo, 1983. 451 p.: bibl.

Judicious statement of Colombian case regarding Venezuelan/Colombian border dispute. Thorough analysis which concludes by urging an international judicial settlement of the matter. Good source for Colombian side.

ECUADOR

7338 Barberis Romero, Jaime O. Nociones generales de geopolítica. Quito: Editorial Instituto Geográfico Militar, 1979. 2 v.: bibl., ill.

Thorough, mechanistic exposition of geopolitical thinking and its "laws." Rehashes history of the approach and only applies it to Ecuador in final chap.

7339 Barrera Valverde, Alfonso. Hombres de paz en lucha. t. 1, El Ecuador ante la agresión peruana de 1981. t. 2, Documentos. Quito: Ediciones J.L.I., 1982. 2 v.

Account of 1981 Ecuador-Peru border conflict from an Ecuadorian perspective. Emphasizes diplomatic initiatives. Vol. 2 consists of good set of documents although selection tends to support author's point of view.

7340 Galarza Zavala, Jaime. El festín del petróleo. 6a ed. Quito: Editorial Alberto Crespo Encalada, 1981. 462 p.: bibl., maps.

Book-length tract by Ecuadorian author that warns his country of dangers of allowing country's oil wealth to be monopolized by foreign oil companies. Sixth ed. of work originally pub. in 1971. Back cover reprints a letter by various prominent persons (Miguel Asturias, Julio Cortázar, Régis Debray, Jean Paul Satre, Gabriel García Márquez, *et al.*) commending book to then-President of Ecuador Rodríguez Lara. [Y. Ferguson]

7341 Mena Villamar, Claudio. Paquisha, toda la verdad. Quito: Letra Nueva, 1981. 175 p.: ill. (Testimonios)

Pro-Ecuadorian account of Peru-Ecuador border conflict of early 1980s. Because account devotes much space to the background (including circumstances of 1942 settlement) and does not focus on specifics of who shot whom, it is of some value.

7342 Oquendo, Diego. En las alturas del Cóndor. S.l.: Consorcio de Consejos Provinciales, 1981. 155 p.: ill.

So little is known outside the region regarding conflict between Ecuador and Peru that this Ecuadorian journalist's account (patriotic to the core) is helpful to those interested. Idiosyncratic.

7343 Ulloa Vernimmen, José. Paquisha, un hito de gloria. Guayaquil, Ecuador: Editorial Cultural y Democracia, 198? 355 p.: ill.

Long journalistic account of background and current situation regarding Peru-Ecuador border situation. Patriotically Ecuadorian but because dispute is little known outside the region, there is some value to work.

Valdez Baquero, Rodrigo. Latinoamérica y el Derecho del Mar. See item **7102.**

7344 Villacrés Moscoso, Jorge W. Peligros para el Ecuador de la integración económica con los estados limítrofes. Guayaquil, Ecuador: Escuela Superior Politécnica del Litoral, 1982. 132 p.: maps (Escuela . . .; 2)

Statement of concern over what author sees as Peruvian and Colombian expansionism.

PARAGUAY

7345 Schley, Michael D. Foreign investment in Paraguay: an analysis of incentives under Law No. 550 (HICLR, 3:1, 1979, p. 177–200)

Naively optimistic account of Paraguayan law and foreign investment incentives. Assures reader of country's political stability and does not mention any problems (including corruption).

7346 Velilla Laconich de Arréllaga, Julia. Paraguay, un destino geopolítico: el informe del Gobernador Fernando de Pinedo. Asunción: Instituto Paraguayo de Estudios Geopolíticos y Relaciones Internacionales, 1982. 315 p.: bibl., ill. (some col.)

In the case of Paraguay, a geopolitical approach is particularly valuable for understanding country's history. Primarily concerned with origins of Paraguay.

PERU

7347 Durán Abarca, Washington. La soberanía y las 200 millas. Lima: Empresa Editora Humboldt, 1983. 116 p.: bibl.

Highly legalistic critique of current Law of the Sea situation with a number of criticisms from Peruvian point of view.

7348 Jaworski C., Helan. Peru: the military government's foreign policy in its two phasaes, 1968–1980 (*in* Latin American nations in world politics [see item **7062**] p. 200–215)

Useful discussion that places in context the International Petroleum Co. takeover and foreign policy which followed over next 12 yrs. However, does not accomplish much in the area of building our theoretical understanding.

7349 Kunimoto, Iyo. Emigración japonesa y sentimiento anti-japonés en América Latina de la época de pre-guerra (Latin American Studies [Univ. of Tsukuba, Japan] 6, 1983, p. 169–180, tables)

Good discussion of anti-Japanese feelings stimulated by Japanese immigration to Latin America prior to World War II. Peru is the particular point of emphasis. Article concludes that Japanese population now has largely been absorbed into Peruvian society.

7350 Mejía Valera, José *et al.* El imperativo de la integración latino americana: a propósito del conflicto de las Malvinas. Lima: Instituto Latinoamericano de Estudios Económicos y Sociales, 1983. 85 p.: bibl.

Peruvian pamphlet espouses continental integration as necessary response to the Malvinas conflict. Pt. 2 is series of *crónicas* written in late 1920s on British and Russian imperialism by Haya de la Torre. [J.M. Hunter]

Nakagawa, Fumio. Japanese-Latin American relations since the 1960s: an overview. See item **7076**.

7351 Ruiz-Eldredge, Alberto. Mar territorial de 200 millas (SP, 8, sept. 1979, p. 61–73)

Legalistic discussion of 200-mile limit and Peruvian constitution.

VENEZUELA

7352 Adueza, José Guillermo. Las potestades del Presidente de la República en materia de política exterior (ACPS/B, 39:89, sept. 1982, p. 161–187)

Legalistic summary of Venezuelan presidency's power in the area of foreign policy.

7353 Braveboy-Wagner, Jacqueline Anne. The Venezuelan-Guyana border dispute: Britain's colonial legacy in Latin America. Boulder, Colo.: Westview Press, 1984. 349 p.: bibl., ill., index (A Westview replica edition)

Useful historical review (up to 1983) of this issue that is thoroughly documented and

includes an excellent bibl. Mostly narrative, weak on analysis. [W. Canak]

Caballero, Manuel. La sección venezolana de la Internacional Comunista: un tema para el estudio de las ideas en el siglo XX venezolano. See *HLAS 46:2913*.

Cabezas, Rodrigo. Crónica de una política petrolera. See item **6392**.

7354 Cardozo, Hilarión. Inquietudes y expectativas de Venezuela sobre las relaciones hemisféricas y el sistema interamericano (VANH/B, 65:260, oct./dic. 1982, p. 829–846)

Thoughtful analysis by Venezuelan diplomat of OAS's future and inter-American system in general. To some extent, author's remarks were generated by Malvinas/Falkland crisis but have broader implications for the future.

7355 Consalvi, Simón Alberto. La política internacional de Venezuela, 1974–1979. Caracas: Editorial Arte, 1979. 271 p., 6 leaves of plates: ports.

Former Venezuelan representative to UN and later Foreign Minister, Consalvi presents his major speeches during 1975–79. Brief introduction (11 p.) provides general (and vague) overview. Good documentary record.

La Cooperación internacional de Venezuela, lo realizado entre 1974–1981, las previsiones, 1982–1985: solidaridad en acción = The International cooperation of Venezuela, achievements between 1974–1981, provisions for 1981–1985: solidarity in action. See item **3467**.

7356 Gitin, L.S. Vneshniaia politika Venesuely: poiski novykh reshenii = The foreign policy of Venezuela: searches for new solutions. Moskva: Mezhdunarodnye otnosheniia, 1981. 103 p. (Bibliotechka mezhdunarodnika)

Not scholarly but useful body of information and good evidence of Soviet ways of thinking about Venezuela. Covers 1959–79. Includes interesting sec. on Venezuelan-Soviet ties (14 p.) as well as numerous footnotes but no bibl. [R.V. Allen]

7357 Gray, William Henry. Venezuela, Uncle Sam, and OPEC: a story for all Ameri-

cans. Austin: O.E.G. Foundation, 1982.
181 p.: bibl.

Rather strange, undocumented (no footnotes) account of Venezuelan history and oil industry's development. Highly sympathetic to Venezuela and moderately critical of some of the more imperialistic efforts of North Americans. Idiosyncratic but interesting.

Grayson, George W. The joint oil facility: Mexican-Venezuelan cooperation in the Caribbean. See item **7137.**

Jongkind, Fred. Venezuelan industrialization, dependent or autonomous?: a survey of national and foreign participation in the industrial development of a Latin American OPEC country. See *HLAS 46:2925.*

7358 Lanza, Eloy. El subimperialismo venezolano. Prólogo de Jerónimo Carrera. Caracas: Fondo Editorial Carlos Aponte, 1980. 215 p.: bibl.

Leftist interpretation of Venezuelan foreign policy which sees country as a subimperialist power in the region. Clear statement of the case with some interesting facts and claims.

7359 Martz, John D. Venezuelan foreign policy and the role of political parties (*in* Latin American nations in world politics [see item **7062**] p. 133–149)

Even-handed discussion of the impact of politics on Venezuelan foreign policy. Excellent although with few theoretical pretensions.

7360 Nweihed, Kaldone G. and María del Valle Vásquez de Martínez. Panorama y crítica del diferendo: el Golfo de Venezuela ante el Derecho del Mar. Caracas: Publicaciones S.A. Venetesa, 1981. 245 p., 8 folded leaves of plates: appendix, bibl., col. maps (Col. internacional)

Detailed study of Colombia-Venezuela boundary dispute from Venezuelan point of view. Good set of eight foldout color maps in the appendix that illustrate various proposals and issues in question.

7361 Ojer, Pablo. La década fundamental en la controversia de límites entre Venezuela y Colombia, 1881–1891. Caracas: Instituto de Derecho Público, Univ. Central de Venezuela, 1982. 618 p.: bibl., index, map.

Excruciatingly detailed discussion of

1881–91 settlement of Venezuelan/Colombian border. Concludes that decision was not just from Venezuela's point of view. For historian's comment, see *HLAS 46:2928.*

————. El Golfo de Venezuela: una síntesis histórica. See *HLAS 46:2929.*

7362 Picón, Delia. Tratados bilaterales de Venezuela. Caracas: Ediciones Centuaro, 1981. 283 p.: bibl.

Useful, elementary introduction to role of treaties in international law accompanies text of Venezuela's most important international agreements. Some interesting insights.

7363 Silva, Elsa Cardozo da. Aproximación al estudio de las relaciones internacionales (Argos [Univ. Simón Bolívar, Div. de Ciencias Sociales y Humanidades, Caracas] 3, 1981,p. 57–91, bibl.)

Study of international relations by a Venezuelan that is perhaps less interesting in itself than as a reflection of the extent to which some of the writings and theoretical concerns of analysts from North America, France, and elsewhere are read and shared in Caracas. [Y. Ferguson]

Venezuela en vísperas de elecciones. See item **6388.**

Vivas Gallardo, Freddy. Venezuela en la Sociedad de las Naciones, 1920–1939: descripción análisis de una actuación diplomática. See *HLAS 46:2938.*

JOURNAL ABBREVIATIONS
INTERNATIONAL RELATIONS

AAFH/TAM The Americas. Academy of American Franciscan History. Washington.

ACPS/B Boletín de la Academia de Ciencias Políticas y Sociales. Caracas.

AEJ/JQ Journalism Quarterly. Assn. for Education in Journalism *with the cooperation of the* American Assn. of Schools, Depts. of Journalism [and] Kappa Tau Alpha Society. Univ. of Minnesota. Minneapolis.

AF/AUR Air University Review. US Air Force. Maxwell Air Force Base, Ala.

AFS   Armed Forces and Society. Univ. of Chicago. Chicago, Ill.

AJC/C   Commentary. American Jewish Committee. New York.

AR   Areíto. Areíto, Inc. New York.

BNCE/CE   Comercio Exterior. Banco Nacional de Comercio Exterior. México.

CM/FI   Foro Internacional. El Colegio de México. México.

CRIA/W   Worldview. Council of Religion and International Affairs. New York.

CRIT   Criterio. Editorial Criterio. Buenos Aires.

CUH   Current History. Philadelphia, Pa.

DEA/IP   International Perspectives: The Canadian Journal on World Affairs. Canada, Dept. of External Affairs. Ottawa.

DIS   Dissent. Dissent Publishing Assn. New York.

FDD/NED   Notes et études documentaires. France, Direction de la documentation. Paris.

FIU/CR   Caribbean Review. Florida International Univ., Office of Academic Affairs. Miami.

FP   Foreign Policy. National Affairs, Inc. [and] Carnegie Endowment for International Peace. New York.

FPRI/O   Orbis. Foreign Policy Research Institute, Philadelphia, Pa. *in association with the* Fletcher School of Law and Diplomacy, Tufts Univ., Medford, Mass.

GU/WQ   The Washington Quarterly. Georgetown Univ., Center for Strategic and International Studies. Washington.

HICLR   Hastings International and Comparative Law Review. Univ. of California, Hastings College of the Law. San Francisco.

IA   International Affairs. Moscow.

IAMEA   Inter-American Economic Affairs. Washington.

ICPHS/D   Diogenes. International Council for Philosophy and Humanistic Studies. Chicago.

IGME/RG   Revista Geográfica. Instituto Geográfico Militar del Ecuador, Depto. Geográfico. Quito.

IRRI/SD   Studia Diplomatica. Institut royal des relations internationales. Bruxelles.

JLAS   Journal of Latin American Studies. Centers or institutes of Latin American studies at the univs. of Cambridge, Glasgow, Liverpool, London and Oxford. Cambridge Univ. Press. London.

LAP   Latin American Perspectives. Univ. of California. Riverside.

LIWA/YWA   Yearbook of World Affairs. London Institute of World Affairs. London.

MR   Monthly Review. New York.

MULINO   Il Mulino. Bologna, Italy.

NACLA   NACLA: Report on the Americas. North American Congress on Latin America. New York.

NS   NS NorthSouth NordSud NorteSur NorteSul. Canadian Assn. of Latin American Studies, Univ. of Ottawa. Ottawa.

NYRB   The New York Review of Books. New York.

NZZ/SRWA   Swiss Review of World Affairs. Neue Zürcher Zeitung. Zurich.

OAS/LE   La Educación. Organización de Estados Americanos, Depto. de Asuntos Educativos. Washington.

OCLAE   OCLAE. Organización Continental Latinoamericana de Estudiantes. La Habana.

PSA/PS   Political Studies. Political Studies Assn. of the United Kingdom. Oxford, England.

PUJ/U   Universitas. Pontificia Univ. Javeriana, Facultad de Derecho y Ciencias Socioeconómicas. Bogotá.

RIB   Revista Interamericana de Bibliografía (Inter-American Review of Bibliography). Organization of American States. Washington.

RIIA/IA   International Affairs. Royal Institute of International Affairs. London.

RIIA/WT   The World Today. Royal Institute of International Affairs. London.

RPC Revista del Pensamiento Centroamericano. Consejo Superior de la Empresa Privada (COSEP). Managua.

SAGE/JIAS Journal of Inter-American Studies and World Affairs. Sage Publication *for the* Center for Advanced International Studies, Univ. of Miami. Coral Gables, Fla.

SECOLAS/A Annals of the Southeastern Conference on Latin American Studies. Kennesaw College. Marietta, Ga.

SP Socialismo y Participación. Ediciones Socialismo y Participación. Lima.

TWF/TWQ Third World Quarterly. Third World Foundation, New Zealand House. London.

UCSB/NS The New Scholar. Univ. of California, Committee on Hispanic Civilization [and] Center for Chicano Studies. Santa Barbara.

UJSC/EA ECA (Estudios Centroamericanos). Univ. Centroamericana José Simeón Cañas. San Salvador.

UNAM/RI Relaciones Internacionales. Revista del Centro de Relaciones Internacionales. Univ. Nacional Autónoma de México, Facultad de Ciencias Políticas y Sociales. México.

UNAM/RMS Revista Mexicana de Sociología. Univ. Nacional Autónoma de México, Instituto de Investigaciones Sociales. México.

UNL/H Humanitas. Univ. de Nuevo León, Centro de Estudios Humanísticos. Monterrey, México.

UP/A Apuntes. Univ. del Pacífico, Centro de Investigación. Lima.

UPB Universidad Pontificia Bolivariana. Medellín, Colombia.

UPR/RCS Revista de Ciencias Sociales. Univ. de Puerto Rico, Colegio de Ciencias Sociales. Río Piedras.

URSS/AL América Latina. Academia de Ciencias de la Unión de Repúblicas Soviéticas Socialistas. Moscú.

USIA/PC Problems of Communism. US Information Agency. Washington.

VANH/B Boletín de la Academia Nacional de la Historia. Caracas.

UWI/SES Social and Economic Studies. Univ. of the West Indies, Institute of Social and Economic Research. Mona, Jamaica.

VANH/B Boletín de la Academia Nacional de la Historia. Caracas.

WQ The Wilson Quarterly. Woodrow Wilson International Center for Scholars. Washington.

SOCIOLOGY

GENERAL

8001 Acedo, Clemy Machado de. Introducción al análisis sociológico. Caracas: Univ. Central de Venezuela, Ediciones de la Biblioteca, 1982. 149 p.: bibl. (Col. Ciencias económicas y sociales; 27)

General treatise on the origins and development of sociological thought. Concludes with analysis of the manner in which various theoretical schools have been articulated by Latin American sociologists. [L. Pérez]

8002 Andrade, Ximena *et al.* Políticas agrarias y urbanas en América Latina. Bogotá: Editorial Impronta, 1981. 391 p.: bibl. (Sociedad Interamericana de Planificación; 3)

Vol. 3 of monographic series sponsored by the Inter-American Planning Society. Emphasis is on agrarian reform, background, laws, mechanisms of implementation, and links with housing reform and policies. Countries covered: Bolivia, Colombia, Cuba, Guatemala, and Peru. [L. Pérez]

8003 Archetti, Eduardo P. Campesinado y estructuras agrarias en América Latina. Quito: Ceplaes, 1981. 328 p.: bibl., ill.

Literate discussion of central issues in regional analysis, logic of peasant economies, and modes of production. Interprets English, French, and Spanish literature, thereby influencing how these issues are likely to be addressed by monolingual Spanish speakers. Case studies, many previously published, are minor part of book. [D. Gilbert]

8004 Arriagada Herrera, Genaro. El pensamiento político de los militares: estudios sobre Chile, Argentina, Brasil y Uruguay. Santiago: Centro de Investigaciones Socioeconómicas, Compañía de Jesús en Chile, 1981? 224 p.: bibl.

Pt. 1 is a review of the literature on the military profession and political role of the military. Pt. 2, the most interesting one, deals with the political doctrine of the military in Southern Cone. Focuses on the "Prussianization" of Chilean army prior to the Depression, influence of geopolitical doctrines on the armies of Argentina, Brazil, and Chile, and doctrine of counterinsurgency warfare in all armies of the Southern Cone. [C.H. Waisman]

8006 Borsotti, Carlos A. La organización social de la reproducción de los agentes sociales, las unidades familiares y sus estrategias. Buenos Aires: Centro de Estudios de Población, 1982. 26 p.: bibl. (Cuaderno del CENEP, 0326–1905; 23)

Review of the literature on family structure and reproductive behavior. Includes interesting discussion of family strategies which are defined as the logic underlying patterns of resource mobilization for the attainment of family goals. [C.H. Waisman]

8007 Cardoso, Fernando H. *et al.* Medina Echavarría y la sociología latinoamericana. Madrid: Ediciones Cultura Hispánica del Instituto de Cooperación Iberoamericana, 1982. 159 p.: bibl.

Cardoso, Stavenhagen, Faletto, and Prebisch are among the 13 prominent social scientists that contributed to this work on the influence of Spanish sociologist Medina Echavarría on Latin American sociology. [L. Pérez]

8008 Castells, Manuel. Capital multinacional, estados nacionales y comunidades locales. México: Siglo Veintiuno Editores, 1981. 127 p., 1 folded leaf of plates: bibl., ill. (some col.) (Arquitectura y urbanismo)

Short book brings together many important ideas developed throughout the years by leading urban sociologist and Latin Americanist. Case studies from Chile, Mexico, Peru, Argentina, and Venezuela provide a comparative perspective. One of the best introductions to the study of urban problems in Latin America. [A. Ugalde]

8009 Cinco estudios sobre la situación de la mujer en América Latina. Santiago: CEPAL; Nueva York: Naciones Unidas, Sec. Ventas, 1982. 178 p.: bibl. (Estudios e informes de la CEPAL; 16)
Five studies comprise the work: 1) women and development; 2) women in the family context; 3) poor women; 4) the educational status of women; and 5) female employment. Concludes with list of recommendations. [L. Pérez]

8010 Díaz Briquets, Sergio. La migración internacional en América Latina y el Caribe: una visión general de algunas de sus características (CPES/RPS, 18:50, enero/mayo 1981, p. 25–64, bibl.)
General work on international migration in Latin America: its determinants, consequences, and the policies adopted by the various governments to regulate it. [L. Pérez]

8011 Dorfman, Ariel. Bread and burnt rice: culture and economic survival in Latin America (Grassroots Development [Interamerican Foundation, Rosslyn, Va.] 8:2, 1984, p. 2–25, ill.)
Highly readable essay on role of culture in process of development, based on author's personal experiences throughout Latin America. Culture can both help and hinder development, and development can have both positive and negative impacts on culture. Optimistic outlook. [L. Pérez]

8012 Economía y población: una reconceptualización crítica de la demografía. Editado por Wim Dierckxsens y Mario E. Fernández. Katty Rochwerger *et al.* Ciudad Universitaria Rodrigo Facio, Costa Rica: Editorial Universitaria Centroamericana, 1979. 345 p.: bibl., ill. (Col. DEI)
Articles of this collection are an attempt to advance a Marxist epistemology for demography: R. Pavon, "Population Problems and Econmic Thought;" K. Rochwerger, "The Limits of the Growth Myth;" W. Dierckxsens, "Demography and the Dialectic of Its Objective and Method;" and "A Historical Interpretation of Population;" A Hernández, "Notes on the Mode of Production and Population Dynamics;" P. Campanario, "Capital Accumulation and the Fetishism of the Family;" M. Fernández, "Capital Dynamics and

Migration;" J. Breilh, "The Inequality of Death: Epistemology and Epidemiology;" and E. Ritcher and P. Campanario, "Capitalist Population Explotation in Latin America." A valient effort that falls short of establishing a theoretical framework by lack of unity of articles and perhaps by a tendency to espouse a traditional view of Marxism. [A. Ugalde]

8013 Elkin, Jidth Laikin. A demographic profile of Latin American Jewry (AJA, 34:2, Nov. 1982, p. 231–248, tables)
Estimates the size of Jewish communities in Latin America, their birth and death rates, and discusses intermarriage. The estimation of Jewish population size is very complex, even in societies where statistical information on religious affiliation is available. Overall, Jewish communities have low birth and death rates, and are declining due to natural demographic procesess and through intermarriage with gentiles. [C.H. Waisman]

8014 Elton, Charlotte. Migración femenina en América Latina: factores determinantes. Santiago: Centro Latinoamericano de Demografía, 1978. 84 p.: bibl. (Serie E; 26)
Given the numerical importance of women in the migration streams to Latin American cities, this brief work synthesizes existing studies regarding the motivations of women in migrating and their economic activities in cities. [L. Pérez]

8015 Ensayos sobre el problema de la vivienda en América Latina. Compilado por Emilio Pradilla Cobos. México: Univ. Autónoma Metropolitana, Unidad Xochimilco, Depto. de Teoría y Análisis, Carrera de Diseño de Asentamientos Humanos, 1982. 472 p.: bibl., ill. (Col. Ensayos)
Readings in urban sociology by 14 scholars discuss housing problems in Guatemala, Mexico, Venezuela, Colombia, Brazil, Ecuador, El Salvador, Cuba, and Latin America in general. Unifying theme: capitalist development creates anarchic conditions in the use of urban space. [L. Pérez]

Fajnzylber, Fernando. Intervención, autodeterminación e industrialización en la América Latina. See item **2843.**

González Casanova, Pablo. América Latina: las críticas a las ciencias sociales y las tareas inmediatas. See *HLAS 46:7513.*

Goyer, Doreen S. and **Eliane Domschke.** The handbook of national population censuses: Latin America and the Caribbean, North America, and Oceania. See *HLAS 46:77.*

8016 International Congress of Human Sciences in Asia and North Africa, *30th, Mexico, 1976.* Asiatic migrations in Latin America. Edited by Luz M. Martínez Montiel. México: El Colegio de México, 1981. 186 p.: bibl., ill.

Valuable anthology of papers presented at seminar held during 30th International Congress of Human Sciences in Asia and North Africa. Each deals with a particular Asian group in a specific nation or locality in Latin America: the Chinese in Sonora (Mexico), Panama, Chincha Islands (Peru), and Cuba; the Japanese in Brazil, São Paulo, and Mexico; Asian Jews in Mexico; Arabs in Tucumán (Argentina) and Mexico; and East Indians in the British Caribbean. Historical treatment predominates. Many of these immigrant groups have traditionally received little attention from Latin Americanists. [L. Pérez]

8018 Kaplan, Marcos. La teoría del Estado en la América Latina contemporánea: el caso del marxismo (FCE/TE, 50[2]:198, abril/junio 1983, p. 677–711)

Discusses the Marxist theory of the State in Latin America, from World War II to present. Analyzes influences of Gramsci, Althusser, the German "logical" school, and other European strains, as well as local developments. Presents a synthetic framework for the analysis of the State as an organization and of the relationship between State and class structure. [C.H. Waisman]

8019 Kronish, Rich. Latin America and the world motor vehicle industry: the turn to exports (*in* Political economy of the Latin American motor vehicle industry. Edited by Rich Kronish and Kenneth S. Mericle. Cambridge: MIT Press, 1983, p. 75–93, tables)

Automobile industry in Latin America is beginning to produce for the world market. This is due to a shift in overall strategy of the multinationals, which now tend to integrate their world-wide operations. Latin American subsidiaries have begun to supply components and finished vehicles to other markets. This change in the strategy of the multinationals requires explanation. [C.H. Waisman]

8020 ——— and Kenneth S. Mericle. The development of the Latin American motor vehicle industry, 1900–1980: a class analysis (*in* Political economy of the Latin American motor vehicle. Edited by Rich Kronish and Kenneth S. Mericle. Cambridge: MIT Press, 1984, p. 261–306, tables)

Discusses automobile industry in Argentina, Brazil, and Mexico throughout the century. Topics include relationship between the multinationals and the host governments, the transition from assembly to manufacturing, labor relations, and state intervention. Interesting analysis of the effect of class struggle on the cost structure and on the development of the market. [C.H. Waisman]

Kuznetsova, Emma. Modernización neocapitalista de la relaciones sociales. See item **6014.**

8020a Latin America, its problems and its promise: a multidisciplinary introduction. Edited by Jan Knippers Black. Boulder, Colo.: Westview Press, 1984. 549 p.: bibl., ill., map, tables.

Commendable effort to provide a comprehensive and multidisciplinary treatment of Latin American societies. Consists of 29 readings by scholars in eight academic fields. Combines a general topical approach to entire region (economics, history, culture, politics, society) with readings in specific nations by the following sociologists: Gilbert W. Merkx, "Social Structure and Social Change in Twentieth-Century Latin America;" Nelson P. Valdés, "The Cuban Revolution;" and Anthony P. Maingot, "The Caribbean: The Structure of Modern Conservative Societies." For bibliographer's comment, see item **124.** [L. Pérez]

8021 Marshall, Adriana. Tendencias estructurales en la migración internacional fuerza de trabajo: el Cono Sur de América Latina (Migraciones Internacionales en las Américas [Centro de Estudios de Pastoral y Asistencia Migratoria, Caracas] 1:1, 1980, p. 133–153, bibl., tables)

Studies migration flows within the Southern Cone, basically from neighboring countries toward Argentina, with a focus on 1970s. Discusses expulsion factors operating in Bolivia, Chile, Paraguay, and Uruguay, and the geographic and economic distribution of the immigrants once in Argentina. [C.H. Waisman]

8021a Mertens, Walter; Adam Przeworski; Hugo Zémelman; and Manuel Mora y Araujo. Reflexiones teórico-metodológicas sobre investigaciones en población. México: El Colegio de México: Consejo Latino-americano de Ciencias Sociales, 1982. 191 p.: bibl.

Four articles by leading demographers discuss methodological shortcomings of survey methods and theoretical approaches to the study of population: W. Mertens Mertens (on research on Latin American population: introduction and evaluation of recent approaches); A. Przeworski (on sociological theory and the study of population: considerations on the activities of CLACSO's Commission on Population and Development; H. Zemelman (on problems explaining reproductive behavior: on measurements); and M. Mora y Araujo (on theory and data: comments on the historical-structural approach). [A. Ugalde]

8022 Miró, Carmen A. and **Daniel Rodríguez.** Capitalismo, relaciones sociales de producción y población en el agro latino-americano: revisión de algunos estudios recientes. México: El Colegio de México: PISPAL, 1981. 154 p.: bibl. (Cuadernos del PISPAL)

Overview and critique of studies that examine relationship between population dynamics and agrarian structure. Studies on Argentina, Uruguay, Brazil, Chile, Peru, and Central America are reviewed. Authors conclude with suggestions on how to further our understanding of the subject. [L. Pérez]

8023 Mora y Araujo, Manuel. Cientificismo e ideologismo: un comentario sobre la lucha de clases, el imperialismo y otras variables ruidosas en la explicación de la sociología argentina (CPES/RPS, 13:35, enero/abril 1976, p. 59–69)

Argues that explanations based on imperialist penetration and the class struggle, so popular in Latin American social science, are in fact an ideology which masks the interests of groups within the academic community and legitimizes their position vis-à-vis other scientific groups. Article is critical of Eliseo Veron's *Imperialismo, lucha de clases y conocimiento.* [C.H. Waisman]

8024 Mouzelis, Nicos. On the demise of oligarchic parliamentarism in the semi-periphery: a Balkan-Latin American comparison (BSA/S, 17:1, Feb. 1983, p. 28–43)

Interesting three-way comparison of political processes in the Cono Sur of Latin America, the Balkan republics and Greece, in which Mouzelis argues that the transition from oligarchic control of parliamentary government to broader forms of political participation took place before industrialization in these "peripheral" societies. As a result the development of both independent trade unions and independent working class parties was frustrated with unions and working class parties either repressed or co-opted by the State. Stresses that the timing of ecnmic political, and social change is as important as the structure of that change. [S. Socolow]

8025 Muñoz, Braulio. Sons of the wind: the search for identity in Spanish American Indian literature. New Brunswick, N.J.: Rutgers Univ. Press, 1982. 321 p.: bibl., index.

Indigenismo was a socio-literary movement that sought the cultural identity of Latin Americans by evoking their Indian ancestry. A logical sequence to the glorification of the past was the cry against discrimination and exploitation of the Indians. Muñoz shows the incongruence of this logic among novelists from Bolivia, Ecuador, Peru, Guatemala and Mexico, who in efforts to improve the economic well-being of the Indians supported their acculturation and the destruction of their cultures. [A. Ugalde]

Nunn, Frederick M. Yesterday's soldiers: European military professionalism in South America, 1890–1940. See *HLAS 46:1911.*

8026 Orrego Vicuña, Claudio. Latin America: a human rights perspective for the 1980s (*in* Latin American prospects for the 1980s: equity, democratization, and development. Edited by Archibald R.M. Ritter and David H. Pollock. New York: Praeger, 1983, p. 40–53)

Discusses prospects for human rights in Latin America in 1980s. At the beginning of the new decade, outlook is much more favorable than in 1970s. Armed insurgency has failed, and massive and arbitrary repression by military regimes in the 1970s has subsided. Focuses on the new awareness regarding human rights and the formation of a substantial human rights movement in the region. For political scientist's comment, see item **7078**. [C. H. Waisman]

8027 Podetti, Humberto A. Política social: objeto y principios básicos, desarrollo social, planificación técnica, política laboral y de la seguridad social, políticas sectoriales. Buenos Aires: Editorial Astrea de A. y R. Depalma, 1982. 390 p.: bibl., ill., index.

Very general work on social problems, development, planning, and social policy in the areas of social security, health, education, housing, family, and population. Apparently intended as a textbook in public administration and planning. [L. Pérez]

8028 Quijano, Aníbal. Sociedad y sociología en América Latina (UPR/RCS, 23:1/2, marzo/junio 1981, p. 225–249, bibl.)

Latin American sociology since early 1960s interpreted against social and political backdrop of the times by one of Peru's most sophistical practitioners. [D. Gilbert]

8029 Las Relaciones laborales en las empresas estatales de América Latina. Dirección, Arturo S. Bronstein. Geneva: OIT, 1981. 193 p.: bibl.

Comparative study of labor-management relations in state enterprises in Latin America. Emphasis on collective bargaining and resolution of disputes. Three national case studies are presented: Peru, Venezuela, and Mexico. [L. Pérez]

8030 Rodríguez, Atahualpa. Los científicos sociales latinoamericanos como nuevo grupo de intelectuales (FCE/TE, 50(2):198, abril/junio 1983, p. 939–962)

Discusses social scientists as a new type of Latin American intellectual. Distinguishes three groups: critical intellectuals, social scientists linked to "northern" academic institutions and style of research, and technocrats. Considers the institutionalization of research through different types of organization (universities, centers, etc.), and the ideological orientations of Latin American social scientists. [C.H. Waisman]

8031 Sánchez, Domingo; Monica Leyton; and Mónica Pregar. Migraciones internacionales desde los países del Cono Sur de América Latina hacia el Brasil (Migraciones Internacionales en las Américas [Centro de Estudios de Migración, Centro de Estudios de Pastoral y Asistencia Migratoria, Caracas] 1:1, 1980, p. 155–172, bibl., tables)

Studies immigration from Southern Cone countries to Brazil. Concludes that the limited volume of this immigration is due to the land tenure system, the weight of the primary sector, and the age structure of the population in Brazil. [C.H. Waisman]

8032 Santagada, Osvaldo D. *et al.* Sectas en América Latina. Bogotá: Consejo Episcopal Latinoamericano (CELAM), 1981? 299 p.: bibl. (CELAM; 50)

Collection of papers written by Latin American Episcopal clergy on "the challenge" posed to their ecumenical work by "sects" and independent religious groups. Some papers focus on specific groups: Mormons, Jehovah's Witnesses, Baptists, Adventists, and Pentecostals. [L. Pérez]

8033 Simmons, Alan B. Social inequality and the demographic transition (*in* Latin American prospects for the 1980s: equity, democratization, and development. Edited by Archibald R.M. Ritter and David H. Pollock. New York: Praeger, 1983, p. 85–110, tables)

Offers new consideration to the classic transition model of development used to analyze changing mortality, population growth, and urbanization patterns in Latin America. Argues that assumptions of model derive from Western industrialized nations' historical experiences rather than Latin America's. Adds the variables of the specific kinds of technology, income distribution, and shift to salaried work as important to Latin American historical context and, therefore, more essential to a model which explains change over time on a number of social and economic indicators. [K.J. Healy]

8034 Simposio Regional sobre la Pobreza Crítica en la Niñez, *Santiago, 1979.* Pobreza crítica en la niñez: América Latina y el Caribe. Compilado por Fernando Galofré. Santiago: CEPAL: UNICEF, 1981. 422 p.: bibl., ill.

Consists of 18 papers presented at 1979 symposium sponsored by CEPAL and UNICEF. High quality papers by specialists in various fields related to childhood poverty. Wide ranging, covering origins of the problem, consequences of poverty in children, alternative programs and policies, and evaluations of existing intervention efforts. [L. Pérez]

8035 Social responsibility & Latin America. Nancy T. Baden, vol. ed. San Diego, Calif.: Campanile Press, 1981. 191 p.: bibl., ill. (*Proceedings of the Pacific Coast Council on Latin American Studies;* 8, 1981–82)

Papers that comprise these PCCLAS proceedings are a varied lot: banditry and messianism in Brazil, English language education in Trinidad, struggle of Free Coloreds in Grenada and St. Kitts, Christian Left in Argentina and Chile, deforestation in the neotropics, nationalism in Peru and the IMF, as well as photographic essays, art, documents on the Mexican Revolution, and a bibliography of family life. Of special interest to sociologists: Kathleen Logan's "Fraccionamientos as a Means of Urban Integration" and Manuel J. Carlos's "Agrarian Policies in Mexico during the Luis Echeverría Regime, 1970–1976: Rebirth and Decline of Agrarismo." [L. Pérez]

8036 Sociedad y utopía. Compilado por Eleonora Masini, Johan Galtung y Bibiano F. Osorio. Herb Addo *et al.* México: CEESTEM: Editorial Nueva Imagen, 1983. 287 p.: bibl., ill. (Serie CEESTEM-Nueva Imagen)

In 1979 the World Federation for Studies of the Future and CEESTEM organized a conference on "Alternative Visions of Desirable Societies." This book compiles 13 papers presented by reknown international figures such as Johan Galtung (on escatology, cosmology, and the formation of visions); Marcos Kaplan (on world models and social participation); Mihailo Markovic (on scientific predictions and visions of the future); Leopoldo Zea (on vision on a desirable society). Should be of interest to those concerned with social change and development. [A. Ugalde]

Suárez, Orozco and **Alan Dundes.** The *piropo* and the dual image of women in the Spanish-speaking world. See item **990.**

8037 Szlajfer, Henryk. Modernizacja zalezności: kapitalizm i rozwój w Ameryce Lacińskiej = Modernizing dependency: capitalism and development in Latin America. Wrocław, Poland: Zakład Narodowy im. Ossolińskich, 1985. 252 p.: bibl., tables.

Insightful and competent critique of dependency theory by Polish sociologist. [K. Complak]

8038 Technical change and social conflict in agriculture: Latin American perspectives. Edited by Martín Piñeiro and Eduardo Trigo. Boulder, Colo.: Westview Press, 1983. 248 p.: bibl., ill., graphs, tables.

Represents efforts of a multinational network of independent research teams working on interpreting the process of technological change in Latin American agriculture. Proposes an analytical framework that stresses the broad social context and not just economic factors. [L. Pérez]

8039 Torres Abrego, José Eulogio. Contribución al estudio del subdesarrollo: de la monoproducción a la oligarquía moderna. México: Impresora Herrerana, 1981. 153 p.: bibl.

Orthodox Marxist looks at key theoretical concepts: social classes, process of production, and nature of the State. Deviance from traditional Marxian thought, particularly by Latin American leftist scholars, is criticized by references to authority more than by empirical data. [A. Ugalde]

Torres-Rivas, Edelberto. Estado y nación en la historia latinoamericana. See *HLAS 46:1790.*

8040 United Nations Children's Fund (UNICEF). Regional Office for the Americas. Situación de la infancia en América Latina y el Caribe. Coordinación, Juan Pablo Terra. Santiago: La Oficina, 1979. 630 p.: bibl., graphs.

Prepared by UNICEF's Latin American office, this massive work is packed with statistical analyses covering a wide range of social, economic, and political factors that affect the welfare of children. Emphasis on sociodemographic conditions, level of living, public policy, and educational and health services. Excellent reference work. [L. Pérez]

8041 Vitale, Luis. Historia y sociología de la mujer latinoamericana. Barcelona, Spain: Fontamara, 1981. 122 p.: bibl. (Col. Ensayo contemporáneo)

Short work with ambitious scope: history of the role of women in Latin America since precolumbian days, with emphasis on 20th century and the emergence of feminist movement. Theme is the exploitation and alienation of women. [L. Pérez]

8042 La Vivienda a bajo costo en América Latina. Políticas del Estado en materia de vivienda en América Latina. Bogotá: Sociedad Colombiana de Planificación, s.d. 2 v. (300, 288 p.): bibl. (Sociedad Interamericana de Planificación; 1–2)

Results of comparative multinational study on low-cost housing issued as part of monographic series sponsored by the Inter-American Planning Society (see item **8002**). Emphasis in these two volumes is on housing policies, agrarian reform and rural housing, urban housing, and markets. Countries covered: Colombia, El Salvador, Costa Rica, Guatemala, Mexico, Paraguay, and Venezuela. [L. Pérez]

8043 Wiarda, Iêda Siqueira and Judith F. Helzner. Women, population, and international development in Latin America: persistent legacies and new perceptions for the 1980s. Amherst: International Area Studies Programs, Univ. of Massachusetts at Amherst, 1981. 40 p.: bibl. (Occasional papers series; 13)

Authors argue that in the formulation of international development policy and family planning programs the participation of women has been excluded. Conclude with recommendations on how to remedy the situation. [L. Pérez]

8044 World Congress of the International Federation for Parent Education, *11th,* *Mexico, 1980.* El niño y la familia: compendio. México: Asociación Científica de Profesionales para el Estudio Integral del Niño, 1982. 522 p.: bibl.

Proceedings from the 1980 World Congress of the International Federation for Parents' Education held in Mexico City. Of the 54 contributions, 27 are from Mexico, three from Argentina, one from Peru, and one from Uruguay. Articles are grouped under four chapters which provide an idea of content: "The Family: General Considerations," "The Family, Society, and Culture," "The Role of the Family and the Education of parents," and "The Family Conflict: Diagnosis and Treatment." Interdisciplinary and of mixed quality. [A. Ugalde]

MEXICO AND CENTRAL AMERICA

ANTONIO UGALDE, *Professor of Sociology, University of Texas, Austin*

AN IMPORTANT NEW TREND in Mexican publications reviewed for this volume of the *Handbook* is the increase in regional studies which probably reflects the decentralization and expansion of universities and research centers such as the Colegio de Michoacán (Zamora), the Colegio de Jalisco, the Instituto de Investigaciones Sociológicas of the Oaxaca Autonomous Univ., Instituto Michoacano de Estudios Sociales (Morelia), and the Centro de Estudios Fronterizos del Norte de México (Tijuana), to mention a few. While the decentralization policy began a decade ago, the quality and quantity of regional studies that is now surfacing suggests that the policy has been successful. The most outstanding studies in this regard are one edited by R. Benítez (item **8104**) and one by I. Menéndez (item **8082**).

The same interest in Mexican migration to the US that existed in the previous biennium continues, and such is the case also for the political economy of rural development: almost half of the works annotated below are related to these topics. We noticed a decrease in demographic studies and the beginning of research on drug addiction, an indication perhaps that drug abuse is becoming a social problem in Mexico (see items **8051, 8085** and **8093**). It should be added that the field of criminology remains totally neglected from a sociological point of view, and in this vacuum the volume edited by J. Piña y Palacios (item **8086**) is a welcome and solid contribution. For the reader who wants to update his/her knowledge of the socioeconomic and political problems facing Mexico, the collection of essays edited by *Nexos* and written by well-known experts will be of invaluable assistance (item **8045a**).

In the area of methodology we have detected in Mexico, as well as in Central America, a concern to involve the peasantry in the study of its own social conditions, or as some will put it "in the democratization of social science research." This progressive approach has been incorporated in a number of works that collect peasants' autobiographies or lengthy narrations. The most ambitious project is the one embarked upon by the Escuela de Planificación y Promoción Social of the National Univ. of Costa Rica (see items **8140** and **8118**) which collected 802 autobiographies and classified their contents following Murdock's Thesaurus. Other studies that exhibit similar methodological tendencies are by C. Castro (item **8057**), by J.A. Alonso *et al.* (item **8107**), a compilation edited by L.P. Paredes and J. Moguel (item **8101**) in Mexico, and works by R. Falla (item **8126**) and J. Meléndez (item **8133**) in Central America. The UN funded project of Cine Obrero in Nicaragua (see item **8121**) shows the same participatory orientation through a different modality of social action.

What appears to be a healthy though surprising development—if one takes into account the frequency with which the region makes the headlines—is the scanty participation of US researchers in Central America. Indeed, of all the materials reviewed only four have been written by US scholars. That native writers are examining the issues and problems of their own societies is bound to provide a more accurate and less distorted view of them. The interests of Central American sociologists is centered around the conflict among factions of the bourgeoisie and the role that the middle class may play in the revolutionary movements that are shaking the region. The most outstanding studies on this topic are those by: Equipo de Investigadores de CIDCA (item **8125**), S. Montes (item **8134**), M. Posas (item **8136**), J. Rovira (item **8138**), and E. Torres (item **8142**). There is an almost total consensus among these writers that the ongoing violence is the result of efforts of the oligarchy supported by the US government to defer their impending demise.

MEXICO

8045 Abella, María Isabel. Estado e intelectuales en México: los escritores como servidores políticos o burócratas, 1876–1967 (CM/RE, 3:11, Verano 1982, p. 65–88, bibl., tables)

Classifies 209 creative writers according to degree and type of participation in the political system: elected offices, bureaucratic and university appointments. Discusses the nature of this cooptation and questions the possibility of a non-biased intellectual class in Mexico.

Adame Goddard, Jorge. El pensamiento político y social de los católicos mexicanos, 1867–1914. See *HLAS 46:7540.*

L'Agriculture, la pêche et l'artisanat au Yucatan: prolétarisation de la paysannerie mayan au Mexique. See item **5082.**

8045a Aguilar, H. *et al.* El desafío mexicano. México: Ediciones Océano, 1982. 354 p.: bibl.

Outstanding compendium with 33 critical short essays by distinguished scholars and journalists on basic political, social, economic, and moral issues facing Mexico today. Contributors include: H. Aguilar (political transition); A. Aguilar (national security); I. Almada (health); R. Bartra (nationalism); G. Bonfil (ethnic minorities); J. Bustamante (northern border); J. Blanco (public morality); A. Cantú (national planning); R. Cordera (modernization); R. Cremoux (mass communications); F. de Alba (population); E. Florescano (political culture); G. Gordillo (peasantry); G. Guevara (higher education); M.A. Granados (municipal governments); R. Granados (army); R. Green (foreign debt); S. Loaeza (middle classes); A. Lazcano (science research policies), C. Monsivais (nationalism); A. Mori (urbanization); A. Moreno (decentralization); R. Pérez Tamayo (CONACYT): J.L. Rhi Sauci (workers); F. Rello (food); C. Tello (foreign debt); A. Warman (modernization); and I. Zavala (labor unions).

8046 Alegría, Juana Armanda. Emancipación femenina en el subdesarrollo. México: Editorial Diana, 1982. 213 p.

Potpourri of interviews with feminist leaders, anecdotes, testimonials, and short essays on a variety of topics such as the portrait of woman in Latin American novels, in popular Mexican songs, female sexual fantasies, and single mothers organizations.

8047 Allub, Leopoldo and Marco A. Michel. Migración y estructura ocupacional en una región petrolera (UNAM/RMS, 44:1, enero/marzo 1982, p. 151–166, tables)

Due to the oil industry, Tabasco state has experienced a different migration pattern than other regions in Mexico. Contrary to employment situations elsewhere, migrants tend to occupy higher paid and more productive jobs than natives, and are also better educated. Based on a large 1979 survey of labor force.

8048 Una Aproximación a la problemática rural juvenil. México: Consejo Nacional de Recursos para la Atención de la Juventud, Dirección de Planeación, 1982. 194 p.: bibl., ill. (Serie Juventud rural; 2)

Title of book is misleading. Problems of rural youth are touched only tangentially during general discussions of rural development and education in Mexico. Even the treatment of these topics is too broad to be of interest to specialists.

8049 Arias, Patricia; Alfonso Castillo; and Cecilia López. Radiografía de la Iglesia Católica en México, 1970–1978. México: UNAM, 1981. 123 p. (Cuaderno de investigación social; 5)

Looking at the Catholic Church as a complex organization, authors examine the nature, roots, and outcome of conflicts between different groups within the Church (bishops and clergy, bishops and laity) and between Church and State in 1970s. Very informative, a necessary reference for students of Mexican political sociology.

8050 Arizpe S., Lourdes. La migración por relevos y la reproducción social del campesinado. México: Centro de Estudios Sociológicos, El Colegio de México, 1980. 38 p.: bibl., ill. (Cuadernos del CES; 28)

Arizpe has been studying the economics of migration of the Mazahuas since the early 1970s (see *HLAS 39:9088*). In this monograph she demonstrates that seasonal and temporary migration are the only available means for rural households of obtaining additional resources to keep on farming. Data from a 1976 two-village survey of 144 households.

8051 Azaola de Hinojosa, Elena. Conducta antisocial en una unidad habitacional. México: Instituto Nacional de Ciencias Penales, 1978. 127 p.: bibl. (Cuadernos del Instituto; 4)

Tlatelolco in Mexico City, the site of this study, houses one of the largest public urban projects in Latin America: over 120,000 persons live in 102 buildings. Perhaps more than a contribution to criminology, this is an informative account of urban conditions and social problems, including crime and juvenile delinquency. Survey of 120 statistically selected respondents add data to the information gathered through participation and observation.

8052 Bartra, Roger. Campesinado y poder político en México. México: Ediciones Era, 1982. 127 p.: bibl. (Col. Problemas de México)

Most essays in the collection were published in mid-1970s. Last article, "Notes for an Agrarian Program," was presented in 1974 at a plenary session of the Mexican Communist Party and is published now for the first time. The original versions have been slightly edited. Those not acquainted with Bartra's work will find this volume a useful introduction to his scholarly interpretation of contemporary agrarian history.

8053 Bizberg, Ilán. La acción obrera en Las Truchas. México: El Colegio de México, 1982. 321 p.: bibl., ill.

Case study of labor force and union politics in one of the newest regional poles of development in Michoacán. Pt. 1 is a description of the steel mill union organization, social stratification of workers, labor bargaining with management (in this case the Federal Government), elections and a 1979 strike. Pt. 2 looks at attitudes of workers through a random sample survey of 238 respondents.

The Border that joins: Mexican migrants and U.S. responsibility. See item **3095.**

8054 Camp, Roderic A. Family relationsihps in Mexican politics: a preliminary view (SPSA/JP, 44:3, Aug. 1982, p. 848–862, tables)

Study of the influence of family ties on the recruiting of political leaders since 1935 shows that the importance of kinship relations has not decreased. Ends by questioning the political "modernization" of Mexico, whatever the term may mean.

8055 ———. The influence of European and North American ideas on students at Mexico's National School of Law and Economics (UCSB/NS, 8, 1982, p. 289–308)

Following his early work on Mexican political elites and data bank (see *HLAS 43: 6103–6104*), Camp identifies foreign intellectual influences on those 1920–40 students of UNAM Law and Economic Schools, who later became political leaders. List includes Durkheim, Bergson, Spencer, Spengler, Gumplowicz, Adam Smith, Ricardo, Marshall, Webb, Keynes, and Marx.

8056 Castellanos Guerrero, Alicia. Ciudad Juárez, la vida fronteriza. México: Editorial Nuestro Tiempo, 1981. 225 p.: bibl. (Col. Estudios regionales)

Secondary sources and author's own 360 interviews of workers are the data base of this study on urban growth and international migration. No information is presented on the nature of questionnaire, and sample procedures and methodology are briskly explained in a few lines. The tone of the book is more argumentative than academic.

8057 Castro, Carlo Antonio. Siluetas mexicanas. Jalapa, México: Editorial Amate, 1980. 107 p.

Two peasant life histories, one from Papaloapán and the second from the municipality of Altotonga in Veracruz. No information is given about methodology, editing procedures or even year of recording, which probably took place in late 1950s or early 1960s. Male narration includes aspects of land reform and local politics. Female life history, which appears to be of a young woman (no age is provided), is centered around the household.

Christopherson, Susan. Female labor force participation and urban structure: the case of Ciudad Juárez, Mexico. See item **5083**.

8058 Clasificación mexicana de ocupaciones, 1980. v. 1, Ordenamiento por grupos de actividad. v. 2, Ordenamiento alfabético. México: Coordinación General de los Servicios Nacionales de Estadística, Geografía e Informática, 1982. 2 v.: bibl.

Vol. 1 includes the criteria for classifying occupations, definitions of groups and subgroups, listings of occupations by occupational groups, and the relations between 1970 and 1980 censuses. Vol. 2 is an alphabetical listing of 11,891 occupations.

Clawson, David L. Religious allegiance and economic development in rural Latin America. See item **5084**.

Cockcroft, James D. Immiseration, not marginalization: the case of Mexico. See *HLAS 46:2186*.

8059 El Colegio de Etnólogos y Antropólogos Sociales, *México.* Dominación ideológica y ciencia social: el I.L.V. en México: declaración José Carlos Mariátegui. México: Nueva Lectura, 1979. 134 p.: bibl., facsims., ill.

Contains report prepared by the Colegio de Etnólogos y Antropólogos on the activities of the controversial Summer Institute of Linguistics. The declaration finds the SIL a vehicle for the penetration of US capitalism and values, and responsible for the destruction of Indian cultures. The last 100 p. of the book are documents supporting the claims in Mexico and in other Latin American countries.

8060 Cornelius, Wayne A. Interviewing undocumented immigrants: methodological reflections based on fieldwork in Mexico and the U.S. (CMS/IMR, 16:2, 1982, p. 378–410, bibl.)

Suggests methodological tips for improving reliability and validity of responses. With annotated bibliography of recent studies of undocumented workers.

8061 Cross, Harry E. and James A. Sandos. Across the border: rural development in Mexico and recent migration to the United States. Berkeley: Institute of Governmental Studies, Univ. of California, 1981. 198 p.: bibl., map.

This comprehensive study has been written in a theoretical vacuum, and consequently, migration is viewed primarily as the result of rural poverty in Mexico. Conclusions and recommendations reflect this approach and contrast with those advanced by Mexican and other US scholars.

8062 Elementos históricos y actuales del trabajo social mexicano. Lima: Centro Latinoamericano de Trabajo Social, 1980. 70 p.: bibl. (Cuadernos CELATS; 27)

History of ideological and theoretical influences on social work as a profession and a discipline. Also describes evolution and growth of the profession and the roles adscribed to social workers.

8063 Farriss, Nancy M. Maya society under colonial rule: the collective enterprise of survival. Princeton, N.J.: Princeton Univ. Press, 1984. 585 p.: bibl., index, maps, photos, tables.

Scholarly study of social organization (economy, family, religion and world view, politics, ethnic relations and population changes) of the Maya of Yucatan from late preconquest to 1820. What allowed the Maya to survive, while most other Indian cultures succumbed, is the question that runs through the pages and threads the chapters of this classic work.

8064 Fernández Christlieb, Fátima. Los medios de difusión masiva en México. México: J. Pablos, 1982. 330 p.: bibl.

History of political conflict between Mexican government and private sector for control of newspapers, radio, and television up to 1980. Provides insightful observations about mechanisms used by government for controlling radio and newspapers, and explains reasons for success of private sector efforts in keeping television under its dominion.

8065 Finkler, Kaja. Dissident sectarian movements, the Catholic Church, and social class in Mexico (CSSH, 25:2, April 1983, p. 277–305, tables)

From participant-observation of four spiritualist centers near Mexico City and in-depth interviews of participants, author describes organization, rituals, and socioeconomic characteristics of believers. Finds that social differentiation is a major factor in membership and theorizes that spirtualism is adaptive and fosters positive male-female relations within the family.

8066 García, Brígida; Humberto Muñoz; and Orlandina de Oliveira. Hogares y trabajadores en la Ciudad de México. México: El Colegio de México; Ciudad Universitaria: Instituto de Investigaciones Sociales, UNAM, 1982. 202 p.: bibl.

Data from an earlier large survey on migration (1970) are used for a demographic treatment of household composition (size, sex of head, and family type). Employment of head of household is classified in self-employed, manual salaried worker and nonmanual salaried worker, and these categories are cross-tabulated with the demographic ones.

8067 García Canclini, Néstor. Las culturas populares en el capitalismo. México: Editorial Nueva Imagen, 1982. 224 p., 32 p. of plates: bibl., ill. (Serie El arte en la sociedad)

Essay on the manipulation of crafts, local markets, and popular *fiestas* by commercial interests. Case studies from Tarascan villages are used to illustrate exploitation of traditions and artisans and the inadequacy of public policies.

8068 Gates, Marilyn. Partial proletarianization and reinforcement of peasantry in the Mexican ejido (NS, 6:12, 1981, p. 63–79, charts, map)

Critique of the National Plan of Small Irrigation Works in Campeche. Plan began in 1968 and was partially financed by the IDB. Contrasting views of bureaucrats and peasants on results and problems of project suggest that rural dwellers are no longer willing to accept capital infussion that benefits someone else.

8069 Gereffi, Gary. The pharmaceutical industry and dependency in the Third World. Princeton, N.J.: Princeton Univ. Press, 1983. 291 p.: bibl., tables.

Contains a four-chap. case study on the hormone industry in Mexico. Documents displacement of national firms by multinationals and effects of the take-over on prices. Excellent example of the conflict between national interests and MNCs.

8070 Gomezjara, Francisco A. La lucha por la tierra debe ser contra el capital. México: Ediciones Nueva Sociología; Coyoacán, México: Distribución Fontamara, 1982. 410 p.: bibl. (Investigaciones sociales)

Collection of 11 essays by keen analyst of rural problems, previously published in mid and late 1970s in professional journals and newspapers. Includes a lengthy essay (170 p.) on "Agricultural Education and Multinationals" and shorter articles on peasant struggles in the states of Sinaloa, Guerrero, Oaxaca, Veracruz, Morelos, and San Luis de Potosí.

8071 Goulet, Denis. Mexico, development strategies for the future. Notre Dame, Ind.: Univ. of Notre Dame Press, 1983. 191 p.: bibl., index.

Excellent review of Mexico's fundamental social, political and economic problems with emphasis on 1976–82 period. Views by prominent Mexican scholars such as Cordera, Tello, Solís, Stavenhagen, and Esteva on development strategies are summarized. Endorses a pluralistic approach which will achieve economic growth, redistribution, and at the same time satisfy basic human needs.

Granados Chapa, Miguel Angel. Examen de la comunicación en México. See item **6066.**

Gutiérrez, Phillip R. The channelization of Mexican nationals to the San Luis Valley of Colorado. See item **5095.**

Hamilton, Nora. The State and the national bourgeoisie in post-revolutionary Mexico: 1920–1940. See HLAS 46:2211.

8072 Hellman, Judith Alder. The role of ideology in peasant politics: peasant mobilization and demobilization in the Laguna Region (SAGE/JIAS, 25:1, Feb. 1983, p. 3–30, bibl.)

How independent political leaders are able to keep followers in a clientelistic political system, is the question that directs author to compare a Marxist and an "agrarian" peasant organization. The ideology of Marxism creates a class consciousness that maintains members together in times of crisis more easily than the non-ideological agrarian movement. For political scientist's comment, see item **6069.**

Hendricks, Janet and **Arthur D. Murphy.** From poverty to poverty: the adaptation of young migrant households in Oaxaca, México. See item **938.**

8073 Hicks, Whitney; Romeo Madrigal; and **Raymundo Rodríguez.** Determinantes de la anticoncepción: el caso de las mujeres

casadas o unidas que no desean más hijos. Nuevo León, México: Univ. Autónoma de Nuevo León, Facultad de Economía, Centro de Investigaciones Económicas, 1980. 16 leaves: bibl., ill.

R.E. Easterlin's model of fertility is applied to a subsample of females (ages 15–49) of the *First National Survey of Prevalence of Uses of Birth Control Methods* (1978). According to findings, probability of birth control use increases with size of place of residence and with level of education of female and decreases with age.

8074 Hodges, Donald Clark and **Ross Gandy.** Mexico, 1910–1982: reform or revolution? 2nd ed. London: Zed Press, 1983. 250 p.: bibl., index.

Marxist introduction to Mexican political sociology. Two chapters are devoted to other Latin American revolutionary ideologies including Aprismo, populism, and military-populist regimes. Review and criticism of leftist literature is useful for the scholar but too detailed for the layman.

Holian, John. Fertility differentials in Mexico: an individual level analysis. See item **1662.**

Jones, Richard C. Recent patterns of undocumented migration from Mexico to South Texas. See item **5100.**

8075 Krotz, Esteban. La cooperación agropecuaria en México: elementos para el estudio y la evaluación de la situación de la población rural (Iztapalapa [Univ. Autónoma Metropolitana, Iztapalapa, México] 1:1, julio/dic. 1979, p. 116–149, bibl., ill.)

Helpful review of the cooperative movement. Exposes the government interferences and suggests that in the Mexican case cooperativism has been a vehicle of capitalist penetration.

8076 Linck, Thierry. Estrategias campesinas y agropolítica: un caso en la meseta tarasca (CM/RE, 3:9, invierno 1982, p. 49–96)

Critical evaluation of recent official agricultural policies (1980–85) such as SAM (*Sistema Alimentario Mexicano*) and LFA (*Ley de Fomento Agropecuario*). Using the village of San Felipe as a case study, author shows the technical problems and bureaucratic snarls in the application of "modern" agricultural technologies advanced by official policies.

8077 Logan, Kathleen. *Fraccionamientos* as a means of urban integration (PCCLAS/P, 8, 1981/1982, p. 75–92) Rev. version of *HLAS 43:8105.*

8078 Macías, Anna. Against all odds: the feminist movement in Mexico to 1940. Westport, Conn.: Greenwood Press, 1982. 195 p.: bibl., index (Contributions in women's studies, 0147–104X; 30)

History of feminist movement from mid 1800s to 1940 is narrated in sequential format. Two chapters are dedicated to Yucatan women's movement. Concludes with bibiographical essay on the topic (22 p.). Well written and thorough, this monograph should become a standard reference. For historian's comment, see *HLAS 46:2230.*

8079 Margolis, Jane. El papel de la mujer en la agricultura del bajío (Iztapalapa [Univ. Autónoma Metropolitana, Iztapalapa, México] 1:1, julio/dic. 1979, p. 158–169, tables)

Applies theoretical principles of Chayanov, Meillassoux and Luxemburg to the study of labor in small village of Magdalena (Guanajuato). Male migration to US leaves agricultural work to females and children. Findings from field research suggest that exploitation of females and children is necessary for the reproduction of labor force and household maintenance, and that it benefits only capitalism.

8080 Martínez, Marielle P.L.; Luis Foncerrada; and Esperanza Oteo Bautista. Los caminos de mano de obra como factores de cambio socioeconómico: análisis de una encuesta a 423 familias campesinas mexicanas. México: Centro de Estudios Sociológicos, El Colegio de México, 1980. 69 p. (Cuadernos del CES; 27)

Carefully designed survey of 14 small communities in Chiapas, Durango, Guerrero, Jalisco, Nuevo León, Veracruz, Oaxaca, and Yucatán assesses economic impact of improvement and construction of rural feeding roads with local labor. There were no major changes in agricultural output but more employment opportunities (besides road construction) and increases in consumerism. The wealthy local families profited more than the rest.

8081 Menéndez, Eduardo L. Poder, estratificación y salud: análisis de las condiciones sociales y económicas de la enfermedad en Yucatán. México: Centro de Investigaciones y Estudios Superiores en Antropología Social, 1981. 590 p.: bibl., tables (Ediciones de la Casa Chata; 13)

Comprehensive study of health conditions and practices, organization of health services, and health statistics from early part of the century to 1977. Changes in health status and practices are analyzed from the perspective of political sociology. Solid contribution to public health and medical sociology.

8082 Menéndez, Iván. Lucha social y sistema político en Yucatán. Prólogo, Horacio Labastida. México: Editorial Grijalbo, 1982. 250 p.

One of the first political sociology studies of contemporary Yucatán with emphasis on 1970–76 Echeverría administration. Written from a dependency theoretical framework, this excellent monograph includes chapters on independent labor unions and rural social and political movements. Important reference for the study of regional Mexican politics.

8083 Moguel, Julio *et al.* Ensayos sobre la cuestión agraria y el campesinado. México: J. Pablos Editor, 1981. 189 p.: bibl., ill.

Four theoretical essays and an excellent historical review of the independent rural organization movement. Topics of titles suggest content and theoretical orientation of contributors: J. Moguel (the agrarian question in Marx's writings), B. Rubio and J. Moguel (land value and rent in political economy and in Marx), J. Veraza (land rent in the 1844 manuscripts of Marx), J. Moguel (peasants and landlords, a critique of the structuralist view of social classes), R. Robles (independent peasants' organizations in Mexico), and F. Omar (salaries and the Reserve Labor Army in the Mexican countryside).

8084 Morales, Patricia. Indocumentados mexicanos. México: Editorial Grijalbo, 1982. 270 p.: bibl.

Push and pull factors for migration are comprehensively analyzed from the 19th century to present. The capitalist economies of US and Mexico are blamed for social problems encountered by migrants. Based on secondary analysis of most important works.

8085 Münch, Guido. Etnografía de la colonia Las Aguilas (UNAM/AA, 18, 1981, p. 139–172, graphs, ill., tables)

Traditional ethnographic report of a large socially mixed neighborhood in Mexico City. Tables are based on a 43 household survey. Original intent of research was to study drug abuse, but had to be discontinued because of risks. Contains some information on this topic.

8086 La Mujer delincuente: curso impartido en el Instituto de Investigaciones Jurídicas de la UNAM, en febrero de 1980. Coordinador, Javier Piña y Palacios. México: El Instituto, 1983. 299 p.: bibl., ill. (Serie E. Varios; 15)

In 1980 the UNAM's Instituto de Investigaciones Jurídicas organized a course on female delinquency. The 19 lectures presented are pub. in this vol. Professionals and administrators of penal institutions provide an excellent collection of materials about a topic seldom discussed in Latin America and expose violation of human rights and brutality of law enforcement agencies.

8087 Ordorica, Manuel and Joseph E. Potter. Evaluation of the Mexican fertility survey, 1976–77. Voorburg, Netherlands: International Statistical Institute; London: World Fertility Survey, 1981. 29 p.: bibl. (Scientific reports; 21)

The World Fertility Survey is an international program whose purpose is to assess the state of human fertility. In Mexico, like in other countries, an evaluation of the survey was carried out to verify quality of data on age, nuptiality, fertility, mortality, and births. Procedures included tests of internal consistency, and comparisons with national censuses and with the 1978 *Contraceptive Prevalence Survey*.

8088 Paradowska, Maria. Polacy w Meksyku i Ameryce Srodkowej = The Poles in Mexico and Central America. Wrocław, Poland: Zakład Narodowy im. Ossolińskich, 1985. 384 p.: bibl., ill., index.

Polish ethnographer is author of first book entirely devoted to the role of Polish immigrants in Mexico and Central America. Designed for the lay reader but useful for specialists. [K. Complak]

8089 Peña, Sergio de la. Acumulación originaria y negación de la sociedad indígena en México (BAA, 6, dic. 1982, p. 37–52)

Brief historical survey of modes of production from colonial days to present. Dates formation of bourgeoisie to end of 18th century, however, argues that capital accumulation began in early colonial days.

8090 Pérez Castro, Ana Bella. Movimiento campesino en Simojovel, Chiapas, 1936–1978: problema étnico o de clases sociales (UNAM/AA, 19, 1982, p. 207–229, bibl., charts)

Lengthy historical description of land conflict in Chiapas precedes the narration of 1972 movement caused by demographic pressures, corruption, and abuses by official leaders and bureaucrats. Tactics used by landlords and Indians are described in some detail. According to author, in the struggle for land, class consciousness among Indians overrides ethnic considerations.

8091 Piho, Virve. La obrera textil. 2a ed. México: Facultad de Ciencias Políticas y Sociales, Centro de Estudios del Desarrollo, UNAM, 1982. 199 p.: bibl., ill. (Acta sociológica; 4. Serie La industria)

Written in 1970 and first pub. in 1974, Piho's monograph has survived the test of time. Anthropological in her methodology, author has put together an excellent ethnography of the life and work of female laborers in a Mexico City factory. Sociodemographic characteristics of workers, organization of labor, employer-employee relations, income and housing, and family life are treated in depth.

8092 Porras M., Agustín. Desarrollo agrario y cambio demográfico en tres regiones de México. La Jolla: Program in US-Mexican Studies, Univ. of California, San Diego, 1981. 43 leaves: bibl. (Working papers in US-Mexican studies; 18)

Non-random fertility survey of municipalities in La Laguna, El Bajío, and Sierra Norte de Puebla finds that fertility is lower in the less developed region with less knowledge and use of birth control. Possible explanation for incongruency is the lengthier breast feeding practices in the poor region. Methodological procedures and analysis of data are somewhat unclear.

8093 Problemas de organización social: farmacodependencia, alcoholismo y violencia en jóvenes veracruzanos. México: Consejo Nacional de Recursos para la Atención de la Juventud, Dirección de Planeación, 1982. 218 p., 16 leaves of plates: ill. (Serie Salud; 2)

Three youth groups (ages 12 to 24) in Xalapa, Coatepec, and Coatzacoalcos are the object of analysis: univ. students, blue collar workers, and slum dwellers. Sample techniques and size for each group and city are poorly explained. Different research teams carried out the surveys in each city for each group and it is not clear if the same instruments were used. Comparability of findings and conclusions suffer from these shortcomings.

8094 Ramírez Mac Naught, Darío Edgar.
Algunas características del trabajo y su comportamiento con factores de organización entre diferentes poblaciones urbanas de México. México: s.n., 1982. 178 leaves: bibl., ill.

Doctoral dissertation that examines the relation between labor productivity and city size in metal industries in Monterrey, Querétaro, Mexico City, and Veracruz. Factorial analysis of 820 questionnaires of metal workers shows an inverse correlation between productivity and size.

La Reforma política y la izquierda. See item 6087.

8095 Reseña comentada sobre estudios de migración en México. México: SPP, Coordinación General de los Servicios Nacionales de Estadística, Geografía e Informática, 1980. 156 p.: bibl.

Annotated bibliography of national and international migration which includes a useful classification of entries by methodologies, sources of data, and variables studied.

8096 Roberts, Kenneth D. and **Gustavo Treviño Elizondo.** Agrarian structure and labor migration in rural Mexico: the case of circular migration of undocumented workers to the U.S. Austin: Institute of Latin American Studies, Univ. of Texas; Mexico: Centro Nacional de Investigaciones Agrarias, 1980. 294 p.: bibl., ill. (Mexico-US migration research reports)

Specific agricultural conditions which cause migration to the US were studied in Las Huastecas (San Luis de Potosí), Mixteca Baja (Oaxaca), Valsequillo (Puebla), and Bajío (Guanajuato). The surprising conclusion from this study is that regional agricultural development will not necessarily stem the flow of migration.

Rohner, Ronald P.; Samuel Roll; and Evelyn C. Rohner. Perceived parental acceptance-rejection and personality organization among Mexican and American elementary school children. See item **977.**

8097 Rothstein, Frances. Women and men in the family economy: an analysis of the relations between the sexes in three peasant communities (CUA/AQ, 56:1, Jan. 1983, p. 10–23, tables)

Male-female relations in three villages are compared: author's study of San Cosme, Lewis's Tepoztlan, and Beals's Cheran. Concludes that contrary to the latter authors' observations, economic relations among sexes are egalitarian. Raises an interesting question about reliability of field methods.

8098 Roxborough, Ian and **Ilán Bizberg.**
Union in locals in Mexico: the new unionism in steel and automobiles (JLAS, 15:1, May 1983, p. 117–135, tables)

Examines the nature of union militancy and its implications for Mexican politics in two modern industries: steel production, organized as an industrial union (see item **8053**) and auto production, organized as part of national confederations of labor unions. Differences in organization have implications for militancy, relations between local and national bosses, and internal democracy.

8099 Saldaña Harlow, Adalberto. El Estado en la sociedad mexicana: filosofía, estructura, influencia y perspectivas del sistema del Estado. México: Editorial Porrúa, 1981. 534 p.: ill.

Lengthy, formal and at times heavy treatise on the political system. Contains some useful insights but the text is short on data and references to the many outstanding books and articles on the topic.

8100 Sández Parma, Rodrigo. Nosotros los bajacalifornianos. México: Rotopunto Color, 1979. 192 p.

Collection of vignettes of political leaders and socialites, and anecdotes about the life and culture of the region.

8101 Santa Gertrudis: testimonios de una lucha campesina. Compilado por Lorena Paz Paredes y Julio Moguel. México: Ediciones Era, 1979. 106 p.

Slightly modified version of script for Gilles Groulx's movie *La Primera pregunta sobre la felicidad* (1977?) about agrarian struggles and political conflict in a Oaxacan village. Includes section on the operation of local *ejido*. Narrative by caciques and peasants presents contrasting views on land conflicts and social problems.

8102 Seligson, Mitchell A. and Edward J. Williams. Maquiladoras and migration: workers in the Mexico-United States border industrialization program. Austin: Mexico-US Border Research Program, Univ. of Texas, 1981. 202 p.: bibl., index.

The Border Industrialization Program (BIP) in Mexico through US run-away-shops has been the object of political debate and academic research for several years. This book is a welcome contribution to the topic with information on sociodemographic, economic and migration characteristics of workers. Findings negate the view that BIP fosters Mexican migration to US. Data from interviews with 839 workers in 82 plants and eight cities.

8103 Seligson Berenfeld, Silvia. Los judíos en México: un estudio preliminar. México: SEP, 1983. 200 p.: appendix (Cuadernos de la Casa Chata; 88)

Published dissertation divided in two pts.: 1) historical overview of Jewish international migration in 19th and 20th centuries; and 2) Jewish migration to Mexico, Mexican migration policies in general and towards Jews in particular, as well as social organization and adaptation of migrants (70 p.). Appendix includes original data gathered by author about Jewish community in Guadalajara that is not analyzed in the text.

8104 Sociedad y política en Oaxaca, 1980. Compilación de Raúl Benítez Zenteno. Moisés J. Bailón Corres *et al.* Oaxaca, México: Instituto de Investigaciones Sociológicas, 1982. 349 p., 2 p. of plates: bibl., maps.

One of the first publications of the new Instituto de Investigaciones Sociológicas of the Autonomous Univ. of Oaxaca brings together 15 articles from theses of graduating students. Topics include issues on rural development, migration, social organization of local villages, and the political conflict of the 1970s in Oaxaca. While mostly descriptive, articles are of high quality.

8105 Sommerlad, Ernest Lloyd; Gustavo Esteva; and María Angélica Luna Parra. Políticas y sistemas nacionales de comunicación social. México: Coordinación General de Comunicación Social, Presidencia de la República, 1981. 143 p.: bibl. (Col. Aportes de comunicación social; 1)

First article (two-thirds of book) by E. Sommerlad, "National Communications Systems" originally published by UNESCO in 1975, is a general introduction to the functions, effects, potential of media, and limitations imposed by interests groups, no mention made to Mexico. G. Esteva's "Social Communication Policies in Mexico" affirms that poor bureaucratic coordination and private monopolies are responsible for the lack of a national policy. In the last article, "A Proposal for National Communication Policies," A. Luna argues that TV more than the other media fosters foreign cultural penetration and private interests.

Story, Dale. Industrial elites in Mexico: political ideology and influence. See *HLAS 46:2287.*

8106 Tamayo, Jaime E. Apuntes para el estudio de la clase obrera y el movimiento sindical en Jalisco (CM/RE, 3:10, Primavera 1982, p. 87–98)

Gives reasons for low percentage of unionized workers in a state with second largest salaried working force. Each sector of economy is discussed separately. Ends with brief description of role of official labor unions and reason for growth of industry's control of white unions (*sindicatos blancos*).

8107 Trabajadores de Michoacán: historia de un pueblo migrante. Coordinador, James D. Cockcroft. José Antonio Alonso *et al.* Morelia, México: IMISAC, 1982. 112 p.: ill.

Ethnography of La Purisima, small village on a former hacienda, with emphasis on history of land struggle and migration to US. Ends with a critical comment on Reagan's proposal for the Mexican "guest workers" program. Useful contribution to the study of Mexican-US migration.

8108 Los Trabajadores mexicanos en Estados Unidos: resultados de la *En-*

cuesta Nacional de Emigración a la Frontera Norte del País y a los Estados Unidos. México: Secretaría del Trabajo y Previsión Social, CENIET, 1982.

Summary of scope, methodology, and findings of the study carried out in 1977 by CENIET. For more findings drawn from this important data base, see item **8115**, *HLAS 45:8070*, and *HLAS 45:8093–8094*.

Varela, Roberto. Proceso políticos en Tlayacapan, Morelos. See item **997**.

8109 Velázquez Guzmán, María Guadalupe. Afectaciones petroleras en Tabasco: el movimiento del Pacto Ribereño (UNAM/RMS, 44:1, enero/marzo 1982, p. 167–187)

Ecological destruction of farm land in Tabasco and PEMEX unwillingness to pay damages to affected peasants gave birth to a large movement. Author explains ensuing conflict and tactics used by both government and peasants, including government violence and intimidation.

8110 Vélez-Ibañez, Carlos G. Bonds of mutual trust: the cultural systems of rotating credit associations among urban Mexicans and Chicanos. New Brunswick, N.J.: Rutgers Univ. Press, 1983. 180 p.: bibl., ill., index.

Study of organization and functions of rotating credit assns. According to author, associations are widespread in urban settings and cut across social classes, age groups, and sex. Reports on 90 assns., with 4000 members in 17 US and Mexican cities. Data are gathered throughout 1970s by informal interviews and participant observation.

8111 Wessman, James W. Campesinos, capitalistas y el Estado: la cambiante política agrícola mexicana y el Proyecto Hungaro (CM/RE, 3:12, otoño 1982, p. 67–90)

Evaluation of SAM and LFA (for acronyms, see item **8076**) in two *ejidos* in Jalisco state. In-fighting and incompetence of federal bureaucracy reduced significantly the benefits to be provided by Hungarian technical assistance to *ejidos*.

8112 Yamada, Mutsuo. Mexico City: development and urban problems after the Revolution, 1910–1970 (Latin American Studies [Univ. of Tsukuba, Sakura-Mura, Japan] 7, 1983, p. 49–75, maps, tables)

Very competent ecological analysis of spatial and demographic growth with empha-

sis on water and drainage problems, air pollution, and public health. For historian's comment, see *HLAS 46:2299*.

8113 ———. Mexico City: development and urban problems before the Revolution (Latin American Studies [Univ. of Tsukuba, Sakura-Mura, Japan] 7, 1983, p. 1–47, ill., maps, tables)

Historical survey of ecological problems in the basin of Mexico from preconquest to 1910. Particular attention is given to soil erosion, water, sewage and drainage, and air pollution. Also explores effects of ecological changes on population, food availability, public health, and natural disasters. For historian's comment, see *HLAS 46:2300*.

8114 Zazueta, Carlos H. Consideraciones acerca de los trabajadores mexicanos indocumentados en los Estados Unidos: mitos y realidades (MSTPS/R, 2, 1979, p. 15–45, bibl., graph, tables)

Provocative and well documented essay that suggests political motivations behind US Immigration and Naturalization Service's official increment of illegal migrant figures. Also questions US studies on costs of illegal migrants' use of social services and the volume of remittances from US to Mexico. Data drawn from 1977 and 1978 surveys (see *HLAS 45:8093–8094*).

8115 Zazueta, César *et al.* Sindicalismo y ramas industriales de juridsicción federal: México, 1978. México: Secretaría del Trabajo y Previsión Social, CENIET, 1982. 313 p.: bibl., ill. (Serie Estudios; 11)

Recasting of previous publications (see *HLAS 45:8095–8096*).

CENTRAL AMERICA

8116 Abarca, Carlos A. *et al.* Desarrollo del movimiento sindical en Costa Rica. San José: Editorial Univ. de Costa Rica, 1981. 193 p.: bibl., ill.

M. Bolaños's first article on the development of the labor movement in Costa Rica is a solid review of the movement (1880–1978); C. Albarca's on popular struggles and labor organization in Costa Rica (1950–60) describes the intense post-civil war conflict between labor and management; O. Cuellar's and S. Quevedo's on preconditions for the development of unions in Costa Rica deals with

levels of unionism by types of occupations;
L. Herrera's and R. Santos's article is part of
item **8128**; and D. Camacho *et al.*'s on ideological domination and popular movements
in Costa Rica presents the results of a survey
of 73 labor leaders financed by USAID on
class consciousness. Concludes with a 60-
item bibliography.

Anderson, Thomas P. The war of the dispossessed: Honduras and El Salvador, 1969.
See item **6100**.

8117 Argüello, Manuel. Los más pobres en
        lucha. Heredia, Costa Rica: Editorial
de la Univ. Nacional (EUNA), 1981. 282 p.:
bibl., ill. (Col. Barva. Serie Sociedad. Subserie
Ensayo)
    Comprehensive study of urbanization
of Puntarenas (Costa Rica) and neighboring
villages which includes population growth,
housing arrangements, occupation and income of residents, migration patterns, and
political participation and conflict.

Argueta, Mario R. Algunas obras de referencia hondureña en el campo de las ciencias sociales. See *HLAS 46:8.*

8118 Autobiografías campesinas. v. 1,
        Alajuela. v. 2, Cartago y Limón. v. 3,
Heredia. v. 4, Puntarenas y Guanacaste. v. 5,
San José. Heredia, Costa Rica: Editorial de la
Univ. Nacional (EUNA), 1983. 5 v. (Col.
Barva. Serie Sociedad. Subserie Autobiografía)
    The National Univ. of Costa Rica
(College of Social Sciences) organized in
1976–78 a contest of peasant autobiographies. Of the 802 received, 27 were selected
for publication in five volumes. Useful approach to understanding culture and social
problems of the peasantry.

Barry, Tom; Beth Wood; and Deb Preusch.
Dollars and dictators: a guide to Central
America. See item **6102**.

**8119 Bermúdez Méndez, Vera; Carlos Raabe
        Cercone; and Laura Ortiz Malavassi.**
Embarazo entre los adolescentes: resultados
de una encuesta realizada en la ciudad de
Limón, 1980. San José: Asociación Demográfica Costarricense, 1982. 94 p.: bibl., ill.
    Compares sample of 264 pregnant
women (ages 15 to 19) to control group. Independent variables are: age, religion, size of
family, education, marital status, employment, head of household, and household in-

come. Also includes respondents' knowledge
and use of birth control, economic and social
impact of pregnancy, and their attitudes and
knowledge about sexuality. For anthropologist's comment, see item **1823**.

Brockett, Charles D. Malnutrition, public
policy, and agrarian change in Guatemala. See
item **5062**.

Browning, David. Agrarian reform in El Salvador. See item **5059**.

8120 Cid V., Rafael del. Las clases sociales y
        su dinámica en el agro hondureño
(CSUCA/ESC, 18, sept./dic. 1977, p. 119–
155, tables)
    The outcome of the transformation
from hacienda to modern agricultural production for exports is the topic of this essay.
According to author, it does not lead to the
development of a proletarian rural class but
to dual agricultural economies.

8121 Cine obrero sandinista (Cuadernos de
        Comunicación Alternativa [Centro de
Integración de Medios de Comunicación Alternativa, La Paz] 1, mayo 1983, p. 23–28)
    Description of experimental UN
funded program to train Nicaraguan workers
in film making. Program's ultimate objective
was to allow workers the use of this media to
express their own views.

8122 Coelho, Ruy Galvao de Andrade. Los
        negros caribes de Honduras. Traduc-
ción, Guadalupe Carías Zapata. Tegucigalpa:
Editorial Guaymuras, 1981. 208 p. (Col.
Codices. Ciencias sociales)
    Spanish translation of traditional eth-
nography published originally in English in
1955. Includes information on social organization, the economy, kinship, and belief
systems.

**8123 Congreso Nicaragüense de Ciencias
        Sociales Carlos Manuel Galves,** 2nd,
Managua, 1981. Estado y clases sociales en
Nicaragua. Paul Oquist *et al.* Managua:
Asociación Nicaragüense de Científicos So-
ciales, 1982. 254 p.: bibl., ill. (Col. Blas real
espinales)
    Titles of papers presented at the II
Nicaraguan Congress of Social Sciences give
an idea of book's content: P. Oquist, "Social
Sciences and Revolution in Nicaragua;" Jaime
Wheelock, "A Welcome Address;" S. Ramírez,
"Survivals of the Collapse" (describes at-

tempts by former oligarchs to fight the revolution); C. Villas, "The Contradictions of the Transition: Classes, Nation and State in Nicaragua;" O. Núñez, "Ideology as a Material Force and Youth as an Ideological Force;" M. Villagra, "Social Forces and Revolutionary Projects;" M. Ortega, "The Ethnia-Nation Conflict in Nicaragua;" M. de Castilla "Education as Power, Crisis without Solution in the Revolutionary Transition: The Case of Nicaragua, 1978–81." Useful for understanding postrevolutionary dilemmas.

Corbett, Jack and **Scott Whiteford.** State penetration and development in Mesoamerica, 1950–1980. See item **909.**

8124 Early, John D. The demographic structure and evolution of a peasant system: the Guatemalan population. Boca Raton: Univ. Presses of Florida, 1982. 207 p.: bibl., ill., maps.

Scholarly monograph that combines quantitative (1950, 1964, and 1973 censuses) and qualitative (ethnographic reports) methodologies in efforts to study the demographic transition. Mortality, fertility, population growth, migration, and acculturation are examined at the national level and in selected villages.

8125 Equipo Investigadores de CIDCA. El Estado, la lucha de clases y la violencia en Guatemala (CSUCA/ESC, 8:23, mayo/agosto 1979, p. 49–83, tables)

Brief history of class struggle in Costa Rica is followed by a discussion of violence. Authors develop a useful classification of social violence: institutional, paramilitary, terrorism, insurgency, and counter insurgency. Second half is dedicated to illustrating and quantifying various types of violence in Guatemala.

Everitt, John C. Mennonites in Belize. See item **5048.**

8126 Falla, Ricardo. Masacre de la finca San Francisco, Huehuetenango, Guatemala: 17 de julio de 1982. Copenhague: International Work Group for Indigenous Affairs, 1983. 117 p.: ill. (Documento IWGIA, 0108–9927; 1)

On July 17, 1982, 302 inhabitants of the San Francisco hamlet were massacred by the army. In a Guatemalan refugee camp in Chiapas (Mexico), Falla, a Jesuit anthropologist, met the few survivors who had witnessed the tragedy. Their taped account is reproduced in this book which also includes author's interpretation. A horror story that should be read by those who are concerned about violence in the region.

8127 Gudmundson, Lowell. Costa Rica before coffee: occupational distribution, wealth inequality and elite society in the village economy of the 1840s (JLAS, 15:2, Nov. 1983, p. 427–452, tables)

Refutes the commonly held view that before the coffee boom, Costa Rican social structure was characterized by dispersed small landholders and low stratification. Scholarly analysis of census data shows that a pre-capitalist elite and significant division of labor and inequality were prevalent before the boom.

Guidos Véjar, Rafael. Ascenso del militarismo en El Salvador. See item **6152.**

8128 Herrera, Liliana and **Raimundo Santos.** Del artesano al obrero fabril. San José: Editorial Porvenir, 1979. 169 p. (Col. Debate)

Economic history of Costa Rica's industrialization is followed by examination of labor union formation, history of labor participation in politics and social movements, and by account of labor demands and bargaining. Contrary to theory, authors conclude, industrial labor force does not lead other workers in class struggle.

Hunter, John M. and **Renate De Kleine.** Geography in Central America. See item **5067.**

8129 Kerns, Virginia. Women and the ancestors: Black Carib kinship and ritual. Urbana: Univ. of Illinois Press, 1983. 229 p., 24 p. of plates: bibl., ill., index.

Rituals recognizing obligations to ancestors are at the center of culture and social organization of Black Caribs in Belize. Field research focuses on older women, the managers of the rituals. Meticulous and comprehensive treatment. [L. Pérez]

Koechert, Andreas. Die guatemaltekische *comunidad indígena.* See item **5069.**

Leis, Raúl. Radiografía de los partidos. See item **6202.**

López Vallacillos, Italo. Trayectoria y crisis del Estado salvadoreño: 1918–1981. See *HLAS 46:2413.*

8130 López y Rivas, Humberto. Nicaragua: diario de campo de un antropólogo (Iztapalapa [Univ. Autónoma Metropolitana, Div. de Ciencias Sociales y Humanidades, Iztapalapa, México] 2 : 3, julio/dic. 1980, p. 212–227)

In early 1980, the author, a Mexican anthropologist, spent two months in Nicaragua working as a volunteer on the Oral History of the Sandinista Insurrection Project. His diary is an interesting and candid account of his experiences, with useful information on the struggles of the Sandinista government to consolidate the revolution.

8131 Martín Baró, Ignacio. Aspiraciones del pequeño burgués salvadoreño (UJSC/ECA, 36 : 394, agosto 1981, p. 773–788, bibl., ill., tables)

Responses elicited from an urban middle-class sample (n = 1114) about the need for selected household appliances and automobiles is the basis for author's consumerism index. Through step regression analysis the predictors of consumerism are identified. Findings show that socioeconomic variables are better predictors than personal and demographic ones. Questions the economy's capability to satisfy middle-class aspirations. For political scientist's comment, see item **6156.**

8132 Materno Vásquez, Juan. Investigaciones sobre la naturaleza del ser panameño. Panamá: Ediciones Olga Elena, 1981. 376 p.: bibl.

Hodge-podge of materials and essays that touch on a large variety of issues: demography, urbanization, religion, economics, history, international relations, art, language, social classes, etc. Based on author's personal reflections more than on data.

8133 Meléndez Ibarra, José. Los campesinos cuentan. San José: Editorial Costa Rica, 1983. 105 p.

Collection of short stories as narrated by Costa Rican peasants and edited by a seasoned organizer and member of the executive board of the Federación Nacional Campesina. Presents insightful and forceful view of social problems, abuses, and exploitation of the peasantry. Fails to indicate the method used in editing the materials.

8134 Montes, Segundo. Los sectores medios en El Salvador: historia y perspectivas (UJSC/ECA, 36 : 394, agosto 1981, p. 753–772, ill., tables)

After identifying the occupational groups that can be classified as middle class, author studies the political and economic roles that capitalism ascribed to them. Concludes with scenario in which a revolutionary movement has achieved power and a discussion of difficulties that the middle class will encounter in adapting to the new social order.

Murga Franssinetti, Antonio. Estado y burguesía industrial en Honduras. See *HLAS* 46:2425.

8135 Navarro Solano, Sonia. Estigmatización, conducta desviada y victimización en una zona marginada. San José: Instituto Latinoamericano de las Naciones Unidas para la Prevención del Delito y Tratamiento del Delincuente, 1983. 135 p.: ill.

Random survey of 318 inhabitants of a poor neighborhood in San José on their attitudes towards crime, judicial system, and police. Controls include age, sex, education, and occupation. Information is also obtained on number of types of crimes suffered by respondents.

Palacio, Joseph. Food and social relations in a Belizean Garifuna village. See item **1797.**

Paradowska, Maria. Polacy w Meksyku i Ameryce Srodkowej = The Poles in Mexico and Central America. See item **8088.**

8136 Posas, Mario. Política estatal y estructura agraria en Honduras: 1950–1978 (CSUCA/ESC, 8 : 24, sept./dic. 1979, p. 37–116, tables)

Well documented and in-depth critique of agricultural policies. According to author, land reforms have left intact latifundia and only marginally touched US fruit companies. Main beneficiaries of colonization projects have been cooperatives which engage in cash crops for exports and cattle ranchers. Policies have resulted in Honduras's insertion in a new international division of labor.

8137 Richter, Ernesto. La contradicción capital-suelo como determinante de las formas de explotación de la fuerza de trabajo en la agricultura (CSUCA/ESC, 8 : 24, sept./dic. 1979, p. 203–245)

Orthodox Marxist theorizes about exploitation of labor force under the new modality of capitalism in Central America: the industrialization of agriculture.

8138 Rovira Mas, Jorge. Estado y política económica en Costa Rica, 1948–1970. San José: Editorial Porvenir, 1982. 224 p.: bibl. (Col. Debate)

Lucid political history by Marxist scholar written without jargon. Focuses on economic policy formation and implementation. Shows that progressive reforms by National Liberation Party, including nationalization of banks, reinforced economy's capitalist orientation.

8139 Seminario de Trabajo Social en Nicaragua, 1st, *Managua, 1982.* Política social y trabajo social. Lima: Centro Latinoamericano de Trabajo Social, 1982. 137 p.: bibl. (Cuadernos Celats; 39)

Collection of papers presented at the First National Seminar on Social Work held in Nicaragua. Each paper describes the roles of social workers in one social sector of the country: mental health and disability, health, social security, education, housing, and vocational training.

Sewastynowics, James. Community power brokers and national political parties in rural Costa Rica. See item **6135.**

8140 Sobrado Chaves, Miguel A. Introducción a los resultados del Primer Concurso Nacional de Autobiografías Campesinas, CONAUCA, y una reflexión obligada sobre el desarrollo de las ciencias sociales (CSUCA/ESC, 8:24, sept./dic. 1979, p. 353–383, tables)

Pt. 1 reports on the conflict between groups of social scientists in Costa Rica with different theoretical and methodological approaches. Pt. 2 explains purpose and methodology used in the oral history of peasants project (see item **8118**).

Solís R., Luis Guillermo. La dinastía de los colonizadores: *vecinismo* en San Isidro de Pérez Zeledón, Costa Rica. See *HLAS 46:2443.*

8141 Suazo, Margarita *et al.* Honduras: *Encuesta Nacional de Prevalencia del Uso de Anticonceptivos:* resultados generales. Tegucigalpa: Ministerio de Salud Pública y Asistencia Social, Dirección General de Estadística y Censos, 1982? 163 p.: forms, ill.

Standard national survey of 4914

households provides information on attitudes towards family size, and knowledge and use of birth control methods. Control variables are age, level of education, number of children, and place of residence. Includes chapters on birth control programs in Honduras and on breast feeding, place of delivery, and immunizations.

8142 Torres Rivas, Edelberto. Derrota oligárquica, crisis burguesa, revolución popular: notas sobre la crisis en Centroamérica (FCE/TE, 50[2]:198, abril/junio 1983, p. 991-1018, tables)

Following a neo-Marxist approach, author suggests that the traditional landed oligarchy has maintained political control because of region's limited industrialization. However, lack of modernization in agriculture has opened a rift between the oligarchy and petty bourgeoisie, and placed the former on the brink of collapse.

Tripp, Robert. Domestic organization and access to property in a town in eastern El Salvador. See item **994.**

8143 Vargas Escobar, Oscar René. Notas sobre el nuevo eje de acumulación capitalista en Centroamérica: el caso de Nicaragua (CSUCA/ESC, 8:22, enero/abril 1979, p. 251–272)

Written before the Sandinista victory, article examines the conflict between competing groups of the oligarchy: the new industrialists and the old landed oligarchy. Unfortunately, does not present empirical data to support many of the interesting propositions advanced.

8144 Vicente, José *et al.* Personality correlates of ordinal family position in Panamanian adolescents (JSP, 120, June 1983, p. 7–12, bibl.)

Sample of 804 Panamanian adolescents suggests that first-born females exceed later-born females in need of approval, and marginally, in empathy. First-born males show less empathy than later-born males.

8145 Wasserstrom, Robert. Revolución en Guatemala: campesinos y políticos durante el gobierno de Arbenz (CSUCA/ESC, 18, sept./dic. 1977, p. 25–64, tables)

Reexamination of the historically important presidencies of Arévalo and Arbenz through secondary analysis of ethnographic reports written during the 1944–53 period. Reports show that Indian communities were stratified and, according to author, Arbenz's land reform failed to take this fact into account which intensified rural strife.

8146 Wilson, Everett A. Sanguine saints: Pentecostalism in El Salvador

(ASCH/CH, 52:2, June 1983, p. 186–198, table)

Last three decades growth of Pentecostalism in El Salvador is attributed to its popular institutional authority, internal cohesion and stability, and acceptance of social change, and less to the emergence of a mass society.

THE CARIBBEAN AND THE GUIANAS

LISANDRO PEREZ, *Chairperson and Associate Professor, Department of Sociology and Anthropology, and Director, Graduate Program in International Studies, Florida International University*

INTERNATIONAL MIGRATION continues to be the topic of greatest interest among sociologists studying the Caribbean. A large proportion of the literature examined during the past biennium deals with either immigration or emigration (items **8149, 8157, 8170, 8171, 8175, 8178, 8193, 8203, 8204, 8205, 8208, 8212, 8216, 8218,** and **8219**). Typically, works on immigration tend to be historical, documenting the origins of established ethnic communities (e.g., Arabs, East Indians, Galicians, European Jews). Works on emigration, however, usually deal with more contemporary migrations, especially to the US. Analyses on Haiti and the Commonwealth Caribbean accounted for most of the emigration studies, but the Hispanic Caribbean was also represented. As noted in *HLAS 45* (p. 623–624), the emphasis on migration does not extend to internal migration: there is still little evidence of interest in that topic among Caribbeanists.

Studies on the status of women continue to proliferate (items **8160, 8173, 8177, 8198, 8202,** and **8220**). This is especially evident in the English-speaking Caribbean, where the Women in the Caribbean Project at the Institute of Social and Economic Research of the Univ. of the West Indies has spearheaded the research efforts in that field.

In fact, it seems that the Commonwealth Caribbean has been attracting the bulk of the sociological attention focused on the region. There has been an extraordinary increase in the number of such works over the past few years as new perspectives and topics are explored imparting to the literature a dynamic and innovative character. Note, for example, recent attempts to redefine the concept of the peasantry in a Caribbean context (items **8162, 8199,** and **8213**), as well as the continuation of the exciting efforts (noted in *HLAS 45,* p. 625) to come to grips with the problems of governance, order, and social integration in the postcolonial era (items **8159, 8169, 8183, 8184, 8186, 8191, 8192, 8207,** and **8215**). At press time, it was still too soon for the academic literature of this biennium to reflect the intellectual impact of events in Grenada (item **8201**).

With a few notable exceptions, there seemed to be a decline of interest in the Dominican Republic and Puerto Rico in this biennium. The literature was scanty and without a defined emphasis. For Cuba, there was a marked interest in issues of health and mortality and in evaluating the government's performance in improving the well-being of the population (items **8147, 8153, 8155, 8172, 8180, 8181,** and

8217). It is also apparent that the works of Miguel Barnet have been influential: the *testimonio* as a tool of social research is increasingly evident in the literature (items **8166** and **8203**). The expected release of the results of Cuba's 1981 population and housing census (item **8163**) should stimulate considerable research.

Largely because of its scope, it is worthwhile to single out here the two volumes edited by Susan Craig (item **8165**). It is a commendable effort to provide a sociological work that encompasses the entire region.

8147 Abascal López, Jesús. Dime lo que comes . . . (Cuba Internacional [Prensa Latina, La Habana] 16:178, sept. 1984, p. 20–27, ill.)

Intention is to refute the claim that there is scarcity of food in Cuba. Value lies in the large amount of statistical data presented on food production and consumption.

8148 Alemán, José Luis. 27 ensayos sobre economía y sociedad dominicanas. Santiago, República Dominicana: Univ. Católica Madre y Maestre (UCMM), 1982. 561 p.: bibl, ill. (Col. Estudios; 74)

Collection of previously published essays. Most appeared in *Estudios Sociales*. Emphasis on rural problems, economic institutions, regional development, and population. Best essays are those dealing with agrarian structure.

8149 Allman, James. L'emigration haitienne vers l'étranger de 1950 à 1980 (IFH/C, 157, mars 1983, p. 65–68, tables)

Using foreign-born data found in population censuses of various countries, author estimates levels of Haitian emigration (1950–80).

8150 Aprueba el Comité Ejecutivo del Consejo de Ministros Proyecto de Ley General de la Vivienda (Bohemia [La Habana] 76:45, nov. 1984, p. 20–33, ill.)

Complete text of comprehensive housing law that went into effect Jan. 1, 1985. Introductory note outlines major provisions.

Ashton, Guy T. Migration and the Puerto Rican support system. See item **1009.**

8151 Austin, Diane J. Urban life in Kingston, Jamaica: the culture and class ideology of two neighborhoods. New York: Gordon & Breach Science Publishers, 1984. 282 p.: bibl., ill., indexes (Caribbean studies, 0275–5793; 3)

Detailed and comprehensive study of two Kingston neighborhoods. Because of the marked socioeconomic differences between residents of the two communities, a major theme of the work is social class ideology and cultural hegemony. For anthropologist's comment, see item **1011.**

8152 Barros, Jacques. Haïti, de 1804 à nos jours. Paris: Editions L'Harmattan, 1984. 2 v. (915, 52 p.): bibl., ill.

Broad reflections on Haiti's sociopolitical difficulties, based on author's long stay in the country. [A. Pérotin-Dumon]

Beckford, George L. Socioeconomic change and political continuity in the Anglophone Caribbean. See item **3300.**

Bellegarde-Smith, Patrick. Class struggle in contemporary Haitian politics: an interpretative study of the campaign of 1957. See item **6269.**

8153 Benjamin, Medea; Joseph Collins; and Michael Scott. No free lunch: food and revolution in Cuba today. San Francisco: Institute for Food and Development Policy, 1984. 240 p.: graphs, ill., tables.

Comprehensive look at subject often mentioned but seldom studied: food in socialist Cuba. Overall, a positive view of government's policies but negative view of the population's food-related cultural practices. Valuable work despite occasional and unnecessary polemics and the absence of statistical comparisons with the pre-revolutionary period.

8154 Berube, Maurice R. Education and poverty: effective schooling in the United States and Cuba. Westport, Conn.: Greenwood Press, 1984. 163 p.: bibl., index (Contributions to the study of education, 0196–707X; 13)

Comparative study of educational systems of US and Cuba, with goal of learning what can be applied here from Cuban experience. Analysis of Cuban education largely superficial and unoriginal. Argues that Cuba's case is relevant to US because of the presence of a "significant black population."

8155 Bianchi Ross, Ciro. El derecho a la vida (Cuba Internacional [Prensa Latina, La Habana] 16 : 176, julio 1984, p. 36–43, ill.)

Describes in detail services, facilities, and accomplishments of large obstetrics-gynecology hospital in Havana. Author's point is that Cuba's low infant mortality rate is no accident.

8156 ———. Dueños de la tierra (Cuba Internacional [Prensa Latina, La Habana] 16 : 174, mayo 1984, p. 20–27, table, ill.)

Views transformation of Cuba's agrarian system through the experience of a cooperative in Havana province. Praises cooperatives and presents national-level figures on their growth and characteristics.

8157 A Bibliography of Caribbean migration and Caribbean immigrant communities. Compiled and edited by Rosemary Brana-Shute and Rosemarijn Hoefte. Gainesville: Reference and Bibliographic Dept., Univ. of Florida Libraries: *in cooperation with the* Center for Latin American Studies, Univ. of Florida, 1983. 339 p.: bibl., indexes (Bibliographic series; 9)

Includes more than 2,500 works with subject, author, and geographical indexes. Comprehensive listing of works on migration into, within, and out of all Caribbean islands, Belize, and The Guianas. Also includes works on communities of Caribbean emigrants. For bibliographer's comment, see item 22.

8158 Bosch, Juan. Clases sociales en la República Dominicana. Santo Domingo: Editora Corripio, 1982. 259 p.

Collection of essays culled from two Dominican periodicals (1974–82). Author's introduction warns that it is not a work written in the "language of sociologists." It can perhaps best be regarded as a loosely-integrated collection of insightful reflections on the Dominican class system.

8159 Brathwaite, Farley. Unemployment and social life: a sociological study of the unemployed in Trinidad. Bridgetown: Antilles Publications, 1983. 165 p.: bibl., index, map.

Discusses pervasive problem of unemployment in Trinidad through a national sample of unemployed persons. Examines levels of living, subjective definitions of un-employment, survival strategies, family life, and political culture among the unemployed. Emphasizes issue of unemployment and "social breakdown." For anthropologist's comment, see item 1021.

8160 Brodber, Erna. Perceptions of Caribbean women: towards a documentation of stereotypes. Introduction by Merle Hodge. Cave Hill, Barbados: Institute of Social and Economic Research, Eastern Caribbean, Univ. of the West Indies, 1982. 62 p.: bibl. (Women in the Caribbean project; 4)

Using newspapers and church documents, author examines the development of stereotypes about women among the press and clergy. Interest is in the creation of images that negatively affect the development of women.

8161 Cabrera, Lydia. La medicina popular en Cuba: médicos de antaño, curanderos, santeros y paleros de hogaño. Miami: Ultra Graphics Corp., 1984. 270 p.: bibl. (Col. del Chicherekú en el exilio)

Noted Cuban anthropologist turns her attention to the history and practice of Cuban folk medicine. Lengthy glossary of herbs and medicinal plants and detailed descriptions of remedies.

8162 Castor, Susy. Estructuras de dominación y de existencia campesina en Haití (CEDLA/B, 35, dic. 1983, p. 71–84)

Details the mechanisms through which the Haitian peasant has historically been exploited. Outlines forms of resistance, both passive and active, to that oppression.

Cato, John D. The People's Temple: a socio-religious analysis. See item 1026.

8163 Censo de población y viviendas, 1981: cifras preliminares. La Habana: Comité Estatal de Estadísticas, 1981. 196 p.: ill., tables.

Issued only two months after the 1981 *Census* was taken, this mimeographed volume presents preliminary results. Limited only to number of inhabitants in each civil-administrative division by sex, rural/urban residence, and broad age categories. Also data on housing by *municipio* and rural/urban residence.

Chevannes, Barry. Some notes on African religious survivals in the Caribbean. See item 1028.

8164 Collinwood, Walter. Terra Incognita: research on modern Bahamian society (Journal of Caribbean Studies [Assn. of Caribbean Studies] 2:2/3, Autumn/Winter 1981, p. 284–297)

Argues that social scientists have ignored the Bahamas, largely because it is not considered a Caribbean country. Proposes that the Bahamas be treated as an integral part of the Caribbean community.

8165 Contemporary Caribbean: a sociological reader. Edited by Susan Craig. St. Augustine, Trinidad and Tobago?: The Author; Maracas, Trinidad and Tobago: College Press, 1982. 2 v.: bibl., ill.

Two-volume anthology with 31 readings on Caribbean society (three-fourths of them appear in print for the first time). Excellent coverage: there is at least one reading on every nation and major island in the region. Divided into six parts, each with own editor and introduction: population and migration, class and race, agrarian structures and peasant movements, developments within the working class, theory and ideology, and societies in crisis.

Craig, Dennis R. Language identity and the West Indian child. See item **1034.**

8166 Cruz Díaz, Rigoberto. Chicharrones: la Sierra Chiquita. Santiago, Cuba: Oriente, 1982. 160 p.: ill.

Collection of *testimonios* by residents of a poor neighborhood in Santiago de Cuba. No structure, unity, nor purpose to the work beyond depicting the struggles of a class "that made the Revolution."

8167 Cuba. Ministerio de Cultura. Dirección de Cultura Masiva. Antecedentes de la cultura popular masiva: Cuba, 1902–1978 (*in* La Cultura en Cuba socialista. La Habana: Editorial Letras Cubanas, 1982, p. 63–89)

Title gives 1902–78 as period covered, but first 56 years are dispatched in less than three pages. Concentrates on institutional efforts of the revolutionary government to promote various manifestations of popular culture and folklore.

8169 Danns, George. Decolonization and militarization in the Caribbean: the case of Guyana (*in* The Newer Caribbean: decolonization, democracy, and development.

Philadelphia, Pa.: Institute for the Study of Human Issues, 1983, p. 63–93, bibl.)

Principal theoretical issue examined is the continuity of colonial authoritarianism into the postcolonial period. The crisis of legitimacy of newly-independent nations leads to the development of instruments of coercion. Examines Guyana's case and concludes that decolonization made inevitable the militarization process, which serves many functions for the ruling elite and society.

8170 De Frank Canelo, Juan. Dónde, por qué, de qué, cómo viven los dominicanos en el extranjero: un informe sociológico sobre el proceso migratorio nuestro, 1961–82. Santo Domingo: Editora Alfa y Omega, 1982. 254 p.: ill.

Title says it all. Valuable only because so little is available on Dominican emigration and Dominican communities in US. Unfortunately, approach is impressionistic with little empirical support.

8171 Díaz-Briquets, Sergio. Demographic and related determinants of recent Cuban emigration (CMS/IMR, 17:1, Spring 1983, p. 95–119, bibl., tables)

Analyzes demographic and labor force pressures for Cuban emigration. Greatest contribution is in including temporary "labor migration" to socialist countries in discussion of Cuban emigration.

8172 ———. The health revolution in Cuba. Austin: Univ. of Texas Press, 1983. 227 p.: bibl., ill., index, tables.

Excellent work on factors responsible for a revolution that took place in Cuba considerably before 1959: the mortality decline. Emphasizing 1899–1953 period, author weights the relative impact of health reforms and socioeconomic development. Concludes with observations on the impact of the 1959 Revolution on mortality. For anthropologist's comment, see *HLAS 45:1667.*

Dodd, David J. Rule-making and rule-enforcement in plantation society: the ideological development of criminal justice in Guyana. See item **1046.**

8173 Driver, Edwin D. and Aloo E. Driver. Gender, society, and self-conceptions: India, Iran, Trinidad-Tobago, and the United States (YU/IJCS, 24:3/4, Sept./Dec. 1983, p. 200–217, bibl., tables)

Trinidad-Tobago is included in this

comparative analysis of sex role definitions that portray women as subordinate and effect of those definitions on the self-concept of men and women.

8174 Earnhardt, Kent C. Population research, policy, and related studies in Puerto Rico: an inventory. Río Piedras: Editorial de la Univ. de Puerto Rico, Graduate Program in Planning, 1984. 132 p.: indexes (Planning series; S-6)

Extensive and useful inventory of works published up to 1976 on population research and policy in Puerto Rico. With annotations and tables cross-referenced by subject.

8175 Eichen, Josef David. Sosúa: una colonia hebrea en la República Dominicana. Santiago, República Dominicana: Univ. Católica Madre y Maestra (UCMM), Depto. de Publicaciones, 1980. 126 p.: ill., ports. (Col. Estudios; 54)

Description of a Jewish community near Puerto Plata. Author is member of community which was established by immigrants during World War II.

8176 Fernández, Manuel. Religión y revolución en Cuba: veinticinco años de lucha ateísta. Miami, Fla.: Saeta Ediciones, 1984. 247 p.: bibl., tables (Col. Realidades)

Personal account of conflict between the Catholic Church and the Cuban Revolution. Sympathetic to the Church, author provides a fresh perspective on a number of issues, especially the origins of the conflict. Includes texts of most relevant documents.

Fisher, Lawrence E. Colonial madness: mental health in the Barbadian social order. See item **1054.**

8177 Forde, Norma Monica. Women and the law. Cave Hill, Barbados: Institute of Social and Economic Research, Eastern Caribbean, Univ. of the West Indies, 1981. 125 p.: bibl. (Women in the Caribbean project, research papers. Phase I; 1)

Straightforward presentation of laws of the Commonwealth Caribbean that especially affect women: marriage laws, divorce, support, matrimonial property, inheritance, equality of employment, and relevant criminal provisions.

Forsythe, Dennis. Rastafari, for the healing of the nation. See item **1055.**

8177a García del Cueto, Mario. Historia, economía, y sociedad en los pueblos de habla ingles del Caribe. La Habana: Editorial de Ciencias Sociales, 1982. 106 p.: bibl.

Intended as a brief overview for Cuban readers on the social history of their English-speaking Caribbean neighbors.

8178 Gemmink, Johan. De europeesche landbouwkolonisatie in Suriname: 1845–1950 = The Dutch rural settlers in Surinam, 1845–1950. Zuidwolde, The Netherlands: s.n., 1980. 296 p. (Socio-demographische studien; 5)

Comprehensive historical and demographic analysis of the settlement of Dutch agriculturalists in Surinam (1845–1950). Includes numerous tables with censal data. Fairly extensive English summary.

8179 Gurak, Douglas T. and **Mary M. Kritz.** Female employment and fertility in the Dominican Republic: a dynamic perspective (ASA/ASR, 47:6, Dec. 1982, p. 810–818, bibl., tables)

Married urban women were surveyed to test relationship between female employment and fertility. No proximate relationship was found between the two, and authors argue that in the Domincan Republic motherhood and employment may not be as incompatible as in the US.

8180 Gutiérrez, Héctor. La mortalité par cause à Cuba, avant et aprés la Révolution (INED/P, 39:2, mars/avril 1984, p. 383–388, bibl., tables)

Cause-of-death analysis comparing the pre-revolutionary and post-revolutionary periods. Contrast explained largely by the decline in infant mortality which is attributed to social and health reforms.

8181 Gutiérrez Muñiz, José; José Camarós Fabián; José Cobas Manríquez; and **Rachelle Hartenberg.** The recent worldwide economic crisis and the welfare of children: the case of Cuba (WD, 12:3, March 1984, p. 247–260, bibl., tables)

Presents evidence to support claim that despite scarce resources, Cuban government has given priority to redistributive policies that have greatly advanced the health, diet, education, and housing of children.

8182 Haiti. Institut haïtien de statistique et d'informatique. Div. d'analyse et de recherches démographiques. Le recensement

Haïtien de 1982 (INED/P, 38:6, nov./déc. 1983, p. 1055–1059, tables)

Brief overview of results of 1982 Haitian population census emphasizes regional intercensal growth rates.

Halberstein, Robert A. and **John E. Davies.** Biosocial aspects of high blood pressure in people of the Bahamas. See item **1832.**

8183 Henry, Paget. Decolonization and cultural underdevelopment in the Commonwealth Caribbean (in The Newer Caribbean: decolonization, democracy, and development. Philadelphia, Pa.: Institute for the Study of Human Issues, 1983, p. 95–120)

Sociohistorical analysis of cultural decolonization in the Commonwealth Caribbean. Author views cultural decolonization as an important process, but feels it has been hindered by the dependent nature of Caribbean economy and society in the postcolonial period.

8184 Hintzen, Percy C. Bases of elite support for a regime: race, ideology, and clientelism as bases for leaders in Guyana and Trinidad (CPS, 16:3, Oct. 1983, p. 363–392, bibl., tables)

Examines ideological, clientelistic, and racial bases of regime support among the elite. Guyana and Trinidad are compared because they differ in their post-independence political paths, yet are similar in racial and ethnic composition and pre-independence institutions. Finds that clientelism was crucial for elite support, while race and ideology were not, so that elites that support the opposition on racial and ideological grounds can be co-opted by ruling parties, regardless of the development path undertaken. Seminal work.

—— and **Ralph R. Premdas.** Race, ideology, and power in Guyana. See item **6263.**

8185 Hollerbach, Paula E. and **Sergio Díaz-Briquets.** Fertility determinants in Cuba. Washington: National Academy Press, 1983. 242 p.: graphs, maps, tables (Committee on Population and Demography, National Research Council Report; 26)

Exhaustive and definitive study of Cuban fertility, especially since 1953. Includes: descriptions of trends, proximate determinants (nuptiality, contraception, and abortion), and social and economic determinants (economic conditions and policies, education, health, and housing). There is also

an abridged ed. (New York: The Population Council, 1983. 106 p.: tables [Center for Policy Studies working papers; 102]).

Hope, Margaret. Journey in the shaping: report of the First Symposium on Women in the Caribbean Culture, July 24, 1981. See *HLAS 46:102.*

8186 Horowitz, Irving Louis. Democracy and development: policy perspectives in a post-colonial context (in The Newer Caribbean: decolonization, democracy, and development. Philadelphia, Pa.: Institute for the Study of Human Issues, 1983, p. 221–233)

Examines prospects for democracy in the Third World, especially the Caribbean, by focusing on the relationship between the process of development and democracy. Places discussion within broader theoretical issue of the link between economic systems and political structures.

8187 Hospice, Marlène. Pas de pitié pour Marny: une affaire martiniquaise. Fort-de-France: Editions Désormeaux, 1984. 163 p.: ill.

True story of enigmatic young Martinican, delinquent from age three, permanently expelled from school at eight. As adolescent, he becomes the close companion of an elderly priest. Later, betrayed by his former comrades in crime, the youth seeks revenge which leads to a sentence of life imprisonment. Author sees her protagonist as a victim of the social structure of Martinique and the French colonial system rather tan as an incorrigible culprit! Psychological study of an interesting social phenomenon. [E.O. Davie]

8189 Ibarra, Jorge. Nación y cultura nacional. La Habana: Editorial Letras Cubanas, 1981. 222 p.: bibl. (Col. Crítica)

Traces evolution of a Cuban national culture, as manifested in poetry, fiction, music, and art through various stages of Cuban history. Evaluates negatively the impact of the republican period on Cuban culture.

Immink, Maarten D.C.; Diva Sanjur; and **María Burgos.** Nutritional consequences of US migration patterns among Puerto Rican women. See item **1782.**

8190 Jolivet, Marie-José. La question créole: essai de sociologie sur la Guyane française. Paris: Editions de l'Office de la

recherche scientifique et technique Outre-
mer, 1982. 502 p.: appendices, ill., maps.

Sociological interpretation of the society of French Guiana, stressing three long-
term factors: slavery, gold-search (orpaillage);
and départementalisation. Well informed
synthesis. [A. Pérotin-Dumon]

8191 Jones, Edwin. Class and administrative
development doctrines in Jamaica
(UWI/SES, 30:3, Sept. 1981, p. 1–20, bibl.)

Interesting examination of ideological
and class influences in the system of public
administration that has predominated in Jamaica. Emphasizes the colonial legacy.

8192 Jones, Howard. Crime in Guyana:
some problems of comparative study
in the Caribbean (UWI/SES, 29:1, March
1980, p. 60–68, tables)

Using official crime data, author compares Guyana with Great Britain, Jamaica,
Barbados, and Trinidad-Tobago to test widely
held assumption that Guyana is a violent and
lawless country. Despite problems with data
comparability, it appears that Guyana does
not have a higher rate of violent crime.

8193 Kempeneers, Marianne and **Jean
Poirier.** Economie et population en
Guadeloupe: la baisse de la fécondité et
l'accroissement de l'émigration: les tendances d'une même processus. Montréal, Canada: Univ. de Montréal, Centre de recherches
caraïbes, 1981. 112 p.: bibl., ill.

Brief but interesting work by investigators at the Center for Caribbean Studies
at the Univ. of Montreal. Emigration and the
decline in fertility are interpreted within the
broader context of profound socioeconomic
changes taking place in Guadeloupe.

8194 La Rosa, Gabino. El apalencamiento
(Bohemia [La Habana] 76:32, agosto
10, 1984, p. 82–89, ill., map, tables)

Valuable description of the origins and
characteristics of palenques, clandestine
communities of runaway slaves. Includes
listing of locations of palenques known to
exist between 1800 and 1850 in remote areas
of Cuba.

8195 Landolfi, Ciriaco. Evolución cultural
dominicana, 1844–1899. Santo Do-
mingo: Univ. Autónoma de Santo Domingo,
1981. 292 p.: bibl. (Univ. . . .; 290. Col. Historia y sociedad; 21)

By focusing on a critical period in the

social history of the Dominican Republic,
author traces origins of nation's cultural and
social patterns.

8196 Layng, Anthony. The Carib Reserve:
identity and security in the West Indies. Foreword by Leo A. Despres. Washington: Univ. Press of America, 1983. 177 p.:
bibl., ill., index.

Community study of Carib Reserve in
eastern Dominica. Descriptions of inhabitants' history, social structure, religion, education, economy, relations with outsiders,
and ethnic identity.

Levine, Suzanne. Food production and
population size in the Lesser Antilles. See
item **1790.**

McKee, David L. Some specifics on the loss
of professional personnel from the Commonwealth Caribbean. See item **3326.**

8198 Massiah, Joycelin. Women as heads
of households in the Caribbean: family structure and feminine status. Paris:
UNESCO, 1983. 69 p.: bibl., ill. (Women in a
world perspective)

Good empirical study of the extent
and economic consequences of females being
heads of households in the English-speaking
Caribbean.

8199 Mintz, Sidney W. Reflections on Caribbean peasantries (NWIG, 57:1/2,
1983, p. 1–17, bibl.)

Originally written as a lecture, article
gives excellent overview of the development
of the study of the peasantry in the Caribbean, especially its link with plantation
studies. Argues that the importance of
understanding the peasantry remains
undiminished.

8200 Morenc, J. Agricultural cooperatives in
Surinam: complex problems and
policy responses (CEDLA/B, 3, dic. 1983,
p. 51–70, bibl., map, table)

Fairly comprehensive piece, combines
a theoretical interpretation of the development of cooperatives with discussion of specific cooperatives and government policies.

8201 Naipaul, V.S. An island betrayed: Grenada's revolution never got beyond slogans and texts, amid the heat and torpor,
language and intentions blurred (Harper's
Magazine [New York] 268:1606, March 1984,
p. 61–72, ill.)

Impressionistic first-person account of what went wrong with the Grenadian Revolution. Based largely on the well known author's visit to Grenada 17 days after the invasion. For political scientist's comment, see item **7246.**

8202 Nazzari, Muriel. The "woman question" in Cuba: analysis of material constraints on its solution (UC/S, 9:2, Winter 1983, p. 246–263)

Unlike most of the literature on women in revolutionary Cuba, rhetoric and ideology are not the focus here, but rather a realistic assessment of the negative impact of the economic reforms of the 1970s on women's equality at work and at home.

8203 Neira Vilas, Xosé. Gallegos en el Golfo de México. La Habana: Editorial Letras Cubanas, 1983. 197 p., 15 p. of plates: ill.

In-depth interviews with 16 elderly Spanish (Galician) immigrants on their early experiences in Cuba, their lives as fishermen, ideology and values, and community life in Casablanca, a town within Greater Havana.

8204 Nevadomsky, Joseph. Social change and the East Indians in rural Trinidad: a critique of methodologies (UWI/SES, 31:1, March 1982, p. 90–126, bibl.)

Interesting and balanced critique of different perspectives on social change among East Indians in Trinidad, with focus on relative role of cultural differentiation vs. socioeconomic adaptation and integration.

8205 Nicholls, David. Los árabes en el Caribe: República Dominicana, Haití y Trinidad (MHD/B, 11:18, 1983, p. 159–176, graph)

Well researched and documented analysis of origins and development of the populations of Arab origin residing in the Dominican Republic, Haiti, and Trinidad. Extensive use of censal data and historical documents.

8205a Nieves-Falcón, Luis et al. Huelga y sociedad. Río Piedras, Puerto Rico: Editorial Edil, 1982. 275 p., 59 p. of plates: ill., photos.

Interesting analysis of the origins and development of the strike and disturbances at the Univ. of Puerto Rico (1980–81). Emphasizes role of the media and public opinion. Includes chronology of events and photographic essay.

8206 Oberg, Larry R. Human services in postrevolutionary Cuba: an annotated international bibliography. Westport, Conn.: Greenwood Press, 1984. 433 p.: indexes.

Extremely useful and comprehensive annotated bibliography of literature on Cuban education, public health, housing, youth, women, and ethnic minorities (1959–82) published internationally. Includes official publications and articles in Cuban periodicals in addition to international journals and monographs. Total of 2,027 items plus author, title, and subject indexes.

Paley, William. Haiti's dynastic despotism: from father to son . . . See item **6271.**

8207 Perspectives on Jamaica in the seventies. Edited by Carl Stone and Aggrey Brown. Kingston: Jamaica Publishing House, 1981. 486 p.: bibl., ill.

Valuable and informative collection of essays by 14 social scientists focusing on political economy, elections and voting, role of the media in political and social change, and social trends. Editors identify themselves as supporters of "left-of-centre approaches to policy change" while recognising many of the shortcomings of the PNP's socialist initiative." For political scientist's comment, see item **6283.**

8208 Perusek, Glenn. Haitian emigration in the early twentieth century (CMS/IMR, 18:1, Spring 1984, p. 4–18, bibl., tables)

Using both documents and official statistics, author gives a good overview of Haitian labor migrations to Cbua and the Dominican Republic during early 20th century.

Pirez, Pedro. Estado y configuración espacial en el período de la organización nacional en América Latina. See *HLAS 46:1783.*

Powell, Dorian. The role of women in the Caribbean. See item **3332.**

Quamina, Odida T. The social organization of Plantation Mackenzie: an account of life in the Guyana mining enterprises. See item **1114.**

8209 Ramírez de Arellano, Annette B. and **Conrad Seipp.** Colonialism, Catholicism, and contraception: a history of birth control in Puerto Rico. Chapel Hill: Univ. of North Carolina Press, 1983. 219 p.: bibl., index.

Excellent and balanced treatment of a controversial topic. Colonialism, Catholicism, and contraception are regarded as the three important currents in a profound process of social change that has shaped the history of birth control in Puerto Rico. Well researched and extensively documented.

8210 Ríos Massabot, N.E. Sistema de información de estadísticas vitales en Cuba (Revista Cubana de Administración de Salud [La Habana] 9:1, enero/marzo 1983, p. 16–31, bibl., ill., table)
Detailed description of Cuban vital statistics registration system. Includes copies of birth and death certificates. Essential for analysts of Cuban fertility and mortality.

8211 Rioseco López-Trigo, Pedro. Sin bola de cristal (Bohemia [La Habana] 75:50, 16 dic. 1983, p. 3–11, ill., map)
Interesting report on Havana's future as seen by its planning office. Enumerates the city's chief physical problems and discusses planning options, including decentralization of retail commerce, new parks, stricter industrial zoning, and even a metro.

8212 Rosario Natal, Carmelo. Exodo puertorriqueño: las emigraciones al Caribe y Hawaii, 1900–1915. San Juan: The Author, 1983. 136 p., 4 leaves of plates: bibl., ill., ports.
Historical treatment of Puerto Rican emigration, with emphasis on little known, but significant, migration stream from Puerto Rico to Hawaii.

8213 Sebastien, Raphael. A typology of the Caribbean peasantry: the development of the peasantry in Trinidad, 1845–1917 (UWI/SES, 29:2, June 1980, p. 107–133, tables)
By focusing on the pivotal 1845–1917 period, author arrives at a typology of the Trinidadian peasantry which he elaborates in the context of both Marxist theories of the peasantry and the existing body of literature on Caribbean peasantries in general.

Serbín, Andrés. Nacionalismo, etnicidad y política en la República Cooperativa de Guyana. See item **6266.**

8214 Sosa, Enrique. Los ñáñigos: ensayo. La Habana: Casa de las Américas, 1982. 464 p., 44 p. of plates: bibl., ill.
Detailed and straightforward descrip-

tion of the origins, organization, rituals, importance, and adaptations of African religious practices in Cuba. Reflects extensive field work and bibliographic research. There is, however, not one reference to any work published by Lydia Cabrera after 1959.

8215 Sudama, Trevor. Class, race, and the state in Trinidad and Tobago (LAP, 10:4, Fall 1983, p. 75–96, bibl.)
Marxist-based explanation of the evolution of the State in postcolonial Trinidad and Tobago. Argues for the incorporation of the racial factor into traditional class analyses.

8216 Tobias, Peter M. The social context of Grenadian emigration (UWI/SES, 29:1, March 1980, p. 40–59, bibl.)
Sociocultural explanation of Grenadian emigration. In a society in which "manliness" is associated with success, emigration, perceived as a vehicle for success, becomes a "rite of passage." Maintaining an image of success after emigrating precludes communicating the hardships encountered abroad, thereby perpetuating emigration.

8217 Waitzkin, Howard. Health policy and social change: a comparative history of Chile and Cuba (SSSP/SP, 31:2, Dec. 1983, p. 235–248, bibl.)
Compares Cuba and Chile to demonstrate importance of broad social change in developing a national public health service. Analysis of Cuba is superficial, derived almost exclusively from a few secondary sources.

8218 Watson, Hilbourne. Theoretical and methodological problems in Commonwealth Caribbean migration research: conditions and casuality (UWI/SES, 31:1, March 1982, p. 165–206, bibl.)
Seeks a theoretical reformulation of Commonwealth Caribbean migration research away from the traditional explanations based on human capital factors and demographic processes to a framework based on post World War II capitalist development and the international division of labor.

8219 Westerman, George W. Los inmigrantes antillanos en Panamá. Panamá?: The Author, 1980. 183 p.: bibl., ill.
Informative look at history and social life of a West Indian community in Panama. Tracing its origins to the demand for labor in

banana plantations and in building the Canal, author describes the present-day community and problems it has encountered overcoming racism and discrimination.

8220 Women and the family. Cave Hill, Barbados: Institute of Social and Economic Research, Eastern Caribbean, Univ. of the West Indies, 1982. 162 p.: bibl., ill. (Women in the Caribbean project, research papers. Phase I; 2)

One of a series of publications from a three-year study on the role of women in English-speaking Caribbean. Contains four papers written from different perspectives: anthropology, psychology, sociology, and demography, and dealing with the role of women within the family. For ethnologist's comment, see item **1149.**

COLOMBIA AND VENEZUELA

WILLIAM L. CANAK, *Assistant Professor of Sociology, Tulane University*

THANKS TO THE EFFORTS OF Colombian sociologists, the Colombian Sociological Assn. was reborn in 1979. In the past five years, this hard-working and talented body of Colombian scholars has reconfirmed the institutional vitality of the discipline. There have been several National Congresses (the third in 1980, the fourth in 1982, etc.) and a number of publications have been brought out under the aegis of the organization. A compilation of papers from the IV Congreso Nacional, held in Cali, is annotated below (item **8227**). Although intellectual life in Colombia has continued to be a turbulent environment, the National Univ. in Bogotá being closed for a good part of 1984, one can anticipate that this newly reorganized national association will provide an organization that may help stabilize the volatile environment.

For many years Colombian sociologists have been recognized for their superior research in areas of urban and rural sociology and Colombians have been at the intellectual forefront of the "action research" movement among Latin American social scientists. This heritage is well served by Colombian sociologists currently working in these fields. But perhaps most notable in recent years is the development of "Women's Studies" as an area in which Colombian sociology, represented by a well trained, insightful and productive group of women sociologists, has made a mark. Annotated below are three volumes of research by sociologists, mostly by Colombian women sociologists, which establish a real benchmark for Latin American studies in this field (item **8228**).

Venezuela continues to be strong in the area of demographic research. The Chi-Yi Chen and M. Picouet study noted below (item **8245**) is one of the most significant documents of population research yet produced in Latin America. Venezuelan sociology, historically, has produced many studies focusing on social values, electoral political behavior, and criminology. These continue to be strong areas of research in the nation, partly due to the institutional support available for such studies within the university system. In this, Venezuela contrasts with Colombia where much of the best research continues to take place in private research institutes often funded by foreign foundations and international agencies.

COLOMBIA

8221 Adelman, Alan H. Colombian friendship groups: constraints on a rural development acquisition system (JDA, 15:3, April 1981, p. 457–470, ill., table)

Based on secondary analysis. Examines varied impact of FEDERACAFE "friendship groups" on rural social relations, focusing on constraints imposed by the larger social system's institutions and policies. Also focuses on the micro level of "friendship group" organization and problem solving and concludes that they do not develop autonomous analytic abilities of members.

Ayala, Ulpiano. El empleo en las grandes ciudades colombianas. See item **3377.**

8222 ——— *et al.* La problemática urbana hoy en Colombia. Bogotá: Centro de Investigaciones y Educación Popular, 1982. 332, 6 p.: bibl., ill. (Serie Teoría y sociedad; 7)

Consists of 14 essays by Colombian sociologists on urban problems (e.g., social movements, the informal economy, housing and policy). Overall, essays give evidence of the sophistication and insight of Colombian urban studies.

8223 Bohman, Kristina. Women, resources and magic: a case-study from a Colombian "barrio" (SEM/E, 46:3/4, 1981, p. 230–262)

Based on a biographical case study, analyzes women's power from a control perspective with special attention to the use of magic in "efforts to control and influence events" in the family. Concludes that class status determines opportunities and resources in ways that lead poor women to adopt magic as a coping behavior.

8224 Bonilla de Ramos, Elssy. La madre trabajadora. Bogotá: Centro de Estudios sobre Desarrollo Económico, Facultad de Economía, Univ. de los Andes, 1981. 139 p.: bibl. (Documento; 066)

Policy evaluation research focuses on the Centros de Atención Integral al Prescolar (CIAP) begun in 1974 as part of the Instituto Colombiano de Bienestar Familiar (ICBF) and their impact on women, preschool children, and families. Also analyzes programs directly aimed at promoting women's interests. Based on a stratified (income) sample of Bogotá mothers participating in program at 15 centers.

8225 Browner, Carole and Ellen Lewin. Female altruism reconsidered: the Virgin Mary as economic woman (AES/AE, 9:1, Feb. 1982, p. 61–75, bibl.)

Comparative study of working-class women in Cali, Colombia, and San Francisco, US, based on ethnographic data. Concludes the wife-mother role complex is similar in each setting, while behavior differences are determined by economic and social resources available to women in each city.

8226 Carvallo, Gloria and Fernando Ramírez. The improvement of the situation of women and its impact on the welfare of children: case study based on a project in Cartagena, Colombia. New York: UNICEF Reginal Office for the Americas, 1980. 21 p., 4 leaves of plates: bibl., ill. (Working documents on programmes benefitting women. UNICEF/TARO/PM/80/6)

Case study of UNICEF-aided Cartagena project aimed at improving women's and children's welfare via schooling services, employment training, and creation of enterprises, improved housing, and hygiene.

Colombia 2000: estrategias de desarrollo para satisfacer las necesidades humanas esenciales en Colombia. See item **3387.**

8227 Congreso Nacional de Sociología, 4th, Bogotá, 1980. La sociedad colombiana y la investigación sociológica: memoria. Bogotá: Asociación Colombiana de Sociología: Depto. de Sociología, Univ. del Valle, 1983. 350 p.: appendix, bibl., ill. (Serie de memorias de eventos científicos colombianos, 0120–5009; 6)

Consists of 13 papers from the 1982 IV National Sociology Congress held in Cali and organized into sections on: 1) the Urban and Rural World; 2) Education and Society; 3) Knowledge, Communication, and Culture; 4) Women and Society. Contains appendix with documents related to the congress.

8228 Debate sobre la mujer en América Latina y el Caribe: discusión acerca de la unidad producción-reproducción. v. 1, La realidad colombiana. v. 2, Las trabajadoras del agro. v. 3, Sociedad subordinación y feminismo. Edición de Magdalena León de Leal. Bogotá: Asociación Colombiana para el Estudio de la Población, 1982. 3 v.: bibl., ill.

Important multi-volume work initiates series entitled *Debate on women in Latin America and the Caribbean*. Vol. 1 consists of 13 essays covering four topics: 1) the peasant economy and agribusiness; 2) production and reproduction of the urban labor force; 3) aspects of sexuality; and 4) ideology and politics. Vol. 1's introductory essay links content of all three volumes to broader movement in women's studies. Contributions by many of the best Latin American and North American scholars working in this field. Vol. 2 contains 18 essays on: 1) elements of a theoretical debate: subsistence, accumulation, and reproduction; 2) the peasant economy, agribusiness, sexual division of labor and subordination; 3) rural development, agrarian reform, and political planning. Like vol. 1, essential reading with many significant articles. Vol. 3 consists of 14 articles grouped in four subject areas: 1) paternalism and the family; 2) women and development; 3) capital, labor and women in urban contexts; and 4) feminist perspectives and struggles. In brief, a landmark multi-volume work which attests to the significant advances made in this area of scholarship in recent years.

8229 Deere, Carmen Diana and **Magdalena León de Leal.** Women in Andean agriculture: peasant production and rural wage employment in Colombia and Peru. Geneva: ILO, 1982. 172 p.: bibl., ill., maps (Women, work and development, 0253–2042; 4)

Based on data from three regions of Colombia and Peru, study traces the impact of the agrarian transition of women's work. Provides evidence of the diversity and range of women's work, their overall economic participation and family/community status. Data and conclusions counter recent census/demographic studies on the declining role of women in agriculture and document the egalitarian family farming system.

Fajardo, D. *et al.* Campesinado y capitalismo en Colombia. See item **3401.**

8230 Gómez J., Alcides and **Luz Marina Díaz Mesa.** La moderna esclavitud: los indocumentados en Venezuela. Bogotá: Fines: Editorial Oveja Negra, 1983. 348 p.: bibl., ill., maps, tables.

Important contribution to the literature on international labor migration within Latin America. Pt. 1 draws on a historical political-economic analysis and focuses on contemporary migration characteristics, including income, conditions of labor in Venezuela, and living conditions among Colombian migrants.

8231 Guzmán B., Alvaro. La acción comunal y los pobladores de Cali (Boletín de Coyuntura Socio-Económica [Univ. del Valle, Cali, Colombia] 8, sept. 1982, p. 1–29)

Historical analysis of the development of the "Communal Action" program in the "marginal (i.e., poor) neighborhoods of Cali. Concludes that in Cali there are objective possibilities for a State-initiated effective organization representing and organizing the interests of the popular classes. Theoretically informed and insightful preliminary evaluation of this type of program and contrasts with findings elsewhere in Latin America where State led programs are seen as only cooptive.

Izard, Miguel. Ni cuatreros ni montoneros: llaneros. See *HLAS 46:2642.*

8232 Marmora, Lelio. Características de la política de migraciones laborales en Colombia (Migraciones Internacionales en las Américas [Centro de Estudios de Migración, Centro de Estudios de Pastoral y Asistencia Migratoria, Caracas] 1:1, 1980, p. 89–111, bibl.)

Useful brief overview of the dominant migration streams within and from Colombia by the Minister of Labor and Social Security. As a summary of policy and an analysis of the sources of "expulsion," this work is valuable, but its analysis is limited.

8233 Osorio, Iván Darío; Luis H. Saldarriaga; and **Remberto Rhenals.** El sindicalismo antioqueño hoy (RAE, 7:3, 1982, p. 97–113, plates, tables)

Report based on the 1981 Census of labor organizations in three Colombian depts.: Antioquia, Caldas, and Risaralda. Contains detailed descriptive data and an analysis that related these organizations to national economic development. Substantial contribution to the literature on contemporary Colombian labor.

Palacios, Marco. La fragmentación regional de las clases dominantes en Colombia: una perspectiva histórica. See *HLAS 46:2905.*

8234 Parra Escobar, Ernesto. La investigación-acción en la Costa Atlántica:

evaluación de la Rosca, 1972–1974. Cali, Colombia: Fundación para la Comunicación Popular, 1982. 218 p.: bibl., ill.

Case study report of a participant "action investigation" that began in Córdoba in 1976 and was associated with peasant struggles for land and was principally linked to the Asociación Nacional de Usuarios Campesinos (ANUC). Good example of this type of action research which has numerous supporters in Colombia.

8235 Parra Sandoval, Rodrigo and Leonor Zubieta. Escuela, marginalidad y contextos sociales en Colombia (CPES/RPS, 19:54, mayo/agosto 1982, p. 21–34)

Based on two field studies in Colombia, one urban and one rural, this theoretical article discusses the socialization functions of formal educational institutions and the teacher-student relation in terms of: 1) relation between peasant and urban marginal communities and the larger national culture; and 2) internal relations of these communities.

8236 Rivera Cusicanqui, Silvia. Política e ideología en el movimiento campesino colombiano: el caso de la ANUC, Asociación Nacional de Usuarios Campesinos. Bogotá: CINEP; New York: UN Research Institute for Social Development, 1982. 188 p.: appendix, bibl. (Colombia agraria; 7)

Historical analysis of origins and political development of the ANUC. Organized in two parts: 1) chronological discussion of Colombian politics since 1930; and 2) chronological review of ANUC itself. Contains good appendix on bibliographic and archival sources. Good introduction to the subject.

8237 Rubbo, Anna and Michael Taussig. Up off their knees: servanthood in southwest Colombia (LAP, 10:4, 1983, p. 5–23, bibl.)

Insightful analysis of how female domestic service in the Cauca Valley of Colombia links the macro-structure of political life to the micro-structure of interpersonal relations and functions to reproduce social roles. Presents thoughtful approach to study changes in economic development structure, female income opportunities, and servanthood itself.

8238 Segura de Camacho, Nora. Reproducción social, familia y trabajo: Cali, historias de caso (Boletín de Coyuntura Socio-Económica [Univ. del Valle, Cali, Colombia] 8, sept. 1982, p. 30–67, charts)

Analysis of women's labor and family activity in Cali. Contains overview based on Colombian government data and detailed study of 17 cases (i.e., seven in the manufacturing, 10 in the service, eight in the formal, and nine in the informal sectors of the economy).

8239 Thornton, W. Philip. Resocialization: Roman Catholics becoming Protestants in Colombia, South America (CUA/AQ, 57:1, Jan. 1984, p. 28–37, bibl.)

Analysis of the resocialization process experienced by Colombian Roman Catholics who join Protestant sects. Focuses on the following aspects: 1) joining; 2) staying; and 3) leaving.

8240 Zamosc, León. Los usuarios campesinos y las luchas por la tierra en los años 70. Bogotá: Centro de Investigación y Educación Popular; New York: UN Research Institute for Social Development, 1982? 307 p.: appendices, bibl. (Colombia agraria; 8)

Another (see item **8236**) close analysis of ANUC. Focuses on its relation to the State, its internal transformations and impact on Colombian society since its origins in 1967. Impressive study of reformist policies and evolution of a movement. Appendices include: data on peasant land invasions 1971–78 and extensive bibliography and review of primary sources.

VENEZUELA

8241 Ayerra, Jacinto. Los Protestantes en Venezuela: quiénes son, qué hacen. Caracas: Ediciones Trípode, 1980. 299 p.: bibl. (Iglesia y sociedad; 14)

Brief descriptions of Venezuelan Protestant groups includes analysis of organization and strategies. Useful introduction to topic written from a Roman Catholic viewpoint.

8242 Brigé Pinedo, Lucía; Norma González de Piñango; and Rosalind Greaves de Pulido. Estadísticas sociales: información comparativa. Caracas: Despacho de la Ministro de Estado para la Participación de la Mujer en el Desarrollo, 1983. 2 v.: bibl., tables.

Two volumes of useful background statistical information designed to address the needs of planners and researchers. Draws on a variety of data sources (censuses, national housing surveys, national fertility survey, government reports) to provide information on employment, education, health, and participation in politics and labor organizations, all of it (relate to the study of family and women in Venezuela).

8243 Carrera Damas, Felipe. La pareja sexual venezolana. Caracas: Ediciones ANAFESI, 1983. 227 p.

Based on 1983 sample of 1,306 males, 1,248 females, and 1,625 couples, this study reports survey findings on sexual values and behavior. First Venezuelan national survey on this topic and presents important benchmark data for future research.

8244 Chen, Chi-Yi *et al.* Dinámica de la población: caso de Venezuela. Caracas: Univ. Católica Andrés Bello: ORSTOM, 1979. 735 p.: bibl., ill., indexes, col. maps.

A major work. The most comprehensive and extensive demographic study of Venezuela available. An essential document for anyone studying Venezuela. An exemplar for demographers working elsewhere.

8245 ———— and Michel Picouet. Migración internacional en Venezuela: evolución y características socio-demográficas (Migraciones Internacionales en las Américas [Centro de Estudios de Migración, Centro de Estudios de Pastoral y Asistencia Migratorias, Caracas] 1:1, 1980, p. 41–62, bibl., graphs, tables)

Succinct descriptive summary of Venezuela immigration patterns since 1940s. Two primary migration streams are analyzed: European and Colombian. Also discusses immigration from the Pacific and Caribbean regions. Contains base line data on socioeconomic and demographic characteristics of Venezuelan immigrants.

Jongkind, Fred. Venezuelan industrialization, dependent or autonomous?: a survey of national and foreign participation in the industrial development of a Latin American OPEC country. See *HLAS 46:2925.*

8246 Marta Sosa, Joaquín. Venezuela: elecciones y transformación social. Caracas: Ediciones Centauro, 1984. 483 p.: bibl., ill.

Important study of democratic electoral politics that hypothesizes how electoral politics serve to perpetuate and legitimate existing institutional structures and hegemony. Analysis focuses on contemporary Venezuela, especially 1978. Useful bibliography.

8247 Ramírez, Erasmo. Aspectos demográficos de la región de los Andes. Mérida, Venezuela: Univ. de los Andes, Facultad de Economía, Instituto de Investigaciones Económicas, 1979. 81 leaves: bibl., ill.

Historical demographic data (1936–75) covers population distribution, composition, and related political-economic descriptive statistics for the Andean region of Venezuela. Includes some time-series breakdowns by region, state, and nation.

8248 Recagno-Puente, Ileana. Hábitos de crianza y marginalidad. Caracas: Facultad de Humanidades y Educación, Univ. Central de Venezuela, 1982. 286 p.: ill.

Based on sample of 101 mothers in Caracas and using a control group, this survey focuses on effects of family and socialization patterns on children's (ages 1–6) intellectual development. Concludes that mothers who introduce childcare principles modify their children's behavior, especially educational and social problem behavior.

8249 Rofman, Alejandro. Revisión crítica de la política de desconcentración espacial de la economía (CPES/RPS, 16:46, sept./dic. 1979, p. 25–47, tables)

Policy evaluation study of Venezuelan government actions aimed at alleviating spatial concentration of population and industry. Valuable description and analysis of policy's structure, implementation, and sociopolitical outcomes.

8250 Roseberry, William. Coffee and capitalism in the Venezuelan Andes. Austin: Univ. of Texas Press, 1983. 256 p.: bibl., ill., index (Latin American monographs; 59)

Important contribution to rural sociology and peasant studies that is based on fieldwork (1974–76) in a Venezuelan coffee-producing region. Presents social, economic, and political history of the area with special attention to the formation and transformation of a property-owning, commodity-producing peasantry.

8251 Sassen-Koob, Saskia. Crecimiento económico e inmigración en Venezuela (Migraciones Internacionales en las Américas [Centro de Estudios de Migración, Centro de Estudios de Pastoral y Asistencia Migratoria, Caracas] 1 : 1, 1980, p. 63–87, bibl., tables)

Excellent analysis of political, economic, and social contexts affecting Venezuelan immigration and emigration policies

since 1940s, with emphasis on 1970s, Colombian immigrants, and related policies.

8252 Serbin, Andrés. Estado, indigenismo e indianidad en Venezuela, 1946–1979 (CEDLA/B, 34, junio 1983, p. 17–40, bibl.)

Description and analysis of development of an Indian (original native population of Venezuela) ideology (1946–79) of State policy in this period, and finally the development of ethnic identity and social movement.

ECUADOR AND PERU

DENNIS GILBERT, *Associate Professor, Department of Rural Sociology, Cornell University*
BARBARA DEUTSCH LYNCH, *Assistant Coordinator, Water Management Synthesis II Project, Cornell University*
PATRICIA GARRETT, *Associate Professor, Department of Rural Sociology, Cornell University*

IN BOTH PERU AND ECUADOR, the capitalist penetration of rural society has been a central focus of social research. Closely related concerns are the modernization of the latifundio, agrarian reform, the differentiation of peasant communities and the proletarianization of the rural labor force. These themes are broadly treated in the FLACSO collection (item **8256**) and Guerrero's article (item **8261**) for Ecuador and in Sánchez's (item **8295**) and Montoya's (item **8286**) for Peru. Mallon (item **8284**), in a subtle and pathbreaking work, treats capitalist expansion from the perspective of the peasant community. The unit of analysis for recent studies of the Sierra has shifted away from the commuity to the household (item **8288**) and to social and economic networks within a regional context (items **8281** and **8284**).

Much of the Peruvian literature reviewed here attempts to come to terms with the revolution of the early 1970s. Gorman's (item **8293**) collection is broadest effort to define the long-term significance of the transformation. Becker (item **8266**) presents an especially radical interpretation, arguing that relations among the State, foreign enterprise, and the bourgeoisie were fundamentally altered. (For a more skeptical interpretation, see Dennis Gilbert's "The End of the Peruvian Revolution: a Class Analysis," in *Studies in Comparative International Development*, 15 : 1, 1980, p. 15–38). Several authors focus on the agrarian reform. Caballero (item **8268**), McClintock (item **8283**), and Petras and Havens (item **8291**) treat the contradictions in agrarian cooperative policy and the problems of post-reform agricultural production.

The role of women has been receiving increased research attention throughout Latin America. The economic role and position of Peruvian women have been discussed in recent contributions ranging from Wilson's (item **8298**) treatment of elite women as managers of family estates to studies of the economic contribution of peasant women (items **8272** and **8294**). Of particular interest is the collection of autobiographical accounts published by the Cuzco Domestic Workers' Union (Sindicato de Trabajadores del Hogar; see item **8296a**).

The growth and politics of urban shanty towns, a traditional staple of Peruvian studies, continues to attract research interest. However, the urban informal sector, employer of much of the shanty-town population, has still not received the attention it merits (in contrast to the many detailed studies of the peasant economy). Another *lacuna* for both countries is the study of contemporary social movements.

ECUADOR

8253 Barsky, Osvaldo. Acumulación campesina en el Ecuador: los productores de Papa del Carchi. Quito: FLACSO, 1984. 136 p.: bibl., tables (Col. Investigaciones; 1)

Important theoretical and empirical analysis of capital accumulation by small holders. Emphasizes economic, political, and technological context of differentiation in one country, combining historical interpretation with the analysis of agricultural census and survey data. Illustrative of one position in the contemporary Ecuadorian debate concerning class formation in agricultural sector.

8254 Belote, Linda Smith and **Jim Belote.** Drain from the bottom: individual ethnic identity change in southern Ecuador (SF, 63:1, Sept. 1984, p. 24–50, table)

Fascinating analysis based on episodic field research during 20 years. Analyzes transculturation among poor Indians and whites in Saraguro, where changes in ethnic identity require neither geographic mobility nor deceit.

8255 Carrasco A., Eulalia. Salasaca: la organización social y el alcalde. Ilustraciones de Segundo Obando. S.l.: Mundo Andino, 1982. 135 p.: ill.

Competent bachelor's thesis based on secondary data and limited field research.

Chiriboga, Manuel *et al.* Ecuador agrario: ensayos de interpretación. See item **3433.**

8256 Ecuador: cambios en el agro serrano. Introducción, Miguel Murmis. Quito: FLACSO: Centro de Planificación y Estudios Sociales (CEPLAES), 1980. 531 p.: bibl., tables.

Landmark collection inspired by Marxist theory and informed by historical analysis. Brilliant introduction by Miguel Murmis of the development of capitalism in highland estates. Original studies by young intellectuals cover several regions and policies, notably agrarian reform. Updates "Transformaciones Agrarias en el Altiplano Andino"

(special issue of *Revista Ciencias Sociales,* 11:5, 1978).

8257 Espinosa Tamayo, Alfredo. Psicología y sociología del pueblo ecuatoriano. Estudio introductorio, Arturo Andrés Roig. Quito: Banco Central del Ecuador: Corporación Editora Nacional, 1979. 363 p.: bibl. (Biblioteca básica del pensamiento ecuatoriano; 2)

Important book for intellectual historians. New edition of 1918 essay by Espinosa Tamayo, plus lengthy introduction by Roig.

8258 El Estado y la economía: políticas económicas y clases sociales en el Ecuador y América Latina. Introducción y compilación de Lucas Pacheco. Cristian Sepúlveda *et al.* Quito: Instituto de Investigaciones Económicas, Pontificia Univ. Católica del Ecuador (PUCE), 1983. 443 p.: bibl.

Collection of articles, covering 1960–82, predominantly critical of status quo. Likely to be of historical interest, since such critiques have come late to Ecuador.

8259 Estructuras agrarias y reproducción campesina: lecturas sobre transformaciones capitalistas en el agro ecuatoriano. Edición de Cristian Sepúlveda. Quito: Pontificia Univ. Católica del Ecuador (PUCE), 1982. 295 p.: ill., tables.

Interesting analyses developed at the Instituto. Initial articles largely theoretical; final selections more empirical. Noteworthy important study of artisan/agricultural activities in Otavalo by Meier. For economist's comment, see item **3438.**

8260 Farrell, Gilda and **Sara da Ross.** El acceso a la tierra del campesino ecuatoriano. Ilustraciones de Tonino Clemente. S.l.: Mundo Andino; s.l.: Fundación Ecuatoriana Populorum Progressio, 1983. 132 p.: ill.

Useful summary of agricultural census data by major regions. Minimal analysis supports structuralist analysis of why reform is needed.

8261 Guerrero, Andrés. La producción del productor: conversaciones entre C.

Meillassoux y A. Guerrero (CLACSO/ERL, 2:2, 1979, p. 157–172)

Accessible introduction to the ideas of an influential theorist and educator.

8262 Martínez, Luciano. De campesinos a proletarios: cambios en la mano de obra rural en la Sierra Central del Ecuador. Quito: Editorial El Conejo, 1984. 200 p.: maps, tables.

Major analysis of how changes in large farm sector affect proletarianization. Theoretical analysis reflects contemporary literature; historical framework derives partially from archival research; case studies selected contrasting regions of Cotopaxi. Lucid conclusions.

8263 Naranjo, Marcelo Fernando. Etnicidad, estructura social y poder en Manta, occidente ecuatoriano. Otavalo, Ecuador: Instituto Otavaleño de Antropología, 198? 329 p.: ill. (Col. Pendoneros; 36. Serie Antropología social)

Revised dissertation in urban anthropology focusing on seaport of one coastal province. Applies predominantly North American concerns to Ecuadorian case study.

8264 Santana, Roberto. Campesinado indígena y el desafío de la modernidad. Quito: Centro Andino de Acción Popular, 1983. 209 p.: bibl., ill. (Cuaderno de discusión popular; 7)

Strong argument in favor of the primacy of ethnicity over other bases for social change and mobilization. Informed critique of many private and publicly financed development programs, from the old Mission Andino to the contemporary Integrated Rural Development Projects. Well researched but poorly organized and written.

PERU

8266 Becker, David G. The new bourgeoisie and the limits of dependency: mining, class, and power in "revolutionary" Peru. Princeton, N.J.: Princeton Univ. Press, 1983. 419 p.: bibl., index.

Unorthodox interpretation of early 1970s based on close examination of mining sector. Concludes that revolution modernized the State, the bourgeoisie, the middle class, and modern-sector working class, while creating new foundations for liberal democracy. The modern transnational corporation gets much of the credit for this transformation.

Bedoya Garland, Eduardo. Ocupaciones de tierras en el fundo Saipai: antecedentes e historia del movimiento. See *HLAS 46:2956.*

8267 Bradby, Barbara. "Resistance to capitalism" in the Peruvian Andes (*in* Ecology and exchange in the Andes [see item 1400] p. 97–122, bibl.)

Looks at community organization and exchange relationships between communities in different vertical zones. Upending earlier assumptions, suggests the money use does not necessarily signify capitalist penetration and that intercommunal exchange may be an indicator of the breakdown of direct community control of resources from different altitudinal zones.

Brass, Tom. Class formation and class struggle in La Convención, Perú. See *HLAS 46:2963.*

8268 Caballero, José María. Agricultura, reforma agraria y pobreza campesina. Lima: Instituto de Estudios Peruanos, 1980. 158 p.: bibl. (Col. Mínima; 6)

Stresses inherent contradictions between economic and social goals of the reform and outlines partisan approaches to agricultural issues. Four general essays on the agrarian reform and peasantry in the national economy.

8269 Cathelat, Marie-France and **Teresa Burga.** Perfil de la mujer peruana, 1980–1981. Lima?: Investigaciones Sociales Artísticas; Lima: Fondo del Libro del Banco Industrial del Perú, 1981? 340 p.: bibl., ill.

Comprehensive survey of middle-class women (ages 25–29) in metropolitan Lima. Ranges from anthropometric/clinical matters to fertility behavior and attitudes on diverse topics. Long on data, short on interpretation.

8270 Congreso de Investigación acerca de la Mujer en la Región Andina, Lima, *1982.* Informe final. Auspició, Univ. Católica del Perú, AMIDEP. Edición de Jeanine Anderson de Velasco. Lima: Asociación Perú-Mujer, 1983. 205 p.

Informative collection of very short summaries. Conference participants were disproportionately South Americans with identifiable North American connections. Papers reflect fundamentally feminist perspectives lacking class analysis.

8271 Cotler, Julio. Clases, estado y nación en el Perú. 2a ed. México: UNAM, Instituto de Investigaciones Sociales, 1982. 339 p.: ill.

Interpretive history of Peru from the conquest to 1968, seeking the roots of the crisis of the old order that culminated in Gen. Velasco's coup. Emphasizes the dependent context of Peruvian history, relative weakness of propertied classes, and uneven development of Peruvian society.

8272 Deere, Darmen Diana and **Alain de Janvry.** Demographic and social differentiation among northern Peruvian peasants (JPS, 8:3, Apri1 1981, p. 335–366, bibl., graphs, tables)

Deere finds that Peruvian census data underestimates women's agricultural participation and that women's participation in agricultural labor and decision making is greatest in poor households. In these households agriculture is a family activity making a relatively minor contribution to the total subsistence strategy.

——— and **Magdalena León Leal.** Women in Andean agriculture: peasant production and rural wage employment in Colombia and Peru. See item **8229.**

8273 Dietz, Henry A. Poverty and problem-solving under military rule: the urban poor in Lima, Peru. Austin: Univ. of Texas Press, 1980. 286 p.: bibl., ill., index (Latin American monographs; 51)

Study of relationship between the Velasco government and urban poor in six neighborhoods in and around Lima. Analyzes meaning of political participation by the poor as an extension of authoritarian government policy, using long open-ended survey instruments to elicit perceptions of government programs by urban poor and to examine their behavior and survival mechanisms.

8274 Fernández de la Gala, Angel; José Vélez Castellanos; and **Germán Torre Villafañe.** Crisis y modalidades de reestructuración en las cooperativas agrarias no azucareras: informe preliminar. Chiclayo, Perú: Centro de Estudios Sociales Solidaridad, 1982. 69 p.: bibl., ill.

Survey of non-sugar agrarian cooperatives formed during 1969 reform, covering technical, financial, and human aspects of their operations. Examines issues of individual parcels within cooperatives, use of seasonal workers, administrative control, and parcelization. Rich in data on cooperatives and quotations from *campesinos.*

8275 Ferner, Anthony. La burguesía industrial en el desarrollo peruano. Traducción, Luz María Fort de Acha. Lima: Editorial ESAN, 1982. 293 p.: bibl.

Reactions of different sectors of the industrial bourgeoisie to economic development model promoted by the Velasco regime. Based on interviews with industrialists and analyses of positions taken by empresarial organizations.

Gilbert, Dennis. Cognatic descent groups in upper-class Lima, Peru. See *HLAS 46:2975.*

8276 González, José Luis and **Teresa María van Ronzelen.** Religiosidad popular en el Perú: bibliografía: antropología, historia, sociología y pastoral. Lima: Centro de Estudios y Publicaciones, 1983. 375 p.: ill.

Annotated bibliography of Spanish, French, and English langauge works on religions and popular religious institutions and beliefs, arranged by theme and cross referenced by department.

Langton, Kenneth P. The influence of military service on social consciousness and protest behavior: a study of Peruvian mine workers. See item **6432.**

8277 Lausent, Isabelle. Pequeña propiedad, poder y economía de mercado: Acos, Valle de Chancay. Lima: Instituto de Estudios Peruanos, 1983. 424 p.: figures, maps, tables (Estudios etnológicos del Valle de Chancay; 7)

Community study focused on changing land tenure and power relationships which accompany a shift in production from livestock to alfalfa and later to commercial fruit production. Although means of production are becoming concentrated in the hands of small merchants who control marketing, small holders from "legitimate families" maintain a conservative ideology, respectful of private property.

8278 Lima: una metrópoli, 7 debates. Edición de Abelardo Sánchez León y Luis Olivera C. Julio Calderón et al. Lima: DESCO, 1983. 274 p.: bibl., maps.

Seven papers and critical commentaries by social scientists and city planners from 1983 conference on problems of metropolitan Lima, sponsored by DESCO. Topics covered: growth of metropolitian Lima, employment in informal sector, water, transportation, housing, city administration, and popular participation in local government. For economist's comment, see item **3595.**

8279 Lloyd, Peter Cutt. The "young towns" of Lima: aspects of urbanization in Peru. Cambridge, England: Cambridge Univ. Press, 1980. 160 p.: bibl., index, maps (Urbanization in developing countries)

General introduction to Lima shantytowns, centered on a case study of Medalla Milagrosa, a relatively small, older (1961) barriada near Magdalena del Mar. Covers work, family life, community organization, relationship to larger metropolis, and meaning of marginality.

8280 Lobo, Susan B. A house of my own: social organization in the squatter settlements of Lima, Peru. Tucson: Univ. of Arizona Press, 1982. 190 p.: bibl., ill., maps.

Examines how kinship and preexisting community ties create social patterns in the lives of residents of two *pueblos jóvenes* near Callao. Using an ethnographic approach to the study of these new settlements, focuses on residence patterns, value systems, and social structure and finds an extremely high level of social density coupled with positive adaptation to urban life.

8281 Long, Norman and **Bryan Roberts.** Miners, peasants, and entrepreneurs: regional development in the central highlands of Peru. Cambridge, England: Cambridge Univ. Press, 1984. 288 p.: bibl., index (Cambridge Latin American studies; 48)

Important and thorough study of the relationship between mining activities and village economy and society in Junín. Uses a regional framework to show systematic relationships between different economic sectors and social classes and to explain how peripheral regions survive when faced with increasing centralization. Themes include impact of mining on village class relations, migration, development of informal sector, roles of regional associations, and rural-urban household linkages.

8282 Lusk, Mark W. Peuvian higher education in an environment of develop-

ment and revolution. Logan: Utah State Univ., Dept. of Sociology, 1984. 1 v. (Research monograph; 1)

Provides unique examination of crisis confronting Peruvian universities resulting from the rapid expansion of the student body, politicization of faculty and students, and evaporation of financial resources for education.

8283 McClintock, Cynthia. Peasant cooperatives and political change in Peru. Princeton, N.J.: Princeton Univ. Press, 1981. 418 p.: bibl., ill., index.

On basis of attitudinal surveys conducted at five sites on north coast and Junín, concludes that Velasco's self-management policies have produced "group egoism"— political commitment which does not extend beyond the enterprise.

8284 Mallon, Florencia. The defense of community in Peru's central highlands: peasant struggle and capitalist transition, 1860–1940. Princeton, N.J.: Princeton Univ. Press, 1983. 384 p.: maps.

Mallon presents an illuminating analysis of shifting institutional forms of *comunidad* which accompany the development of export mining and the emergence of capitalist class relations within agricultural villages. Focus is on changing class relations in four communities in Junín in relation to development, internationalization, and depression in mining sector.

8285 Martínez, Héctor. Los estudios acerca de la migración y ocupación selvática peruana (CAAAP/AP, 5:9, julio 1983, p. 7–12, bibl.)

Review of the demographic statistics of Amazonian Peru in contrast to the rest of Peru to characterize process of occupation. [W.H. Kracke]

8286 Montoya, Rodrigo. Class relations in the Andean countryside (LAP, 9[34]:3, Summer 1982, p. 62–78, bibl.)

After a century of capitalist penetration of the Peruvian sierra and transition to an economy based on relationships of exchange, Montoya argues, Peru has become transformed into a bourgeois state. Finds increasing association of rural wealth with commercial activity, a tendency toward small holding and semi-proletarianization of the peasantry, consolidation and growth of an agrarian petit bourgeoisie, and subordination of small holdings to capital.

8287 Movimiento de pobladores y lucha de clases: balance y perspectivas. Lima?: Círculo de Estudios Alejandro Quijano, 1982. 89 p.: bibl., ill.

History of *barrio* movements (1945–82) written by leftist activitists.

8288 Orlove, Benjamin S.and Glynn Custred. The alternative model of agrarian society in the Andes: households, networks, and corporate groups (*in* Land and power in Latin America: agrarian economies and social processes in the Andes. Edited by Benjamin S. Orlove and Glynn Custred. New York: Holmes & Meier Publishers, 1980, p. 31–54)

Introductory chapters present new framework for analysis of Andean rural societies based on the household and develops framework for study of interhousehold ties in the form of network or corporate groups. Other chapters treat interactions of ideology and peasant reality over time, patterns of class differentiation, and the nature of various interhousehold networks.

8289 Participación económica y social de la mujer peruana. Lima: UNICEF, 1981. 388 p.: bibl., ill.

Analyzes value of women's work in agriculture and cottage textile industry and evaluates impacts on women of integrated service programs supported by UNICEF in Puno and in *pueblos jóvenes* in metropolitan Lima. Recommends reexamination of women's productive roles, end to discrimination in extension programs, and participation of women in development of programs designed to serve them.

8290 Peirano Falconi, Luis and **Tokihiro Kudó.** La investigación en comunicación social en el Perú. Lima: DESCO, 1982. 182 p.: indexes (Serie Estudios)

Thoughtfully annotated bibliography of the mass media in Peru containing approximately 500 items. Usefully indexed.

8291 Petras, James and **Eugene Havens.** Comportamiento campesino y cambio social en Perú: cooperativas y tenencia individual de la tierra (CLACSO/ERL, 4:2, mayo/agosto 1981, p. 165–179, bibl., tables)

Petras and Havens evaluate peasant support for the dissolution of agricultural co-

operatives created by 1970s' agrarian reform. They conclude that member opposition to cooperatives is economically rational behavior, but that decentralization of cooperative management, rather than atomization of peasant holdings, is the most promising solution to Peruvian agrarian problem.

8292 Plaza J., Orlando and **Marfil Francke.** Formas de dominio, economía y comunidades campesinas. Lima: DESCO, 1981. 127 p.: bibl. (Serie Estudios)

Study's objective is to provide a theoretically coherent perspective on the community of Peruvian rural development programs. Authors review peasant community literature, discuss communal organization and communal-household dialectic, and recommend development of methods for intercommunal cooperation based on peasant family needs.

8293 Post-revolutionary Peru: the politics of transformation. Edited by Stephen M. Gorman. Boulder, Colo.: Westview Press, 1982. 25 p. (Westview special studies on Latin America and the Caribbean)

Policies of Velasco and Morales Bermúdez governments and the future of Peruvian society. Authors examine intellectual foundations of the Velasco revolution, 1980 transition to civilian rule, party politics, the economy, agriculture, social property, foreign policy, military affairs, urban poor, and organized labor.

8294 Rubín de Celis T., Emma; Blanca Fernández Montenegro; and **Luisa Guarnizo de Erazo.** Rol económico de la mujer campesina: informe final del proyecto de investigación y promoción "Rol de la Mujer Campesina en el Desarrollo Económico," apoyado por CIPCA. Piura, Perú: CIPCA, Depto. de Publicaciones, 1982. 210 p.: bibl., map.

Participant observation, unstructured interview and survey data from Piura agricultural community are used to determine economic activities of peasant women, needs of the peasant family, and how women help to meet these needs. Rubín emphasizes central role of women in the articulation of capitalist and non-capitalist systems of relations of production, the problem of sociosexual domination.

8295 Sánchez, Rodrigo. The Andean economic system and capitalism (*in* Ecology and exchange in the Andes [see item **1400**] p. 157–190, map, tables]

Author argues that peasant economic relationships in parts of the Peruvian Andes cannot be considered apart from the capitalist mode of production, and that Andean peasant activities are consistent with logic of the capitalist system within which they are integrated. Andahuaylas economic data show proletarianization of peasants as wage laborers, intensification of family production, and differentiation among peasant strata.

8296 La Selva y su ley: caso, lavadores de oro. Sicuani, Perú: Comité de Defensa de los Derechos Humanos de las Provincias Altas, 1983. 128 p.: ill.

Vivid description of working and living conditions of migrant gold washers in the selva of Canchis prov., Madrid de Díos. Considers reasons for migration and critically examines *enganche* system and living conditions of migrants.

8296a Sindicato de Trabajadoras del Hogar, *Cusco.* Basta, testimonios. Cusco: Centro de Estudios Rurales Andinos Bartolomé de las Casas, 1982. 154 p.: ill. (Biblioteca de la tradición oral andina; 4)

Transcribed biographical statements by members of the Cusco Syndicate of Domestic Workers cover transition from rural to urban life, conditions of recruitment and employment, consciousness raising and role of union's importance and its organizer, Egidia

Laime Jancco. They provide a vivid portrayal of the ideological, physical, and psychological pressures faced by maids in isolation and the role of this sector and the union in the class struggle.

8297 Verdera, Francisco. El empleo en el Perú: un nuevo enfoque. Lima: Instituto de Estudios Peruanos, 1983. 158 p.: tables.

Critical examination of employment concepts and statistics. Finds category of "underemployment" (*subempleo*), as currently defined, empirically and conceptually misleading.

8298 Wilson, Fiona. Marriage, poverty, and the position of women in the Peruvian Central Andes (*in* Kinship, ideology and practice in Latin America [see item **259**] p. 297–325, bibl.)

Analysis of gender and property in 19th-century Tarma elites based on study of wills and contracts. Concludes that the fundamental gender inequality in benefits derived from land ownership enabled families to reproduce themselves socially; that widows exerted enhanced control over property and spent their income on children rather than investing in productive activities; and that capitalist development in the *montaña* circumscribed women's opportunities for entrepreneurship. For ethnologist's comment, see item **1514**.

BOLIVIA AND PARAGUAY

KEVIN J. HEALY, *Foundation Representative, Inter-American Foundation, Rosslyn, Virginia*

THE STEADY STREAM OF SOCIOLOGICAL literature in Bolivia during 1984 was a remarkable development in view of the country's unprecedented economic crises. An official inflation rate of 2800 percent and constant currency devaluations made imported paper both scarce and costly. These changes presented great obstacles to publishing houses and their readership alike. Nonetheless, the Centro de Estudios de la Realidad Económica y Social (CERES) forged ahead to increase its output with the addition of several important works. And despite the crises, another important social science publishing group emerged in Bolivia, the Instituto de Historia Social Boliviana (HISBOL).

Several works by Albó and Barnadas (item **8300**), Calderón and Dandler (item **8304**), and Rivera (item **8312**) mark the emergence of an updated body of literature on the Bolivian agrarian reform and peasant syndicate movement. It includes fascinating and compelling new interpretations. This literature gives a more recent, revised, and refined view of the evolution of the peasant syndicates which have resumed their political role as a national pressure group in the new democratic order. There is also a set of works on Bolivia's agrarian structure (items **8301, 8307, 8311,** and **8313**) which contributes new levels of understanding to the rural social systems, especially in the Dept. of Santa Cruz.

Two recent books by CERES (items **8302** and **8303**) shed light on the small farmers in the Chapare region, a major center of coca-leaf production which has experienced increasingly rapid expansion of production as a result of the growth in cocaine consumption in the US.

In Paraguay the theme of rural colonization continues to hold a prominent place in sociological studies (items **8315, 8316,** and **8320**). This thematic rubric is broad given the diversity of institutional patterns associated with colonization. Colonization in this context encompasses subjects that range from commonplace small-farmer resettlement and reproduction of the subsistence economy to the actions of Brazilian enterprises and farmers in Paraguayan territory. Another important reference book provides a quantitative and comprehensive national view of the distribution of land and land-tenancy patterns that make up today's agrarian structure. This work includes especially important detail on ethnic minority groups subject to the worst discrimination and exploitation among Paraguay's rural population (see item **8319**).

BOLIVIA

8299 Aguiló, Federico. Religiosidad de un mundo rural en proceso de cambio: estudio socio-antropológico del proceso de cambio en la religiosidad del campesino de Potosí, Chuquisaca y Tarija. Sucre, Bolivia: Talleres Gráficas Q'ori Llama, 1981. 235 p.: bibl.

Study by Spanish Jesuit of religious values and attitudes found among sample of campesinos from 66 communities in the three southern depts. of Chuquisaca, Potosí, and Tarija. Author uses anthropological rather than survey techniques to obtain his data. Examines interaction between religious and secular change, religious attitudes toward fatalism and ethical responsibility, impact of external world upon religious values of Quechua-speakers, and various forms of religious imagery and content found in this area of rural Bolivia. Epilogue section contains excerpts from extensive interviews with campesino interviewees.

8300 Albó, Xavier and **Josep M. Barnabas.** La cara campesina de nuestra historia. La Paz: UNITAS, 1985. 306 p.: ill.

"Revisionist" view of Bolivian history from the standpoint of campesino protagonists. Rich and lucid interpretation and

overview of the campesino and rural syndicate's road to Bolivia's contemporary political platform. Written to serve as a pedagogical instrument for work in political education with peasant syndicates.

8301 Ambaná, tierras y hombres: Provincia de Camacho, Departamento de La Paz, Bolivia. Lima: Instituto Francés de Estudios Andinos (IFEA), Comité Nacional de Bolivia, Programa El Hombre y la Biósfera (MAB), 1980. 249 p.: bibl., ill., plates. 249 p. (Travaux de l'IFEA; 21 : 1)

Superb socioeconomic profile of Ambaná region in the La Paz dept., prov. of Camacho. Done by multidisciplinary team. Covers ethnohistory, ecology, land tenure, migration, social structure, agricultural production, and animal husbandry. Demonstrates potential of this type of study which can be extremely useful for non-government and government development programs in this zone.

Arze, José Roberto. Algunos antecedentes ideológicos de la cuestión agraria. See item **1419.**

8302 Blanes, José. De los valles al Chaparé: estrategias familiares en un contexto de cambios. Cochabamba, Bolivia: CERES, 1983. 191 p.: bibl., ill., maps (Serie Cochabamba; 4)

Discusses various social and economic facets of the household during the process of colonization and settlement in the Chaparé region. Examines family survival strategy as a work unit, its market participation, women's economic role and income levels. First mini-book in CERES's monographic series on the Chaparé.

——. Desarrollo económico y sectores sociales en Bolivia: análisis de algunos aspectos estructurales. See item **3626.**

8303 —— and **Gonzalo Flores.** ¿Dónde va el Chaparé? Cochabamba, Bolivia: CERES, 1984. 273 p.

Second work in CERES mini-series (see item **8302**) to examine the colonization and resettlement process by highland families in the tropical Chaparé region. Principal focus is on the "coca boom" and numerous and rapid social and economic changes set in motion. Provides a fascinating development analysis of the consequences of this peculiar form of "dependent development."

8304 Bolivia: la fuerza histórica del campesinado: movimientos campesinos y etnicidad. Fernando Calderón y Jorge Dandler, comps. Geneva: UN Research Institute for Social Development (UNRISD); La Paz: CERES, 1984. 625 p.: ill. (Report. UNRISD; 84.1. Serie Movimientos sociales. CERES; 2)

Important series of articles which brings together recent major research on the Bolivian peasant movement covering the period between the origins of 1952 agrarian mobilization and early 1980s. First major work of the new literature to emerge after the publication of various books documenting the 1952 agrarian changes. Includes Bolivia's foremost writers on recent agrarian change.

8305 Calderón G., Fernando. Conflicto y políticas urbanas en Bolivia en el contexto de las relaciones clase-Estado, 1952–1976 (CPES/RPS, 18:51, junio/sept. 1981, p. 43–58)

Discusses various dimensions of Bolivia's "urban crisis" during 1952–71. Presents an urban view of the sequence of urban reforms and popular pressures resulting from State policy that began with the 1952 revolution. Concludes that capital accumulation in urban sectors has failed to satisfy the majority of the population's basic consumption and job opportunity needs.

8306 —— and **Gonzalo Flores Céspedes.** Urbanización y desarrollo: necesidades básicas en áreas periféricas. Tarija, Bolivia: UNICEF, 1981. 96 p.: bibl. (Serie Documentos; 2)

Through a survey of residents in La Paz's peripheral urban settlements, authors present broad-ranging conclusions on sociodemographic characteristics, economic activity, level of living, adequacy of services, effectiveness of public agencies. Conclude with recommendations to alleviate shortcomings of public policy towards urban marginality in Latin America. [L. Pérez]

Canelas Orellana, Amado and **Juan Carlos Canelas Zannier.** Bolivia: coca, cocaína, subdesarrollo y poder político. See item **3630.**

8307 Eckstein, Susan. El capitalismo mundial y la revolución agraria en Bolivia (UNAM/RMS, 41, 1979, p. 457–478)

Analysis of the Bolivian agrarian reform's impact on agricultural sectors. Indicates an increased dependency on world markets for agricultural commodities as well as State and international support for an emerging privileged class of commercial farmers. This development exacerbated regressive income distribution patterns and higher discriminatory policies concerning the consumption and production needs of the rural majority located in the highlands. Stresses importance of international and national, political and economic variables in analytical framework and tests theoretical propositions from Wallerstein and Gunder Frank.

8308 Eddy de Arellano, Bambi. Integrating women into rural cooperatives: pluses and minuses (in Latin American woman: the meek speak out. Edited by June H. Turner. Silver Spring, Md.: International Educational Development, 1980, p. 112–122, plate)

Balanced overview of the Bolivian government's National Community Development Services Agency program in rural Bolivia in terms of women's participation. A professional administrator of this program, the author gives her personal assessment of its flaws and positive features. Concludes that "team approaches" in rural development programs which incorporate men and women together are more effective and that programs with foreign governmental funding which expand too fast can undermine women's participation in decision-making.

8309 Iriarte, Gregorio. Los mineros: sus luchas, frustraciones y esperanzas. La Paz: Puerta del Sol, 1983. 298 p.: bibl., ill. (Col. Luces y sombras; 4)

Polemical treatment of the social conditions and political struggles of Bolivian mine workers. Contains interesting statistics and analysis of the Bolivian State Mining Corp.'s (COMIBOL) decline during 1970s and discussion of experiences and prospects for co-management between government officials and elected mine workers.

8310 Laserna, Roberto. Espacio y sociedad regional: constitución y desarrollo del mercado interno en Cochabamba. Cochabamba, Bolivia: CERES, 1984. 266 p.: bibl., ill., maps (Serie Cochabamba; 9)

Work constitutes a social and economic profile of the Dept. of Cochabamba. Author briefly examines historical changes and aspects such as market expansion, colonization, commerce and services, industrial and agricultural production. Underscores peculiar patterns of small and medium scale operations for production commerce and trade as the central distinctive characteristic of this regional economy.

8311 Paz Ballivián, Danilo. Estructura agraria boliviana. La Paz: Librería Editorial Popular, 1983. 163 p.: bibl.

Attempts a comprehensive analysis of Bolivia's agrarian structure and describes the State's role in the political economy. Emphasizes agrarian reform, colonization of the lowlands by highland farmers, and capitalist expansion by large commercial farms in the eastern tropics. Interesting book conceptually that provides very meager new data.

8312 Rivera Cusicanqui, Silvia. "Oprimidos pero no vencidos:" luchas del campesinado aymara y qhechwa en Bolivia, 1900–1980. La Paz: UN Research Institute for Social Development (UNRISD), 1984. 201 p.: bibl.

Very important overview of highland Bolivia campesino revolts against the State since 1900. Author makes some controversial interpretations of the 1952 agrarian reform in her arguments that Aymara altiplano ayllu structures were undermined by reformist measures and disproportionate influence of

Cochabamba peasant syndicates. Includes in-depth examination of the Tupak Katari movement's origins and trajectory as a social and ethnic force for change in contemporary Bolivia.

Rivera P., Alberto. Pachamama expensive: el contexto territorial urbano y la diferenciación social en la ciudad de La Paz, 1971–1986. See item **3645.**

Tendler, Judith; Kevin Healy; and Carol Michaels O'Laughlin. What to think about cooperatives: a guide from Bolivia. See item **3648.**

8313 Tierra, estructura y poder en Santa Cruz. La Paz: Grupo de Estudios Andrés Ibáñez, 1983. 169 p.: bibl.

Describes changes in agrarian structure in Dept. of Santa Cruz which has experienced rapid agricultural growth during past two and a half decades. Includes important wealth concentration data and findings concerning political and social articulation of regional economic elites. Regional political economy variables include credit, agroindustrial expansion, land distribution, labor relations, etc. Book is rich on data and short on analysis and elaboration.

PARAGUAY

8314 Ciudad y vivienda en el Paraguay. Asunción: Sociedad de Análisis, Estudios y Proyectos (SAEP), 1984. 331 p., 2 p. of plates: bibl., ill.

Series of articles by Paraguayan social scientists focusing on Asunción and dealing with housing, demographics, historical processes of urbanization, urban neighborhoods, and social conditions of low-income sectors. Represents social analysis and interpretations of Paraguay's best urban sociologists on recent urban changes.

8315 Fogel, Ramón. Colonización agraria y distribución espacial de la población: características del proceso (CPES/RPS, 16:44, enero/abril 1979, p. 109–164)

Comparative analysis of different types of internal colonization of agricultural areas in Paraguay. Gives historical overview from the beginning of 20th century to present. Demonstrates contrast between earlier 1960s colonization undertaken by subsistence farmers and the one during 1970s via Brazilian agro-businesses and involving considerable social and ecological cost.

8316 Herken Krauer, Juan Carlos. La inmigración en el Paraguay de posguerra: el caso de los *Lincolnshire farmers*: 1870–1873 (CPES/RPS, 18:52, sept./dic. 1981, p. 33–107, tables)

Analysis of a case study of British emigrants who attempted resettlement and agricultural development in Paraguay during early 1870s . Documents this foiled attempt at resettlement despite substantial material support and the consequences this episode had for subsequent migration during late 19th and early 20th centuries. Compares Paraguay's influx of foreign migrants with Argentina's and Uruguay's in setting the economic and social framework for the analysis. For historian's comment, see *HLAS 46:3387*.

Miranda, Aníbal. Desarrollo y pobreza en Paraguay. See item **3661.**

Peters, Heinz. Das Paraguayische Erziehungswesen von 1811 bis 1865: Schule und Staat in einem Modell autozentrierter Entwicklung. See *HLAS 46:3397*

8317 Schoemaker, Juan. Participación laboral femenina y fecundidad en Paraguay. Santiago: CELADE, 1981. 72, 20 p.: bibl. (Serie D. CELADE; 98)

Study of fertility and female participation in the labor force in Paraguay, based on a large sample (N=4,622). Topics include age and work status (yes/no) at the time of marriage, and their relationship with fertility patterns during marriage. Findings confirm existing propositions: women who work have less children than those who do not, fertility is lower in urban than in rural settings. etc. [C.H. Waisman]

8318 Schvartzman, Mauricio. El "indio" y la sociedad: los prejuicios étnicos en el Paraguay (UCNSA/SA, 18:1, 1983, p. 17?–246, bibl., tables)

Discussion of ethnic prejudice against "Indians" in Paraguay. Survey data indicate that most individuals who define themselves as "white" have a latent prejudice against "Indians." About a fourth displays manifest forms of prejudice. Pioneer study. [C.H. Waisman]

8319 Tierra y sociedad: problemática de la tierra urbana, rural e indígena en el Paraguay. Asunción: Conferencia Episcopal Paraguaya, Equipo Nacional de Pastoral Social, 1984. 402 p.: bibl.: ill. (Cuadernos de pastoral social; 4)

Comprehensive analysis of land problems of Paraguay's urban poor, peasants, and indigenous populations. For urban areas, study presents case studies and derives typologies of land conflicts. For indigenous groups, it offers an exhaustive treatment of landholding situations of different ethnicities scattered throughout rural areas. In relation to the peasant population, this work emphasizes variables of land concentration and forms of land tenancy and colonization programs and discusses them within a framework of broader social and economic changes, such as the rapid economic growth of the past decade. This book constitutes an admirable and impressive effort, in a politically tight social research setting, presenting both a regionally specific and national view of the control over the distribution of land in urban and rural Paraguay.

8320 Ziche, Joachim. El desarrollo de la situación socio-económica de los colonos en el Eje Norte de Colonización, Paraguay (CPES/RPS, 16:45, mayo/agosto 1979, p. 37–56, graph, map, tables)

Survey uses variables such as credit dependency, family budgets, size of landholdings, health and nutrition status to compare socioeconomic conditions of peasant colonists in a decade (1968–78). Results reveal very little socioeconomic change in individual households.

THE SOUTHERN CONE: ARGENTINA, CHILE, AND URUGUAY

CARLOS H. WAISMAN, *Associate Professor of Sociology, University of California, San Diego*

WITH THE REESTABLISHMENT OF LIBERAL democracy in Argentina and Uruguay, sociology has reemerged in these countries. Research centers and other "catacombs" which, in very difficult conditions, protected the survival of social research will continue to serve as the backbone of the profession. For now, at last, sociology and other "suspect" disciplines are once again permitted to share the impure but nonetheless healthy air of open intellectual life in the universities and other public fora. Underground or *zamisdat* social science literature is now a thing of the past, and books on controversial sociological subjects can be published again. The limitations which confront the social sciences today in the newly democratic countries are not political but economic: stagnant, debt-ridden economies that can hardly support a solid research establishment.

In Chile where social scientists continue to work under a dictatorship, a remarkable network of research centers exists allowing sociologists not only to remain in the country but to turn out high quality work. Paradoxically, some of the most interesting research in the Southern Cone is being conducted in Pinochet's Chile, as can be gleaned from the publications annotated below (items **8338–8352**). Overall, Chilean contributions focus on the social and economic changes brought about by the military regime. For the first time, we list items on cultural issues, including a fascinating semiotic analysis of authoritarian discourse (item **8344**).

Due to the obvious time lag, Argentine and Uruguayan works selected below do not reflect these countries' recent political changes. Argentine publications mostly concern descriptive demography, one of the few "safe" topics under the military regime. Other entries exemplify a traditional genre in Argentine sociology: the sociopolitical essay. The challenge in Argentine sociology, as in sociology in general, is how to link both types of research in a cohesive and organic manner. Uruguayan publications are overall professional and they do provide an overview of the society. They consist principally of demographic works—emphasizing a phenomenon that worries Uruguayans, emigration—and secondly of analytical descriptions of class structure.

ARGENTINA

8321 Alimonda, Héctor A. "Paz y administración"—"Ordem e progresso:" notas para un estudio comparativo de los Estados Oligárquicos argentino y brasileño (UNAM/RMS, 44:4, oct./dic. 1982, p. 1323–1350, bibl., tables)

Sophisticated comparative analysis of the Oligarchic State in Argentina and Brazil in the period of externally-led economic growth. Author studies effects of the countries' different forms of integration into the world market, different social structures, differences in the division of labor and the distribution of power, and styles of political conflict.

Bertinotti de Petrei, Nelva M. Las migraciones en Argentina en el período 1970–1980. See item **3693**.

8322 Blackwelder, Julia Kirk and Lyman L. Johnson. Changing criminal patterns in Buenos Aires, 1890 to 1914 (JLAS, 14:2, Nov. 1982, p. 359–379, tables)

Discussion of criminal behavior and policing practices in Buenos Aires (1880–1914). Authors relate crime and law enforcement to salient economic and political issues of the period, especially with the city's demographic and spatial expansion. At the time, Buenos Aires was perceived as a dangerous place and European immigrants as the direct cause.

8323 Boleda, Mario. El proceso emigratorio misionero en la últimas tres décadas (IDES/DE, 23:90, julio/sept. 1983, p. 287–298, maps, tables)

In a pattern well known in the Southern Cone, the prov. of Misiones shifted, from serving as a pole of attraction to European immigrants, to becoming a region of emigration. Immigration ended in 1930, and emigration began in 1940s. Well documented work.

8324 Carrón, Juan M. Factores de atracción de la inmigración de origen limítrofe existente en la Argentina (Migración Internacionales en las Américas [Centro de Estudios de Migración (CEMPAM), Centro de Estudios de Pastoral y Asistencia Migratoria, Caracas] 1:1, 1980, p. 113–131, bibl., tables)

Discussion of attraction factors that draw immigration from neighboring countries into Argentina. Up to mid-1940s, immigrants settled in areas whose output and employment were expanding. As of the 1950s, immigrants began moving to depressed areas where they fill low-level positions at wages that are unattractive to locals.

8325 Catholic Church. Conferencia Episcopal Argentina. Documentos del Episcopado Argentino, 1965–1981: colección completa del magisterio postconciliar de la Conferencia Episcopal Argentina. Buenos Aires: Editorial Claretiana, 1982. 492 p.: bibl., indexes.

Collection of documents issued by Argentina's Catholic Bishops since mid-1960s. The Church endeavors to appear as the representative of the nation and as such, issues statements about political and economic questions in addition to specifically religious ones. In periods of military rule, when political parties were banned and trade union activity was restricted, the Church serves as intermediary between labor and the State.

8326 Catterberg, Edgardo and Luis Aznar. Coaliciones sociales y orden político en la Argentina: un ensayo sobre la inestabilidad del peronismo, 1973–76 (CPES/RPS, 14:38, enero/abril 1988, p. 39–51)

One of peronism's main characteristics as a movement is the fact of its strength when in opposition and weakness when in power. Discusses social coalitions which made up the social base of peronism at different stages, its political culture and its role as an opposition party.

Censo nacional de población y vivienda, 1980. See item **6511.**

Ciria, Alberto. Política y cultura popular: la Argentina peronista, 1946–1955. See *HLAS 46:3205.*

8327 Cuevillas, Fernando N. *et al.* Ser y no ser de los argentinos: sociología para nosotros. Buenos Aires: Ediciones Macchi, 1979. 537 p.: bibl.

Sociology textbook with a traditional, essay-type approach. Authors show little awareness of contemporary sociology, even of the type practiced in Argentina. Includes remarkable propositions for an academic textbook (e.g., "It is, then, evident that man knows primitively through revelation and only through revelation," p. 80).

8328 Delich, Francisco. Después del diluvio, la clase obrera (*in* Argentina, hoy. Alain Rouquié, comp. México: Siglo Veintiuno Editores, 1982, p. 129–150 [Serie Historia inmediata])

Discusses the labor movement under the military regime established in 1976. Topics include the effects of free market economic policies, political repression, the new labor legislation, and the limited opportunities for workers' demands.

8329 Deutsch, Mario *et al.* Eva Perón: una aproximación psicoanalítica. Montevideo: Imago, 1983. 77 p.: ill.

Psychoanalytic study of Eva Perón. Authors conclude that the character developed both masculine and feminine traits, a factor conducive to massive identification and projection. Evita displayed a very narcissistic libidinal orientation, and a strong ideal ego. Although the analysis is hampered by lack of information about her childhood, it is a pioneer study.

Di Tella, Guido. Argentina under Perón, 1973–76: the nation's experience with a labour-based government. See item **6516.**

Elkin, Judith Laikin. A demographic profile of Latin American Jewry. See *HLAS 46:1904.*

8330 Escala, Alberto. Argentina, estructura social y sectores intermedios. Buenos Aires: Ediciones Estudio, 1982. 136 p.: bibl., ill.

Marxist examination of the structure of the middle class in different settings. Author is clearly an amateur sociologist, his Marxism is of the textbook type, his sources well known, and yet the book is one of the few on Argentina's largest social class.

8331 Evans, Judith; Paul Heath Hoeffel; and Daniel James. Reflections on Argentine auto workers in their unions (in Political economy of the Latin American motor vehicle industry. Edited by Rich Kronish and Kenneth S. Mericle. Cambridge: MIT Press, 1984, p. 133–159)

Argentine auto workers have displayed an unusually high level of militancy. This chapter examines their union organization, ideologies, and strategies as of 1955. Stresses the importance of understanding the social context of both auto plants and the wider working-class community.

Marshall, Adriana. Tendencias estructurales en la migración internacional fuerza de trabajo: el Cono Sur de América Latina. See item **8021.**

8332 Martín de Rover, Matilde. Características generales del suicidio en la Provincia de Mendoza, 1972–1981. Mendoza, Argentina: Dirección de Estadísticas e Investigaciones Económicas, Ministerio de Economía, 1983. 32 p.: ill. (Publicaciones estadísticas. Serie Estudios sociales; 132)

Analysis of suicide by sex, age, procedure employed, and geographic location in the province of Mendoza, a "modern" region of the Argentine interior. Paper also has suicide rates for the country as a whole: Argentine rates are higher than in Latin America as a whole and lower than in the US.

8333 Merlo Flores de Ezcurra, Tatiana and Ana María Rey. La televisión, ¿forma o deforma?: investigación con 2000 niños argentinos. Buenos Aires: Ediciones Culturales Argentinas, Secretaría de Cultura, Presidencia de la Nación, 1983. 184 p.: ill.

Survey of TV viewing by Argentine children. Research is based on a random sample (N=1,590). Author focuses on three issues: time spent on TV viewing, preference for program contents, and effects of social class. In relation to the latter, children were asked which characters they prefer. Middle-upper class children favored imaginary characters, lower-class children real ones. Interesting monograph.

8334 Nilo Pelegrino, Antonio. Población actual, 1978, y futura de la Argentina. Buenos Aires: Oikos Asociación para la Promoción de los Estudios Territoriales y Ambientales, 1980. 32 leaves: bibl., ill., maps (Contribuciones, 0325–4259; 2–07)

Estimates of the Argentine population in 1978 and projections up to the end of the century. Author forecasts a population of 32.9 million for the year 2000, an increment of only 24 percent with respect to 1978 (vs. a growth of 78 percent in Brazil and 46 percent in Chile).

8335 Pantelides, Edith Alejandra. Evolución de la fecundidad en la Argentina. Buenos Aires: Centro de Estudios de Población; Santiago: Centro Latinoamericano de Demografía, 1979. 51 p.: bibl., ill.

Analysis of the evolution of fertility, based on 1970 census. Author shows that the number of children can be used for a retrospective estimation of fertility rates. Her substantive findings are interesting: fertility declined since the beginning of the century, was relatively stable in 1940–55, and continued to fall thereafter.

Perón, Juan Domingo. Manual de adoctrinamiento peronista: materias fundamentales y básicas: apuntes doctrinarios para una historia del peronismo. See item **6530.**

8336 Pion-Berlin, David. Political repression and economic doctrines: the case of Argentina (CPS, 16:1, April 1983, p. 37–66, bibl., ill.)

Argues that the use of force by Argentina's military regimes is a function of shifts in economic stabilization policies from structuralism to monetarism, and of linkages between domestic elites and international institutions partial to deflationary policies. Based on a time-series analysis.

8337 Waldmann, Peter. Anomía social y violencia (in Argentina, hoy. Alain Rouquié, comp. México: Siglo Veintiuno Editores, 1982, p. 206–248, tables [Serie Historia inmediata])

Explores causes in the 1930s that led to the emergence of guerrillas in Argentina.

Hypothesizes that in the 1960s and 1970s traditional values were weakened as the society became more secular. The origin of the phenomenon lies in the tension between a modern economic structure and traditional ideologies. The result is anomie. Indicators are the rise in crime, divorce rates, and the decline in the number of priests.

CHILE

8338 Barrera, Manuel. Estructura educativa de la fuerza de trabajo chilena (CPES/RPS, 15:41, enero/abril 1978, p. 57–75, bibl., tables)

Discussion of the education of the Chilean active population in 1970. Levels of schooling are related to gender, rural-urban location, occupational category, and branch of the economy. Analysis is based on census data.

8339 Batallán, Graciela. Las comunidades agrícolas del Norte Chico chileno (CPES/RPS, 18:50, enero/mayo 1981, p. 89–139, bibl., maps, tables)

Studies peasant community development projects in area of Chile known as "Norte Chico." Discusses history of these communities, describes their current structural characteristics, their organization of labor, and their culture.

8340 Bengoa, José. El campesinado chileno después de la reforma agraria. Santiago: Ediciones Sur, 1983. 204 p.: ill. (Col. Estudios sociales)

Consists of discussion of changes in the structure of the Chilean peasantry since the inception of the 1960s land reforms. After the establishment of the military regime in 1973, reform plans ended and cooperative settlements were transformed into private landholdings. The application of free-market policies led to a large-scale differentiation of the peasantry. A substantial proportion of the agrarian population underwent processes of marginalization.

8341 Calvo, Roberto. La doctrina militar de la seguridad nacional: autoritarismo político y neoliberalismo económico en el Cono Sur. Caracas: Univ. Católica Andrés Bello, 1979. 335 p.: bibl., index. (Col. Manoa; 24)

Good summary of the "national security doctrine" of the armed forces in Brazil and Chile, and a discussion of the economic policies implemented by the military regimes in these countries. Includes valuable bibliography (over 100 p.) on national security and militarism in several Latin American countries.

8342 Campero, Guillermo and **José A. Valenzuela.** El movimiento sindical chileno en el capitalismo autoritario, 1973–1981. Santiago: Instituto Latinoamericano de Estudios Transnacionales (ILET), Oficina de Santiago: Academia de Humanismo Cristiano (AHC), Programa de Economía del Trabajo (PET), 1981. 605 p.: bibl.

Study of the structure of the working class, labor movement, and relationship between State and labor under the military regime established in 1973. Topics include changes in the organization of production, employment and wages, labor laws, unionization, and the emergence of labor mobilization. First-rate analysis.

8343 Coeymans, Juan Eduardo. Determinantes de la migración rural-urbana en Chile según origen y destino. Santiago: Pontificia Univ. Católica de Chile, Instituto de Economía, Oficina de Publicaciones, 1982. 82 p.: bibl. (Documento de trabajo; 81)

Equation model of the determinants of rural-urban migration, based on 1970 data. The level of rural poverty is the most important expulsion factor, and the selection of the area of destinations is determined by the per-capita income differential, and by the availability of educational opportunities and health care facilities.

8344 The Discourse of power: culture, hegemony, and the authoritarian State. Introduced and edited by Neil Larsen. Minneapolis: Institute for the Study of Ideologies and Literature, 1983. 193 p.: bibl.

This path-breaking study links contemporary literary techniques and the sociological study of military regimes in the Southern Cone. Most papers are semiological analyses of the official discourse. Vidal's study of the statement of principles of the Chilean junta and Munizaga and Ochsenius's content analysis of Pinochet's speeches are especially noteworthy.

Escobar, Roberto. Teoría del chileno. See *HLAS 46:3078.*

8345 Foxley, Alejandro and **Dagmar Raczynski.** Vulnerable groups in recessionary situations: the case of children and the young in Chile (WD, 12:3, March 1984, p. 223–246, bibl., tables)

Discusses effects of Chile's deep recession on a particularly vulnerable age group: children and the young. Also evaluates the success of programs designed to shelter children from adverse economic conditions. In the period under analysis, infant mortality fell, but the situation of the young deteriorated significantly.

8346 Fuenzalida, Edmundo F. The reception of "scientific sociology" in Chile (LARR, 18:2, 1983, p. 95–112, bibl.)

Interesting account of the institutionalization of social research in Chile. Author discusses the traditional essay-type literature and the development of three institutes: the Institute of Social Research of the Univ. of Chile, FLACSO, and the Center for Social Research of the Catholic Univ. Each of these organizations represents a different style of sociological work.

8347 Galilea W., Carmen. Valores en el Chile de hoy. Santiago: Centro Bellarmino, Depto. de Investigaciones Sociológicas, 1983. 131 p.: bibl.

Concerns answers to a questionnaire applied to a sample of 800 Chileans and carried out by a Catholic research organization. Questions deal with values in different areas of social life: politics, religion, family work, etc. Some demographic characteristics of the interviewees are presented.

Gariazzo, Alicia. Orígenes ideológicos de los movimientos obreros chileno y argentino. See *HLAS 46:3088.*

Godoy Urzúa, Hernán. El carácter chileno: estudio preliminar y selección de ensayos. See *HLAS 46:3091.*

8348 ———. La cultura chilena: ensayo de síntesis y de interpretación sociológica. Santiago: Editorial Universitaria, 1982. 553 p.: bibl., ill. (some col.)

Illustrated textbook of Chilean cultural history, which is understood as the history of artistic genres and of studies in the humanities. Both the discussion of culture and references to the social and political context are at a popularization level.

Grenier, Philippe. Chiloé et les chilotes: marginalité et dépendance en Patagonia chilienne, étude de géographie humaine. See item **5154.**

8349 Kay, Cristóbal. Political economy, class alliances and agrarian changes in Chile (JPS, 8:4, July 1981, p. 485–513)

Sophisticated discussion of the "agrarian question" in Chile. It arose after 1930, as a transition to capitalist social relations began taking place. The agrarian reform policies of 1967–73 attempted to solve the problem in a cooperative direction, while the policies of the Pinochet regime emphasize private farming at labor's expense. For economist's comment, see item **3547.**

Krebs, Ricardo *et al.* Catolicismo y laicismo: las bases doctrinarias del conflicto entre la Iglesia y el Estado en Chile, 1875–1885: seis estudios. See *HLAS 46:3104.*

8350 Lira, Luis Felipe. Estructura agraria, crecimiento de la población y migraciones: el caso de la zona central de Chile, 1952–1970 (CPES/RPS, 13:37, set./dic. 1976, p. 49–88, tables)

Examines changes in the agrarian structure of Chile's central zone and their effect on emigration flows. Structural changes are analyzed on the basis of the agrarian censuses of 1936, 1955, and 1965. Emigration is discussed for the 1950–70 period. Serious work.

McCaa, Roberto. Marriage and fertility in Chile: demographic turning points in the Petorca Valley, 1840–1976. See *HLAS 46:3107.*

8351 Rivera, Anny. Transformaciones culturales y movimiento artístico en el orden autoritario: Chile, 1973–1982. Santiago: Centro de Indagación y Expresión Cultural y Artística (CENECA), 1983. 156, 4 p.: bibl. (Cultura y autoritarismo; 33)

Interesting study of artistic movements in Chile, both before and after the military coup of 1973. Emphasizes the relationship between authoritarianism and artistic expression. What author calls the unofficial artistic movement developed and attained considerable success under the harsh conditions of Pinochet's regime.

Ruiz, Carlos. Notes on authoritarian ideologies in Chile. See *HLAS 46:7617*.

8352 Waitzkin, Howard. Health policy and social change: a comparative history of Chile and Cuba (SSSP/SP, 31:2, Dec. 1983, p. 235–248, bibl.)

Compares the social history of health care in Cuba and Chile. When Allende took power in Chile, the country had a tradition of public health care. At the time of the Cuban Revolution by contrast, the island's health care was rudimentary. However, Cuba succeeded in creating a radically different health care system, and one superior to Chile's. Author argues that basic changes in society are a prerequisite for the transformation of health care (see also item **8217**).

URUGUAY

8353 Aguiar, César A. Uruguay, país de emigración. Montevideo: Ediciones de la Banda Oriental, 1982. 130 p. (Temas del siglo XX; 3)

Uruguay is a country of emigration: during 1963–75, it lost about 10 percent of its population. In 1981, a fourth of the population said it was considering emigration. The proportion among young people (18 to 25) was 45 percent. About half of the emigrants go to Argentina. Book is a discussion of statistical and survey materials.

Araujo, Ana María. Tupamaras. See item **6547**.

Casal, Pedro M. Alimentación en el Uruguay. See item **1759**.

Castagnola, José Luis and **Martín Gargiulo Blanco.** Roles ocupacionales asalariados en la producción ganadera. See item **3673**.

8354 Grupo de Estudios sobre la Condición de la Mujer (GRECMU), *Montevideo.* La mujer en el Uruguay: ayer y hoy. Montevideo: Ediciones de la Banda Oriental, 1983. 142 p. (Temas del siglo XX; 15)

Series of papers on the status of women in Uruguay that discuss: female labor in a period of economic crisis; the family and the economic status of rural women; the social creation of a female stereotype throughout the educational system; the ideology of female subordination; female labor in Montevideo during the period of externally-led growth; and images of women at the beginning of the century. Solid papers.

8355 Martorelli, Horacio. La sociedad rural uruguaya. Montevideo: Fundación de Cultura Universitaria: Centro Interdisciplinario de Estudios sobre el Desarrollo Uruguay, 1982. 48 p.: bibl., ill. (Col. Temas nacionales; 5)

Description of the rural sector of Uruguayan society. Topics include its economic bases, characteristics of its social structure, land tenure, income distribution, and stratification. Emphasizes the heterogeneity of rural society. Useful summary.

8356 Merino, Francisco Melitón. El negro en la sociedad montevideana. Montevideo: Ediciones de la Banda Oriental, 1982. 103 p.: bibl. (Temas del siglo XX; 7)

Popular essay on Uruguay's blacks. Topics include organization of the black community, white perceptions of blacks, Afro-Uruguayan ceremonies and folklore, blacks in sports, discrimination, etc.

8357 Picerno, Alfredo and **Pablo Mieres.** Uruguay, indicadores básicos. Montevideo: Centro Latinoamericano de Economía Humana (CLAEH), 1983. 85, 11 p.: bibl., ill.

Useful compendium of Uruguayan statistics. Topics include composition of GDP, international trade, financial statistics, wages, income distribution, demographic indicators, housing, health, employment, education, organization of households, religion media, social security, and electoral data.

Rama, Germán W. Dependencia y segmentación en Uruguay en el siglo XIX. See *HLAS 46:3438*.

8358 Rial Roade, Juan. Situación de la vivienda de los sectores populares de Montevideo, 1889–1930. Montevideo: Centro de Informaciones y Estudios del Uruguay, 1982. 73 p.: bibl., ill. (Cuaderno; 44)

Study of housing conditions of the Montevideo lower classes in the period of externally-led growth (1889–1930). Topics include characteristics of housing units, localization of lower class housing, transportation, *conventillos* (tenements), private-built housing projects, and housing policy of the Uruguayan government at the time. Serious work.

8359 Rivero Herrera, José. Psiquiatría y dictadura en el Uruguay (SP, 6, 1979, p. 155–157)

Author calls this paper "a reflection of madness and fascism." It discusses psychosocial disturbances and psychiatric disorders generated by the institutions of the military regime. Based on clinical observation and documents. Symptoms are generalized fear, danger of denunciation, personal insecurity, isolation, and impotence.

8360 Rodríguez Villamil, Silvia and Graciela Sapriza. La inmigración europea en el Uruguay: los italianos. Montevideo: Ediciones de la Banda Oriental, 1982. 144, 8 p.: bibl., ill.

Well documented study of Italian immigration to Uruguay before 1930. During 1880–1930, Uruguay received over a quarter of a million European immigrants, a third of whom were Italian. Topics include a general discussion of immigration, competition with Argentina as a pole of attraction, motivations of immigrants, labor market and wages in Montevideo and in the interior at the time of mass immigration, and post-immigration mobility patterns.

8361 Solari, Aldo and Rolando Franco. Equality of opportunities and elitism in the Uruguayan university (NS, 6:11, 1981, p. 1–16)

The Uruguayan university has been organized on the basis of a democratic ideology, which emphasizes free access to higher education. Three-fourths of high school graduates enter the university. Selection, however, takes place at lower levels of the educational system. About 30 percent of students do not finish elementary school, and a large proportion of those entering high school do not ob-

tain the certificate enabling them to pursue university studies.

8362 Uruguay. Presidencia. Secretaría de Planeamiento, Coordinación y Difusión. Dirección General de Estadística y Censos. Encuesta de migración internacional: noviembre 1981-mayo 1982. Montevideo: La Dirección, 1982. 78 p., 2 p. of plates: ill.

Survey of emigration and return migration, based on a sample of 12,000 Montevideo households. Data include rise of emigration flows, countries of destination, selectivity of emigration by gender, age, marital status, education, and occupation, and reasons for returning.

8363 Veiga, Danilo. Socioeconomic structure and population displacements: the Uruguayan case (NS, 6:12, 1981, p. 1–25, bibl., graphs, ill., maps, tables)

Discusses migration within and emigration from Uruguay. Interprets internal population movements of the basis of the center-periphery paradigm. Stagnation produced a shift, from rural-urban migration to emigration. This shift is facilitated by the fact that Montevideo is both the pole of attraction for domestic migrants and the link with Argentina and other countries which receive Uruguayan emigrants.

8364 ———. Tipología departamental y desarrollo regional en el Uruguay. Montevideo: Centro de Informaciones y Estudios del Uruguay, 1978. 95 p.: ill.

Typology of Uruguayan departments based on the factor analysis of indicators of economic and social development (manufacturing GDP, energy production, per capital GDP, secondary education, urbanization, physicians per capita, telephones per capita).

BRAZIL

JOHN V.D. SAUNDERS, *Professor of Sociology, Mississippi State University*

RACE, RELIGION, AND THE NORTHEAST are of abiding interest to Brazilian social scientists. These topics are, in many ways, central to the Brazilian national ethos, and are represented by 20 of the 45 works annotated in this section.

Demographic and population studies are the subject of nine entries listed below, also an important category in *HLAS 45* (p. 659–669). The prevalence of this subject partly reflects the availability of data from national sample household surveys and partly the publication of results of the 1980 census. However, this would not have occurred had it not been for the expansion of opportunities for the study of demography both in Brazil and abroad which began in the late 1960s.

The remaining works annotated below deal with ethnic groups (Germans, Italians, Japanese), women, women's issues and social problems. One third of the annotations fall into a miscellaneous category.

8366 Almeida, Ana Maria Chiarotti de. Participação social dos operários de origem rural em área urbana, Londrina, Pr. Curitiba: Grafipar, 1981. 118 p.: ill (Estudos paranaenses; 6)

Focuses on the social participation of urban workers in the municipio of Londrina who are rural migrants. Most social participation occurs in informal and semi-formal groups rather than in organized groups such as political parties. It is positively associated with educational attainment, longevity on the job and is greater among single than among married workers. No association was found between social participation and length of residence in the city or with income.

8367 Análise demográfica regional: o perfil populacional do Estado de São Paulo, segundo o censo de 1980. São Paulo: Fundação Sistema Estadual de Análise de Dados (SEADE), 1982. 54 p.: bibl., ill.

Study devoted to population growth, the economically active population and households. Worthy of note are an annual growth rate of the population of 3.49 percent, net migration that accounts for 42 percent of population growth (1970–80), reduction of Northeastern migrants and increase of migrants from the southern region, and increase of the use of oral contraceptives among married women of childbearing age in the municipio of São Paulo from six percent in 1965 to 30 percent in 1978.

8368 Araújo, Silvia Maria Pereira de. Imposição de classes sociais: migrantes rurais em processo de alfabetização de adultos (UFP/EB, 5:9, junho 1980, p. 13–26, bibl.)

Studies the behavior of teachers whose students are illiterate adult rural migrants. Selects from analysis the manifestations of social class prejudice and stereotypes in the classroom.

8369 Arruda, Rinaldo Sergio Vieira. Pequenos bandidos. São Paulo: Global Editôra, 1983. 175 p. (Tesis; 12. Sociologia)

Examines characteristics, histories, family backgrounds of juvenile delinquents

in the city of São Paulo. Interviews and observations are main concerns of this volume which focuses on the delinquent as he is processed through a system of agencies established on his behalf.

Azevedo, Eliane S. Sobrenomes no Nordeste e suas relações com a heterogeneidade étnica. See item **5216.**

8370 Baiocchi, Mari de Nasaré. Negros de Cedro: estudo antropológico de um bairro rural de negros em Goiás. São Paulo: Editôra Atica: em convênio com o Instituto Nacional de Libro, Fundação Nacional Pró-Memória, 1983. 201 p.: bibl., ill. (Ensaios; 97)

Studies in detail a rural neighborhood almost entirely populated by blacks. Describes and analyzes the community, its economy, family institutions, religion, medicine, and leisure activities.

8371 Bandeira de Alairá: outros escritos sobre a religião dos orixás. Organização de Carlos Eugênio Marcondes de Moura. Roberto Motta et al. São Paulo: Noble, 1982. 191 p.: bibl., ill.

Consists of four papers and a bibliography devoted to Afro-Brazilian religions: Roberto Motta's "Bandeira de Alairá: A Festa de Xangô-São João" deals with religious syncretism; Claude Levine's "Análise Formal do Panteão Nagô" is largely devoted to ritual objects, foods and sacrifices, and contains a useful glossary; Octavio da Costa Eduardo's "O Tocador de Atabaque nas Casas de Culto Afro-Maranhenses" is a succinct analysis of the functions of the players of these percussion instruments; and Vivaldo da Costa Lima's "Organização do Grupo de Candomblé: Estratificação, Senioridade e Hierarquia," extracted from his MA thesis, is based on extensive field work and chiefly concerns the social organization of a candomblé group in Salvador. While the bibliography by Carlos Eugênio Marcondes de Moura is not annotated, 50 subject headings are used which enhance its utility.

8372 Barreto, Maria Theresinha Sobierajski. Poloneses em Santa Catarina: a colonização do Alto Vale do Rio Tijucas. Prefácio de Maria Luiza Marcílio. Florianópolis: Editôra da Univ. Federal de Santa Catarina: Editôra Lunardelli, 1983. 143 p.: bibl., ill., maps.

Author applied techniques of historical demography and of oral history to area colonized by Polish immigrants, beginning in 1890, producing a volume rich in detail. Among its primary concerns are fertility, birth intervals, endogamy, exogamy, and assimilation.

8372a Berquó, Elza et al. Estudos de população: estudo de caso—dinâmica populacional, transformações sócio-econômicas, atuação das instituições. v. 4–8. São Paulo: CEBRAP, 1982. 5 v.: ill.

These volumes follow similar outlines. A section on population growth and change is followed by a discussion of area's social and economic history. They conclude with a section devoted to social institutions (e.g., the Church) and agencies (e.g., the health delivery system) as they affect reproduction. Vol. 8 contains summaries of findings of prior studies. Competently done.

Blay, Eva Alterman. As prefeitas: a participação política da mulher no Brasil. See item 6614.

Brandão, Carlos Rodrigues. "Casa de escola:" cultura camponesa e educação rural. See item 4528.

8373 Brazil. Presidência. Secretaria de Planejamento. Fundação Instituto Brasileiro de Geografia e Estatística (IBGE). Censo demográfico: dados gerais, migração, instrução, fecundidade, mortalidade. v. 26. Rio de Janeiro: IBGE, 1983. 1 v. (IX recenseamento geral do Brasil, 1980; 1:4)

Vol. 1, pts. 1–2 of this set were devoted to preliminary and to advance data based on samples of returns. Pts. 3–6 are definitive. Pt. 3 contains district level data. Pts. 4–6, data for meso-regions, micro-regions, and municipios. Vol. 26 contains general population characteristics followed by sets of tables devoted to migration, to education and to fertility. This set contains the most complete data on these topics to date. Pt. 5 will be devoted to labor force and pt. 6 to characteristics of families and households.

8374 ——. ——. ——. ——. Perfil estatístico de crianças e mães no Brasil: características sócio-demográficas, 1970–1977. Rio de Janeiro: IBGE, 1982. 424 p.: bibl., col. ill., tables.

Children, youth, and mothers are the main concern of this compilation of tables based on the 1970 census and the 1977 national sample household interview survey. Data on fertility are presented in relation to income, education, and marital status; on mortality in relation to rural-urban residence and socioeconomic status. Comparable data are also presented for families. Data are either national, for the Northeast or for the state or city of São Paulo.

Brazil: an interim assessment of rural development programs for the Northeast. See item 3750.

Calvo, Roberto. La doctrina militar de la seguridad nacional: autoritarismo político y neoliberalismo económico en el Cono Sur. See item 8341.

8375 Carvalho, Rejane Vasconcelos Accioly de. Justiça social e acumulação capitalista: o PROTERRA [i.e. Programa de Redistribuição de Terras]. Fortaleza: Edições Univ. Federal do Ceará: Programa de Estímulo à Agro-Indústria no Norte e Nordeste (PROEDI), 1982. 169 p.: bibl., map.

Program of land redistribution and development of agro-industries in the north and Northeast is the focus of this study which uses a Marxist analytical perspective. Concludes that land redistribution goals were subordinated to those of "modernization."

8376 Chaloult, Yves. Questão agrária e política do Estado: o Polonordeste (BNB/REN, 11:4, out./dez. 1980, p. 527–564, bibl., tables)

Analyzes rural development program of POLONORDESTE (Programa de Desenvolvimento de Areas Integradas no Nordeste), a governmental agency. Concludes that while the program benefits thousands of small farmers, because it operates within the context of a market economy, it benefits even more those who control large amounts of capital.

8377 Costa, Eda Maranhão Pessoa da. Expansão urbana e organização espacial. Recife: Univ. Federal de Pernambuco, Editôra Universitária, 1982. 248 p.: bibl., ill.

Coastal zone located in the municipios of Olinda and Paulista, part of the Recife metropolitan area is the object of this study. Analyzes area's transformation from rural to urban economy and from rural to urban land use patterns.

8378 Costa, Iraci del Nero da. Populações mineiras: sobre a estrutura populacional de alguns núcleos mineiros no alvorecer do século XIX. São Paulo: Instituto de Pesquisas Econômicas, 1981. 335 p.: bibl., ill., tables (Série Ensaios econômicos; 7)

Excellent historical demography principally of Vila Rica (Ouro Prêto), an important administrative and mining center, at the beginning of 19th century. Also includes nine other communities in Minas Gerais. Replete with graphs and nearly 200 tables.

8379 Dasilva, Fabio B. and **Evandro Camara.** Music and society in Brazil: the recent experience (International Review of the Aesthetics and Sociology of Music [Muzicka Akademija u Zagreby, Institute of Musiciology, Zagreb, Yugoslavia] 15:1, 1984, p. 15–29)

Relates the recent past in Brazilian political development to the lyrics of major popular songs. This period is divided into the years just immediately before and following 1964 coup, characterized by subjects such as peasants and exploitation; a second period from middle 1960s through 1970s, which gave vent to frustration at the political situation, and a third period reflecting disillusionment and an eclecticism of subject matter.

8380 De Boni, Luís Alberto and **Rovílio Costa.** Os Italianos do Rio Grande do Sul. Pôrto Alegre: Escola Superior de Teologia São Lourenço de Brindes; Caxias do Sul: Univ. de Caxias do Sul, 1979. 280 p.: bibl.

Examines Italian immigration to Rio Grande do Sul, consisting largely of agriculturists, from the standpoint of social organization and acculturation.

8381 Dinâmica das microrregiões de intensa atividade migratória. Coordenadores, Manuel Correia de Andrade, Gisélia Franco Potengi. Recife: SUDENE, Depto. de Recursos Humanos, 1980. 4 v.: graphs, ill., tables (Série População e emprego; 9)

Follows standard format for the presentation of data on each of 12 micro-regions of the Northeast. A description of the micro-

region's physical geography is followed by discussion of size of agricultural holdings, labor force characteristics, agriculture, and industry. Text is supplemented by 10 tables and three graphs related to these topics. Useful reference.

Dowbor, Ladislau. La formation du capitalisme dépendant au Brésil. See item **3767.**

Estratos ocupacionais de baixa renda. See item **3771.**

8382 Faria, Vilmar. Una tipología empírica de las ciudades brasileñas (UNAM/RMS, 44:1, enero/marzo 1982, p. 53–79, tables)

Data for all municipios having 30,000 or more urban inhabitants in 1970 were factor-analyzed. Eight factors were found which explained 72 percent of the variance; four of these explained 52 percent. Factors which reflect socioeconomic structure (level of development, industrial employment, functional specialization) were found to account for 40 percent of the variance. Factors related to population change and migration explained 29 percent of the variance. These data were used to classify cities into eight principal groups containing 14 subgroups.

8383 Foot, Francisco and **Victor Leonardi.** História da indústria e do trabalho no Brasil: das origens aos anos vinte. São Paulo: Global Editôra, 1982. 416 p.: bibl., ill., ports (Teses; 6)

Begins with the industrial revolution in Britain and the establishment of the first factories in Brazil. Proceeds to the formation of the bourgeoisie and the proletariat, working conditions, and characteristics of working class. Ends with political movements of working class, notably socialism and anarchosindicalism. Written from a Marxist perspective.

8384 García-Zamor, Jean-Claude. El marginalismo del negro brasileño (CPES/RPS, 19:54, mayo/agosto 1982, p. 67–77)

Competent review of the history of race relations in Brazil ends with an assessment of the situation as of about 1970.

Gomes, Eduardo Rodrigues. Campo contra cidade: o ruralismo e a crise oligárquica no pensamento político brasileiro, 1910–1935. See *HLAS 46:7627.*

Gouveia, Aparecida Joly. Democratização do ensino e oportunidades de emprego. See item **4557.**

Humphrey, John. The growth of female employment in the Brazilian manufacturing industry in the 1970s. See item **3789.**

Incao, Maria da Conceição d'. O *bóia-fria*: acumulação e miséria. See item **5261.**

8385 Informações demográficas de Pernambuco: evolução da fecundidade, 1930–1978. Recife: Governo de Pernambuco, Secretaria de Planejamento, Fundação de Informações para o Desenvolvimento de Pernambuco, 1981. 47 p.: bibl., ill.

Age-specific birth rates for females and total fertility rates were calculated based on census data and on the 1978 national household sample survey. Fertility per states was found to be substantially higher than overall fertility for the nation. However, declines in fertility began in 1968 and were greater in urban than in rural areas and inversely related to income.

8386 José, Oiliam. Racismo em Minas Gerais. Belo Horizonte: Imprensa Oficial de Minas Gerais, 1981. 258 p., 12 leaves of plates: bibl., ill., index.

Extensive review of the literature on racism and on blacks in Minas Gerais. Glossary.

8387 Küchemann, Berlindes Astrid. O minifúndio gaúcho: ajuda técnica como alternativa? Caxias do Sul: Univ. de Caxias do Sul; Pôrto Alegre: Escola Superior de Teologia São Lourenço de Brindes, 1980. 251 p.: bibl., ill. (Col. Temas gaúchos; 22)

Brief analysis of the agrarian structure of Brazil is sandwiched between sections dealing with West German international technical assistance programs and a large section devoted to an analysis of the outcome of one of them, the Jungbauernprogramm under which 282 young Brazilian farmers, mostly from Rio Grande do Sul, were taken to Germany for training. Of these, at the time of the study, 43 percent practiced agriculture and of them 46 percent owned land. Concludes that program's effect on the development of agriculture was negligible.

Lamounier, Bolívar. 1970–1980: structures sociales, élections et changements politique au Brésil. See item **6568.**

8388 Lemgruber, Julita. Cemitério dos vivos: análise sociológica de uma prisão de mulheres. Rio de Janeiro: Achiamé, 1983. 142 p.: ill.

Combines the concept of total institution with labeling theory to produce a competent study of a woman's prison in Rio de Janeiro.

8389 Lepargneur, François Hubert. Demografia, ética e Igreja. São Paulo: Editôra Atica, 1983. 169 p.: bibl. (Ensaios; 91)

Examines problems presented by rapid population growth and unwanted fertility against Catholic policies regarding these issues. Rejects abortion but supports a national family planning program.

Luyten, Sonia Maria Bibe. Comunicação e aculturação: a colonização holandesa no Paraná. See item **5276.**

8390 Maeyama, Takashi. Religion, kinship, and the middle classes of the Japanese in urban Brazil (Latin American Studies [Univ. of Tsukuba, Special Research Project on Latin America, Sakura-Mura, Japan] 5, 1983, p. 57–82, bibl., charts)

Excellent analysis of the assimilation and accommodation patterns of Japanese immigrants to social class structure and to religious ideologies and institutions and how these relate, in particular, to social class ascription and achievement.

8391 ——— and Robert J. Smith. Omoto: a Japanese "new religion" in Brazil (Latin American Studies [Univ. of Tsukuba, Special Research Project on Latin America, Sakura-Mura, Japan] 5, 1983, p. 83–102, bibl., tables)

Describes transfer to Brazil of Omoto, a Japanese sect and its lack of development due to weak ties with home headquarters and a tendency to syncretism with Catholicism and spiritism. Analyzes in detail petitions made to the sect by believers, more than 90 percent of whom are of Brazilian rather than Japanese origin.

8392 Moll, Peter. Base communities: helping the poor (INDEX, 12:5, Oct. 1983, p. 15–17)

First-hand journalistic and enlightening account of experience with *comunidades eclesiais de base*, as they attempt to help the poor help themselves.

8393 A Morte e os mortos na sociedade brasileira. Edited by José de Souza Martins. São Paulo: Editôra HUCITEC, 1983. 339 p.: bibl., ill.

Consists of 23 articles on attitudes toward and beliefs about death throughout Brazilian history and in present-day Brazilian society (e.g., in literature, among Afro-Brazilians, indigenous Brazilians and in Caipira and Caboclo peasant groups). [W.H. Kracke]

Novaes, Maria Eliana. Professora primária: mestre ou tia? See item **4568.**

Paiva, Vanilda. Pedagogia e luta social no campo paraibano. See item **4572.**

8394 Pastore, José; Hélio Zylberstajn; and Carmen Silvia Pagotto. Mudança social e pobreza no Brasil, 1970–1980: o que ocorreu com a família brasileira? São Paulo: Fundação Instituto de Pesquisas Econômicas (FIPE): Livraria Pioneira Editôra, 1983. 152 p.: bibl. (Biblioteca Pioneira de ciências sociais. Economia. Estudos econômicos)

Imaginative analysis of family units uses 1970 and 1980 census data, both published and unpublished, to examine poverty. Uses definition based on per-capita share of the minimum salary to establish that 18 percent of all families were poor. Poor families were large, young, and frequently headed by women. Between 1970–80 unemployment among poor families increased to the point that one fifth of them did not have a single member employed. During the decade poverty increased in the Northeast and decreased in the southeast. Important study.

8395 Pena, Maria Valéria Junho. Mulheres e trabalhadoras: presença feminina na constituição do sistema fabril. Rio de Janeiro: Paz e Terra, 1981. 227 p.: bibl. (Col. O Mundo, hoje; 40)

Examines social history of Brazil's female labor force (1850–1950), with particular attention being paid to factory labor and the State's role, labor legislation, and women's rights. Regards women as the victims of an alliance between capitalism and patriarchalism.

8396 Pereira, João Baptista Borges. Estudos antropológicos e sociológicos sobre o negro no Brasil (in Contribuções à antropologia em homenagem ao Professor Egon Schaden [see item **1215**] p. 193–206, bibl.)

Review of "anthropological and socio-logical studies of the *negro* in Brazil," distinguishes historically between those that view the *negro* as a manifestation of "race," "culture," or "society." [W.H. Kracke]

Pereira, Luiz Carlos Bresser. Development and crisis in Brazil, 1930–1983. See item **3823.**

8397 Pesquisa acerca dos hábitos e atitudes sexuais dos brasileiros. A pesquisa, Instituto Paulista de Pesquisas de Mercado e Antônio Leal de Santa Inez. Os estudos, Alyrio Cavallieri et al. São Paulo: Editôra Cultrix, 1983. 175 p.: ill.

Seemingly a study inspired by the *Kinsey Report.* Consists of 4860 interviews conducted in 20 large-to-medium sized cities. Introductory chapter describing research methods contains principal results. It is followed by eight commentaries by as many authors using research results as points of departure.

8398 Pessar, Patricia R. Unmasking the politics of religion: the case of Brazilian millenarianism (UCLA/JLAL, 7:2, Winter 1981, p. 255–277, bibl.)

Analyzes messianic movements in the context of folk religions and rural political culture. Concludes that millenarianists rejected many features of the dominant society but championed the patron-dependent relationship which had been undermined by economic and political change. Thus, while the protest was reactionary, it was also revolutionary in the context of the times.

8399 Pierucci, Antonio Flavio. De l'Eglise traditionnelle aux communautés ecclésiales de base (FDD/NED [Problèmes d'Amérique latine, 65] 4675/4676, 12 juillet 1982, p. 57–80)

Analyzes response and relationships of the Catholic Church to the Brazilian State beginning with the Estado Novo and ending with the first cracks of the *abertura.*

8400 Reesink, E.B. The peasant in the sertão: a short exploration of his past and present. Leiden, The Netherlands: Institute of Cultural and Social Studies, Leiden Univ., 1981. 138 p.: bibl., ill. (ICA publication; 47)

Social history of peasants in the Northeast is followed by discussion of their present social, economic, and political situation.

8401 Ribeiro, Boanerges. Protestantismo e cultura brasileira: aspectos culturais da implantação do Protestantismo no Brasil. São Paulo: Casa Editôra Presbiteriana, 1981. 361, 23 p.: bibl., ill.

Contrary to its title, this volume is largely limited to the arrival and spread of the Presbyterian Church in Brazil. Contains transcriptions of documents as well as narrative accounts. Useful reference.

8402 Ribeiro, René. Antropologia da religião e outros estudos. Recife: Fundação Joaquim Nabuco: Editôra Massangana, 1982. 310 p.: bibl.

Collection of author's papers published in several sources (1945–77). Divided into sections dealing with race relations, especially in the Northeast; Afro-Brazilian religions; and messianic social movements. Valuable compilation of works by major Brazilian social scientist.

Rosemberg, Fúlvia; Regina P. Pinto; and **Esmeralda V. Negrão.** A educação da mulher no Brasil. See item **4580.**

8403 Russell-Wood, A.J.R. The black man in slavery and freedom in colonial Brazil. New York: St. Martin's Press, 1982. 295 p., 8 p. of plates: bibl., ill., index.

Another in author's distinguished series of books on race relations in Brazil. Emphasizes social role of the population of color and its cultural practices and values, particularly the economic and social functions of free blacks and mulattos. Concludes that in matters of race ambiguity and flexibility with regard to social and economic functions and status was a major difference between Portuguese America and English America. For historian's comment, see *HLAS 46:3508.*

8404 Saffioti, Heleieth Iara Bongiovani. Do artesanal ao industrial: a exploração da mulher: um estudo de operárias têxteis e de confecções no Brasil e nos Estados Unidos. São Paulo: Editôra HUCITEC, 1981. 184 p.: ill. (Memória feminina)

Examines sex-based wage discrimination in Brazil and US using macro level data. Concludes with an analysis of research data gathered through interviews with female factory workers in São Paulo and data gathered by Helen Safa in interviews with female factory workers in Bayonne, N.J. Examines positive and negative consequences of industrial employment for female workers and tensions between their roles as women and factory workers.

8405 São Paulo, o povo em movimento. Organizadores, Paul Singer e Vivícius Caldeira Brant. Petrópolis: Editôra Vozes: em co-edição com CEBRAP, 1980. 230 p., 1 p. of plates: ill.

Social movements are the main concern of authors of this volume which discusses labor unions, *comunidades eclesiasis de base,* neighborhood movements, feminism, organizations of blacks, and political parties.

8406 Silva, José Francisco Graziano da. A modernização dolorosa: estrutura agrária, fronteira agrícola e trabalhadores rurais no Brasil. Apresentação de Otávio Guilherme Velho. Rio de Janeiro: Zahar Editores, 1982. 192 p.: bibl., ill. (Col. Agricultura e sociedade)

Contains 10 essays (1976–80) which deal with changes in the structure of agriculture and the expansion of the agricultural frontier. Other topics include the rural labor force, small producers in relations to the modernization of agriculture, and an evaluation of the effects of the rural land tax.

Skidmore, Thomas E. Race and class in Brazil: historical perspectives. See *HLAS 46:3680.*

8407 Superintendência do Desenvolvimento do Nordeste (SUDENE), *Brazil.* Divisão de Estudos Demográficos. Estrutura e dinâmica da população do Nordeste brasileiro, 1940–1970. Prepared by A. Moura *et al.* Recife: A Divisão, 1978. 225 p.: graphs, tables (Série População e emprego; 2)

Six papers by different authors examine population growth, age and sex composition, migration, spatial distribution, and educational status. Well integrated and useful. Includes 65 tables.

8408 Trabalhadoras do Brasil. Organizadoras, Maria Cristina A. Bruschini, Fúlvia Rosemberg. São Paulo: Brasiliense, 1982. 203 p.: bibl.

Set of seven papers that examine in detail the status of women as workers in a variety of settings. Documents the exploitation of female labor in subsistence agriculture and in sophisticated urban settings.

8409 Vangelista, Chiara. Le braccia per la fazenda: immigrati e caipiras nella formazione del mercato del lavoro paulista, 1850–1930. Milano, Italy: F. Angeli, 1982. 272 p.: bibl., ill. (Istituto di scienze politiche G. Solari, Univ. di Torino; 29)

Well balanced economic and social analysis of pressures leading to the opening of São Paulo to Italian immigrants as agricultural laborers and of the outcome of that migration. Emphasizes supply, demand, and remuneration of labor.

8410 Violência e cidade. Organizador, Renato Raul Boschi. Ruben George Oliven *et al.* Rio de Janeiro: Zahar Editores, 1982. 98 p.: bibl., ill. (Série Debates urbanos; 2)

Major paper in set of three, by Kowarick and Ant, presents a pessimistic view of the working and living conditions of Brazil's urban working class. Material success is nearly impossible, illness and injury on the job translate into joblessness. Fear and violence are daily companions compounded by long journeys to work and job insecurity.

Wolff, Egon. Judeus nos primórdios do Brasil-República: visto especialmente pela documentação no Rio de Janeiro. See *HLAS 46:3696.*

8411 Zaluar, Alba. Os homens de Deus: um estudo dos santos e das festas no catolicismo popular. Rio de Janeiro: Zahar Editores, 1983. 127 p.: bibl. (Antropologia social)

Examines practices of folk Catholicism from an anthropological perspective viewing them as symbolic, ideological, and intimately connected to relationships among various social classes. Observed changes are said to reflect the secularization of the relationship between patron and worker and of the latter with land and farm animals. Also discusses connections between expansion of the social horizon and local groups and personal networks.

JOURNAL ABBREVIATIONS
SOCIOLOGY

AES/AE American Ethnologist. American Ethnological Society. Washington.

AJA American Jewish Archives. Cincinnati, Ohio.

ASA/ASR American Sociological Review. American Sociological Assn. Manasha, Wis.

ASCH/CH Church History. American Society of Church History, Univ. of Chicago. Chicago.

BAA Boletín de Antropología Americana. Instituto Panamericano de Geografía e Historia. México.

BNB/REN Revista Econômica do Nordeste. Banco do Nordeste do Brasil, Depto. de Estudos Econômicos do Nordeste. Fortaleza.

BSA/S Journal of the British Sociological Assn. Carendon Press. Oxford, England.

CAAAP/AP Amazonía Peruana. Centro Amazónico de Antropología y Aplicación Práctica, Depto. de Documentación y Publicaciones. Lima.

CEDLA/B Boletín de Estudios Latinoamericanos. Centro de Estudios y Documentación Latinoamericanos. Amsterdam.

CLACSO/ERL Estudios Rurales Latinoamericanos. Consejo Latinoamericano de Ciencias Sociales, Secretaría Ejecutiva [y] la Comisión de Estudios Rurales. Bogotá. Rio de Janeiro.

CM/RE Relaciones. El Colegio de Michoacán. Zamora, México.

CMS/IMR The International Migration Review. Center for Migration Studies. New York.

CPES/RPS Revista Paraguaya de Sociología. Centro Paraguayo de Estudios Sociológicos. Asunción.

CPS Comparative Political Studies. Northwestern Univ., Evanston, Ill. [and] Sage Publications, Beverly Hills, Calif.

CSSH Comparative Studies in Society and History. Society for the Comparative Study of Society and History. The Hague.

CSUCA/ESC Estudios Sociales Centroamericanos. Consejo Superior de Universidades Centroamericanas, Confederación Universitaria Centroamericana, Programa

Centroamericana de Ciencias Sociales. San José.

CUA/AQ Anthropological Quarterly. Catholic Univ. of America, Catholic Anthropological Conference. Washington.

FCE/TE El Trimestre Económico. Fondo de Cultura Económica. México.

FDD/NED Notes et études documentaires. France, Direction de la documentation. Paris.

IDES/DE Desarrollo Económico. Instituto de Desarrollo Económico y Social. Buenos Aires.

IFH/C Conjonction. Institut français d'Haïti. Port-au-Prince.

INDEX Index on Censorship. Writers & Scholars International. London.

INED/P Population. Institut national d'études demographiques. Paris.

JDA The Journal of Developing Areas. Western Illinois Univ. Press. Macomb.

JLAS Journal of Latin American Studies. Centers or institutes of Latin American studies at the universities of Cambridge, Glasgow, Liverpool, London and Oxford. Cambridge Univ. Press. London.

JPS The Journal of Peasant Studies. Frank Cass & Co. London.

JSP Journal of Social Psychology. The Journal Press. Provincetown, Mass.

LAP Latin American Perspectives. Univ. of California. Riverside.

LARR Latin American Research Review. Univ. of North Carolina Press for the Latin American Studies Assn. Chapel Hill.

MHD/B Boletín del Museo del Hombre Dominicano. Santo Domingo.

MSTPS/R Revista Mexicana del Trabajo. Secretaría del Trabajo y Previsión Social. México.

NS NS NorthSouth NordSud NorteSur NorteSul. Canadian Assn. of Latin American Studies. Univ. of Ottawa. Ottawa.

NWIG Nieuwe West-Indische Gids. Martinus Nijhoff. The Hague.

PCCLAS/P Proceedings of the Pacific

Coast Council on Latin American Studies. Univ. of California. Los Angeles.

RAE Revista Antioqueña de Economía. Medellín, Colombia.

SAGE/JIAS Journal of Inter-American Studies and World Affairs. Sage Publication for the Center for Advanced International Studies, Univ. of Miami. Coral Gables, Fla.

SEM/E Ethnos. Statens Etnografiska Museum. Stockholm.

SF Social Forces. Univ. of North Carolina Press by the Williams & Wilkins Co. Baltimore, Md.

SP Socialismo y Participación. Ediciones Socialismo y Participación. Lima.

SPSA/JP The Journal of Politics. Southern Political Science Assn. in cooperation with the Univ. of Florida. Gainesville.

SSSP/SP Social Problems. Society for the Study of Social Problems affiliated with the American and International Sociological Assns. Kalamazoo, Mich.

UC/S Signs. Univ. of Chicago Press. Chicago, Ill.

UCLA/JLAL Journal of Latin American Lore. Univ. of California, Latin American Center. Los Angeles.

UCNSA/SA Suplemento Antropológico. Univ. Católica de Nuestra Señora de la Asunción, Centro de Estudios Antropológicos. Asunción.

UCSB/NS New Scholar. Univ. of California, Committee on Hispanic Civilization [and] Center for Chicano Studies. Santa Barbara.

UFB/EB Estudos Baianos. Univ. Federal de Bahia, Centro Editorial e Didático, Núcleo de Publicações. Bahia.

UJSC/ECA ECA (Estudios Centroamericanos). Univ. Centroamericana José Simeón Cañas. San Salvador.

UNAM/AA Anales de Antropología. Univ. Nacional Autónoma de México, Instituto de Investigaciones Históricas. México.

UNAM/RMS Revista Mexicana de Sociología. Univ. Nacional Autónoma de

México, Instituto de Investigaciones Sociales. México.

UPR/RCS Revista de Ciencias Sociales. Univ. de Puerto Rico, Colegio de Ciencias Sociales. Río Piedras.

UWI/SES Social and Economic Studies. Univ. of the West Indies, Institute of Social and Economic Research. Mona, Jamaica.

WD World Development. Pergamon Press. Oxford, England.

YU/IJCS International Journal of Comparative Sociology. York Univ., Dept. of Sociology and Anthropology. Toronto, Canada.

INDEXES

ABBREVIATIONS AND ACRONYMS

Except for journal acronyms which are listed at: a) the end of each major disciplinary section, (e.g., Anthropology, Economics, Education, etc.); and b) after each serial title in the *Title List of Journals Indexed*, p. 707.

a.	annual
ABC	Argentina, Brazil, Chile
A.C.	antes de Cristo
ACAR	Associação de Crédito e Assistência Rural, Brazil
AD	Anno Domini
A.D.	Acción Democrática, Venezuela
ADESG	Associação dos Diplomados de Escola Superior de Guerra, Brazil
AGI	Archivo General de Indias, Sevilla
AGN	Archivo General de la Nación
AID	Agency for International Development
a.k.a.	also known as
Ala.	Alabama
ALALC	Asociación Latinoamericana de Libre Comercio
ALEC	*Atlas lingüístico etnográfico de Colombia*
ANAPO	Alianza Nacional Popular, Colombia
ANCARSE	Associação Nordestina de Crédito e Assistência Rural de Sergipe, Brazil
ANCOM	Andean Common Market
ANDI	Asociación Nacional de Industriales, Colombia
ANUC	Asociación Nacional de Usuarios Campesinos, Colombia
ANUIES	Asociación Nacional de Universidades e Institutos de Enseñanza Superior, Mexico
AP	Acción Popular
APRA	Alianza Popular Revolucionaria Americana
ARENA	Aliança Renovadora Nacional, Brazil
Ariz.	Arizona
Ark.	Arkansas
ASA	Association of Social Anthropologists of the Commonwealth, London
ASSEPLAN	Assessoria de Planejamente e Acompanhamento, Recife, Brazil
Assn.	Association
Aufl.	Auflage (edition, edición)
AUFS	American Universities Field Staff Reports, Hanover, N.H.
Aug.	August, Augustan
aum.	aumentada
b.	born (nació)
BBE	Bibliografia Brasileira de Educação
b.c.	indicates dates obtained by radiocarbon methods
BC	Before Christ
bibl(s).	bibliography(ies)
BID	Banco Interamericano de Desarrollo
BNDE	Banco Nacional de Desenvolvimento Econômico, Brazil
BNH	Banco Nacional de Habitação, Brazil
BP	before present

b/w	black and white
C14	Carbon 14
ca.	*circa* (about)
CACM	Central American Common Market
CADE	Conferencia Anual de Ejecutivos de Empresas, Peru
CAEM	Centro de Altos Estudios Militares, Peru
Calif.	California
CARC	Centro de Arte y Comunicación
CARICOM	Caribbean Common Market
CARIFTA	Caribbean Free Trade Association
CBD	central business district
CD	Christian Democrats, Chile
CDI	Conselho de Desenvolvimento Industrial
CEBRAP	Centro Brasileiro de Análise e Planejamento, São Paulo
CECORA	Centro de Cooperativas de la Reforma Agraria, Colombia
CEDAL	Centro de Estudios Democráticos de América Latina, Costa Rica
CEDE	Centro de Estudios sobre Desarrollo Económico, Univ. de los Andes, Bogotá
CEDEPLAR	Centro de Desenvolvimento e Planejamento Regional, Belo Horizonte, Brazil
CEDES	Centro de Estudios de Estado y Sociedad, Buenos Aires; Centro de Estudos de Educação e Sociedade, São Paulo, Brazil
CEDI	Centro Ecuménico de Documentos e Informação, São Paulo
CEDLA	Centro de Estudios y Documentación Latinoamericanos, Amsterdam
CEESTEM	Centro de Estudios Económicos y Sociales del Tercer Mundo, México
CELADE	Centro Latinoamericano de Demografía
CELADEC	Comisión Evangélica Latinoamericana de Educación Cristiana
CELAM	Consejo Episcopal Latinoamericano
CEMLA	Centro de Estudios Monetarios Latinoamericanos, Mexico
CENDES	Centro de Estudios del Desarrollo, Venezuela
CENIDIM	Centro Nacional de Información, Documentación e Investigación Musicales, Mexico
CENIET	Centro Nacional de Información y Estadísticas del Trabajo, Mexico
CEPADE	Centro Paraguayo de Estudios de Desarrollo Económico y Social
CEPA-SE	Comissão Estadual de Planejamento Agrícola, Sergipe, Brazil
CEPAL	Comisión Económica para América Latina
CERES	Centro de Estudios de la Realidad Económica y Social, Bolivia
CES	constant elasticity of substitution
cf.	compare
CFI	Consejo Federal de Inversiones, Buenos Aires
CGE	Confederación General Económica, Argentina
CGTP	Confederación General de Trabajadores del Perú
chap.	chapter
CHEAR	Council on Higher Education in the American Republics
Cía.	Compañía
CIA	Central Intelligence Agency
CIDA	Comité Interamericano de Desarrollo Agrícola
CIDE	Centro de Investigación y Desarrollo de la Educación, Chile
CIE	Centro de Investigaciones Económicas, Buenos Aires
CIEDLA	Centro Interdisciplinario de Estudios sobre el Desarrollo Latinoamericano, Buenos Aires
CIEDUR	Centro Interdisciplinario de Estudios sobre el Desarrollo/Uruguay, Montevideo
CIEPLAN	Corporación de Investigaciones Económicas para América Latina, Santiago
CIMI	Conselho Indigenista Missionário, Brazil

CINTERFOR	Centro Interamericano de Investigación y Documentación sobre Formación Profesional
CINVE	Centro de Investigaciones Económicas, Montevideo
CIP	Conselho Interministerial de Preços
CIPCA	Centro de Investigación y Promoción del Campesinado, Bolivia
CLACSO	Consejo Latinoamericano de Ciencias Sociales, Secretaría Ejecutiva, Buenos Aires
CLASC	Confederación Latinoamericana Sindical Cristiana
CLE	Comunidad Latinoamericana de Escritores, Mexico
cm	centimeter
CNI	Confederação Nacional da Industria, Brazil
Co.	Company
COB	Central Obrera Boliviana
COBAL	Companhia Brasileira de Alimentos
Col.	Collection, Colección, Coleção
Colo.	Colorado
COMCORDE	Comisión Coordinadora para el Desarrollo Económico, Uruguay
comp(s).	compiler(s), compilador(es)
CONCLAT	Congresso Nacional de Classe Trabalhadora, Brazil
CONDESE	Conselho de Desenvolvimento Econômico de Sergipe, Brazil
Conn.	Connecticut
COPEI	Comité Organizador Pro-Elecciones Independientes, Venezuela
CORFO	Corporación de Fomento de la Producción, Chile
CORP	Corporación para el Fomento de Investigaciones Económicas, Colombia
Corp.	Corporation
corr.	corregida
CP	Communist Party
CPDOC	Centro de Pesquisa e Documentação, Brazil
CRIC	Consejo Regional Indígena del Cauca, Colombia
CSUTCB	Confederación Sindical Unica de Trabajadores Campesinos de Bolivia
CUNY	City University of New York
CVG	Corporación Venezolana de Guayana
d.	died (murió)
DANE	Departamento Nacional de Estadística, Colombia
DC	developed country; Demócratas Cristianos, Chile
d.C	después de Cristo
déc.	décembre
Dec.	December
Del.	Delaware
dept.	department
depto.	departamento
DESCO	Centro de Estudios y Promoción del Desarrollo, Lima
dez.	dezembre
dic.	diciembre
disc.	discography
div(s).	division(s), división(es), divisão(ões)
DNOCS	Departamento Nacional de Obras Contra as Sécas, Brazil
doc.	document, documento
Dr.	Doctor
Dra.	Doctora
DRAE	*Diccionario de la Real Academia Española*
ECLA	Economic Commission for Latin America
ECOSOC	UN Department of Economic and Social Affairs
ed(s).	edition(s), edición(es), editor(s), redactor(es), director(es)

EDEME	Editora Emprendimentos Educacionais, Florianópolis, Brazil
Edo.	Estado
EEC	European Economic Community
EFTA	European Free Trade Association
e.g.	*exempio gratia* (for example)
ELN	Ejército de Liberación Nacional, Colombia
ENDEF	Estudo Nacional da Despesa Familiar, Brazil
ESG	Escola Superior de Guerra, Brazil
estr.	estrenado
et al.	*et alia* (and others)
ETENE	Escritório Técnico de Estudios Econômicos do Nordeste, Brazil
ETEPE	Escritório Técnico de Planejamento, Brazil
EUDEBA	Editorial Universitaria de Buenos Aires
EWG	Europaische Wirtschaftsgemeinschaft. *See* EEC.
facsim(s).	facsimile(s)
FAO	Food and Agriculture Organization of the United Nations
FDR	Frente Democrático Revolucionario, El Salvador
Feb./feb.	February, febrero
FEDECAFE	Federación Nacional de Cafeteros, Colombia
fev.	fevreiro, février
ff.	following
FMLN	Frente Farabundo Martí de Liberación Nacional, El Salvador
FGTS	Fundo do Garantia do Tempo de Serviço, Brazil
FGV·	Fundação Getúlio Vargas
FIEL	Fundación de Investigaciones Económicas Latinoamericanas, Argentina
film.	filmography
fl.	flourished
Fla.	Florida
FLACSO	Facultad Latinoamericana de Ciencias Sociales
FMI	Fondo Monetario Internacional
fold.	folded
fol(s).	folio(s)
FRG	Federal Republic of Germany
FSLN	Frente Sandinista de Revolución Nacional, Nicaragua
ft.	foot, feet
FUAR	Frente Unido de Acción Revolucionaria, Colombia
FUNAI	Fundação Nacional do Indio, Brazil
Ga.	Georgia
GAO	General Accounting Office, Washington
GATT	General Agreement on Tariffs and Trade
GDP	gross domestic product
GDR	German Democratic Republic
GEIDA	Grupo Executivo de Irrigação para o Desenvolvimento Agrícola, Brazil
Gen.	General
GMT	Greenwich Meridian Time
GPA	grade point average
GPO	Government Printing Office, Washington
h.	hijo
ha.	hectares, hectáreas
HLAS	*Handbook of Latin American Studies*
HMAI	*Handbook of Middle American Indians*
Hnos.	hermanos
IBBD	Instituto Brasileiro de Bibliografia e Documentação
IBGE	Instituto Brasileiro de Geografia e Estatística, Rio de Janeiro
IBRD	International Bank of Reconstruction and Development

ICA	Instituto Colombiano Agropecuario
ICAIC	Instituto Cubano de Arte e Industria Cinematográficas
ICCE	Instituto Colombiano de Construcción Escolar
ICE	International Cultural Exchange
ICSS	Instituto Colombiano de Seguridad Social
ICT	Instituto de Crédito Territorial, Colombia
IDB	Inter-American Development Bank
i.e.	*id est* (that is)
IEL	Instituto Euvaldo Lodi, Brazil
IEP	Instituto de Estudios Peruanos
IERAC	Instituto Ecuatoriano de Reforma Agraria y Colonización
IFAD	International Fund for Agricultural Development
IICA	Instituto Interamericano de Ciencias Agrícolas, San José
III	Instituto Indigenista Interamericana, Mexico
IIN	Instituto Indigenista Nacional, Guatemala
ill.	illustration(s)
Ill.	Illinois
ILO	International Labour Organization, Geneva
IMES	Instituto Mexicano de Estudios Sociales
IMF	International Monetary Fund, Washington
Impr.	Imprenta, Imprimerie
in.	inches
INAH	Instituto Nacional de Antropología e Historia, Mexico
INBA	Instituto Nacional de Bellas Artes, Mexico
Inc.	Incorporated
INCORA	Instituto Colombiano de Reforma Agraria
Ind.	Indiana
INEP	Instituto Nacional de Estudios Pedagógicos, Brazil
INI	Instituto Nacional Indigenista, Mexico
INIT	Instituto Nacional de Industria Turística, Cuba
INPES/IPEA	Instituto de Planejamento Econômico e Social, Instituto de Pesquisas, Brazil
INTAL	Instituto para la Integración de América Latina
IPA	Instituto de Pastoral Andina, Univ. de San Antonio de Abad, Seminario de Antropología, Cuzco, Peru
IPEA	Instituto de Pesquisas Econômico-Social Aplicadas, Brazil
IPES/GB	Instituto de Pesquisas e Estudos Sociais, Guanabara, Brazil
IPHAN	Instituto de Patrimônio Histórico e Artístico Nacional, Brazil
ir.	irregular
IS	Internacional Socialista
ITT	International Telephone and Telegraph
Jan./jan.	January/janeiro, janvier
JLP	Jamaican Labour Party
JUCEPLAN	Junta Central de Planificación, Cuba
Kan.	Kansas
km	kilometers, kilómetres
Ky.	Kentucky
La.	Louisiana
LASA	Latin American Studies Association
LDC(s)	less developed country(ies)
LP	long-playing record
Ltda.	Limitada
m	meters, metros
m.	murió (died)
M	mille, mil, thousand
MAPU	Movimiento de Acción Popular Unitario, Chile

MARI	Middle American Research Institute, Tulane University, New Orleans
Mass.	Massachusetts
MCC	Mercado Común Centro-Americano
Md.	Maryland
MDB	Movimiento Democrático Brasileiro
MDC	more developed country(ies)
MEC	Ministério de Educação e Cultura, Brazil
Mich.	Michigan
mimeo	mimeographed, mimeografiado
min.	minutes, minutos
Minn.	Minnesota
MIR	Movimiento de Izquierda Revolucionaria, Chile
Miss.	Mississippi
MIT	Massachusetts Institute of Technology
ml	milliliter
MLN	Movimiento de Liberación Nacional
mm.	millimeter
MNC's	multinational corporations
MNR	Movimiento Nacionalista Revolucionario, Bolivia
Mo.	Missouri
MOBRAL	Movimento Brasileiro de Alfabetização, Brazil
MOIR	Movimiento Obrero Independiente y Revolucionario, Colombia
Mont.	Montana
MRL	Movimiento Revolucionario Liberal, Colombia
ms.	manuscript
msl	mean sea level
n.	nació (born)
NBER	National Bureau of Economic Research, Cambridge, Massachusetts
N.C.	North Carolina
N.D.	North Dakota
Neb.	Nebraska
neubearb.	neubearbeitet (revised, corregida)
Nev.	Nevada
n.f.	neue Folge
N.H.	New Hampshire
NIEO	New International Economic Order
NIH	National Institutes of Health, Washington
N.J.	New Jersey
N.M.	New Mexico
no(s).	number(s), número(s)
NOIE	Nuevo Orden Económico Internacional
NOSALF	Scandinavian Committee for Research in Latin America
Nov./nov.	November/noviembre, novembre, novembro
NSF	National Science Foundation
N.Y.	New York
OAB	Ordem dos Advogados do Brasil
OAS	Organization of American States
Oct./oct.	October/octubre, octobre
ODEPLAN	Oficina de Planificación Nacional, Chile
OEA	Organización de los Estados Americanos
OIT	See ILO.
Okla.	Oklahoma
Okt.	Oktober
op.	opus
OPANAL	Organismo para la Proscripción de las Armas Nucleares en América Latina

OPEC	Organization of Petroleum Exporting Countries
OPEP	Organización de Países Exportadores de Petróleo
OPIC	Overseas Investment Corporation
Or.	Oregon
OREALC	Oficina Regional de Educación para América Latina y el Caribe
ORIT	Organización Regional Interamericana del Trabajo
out.	outubre
p.	page(s)
Pa.	Pennsylvania
PAN	Partido Acción Nacional, Mexico
PC	Partido Comunista
PCCLAS	Pacific Coast Council on Latin American Studies
PCN	Partido de Conciliación Nacional, El Salvador
PCP	Partido Comunista del Perú
PCR	Partido Comunista Revolucionario, Chile and Argentina
PCV	Partido Comunista de Venezuela
PDC	Partido Demócrata Cristiano, Chile
PDS	Partido Democrático Social, Brazil
PDT	Partido Democrático Trabalhista, Brazil
PEMEX	Petróleos Mexicanos
PETROBRAS	Petróleo Brasileiro
PIMES	Programa Integrado de Mestrado em Economia e Sociologia, Brazil
PIP	Partido Independiente de Puerto Rico
PLANAVE	Engenharia e Planejamento Limitada, Brazil
PLANO	Planejamento e Assesoria Limitada, Brazil
PLN	Partido Liberación Nacional, Costa Rica
PMDB	Partido Movimento Democrático Brasileiro
PNAD	Pesquisa Nacional por Amuestra Domiciliar, Brazil
PNM	People's National Movement, Trinidad and Tobago
PNP	People's National Party, Jamaica
pop.	population
port(s).	portrait(s)
PPP	purchasing power parities
PRD	Partido Revolucionario Dominicano
PREALC	Programa Regional del Empleo para América Latina y el Caribe, Organización Internacional del Trabajo, Santiago
PRI	Partido Revolucionario Institucional, Mexico
PROABRIL	Centro de Projetos Industriais, Brazil
Prof.	Professor(a)
PRONAPA	Programa Nacional de Pesquisas Arqueológicas, Brazil
prov.	province, provincia
PS	Partido Socialista, Chile
pseud.	pseudonym, pseudónimo
PT	Partido dos Trabalhadores, Brazil
pt(s).	part(s), parte(s)
PTB	Partido Trabalhista Brasileiro
pub.	published, publisher
PUC	Pontificia Universidad Católica, Rio de Janeiro
PURSC	Partido Unido de la Revolución Socialista de Cuba
q.	quarterly
rev.	revisada, revised
R.I.	Rhode Island
s.a.	semiannual
SALALM	Seminar on the Acquisition of Latin American Library Materials
sd.	sound

s.d.	*sine datum* (no date, sin fecha)
S.D.	South Dakota
SDR	special drawing rights
sec(s).	section(s), sección(es), secção(ões)
SELA	Sistema Económico Latinoamericano
SENAC	Serviço Nacional de Aprendizagem Comercial, Rio de Janeiro
SENAI	Serviço Nacional de Aprendizagem Industrial, São Paulo
SEP	Secretaría de Educación Pública, Mexico
SEPLA	Seminario Permanente sobre Latinoamérica, Mexico
Sept./sept.	September, septiembre, septembre
SES	socioeconomic status
SESI	Serviço Social de Industria, Brazil
set.	setembre
SI	Socialist International
SIECA	Secretaría Permanente del Tratado General de Integración Centroamericana
SIL	Summer Institute of Linguistics
SINAMOS	Sistema Nacional de Apoyo a la Movilización Social, Peru
S.J.	Society of Jesus
s.l.	*sine loco* (place of publication unknown)
s.n.	*sine nomine* (publisher unknown)
SNA	Sociedad Nacional de Agricultura, Chile
SPP	Secretaría de Programación y Presupuesto, Mexico
SPVEA	Superintendência do Plano de Valorização Econômica de Amazônia, Brazil
sq.	square
SSRC	Social Sciences Research Council, New York
SUDAM	Superintendência de Desenvolvimento da Amazônia, Brazil
SUDENE	Superintendência de Desenvolvimento do Nordeste, Brazil
SUFRAME	Superintendência da Zona Franca de Manaus, Brazil
SUNY	State University of New York
t.	tomo(s), tome(s)
TAT	Thematic Apperception Test
TB	tuberculosis
Tenn.	Tennessee
Tex.	Texas
TG	transformational generative
TL	Thermoluminescent
TNEs	Transnational enterprises
TNP	Tratado de No Proliferación
trans.	translator
UCA	Universidad Centroamericana José Simeón Cañas, San Salvador
UCLA	University of California, Los Angeles
UDN	União Democrática Nacional, Brazil
UK	United Kingdom
UN	United Nations
UNAM	Universidad Nacional Autónoma de México
UNCTAD	United Nations Conference on Trade and Development
UNDP	UN Development Programme
UNEAC	Unión de Escritores y Artistas de Cuba
UNESCO	UN Educational, Scientific and Cultural Organization
UNI/UNIND	União das Nações Indígenas
Univ(s).	university(ies), universidad(es), universidade(s), université(s), universität(s), universitá(s)
uniw.	uniwersytet
UP	Unidad Popular, Chile
URD	Unidad Revolucionaria Democrática

URSS	Unión de Repúblicas Soviéticas Socialistas
US	United States
USAID	*See* AID.
USIA	US Information Agency, Washington
USSR	Union of Soviet Socialist Republics
UTM	Universal Transverse Mercator
v.	volume(s), volumen (volúmenes)
Va.	Virginia
viz.	*videlicet* (that is, namely)
vol(s).	volume(s), volumen (volúmenes)
vs.	versus
Vt.	Vermont
W.Va.	West Virginia
Wash.	Washington
Wis.	Wisconsin
Wyo.	Wyoming
yr(s).	year(s)

TITLE LIST OF JOURNALS INDEXED

Journals that have been included in the *Handbook* as individual items are listed alphabetically by title in the *Author Index*, p. 747.

AEI Foreign Policy and Defense Review. American Enterprise Institute for Public Policy Research. Washington.

Acta Científica Venezolana. Asociación Venezolana para el Avance de la Ciencia. Caracas. (AVAC/ACV)

Acta Endocrinológica. Copenhagen.

Acta Amazônica. Manaus.

Actualidades. Consejo Nacional de la Cultura, Centro de Estudios Latinoamericanos Rómulo Gallegos. Caracas. (CNC/A)

Advances in World Archaeology. Academic Press. New York.

Air University Review. US Air Force. Maxwell Air Force Base, Ala. (AF/AUR)

Allegemeine und Vergleichende Archäologie Beitrage. München, FRG.

Allpanchis. Instituto de Pastoral Andina. Cuzco, Perú. (IPA/A)

A Amazônia Brasileira em Foco. Rio de Janeiro.

Amazonía Peruana. Centro Amazónico de Antropología y Aplicación Práctica, Depto. de Documentación y Publicaciones. Lima. (CAAAP/AP)

América Indígena. Instituto Indigenista Interamericano. México. (III/AI)

América Latina. Academia de Ciencias de la URSS. Moscú. (URSS/AL)

American Anthropologist. American Anthropological Assn. (AAA/AA)

American Antiquity. Society for American Archaeology. Menasha, Wis. (SAA/AA)

The American Economic Review. American Economic Assn. Evanston, Ill. (AEA/AER)

American Ethnologist. American Ethnological Society. Washington. (AES/AE)

American Jewish Archives. Cincinnati, Ohio. (AJA)

American Journal of Clinical Nutrition. American Society for Clinical Nutrition. New York.

The American Journal of Economics and Sociology. Francis Neilson Fund [and] Robert Schalkenbach Foundation. New York. (AJES)

American Journal of Medical Genetics. Alan R. Liss Inc. New York.

American Journal of Physical Anthropology. American Assn. of Physical Anthropologists [and] the Wistar Institute of Anatomy and Biology. Philadelphia. (AJPA)

American Political Science Review. American Political Science Assn. Columbus, Ohio. (APSA/R)

American Sociological Review. American Sociological Assn. Menasha, Wis. (ASA/ASR)

The Americas. Academy of American Franciscan History. Washington. (AAFH/TAM)

Amérique latine. Centre de recherche sur l'Amérique latine et la Tiers mond. Paris.

Anales de Antropología. Univ. Nacional Autónoma de México, Instituto de Investigaciones Históricas. México. (UNAM/AA)

Anales del Instituto de Investigaciones Estéticas. Univ. Nacional Autónoma de México. México. (IIE/A)

Annals of Human Biology. Taylor & Francis. London.

Annals of the Carnegie Museum. Pittsburgh, Pa.

Annals of the Southeastern Conference on Latin American Studies. Kennesaw College, Marietta, Ga. (SECOLAS/A)

Annales de Géographie. Paris.

Annual Review of Anthropology. Annual Review, Inc. Palo Alto, Calif.

Anthropologica. Pontificia Univ. Católica del Perú. Lima.

Anthropological Linguistics. A publication of the Archives of the Languages of the World. Indiana Univ., Anthropology Dept. Bloomington. (IU/AL)

Anthropological Quarterly. Catholic Univ. of

America, Catholic Anthropological Conference. Washington. (CUA/AQ)

Anthropologie et sociétés. Univ. Laval. Québec, Canada.

Anthropology. Dept. of Anthropology. State University of New York. Stony Brook.

Antiquaries Journal. Society of Antiquaries. London.

Antiquity. Antiquity Trust. Cambridge, England. (AT/A)

Antropología Ecuatoriana. Casa de la Cultura Ecuatoriana. Quito.

Antropológica. Fundación La Salle de Ciencias Naturales, Instituto Caribe de Antropología y Sociología. Caracas. (FSCN/A)

Anuário Antropológico. Edições Tempo Brasileiro. Rio de Janeiro.

Anuário de Divulgação Científica. Instituto Goiana de Pré-História e Antropologia, Univ. Católica de Goiás. Goiânia, Brazil.

Anuario de Estudios Americanos. Consejo Superior de Investigaciones Científicas [and] Univ. de Sevilla, Escuela de Estudios Hispano-Americanos. Sevilla. (EEHA/AEA)

Anuario del Instituto Boliviano de Biología de la Altura. La Paz.

Apuntes. Univ. del Pacífico, Centro de Investigación. Lima. (UP/A)

Archaeological Reviews from Cambridge. Dept. of Archaeology, Cambridge Univ. Cambridge, England.

Archaeology. Archaeological Institute of America. New York. (AIA/A)

Archaeology and Anthropology. Walter Roth Museum of Archaeology and Anthropology. Georgetown.

Archaestronomy. Supplement to Journal of the History of Astronomy. Giles, England.

Archiv für Völkerkunde. Museum für Völkerkunde in Wien und von Verein Freunde der Völkerkunde. Wien. (MVW/AV)

Archivos Latinoamericanos de Nutrición. Sociedad Latinoamericano de Nutrición. Caracas. (SLN/ALN)

Archivos Venezolanas de Puericultura y Pediatría. Sociedad Venezolana de Puericultura y Pediatría. Caracas. (SVPP/A)

Areíto. Areíto, Inc. New York. (AR)

Argos. Univ. Simón Bolívar, Div. de Ciencias Sociales y Humanidades. Caracas.

Armed Forces and Society. Univ. of Chicago. Chicago. (AFS)

Arqueología Boliviana. Instituto Nacional de Arqueología. La Paz.

Arstryck. Etnografiska Museum. Göteborg, Sweden. (EM/A)

The Atlantic. Atlantic Monthly Co. Boston.

Baessler-Archiv. Museums für Völkerkunde. Berlin, FRG. (MV/BA)

The Banker. Financial Times Business Publishing. London.

Behavior Science Research. Human Relations Area Files. New Haven. (HRAF/BSR)

Beiträge zur Allgemeinen und Vergleichenden Archäologie. München, FRG.

Belizean Studies. Belizean Institute of Social Research and Action [and] St. John's College. Belize City. (BISRA/BS)

Bijdragen tot de Taal-, Land- en Volkenkunde. Koninklijk Instituut voor Taal-, Land- en Volkenkunde. Leiden, The Netherlands. (KITLV/B)

Biological Conservation. Elsevier Publishing Co. Essex, England.

Bohemia. La Habana.

Boletim do Museo do Indio. Rio de Janeiro.

Boletim Série Ensaios. Instituto de Arqueologia Brasileira. Rio de Janeiro.

Boletín. Museo del Oro, Banco de la República. Bogotá.

Boletín Americanista. Univ. de Barcelona, Facultad de Geografía e Historia, Depto. de Historia de América. Barcelona. (UB/BA)

Boletín Bibliográfico de Antropología Americana. Instituto Panamericano de Geografía e Historia, Comisión de Historia. México. (BBAA)

Boletín de Antropología Americana. See Boletín Bibliográfico de Antropología Americana.

Boletín de Coyuntura Socio-Económica. Univ. del Valle. Cali, Colombia.

Boletín de Estudios Latinoamericanos. Centro de Estudios y Documentación Latinoamericanos. Amsterdam. (CEDLA/B)

Boletin de la Academia de Ciencias Políticas y Sociales. Caracas. (ACPS/B)

Boletín de la Academia Nacional de Historia. Buenos Aires. (ANH/B)

Boletín de la Academia Nacional de Historia. Quito. (EANH/B)

Boletín de la Academia Nacional de la Historia. Caracas. (VANH/B)

Boletín de la Asociación Costarricense de Arqueólogos. San José.

Boletín de la Sociedad Geográfica de Lima. Lima. (SGL/B)

Boletín de Lima. Lima.

Boletín de Prehistoria de Chile. Univ. de Chile, Facultad de Filosofía, Humanidades y Educación, Depto. de Ciencias Socio-

lógicas y Antropológicas. Santiago.
(UC/BPC)

Boletín del Museo del Hombre Dominicano. Santo Domingo. (MHD/B)

Boletín del Programa Arqueología de Rescate. Corpozulia, Univ. del Zulia. Maracaibo, Venezuela.

Boletín del Sistema Bibliotecario de la UNAH. Univ. Nacional Autónoma de Honduras. Tegucigalpa.

Boletín Indigenista Venezolano. Ministerio de Justicia, Comisión Indigenista. Caracas. (VMJ/BIV)

Brenesia. San José.

Bulletin. Institute of Archaeology, Univ. of London. London.

Bulletin. Société suisse des américanistes. Geneva. (SSA/B)

Bulletin de l'Association de géographes français. Paris. (AGF/B)

Bulletin de l'Institute français d'études andines. Lima. (IFEA/B)

Bulletin of Eastern Caribbean Affairs. Univ. of the West Indies, Institute of Social & Economic Research, Eastern Caribbean. Cave Hill, Barbados.

Bulletin of the International Committee on Urgent Anthropological and Ethnological Research. Vienna. (ICUAER/B)

Bulletin of the Pan American Health Organization. Washington. (PAHO/B)

Cadernos de Pesquisa. Fundação Carlos Chagas. São Paulo.

Cahiers de Amériques latines. Paris. (CDAL)

Cahiers des géographie de Québec. Univ. Laval, Institut de géographie. Québec, Canada. (ULIG/C)

Les Cahiers d'outre-mer. Institut de géographie, Faculté des lettres de Bordeaux, Institut de la France d'outre-mer; Société de géographie de Bordeaux *avec le concours* du Centre national de la recherche scientifique [and] VI Section de l'Ecole pratique des hautes études. Bordeaux, France. (SGB/COM)

Cambridge Anthropology.

Canadian Geographer/Le Géographe canadien. Canadian Assn. of Geographers. Toronto, Canada. (CAG/CG)

Caribbean Journal of Education. Univ. of the West Indies. Mona, Jamaica.

Caribbean Journal of Religious Studies. United Theological College of the West Indies. Kingston.

Caribbean Quarterly. Univ. of the West Indies. Mona, Jamaica. (UWI/CQ)

Caribbean Review. Florida International Univ., Office of Academic Affairs. Miami. (FIU/CR)

Caribbean Studies. Univ. of Puerto Rico, Instituto of Caribbean Studies. Río Piedras. (UPR/CS)

Casa de las Américas. Instituto Cubano del Libro. La Habana. (CDLA)

Chungará. Univ. del Norte, Depto. de Antropología. Arica, Chile. (UN/C)

Church History. American Society of Church History, Univ. of Chicago. Chicago. (ASCH/CH)

Cielo Abierto. Lima.

Ciencia Interamericana. Organization of American States, Dept. of Scientific Affairs. Washington. (OAS/CI)

Civilisations. International Institute of Differing Civilizations. Bruxelles. (IIDC/C)

Colombia Journal of World Business. Columbia Univ. New York. (CJWB)

Comercio Exterior. Banco Nacional de Comercio Exterior. México. (BNCE/CE)

Commentary. American Jewish Committee. New York. (AJC/C)

Comparative Education Review. Comparative Education Society. New York. (CES/CER)

Comparative Political Studies. Northwestern Univ., Evanston, Ill. [and] Sage Publications, Beverly Hills, Calif. (CPS)

Comparative Politics. City Univ. of New York, Political Science Program. New York. (CUNY/CP)

Comparative Studies in Society and History. Society for the Comparative Study of Society and History. The Hague. (CSSH)

The Condor. Cooper Ornithological Society. Berkeley, Calif.

Conjonction. Institut français d'Haïti. Port-au-Prince. (IFH/C)

Contemporary Review. Contemporary Review Co. London.

Contribuciones. Konrad-Adenauer-Stiftung A.C. Centro Interdisciplinario de Estudios sobre el Desarrollo Latinoamericano (CIEDLA). Buenos Aires.

Criterio. Editorial Criterio. Buenos Aires. (CRIT)

Croissance des jeunes nations. Paris. (CJN)

Cuadernos de Arquitectura Mesoamericana. Univ. Nacional Autonóma de México. México.

Cuadernos de Comunicación Alternativa. Centro de Integración de Medios de Comunicación Alternativa. La Paz.

Cuadernos de Historia. Depto. de Ciencias Históricas, Univ. de Chile. Santiago.

Cuadernos Políticos. Ediciones Era. México. (CP)

Cuba Internacional. Prensa Latina. La Habana.

Cuba Socialista. La Habana.

Cuban Studies/Estudios Cubanos. Univ. of Pittsburgh, Univ. Center for International Studies, Center for Latin American Studies. Pittsburgh, Pa. (UP/CSEC)

Cuicuilco. Escuela Nacional de Antropología e Historia. México.

Cultura de Guatemala. Univ. Rafael Landívar. Guatemala.

Cultural Survival Quarterly. Cambridge, Mass.

Culture and Agriculture. Anthropological Study Group on Agrarian Systems.

Current Anthropology. Univ. of Chicago. Chicago. (UC/CA)

Current History. A monthly magazine of world affairs. Philadelphia. (CUH)

Debates en Antropología. Pontificia Univ. Católica del Perú, Depto. de Ciencias Sociales. Lima. (PUCP/DA)

Desarrollo Económico. Instituto de Desarrollo Económico y Social. Buenos Aires. (IDES/DE)

Desarrollo Indoamericano. Barranquilla, Colombia.

Development Digest. Washington.

Dialectical Anthropology. New School of Social Research. New York.

Diálogos. El Colegio de México. México. (CM/D)

Diogenes. International Council for Philosophy and Humanistic Studies. Chicago. (ICPHS/D)

Dissent. Dissent Publishing Assn. New York. (DIS)

Docencia. Univ. Autónoma de Guadalajara. México. (UAG/D)

Documentos de Trabajo. Univ. de Tarapacá, Instituto de Antropología y Arqueología. Arica, Chile.

ECA (Estudios Centroamericanos). Univ. Centroamericana José Simeón Cañas. San Salvador. (UJSC/ECA)

Early Human Development. Elsevier Biomedical Press. Amsterdam.

Ecology of Food and Nutrition. Gordon & Breach. London.

Economia Internazionale. Rivista dell'Instituto di Economia Internazionale. Genova, Italy. (IEI/EI)

Economía Política. Univ. Nacional Autónoma de Honduras, Instituto de Investigaciones Económicos y Sociales. Tegucigalpa.

Economía y Desarrollo. Univ. de La Habana, Instituto de Economía. La Habana. (UH/ED)

Economic Botany. New York Botanical Garden *for the* Society for Economic Botany. New York. (SEB/EB)

Economic Development and Cultural Change. Univ. of Chicago, Research Center in Economic Development and Cultural Change. Chicago, Ill. (UC/EDCC)

Economic Survey of Latin America and the Caribbean. United Nations, Economic Commission for Latin America. Santiago.

Económica. Facultad de Ciencias Económicas, Univ. Nacional de La Plata. La Plata, Argentina. (UNLP/E)

Educação & Sociedade. Centro de Estudos de Educação e Sociedade (CEDES). São Paulo.

La Educación. Organization of American States, Dept. of Educational Affairs. Washington. (OAS/LE)

Encontros com a Civilização Brasileira. Editôra Civilização Brasileira. Rio de Janeiro. (ECB)

Ensayos Económicos. Banco Central de la República Argentina. Buenos Aires. (BCRA/EE)

Environmental Conservation. Elsevier Sequoia *for the* Foundation for Environmental Conservation. Lausanne, Switzerland.

Erdkunde. Archiv für Wissenschaftliche Geographie. Univ. Bonn, Geographisches Institut. Bonn, FRG. (UBGI/E)

Estudios Andinos. Univ. of Pittsburgh, Latin American Studies Center. Pittsburgh, Pa. (UP/EA)

Estudios de Ciencias y Letras. Instituto de Filosofía. Montevideo.

Estudios de Cultura Maya. Univ. Nacional Autónoma de México, Centro de Estudios Mayas. México. (CEM/ECM)

Estudios de Cultura Náhuatl. Univ. Nacional Autónoma de México, Instituto de Historia, Seminario de Cultura Náhuatl. México. (UNAM/ECN)

Estudios Latinoamericanos. Polska Akademia Nauk [Academia de Ciencias de Polonia], Instytut Historii [Instituto de Historia]. Warszawa. (PAN/ES)

Estudios Rurales Latinoamericanos. Consejo Latinoamericano de Ciencias Sociales, Secretaría Ejecutiva [and] Comisión de Estudios Rurales. Bogotá. (CLACSO/ERL)

Estudios Sociales Centroamericanos. Consejo Superior de Universidades Centroamericanas, Confederación Universitaria Centroamericana, Programa Centroamericano de Ciencias Sociales. San José. (CSUCA/ESC)

Estudos Baianos. Univ. Federal de Bahia, Centro Editorial e Didático, Núcleo de Publicações. Bahia. (UFB/EB)

Estudos Brasileiros. Univ. Federal do Paraná, Setor de Ciências Humanas, Centro de Estudos Brasileiros. Curitiba. (UFP/EB)

Estudos Econômicos. Univ. de São Paulo, Instituto de Pesquisas Econômicas. São Paulo. (IPE/EE)

Ethnic Groups. Gordon & Breach Science Publishers. New York.

Ethnohistory. American Society for Ethnohistory. Buffalo, N.Y. (ASE/E)

Ethnology. Univ. of Pittsburgh. Pittsburgh, Pa. (UP/E)

Ethnos. Statens Etnografiska Museum. Stockholm. (SEM/E)

Ethos. Univ. of California. Berkeley.

Finance and Development. International Monetary Fund. Washington.

The Florida Anthropologist. Florida Anthropological Society. Gainesville. (FAS/FA)

Foreign Affairs. Council on Foreign Relations. New York. (CFR/FA)

Foreign Policy. National Affairs Inc. [and] Carnegie Endowment for International Peace. New York. (FP)

Foro Internacional. El Colegio de México. México. (CM/FI)

Fragmentos. Centro de Estudios Latinoamericanos Rómulo Gallegos, Depto. de Investigaciones. Caracas.

Freedom at Issue. Freedom House. New York.

Gaceta Arqueológica Andina. Instituto Andino de Estudios Arqueológicos. Lima.

Genetics. Genetics Society of America. Austin, Tex.

Gente. Buenos Aires.

Geoforum. Pergamon Press. Oxford, England.

Geographica Helvetica. Schweizerische Zeitschrift für Länder- und Völkerkunde. Kümmerly & Frey, Geographischer Verlag. Bern. (GH)

The Geographical Magazine. London. (GM)

Geographical Review. American Geographical Society. New York. (AGS/GR)

Geographische Rundschau. Zeitschrift für Schulgeographie. Georg Westermann Verlag. Braunschweig, FRG. (GR)

Geojournal. Wiesbaden, FRG.

The Global Reporter. Anthropology Resource Center. Boston.

Grassroots Development. Inter-American Foundation. Rosslyn, Va.

Guaman-Poma. Centro de Investigación de Ciencias Sociales, Económicas, Administrativas y Humanidades, Univ. Nacional del Centro del Perú. Huancayo.

HISLA. Review latinoamericana de historia económica y social. Lima. (HISLA)

Habitat International. Pergamon Press. Oxford, England.

Harper's Magazine. New York.

Harvard University Gazette. Cambridge, Mass.

Hastings International and Comparative Law Review. Univ. of California, Hastings College of the Law. San Francisco. (HICLR)

Hispanic American Historical Review. Duke Univ. Press for the Conference on Latin American History of the American Historical Assn. Durham, N.C. (HAHR)

Historia Boliviana. La Paz.

Historia Obrera. Centro de Estudios Históricos del Movimiento Obrero Mexicano. México. (CEHSMO)

The Historian. Phi Alpha Theta, National Honor Society in History. Univ. of Pennsylvania. University Park. (PAT/TH)

Historias. Instituto Nacional de Antropología e Historia. México.

Historiografía y Bibliografía Americanista. Escuela de Estudios Hispano-Americanos de Sevilla. Sevilla. (EEHA/HBA)

History of Education Quarterly. New York.

History Workshop. Routledge & Kegan Paul. London.

L'Homme. La Sorbonne, L'Ecole pratique des hautes études. Paris. (EPHE/H)

Human Biology. Official publication of the Human Biology Council. Wayne State Univ., School of Medicine. Detroit, Mich. (WSU/HB)

Human Ecology. Plenum, N.Y.

Human Genetics. Springer Verlag. Hamburg, FRG.

Human Heredity. Basel, Switzerland. (HH)

Human Organization. Society for Applied Anthropology. New York. (SAA/HO)

Humanitas. Univ. de Nuevo León, Centro de Estudios Humanísticos. Monterrey, México. (UNL/H)

Ibero Americana. Scandinavian Assn. for Research on Latin America (NOSALF). Stockholm. (NOSALF/IA)

Ibero-Amerikanisches Archiv. Ibero-

Amerikanisches Institut. Berlin, FRG. (IAA)

Index on Censorship. Writers & Scholars International. London. (INDEX)

Indiana. Beiträge zur Volker-und Sprachenkunde, Archäologie und Anthropologie des Indianischen Amerika. Ibero-Amerikanisches Institut. Berlin, FRG. (IAI/I)

Informaciones Geográficas. Univ. de Chile, Depto. de Geografía. Santiago. (UC/IG)

Informe ODCA. Organización Demócrata Cristiana de América, Secretaría General. Caracas.

Integración Latinoamericana. Instituto para la Integración de América Latina. Buenos Aires. (INTAL/IL)

Inter-American Economic Affairs. Washington. (IAMEA)

Interciencia. Asociación Interciencia. Caracas. (AI/I)

Interior. Ministério do Interior. Brasília.

International Affairs. Moscow. (IA)

International Affairs. Royal Institute of International Affairs. London. (RIIA/IA)

International Journal of American Linguistics. Indiana Univ. *under the auspices of the* Linguistic Society of America, American Anthropological Assn., *with the cooperation of the* Joint Committee on American Native Languages. Bloomington. (IU/IJAL)

International Journal of Comparative Sociology. York Univ., Dept. of Sociology and Anthropology. Toronto, Canada. (YU/IJCS)

International Migration/Migrations internationales/Migraciones Internacionales. Intergovernmental Committee for European Migration [and] the Research Group for European Migration Problems. Geneva. (ICEM/IM)

The International Migration Review. Center for Migration Studies. New York. (CMS/IMR)

International Perspectives: The Canadian Journal of World Affairs. Canada, Dept. of External Affairs. Ottawa. (DEA/IP)

International Review of Administrative Sciences. International Institute of Administrative Sciences. Bruxelles. (IIAS/IRAS)

International Review of Education. UN Educational, Scientific, and Cultural Organization, Institute for Education. Hamburg, FRG. (UNESCO/IRE)

International Review of the Aesthetics and

Sociology of Music. Muzicka Akademija u Zagreby, Institute of Musicology. Zagreb, Yugoslavia.

Iztapalapa. Univ. Autónoma Metropolitana, Div. de Ciencias Sociales y Humanidades. Iztalapa, México.

Jahrbuch für Geschichte von Staat, Wirtschaft und Gesellschaft Lateinamerika. Köln, FRG. (JGSWGL)

Jahrbuch Preussischer Kulturbesitz. Berlin, FRG.

Jamaica Journal. Institute of Jamaica. Kingston. (IJ/JJ)

Journal de la Société des américanistes. Paris. (SA/J)

Journal of American Folklore. American Folklore Society. Washington. (AFS/JAF)

Journal of Anthropological Archaeology. Academic Press. New York.

Journal of Anthropological Research. Univ. of New Mexico, Dept. of Anthropology. Albuquerque. (UNM/JAR)

Journal of Archaeological Science. London.

Journal of Biosocial Science. Oxford, England.

The Journal of Caribbean History. Univ. of the West Indies, Dept. of History [and] Caribbean Universities Press. St. Lawrence, Barbados. (UWI/JCH)

Journal of Caribbean Studies. Assn. of Caribbean Studies. Coral Gables, Fla.

Journal of Commonwealth & Comparative Politics. Univ. of London, Institute of Commonwealth Studies. London. (ICS/JCCP)

Journal of Comparative Family Studies. Calgary, Canada.

Journal of Cultural Geography. Bowling Green State Univ. Bowling Green, Oh.

Journal of Developing Areas. Western Illinois Univ. Press. Macomb. (JDA)

Journal of Developing Economics. North Holland Publishing Co. Amsterdam.

Journal of Development Studies. London. (JDS)

Journal of Economic History. New York Univ., Graduate School of Business Administration *for the* Economic History Assn. Rensselaer, N.Y. (EHA/J)

Journal of Economic Issues. Assn. for Evolutionary Economics. Austin, Tex.

Journal of Ethnic Studies. Western Washington Univ. Bellingham.

Journal of Ethnopharmacology. Elsevier Sequoia. Lausanne, Switzerland.

Journal of Field Archaeology. Boston Univ.

for the Assn. for Field Archaeology. Boston. (AFA/JFA)

Journal of Geography. National Council of Geographic Education. Menasha, Wis. (NCGE/J)

Journal of Historical Geography. Academic Press. London.

Journal of Human Evolution. Academic Press. New York.

Journal of Inter-American Studies and World Affairs. Sage Publications *for the* Center for Advanced International Studies, Univ. of Miami. Coral Gables, Fla. (SAGE/JIAS)

Journal of International Affairs. Colombia Univ., School of International Affairs. New York. (CU/JIA)

Journal of Latin American Lore. Univ. of California, Latin American Center. Los Angeles. (UCLA/JLAL)

Journal of Latin American Studies. Centers or institutes of Latin American studies at the univs. of Cambridge, Glasgow, Liverpool, London and Oxford. Cambridge Univ. Press. London. (JLAS)

Journal of Peace Research. Edited at the International Peace Research Institute. Universitetforlaget. Oslo. (JPR)

Journal of Peasant Studies. Frank Cass & Co. London. (JPS)

Journal of Politics. Southern Political Science Assn. *in cooperation with the* Univ. of Florida. Gainesville. (SPSA/JP)

Journal of Social Psychology. Journal Press. Provincetown, Mass. (JSP)

Journal of the Barbados Museum and Historical Society. Barbados, West Indies. (BMHS/J)

Journal of the British Sociological Association. Carendon Press. Oxford, England. (BSA/S)

Journalism Quarterly. Assn. for Education in Journalism *with the cooperation of the* American Assn. of Schools, Depts. of Journalism [and] Kappa Tau Alpha Society. Univ. of Minnesota. Minneapolis. (AEJ/JQ)

LASA Forum. Latin American Studies Assn. Austin, Tex.

Language. Journal of the Linguistic Society of America. Waverly Press. Baltimore, Md. (LSA/L)

Latin American Indian Literatures. Univ. of Pittsburgh, Dept. of Hispanic Languages and Literatures. Pittsburgh, Pa. (UP/LAIL)

Latin American Perspectives. Univ. of California. Riverside. (LAP)

Latin American Research Review. Univ. of North Carolina Press *for the* Latin American Studies Assn. (LASA). Chapel Hill. (LARR)

Latin American Studies. Univ. of Tsukuba, Special Research Project on Latin America. Sakura-Mura. Japan.

Letras de Guatemala. San Carlos, Guatemala.

El Libro Español. Instituto Nacional del Libro Español (INLE). Madrid.

Linden Lane Magazine. Millburn, N.J.

Lingua. North-Holland Publishing Co. Amsterdam. (LINGUA)

Linguistic Analysis. Elsevier Science Publishing Co. New York.

La Linguistique. Presses universitaires de France. Paris.

Lotería. Lotería Nacional de Beneficiencia. Panamá. (LNB)

Maldoro. Arca Editorial. Montevideo.

of Pennsylvania. Philadelphia.

Man. The Royal Anthropological Institute. London. (RAI/M)

MASCA Journal. Museum Applied Science Center for Archaeology, Univ. Museum, Univ. Medical Anthropology. Redgrave Press. South Salem, N.Y.

Memórias do Instituto Oswaldo Cruz. Rio de Janeiro. (IOC/M)

Mensário do Arquivo Nacional. Ministério da Justiça, Arquivo Nacional, Div. de Publicações. Rio de Janeiro. (MAN)

Mesoamérica. Centro de Investigaciones Regionales de Mesoamérica. La Antigua, Guatemala. (CIRMA/M)

Mexicon. Berlin, FRG.

Migraciones Internacionales en las Américas. Centro de Estudios de Migración, Centro de Estudios de Pastoral y Asistencia Migratoria. Caracas.

Miscelánea Antropológica Ecuatoriana. Guayaquil.

Monetaria. Centro de Estudios Monetarios Latinoamericanos. México. (CEMLA/M)

Monthly Review. New York. (MR)

Il Mulino. Bologna, Italy. (MULINO)

NACLA: Report on the Americas. North American Congress on Latin America. New York. (NACLA)

N&N Ling/Notas y Noticias Lingüísticas. Instituto Boliviano de Cultura, Instituto Nacional de Antropología. La Paz.

NS NorthSouth NordSud NorteSur NorteSul. Canadian Assn. of Latin American Studies, Univ. of Ottawa. Ottawa. (NS)

National Geographic Magazine. National Geographic Society. Washington. (NGS/NGM)

Natural History. American Museum of Natural History. New York. (AMNH/NH)

Naval War College Review. Newport, R.I.

Navy International. Maritime World Ltd. Surrey, England.

The New Scholar. Univ. of California, Committee of Hispanic Civilization [and] Center for Chicano Studies. Santa Barbara. (UCSB/NS)

The New York Review of Books. New York. (NYRB)

The New York Times Magazine. New York.

The New Yorker. New York.

Nieuwe West-Indische Gids. Martinus Nijhoff. The Hague. (NWIG)

Notes e études documentaires. France, Direction de la documentation. Paris. (FDD/NED)

Nova Americana. Giulio Einaudi Editore. Torino, Italy. (GEE/NA)

Nueva Sociedad. San José. (NSO)

Nutrition Reports International. Los Altos, Calif.

Nutrition Research. Pergamon Press. New York.

OCLAE. Organización Continental Latinoamericana de Estudiantes. La Habana. (OCLAE)

OSO. Surinaamse taalkunde, letterkunde en geschiedenis. Paramaribo.

Orbis. Foreign Policy Research Institute, Philadelphia, Pa., in association with the Fletcher School of Law and Diplomacy, Tufts Univ., Medford, Mass. (FPRI/O)

Paideuma. Mitteilungen zur Kulturkunde. Deutsche Gesellschaft für kulturmorphologie von Frobenius Institut au der Johann Wolfgang Goethe—Universität. Wiesbaden, FRG. (PMK)

Paleoetnológica. Buenos Aires.

Pantoc. Instituto de Investigaciones Antropológicas, Univ. Autónoma de Guadalajara. Guadalajara, México.

Peasant Studies. Univ. of Utah, Dept. of History. Salt Lake City. (UU/PS)

Pesquisas. Anuário do Instituto Anchietano de Pesquisas. Pôrto Alegre. (IAP/P)

Pesquisas e Planejamento Econômico. Instituto de Planejamento Econômico e Social. Rio de Janeiro. (IPEA/PPE)

Phylon. Atlanta Univ. Atlanta. (AU/P)

Playboy. Chicago.

Política. Instituto de Ciencia Política, Univ. de Chile. Santiago.

Political Studies. Political Studies Assn. of the United Kingdom. Oxford, England. (PSA/PS)

Politics & Society. Iowa State Univ. Ames. (ISU/PS)

Politics & Society. Los Altos, Calif.

Population. Institut national d'études demographiques. Paris.

Problems of Communism. US Information Agency. Washington. (USIA/PC)

Proceedings. US Naval Institute. Annapolis.

Proceedings of the American Philosophical Society. Philadelphia. (APS/P)

Proceedings of the Pacific Coast Council on Latin American Studies. Univ. of California. Los Angeles. (PCCLAS/P)

Psychoanalytic Anthropology.

Relaciones. El Colegio de Michoacán. Zamora, México. (CM/RE)

Relaciones de la Sociedad Argentina de Antropología. Buenos Aires. (SAA/R)

Relaciones Internacionales. Univ. Nacional Autónoma de México, Facultad de Ciencias Políticas y Sociales, Centro de Relaciones Internacionales. México. (UNAM/RI)

Religião e Sociedade. Rio de Janeiro.

Revista Andina. Centro Bartolomé de las Casas. Cusco, Peru.

Revista Antioqueña de Economía. Medellín, Colombia. (RAE)

Revista Brasileira de Economia. Fundação Getúlio Vargas, Instituto Brasileiro de Economia. Rio de Janeiro. (IBE/RBE)

Revista Brasileira de Estatística. Ministério do Planejamento e Coordenação Geral, Instituto Brasileira de Geografia e Estatística. Rio de Janeiro. (IBGE/RBE)

Revista Brasileira de Estudos Pedagógicos. Instituto Nacional de Estudos Pedagógicos, Centro Brasileiro de Pesquisas Educacionais. Rio de Janeiro. (INEP/RBEP)

Revista Brasileira de Geografia. Conselho Nacional de Geografia, Instituto Brasileiro de Geografia e Estatística. Rio de Janeiro. (IBGE/R)

Revista Brasileira de Mercado de Capitais. Instituto Brasileiro de Mercado de Capitais. Rio de Janeiro. (RMBC)

Revista Brasileira de Política Internacional. Instituto Brasileiro de Relações Internacionais. Rio de Janeiro. (IBRI/R)

Revista Centroamericana de Economía. Univ. Nacional Autónoma de Honduras,

Programa de Postgrado Centroamericano en Economía y Planificación. Tegucigalpa. (UNAH/RCE)

Revista Chilena de Historia y Geográfia. Sociedad Chilena de Historia y Geografía. Santiago. (SCHG/R)

Revista Colombiana de Educación. Univ. Pedagógica Nacional, Centro de Investigaciones. Bogotá. (UPN/RCE)

Revista Cubana de Administración de Salud. La Habana.

Revista Cubana de Pediatría. La Habana.

Revista da Univ. Católica de Pernambuco. Recife.

Revista da Univ. Católica de Petrópolis. Petrópolis.

Revista de Antropología. Casa de la Cultura Ecuatoriana, Núcleo del Azuay. Cuenca, Ecuador. (CCE/RA)

Revista de Antropologia. Univ. de São Paulo, Faculdade de Filosofia, Letras e Ciências Humanas [and] Associação de Antropologia. São Paulo. (USP/RA)

Revista de Arqueologia. Museu Paraense Emílio Goeldi. Belém, Brazil.

Revista de Biblioteconomia de Brasília. Associação dos Bibliotecários do Distrito Federal *com a colaboraco do* Depto. de Biblioteconomia, Faculdade de Estudos Sociais Aplicados, Univ. de Brasília. Brasília.

Revista de Ciencias Sociales. Univ. de Puerto Rico, Colegio de Ciencias Sociales. Río Piedras. (UPR/RCS)

Revista de Economía. Banco de la Provincia de Córdoba. Córdoba, Argentina. (BPC/RE)

Revista de Economia Política. Editôra Brasiliense. São Paulo.

Revista de Economía y Estadística. Univ. Nacional de Córdoba, Facultad de Ciencias Económicas. Córdoba, Argentina. (UNC/REE)

Revista de Estudios Agro-Sociales. Instituto de Estudios Agro-Sociales. Madrid. (IEAS/R)

Revista de Geografía Norte Grande. Pontificia Univ. Católica de Chile, Instituto de Geografía. Santiago.

Revista de Historia. Univ. Nacional de Costa Rica, Escuela de Historia. Heredica, Costa Rica. (UNCR/R)

Revista de Historia de América. Instituto Panamericano de Geografía e Historia, Comisión de Historia. México. (PAIGH/H)

Revista de Historia de las Ideas. Instituto Panamericano de Geografía e Historia. Edi-

torial Casa de la Cultura Ecuatoriana. Quito. (IPGH/RHI)

Revista de Indias. Instituto Gonzalo Fernández de Oviedo [and] Consejo Superior de Investigaciones Científicas. Madrid. (IGFO/RI)

Revista de la Educación Superior. Asociación Nacional de Universidades e Institutos de Enseñanza Superior (ANUIES). México.

Revista de la Universidad de Yucatán. Mérida, Mexico. (UY/R)

Revista de Pré-História. Univ. de São Paulo, Instituto de Pré-História. São Paulo.

Revista de la Universidad. Univ. Nacional Autónoma de Honduras. Tegucigalpa. (HUN/RU)

Revista del Instituto de Cultura Puertorriqueña. San Juan. (ICP/R)

Revista del Museo de La Plata. Univ. Nacional de La Plata, Facultad de Ciencias Naturales y Museo. La Plata, Argentina. (UNLPM/R)

Revista del Museo Nacional. Casa de la Cultura del Perú, Museo Nacional de la Cultura Peruana. Lima. (PEMN/R)

Revista del Pensamiento Centroamericano. Centro de Investigaciones y Actividades Culturales. Managua. (RPC)

Revista do CEPA. Associação Pró-Ensino em Santa Cruz do Sul. Santa Cruz do Sul, Brazil.

Revista Econômica do Nordeste. Banco do Nordeste do Brasil, Depto. de Estudos Econômicos do Nordeste. Fortaleza, Brazil. (BNB/REN)

Revista Estadística. Instituto de Investigaciones Estadísticas (INSIE). La Habana.

Revista Geográfica. Instituto Geográfico Militar del Ecuador, Depto. Geográfico. Quito. (IGME/RG)

Revista Geográfica. Instituto Panamericano de Geografía e Historia, Comisión de Geografía. México. (PAIGH/G)

Revista Geográfica. Univ. de Los Andes. Mérida, Venezuela. (ULA/RG)

Revista Iberoamericana. Instituto Internacional de Literatura Latinoamericana. Patronicada por la Univ. de Pittsburgh. Pittsburgh, Pa. (IILI/RI)

Revista Interamericana de Bibliografía (Inter-American Review of Bibliography). Organization of American States. Washington.(RIB)

Revista Internacional de los Países Socialistas. Ministerio de Educación. La Habana.

Revista Mexicana de Ciencias Políticas y Sociales. Univ. Nacional Autónoma de México, Facultad de Ciencias Políticas y Sociales. México. (UNAM/RMCPS)

Revista Mexicana de Sociología. Univ. Nacional Autónoma de México, Instituto de Investigaciones Sociales. México. (UNAM/RMS)

Revista Mexicana del Trabajo. Secretaría del Trabajo y Previsión Social. México. (MSTPS)

Revista Occidental. Cali, Colombia.

Revista Paraguaya de Sociología. Centro Paraguayo de Estudios Sociológicos. Asunción. (CPES/RPS)

Revista Pernambucana de Desenvolvimento. Instituto de Desenvolvimento de Pernambuco. Recife, Brazil.

Revista/Review Interamericana. Univ. Interamericana. San Germán, P.R. (RRI)

Revue de l'Institut de sociologie. Univ. libre de Bruxelles. Bruxelles. (ULB/RIS)

Rivista Geografia Italiana. Società di Studi Geografici e Coloniali. Firenze, Italy. (SSG/RGI)

Science. American Assn. for the Advancement of Science. Washington. (AAAS/S)

Science and Society. New York. (SS)

Scientific American. Scientific American Inc. New York. (SA)

Semiotica. Association internationale de sémiotique. The Hague.

Signs. Univ. of Chicago Press. Chicago, Ill. (UC/S)

Social and Economic Studies. Univ. of the West Indies, Institute of Social and Economic Research. Mona, Jamaica. (UWI/SES)

Social Forces. Univ. of North Carolina Press *by the* Williams & Wilkins Co. Baltimore, Md. (SF)

Social Problems. Society for the Study of Social Problems *affiliated with the* American and International Sociological Assns. Kalamazoo, Mich. (SSSP/SP)

Social Science and Medicine. Pergamon Press. New York.

Social Thought and Practice. Belgrade.

Socialismo y Participación. Ediciones Socialismo y Participación. Lima. (SP)

Sociologus. Zeitschrift für empirische Soziologie, sozialpsychologische und ethnologische Forschung. Berlin, FRG. (SOCIOL).

South Eastern Latin Americanist. South-

eastern Conference on Latin American Studies. Clemson Univ. Clemson, S.C. (SECOLAS/SELA)

Southeastern Archaeology. Southeastern Archaeological Conference. Gainesville, Fla.

Staff Papers. International Monetary Fund. Washington. (IMF/SP)

Studia Diplomatica. Institut royal des relations internationales. Bruxelles. (IRRI/SD)

Studies in Comparative Communism. Univ. of Southern California, School of International Relations, Von KleinSmid Institute of International Affairs. Los Angeles. (USC/SCC)

Studies in Comparative International Development. Georgia Institute of Technology. Atlanta. (GIT/SCID)

Studies in Family Planning. Population Council. New York.

Suplemento Antropológico. Univ. Católica de Nuestra Señora de la Asunción, Centro de Estudios Antropológicos. Asunción. (UCNSA/SA)

Swiss Review of World Affairs. Neue Zürcher Zeitung. Zurich, Switzerland. (NZZ/SRWA)

Syracuse Scholar. Syracuse Univ. Syracuse, N.Y.

Technology and Culture. Society for the History of Technology. Detroit, Mich.

Temas de Economía Mundial. La Habana.

Tercer Mundo y Economía Mundial. Centro de Estudios Económicos y Sociales del Tercer Mundo. México. (CEESTEM/TM)

Texas Business Review. Univ. of Texas, Bureau of Business Research. Austin.

Third World Quarterly. Third World Foundation, New Zealand House. London. (TWF/TWQ)

This World. Institute for Educational Affairs. New York.

Tiers monde. Univ. de Paris, Institut d'étude de développement économique et social. Paris. (UP/TM)

Transactions. Institute of British Geographers. London. (IBG/T)

Tribus. Veröffentlichungen den Linden-Museums. Museum für Länder- und Völkerkunde. Stuttgart, FRG. (MLV/T)

El Trimestre Económico. Fondo de Cultura Económica. México. (FCE/TE)

Universidad Pontificia Bolivariana. Medellín, Colombia. (UPB)

Universitas. Pontificia Univ. Javeriana, Facultad de Derecho y Ciencias Socioeconómicas. Bogotá. (PUJ/U)

Universitas. Univ. Federal da Bahia. Bahia, Brazil.

Urban Anthropology. State Univ. of New York, Dept. of Anthropology. Brockport. (UA)

Verhandlungen der Naturf. Gesselschaft. Basel, Switzerland.

Vínculos. Museo Nacional de Costa Rica. San José. (MNCR/V)

Vuelta. México.

The Washington Quarterly. Georgetown Univ., Center for Strategic and International Studies. Washington. (GU/WQ)

Weltwirtshaftliches Archiv. Zeitschrift des Instituts für Weltwirtschaft an der Christians-Albrechts-Univ. Kiel. Kiel, FRG. (CAUK/WA)

West Indian Medical Journal. Univ. of the West Indies. Mona, Jamaica.

Western Political Quarterly. Univ. of Utah, Institute of Government *for the* Western Political Science Assn.; Pacific Northwest Political Science Assn.; and the Southern California Political Science Assn. Salt Lake City. (UU/WPQ)

World Archaeology. Routledge & Kegan Paul. London.

World Development. Pergamon Press. Oxford, UK. (WD)

World Policy Journal. New York.

The World Today. Royal Institute of International Affairs. London. (RIIA/WT)

Worldview. Council on Religion and International Affairs. New York. (CRIA/W)

Yaxkin. Instituto Hondureño de Antropología e Historia. Tegucigalpa. (YAXKIN)

Yearbook of Physical Anthropology. Alan R. Liss, Inc. New York.

Yearbook of World Affairs. London Institute of World Affairs. London. (LIWA/YWA)

Zeitschrift für Ethnologie. Deutschen Gesellschaft für Völkerkunde. Braunschweig, FRG. (DGV/ZE)

Zeitschrift für Geomorphologie. Gebrüder Borntraeger. Berlin, FRG. (ZG)

Zeitschrift für Lateinamerika Wien. Osterreichisches Lateinamerika-Institut. Wien. (OLI/ZLW)

SUBJECT INDEX

Accounting. Chile, 3561.
Acculturation. Achuar, 1355. Brazil, 5276.
  Latin America, 8025. Mēkranoti, 1384.
  Mexico, 8063. Tukano, 1170.
Aché (indigenous group), 1264–1265, 1273.
Achuar (indigenous group), 1276, 1283.
Acronyms. Latin America, 104.
Adult Education. Brazil, 4542. Costa Rica,
  4412. Latin America, 4321–4322, 4359b.
  Laws and Legislation, 4447. Mexico, 4447.
  Nicaragua, 4478.
Aeronautics. Accidents, 6393. Argentina,
  7303. Bahamas, 5335. Brazil, 3781, 3788.
  Dominican Republic, 5348. Ecuador, 6393.
  Guatemala, 5398. Laws and Legislation,
  7303. Maps, 5335, 5348, 5398.
Agassiz, Louis, 5172.
Agrarian Reform. Bolivia, 1416, 1424, 1436–
  1437, 8304, 8307, 8311–8312. Brazil, 3794,
  5220, 6557, 8375. Chile, 3542, 3547, 8340,
  8349–8350. Colombia, 3407, 8234, 8240.
  Costa Rica, 3257. Cuba, 8156. Dominican
  Republic, 3265. Ecuador, 3430, 3438, 8256,
  8260. El Salvador, 3205, 3225, 3255, 3262,
  5059, 6142. Guatemala, 5062. Honduras,
  3255. Latin America, 2828, 2839, 2900,
  5009, 5014, 8002–8003, 8042. Mexico,
  6067, 8035, 8070, 8101. Nicaragua, 3215,
  3243, 3245, 5078. Paraguay, 3654, 3658.
  Peru, 3569, 5187, 6411, 6416, 6424, 8268,
  8274, 8291. Venezuela, 3475–3476.
Agricultural Credit. Costa Rica, 3198. Jamaica, 3329.
Agricultural Development. Bolivia, 3629,
  3636, 5145. Brazil, 5259, 5318. Dominican
  Republic, 3275. Mesoamerica, 334. Mexico, 5084. Nicaragua, 3236.
Agricultural Industries. Bolivia, 8313. Brazil,
  5230, 5296. Latin America, 2807.

Agricultural Laborers. Brazil, 3783, 3811,
  5308. Chile, 3566. Dominican Republic,
  3282. Ecuador, 3432. Honduras, 6175.
  Latin America, 2788a, 2839, 2844, 2925.
  Mexico, 8079. Uruguay, 3673. US, 7133.
Agricultural Policy. Argentina, 3724. Bolivia,
  1449. Brazil, 3809, 3812, 3818, 8375. Colombia, 3407, 3415, 5170, 8236. Ecuador,
  3430–3431, 8256. Honduras, 8136. Jamaica, 3337, 5041. Latin America, 6045,
  8038. Mexico, 3131, 3137–3138, 6086,
  8076, 8111. Peru, 3592. Uruguay, 3683.
Agriculture. Amazonia, 1184. Antigua, 6295.
  Argentina, 3698. Belize, 5050. Bolivia,
  1431, 3627, 3633–3634, 5144, 8301–8303,
  8311, 8313. Brazil, 3736, 3742, 3775, 3783,
  3797, 3806–3807, 3810–3811, 3847, 5227,
  5230, 5238, 5248, 5270, 5273, 5281, 5294,
  5308, 5313, 5511, 8406. Central America,
  254, 3171, 5042, 8137. Chile, 3517, 3532,
  3542. Colombia, 743, 3379, 3404, 5165–
  5166, 8229. Cuba, 3364, 6222. Dominican
  Republic, 3271, 5037. Ecuador, 780–781,
  3433, 8253, 8259, 8262, 8264. Guyana,
  3343. Haiti, 5039. Honduras, 5076, 8210.
  Inca, 809. Latin America, 2799, 2835,
  2944–2945, 2986, 5019, 8022, 8038. Maps,
  5511. Maya, 469, 487. Mesoamerica,
  260–261, 337–338, 403, 455, 475–476.
  Mexico, 964, 974, 3135–3136, 5082,
  5089–5090, 5092, 5112, 7130, 8052, 8096.
  Nicaragua, 3244, 5077, 6185. Paraguay,
  3650, 8315. Peru, 1469, 1482a–1483, 1516,
  3582, 3614, 3616, 5181, 8229, 8268, 8274,
  8294. Precolumbian, 265, 286, 659, 817,
  839, 841, 5019, 5110, 5115. South America,
  254. Statistics, 3736, 3797, 3806. Surinam,
  3343, 8178. Uruguay, 3668, 3679. Venezuela, 3456, 3459, 3466.

AUTHOR INDEX

dência do Desenvolvimento da Região
Centro-Oeste, 5474
———. Ministério dos Transportes. Depto.
Nacional de Estradas de Rodagem. Di-
retoria de Planejamento. Grupo de Projetos
Cartográficos, 5475
Brazil: an interim assessment of rural devel-
opment programs for the Northeast, 3750
Brazil and Mexico: patterns in late develop-
ment, 3112
Brazilian geographical studies, 5219
Brazilian Indians and the law, 1173
Bremer, R., 6313
Breton, Yvan, 5082
Briceño Monzillo, José Manuel, 5196
Bricker, Victoria R., 500, 896, 1525
Brigé Pinedo, Lucía, 8242
Bright, William, 1526
Brineman, Elena, 1761
Briones, Guillermo, 3514
Briones Morales, Luis, 701
Brisseau Loaiza, Janine, 5183
British Parliamentary Human Rights Group,
6258
Brito, José Carlos Aguiar, 6607
Brito, Maristella de Azevedo, 5220
Brito, Ney Roberto Ottoni de, 3751
Brito Sansores, William, 508
Britto, Luiz Navarro de, 6621
Britton, John, 7161
Brockett, Charles D., 5062
Brockmann, C. Thomas, 1022
Broda, Johanna, 501
Brodber, Erna, 1023, 8160
Brodersohn, Víctor, 2788a,3170
Bronstein, Arturo S., 8029
Brooks, Reuben H., 5221
Brotherston, Gordon, 502, 505
Browman, David L., 610
Brown, Aggrey, 6283, 8207
Brown, C.G., 6460
Brown, Chester L., 7013
Brown, Juanita, 5007
Brown, Michael F., 1174–1177, 1590
Brown, Peter G., 3095
Browner, C.H., 897
Browner, Carole, 8225
Browning, David, 3205, 5059
Brozek, Josef, 1793
Bruce, Robert D., 972
Bruhns, Karen Olsen, 503, 542
Brumfiel, Elizabeth M., 504
Bruna, Gilda Collet, 5299
Brundenius, Claes, 3348–3349
Brunella, Daniel A., 2789

Brunet, Yves, 5027
Bruschini, Maria A. Cristina, 4523, 8408
Brush, Stephen, 1396, 1469
Bryan, Alan L., 601
Bryant, Douglas Donne, 361
Bucaram: historia de una lucha, 6391
Buchanan, Paul, 6505
Buckley, Tom, 6104
Bueno, Gerardo M., 3062
Bueno Mendoza, Alberto, 804
Buer, Wilhelm P., 1178
Büttner, Thomas Th., 1591
Buira, Ariel, 2790
Bulmer-Thomas, V., 3171
Bunker, Stephen G., 5222, 6558
Burchard, Roderick, 1470
Burga, Teresa, 8269
Burger, Hillel, 364
Burger, Richard L., 610, 805
Burgess, Don, 898
Burgos, María, 1782
Burgos Villasmil, José R., 3461
Burmeister, Hermann, 5223
Burquest, Donald A., 1608
Buschang, Peter H., 1710
Buses y busetas: una evaluación del trans-
porte urbano de Bogotá, 5163
Business Yearbook of Brazil, Mexico & Vene-
zuela, 2791
Bustos M., Patricia, 1751
Butler, Judy, 7014
Butt Colson, Audrey, 1023a, 1178a
Bustamante, Jorge A., 87
Bustamante Belaúnde, Luis, 3594
Bustos-Obregón, Eduardo, 5148
Buzaglo, Jorge D., 3033
Byrne de Caballero, Geraldine, 655
Byron, Michael J., 7214
Caba Fuentes, Angel, 585
Caballero, José María, 6416, 8268
Cabanellas, Guillermo, 7273
Cabarrús, Carlos Rafael, 899
Cabello Carro, Paz, 543
Cabezas, Omar, 6184
Cabezas, Rodrigo, 5561, 6392
Cabieses, H., 3578
Cabonell de Masy, Rafael, 3650
Cabral, Alvaro, 1288
Cabral, Antônio, 7274
Cabral, João Batista Pinheiro, 6048
Cabral, Milton, 7323
Cabrera, Lydia, 8161
Cabrera, Rubén, 481
Cabrero G., María Teresa, 362
Cabrisas, Ricardo, 3350

Daroczi, Isabel, 5593
D'Ascoli, Carlos Alberto, 3471
Dasilva, Fabio B., 8379
Dauelsberg H., Percy, 705–707
Daus, Federico A., 5131
Davidson, Judith R., 811
Davidson, William V., 1039
Davies, H., 5126
Davies, John E., 1832
Davies, Nigel, 285
Davies, Thomas M., Jr., 6450, 7047
Dávila, Violeta Jaramilla de, 5562
Davis, Albert, 2933
Davis, Charles L., 6052, 6056–6057
Davis, E. Wade, 1040
Davis, L. Harlan, 5042
Davis, Martha Ellen, 1041
Davis, Patricia M., 1589
Davis, Ricardo Ffrench. *See* Ffrench-Davis, Ricardo.
Dávita, Carmen Lucía, 740
Davoust, Michel, 1531
Davrieux, Hugo, 3674
Day, Jane Stevenson, 550–551
Daza Valenzuela, Pedro, 7019
De Boni, Luís Alberto, 8380
De Frank Canelo, Juan, 8170
De Kleine, Renate, 5067
De Mille, Richard, 915
Dean, Warren, 5233–5234
Debate sobre la mujer en América Latina y el Caribe: discusión acerca de la unidad producción-reproducción, 8228
Os Debates dos jornalistas brasileiros, *1970–1982*, 6586
Debien, Gabriel, 24
Debret, Jean Baptiste, 5235
XX [i.e. Décimo] Censo Industrial 1976: datos de 1975, desglose de materias primas consumidas por clase de activad, 3146
Decker, David R., 3393, 6515
La Declaración Franco-Mexicana, 7125
Deere, Carmen Diana, 8229, 8272
Déficit fiscal en Colombia: recopilación de las ponencias, comentarios y resúmenes referentes a los dos foros realizados en Medellín y Bogotá en septiembre 7 y 21 respectivamente, 3394
DeHart, Evelyn Hu. *See* Hu-DeHart, Evelyn.
Deheza, José A., 2794
Del Aguila, Juan M., 6217
Del Liberalismo al capitalismo autoritario: contribución de ILADES al "objectivo general" de las Orientaciones Pastorales 1982/85 de la Conferencia Episcopal de Chile, 6468

Del Papa, Paolo, 1226
Deláncer, Víctor Hugo, 4424
Delavaud, Anne Collin. *See* Collin Delavaud, Anne.
Delbosco, Norma, 5439
Delgado, Hernán L., 1761–1764
Delgado, Kenneth, 4491
Delgado, Ribas, Josep María, 2827
Delich, Francisco, 8328
Demarest, Arthur A., 253
Demarquet, Sonia de Almeida, 1227
Demicheli, Tulio H., 7126
d'Emilio, Lucia, 1156
Demografische data, 84
Denevan, William M., 286
Denis, Ferdinand, 5236
Dennis, Philip A., 914
Denslow, David, Jr., 3761
Dependency under challenge: the political economy of the Commonwealth Caribbean, 3310
Los Derechos humanos: sus fundamentos en la enseñanza de la Iglesia, 6008
Derze, Gilberto Ruy, 5482–5483
Desai, I.D., 1714
Desarrollo agrario y la América Latina, 2828
Desarrollo de América Latina y sus repercusiones en la educación: alfabetismo y escolaridad básica, 4314
Desarrollo de las cuentas nacionales en América Latina y el Caribe: documento, 2829
El Desarrollo regional de Bonao: realidad y futuro, 3269
El Desarrollo rural humanista en América: una perspectiva desde el IICA, 2830
Descola, Philippe, 1228
Desenvolvimento capitalista no Brasil: ensaios sobre a crise, 3762
Desigualdes regionais no desenvolvimento brasileiro, 3763
Despradel, Carlos, 3270, 3276
Despradel, Fidelio, 6238
Destéfani, Laurio Hedelvio, 5132, 7281
Destino de ingreso de capitales, 3531
Destler, I.M., 7020
Deústua, José, 1475
Deutsch, Mario, 8329
Devas, Esmond, 26
Développement rural en Haïti et dans la Caraïbe, 1042
Dévieux, Lilian, 1043
Devonish, Hubert, 1044
Dew, Edward, 6311–6312, 7224
Dewey, Kathryn G., 1765–1766